BEST BOOKS FOR CHILDREN

BEST BOOKS
FOR CHILDREN

Preschool Through the Middle Grades

EDITED BY John T. Gillespie
AND Christine B. Gilbert

SECOND EDITION

R. R. Bowker Company / New York & London, 1981

010
G

Published by R. R. Bowker Company
1180 Avenue of the Americas, New York, N.Y. 10036
Copyright © 1981 by Xerox Corporation
Printed and bound in the United States of America

Library of Congress Cataloging in Publication Data
Gillespie, John Thomas, 1928-
   Best books for children, preschool through the middle grades.

   Includes indexes.
   1. Children's literature—Bibliography.
I. Gilbert, Christine Bell, 1909-   joint author.   II. Title.
Z1037.G48   1981   [PN1009.A1]   010   80-29095
ISBN 0-8352-1332-3

Contents

Preface

This is the second edition of *Best Books for Children* in its new format, the first edition being published in 1978. Since the original publication of this title in 1959, *Best Books for Children* has grown from a paperback bibliography of approximately 5,000 titles to this annotated listing of some 13,000 recommended books for use with readers from preschool through the middle grades. The sustained interest by librarians in this selection aid has resulted in greater in-depth coverage and greater accessibility to titles through a more detailed listing of subjects in the contents pages.

As with the 1978 edition, the primary aim of this work is to provide a list of books, gathered from a number of sources, that are highly recommended to satisfy both a child's recreational reading needs and the demands of a typical school curriculum. For greatest depth, coverage has been limited to the age group including preschool children through advanced readers in the sixth grade. Although many of the listed titles indicate use with junior high school students, it is not the intent to give complete coverage for this group.

Of the approximately 13,000 titles included in this book (an increase of more than 3,000 from the previous edition), nearly 10,000 are individual entries. The remainder are related titles covering similar material; they are mentioned in the annotations and can be used with the main entry. When the author of both the main entry and additional title(s) is the same, the author's name is not repeated in the annotation. Instances of similar coverage but differing grade suitability are noted. In fiction areas, multiple listings within the annotations are used primarily for books in a series. However, in cases where it was felt that sequels showed unusual individuality in style and content, separate entries are given. On the other hand, some series are so extensive that, due to space limitations, only representative titles could be included.

For a title to be considered for listing, the basic requirement was multiple recommendations (usually three) in the sources consulted. However, because many of these sources give scant coverage to books that are primarily curriculum-oriented, the number of necessary recommendations for nonfiction titles was sometimes lowered. Beyond this, additional criteria included such obvious considerations as availability, up-to-dateness, accuracy, usefulness, and relevance.

Several sources were used to compile this annotated bibliography. At the outset there was a thorough perusal and evaluation of the entries in the 1978 edition of *Best Books for Children*. All out-of-print titles were dropped, as well as those that were considered no longer relevant or suitable. The other sources consulted were numerous and varied, although a thorough review was made of such retrospective sources as *Children's Catalog* (H.W. Wilson) and *The Elementary School Library Collection* (Bro-Dart). The major tools were current periodicals and annual bibliographies, including: *Children's Books* (Library of Congress), *Notable Children's Books* (Association for Library Service to Children), and *Children's Books* (New York Public Library), as well as semiannual roundups in *School Library Journal* and yearly subject listings such as "Outstanding Science Trade Books for Children" (*Science and Children*) and "Notable Children's Trade Books in the Field of Social Studies" (*Social Education*). Many special subject bibliographies also were used. Current book reviewing periodicals were consulted—specifically those issues from January 1978 through June 1980 of four periodicals: *Booklist, Bulletin of Center for Children's Books, Horn Book*, and *School Library Journal*.

It is our hope that this bibliography will be used in four different ways: (1) as a tool to evaluate the adequacy of existing collections, (2) as a book selection instrument for beginning and expanding collections, (3) as an aid for giving reading guidance to children, and (4) as a tool for the preparation of bibliographies and reading lists. To increase the book's usefulness, particularly in the two latter areas, it was decided to arrange the chosen titles under broad interest areas or, as in the case of nonfiction works, by curriculum-oriented subjects rather than by using the Dewey Decimal Classification System for nonfiction and an alphabetical-by-author entry for fiction. In this way, analogous titles that otherwise would have been separated are brought together and can be seen in relation to other important books on the same broad topic.

A typical entry in the main section contains the following information: (1) author, (2) title, (3) suitable grade levels, (4) indication of illustrations, or illustrator's name where appropriate, (5) date of publication, (6) publisher, (7) price and editions where applicable—LB = library binding, paper = paperback, and (8) annotation. Bibliographical information and prices were verified in *Children's Books in Print*, 1979–1980 (R. R. Bowker Co.) and *Publisher's Trade List Annual*, 1980 (R. R. Bowker Co.).

Titles in the main section of this book are given an entry number. To facilitate quick reference, all listings in the indexes refer the user to the entry number, not the page number. *Best Books for Children* includes four indexes—an index of authors/illustrators; one of book titles; one of biographical subjects (individual biographies in the main section are arranged alphabetically under the name of the person who is the subject of the biography) and a subject index. In this second edition, the author index has been expanded to include the book title(s) as well as the entry number(s).

Dozens of people were involved in the preparation of this bibliography—specifically we would like to mention the contributions of Bette Vander Werf, and our many helpers at Bowker, including Corinne Naden. To all of you many thanks. We hope that our collected efforts have produced a book of value and use.

BEST BOOKS FOR CHILDREN

Alphabet, Counting, and Concept Books

Alphabet Books

1. Anglund, Joan Walsh. *In a Pumpkin Shell* (PS–2). Illus. by author. 1960, Harcourt $5.95; paper $1.95. A Mother Goose ABC book.

2. Anno, Mitsumasa. *Anno's Alphabet: An Adventure in Imagination* (PS–2). 1975, Crowell $8.95; LB $8.79. A most unusual and distinctive alphabet book that shows the letters as pieces of rough-grained wood and, on the opposite pages, objects beginning with that letter. An excellent introduction to art as well.

3. Baskin, Leonard, illus. *Hosie's Alphabet* (PS–1). Words by Hosea Tobias and Lisa Baskin. 1972, Viking $6.95. A highly sophisticated dazzling picture book, which is more of an art experience than an alphabet book.

4. Brown, Marcia. *All Butterflies: An ABC* (PS–K). Illus. by author. 1972, Scribner $6.95. Handsome woodcuts show a variety of creatures in various settings in this delightful alphabet book.

5. Bruna, Dick. *B Is for Bear* (PS–K). Illustrated. 1977, Methuen $4.95. A simple ABC book with a 2-page spread devoted to each letter and a pictured object.

6. Burningham, John. *ABC* (PS–1). Illus. by author. 1967, Bobbs-Merrill $6.95. A simple, handsome ABC book in which the initial letters and the words they accompany are illustrated in facing full-page, color-filled stylizations.

7. Carle, Eric. *All about Arthur: An Absolutely Absurd Ape* (PS–K). Illus. by author. 1974, Watts $5.95. As Arthur travels, he picks up various animals in a variety of cities. An intriguing, nonsensical alphabet book illustrated with woodcuts and photographs.

8. Chess, Victoria. *Alfred's Alphabet Walk* (PS–1). Illus. by author. 1979, Greenwillow $7.95; LB $7.63. Alliteration is used to highlight a boy's walk through the ABCs.

9. Coletta, Irene. *From A to Z: The Collected Letters of Irene and Hallie Coletta* (PS–1). Illus. by Hallie Coletta. 1979, Prentice-Hall $7.95. An ABC book using a variety of objects each accompanied by a rhyme.

10. Crowther, Robert. *The Most Amazing Hide-and-Seek Book* (PS–1). 1978, Kestral/Viking $5.95. Hidden animals are revealed when the reader uses this push/pull alphabet book.

11. Duvoisin, Roger. *A for the Ark* (K–2). Illus. by author. 1952, Lothrop $7.44. A new kind of alphabet book woven around the Old Testament story of the Flood.

12. Eichenberg, Fritz. *Ape in a Cape: An Alphabet of Odd Animals* (PS–1). Illus. by author. 1952, Harcourt paper $1.35. Each letter of the alphabet is represented by a full-page color picture of an animal with a brief nonsense rhyme explaining it.

13. Emberley, Edward. *Ed Emberley's A B C* (PS–1). Illus. by author. 1978, Little $6.95. Each letter is related to an animal in this amusing, often zany treatment.

14. Falls, C. B. *A B C Book* (PS–1). Illus. by author. 1957, Doubleday $4.95; paper $1.49 A lovely alphabet book first published in 1922.

15. Farber, Norma. *As I Was Crossing Boston Common* (K–3). Illus. by Arnold Lobel. 1975, Dutton $8.50. An alphabetical parade of unusual animals crosses Boston Common at a slow stately pace in this humorous, imaginative picture book.

16. Farber, Norma. *This Is the Ambulance Leaving the Zoo* (PS–1). Illus. by Tomie de Paola. 1975, Dutton $5.95. A bright, attractive alphabet book that follows an ambulance through the busy city streets to the zoo and back again.

17. Feelings, Muriel. *Jambo Means Hello: Swahili Alphabet Book* (K–3). Illus. by Tom Feelings. 1974, Dial $5.95; LB $5.47. An alphabet book that concentrates on the positive, beautiful aspects of African-Swahili life.

18. Fife, Dale. *Adam's ABC* (PS–2). Illus. by Don Robertson. 1971, Coward $5.49. The day-by-day activities of a small black boy are pictured in this alphabet book, with illustrations that reflect an urban setting.

19. Gag, Wanda. *The A B C Bunny* (PS–1). Illus. by author. 1933, Coward $5.95; LB $5.49; paper $1.95. Bunny scampers through the alphabet.

20. Greenaway, Kate. *A Apple Pie* (PS–1). Illus. by author. 1886, Warne $6.95. The classic ABC book involving an apple pie and how the alphabet treated it.

21. Grossbart, Francine B. *A Big City* (PS–K). Illus. by author. 1966, Harper $7.89. Objects used in this ABC book are selected from big city life—mailboxes, vending machines, etc.

22. Hoberman, Mary Ann. *Nuts to You and Nuts to Me: An Alphabet of Poems* (PS–K). Illus. by Ronni Solbert. 1974, Knopf $5.99. Verses accompany each letter of the alphabet in this appealing and lively book.

23. Leman, Martin, and Carter, Angela. *Comic and Curious Cats* (1–4). Illus. by Martin Leman. 1979, Harmony $7.95. A cat-centered ABC book that contains highly stylized illustrations.

24. Lisowski, Gabriel. *On the Little Hearth* (K–3). Illus. by author. 1978, Holt $5.95. Based on a Jewish lullaby, this story tells of children learning their ABCs at their teacher's table.

25. McMillan, Bruce. *The Alphabet Symphony: An ABC Book* (PS–3). Illustrated. 1977, Greenwillow $6.25; LB $6.00. Details of musical instruments assume the configurations of letters of the alphabet.

26. Merriam, Eve. *Good Night to Annie* (PS–1). Illus. by John Wallner. 1980, Scholastic $8.95. A bedtime alphabet book that shows how animals rest.

27. Miles, Miska. *Apricot ABC* (K–3). Illus. by Peter Parnall. 1969, Little $6.95. An ABC in which fauna and flora are interspersed with the rhymes about what happens to an apricot.

28. Milne, A. A. *Pooh's Alphabet Book* (1–3). Illus. by Ernest H. Shepard. 1975, Dutton $4.95; paper $1.25. A delightful collection of quotations from Milne's works arranged in alphabet-book format.

29. Munari, Bruno. *Bruno Munari's ABC* (PS–1). Illus. by author. 1960, Collins $5.95; LB $5.91. An ABC book with characteristic, vibrant illustrations.

30. Newberry, Clare Turlay. *Kittens ABC* (PS–1). Illus. by author. 1965, Harper $7.95; LB $8.79.

The lifelike illustrations are bound to enchant children as they learn the alphabet.

31. Niland, Deborah. *ABC of Monsters* (PS–K). Illus. by author. 1978, McGraw $3.95. Monsters perform antics that represent each letter of the alphabet.

32. Oxenbury, Helen. *Helen Oxenbury's ABC of Things* (PS–K). Illus. by author. 1972, Watts $4.95. Groups of unlikely animals and objects are pictured together in this imaginative and humorous alphabet book.

33. Piatti, Celestino. *Celestino Piatti's Animal ABC* (PS–1). English text by Jon Reid. Illus. by author. 1966, Atheneum $4.95. This brilliantly handsome alphabet book pictures familiar animals, often in a whimsical way.

34. Provensen, Alice, and Provensen, Martin., illus. *A Peaceable Kingdom: The Abecedarius* (PS–K). 1978, Viking $8.95. A newly illustrated version of Shaker "Animal Rhymes" first published in 1882.

35. Rey, H. A. *Curious George Learns the Alphabet* (K–2). Illus. by author. 1963, Houghton $7.95. paper $2.45. George makes learning the alphabet a wonderful and amusing game.

36. Rockwell, Anne. *Albert B. Cub and Zebra: An Alphabet Storybook* (K–2). Illustrated. 1977, Crowell $7.95; LB $8.49. An interesting alphabet book in which readers are supposed to identify objects beginning with a specific letter.

37. Rojankovsky, Feodor. *Animals in the Zoo* (PS–1). Illus. by author. 1962, Knopf LB $5.99; paper $.95. Colorful lithographs portray the animals that illustrate each letter of the alphabet.

38. Ruden, Patricia. *Apples to Zippers* (K–1). Illustrated. 1976, Doubleday $5.95. An alphabet book using familar objects.

39. Scarry, Richard. *Richard Scarry's ABC Work Book* (PS–1). Illus. by author. 1970, Random $4.95; LB $5.99. An alphabet book that shows how letters are used in words and names.

40. Schmiderer, Dorothy, illus. *The Alphabeast Book: An Abecedarium* (PS–K). 1971, Holt $4.95. Each letter in this wordless animal ABC book is graphically transformed with familiar animals.

41. Seuss, Dr. *Dr. Seuss' ABC* (K–2). Illus. by author. 1963, Random $3.50; LB $4.39. A master author creates a strikingly popular alphabet book.

42. Tallon, Robert. *Zoophabets* (PS–1). Illus. by author. 1980, Scholastic $1.95. The author has created nonsensical animals to explain the alphabet.

43. Tudor, Tasha. *A Is for Annabelle* (PS–1). Illus. by author. 1954, Walck $4.95; paper $2.50. Two little girls play with an elegant old-fashioned doll in this alphabet book.

44. Wildsmith, Brian. *Brian Wildsmith's ABC* (PS–1). Illus. by author. 1962, Watts $5.95. Jewel-like pictures on brightly colored pages.

45. Yolen, Jane. *All in the Woodland Early: An ABC Book* (PS). Music and lyrics by author. Illus. by Jane Breskin Zalben. 1979, Collins $8.95; LB $8.91. An ABC book in rhyme that uses animals to bring the letters to life.

Counting Books

46. Anno, Mitsumasa. *Anno's Counting Book: An Adventure in Imagination* (PS–K). 1977, Crowell $7.95; LB $8.79. An appealing book on numbers in which the same landscapes are used throughout; houses, birds, trees, and people are added as the seasons progress.

47. Bayley, Nicola. *One Old Oxford Ox* (PS–1). Illus. by author. 1977, Atheneum $6.95. Twelve nonsensical counting rhymes with accompanying intricate paintings.

48. Becker, John. *Seven Little Rabbits* (K–2). Illus. by Barbara Cooney. 1973, Walker $4.95; LB $5.85; Scholastic paper $1.25. A counting book in reverse with charming colored sketches.

49. Boynton, Sandra. *Hippos Go Berserk* (PS–K). Illus. by author. 1979, Little $7.95; paper $3.95. A counting book in rhyme about several hippos.

50. Carle, Eric. *1, 2, 3 to the Zoo* (PS–2). Illus. by author. 1968, Collins $6.95. A counting book illustrated with pictures of animals in a zoo train.

51. Carle, Eric. *The Rooster Who Set Out to See the World* (K–3). Illus. by author. 1972, Watts $5.95. A rooster gathers together a group of animals to explore the world.

52. Cleveland, David. *The April Rabbits* (PS–1). Illus. by Nurit Karlin. 1978, Coward $5.95. The days of the month and a group of rabbits are used in this counting book.

53. Duvoisin, Roger. *Two Lonely Ducks: A Counting Book* (PS–1). Illus. by author. 1955, Knopf $5.99. A drake and duck have a family of 10 little ducklings.

54. Eichenberg, Fritz. *Dancing in the Moon* (PS). Illus. by author. 1955, Harcourt $7.95; paper $1.85. Simple animal nonsense rhymes that use each number from one to 20.

55. Feelings, Muriel. *Moja Means One: Swahili Counting Book* (K–3). Illus. by Tom Feelings. 1971, Dial $5.47; paper $1.75. The sights and sounds of East Africa come alive in this charming counting book.

56. Francoise. *Jeanne-Marie Counts Her Sheep* (PS–1). Illus. by author. 1951, Scribner $9.95. Jeanne-Marie plans for all the things she expects from her lamb's wool.

57. Freschet, Berniece. *Where's Henrietta's Hen?* (PS). Illus. by Lorinda Bryan Cauley. 1980, Putnam $7.95. Henrietta's hen disappears but is finally found in a haystack.

58. Friskey, Margaret. *Chicken Little, Count to Ten* (PS–1). Illus. by Katherine Evans. 1946, Childrens Press $7.35. Not one of the 10 animals questioned can tell Chicken Little how to drink. Also use: *One to Ten, Count Again* by Elaine Livermore (1973, Houghton $4.95).

59. Gretz, Susanna. *Teddy Bears 1 to 10* (PS–1). Illus. by author. 1969, Follett $5.95. Endearing bears provide jolly inspiration for the pre-Modern Math set.

60. Hoban, Russell. *Ten What? A Mystery Counting Book* (PS–K). Illus. by Sylvia Selig. 1975, Scribner $6.95. A counting book in the guise of a mystery story, amusingly illustrated.

61. Hoban, Tana. *Count and See* (PS–K). Illustrated. 1972, Macmillan paper $1.50. Beginning with numbers 1 to 15, then going to 100; clear photographs of familiar objects are easily recognized and fun to count.

62. Hobzek, Mildred. *We Came a-Marching . . . 1,2,3* (K–2). Illus. by William Pene du Bois. 1978, Parents $5.95; LB $5.41. A counting book in 12 different languages.

63. Keats, Ezra Jack. *Over in the Meadow* (K–3). Illus. by author. 1972, Scholastic $8.95. Based on a favorite old rhyme, this counting book involves 10 different sets of animals and insects.

64. Kredenser, Gail. *One Dancing Drum* (PS–1). Illus. by Stan Mack. 1971, Phillips $7.95. Colorful book in which musicians march across the pages in increasing numbers.

65. Kruss, James. *Three by Three* (K–1). Illus. by Eva J. Rubin. 1965, Macmillan $4.75; paper $1.25. A counting book that explores the idea of working with sets of threes.

66. Langstaff, John. *Over in the Meadow* (PS–1). Illus. by Feodor Rojankovsky. 1957, Harcourt $5.95; paper $1.50. Based on an old animal counting song.

67. Le Sieg, Theo. *Wacky Wednesday* (PS–1). Illus. by George Booth. 1974, Random $3.50. In this counting book, every page has a number of things out of place.

68. Little, Mary E. *1 2 3 for the Library* (PS–K). Illus. by author. 1974, Atheneum $5.95. Eleven different children arrive for story hour in this charming counting book.

69. Livermore, Elaine. *Lost and Found* (K–3). Illus. by author. 1975, Houghton $5.95. A puzzle book in which the reader must find items missing in illustrations.

70. Mack, Stan. *10 Bears in My Bed: A Goodnight Countdown* (PS–K). Illustrated. 1974, Pantheon $3.99. In this children's favorite, based on a counting song, when the "little one" says "Roll over, Roll over," one by one the bears leave the bed.

71. McLeod, Emilie W. *One Snail and Me: A Book of Numbers and Animals and a Bathtub* (K–2). Illus. by Walter Lorraine. 1961, Atlantic/Little $6.95. Counting is easy when you start with one little girl in a bathtub and add up the animals bathing with her.

72. Maestro, Giulio. *One More and One Less* (PS–K). Illus. by author. 1974, Crown $5.95. One animal is added on each page up to 10, and then an animal is subtracted as they leave one by one.

73. Obligado, Lilian. *Little Wolf and the Upstairs Bear* (PS–1). Illustrated. 1979, Viking $7.95. Little Wolf adjusts to apartment house life by using the elevator to stop at floors one through 10.

74. Oxenbury, Helen. *Numbers of Things* (PS–2). Illus. by author. 1968, Watts $4.90. An imaginative and intriguing tall counting book with handsome, humorous illustrations.

75. Pavey, Peter. *One Dragon's Dream* (PS–1). Illus. by author. 1979, Bradbury $7.95. A counting book plus the masochistic reveries of a dragon.

76. Peppe, Rodney. *Circus Numbers: A Counting Book* (PS–1). Illus. by author. 1969, Delacorte $5.95; LB $5.47. A number book with a circus theme, from one ringmaster to 100 elephants.

77. Peppe, Rodney. *Odd One Out* (K–2). Illus. by author. 1974, Viking $6.50; LB $1.25; Penguin paper $1.25. Several everyday activities are pictured, but each illustration contains some element that is out of place.

78. Reiss, John J. *Numbers* (PS–1). Illus. by author. 1971, Bradbury $7.95. A number recognition book.

79. Scarry, Richard. *Richard Scarry's Best Counting Book Ever* (PS–3). Illus. by author. 1975, Random $4.95. Willy Bunny counts everything he sees in this counting book that goes to 100.

80. Sendak, Maurice. *Seven Little Monsters* (K–2). Illus. by author. 1977, Harper $3.95; LB $4.79; paper $1.95. A counting book involving monsters that townspeople try to eliminate.

81. Tudor, Tasha. *1 is One* (K–2). Illus. by author. 1956, Rand paper $2.50. Original verses, delicate pastel illustrations. Also use: *1,2,3's* by Brian Wildsmith (1965, Watts $5.95).

82. Wells, Rosemary. *Max's Toys: A Counting Book* (K–1). Illus. by author. 1979, Dial $2.95. A highly original book that uses toys to introduce numbers 1 through 10.

83. Wild, Robin, and Wild, Jocelyn. *The Bears' Counting Book* (K–2). Illustrated. 1978, Lippincott $4.95. A variation on the Goldilocks story is used to introduce numbers.

84. Williams, Garth. *Chicken Book* (PS–1). Illus. by author. 1970, Delacorte $5.95. In this simple counting book a mother hen tells her 5 chicks that they must forage for food.

85. Yeoman, John. *Sixes and Sevens* (PS–2). Illus. by Quentin Blake. 1971, Macmillan $4.95; paper $1.25. As he poles up the river, Barnaby picks up a strange cargo—one thing after another in this ingenious counting book.

86. Youldon, Gillian. *Numbers* (PS–K). Illustrated. 1979, Watts $2.95; LB $4.90. Outdoor scenes and split pages point up the values of various numbers.

87. Ziner, Feenie. *Counting Carnival* (PS–1). Illus. by Paul Galdone. 1962, Coward $4.69. This counting book begins with one boy, and ends up with 12 children of various races and nationalities.

Concept Books

General

88. Balian, Lorna. *Where in the World Is Henry?* (PS). Illustrated. 1980, Abingdon $5.95. A concept book that explains a child's place in the universe.

89. Berenstain, Stanley. *Inside, Outside, Upside Down* (PS–1). Illus. by author. 1968, Random $3.50; LB $4.39. A bear has a brief trip that explains various concepts.

90. Bester, Roger. *Guess What?* (PS). Illustrated. 1980, Crown $6.95. A guessing game featuring common animals.

91. De Regniers, Beatrice S., and Gordon, Isabel. *The Shadow Book* (PS–3). Illus. by author. 1960, Harcourt $5.95. Imaginative prose and photographs depict a child and his shadow at play.

92. Hazen, Barbara S. *The Me I See* (1–2). Illus. by Ati Forberg. 1978, Abingdon $5.21. About how each person is different.

93. Hoban, Tana. *Push, Pull, Empty, Full: A Book of Opposites* (PS). Illus. by author. 1972, Macmillan $6.95. Clear photographs show pictures that illustrate opposites and help young children learn the principle of comparison.

94. Hoberman, Mary Ann. *A House Is a House for Me* (K–2). Illus. by Betty Fraser. 1978, Viking $5.95. This picture book explores the idea that various objects can serve as houses.

95. Holzenthaler, Jean. *My Hands Can* (PS). Illus. by Nancy Tafuri. 1978, Dutton $6.95. All sorts of things that hands can do, such as button buttons.

96. Krauss, Ruth. *A Hole Is to Dig* (PS). Illus. by Maurice Sendak. 1952, Harper $5.95; LB $5.89. Child-perceived definitions, such as "the world is so you have something to stand on," complemented by whimsical drawings.

97. Kuskin, Karla. *James and the Rain* (PS–1). Illus. by author. 1957, Harper $6.89. James asks animals what games can be played on a rainy day.

98. Lewis, Steven. *Zoo City* (K–3). Illus. by author. 1976, Greenwillow $7.25. Commonplace articles are matched with look-alike animals.

99. Scarry, Richard. *Richard Scarry's Best Word Book Ever* (PS–2). Illus. by author. 1963, Golden $4.95; LB $10.89 A diverse, unorthodox picture dictionary for children who like lots of little pictures.

100. Sendak, Maurice. *The Nutshell Library* (PS–3). Illus. by author. 1962, Harper $6.45. Miniature volumes include: an alphabet book, *Alligators All Around*, and a counting book, *One Was Johnny*. (both 1962, 7.89).

101. Spier, Peter. *Fast-Slow, High-Low: A Book of Opposites* (K–2). Illus. by author. 1972, Doubleday $7.95; paper $2.95. Delightful pictures in pairs that represent qualities—some very subtle—that are opposites. No text except headings.

102. Wheeler, Cindy. *A Good Day, A Good Night* (PS). 1980, Lippincott $7.95; LB $7.89. The con-

cepts of night and day are explored in experiences of a cat and a robin.

103. Youldon, Gillian. *Time* (K–1). 1980, Watts $5.45. A split-page book that takes a child hour by hour through a single day.

104. Zolotow, Charlotte. *Someone New* (K–3). Illus. by Erik Blegvad. 1978, Harper $5.95; LB $5.79. In a first-person narrative, a young boy realizes he is changing and growing up.

Colors

105. Haskins, Ilma. *Color Seems* (PS–3). Illus. by author. 1974, Vanguard $5.95. An introduction to the world of color.

106. Hoban, Tana. *Is It Red? Is It Yellow? Is It Blue? An Adventure in Color* (PS). Illustrated. 1978, Morrow $6.95. Without words, this picture book explains the concept of color.

107. Kumin, Maxine. *What Color Is Caesar?* (K–3). Illus. by Evaline Ness. 1978, McGraw $7.95. A book about colors and how to distinguish them.

108. Lionni, Leo. *Little Blue and Little Yellow* (PS–1). Illus. by author. 1959, Astor-Honor $7.95. All the characters are blobs of color in this ingenious story intended to give the young child an awareness of human relations.

109. McGovern, Ann. *Black Is Beautiful* (PS–2). Illus. by Hope Warmfeld. 1969, Scholastic $4.95; LB $4.95. A series of photographs show various objects and natural phenomena stressing the fact that black is beautiful.

110. Pienkowski, Jan. *Colors* (K–1). Illus. by author. 1975, Harvey House $3.79. Ten objects are used as examples of colors.

111. Reiss, John J. *Colors* (PS–1). Illus. by author. 1969, Bradbury $7.95. Boldly designed to attract the youngest, the various hues of the primary and secondary colors, plus white (day) and black (night), are displayed in familiar forms, clearly labeled—just right as a teaching tool.

112. Tison, Annette, and Talus, Taylor. *The Adventures of the Three Colors* (K–3). Illus. by author. 1971, World $5.95. Experimenting with paint, a boy discovers how to obtain secondary colors from primary blue, yellow, and red.

113. Youldon, Gillian. *Colors* (PS–K). Illustrated. 1979, Watts $2.95; LB $4.90. Split pages are used to distinguish various colors.

Perception

114. Aruego, Jose, and Dewey, Ariane. *We Hide, You Seek* (PS). Illus. by author. 1979, Greenwillow $7.95; LB $7.63. An almost wordless picture book in which a rhinoceros sets out to find his friends who are playing hide-and-seek with him.

115. Baylor, Byrd. *The Other Way to Listen* (K–3). Illus. by Peter Parnall. 1978, Scribner $7.95. An old man teaches a young boy how to listen.

116. Brown, Marcia. *Touch Will Tell* (1–4). Illustrated. 1979, Watts $4.95; LB $7.90. A concept book that explores a sense of touch and increases one's awareness.

117. Brown, Marcia. *Walk with Your Eyes* (1–4). Illustrated. 1979, Watts $4.95; LB $7.90. A reader's powers of observation are highlighted through a nature walk.

118. Carle, Eric. *A Very Long Tail: A Folding Book* (PS). Illus. by author. 1972, Crowell paper $1.95. A mouse scampers along what he thinks is a tail, but is actually a snake, in this folding book whose companion volume is *The Very Long Train* (1972, Crowell $1.95).

119. Domanska, Janina. *What Do You See?* (PS–1). Illus. by author. 1974, Macmillan $6.95. The frog, the fly, the fern, and the bat each see the world from a different point of view in this vibrantly illustrated book.

120. Hoban, Tana. *Look Again!* (PS–2). Illus. by author. 1971, Macmillan $6.95. A concept book in which photographs of objects appear in part, as a whole, and then as a part within a composition.

121. Livermore, Elaine. *Find the Cat* (PS–2). Illus. by author. 1973, Houghton $5.95; paper $1.95. A puzzle book with a cat skillfully hidden in a series of pictures.

122. Matthiesen, Thomas. *Things to See: A Child's World of Familiar Objects* (PS–2). Illus. by author. 1966, Platt $2.95. Colored pictures of objects, with brief lines of text facing them.

123. Shaw, Charles G. *It Looked Like Spilt Milk* (K–2). Illus. by author. 1947, Harper $7.89. White material appears on each page, but its identity is not revealed until the end.

124. Spier, Peter. *Crash! Bang! Boom!* (PS–1). Illus. by author. 1972, Doubleday $6.95; paper $2.95. The author captures the visual essence of a variety of sounds that come from inanimate objects.

125. Spier, Peter. *Gobble, Growl, Grunt* (PS–1). Illus. by author. 1971, Doubleday $7.95; paper $2.95. Over 600 colorful animals march across the pages, with text consisting of the sounds each makes.

126. Withers, Carl. *Tale of a Black Cat* (PS–1). Illus. by Alan E. Cober. 1966, Holt $4.95. The storyteller draws the pictures as he tells the story of the adventures of Tommy and Sally with a surprise ending.

127. Zacharias, Thomas, and Zacharias, Wanda. *But Where Is the Green Parrot?* (K–3). Illus. by author. 1968, Delacorte $4.95; LB $4.58; paper $2.75. A puzzle book in which a green parrot is artfully hidden in each of the 9 double-page illustrations.

Size and Shape

128. Brown, Marcia. *Listen to a Shape* (2–4). Illus. by author. 1979, Watts $4.95; LB $7.90. A variety of shapes are explored in simple text and colored photographs.

129. Budney, Blossom. *A Kiss Is Round* (PS–K). Illus. by Vladimir Bobri. 1954, Lothrop $6.96. A picture book that stresses the concept of roundness, with original and humorous illustrations.

130. Charlip, Remy, and Joyner, Jerry. *Thirteen* (1–3). Illus. by author. 1975, Parents $5.95; LB $5.41. A wordless concept book consisting of 13 picture sequences in which shapes evolve into new forms.

131. Emberley, Ed. *Ed Emberley's Amazing Look Through Book* (PS–1). Illus. by author. 1979, Little $4.95. A puzzle book in which youngsters must identify shapes.

132. Emberley, Ed. *The Wing on a Flea: A Book About Shapes* (PS–2). Illus. by author. 1961, Little $6.95. Through rhymes and colorful drawings, children are shown how to identify shapes in everyday objects around them.

133. Hoban, Tana. *Circles, Triangles, and Squares* (PS–2). Illus. by author. 1974, Macmillan $6.95. A series of 5 photographs show the 3 most familiar geometric forms.

134. Hoban, Tana. *Over, Under and Through and Other Spacial Concepts* (K–2). Illus. by author. 1973, Macmillan $6.95. Spacial concepts are conveyed through brief text and photographs.

135. Hoban, Tana. *Shapes and Things* (K–1). 1970, Macmillan $6.95. A recognition book that is a collection of photographs.

136. Kalan, Robert. *Blue Sea* (K–3). Illus. by Donald Crews. 1979, Greenwillow $6.95. Big fish and little fish in the sea convey the idea of size.

137. Kuskin, Karla. *Herbert Hated Being Small* (K–2). 1979, Houghton $6.95. A short boy and tall girl decide to run away. Also use: *Lets Find Out What's Big and What's Small* by Martha Shapp and Charles Shapp (1975, Watts $4.90).

138. Mathews, Louise. *Gator Pie* (1–3). Illus. by Jeni Bassett. 1979, Dodd $6.95. Fractions are taught when 2 alligators decide to cut up a pie for their friends.

139. Myller, Rolf. *How Big Is a Foot?* (K–2). Illus. by author. 1962, Atheneum paper $.95. The problem of relative sizes, humorously and imaginatively described.

140. Reiss, John J. *Shapes* (PS–1). Illus. by author. 1974, Bradbury $7.95. Shapes, such as oval, circle, triangle, rectangle, and square, are presented to young children in vivid primary colors.

141. Schlein, Miriam. *Fast Is Not a Ladybug: A Book about Fast and Slow Things* (K–2). Illus. by Leonard Kessler. 1953, Children's Press $5.95. It involves such disparate elements as a fire engine and a cloud on a lazy day. Also use: *Heavy Is a Hippopotamus* (1954, Childrens Press $5.95).

142. Srivastava, Jane Jonas. *Spaces, Shapes and Sizes* (PS–2). Illus. by Loretta Lustig. 1980, Crowell $7.89. An easily read account that explains the concept of volume.

143. Ungerer, Tomi. *Snail, Where Are You?* (PS–1). Illus. by author. 1962, Harper $7.89. The shape of a snail on the first page is repeated on each succeeding page, where young children delight in finding the shape.

144. Wildsmith, Brian. *What the Moon Saw* (PS–1). Illus. by author. 1978, Oxford $7.95. The Sun shows the Moon many things that involve such basic concepts as numbers and weight. Also use: *Let's Find Out What's Light and What's Heavy* by Martha Shapp and Charles Shapp (1975, Watts $4.90).

145. Youldon, Gillian. *Shapes* (PS–K). Illustrated. 1979, Watts $2.95; LB $4.90. Five basic forms, such as square and circle, are explained and illustrated.

146. Youldon, Gillian. *Sizes* (PS–K). Illustrated. 1979, Watts $2.95; LB $4.90. The relative differences between being big and little are explored in this imaginative picture book.

Nursery Rhymes and Bedtime Books

Nursery Rhymes

147. Alderson, Brian, ed. *Cakes and Custard: Children's Rhymes* (K–4). Illus. by Helen Oxenbury. 1975, Morrow $9.95. A large, bounteous collection that extends from traditional nursery rhymes to the work of contemporary writers.

148. Bayley, Nicola, illus. *Nicola Bayley's Book of Nursery Rhymes* (PS–K). 1977, Knopf $4.95; LB $5.99. A luxuriously illustrated collection of well-known nursery rhymes.

149. Blake, Pamela, ed. *Peep Show: A Little Book of Rhymes* (PS–3). Illustrated. 1973, Macmillan $3.95. This small book of traditional rhymes includes such favorites as "Bobby Shaftoe."

150. Blegvad, Erik, illus. *Burnie's Hill: A Traditional Rhyme* (K–2). 1977, Atheneum $6.95. A traditional British question-and-answer rhyme, beautifully illustrated with luminous watercolor paintings.

151. Blegvad, Lenore, ed. *This Little Pig-a-Wig and Other Rhymes About Pigs* (K–2). Illus. by Erik Blegvad. 1978, Atheneum $7.95. Twenty-two rhymes involved with the doings of pigs.

152. Bodecker, N.M., ed. and illus. *It's Raining Said John Twaining: Danish Nursery Rhymes* (PS–K). 1973, Atheneum $6.95. Comic, detailed drawings illustrate this fresh collection of nursery rhymes that are Danish in origin but universal in appeal.

153. Briggs, Raymond, ed. and illus. *The Mother Goose Treasury* (PS–2). 1966, Coward $9.99. Bold, humorous drawings bring fresh vitality to this collection of 408 rhymes.

154. Brooke, Leslie, illus. *Johnny Crow's Garden* (PS). 1903, Warne $5.95. Amusing nonsense rhyme illustrated with 8 full-page drawings in color and 39 black-and-white pictures. Sequels: *Johnny Crow's Party* (1907, Warne $5.95) and *Johnny Crow's New Garden* (1935, Warne $5.95).

155. Brooke, Leslie, illus. *Ring O'Roses* (PS–2). 1977, Warne $7.95. An action-filled series of pictures gaily illustrate these classic Mother Goose rhymes.

156. Caldecott, Randolph. *Randolph Caldecott's John Gilpin and Other Stories* (K–3). Illus. by author. 1977, Warne $9.95. Subtitle: "Containing: The diverting History of John Gilpin; The House that Jack Built; The Frog He Would a-Wooing Go; The Milkmaid"

157. Chorao, Kay, illus. *The Baby's Lap Book* (PS–K). 1977, Dutton $6.95. Soft pencil drawings illustrate such familiar Mother Goose rhymes as "Jack Be Nimble" and "Old King Cole."

158. De Angeli, Marguerite, illus. *Book of Nursery and Mother Goose Rhymes* (PS–2). 1954, Doubleday $7.95. A collection of 376 rhymes illustrated in soft watercolors.

159. DeForest, Charlotte B. *The Prancing Pony: Nursery Rhymes from Japan* (PS–2). Illus. by Keiko Aida. 1968, Weatherhill $4.50. A visually delightful volume of 53 Japanese nursery songs and rhymes freely adapted into English verse for children, delicately illuminated in a form of rice paper collage.

160. DeKay, Ormonde, trans. *Rimes de la Mere Oie: Mother Goose Rhymes* (2–4). Illus. by Seymour Chwast et al. 1971, Little $8.95. Sixty popular Mother Goose rhymes in French with English translations.

161. Domanska, Janina, illus. *I Saw a Ship A-Sailing* (PS–K). 1972, Macmillan $4.95. Geometric, stylized, bold colorful designs illustrate this well-known rhyme.

162. Domanska, Janina, illus. *If All the Seas Were One Sea* (PS–1). 1971, Macmillan $5.95. Blue and black etchings with red and green overlays create flowing, swirling illustrations that give a new dimension to an old nursery rhyme.

163. Frasconi, Antonio, illus. *The House That Jack Built* (1–4). 1958, Harcourt $6.50. A picture book in French and English, enhanced by modern woodcuts.

164. Fujikawa, Gyo, illus. *Mother Goose* (PS–1). 1968, Grosset $5.95; paper $2.95. An oversize book that contains 300 rhymes.

165. Galdone, Paul, illus. *The House That Jack Built* (K–2). 1961, McGraw $7.95. A joyful interpretation of the familiar old nursery rhyme with colorful pictures.

166. Galdone, Paul, illus. *Old Mother Hubbard and Her Dog* (PS–1). 1960, McGraw $7.95. Lively humorous illustrations accompany this favorite Mother Goose rhyme.

167. Galdone, Paul, illus. *The Old Woman and Her Pig* (K–2). 1960, McGraw $7.95. Delightful, quaint illustrations tell the cumulative story of the old woman who has difficulty getting her pig over the stile and safely home from market.

168. Greenaway, Kate, illus. *Mother Goose: Or, The Old Nursery Rhymes* (K–2). 1882, Warne $3.95. Characteristic drawings in color by the nineteenth-century illustrator.

169. Hogrogian, Nonny, illus. *One I Love, Two I Love: And Other Loving Mother Goose Rhymes* (PS). 1972, Dutton $5.95. Seventeen nursery rhymes on the subject of love, illustrated with warmth and humor.

170. Ivimey, John W. *Complete Version of Ye Three Mice* (PS–2). Illus. by Walton Corbould. 1979, Warne $6.95. The traditional English nursery rhyme in an edition first published in 1904.

171. Jeffers, Susan, ed. and illus. *If Wishes Were Horses and Other Rhymes* (K–1). 1979, Dutton $9.95. Eight Mother Goose rhymes involving horses.

172. Jeffers, Susan, ed. and illus. *Three Jovial Huntsmen* (K–2). 1973, Bradbury $7.95. All sorts of animals are well hidden in the forest picture as 3 hunters forage for their dinner.

173. Jensen, Virginia Allen, trans. *Old Mother Hubbard and Her Dog* (PS–K). Illus. by Ib Spang Olsen. 1976, Coward $6.95. A delightfully illustrated Swedish version of the old nursery rhyme.

174. Kepes, Juliet, illus. *Lady Bird, Quickly* (PS–1). 1964, Atlantic/Little $5.95. Picture-book version of the familiar rhyme.

175. Lobel, Arnold, illus. *Gregory Griggs and Other Nursery Rhyme People* (PS–1). 1978, Greenwillow $7.95; LB $7.35. Out-of-the-ordinary nursery rhymes are included in this refreshingly different collection.

176. Marshall, James. *James Marshall's Mother Goose* (PS–1). Illus. by author. 1979, Farrar $8.95. An ebullient, breezy treatment of traditional material.

177. Mayer, Mercer. *Little Monster's Mother Goose* (K–2). Illus. by author. 1979, Golden $3.95; LB $7.62. Within the framework of a stage show, popular monsters illustrate Mother Goose rhymes.

178. Miller, Mitchell, ed. and illus. *One Misty Moisty Morning: Rhymes From Mother Goose* (PS–1). 1970, Farrar $2.95. Twenty-one little-known Mother Goose rhymes with full-page, storytelling pictures.

179. Ness, Evaline, illus. *Old Mother Hubbard and Her Dog* (PS–3). 1972, Holt $4.95; paper $1.45. Thirteen verses about this improbable pair, deftly illustrated with infectious humor.

180. Opie, Iona, and Opie, Peter., eds. *The Oxford Nursery Rhyme Book* (K–3). Illus. by Joan Hassall. 1955, Oxford $15.95. The most complete Mother Goose collection, with 800 rhymes for reading aloud. Also use: *The Opies Oxford Dictionary of Nursery Rhymes* (1951, Oxford $22.50).

181. Peppe, Rodney, ed. and illus. *Hey Riddle Diddle!* (PS–3). 1971, Penguin paper $2.50. Forty-five Mother Goose rhymes surrounded with detailed collages that will offer surprises long after the riddles themselves have been solved.

182. Petersham, Maud, and Petersham, Miska., illus. *The Rooster Crows: A Book of American Rhymes and Jingles* (K–2). 1945, Macmillan $5.95; paper $.95. Rope skipping, counting, and other game rhymes form the bulk of this jaunty collection.

183. Provensen, Alice, and Provensen, Martin., illus. *The Mother Goose Book* (PS–K). 1976, Random $6.95. The familiar old favorites in eighteenth-century dress.

184. Rackham, Arthur, illus. *Mother Goose Nursery Rhymes* (PS–3). 1975, Viking $7.95. A modern edition of a book first published in 1913.

185. Roffey, Maureen. *The Grand Old Duke of York* (PS–K). Illus. by author. 1978, Bodley $4.25. A traditional rhyme illustrated with verve and daring.

186. Rojankovsky, Feodor, illus. *The Tall Book of Mother Goose* (PS). 1942, Harper $4.95; LB $5.49. These 100 old favorites are presented in an unusual format with bold illustrations.

187. Sendak, Maurice, illus. *Hector Protector, and As I Went over the Water* (K–1). 1965, Harper $8.95; LB $8.79. Two brief Mother Goose rhymes expanded with many drawings that make them both humorous and appealing.

188. Spier, Peter. *"Hurrah, We're Outward Bound."* (K–3). Illus. by author. 1968, Doubleday $3.95. Minutely detailed illustrations highlight this handsome edition of a Mother Goose rhyme.

189. Spier, Peter, illus. *London Bridge Is Falling Down!* (K–3). 1967, Doubleday $6.95; paper $1.49. The old rhyme colorfully depicted against the background of a bustling London town; musical score included.

190. Stanley, Diane, illus. *Fiddle-I-Fee: A Traditional American Chant* (PS–1). 1979, Little $7.95. A young girl welcomes all her animal friends to dinner in this cumulative chant.

191. Tarrant, Margaret Winifred. *Nursery Rhymes* (PS–2). Illustrated. 1978, Crowell $6.95. One hundred favorite rhymes illustrated with the world-famous old pictures of Tarrant.

192. Tucker, Nicholas, ed. *Mother Goose Abroad* (K–3). Illus. by Trevor Stubley. 1975, Crowell $6.50; LB $7.39. Engaging nursery rhymes from Europe.

193. Tudor, Tasha, illus. *Mother Goose* (PS–2). 1944, Walck $6.95. A collection of 77 nursery rhymes with colored illustrations.

194. Wildsmith, Brian, illus. *Brian Wildsmith's Mother Goose: A Collection of Nursery Rhymes* (PS–2). 1964, Watts $6.90; paper $4.95. Original artistic conceptions of the old rhymes with wonderful action in brilliantly colored animal and human figures.

195. Wright, Blanche Fisher, illus. *Real Mother Goose* (PS–3). 1916, Rand $5.95; LB $5.97. Golden anniversary edition with introduction by May Hill Arbuthnot.

Bedtime Books

196. Barrett, Judith. *I Hate to Go to Bed* (K–3). Illus. by Ray Cruz. 1977, Four Winds $5.50. Various excuses for not going to sleep are exposed in a humorous text with detailed illustrations.

197. Berends, Polly. *Ladybug and Dog and the Night Walk* (PS–1). Illus. by Cyndy Szekeres. 1980, Random $4.95; LB $4.99. A bedtime tale about Dog and Ladybug who watch the nighttime world.

198. Bottner, Barbara. *There Was Nobody There* (K–3). Illus. by author. 1978, Macmillan $6.95. A child fantasizes about being completely alone in the world at night.

199. Brown, Margaret Wise. *A Child's Good Night Book* (PS–K). Illus. by Jean Charlot. 1950, Addison $6.95. Animals and children prepare for bed in this rhythmically told story.

200. Brown, Margaret Wise. *Goodnight Moon* (PS). Illus. by Clement Hurd. 1947, Harper $4.95; LB $5.79; paper $1.95. A soothing go-to-sleep story.

201. Burningham, John. *The Blanket* (PS–1). Illus. by author. 1976, Crowell $3.79. One night a young child can't find his blanket.

202. Coker, Gylbert. *Naptime* (K–2). Illustrated. 1978, Delacorte $5.95; LB $5.47. A preschool situation about a young child's nap.

203. Crowley, Arthur. *The Boogey Man* (K–3). Illus. by Annie Gusman. 1978, Houghton $6.95. Sonny won't eat his liver, and as a result the boogey man arrives.

204. Fregosi, Claudia. *Are There Spooks in the Dark?* (K–3). Illus. by author. 1977, Four Winds $5.95. A brother and sister look for spooks.

205. Goffstein, M. B. *Sleepy People* (PS–1). Illustrated. 1979, Farrar $5.95. A nighttime book bound to induce sleep.

206. Hurd, Edith Thacher. *The Quiet Evening* (K–2). Illus. by author. 1978, Greenwillow $5.95; LB $5.71. A mood piece in which all forms of life quiet down after a busy day.

207. Marzollo, Jean. *Close Your Eyes* (PS–2). Illus. by Susan Jeffers. 1978, Dial $7.95; LB $7.45. A sleep book that tells 2 stories at the same time.

208. Mayer, Mercer. *There's a Nightmare in My Closet* (K–3). Illus. by author. 1968, Dial $6.46. A boy brings a creature out of the closet into a more friendly atmosphere.

209. Segal, Joyce. *It's Time to Go to Bed* (PS–1). Illus. by Robin Eaton. 1979, Doubleday $6.95. A bedtime story for those who don't want to go to bed.

210. Sharmat, Marjorie W. *Goodnight, Andrew, Goodnight, Craig* (PS–3). Illus. by Mary Chalmers. 1969, Harper $6.89. Two brothers in bunk beds can't get to sleep.

211. Ward, Andrew. *Baby Bear and the Long Sleep* (PS–2). Illus. by John Walsh. 1980, Little $8.95. A young bear has difficulty going to sleep in the winter.

212. Watson, Clyde. *Midnight Moon* (PS–1). Illus. by Susanna Natti. 1979, Collins $6.95; LB $6.91. The sandman takes a child to visit the Man in the Moon in this sleepy-time book.

213. Willoughby, Elaine Macmann. *Boris and the Monsters* (PS–1). Illus. by Lynn Munsinger. 1980, Houghton $7.95. Boris makes up many excuses because he is afraid to go to bed.

214. Zagone, Theresa. *No Nap for Me* (PS–K). Illus. by Lillian Hoban. 1978, Dutton $5.95. On her fourth birthday, Fay decides she no longer needs a nap.

215. Zalben, Jane Breskin. *Norton's Nighttime* (PS–K). Illus. by author. 1979, Collins $5.95; LB $5.91. Norton's nighttime fears are allayed by Rabbit and Possum.

216. Zolotow, Charlotte. *I Have a Horse of My Own* (PS–K). Illus. by Yoko Mitsuhashi. 1980, Crowell $7.89. At night a little girl and her horse share magical adventures.

217. Zolotow, Charlotte. *The Summer Night* (PS–K). Illus. by Ben Shecter. 1974, Harper $7.95; LB $7.89. A comfortable and comforting story about a little girl who goes to her father when she can't sleep, and they enjoy the night's sights and sounds together until she is ready for bed.

218. Zolotow, Charlotte. *The Sleepy Book* (1–3). Illus. by Vladimir Bobri. 1958, Lothrop $6.00. How children and various animals go to sleep; rich, dusky blue illustrations.

Stories without Words

219. Alexander, Martha. *Bobo's Dream* (PS–2). Illus. by author. 1970, Dial $4.95; LB $4.58; paper $1.75. A small dachshund's dream becomes reality as the outstanding illustrations unfold the tale.

220. Alexander, Martha. *Out, Out, Out!* (PS–1). Illus. by author. 1968, Dial $4.58. A pigeon enters through the open window, and the clever, unruffled child—unlike the adults in this amusing situation—lures it out of the house; a pantomime for preschoolers with simple lilac and gray wash drawings.

221. Anno, Mitsumasa. *Anno's Italy* (PS–4). Illustrated. 1980, Collins $8.91. The Japanese artist sensitively portrays the cities and countryside of Italy.

222. Anno, Mitsumasa. *Anno's Journey* (1–3). Illus. by author. 1978, Collins $6.95; LB $6.91. A journey through town and country with many visual delights.

223. Anno, Mitsumasa. *Topsy-Turvies: Pictures to Stretch the Imagination* (PS–2). Illus. by author. 1970, Weatherhill $6.50. A picture book full of visual tricks and puzzles. See also the sequel: *Upside-Downers: More Pictures to Stretch the Imagination* (1971, Weatherhill $6.50).

224. Aruego, Jose. *Look What I Can Do* (K–2). Illus. by author. 1971, Scribner $6.95; paper $2.95. Almost wordless picture book about the antics that result when one carabao challenges another.

225. Bang, Molly. *The Grey Lady and the Strawberry Snatcher* (1–3). 1980, Four Winds $10.95. An exciting story of how the Grey Lady escapes the Strawberry Snatcher.

226. Barton, Byron. *Harry Is a Scaredy-Cat* (K–2). Illus. by author. 1974, Macmillan $5.95. Harry is afraid of everything until one fateful day he and his father go to the circus.

227. Briggs, Raymond. *The Snowman* (K–3). Illus. by author. 1979, Random $4.95. A small boy has adventures with the snowman he has made.

228. Burton, Marilee Robin. *The Elephant's Nest: Four Wordless Stories* (K–2). Illus. by author. 1979, Harper $7.95; LB $8.79. A series of fantasies that will appeal to imaginative youngsters.

229. Carle, Eric. *Do You Want to Be My Friend?* (PS–K). Illus. by author. 1971, Crowell $8.95. The end of an animal's tail appears on each page, and the child must guess the animal before turning the page to see the front end.

230. Carroll, Ruth. *What Whiskers Did* (K–3). Unpaged, color illustrations. 1950, Walck $5.95; Scholastic paper $1.25. A runaway puppy is befriended by a family of rabbits.

231. Crews, Donald, illus. *Truck* (1–3). 1980, Greenwillow $7.95; LB $7.63. The picture book that traces a truck trip from loading dock to its San Francisco destination.

232. de Groat, Diane. *Alligator's Toothache* (K–2). Illus. by author. 1977, Crown $4.95. An alligator is tricked into seeing a dentist to end his toothache.

233. de Paola, Tomie. *Flicks* (PS–1). Illustrated. 1979, Harcourt $5.95. Five stories are told as if they were silent screen epics.

234. Freeman, Don. *The Chalk Box Story* (PS–2). Illus. by author. 1976, Lippincott $5.95. Eight sticks of chalk create a series of pictures that tell a story.

235. Fromm, Lilo. *Muffel and Plums* (PS–K). Illus. by author. 1972, Macmillan $4.95. The misadventure of Plums, a rabbit, and his rescue from mishaps by Muffel, a lion, are portrayed in cartoonlike style.

236. Goodall, John S. *The Adventures of Paddy Pork* (PS–1). Illus. by author. 1968, Harcourt $4.95. A cleverly designed book that shows what befalls a young pig after he runs away to join a traveling circus. Its sequel is *The Ballooning Adventures of Paddy Pork* (1969, Harcourt $4.75). See also (Atheneum $4.95): *Paddy's Evening Out* (K–3) (1973) and *Paddy Pork's Holiday* (PS–K) (1976).

237. Goodall, John S. *Creepy Castle* (PS–K). Illus. by author. 1975, Atheneum $4.95. Depicted in a medieval setting, this concerns the adventures of 2 mice who get locked in a castle, are rescued, and foil the villain.

238. Goodall, John S. *An Edwardian Summer* (K–2). Illus. by author. 1976, Scribner $6.95.

Brother and sister have leisurely experiences on their way to and from school.

239. Goodall, John S. *Jacko* (PS–K). Illus. by author. 1972, Harcourt $4.75. Jacko, an·organ-grinder's monkey, escapes from his master and inadvertently stows away on a sailing ship, hidden in a sea chest. When pirates attack the ship, Jacko escapes and returns once more to his jungle home.

240. Goodall, John S. *The Midnight Adventures of Kelly, Dot and Esmeralda* (PS–2). Illus. by author. 1973, Atheneum $4.95. A koala bear, a rag doll, and a mouse journey together into a magic land.

241. Goodall, John S. *Naughty Nancy* (PS–K). Illus. by author. 1975, Atheneum $4.95. Nancy, a móuse, is the flower girl at her sister's wedding, with disastrous, although humorous, results.

242. Goodall, John S. *The Surprise Picnic* (PS–K). Illus. by author. 1977, Atheneum $4.95. A cat and 2 kittens set off on a picnic and run into many complications. Lots of fun and adventure in this easy-to-follow plot.

243. Hartelius, Margaret A. *The Chicken's Child* (K–1). 1975, Doubleday $5.95. A hen hatches an alligator's egg.

244. Hauptmann, Tatjana. *Day in the Life of Petronella Pig* (1–3). Illus. by author. 1980, Mayflower $12.95. The adventures of a mother pig and her mischievous son.

245. Hoban, Tana. *Big Ones, Little Ones* (PS). Illus. by author. 1976, Greenwillow $6.25. A photographic wordless book that shows adult and young animals, some tame and some wild.

246. Hoban, Tana. *Where Is It?* (PS). Illus. by author. 1974, Macmillan $5.95. Large photographs show a rabbit searching for food—where will he find it?

247. Hogrogian; Nonny. *Apples* (PS–2). Illus. by author. 1972, Macmillan $4.95. A book on the beginnings of an apple orchard, which starts when various animals discard their apple cores.

248. Hughes, Shirley. *Up and Up* (K–2). Illustrated. 1979, Prentice-Hall $7.95. After many attempts, a young girl in fantasy achieves her goal to fly.

249. Hutchins, Pat. *Changes, Changes* (PS–1). Illus. by author. 1971, Macmillan $5.95. A wooden doll couple rearranges a set of building blocks to suit different situations.

250. Keats, Ezra Jack. *Psst! Doggie* (K–2). Illus. by author. 1973, Watts $4.95. A dog story illustrated by a master.

251. Kent, Jack. *The Egg Book* (PS–K). Illus. by author. 1975, Macmillan $5.95. A hen tries desperately to hatch a few eggs, but keeps getting baby creatures that are not chicks. Success finally crowns her efforts, and there is a happy chick following her around.

252. Kessler, Ethel, and Kessler, Leonard. *Big Red Bus* (K–2). Illus. by author. 1957, Doubleday $6.95. Pictures recount all of the many sights on a bus ride.

253. Krahn, Fernando. *Catch That Cat!* (4–6). Illustrated. 1978, Dutton $5.95. A boy chases a cat and has a sea adventure.

254. Krahn, Fernando. *A Funny Friend from Heaven* (1–3). Illus. by author. 1977, Lippincott $6.95. An angel and a hobo are changed into clowns. Also use: *April Fools* (1974, Dutton $5.95).

255. Krahn, Fernando. *The Mystery of the Giant's Footprints* (PS–1). Illus. by author. 1977, Dutton $5.95. A family tracks down the origins of giant footsteps in the snow. Also use: *Self-Made Snowman* (1974, Lippincott $5.95).

256. Krahn, Fernando. *Robot-Bot-Bot* (1–3). Illustrated. 1979, Dutton $5.95. A little girl decides to rewire a robot who has been doing housework.

257. Krahn, Fernando. *Who's Seen the Scissors?* (PS–1). Illus. by author. 1975, Dutton $5.95. A self-propelled pair of scissors causes havoc in town.

258. Mari, Iela, and Mari, Enzo. *The Apple and the Moth* (PS–K). Illus. by Iela Mari. 1970, Pantheon $4.99. A moth larva feeding within the apple emerges, spins a cocoon, flies off, and lays an egg on an apple blossom. A clear presentation of the reproductive cycle.

259. Mari, Iela, and Mari, Enzo. *Chicken and the Egg* (PS–K). Illus. by author. 1970, Pantheon $4.99. Wordless story of a chicken from egg to young chick.

260. Mayer, Mercer. *Ah-Choo* (K–2). Illus. by author. 1976, Dial $4.95; LB $4.58. A humorous tale told in imaginative pictures.

261. Mayer, Mercer. *A Boy, a Dog and a Frog* (PS–1). Illus. by author. 1967, Dial $3.95; LB $3.69. Engaging pen-and-ink drawings will delight youngsters into supplying the story line for the boy and his dog on their frog hunt. Sequel: *Frog, Where Are You?* (1969, Dial $3.95; LB $3.69). Also use (Dial $3.95; LB $3.69): *A Boy, a Dog, a Frog and a Friend* (1971), *Frog on His Own* (1973), and *Frog Goes to Dinner* (1974).

262. Mayer, Mercer. *The Great Cat Chase: A Wordless Book* (PS–K). 1975, Scholastic $3.95. A cat, who rebels against being dressed up and taken for a ride in a baby carriage, leads 3 children on a wild chase as he tries to make his escape.

263. Mayer, Mercer. *Two Moral Tales* (K–2). Illus. by author. 1974, Scholastic $3.95. Two fables illustrated with humor and style. Also use: *Two More Moral Tales* (1974, Scholastic $3.95).

264. Mayer, Mercer, and Mayer, Marianna. *One Frog Too Many* (PS–K). Illus. by author. 1975, Dial $3.50; LB $3.39. This describes Frog's attempts to rid himself of a new rival—another small frog.

265. Oakley, Graham. *Graham Oakley's Magical Changes* (K–6). Illustrated. 1980, Atheneum $12.95. Split pages create a multitude of new objects and shapes.

266. Turkle, Brinton. *Deep in the Forest* (PS–1). Illus. by author. 1976, Dutton $5.95. In a reversal of the Goldilocks story, a mischievous bear tries the porridge, chairs, and beds.

267. Ueno, Noriko. *Elephant Buttons* (PS). Illus. by author. 1973, Harper $5.95; LB $6.89. An amusing book that shows all elephants with numerous buttons. As the buttons pop open, they reveal another animal and so on until finally a little mouse's buttons pop open, and an elephant balloons out!

268. Van Soelen, Philip. *Cricket in the Grass, and Other Stories* (K–3). Illus. by author. 1979, Sierra $9.95; LB $4.95. The food chain told in 5 picture stories.

269. Ward, Lynd. *The Silver Pony: A Story in Pictures* (2–4). Illus. by author. 1973, Houghton $7.95. Handsome pictures grace this story about a farm boy's imaginative adventures on a magnificent winged horse.

270. Wezel, Peter. *The Good Bird* (PS–1). Illus. by author. 1966, Harper $7.89. A picture story of a friendly pink bird who shares a worm with a goldfish.

Picture Books

Imaginative Stories

Imaginary Animals

271. Alexander, Martha. *And My Mean Old Mother Will Be Sorry, Blackboard Bear* (PS–2). Illus. by author. 1972, Dial $4.95; LB $4.58. Anthony and his friendly bear run away and spend an uncomfortable night in a cave.

272. Alexander, Martha. *Blackboard Bear* (PS–1). Illus. by author. 1969, Dial $4.95; LB $4.58; paper $1.50. Spurred on by the older children and told to play with his teddy bear, a small boy defiantly tosses the bear out of the window and then draws a picture of a big bear on his blackboard. The bear steps right down and becomes his playmate in this engaging picture book.

273. Alexander, Martha. *I Sure Am Glad to See You, Blackboard Bear* (PS–1). Illus. by author. 1976, Dial $4.95; paper $1.75. A boy and his imaginary friend, a teddy bear, put his tormentors in their place.

274. Alexander, Martha. *We're in Big Trouble, Blackboard Bear* (PS–1). Illus. by author. 1980, Dial $6.95; LB $6.46. Bear steals some food and gets into real trouble.

275. Allard, Harry. *Bumps in the Night* (K–3). Illus. by James Marshall. 1979, Doubleday $6.95; LB $7.90. Dudley the Stork thinks his house is haunted.

276. Allard, Harry. *I Will Not Go to Market Today* (PS–1). Illus. by James Marshall. 1979, Dial $6.95; LB $6.46. A chicken, whose first name is Fenimore, seems destined not to get to market.

277. Allard, Harry. *It's So Nice to Have a Wolf Around the House* (PS–2). Illus. by James Marshall. 1977, Doubleday $5.95. When an elderly man and his pets decide they need a fresh face about the place, a wolf who is a former bank robber pretends to be a dog and applies for the post.

278. Allen, Pamela. *Mr Archimedes' Bath* (PS–2). Illustrated. 1980, Lothrop $8.95; LB $8.59. Every time he and his animal friends take a bath together, the tub overflows.

279. Anderson, Lonzo. *Mister Biddle and the Birds* (1–3). Illus. by Adienne Adams. 1971, Scribner $5.95. Mister Biddle gets 4 birds to help him to fly.

280. Annett, Cora. *The Dog Who Thought He Was a Boy* (K–3). Illus. by Walter Lorraine. 1965, Houghton $6.95; paper $.95. A puppy thinks he is his owner's little brother in a fun-filled story.

281. Artis, Vicki. *Brown Mouse and Vole* (1–3). Illus. by author. 1975, Putnam $5.29. Two friends and their amazing adventures.

282. Asch, Frank. *Macgooses' Grocery* (PS–1). Illus. by James Marshall. 1978, Dial $5.95; LB $5.47. A family decides to give up their duties and let an unhatched chick fend for itself.

283. Asch, Frank. *Moon Bear* (PS–K). Illus. by author. 1978, Scribner $7.95. A bear learns about the phases of the moon.

284. Asch, Frank. *Sand Cake* (K–2). Illus. by author. 1979, Parents $4.99. On the beach, Papa Bear makes a sand cake.

285. Asch, Frank. *Turtle Tale* (PS–2). Illus. by author. 1978, Dial $6.50; LB $6.29. Whether his head is in or out of his shell, the important thing is that the turtle has a choice.

286. Bach, Alice. *The Most Delicious Camping Trip Ever* (K–2). Illus. by Steven Kellogg. 1976, Harper $5.95; LB $6.89; Dell paper $.95. Two bear cubs and Aunt Bear prepare for a camping trip, which turns out to be more fun than they had expected.

287. Bach, Alice. *Smartest Bear and His Brother Oliver* (2–4). Illus. by Steven Kellogg. 1975, Harper $5.95; Dell paper $.95. Ronald learns the contents of a whole encyclopedia to be smarter than his brother.

288. Baker, Alan. *Benjamin's Dreadful Dream* (1–3). Illus. by author. 1980, Lippincott $7.95. A bespectacled mouse has a series of strange adventures, but finally gets back to his own bed.

289. Bate, Lucy. *Little Rabbit's Loose Tooth* (PS–K). Illus. by Diane deGroat. 1975, Crown $5.95; Scholastic paper $1.50. Little Rabbit loses her first tooth and makes the most of it in this beguiling story.

290. Baumann, Hans. *The Hare's Race* (K–3). Illus. by Antoni Boratynski. 1976, Morrow $6.00. A mole challenges a hare to a race in which the latter predictably loses.

291. Bennett, R. *The Secret Hiding Place* (K–3). Illus. by author. 1960, Collins $5.21. Little Hippo attempts to find his own secret place where he can be alone.

292. Berson, Harold. *Henry Possum* (K–2). Illus. by author. 1973, Crown $5.95. Henry Possum is always too busy watching butterflies and humming birds to pay attention to the safety lessons his mother is trying to teach him.

293. Berson, Harold. *I'm Bored, Ma!* (K–2). Illus. by author. 1976, Crown $4.95. Steve, a bored rabbit, learns a lesson in resourcefulness from a pack rat.

294. Berson, Harold. *Joseph and the Snake* (K–1). Illus. by author. 1979, Macmillan $6.95. Joseph saves an ungrateful snake but is helped by a canny fox.

295. Berson, Harold. *A Moose Is Not a Mouse* (K–2). 1975, Crown $6.95. To this young mouse, a moose is just an oversize mouse, and so Victor grows in daring and attacks the cat, with almost disastrous results.

296. Bornstein, Ruth. *Little Gorilla* (PS). Illus. by author. 1976, Seabury $6.95. Even though Little Gorilla grows into a big gorilla, everyone still loves him.

297. Boynton, Sandra. *Hester in the Wind* (PS–2). Illus. by author. 1979, Harper $6.95; LB $7.89. Hester, the pig, has bad luck when she tries camping and canoeing.

298. Boynton, Sandra. *If at First . . .* (1–3). Illustrated. 1980, Little $6.95; paper $3.95. A little brown mouse must get an elephant up a hill.

299. Brandenberg, Franz. *Fresh Cider and Pie* (K–3). Illus. by Aliki. 1973, Macmillan $4.95. A fresh retelling of the story of the spider and the fly.

300. Brandenberg, Franz. *Nice New Neighbors* (K–2). Illus. by Aliki. 1977, Greenwillow $5.95; LB $5.71. A family of mice children generously include their neighbors who formerly spurned them when they decide to give a play—*The Three Blind Mice.*

301. Bridwell, Norman. *Clifford's Good Deeds* (PS–1). Illus. by author. 1976, Scholastic $4.95. Clifford is a large shaggy dog whose efforts to be helpful result in comic mishaps. Also use: *Clifford, the Big Red Dog* (1969, Scholastic, paper .95).

302. Brock, Betty. *No Flying in the House* (2–4). Illus. by Wallace Tripp. 1970, Harper $5.95; LB $5.79; Avon paper $.95. A small dog seeks shelter for herself and her human friends.

303. Brown, Margaret Wise. *The Runaway Bunny* (PS–K). Illus. by Clement Hurd. 1972, Harper $4.95; LB $5.79; paper $1.50. With 9 colorful illustrations, this new edition of an old favorite is a charming story of mother bunny's love for her restless youngster, who keeps trying to escape but is always found.

304. Browne, Anthony. *Bear Hunt* (PS–K). Illustrated. 1980, Atheneum $7.95. A white bear draws pictures to get himself out of tight scrapes.

305. De Brunhoff, Jean. *The Story of Babar, the Little Elephant* (PS). Illus. by author. 1933, Random $4.95; LB $5.99. A time-tested reading favorite about the little French elephant. Also use: *The Travels of Babar* (1937, $4.95; LB 5.99) and *Babar and Father Christmas* (1949, $4.95; LB $5.99).

306. De Brunoff, Laurent. *Babar's Mystery* (PS–1). Illus. by author. 1978, Random $3.95; LB $4.99. Babar helps capture a robber in this more recent addition to the vast Babar series.

307. Burningham, John. *Would You Rather . . .* (PS–2). 1978, Crowell $8.95; LB $8.49. Riding a bull into a supermarket is one of the imaginative situations described in this humorous book.

308. Byars, Betsy. *The Last Snail* (K–2). Illus. by author. 1975, Viking $5.95. How does a snail make lace? Snail doesn't know, but she is glad to give some to each animal that asks, as long as it lasts.

309. Calhoun, Mary. *Cross-Country Cat* (K–2). Illus. by Erick Ingraham. 1979, Morrow $6.95; LB $6.67. A Siamese named Henry sets out on a cross-country skiing adventure.

310. Cameron, John. *If Mice Could Fly* (PS–1). Illustrated. 1974, Atheneum $8.95. This amusing picture book explores the possible consequences if mice became as powerful as cats.

311. Carle, Eric. *The Grouchy Ladybug* (PS–K). Illus. by author. 1977, Crowell $7.95; LB $7.89. A grouchy ladybug, who is looking for a fight, challenges every insect and animal she meets regardless of size. Brilliantly illustrated in collage, the pages vary in size with the size of the animal.

312. Carlson, Natalie Savage. *Time for the White Egret* (K–2). Illus. by Charles Rovinson. 1978, Scribner $7.95. A young egret's adventures in the search of Time.

313. Charmatz, Bill. *The Cat's Whiskers* (K–2). Illus. by author. 1969, Macmillan $5.95. A cat works wonders with his whiskers.

314. Clymer, Eleanor. *Horatio Goes to the Country* (K–2). Illus. by Robert Quackenbush. 1978, Atheneum $6.95. Horatio, the cat, takes an instant dislike to country living and longs to go back to the city.

315. Clymer, Eleanor. *Horatio Solves a Mystery* (K–2). Illus. by Robert Quackenbush. 1980, Atheneum $8.95. Horatio, the cat, discovers that a mischievous monkey is responsible for some mysterious thefts.

316. Clymer, Eleanor. *Horatio's Birthday* (PS–1). Illus. by Robert Quackenbush. 1976, Atheneum $6.95. Horatio, a large black cat, is bored with his life and goes out on the town one evening. The next day, when he celebrates his birthday, he has a new companion, a small yellow cat, to share his domestic life.

317. Clymer, Eleanor. *Leave Horatio Alone* (PS–1). Illus. by Robert Quackenbush. 1974, Atheneum $6.95. Horatio, a middle-aged cat, is annoyed when other homeless animals are brought into the household, and he runs away. He finds a family with no pets but several children, and is happy to return to his original home.

318. Cole, Brock. *No More Baths* (PS–1). Illus. by author. 1980, Doubleday $7.95; LB $8.90. Jessie thinks she would rather live with animals than take baths.

319. Conford, Ellen. *Eugene the Brave* (1–3). Illus. by John Larrecq. 1978, Little $5.95. Possum Geraldine pokes fun at her brother's fear of the dark but appreciates his help when she falls in a hole.

320. Conford, Ellen. *Impossible Possum* (1–3). Illus. by Rosemary Wells. 1971, Little $5.95. Tale of a young possum who has an impossible time learning to hang by his tail.

321. Conford, Ellen. *Just the Thing for Geraldine* (K–2). Illus. by John Larrecq. 1974, Little $5.95. "Do your own thing" is the message. Poor Geraldine didn't seem to have any artistic accomplishments until her family found out that she excelled as a juggler.

322. Coombs, Patricia. *Tilabel* (1–3). Illus. by author. 1978, Lothrop $5.95; LB $5.71. A takeoff on the Rumpelstiltskin story.

323. Craft, Ruth. *Winter Bear* (PS–1). Illus. by Erik Blegvad. 1975, Atheneum $7.95; paper $2.50. Three children on a wintry day come upon a toy bear, which they take home and lovingly wash, dry, and dress.

324. Cressey, James. *Fourteen Rats and a Rat-Catcher* (1–3). Illus. by Tamasin Cole. 1978, Prentice-Hall $6.95. A rat catcher resolves a difference between an old lady and her rats.

325. Cressey, James. *Pet Parrot* (K–2). Illus. by Tamasin Cole. 1979, Prentice-Hall $6.95. A humorous tale of how a pet parrot helps out around the house.

326. Dahl, Roald. *The Enormous Crocodile* (K–3). Illus. by Quentin Blake. 1978, Knopf $4.95; LB $5.99. Animals band together to save a group of children from becoming a crocodile's lunch.

327. Dauer, Rosamond. *Bullfrog Builds a House* (1–3). Illus. by Byron Barton. 1977, Greenwillow $5.95; LB $5.71. Bullfrog gets assistance from Gertrude in building a house, but finds it is not complete until she comes to live with him.

328. Daugherty, James. *Andy and the Lion* (1–4). Illus. by author. 1938, Viking $6.95; Penguin paper $1.75. A popular, modern version of the story of Androcles and the lion.

329. Davis, Douglas F. *There's an Elephant in the Garage* (K–2). Illus. by Steven Kellogg. 1979, Dutton $7.95. April, her cat Zelda, and 2 bears hunt elephants.

330. Delaney, Ned. *Bert and Barney* (5–7). Illus. by author. 1979, Houghton $7.95. Two friends, a frog and an alligator, quarrel but make up.

331. Delton, Judy. *Brimhall Turns to Magic* (1–3). Illus. by Bruce Degen. 1979, Morrow $4.95; LB $4.76. Brimhall has trouble at magic classes even when Bear helps.

332. Delton, Judy. *On a Picnic* (K–2). Illus. by Mamoru Funai. 1979, Doubleday $4.95; LB $5.90. A goose and a gorilla realize their imperfections but end by accepting themselves.

333. Delton, Judy. *Penny-Wise, Fun-Foolish* (1–3). Illus. by Giulio Maestro. 1977, Crown $6.95. An ostrich learns that there is more to life than saving money.

334. Delton, Judy. *Two Good Friends* (1–2). Illus. by Giulio Maestro. 1974, Crown $5.50. Bear and Duck have different ways of keeping house—Duck is tidy but no cook; Bear is a good baker but very sloppy.

335. Delton, Judy. *Two Is Company* (K–2). Illus. by Giulio Maestro. 1976, Crown $4.95. Three isn't always a crowd, as Bear finds out after Chipmunk has been welcomed by Duck and becomes a valuable member of the group.

336. Dennis, Wesley. *Flip* (K–2). Illus. by author. 1941, Viking $2.75; Penguin paper $1.50. A young horse achieves his desire to jump across a brook in his pasture. Also use the sequel: *Flip and the Morning* (1951), Viking $3.95; Penguin paper $2.25.

337. de Paola, Tomie. *The Knight and the Dragon* (1–3). Illus. by author. 1980, Putnam $8.95; paper $3.95. An inexperienced knight and an inexperienced dragon prepare themselves to do battle.

338. du Bois, William Pene. *Bear Circus* (PS–2). Illus. by author. 1971, Viking $4.95; Penguin paper $1.50. The teddy bears of Koala Park put on a circus to repay their dear friends, the kangaroos, for saving their lives.

339. du Bois, William Pene. *Lion* (1–3). Illus. by author. 1956, Viking $5.95; Penguin paper $1.50. Brilliant picture book about a designer of animals who had great difficulty in making the word *lion* and the animal lion match.

340. Dumas, Philippe. *Lucie: A Tale of a Donkey* (K–3). 1980, Prentice-Hall $7.95. Lucie and a little boy named Louis see Paris together in this sequel to *The Story of Edward*.

341. Dumas, Philippe. *The Story of Edward* (K–3). Illus. by author. 1977, Parents $5.95; LB $5.41; paper $1.95. In this French picture book, Edward discovers that trying to disguise the fact that he is a donkey is self-defeating.

342. Duvoisin, Roger. *The Crocodile in the Tree* (K–3). Illus. by author. 1973, Knopf $5.99. Farm animals band together to protect a friendly crocodile.

343. Duvoisin, Roger. *Crocus* (PS–1). Illus. by author. 1977, Knopf $5.95; LB $6.99. Vain Crocus Crocodile has his teeth pulled, but is assuaged by receiving beautiful false ones.

344. Duvoisin, Roger. *Jasmine* (PS–K). Illus. by author. 1973, Knopf $5.99. Jasmine is a captivating plump pink cow who finds an old flower-bedecked bonnet, which she promptly wears. This upsets the other barnyard animals, who can't adjust to a cow that wants to be different.

345. Duvoisin, Roger. *Petunia* (K–2). Illus. by author. 1950, Knopf $5.99; paper $1.25. Petunia, the silly goose, finds a book and carries it around believing this will make her wise, until her own foolishness proves her wrong. More adventures at same price: *Petunia Takes a Trip* (1953) and *Petunia, I Love You* (1965).

346. Duvoisin, Roger. *Snowy and Woody* (3–5). Illus. by author. 1979, Random $6.95; LB $6.99. A polar bear moves south to a warmer climate but quarrels with a resident, Woody, the brown bear.

347. Duvoisin, Roger. *Veronica* (K–3). Illus. by author. 1961, Knopf $5.99; paper $.95. Picture story of a rugged individualist hippopotamus. Also use: (Knopf $5.99) *Our Veronica Goes to Petunia's Farm* (1962, also paper $1.25) and *Veronica and the Birthday Present* (1971).

348. Erickson, Russell E. *A Toad for Tuesday* (K–2). Illus. by Lawrence Di Fiori. 1974, Lothrop $5.09. Warton, a toad, is captured by Owl, who considers Warton perfect for his birthday dinner —on Tuesday. Wharton escapes, but finds that, after all, Owl has become his friend.

349. Erickson, Russell E. *Warton and Morton* (1–3). Illus. by Lawrence Di Fiori. 1976, Lothrop $4.95; Dell paper $.95. Two toads become separated in a swamp during an adventure-filled hike.

350. Erickson, Russell E. *Warton and the King of the Skies* (2–4). Illus. by Lawrence Di Fiori. 1978, Lothrop $5.95; LB $5.71. Two toads take off in a skyborne washtub.

351. Erickson, Russell E. *Warton and the Traders* (1–3). Illus. by Lawrence Di Fiori. 1979, Lothrop $5.95; LB $5.71. Warton the toad offers to help two wood rats get rid of a wildcat in exchange for a favor.

352. Ernst, Kathryn F. *Owl's New Cards* (K–2). Illus. by Diane deGroat. 1977, Crown $5.95. Owl tests his new set of playing cards on Beaver and Weasel with disastrous but amusing results.

353. Erskine, Jim. *The Snowman* (1–3). 1978, Crown $5.95. Two bear cubs quarrel over the snowman they have made.

354. Ets, Marie Hall. *Elephant in a Well* (PS–K). Illus. by author. 1972, Viking $4.50. Penguin paper $.75. A cumulative tale about the efforts of a horse, cow, goat, pig, lamb, dog, and finally a mouse to rescue an elephant, who has fallen into the well.

355. Ets, Marie Hall. *In the Forest* (PS). Illus. by author. 1944, Viking $5.95; Penguin paper $1.95. A small boy's adventures with his forest friends. Another animal story by the author: *Another Day* (1953, Viking $2.50).

356. Evans, Mari. *Jim Flying High* (3–4). Illus. by Ashley Bryan. 1979, Doubleday $7.95; LB $8.90. A flying fish lands in a tree and causes problems.

357. Farber, Norma. *How the Left-Behind Beasts Built a Raft* (1–3). Illus. by Antonio Frasconi.

1978, Walker $7.50; LB $7.45. The story of those animals left behind by Noah.

358. Fatio, Louise. *The Happy Lion's Vacation* (K–3). Illus. by Roger Duvoisin. 1967, McGraw $6.84. Instead of a planned vacation at the seashore, the Happy Lion finds himself in jail. Others in this series are: *The Happy Lion Roars* (1957, $6.84), *The Three Happy Lions* (1959, $6.84), *The Happy Lion's Quest* (1961, $6.84), and *The Happy Lion's Treasure* (1970, $5.72).

359. Fatio, Louise, and Duvoisin, Roger. *Marc and Pixie and the Walls in Mrs. Jones' Garden* (1–3). Illus. by Roger Duvoisin. 1975, McGraw $5.95; LB $5.72. Pixie, a Siamese cat, sets out to hurt the chipmunks, particularly fat Marc, who have invaded the garden.

360. Flack, Marjorie. *Ask Mr. Bear* (PS–1). Illus. by author. 1958, Macmillan $3.95; paper $1.25. To find a present for his mother's birthday, Danny asks a variety of animals for suggestions, with little success until he meets Mr. Bear.

361. Flora, James. *Sherwood Walks Home* (PS–1). Illus. by author. 1966, Harcourt $6.95. A very humorous story of Sherwood, a toy bear, who has to find someone to wind him up, and then he tries to reach home before the motor runs down.

362. Flora, James. *Stewed Goose* (K–3). Illus. by author. 1973, Atheneum $4.95. A zany story of the ways Benjamin B. Bear tries to trap Wacker, a silly goose. Also use: *Little Hatchy Hen* (1969; Harcourt $5.95).

363. Freeman, Don. *Beady Bear* (K–2). Illus. by author. 1954, Viking $4.95; Penguin paper $1.25. A toy bear is unhappy living in a cave like other bears and becomes happy when his young owner finds him.

364. Freeman, Don. *Corduroy* (PS–1). Illus. by author. 1968, Viking $6.50; Penguin paper $1.95. The amusing story of a toy bear whose one missing button from his green corduroy overalls almost costs him the opportunity of belonging to someone.

365. Freeman, Don. *Dandelion* (K–2). Illus. by author. 1964, Viking $6.50. A vain lion goes to a barber shop before a party and makes himself unrecognizable to his friends.

366. Freeman, Don. *Hattie the Backstage Bat* (K–2). Illus. by author. 1970, Viking $6.95. Hattie plans her debut for an opening night audience.

367. Freeman, Don. *Norman the Doorman* (PS–2). Illus. by author. 1959, Viking $6.95; Penguin paper $1.95. Norman is the doorman at the basement of the art museum and enjoys showing his rodent friends through its treasures.

368. Freeman, Don. *Penguins, of All People* (1–3). Illus. by author. 1971, Viking $4.95; LB $4.53. Ambassador Peary Byrd Penguin is called to the UN from Antarctica to help solve the problems of the world, but the mission turns into rollicking fun when a penguin delegation arrives to support the ambassador.

369. Freeman, Don. *A Pocket for Corduroy* (PS–1). Illus. by author. 1978, Viking $6.95. The adventures of the famous pet bear at the self-service laundry.

370. Freeman, Don. *Will's Quill* (K–2). Illus. by author. 1975, Viking $6.95; Penguin paper $1.95. Willoughby Waddle, a country goose, goes to Elizabethan London and there meets and helps Shakespeare write his new play with one of Willoughby's own quills.

371. Freschet, Berniece. *Bear Mouse* (K–2). Illus. by Donald Carrick. 1973, Scribner $6.95; Scholastic paper $1.25. The efforts of a bear, or meadow, mouse to sustain herself and her young family in winter are described, as well as her need to ward off predators who are also in search of food.

372. Freschet, Berniece. *Bernard of Scotland Yard* (K–3). Illus. by Gina Freschet. 1978, Scribner $7.95. Bernard, the mouse, fresh from *Bernard Sees The World*, is on the trail of some English jewel thieves.

373. Freschet, Berniece. *Bernard Sees the World* (K–3). Illus. by Gina Freschet. 1976, Scribner $5.95. Bernard, a mouse, decides to see the world, about which he has read so much, and he even makes a trip to the moon, returning home in time for Christmas with a tiny moon rock to add to the holiday decorations.

374. Freschet, Berniece. *Elephant and Friends* (1–3). Illus. by Glen Rounds. 1978, Scribner $6.95. A group of animals seek a new home in the forest.

375. Freschet, Berniece. *The Happy Dromedary* (1–3). Illus. by Glen Rounds. 1977, Scribner $5.95. An original story about how the dromedary got his characteristic appearance.

376. Freschet, Berniece. *Little Black Bear Goes for a Walk* (1–2). Illus. by Glen Rounds. 1977, Scribner $5.95. Little bear takes his first trip alone and encounters many predicaments, but returns home to be comforted by mother—having learned a measure of independence.

377. Friskey, Margaret. *Seven Diving Ducks* (1–3). Illus. by Jean Morey. 1965, Childrens Press $6.00. A frightened little duck conquers his fear of the water.

378. Gackenbach, Dick. *Hound and Bear* (PS–3). Illus. by author. 1976, Seabury $5.95. Hound finally agrees to stop playing tricks on long suffering Bear.

379. Gackenbach, Dick. *Pepper and All the Legs* (PS–2). Illus. by author. 1978, Seabury $6.95. The dachshund who appeared in *Claude the Dog* (1974) and *Claude and Pepper* (1976) (both Seabury $6.95) explores his leg's-eye view of people.

380. Gackenbach, Dick. *The Pig Who Saw Everything* (K–3). 1978, Seabury $6.95. Henry, a curious pig, explores the world outside the barnyard.

381. Gantos, Jack. *Rotten Ralph* (K–3). Illus. by author. 1976, Houghton $6.95. Ralph is truly a nasty cat—mean and disruptive—until he is reformed under unusual circumstances.

382. Gantos, Jack. *Worse Than Rotten, Ralph* (1–3). Illus. by Nicole Rubel. 1978, Houghton $6.95. Ralph again goes on the rampage.

383. Ginsburg, Mirra. *The Chick and the Duckling* (PS–K). Trans. and adapted from the Russian by V. Suteyev. Illus. by Jose Aruego and Ariane Dewey. 1972, Macmillan $5.95. A duck and a chick who hatch at the same time become constant companions, with the chick copying everything the duck does until they go for a swim, and then the chick changes his refrain from "me too" to "not me."

384. Ginsburg, Mirra. *Which Is the Best Place?* (PS–1). Illus. by Roger Duvoisin. 1976, Macmillan $6.95. A series of animals argue about which place is the best to rest.

385. Godden, Rumer. *A Kindle of Kittens* (K–2). Illus. by Lynne Byrnes. 1979, Viking $8.95. A mother cat must find homes for her kittens.

386. Graham, Al. *Timothy Turtle* (K–2). Illus. by Tony Palazzo. 1940, Harcourt $5.95; paper $1.35. Humorous verses and pictures describe what happens when Timothy Turtle decides to be an adventurer.

387. Graham, Margaret B. *Be Nice to Spiders* (PS–2). Illus. by author. 1967, Harper $5.95; LB $5.79. Helen, Billy's pet spider, makes all the animals at the zoo happy when she spins webs and catches flies for them.

388. Graham, Margaret B. *Benjy and the Barking Bird* (PS–1). Illus. by author. 1971, Harper $5.79. Tilly the parrot can bark like a dog, and Benjy, a small sensitive dog, is very jealous and takes revenge.

389. Gretz, Susanna. *The Bears Who Went to the Seaside* (K–2). Illus. by author. 1973, Follett $4.95; LB $5.97; Scholastic paper $1.50. Five bears and Fred, their dalmatian friend, have fun at the beach. Also use: *The Bears Who Stayed Indoors* (1970, Follett $5.95; LB $5.97).

390. Hale, Irina. *Chocolate Mouse and Sugar Pig* (PS–K). 1979, Atheneum $8.95. Subtitle: "How They Ran Away to Escape Being Eaten."

391. Hall, Malcolm. *Forecast* (1–3). Illus. by Bruce Degen. 1977, Coward $4.99. Caroline Porcupine of the *Claws n' Paws* newspaper staff takes over the job of weather forecasting with amusing results.

392. Hayes, Geoffrey. *Patrick Comes to Puttyville* (K–3). Illus. by author. 1978, Harper $5.95; LB $5.79. Five adventures of the stuffed bear who also appeared in the author's *Bear by Himself* (1976, Harper $4.95; LB $5.89).

393. Heide, Florence Parry, and Van Clief, Sylvia Worth. *Fables You Shouldn't Pay Any Attention To* (K–3). Illus. by Victoria Chess. 1978, Lippincott $6.95. An irreverent collection of fables where the moral of the stories are reversed.

394. Heine, Helme. *The Pig's Wedding* (PS–3). Illus. by author. 1979, Atheneum $7.95. Curlytail and Porker say "I do."

395. Hellsing, Lennart. *The Wonderful Pumpkin* (PS–3). Illus. by Svend Otto. 1977, Atheneum $5.95. Two bears first use their giant pumpkin as a yacht and then as a balloon as they set out to see the world.

396. Henstra, Friso. *Wait and See* (1–3). Illus. by author. 1978, Addison $7.95. A man tries to feel important and succeeds in inventing the lowly safety pin.

397. Heuck, Sigrid. *The Stolen Apples* (K–3). Illus. by author. 1979, Hart $5.95. A horse searches for the thief who has stolen his apples.

398. Hoban, Lillian. *Harry's Song* (1–3). Illus. by author. 1980, Greenwillow $7.95; LB $7.63. Harry makes an unusual contribution to the rabbits' winter provisions.

399. Hoban, Russell. *Dinner at Alberta's* (K–2). Illus. by James Marshall. 1975, Crowell $5.50; LB $6.50. Arthur, a really sloppy crocodile, valiantly practices his table manners in preparation for dinner at Alberta's, with whom he is smitten.

400. Hoban, Russell. *The Little Brute Family* (K–3). Illus. by Lillian Hoban. 1969, Macmillan $4.50; paper $1.25. The Brute family and their equally disagreeable home are transformed by the actions of Baby Brute.

401. Hogrogian, Nonny. *Carrot Cake* (PS–3). Illus. by author. 1977, Greenwillow $6.95; LB $6.95. Two married rabbits have marital problems in this humorous story.

402. Holl, Adelaide. *Minnikin, Midgie and Moppet: A Mouse Story* (K–2). Illus. by Pricilla Hillman. 1977, Western $4.95; paper $1.95. Mrs. Mouse encounters all sorts of dangers when she tries to visit her young children.

403. Holl, Adelaide. *The Remarkable Egg* (K–2). Illus. by Roger Duvoisin. 1968, Lothrop $6.43. A series of birds are asked if they own the mysterious egg that has been placed in a nest.

404. Hutchins, Pat. *Good-Night, Owl* (PS–K). Illus. by author. 1972, Macmillan $4.95; paper $1.95. Owl is kept awake by different animal noises, as various animals perch on a branch of his tree; but when darkness falls, Owl has his turn and wakes everyone with his screeches.

405. Hutchins, Pat. *The Surprise Party* (PS–1). Illus. by author. 1969, Macmillan $6.95; paper $.95. In a clever takeoff on the childhood game "pass it on," the rabbit's colorful stylized animal friends so distort his invitation to a party that it really turns out to be quite a surprise. Another, about an inattentive hen: *Rosie's Walk* (1968, Macmillan $4.95; paper $1.25).

406. Jeschke, Susan. *Angela and Bear* (K–2). Illus. by author. 1979, Holt $6.95. Angela's bear steps out of the picture she has drawn with magic crayons, and they share adventures.

407. Jeschke, Susan. *Sidney* (K–3). Illus. by author. 1975, Holt $4.95. A chicken named Sidney pretends to be a fox and actually turns into one.

408. Joerns, Consuelo. *The Lost and Found Mouse* (K–2). Illus. by author. 1979, Four Winds $5.95. Cricket, a mouse, finds a new home in a doll's house.

409. Johnston, Tony. *Five Little Foxes and the Snow* (PS–K). Illus. by Cyndy Szekeres. 1977, Putnam $6.95. Gramma knits mittens for her young foxes so they can enjoy themselves in the snow.

410. Jones, Harold. *There and Back Again* (PS–3). Illus. by author. 1977, Atheneum $5.95. A toy rabbit left behind by children leaves on his own adventure.

411. Joslin, Sesyle, and Weisgard, Leonard. *Baby Elephant and the Secret Wishes* (K–2). Illus. by Leonard Weisgard. 1962, Harcourt $6.50. Fun with Baby Elephant for young readers.

412. Joslin, Sesyle, and Weisgard, Leonard. *Brave Baby Elephant* (K–2). Illus. by Leonard Weisgard. 1960, Harcourt $4.95. Baby Elephant prepares for a long trip, which is actually upstairs to bed.

413. Kellogg, Steven. *The Mysterious Tadpole* (K–3). Illus. by author. 1977, Dial $6.95; LB $6.46. When a tadpole grows at an alarming rate, Louis discovers his new pet is really a baby Loch Ness Monster.

414. Kepes, Juliet. *Run, Little Monkeys! Run, Run, Run!* (K–3). Illus. by author. 1974, Pantheon $5.99. Three jolly monkeys begin a wild humorous chase through the jungle.

415. Krahn, Fernando. *The Family Minus* (1–3). Illus. by author. 1977, Parents $5.95; LB $5.41. Eight furry youngsters find excitement in having a genius-inventor for a mother.

416. Kraus, Robert. *Another Mouse to Feed* (1–3). Illus. by Jose Aruego and Ariane Dewey. 1980, Windmill $8.95. A wacky mouse family finds it has another mouth to feed.

417. Kraus, Robert. *Boris Bad Enough* (K–2). Illus. by Jose Aruego and Ariane Dewey. 1976, Windmill $7.95. Boris, a young elephant, plays so many tricks on people that he becomes the despair of his parents.

418. Kraus, Robert. *Herman the Helper* (PS–K). Illus. by Jose Aruego and Ariane Dewey. 1974, Windmill $6.95. Herman, a green octopus, with his many arms is especially helpful to family and friends, and learns to help himself as well.

419. Kraus, Robert. *Leo the Late Bloomer* (PS–K). Illus. by Jose Aruego. 1973, Windmill $2.95. Leo, a lion, is just a late bloomer, as Mother tells Father, but Father is worried. But finally Leo blooms—he can read, write, and eat neatly. A beguiling, humorous story.

420. Kraus, Robert. *Milton the Early Riser* (PS–K). Illus. by Jose Aruego and Ariane Dewey. 1972, Windmill $7.95. A nonsensical story of Milton, a little panda bear who wakes up early one morning and finds all the other animals asleep. Finally by his sneezing he gets them awake, only to be so worn out that he falls asleep.

421. Kraus, Robert. *Noel the Coward* (PS–K). Illus. by Jose Aruego and Ariane Dewey. 1977, Windmill $7.95. Timidity triumphs in this story of a father and son who study self-defense together.

422. Kraus, Robert. *Owliver* (PS–1). Illus. by Jose Aruego and Ariane Dewey. 1974, Windmill $6.95. A fresh, funny, and engaging story of a small owl who imitates and play-acts whatever his mother or father want him to be—a doctor, lawyer, or actor —and then makes his own decision.

423. Kraus, Robert. *Whose Mouse Are You?* (PS–1). Illus. by Jose Aruego. 1970, Macmillan $5.95; paper $1.25. A young mouse is asked 8 questions by his family—which should delight young children who are asked similar questions by their families.

424. Lathrop, Dorothy P. *Who Goes There?* (K–2). Illus. by author. 1963, Macmillan $4.95. Two little children decide to give the animals a picnic.

425. Leaf, Munro. *Noodle* (K–2). Illus. by Ludwig Bemelmans. 1969, Four Winds $4.95; paper $.95. Noodle, the dachshund, tries to find a shape that is better for digging than his own.

426. Leaf, Munro. *The Story of Ferdinand* (K–4). Illus. by Robert Lawson. 1936, Viking $6.95. Penguin paper $1.50. The classic story of the bull who wants only to sit and smell flowers.

427. Le-Tan, Pierre. *Happy Birthday Oliver!* (K–2). Illus. by author. 1979, Random $2.95; LB $4.99. Oliver is convinced that everyone has forgotten his birthday.

428. Levitin, Sonia. *Nobody Stole the Pie* (K–3). Illus. by Fernando Krahn. 1980, Harcourt $7.95. Slowly a number of animals pick away at a pie intended for a special celebration until there is only one piece left.

429. Lionni, Leo. *Alexander and the Wind-Up Mouse* (K–2). Illus. by author. 1969, Pantheon $5.99; paper $1.45. Alexander, a real mouse, envies Willy, a toy, windup mouse, who is loved and cuddled.

430. Lionni, Leo. *The Biggest House in the World* (PS–2). Illus. by author. 1968, Pantheon $6.99. A young snail, desiring a larger shell, receives fatherly advice and decides that small accommodations are an asset in regaining his mobility; gaily colored illustrations.

431. Lionni, Leo. *Fish Is Fish* (K–2). Illus. by author. 1970, Pantheon $5.99; paper $1.45. A fable about a fish who learns from a frog how to be happy just being himself.

432. Lionni, Leo. *A Flea Story: I Want to Stay Here! I Want to Go There!* (PS–1). Illus. by author. 1977, Pantheon $5.95; LB $6.99. Two fleas try living on a variety of animals, but homebody flea prefers his old friend the dog.

433. Lionni, Leo. *Geraldine, the Music Mouse* (PS–K). Illus. by author. 1979, Pantheon $6.95; LB $6.99. A mouse learns to play lovely music using her tail.

434. Lionni, Leo. *The Greentail Mouse* (PS–3). Illus. by author. 1973, Pantheon $5.99. A group of field mice assume new identities when they put on masks.

435. Lionni, Leo. *Inch by Inch* (PS–2). Illus. by author. 1960, Astor-Honor $4.95. When the birds demand that he measure the length of a nightingale's song, this clever, captive inchworm inches his way to freedom.

436. Lionni, Leo. *Swimmy* (PS–1). Illus. by author. 1963, Pantheon $5.99; paper $1.25. A remarkable little fish instructs the rest of his school in the art of protection; swim in the formation of a gigantic fish! Beautiful, full-color illustrations.

437. Lionni, Leo. *Theodore and the Talking Mushroom* (K–3). Illus. by author. 1971, Pantheon $5.95. Theodore is an unusual little mouse who claims he has been proclaimed king of the animals —by a talking mushroom!

438. Lipkind, William. *Nubber Bear* (K–1). Illus. by Roger Duvoisin. 1966, Harcourt $5.50. Nubber, a young bear, tries to devise a way of entering the forbidden Middle Wood to collect honey.

439. Lipkind, William, and Mordvinoff, Nicolas. *The Little Tiny Rooster* (PS–1). Illus. by Nicolas Mordvinoff. 1960, Harcourt $6.50. The little tiny rooster is spurned by all the other barnyard animals because of his size, until they realize the value of his crowing to announce the coming of dawn.

440. Lobel, Arnold. *Zoo for Mister Muster* (PS–1). Illus. by author. 1962, Harper $6.89. When Mr. Muster can't go to the zoo to visit his animal friends, they all come to visit him in bed in his house until he is made assistant zookeeper. Also use: *Holiday for Mister Muster* (1963, Harper $5.79).

441. Low, Joseph. *Trust Reba* (K–2). Illus. by author. 1974, McGraw $5.95; LB $5.72. Reba, a domesticated bear, shares the household chores with members of a human family.

442. MacGregor, Ellen. *Theodore Turtle* (K–2). Illus. by Paul Galdone. 1955, McGraw $6.95. Theodore has difficulty getting organized for a trip downtown.

443. McLeod, Emilie W. *The Bear's Bicycle* (PS–2). Illus. by David McPhail. 1975, Little $6.95; paper $1.75. A small boy and his teddy bear have an exciting bicycle ride as he gives the bear safety lessons. When the bear, grown to grizzly bear proportions, does not follow the safety rules, the bear suffers the consequences.

444. McNulty, Faith. *Congo, the Elephant Who Couldn't Forget* (1–3). Illus. by Marc Simont. 1980, Harper $5.95; LB $6.89. A moral lesson about an elephant who was unable to forgive and forget.

445. McPhail, David. *The Bear's Toothache* (PS–K). Illus. by author. 1972, Little $7.95. A very funny story of a little boy's attempt to help extract a bear's tooth and rid him of his toothache.

446. McPhail, David. *Captain Toad and the Motorbike* (1–3). Illus. by author. 1978, Atheneum $9.95. A retired Navy officer wins a motorcycle race.

447. McPhail, David. *Stanley, Henry Bear's Friend* (2–4). Illus. by author. 1979, Little $6.95. After a harrowing time in jail, a young raccoon forms a friendship with Henry Bear.

448. McPhail, David. *Where Can an Elephant Hide?* (PS–K). Illus. by author. 1979, Doubleday $6.95; LB $7.90. Several creatures suggest ways in which Morris can hide from approaching hunters.

449. Maestro, Betsy. *Harriet Goes to the Circus* (PS–1). Illus. by Giulio Maestro. 1977, Crown $6.95. Harriet, an elephant, is determined to be first in line for the best circus seats, in this charming story.

450. Maestro, Betsy, and Maestro, Giulio. *Where Is My Friend?* (PS–K). Illus. by Giulio Maestro. 1976, Crown $6.95. Harriet, an elephant, searches for her friend, a mouse, in this simply told story.

451. Maestro, Giulio. *Leopard and the Noisy Monkeys* (1–3). Illus. by author. 1979, Greenwillow $5.95; LB $5.71. Leopard's mistake in letting a group of chittering monkeys use his treehouse overnight affects all the jungle animals. Also use: *Leopard Is Sick* (1978, Greenwillow $5.95; LB $5.71).

452. Marshall, James. *George and Martha* (PS–1). Illus. by author. 1972, Houghton $6.96; paper $1.95. The friendship of 2 hippos leads to some very humorous situations. Also use the sequel: *George and Martha Encore* (K–3), (1973, Houghton $6.95; paper $1.95).

453. Marshall, James. *George and Martha One Fine Day* (1–3). Illus. by author. 1978, Houghton $5.95. Five funny stories involving the hippo friends.

454. Marshall, James. *Portly McSwine* (K–2). Illus. by author. 1979, Houghton $5.95. Portly worries about his National Snout Day party.

455. Marshall, James. *What's the Matter with Carruthers? A Bedtime Story* (K–3). Illus. by author. 1972, Houghton $4.95. Carruthers, a very large bear, gets grumpy because it's time for his sleep.

456. Marshall, James. *Willis* (PS–K). Illus. by author. 1974, Houghton $6.95. Willis, an alligator, has sensitive eyes and needs sunglasses when he goes sunbathing, but he has no money to buy them. His friends Bud, Snake, and Lobster, devise very funny ingenious jobs to help him earn the money—19¢ for a pair of glasses!

457. Marshall, James. *Yummers!* (PS–K). Illus. by author. 1973, Houghton $5.95. Emily Pig is worried about her weight, so she goes for a walk for exercise. Unfortunately, the walk is interrupted for several snacks, and the resulting stomachache, Emily Pig suggests, is due to the exercise, not the food!

458. Mayer, Mercer. *Appelard and Liverwurst* (K–2). Illus. by Steven Kellogg. 1978, Four Winds $8.95. Liverwurst, a rhino, helps Appelard plow his fields and raise a bumper crop.

459. Meddaugh, Susan. *Maude and Claude Go Abroad* (PS–1). Illustrated. 1980, Houghton $7.95. A rhyming story about 2 foxes and an eventful transatlantic crossing.

460. Meshover, Leonard, and Feistel, Sally. *The Monkey that Went to School* (PS–K). Illus. by Eve Hoffmann. 1978, Follett $5.97; paper $3.95. A spider monkey is taken to school and has many adventures.

461. Miles, Miska. *Chicken Forgets* (PS–K). Illus. by Jim Arnosky. 1976, Little $5.95. Chicken is told not to be forgetful this time and to fill his basket with wild blackberries, but he is easily diverted until robin helps him out by advising what berries are best.

462. Miles, Miska. *Mouse Six and the Happy Birthday* (1–3). Illus. by Leslie Morrill. 1978, Dutton $5.95. When Mouse Six goes out to buy a birthday present for his mother, others think he has run away.

463. Miles, Miska. *Noisy Gander* (PS–K). Illus. by Leslie Morrill. 1978, Dutton $5.95. A little gosling becomes proud of her honking father when he saves the barnyard animals.

464. Miller, Edna. *Mousekin's Family* (1–3). Illus. by author. 1969, Prentice-Hall $5.95; paper $1.50. Complications occur when a little whitefoot mouse mistakenly believes she has found a relative.

465. Moeri, Louise. *How the Rabbit Stole the Moon* (K–3). Illus. by Marc Brown. 1977, Houghton $7.95. A story about how a rabbit stole a piece of the sun and was responsible for the creation of the moon and stars.

466. Most, Bernard. *If the Dinosaurs Came Back* (1–3). Illus. by author. 1978, Harcourt $5.95. All the things that might happen if dinosaurs came back to the world.

467. Murphy, Jim. *Harold Thinks Big* (1–3). Illus. by Susanna Natti. 1980, Crown $6.95. In spite of losing his love to a football hero, Harold, a pig, finds another girl friend.

468. Murphy, Shirley. *The Flight of the Fox* (1–3). 1978, Atheneum $8.95. A kangaroo rat repairs a model airplane and becomes a pilot.

469. Nakatani, Chiyoko. *My Teddy Bear* (PS–2). Illus. by author. 1976, Crowell $7.89. A little boy tells how he spends his time with his best friend, a teddy bear.

470. Newberry, Clare Turlay. *Marshmallow* (K–3). Illus. by author. 1942, Harper $8.95. Oliver, a bachelor cat, and Marshmallow, a soft white bunny, become playmates. Another cat story illustrated by the author is *April's Kittens* (1940, Harper $5.95; LB $5.11).

471. Nicholson, William. *Clever Bill* (1–3). Illus. by author. 1977, Farrar $5.95. Reprint of a classic first published in England in 1926.

472. Nixon, Joan Lowery. *Bigfoot Makes a Movie* (K–2). Illus. by Syd Hoff. 1979, Putnam $7.95. A delightful mix-up in which a Bigfoot accidentally disrupts the making of a movie.

473. Oakley, Graham. *The Church Cat Abroad* (K–3). Illus. by author. 1973, Atheneum $6.95. Sampson, the tomcat of *The Church Mouse*, sails to the South Seas to appear in a cat food advertisement.

474. Oakley, Graham. *The Church Mice and the Moon* (K–3). Illus. by author. 1974, Atheneum $6.95. Two of the church mice are captured by scientists and are being readied for a space flight when they are rescued by Samson, the church cat. Also use: *The Church Mice Spread Their Wings* (1976, Atheneum $7.95).

475. Oakley, Graham. *The Church Mice at Bay* (K–2). Illus. by author. 1978, Atheneum $8.95. Sampson, the church cat, and his mice face new problems when a substitute curate appears.

476. Oakley, Graham. *The Church Mouse* (K–2). Illus. by author. 1972, Atheneum $7.95. The humorous escapades of Arthur, the church mouse, and Samson, the church cat. All goes well, until one Sunday when Samson, who is dreaming, chases some mice and disrupts the service, much to the dismay of the congregation.

477. Ormondroyd, Edward. *Broderick* (PS–3). Illus. by John Larrecq. 1969, Parnassus $5.95; LB $4.77. Broderick, a mouse, loves to chew books, until one night he stops chewing and reads one. The book is on surfing, and it changes his life!

478. Ormondroyd, Edward. *Theodore* (PS–2). Illus. by John Larrecq. 1966, Parnassus $5.95; LB $4.59. A toy bear accidentally gets washed clean, and his little girl owner does not recognize him until he is properly dirty again. Also use: *Theodore's Rival* (1971, Parnassus $4.50; LB $4.38).

479. Oxenbury, Helen. *Pig Tale* (K–3). Illus. by author. 1973, Morrow $6.96. Sudden wealth produces complications for 2 bored pigs.

480. Panek, Dennis. *Catastrophe Cat* (K–2). Illus. by author. 1978, Bradbury $7.95. A mischievous cat has an unexpected adventure.

481. Parker, Nancy W. *The Crocodile under Louis Finneberg's Bed* (1–3). Illus. by author. 1978, Dodd $5.50. The Finnebergs give a talking crocodile to a zoo in memory of their missing son.

482. Parker, Nancy W. *The Ordeal of Byron B. Blackbear* (K–2). Illus. by author. 1979, Dodd $6.95. Byron fools scientists who are out exploring animal hibernation.

483. Patz, Nancy. *Nobody Knows I Have Delicate Toes* (PS–3). Illustrated. 1980, Watts $4.95; LB $6.90. Ben and Elephant of *Pumpernickel Tickle and Mean Green Cheese* (1978, Watts $4.95; LB $6.90) are back in another hilarious adventure.

484. Payne, Emmy. *Katy No-Pocket* (PS–1). Illus. by H. A. Rey. 1944, Houghton $8.95; paper $2.25. Until Katy finds an apron with pockets, she is very sad, for she has no way in which to carry her baby.

485. Pearson, Susan. *Izzie* (PS–K). Illus. by Robert Andrew Parker. 1975, Dial $6.95; LB $6.46. When Cary's favorite stuffed cat Izzie is cleaned up, he looks like new, but by that time Cary is off to school, and although she misses Izzie, she no longer needs him.

486. Peet, Bill. *Cowardly Clyde* (K–2). Illus. by author. 1979, Houghton $8.95. A horse named Clyde quivers in fear at the thought of fighting a dragon with his master, Sir Galavant.

487. Peet, Bill. *Eli* (1–3). Illus. by author. 1978, Houghton $7.95. An old lion is saved from hunters by playing dead.

488. Peet, Bill. *Whingdingdilly* (2–4). Illus. by author. 1970, Houghton $7.95. Scamp, tired of leading a dog's life, is transformed by a witch.

489. Petersham, Maud, and Petersham, Miska. *The Box with Red Wheels: A Picture Book* (PS–1). Illus. by author. 1949, Macmillan $3.95; paper $1.25. A sleeping baby is discovered by curious barnyard animals when they investigate a box.

490. Petersham, Maud, and Petersham, Miska. *The Circus Baby* (PS–1). Illus. by author. 1950, Macmillan $4.95. A circus elephant decides that the baby must learn to eat as the clown's family does, with rather disastrous results.

491. Phillips, Louis. *The Brothers Wrong and Wrong Again* (K–3). Illus. by J. Winslow Higginbottom. 1979, McGraw $7.95. A humorous story of 2 brothers who inadvertently tame a dragon who has ravaged the countryside.

492. Piatti, Celestino. *The Happy Owls* (K–3). Trans. from the German. Illus. by author. 1964, Atheneum $7.95. Two wise owls try to explain their joy in the changing seasons to the barnyard fowl.

493. Pinkwater, D. Manus. *Blue Moose* (1–3). Illus. by author. 1975, Dodd $5.25; Dell paper $.95. A restaurant owner takes in a blue moose as his maitre d' in this comic tale.

494. Pinkwater, D. Manus. *Pickle Creature* (K–3). Illus. by author. 1979, Four Winds $7.95. Instead of pickles, Conrad brings home a pickle creature from the supermarket.

495. Pinkwater, D. Manus. *The Wuggie Norple Story* (1–3). Illus. by Tomie de Paola. 1980, Scholastic $9.95. A nonsense story about the size of animals.

496. Pomerantz, Charlotte. *The Piggy in the Puddle* (PS–K). Illus. by James Marshall. 1974, Macmillan $4.95. Amusing story of the antics of a pig family enjoying a mud puddle.

497. Potter, Beatrix. *The Sly Old Cat* (PS–K). Illus. by author. 1972, Warne $3.95. How Rat outwits Cat, who had planned to eat him for dessert, is described with sly humor.

498. Potter, Beatrix. *The Tale of Peter Rabbit* (K–2). Illus. by author. 1903, Warne $3.95. This miniature book is an all-time favorite with little children. The complete series of 23 titles includes: *The Tale of Squirrel Nutkin* ($2.95), *The Tailor of Gloucester* ($4.95), *The Tale of Benjamin Bunny* ($2.95), and *The Tale of Two Bad Mice* ($2.95).

499. Potter, Beatrix. *The Tale of the Faithful Dove* (K–2). Illus. by Marie Angel. 1970, Warne $2.50. A gentle story of a little pigeon who is chased into a chimney by a hawk. A posthumous manuscript, illustrated and printed in the style and format of the other Potter books.

500. Potter, Beatrix. *A Treasury of Peter Rabbit and Other Stories* (K–2). Illus. by author. 1978, Watts $6.90. A collection of 5 tales.

501. Prelutsky, Jack. *The Mean Old Mean Hyena* (K–3). Illus. by Arnold Lobel. 1978, Greenwillow $6.95; LB $6.67. The animals who have been victimized by the hyena plan their revenge.

502. Preston, Edna Mitchell, and Cooney, Barbara. *Squawk to the Moon, Little Goose* (K–2). Illus. by Barbara Cooney. 1974, Viking $5.95; Penguin paper $1.50. A silly but resourceful goose uses her fear of the moon, which she is sure has fallen into the pond, to escape from the clutches of Mr. Fox. A lovely book to read aloud.

503. Preston, Edna Mitchell. *Where Did Mother Go?* (K–2). Illus. by Chris Conover. 1978, Four Winds $7.95. Little Cat searches all over town for his mother.

504. Quackenbush, Robert. *Moose's Store* (1–3). Illus. by author. 1979, Morrow $4.95; LB $4.76. Beaver decided to modernize Moose's old-fashioned store.

505. Raskin, Ellen. *And It Rained* (K–2). Illus. by author. 1969, Atheneum $6.95. Cleverly designed to amuse, the illustrations reveal a comically romantic subplot while some animals try to solve their problems.

506. Raskin, Ellen. *Moose, Goose and Little Nobody* (PS–3). Illus. by author. 1974, Parents $5.95; LB $5.41. Moose and Goose adopt a homeless waif.

507. Rayner, Mary. *Garth Pig and the Ice Cream Lady* (K–3). Illus. by author. 1977, Atheneum $8.95. A wolf disguised as an ice-cream vendor almost succeeds in making a piglet dinner out of Garth.

508. Rayner, Mary. *Mr. and Mrs. Pig's Evening Out* (PS–K). Illus. by author. 1976, Atheneum $8.95. When Mr. and Mrs. Pig go out for the evening, Mrs. Wolf is sent to baby-sit with the 10 piglets, with almost disastrous results.

509. Rey, H. A. *Cecily G and the Nine Monkeys* (K–2). Illus. by author. 1942, Houghton paper $1.95. A lonely giraffe and 9 homeless monkeys share some uproarious adventures.

510. Rey, H. A. *Curious George* (K–4). Illus. by author. 1941, Houghton paper $1.95. A small monkey finds himself in difficulties due to his mischievous curiosity. Some other books about George by the same author (Houghton, paper $1.95) are: *Curious George Takes a Job* (1947), *Curious George Rides a Bike* (1952), and *Curious George Gets a Medal* (1957).

511. Rey, Margaret. *Curious George Flies a Kite* (K–2). Illus. by H. A. Rey. 1958, Houghton $5.95; paper $2.45. More predicaments are encountered by this fun-loving monkey. Also use: *Curious George Goes to the Hospital* (1966, Houghton $5.95).

512. Richter, Mischa. *Quack?* (1–3). Illus. by author. 1978, Harper $5.95; LB $5.79. A duck seeks a proper response to his "quack" but hears only sounds like hoots and hee-haws.

513. Robinson, Marileta. *Mr. Goat's Bad Good Idea* (K–2). Illus. by Arthur Getz. 1979, Crowell $6.95; LB $6.89. Three amusing animal stories that use a Navajo setting.

514. Robinson, Tom. *Buttons* (K–1). Illus. by Peggy Bacon. 1976, Penguin $1.25. An alley cat joins the British upper crust.

✓**515.** Roche, P. K. *Good-Bye, Arnold!* (K–2). Illus. by author. 1979, Dial $6.95; LB $6.46. Webster's big brother goes away for a week, and Webster realizes how much he misses him.

516. Rockwell, Anne. *Henry the Cat and the Big Sneeze* (1–3). Illus. by author. 1980, Greenwillow $5.95; LB $5.71. When Henry the Cat falls into a deep hole, he must use trickery to get out.

517. Seuss, Dr. *Horton Hears a Who!* (K–3). Illus. by author. 1954, Random $4.95; LB $5.99. The children's favorite elephant discovers a whole town of creatures so small that they live on a speck of dust. Other titles by Dr. Seuss (Random $4.95): *Horton Hatches the Egg* (1940), *Thidwick, the Big Hearted Moose* (1948), *If I Ran the Zoo* (1950), *If I Ran the Circus* (1956), and *Yertle the Turtle and Other Stories* (1958, also LB $5.99).

518. Sharmat, Marjorie W. *I'm Terrific* (PS–1). Illus. by Kay Chorao. 1977, Holiday $5.95; paper $1.25. An amusing story of a bear cub who thinks he is marvelous and insists on telling everyone so.

519. Sharmat, Marjorie W. *Mr. Jameson & Mr. Phillips* (K–3). Illus. by Bruce Degen. 1979, Harper $7.95; LB $7.89. Two animal friends, leaving the big city, sail away to find a tropical island.

520. Sharmat, Marjorie W. *Mitchell Is Moving* (1–3). Illus. by Jose Aruego and Ariane Dewey. 1978, Macmillan $6.95. Mitchell, the dinosaur, moves, but unexpectedly misses his neighbor Margo.

521. Sharmat, Marjorie W. *Say Hello, Vanessa* (5–7). Illus. by Lillian Hoban. 1979, Holiday $5.95. A shy mouse manages to answer teacher's questions out loud.

522. Sharmat, Marjorie W. *The 329th Friend* (K–3). Illus. by Cyndy Szekeres. 1979, Four Winds $8.95. Emery Raccoon invites 328 guests to lunch and ends up making friends with himself.

523. Sharmat, Marjorie W. *Taking Care of Melvin* (1–3). Illus. by Victoria Chess. 1980, Holiday $6.95. When Melvin gets sick, his friends take care of him and he learns a lesson.

524. Shecter, Ben. *The Hiding Game* (PS–3). Illus. by author. 1977, Parents $5.95; LB $5.41. A hippo and rhinoceros play a hide-and-seek game.

525. Singer, Marilyn. *The Dog Who Insisted He Wasn't* (K–2). Illus. by Kelly Oechsli. 1976, Dutton $5.95. A very funny story about Konrad, a dog who insists he isn't a dog at all and acts like a human, sitting at the dining-room table and going to school. The other dogs soon follow his example with tumultuous results.

526. Smith, Jim. *Alphonse and the Stonehenge Mystery* (1–3). Illustrated. 1980, Little $7.95. Alphonse le Flic and sidekick Marlo McGrath discover criminals stealing the rocks from Stonehenge.

527. Smith, Jim. *The Frog Band and the Mystery of the Lion Castle* (1–3). Illus. by author. 1979, Brown $7.95. Alphonse the detective solves the mystery of Clarence the Lion's disappearance.

528. Smith, Jim. *The Frog Band and the Onion Seller* (1–3). Illus. by author. 1977, Little $6.95. A frog detective, Alphonse le Flic, sets out to recover a treasure chest in this detective story spoof.

529. Steig, William. *Amos and Boris* (K–2). Illus. by author. 1971, Farrar $6.95; Penguin paper $1.95. The friendship between Amos, a seafaring mouse, and Boris, his whale rescuer, whose life, in turn, Amos manages to save.

530. Steig, William. *Farmer Palmer's Wagon Ride* (K–2). Illus. by author. 1974, Farrar $6.95; Penguin paper $2.25. Farmer Palmer, a pig, and the hired hand, a donkey, have a disastrous ride home from the market in this engaging nonsensical bit of fun.

531. Steig, William. *Sylvester and the Magic Pebble* (K–3). Illus. by author. 1969, Simon & Schuster $6.95; LB $6.70; Dutton paper $2.95. A donkey who collects pebbles finds a red stone that will grant wishes—and off Sylvester goes on a series of adventures. Caldecott Medal, 1969. Also use: *Roland the Minstrel Pig* (1968, Harper $8.95); LB $9.89; Dutton, paper $2.95).

532. Steig, William. *Tiffky Doofky* (K–2). Illus. by author. 1978, Farrar $7.95. A canine garbage collector awaits a fortune-teller's prophecy to come true.

533. Steiner, Jorg, ed. *The Bear Who Wanted to Be a Bear* (K–3). Illus. by Jorg Muller. 1976, Atheneum $7.95. Amusing colorful pictures enhance this story, first published in Switzerland, of a bear who did not want to be anything other than a bear.

534. Stevens, Carla. *Hooray for Pig!* (K–2). Illus. by R. Bennett. 1974, Seabury $5.95. With the help of Otter, Pig conquers his fear of the water and learns to swim.

535. Stevenson, James. *The Bear Who Had No Place to Go* (K–3). Illus. by author. 1972, Harper $6.89. What happens to a bear when he is displaced from the circus by a seal who plays a horn? Finally, Ralph settles down comfortably in a wildlife community where his act is appreciated.

536. Stevenson, James. *Howard* (PS–1). Illus. by author. 1980, Greenwillow $7.95; LB $7.63. A duck named Howard looses his way and spends the winter in New York City.

537. Stevenson, James. *Monty* (K–2). Illus. by author. 1979, Greenwillow $7.95; LB $7.63. Monty, a crocodile, thinks he is being taken for granted by his friends and goes on a vacation.

538. Stevenson, James. *Wilfred the Rat* (K–2). Illus. by author. 1977, Greenwillow $6.00; Penguin paper $1.95. Wilfred is lonely until he finds 2 friends, Wayne, a squirrel, and Ruppert, a chipmunk, and he forsakes an opportunity to work in the carnival to be with his friends. Lively cartoon-type illustrations add to the humor of the text.

539. Stevenson, James. *Winston, Newton, Elton and Ed* (1–3). Illus. by author. 1978, Greenwillow $5.95; LB $5.71. Two stories—one about a squabbling walrus and a marooned penguin.

540. Sutton, Eve. *My Cat Likes to Hide in Boxes* (PS–2). Illus. by Lynley Dodd. 1974. Parents, $5.95; LB $5.41. Kitten antics will delight the youngest readers.

541. Sutton, Jane. *What Should a Hippo Wear?* (K–2). Illus. by Lynn Munsinger. 1979, Houghton $6.95. Bertha has trouble deciding what to wear when invited to a dance by Fred, the giraffe.

542. Taylor, Mark. *The Case of the Missing Kittens* (1–3). Illus. by Graham Booth. 1978, Atheneum $7.95. An intrepid dog sets out to find the kittens so cleverly hidden by their mother.

543. Thomas, Patricia. *"There Are Rocks in My Socks!" Said the Ox to the Fox* (1–3). Illus. by Mordecai Gerstein. 1979, Lothrop $6.95; LB $6.67. An ox has many problems and so consults his friend, a fox.

544. Titus, Eve. *Anatole and the Cat* (K–2). 1965, McGraw $6.95. One book in the series about an enterprising mouse. Also use (all $6.95): *Anatole and the Piano* (1966), *Anatole and the Thirty Thieves* (1969), and *Anatole in Italy* (1973).

545. Titus, Eve. *Anatole and the Pied Piper* (K–3). Illus. by Paul Galdone. 1979, McGraw $7.95. Anatole's mouse wife, Dourette, tries to rescue 24 schoolmice spirited away by Gussac, a flute player.

546. Tompert, Ann. *Little Fox Goes to the End of the World* (K–2). Illus. by John Wallner. 1976, Crown $6.95; Scholastic paper $1.50. A fox cub pretends that she travels afar and outwits other animals.

547. Tresselt, Alvin. *The Frog in the Well* (K–3). Illus. by Roger Duvoisin. 1958, Lothrop $6.96. A foolish but happy frog learns that there is more to the world than just his cool, green moss-covered home.

548. Ungerer, Tomi. *Crictor* (PS–2). Illus. by author. 1958, Harper $6.95; LB $7.89; Scholastic paper $1.25. A boa constrictor becomes the hero of a small French town after he captures a burglar.

549. Ungerer, Tomi. *No Kiss for Mother* (1–3). Illus. by author. 1973, Harper $6.95; LB $5.79; Dell paper $.95. Piper Paw, a untidy kitten, learns a lesson at the hands of a tough school nurse.

550. Van Horn, William. *Harry Hoyle's Giant Jumping Bean* (K–2). Illus. by author. 1978, Atheneum $7.95. Harry the pack rat's enormous collection of oddments is endangered by a giant jumping bean.

551. Van Leeuwen, Jean. *Tales of Oliver Pig* (K–2). Illus. by Arnold Lobel. 1979, Dial $5.89; paper $1.95. Five charming stories about Oliver's adventures.

552. Van Woerkom, Dorothy O. *Donkey Ysabel* (1–2). Illus. by Normand Chartier. 1978, Macmillan $6.95. A donkey is afraid that the automobile purchased by her owners will replace her.

553. Waber, Bernard. *An Anteater Named Arthur* (PS–2). Illus. by author. 1967, Houghton $7.95; paper $2.45. A mother anteater despairs of her son Arthur, who has problems very much like those of a young boy's. Also use: *A Firefly Named Torchy* (1970, Houghton $5.95).

554. Waber, Bernard. *Good-Bye, Funny Dumpy-Lumpy* (PS–2). Illus. by author. 1977, Houghton $6.95. Five chapter stories in the life of a Victorian cat family poke fun at family foibles.

555. Waber, Bernard. *The House on East 88th Street* (K–2). Illus. by author. 1962, Houghton $7.95; paper $1.95. Adventures of a pet crocodile (Lyle) who lives with a family in a New York brownstone. Other books about Lyle by the same author and publisher: *Lyle, Lyle, Crocodile* (1965, $6.95; paper $1.95), *Lyle and the Birthday Party* (1966, LB $6.95; paper $1.95), *Lovable Lyle* (1969, $6.95; paper $1.95), and *Lyle Finds His Mother* (1974, $7.95).

556. Waber, Bernard. *I Was All Thumbs* (K–2). Illus. by author. 1975, Houghton $6.95. The amusing adventures of Legs, a young octopus who goes from a laboratory tank to sea, with its attendant dangers.

557.   Waber, Bernard. *The Snake: A Very Long Story* (PS). Illus. by author. 1978, Houghton $7.95. A long trip brings the snake back home again.

558.   Waber, Bernard. *You Look Ridiculous, Said the Rhinoceros to the Hippopotamus* (K–2). Illus. by author. 1966, Houghton $7.95. The hippopotamus is discontented with her shape and imagines herself with many of the appendages of neighboring animals.

559.   Wagner, Jenny. *The Bunyip of Berkeley's Creek* (PS–2). Illus. by Ron Brooks. 1977, Bradbury $7.95; Penguin paper $2.25. A strange creature called bunyip thinks he is unwanted until he meets his female counterpart.

560.   Wagner, Jenny. *John Brown, Rose and the Midnight Cat* (PS–1). Illus. by Ron Brooks. 1978, Bradbury $7.95. A widow and her dog accept a cat into their household.

561.   Wahl, Jan. *Doctor Rabbit's Lost Scout* (PS–1). Illus. by Cyndy Szekeres. 1979, Random $4.95; LB $5.99. A group of animals search for their chipmunk friend who is lost in a forest.

562.   Wahl, Jan. *Sylvester Bear Overslept* (1–2). Illustrated. 1979, Parents $4.95; LB $4.99. Sylvester overhibernates and almost loses his mate, Phyllis.

563.   Walsh, Ellen Stoll. *Brunus and the New Bear* (PS–K). 1979, Doubleday $7.95; LB $8.90. A favorite stuffed bear becomes jealous when a new arrival tries to take his place.

564.   Wateron, Betty. *A Salmon for Simon* (K–3). 1980, Atheneum $5.95. A small Canadian Indian has a great adventure with a live salmon.

565.   Watson, Wendy. *Has Winter Come?* (PS–1). Illus. by author. 1978, Collins $6.95; LB $6.91. A family of woodchucks prepares for hibernation.

566.   Watson, Wendy. *Lollipop* (PS). Illus. by author. 1976, Crowell $5.79; Penguin paper $1.95. A rabbit begs for a lollipop and when his mother says no, he takes one of his pennies and runs off to the store to buy one—but he is so small, no one sees or hears his pleas for a lollipop.

567.   Weil, Lisl. *Gertie and Gus* (K–2). Illus. by author. 1977, Parents $5.95; text ed. $5.41. Two bears, Gertie and Gus, abandon their simpler life to pursue wealth and material things.

568.   Weil, Lisl. *Gillie and the Flattering Fox* (K–2). Illus. by author. 1978, Atheneum $7.95. The classic tale of the rooster fooled by a flattering fox.

569.   Weiss, Leatie. *Funny Feet!* (1–2). Illus. by Ellen Weiss. 1978, Watts $4.90. Priscilla, the penguin, tries to cure her awkwardness.

570.   Wells, Rosemary. *Don't Spill It Again, James* (PS–1). Illus. by author. 1977, Dial $5.95; LB $5.47. Three short episodes about 2 endearing animal children in which the elder brother tenderly cares for James, the younger.

571.   Wells, Rosemary. *Max's First Word* (PS). Illus. by author. 1979, Dial $2.95. A short book that features a charming hero, a young rabbit named Max. Other titles are: *Max's Ride* (1979, $2.95) and *Max's New Suit* (1979, $2.95).

572.   Wells, Rosemary. *Noisy Nora* (PS–1). Illus. by author. 1973, Dial $4.95; LB $4.58; Scholastic paper $.95. Young readers will enjoy the adventures of Nora, who is always loud.

573.   Wells, Rosemary. *Stanley and Rhoda* (PS–K). Illus. by author. 1978, Dial $5.95; LB $5.47. Stanley copes with the problem of getting along with a difficult younger sister.

574.   Wildsmith, Brian. *Hunter and His Dog* (K–2). Illus. by author. 1979, Oxford $7.95. A hunter's dog protects a flock of wild ducks.

575.   Wildsmith, Brian. *The Lazy Bear* (PS–K). Illus. by author. 1974, Watts $5.95. A bear who loves to coast downhill finds it difficult to push his wagon uphill. He then invites all his friends to join him, but demands they push the wagon up while he rides. How they manage to get even makes an entertaining story.

576.   Wildsmith, Brian. *The Little Wood Duck* (K–3). Illus. by author. 1973, Watts $5.95. A duckling is scorned because, with one foot larger than the other, he always swims in circles.

577.   Wildsmith, Brian. *The Owl and the Woodpecker* (K–3). Illus. by author. 1972, Watts $5.95. An amusing quarrel between an owl and a woodpecker concerning their different hours for work and play.

578.   Wildsmith, Brian. *Python's Party* (K–2). Illus. by author. 1975, Watts $5.95. Hungry python invites several jungle animals to a party—and near extinction. Vibrant, brilliant illustrations add to the beauty of the book.

579.   Wilson, Lionel. *The Mule Who Refused to Budge* (K–3). Illus. by Harold Berson. 1975, Crown $5.95. In this cumulative tale, 5 animals unite to rid themselves of an unwanted intruder.

580. Woldin, Beth Weiner. *Benjamin's Perfect Solution* (PS–1). Illus. by author. 1979, Warne $6.95. Benjamin doesn't have quills like other porcupines.

581. Yeoman, John. *Mouse Trouble* (PS–3). Illus. by Quentin Blake. 1973, Macmillan $4.95; paper $1.95. A miller brings in a cat to control the mice who have taken over his mill.

582. Yolen, Jane. *Spider Jane on the Move* (1–3). Illus. by Stefen Bernath. 1980, Coward $6.29. Humorous adventures of a feisty heroine and her friend Bert Bluebottle.

583. Zalben, Jane Breskin. *Penny and the Captain* (K–2). Illus. by author. 1978, Collins $5.95; LB $6.91. A penguin and a walrus share simple adventures in this episodic series of stories.

584. Zolotow, Charlotte. *Mr. Rabbit and the Lovely Present* (PS–3). Illus. by Maurice Sendak. 1962, Harper $6.89; paper $1.95. A little girl meets Mr. Rabbit, and together they find the perfect birthday gift for her mother.

Fantasies

585. Adshead, Gladys L. *Brownies—Hush!* (K–3). Illus. by Elizabeth Orton Jones. 1938, Walck $5.50; paper $1.50. The Brownies help an old couple with their work.

586. Ahlberg, Janet, and Ahlberg, Allan. *Each Peach Pear Plum* (PS). Illus. by author. 1979, Viking $8.95. A pictorial guessing game revealed in pictures and rhymes.

587. Anderson, Lonzo, and Adams, Adrienne. *Two Hundred Rabbits* (1–3). Illus. by Adrienne Adams. 1968, Penguin paper $.95. A poor boy makes good at the king's court in this modern fairy tale with a medieval setting.

588. Anno, Mitsumasa. *Dr. Anno's Magical Midnight Circus* (K–2). Illus. by author. 1972, Weatherhill $6.50. The little people come out at midnight and perform as they would in a real circus.

589. Anno, Mitsumasa. *The King's Flower* (K–3). Illus. by author. 1979, Collins $7.95; LB $7.91. A king wants to own the largest of everything, including the world's biggest flower.

590. Balian, Lorna. *The Sweet Touch* (K–3). Illus. by author. 1976, Abingdon $8.95. Piggy is granted a wish to turn everything she touches to candy.

591. Bauer, John. *In the Troll Wood* (K–3). Illus. by author. 1978, Methuen $7.95. Fifteen of this Swedish illustrator's works are the basis of this fanciful, slight story.

592. Bishop, Claire Huchet. *The Man Who Lost His Head* (K–3). Illus. by Robert McCloskey. 1942, Viking $4.95. A man tries several unsatisfactory substitutes for the head he has lost.

593. Bowden, Joan Chase. *Why the Tides Ebb and Flow* (1–3). Illus. by Marc Brown. 1979, Houghton $7.95. In her search for a hut, Old Woman causes the tides.

594. Briggs, Raymond. *Jim and the Beanstalk* (4–7). Illus. by author. 1970, Coward $5.89. A humorous, fast-moving sequel to the well-known tale.

595. Bright, Robert. *Georgie and the Robbers* (K–2). Illus. by author. 1963, Doubleday $5.95. Adventures of Georgie, the friendly little ghost who haunted the Whittaker's attic. Also use (Doubleday $5.95; paper $1.95): *Georgie* (1944) and *Georgie to the Rescue* (1956).

596. Bright, Robert. *My Red Umbrella* (PS–1). Illus. by author. 1973, Morrow $5.32. A little girls' umbrella grows so that everyone who wants to can get under it.

597. Brown, Jeff. *Flat Stanley* (1–3). Illus. by Tomi Ungerer. 1964, Harper $6.89. Dell paper $1.50. A falling bulletin board flattens Stanley so he is only one-half-inch thick.

598. Burch, Robert. *Jolly Witch* (2–3). Illus. by Leigh Grant. 1975, Dutton $5.95. Cluny, a happy witch, faces challenges involving an angry old woman.

599. Burningham, John. *Come Away from the Water, Shirley* (K–2). Illus. by author. 1977, Crowell $6.95; LB $7.95. While her parents nap on the beach, Shirley goes adventuring at sea—in her imagination.

600. Carrick, Carol. *Old Mother Witch* (1–3). Illus. by Donald Carrick. 1975, Seabury $7.95. A prank on a supposed witch and its aftermath.

601. Calhoun, Mary. *Hungry Leprechaun* (K–3). Illus. by Roger Duvoisin. 1962, Morrow $6.01. A fantasy about how a hungry leprechaun changes rocks into the first potatoes found in Ireland.

602. Calhoun, Mary. *The Witch Who Lost Her Shadow* (K–2). 1979, Harper $7.95; LB $7.89. A lovable old lady loses her cat.

603. Calhoun, Mary. *Wobble the Witch Cat* (PS–1). Illustrated. 1958, Morrow $4.09. A cat hides a witch's broomstick because he can't ride it.

604. Chapman, Carol. *Barny Bipple's Magic Dandelions* (K–3). Illus. by Steven Kellogg. 1977,

Dutton $6.95. Barny gets 3 magic dandelions and 3 accompanying wishes.

605. Clifton, Lucille. *Three Wishes* (K–3). Illus. by Stephanie Douglas. 1976, Viking $6.95; paper $.85. A lucky penny brings 3 wishes to Zenobia, and they all come true.

606. Coombs, Patricia. *Dorrie and the Birthday Eggs* (K–3). Illus. by author. 1971, Lothrop $6.00. Magic spells and the birthday theme combine in an enchanting story of little Dorrie and her adventures. Also use: *Dorrie and the Blue Witch* (1964, Lothrop $5.49; Dell, paper n.p.) and *Dorrie and the Goblin* (1972, Lothrop $6.00.).

607. Coombs, Patricia. *Dorrie and the Screebit Ghost* (2–4). Illus. by author. 1979, Lothrop $5.95; LB $5.71. Dorrie calls forth a playful witch/companion who likes Big Witch's magic ring.

608. Coville, Bruce, and Coville, Katherine. *The Foolish Giant* (1–3). 1978, Lippincott $4.95. In spite of not being too bright, a giant named Harry saves a town from a wicked wizard.

√ **609.** de Paola, Tomie. *Bill and Pete* (K–2). Illus. by author. 1978, Putnam $7.95; paper $2.95. Pete is a toothbrush (alias a bird) who helps young Bill in a series of world misadventures.

610. de Paola, Tomie. *Songs of the Fog Maiden* (PS–K). Illus. by author. 1979, Holiday $8.95. Poems about the magic of Fog Maiden.

611. D'Ignazio, Fred. *Katie and the Computer* (2–4). Illus. by Stan Gilliam. 1980, Creative Computing $6.95. Katie enters the world of computers and learns their language.

612. Flora, James. *The Great Green Turkey Creek Monster* (K–4). Illus. by author. 1976, Atheneum $7.95. The monster is really a many-headed vine that grows out of control in this tall tale.

613. Flora, James. *My Friend Charlie* (K–3). Illus. by author. 1964, Harcourt LB $5.95; paper $1.25. Friend Charlie's fabulous escapades: talking to fish, skating on his head while eating noodles, and finding a submarine caught in a wad of bubble gum. Also use: *Grandpa's Farm* (1965, Harcourt $6.95).

614. Flora, James. *Pishtosh, Bullwash and Wimple* (K–4). Illus. by author. 1972, Atheneum $4.50. A wonderful nonsense tale that involves, among other adventures, returning the stolen North Pole to its rightful position.

615. Freeman, Don. *Tilly Witch* (1–3). Illus. by author. 1969, Viking $4.95. Tilly attends Miss Fitch's Finishing School for Witches.

616. Gage, Wilson. *Mrs. Gaddy and the Ghost* (1–3). Illus. by Marylin Hafner. 1979, Greenwillow $5.95; LB $5.71. Mrs. Gaddy tries to get rid of a ghost but relents when she realizes how gentle it is.

617. Galdone, Paul. *The Magic Porridge Pot* (K–3). Illus. by author. 1976, Seabury $6.95. The familiar tale of the magic pot that produces porridge but runs amuck when the words that stop it are forgotten.

618. Garrison, Christian. *Little Pieces of the West Wind* (PS–1). Illus. by Diane Goode. 1975, Bradbury $7.95. In this cumulative tale, various people imprison parts of the West Wind until it becomes only a breeze.

619. Goffstein, M. B. *Me and My Captain* (K–2). Illus. by author. 1974, Farrar $3.95. A small wooden doll dreams that the captain of a toy boat on the shelf below her comes to visit and asks to marry her.

620. Haas, Irene. *The Maggie B* (K–2). Illus. by author. 1975, Atheneum $7.95. Beautiful watercolors enhance this story of a little girl and her adventures on an imaginary ship named for her—The Maggie B.

621. Horwitz, Elinor. *When the Sky Is Like Lace* (K–2). Illus. by Barbara Cooney. 1975, Lippincott $6.95. A dreamlike story involving 3 little girls and magical powers.

622. Hurd, Edith Thacher. *The So-So Cat* (2–4). Illustrated. 1965, Harper $6.90. A cat hides a witch's equipment but returns them to aid a tiny witch.

623. Jacobs, Joseph. *Coo-My-Dove, My Dear* (K–3). Illus. by Marcia Sewall. 1976, Atheneum $5.95. A young girl is visited by her lover disguised as a dove in this fairy tale.

624. Jacques, Faith. *Tilly's House* (K–2). Illus. by author. 1979, Atheneum $8.95. Tilly, tired of being a kitchen maid in the dollhouse, decides to set out on her own.

625. Jeschke, Susan. *Mia, Grandma and the Genie* (1–3). Illus. by author. 1977, Winston $6.95. It's so nice to have a genie around the house to fulfill any number of tasks.

626. Johnston, Tony. *Four Scary Stories* (K–2). Illus. by Tomie de Paola. 1978, Putnam $7.95. An imp, a goblin, a scalawag, and a young boy each tell an amusing story.

627. Kennedy, Richard. *The Leprechaun's Story* (K–3). Illus. by Marcia Sewall. 1979, Dutton $8.95. A wily leprechaun wins his freedom from his captor.

628. Kennedy, Richard. *The Lost Kingdom of Karnica* (1–3). Illus. by Uri Shulevitz. 1979, Scribner $8.95. A king is warned that removal of a precious stone from the earth will destroy his kingdom.

629. Kennedy, Richard. *The Porcelain Man* (1–3). Illus. by Marcia Sewall. 1976, Little $6.95. A timid young girl fashions broken bits of porcelain into different figures.

630. Kimmel, Margaret Mary. *Magic in the Mist* (1–3). Illus. by Trina Schart. 1975, Atheneum $5.95. A young Welsh boy and his toad Jeremy find a dragon.

631. Krauss, Ruth. *Carrot Seed* (K–1). Illus. by Crockett Johnson. 1945, Harper $4.95; paper $1.25. A young boy is convinced that the seed he plants will grow, in spite of his family's doubts.

632. Kroll, Steven. *The Candy Witch* (PS–1). Illustrated. 1979, Holiday $7.95. A family of witches perform good works except the youngest, who undoes their work.

633. Kroll, Steven. *The Tyrannosaurus Game* (PS–3). Illus. by Tomie de Paola. 1976, Holiday $6.95. A group of first-graders plays a game involving an imaginary purple tyrannosaurus.

634. Lareuse, Jean. *Devils in the Castle* (K–3). Illus. by author. 1979, Scribner $8.95. Some boys discover that a group of fun-loving devils have taken over a chateau.

635. Laughlin, Florence. *Little Leftover Witch* (2–4). Illustrated. 1960, Macmillan $4.95. Felina is stranded on earth when her broomstick breaks.

636. Lobel, Anita. *A Birthday for the Princess* (K–3). Illus. by author. 1973, Harper $5.95; LB $6.49. Written in the fairy-tale tradition, this is the story of an unloved and unnoticed princess who rebels and runs away on her birthday with a friendly organ-grinder, never to return because the king and queen are really mean.

637. Lobel, Anita. *Troll Music* (1–3). Illus. by author. 1966, Harper $7.89. A mischievous troll casts a spell over a group of musicians, who thereafter can only produce animal sounds from their instruments. Also use: *Sven's Bridge* (1965, Harper $5.79).

638. McCrady, Lady. *Miss Kiss and the Nasty Beast* (K–2). Illus. by author. 1979, Holiday $7.95. Everyone in Kiss City loves one another until Nasty Beast disrupts their smooching existence.

639. McMillan, Bruce. *The Remarkable Riderless Runaway Tricycle* (1–3). Illus. by author. 1978, Houghton $6.95. A discarded tricycle finds its way home from the town dump.

640. McPhail, David. *The Magical Drawings of Moony B. Finch* (1–3). Illus. by author. 1978, Doubleday $6.95; LB $7.90. Moony's drawings come to life in this fantasy.

641. McPhail, David. *The Train* (3–6). Illus. by author. 1977, Atlantic/Little $5.95; LB $4.99. This fantasy begins with the breaking of an electric train.

642. Mahy, Margaret. *A Lion in the Meadow* (PS–1). Illus. by Jenny Williams. 1969, Watts $4.90. A small boy reports the sighting of a lion in his usual play spot, and his doubting mother responds with a dragon of her own in this original, slight fantasy, a gaily illustrated charmer for story hour.

643. Mahy, Margaret. *The Witch in the Cherry Tree* (K–2). Illus. by Jenny Williams. 1974, Parents $5.95; LB $5.41. A witch perched in a cherry tree tries to trick David and his mother out of their freshly baked cakes.

644. Noble, Trinka Hakes. *The King's Tea* (K–2). Illus. by author. 1979, Dial $7.50; LB $7.28. Each character blames the other when the milk in the king's tea is found to be sour.

645. Olsen, Ib Spang. *The Boy in the Moon* (PS–4). Illus. by author. 1977, Parents $5.95; LB $5.41. A moonboy sets out to gather the reflection of the moon in this translation from the Danish.

646. Palazzo, Tony. *Magic Crayon* (K–2). Illus. by author. 1967, Lion $4.95; LB $4.59. Imaginative fun for very young readers.

647. Peet, Bill. *Big Bad Bruce* (K–3). Illus. by author. 1977, Houghton $7.95. Bruce encounters a witch and is shrunk to the size of a chipmunk.

648. Pienkowski, Jan. *Haunted House* (K–2). Illus. by Jane Walmsley. 1979, Dutton $7.95. All kinds of ghosts emerge from various places in this unusual house.

649. Plath, Sylvia. *The Bed Book* (PS–3). Illus. by Emily McCully. 1976, Harper $5.95. Lyric verses that investigate the characteristics of a variety of beds.

650. Postma, Lidia. *The Witch's Garden* (K–3). Illus. by author. 1979, McGraw $7.95. Seven children pay a visit to a witch and meet an elf.

651. Raskin, Ellen. *Franklin Stein* (K–2). Illus. by author. 1972, Atheneum $5.95; paper $1.50. Franklin makes himself an ingenious contraption, which he calls Fred. Everyone sneers at it until it is judged best in the pet show.

652. Raskin, Ellen. *Ghost in a Four-Room Apartment* (K–2). Illus. by author. 1969, Atheneum

$7.27. The story of a poltergeist who haunts a 4-room apartment is told on one page and the reactions of the haunted family are recounted on the facing page.

653. Russ, Lavinia. *Alec's Sand Castle* (K–3). Illus. by James Stevenson. 1972, Harper $6.89. Everyone in the family wants to help Alec build his sand castle, but Alec is bored with their efforts and builds a sand castle in his imagination, which not even the rain can wash away.

654. Robb, Brian. *My Grandmother's Djinn* (1–3). Illus. by author. 1978, Parents $5.95; LB $5.41. An old Englishman sets out with his sister to free the djinns.

655. Ryan, Cheli D. *Hildilid's Night* (K–2). Illus. by Arnold Lobel. 1971, Macmillan $4.50; paper $.95. A little old lady who hates the night tries vainly to chase it away, in this amusing story.

656. Sandburg, Carl. *The Wedding Procession of the Rag Doll and the Broom Handle and Who Was In It* (1–3). Illus. by Harriet Pincus. 1967, Harcourt $6.50. Illustrated edition of one of the *Rootabaga Stories*.

657. Sendak, Maurice. *In the Night Kitchen* (K–3). Illus. by author. 1970, Harper $8.95; LB $8.79. Mickey discovers that the "night kitchen" is where the wild snacks are.

658. Sendak, Maurice. *Maurice Sendak's Really Rosie* (1–4). Illus. by author. 1975, Harper $5.95. A book based on the TV presentation, including 7 songs used in the program.

659. Sendak, Maurice. *Where the Wild Things Are* (K–3). Illus. by author. 1963, Harper $6.95; LB $6.79. The few moments' wild reverie of a small unruly boy who has been sent supperless to his room. 1964 Caldecott Award.

660. Seuss, Dr. *The 500 Hats of Bartholomew Cubbins* (K–3). Illus. by author. 1938, Vanguard $4.29. Everytime Bartholomew takes off his hat before the king, a new one appears. Also use: *And to Think that I Saw It on Mulberry Street* (1937, $3.95), *McElligot's Pool* (1947, $4.99), and *Bartholomew and the Oobleck* (1949, $5.99).

661. Sharmat, Marjorie W. *What Are We Going to Do about Andrew?* (PS–1). Illus. by Ray Cruz. 1980, Macmillan $7.95. Andrew's ability to fly and become a hippopotamus at will causes family problems and social problems.

662. Shulevitz, Uri. *One Monday Morning* (PS–1). Illus. by author. 1967, Scribner $8.95; paper $2.95. Royal visitors right out of a small boy's colorful daydream brighten his drab tenement on a rainy day.

663. Slobodkin, Louis. *Magic Michael* (K–1). Illus. by author. 1944, Macmillan $4.95; paper $1.95. Michael has a vivid imagination and pretends to be all sorts of different people, but the gift of a bicycle changes everything.

664. Spier, Peter. *Bored—Nothing to Do!* (K–3). Illus. by author. 1978, Doubleday $6.95; LB $7.90. Two bored boys put together an airplane and fly it.

665. Steig, William. *Caleb and Kate* (PS–3). Illus. by author. 1977, Farrar $7.95. Scholastic paper $1.50. Because he constantly quarrels with his wife, Caleb is transformed into a dog by a witch.

666. Stern, Simon. *Mrs. Vinegar* (PS–1). Illustrated. 1979, Prentice-Hall $7.95. When the Vinegars lose their home, they set out to find another.

667. Stevenson, James. *The Worst Person in the World* (1–3). Illus. by author. 1978, Greenwillow $6.95; LB $6.67. A visiting monster named Ugly makes a grouch change his ways.

668. Storm, Theodor. *Little John* (PS–3). Illus. by Anita Lobel. 1972, Farrar $4.50. A boy and his trundle bed have several wonderful nocturnal adventures in this nineteenth-century nursery tale.

669. Talbot, Toby. *A Bucketful of Moon* (1–4). Illus. by Imero Gobbato. 1976, Lothrop $6.00. An active old woman tries to capture the moon in this rollicking story.

670. Thayer, Jane. *Andy and the Wild Worm* (PS–K). Illus. by Beatrice Darwin. 1973, Morrow $6.25; LB $6.00. After watching a worm in the garden, Andy announces that there is a wild animal in the house and asks his mother to guess what it is. After keeping the guessing game going for a long while, Andy finally admits it is the worm just like the one he observed outdoors. Also use: *Andy and the Runaway Horse* (1963, Morrow $5.49).

671. Thayer, Jane. *Gus and the Baby Ghost* (K–2). Illus. by Seymour Fleishman. 1972, Morrow $6.48. Gus, the friendly ghost, adopts a baby ghost that he finds on his doorstep and takes the baby to live with him in the historical museum, much to the delight of the visitors.

672. Tobias, Tobi. *Chasing the Goblins Away* (PS–1). Illus. by Victor G. Ambrus. 1977, Warne $6.95. With the help of his dog, Jimmy fights a nightly invasion of goblins that disturb his sleep.

673. Tobias, Tobi. *Jane, Wishing* (1–3). Illus. by Trina Schart Hyman. 1977, Viking $6.95. Black and white represent realities, but Jane's delightful fantasies are in glorious color.

674. Tresselt, Alvin. *The World in the Candy Egg* (PS–2). Illus. by Roger Duvoisin. 1967, Lothrop $6.96. The magic world inside a spun-sugar egg is revealed in a gentle story combining prose and poetry enhanced by elaborate full-color collage illustrations.

675. Udry, Janice May. *The Moon Jumpers* (K–2). Illus. by Maurice Sendak. 1959, Harper $8.95; LB $8.79. The pleasure and enjoyment of 4 children as they dance in the moonlight.

676. Ungerer, Tomi. *The Three Robbers* (PS–1). Illus. by author. 1962, Atheneum LB $7.43 paper $1.95. A little orphan captured by robbers is delighted to live with them rather than with her wicked aunt, and she persuades them to spend their loot building a new village for other poor orphans.

677. Ungerer, Tomi. *Zeralda's Ogre* (K–2). Illus. by author. 1967, Harper $8.79. Even a child-eating ogre can be reformed if he meets a cook with Zeralda's skill.

678. Ventura, Piero. *The Magic Well* (K–4). Illus. by author. 1976, Random $5.95; LB $6.99. The villagers of Pozzo try different methods to rid their town of a plague of yellow balls that come from their well.

679. Waber, Bernard. *You're a Little Kid with a Big Heart* (PS–2). Illus. by author. 1980, Houghton $8.95. A little girl is granted her wish—to be an adult.

680. Williams, Jay. *The City Witch and the Country Witch* (K–3). Illus. by Ed Renfro. 1979, Macmillan $8.95. A city witch trades places with her country counterpart and finds that her powers are inappropriate.

681. Williams, Jay. *One Big Wish* (K–2). Illus. by John O'Brien. 1980, Macmillan $7.95. The idea of having an unlimited number of wishes fails to satisfy Fred Butterspoon.

682. Williams, Jay. *The Practical Princess* (1–3). Illus. by Friso Henstra. 1969, Parents $8.50; LB $7.61. A modern spoof on the traditional princess tale; Bedelia outwits a dragon and finds her true love. Ornately illustrated.

683. Yolen, Jane. *The Boy Who Had Wings* (1–3). Illus. by Helga Aichinger. 1974, Crowell $8.79. Actos uses his gift of possessing wings to help rescue his father.

684. Yolen, Jane. *The Girl Who Loved the Wind* (K–3). Illus. by Ed Young. 1972, Crowell $8.95. An overly protected child discovers that life is not always happy.

685. Yolen, Jane. *The Witch Who Wasn't* (K–2). Illus. by Arnold Roth. 1964, Macmillan $4.95. As an apprentice witch, Isabel is a dismal failure.

686. Zemach, Harve, and Zemach, Kaethe. *The Princess and Froggie* (PS–2). Illus. by Margot Zemach. 1975, Farrar $5.95. These brief tales are charmingly presented by the Zemachs and their teenage daughter.

Realistic Stories

Real and Almost Real Animals

687. Alexander, Martha. *No Ducks in Our Bathtub* (PS–1). Illus. by author. 1973, Dial $4.95; paper $1.50. David wanted a pet and finally his mother agreed to let him have some fish eggs to hatch. Much to everyone's surprise, and David's joy, 103 tadpoles inhabit the bathtub!

688. Aliki. *At Mary Bloom's* (K–2). Illus. by author. 1976, Greenwillow $6.95. When her pet mouse has babies, a little girl shares the excitement with a neighbor's household.

689. Anderson, Clarence W. *Billy and Blaze* (K–2). Illus. by author. 1962, Macmillan $4.95; paper $1.95. An old favorite about Billy who loved horses and his pony Blaze.

690. Barnhart, Peter. *The Wounded Duck* (1–3). Illus. by Adrienne Adams. 1979, Scribner $9.95. An old woman stays home to take care of a wounded duck until her own death.

691. Bartoli, Jennifer. *In a Meadow, Two Hares Hide* (PS–1). Illus. by Takeo Ishida. 1978, Whitman $7.50. Two rabbits help each other survive from their natural enemies.

692. Bell, Anthea. *The Great Menagerie* (2–6). 1980, Viking $7.95. A variety of animals come to life in this pop-up book from the nineteenth century.

693. Binzen, William. *The Rory Story* (1–3). Illus. by author. 1974, Doubleday $4.95. Rory, a golden retriever pup, matures until, at the end of the book, he is fully grown.

694. Birnbaum, A. *Green Eyes* (PS–K). Illus. by author. 1973, Golden $9.15. A large white cat tells about the first year of his life in this dramatically illustrated book.

695. Bishop, Claire Huchet. *The Truffle Pig* (1–3). Illus. by Kurt Wiese. 1971, Coward $4.99. Pierre, the pet pig, can detect truffles, leading to a new life for the family who had originally purchased him for sausage.

696. Bourne, Miriam Anne. *Raccoons Are for Loving* (PS–1). Illus. by Marion Morton. 1968, Random $5.39. A black child holds a raccoon in her arm as her grandmother did many years before.

697. Brown, Marcia. *How Hippo!* (K–1). Illus. by author. 1969, Scribner $6.95; paper $.95. Mother Hippo saves the day for her venturesome Little Hippo, just learning the proper grunts and roars, when a crocodile threatens. Eye-filling, double-page woodcuts.

698. Brown, Margaret Wise. *When the Wind Blew* (PS–2). Illus. by Geoffrey Hayes. 1977, Harper $3.95; LB $4.89. A reissue with new illustrations of the story about an old woman with 17 cats.

699. Burch, Robert. *Joey's Cat* (PS–2). Illus. by Don Freeman. 1969, Viking $5.95. Joey's mother finally lets her pet cat and her 4 kittens into the house.

700. Burningham, John. *Cannonball Simp* (K–2). Illus. by author. 1979, J. Cape $6.95. An abandoned dog and a circus clown team up.

701. Burningham, John. *Harquin: The Fox Who Went Down to the Valley* (K–2). Illus. by author. 1979, J. Cape $6.95. During a hunt, a fox cub saves his family and acquires the squire's cap.

702. Caras, Roger. *Skunk for a Day* (K–2). Illus. by Diane Paterson. 1976, Windmill $5.95. A skunk's night activities are dramatically told from the skunk's point of view.

703. Carle, Eric. *Have You Seen My Cat?* (PK–K). Illus. by author. 1973, Watts $5.95. A small boy in search of his cat keeps finding various members of the feline family, but only when he returns home does he find his own missing cat, who has had kittens.

704. Carrick, Carol. *Lost in the Storm* (K–3). Illus. by Donald Carrick. 1974, Seabury $6.95. The story of a dog, lost overnight in a storm, who is found in the morning by his owner and safely sheltered under a flight of stairs.

705. Carrick, Carol. *A Rabbit for Easter* (1–3). Illus. by Donald Carrick. 1979, Greenwillow $6.95; LB $6.67. During Easter vacation, Paul has adventures with the rabbit from kindergarten.

706. Chaffin, Lillie D. *Bear Weather* (PS–1). Illus. by Helga Aichinger. 1969, Macmillan $4.95. Drawings in frosty blues and earthy browns are combined with lilting verse about baby and mother bear who bed down from winter until spring, when the promise of honey beckons.

707. Chen, Suzanne Noguere, and Chen, Tony. *Little Koala* (K–2). Illus. by Tony Chen. 1979, Holt $6.95. The life and environments of an appealing koala in Australia.

708. Coatsworth, Elizabeth. *Under the Green Willow* (K–2). Illus. by Janina Domanska. 1971, Collier $4.50. The sun describes a place where a variety of animals await food.

709. d'Aulaire, Ingri, and d'Aulaire, Edgar P. *Animals Everywhere* (PS). Illus. by author. 1954, Doubleday $4.50. Animals in their native settings, from the polar regions to the African jungles. Also use: *Don't Count Your Chicks* (1943, Doubleday $6.95; paper $1.95).

710. de Paola, Tomie. *The Kids' Cat Book* (1–3). Illus. by author. 1979, Holiday $7.95. Patrick learns about the care, feeding, and history of cats when he decides to adopt one.

711. Dobrin, Arnold. *Jillions of Gerbils* (K–3). Illus. by author. 1973, Lothrop $5.95; LB $5.49. When they moved, somehow Herbert the gerbil got lost, and then Max, a replacement, also disappeared. However, they were found hiding in a tiny nook and evidently were misnamed, for baby gerbils began to appear. Also use: *Josephine's Imagination* (1973, Four Winds $5.95; Scholastic, paper $1.50).

712. Doiseau, Robert. *The Boy and the Dove* (1–3). Illustrated. 1978, Workman $7.95; paper $3.95. A boy has a dove for a pet in this story that is well illustrated with photographs.

713. Duncan, Jane. *Janet Reachfar and Chickabird* (K–2). Illus. by Mairi Hedderwick. 1978, Seabury $7.95. Janet, a Scottish farm girl, helps an injured baby chick.

714. Ernst, Kathryn F. *Charlie's Pets* (K–2). Illus. by Arthur Cumings. 1978, Crown $4.95. Charlie decides to make pets of some cockroaches.

715. Ets, Marie Hall. *Just Me* (PS–K). Illus. by author. 1965, Viking $2.50; Penguin paper $1.95. A little boy imagines he can match the antics of his animal friends as he spends an afternoon at solitary play.

716. Ets, Marie Hall. *Play with Me* (PS–K). Illus. by author. 1953, Viking $4.95; LB $7.95; Penguin paper $1.95. A little girl finds a playmate among the meadow creatures when she finally learns to sit quietly and not frighten them.

717. Fatio, Louise. *Hector and Christina* (K–2). Illus. by Roger Duvoisin. 1977, McGraw $7.95. Two animals are rescued from a zoo and allowed to return to their forest home.

718. Feder, Jane. *Beany* (PS–K). Illus. by Karen Gundersheimer. 1979, Pantheon $4.95. The story of a young boy's love for his cat.

719. Fisher, Aileen. *Listen Rabbit* (K–2). Illus. by Symeon Shimin. 1964, Crowell $8.79. A delightful picture-poetry book describing a small boy's efforts to make friends with a rabbit.

720. Flack, Marjorie. *Angus and the Ducks* (K–2). Illus. by author. 1939, Doubleday $5.95; paper $1.95. Angus, the Scotch terrier, and his amusing adventures. Other titles in this series are: *Angus and the Cat* (PS–1) (1931, $4.95; paper $1.49) and *Angus Lost* (K–2) (1941, $4.50; paper $1.49).

721. Freeman, Don. *Fly High, Fly Low* (K–3). Illus. by author. 1957, Viking $6.95; paper $1.50. Two pigeons make their home in a San Francisco hotel sign.

722. Fregosi, Claudia. *The Happy Horse* (PS–3). Illus. by author. 1977, Greenwillow $8.25; LB $6.96. In this joyful book a carefree horse spends a lovely day in a meadow.

723. Freschet, Berniece. *Grizzly Bear* (1–3). Illus. by Donald Carrick. 1975, Scribner $7.95. A year in the life of a grizzly bear and her young cubs is well described and handsomely illustrated in watercolors.

724. Gackenbach, Dick. *Do You Love Me?* (K–2). Illus. by author. 1975, Seabury $6.95. Walter has no one to play with, and so he tries to make pets of some insects, but realizes that wild things need freedom. At last he gets a puppy that needs his love and attention and that he can fondle and cuddle.

725. Gag, Wanda. *Millions of Cats* (PS–1). Illus. by author. 1928, Coward $4.95; paper $1.50. A wonderful picture book about an old man looking for a cat who suddenly finds himself with millions. Also use (Coward $3.99): *The Funny Thing* (1929) and *Snippy and Snappy* (1931).

726. George, Jean Craighead. *The Wentletrap Trap* (1–3). Illus. by Symeon Shimin. 1978, Dutton $5.95. Denis tries to catch the Wentletrap and learns to accept defeat.

727. George, Jean Craighead. *The Wounded Wolf* (1–3). Illus. by John Schoenherr. 1978, Harper $4.95; LB $5.49. A simple story that abounds in the author's knowledge of animal lore.

728. Ginsburg, Mirra. *Mushroom in the Rain* (K–2). Adapted from the Russian of V. Suteyev.

Illus. by Jose Aruego and Ariane Dewey. 1974, Macmillan $4.95. An ant, huddling under a mushroom in the rain, makes room for a butterfly, a mouse, a sparrow, and finally a rabbit who is being chased by a fox.

729. Goble, Paul. *The Girl Who Loved Wild Horses* (K–2). Illus. by author. 1978, Bradbury $8.95. A mystical story of a girl and her love for a black stallion. Caldecott Medal, 1979.

730. Graham, John. *I Love You, Mouse* (K–2). Illus. by Tomie de Paola. 1976, Harcourt $4.50; paper $1.75. A tender book about how a young boy would feel if he were several different animals.

731. Graham, Margaret B. *Benjy's Boat Trip* (PS–3). Illus. by author. 1977, Harper $6.95; LB $7.89. A dachshund refuses to be left behind and sets out to find his family who have left on a summer vacation.

732. Graham, Margaret B. *Benjy's Dog House* (PS–K). Illus. by author. 1973, Harper $7.95; LB $7.89. Benjy is an amiable dog, and when put out of the house where he has been sleeping with Jimmy and Linda, he finds a cozy berth in a bakery. Evicted from that, he returns home once more to enjoy happy nights in the children's beds.

733. Hazen, Barbara S. *Where Do Bears Sleep?* (PS–2). Illus. by Ian E. Staunton. 1970, Addison $6.95. Questions and answers about where various animals sleep; good for storytelling or beginning readers.

734. Hazen, Barbara S. *Look Tight Times* (2–3). Illus. by Trina S. Hyman. 1979, Viking $5.95. A child is allowed to keep a stray kitten even though there are hard times in the household.

735. Hewett, Joan. *The Mouse and the Elephant* (1–3). Illus. by Richard Hewett. 1977, Little $5.95. Photographs answer the question, What if a mouse lived with an elephant?

736. Hoban, Tana. *One Little Kitten* (PS–1). Illustrated. 1979, Greenwillow $6.95; LB $6.67. The activities of a kitten in text and unusual photographs.

737. Holl, Adelaide. *The Rain Puddle* (PS–K). Illus. by Roger Duvoisin. 1965, Lothrop $6.96. When the barnyard animals see their reflections in a rain puddle, each believes that one of his own kind has fallen into the water.

738. Ipcar, Dahlov. *A Flood of Creatures* (K–3). Illus. by author. 1973, Holiday $6.95. An old lady's house is invaded by a host of animals fleeing a flood.

739. Ipcar, Dahlov. *Hard Scrabble Harvest* (K–2). Illus. by author. 1976, Doubleday $6.95. Brisk, colorful illustrations and lilting verses describe the assault made on a farmer's crops by both wild and domesticated animals.

740. Kahl, Virginia. *Whose Cat Is That?* (K–2). Illus. by author. 1979, Scribner $7.95. Seven different households adopt the same pretty white cat.

741. Keats, Ezra Jack. *Hi, Cat!* (K–2). Illus. by author. 1969, Macmillan $6.95; paper $1.95. Archie meets a stray cat on his way to see Peter, and when the cat interferes with their show, Archie acknowledges that it "just kinda liked me!" Also with the same central characters: *Pet Show* (PS–2). Illus. by author. (1972, Macmillan $4.95; paper $1.25).

742. Keith, Eros. *Rrra-ah* (1–3). Illus. by author. 1969, Bradbury $6.95. Rrra-ah, a toad, is overjoyed when he is eventually released after being captured by children.

743. Kellogg, Steven. *Pinkerton, Behave!* (K–3). Illus. by author. 1979, Dial $7.95; LB $7.45. A mischievous Great Dane puppy foils a burglary attempt.

744. Knight, Hilary. *Where's Wallace* (PS–K). Illus. by author. 1964, Harper $7.95; LB $8.79. A little orangutan escapes from the zoo and explores the outside world. Chidlren will find him hidden in the pictures of the various places he explores.

745. Knotts, Howard. *The Winter Cat* (K–2). Illus. by author. 1972, Harper $6.95; LB $6.89. A wild gray cat succumbs to the kindness of a family and is brought into a home far from the rigors of a severe winter.

746. Lipkind, William, and Mordvinoff, Nicolas. *Finders Keepers* (K–3). Illus. by author. 1951, Harcourt $6.50; paper $1.35. Two dogs have a dispute over one bone, but unite against a common enemy. Caldecott Medal, 1952.

747. Lipkind, William, and Mordvinoff, Nicolas. *The Two Reds* (PS–1). Illus. by author. 1950, Harcourt $6.50. The "two reds" are Joey, a redheaded boy, and a red cat whom Joey rescues from a gang in New York City.

748. Low, Joseph. *My Dog, Your Dog* (K–2). Illus. by author. 1979, Macmillan $5.95. Positive and negative views of the same dogs.

749. McCloskey, Robert. *Make Way for Ducklings* (PS–3). Illus. by author. 1941, Viking $7.95; Penguin paper $2.50. The Mallard family creates a commotion as they search for and find a permanent home in Boston. Caldecott Medal, 1942.

750. McNulty, Faith. *Mouse and Tim* (K–2). Illus. by Marc Simont. 1978, Harper $5.95; LB $5.49. Tim adopts an abandoned deer mouse as a pet.

751. Martin, Patricia Miles. *The Rice Bowl Pet* (K–2). Illus. by Ezra Jack Keats. 1962, Crowell $7.89. A boy who lives in a small apartment searches for a pet to keep in a rice bowl.

752. Miles, Miska. *Nobody's Cat* (1–3). Illus. by John Schoenherr. 1969, Atlantic/Little $6.95. Episodes in the life of an independent, dignified cat with a keen knowledge of his rough urban environment and how best to cope with it—superb, dramatic drawings.

753. Miles, Miska. *Small Rabbit* (PS–K). Illus. by Jim Arnosky. 1977, Atlantic/Little $5.95. A nature tale about a young rabbit encountering imaginary enemies on her first run alone in the woods.

754. Modell, Frank. *Seen Any Cats?* (PS–1). Illus. by author. 1979, Greenwillow $6.95; LB $6.67. Two enterprising boys decide to put on their own circus by training their cats.

755. Modell, Frank. *Tooley! Tooley!* (K–3). Illus. by author. 1979, Greenwillow $6.95; LB $6.67. Milton and Marvin set out to find Tooley, a lost dog.

756. Moskin, Marietta D. *Toto* (K–3). Illus. by Rocco Negri. 1972, Coward $4.69. Toto, a curious baby elephant with wanderlust, is brought back to the herd by a young boy.

757. Munari, Bruno. *Bruno Munari's Zoo* (PS–K). Illus. by author. 1963, World $6.95; LB $6.91. Bold and brilliantly colorful animals.

758. Murschetz, Luis. *Mister Mole* (PS–3). Illus. by author. 1976, Prentice-Hall $5.95. Mister Mole's idyllic life ends when humans decide to construct apartment buildings in his meadow.

759. Nakatani, Chiyoko. *My Day on the Farm* (PS–3). Illus. by author. 1977, Crowell $7.95; LB $7.89. A very small boy visits a farm and meets a number of animals.

760. Nakatani, Chiyoko. *The Zoo in My Garden* (K–2). Illus. by author. 1973, Crowell $7.89. Such familiar plants and animals as tulips and cats become a youngster's first introduction to zoos.

761. Orbach, Ruth. *Please Send a Panda* (K–3). Illus. by author. 1978, Collins $6.95; LB $6.91. Agatha thinks she is going to get an exotic pet, but receives a cat.

762. Parker, Nancy W. *Puddums, the Cathcarts' Orange Cat* (2–4). Illus. by author. 1980, Atheneum $8.95. Puddums, the cat, gets mysteriously ill and frightens the Cathcarts.

763. Politi, Leo. *Song of the Swallows* (K–3). Illus. by author. 1949, Scribner $8.95; paper $.95. Juan rings the mission's bells to welcome the swallows back to San Juan Capistrano. Caldecott Medal, 1950.

764. Provensen, Alice, and Provensen, Martin. *My Little Hen* (PS–1). Illus. by author. 1974, Random $4.99. A little girl's pet hen hatches an egg, and the problems begin. Also use: *Our Animal Friends at Maple Hill Farm* (1974, Random $4.99).

765. Provensen, Alice, and Provensen, Martin. *The Year at Maple Hill Farm* (PS–1). Illus. by author. 1978, Atheneum $5.95. Month-by-month activities of the animals on a farm.

766. Rice, Eve. *Sam Who Never Forgets* (PS–1). Illus. by author. 1977, Greenwillow $6.95; LB $6.67; Penguin paper $2.25. Sam, the zoo keeper, feeds all the animals each day, but one day there appears to be nothing for the elephant.

767. Rockwell, Anne. *Willy Runs Away* (4–6). Illustrated. 1978, Dutton $6.95. A little dog gets lost.

768. Rojankovsky, Feodor. *Animals on the Farm* (K–2). Illus. by author. 1967, Knopf $5.99. Nineteen common farm animals are pictured and identified.

769. Rosen, Winifred. *Henrietta and the Day of the Iguana* (K–3). Illus. by Kay Chorao. 1978, Four Winds $5.95. A willful child decides that she wants an iguana for a pet.

770. Ross, George M. *When Lucy Went Away* (K–3). Illus. by Ingrid Fetz. 1976, Dutton $5.95. A tender story about the disappearance of a pet cat and the children's adjustment to their loss.

771. Roy, Donald. *A Thousand Pails of Water* (K–2). Illus. by VoDinh Mai. 1978, Knopf $4.95; LB $4.99. A small Japanese boy helps save a beached whale.

772. Roy, Ron. *Three Ducks Went Wandering* (PS–1). Illus. by Paul Galdone. 1979, Seabury $8.94. Three ducks are oblivious to the dangers all around them when they take a walk.

773. Schlein, Miriam. *What's Wrong with Being a Skunk?* (K–3). Illus. by Ray Cruz. 1974, Four Winds $5.95. Shunks are really good-natured animals and only spray when in danger. Their hibernation and feeding habits are well described.

774. Schneider, Gerlinde. *Uncle Harry* (PS–1). Adapted from the German by Elizabeth Shub. Illus. by Lilo Fromm. 1972, Macmillan $3.95. Kindly Uncle Harry is the only one who will give the stray kitten a home.

775. Schoenherr, John. *The Barn* (1–3). Illus. by author. 1968, Atlantic/Little $3.95. The tension of a skunk finding itself prey to an owl is delicately captured in words and pictures in this compelling nature drama.

776. Schweitzer, Byrd Baylor. *Amigo* (K–3). Illus. by Garth Williams. 1963, Macmillan $5.95; paper $.95. Francisco, who longs for a pet, finds a wild prairie dog who wishes to tame a boy.

777. Sewell, Helen. *Blue Barns* (1–3). Illus. by author. 1961, Macmillan $3.95. Subtitled: *The Story of 2 Big Geese and 7 Little Ducks.*

778. Sharmat, Marjorie W. *Morris Brookside, a Dog* (K–3). Illus. by Ronald Himler. 1973, Holiday $4.95. An elderly couple adopt a stray dog, Morris, who insists on making friends with another very dirty female stray, and finally the old couple relent and adopt her too. Sequel: *Morris Brookside Is Missing* (1974, Holiday $4.95).

779. Skorpen, Liesel Moak. *Bird* (K–3). Illus. by Joan Sandin. 1976, Harper $5.79. A small boy finds a baby bird and cares for it through one summer until it is ready to fly.

780. Skorpen, Liesel Moak. *His Mother's Dog* (1–3). Illus. by M. E. Mullin. 1978, Harper $6.95; LB $6.79. A little boy is crushed when his new dog prefers his mother.

781. Skorpen, Liesel Moak. *Old Arthur* (PS–2). Illus. by Wallace Tripp. 1972, Harper $8.97. Old Arthur becomes too old to work on the farm and ends up in the dog pound. All is not lost, however, for young William chooses Arthur for his pet, and a lovely friendship develops.

782. Turner, Dona. *My Cat Pearl* (PS–2). Illus. by author. 1980, Crowell $7.89. A description of the everyday activities of a young girl and her cat.

783. Uchida, Yoshiko. *The Rooster Who Understood Japanese* (1–3). Illus. by Charles Robinson. 1976, Scribner $6.95. Little Miyo spends her after school hours with Mrs. Kitamura, who speaks Japanese to her many pets.

784. Wagner, Jenny. *Aranea: A Story about a Spider* (K–3). Illus. by Ron Brooks. 1978, Bradbury $6.95. Tells about the painstaking work of spinning a perfect spider's web.

785. Willard, Nancy. *Papa's Panda* (K–2). Illus. by Lillian Hoban. 1979, Harcourt $5.95. James realizes that it's better to live with a toy panda than a real one.

786. Yashima, Mitsu, and Yashima, Taro. *Momo's Kitten* (K–3). Illus. by author. 1961, Penguin paper $1.25. Momo must give away her pet cat's 5 kittens.

787. Ylla. *Two Little Bears* (PS–1). Illus. by author. 1954, Harper $7.89; paper $1.95. Photographic story of 2 cubs.

788. Zimelman, Nathan. *The Lives of My Cat Alfred* (K–3). Illus. by Evaline Ness. 1976, Dutton $5.95. Alfred thinks his cat is so special and wise that he might have participated in any number of important events, engagingly illustrated.

Family Stories

789. Adoff, Arnold. *Black Is Brown Is Tan* (K–3). Illus. by Emily McCully. 1973, Harper $4.95; LB $5.49. A story in rhyme, which needs to be read aloud for greater understanding, depicts the warmth and companionship of an interracial family.

790. Alexander, Martha. *I'll Be the Horse If You'll Play with Me* (PS–2). Illus. by author. 1975, Dial $5.95; LB $5.47. Bonnie issues her own declaration of independence in this humorous story.

791. Alexander, Martha. *Nobody Asked Me If I Wanted a Baby Sister* (PS–1). Illus. by author. 1971, Dial $4.95; LB $4.58. A young boy discovers that he does love his baby sister in spite of the fact that he thinks there is much too much fuss made over her.

792. Alexander, Martha. *We Never Get to Do Anything* (K–2). Illus. by author. 1970, Dial $4.95; LB $4.58. On a hot summer day, Adam's plans to go swimming are foiled, but rainfall helps ease the situation.

793. Alexander, Martha. *When the New Baby Comes, I'm Moving Out* (PS–K). Illus. by author. 1979, Dial $5.95; LB $5.47. Oliver has many reasons to resent his place being usurped by a new baby.

794. Asch, Frank. *Monkey Face* (1–3). Illus. by author. 1977, Parents $5.95; LB $5.41. Is it really true that only a mother could love this portrait?

795. Baldwin, Anne Norris. *Sunflowers for Tina* (1–3). Illus. by author. 1970, Scholastic paper $1.25. How Tina finds a "garden" of sunflowers and shares her joy with her grandmother.

796. Bartoli, Jennifer. *Nonna* (K–3). Illus. by Joan Drescher. 1975, Harvey House $5.99. A warm gentle story of an Italian-American family and of the grandmother's death, as seen from the child's point of view.

797. Barton, Pat. *A Week Is a Long Time* (PS–2). Illus. by Jutta Ash. 1980, Academy $5.95. Honey

Brown wonders if she will enjoy her week-long visit with Great Aunt Em.

798. Baylor, Byrd. *Guess Who My Favorite Person Is* (1–3). Illus. by Robert Andrew Parker. 1977, Scribner $7.95. A sensitive book that celebrates the joy and happiness in listing favorites.

799. Behrens, June. *Fiesta!* (1–3). Illus. by Scott Taylor. 1978, Childrens Press $7.35. The fun of celebrating a Mexican-American family holiday—Cinco de Mayo.

800. Blaine, Marge. *The Terrible Thing that Happened at Our House* (K–2). Illus. by John Wallner. 1975, Parents $5.95; LB $5.41. Chaos reigns when mother decides to go back to work and the children have to learn to "cope."

801. Borack, Barbara. *Grandpa* (PS–2). Illus. by Ben Shecter. 1967, Harper $6.79. Marilyn enjoys a visit with her grandparents and has an especially good time with her grandfather.

802. Brandenberg, Franz. *I Wish I Was Sick Too!* (K–3). Illus. by Aliki. 1976, Greenwillow $6.95; LB $6.43; Penguin paper $1.95. Elizabeth is jealous when her brother's illness gets him all sorts of special attention.

803. Buckley, Helen E. *Grandmother and I* (PS–1). Illus. by Paul Galdone. 1961, Lothrop $6.43. A small girl explains the reasons why Grandmother's lap is better than anyone else's. Also use: *Grandfather and I* (1959, Lothrop $6.43).

804. Bunin, Catherine, and Bunin, Sherry. *Is That Your Sister? A True Story of Adoption* (K–3). Illus. by author. 1976, Pantheon $4.95; LB $5.99. Six-year-old Catherine and her sister Carla, both black, are adopted into a white family with 2 boys.

805. Byars, Betsy. *Go and Hush the Baby* (PS–1). Illus. by Emily McCully. 1971, Viking $5.95. A clever young boy tries to quiet his baby brother.

806. Caines, Jeannette Franklin. *Abby* (PS–1). Illus. by Steven Kellogg. 1973, Harper $5.95; LB $6.89. Abby, a little black girl, is adopted and enjoys hearing about the day she became part of her warm, loving family.

807. Carle, Eric. *The Secret Birthday Message* (PS–1). Illus. by author. 1972, Crowell $6.95; LB $6.85. In a brightly illustrated picture book with intriguing cutouts, a little boy has to decipher the coded message to find his birthday present.

808. Castiglia, Julie. *Jill the Pill* (K–3). Illus. by Steven Kellogg. 1979, Atheneum $6.95. Pat the Brat describes all the things he dislikes about his older sister.

809. Clifton, Lucille. *Amifika* (PS–1). Illus. by Thomas D. Grazia. 1977, Dutton $5.95. Poor Amifika misunderstands a remark and thinks his family wants to get rid of him.

810. Clifton, Lucille. *Don't You Remember?* (PS–K). Illus. by Evaline Ness. 1973, Dutton $6.50. Four-year-old Denise remembers everything and is very upset when her parents keep putting off what they had promised her.

811. Clifton, Lucille. *Everett Anderson's Nine Month Long* (K–2). Illus. by Ann Grifalconi. 1978, Holt $6.95. Everett, a young black boy, must adjust to a new stepfather.

812. Clifton, Lucille. *My Brother Fine with Me* (K–3). Illus. by M. Barnett. 1975, Holt $5.50. Johnetta's brother, Baggy, decides to run away in this amusing story told in black English.

813. Delton, Judy. *My Mom Hates Me in January* (K–2). Illus. by John Faulkner. 1977, Whitman $5.95. Mother really doesn't hate Lee Henry in January. What she hates is the weather in January, a sentiment echoed by many adults.

814. de Paola, Tomie. *Watch Out for the Chicken Feet in Your Soup* (K–2). Illus. by author. 1974, Prentice-Hall $5.95; paper $1.50. Joey is a little embarrassed to take his friend Eugene to his old-fashioned Italian grandmother's for a visit, but in spite of her strange foreign ways, both boys pronounce the visit a great success.

815. Dickenson, Louise. *Good Wife, Good Wife* (1–3). Illus. by Ronald Himler. 1977, McGraw $9.95; LB $7.95. A couple's ways change with the arrival of their first baby.

816. Edwards, Dorothy. *A Wet Monday* (K–3). Illus. by Jenny Williams. 1976, Morrow $6.00; paper $2.95. Everything seems to go wrong for a household on a particularly wet Monday.

817. Ehrlich, Amy. *Zeek Silver Moon* (PS–3). Illus. by Robert Andrew Parker. 1972, Dial $5.95; LB $5.47. The happiness encountered in everyday living is revealed in scenes of the first 5 years of Zeek Silver Moon's life.

818. Everton, Macduff. *Elcirco Magico Modelo: Finding the Magic Circus* (K–4). Illus. by author. 1979, Carolrhoda $7.95. Ricky spends a summer in Yucatan with his father, a former circus performer.

819. Farber, Norma. *How Does It Feel to Be Old?* (1–3). Illus. by Trina Schart Hyman. 1979, Dutton $7.95. Grandmother tries to explain to a young girl what it is like to be old.

820. Fenton, Edward. *Fierce John* (K–2). Illus. by William Pene du Bois. 1974, Dell paper $.75.

After seeing a lion in a zoo, John spends the day pretending that he is as fierce.

821. Flack, Marjorie. *Wait for William* (1–3). Illus. by A and R. A. Holberg. 1935, Houghton $6.95. William is left behind by his brother and sister, but all is well when he is allowed to ride in the circus parade.

822. Goffstein, M. B. *Family Scrapbook* (K–3). Illus. by author. 1978, Farrar $5.95. Vignettes of a Jewish family, told by one of the 2 children.

823. Goffstein, M. B. *Fish for Supper* (PS). Illus. by author. 1976, Dial $4.95; LB $4.58. Grandmother enjoys fishing more than anything else and spends each day doing just that. Caldecott Honor Book.

824. Goffstein, M. B. *My Crazy Sister* (K–3). Illus. by author. 1976, Dial $5.95; LB $5.47. Two sisters and a baby live in harmony in spite of the preposterous doings of one of the girls.

825. Goldman, Susan. *Cousins Are Special* (K–2). Illus. by author. 1978, Whitman $5.50; LB $4.13. A warm friendship is depicted between 2 cousins.

826. Gray, Genevieve. *Send Wendell* (K–3). Illus. by Symeon Shimin. 1974, McGraw $6.84. It is always 6-year-old Wendell whose services are called upon to run errands for his older brothers and sisters in this happy black family.

827. Greenfield, Eloise. *First Pink Light* (K–3). Illus. by M. Barnett. 1976, Crowell $6.50. A mother's wisdom subdues the willful intent of a young boy on waiting up until his father returns.

828. Greenfield, Eloise. *She Come Bringing Me That Little Baby Girl* (K–2). Illus. by John Steptoe. 1974, Lippincott $8.95. Kevin resents all the attention the new baby is getting; most of all he resents the fact that she is a girl.

829. Hamilton, Morse, and Hamilton, Emily. *My Name Is Emily* (PS–1). Illus. by Jenni Oliver. 1979, Morrow $6.95; LB $6.67. When Emily returns home after running away, her father pretends not to recognize her.

830. Hapgood, Miranda. *Martha's Mad Day* (K–2). Illus. by Emily McCully. 1977, Crown $3.95. In spite of her parents' patience, Martha continues to be generally obnoxious during her awful day.

831. Hautzig, Deborah. *The Handsomest Father* (K–2). Illus. by Muriel Batherman. 1979, Greenwillow $5.95; LB $5.71. At school, a young girl has fears that her father won't match up to her friends' parents on visiting day.

832. Hazen, Barbara S. *If It Weren't for Benjamin I'd Always Get to Lick the Icing* (PS–2). Illus. by Laura Hartman. 1979, Human Sciences $6.95. A younger sibling recounts the reasons for his sense of injustice.

833. Hill, Elizabeth Starr. *Evan's Corner* (K–3). Illus. by Nancy Grossman. 1967, Holt $5.95; paper $1.45. Evan longs for a place of his own, until his mother points out that there are 8 corners in their 2-room apartment—one for him and each member of the family.

834. Hirsch, Karen. *My Sister* (K–2). Illus. by Nancy Inderieden. 1977, Carolrhoda $4.95. A narrator introduces her sister, a retarded girl, whom she loves and protects.

835. Hoban, Russell. *The Sorely Trying Day* (K–3). Illus. by Lillian Hoban. 1964, Harper $6.89. After a bad day at the office, father has an equally trying time when he returns home.

836. Hutchins, Pat. *Happy Birthday, Sam* (1–3). Illus. by author. 1979, Greenwillow $6.67. Sam is disappointed on his birthday morning to discover that he hasn't grown at all.

837. Hutchins, Pat. *Titch* (K–3). Illus. by author. 1971, Macmillan $5.95; paper $.95. Titch, the youngest in the family, enjoys a moment of triumph.

838. Keats, Ezra Jack. *Peter's Chair* (PS–1). Illus. by author. 1967, Harper $7.95; LB $7.89. Distinctive collage technique and a gentle story show Peter emerging from his jealousy of a recent addition to the family to the acceptance of his new role as big brother.

839. Kellogg, Steven. *Can I Keep Him?* (K–2). Illus. by author. 1971, Dial $4.95; paper $1.95. Arnold, an incorrigible animal lover, constantly distresses his mother with a wide assortment of pets —real, imaginary, and human.

840. Klein, Norma. *If I Had My Way* (K–2). Illus. by Ray Cruz. 1974, Pantheon $5.99. Ellie dreams of all the things she would do if she were in charge and her parents had to obey her.

841. Knotts, Howard. *Great-Grandfather, the Baby and Me* (K–2). Illus. by author. 1978, Atheneum $5.95. Great-grandfather helps a young boy adjust to the arrival of a baby sister in the family.

842. Kroll, Steven. *If I Could Be My Grandmother* (PS–K). Illus. by Lady McCrady. 1977, Pantheon $5.95; LB $5.99. A little girl pretends that she is a grandmother and imitates her real-life counterpart.

843. Langner, Nola. *Freddy My Grandfather* (2–3). Illus. by author. 1979, Four Winds $6.95. A warm account of a young girl's reflections on her grandfather who lives in her home.

844.   Lapsley, Susan. *I Am Adopted* (PS–K). Illus. by Michael Charlton. 1975, Bradbury $4.95. "Adoption means belonging" is the theme of this very simple story of 2 children who know they are adopted.

845.   Lasker, Joe. *Lentil Soup* (K–3). Illus. by author. 1977, Whitman $5.75. Meg finds it impossible to make lentil soup exactly as her mother-in-law used to make.

846.   Lasky, Kathryn. *My Island Grandma* (K–2). Illus. by Emily McCully. 1979, Warne $7.95. An idyllic summer spent by Abbey with her grandmother.

847.   Lexau, Joan M. *Benjie* (PS–1). Illus. by Don Bolognese. 1964, Dial $6.95; LB $6.46. Benjie is painfully shy until he forces himself to go out alone to look for Granny's lost earring. Also use: *Benjie on His Own* (1970, Dial $5.95; LB $5.47).

848.   Lexau, Joan M. *Emily and the Klunky Baby and the Next-Door Dog* (K–2). Illus. by Martha Alexander. 1972, Dial $5.95; LB $5.47. A little girl takes her baby brother for a ride on a sled and becomes lost. Since she is not allowed to cross streets, she eventually returns home and is not lost at all.

849.   Lexau, Joan M. *Me Day* (K–3). Illus. by Robert Weaver. 1971, Dial $4.95; LB $4.58. A poignant story tells of Rafer's birthday and his surprise—a meeting with his divorced father whom he misses very much.

850.   Lobel, Arnold. *A Treeful of Pigs* (K–2). Illus. by Anita Lobel. 1978, Greenwillow $7.95; LB $7.63. A canny wife cures her husband of laziness.

851.   McCloskey, Robert. *One Morning in Maine* (1–3). Illus. by author. 1952, Viking $7.95; Penguin paper $1.95. An exciting day, the loss of Sal's first tooth, is realistically recaptured by this fine storyteller and in the large, extraordinary blue pencil drawings of Penobscot Bay. Also use: *Blueberries for Sal* (1948, Viking $5.95; Penguin, paper $1.95).

852.   MacLachlan, Patricia. *The Sick Day* (K–2). Illus. by William Pene du Bois. 1979, Pantheon $6.95; LB $6.99. When Emily is sick, her father takes care of and amuses her.

853.   Mahood, Kenneth. *Why Are There More Questions Than Answers, Grandad?* (PS–2). Illus. by author. 1974, Bradbury $6.95. A young boy gets help from picture-book characters in cleaning up an attic.

854.   Merriam, Eve. *Mommies at Work* (K–1). Illus. by Beni Montresor. 1973, Scholastic paper $1.50. Why mommy can be like other people and hold down a job.

855.   Milgram, Mary. *Brothers Are All the Same* (1–3). Illus. by Rosmarie Hauscherr. 1978, Dutton $6.95. About adoption and acceptance of a foster brother.

856.   Mizumura, Kazue. *If I Were a Mother* (PS–1). Illus. by author. 1968, Crowell $7.89. A tender, warm story about a little girl's imagining what kind of mother she would be, in terms of animal mothers she knows.

857.   Naylor, Phyllis Reynolds. *How Lazy Can You Get?* (2–4). Illus. by Alan Daniel. 1979, Atheneum $7.95. Three children adjust slowly to their strict professional caretaker, Miss Brasscoat.

858.   Ness, Evaline. *Do You Have the Time, Lydia?* (K–3). Illus. by author. 1971, Dutton paper $1.25. Lydia never has time to complete any of her projects until, through her baby brother, she learns a valuable leason.

859.   Ness, Evaline. *Yeck Eck* (1–3). Illus. by author. 1974, Dutton $6.95. Tana Jones gets her wish to adopt babies in this delightfully daffy tale.

860.   Nolan, Madeena Spray. *My Daddy Don't Go to Work* (1–3). Illus. by Jim LaMarche. 1978, Carolrhoda $4.95. A black girl tells of family problems caused by her father's unemployment.

861.   Ostrovsky, Vivian. *Mumps!* (K–1). Illus. by Rose Ostrovsky. 1978, Holt $6.95. The whole family is dislocated when Booboo Fitzleberry gets the mumps.

862.   Parson, Ellen. *Rainy Day Together* (PS–2). Illus. by Lillian Hoban. 1971, Harper $6.89. A quiet, tender picture book about a young girl's rainy day spent at home with her family.

863.   Pearson, Susan. *That's Enough for One Day, J.P.!* (K–2). Illus. by Kay Chorao. 1977, Dial $5.95; LB $5.47. John Philip obeys his mother and goes out to play, with humorous results.

864.   Peterson, Jeanne Whitehouse. *I Have a Sister: My Sister Is Deaf* (PS–2). Illus. by Deborah Ray. 1977, Harper $6.95; LB $6.89. A simple direct story in which it is pointed out that deaf children can be alert, intelligent, and sensitive.

865.   Pincus, Harriet. *Minna and Pippin* (PS–3). Illus. by author. 1972, Farrar $3.95. The pleasures a young girl named Minna receives from naming Pippin, a new doll.

866.   Politi, Leo. *Three Stalks of Corn* (K–4). Illus. by author. 1976, Scribner $6.95. Chicano culture, including some recipes, are included in this story of a girl and her grandmother.

867. Power, Barbara. *I Wish Laura's Mommy Was My Mommy* (1–3). Illus. by Marylin Hafner. 1979, Lippincott $7.95; LB $7.89. When roles are reversed, Jennifer is glad to have her own mommy back.

868. Rice, Eve. *New Blue Shoes* (PS–K). Illus. by author. 1975, Macmillan $7.95; Penguin paper $1.95. Rebecca insists on blue as the color for her new shoes, but after purchasing them, doubts assail her.

869. Rice, Eve. *What Sadie Sang* (PS). Illus. by author. 1976, Greenwillow $5.04; LB $4.59. What Sadie, a very young child, sang was a song according to her mother.

870. Rockwell, Anne. *Blackout* (2–3). Illus. by author. 1979, Macmillan $6.95. How a family lives through a long power blackout.

871. Ruffins, Reynold. *My Brother Never Feeds the Cat* (PS–K). Illus. by author. 1979, Scribner $7.95. A young girl complains that her brother doesn't have the chores that she has.

872. Schermer, Judith. *Mouse in House* (PS–K). Illus. by author. 1979, Houghton $6.95. Mama and Dad turn the house inside out to find a mouse.

873. Schick, Alice, and Schick, Joel. *Viola Hates Music* (PS). Illus. by author. 1977, Lippincott $4.95. Everyone in the Osborne family makes music, which only causes Viola, the dog, to howl in anguish.

874. Schick, Eleanor. *Peggy's New Brother* (K–2). Illus. by author. 1970, Macmillan $4.95. Peggy's status changes with the arrival of a brother, but she manages to find a unique way she can help her mother.

875. Scott, Ann H. *Sam* (PS–1). Illus. by Symeon Shimin. 1967, McGraw $5.95; LB $5.72. Each member of this black family is too preoccupied to give any attention to Sam, until they notice his dejection and provide a satisfying job for him to do.

876. Segal, Lore. *Tell Me a Mitzi* (K–2). Illus. by Harriet Pincus. 1970, Farrar $4.95. Three hilarious stories about the antics of a city family; a mad trip to Grandma's house, coming down with a cold, and a meeting with the president.

877. Segal, Lore. *Tell Me a Trudy* (PS–3). Illus. by Rosemary Wells. 1977, Farrar $8.95. A zany family undergoes ordinary situations that somehow become most unusual.

878. Sharmat, Marjorie W. *I Don't Care* (PS–K). Illus. by Lillian Hoban. 1977, Macmillan $6.95. Jonathan stoutly insists he doesn't care when his blue balloon drifts off into the sky, but he does and goes to his bedroom crying over his loss.

879. Sharmat, Marjorie W. *I Want Mama* (K–2). Illus. by Emily Arnold McCully. 1974, Harper $6.89. When her mother goes to the hospital, the little girl is very lonesome and even though daddy says mother will be home soon, soon seems like forever.

880. Sharmat, Marjorie W. *Sometimes Mama and Papa Fight* (K–3). Illus. by Kay Chorao. 1980, Harper $7.95; LB $7.89. Two youngsters react to their parents' quarreling.

881. Shulevitz, Uri. *The Treasure* (K–2). Illus. by author. 1979, Farrar $7.95. A man discovers that the most valuable things in life are usually found at home.

882. Simon, Norma. *I'm Busy Too* (PS–1). Illus. by Dora Leder. 1980, Whitman $6.25. The work activities of preschool children and parents are compared in this picture book.

883. Skorpen, Liesel Moak. *Mandy's Grandmother* (K–2). Illus. by Martha Alexander. 1975, Dial $4.95; LB $4.98. Mandy learns to love her grandmother as much as her grandmother loves her.

884. Smith, Lucia B. *My Mom Got a Job* (1–3). Illus. by C. Christina Johanson. 1979, Holt $5.95. A young girl weighs the pros and cons of her mother's new job.

885. Sonneborn, Ruth A. *Friday Night Is Papa Night* (K–3). Illus. by Emily McCully. 1970, Viking $5.95; paper $2.40. Story of a Puerto Rican family, in which Pedro and his brothers and sister wait for "Papa night" (Friday), when Papa is home from his 2 jobs. Also use: *Seven in a Bed* (1968, Viking $3.95).

886. Steptoe, John. *Daddy Is a Monster . . . Sometimes* (K–3). Illustrated. 1980, Lippincott $8.95; LB $8.79. Two boys talk about their fathers and agree that they are not so mean after all.

887. Steptoe, John. *Stevie* (PS–2). Illus. by author. 1969, Harper $7.95; LB $7.89. A small black boy eloquently expresses his resentment at having to share his possessions and mother with a temporary younger boarder who became "kinda like a little brother," illustrated in bold line and color.

888. Strete, Craig Kee. *When Grandfather Journeys into Winter* (1–3). Illus. by Hal Frenck. 1979, Greenwillow $6.95. The touching relationship between an American Indian boy and his grandfather.

889. Thomas, Ianthe. *Walk Home Tired, Billy Jenkins* (K–2). Illus. by Thomas DiGrazia. 1974, Harper $6.89. Poor sister Nina tries everything to coax weary Bill Jenkins to walk home, in this warm, tender story.

890. Tobias, Tobi. *A Day Off* (K–2). Illus. by Ray Cruz. 1973, Putnam $5.69. A little boy enjoys his one day of sickness, for he is just sick enough to stay home from school and get more than the usual amount of attention from mother.

891. Tobias, Tobi. *Moving Day* (PS–K). Illus. by William Pene du Bois. 1976, Knopf $4.95; LB $5.99. A stuffed toy bear helps comfort a little girl through the turmoil and fears of moving day.

892. Udry, Janice May. *What Mary Jo Wanted* (K–2). Illus. by Eleanor Mill. 1968, Whitman $5.95. Mary Jo fulfills her promise to take full responsibility for the care and training of her long-desired pup. Attractive, realistic drawings of a black family. Also use: *What Mary Jo Shared* (1966, $5.95) and *Mary Jo's Grandmother* (1970, $4.95).

893. Van Leeuwen, Jean. *Too Hot for Ice Cream* (K–2). Illus. by Martha Alexander. 1974, Dial $4.78. Everything goes wrong for Sara on this particular day.

894. Vineberg, Ethel. *Grandmother Came from Dworitz: A Jewish Story* (2–4). Illus. by Rita Briansky. 1978, Tundra paper $2.95. A simple retelling of an immigration story from Poland to Canada.

895. Viorst, Judith. *Alexander and the Terrible, Horrible, No Good, Very Bad Day* (K–3). Illus. by Ray Cruz. 1972, Atheneum $1.95. Alexander wakes up to a bad day and things get progressively worse as the hours wear on, until he thinks he may escape it all and go to Australia.

896. Waber, Bernard. *But Names Will Never Hurt Me* (PS–1). Illus. by author. 1976, Houghton $6.95. Alison is teased about her last name, but after her family tells her the story of how she was named, she feels better and can even joke about it.

897. Watts, Bernadette. *David's Waiting Day* (PS–1). 1978, Prentice-Hall $6.95. David is delighted when his mother brings home a new baby.

898. Wells, Rosemary. *Unfortunately Harriet* (PS–3). Illus. by author. 1972, Dial $4.95; LB $4.58. Harriet faces problems when she spills varnish in the middle of the family's new rug.

899. Williams, Barbara. *Kevin's Grandma* (K–2). Illus. by Kay Chorao. 1975, Dutton $6.95. Kevin's grandma is an unforgettable personality—a real "swinger" when compared with the traditional grandmother type.

900. Williams, Barbara. *Someday, Said Mitchell* (K–3). Illus. by Kay Chorao. 1976, Dutton $5.95. Mother and young son discuss everyday matters while the boy dreams of how things might be someday.

901. Williams, Jay. *A Bag Full of Nothing* (K–2). Illus. by Tom O'Sullivan. 1974, Parents $5.95; LB $5.41. When Tip and his father go walking, they find a brown paper bag. Mr. Wellcome is sure it is "a bag full of nothing," but Tip thinks it is a bag full of magic, and his father is forced to agree with him.

902. Williams, Vera B. *The Great Watermelon Birthday* (K–2). Illustrated. 1980, Greenwillow $7.95; LB $7.63. An elderly couple celebrate the birth of a great-grandchild by giving away watermelon.

903. Winthrop, Elizabeth. *Are You Sad, Mama?* (K–2). Illus. by Donna Diamond. 1979, Harper $5.95; LB $6.49. A young girl tries to cheer up her mother.

904. Winthrop, Elizabeth. *I Think He Likes Me* (PS–1). Illus. by Denise Saldutti. 1980, Harper $7.95; LB $7.89. Eliza adjusts to a new baby.

905. Zemach, Margot. *To Hilda for Helping* (K–2). Illus. by author. 1977, Farrar $7.95. Hilda receives a little tin medal from her father for helping around the house, and her sister becomes jealous.

906. Zolotow, Charlotte. *Do You Know What I'll Do?* (PS–1). Illus. by Garth Williams. 1958, Harper $7.95. A little girl explains all the lovely things she is going to do for her baby brother.

907. Zolotow, Charlotte. *A Father Like That* (K–2). Illus. by Ben Shecter. 1971, Harper $5.95; LB $6.89. A fatherless boy describes the kind of father he would like to have in this tender story.

908. Zolotow, Charlotte. *If It Weren't for You* (1–3). Illus. by Ben Shecter. 1966, Harper $5.95; LB $6.49. A young boy lists all of the nice things life would provide if he just didn't have a baby brother.

909. Zolotow, Charlotte. *May I Visit?* (K–2). Illus. by Erik Blegvad. 1976, Harper $4.95; LB $5.89. A little girl imagines what it would be like to be grown up and asks her mother if she may come back for a visit at that time.

910. Zolotow, Charlotte. *My Grandson Lew* (K–3). Illus. by William Pene du Bois. 1974, Harper $4.95. Lew and his mother discuss their memories of grandpa in a gentle, poignant story of a family member who has died.

911. Zolotow, Charlotte. *The Quarreling Book* (K–2). Illus. by Arnold Lobel. 1963, Harper $3.95; LB $3.79. Father's failure to kiss mother one morning triggers a series of quarrels, but the pet dog sets things right. Also use: *The Hating Book* (1969, Harper $3.95).

912. Zolotow, Charlotte. *When the Wind Stops* (1–3). Illus. by Howard Knotts. 1975, Harper $4.50; LB $4.79. A mother answers some of her child's simple questions.

913. Zolotow, Charlotte. *William's Doll* (PS–3). Illus. by William Pene du Bois. 1972, Harper $6.95; LB $7.89. William wanted a doll, much to his father's dismay, but when Grandma comes to visit she presents William with a doll, saying that now he will have an opportunity to practice being a good father.

Friendship Stories

914. Battles, Edith. *What Does the Rooster Say, Yoshio?* (PS–K). Illus. by Toni Hormann. 1978, Whitman $5.50; LB $4.13. A Japanese boy and an American girl have difficulty communicating.

915. Charlip, Remy, and Supree, Burton. *Harlequin and the Gift of Many Colors* (K–3). Illus. by Remy Charlip. 1973, Parents $5.95. Harlequin can't go to the carnival because he is too poor to have a costume. His friends give Harlequin pieces of their costumes, and when they are sewn together, he becomes a rainbow of colors, clothed "in the love of his friends."

916. Desbarats, Peter. *Gabrielle and Selena* (K–3). Illus. by Nancy Grossman. 1968, Harcourt $5.50; paper $.95. When 8-year-old girls, one black, the other white, show up in each other's homes in an exchange of identity for the evening, to their surprise their parents amusingly turn the joke on them by attributing to each girl strange and previously undiscovered likes and dislikes.

917. Erskine, Jim. *Bert and Susie's Messy Tale* (PS–K). Illus. by author. 1979, Crown $5.95. Bert and a friend play in a mud puddle and almost miss the flower show.

918. Goffstein, M. B. *Neighbors* (1–3). Illus. by author. 1979, Harper $6.95; LB $6.89. After several false starts, two women gradually become friends.

919. Hays, Wilma Pitchford. *Yellow Fur and Little Hawk* (2–4). Illus. by Anthony Rao. 1980, Coward $6.29. Two friends—one American Indian, one white—and the story of a devastating drought.

920. Hazen, Barbara S. *Why Couldn't I Be an Only Kid Like You, Wigger* (PS–2). Illus. by Leigh Grant. 1975, Atheneum $6.96; paper $1.95. Two different views on the advantages and disadvantages of being an only child are whimsically presented.

921. Hickman, Martha Whitmore. *My Friend William Moved Away* (PS–1). Illus. by Bill Myers. 1979, Abingdon $6.95. Jimmy misses his friend William in this companion piece to *I'm Moving* (1975, Abingdon $5.25).

922. Hirsh, Marilyn. *Captain Jiri and Rabbi Jacob* (1–4). Illus. by author. 1976, Holiday $6.95. Two different men find they can work together and profit from each other's company.

923. Hoffman, Phyllis. *Steffie and Me* (K–3). Illus. by Emily McCully. 1970, Harper $6.89. Two children, one black, the other white, enjoy everyday activities together.

924. Hurwitz, Johanna. *Busybody Nora* (K–2). Illus. by Susan Jeschke. 1976, Morrow $4.95; Dell paper $.95. Six-year-old Nora lives in an apartment building in New York City and wants to know all her neighbors. Most of them are friendly except for one woman who calls her a busybody.

925. Hurwitz, Johanna. *New Neighbors for Nora* (2–3). Illus. by Susan Jeschke. 1979, Morrow $5.95; LB $5.71. Nora, hoping to make a new friend, is not too happy when Eugene Spencer Eastman moves into her building.

926. Kantrowitz, Mildred. *Maxie* (PS–3). Illus. by Emily McCully. 1970, Parents $5.95; LB $5.41. Maxie is a little old lady who keeps the entire neighborhood on its toes—everyone sets their clocks by her, until one morning Maxie stays in bed.

927. Keats, Ezra Jack. *Apt. 3* (PS–3). Illus. by author. 1971, Macmillan $5.95. Two brothers, investigating the various sounds of an apartment building, find a friend in Mr. Muntz, the blind man behind the door of Apt. 3.

928. Keats, Ezra Jack. *Goggles* (K–2). Illus. by author. 1969, Macmillan $5.50; paper $1.25. Dachshund Willie outmaneuvers some neighborhood bullies trying to confiscate the motorcycle goggles found by Peter. Bold collage paintings perfectly capture inner-city neighborhood scenes. Also use: *Whistle for Willie* (1964, Viking $5.95; Penguin, paper $2.25).

929. Keats, Ezra Jack. *A Letter to Amy* (1–3). Illus. by author. 1968, Harper $5.95; LB $6.49. The dilemma faced by a boy who wants to invite a girl to his all-boy birthday party.

930. Kingman, Lee. *Peter's Long Walk* (PS–1). Illus. by Barbara Cooney. 1953, Doubleday $4.95.

Peter searches for new playmates, told in repetitive text and charming pictures.

931. Lund, Doris. *You Ought to See Herbert's House* (1–3). Illus. by Steven Kellogg. 1973, Watts $4.90. Herbert tells tall tales about his house when in reality it is like everyone else's.

932. Oppenheim, Joanne. *On the Other Side of the River* (K–3). Illus. by Aliki. 1972, Watts $4.90. Quarreling inhabitants in a village learn to live together.

933. Park, W. B. *Jonathan's Friends* (PS–1). Illus. by author. 1977, Putnam $7.95. Michael tries to shake his younger brother's belief in the existence of fairies, witches, and Santa Claus.

934. Politi, Leo. *Moy Moy* (PS–3). Illus. by author. 1960, Scribner $7.95. Appealing picture of Moy Moy's life in a Los Angeles Chinese neighborhood.

935. Politi, Leo. *Pedro, the Angel of Olivera Street* (1–3). Illus. by author. 1946, Scribner $8.95. Olivera Street in Los Angeles is the setting for this story of a small boy who is chosen to play the part of an angel in the Mexican Christmas celebration.

936. Schulman, Janet. *The Great Big Dummy* (K–2). Illus. by Lillian Hoban. 1979, Greenwillow $5.95. Out of old clothes and other objects, a girl creates a playmate.

937. Sharmat, Marjorie W. *Gladys Told Me to Meet Her Here* (K–2). Illus. by Edward Frascino. 1970, Harper $6.89. Irving is waiting for his friend Gladys, who is 10 minutes late.

938. Sharmat, Marjorie W. *I'm Not Oscar's Friend Anymore* (K–2). Illus. by Tony DeLuna. 1975, Dutton $5.95. Oscar's best friend tells all the reasons why they aren't friends anymore, but Oscar doesn't even remember they had a fight, and normal relations are happily resumed.

939. Sherman, Ivan. *I Do Not Like It When My Friend Comes to Visit* (PS–2). Illus. by author. 1973, Harcourt $6.25. A little girl voices her displeasure when her friend comes to visit and gets the lion's share of the toys and attention.

940. Uchida, Yoshiko. *The Birthday Visitor* (1–3). Illus. by Charles Robinson. 1975, Scribner $5.95. At first, Emi, a Japanese-American girl, resents having a visitor from Japan on her birthday.

941. Udry, Janice May. *Let's Be Enemies* (PS–2). Illus. by Maurice Sendak. 1961, Harper $4.95; Scholastic paper $.95. John is tired of James and his bossiness and decides to tell him so, but things are patched up and they remain friends.

942. Winthrop, Elizabeth. *That's Mine!* (PS–K). Illus. by Emily McCully. 1977, Holiday $5.95. Two children who quarrel over a block learn the necessity of sharing.

943. Wittman, Sally. *A Special Trade* (1–3). Illus. by Karen Gundersheimer. 1978, Harper $7.95; LB $7.89. Nelly, now grown, takes Old Bartholomew out for a walk as he once took her.

944. Zolotow, Charlotte. *Janey* (1–3). Illus. by Ronald Himler. 1973, Harper $5.95; LB $6.89. A little girl misses her best friend who has moved away and reminisces about the things they used to do together.

945. Zolotow, Charlotte. *The Unfriendly Book* (K–3). Illus. by William Pene du Bois. 1975, Harper $4.95. Bertha finds fault with many of her friends, but Judy always has a compliment for each. Finally, Bertha accuses Judy of liking everyone, and Judy replies, "No—I don't like everyone. In fact, I don't like you!"

School Stories

946. Alexander, Martha. *Sabrina* (PS–2). Illus. by author. 1971, Dial $5.95. Sabrina's companions at nursery school make fun of her name until they realize it is the name of a princess.

947. Allard, Harry. *Miss Nelson Is Missing!* (K–2). Illus. by James Marshall. 1977, Houghton $6.95. When Miss Nelson's students in Room 207 misbehave, she disappears and is replaced by a martinet, Miss Viola Swamp, much to the dismay of the children.

948. Anderson, Eloise A. *Carlos Goes to School* (PS–2). Illus. by Harold Berson. 1973, Warne $4.95. Carlos, a 6-year-old, is apprehensive about going to school but finds the experience interesting and enjoyable.

949. Barkin, Carol, and James, Elizabeth. *Sometimes I Hate School* (K–2). Photos by Heinz Kluetmeier. 1975, Raintree $7.33. Surprisingly, the substitute teacher turns out to be fun and will be missed when the regular teacher returns.

950. Breinburg, Petronella. *Shawn Goes to School* (PS–1). Illus. by Errol Lloyd. 1974, Crowell $7.89. Shawn's first day at school is described by his older sister, in a story written by a South American author and illustrated by a Jamaican. Also use: *Doctor Shawn* (1975, Crowell $5.95; LB $6.95) and *Shawn's Red Bike* (1976, Crowell $6.95).

951. Brooks, Ron. *Timothy and Gramps* (1–3). 1979, Bradbury $6.95. Gramps' visit to school changes Timothy's classroom status.

952. Caudill, Rebecca. *A Pocketful of Cricket* (1–3). Illus. by Evaline Ness. 1964, Holt $5.95; paper $1.65. A small boy delights in the countryside around his home, and one day his pet cricket goes to school in his pocket.

953. Chorao, Kay. *Molly's Lies* (K–2). Illus. by author. 1979, Seabury $7.50. Molly copes with the first day of school by telling fibs.

954. Cohen, Miriam. *Best Friends* (PS–K). Illus. by Lillian Hoban. 1971, Macmillan $5.95; paper $.95. Kindergarten is the setting for this story of the friendship and disagreements between 2 boys.

955. Cohen, Miriam. *The New Teacher* (PS–1). Illus. by Lillian Hoban. 1972, Macmillan paper $1.25. June was very apprehensive about the new teacher, but she turned out to be enthusiastic and fun. A good story for reading aloud.

956. Cohen, Miriam. *Touch Jim* (PS–1). Illus. by Lillian Hoban. 1974, Macmillan $4.95. The first-grade class has a costume party, and Jim comes as the strongest man in the world. But he has to prove his toughness when a bully from the third grade appears.

957. Cohen, Miriam. *Will I Have a Friend?* (PS–K). Illus. by Lillian Hoban. 1967, Macmillan $4.95; paper $1.25. Jim, a kindergartner, lives out the actual concerns that small children have about finding a friend on the first day of school.

958. Isadora, Rachel. *Willaby* (K–2). Illus. by author. 1977, Macmillan $6.95. Willaby's desire to express himself in drawing causes school complications.

959. Johnston, Johanna. *Speak Up, Edie!* (K–3). Illus. by Paul Galdone. 1974, Putnam $5.29. Edie is a talker and annoys everyone with her prattle. When she is chosen as the narrator for the class play, she becomes tongue-tied and suddenly realizes what her incessant chatter does to other people.

960. Johnston, Johanna. *That's Right, Edie* (K–3). Illustrated. 1966, Putnam $5.99. More adventures of spirited Edie.

961. Rockwell, Harlow. *My Nursery School* (PS). Illus. by author. 1976, Greenwillow $6.43. Clear, simple pictures show the daily activities of a nursery school.

962. Tester, Sylvia Root. *We Laughed a Lot, My First Day of School* (PS–1). Illus. by Frances Hook. 1979, Childrens Press $5.50. A Mexican-American boy has an unexpectedly pleasant first day at school.

963. Udry, Janice May. *Glenda* (K–3). Illus. by Marc Simont. 1969, Harper $5.95; LB $5.79; Archway paper $.95. Glenda, a witch in the guise of a schoolgirl, brews malicious mischief in the classroom—envy, tale carrying, currying favor—but she fails amusingly in a successful comic mirror of middle-grade social structure.

964. Welber, Robert. *Goodbye, Hello* (PS–K). Illus. by Cyndy Szekeres. 1974, Pantheon $4.99. A little boy and his mother walk through the woods and address each animal with a hello and then on leave-taking, a goodbye. At the end the little boy says, "Goodbye Mother—Hello Teacher."

965. Wellman, Alice. *Tatu and the Honeybird* (K–3). Illus. by Dale Payson. 1972, Putnam $4.89. A lucky find of honey allows Tatus's sister to attend school in this tale set in Africa.

966. Whitney, Alma Marshak. *Just Awful* (K–2). Illus. by Lillian Hoban. 1971, Addison $6.95. James cuts his finger and goes to the school nurse for the first time, with satisfactory results.

967. Wolf, Bernard. *Adam Smith Goes to School* (PS–1). Illustrated. 1978, Lippincott $6.95. Adam's first day in the first grade.

968. Yashima, Taro. *Crow Boy* (K–3). Illus. by author. 1955, Viking $5.95; Penguin paper $2.25. Distinguished picture book about a shy little Japanese boy who feels like an outsider at school.

Adventure Stories

969. Adoff, Arnold. *Where Wild Willie* (K–2). Illus. by Emily McCully. 1978, Harper $6.95; LB $6.79. Willie stays out late exploring the neighborhood.

970. Ambrus, Victor G. *Mishka* (1–3). 1978, Warne $6.95. A boy plays his fiddle and wins applause with a circus.

971. Anglund, Joan Walsh. *Cowboy and His Friend* (K–3). Illus. by author. 1961, Harcourt $3.95; paper $1.95. Adventures of a small cowboy who has an imaginary bear for a playmate. See also (Harcourt $3.95): *The Brave Cowboy* (1959, also paper $1.95) and *Cowboy's Secret Life* (1963).

972. Ardizzone, Edward. *Tim's Last Voyage* (K–3). Illus. by author. 1972, Walck $6.95. When Tim and Ginger sign for a 3-day voyage, it is Tim who saves the crew when shipwreck is imminent. This will be his last trip to sea until he grows up, Tim promises his mother. Also use: *Little Tim and* *the Brave Sea Captain* (1936, $8.95), *Tim to the Rescue* (1949, $6.95), *Tim All Alone* (1957, $6.95).

973. Ardizzone, Edward. *Ship's Cook Ginger* (2–3). Illus. by author. 1978, Macmillan $7.95. Two young boys save a ship when the entire crew falls ill.

974. Austin, Margot. *Barney's Adventure* (K–2). Illus. by author. 1941, Dutton $4.95; paper $.85. An enterprising boy and his dog earn tickets to the circus.

975. Berson, Harold. *The Boy, the Baker, the Miller and More* (K–3). Illus. by author. 1974, Crown $5.95. A cumulative tale that begins when a boy asks the baker's wife for a piece of bread.

976. Blake, Quentin. *Snuff* (K–2). Illus. by author. 1973, Lippincott $5.95. Snuff is a page who can't seem to master any of the skills needed to become a knight, but he uses his brain to foil some robbers and thus demonstrates his ability after all.

977. Bornstein, Ruth. *Of Course a Goat* (PS–K). Illustrated. 1980, Harper $7.95; LB $7.89. A boy imagines a journey to the top of a mountain.

978. Brenner, Barbara. *Barto Takes the Subway* (2–3). Illus. by Sy Katzoff. 1961, Crowell $4.69. Barto, from Puerto Rico, takes his first subway ride in New York City.

979. Burningham, John. *Mr. Gumpy's Motor Car* (K–3). Illus. by author. 1976, Crowell $7.95; LB $8.50; Penguin paper $1.95. Mr. Gumpy takes his daughter and an assortment of animals for a ride in the country in his old-fashioned touring car. Companion to: *Mr. Gumpy's Outing* (1971, Holt $5.95.)

980. Byfield, Barbara. *The Haunted Churchbell* (K–3). Illus. by author. 1971, Doubleday $4.95. Suspense in a mountain village when Sir Roger de Rudisill solves the mystery of the tolling church bell—with the aid of a snowball, a cello, and a lonely hermit.

981. Calhoun, Mary. *Euphonia and the Flood* (K–3). Illus. by Simms Taback. 1976, Parents $5.95; LB $5.41; paper $1.95. Euphonia puts her motto—If a thing is worth doing, it's worth doing well—to good use when she, her broom Briskly, and her pig Fatly, ride along in a flood rescuing animals, whether they want to be rescued or not!

982. Carle, Eric. *The Rooster Who Set Out to See the World* (K–3). Illus. by author. 1972, Watts $5.95. On his trip, the rooster accumulates friends who desert him when night falls and they get hungry.

983. Carrick, Carol. *Sleep Out* (1–3). Illus. by Donald Carrick. 1973, Seabury $5.95. Christo-pher has an unsettling experience when he spends his first night outdoors in his sleeping bag.

984. Carrick, Carol. *The Washout* (1–3). Illus. by Donald Carrick. 1978, Greenwillow $6.95; LB $6.67. Christopher has an unexpected adventure after a summer storm.

985. Chorao, Kay. *Lester's Overnight* (PS–1). Illus. by author. 1977, Dutton $5.95. All of the fun and fears of the first night spent away from home are captured in this charmingly gentle picture book.

986. Cleary, Beverly. *The Real Hole* (PS–1). Illus. by Mary Stevens. 1960, Morrow $6.00. Four-year-old Jimmy digs a big hole and puts it to good use.

987. Cohen, Miriam. *Lost in the Museum* (K–1). Illus. by Lillian Hoban. 1978, Greenwillow $7.25; LB $6.95. Jim and his friends wander away from the group and get lost in the American Museum of Natural History.

988. Craft, Ruth. *Carrie Hepple's Garden* (K–2). Illus. by Irene Haas. 1979, Atheneum $9.95. In this rhyming picture book 3 children visit a forbidden garden.

989. Credle, Ellis. *Down, Down This Mountain* (K–3). Illustrated. 1961, Nelson $4.95. Two poor children from the Blue Ridge Mountains sell turnips to get new shoes.

990. de Leeuw, Adele. *Horseshoe Harry and the Whale* (K–4). Illus. by Quentin Blake. 1976, Parents $5.95; LB $5.41. Horseshoe Harry, a cowboy, is shanghaied aboard a Boston whaler and has many adventures at sea.

991. De Regniers, Beatrice S. *Laura's Story* (K–2). Illus. by Jack Kent. 1979, Atheneum $7.95. A reversal story in which a young girl tells her mother a bedtime story.

992. Devlin, Wende, and Devlin, Harry. *Hang on Hester!* (K–2). Illus. by author. 1980, Lothrop $6.95; LB $6.67. A spunky heroine finds adventure in a flood.

993. Dyke, John. *Pigwig and the Pirates* (K–2). 1979, Methuen $6.95. Pigwig sets out to rescue his nephew, who has been kidnapped by pirates.

994. Emberley, Ed. *Klippity Klop* (PS–1). Illus. by author. 1974, Little $4.95. Prince Krispin and his horse Dumpling go adventuring and discover a fierce dragon, which sends them "klickity klackity" back to the castle and safety.

995. Gantos, Jack, and Rubel, Nicole. *Greedy Greeny* (PS–1). Illustrated. 1979, Doubleday $7.95; LB $8.90. Greeny Monster eats all the food available in the kitchen, including a watermelon, and then has a nightmare.

996. Gibbons, Gail. *The Missing Maple Syrup Sap Mystery* (K–1). Illustrated. 1979, Warne $8.95. Mr. and Mrs. Mapleworth solve the mystery of the missing maple sap in an account that also explains how maple syrup is made.

997. Hoff, Syd. *Slugger Sal's Slump* (1–3). 1979, Windmill $5.95. Sal's baseball career is saved by a last-minute reversal.

998. Hutchins, Pat. *One-Eyed Jake* (1–3). Illus. by author. 1979, Greenwillow $7.95; LB $7.63. A terrifying old buccaneer meets a watery end.

999. Keats, Ezra Jack. *Maggie and the Pirate* (1–3). Illus. by author. 1979, Four Winds $8.95. Maggie tries to find the kidnapper of her pet cricket.

1000. Kellogg, Steven. *The Mystery of the Magic Green Ball* (1–3). Illus. by author. 1978, Dial $4.95; LB $4.58. A humorous mystery in which Tommy loses his big green ball.

1001. LaFarge, Phyllis. *Joanna Runs Away* (K–2). Illus. by Trina Schart Hyman. 1973, Holt $5.95. A lonely big-city child hides inside a vegetable peddler's cart.

1002. Lloyd, Errol. *Nini at Carnival* (1–3). Illustrated. 1979, Crowell $6.95. A little Jamaican girl enjoys Carnival in this festive book.

1003. McPhail, David. *Mistletoe* (1–3). Illus. by author. 1978, Dutton $6.95. A little girl wants a real horse but gets a wooden rocking horse instead.

1004. Miles, Miska. *Swim Little Duck* (PS–K). Illus. by Jim Arnosky. 1976, Little $5.95. A little duck goes out to see the world and is joined by a frog, a pig, and a rabbit, but finds that his own pond is the best after all.

1005. Myers, Walter Dean. *The Black Pearl and the Ghost: Or, One Mystery after Another* (2–4). Illus. by Robert Quackenbush. 1980, Viking $6.95. Two brief mystery stories involving Dr. Aramy and Mr. Dibble.

1006. Parish, Peggy. *Granny and the Desperadoes* (K–2). Illus. by Steven Kellogg. 1970, Macmillan $4.95; paper $.95. Granny captures 2 outlaws with her gun that doesn't shoot.

1007. Parkin, Rex. *Red Carpet* (K–2). Illus. by author. 1948, Macmillan $5.95. When the red carpet is unrolled to welcome a visiting duke, it keeps on rolling, bringing excitement wherever it goes.

1008. Peet, Bill. *The Caboose Who Got Loose* (K–3). Illus. by author. 1971, Houghton $8.95. When Katy Caboose is jarred loose from the rest of the

train, she gets her wish to be a "cabin in the trees," free from noise and smoke.

1009. Peet, Bill. *Jennifer and Josephine* (1–3). Illus. by author. 1967, Houghton $8.95. Jennifer, an old touring car, is driven through several adventures by a reckless driver and is accompanied by a friendly cat named Josephine.

1010. Quackenbush, Robert. *Detective Mole and the Tip-Top Mystery* (1–3). Illus. by author. 1978, Lothrop $4.95; LB $4.76. Mole investigates why guests are being disturbed at the Tip-Top Inn.

1011. Robison, Nancy. *UFO Kidnap!* (1–3). Illus. by Edward Franklin. 1978, Lothrop $4.95; LB $4.76. Two friends find a giant Frisbee and later discover that it is a UFO.

1012. Saari, Kaye. *The Kidnapping of the Coffee Pot* (1–3). Illus. by Henri Galeron. 1974, Harlin Quist $6.95. "Long ago in a forgotten corner of a city dump—lived a Lawn Mower, a Coffee Pot and a Pair of old shoes." How the objects rescue Coffee Pot is simply told and brilliantly illustrated.

1013. Schulman, Janet. *Camp Keewee's Secret Weapon* (1–3). Illus. by Marilyn Hafner. 1978, Greenwillow $5.95; LB $5.71. In spite of herself, Jill enjoys summer camp when she becomes the baseball team's pitcher.

1014. Shire, Ellen. *The Mystery at Number Seven Rue Petite* (1–3). Illus. by author. 1978, Random $3.95; LB $4.99. Two Parisians solve the mystery of an art forgery and collect the reward.

1015. Shortall, Leonard. *Sam's First Fish* (1–2). Illus. by author. 1965, Morrow $6.48. The very special event of a 7-year-old boy who catches his first fish. Also use: *Ben on the Ski Trail* (1965, Morrow $6.75).

1016. Stevenson, James. *"Could Be Worse!"* (K–2). Illus. by author. 1977, Greenwillow $6.96. Grandpa's response to all minor catastrophes is always the same.

1017. Stevenson, James. *The Sea View Hotel* (K–2). Illus. by author. 1978, Greenwillow $6.95; LB $6.67. A young child's vacation boredom is relieved by an unexpected airplane ride.

1018. Taylor, Mark. *Henry the Explorer* (K–2). Illus. by Graham Booth. 1966, Atheneum paper $1.95. Henry leaves home on an exploring expedition, but finds at nightfall that he is hopelessly lost. Also use: *Henry Explores the Jungle* (1968, $7.95), *Henry the Castaway* (1973, paper $1.95), and *Henry Explores the Mountains* (1975, $9.95).

1019. Van Allsburg, Chris. *The Garden of Abdul Gasazi* (K–3). Illus. by author. 1979, Houghton

$8.95. Young Alan wanders into the garden of a retired magician with unexpected results.

1020. Ward, Lynd. *The Biggest Bear* (K–3). Illus. by author. 1952, Houghton $7.95; paper $1.95. A popular Caldecott Award picture book. Johnny wanted a bearskin on his barn so he went looking for the biggest bear.

1021. Yeoman, John. *Beatrice and Vanessa* (K–2). Illus. by Quentin Blake. 1975, Macmillan $5.95. An owl and a nanny goat have adventures in the woods.

Personal Problems

1022. Arthur, Catherine. *My Sister's Silent World* (1–3). Illus. by Nathan Talbot. 1979, Childrens Press $5.95. An older girl tells about her 8-year-old deaf sister, Heather.

1023. Babbitt, Natalie. *The Something* (PS–3). Illus. by author. 1970, Farrar $2.95. Fear of the dark—common in childhood—underlies this fantasy in which the unusual-looking hero Milo comes face-to-face with the dreaded "something."

1024. Barrett, Judith. *I Hate to Take a Bath* (PS–1). Illus. by Charles B. Slackman. 1975, Four Winds $5.50. A humorous exploration of the pros and cons of taking a bath.

1025. Baylor, Byrd. *Everybody Needs a Rock* (K–3). Illus. by Peter Parnall. 1974, Scribner $7.95; paper $2.95. Everyone needs a rock—one that is just the right shape and size, color, and smell, to suit its owner. Beautiful earth-tone illustrations accompany this sensitive text.

1026. Beim, Jerrold. *The Smallest Boy in the Class* (1–3). Illus. by Meg Wohlberg. 1949, Morrow $6.48. A little boy who rebelled against being called "tiny" learns that bigness is not always measured in inches.

1027. Carrick, Carol. *The Accident* (K–3). Illus. by Donald Carrick. 1976, Seabury $6.95. A story that deals sympathetically and realistically with a child's reaction to the death of his pet dog.

1028. Carrick, Carol. *The Foundling* (PS–3). Illus. by Donald Carrick. 1977, Seabury $6.95. Young Christopher has difficulty adjusting to his dog's death and getting a replacement.

1029. Carrick, Carol. *The Highest Balloon on the Common* (K–3). Illus. by Donald Carrick. 1977, Greenwillow $7.25; LB $6.43. A young boy becomes frightened when separated from his father during a holiday celebration on a village common.

1030. Carrick, Carol. *Paul's Christmas Birthday* (K–2). Illus. by Donald Carrick. 1978, Greenwillow $6.95; LB $6.67. Paul's family helps him adjust to having a birthday just before Christmas.

1031. Bulla, Clyde Robert. *Keep Running, Allen!* (PS–1). Illus. by Satomi Ichikawa. 1978, Crowell $6.95. Little Allen usually has trouble keeping up with his brothers and sister.

1032. Bunting, Eve. *The Big Red Barn* (2–3). Illus. by Howard Knotts. 1979, Harcourt $4.95; paper $1.95. When a boy's barn burns one night, he must adjust to a new aluminum one.

1033. de Paola, Tomie. *Andy: That's My Name* (PS–K). Illus. by author. 1973, Prentice-Hall $4.95; paper $1.25. The big boys borrow Andy's name, affixed to his wagon, and in a play on words, add and subtract letters and make other words out of his name. Finally, Andy has had enough and marches off with his wagon, murmuring that although he may be little, he is no less important.

1034. de Paola, Tomie. *Nana Upstairs and Nana Downstairs* (PS–K). Illus. by author. 1973, Putnam $5.29; Penguin paper $1.95. The love of a child for his grandmother and Tommy's adjustment to her death are told in tender, comfortable terms.

1035. De Regniers, Beatrice S. *A Little House of Your Own* (PS). Illus. by Irene Haas. 1954, Harcourt $4.95. An exploration of the many places in which a child can have a secret house.

1036. De Regniers, Beatrice S. *Snow Party* (K–3). Illus. by Reiner Zimmik. 1959, Pantheon $4.99. When a heavy snow blocks the roads, unexpected visitors come to the home of a lonely old man and woman on their prairie farm.

1037. Dragonwagon, Crescent. *Will It Be Okay?* (K–2). Illus. by Ben Shecter. 1977, Harper $6.95; LB $6.89. Mother comforts her daughter by giving her lots of love and suggestions for overcoming her fears.

1038. Felt, Sue. *Rosa-Too-Little* (K–2). Illus. by author. 1950, Doubleday $7.95. Appealing picture book about a little girl who wants to have her own library card.

1039. Goodsell, Jane. *Katie's Magic Glasses* (K–3). Illus. by Barbara Cooney. 1965, Houghton $5.95; paper $2.25. Katie's sight problems are solved when she gets her first glasses.

1040. Gordon, Sheila. *A Monster in the Mailbox* (2–4). Illus. by Tony DeLuna. 1978, Dutton $6.95. A young boy sends away for a mail-order monster.

1041. Greenberg, Barbara. *The Bravest Babysitter* (PS–2). Illus. by Diane Paterson. 1977, Dial $5.95; LB $5.47. A baby-sitter's young charge helps her overcome her fear of thunder and lightning.

1042. Greenfield, Eloise. *Me and Nessie* (1–3). Illus. by M. Barnett. 1975, Crowell $6.49. A little girl outgrows her need for an imaginary friend in this story told partly in black English.

1043. Hanlon, Emily. *What If a Lion Eats Me and I Fall into a Hippopotamus' Mud Hole?* (PS–3). Illus. by Leigh Grant. 1975, Delacorte $5.95. Barney manages to convince Stuart that nothing terrible will happen to him on his first trip to the zoo.

1044. Hann, Jacquie. *Up Day, Down Day* (K–3). Illus. by author. 1978, Four Winds $5.95. Good days and bad days are experienced by our hero and his friend.

1045. Hazen, Barbara S. *Two Homes to Live In: A Child's-Eye View of Divorce* (K–2). Illus. by Peggy Luks. 1978, Human Sciences $6.95. A reassuring view of divorce because now there are 2 homes where there is love.

1046. Hughes, Shirley. *David and Dog* (PS–K). Illus. by author. 1978, Prentice-Hall $7.95. David loses his favorite toy, a stuffed dog, in this English picture book that won the Greenaway Medal.

1047. Hughes, Shirley. *Moving Molly* (1–3). Illus. by author. 1979, Prentice-Hall $7.95. At first Molly is very lonely when her family moves, but things change when she makes new friends of animals and children.

1048. Isadora, Rachel. *Ben's Trumpet* (K–3). Illus. by author. 1979, Greenwillow $6.95. A young black boy dreams of becoming a trumpet player and eventually is taken to a jazz club by a musician.

1049. Jensen, Virginia Allen. *Sara and the Door* (1–3). Illus. by Ann Strugnell. 1977, Addison $4.95. A big problem is solved by a little black girl when her coat gets caught in a door.

1050. Jensen, Virginia Allen, and Haller, Dorcas. *What's That?* (PS). Illustrated. 1979, Collins $9.95. Embossed shapes tell a story in this picture book intended primarily for blind children.

1051. Jewell, Nancy. *Bus Ride* (1–3). Illus. by Ronald Himler. 1978, Harper $5.95; LB $6.49. Janie is fearful of riding the bus alone but soon makes a friend.

1052. Kay, Helen. *One Mitten Lewis* (K–3). Illus. by Kurt Werth. 1955, Lothrop $6.48. Lewis is always losing a mitten until his exasperated mother comes up with a solution.

1053. Keats, Ezra Jack. *Louie* (PS–K). Illus. by author. 1975, Greenwillow $7.25; LB $6.96; Scholastic paper $1.95. Louie, a silent child, makes his first friend, a puppet, and is allowed to keep it for his very own.

1054. Kellogg, Steven. *Much Bigger Than Martin* (K–2). Illus. by author. 1976, Dial $5.95; LB $5.47. Henry is upset because his older brother is so much bigger than he is, and Henry tries many ways to overcome this.

1055. Klein, Norma. *Girls Can Be Anything* (1–3). Illus. by Roy Doty. 1973, Dutton $5.95; paper $1.95. Marina convinces Sean that one day she could be a doctor, pilot, or president.

1056. Klein, Norma. *Visiting Pamela* (PS–1). Illus. by Kay Chorao. 1979, Dial $6.95; LB $6.46. Because of her mother's ultimatum, Carrie emerges from her shell and visits a friend.

1057. Krauss, Ruth. *A Very Special House* (PS–K). Illus. by Maurice Sendak. 1953, Harper $7.95; LB $7.89. A little boy tells what it would be like in his very special house—no one would ever say "Stop, Stop."

1058. Larson, Hanna. *Don't Forget Tom* (1–3). Illustrated. 1978, Crowell $5.97. A six-year-old mentally retarded child copes with his handicap.

1059. Little, Lessie Jones, and Greenfield, Eloise. *I Can Do It by Myself* (K–2). Illus. by Carole Byard. 1978, Crowell $7.95; LB $7.89. A young boy is successful in his first bid for independence.

1060. Marino, Barbara Pavis. *Eric Needs Stitches* (PS–3). Illustrated. 1979, Addison $6.95. A boy must conquer his fears when the doctor says he must have stitches on his knee.

1061. Mayer, Mercer. *You're the Scaredy-Cat* (K–2). Illus. by author. 1974, Parents $5.95. Two young boys decide to spend the night in the backyard camping out, but after telling spooky stories to each other, one by one they creep back into the safety of their own beds.

1062. Meddaugh, Susan. *Too Short Fred* (1–3). Illus. by author. 1978, Houghton $5.95. Fred masters situations despite his small stature.

1063. Ness, Evaline. *Sam, Bangs & Moonshine* (K–2). Illus. by author. 1966, Holt $5.95; paper $1.45. A little girl learns to distinguish truth from "moonshine" only after her cat and playmate nearly meet tragedy. Caldecott Medal, 1967.

1064. Perrine, Mary. *Salt Boy* (K–3). Illus. by Leonard Weisgard. 1968, Houghton paper $.95. Salt Boy, a Navajo, wants to learn how to rope the big black horse, but his father thinks he is too young.

1065. Peterson, Esther Allen. *Frederick's Alligator* (K–2). Illus. by Susanna Natti. 1979, Crown $6.95. A young boy given to telling tall tales really does have an alligator under his bed.

1066. Peterson, Jeanne Whitehouse. *I Have a Sister, My Sister Is Deaf* (1–3). Illus. by Deborah Ray. 1978, Harper $4.95. About a young girl's adjustment to deafness.

1067. Raskin, Ellen. *Spectacles* (K–3). Illus. by author. 1968, Atheneum $5.93; paper $1.95. A spectacle not to be missed is Iris Fogel's misinterpretation of everything she sees . . . until her myopia is corrected. Cleverly illustrated. Meet Iris's friend Chester in: *Nothing Ever Happens on My Block* (1966, Atheneum $6.95; paper $1.95; Scholastic, paper 95¢).

1068. Sharmat, Marjorie W. *A Big Fat Enormous Lie* (PS–1). Illus. by David McPhail. 1978, Dutton $5.95. A small lie becomes a monster that haunts a youngster until he tells the truth.

1069. Shortall, Leonard. *Tony's First Dive* (1–3). Illus. by author. 1972, Morrow $6.75. Six-year-old Tony is frightened of the water, but with the help of a sympathetic lifeguard, he overcomes his fear and learns to swim.

1070. Simon, Norma. *I Was So Mad!* (K–3). Illus. by Dora Leder. 1974, Whitman $5.50. Children catalog the things that make them mad and learn that adults get angry too. They are helped to realize why they get angry and how to handle their frustrations.

1071. Smith, Lucia B. *A Special Kind of Sister* (K–3). Illus. by Chuck Hall. 1979, Holt $5.95. A seven-year-old girl's mixed emotions toward her retarded young brother.

1072. Tester, Sylvia Root. *Sometimes I'm Afraid* (PS–1). Illus. by Frances Hook. 1979, Childrens Press $5.50. An understanding treatment of the fears of a young child.

1073. Thomas, Ianthe. *Eliza's Daddy* (1–3). Illustrated. 1976, Harcourt paper $1.65. A small black girl tries to cope with her parents' divorce.

1074. Tobias, Tobi. *Petey* (1–3). Illus. by Symeon Shimin. 1978, Putnam $5.95. Emily adjusts to the death of her pet gerbil, Petey.

1075. Viorst, Judith. *The Tenth Good Thing about Barney* (K–2). Illus. by Erik Blegvad. 1971, Atheneum $7.95; paper $1.95. At a backyard funeral, a little boy tries to think of 10 good things to say about his cat, Barney—but at first can only come up with 9.

1076. Waber, Bernard. *Ira Sleeps Over* (PS–2). Illus. by author. 1972, Houghton $7.95; paper $1.95. When Ira is invited to sleep overnight at Reggie's house, he wants to go, but should he or shouldn't he take along his teddy bear?

1077. Watanabe, Shigeo. *How Do I Put It On?* (PS). Illus. by Yasuo Ohtomo. 1979, Collins $6.95; LB $6.91. How to dress oneself told in simple, noncondescending terms.

1078. Watson, Wendy. *Moving* (PS–K). Illus. by author. 1978, Crowell $4.95. Muffin hates to leave her old home but will give her new one a trial.

1079. Welber, Robert. *The Train* (K–2). Illus. by Deborah Ray. 1972, Pantheon $4.99. A small black girl is anxious to cross the field to see the trains go by, but she is afraid of what may lie in the meadow. Conquering her fears with the help of her family, she makes a successful trip and is proud and pleased with herself.

1080. White, Paul. *Janet at School* (2–4). Illus. by Jeremy Finlay. 1978, Crowell $5.79. Janet, a victim of spina bifida, is shown, through photographs and text, engaging in various activities.

1081. Williams, Barbara. *Whatever Happened to Beverly Bigler's Birthday?* (2–3). Illus. by Emily McCully. 1979, Harcourt $5.95; paper $1.95. Beverly decides to run away when she thinks everyone has forgotten her birthday.

Other Times, Other Places

1082. Adoff, Arnold. *Ma nDa la* (PS–1). Illus. by Emily McCully. 1971, Harper $6.95; LB $7.89. The joy of African family life is celebrated in this poem of sounds.

1083. Anderson, Lonzo. *Izzard* (2–4). Illus. by Adrienne Adams. 1973, Scribner $8.95. James, who lives in the West Indies, has a pet lizard that follows him everywhere until James sets her free. Beautiful, soft illustrations and an effective text make this an appealing story of a boy and his pet.

1084. Ayer, Jacqueline. *A Wish for Little Sister* (K–2). Illus. by author. 1960, Harcourt $6.50. Picture stories from Siam.

1085. Balet, Jan. *Joanjo: A Portuguese Tale* (K–2). Illus. by author. 1967, Delacorte $4.95; LB $4.58. The small son of a Portuguese fisherman dreams of a different life in this brilliantly illustrated picture book.

1086. Bemelmans, Ludwig. *Madeline's Rescue* (K–3). Illus. by author. 1953, Viking $8.95; Penguin paper $2.50. This Paris adventure of the inimitable Madeline won the 1954 Caldecott Medal.

Also use: *Madeline* (1939, Viking $7.95; Penguin, paper $2.50), *Madeline and the Bad Hat* (1957, Viking $8.95; Penguin, paper $2.50), *Madeline and the Gypsies* (1959, Viking $6.95; Penguin, paper $1.95), and *Madeline in London* (1961, Viking $5.95; Penguin, paper $2.50).

1087. Beskow, Elsa. *Pelle's New Suit* (PS–3). Illus. by author. 1929, Harper $8.79; Scholastic paper $1.50. A Swedish story of the steps in getting a new suit for a small boy, from shearing the lamb to tailoring.

1088. Beskow, Elsa. *Peter's Adventures in Blueberry Land* (PS–2). Illus. by author. 1975, Delacorte $6.95; LB $6.46. A commonplace text but imaginative pictures in this Swedish tale of a boy's adventures looking for blueberries.

1089. Bradley, Helen. *The Queen Who Came to Tea* (1–3). Illus. by author. 1979, Merrimack $9.95. A fond recollection of the great stir when Queen Victoria visited Manchester in 1901.

1090. Brown, Marcia. *Felice* (K–3). Illus. by author. 1958, Scribner $6.95. A lonely little cat is befriended by a Venetian boy who is learning to be a gondolier.

1091. Brown, Margaret Wise. *Wheel on the Chimney* (1–3). Illus. by Tibor Gergely. 1954, Lippincott $8.95. Life-cycle story of a pair of storks, from nesting in Hungary, to their flight to Africa, to their return.

1092. Chonz, Selina. *A Bell for Ursli* (1–4). Illus. by Alois Carigiet. 1953, Walck $9.50. The spring festival in a tiny Swiss mountain village brings adventure to a small boy.

1093. Clifton, Lucille. *All of Us Come Cross the Water* (1–3). Illus. by John Steptoe. 1973, Holt $5.95. Beautifully illustrated and told in rhythmic black prose. The poet describes a little boy's answer to his teacher's question about where his people came from and his conclusion that all Americans have "come cross the water."

1094. Cole, Brock. *The King at the Door* (K–2). Illus. by author. 1979, Doubleday $7.95; LB $8.90. Kindness and helpfulness are rewarded in this folklike tale.

1095. d'Aulaire, Ingri, and d'Aulaire, Edgar. *Ola* (K–3). Illus. by author. 1939, Doubleday $6.95. A little Norwegian boy skis off to adventure.

1096. de Paola, Tomie. *The Lady of Guadalupe* (K–3). Illus. by author. 1980, Holiday $10.95; paper $4.95. The legend of the patron saint of Mexico is retold in this excellent picture book.

1097. Ets, Marie Hall. *Gilberto and the Wind* (PS–1). Illus. by author. 1963, Viking $4.95; Penguin paper $1.75. A small Mexican boy learns to play with and understand the moods of the wind.

1098. Feelings, Muriel. *Zamani Goes to Market* (K–3). Illus. by Tom Feelings. 1970, Seabury $6.95. The sights and adventures of a young East African boy's first trip to market with his father and brothers, brilliantly illustrated.

1099. Flack, Marjorie. *The Story about Ping* (PS–3). Illus. by Kurt Wiese. 1933, Viking $5.95; Penguin paper $1.50. A little Peking duck spends a harrowing night on the Yangtze River after he is accidently separated from his family.

1100. Francoise. *Minou* (PS–2). Illus. by author. 1962, Scribner $5.95. A little girl journeys through Paris in search of her pet cat. Also: *Springtime for Jeanne-Marie* (1955, Scribner $5.95).

1101. Goffstein, M. B. *My Noah's Ark* (K–2). Illus. by author. 1978, Harper $5.95; LB $6.44. An old woman reminisces about an ark and animals that her grandfather had carved.

1102. Graham, Lorenz. *Song of the Boat* (K–3). Illus. by Leo Dillon and Diane Dillon. 1975, Crowell $7.95; LB $7.89. Momolu helps his father find just the right tree for making a magnificent boat to replace the canoe broken by the alligator.

1103. Green, Norma B. *The Hole in the Dike* (K–2). Illus. by Eric Carle. 1975, Crowell $8.95; LB $8.79; Scholastic paper $1.50. Brilliant illustrations accompany this simple retelling of the Mary Mapes Dodge story of the boy who puts his finger in the dike and saves his Dutch town.

1104. Hall, Donald. *Ox-Cart Man* (K–3). Illus. by Barbara Cooney. 1979, Viking $8.95. The cycle of production and sale of goods in nineteenth-century New England is pictured in human terms. Caldecott Medal, 1980.

1105. Handforth, Thomas. *Mei Li* (1–3). Illus. by author. 1938, Doubleday $6.95. Adventures of a little Chinese girl who decided to go to the New Year's fair in the city. Caldecott Medal, 1939.

1106. Hirsh, Marilyn. *Hannibal and His 37 Elephants* (1–3). Illus. by author. 1977, Holiday $5.95. Hannibal crosses the Alps with earmuffed elephants in this humorous view of history.

1107. Krasilovsky, Phyllis. *The Cow Who Fell in the Canal* (PS–1). Illus. by Peter Spier. 1957, Doubleday $5.95; paper $1.49. Detailed watercolor scenes illustrate this amusing tale of Hendrika, a not-so-contented Dutch cow who floated on a raft to the city.

1108. Lamorisse, Albert. *The Red Balloon* (1–3). Illus. by author. 1956, Doubleday $5.95; paper $1.95. Pascal possesses a magical balloon that leads him on a tour of Paris, and he must defend the balloon from a gang of boys bent on bursting it.

1109. Lasker, David. *The Boy Who Loved Music* (1–3). Illus. by Joe Lasker. 1979, Viking $9.95. Karl, a young horn player for Prince Esterhazy, meets Joseph Haydn.

1110. Leaf, Munro. *Wee Gillis* (1–4). Illus. by Robert Lawson. 1938, Viking $5.95. Wee Gillis, a Scottish boy, has to choose between raising cows in the valley or stalking stags in the Highlands.

1111. Leech, Jay, and Spencer, Zane. *Bright Fawn and Me* (K–2). Illus. by Glo Coalson. 1979, Crowell $6.95; LB $6.89. A Cheyenne girl takes care of her little sister at a tribal fair set in the nineteenth century.

1112. Lindgren, Astrid. *The Tomten* (PS–2). Illus. by Harald Wiberg. 1961, Coward $6.50; LB $5.89; paper $2.50. The friendly troll speaks in Tomten language only animals and children understand. Also by the same author and illustrator: *The Tomten and the Fox* (1965, Coward $5.89; paper $2.50).

1113. Lindman, Maj. *Snipp, Snapp, Snurr and the Red Shoes* (PS–1). Illus. by author. 1932, Whitman $5.25. Snipp, Snapp, Snurr, triplets, have long been great favorites of Swedish children. This story tells how they earned enough money to buy their mother the birthday present she wanted.

1114. McClenathan, Louise. *My Mother Sends Her Wisdom* (K–3). Illus. by Rosekrans Hoffman. 1979, Morrow $7.95; LB $7.63. A folklike story set in old Russia about a clever peasant woman.

1115. Marceau, Marcel. *The Story of Bip* (PS–3). Illus. by author. 1976, Harper $6.95; LB $6.79. Bip sprouts wings and soars over the city of Paris before returning to earth.

1116. Parker, Dorothy D. *Liam's Catch* (K–3). Illus. by Robert Andrew Parker. 1972, Viking $5.95. Ten-year-old Liam is given responsibilities during the salmon-netting season in this story set in Ireland.

1117. Paterson, A. B. *Mulga Bill's Bicycle* (K–3). Illus. by Kilmeny Niland and Deborah Niland. 1975, Parents $5.95; LB $5.41. This is a story set in Australia when bicycles were new there. It tells in rhyme about Mulga Bill's mad ride through the countryside on his newly purchased vehicle.

1118. Politi, Leo. *Little Leo* (K–2). Illus. by author. 1951, Scribner $6.95. Little Leo, decked out in a brand-new Indian chief suit, leaves San Fran-

cisco to live in Italy and creates great excitement among the children in the town with his tales of the West.

1119. Quin-Harkin, Janet. *Peter Penny's Dance* (K–2). Illus. by Anita Lobel. 1976, Dial $7.95; LB $7.47; paper $2.50. Based on an old English ballad, this is the rollicking tale of how Peter Penny danced the hornpipe around the world in 5 years.

1120. Sandberg, Inger. *The Boy with Many Houses* (K–2). Illus. by Lasse Sandberg. 1970, Delacorte $5.95. Matthew, a small Swedish boy, tries to construct a playhouse in every room in his home and finally settles for a permanent house in the woods.

1121. Scott, Ann H. *On Mother's Lap* (PS–K). Illus. by Glo Coalson. 1972, McGraw $6.95; LB $7.95. A very warm, tender story of an Eskimo family and of a young boy's realization that there is enough room on mother's lap for both him and his sister to snuggle together under the reindeer blanket.

1122. Steptoe, John. *Birthday* (1–3). Illus. by author. 1972, Holt $5.27. Javaka's eighth birthday is a very special occasion, for he is the firstborn child in the black land of Yoruba, and the whole village joins in on the celebration.

1123. Surany, Anico. *Ride the Cold Wind* (1–3). Illus. by Leonard Everett Fisher. 1964, Putnam $5.39. A Peruvian Indian shepherd boy longs to escape the boredom of his work to become a fisherman and ride the cold wind.

1124. Tamchina, Jurgen. *Dominique and the Dragon* (K–3). Illus. by Heidrun Petrides. 1969, Harcourt $6.50. A misunderstood dragon terrifies the townspeople until Dominique shows them he is harmless. Beautiful full-color pictures of Avignon and the Rhine River area enhance the story.

1125. Varner, Velma. *Animal Frolic* (K–3). Illus. by Toba Sojo. 1954, Putnam $4.69. Toba Sojo's illustrations for the twelfth-century Japanese *Scroll of Animals* makes this a most interesting book.

1126. Ward, Leila. *I Am Eyes Ni Macho* (PS–1). Illus. by Nonny Hogrogian. 1978, Greenwillow $7.95. A new day and all of nature's wonders are greeted by a Kenyan child.

1127. Yarbrough, Camille. *Cornrows* (1–3). Illus. by Carole Byard. 1979, Coward $7.95. Past and present mingle in this discussion of an unusual hair style.

1128. Yashima, Taro. *The Village Tree* (PS–K). Illus. by author. 1953, Penguin paper $1.25. A picture of the author's childhood in Japan and the fun he and his friends had by the river where the great tree stood.

1129. Yolen, Jane. *The Seeing Stick* (K–3). Illus. by Remy Charlip and Demetra Maraslis. 1977, Crowell $6.95; LB $6.79. By carving pictures on a stick, an old man helps a blind girl to "see" in this tale set in ancient Peking.

Humorous Stories

1130. Ahlberg, Janet, and Ahlberg, Allan. *The Vanishment of Thomas Tull* (2–4). 1979, Scribner $6.95. No one seems able to stop the shrinking of 7-year-old Thomas Tull.

1131. Aitken, Amy. *Ruby!* (K–2). Illus. by author. 1979, Bradbury $6.95. Ruby daydreams of becoming a rock star, movie queen, and even president.

1132. Alexander, Sue. *Marc the Magnificent* (1–3). Illus. by Tomie de Paola. 1978, Pantheon $4.95; LB $4.99. Marc dreams of being a great magician, but he can't master the first trick.

1133. Alexander, Sue. *Seymour the Prince* (1–2). Illus. by Lillian Hoban. 1979, Pantheon $3.95; LB $4.99. A young boy chosen to be the prince in a production of *Sleeping Beauty* balks at kissing the princess.

1134. Allard, Harry, and Marshall, James. *The Stupids Have a Ball* (K–3). Illus. by James Marshall. 1978, Houghton $5.95. The whole Stupid family decides to celebrate when the children bring home terrible report cards from school.

1135. Armitage, Ronda, and Armitage, David. *"Don't Forget, Matilda!"* (PS–K). Illus. by author. 1979, Dutton $6.95. An unusual day in the Bear family when everyone forgets things.

1136. Asch, Frank. *Good Lemonade* (K–3). Illus. by Marie Zimmerman. 1976, Watts $4.90. A young boy decides to improve business at the lemonade stand by using advertising techniques.

1137. Aylesworth, Jim. *Hush Up!* (1–3). Illus. by Glen Rounds. 1980, Holt $6.95. Lazy Jasper Walker is rudely awakened from his nap.

1138. Barrett, Judith. *Animals Should Definitely Not Wear Clothes* (PS–1). Illus. by Ron Barrett. 1970, Atheneum $7.95; paper $1.95. Humorous idea expressed in brief text and comic drawings.

1139. Barrett, Judith. *Benjamin's 365 Birthdays* (K–2). Illus. by Ron Barrett. 1974, Atheneum $7.95; paper $1.95. Benjamin, a bear, is so delighted with his birthday presents that he decides to rewrap them so that he can enjoy one each day throughout the ensuing months.

1140. Bishop, Claire Huchet. *Five Chinese Brothers* (1–3). Illus. by Kurt Wiese. 1938, Coward $5.95; LB $4.79. Physically identical in every way, each of the 5 Chinese brothers has one distinguishing trait that saves the lives of all of them.

1141. Blake, Quentin. *Mister Magnolia* (PS). Illustrated. 1980, Merrimack $8.95. A silly rhyming tale about a bumpkin and his adventures.

1142. Bottner, Barbara. *Messy* (K–3). Illus. by author. 1979, Delacorte $6.95; LB $6.46. Harriet tries to reform and be neat and clean to take a part in a dance recital.

1143. Bulla, Clyde Robert. *The Stubborn Old Woman* (2–3). Illus. by Anne Rockwell. 1980, Crowell $7.95; LB $7.89. Only by trickery is an old woman convinced that she must leave her crumbling home.

1144. Bunting, Eve. *Barney the Beard* (PS–3). Illus. by Imero Gobbato. 1975, Parents $5.95; LB $5.41. Barney, a hard-working baker, tries various styles with his beard.

1145. Burningham, John. *Time to Get Out of the Bath, Shirley* (K–2). Illus. by author. 1978, Crowell $6.95; LB $6.79. While taking a bath, Shirley daydreams of knights and castles.

1146. Caudill, Rebecca, and Ayars, James S. *Contrary Jenkins* (K–3). Illus. by Glen Rounds. 1969, Holt $5.95. "Contrary" was the name for Ebenezer Jenkins, a character in old Appalachia, who always said yes when others said no, with humorous results.

1147. Chorao, Kay. *Molly's Moe* (PS–K). Illus. by author. 1976, Seabury $6.50. Molly is continually losing things, and when she loses her pet stuffed animal Moe, a stegosaurus, she is disconsolate, until she finds him in a bag of potatoes!

1148. Christian, Mary Blount. *The Devil Take You, Barnabas Beane* (1–3). Illus. by Ann Burgess. 1980, Crowell $6.89. Mean old Barnabas Beane thinks he has been placed under a curse.

1149. Clymer, Eleanor. *Hamburgers—and Ice Cream for Dessert* (K–2). Illus. by Roy Doty. 1975, Dutton $7.95. The fun in a variety of diets is the theme of this screwball adventure.

1150. Crowe, Robert L. *Clyde Monster* (PS–2). Illus. by Kay Chorao. 1976, Dutton $5.95. A humorous reassuring story about an engaging monster named Clyde, who is afraid of the dark.

1151. Cutler, Ivor. *The Animal House* (K–3). Illus. by Helen Oxenbury. 1977, Morrow $7.25; LB $6.96. Zoo animals come to the rescue when Diamond's house is blown away in a severe windstorm. An imaginative and nonsensical story.

1152. Cutler, Ivor. *Elephant Girl* (PS). Illus. by Helen Oxenbury. 1976, Morrow $5.25; LB $5.04. A nonsense story about a little girl who digs up an elephant in the garden with her teaspoon.

1153. de Paola, Tomie. *Helga's Dowry: A Troll Love Story* (K–2). Illus. by author. 1977, Harcourt $7.95; paper $2.95. Helga cannot marry Lars because she has no dowry in this humorous account of how she acquires one.

1154. de Paola, Tomie, illus. *Pancakes for Breakfast* (PS–2). 1978, $7.95; paper $1.95. The trials and travails of a country woman who decides to make some pancakes.

1155. De Regniers, Beatrice S. *May I Bring a Friend?* (PS–2). Illus. by Beni Montresor. 1964, Atheneum $6.95. The king and queen invite a small boy to tea, and each time he goes, he takes a friend—a seal, a hippopotamus, and several lions. Caldecott Medal, 1965.

1156. Elkin, Benjamin. *The Loudest Noise in the World* (1–3). 1954, Viking $6.95. A prince wants the loudest noise in the world for a birthday present.

1157. Freeman, Don. *Mop Top* (K–2). Illus. by author. 1955, Viking $6.95. Moppy changes his mind about a haircut after being mistaken for a floor mop by a nearsighted shopper.

1158. Getz, Arthur. *Hamilton Duck* (PS). Illus. by author. 1972, Golden $7.15. A humorous read-a-loud story of a silly duck who goes to the pond for a swim, only to find it iced over, and then he realizes winter has come.

1159. Getz, Arthur. *Hamilton Duck's Springtime Story* (PS–K). Illus. by author. 1974, Golden $7.15. Large colorful illustrations are used effectively in this story in which Hamilton Duck awaits the arrival of spring.

1160. Gray, Nigel. *It'll Come Out in the Wash* (PS–1). 1979, Harper $6.95; LB $6.89. No matter how large the stains and spills created by the young heroine, Dad has a pat answer.

1161. Hoban, Russell C. *Arthur's New Power* (K–3). Illus. by Byron Barton. 1978, Crowell $5.95; LB $5.79. Arthur blows a fuse when he plugs in a new amplifier for his electric guitar.

1162. Haywood, Carolyn. *The King's Monster* (2–3). Illus. by Victor G. Ambrus. 1980, Morrow $7.95; LB $7.63. A young knight discovers that the dread monster in the dungeon is only a mouse.

1163. Hazen, Barbara S. *The Gorilla Did It* (PS–1). Illus. by Roy Cruz. 1974, Atheneum $6.95; paper $1.95. A child keeps blaming an imaginary animal—a gorilla—for all the messes in his room.

1164. Heide, Florence Parry. *The Shrinking of Treehorn* (1–3). Illus. by Edward Gorey. 1971, Holiday $5.95. Treehorn has a special talent—he can become smaller by the moment—but nobody notices.

1165. Hoban, Russell C. *How Tom Beat Captain Najork and His Hired Sportsmen* (1–3). Illus. by Quentin Blake. 1974, Atheneum paper $1.95. Impish fun in both text and illustrations in this story of Tom, who triumphs over those intent on punishing him for his constant fooling around.

1166. Hoban, Russell C. *A Near Thing for Captain Najork* (1–3). Illus. by Quentin Blake. 1976, Atheneum $7.95. Tom builds a jam-powered frog vehicle and is pursued by his enemy in this sequel to *How Tom Beat Captain Najork and His Hired Sportsmen.*

1167. Hughes, Shirley. *George the Babysitter* (1–3). Illus. by author. 1977, Prentice-Hall $6.95. Life becomes a sudden adventure when the new babysitter arrives.

1168. Hutchins, Pat. *Clocks and More Clocks* (1–3). Illus. by author. 1970, Macmillan $6.95; paper $.95. An old gentleman has difficulty acquiring a clock that tells the correct time.

1169. Hutchins, Pat. *Don't Forget the Bacon* (K–2). Illus. by author. 1976, Greenwillow $7.25; Penguin paper $1.95. An absent-minded child has trouble remembering the shopping list, and the one thing—"don't forget the bacon"—that he does remember, he forgets to bring home.

1170. Isadora, Rachel. *Max* (K–2). Illus. by author. 1976, Macmillan $5.95. Max, an avid baseball player, finds that joining his sister's dancing class makes an excellent warmup for the game.

1171. Jeschke, Susan. *The Devil Did It* (K–3). Illus. by author. 1975, Holt $5.95. Nana is always being blamed for her devil's pranks in this engaging story.

1172. Jeschke, Susan. *Firerose* (K–3). Illus. by author. 1974, Holt $4.95. What happens when a foundling child, who turns out to be a dragon, can't be admitted to school because of her tail.

1173. Keats, Ezra Jack. *Jenny's Hat* (K–2). Illus. by author. 1966, Harper $8.95; LB $8.79. Jenny's drab new hat is decorated by her bird friends who become its trimming.

1174. Kellogg, Steven. *The Mystery of the Missing Red Mitten* (PS–K). Illus. by author. 1974, Dial $4.95; LB $4.58; paper $1.50. While playing in the snow, a child loses her red mitten, and in searching for it, she imagines how the mitten might be used for other purposes.

1175. Kent, Jack. *There's No Such Thing as a Dragon* (K–2). Illus. by author. 1975, Western $6.08; paper $.95. In spite of mother's insistence that there is no such thing as a dragon, this dragon poses many problems for mother in a highly amusing story.

1176. Krasilovsky, Phyllis. *The Man Who Didn't Wash His Dishes* (K–2). Illus. by Barbara Cooney. 1950, Doubleday $6.95; paper $1.95. A man learns his lesson when his home becomes so full of dirty dishes that there is no place to sit down.

1177. Krasilovsky, Phyllis. *The Man Who Tried to Save Time* (K–2). Illus. by Marcia Sewall. 1979, Doubleday $4.95; LB $5.90. All of a man's strategems for time saving—like eating breakfast the night before—backfire.

1178. Kuskin, Karla. *A Boy Had a Mother Who Bought Him a Hat* (K–3). Illus. by author. 1976, Houghton $5.95. A humorous cumulative poem about a boy receiving an amazing array of new possessions.

1179. Laurin, Anne. *Little Things* (K–3). Illus. by Marcia Sewall. 1978, Atheneum $5.95. When Mrs. B's knitting begins to take over the house, Mr. B rebels.

1180. Levitin, Sonia. *A Single Speckled Egg* (K–3). Illus. by John Larrecq. 1976, Parnassus $6.95. Three foolish farmers are outwitted by their wives in this ridiculous tale told in the folk tradition.

1181. Levitin, Sonia. *Who Owns the Moon?* (K–2). Illus. by John Larrecq. 1973, Parnassus $6.95; LB $5.38. Each of three noodle-headed farmers claims to own the moon and is dismayed when it moves—someone has stolen a piece of it! How the sage of the village resolves their quarrel makes a very humorous story.

1182. Lindgren, Astrid. *Of Course Polly Can Do Almost Everything* (K–2). Illus. by Ilon Wikland. 1978, Follett $6.95; LB $6.99. Polly has many skills—some, however, still need polishing.

1183. Lobel, Arnold. *The Man Who Took the Indoors Out* (K–2). 1974, Harper $7.95; LB $7.89. A nonsense story in verse of the absurd situation that develops when a kindly old man who loves the outdoors invites all his household objects to share the beautiful day with him, and then they won't go back into the house when winter comes!

1184. McCloskey, Robert. *Burt Dow, Deep-Water Man* (K–3). Illus. by author. 1963, Viking $8.95. The humorous tale of an old Maine fisherman who caught a whale by the tail and then used a multicoloral Band-Aid to cover the hole.

1185. McCloskey, Robert. *Lentil* (K–3). Illus. by author. 1940, Viking $7.95; paper $1.95. Tale of a boy who can't carry a tune, yet learns to play the harmonica.

1186. McGovern, Ann. *Mr. Skinner's Skinny House* (1–3). Illus. by Mort Gerberg. 1980, Scholastic $7.95. A skinny man finds a perfect mate in Ms. Thinner.

1187. Mahy, Margaret. *The Boy Who was Followed Home* (K–2). Illus. by Steven Kellogg. 1975, Watts $5.90. Robert likes hippopotamuses and is delighted when one follows him home.

1188. Merriam, Eve. *Unhurry Harry* (K–2). Illus. by Gail Owens. 1978, Four Winds $5.95. A natural-born dawdler finds ways to avoid being in a hurry.

1189. Newell, Hope. *The Little Old Woman Who Used Her Head* (1–3). Illus. by Margaret Ruse. 1935, Nelson $6.95. Ten amusing but taxing problems are solved through thought by a little old woman.

1190. Nixon, Joan Lowery. *Alligator under the Bed* (K–3). Illus. by John Hughes. 1974, Putnam $6.95. Jill claims she can't go to sleep because of the alligator under her bed, but her parents think it is all her imagination.

1191. Oxenbury, Helen. *The Queen and Rosie Randall* (K–3). Illus. by author. 1979, Morrow $6.95; LB $6.67. A young girl helps her queen entertain the king of Wottermazzy.

1192. Park, Ruth. *The Gigantic Balloon* (K–4). Illus. by Kilmeny Niland and Deborah Niland. 1976, Parents $5.95; LB $5.41; paper $1.95. A storekeeper tries to prevent his rival from advertising by using a balloon in this Australian farce.

1193. Parker, Nancy W. *Love from Uncle Clyde* (PS). Illus. by author. 1977, Dodd $5.95. Uncle Clyde's birthday gift to Charlie is Elfreda, a purple hippopotamus.

1194. Parker, Nancy W. *Poofy Loves Company* (4–6). Illus. by author. 1980, Dodd $7.95. On a visit to a neighbor's house, Sally runs afoul of a large shaggy dog named Poofy.

1195. Parnall, Peter. *A Dog's Book of Birds* (1–3). Illus. by author. 1977, Scribner $5.95. A humorous dog's-eye view of all sorts of birds.

1196. Pinkwater, D. Manus. *The Big Orange Splot* (K–2). Illus. by author. 1977, Hastings $6.95; Scholastic paper $1.95. A cumulative story about the effects of dropping a can of orange paint on the roof of Mr. Plumbean's home.

1197. Preston, Edna Mitchell. *Pop Corn and Ma Goodness* (K–3). Illus. by Robert Andrew Parker. 1969, Penguin paper $1.25. Rhythmical nonsensical words and vigorous watercolor illustrations tell the hilarious folksy story of the courtship and married life of Ma and Pa Goodness.

1198. Raskin, Ellen. *Who, Said Sue, Said Whoo?* (PS–2). Illus. by author. 1973, Atheneum $6.95; paper $1.95. A little girl, while driving through a jungle, encounters an ever-increasing menagerie of animals.

1199. Rose, Anne. *As Right as Right Can Be* (K–3). Illus. by Arnold Lobel. 1976, Dial $5.95; LB $5.47; paper $1.95. Acquiring new shoelaces leads to buying a new house and furnishings to match, in this nonsense story.

1200. Ross, David. *A Book of Hugs* (1–3). Illus. by author. 1980, Crowell $5.95. The author describes a variety of hugs, such as people hugs and blanket hugs.

1201. Scheer, Julian, and Bileck, Marvin. *Rain Makes Applesauce* (K–2). Illus. by author. 1964, Holiday $7.95. A series of silly statements nonsensically presented and accompanied by humorous detailed pictures.

1202. Segal, Lore. *All the Way Home* (K–3). Illus. by James Marshall. 1973, Farrar $4.95. Juliet's wailing attracts the attention of some animal friends in this amusing story of a day in the park.

1203. Skorpen, Liesel Moak. *Outside My Window* (PS–2). Illus. by Mercer Mayer. 1968, Harper $5.89. Words and pictures capture the amusingly desperate attempts of a boy to disguise the unacceptable pet—a small bear cub—that he invited in one night.

1204. Skurzynski, Gloria. *Martin by Himself* (1–3). Illus. by Lynn Munsinger. 1979, Houghton $6.95. Martin makes do when his mother goes to work.

1205. Slobodkina, Esphyr. *Caps for Sale* (K–3). Illus. by author. 1947, A. & W. $5.95; Scholastic paper $1.25. When some monkeys engage in a bit of monkey business, the cap peddler must use his imagination to retrieve his wares.

1206. Spier, Peter. *Oh, Were They Ever Happy!* (1–3). Illus. by author. 1978, Doubleday $6.95; LB $7.90. Three children go on a painting spree.

1207. Steig, William. *The Amazing Bone* (K–2). Illus. by author. 1976, Farrar $7.95; Penguin paper $1.95. A bone that talks saves a piglet from being eaten by a fox in this nonsensical and witty story. Caldecott Honor Book.

1208. Suhl, Yuri. *Simon Boom Gives a Wedding* (K–3). Illus. by Margot Zemach. 1972, Four Winds $6.95; LB $6.72. Simon Boom thinks everything should be the very best for his daughter's wedding, with humorous results.

1209. Taback, Simms. *Joseph Had a Little Overcoat* (PS–K). Illus. by author. 1977, Random $3.95. Joseph's coat gets smaller as it is transformed into other articles of clothing until it finally disappears.

1210. Tapio, Pat Decker. *The Lady Who Saw the Good Side of Everything* (K–2). Illus. by Paul Galdone. 1975, Seabury $6.95. An amusing story of a little old lady who was always cheerful in spite of difficulties.

1211. Thaler, Michael C. *Madge's Magic Show* (1–2). Illus. by Carol Nicklaus. 1978, Watts $3.95. Madge has difficulty pulling a rabbit from her hat, particularly when Jimmy heckles her.

1212. Tierney, Hanne. *Where's Your Baby Brother, Becky Bunting?* (5–8). Illus. by Paula Winter. 1979, Doubleday $6.95; LB $7.90. A comic view of sibling rivalry brilliantly illustrated.

1213. Tobias, Tobi. *The Quitting Deal* (K–3). Illus. by Trina Schart Hyman. 1975, Viking $5.95. Thumb-sucking Jenny and cigarette-smoking Mom decide to give up their habit.

1214. Tolstoy, Alexei. *The Great Big Enormous Turnip* (K–2). Illus. by Helen Oxenbury. 1969, Watts $3.90. The humorous, modern folktale about the united efforts of an entire family to pull a huge turnip from the ground.

1215. Tworkov, Jack. *The Camel Who Took a Walk* (K–3). Illus. by Roger Duvoisin. 1951, Dutton paper $2.95. A beautiful young camel decides to take a walk one morning, unaware that a terrible tiger has plans to pounce on her.

1216. Ungerer, Tomi. *Beast of Monsieur Racine* (K–3). Illus. by author. 1971, Farrar $6.95. Monsieur Racine catches the strange creature that was stealing the fruit from his prize pear tree—when the creature reveals his true identity, a surprise is in store.

1217. Van Woerkom, Dorothy O. *Meat Pies and Sausages* (1–4). Illus. by Joseph Low. 1976, Greenwillow $5.71. Three marvelously funny tales involving Fox and Wolf.

1218. Ventura, Piero, and Ventura, Marisa. *The Painter's Trick* (K–2). Illus. by author. 1977, Random $5.95; LB $6.99. Gullible monks are tricked by an itinerant painter in this engaging story.

1219. Viorst, Judith. *My Mama Says There Aren't Any Zombies, Ghosts, Vampires, Creatures, Demons,*

Monsters, Fiends, Goblins or Things (PS–1). Illus. by Kay Chorao. 1973, Atheneum $6.95; paper $1.95. A humorous story concerned with a child's vivid description of imaginary monsters and his mother's reassurance that they don't exist.

1220. Waber, Bernard. *Nobody Is Perfick* (K–3). Illus. by author. 1971, Houghton $6.95. A nonsense book that explains 8 topics true to childhood, such as a secret diary and a fantastic dream.

1221. Watson, Nancy. *The Birthday Goat* (K–2). Illus. by Wendy Watson. 1974, Crowell $5.95; LB $6.79; paper $2.95. A goat family enjoys their day at the carnival until Baby Souci, the youngest goat, is kidnapped.

1222. Wells, Rosemary. *Abdul* (K–2). Illus. by author. 1975, Dial $5.95; LB $5.47. Feisal is very fond of his camel Gilda, but when she gives birth to Abdul, an animal strangely resembling a horse, he feels disaster has struck.

1223. Willard, Nancy, and de Paola, Tomie. *Simple Pictures Are Best* (PS–3). Illus. by Tomie de Paola. 1977, Harcourt $7.95; paper $2.95. Over a weary photographer's warnings, a couple insist on cluttering their anniversary portrait with all their worldly goods.

1224. Williams, Barbara. *Albert's Toothache* (K–2). Illus. by Kay Chorao. 1974, Dutton $6.95; paper $1.95. Albert, a turtle, claims he has a toothache, but not until grandma asks him where his tooth aches does Albert realize he is toothless.

1225. Williams, Barbara. *Jeremy Isn't Hungry* (PS–1). Illus. by Martha Alexander. 1978, Dutton $5.95. Davy tries unsuccessfully to pacify his younger brother.

1226. Williams, Jay. *Everyone Knows What a Dragon Looks Like* (K–3). Illus. by Mercer Mayer. 1976, Four Winds $8.95. In this humorous tale told in the folk tradition, the leaders argue about what a dragon looks like, but the people know—"a small, fat, bald old man."

1227. Yaffe, Alan. *The Magic Meatballs* (K–2). Illustrated. 1979, Dial $6.46. Marvin tries to change his family's habits through using some magic meat a stranger gives him.

1228. Yeoman, John. *The Wild Washerwomen: A New Folk Tale* (K–3). Illus. by Quentin Blake. 1979, Greenwillow $8.95; LB $8.59. Seven washerwomen are dissatisfied with their jobs and become the terrors of the neighborhood.

1229. Yolen, Jane. *No Bath Tonight* (PS–1). Illus. by Alice Provensen and Martin Provensen. 1978, Viking $8.95. Grandmother manages to foil Jeremy's decision not to take a bath.

1230. Zemach, Harve. *The Judge: An Untrue Tale* (1–3). Illus. by Margot Zemach. 1969, Farrar $6.95. A foolish judge, who would not believe the frantic reports of an unusual, threatening monster in the vicinity, gets his comeuppance in this rhyming tale with catchy refrain.

1231. Zemach, Harve. *A Penny a Look: An Old Story Retold* (K–3). Illus. by Margot Zemach. 1971, Farrar $5.95. A rascal tries to exploit his brother in a wild money-making scheme.

1232. Zimelman, Nathan. *Walls Are to Be Walked* (K–2). Illus. by Donald Carrick. 1977, Dutton $6.95. An affectionate satire poking fun at a child's frequent aimless wandering.

1233. Zion, Gene. *Dear Garbage Man* (K–2). Illus. by Margaret B. Graham. 1957, Harper $7.89. Stan, the new garbage man, finds it impossible to throw away what he has collected.

1234. Zion, Gene. *The Plant Sitter* (PS–2). Illus. by Margaret B. Graham. 1959, Harper $7.89; Scholastic paper $1.25. Tommy learns a lot about plants when he volunteers to take care of the neighbors' plants when they go on vacation.

1235. Zion, Gene. *Summer Snowman* (1–3). Illus. by Margaret B. Graham. 1955, Harper $7.89. Henry keeps a snowman in the freezer and brings him out on the Fourth of July. Also use: *Really Spring* (1956, Harper $5.79).

Community and Everyday Life

1236. Burton, Virginia L. *The Little House* (1–3). Illus. by author. 1942, Houghton $8.95; paper $2.25. Story of a little house in the country that over the years witnesses changes and progress. Caldecott Medal, 1943.

1237. Brodsky, Beverly. *Secret Places* (1–3). Illus. by author. 1979, Lippincott $8.95. A recollection in text and pictures of a city childhood.

1238. Corey, Dorothy. *Tomorrow You Can* (PS–K). Illus. by Lois Areman. 1977, Whitman $5.50. A picture book reassuring youngsters that, although today they might not be able to accomplish a great deal, tomorrow they can.

1239. Fisher, Aileen. *Going Barefoot* (K–2). Illus. by Adrienne Adams. 1960, Crowell $8.79. A description of the joys of going barefoot and of a child's envy of the many animals and birds that do not have to wear shoes.

1240. Getz, Arthur. *Tar Beach* (K–3). Illustrated. 1979, Dial $7.50; LB $7.28. Summer in the city including open hydrants and rooftop sunbathing.

1241. Hoberman, Mary Ann. *I Like Old Clothes* (PS–2). Illus. by Jacqueline Chwast. 1976, Knopf $4.95; LB $5.99. The joys of hand-me-downs are explored in rhymes and pictures. Also use: *All My Shoes Come in Twos* (1957, Little $4.50).

1242. Keats, Ezra Jack. *Dreams* (PS–2). Illus. by author. 1974, Macmillan $5.95; paper $2.50. Roberto has difficulty going to sleep on a hot summer night in the city.

1243. Knab, Linda Z. *The Day Is Waiting* (PS–K). Illus. by Don Freeman. 1980, Viking $8.95. A celebration of life in rhyme and paintings.

1244. Leiner, Katherine. *Ask Me What My Mother Does* (K–2). Illustrated. 1978, Watts $4.90. A wide variety of occupations are pictured and discussed.

1245. Lenski, Lois. *The Little Farm* (PS–3). Illus. by author. 1942, Walck $5.25; ITA ed. $3.50; paper $1.50. One in the series of Mr. Small and his family stories enjoyed by young children. Also use (by Walck $5.25; $3.50): *Cowboy Small* (1949) and *Papa Small* (1951).

1246. MacDonald, Golden. *Red Light, Green Light* (K–2). Illus. by Leonard Weisgard. 1944, Doubleday $5.95. A variety of objects, animals, and a boy learn that it is important to obey traffic signals.

1247. Mizumura, Kazue. *If I Built a Village* (1–3). Illus. by author. 1971, Crowell $7.95; LB $7.89. A quiet, idealistic view of what the world could be like if love and beauty were paramount in the human mind; a plea for conservation.

1248. Murphy, Shirley, and Murphy, Pat. *Mrs. Tortino's Return to the Sun* (PS–2). Illus. by Lee Wiggins. 1980, Lothrop $7.95; LB $7.63. Entertainment for younger readers.

1249. Rockwell, Anne, and Rockwell, Harlow. *The Supermarket* (PS–K). Illus. by author. 1979, Macmillan $6.95. Familiar objects and situations are explored in a trip to a supermarket.

1250. Rockwell, Anne. *I Like the Library* (PS–3). Illus. by author. 1977, Dutton $6.50. A small boy describes the joys he experiences during his weekly visit to the public library.

1251. Rockwell, Harlow. *My Kitchen* (PS). Illus. by author. 1980, Greenwillow $7.95; LB $7.63. A simple presentation of the contents of a kitchen and their uses.

1252. Schick, Eleanor. *City in the Summer* (1–3). Illus. by author. 1969, Macmillan $5.95; paper $.95. City summer activities grouped around an old man's trip to the beach with a young boy. Also use: *City in the Winter* (1970, Macmillan $5.95; paper 95¢).

1253. Schick, Eleanor. *Peter and Mr. Brandon* (PS–1). Illus. by Donald Garrick. 1973, Macmillan $5.95. Peter accompanies Mr. Brandon on a tour of the big city.

1254. Thomas, Ianthe. *My Street's a Morning Cool Street* (K–2). Illus. by Emily McCully. 1976, Harper $4.95; LB $4.79. A young boy describes in black English what he sees on his way to school.

1255. Welber, Robert. *The Winter Picnic* (PS–2). Illus. by Deborah Ray. 1970, Pantheon $4.99. In spite of his mother's advice that summer is the proper time for a picnic, Adam plans a picnic in the snow.

1256. Yashima, Taro. *Umbrella* (PS–1). Illus. by author. 1958, Viking $7.95; Penguin paper $1.75. A 3-year-old Japanese-American girl, born in New York, longs for a rainy day so she can use her new blue umbrella and red rubber boots.

Transportation and Machines

1257. Brown, Margaret Wise. *The Steamroller* (K–2). Illus. by Evaline Ness. 1974, Walker $5.95; LB $5.85. Daisy got a big giant steamroller for Christmas, and when she climbed aboard and pushed all the buttons, it flattened everything in its path—people, animals, cars, and all.

1258. Burton, Virginia L. *Mike Mulligan and His Steam Shovel* (1–3). Illus. by author. 1939, Houghton $7.95; paper $1.95. Thrilling race against time as Mike Mulligan and his steam shovel dig a cellar in one day. Also use: *Katy and the Big Snow* (1943, Houghton $5.95; paper 95¢).

1259. Ehrlich, Amy. *The Everyday Train* (PS–K). Illus. by Martha Alexander. 1977, Dial $4.95; LB $4.58. Jane runs across the field every day to watch the train go by and wave to the engineer.

1260. Gramatky, Hardie. *Hercules: The Story of an Old-Fashioned Fire Engine* (K–3). 1940, Putnam $5.79. A horse-drawn fire engine becomes a hero when it saves City Hall. Also use: *Loopy* (1941, Putnam $5.79).

1261. Gramatky, Hardie. *Little Toot* (K–3). Illus. by author. 1939, Putnam $5.49; paper $2.50. Little Toot, son of the mightiest tug in the harbor, had no ambition until he became a hero during a raging storm. Also use: *Little Toot on the Thames* (1964, $4.50; LB $5.79) and *Little Toot on the Mississippi* (1973, $6.95; LB $4.97).

1262. Lasky, Kathryn. *Tugboats Never Sleep* (1–3). Illus. by author. 1977, Little $7.95. A young boy visits a tugboat and learns rope talk.

1263. Lenski, Lois. *Little Auto* (K–3). Illus. by author. 1934, Walck $5.25; ITA ed. $3.50. Adventures of popular Mr. Small. Also use: *Little Train* (1940, Walck $5.95; paper $2.50).

1264. Olsen, Ib Spang. *Little Locomotive* (1–4). Illus. by author. 1976, Coward $6.95. A locomotive leaves its engine behind to explore the joys of the countryside alone.

1265. Piper, Watty. *The Little Engine That Could* (K–2). Illus. by George Hauman and Doris Hauman. 1954, Platt $4.95; Scholastic paper $1.75. Little engine saves the day.

1266. Rockwell, Anne, and Rockwell, Harlow. *Thruway* (PS–1). Illus. by author. 1972, Macmillan $5.95. Pictures and text describe a small boy's adventures riding on a major highway to the city.

1267. Steptoe, John. *Train Ride* (K–3). Illus. by author. 1971, Harper $7.95; LB $7.89. The adventures of a group of boys, from Brooklyn to Times Square.

1268. Swift, Hildegarde. *Little Red Lighthouse and the Great Gray Bridge* (1–3). Illus. by Lynd Ward. 1942, Harcourt $6.95; paper $1.95. The beacon of the little red lighthouse at the base of the George Washington Bridge in New York City is still needed even after the bridge is built.

1269. Young, Miriam. *If I Drove a Truck* (PS–1). Illus. by Robert Quackenbush. 1967, Lothrop $6.48. Big, bold illustrations and simple descriptions of various kinds of trucks will appeal to young readers who dream of driving them. Also use (Lothrop, $6.48): *If I Flew a Plane* (1970) and *If I Sailed a Boat* (1971).

Nature and Science

1270. Anderson, Lonzo. *The Day the Hurricane Happened* (K–3). Illus. by Ann Grifalconi. 1974, Scribner $6.95. A family copes with a hurricane and finds solidarity in this dramatic story set in the Virgin Islands.

1271. Barrett, Judith. *The Wind Thief* (PS–2). Illus. by Diane Dawson. 1977, Atheneum $7.95. In this amusing romp the wind decides that it wants a hat to keep warm.

1272. Baylor, Byrd. *We Walk in Sandy Places* (K–2). Illus. by Marilyn Schweitzer. 1976, Scribner $6.95. The closeness that desert dwellers feel for their environment and its creatures is beautifully described in this photographic prose poem.

1273. Baylor, Byrd. *Your Own Best Secret Place* (2–4). Illus. by Peter Parnell. 1979, Scribner $9.95. A girl shows her secret hiding place, a hollow tree, to other children.

1274. Blor, Charles, and Link, Martin. *The Goat in the Rug* (K–3). Illus. by Nancy W. Parker. 1976, Parents $5.95; LB $5.41. Geraldine, a goat whose hair is used to make a traditional Navajo rug, tells the story of the step-by-step process.

1275. Bodecker, N. M. *The Mushroom Center Disaster* (K–2). Illus. by Erik Blegvad. 1974, Atheneum $6.95. Beetle comes to Mushroom Center to find a haven, and when disaster strikes, he devises ways of restoring the ecology of the community.

1276. Brown, Margaret Wise. *The Country Noisy Book* (PS). Illus. by Leonard Weisgard. 1940, Harper $7.89; paper $1.95. The sounds made by country animals, many of which are left for the child to supply. Also use: *The Indoor Noisy Book* (1942, Harper $7.89; paper $1.95).

1277. Brown, Margaret Wise. *Wait Till the Moon Is Full* (PS–1). Illus. by Garth Williams. 1948, Harper $5.95; LB $6.49. The fears of night are dispelled in this story about raccoons.

1278. Bunting, Eve. *Winter's Coming* (1–2). Illus. by Howard Knotts. 1977, Harcourt $4.95; paper $1.65. A family makes preparations in the fall for the advent of winter.

1279. Carle, Eric. *The Very Hungry Caterpillar* (PS–2). Illus. by author. 1971, Crowell $7.95; LB $7.91. This caterpillar is so hungry he eats right through the pictures on the pages of the book—and after leaving many holes, emerges as a beautiful butterfly on the last page.

1280. Clifton, Lucille. *The Boy Who Didn't Believe in Spring* (K–2). Illus. by Brinton Turkle. 1973, Dutton $7.95; paper $1.95. An account of a black child's determination to "get me some of this spring."

1281. de Paola, Tomie. *Charlie Needs a Cloak* (PS–1). Illus. by author. 1974, Prentice-Hall $4.95; Scholastic paper $1.25. The facts about cloth making are humorously presented in this story of Charlie, a shepherd who shears his sheep, washes the wool, dries it, spins it into cloth, and makes himself a beautiful red cloak.

1282. de Paola, Tomie. *Four Stories for Four Seasons* (2–3). Illus. by author. 1977, Prentice-Hall $7.95. Dog, Cat, Frog, and Pig are involved in activities for each of the seasons in this inviting, easily read picture book.

1283. de Paola, Tomie. *The Quicksand Book* (1–3). Illus. by author. 1977, Holiday $7.95. Science is both informative and entertaining in this story of Jungle Girl who falls into a patch of quicksand

and, while being rescued by Jungle Boy, receives a long lecture on the properties of quicksand and how to rescue oneself.

1284. Domanska, Janina. *Spring Is* (K–3). Illus. by author. 1976, Greenwillow $7.25; LB $6.96. A book about the seasons as seen by a dachshund.

1285. Dos Santos, Joyce Audy. *Sand Dollar; Sand Dollar* (1–3). Illus. by author. 1980, Lippincott $7.89. Peter makes a wish on a sand dollar he finds at the beach.

1286. Elliott, Alan C. *On Sunday the Wind Came* (K–2). Illus. by Susan Bonners. 1980, Morrow $7.95. A week of different kinds of winter weather is described.

1287. Ernst, Kathryn F. *Mr. Tamarin's Trees* (K–2). Illus. by Diane deGroat. 1976, Crown $5.95. Mr. Tamarin becomes so irritated with the trees on his property—they keep dropping leaves —that he chops them down.

1288. Fisher, Aileen. *I Stood upon a Mountain* (1–3). Illus. by Blair Lent. 1979, Crowell $9.95; LB $9.79. A little girl questions the origins of the earth and receives many differing answers.

1289. Fisher, Aileen. *We Went Looking* (1–3). Illus. by Marie Angel. 1968, Crowell $7.95. A walk in the wilds produces glimpses of all sorts of animals in this work illustrated with small, detailed pictures.

1290. Garelick, May. *Down to the Beach* (K–2). Illus. by Barbara Cooney. 1973, Four Winds $7.95; paper $1.50. Beautiful, soft watercolor paintings highlight this simple story of a summer day at the beach.

1291. Garelick, May. *Where Does the Butterfly Go When It Rains?* (K–2). Illus. by Leonard Weisgard. 1961, A. & W. $6.95; Scholastic paper $1.50. Mist-like pictures illustrate how a variety of animals protect themselves from the rain.

1292. Goffstein, M. B. *Natural History* (1–3). Illus. by author. 1979, Farrar $6.95. A gentle look at the earth, its inhabitants, and its problems.

1293. Goudey, Alice E. *The Day We Saw the Sun Come Up* (PS–1). Illus. by Adrienne Adams. 1961, Scribner $8.95. This lovely picture book captures all the wonder of sunrise.

1294. Hader, Berta, and Hader, Elmer. *The Big Snow* (PS–3). Illus. by author. 1948, Macmillan $6.95; paper $2.50. How all the little animals of a country hillside survive a heavy winter storm. Caldecott Medal, 1949.

1295. Himler, Ronald. *Wake Up, Jeremiah* (PS–1). Illus. by author. 1979, Harper $7.95; LB $7.89. A young boy greets a new day.

1296. Hutchins, Pat. *The Wind Blew* (PS–K). Illus. by author. 1974, Macmillan $6.95. A cumulative story in rhyme describes the havoc wrought by a stiff wind and all the objects it carries away.

1297. Kalan, Robert. *Rain* (PS–1). Illus. by Donald Crews. 1978, Greenwillow $6.96; LB $6.67. A rainstorm described in pictures and brief text.

1298. Keats, Ezra Jack. *The Snowy Day* (PS–1). Illus. by author. 1962, Viking $6.95. The Caldecott Medal winner that describes a young black boy's delight during his first snowfall.

1299. Krauss, Ruth. *The Growing Story* (PS–2). Illus. by Phyllis Rowand. 1947, Harper $8.95; LB $7.89. A little boy watches things grow but doesn't realize until fall that he, too, has grown.

1300. Kuskin, Karla. *A Space Story* (K–2). Illus. by Marc Simont. 1978, Harper $6.95; LB $7.49. A simple but accurate presentation of material about the solar system.

1301. Lapp, Eleanor J. *In the Morning Mist* (K–3). Illus. by David Cunningham. 1978, Whitman $4.25; LB $3.19. A pensive account of a boy and his grandfather on an early morning fishing trip.

1302. Lenski, Lois. *Spring Is Here* (K–3). Illus. by author. 1945, Walck $5.95. A small picture book with the delights of the season extolled in verse. Also use (Walck $5.95): *I Like Winter* (1950) and *On a Summer Day* (1953).

1303. McCloskey, Robert. *Time of Wonder* (1–4). Illus. by author. 1957, Viking $8.95; Penguin paper $1.95. Full-color watercolors illustrate this poetic text describing a summer on the Maine coast and the hurricane that hits it. Caldecott Medal, 1958.

1304. Mack, Gail. *Yesterday's Snowman* (K–2). Illus. by Erik Blegvad. 1979, Pantheon $6.95; LB $6.99. A beautiful snowman is made by a family, but because of rain, the next day it is gone.

1305. Munari, Bruno. *The Circus in the Mist* (1–3). Illus. by author. 1969, Collier $6.95; LB $6.91. A uniquely designed picture book that gives the reader the feel of a misty, foggy day, and then the return of the sunshine.

1306. Parnall, Peter. *The Mountain* (K–3). Illus. by author. 1971, Doubleday $6.95. What happens to a beautiful western mountain when tourists invade it and devastate it, told in vivid expressive pictures.

1307. Peet, Bill. *The Wump World* (1–3). Illus. by author. 1970, Houghton $7.95. An animal parable in which pollution and the waste of natural resources are the main themes.

1308. Rand, Ann, and Rand, Paul. *I Know a Lot of Things* (PS–1). Illus. by author. 1956, Harcourt $6.95. A book to help children develop greater awareness and appreciation of their environment.

1309. Ryder, Joanne. *Fog in the Meadow* (K–3). Illus. by Gail Owens. 1979, Harper $7.49. Small animals find ways to react to the coming of a fog.

1310. Seuss, Dr. *The Lorax* (K–3). Illus. by author. 1971, Random $4.95; LB $5.99. The Lorax, a little brown creature, has tried in vain to ward off pollution and ecological blight, but Onceler, who wanted the trees for his business, would not heed the warning.

1311. Shulevitz, Uri. *Dawn* (PS–2). Illus. by author. 1974, Farrar $6.95. A rare, beautiful book describing in simple poetic terms the coming of dawn.

1312. Shulevitz, Uri. *Rain, Rain, Rivers* (PS–2). Illus. by author. 1969, Farrar $7.95. A little girl sits in her attic bedroom while the rain falls, and her imagination takes her to the places touched by the rain—the city, streams, and sea.

1313. Suteyev, V. *Mushroom in the Rain* (K–2). Illus. by Jose Aruego and Ariane Dewey. 1974, Macmillan $5.95; LB $4.95. An ant and several other forms of animal life take refuge from the rain under a mushroom.

1314. Tobias, Tobi. *At the Beach* (K–2). Illus. by Gloria Singer. 1978, McKay $5.95. A child's happy day at the beach.

1315. Tresselt, Alvin. *Hi, Mister Robin!* (K–2). Illus. by Roger Duvoisin. 1950, Lothrop $6.48. A young boy watches the landscape transform itself as spring arrives after he has seen his first robin. Also use: *Johnny Maple Leaf* (1948, Lothrop $6.96).

1316. Tresselt, Alvin. *Hide and Seek Fog* (K–2). Illus. by Roger Duvoisin. 1965, Lothrop $6.00. Pastel watercolors quietly reflect obscure seashore scenes as the mysterious, deepening fog rolls in from the sea.

1317. Tresselt, Alvin. *It's Time Now!* (1–2). Illus. by Roger Duvoisin. 1969, Lothrop $7.25. The changing seasons in beautiful drawings and simple text.

1318. Tresselt, Alvin. *Rain Drop Splash* (K–3). Illus. by Leonard Weisgard. 1946, Lothrop $6.48. How the raindrops form a puddle that grows from pond to river and finally joins the sea.

1319. Tresselt, Alvin. *What Did You Leave Behind?* (K–3). Illus. by Roger Duvoisin. 1978, Lothrop $6.95; LB $6.43. Nature's beauties are explored in poetic text and brilliant pictures.

1320. Tresselt, Alvin. *White Snow, Bright Snow* (PS–1). Illus. by Roger Duvoisin. 1947, Lothrop $7.25; LB $6.96. Puts into words and distinguished pictures the silent fall of snowflakes and the excitement that snow brings to children. Caldecott Medal, 1948.

1321. Udry, Janice May. *A Tree Is Nice* (PS). Illus. by Marc Simont. 1956, Harper $6.95; LB $7.89. The many delights to be had in, with, or under a tree, picking apples, raking leaves, swinging, or just sitting in the shade. Caldecott Medal, 1957.

Books for Beginning Readers

1322. Alexander, Sue. *More Witch, Goblin and Ghost Stories* (1–3). Illus. by Jeanette Winter. 1978, Pantheon $3.95; LB $4.99. Three friends involved in 6 entertaining stories.

1323. Alexander, Sue. *Witch, Goblin and Sometimes Ghost: Six Read-Alone Stories* (1–2). Illus. by Jeanette Winter. 1976, Pantheon $3.95; LB $4.99. Six easy-to-read stories especially useful for beginning readers, since they are built on experiences familiar to young children.

1324. Averill, Esther. *Captains of the City Streets: A Story of the Cat Club* (1–3). Illus. by author. 1972, Harper $5.95; LB $5.89; paper $.95. Two young tramp cats, in spite of their avowed independence, are gradually drawn into the Cat Club.

1325. Averill, Esther. *Jenny and the Cat Club: A Collection of Favorite Stories about Jenny Linsky* (2–4). Illus. by author. 1973, Harper $5.79. Five favorite stories about Jenny, the appealing black cat, are brought together in this collection. Also use: *Jenny's Birthday Book* (1954, $5.95), *Jenny's Bedside Book* (1959, $5.95), and *The Fire Cat* (1960, $5.95; LB $6.89).

1326. Baker, Betty. *Partners* (1–2). Illus. by Emily McCully. 1978, Greenwillow $5.95; LB $5.71. Three Southwest Indian stories about Coyote and Badger are included in this entertaining beginner's book.

1327. Benchley, Nathaniel. *The Deep Dives of Stanley Whale* (K–3). Illus. by Mischa Richter. 1973, Harper $6.89. A cautionary tale about a young whale who disobeys his mother, but who unintentionally rescues Uncle Moby.

1328. Benchley, Nathaniel. *Feldman Fieldmouse: A Fable* (2–4). Illus. by Hilary Knight. 1970, Harper $6.89; paper $1.50. Beginning readers will enjoy this tale of an orphaned mouse who is rescued by a boy who understands mice.

1329. Benchley, Nathaniel. *A Ghost Named Fred* (1–3). Illus. by Ben Shecter. 1968, Harper $5.95; LB $6.89. To get out of the rain, George enters an empty house and meets Fred, an absent-minded ghost.

1330. Benchley, Nathaniel. *Oscar Otter* (K–2). Illus. by Arnold Lobel. 1966, Harper $6.89. Hilarious words and pictures describe Oscar's fun on the long and perilous slide he builds to get to his pool.

1331. Benchley, Nathaniel. *Red Fox and His Canoe* (1–2). Illus. by Arnold Lobel. 1964, Harper $6.89; Scholastic paper $.95. Red Fox gets himself a large canoe and picks up so many unusual passengers that it capsizes. Also use: *The Strange Disappearance of Arthur Cluck* (1967, Harper $5.95; LB $6.89).

1332. Benchley, Nathaniel. *The Several Tricks of Edgar Dolphin* (1–2). Illus. by Mamoru Funai. 1970, Harper $5.95; LB $6.89. When Edgar is captured, he entertains humans with his tricks.

1333. Berenstain, Stanley, and Berenstain, Janice. *Bears in the Night* (1–2). Illus. by author. 1971, Random $3.50; LB $4.39. Bear cubs go on a rampage after being put to bed. The lively cartoon style and simple phrases make this a good book for beginning readers. Also use (Random): *Bears on Wheels* (1969, $3.50; LB $4.39) and *The Bear's Almanac* (1973, $3.95; LB $5.99).

1334. Boegehold, Betty. *Pippa Pops Out: Four Read-Aloud/Read Alone Stories* (K–2). Illus. by Cyndy Szekeres. 1979, Knopf $4.95. A group of stories about an adventurous mouse.

1335. Boegehold, Betty. *Small Deer's Magic Tricks* (1–3). Illus. by Jacqueline Chwast. 1977, Coward $4.99. Four easily read tales about an Indonesian trickster who, although small, can outwit her jungle enemies.

1336. Boegehold, Betty. *Three to Get Ready* (1–2). Illus. by Mary Chalmers. 1965, Harper $6.89. Four humorous stories about 3 mischievous kittens and their mother.

1337. Bonsall, Crosby N. *And I Mean It, Stanley* (1–2). Illus. by author. 1974, Harper $5.95; LB $6.89. A small girl playing alone with a pile of junk keeps up a monologue with Stanley, who is behind the fence, telling him of the great "thing" she is making.

1338. Bonsall, Crosby N. *The Case of the Scaredy Cats* (1–2). Illus. by author. 1971, Harper $5.95; LB $6.89. What do you do when you find a bevy of girls in your secret clubhouse?

1339. Bonsall, Crosby N. *The Day I Had to Play with My Sister* (K–2). Illus. by author. 1972, Harper $5.95; LB $6.89. An older brother impatiently tries to teach his little sister how to play hide-and-seek, but she can't seem to get the idea of the game.

1340. Bonsall, Crosby N. *Mine's the Best* (1–2). Illus. by author. 1973, Harper $5.95; LB $6.89. Two small boys discover they have identical balloons, and then begins the argument—whose is the best?

1341. Bonsall, Crosby N. *Piggle* (1–2). Illus. by author. 1973, Harper $5.95; LB $6.89. Homer goes in search of someone to play games and finds Bear, who enjoys "Piggle" with him. This rhyming spree of nonsense words will please beginning readers.

1342. Bonsall, Crosby N. *Tell Me Some More* (1–3). Illus. by Fritz Siebel. 1961, Harper $6.89. Andrew introduces his friend to the magic of the library.

1343. Bonsall, Crosby N. *Who's a Pest* (1–3). Illus. by author. 1962, Harper $6.89. Even though his 4 sisters, a lizard, a rabbit, and a chipmunk insist that he's a pest, Homer refuses to believe it.

1344. Bonsall, Crosby N. *Who's Afraid of the Dark?* (1–3). 1980, Harper $6.89. A small boy projects his fear of the dark onto his dog.

1345. Bowden, Joan Chase. *The Bean Boy* (K–2). Illus. by Sal Murdocca. 1979, Macmillan $6.95. A sequential yarn that starts with a bean boy being eaten by a rooster.

1346. Bram, Elizabeth. *Woodruff and the Clocks* (K–2). Illustrated. 1980, Dial $5.89; paper $1.95. The story of a boy who enjoys inventing adventures.

1347. Brandenberg, Franz. *Everyone Ready?* (2–3). Illus. by Aliki. 1979, Greenwillow $5.95; LB $5.71. The Fieldmouse children are on a train without their parents.

1348. Brandenberg, Franz. *A Picnic, Hurrah!* (1–4). Illus. by Aliki. 1978, Greenwillow $5.95; LB $5.49. Three short chapters on planning the first picnic of the season.

1349. Brandenberg, Franz. *Six New Students* (1–3). Illus. by Aliki. 1978, Greenwillow $5.95. Six field mice spend their first day at school.

1350. Brandenberg, Franz. *What Can You Make of It?* (1–2). Illus. by Aliki. 1977, Greenwillow $5.71. Mr. and Mrs. Fieldmouse have collected too many things, and there is no room when visitors come. Uncle Alfred suggests that there are many things one can do with rubbish, and proceeds to demonstrate.

1351. Brenner, Barbara. *The Five Pennies* (K–3). Illus. by Erik Blegvad. 1964, Knopf $4.69; paper $.95. Mickey tries to buy a pet with his 5 pennies. Also use: *Beef Stew* (1965, Knopf $4.99).

1352. Brenner, Barbara. *Wagon Wheels* (1–3). Illus. by Don Bolognese. 1978, Harper $4.95; LB $4.79. The adventures of a black family of Kansas in the 1870s.

1353. Bulla, Clyde Robert. *Daniel's Duck* (1–3). Illus. by Joan Sandin. 1979, Harper $5.95; LB $6.89. In this story for beginning readers, a young boy is hurt when people make fun of his wood carving of a duck.

1354. Carrick, Malcolm. *Mr. Tod's Trap* (1–3). Illus. by author. 1980, Harper $6.89. A male chauvinist fox trades places with his wife.

1355. Chapman, Carol. *Ig Lives in a Cave* (1–2). Illus. by Bruce Degen. 1979, Dutton $5.95. A young boy growing up in prehistoric times has problems not too different from those of today's children.

1356. Child Study Association, comp. *Read to Me Storybook* (K–2). Illus. by Lois Lenski. 1947, Crowell $5.95. A delightful assortment of easy-to-read stories and poems, also found in: *Read Me More Stories* (K–2), illus. by Barbara Cooney (1951, $5.95) and *Read to Me Again* (PS–3), illus. by Garry Mackenzie (1961, $6.89).

1357. Christian, Mary Blount. *The Lucky Man* (1–3). Illus. by Glen Rounds. 1979, Macmillan $6.95. A hard-luck hillbilly finally gets the law on his side.

1358. Cohen, Miriam. *When Will I Read?* (1–2). Illus. by Lillian Hoban. 1977, Greenwillow $7.25. Jim, a first-grader, experiences the joys of learning to read.

1359. Croll, Carolyn. *Too Many Babas* (1–3). Illustrated. 1979, Harper $5.95; LB $6.89. Too many cooks spoil the meal in this simple narrative.

1360. Dauer, Rosamond. *Bullfrog Grows Up* (1–4). Illus. by Byron Barton. 1976, Greenwillow $5.71. An easily read story about a frog that 2 mice bring home from a pond.

1361. Degen, Bruce. *The Little Witch and the Riddle* (1–3). Illustrated. 1980, Harper $5.95; LB

$6.89. Little Lily attempts to solve a riddle to open her grandmother's book of spells.

1362. Eastman, P. D. *Are You My Mother?* (1–3). Illus. by author. 1960, Random $3.50; LB $4.39. A small bird falls from his nest and wanders about looking for his mother. Also use: *Go, Dog, Go* (1961, Random $3.50; LB $4.39).

1363. Farley, Walter. *Little Black, a Pony* (1–3). Illus. by James Schucker. 1961, Random $3.50; LB $4.39. The story of a boy and a pony who wishes it were big.

1364. Feder, Paula Kurzband. *Where Does the Teacher Live?* (1–2). Illus. by Lillian Hoban. 1979, Dutton $5.95. Three young people try to find out where their teacher lives.

1365. Firmin, Peter. *Basil Brush Finds Treasure* (1–2). Illus. by author. 1979, Prentice-Hall $5.95. Basil and friend Harry search a seashore for treasure.

1366. Firmin, Peter. *Basil Brush Goes Flying* (1–3). Illus. by author. 1977, Scholastic paper $1.25. An intrepid fox tries several methods in his unsuccessful try at flying.

1367. Freschet, Berniece. *Moose Baby* (1–2). Illus. by Jim Arnosky. 1979, Putnam $6.29. Simple text and appropriate pictures enhance 4 short stories about the first experiences of a moose child.

1368. Gackenbach, Dick. *Hattie Be Quiet, Hattie Be Good* (1–3). Illustrated. 1977, Harper $5.95; LB $6.89. In the first of the stories, Hattie Rabbit valiantly tries to be quiet for an hour; in the second, she visits a sick friend.

1369. Gackenbach, Dick. *More from Hound and Bear* (1–3). Illus. by author. 1979, Clarion $7.95. Three humorous stories that continue the adventures begun in *Hound and Bear* (1976, Seabury $6.95).

1370. Gage, Wilson. *Squash Pie* (1–3). Illus. by Glen Rounds. 1976, Greenwillow $5.95; LB $5.71. A mystery: Who is stealing the squash crop? The solution: Who hates squash pie?

1371. Gilchrist, Theo E. *Halfway Up the Mountain* (1–3). Illus. by Glen Rounds. 1978, Lippincott $4.95. An old man and a half-blind woman drive off a bandit.

1372. Guilfoile, Elizabeth. *Nobody Listens to Andrew* (1–3). Illus. by Mary Stevens. 1957, Follett $3.39; paper $1.50. The reaction of Andrew's elders when he tells them there is a bear in his bed.

1373. Harper, Anita. *How We Work* (1–3). Illus. by Christine Roche. 1977, Harper $4.95; LB $5.11. Comic-strip type illustrations portray various ways and conditions of human work. Also use: *How We Live* (1977, Harper $4.95; LB $5.11).

1374. Heilbroner, Joan. *This Is the House Where Jack Lives* (1–2). Illus. by Aliki. 1962, Harper $6.89. The house is involved in a chain of amusing events. Also use: *The Happy Birthday Present* (1961, Harper $6.89).

1375. Hoban, Lillian. *Arthur's Honey Bear* (1–3). Illus. by author. 1974, Harper $5.95; LB $6.89. Arthur, a chimp, decides to sell all his old toys except his bear, but his sisters bribe him into parting with Honey Bear. Also use: *Arthur's Pen Pal* (1976, Harper $5.95; LB $6.89).

1376. Hoban, Lillian. *Arthur's Prize Reader* (1–2). Illus. by author. 1978, Harper $4.95; LB $5.79. Arthur, the chimp, must adjust to the fact that his sister Violet can read and he can't.

1377. Hoban, Lillian. *Mr. Pig and Sonny Too* (1–3). Illus. by author. 1977, Harper $5.95; LB $6.89. A dutiful son helps his father in this slapstick delight.

1378. Hoban, Lillian. *Stick-in-the-Mud Turtle* (2–4). Illus. by author. 1977, Greenwillow $5.95; LB $5.71. Fred's family wants to keep up with the Joneses when a new turtle family moves next door and fixes up their mudhole.

1379. Hoban, Russell. *Arthur's New Power* (2–3). 1978, Crowell $5.95. The lovable chimp faces a situation where father states there is to be no more electricity in the house.

1380. Hoban, Russell. *Bedtime for Frances* (1–2). Illus. by Garth Williams. 1960, Harper $6.95; LB $6.89. Frances, a badger, tries every familiar trick to tease her way past bedtime. Also use: *Bread and Jam for Frances* (1964, $6.95; LB $6.89; paper $1.25) and *Bargain for Frances* (1970, $5.95; LB $6.89; paper $1.95).

1381. Hoban, Russell. *Best Friends for Frances* (1–2). Illus. by Lillian Hoban. 1969, Harper $6.95; LB $6.81; paper $1.95. When friend Albert decides that he must exclude girls from his "wondering day" and baseball game, Frances chooses younger sister Gloria as a companion. Also use: *A Baby Sister for Frances* (1964, Harper $6.95; LB $6.89; paper $1.95).

1382. Hoff, Syd. *Albert the Albatross* (1–2). Illus. by author. 1961, Harper $5.95; LB $6.89. A seabird's unsuccessful search for the ocean is rewarded by accompanying a lady who is going on an ocean trip.

1383. Hoff, Syd. *Barkley* (1–3). Illus. by author. 1975, Harper $5.95; LB $6.89. An easily read story about a forcibly retired, aging circus dog.

1384.   Hoff, Syd. *Danny and the Dinosaur* (K–2). Illus. by author. 1958, Harper $5.95; LB $6.89; paper $1.95. Danny wanted to play and so did the dinosaur. What could have been more natural than for them to leave the museum together? Also use: *Sammy the Seal* (1959, Harper $5.95; LB $6.89) and *Oliver* (1960, Harper $6.89).

1385.   Hoff, Syd. *Grizzwold* (1–2). Illus. by author. 1963, Harper $6.89. After foresters have destroyed his home, a bear sets out to find a new one.

1386.   Hoff, Syd. *Stanley* (1–3). Illus. by author. 1962, Harper $6.89; paper $1.95. A cave man finds a new home in this inventive tale.

1387.   Holland, Marion. *A Big Ball of String* (1–3). Illus. by author. 1958, Beginner Books $4.39. A child dreams of what he would do with a ball of string, and then receives one.

1388.   Hurd, Edith Thacher. *Come and Have Fun* (1–2). Illus. by Clement Hurd. 1962, Harper $6.89. A mouse refuses the cat's invitation to join him in a series of activities.

1389.   Hurd, Edith Thacher. *Johnny Lion's Rubber Boots* (1–2). Illus. by Clement Hurd. 1972, Harper $6.89. A lion cub tries to amuse himself indoors on a rainy day. Also use (Harper $6.89): *Johnny Lion's Book* (1965) and *Johnny Lion's Bad Day* (1970).

1390.   Hurd, Edith Thacher. *Last One Home Is a Green Pig* (PS–2). Illus. by Clement Hurd. 1959, Harper $6.89. A lively race between a duck and a monkey. Also use (Harper $5.95; LB $6.89): *Hurry, Hurry* (1960) and *Stop, Stop* (1961).

1391.   Hutchins, Pat. *The Best Train Set Ever* (K–2). Illus. by author. 1978, Greenwillow $5.95; LB $5.49. Three stories that deal with various crises surrounding celebrations.

1392.   Jaspersohn, William. *How the Forest Grew* (2–4). Illus. by Chuck Eckart. 1979, Greenwillow $5.95; LB $5.71. Two hundred years in the life of the forest told simply but with lyricism.

1393.   Johnson, Crockett. *Harold and the Purple Crayon* (K–2). Illus. by author. 1955, Harper $4.95; LB $5.89. A little boy draws all of the things necessary for him to go for a walk. Also use: *Harold's Trip to the Sky* (1957, Harper $5.89) and *A Picture for Harold's Room* (1960, Harper $5.95; LB $6.89; Scholastic, paper 95¢).

1394.   Johnston, Tony. *Odd Jobs* (1–3). Illus. by Tomie de Paola. 1977, Putnam $4.99. Odd Jobs undertakes some very unusual tasks in this freewheeling, laughable comedy of errors.

1395.   Kennedy, Richard. *The Mouse God* (2–4). Illus. by Stephen Harvard. 1979, Atlantic $6.95. Mice build a church out of a crate on the advice of their mouse god, the cat in disguise.

1396.   Kent, Jack. *Hoddy Doddy* (2–3). Illus. by author. 1979, Greenwillow $5.95; LB $5.71. Three cheerful Danish tales about hoddy doddies, or very foolish people.

1397.   Kessler, Leonard. *Here Comes the Strike-Out* (1–2). Illus. by author. 1965, Harper $5.95; LB $6.89; paper $1.95. Bobby always strikes out at bat until his friend Willie helps him to improve his game.

1398.   Kessler, Leonard. *Kick, Pass and Run* (1–2). Illus. by author. 1966, Harper $5.95; LB $6.89; paper $1.95. Football rules and terms are tackled in easy-to-read, easy-to-remember terms, reinforced by the illustrated glossary that follows the comic story of animal teams imitating the New York Giants and Jets.

1399.   Kessler, Leonard. *On Your Mark, Get Set, Go!* (1–2). Illus. by author. 1972, Harper $5.95; LB $6.89. Subtitled *The First All-Animal Olympics*, this is the humorous story of a variety of animals and their attempt to organize a sports meet. Also use: *Last One in Is a Rotten Egg* (1969, Harper $5.95; LB $6.89).

1400.   Landshoff, Ursula. *Okay, Good Dog* (1–3). Illus. by author. 1978, Harper $4.95; LB $5.79. An introduction to the principles of successful dog training, simply told.

1401.   Lapp, Eleanor J. *The Mice Came In Early This Year* (1–2). Illus. by David Cunningham. 1976, Whitman $5.50. When mice come in early, it means winter is near, said grandmother, and preparations are made for the cold season ahead.

1402.   Lawrence, James. *Binky Brothers, Detectives* (1–2). Illus. by Leonard Kessler. 1968, Harper $6.89; paper $1.95. Dinky is younger brother to Pinky with the status of "helper" in their Binky Brothers Detective Agency, until he solves the case of the missing catcher's mitt and becomes a full partner. Also use: *Binky Brothers and the Fearless Four* (1970, Harper $4.95; LB $6.89).

1403.   Le Sieg, Theo. *Ten Apples Up on Top* (K–1). Illustrated. 1961, Random $3.50; LB $4.39. Three bears try to pile apples on their heads in this nonsense story. Also use (Random $3.50; LB $4.39): *I Wish That I Had Duck Feet* (1965) and *Eye Book* (1968).

1404.   Leverich, Kathleen. *The Hungry Fox and the Foxy Duck* (1–2). Illus. by Paul Galdone. 1979, Parents $4.95; LB $4.99. A fox invites a duck to breakfast with unexpected results.

1405. Levitin, Sonia. *A Sound to Remember* (1–3). Illus. by Gabriel Lisowski. 1979, Harcourt $6.95. An awkward boy is chosen to blow the ram's horn at Rosh Hashanah.

1406. Lexau, Joan M. *I Hate Red Rover* (1–3). Illus. by Gail Owens. 1979, Dutton $5.95. Jill hates the ridicule when she fails in the game of red rover.

1407. Lexau, Joan M. *Olaf Reads* (1–3). Illus. by Harvey Weiss. 1961, Dial $4.58. Olaf's mistakes as he struggles to learn to read are both hilarious and instructive.

1408. Lexau, Joan M. *The Rooftop Mystery* (1–2). Illus. by Syd Hoff. 1968, Harper $6.89. Trying desperately to avoid transporting sister's doll on moving day, Sam and Albert lose it instead, and in the end prove their worth as junior detectives. Also use: *The Homework Caper* (1966, Harper $6.89).

1409. Lobel, Arnold. *Days with Frog and Toad* (1–2). Illus. by author. 1979, Harper $5.95; LB $6.89. The friendship of Frog and Toad survives 5 incidents such as trying to fly a kite.

1410. Lobel, Arnold. *Frog and Toad All Year* (1–2). Illus. by author. 1976, Harper $5.95; LB $6.89. Five short stories about 2 old friends, Frog and Toad, and their humorous adventures during different seasons of the year, ending with the celebration of Christmas Eve.

1411. Lobel, Arnold. *Frog and Toad Are Friends* (K–2). Illus. by author. 1970, Harper $5.95; LB $6.89. Two new friends for the independent reader.

1412. Lobel, Arnold. *Frog and Toad Together* (K–2). Illus. by author. 1972, Harper $5.95; LB $6.89; paper $1.95. A sequel to *Frog and Toad Are Friends* presents 5 more adventures of the 2 best friends.

1413. Lobel, Arnold. *Grasshopper on the Road* (1–2). Illus. by author. 1978, Harper $4.95; LB $5.79. A series of short stories, each with a vital message.

1414. Lobel, Arnold. *How the Rooster Saved the Day* (K–2). Illus. by Anita Lobel. 1977, Greenwillow $6.95; LB $6.67. A smart rooster outwits a thief with a series of clever ruses in this humorous story with beautifully detailed illustrations.

1415. Lobel, Arnold. *Mouse Soup* (1–2). Illus. by author. 1977, Harper $5.95; LB $6.89. When mouse is caught by weasel, who plans to use him for soup, he convinces his captor that "mouse soup must be mixed with stones to make it taste really good."

1416. Lobel, Arnold. *Mouse Tales* (1–2). Illus. by author. 1972, Harper $5.95; LB $6.89; paper $1.95. Seven bedtime stories told by papa mouse to his 7 sons. Lively little drawings add to the humor.

1417. Lobel, Arnold. *Owl at Home* (1–2). Illus. by author. 1975, Harper $5.95; LB $6.89. Five chapter stories dealing with the humorous and bungling attempts of Owl to be helpful.

1418. Lobel, Arnold. *Small Pig* (K–2). Illus. by author. 1969, Harper $6.89. A dirty little pig in a search for mud ends up in cement.

1419. Lopshire, Robert. *It's Magic* (2–4). Illus. by author. 1969, Macmillan $4.95. Tad the Great fools Boris the Bear over and over again with tricks using ordinary materials.

1420. Lopshire, Robert. *Put Me in the Zoo* (1–3). Illus. by author. 1960, Beginner Books $3.50; LB $4.39. An unusual dog thinks he should be in a zoo, but his talents really mean he should be in a circus.

1421. Low, Joseph. *Benny Rabbit and the Owl* (K–2). Illus. by author. 1978, Greenwillow $5.95; LB $5.49. Benny insists there is an owl in his closet.

1422. McClintock, Mike. *A Fly Went By* (1–3). Illus. by Fritz Siebel. 1958, Random $3.50; LB $4.39. A cumulative tale about a merry chase started by a fly and involving a cat, dog, sheep, and other animals. Also use: *Stop That Ball!* (1958, Random $3.50; LB $4.39) and *What Have I Got?* (1961, Harper $6.89).

1423. McKie, Roy, and Eastman, P. D. *Snow* (1–3). Illustrated. 1962, Random $3.50; LB $4.39. A series of snow adventures, including making a snowman, are gently pictured in this homey story.

1424. McLenigham, Valjean. *You Are What You Are* (1–3). Illus. by Jack Reilly. 1977, Follett $2.97; paper $1.50. An amusing fairy-tale spoof. Also use: *You Can Go Jump* (1977, Follett $3.39; paper $1.50).

1425. Maestro, Betsy. *Lambs for Dinner* (K–3). Illus. by Giulio Maestro. 1978, Crown $6.95. A variation on "The Wolf and the 7 Little Kids" written for beginning readers.

1426. Margolis, Richard J. *Big Bear to the Rescue* (1–3). Illus. by Robert Lopshire. 1975, Greenwillow $5.71; paper $.95. An easily read cumulative story about a bear's attempt to rescue Mr. Mole from an unused well.

1427. Marshall, Edward. *Troll Country* (1–2). Illus. by James Marshall. 1980, Dial $5.89; paper

$1.95. Elsie Fay wanders into the woods and out-smarts a troll.

1428. Michel, Anna. *Little Wild Chimpanzee* (1–3). Illus. by Peter Parnall and Virginia Parnall. 1978, Pantheon $3.95. A description of a chimp grow-ing up in a tropical forest.

1429. Minarik, Else Holmelund. *Little Bear* (K–2). Illus. by Maurice Sendak. 1957, Harper $5.95; LB $6.89; paper $1.95. Humorous adven-ture stories of Mother Bear and Little Bear. Also use ($5.95; LB $6.89): *Little Bear's Friend* (1960), *Little Bear's Visit* (1961, also paper $1.95), and *A Kiss for Little Bear* (1968).

1430. Minarik, Else Holmelund. *No Fighting, No Biting!* (PS–3). Illus. by Maurice Sendak. 1958, Harper $5.95; LB $6.89; paper $1.95. Light-foot and Quick-foot, 2 little alligators, teach Rosa and Willy a lesson.

1431. Moore, Lilian. *Everything Happens to Stuey* (1–3). Illus. by Mary Stevens. 1960, Random $4.39; paper $1.95. Stuey's chemistry experi-ments always backfire. Also use: *The Snake That Went to School* (1957, Random $4.39).

1432. Moore, Lilian. *Little Raccoon and the Thing in the Pool* (1–2). Illus. by Gioia Fiammenghi. 1963, McGraw $5.95. Little Raccoon overcomes his fears of the pool and catches crayfish for dinner.

1433. Myrick, Mildred. *The Secret Three* (1–2). Il-lus. by Arnold Lobel. 1963, Harper $6.89. Two boys on the mainland and one on an island light-house exchange messages in a bottle carried by the tide.

1434. Nodset, Joan I. *Come Here, Cat* (K–3). Il-lus. by Steven Kellogg. 1973, Harper $6.89. A young girl chases a cat around her house and onto the roof in this simple but enjoyable story. Also use: *Go Away, Dog* (1963, Harper $6.89; Scholas-tic, paper 85¢).

1435. Nodset, Joan I. *Who Took the Farmer's Hat?* (1–2). Illus. by Fritz Siebel. 1963, Harper $7.89; Scholastic paper $1.25. When the wind blows away the farmer's hat, all of the animals think they saw it.

1436. Parish, Peggy. *Amelia Bedelia Helps Out* (1–3). Illus. by Lynn Sweat. 1979, Greenwillow $5.95; LB $5.71. More puns taken literally in this addition to the popular series, which also includes *Good Work Amelia Bedelia* (1976, Greenwillow $5.95).

1437. Parish, Peggy. *Good Work, Amelia Bedelia* (1–4). Illus. by Lynn Sweat. 1976, Greenwillow $5.95; LB $5.71. An easily read continuation of the adventures of the housemaid who takes every-thing literally. Also use: *Thank You, Amelia Bedelia* (1964, Harper $4.95; LB $6.89), *Amelia Bedelia and the Surprise Shower* (1966, Harper $5.95; LB $6.89), and *Teach Us, Amelia Bedelia* (1977, Green-willow $5.95; LB $5.71).

1438. Parish, Peggy. *Play Ball, Amelia Bedelia* (1–3). Illus. by Wallace Tripp. 1972, Harper $5.95; LB $6.89. Amelia Bedelia has trouble with baseball lingo, and her literal-minded and humor-ous interpretation of the plays will bring chuckles to young readers. Also use: the first in the series, *Amelia Bedelia* (1963, Harper $5.95; LB $6.89; Scholastic, paper 95¢) and *Come Back, Amelia Bedelia* (1971, Harper $5.95; LB $6.89; paper $1.95).

1439. Parish, Peggy. *Too Many Rabbits* (1–3). Il-lus. by Leonard Kessler. 1974, Macmillan $5.95; Scholastic paper $.95. Shortly after Miss Molly takes in a stray rabbit, her house is overrun with rabbits and she must find a new home for them.

1440. Pearson, Susan. *Molly Moves Out* (1–3). Il-lus. by Steven Kellogg. 1979, Dial $5.89; paper $1.95. Molly, a rabbit, moves to her own home for peace and quiet but soon gets lonely.

1441. Peterson, Jeanne Whitehouse. *That Is That* (2–4). Illus. by Deborah Ray. 1979, Harper $7.95; LB $7.89. Only time can heal the hurt when a girl's father leaves home.

1442. Platt, Kin. *Big Max* (1–2). Illus. by Robert Lopshire. 1965, Harper $6.89; paper $1.95. A modest detective unravels the case of the king's missing elephant in this Mystery I Can Read book.

1443. Prager, Annabelle. *The Surprise Party* (1–3). Illus. by Tomie de Paola. 1977, Pantheon $3.95; LB $4.99. Nicky plans his own surprise party but receives a real surprise in this easily read picture book.

1444. Rice, Eve. *Papa's Lemonade and Other Stories* (1–2). Illus. by author. 1976, Greenwillow $5.95; LB $5.71. Five humorous stories about papa and mama and their 5 children—puppies who seem to be a cross between dogs and bears.

1445. Richter, Alice, and Numeroff, Laura Joffe. *You Can't Put Braces on Spaces* (2–4). Illus-trated. 1979, Greenwillow $5.95; LB $5.71. A boy has doubts about his looks when he has to wear braces.

1446. Rockwell, Anne. *The Bump in the Night* (1–3). Illus. by author. 1979, Greenwillow $5.95; LB $5.71. Toby befriends a ghost and uncovers a hidden treasure.

1447. Rockwell, Anne. *The Gollywhopper Egg* (2–4). Illus. by author. 1974, Macmillan $4.50; pa-per $2.50. A gullible farmer tries to hatch a coconut, thinking that it is a gollywhopper's egg, in this easily read book.

1448. Rockwell, Anne. *The Story Snail* (2–4). Illus. by author. 1974, Macmillan $4.95. John has amazing adventures looking for a magical snail.

1449. Rockwell, Anne. *Timothy Todd's Good Things Are Gone* (K–2). Illus. by author. 1978, Macmillan $6.95. Timothy's refuge in an old man's house costs him part of his belongings.

1450. Roy, Ron. *Awful Thursday* (1–2). Illus. by Lillian Hoban. 1979, Pantheon $3.95; LB $4.99. Jack is fearful that he has ruined his teacher's tape recorder.

1451. Schick, Eleanor. *Home Alone* (2–3). Illustrated. 1980, Dial $5.89; paper $1.95. A boy copes with the time between getting out of school and his mother's return from work.

1452. Schick, Eleanor. *Neighborhood Knight* (1–4). Illus. by author. 1976, Greenwillow $5.71. A young boy thinks he is a knight and his city building is a castle in this imaginative story.

1453. Schick, Eleanor. *Summer at the Sea* (1–3). Illus. by author. 1979, Greenwillow $5.95; LB $5.71. A series of gentle, simple experiences of a girl during a seaside summer.

1454. Schulman, Janet. *The Big Hello* (1–2). Illus. by Lillian Hoban. 1976, Greenwillow $5.95; LB $5.71. A good book for independent readers about a small girl who prattles to her doll, her dog, and her mother.

1455. Schulman, Janet. *Jack the Bum and the Haunted House* (1–3). Illus. by James Stevenson. 1977, Greenwillow $5.95; LB $5.71. A hobo goes to live in a haunted house, discovers a jewel thief hiding there, and is rewarded with a steady job in this amiable picture book.

1456. Seuss, Dr. *The Cat in the Hat* (1–3). Illus. by author. 1957, Random $3.50; LB $4.39. The story of the fabulous cat that came to visit one rainy day when Mother was away. Also use (Random $3.50; LB $4.39): *The Cat in the Hat Comes Back!* (1958) and *Foot Book* (1968).

1457. Seuss, Dr. *Hop on Pop* (1–2). Illus. by author. 1963, Random $3.50; LB $4.39. One of the many entertaining, controlled vocabulary stories of Dr. Seuss. Also use (Random $3.50; LB $4.39): *One Fish, Two Fish, Red Fish, Blue Fish* (1960) and *Fox in Sox* (1965).

1458. Seuss, Dr. *I Can Read with My Eyes Shut!* (1–2). Illus. by author. 1978, Random $3.50; LB $4.39. The cat in the hat tells us of all the joys of reading.

1459. Seuss, Dr. *Oh Say Can You Say?* (1–3). Illus. by author. 1979, Random $3.50; LB $4.39. Tongue-twisting verses presented by a variety of imaginative creatures.

1460. Sharmat, Marjorie. *Griselda's New Year* (1–2). Illus. by Normand Chartier. 1979, Macmillan $6.95. Six charming misadventures of a goose named Griselda.

1461. Sharmat, Marjorie W. *Mooch the Messy* (1–2). Illus. by Ben Shecter. 1976, Harper $5.95; LB $6.89. Mooch the rat lives in his messy rat hole, much to the disgust of his father, who comes to visit and tries to reform him but is successful only temporarily.

1462. Sharmat, Marjorie W. *Mooch the Messy Meets Prudence the Neat* (1–3). Illus. by Ben Shecter. 1979, Coward $5.99. Sloppy Mooch is fearful that new neighbor, superneat Prudence, will clean up his untidy domain.

1463. Sharmat, Marjorie W. *Nate the Great* (1–3). Illus. by Marc Simont. 1972, Coward $4.99; Dell paper $1.50. Nate, a boy detective, puts on his Sherlock Holmes outfit and sets out confidently to solve the mystery of the missing painting. Also use: *Nate the Great Goes Undercover* (1974, Coward $4.99; Dell, paper $1.50) and *Nate the Great and the Phony Clue* (1977, Coward $5.29).

1464. Sharmat, Marjorie W. *Nate the Great and the Sticky Case* (2–3). Illus. by Marc Simont. 1978, Coward $4.69. Nate solves a mystery involving a lost stamp.

1465. Sharmat, Marjorie W. *The Trolls of Twelfth Street* (1–3). Illus. by Ben Shecter. 1979, Coward $6.29. A troll family is let loose in Manhattan with amazing results.

1466. Sharmat, Marjorie W. *Uncle Boris and Maude* (1–2). Illus. by Sammis McLean. 1979, Doubleday $4.95; LB $5.90. Maude Mole tries to rescue Uncle Boris from his frequent attacks of boredom.

1467. Shecter, Ben. *Hester the Jester* (1–3). Illus. by author. 1977, Harper $5.95; LB $6.89. In this amusing book, Hester causes an uproar when she declares she wants to be a jester like her father.

1468. Shub, Elizabeth. *Seeing Is Believing* (1–3). Illus. by Rachel Isadora. 1979, Greenwillow $5.95; LB $5.71. Two folktales about leprechauns and pixies retold simply.

1469. Sleator, William. *Once, Said Darlene* (1–3). Illus. by Steven Kellogg. 1979, Dutton $5.95. Darlene tells too many tall tales and her friends revolt.

1470. Stadler, John. *Cat at Bat* (1–2). Illus. by author. 1979, Dutton $5.95. Simple rhyming words (cub, tub, scrub, etc.) are cleverly used for humorous effect.

1471. Stevens, Carla. *Pig and the Blue Flag* (1–3). Illus. by R. Bennett. 1977, Seabury $6.95. Pig hates gym and is always chosen last for teams; nevertheless, he unexpectedly gains status as an athlete.

1472. Stevenson, James. *Fast Friends: Two Stories* (1–3). Illus. by author. 1979, Greenwillow $5.95; LB $5.71. Two short stories involving friendless turtles.

1473. Stolz, Mary. *Emmet's Pig* (1–3). Illus. by Garth Williams. 1959, Harper $6.89. Although he lives in a city apartment, Emmet's greatest wish is to own his own pig.

1474. Thomas, Ianthe. *Hi, Mrs. Mallory* (1–3). Illus. by Ann Toulmin-Rothe. 1979, Harper $7.95; LB $7.89. A little girl's friendship with an old lady who later dies.

1475. Ungerer, Tomi. *One, Two, Where's My Shoe?* (1–3). Illus. by author. 1964, Harper $6.89. All kinds of shoes are hidden within the pictures of this almost text-free puzzle book.

1476. Van Woerkom, Dorothy O. *Becky and the Bear* (1–3). Illus. by Margot Tomes. 1975, Putnam $5.29. Eight-year-old Becky, left alone in her Maine home while her father and brother are hunting, copes when a bear appears; an excellent and exciting story for beginning readers.

1477. Van Woerkom, Dorothy O. *Harry and Shellburt* (1–3). Illus. by Erick Ingraham. 1977, Macmillan $6.95. The hare and the tortoise engage in a rematch, but in spite of fresh twists, the results are the same.

1478. Viorst, Judith. *Alexander, Who Used to Be Rich Last Sunday* (K–2). Illus. by Ray Cruz. 1978, Atheneum $6.95. Alexander spends his dollar gift foolishly penny by penny.

1479. Vreeken, Elizabeth. *Boy Who Would Not Say His Name* (K–2). Illus. by Leonard Shortall. 1959, Follett $2.50; LB $2.97; paper $1.50. Bobby uses another name, until one day after getting lost, he must identify himself to get home.

1480. Wahl, Jan. *The Teeny, Tiny Witches* (1–3). Illus. by Margot Tomes. 1979, Putnam $6.95. Ma, Pa, and Sam Witch set out to find a new home.

1481. Wiess, Ellen. *Millicent Maybe* (1–3). Illus. by author. 1979, Watts $3.95; LB $5.90. A crocodile named Millicent has trouble making up her mind.

1482. Wiseman, Bernard. *Morris and Boris* (PS–1). Illus. by author. 1974, Dodd $4.95. Serious Boris, the bear, becomes impatient when he unsuccessfully tries to teach silly Morris, the moose, how to play games.

1483. Wiseman, Bernard. *Morris Tells Boris Mother Moose Stories and Rhymes* (1–3). Illus. by author. 1979, Dodd $5.95. Morris attempts to supply a bedtime story with amusing results. Also use: *Morris Has a Cold* (1978, Dodd $5.25).

1484. Wyler, Rose, and Ames, Gerald. *Magic Secrets* (1–3). Illus. by Talivaldis Stubis. 1968, Harper paper $1.25. Easy tricks for the beginning magician.

1485. Yolen, Jane. *The Giant's Farm* (1–4). Illus. by Tomie de Paola. 1977, Seabury $6.95. A simple easy-to-read book of 4 stories each involving the 5 giants who run Fe-Fi-Fo-Farm.

1486. York, Carol Beach. *The Midnight Ghost* (1–3). Illus. by Charles Robinson. 1973, Coward $4.99. When Andrew receives a spyglass and a badge with the word *Detective* on it, naturally he has to look around for a mystery to solve.

1487. Zion, Gene. *Harry and the Lady Next Door* (PS–3). Illus. by Margaret B. Graham. 1960, Harper $5.95; LB $6.89. Harry, a dog, tries to stop the lady next door from singing. Also use: *Harry the Dirty Dog* (1956) and *No Roses for Harry* (1958) (both $5.95; LB $6.89; paper $1.95) and *Harry by the Sea* (1965 $6.89; paper $1.95).

Fiction

Animal Stories

1488. Aaron, Chester. *An American Ghost* (5–9). Illus. by David Gwynee Lemon. 1973, Harcourt $5.95. A tender story about a boy's close relationship with a mountain lion in pre–Civil War Wisconsin.

1489. Anderson, Clarence W. *A Pony for Linda* (1–3). 1951, Macmillan $6.95. How 7-year-old Linda cares for a horse named Daisy and enters her in a horse show. Also use: *Pony for Three* (1958, Macmillan $5.95).

1490. Anderson, Clarence W. *Salute* (3–5). Illus. by author. 1940, Macmillan $3.95. Peter takes a broken-down racehorse and restores it to health and strength. Also use: *Afraid to Ride* (1962, Macmillan $4.95).

1491. Anderson, LaVere. *Balto, Sled Dog of Alaska* (3–5). Illus. by Herman Vestal. 1976, Garrard $4.40. Based on fact, this is the story of a heroic sled dog and a race to bring serum to a town in Alaska.

1492. Annixter, Jane, and Annixter, Paul. *Sea Otter* (5–7). Illus. by John Hamberger. 1972, Holiday $4.95. A great deal of lore about the otter is revealed incidentally in the story of one sea otter, Lutra, from birth to maturity. Also use: *Trumpeter: The Story of a Swan* (1973, Holiday $3.95).

1493. Annixter, Jane, and Annixter, Paul. *Wapootin* (3–5). Illus. by John Schoenherr. 1976, Coward $4.95. The saga of an Alaskan bull moose from birth to full maturity.

1494. Annixter, Jane, and Annixter, Paul. *The Year of the She-Grizzly* (5–7). Illus. by Gilbert Riswold. 1978, Coward $5.95. A year in the life of a Montana grizzly, which includes rearing her cub, Bilbo.

1495. Bagnold, Enid. *National Velvet* (6–9). Illus. by Paul Brown. 1949, Morrow $7.44; paper $1.75. The famous novel about a girl who raced her beloved horse in the Grand National.

1496. Baker, Betty. *Dupper* (4–6). Illus. by Chuck Eckart. 1976, Greenwillow $6.96. A talking-animal story in which a prairie dog tries to save his colony from the attacks of a rattlesnake.

1497. Baker, Charlotte. *Cockleburr Quarters* (3–7). Illus. by Robert Owens. 1972, Prentice-Hall paper $1.50. A young black boy tries to save a family of dogs from extermination.

1498. Balch, Glenn. *Buck, Wild* (4–6). Illus. by Ruth Sanderson. 1976, Crowell $7.95. The life story of a wild mustang in Idaho that would rather face death than live in captivity. Also use: *Horse of Two Colors* (1969, Crowell $7.95).

1499. Ball, Zachary. *Bristle Face* (5–7). 1962, Holiday $6.95; Scholastic paper $.95. A humorous story about an irrepressible dog.

1500. Baudouy, Michel-Aime. *Old One Toe* (5–7). Trans. by Marie Ponsot. Illus. by Johannes Troyer. 1959, Harcourt $6.50. Piet, a clever, marauding old fox, who learns how to observe animal life in the forest, and Commandant, a skillful hunter, are the main characters in this exciting story.

1501. Baylor, Byrd. *Coyote Cry* (3–5). Illus. by Symeon Shimin. 1972, Lothrop $6.96. A young shepherd witnesses a coyote trying to raise a collie pup.

1502. Baylor, Byrd. *Hawk, I'm Your Brother* (3–5). Illus. by Peter Parnall. 1976, Scribner $6.95; paper $2.95. A desert boy captures a young hawk, hoping it will teach him how to fly.

1503. Beatty, Patricia. *The Staffordshire Terror* (4–7). 1979, Morrow $7.95; LB $7.63. Cissie tries to find her lost dog Spook, a Staffordshire terrier.

1504. Benchley, Nathaniel. *Kilroy and the Gull* (5–7). Illus. by John Schoenherr. 1977, Harper $6.95; LB $6.89; paper $1.95. Kilroy, a young killer whale, escapes from an aquarium with the help of Morris, a seagull. Also use: *Feldman Field Mouse* (1971, Harper $6.89; paper $1.50).

1505. Benedict, Dorothy P. *Pagan the Black* (5–7). 1960, Pantheon $4.99. A beautiful stallion turns killer when his master is threatened.

1506. Berends, Polly. *The Case of the Elevator Duck* (3–5). Illus. by James K. Washburn. 1973, Random $5.99; paper $.95. In spite of the rule that no pets are allowed in his housing development, little Gilbert decides to keep a duck in an elevator.

1507. Bernsen, Paul. *The Goose That Went to Hollywood* (4–6). Illus. by Richard E. Amundsen. 1976, McKay $7.95. The adventures of a Canadian goose migrating from northern Canada to southern California.

1508. Brady, Irene. *Doodlebug* (2–5). Illus. by author. 1977, Houghton $5.95. Jennifer heals an injured pony and shapes it into a beautiful animal that pulls a cart as if it were trained to do so.

1509. Brenner, Barbara. *Lizard Tails and Cactus Spines* (4–7). Illustrated. 1975, Harper $6.89. Within a loose fictional framework, the author writes lovingly about desert flora and fauna.

1510. Burch, Robert. *The Hunting Trip* (3–6). Illus. by Susanne Suba. 1971, Scribner $5.05. A charming story of how a husband and wife deliberately spare the lives of the animals they encounter on their hunting trip and return home to a delicious vegetarian dinner.

1511. Burkett, Molly, and Burkett, John. *Foxes Three* (4–6). Illus. by Pamela Johnson. 1975, Lippincott $7.95. Young John cares for 3 abandoned foxes in this appealing animal story.

1512. Burnford, Sheila. *The Incredible Journey* (6–9). Illus. by Carl Burger. 1961, Little $6.95; Bantam paper $1.95. The adventures of a Labrador retriever, a terrier, and a Siamese cat, who journey 250 miles through the Canadian wilderness to return home.

1513. Burnham, Sophy. *Buccaneer* (5–7). Illus. by Mike Eagle. 1977, Warne $6.95. Julie's dream comes true when her mother agrees to stable a beautiful blond bay named Buccaneer.

1514. Byars, Betsy. *The Midnight Fox* (4–6). Illus. by Ann Grifalconi. 1968, Viking $5.95; Avon paper $1.50. When Tom spends 2 months on a farm with his aunt and uncle, he never expects that a black fox will become the focus of his life.

1515. Callen, Larry. *Pinch* (5–7). Illus. by Marvin Friedman. 1976, Little $6.95. Training hunting pigs in rural Louisiana is the theme of this amusing story of a boy and his pig, Homer.

1516. Carroll, Jeffrey. *Climbing to the Sun* (6–8). 1977, Seabury $6.95. After being swept into a valley, 3 mountain goats journey back to their mountain home.

1517. Carlson, Natalie Savage. *Jaky or Dodo* (3–5). Illus. by Gail Owens. 1978, Scribner $6.95. A dog leads a double life in Paris.

1518. Carner, Charles. *Tawny* (5–7). Illus. by Donald Carrick. 1978, Macmillan $7.95. A 12-year-old boy adjusts to the death of his twin brother through the love of a doe.

1519. Catherall, Arthur. *Freedom for a Cheetah* (3–5). Illus. by Shyam Varma. 1971, Lothrop $5.95. When the chief trainer becomes ill, young Ahar Lai must take care of the prize cheetah in this story set in India. Also use: *Big Tusker* (1970, Lothrop $6.00).

1520. Chambers, John W. *Fritzi's Winter* (4–6). Illus. by Carole Kowalchuk Odell. 1979, Atheneum $8.95. A Siamese cat fends for herself on Fire Island when her owners leave her behind.

1521. Clark, Ann Nolan. *Hoofprint on the Wind* (5–7). Illus. by Robert Andrew Parker. 1972, Viking $5.50. Patchun has difficulty convincing the Irish coastal folk that he has seen a wild horse on his rocky island.

1522. Coatsworth, Elizabeth. *The Cat and the Captain* (3–4). Illus. by Bernice Loewenstein. 1974, Macmillan $4.95. In this novel, originally published in 1927 and the author's first book for children, Cat saves her master, the Captain, from Mate, a would-be robber.

1523. Cohen, Peter Z. *Bee* (3–5). Illus. by Richard Cuffari. 1975, Atheneum $6.95. A young boy helps to train a horse and catch a gang of cattle rustlers in this story set in Wyoming.

1524. Cohen, Peter Z. *Deadly Game at Stony Creek* (5–7). Illus. by Michael Deas. 1978, Dial $6.46. Cliff is forced to join a hunt for wild dogs that terrorize the countryside.

1525. Cone, Molly. *Mishmash* (3–5). Illus. by Leonard Shortall. 1962, Houghton $6.95; paper $1.25. A dog, Mishmash, moves in, takes over, and then helps his owner to adjust to a new home. Also use: *Mishmash and the Venus Flytrap* (1976, Houghton $6.95).

1526. Corbin, William. *Golden Mare* (5–7). Illus. by Pers Crowell. 1955, Coward $5.95. Robin and his horse Magic have adventures together, but eventually the boy must face the death of his beloved companion.

1527. Corbin, William. *Smoke* (5–7). 1967, Coward $7.95. A remarkable story of a boy and a pitiful stray dog he feeds and calls Smoke. Through the help of the stepfather the boy had resented, the dog is restored to health.

1528. Corcoran, Barbara. *Me and You and a Dog Named Blue* (6–8). 1979, Atheneum $7.95. An older woman tries to dominate 15-year-old Maggie.

1529. Corcoran, Barbara. *Sasha, My Friend* (5–9). Illus. by Richard L. Shell. 1959, Atheneum $7.95; paper $.95. From Los Angeles to a remote Montana tree farm is a difficult adjustment for a young girl, but it is aided by her attachment to a pet wolf cub.

1530. DeJong, Meindert. *The Almost All-White Rabbity Cat* (3–6). Illus. by Herman Vestal. 1972, Macmillan $4.95. A young boy's boredom is lifted when he meets an apartment-house cat.

1531. DeJong, Meindert. *Along Came a Dog* (4–7). Illus. by Maurice Sendak. 1958, Harper $7.89. The friendship of a timid, lonely dog and a toeless little red hen is the basis for a very moving story, full of suspense.

1532. DeJong, Meindert. *The Singing Hill* (3–5). Illus. by Maurice Sendak. 1962, Harper $7.89. A small boy gains self-confidence through his love for an old horse.

1533. Denzel, Justin F. *Snowfoot: White Reindeer of the Arctic* (3–5). Illus. by Taylor Oughton. 1976, Garrard $4.40. A Lapp boy assumes the responsibility of raising a wounded white fawn.

1534. Dinneen, Betty. *A Lurk of Leopards* (6–8). Illus. by Charles Robinson. 1972, Walck $6.50. An adventure set in an African game park in which a young girl's dream of having a leopard as a pet comes true. Also use: *Lion Yellow* (1975, Walck $6.95).

1535. Disney, Walt. *The Hundred and One Dalmatians* (4–8). Illus. by author. 1976, Western $4.92. Pongo and Missis, a pair of dalmatians, are aided by all the dogs in England when their 15 puppies are stolen to be made into a fur coat.

1536. Dixon, Paige. *Summer of the White Goat* (5–7). Illus. by Grambs Miller. 1977, Atheneum $5.95. Gordon spends a summer in Glacier National Park observing the mountain goats that live on the high slopes.

1537. Dolan, Sheila. *The Wishing Bottle* (4–5). Illus. by Leslie Morrill. 1979, Houghton $6.95. A girl gets part of her wish and has partial ownership of a pony.

1538. Doty, Jean Slaughter. *Winter Pony* (3–5). Illus. by Ted Lewin. 1975, Macmillan $5.95. Ginny finds that owning her pony Monkey in the winter produces many joys and problems. Sequel to *Summer Pony* (1973, Macmillan $6.95; paper $1.95).

1539. Duncan, Lois. *Hotel for Dogs* (4–6). Illus. by Leonard Shortall. 1971, Avon paper $1.25. Bruce and Liz Walker accumulate so many stray dogs that they set up a hotel for them in an abandoned house.

1540. Dunlop, Eileen. *Fox Farm* (4–6). 1979, Holt $7.95. Two boys become friends through their mutual love for an orphaned animal they believe to be a fox.

1541. Eckert, Allan W. *Incident at Hawk's Hill* (6–9). Illus. by John Schoenherr. 1971, Little $5.95; Dell paper $1.25. A 6-year-old boy wanders away from home and is nurtured and protected by a badger. This novel is based on fact and takes place in western Canada during the 1870s.

1542. Ellis, Melvin R. *Flight of the White Wolf* (5–9). 1970, Holt $4.95. A wolf acting upon natural instinct kills a taunting dog, but is condemned by human laws. Also use: *Wild Horse Killers* (1971, Holt $6.95).

1543. Estes, Eleanor. *Ginger Pye* (4–6). Illus. by author. 1972, Harcourt $6.95; paper $2.15. Ginger is the Pye family's engaging puppy who mysteriously disappears. Newbery Award winner. Also use: *Pinky Pye* (1958, Harcourt $7.50; paper $1.75).

1544. Farley, Walter. *Black Stallion* (5–8). 1941, Random $3.95; LB $5.99; paper $1.75. A wild Arabian stallion and the boy who trained him. Also use: *The Black Stallion Returns* (1945, $5.99; paper $1.75), *Son of the Black Stallion* (1947, $3.95; LB $5.99; paper $1.75), and others in the series.

1545. Fenner, Phyllis. *A Dog's Life* (6–9). Illus. by Lloyd Bloom. 1978, Morrow $6.95; LB $6.67. Subtitle: *Stories of Champions, Hunters and Faithful Friends.*

1546. Flack, Marjorie. *Walter the Lazy Mouse* (2–4). Illus. by Cyndy Szekeres. 1937; 1963 Doubleday $5.95. Walter is so lazy, he never gets anywhere on time.

1547. Fox, Michael. *Ramer and Chennai: Brothers of the Wild* (4–7). Illus. by Michael Hampshire. 1975, Coward $6.95. Set in India, the tender story of a young boy and his love for a pet wild dog.

1548. Fox, Michael. *Whitepaws: A Coyote-Dog* (5–7). Illus. by Stephen Gammell. 1979, McCann $7.50. Two youngsters realize that their pet must be given his freedom in the Maine woods.

1549. Fox, Michael. *Wild Dogs Three* (5–6). Illustrated. 1977, Coward $6.95. The life of 3 wild dogs in a big city.

1550. Fox, Paula. *Dear Prosper* (4–6). Illus. by Steve McLachlin. 1968, David White $3.95; LB

$3.76. A retrospective letter, written by an aging, independent, and endearing canine to his abandoned but favorite, next-to-last owner, will be an amusing offering for young dog fanciers.

1551.   Fox, Paula. *The King's Falcon* (4–7). Illus. by Eros Keith. 1969, Bradbury $4.95. King Philip, discontent with the condition of his poor, tiny country, forsakes his kingdom to pursue his real joy in life—falconry.

1552.   Freschet, Berniece. *The Watersnake* (3–4). Illus. by Susanne Suba. 1979, Scribner $7.95. Three boys, a pond, and a snake are the chief ingredients in a thoughtful, slow-moving story.

1553.   Gates, Doris. *A Morgan for Melinda* (5–7). 1980, Viking $8.95. In spite of her misgivings, Melinda accepts the responsibility of taking care of a horse.

1554.   George, Jean Craighead. *The Cry of the Crow* (5–7). 1980, Harper $7.89. Mandy finds a helpless baby crow in the woods and tames it.

1555.   Gipson, Fred. *Old Yeller* (6–9). Illus. by Carl Burger. 1956, Harper $9.95; LB $9.89. A powerful story set in the Texas hill country about a 14-year-old boy and the ugly stray dog he comes to love. Also use: *Savage Sam* (1962, Harper $9.95; LB $9.89; paper $1.75).

1556.   Girion, Barbara. *Misty and Me* (4–7). 1979, Scribner $8.95. Unknown to her parents, Kim adopts a puppy from the pound.

1557.   Griffiths, Helen. *Grip: A Dog Story* (6–8). 1978, Holiday $6.95. The English moors, a cruel father, and the love of a dog are elements in this story of the 1930s.

1558.   Griffiths, Helen. *Just a Dog* (5–7). Illus. by Victor G. Ambrus. 1975, Holiday $6.95; paper $1.50. A stray dog roams the streets of Madrid seeking a permanent home.

1559.   Griffiths, Helen. *Running Wild* (6–9). Illustrated. 1977, Holiday $6.95. Pablo, a young Spanish boy, tries to hide his dog's puppies for fear his grandfather will drown them.

1560.   Guillot, Rene. *Grishka and the Bear* (5–7). Trans. by Gwen Marsh. Illus. by Joan Kiddell Monroe. 1960, Abelard $6.95. The haunting story of a Siberian boy and his bear cub who escape to the forest together when the bear is to be sacrificed as village ritual demands.

1561.   Hall, Lynn. *The Mystery of Pony Hollow* (3–5). Illus. by Ruth Sanderson. 1978, Garrard $4.40. Sarah puts a prize pony's ghost to rest in this adventure story.

1562.   Hall, Lynn. *Stray* (4–7). Illus. by Joseph Cellini. 1974, Follett $4.95; LB $5.95; Avon paper $.95. A lovely girl and a stray dog form a temporary and touching relationship.

1563.   Hall, Lynn. *The Whispered Horse* (5–7). 1979, Follett $6.95; LB $6.99. A supernatural story of a young girl, her mother's murder, and a special horse.

1564.   Hallard, Peter. *Puppy Lost in Lapland* (5–9). Illus. by Wallace Tripp. 1971, Watts $4.90. An injured puppy lost in the wilderness becomes leader of a wolf pack and faces a conflict of instincts when the pack begins tracking a human.

1565.   Hanson, June Andrea. *Summer of the Stallion* (6–8). Illus. by Gloria Singer. 1979, Macmillan $7.95. Janey's relations with her grandfather are highlighted in this fine love story.

1566.   Henry, Marguerite. *King of the Wind* (5–8). Illus. by Wesley Dennis. 1948, Rand $5.95; deluxe ed. $10.00; LB $5.97; paper $2.95. The horse, Godolphin Arabian, ancestor of Man O'War and founder of the thoroughbred strain. Newbery Award, 1949. Also use: *Born to Trot* (1950, Rand $4.95; LB 4.79; paper $2.95) and *Black Gold* (1957, Rand $5.95; paper $2.95).

1567.   Henry, Marguerite. *Mustang, Wild Spirit of the West* (6–8). Illus. by Robert Lougheed. 1966, Rand $5.95. An excellent horse story written by a master.

1568.   Henry, Marguerite. *San Domingo: The Medicine Hat Stallion* (4–6). Illus. by Robert Lougheed. 1972, Rand $4.95. Set in the west during mid-nineteenth century, this is the story of a young man who rights a wrong inflicted on his father. Also use (from Rand): *Misty of Chincoteague* (1947, $5.95; LB $4.97; paper $2.95), *Justin Morgan Had a Horse* (1954, $4.95; paper $2.95), and *Brighty of the Grand Canyon* (1953, $4.95; LB $4.79; paper $2.95).

1569.   Henry, Marguerite. *White Stallion of Lipizza* (5–6). Illus. by Wesley Dennis. 1964, Rand $4.95; LB $4.79. Hans Haupt, baker's son, desires to be a riding master at the famous Spanish Court Riding School in Vienna and is eventually admitted as an apprentice. Also use (from Rand): *Sea Star* (1949, $4.95; paper $2.95) and *Stormy, Misty's Foal* (1963, $5.95; LB $5.97; paper $2.95).

1570.   Holland, Isabelle. *Alan and the Animal Kingdom* (5–7). 1977, Lippincott $8.95; Dell paper $1.50. Twelve-year-old Sean tries to hide the death of his great aunt (with whom he has been living) so that he can keep his pets.

1571.   Holmes, Efner Tudor. *Amy's Goose* (2–4). Illus. by Tasha Tudor. 1977, Crowell $5.95; LB

$6.49. Amy nurses a wild goose back to health, but in the spring she must let it go.

1572. Houston, James. *Wolf Run: A Caribou Eskimo Tale* (4–6). Illus. by author. 1971, Harcourt $5.75. A forceful tale about a 13-year-old Eskimo boy who sets out into the wilderness to find food for his starving family and receives unexpected help from 2 wolves.

1573. Hunter, Kristin. *Boss Cat* (2–5). Illus. by Harold Franklin. 1971, Scribner $5.95. Avon paper $.95. When Paraoh, a cat, moves in with the Tanners, a black family, Mr. Tanner must get his wife used to the idea.

1574. Hurd, Edith Thacher. *The Black Dog Who Went into the Woods* (3–4). Illus. by Emily McCully. 1980, Harper $7.95; LB $7.89. A family accepts the death of the beloved pet dog.

1575. James, Will. *Smoky* (6–8). 1926, Scribner $8.95. The classic horse story; winner of the Newbery Award, 1927.

1576. Kalnay, Francis. *Chucaro: Wild Pony of the Pampa* (5–8). Illus. by Julian de Miskey. 1958, Harcourt $5.50. A 12-year-old boy and a cowboy have many adventures when they try to keep a wild pony from the Argentine pampa for themselves.

1577. Kipling, Rudyard. *Elephant's Child* (3–5). Illus. by Rosemary Wells. 1970, Walker $7.95; LB $7.85. A young elephant gains a lesson and a trunk from a crocodile. Also use: *How the Leopard Got His Spots* (1972, Walker $7.85).

1578. Kipling, Rudyard. *How the Rhinoceros Got His Skin* (3–5). Illus. by Leonard Weisgard. 1974, Walker $7.95; LB $7.85. Colorful illustrations complement the humor of a favorite Kipling story for children.

1579. Kipling, Rudyard. *Jungle Book* (4–7). Illus. by Fritz Eichenberg. 1950, Grosset $5.95; LB $2.95; deluxe ed. $7.95; Airmont paper $1.95. One of many recommended editions of this classic.

1580. Kipling, Rudyard. *Just So Stories* (4–6). Illus. by Etienne Delessert. 1972, Doubleday $12.50. This seventy-fifth anniversary edition of this classic has been illustrated effectively by the eminent Swiss artist. Also use: *New Illustrated Just So Stories* (1952, Doubleday $7.95).

1581. Kjelgaard, James A. *Big Red* (6–9). Illus. by Bob Kuhn. 1945, Holiday $7.95; Bantam paper $1.95. Adventures of a champion Irish setter and a trapper's son. Also use (at same prices): *Irish Red: Son of Big Red* (1951) and *Outlaw Red* (1953).

1582. Kjelgaard, James A. *Haunt Fox* (4–8). Illus. by Glen Rounds. 1954, Holiday $5.95. A fox is pursued by a boy and his dog; interest shifts from hunter to hunted. Also use: *Wolf Brother* (1957, Holiday $5.95).

1583. Knight, Eric. *Lassie Come Home* (4–7). Illus. by Don Bologenese. 1940, Holt $6.95; Dell paper $1.75. The classic that conveys the beautiful relationship between a boy and his loyal dog, and the lives of the people of Yorkshire as well.

1584. Lea, Alec. *Temba Dawn* (5–7). 1975, Scribner $5.95. Rob's tenth birthday present is a calf, Temba Dawn, in this simple story about farm life in Scotland.

1585. Leitch, Paticia. *The Fields of Praise* (6–9). 1978, Lippincott $7.90. Gillian fulfills her dream and rides in the horse-of-the-year competition.

1586. Link, Ruth. *A House Full of Mice* (3–5). Illus. by Marianne Dombret. 1970, Atheneum $4.25. Jimmy takes care of the pet mice of his brother's friend, but they multiply until he has 34 to tend.

1587. Lippincott, Joseph. *Wilderness Champion* (5–8). Illus. by Paul Branson. 1944, Lippincott $6.95; LB $4.82. A puppy becomes leader of a wolf pack but is finally reunited with his master. Also use: *The Wahoo Bobcat* (1950, Lippincott $10.00).

1588. Little, Mary E. *Old Cat and the Kitten* (3–5). Illus. by author. 1979, Atheneum $6.95. Joel must decide the fate of his 2 new pet cats.

1589. London, Jack. *Call of the Wild* (6–9). Illus. by Karen Kezer. 1965, Macmillan $3.95; paper $.95. One of the many recommended editions.

1590. London, Jack. *White Fang* (5–9). 1935, Macmillan $5.95. The classic dog story.

1591. Miklowitz, Gloria D. *Save That Raccoon* (2–4). Illus. by St. Tamara. 1978, Harcourt $5.95; paper $1.95. A raccoon tries to escape a forest fire but is trapped by humans.

1592. Miles, Miska. *Jenny's Cat* (3–4). Illus. by Wendy Watson. 1979, Dutton $6.95. Rather than give up her pet cat, Jenny decides to run away with it.

1593. Miles, Miska. *Mississippi Possum* (2–4). Illus. by John Schoenherr. 1965, Atlantic/Little $6.95. A black family and a little gray possum share the same tent when the mighty Mississippi overflows.

1594. Miles, Miska. *Otter in the Cove* (3–5). Illus. by John Schoenherr. 1974, Atlantic/Little $5.95. In a story that contains much fascinating otter lore, Maggie tries to save from extinction a small herd of otters that swims into her father's cove.

1595. Miles, Miska. *Wharf Rat* (2–4). Illus. by John Schoenherr. 1972, Atlantic/Little $5.95. The survival story of an animal despised by humans.

1596. Moeri, Louise. *A Horse for X.Y.Z.* (4–6). Illus. by Gail Owens. 1977, Dutton $6.95. Young Solveig's desire to ride the superb horse Snake Dancer leads to an unplanned adventure.

1597. Montgomery, Rutherford. *Kildee House* (4–6). Illus. by Barbara Cooney. 1949, Archway paper $.75. An amusing story of Jerome Kildee, who wanted to be a hermit and had to share his privacy with a skunk and a raccoon.

1598. Moody, Ralph. *Come on Seabiscuit* (5–7). Illus. by Robert Riger. 1963, Houghton $6.95. A little man without much capital has faith in the grandson of Man O'War, an undersized, knobby-kneed colt.

1599. Morey, Walt. *Gentle Ben* (5–7). Illus. by John Schoenherr. 1965, Dutton $6.95. Avon paper $1.50. A warm story of the deep trust and friendship between a boy and an Alaskan bear.

1600. Morey, Walt. *Sandy and the Rock Star* (5–8). 1979, Dutton $7.95. A teenage boy and a cougar share adventures in an island wilderness.

1601. Morey, Walt. *Scrub Dog of Alaska* (4–8). 1971, Dutton $6.95. A pup, abandoned because of his small size, turns out to be a winner. Also use: *Kavik, the Wolf Dog* (1968, Dutton $6.95; paper $1.95).

1602. Morey, Walt. *Year of the Black Pony* (5–7). 1976, Dutton $7.95. Scholastic paper $1.25. A family story about a boy's love for his pony in rural Oregon at the turn of the century. Also use: *Runaway Stallion* (1973, Dutton $7.95).

1603. Morgan, Alison. *A Boy Called Fish* (4–6). Illus. by Joan Sandin. 1973, Harper $6.79; paper $1.25. A lonely, misunderstood boy adopts a stray dog that is later accused of killing sheep, in this novel set in rural Wales.

1604. Morgenroth, Barbara. *Impossible Charlie* (4–6). Illus. by Velma Ilsley. 1979, Atheneum $8.95. A young girl receives as a gift a seemingly untrainable horse named Charlie.

1605. Morgenroth, Barbara. *Ride a Proud Horse* (6–8). 1978, Atheneum $7.95. When Corey begins riding lessons with her horse, she finds unexpected benefits.

1606. Moser, Don. *A Heart to the Hawks* (6–8). 1975, Atheneum $6.95. Two friends share an interest in nature study and conservation.

1607. Mowat, Farley. *The Dog Who Wouldn't Be* (4–7). Illus. by Paul Galdone. 1957, Little $6.95; B.J. Pub. paper $1.25. The humorous story of Mutt, a dog of character and personality, and his boy.

1608. Mowat, Farley. *Owls in the Family* (4–6). Illus. by Robert Frankenberg. 1962, Atlantic/Little $6.95. The many adventures of a family that adopts 2 owls.

1609. Mukerji, Dhan Gopal. *Gay Neck: The Story of a Pigeon* (4–8). Illustrated. 1927; 1968 Dutton $7.95. The Newbery Award winner, 1928. This is the story of a boy from India and his brave carrier pigeon during World War I. Also use: *Kari: The Elephant* (1922, Dutton $7.95).

1610. North, Sterling. *Rascal: A Memoir of a Better Era* (6–8). Illus. by John Schoenherr. 1963, Dutton $7.95; Avon paper $1.25. Autobiographical memoir of the beauties of nature as experienced by an 11-year-old and his pet raccoon.

1611. O'Hara, Mary. *My Friend Flicka* (6–9). Illus. by Dave Blossom. 1973, Lippincott $7.95. The wonderful story of a young boy and his horse.

1612. Ottley, Reginald. *Boy Alone* (6–8). Illus. by Clyde Pearson. 1966, Harcourt $6.95. The extreme loneliness of life on an Australian cattle station is depicted in this story of a boy and a pup. Also use: *The Roan Colt* (1967, Harcourt $5.50).

1613. Perovskaya, Olga. *The Wolf in Olga's Kitchen* (4–6). Illus. by Angie Culfogienis. 1969, Bobbs-Merrill $5.50. Russian stories about the menagerie that Olga's father brings home.

1614. Pearce, Ann Philippa. *The Battle of Bubble and Squeak* (4–6). Illus. by Alan Baker. 1979, Deutsch/Dutton $5.95. A family story centering around Sid's battle to keep 2 pet gerbils.

1615. Peyton, K. M. *The Team* (6–7). Illus. by author. 1976, Crowell $7.95. Ruth's position on the pony club's team is uncertain, particularly because of Peter's competition.

1616. Polseno, Jo. *This Hawk Belongs to Me* (4–7). 1977, McKay $6.95. While playing hooky from school, an 11-year-old boy finds a kestrel on a wildlife preserve on Long Island in New York State.

1617. Rawlings, Marjorie K. *The Yearling* (6–9). Illus. by N. C. Wyeth. 1938, Scribner $12.50; text ed. $5.56; paper $3.95. The contemporary classic of a boy and a fawn growing up together in the backwoods of Florida.

1618. Rawls, Wilson. *Where the Red Fern Grows* (4–7). 1961, Doubleday $6.95. A young boy saves money to buy 2 coon dogs and faces heartbreak when they die.

1619. Rivers-Coffey, Rachel. *A Horse Like Mr. Ragman* (5–7). 1977, Scribner $6.95. A fresh treatment of a tired plot concerning a girl's efforts to change her rundown horse into a winner.

1620. Robertson, Keith. *In Search of a Sandhill Crane* (5–8). Illus. by Richard Cuffari. 1973, Viking $7.95; Penguin paper $1.95. Fifteen-year old Link spends an unexpectedly gratifying summer visiting an aunt in the north woods in Michigan.

1621. Rounds, Glen. *The Blind Colt* (4–6). Illus. by author. 1941; 1960 Holiday $7.95. Born blind, a mustang colt learns to "see" with his ears and nose. Also use: *Stolen Pony* (1969, Holiday $6.95).

1622. Salten, Felix. *Bambi: A Life in the Woods* (5–8). 1926, Simon & Schuster $5.95. The growing to maturity of an Austrian deer.

1623. Savitt, Sam. *The Dingle Ridge Fox and Other Stories* (5–7). Illus. by author. 1978, Dodd $5.95. General, appealing stories chiefly about dogs and horses.

1624. Sewell, Anna. *Black Beauty* (4–6). Illus. by Fritz Eichenberg. n.d., Grosset LB $5.95; paper $1.50. There are several recommended editions of this classic horse story.

1625. Shura, Mary Francis. *Mister Wolf and Me* (5–7). Illus. by Konrad Hack. 1979, Dodd $5.95. A German shepherd is accused of sheep killing.

1626. Shura, Mary Francis. *Topcat of Tam* (4–6). Illus. by Charles Robinson. 1972, Holiday $4.50. A beautiful Russian blue cat is adopted as a class pet.

1627. Smith, Gene. *The Hayburners* (5–8). Illus. by Ted Lewin. 1972, Delacorte $5.95; LB $5.47; Dell paper $.75. Will falls heir to 2 "hayburners" —an ungainly steer and a mentally retarded hired hand.

1628. Stoneley, Jack. *Scruffy* (4–6). 1979, Random $6.95; LB $6.99. A dog's life from birth to eventual rescue from a dog pound.

1629. Stong, Phil. *Honk, the Moose* (4–6). Illus. by Kurt Wiese. 1935; 1963 Dodd $6.95. In a Minnesota town, two little boys of Finnish parentage find a moose in a stable.

1630. Stranger, Joyce. *The Fox at Drummer's Darkness* (4–6). Illus. by William Geldart. 1977, Farrar $5.95. Against his instincts, a starving fox is forced to search for food in human territory.

1631. Street, James. *Good-Bye, My Lady* (6–8). 1954, Lippincott $9.95. Skeeter must part with the beautiful dog he found in the Mississippi swamp where he lives with Uncle Jess.

1632. Terhune, Albert Payson. *Lad: A Dog* (6–9). Illustrated. 1959, Dutton $8.95; NAL paper $1.75. One of the best-loved dog stories of all times.

1633. Thiele, Colin. *Storm Boy* (4–6). Illus. by John Schoenherr. 1978, Harper $7.95; LB $7.89. A boy grieves when his pet pelican is shot by a hunter in this story set in rural Australia.

1634. Thiele, Colin. *Fight against Albatross Two* (6–8). 1976, Harper $5.95; LB $5.79. The tragedy to wildlife caused by an oil spill in offshore Australia is explored through the eyes of 14-year-old Link and his younger sister.

1635. Trevino, Elizabeth de. *Nacar, the White Deer* (5–7). Illus. by Enrico Arno. 1963, Farrar $3.95. Lalo, a mute herder, nurses a sickly white deer until the inevitable parting causes a crisis.

1636. Walker, David. *Big Ben* (4–6). Illus. by Victor Ambrus. 1969, Houghton $5.95. An ungainly St. Bernard becomes the Bruce's dog on their farm, but a mean neighbor causes problems.

1637. Walker, Diana. *Mother Wants a Horse* (6–9). 1978, Crowell $6.95; LB $6.79. While training a horse, 16-year-old Joanne gains maturity.

1638. Wallace, Barbara Brooks. *Palmer Patch* (4–6). Illus. by Lawrence DiPiori. 1976, Follett $5.95; LB $5.97. Palmer, the skunk, leads all the pets of the Patch family to freedom when they fear that they will be given away.

1639. Wallin, Mari-Louise. *Tangles* (6–8). Trans. by Gerry Bothmer. 1977, Delacorte $7.95; Dell paper $1.50. Ingeborg gains confidence through learning to ride and to take care of her horse Tangles.

1640. Warburg, Sandol Stoddard. *Growing Time* (3–4). Illus. by Leonard Weisgard. 1969, Houghton $7.95; paper $1.50. Death is sensitively treated as Jamie's shock, grief, and anger begin slowly to abate when he accepts the helpless new pup and, consequently, the loss of his beloved collie.

1641. White, Anne H. *Junket* (4–6). Illus. by Robert McCloskey. 1955, Archway paper $1.25. A dog attempts to reeducate a family to a dog's-eye view of rural living.

1642. Wier, Esther. *King of the Mountain* (5–7). 1975, Walck $7.95. Eleven-year-old Orph and his father try to save the endangered bighorn in the Rockies.

1643. Yates, Elizabeth. *The Seventh One* (6–9). Illus. by Diana Charles. 1978, Walker $6.95. The story of a man and the 7 dogs he has owned.

1644. Young, Miriam. *Christy and the Cat Jail* (3–5). Illus. by Pat Grant Porter. 1972, Lothrop $6.50. Christy's hatred of cats changes as she learns to love Patches and her litter.

1645. Zimmik, Reiner. *The Bear and the People* (4–7). Illus. by author. 1970, Harper $6.89. A tale of compassion and friendship between a juggler and his dancing bear.

Family Stories

1646. Adler, Carole S. *The Silver Coach* (4–6). 1979, Coward $7.95. Chris and her sister adjust to their parents' imminent divorce during a summer with their grandmother.

1647. Alcott, Louisa May. *Eight Cousins* (5–7). 1971, Grosset $4.95. One girl and 7 boy cousins have fun and get into a great deal of mischief. Also use its sequel: *Rose in Bloom* and *Jack and Jill* (both 1971, Grosset $4.95).

1648. Alcott, Louisa May. *Little Women* (4–7). Illus. by Anna M. Magagna and Louis Jambor. 1947, Grosset $6.95; deluxe $8.95. One of the many fine editions of this enduring story. Also use the sequels (both $5.95; deluxe $7.95): *Little Men* (n.d.) and *Jo's Boys* (1949).

1649. Aliki. *The Two of Them* (K–3). Illus. by author. 1979, Greenwillow $7.95; LB $7.63. A moving story of a tender relationship between a child and her grandfather, and of the death of the old man.

1650. Alter, Judy. *After Pa Was Shot* (5–7). 1978, Morrow $6.95; LB $6.43. Ellsberg's new stepfather turns out to be a dud in this story set in turn-of-the-century Texas.

1651. Amoss, Berthe. *Secret Lives* (5–8). 1979, Little $7.95. Through some sleuthing, Addie uncovers some unusual information about her dead mother.

1652. Anckarsvard, Karin. *Doctor's Boy* (4–6). Illus. by Rocker Fermin. 1965, Harcourt $5.50. To 10-year-old Jon, the most exciting part of life is accompanying his father, a doctor in rural Sweden, on his rounds in the horse and buggy.

1653. Armstrong, William H. *Sounder* (6–9). Illus. by James Barkley. 1969, Harper $6.95; LB $6.89; paper $1.50. Harsh customs and hard circumstances cripple the bodies of both the dog Sounder and his master, but their invincible spirit

passes to the boy who shared and witnessed their adversity. Black stoicism and resilience forged in the Old South. Newbery Award winner.

1654. Avery, Gillian. *To Tame a Sister* (6–8). Illus. by John Verney. 1973, Viking $5.95. Margaret has problems adjusting to her cousins with whom she is staying in the country, in this quaint novel set in Victorian times.

1655. Babbitt, Natalie. *The Eyes of the Amaryllis* (4–6). 1977, Farrar $6.95. An 11-year-old girl is drawn into her grandmother's obsession, in this story set in an Atlantic coastal village during the late nineteenth century.

1656. Bach, Alice. *A Father Every Few Years* (6–8). 1977, Harper $5.95; LB $6.89; Dell paper $1.50. Love and anger at an absent stepfather are the focus of this story of adolescence.

1657. Bates, Betty. *Bugs in Your Ears* (5–7). 1977, Holiday $5.95. An eighth-grader named Carrie adjusts to her new stepfather and his 3 sons.

1658. Bates, Betty. *My Mom, the Money Nut* (5–7). 1979, Holiday $6.95. Slowly Fritzi understands why her mother stresses economic security as a future goal.

1659. Bawden, Nina. *The Peppermint Pig* (4–6). 1975, Lippincott $8.95. Penguin paper $1.95. This turn-of-the-century novel set in England recounts the adventures of 9-year-old Poll and his family after they move from London to Norfolk.

1660. Beatty, Patricia. *By Crumbs, It's Mine!* (6–8). 1976, Morrow $6.96. After 14-year-old Damaris Boyd and his family are given a rundown hotel in the Arizona Territory of 1882, the fun begins.

1661. Behn, Harry. *The Two Uncles of Pablo* (4–7). Illus. by Mel Silverman. 1959, Harcourt $4.95. A humorous and sympathetic portrait of a young Mexican boy and his 2 very dissimilar uncles.

1662. Bourne, Miriam Anne. *What Is Papa Up to Now?* (2–3). Illus. by Dick Gackenbach. 1977, Coward $4.99. Ben Franklin's small daughter Sally describes her father's excitement and pleasure at each new discovery he makes while experimenting with electricity. More fictional than biographical. Also use: *Nabby Adams' Diary* (1974, Coward $5.95).

1663. Bradbury, Bianca. *In Her Father's Footsteps* (4–6). Illus. by Richard Cuffari. 1976, Houghton $6.95. Scholastic paper $1.25. Brana adjusts to a new stepmother while continuing to aim at becoming a veterinarian like her father.

1664.   Bunting, Eve. *Blackbird Singing* (5–7). Illus. by Stephen Gammell. 1980, Macmillan $7.95. A division between his parents puts poor Marcus in the middle.

1665.   Branscum, Robbie. *Johnny May* (6–9). Illus. by Charles Robinson. 1975, Doubleday $4.95; Avon paper $1.25. A girl in the Arkansas hill country reaches physical maturity within a household consisting of her grandparents and 2 aunts.

1666.   Branscum, Robbie. *Toby, Granny and George* (6–8). Illus. by Glen Rounds. 1976, Doubleday $6.95; Avon paper $1.25. A heartwarming story set in rural Arkansas about a young girl's search for identity.

1667.   Brelis, Nancy. *The Mummy Market* (4–6). Illus. by Ben Shecter. 1966, Harper paper $1.50. Three orphan children shop to find just the right mother in this engaging and fanciful story.

1668.   Bridgers, Sue Ellen. *Home before Dark* (6–9). 1977, Knopf $6.95. Fourteen-year-old Stella and her family settle down on a tobacco farm after years as migrant workers.

1669.   Brink, Carol. *Caddie Woodlawn* (4–6). Illus. by Trina Schart Hyman. 1973, Macmillan $7.95; paper $1.95. The delightful escapades of a red-haired tomboy and her brothers in early Wisconsin. Newbery Award, 1936. Also use: *Magical Melons* (1944, Macmillan $5.95; paper $1.25).

1670.   Burton, Hester. *In Spite of All Terror* (6–9). Illus. by Victor G. Ambrus. 1969, Collins $5.91. A World War II novel set in England in which a young girl is evacuated to live with a rural family and gets involved with the rout at Dunkirk.

1671.   Canfield, Dorothy. *Understood Betsy* (4–6). Illus. by Martha Alexander. 1946, Avon paper $1.50. A new edition of the old favorite about Elizabeth Ann and the fearful new way of life that awaits her when she goes to live in the wilds of Vermont.

1672.   Carlson, Natalie Savage. *The Half Sisters* (4–6). Illus. by Thomas Di Grazia. 1970, Harper $6.89; paper $1.95. Six sisters growing up on a Maryland farm in 1915.

1673.   Cate, Dick. *Never Is a Long, Long Time* (4–6). Illus. by Trevor Stubley. 1977, Nelson $5.95. Young Billy witnesses many changes in his family and tries to adjust to the absence of his grandmother because of her serious illness. Also use another story of the same family: *Flying Free* (1977, Nelson $5.95).

1674.   Caudill, Rebecca. *The Best-Loved Doll* (2–4). Illus. by Elliott Gilbert. 1962, Holt $6.95. Betsy's doll Jennifer wins the prize because—being the most worn—she is the best loved.

1675.   Chaikin, Miriam. *I Should Worry, I Should Care* (3–5). Illus. by Richard Egielski. 1979, Harper $7.95; LB $7.89. The story of a Jewish family's move to a new apartment in Brooklyn.

1676.   Clark, Mavis Thorpe. *Spark of Opal* (6–9). 1973, Macmillan $4.95. A stark novel about a poor family of Australian opal miners who must face leaving their home and moving to Adelaide to be near adequate schools.

1677.   Cleary, Beverly. *Ramona and Her Mother* (3–5). Illus. by Alan Tiegreen. 1979, Morrow $6.75; LB $6.48. Ramona expects to receive her mother's time and affection even after Mrs. Quimby goes out to work.

1678.   Cleary, Beverly. *Ramona and Her Father* (3–5). Illus. by Alan Tiegreen. 1977, Morrow $6.75; LB $6.48; Dell paper $1.75. An addition to this charming, humorous series; Ramona, now in the second grade, and her family face problems when daddy loses his job.

1679.   Cleary, Beverly. *Ramona the Brave* (3–5). Illus. by Alan Tiegreen. 1975, Morrow $6.75; LB $6.48; Scholastic paper $.95. All the humor and pathos of the earlier *Ramona the Pest* are here as the young heroine experiences the glories and difficulties of being in the first grade and also having a room of her own.

1680.   Cleary, Beverly. *Ramona the Pest* (3–5). Illus. by Louis Darling. 1968, Morrow $6.75; LB $6.48; Scholastic paper $.95. The fine addition to this popular series follows spirited Ramona Quimby, sister to Beezus and neighbor to Henry, through her kindergarten escapades. Also use: *Beezus and Ramona* (1955, Morrow $6.75; LB $6.48; paper $1.50) and *Ribsy* (1964, Morrow $7.25; LB $6.96; Archway, paper $1.50).

1681.   Cleary, Beverly. *Sister of the Bride* (6–8). Illus. by Beth Krush and Joe Krush. 1963, Morrow $7.44. All the excitement and confusion an approaching wedding brings to a household.

1682.   Cleary, Beverly. *Socks* (4–6). Illus. by Beatrice Darwin. 1973, Morrow $6.75; LB $6.48. What happens when the family cat Socks realizes that his position of importance is threatened by the arrival of a baby.

1683.   Cleaver, Vera, and Cleaver, Bill. *I Would Rather Be a Turnip* (5–7). 1971, Lippincott $8.95. Annie prepares to welcome into her household a precocious young boy, Calvin, who is her sister's illegitimate son.

1684.   Cleaver, Vera, and Cleaver, Bill. *The Mock Revolt* (6–9). 1971, Lippincott $7.89; NAL paper $1.25. During the Great Depression, 13-year-old Ussy tries to avoid becoming part of the Establishment and gains an understanding of his wish to revolt through his friendship with a migrant family.

1685. Cleaver, Vera, and Cleaver, Bill. *Queen of Hearts* (6–9). 1978, Lippincott $8.95. A young girl must take care of her salty old grandmother after she has a stroke.

1686. Cleaver, Vera, and Cleaver, Bill. *Trial Valley* (6–9). 1977, Lippincott $8.95. In this sequel to *Where the Lilies Bloom*, Mary Call, now 16, copes with 2 suitors, an abandoned waif, and the day-to-day struggle of keeping her family together.

1687. Cleaver, Vera, and Cleaver, Bill. *Where the Lilies Bloom* (6–9). Illus. by James J. Spanfeller. 1969, Lippincott $8.95; NAL paper $1.50. Gutsy, sharp Mary Call is determined to fulfill her dying sharecropper father's last requests to keep the family together and prevent Devola from marrying Kaiser Pease, their landlord. Mary plans and schemes to bring them out of poverty and defeat in a memorable story set in today's Great Smokies.

1688. Clifton, Lucille. *The Lucky Stone* (3–5). Illus. by Dale Payson. 1979, Delacorte $6.95; LB $6.46. Several stories in the life of a girl's great-grandmother linked by the power of a stone.

1689. Clifton, Lucille. *The Times They Used to Be* (5–6). Illus. by Susan Jeschke. 1974, Holt $4.95; Dell paper $.95. In a series of reminiscences, a young black girl learns about her mother's childhood.

1690. Clymer, Eleanor. *The Get-Away Car* (4–6). 1978, Dutton $7.50. Grahm and Maggie plan to escape from domineering Aunt Ruby, who has plans for their future they don't like.

1691. Clymer, Eleanor. *How I Went Shopping and What I Got* (3–5). Illus. by Trina Schart Hyman. 1972, Holt $4.95. Debbie takes her little sister, Judy, shopping, but Judy becomes lost.

1692. Clymer, Eleanor. *Me and the Eggman* (3–5). Illus. by David K. Stone. 1972, Dutton $6.95. When everything seems to go wrong at home, Donald runs away in the eggman's truck. By hard work, he helps the eggman on his farm and also brings harmony to his family.

1693. Cohen, Barbara. *Benny* (4–6). 1977, Lothrop $6.25; LB $6.00. Twelve-year-old Benny must assume added family responsibilities and make sacrifices when his mother has an operation.

1694. Cohen, Barbara. *The Carp in the Bathtub* (3–4). Illus. by Joan Halpern. 1972, Lothrop $6.25; LB $6.00; Dell paper $.95. Two Jewish children decide that the carp in the bathtub

should be rescued before it becomes Passover gefilte fish.

1695. Cohen, Barbara. *The Innkeeper's Daughter* (6–9). 1979, Lothrop $6.95; LB $6.67. A gently paced novel of a young girl, her family, and the small hotel that her mother manages.

1696. Cone, Molly. *Call Me Moose* (4–6). Illus. by Bernice Lowenstein. 1978, Houghton $6.95. Awkward Martha tries to find a place in her athletic family.

1697. Conford, Ellen. *And This Is Laura* (4–6). 1977, Little $6.95; Archway paper $1.25. A very ordinary girl discovers that she possesses psychic powers.

1698. Conford, Ellen. *The Luck of Pokey Bloom* (4–6). Illus. by Bernice Lowenstein. 1975, Little $6.95; Archway paper $1.25. The warm, sunny family story about a young girl who has a compulsive interest in contests and her brother who is undergoing the pangs of first love.

1699. Coolidge, Olivia. *Come by Here* (5–7). Illus. by Milton Johnson. 1970, Houghton $5.95. In turn-of-the-century Baltimore, 7-year-old, black Minty Lou learns the difference between visiting relatives and living with them when her parents are killed.

1700. Cooper, Gordon. *A Second Springtime* (6–8). 1975, Nelson $6.50. In 1873, 11-year-old Hester and a group of other orphans travel to Nova Scotia to be adopted.

1701. Cretan, Cladys Yessayan. *All except Sammy* (2–5). Illus. by Symeon Shimin. 1966, Little $3.95. Everyone in Sammy's family is musical—except Sammy—but he is a champion baseball player. However, he finds his true niche as an artist.

1702. Cunningham, Julia. *Tuppeny* (6–8). 1978, Dutton $6.95. A strange girl affects the lives of 3 couples, each of whom has lost a daughter.

1703. D'Aulaire, Ingri, and D'Aulaire, Edgar. *Children of the Northlights* (3–5). Illus. by author. 1935, Viking $6.50. A charming book about living in Lapland, as revealed by the lives of 2 children.

1704. De Angeli, Marguerite. *Fiddlestrings* (4–6). Illustrated. 1974, Doubleday $4.95. In this turn-of-the-century novel, a young boy spends a summer with his father on the Steel Pier at Atlantic City.

1705. De Angeli, Marguerite. *Thee, Hannah!* (4–6). Illus. by author. 1940, Doubleday $6.95. Hannah, the youngest in a large Quaker family, loves fine things and has difficulty fitting into the conservative pattern her elders embrace.

1706. Duncan, Jane. *Brave Janet Reachfar* (4–6). Illus. by Mairi Hedderwick. 1975, Seabury $6.95. Scottish farm life is depicted through the adventures of young Janet and her relationship with her tryannical grandmother.

1707. Edmonds, Walter. *Bert Breen's Barn* (6–9). 1975, Little $7.95. Upstate New York at the turn of the century is the setting for this quaint story of a boy determined to raise a barn on his family's land. Also use: *Cadmus Henry* (1949, Dodd $3.95).

1708. Edmonds, Walter. *Two Logs Crossing: John Haskell's Story* (5–7). Illus. by Tibor Gergely. 1943, Dodd $4.50. In upstate New York in 1830, a teen-age boy takes charge of his family at the death of his father.

1709. Eisenberg, Phyllis Rose. *A Mitzvah Is Something Special* (2–4). Illus. by Susan Jeschke. 1978, Harper $6.95; LB $6.79. Lisa brings her 2 very different grandmothers together.

1710. Embry, Margaret. *Shadi* (6–9). 1971, Holiday $4.95. As a shadi—Navajo for older sister— Emma must take care of her family when her father deserts them and her mother dies.

1711. Engebrecht, P. A. *Under the Haystack* (6–8). 1973, Nelson $6.95. Sandy and her 2 younger sisters adjust to the absence of their mother and try to perform the necessary duties on their farm.

1712. Enright, Elizabeth. *Thimble Summer* (4–6). 1976, Holt $5.95; Dell paper $1.25. A small girl on a Wisconsin farm finds a magic thimble. Newbery Award, 1939.

1713. Erwin, Betty K. *Behind the Magic Line* (4–6). Illus. by Julia Iltis. 1969, Little $7.95. Dozie, the oldest girl in a large black family, gets her wish when they are able to move to a new home.

1714. Estes, Eleanor. *The Moffats* (4–6). Illus. by Louis Slobodkin. 1941, Harcourt $6.50; paper $2.25. Lively adventures of 4 Connecticut children, their family, and friends. Sequels are: *The Middle Moffat* (1942, $6.95; paper $2.95) and *Rufus M* (1943, $6.95).

1715. Eunson, Dale. *The Day They Gave Babies Away* (4–7). Illus. by Douglas Gorsline. 1970, Farrar $3.95. This story, based on fact, tells of the efforts of a young boy to place his brothers and sisters in foster homes after they are orphaned.

1716. Fitzhugh, Louise. *Nobody's Family Is Going to Change* (5–8). 1974, Farrar $7.95; Dell paper $1.50. There is considerable misunderstanding within a middle-class black family, but also much humor and warmth.

1717. Fox, Paula. *Maurice's Room* (2–4). Illus. by Ingrid Fetz. 1966, Macmillian $4.95; paper $.95.

A city boy's room is cluttered with junk and small animals until his family moves to the country where an old barn proves the ideal place for his collection.

1718. Friedman, Frieda. *Janitor's Girl* (4–6). Illustrated. 1956, Morrow $6.48. Father's new job as a janitor in a building on Riverside Drive in New York City produces a new and exciting environment for the rest of the family. Also use: *Dot for Short* (1947, Morrow $6.95).

1719. Gage, Wilson. *Big Blue Island* (5–7). Illus. by Glen Rounds. 1964, Collins $5.95; Archway paper $1.25. Darrell, a city orphan, moves to a lonely island on the Tennessee River and gradually learns to understand and appreciate the quiet, primitive life.

1720. Gaines, Ernest J. *A Long Day in November* (4–6). Illus. by Don Bolognese. 1971, Dial $5.95; LB $5.47. The events of a day as seen through the eyes of a child on a southern sugarcane plantation during the 1940s.

1721. Galbraith, Kathryn Osebold. *Come Spring* (4–6). 1979, Atheneum $8.95. A simple story of the effects on a family of their possible relocation.

1722. Gardam, Jane. *A Few Fair Days* (4–6). Illus. by Peggy Fortnum. 1972, Macmillan $4.95. Nine everyday episodes in a child's life in pre–World War II Yorkshire.

1723. Garner, Alan. *The Stone Book* (3–5). Illus. by Michael Foreman. 1978, Collins $6.95. An English stonemason shows his daughter a record of history revealed in marks on rocks.

1724. Garner, Alan. *Tom Fobble's Day* (3–5). Illus. by Michael Foreman. 1979, Collins $6.95. William, grandson of the hero of *Granny Deardun*, lives through World War II in England.

1725. Gates, Doris. *Blue Willow* (4–6). Illus. by Paul Lantz. 1940, Viking $5.95; Penguin paper $1.50. Janey, a child of migrant workers in the San Joaquin Valley of California, longs for a lasting home to "stay" in.

1726. Geras, Adele. *The Girls in the Velvet Frame* (5–7). 1979, Atheneum $6.95. A warm family story set in Jerusalem in pre–World War I times.

1727. Gerson, Corinne. *Son for a Day* (4–6). Illus. by Velma Ilsley. 1980, Atheneum $8.95. Eleven-year-old Danny finds he can be easily "adopted" by families when he visits the Bronx Zoo.

1728. Glaser, Dianne. *Summer Secrets* (5–7). 1977, Holiday $5.59. While spending a summer with a great-aunt, Worthy gradually learns about her family and particularly about her dead mother.

1729. Goffstein, M. B. *Two Piano Tuners* (3–4). Illus. by author. 1970, Farrar $5.95. Debbie wants to become a piano tuner like her grandfather, but Grandpa wants her to become a concert pianist.

1730. Goins, Ellen H. *Big Diamond's Boy* (5–7). 1977, Nelson $6.95. Cotton learns that his gambling father has feet of clay in this novel set in the rural South during the Great Depression.

1731. Green, Phyllis. *Nicky's Lopsided, Lumpy but Delicious Orange* (4–6). 1978, Addison $7.95. Nicky has trouble accepting the imperfections in her mother and stepfather.

1732. Greene, Constance C. *I and Sproggy* (4–6). Illus. by Emily McCully. 1978, Viking $7.95. Adam gradually grows to like his English stepsister, Sproggy.

1733. Greenfield, Eloise. *Sister* (5–7). Illus. by M. Barnett. 1974, Crowell $6.95. Four years in a black girl's life, as revealed through scattered diary entries, during which she shows maturation, particularly in her attitudes toward her sister.

1734. Greenfield, Eloise. *Talk about a Family* (3–5). Illus. by James Calvin. 1978, Lippincott $6.95. Genny is hoping that her brother's return from the army will bring her family back together.

1735. Gordon, Shirley. *The Boy Who Wanted a Family* (2–4). Illus. by Charles Robinson. 1980, Harper $7.95; LB $7.89. Michael spends the first year with his adoptive parent, Miss Gilbert, and finally finds a home.

1736. Hagy, Jeannie. *And Then Mom Joined the Army* (3–5). Illus. by David K. Stone. 1976, Abingdon $4.75. Scott is ashamed when his mother joins the WACs.

1737. Hamilton, Gail. *Love Comes to Eunice K. O'Herlihy* (6–8). 1977, Atheneum $5.95. A Hawaiian family encounters problems when they move to rural Montana.

1738. Hamilton, Gail. *Titania's Lodestone* (6–8). 1975, Atheneum $7.95. Priscilla is amazed when the residents of a New England town accept her hippie parents.

1739. Hamilton, Virginia. *M. C. Higgins the Great* (6–8). 1974, Macmillan $7.95. The Newbery Award winner about a 13-year-old black boy growing up in Appalachia as part of a loving family whose future is threatened by a possible mountain slide.

1740. Hamilton, Virginia. *Justice and Her Brothers* (6–8). 1978, Greenwillow $7.95; LB $7.63. A slow-moving but compelling study of a young girl's relationship with her older twin

brothers. The story is continued in *Dustland* (1980, Greenwillow $8.95; LB $8.59).

1741. Hartling, Peter. *Oma* (4–6). Illustrated. 1977, Harper $6.95; LB $6.79. In an episodic narrative, Kalle shares many warm experiences with his 67-year-old grandmother, Oma.

1742. Hazen, Barbara S. *Amelia's Flying Machine* (3–4). Illus. by Charles Robinson. 1977, Doubleday $6.95. A story about a mischievous girl, based on an actual incident in the life of Amelia Earhart.

1743. Hellberg, Hans-Eric. *Grandpa's Maria* (3–4). Illus. by Joan Sandin. 1974, Morrow $6.75. Maria weathers many trials, including her mother's nursing home confinement and her divorced father's new family, principally because she has a wonderful grandpa on whom to lean.

1744. Herman, Charlotte. *On the Way to the Movies* (5–7). 1980, Dutton $7.95. Simon proves to be less courageous than his younger brother in this humorous story.

1745. Herman, Charlotte. *Our Snowman Had Olive Eyes* (5–7). 1977, Dutton $6.50. This effective novel explores the relationship between a girl and her grandmother when the elderly lady comes to live with the family.

1746. Hopkins, Lee Bennett. *Mama* (3–5). 1977, Knopf $4.95; LB $5.99; Dell paper $1.25. A young boy realizes that his mother has become a thief so that her family can have the things they need.

1747. Houston, James. *Akavak, an Eskimo Journey* (5–7). Illus. by author. 1968, Harcourt $5.95; LB $4.95. A young Eskimo takes his grandfather on a journey so that the old man can see his brother one last time. Also use: *Eagle Mask* (1965, Harcourt $5.50; LB $5.50), *The White Archer* (1967, Harcourt $6.50; paper $2.95), and *Ghost Paddle* (1972, Harcourt $5.50).

1748. Hunt, Irene. *William* (5–7). 1977, Scribner $7.95; Grosset paper $1.50. An orphan black boy, his 2 sisters, and an older girl join forces to produce a self-made family.

1749. Hunt, Mabel Leigh. *Miss Jellytot's Visit* (3–5). Illustrated. 1955, Lippincott $7.89. Katie visits her new home.

1750. Hunter, Evan. *Me and Mr. Stenner* (5–8). 1976, Lippincott $7.95. Abby's attitudes toward her new stepfather gradually change from resentment to love.

1751. Hurmence, Belinda. *Tough Tiffany* (6–8). 1980, Doubleday $7.95; LB $8.90. Tiffany Cox, an 11-year-old black girl, sorts out her feelings toward her family.

1752. Hurwitz, Johanna. *The Law of Gravity* (4–6). Illus. by Ingrid Fetz. 1978, Morrow $6.95; LB $6.43. Margot tries to get her recluse mother to come out of her shell.

1753. Inkiow, Dimiter. *Me and My Sister Clara* (4–6). 1979, Pantheon $2.95; LB $3.99. A translation from the German of stories about a small boy and his sister that is followed by *Me and Clara and Casimir the Cat* (1979, Pantheon $2.95; LB $3.99).

1754. Jackson, Jacqueline. *The Taste of Spruce Gum* (5–7). Illus. by Lilian Obligado. 1966, Little $6.95. After her father's death, Libby and her mother return to rural Vermont and her father's family whom she never really knew.

1755. Jackson, Louise A. *Grandpa Had a Windmill, Grandma Had a Churn* (2–4). Illus. by George Ancona. 1977, Parents $6.25; LB $5.71. A little girl, visiting her grandparents on a farm, describes their life and some of the objects and tools they use.

1756. Johnston, Norma. *The Keeping Days* (6–8). 1973, Atheneum $6.95. Growing up in an unpredictable family in turn-of-the-century Yonkers, New York, as seen by 14-year-old Tish Sterling. Also use the sequel: *Glory in the Flower* (1974, $6.95).

1757. Jordan, June. *New Life: New Room* (2–4). Illus. by Ray Cruz. 1975, Crowell $7.89. Three enterprising black children make room for a new baby in the family.

1758. Kaplan, Bess. *The Empty Chair* (5–7). 1978, Harper $7.95; LB $7.89. Beth is dismayed when her Jewish relatives help plan her father's remarriage.

1759. Kingman, Lee. *Georgina and the Dragon* (2–5). Illus. by Leonard Shortall. 1972, Houghton $6.95; Archway paper $1.25. In this amusing story, an impressionable but engaging young girl tries to earn money for a trip from Ohio to Idaho.

1760. Kingman, Lee. *The Year of the Racoon* (5–8). 1966, Houghton $8.95. The responsibility and discipline of caring for a pet raccoon ease the inferiority complex that 15-year-old Joey has acquired as the average boy among talented brothers in this excellent family story.

1761. Klein, Norma. *Confessions of an Only Child* (4–6). Illus. by Richard Cuffari. 1974, Pantheon $5.95; LB $5.99; Dell paper $.95. Antonia—Toe for short—undergoes many emotional problems anticipating a baby in the family. Also use: *What It's All About* (1975, Dial $5.95).

1762. Klein, Norma. *Mom, The Wolfman and Me* (5–8). 1972, Pantheon LB $5.99; Avon paper $1.50. Brett has a most unusual mother and,

therefore, doesn't mind the state of being fatherless, but the Wolfman changes things.

1763. Klein, Norma. *Naomi in the Middle* (2–4). Illus. by Leigh Grant. 1974, Dial $5.95; LB $5.47; Archway paper $1.25. What will it be like to be the middle child when the new baby arrives, ponders 7-year-old Naomi in this frank discussion of pregnancy.

1764. Kruss, James. *My Great-Grandfather and I* (4–6). Illus. by Jochen Bartsch. 1964, Atheneum $6.95. Great-grandfather has a passion for words and rhymes, and encourages his grandson to match his skill.

1765. LaFarge, Phyllis. *Abby Takes Over* (4–6). Illus. by Glo Coalson. 1974, Lippincott $7.95. Dell paper $.95. Eleven-year-old Abby takes charge of the household when her mother visits a friend.

1766. Landis, James David. *The Sisters Impossible* (5–7). 1979, Knopf $6.95; LB $6.99. Despite her initial aversion to ballet, Lily changes when she begins to take lessons with her sister.

1767. Lee, Virginia. *The Magic Moth* (4–6). Illus. by Richard Cuffari. 1972, Seabury $6.95. A family's adjustment to the death of Maryanne, one of 5 children, as seen principally through the experiences of her 6-year-old brother.

1768. Leigh, Frances. *The Lost Boy* (5–7). 1976, Dutton $6.95. Three children spending Christmas with their father in Malaysia find a young boy who could be their long-lost brother.

1769. L'Engle, Madeleine. *Meet the Austins* (5–7). 1961, Vanguard $5.95. The story of a country doctor's family, told by the 12-year-old daughter, and their reaction to having Maggie, a spoiled orphan, come to live with them.

1770. LeRoy, Gen. *Emma's Dilemma* (4–6). 1975, Harper $6.89; paper $1.50. Emma's problem is that she loves her dog, Pearl, but unfortunately Grandma, who comes to stay, is allergic to dogs.

1771. LeRoy, Gen. *Hotheads* (5–7). 1977, Harper $6.95; LB $7.89. The 2 hotheads in the Michellini family—12-year-old Geneva and her grandfather —work out their problems.

1772. Levoy, Myron. *The Witch of Fourth Street and Other Stories* (4–7). 1972, Harper paper $1.25. Eight stories about growing up poor on the lower East Side of New York City.

1773. Lexau, Joan M. *Striped Ice Cream* (2–5). Illus. by John Wilson. 1968, Lippincott $6.95; Scholastic paper $.95. The conquest of poverty is realistically portrayed in this warmly told story about a fatherless black family as they work together.

1774. Lindquist, Jennie D. *The Golden Name Day* (3–5). Illus. by Garth Williams. 1955, Harper $7.89; paper $1.50. Nancy longs to celebrate her own name day when she spends a summer with her Swedish-American grandparents.

1775. Lingard, Joan. *The Resettling* (6–9). 1976, Nelson $6.95. In this sequel to *The Clearance* (1974, $5.95), Maggie and her Scottish family must move to a high-rise apartment in the suburbs.

1776. Lively, Penelope. *The House in Norham Gardens* (6–9). 1974, Dutton $6.95. Fourteen-year-old Clare enjoys taking care of a huge old house, 2 elderly adults, and some roomers.

1777. Love, Sandra. *But What about Me?* (3–6). Illus. by Joan Sandin. 1976, Harcourt $5.95. A sixth-grader must adjust to her mother's return to work and the discomforts this produces.

1778. McGraw, Eloise. *Moccasin Trail* (6–9). Illus. by Paul Galdone. 1952, Coward $8.50. Dramatic story of a boy's life with the Indians who adopted him and his readjustment after returning to his family.

1779. Madison, Winifred. *Call Me Danica* (5–7). 1977, Four Winds $6.95. Danica and her Croatian family must begin a painful adjustment to life in Canada.

1780. Madison, Winifred. *The Party That Lasted All Summer* (4–6). Illus. by Meiling. 1976, Little $6.95. A period piece set in 1925 at a seaside resort, about a young girl who believes that her neighbor is a princess.

1781. Maguire, Gregory. *The Lightning Time* (5–7). 1978, Farrar $7.95. After the illness of his mother, David moves to his grandmother's home in northern New York State.

1782. Mathis, Sharon Bell. *The Hundred Penny Box* (3–5). Illus. by Leo Dillon and Diane Dillon. 1975, Viking $6.95. Old and frail Aunt Dew tells Michael about her experiences through a box that contains a penny for each year of her life.

1783. Mazer, Harry. *The Dollar Man* (6–9). 1974, Delacorte $5.95; Dell paper $.95. Fat, clumsy Marcus hopes things will change when he is able to track down his father, whom he has nicknamed the Dollar Man.

1784. Mearian, Judy Frank. *Someone Slightly Different* (6–8). 1980, Dial $7.95; LB $7.45. Marty Trevor's grandmother comes to take over the household.

1785. Mearian, Judy Frank. *Two Ways about It* (5–7). 1979, Dial $7.95; LB $7.45. Eleven-year-old Annie decides that having her older cousin Lou spend summers with her has a lot of hidden rewards.

1786. Miles, Betty. *Just the Beginning* (4–7). 1976, Knopf $5.95; LB $6.39. Being relatively poor in an upper-class neighborhood causes problems for 13-year-old Catherine Myers.

1787. Miles, Miska. *Aaron's Door* (2–5). Illus. by Alan E. Cober. 1977, Atlantic/Little $5.95. Aaron and his sister are adopted, and they react quite differently toward their new parents.

1788. Nagenda, John. *Mukasa* (4–6). Illus. by Charles Lilly. 1973, Macmillan $4.95. This story of a boy growing up in Uganda of the 1940s is based on the author's experiences.

1789. Neville, Emily. *It's Like This, Cat* (6–9). Illus. by Emil Weiss. 1963, Harper $6.95; LB $6.79; paper $1.50. Good picture of New York and city living is presented in the story of Dave and his relationships with his friends and family. Newbery Award, 1964. Also use: *Berries Goodman* (1965, Harper, LB $7.89; paper $1.50).

1790. Nostlinger, Christine. *Girl Missing* (6–8). 1976, Watts $5.90. Erika tells of her feelings toward her older, more attractive sister, Ilse, whom she adores, but who deceives her.

1791. Orgel, Doris. *A Certain Magic* (4–6). 1976, Dial $7.95; paper $1.50. Jenny's reading from her aunt's childhood diary leads to her tracking down some of her aunt's lost friends.

1792. Panetta, George. *Sea Beach Express* (4–6). Illus. by Emily McCully. 1966, Harper $5.79. A fun-filled trip by Tony Buccaccio and his family via subway to Coney Island in New York City.

1793. Parker, Richard. *The Runaway* (6–8). 1977, Nelson $6.95. Hugo Prescott is so tired of his parents' constant quarreling that he tries to divert them by faking his own kidnapping.

1794. Pascal, Francine. *The Hand-Me-Down Kid* (5–7). 1980, Viking $9.95. Eleven-year-old Ari feels that other people, including her older sister, are taking advantage of her.

1795. Perl, Lila. *Pieface and Daphne* (5–7). 1980, Houghton $7.95. Pamela feels a strange resentment against Daphne, an older cousin who comes to spend the summer.

1796. Pevsner, Stella. *And You Give Me a Pain, Elaine* (5–7). 1978, Seabury $7.50. Andrea tries to get along with her older sister while trying to adjust to her mother's death.

1797. Pfeffer, Susan Beth. *Kid Power* (4–6). Illus. by Leigh Grant. 1977, Watts $5.90; Scholastic paper $.95. A spunky young girl organizes an employment agency for herself and friends when her mother loses her job.

1798. Phipson, Joan. *The Family Conspiracy* (5–6). 1965, Harcourt $5.95; paper $.65. Some Australian children try to collect enough money for their mother's operation.

1799. Phipson, Joan. *Threat to the Barkers* (5–7). Illus. by Margaret Horder. 1965, Harcourt $4.95. Anxiety and excitement mount on an Australian sheep ranch when it is learned that a band of robbers is in the area.

1800. Pritchard, Katharine Susannah. *The Wild Oats of Han* (4–6). Illus. by Genevieve Melrose. 1973, Macmillan $4.95. An old (1928) novel about Han, age 12, and his siblings growing up in a Tasmanian village.

1801. Rabin, Gil. *Changes* (6–9). 1973, Harper $6.89. Chris finds many things difficult to adjust to, including his mother's move to Brooklyn and placing his grandfather in a nursing home.

1802. Read, Elfrieda. *Brothers by Choice* (6–9). 1974, Farrar $5.95. Brett tries to resolve the difficulties between his pompous and difficult father and his alienated and older adopted brother, Rocky.

1803. Reynolds, Pamela. *Will the Real Monday Please Stand Up* (6–9). 1975, Lothrop $7.25; LB $6.96; Archway paper $1.25. Through tape recordings in which she talks about herself and her family, 14-year-old Monday Holliday tells of her brother's encounters with drugs and her growing alienation from her family.

1804. Rich, Louise Dickinson. *Summer at High Kingdom* (5–8). 1975, Watts $5.88. A 13-year-old boy and his family react to the presence of a hippie commune in rural Maine.

1805. Rich, Louise Dickinson. *Three of a Kind* (4–6). Illus. by William M. Hutchinson. 1970, Watts $4.90. Life in her ideal foster home changes for Sally when 4-year-old, withdrawn Benjie arrives.

1806. Richard, Adrienne. *Wings* (5–6). 1974, Little $5.95; Dell paper $1.25. An episodic story about Pip who, in the 1920s, is living with her mother and brother in a California valley town.

1807. Rinaldo, C. L. *Dark Dreams* (6–9). 1974, Harper $6.95. In this novel set during World War II, Carlo adjusts to a new life with his grandmother and being bullied by local toughs, through the help of a retarded man and a letter from his absent father.

1808. Rodowsky, Colby F. *Evy-Ivy-Over* (5–7). 1978, Watts $7.90. Slug's grandmother has an unusual gift, which causes embarrassment for the young girl.

1809. Rogers, Pamela. *The Rare One* (4–6). 1974, Nelson $5.95. Josh's tragedy and guilt over the death of an old man he has befriended brings him closer to his own family.

1810. Sachs, Marilyn. *Dorrie's Book* (5–6). Illus. by Ann Sachs. 1975, Doubleday $5.95. For a school assignment, Dorrie writes on how her comfortable "only child" status was upset with the arrival of triplets.

1811. Sachs, Marilyn. *The Truth about Mary Rose* (4–7). Illus. by Louis Glanzman. 1973, Doubleday $4.95; Dell paper $1.25. Mary Rose, Veronica Ganz's daughter, tries to find out about her namesake, an aunt who died in a fire when she was only a child.

1812. Sargent, Sarah. *Edward Troy and the Witch Cat* (3–5). Illus. by Emily McCully. 1978, Follett $6.99. Edward discovers that he can't depend on his father.

1813. Sheifman, Vicky. *Mindy* (3–5). Illus. by Lisl Weil. 1974, Macmillan $4.95. An only child's reaction to the arrival of a new baby.

1814. Shore, June Lewis. *Summer Storm* (6–8). 1977, Abingdon $4.95. The effects of a tornado on a family and their guests, set in pre–World War II Kentucky.

1815. Shotwell, Louisa R. *Magdalena* (5–7). Illus. by Lilian Obligado. 1971, Viking $5.95. Generation and cultural conflicts in a Puerto Rican family involving Magdalena, her grandmother, and the girl's desire to have her pigtails cut.

1816. Shotwell, Louisa R. *Roosevelt Grady* (4–6). Illus. by Peter Burchard. 1963, Collins $5.95. Candor and the simplicity that commands attention mark this story of the 9-year-old son of migrant farm workers who longs for and achieves a permanent home.

1817. Silman, Roberta. *Somebody Else's Child* (3–5). Illus. by Chris Conover. 1976, Warne $5.95. An adopted child explores his position in his surrogate family in this nicely illustrated story.

1818. Simon, Norma. *How Do I Feel?* (4–6). Illus. by Joe Lasker. 1970, Whitman $5.95. A small boy has tangled emotional problems with his twin and his older brother.

1819. Skolsky, Mindy Warshaw. *Carnival and Kopeck and More about Hannah* (3–5). Illus. by Karen Ann Weinhaus. 1979, Harper $7.95; LB $7.89. Hannah's relationship with her grandmother is realistically treated in this convincing novel.

1820. Smith, Alison. *Reserved for Mark Anthony Crowder* (5–7). 1978, Dutton $6.95. Mark, a misfit sixth-grader, is able to prove himself to his father.

1821. Sorensen, Virginia. *Miracles on Maple Hill* (4–6). Illus. by Beth Krush and Joe Krush. 1956, Harcourt $5.95; paper $1.95. The story of a troubled family drawn together by the experience of a year of country living. Newbery Award, 1957.

1822. Spyri, Johanna H. *Heidi* (4–6). Illus. by Greta Elgaard. 1962, Macmillan $4.95. A Swiss girl must leave her beloved grandfather. One of many recommended editions of this classic.

1823. Stren, Patti. *There's a Rainbow in My Closet* (4–6). 1979, Harper $8.79. During a visit, Emma's grandmother helps the young girl understand why it's good to be different.

1824. Stolz, Mary. *Go and Catch a Flying Fish* (6–8). 1979, Harper $7.95; LB $7.89. Three children face a disturbing future when their mother abandons them.

1825. Stolz, Mary. *Lands End* (5–8). Illus. by Dennis Hermanson. 1973, Harper $7.95; LB $7.89; paper $1.50. Josh finds an intriguing contrast between his family structure and the casual, relaxed life-style of his new neighbors, the Arthurs.

1826. Strang, Celia. *Foster Mary* (6–8). 1979, McGraw $7.95. The story of Aunt Foster Mary, her husband Alonzo, and the 4 unrelated, unwanted children they have taken in.

1827. Sunderlin, Sylvia. *Antrim's Orange* (2–4). Illus. by Diane de Groat. 1976, Scribner $6.95. During World War II, a young boy receives a precious orange from visiting grandmother.

1828. Sypher, Lucy Johnston. *The Spell of the Northern Lights* (4–6). Illus. by Ray Abel. 1975, Atheneum $7.95. Lucy, of *The Edge of Nowhere*, discovers that she possesses courage in this story set in a North Dakota town during 1916. The series also contains *Cousins and Circuses* (1974, $6.95) and is completed by *The Turnabout Year* (1976, $8.50).

1829. Talbot, Toby. *Dear Greta Garbo* (6–8). 1978, Putnam $6.95. Through their friendship, a young girl and her grandmother adjust to grandfather's death.

1830. Taylor, Mildred D. *Roll of Thunder, Hear My Cry* (6–8). Illus. by Jerry Pinkney. 1976, Dial $7.95. Set in rural Mississippi during the Depression, this Newbery Award winner continues the story about black Cassie Logan and her family begun in *Song of the Trees*.

1831. Taylor, Mildred D. *Song of the Trees* (3–5). Illus. by Jerry Pinkney. 1975, Dial $5.95; LB $5.47. The first novel about the Logans, a poor black family living in rural Mississippi, as told by Cassie, one of the 4 children.

1832. Taylor, Sydney. *All-of-a-Kind Family* (3–6). Illus. by Helen John. 1951, Follett $4.95; LB $5.97; Dell paper $1.25. Warm and moving stories of Jewish family life in New York City. Also use: *More All-of-a-Kind Family* (1954, Follett $4.95; LB $4.98; Dell, paper $1.25).

1833. Taylor, Sydney. *All-of-a-Kind Family Downtown* (3–6). Illus. by Beth Krush and Joe Krush. 1972, Follett $4.95; LB $6.99; Dell paper $1.25. Mischievous adventure of 5 little girls and their younger brother on the lower East Side of New York City at the turn of the century. Also use: *All-of-a-Kind Family Uptown* (1968, Dell, paper $1.25).

1834. Taylor, Sydney. *Ella of All-of-a-Kind Family* (4–6). Illus. by Gail Owens. 1978, Dutton $7.95. The oldest daughter of this famous New York City family caught between a singing career and home life.

1835. Thiele, Colin. *February Dragon* (5–7). 1976, Harper $5.95; LB $5.79. The Pine family face a new life in rural Australia after their home is destroyed by the February dragon, a brush fire that gets out of control.

1836. Thomas, Jane Resh. *Elizabeth Catches a Fish* (2–4). Illus. by Joseph Duffy. 1977, Seabury $6.95. For her seventh birthday, Elizabeth receives fishing gear and, with her father, goes on a day-long fishing trip.

1837. Thompson, Jean. *Don't Forget Michael* (3–4). Illus. by Margot Apple. 1979, Morrow $6.95; LB $6.67. Four short stories about Michael and his large family.

1838. Trasher, Crystal. *Between Dark and Daylight* (5–8). 1979, Atheneum $8.95. When a family's car breaks down during a move, they decide to take over an abandoned house. Companion to *The Dark Didn't Catch Me*.

1839. Thrasher, Crystal. *The Dark Didn't Catch Me* (5–7). 1975, Atheneum $7.95. Young Seely is determined to survive and not let the dark catch her, in spite of monumental problems and hardships that beset her family during the Great Depression.

1840. Tobias, Tobi. *How Your Mother and Father Met, and What Happened After* (3–4). Illus. by Diane de Groat. 1978, McGraw $6.95. A story of courtship, marriage, and the arrival of the first child.

1841. Tolan, Stephanie S. *Grandpa and Me* (4–6). 1978, Scribner $6.95. A young girl must face life with a senile grandfather.

1842. Townsend, John R. *Noah's Castle* (6–9). 1976, Lippincott $7.95. Interpersonal conflicts within a family are realistically portrayed in this novel set in England in the near future.

1843. Vestly, Anne-Cath. *Hello, Aurora* (3–5). Illus. by Leonard Kessler. 1974, Crowell $7.95. Father, a doctoral student, changes places with his wife, a lawyer, and stays home to care for Aurora and the new baby. Also use the sequel: *Aurora and Socrates* (1977, $7.95).

1844. Vogel, Ilse-Margret. *Dodo Every Day* (2–4). Illus. by author. 1977, Harper $5.95; LB $6.89. A quiet book in which the author pays tribute to her grandmother. Also use: *The Rainbow Dress* (1975, Harper $5.95; LB $6.89).

1845. Walker, Diana. *The Hundred Thousand Dollar Farm* (6–8). 1977, Abelard $6.95. An abandoned Australian boy seeks shelter with a Prince Edward Island farm family.

1846. Walker, Diana. *The Year of the Horse* (5–7). 1975, Abelard $6.95. Joanna's year on her grandmother's farm in Ontario provides unexpected rewards.

1847. Wallace, Barbara Brooks. *Julia and the Third Bad Thing* (5–7). Illus. by Mike Eagle. 1975, Follett $5.95; LB $5.97. Two bad things happen, and Julia's grandmother has said that they always come in threes.

1848. Wells, Rosemary. *Leave Well Enough Alone* (6–8). 1977, Dial $7.95; Archway paper $1.50. Fourteen-year-old Dorothy takes a summer job with a wealthy family in Pennsylvania, caring for their spoiled children.

1849. Wiggin, Kate Douglas. *Rebecca of Sunnybrook Farm* (4–7). Illus. by Lawrence Beall Smith. 1962, Macmillan $4.95. Rebecca is a spunky curious girl living in a quiet Maine community of the nineteenth century.

1850. Wilder, Laura Ingalls. *Little House in the Big Woods* (4–7). Illus. by Garth Williams. 1932, Harper $7.95; LB $8.79; paper $2.50. Outstanding story of a log-cabin family in Wisconsin in the late 1800's. Also use (all Harper, $7.95; LB $8.79; paper $2.50): *Farmer Boy* (1933, 1953), *Little House on the Prairie* (1935, 1953), *On the Banks of Plum Creek* (1937, 1953), *By the Shores of Silver Lake* (1939, 1953), *Long Winter* (1940, 1953), *Little Town on the Prairie* (1941, 1953), and *These Happy Golden Years* (1943, 1953).

1851. Wilder, Laura Ingalls. *West from Home: Letters of Laura Ingalls Wilder, San Francisco* (6–9). 1974, Harper $6.95; LB $6.79; paper $1.95. Laura visited her daughter Rose in San Francisco in the year that the city was preparing a world's fair, and she wrote about her experiences to her husband.

1852. Willard, Barbara. *Happy Families* (6–8). Illus. by Krystyna Turska. 1974, Macmillan $6.95. A collection from writers of both juvenile and adult fiction and nonfiction, past and present, which explores various aspects of family life.

1853. Willard, Barbara. *Storm from the West* (5–7). Illus. by Douglas Hall. 1964, Harcourt $5.95. The mother of 2 English children marries an American father of 4 teenagers. When the 2 households merge, problems arise.

1854. Yep, Laurence. *Child of the Owl* (6–9). 1977, Harper $6.95; LB $7.89. Because of family problems, Casey is sent to live with her grandmother in San Francisco's Chinatown.

1855. Zindel, Bonnie, and Zindel, Paul. *A Star for the Latecomer* (6–9). 1980, Harper $7.95; LB $7.89. A girl's relations with her terminally ill mother are explored in this novel with a ballet setting.

Friendship Stories

1856. Adler, Carole S. *The Magic of the Glits* (5–7). Illus. by Ati Forberg. 1979, Macmillan $7.95. Jeremy, age 12, takes care of 7-year-old Lynette for the summer.

1857. Angell, Judie. *Ronnie and Rosie* (5–7). 1977, Bradbury $7.95. Ronnie, a girl, and Rosie, a boy, form a close friendship, particularly after the death of Ronnie's father.

1858. Angell, Judie. *Secret Selves* (6–8). 1979, Bradbury $7.95. A prank phone call leads to two youngsters developing a secret friendship.

1859. Angell, Judie. *Tina Gogo* (5–8). 1978, Bradbury $7.95. Sarajane becomes friendly with an outlandish, irresponsible, but basically insecure young girl.

1860. Angell, Judie. *A Word from Our Sponsor or My Friend Alfred* (5–7). 1979, Bradbury $6.95. A message about consumerism is delivered in this entertaining novel about a group of boys who take on big business.

1861. Anker, Charlotte. *Last Night I Saw Andromeda* (4–6). Illus. by Ingrid Fetz. 1975, Walck $6.95. Jenny, a white girl, and Toby, a black boy, work together to solve their problems.

1862. Barford, Carol. *Let Me Hear the Music* (6–8). 1979, Seabury $7.95. A young girl bemoans the death of her gentle friend, Benny Kretchar.

1863. Beckman, Delores. *My Own Private Sky* (6–8). 1980, Dutton $7.95. A young boy helps his 68-year-old friend recover after an automobile accident.

1864. Berger, Terry. *Special Friends* (3–5). Illustrated. 1979, Messner $6.97. The story of a friendship between a young girl and an elderly woman.

1865. Billington, Elizabeth. *Part-Time Boy* (4–6). 1980, Warne $6.95. Jamie, a quiet boy, gains self-confidence through a friendship with a most unusual young woman.

1866. Bosse, Malcolm J. *The 79 Squares* (6–9). 1979, Crowell $7.95; LB $7.89. An unusual story of a friendship between a young boy and a dying ex-convict.

1867. Brink, Carol. *Louly* (4–6). Illus. by Ingrid Fetz. 1974, Macmillan $5.95. Louly and Chrys, the 2 girl companions of *Two Are Better Than One* (1968, Macmillan $6.95), are now 13 and continue their friendship in this mild story involving backyard camping among other things.

1868. Bulla, Clyde Robert. *Last Look* (3–5). Illustrated. 1979, Crowell $7.95; LB $7.89. Monica's indifference to the needs of a newcomer causes emotional problems.

1869. Bunting, Eve. *One More Flight* (4–8). 1976, Warne $5.95; Dell paper $1.25. A runaway boy finds help and direction in his life from meeting Timmie, who nurses injured birds of prey.

1870. Burch, Robert. *Two That Were Tough* (4–6). Illus. by Richard Cuffari. 1976, Viking $6.95. A story set in rural Georgia about an old man's attachment to children who, like himself, crave independence.

1871. Byars, Betsy. *The Pinballs* (5–7). 1977, Harper $6.95; LB $6.79. Three misfits in a foster home band together to help lessen their problems.

1872. Calhoun, Mary. *Katie John* (4–6). Illus. by Paul Frame. 1960, Harcourt $7.89; paper $1.95. In spite of her worst fears, Katie John has a pleasant time and makes new friends during a summer in a small southern town.

1873. Callen, Larry. *Sorrow's Song* (5–7). Illus. by Marvin Friedman. 1979, Atlantic/Little $7.95. In a Four Corners story, Pinch and his friend Sorrow try to save a whooping crane.

1874. Carlson, Natalie Savage. *Ann Aurelia and Dorothy* (4–6). Illus. by Dale Payson. 1968, Harper $7.89. Foster child Ann Aurelia must decide between her foster home with its experiences of sharing in her black friend Dorothy's stable home life and her mother.

1875. Carlson, Natalie Savage. *Carnival in Paris* (2–4). Illus. by Fermin Rocker. 1962, Harper $8.79. Children of carnival workers spend their Easter vacation at the Gingerbread Fair.

1876. Carlson, Natalie Savage. *Family under the Bridge* (3–5). Illus. by Garth Williams. 1958, Harper $7.89. Old Armand, a Paris hobo, finds 3 children huddled in his hideaway under the bridge, and befriends them.

1877. Child Study Children's Book Committee, ed. *Friends Are Like That! Stories to Read to Yourself* (2–3). Illus. by Leigh Grant. 1979, Crowell $7.95; LB $7.89. Nine stories and 2 poems celebrate friendship in its many facets.

1878. Carrick, Carol. *Some Friend!* (3–5). Illus. by Donald Carrick. 1979, Houghton $6.95. It is difficult for Mike to accept his friend Rob's overbearing behavior.

1879. Conford, Ellen. *Me and the Terrible Two* (4–6). Illus. by Charles Carroll. 1978, Little $6.95; Archway paper $1.25. The *Me* of the title, Dorrie, wages an undeclared war on twin boys who move next door, until she becomes ill and they become her only real friends.

1880. Cooper, Susan. *Dawn of Fear* (5–6). Illus. by Margery Gill. 1970, Harcourt $5.95. Reality must be faced by a group of English boys when one of their friends is killed in an air raid during World War II.

1881. Corcoran, Barbara. *The Winds of Time* (5–7). Illus. by Gail Owens. 1974, Atheneum $7.95. When Gail runs away rather than be forced to live with her Uncle Chad, whom she dislikes, she stumbles into a new life and unexpected kindness and understanding.

1882. Cresswell, Helen. *The Bongleweed* (4–6). 1973, Macmillan $4.95. In this English story, Becky and her friend try to save a strange plant they call the "bongleweed."

1883. Cresswell, Helen. *The Night Watchmen* (4–6). Illus. by Gareth Floyd. 1970, Macmillan $5.95. Henry has time on his hands until he meets 2 fascinating tramps, Josh and Caleb.

1884. Delton, Judy. *Kitty in the Middle* (3–4). Illus. by Charles Robinson. 1979, Houghton $6.95. An episodic account of 3 fourth-grade girls living through the war in 1942.

1885. Epstein, Anne Merrick. *Good Stones* (5–7). Illus. by Susan Meddaugh. 1977, Houghton $6.95. During the 1930s in New Hampshire, 2 outcasts—a young part-Indian girl and an ex-convict—try to find a better world together.

1886. Farrar, Susan Clement. *Samantha on Stage* (5–6). Illus. by Ruth Sanderson. 1979, Dial $7.95; LB $7.45. Lizinska and Sam study ballet together.

1887. Feil, Heila. *The Ghost Garden* (4–6). Illus. by Thomas Quirk. 1976, Atheneum $7.95. Death separates 2 girls whose friendship had grown one summer on Cape Cod.

1888. Fine, Anne. *The Summer-House Loon* (6–9). 1979, Crowell $6.95. An English story that takes place in 24 hours in the lives of two lonely, misunderstood young people.

1889. Franco, Marjorie. *So Who Hasn't Got Problems?* (6–8). 1979, Houghton $6.95. Thirteen-year-old Jennifer and her 2 friends have trouble growing up in a North Side Chicago neighborhood.

1890. Friedman, Frieda. *Ellen and the Gang* (5–6). Illus. by Jacqueline Tomes. 1963, Morrow $6.96. A compelling portrayal of an insecure city girl who finds that new, false friends have been framing her as the thief in a series of newsstand thefts.

1891. Garrigue, Sheila. *Between Friends* (4–6). 1978, Bradbury $6.95. A dog-watching job brings new friends to Dede.

1892. Giff, Patricia Reilly. *The Girl Who Knew It All* (3–5). Illus. by Leslie Morrill. 1979, Delacorte $6.95; LB $6.46. Tracy faces up to the fact that she has reading problems.

1893. Gilbert, Nan. *The Strange New York across the Street* (4–6). 1979, Avon $1.50. Withdrawn Robbie makes friends with Janet and her family across the street.

1894. Godden, Rumer. *Diddakoi* (5–7). 1972, Viking $5.95. Kizzy, who is a half-gypsy—a diddakoi, finds that her life comes apart when old Gran dies.

1895. Godden, Rumer. *Mr. McFadden's Hallowe'en* (4–6). 1975, Viking $6.95. Eight-year-old Selina tackles a formidable task—to persuade crusty Mr. McFadden to deed some of his land to the village for a park.

1896. Greene, Bette. *Philip Hall Likes Me, I Reckon Maybe* (4–6). Illustrated. 1974, Dial $6.95; LB $6.46; Dell paper $1.25. Beth finds that letting Philip Hall get first place in their class turns out not to be the best way to gain his affection.

1897. Greene, Constance C. *Getting Nowhere* (6–8). 1977, Viking $6.95. Fourteen-year-old Mark's bottled-up hatred turns to self-loathing in this powerful novel.

1898. Greene, Constance C. *A Girl Called Al* (5–7). Illus. by Byron Barton. 1969, Viking $5.95; Dell paper $1.25. The friendship between 2 seventh-graders and their apartment building superintendent is humorously and deftly recounted.

1899. Greene, Constance C. *The Unmaking of Rabbit* (4–6). 1972, Viking $6.95; Dell paper $.95. The class outsider overcomes many disappointments and slights to gain a measure of acceptance by his peers and a feeling of confidence.

1900. Grimes, Nikki. *Growin'* (4–6). Illus. by Charles Lilly. 1977, Dial $6.95; LB $6.46. Yolanda tames the class bully in this story of the friendship of 2 black children.

1901. Gripe, Maria. *Elvis and His Secret* (4–6). 1976, Delacorte $6.95; LB $6.46. A boy of 6 learns to accept himself and find his own identity with the help of a friend in this Swedish novel.

1902. Gripe, Maria. *Julia's House* (5–6). Illus. by Harold Gripe. 1975, Delacorte $5.95; LB $5.47; Dell paper $1.25. Alternate chapters written by Julia and her nighttime baby-sitter, Peter, deal with many matters, including the threatened destruction of their house in this sequel to *The Night Daddy* (1971, Delacorte, LB $4.58; Dell, paper $1.25).

1903. Grohskopf, Bernice. *Children in the Wind* (6–8). 1977, Atheneum $8.95. Lenora makes friends with 2 different but fascinating girls.

1904. Hahn, Mary Dorning. *The Sara Summer* (4–6). 1979, Houghton $7.95. Two young girls, Sara and Emily, form a friendship one summer.

1905. Hanlon, Emily. *The Swing* (5–7). 1979, Bradbury $7.95. Two youngsters, one deaf and the other grieving for a dead father, are brought together at the swing.

1906. Hart, Carole. *Delilah* (3–4). Illus. by Edward Frascino. 1973, Harper $6.89. A friendly, cozy book about the everyday adventures of an unusual heroine.

1907. Hoban, Lillian. *I Met a Traveller* (5–7). 1977, Harper $6.95; LB $6.79. Josie and her newly divorced mother have an extended visit to Israel, where Josie conquers her loneliness.

1908. Hodges, Margaret. *The Freewheeling of Joshua Cobb* (4–7). Illus. by Richard Cuffari. 1974, Farrar $5.95. Josh spends an interesting summer vacation on a bicycle camping trip with a group of friends and the enigmatic Cassandra.

1909. Holmes, Efner Tudor. *Carrie's Gift* (2–4). Illus. by Tasha Tudor. 1978, Collins $5.95; LB $6.49. The story of the friendship between a young girl and a lonely old man.

1910. Howell, Ruth Rea. *The Dome People* (5–8). Illus. by Arline Strong. 1974, Atheneum $5.25. An instructional book with fictional trappings about how a group of young people construct a dome clubhouse.

1911. Jones, Adrienne. *The Hawks of Chelney* (6–9). Illus. by Stephen Gammell. 1978, Harper $7.95; LB $7.89. A strong, introspective story of an outcast from his tribe and his love for a shipwrecked girl.

1912. Keller, Beverly. *Fiona's Bee* (2–3). Illus. by Diane Paterson. 1975, Coward LB $4.69; paper $1.50. Fiona accidently makes a number of friends when she saves a bee from drowning.

1913. Kemp, Gene. *Turbulent Term of Tyke Tiller* (4–6). Illus. by Carolyn Diman. 1980, Faber $8.50. A humorous English story about Tyke's friendship with Danny, a boy with a speech impediment.

1914. Kerr, M. E. *The Son of Someone Famous* (6–9). 1979, Harper $7.89. Adam Blessing and Brenda Belle Blossom are 2 outsiders whose problems bring them together in a small-town environment.

1915. Kidd, Ronald. *That's What Friends Are For* (6–8). 1978, Nelson $6.95. A tribute by a young boy to a friend who has just died of leukemia.

1916. Konigsburg, E. L. *Jennifer, Hecate, Macbeth, William McKinley, and Me, Elizabeth* (4–6). Illus. by author. 1967, Atheneum $6.95; paper $1.95. Black Jennifer hazes white newcomer, Elizabeth, her apprentice witch, and their amusing amateur sorcery leads to the magic of a firm friendship for 2 loners.

1917. LeGuin, Ursula. *Very Far from Anywhere Else* (6–8). 1976, Atheneum $6.95. A loner, attending a college he dislikes, forms a friendship with an equally independent girl.

1918. Levoy, Myron. *Alan and Naomi* (6–8). 1977, Harper $6.95; LB $6.79; Dell paper $1.50. A young boy tries to bring a traumatized Jewish refugee out of her withdrawn state.

1919. Line, David. *Soldier and Me* (6–8). 1965, Harper $6.79. An English schoolboy befriends a Hungarian refugee, and they join forces in an effort to prevent murder.

1920. Lingard, Joan. *The Pilgrimage* (6–9). 1977, Nelson $6.95. Maggie causes her boyfriend to become jealous when she forms a friendship with a young Canadian on a bike trip in Highland Scotland, in the third of these novels about Maggie McKinley.

1921. Lipsyte, Robert. *One Fat Summer* (6–9). 1977, Harper $5.95; LB $6.89. Bobby has a weight problem, and Joanie has a big nose. Together they help solve each other's problems.

1922. Little, Jean. *Look through My Window* (4–6). Illus. by Joan Sandin. 1970, Harper $7.89; paper $2.95. Emily's horizons change when Aunt Deborah's 4 children come to live with Emily's family.

1923. Little, Jean. *Stand in the Wind* (4–6). Illustrated. 1975, Harper $7.89. Four young girls share a lake cottage during one summer and gradually lose their animosities.

1924. Lively, Penelope. *Boy without a Name* (4–6). Illus. by A. Dalton. 1975, Parnassus $5.95; LB $4.77. A nameless orphan finds a home with a stonemason in this English novel set in the time of Charles Stuart.

1925. Lorenzo, Carol Lee. *Heart-of-Snowbird* (6–8). 1975, Harper $5.95; LB $5.79. Laurel's longing to leave the southern town of Snowbird Gap is assuaged somewhat by her friendship with Hank Bearfoot.

1926. Madison, Winifred. *The Mysterious Caitlin McIver* (6–9). 1975, Follett $6.95; LB $6.99. James Jamison encounters a young Scottish temptress who changes his life in this tale of adolescence set in San Francisco.

1927. Mark, Jan. *Thunder and Lightnings* (6–9). 1979, Crowell $7.95; LB $7.89. Two English boys form a fast friendship in this story set in Norfolk, which won the Carnegie Medal, 1976.

1928. Mazer, Harry. *Snowbound* (5–7). 1973, Delacorte $6.95; paper $1.25. In this survival story, Tony and Cindy spend 11 days together snowbound.

1929. Micklish, Rita. *Sugar Bee* (3–7). Illus. by Ted Lewin. 1972, Delacorte $5.95; LB $5.47. The tender story of the friendship between a blind girl and Sugar Bee, an underprivileged black girl.

1930. Miles, Betty. *The Trouble with Thirteen* (6–8). 1979, Knopf $6.95; LB $6.99. Both Annie and Rachel find that 13 is a troublesome age.

1931. Myers, Walter Dean. *Fast Sam, Cool Clyde and Stuff* (6–9). 1975, Viking $6.95. Stuff tells the story of the 116th St. Good People, a group of Harlem teenagers who help each other face problems of growing up.

1932. Neville, Emily. *Garden of Broken Glass* (6–9). 1975, Delacorte $6.95; LB $6.46. Brian, unhappy with an alcoholic mother and no father, receives help from some black classmates who take him into their lives.

1933. Neville, Emily. *The Seventeenth-Street Gang* (5–7). Illus. by author. 1966, Harper $6.89; paper $1.95. Hollis and her crew find problems accepting Irving, a new boy in their New York City neighborhood.

1934. Norris, Gunilla B. *Standing in the Magic* (3–5). Illus. by Richard Cuffari. 1974, Dutton $5.95. Two poor boys, Joel and Brady, spend a summer together in the hot city.

1935. O'Connor, Jane. *Your's Till Niagara Falls* (4–6). Illus. by Margot Apple. 1979, Hastings $6.95. Abby's summer at camp proves to be unexpectedly rewarding.

1936. Paterson, Katherine. *Bridge to Terabithia* (6–8). Illus. by Donna Diamond. 1977, Crowell $7.95; Avon paper $1.50. Jess becomes a close friend of Leslie, a new girl in his school, and suffers agony after her accidental death. Newbery Award winner.

1937. Peck, Richard. *Dreamland Lake* (5–8). 1973, Holt $5.95. Two deaths—one of a vagrant and the other of a friendless boy—are experienced by Bryan and Flip in this perceptive tale of growing up.

1938. Peck, Robert Newton. *Soup* (5–7). Illus. by Charles C. Gehm. 1974, Knopf $4.95; LB $5.99; Dell paper $1.25. Rural Vermont in the 1920s is recreated in these reminiscences of the author of the times he spent with his friend Soup. Also use: *Soup and Me* (1975, Knopf $4.95; LB $5.95; Dell, paper $1.25).

1939. Peck, Robert Newton. *Soup for President* (5–7). Illus. by Ted Lewin. 1978, Knopf $5.95; LB $5.99. Soup competes against Norma Jean Bissell in a race for the school presidency.

1940. Phipson, Joan. *Horse with Eight Hands* (5–7). 1974, Atheneum $7.50. Four children help a German immigrant, Horst, to open an antique shop in this satisfying novel set in Australia.

1941. Rock, Gail. *Addie and the King of Hearts* (4–6). Illustrated. 1976, Knopf $4.95; LB $5.99; Bantam paper $1.75. Addie Mills, a seventh-grader, tries to avoid Billy, who has a crush on her. Also use: *A Dream for Addie* (1975, Knopf $4.95; LB $5.69; Bantam, paper $1.75).

1942. Rockwell, Thomas. *The Thief* (4–5). Illus. by Gail Rockwell. 1977, Delacorte $5.95; LB $5.47. A young boy discovers that his only true friend is a thief.

1943. Shreve, Susan. *The Nightmares of Geranium Street* (4–6). 1977, Crowell $5.95; LB $6.99. A gang of waifs growing up in the Germantown section of Philadelphia solve the mystery of strange doings at Aunt Ress's home.

1944. Shura, Mary Francis. *The Barkley Street Six-Pack* (5–7). 1979, Dodd $6.95. Instant friendship with scheming Natalie proves to be ultimately unsatisfactory for Jane.

1945. Simmons, Anthony. *The Optimists of Nine Elms* (5–6). Illus. by Ben Stahl. 1975, Pantheon $4.50; LB $5.99. A family story set in England in which 2 children form a tender relationship with an old man and his dog.

1946. Singer, Marilyn. *No Applause, Please* (5–7). 1977, Dutton $7.50. Ruthie and Laurie try to remain friends in spite of rivalry about a singing career.

1947. Snyder, Zilpha Keatley. *The Egypt Game* (5–7). Illus. by Alton Raible. 1967, Atheneum $8.95; paper $2.50. Humor and suspense mark an outstanding story of city children whose safety while playing at an unsupervised re-creation of an Egyptian ritual is threatened by a violent lunatic.

1948. Snyder, Zilpha Keatley. *The Velvet Room* (5–6). Illus. by Alton Raible. 1965, Atheneum $7.95; paper $1.95. Robin's search to escape the realities of life in a sharecropper's family leads her to new friendships and insights.

1949. Southall, Ivan. *Josh* (5–8). 1972, Macmillan $5.95. Josh's hoped-for visit at his aunt's home in rural Australia turns sour when he encounters hostility instead of friendship from boys his own age. Carnegie Medal winner.

1950. Stolz, Mary. *The Bully of Barkham Street* (4–8). Illus. by Leonard Shortall. 1963, Harper $7.50; LB $6.89; Dell paper $1.25. Eleven-year-old Martin goes through a typical phase of growing up—feeling misunderstood. Also use: *A Dog on Barkham Street* (1960, Harper $6.89; Dell paper .95¢).

1951. Stolz, Mary. *Cider Days* (4–5). 1978, Harper $7.95. A friendship between 2 very different girls matures in this sequel to *Ferris Wheel*.

1952. Stolz, Mary. *Juan* (4–6). Illus. by Louis Glanzman. 1970, Harper $5.95; LB $5.79. Orphanage life in a small Mexican town as experienced principally by 2 children.

1953. Stolz, Mary. *The Noonday Friends* (4–6). Illus. by Louis Glanzman. 1965, Harper $6.89; paper $1.95. Eleven-year-old Franny's unskilled father is out of work, and the demanded family teamwork leaves her free from chores only during lunch periods. Inner-city realities in a skillful family story.

1954. Stolz, Mary. *A Wonderful, Terrible Time* (4–6). 1967, Harper $6.89. Clear characterizations perceptively reveal the different reactions to a summer camp for 2 black girl friends of lower-income urban families.

1955. Streatfeild, Noel. *Ballet Shoes* (4–6). Illus. by Richard Floethe. 1937, Random $6.99. Three small girls are adopted by an elderly professor and educated for the stage in a London school of dancing.

1956. Tate, Joan. *Wild Boy* (5–7). Illus. by Susan Jeschke. 1973, Harper LB $6.89. The friendship between 2 boys—one quiet and restrained, the other wild and untamed.

1957. Taylor, Theodore. *The Cay* (5–8). 1969, Doubleday $5.95; Avon paper $1.50. Themes of growing up and survival, black versus white, innocence and distrust versus wisdom and respect, are deftly woven into the saga of a young blind American boy and an old West Indian native, both stranded on a Caribbean cay.

1958. Teal, Mildred. *Bird of Passage* (6–8). Illus. by Ted Lewin. 1977, Little $6.95. The flight of the great blue heron becomes the symbol of strength for 2 troubled youngsters.

1959. Terris, Susan. *Two P's in a Pod* (5–7). 1977, Greenwillow $7.25; LB $6.96. Sixth-grader Pru finds she is being dominated by her look-alike friend, Penny Hoffman.

1960. Thiele, Colin. *The Shadow on the Hills* (5–8). 1978, Harper $6.95; LB $6.79. Farm life in rural Australia is highlighted in this story of a young boy and his encounters with a half-crazed hermit.

1961. Towne, Mary. *The Glass Room* (5–7). Illus. by Richard Cuffari. 1971, Farrar $5.95. A story of 2 boys drawn together by the difficulties in their life patterns and families.

1962. Wallace, Barbara Brooks. *Victoria* (5–7). 1972, Follett $5.97; Dell paper $1.25. A disturbed, complex girl causes problems for her friends and roommates at a private school in this perceptively written story.

1963. Watson, Simon. *The Partisan* (5–7). 1975, Macmillan $4.95. What begins as a group of innocent friends degenerates into a brutish gang in this English novel with overtones of *Lord of the Flies.*

1964. Westall, Robert. *The Machine Gunners* (5–9). 1976, Greenwillow $7.25; LB $6.96; GID paper $1.75. Charles and his young friends conceal a machine gun and a German prisoner in this Carnegie award-winning novel set in a small town during World War II.

1965. White, Dori. *Sarah and Katie* (4–6). Illus. by Trina Schart Hyman. 1972, Harper paper $1.95. A new girl in their sixth-grade class disturbs the friendship of Sarah and Katie.

1966. Willard, Barbara. *The Miller's Boy* (4–6). Illus. by Gareth Floyd. 1976, Dutton $7.95. Thomas, a lowly orphan, becomes friends with a squire in this novel of fifteenth-century England.

1967. Winthrop, Elizabeth. *Walking Away* (5–7). Illus. by Noelle Massena. 1973, Harper $6.89; Dell paper $.95. Emily's friend Nina doesn't fit in as expected when the 2 girls spend a summer with Emily's grandparents.

School Stories

1968. Beim, Jerrold. *Trouble after School* (5–7). Illus. by Don Sibley. 1957, Harcourt $5.50. Lee begins to run around with a rough crowd, and his grades start to slip.

1969. Branscum, Robbie. *The Three Wars of Billy Joe Treat* (5–7). 1975, McGraw $5.95; LB $5.72. During World War II, 13-year-old Billy Joe is waging 2 other wars, one against his mother who still treats him as a child and the other against his new teacher.

1970. Branscum, Robbie. *To the Tune of a Hickory Stick* (4–6). 1978, Doubleday $6.95. Two children, while escaping a cruel guardian, find refuge in a deserted schoolhouse.

1971. Byars, Betsy. *The 18th Emergency* (4–6). Illus. by Robert Grossman. 1973, Avon paper $1.25. A young boy, nicknamed Mousi, incurs the wrath of the school bully and awaits his inevitable punishment with fear.

1972. Carlson, Natalie Savage. *The Empty Schoolhouse* (3–5). Illus. by John Kaufmann. 1965, Harper $7.89. A 10-year-old black girl in a small Louisiana town endures loneliness and abuse as the first to integrate her school.

1973. Carlson, Natalie Savage. *Luvvy and the Girls* (4–6). Illus. by Thomas Di Grazia. 1971, Harper $5.95; LB $6.89; paper $1.50. In this novel, a sequel to *The Half Sisters* (1970, $6.89; paper $1.95), Luvvy Savage adjusts, sometimes with difficulty, to life at Visitation Academy.

1974. Caudill, Rebecca. *Did You Carry the Flag Today, Charley?* (2–5). Illus. by Nancy Grossman. 1966, Holt $5.95; paper $1.65. Contemporary Appalachia is the setting for the activities of Charley, an irrepressibly curious kindergartner who finally achieves the honor of carrying the school flag for his class—a signal of his early commitment to education.

1975. Colman, Hila. *The Case of the Stolen Bagels* (2–4). Illus. by Pat Grant Porter. 1977, Crown $5.95. Paul must prove his innocence when he becomes the prime suspect after the school's bagel supply is crumbled.

1976. Conford, Ellen. *Dear Lovey Hart, I Am Desperate* (6–7). 1975, Little $6.95; Scholastic paper $1.25. Freshman reporter Carrie Wasserman gets into trouble with her advice column in the school newspaper. A sequel is *We Interrupt This Semester for an Important Announcement* (1979, $7.95).

1977. Conford, Ellen. *The Revenge of the Incredible Dr. Rancid and His Youthful Assistant Jeffrey* (5–7). 1980, Brown $7.95; paper $4.95. An 11-year-old boy tries to cope with the class bully.

1978. Corcoran, Barbara. *Sam* (5–8). Illus. by Barbara McGee. 1967, Atheneum paper $1.25. Until her junior year in high school, Sam had been taught at home on an island. When she leaves the island, Sam must learn to adjust to school, friends, and life in general.

1979. Danziger, Paula. *The Cat Ate My Gymsuit* (6–8). 1974, Delacorte $6.95; LB $6.46. Marcy will go to any lengths to get out of going to gym and to defend an English teacher she feels has been wrongly dismissed.

1980. Estes, Eleanor. *The Hundred Dresses* (3–5). Illus. by Louis Slobodkin. 1944, Harcourt $6.95; paper $1.50. A little Polish girl in an American school finally wins acceptance by her classmates.

1981. Fitzhugh, Louise. *Harriet the Spy* (4–6). Illus. by author. 1964, Harper $7.95; LB $7.89; Dell paper $1.50. Precocious, overprivileged Harriet darts around her Manhattan neighborhood ferreting out and writing down the worst and best on her scene, sparing no one. A provocative sequel, primarily about Harriet's friend Beth, is: *The Long Secret* (1965, Harper $8.95; LB $8.79; Dell, paper $1.50).

1982. Giff, Patricia Reilly. *Fourth-Grade Celebrity* (3–5). Illus. by Leslie Morrill. 1979, Delacorte $6.95; LB $6.46. Casey decides that she wants to become famous, and she does, in a most surprising way.

1983. Giff, Patricia Reilly. *Today Was a Terrible Day* (1–3). Illus. by Susanna Natti. 1980, Viking $6.95. Ronald is having a terrible day until his teacher writes him an understanding note.

1984. Girion, Barbara. *Joshua, the Czar and the Chicken Bone* (4–6). Illus. by Richard Cuffari. 1978, Scribner $7.95. Awkward Joshua gets help from Nicholai Romanoff, Czar of Markova.

1985. Gonzalez, Gloria. *The Glad Man* (4–6). 1975, Knopf $5.99; Dell paper $1.50. About trying to make the school baseball team and stopping an elderly man's eviction from the old school bus he calls home.

1986. Gray, Genevieve. *Sore Loser* (4–6). Illus. by Beth Krush and Joe Krush. 1974, Houghton $5.95. Told mostly through letters to a friend, this story has young Loren Ramsey recount his adventures adjusting to the sixth grade in a new school.

1987. Haywood, Carolyn. *"B" Is for Betsy* (3–4). Illus. by author. 1939, Harcourt $6.95; paper $1.95. Betsy's adventures in the first grade. Also use: *Betsy and Billie* (1941, $6.95), *Back to School with Betsy* (1943, $7.95; paper $1.95), and *Betsy and the Boys* (1945, $6.95; paper $1.95).

1988. Haywood, Carolyn. *Betsy's Play School* (3–5). Illus. by James Griffin. 1977, Morrow $6.95; LB $6.43. In this Betsy book, the young heroine manages a summer play school for neighborhood children. Also use: *Betsy's Busy Summer* (1956, $6.96), *Betsy's Winterhouse* (1958, $6.96), and *Snowbound with Betsy* (1962, $7.25; LB $6.96).

1989. Haywood, Carolyn. *"C" Is for Cupcake* (2–4). Illus. by author. 1974, Morrow $6.96. Cupcake is a pet rabbit that is brought to school and stays in the schoolroom with first-grade children. An excellent "chapter" story for independent readers in the primary grades.

1990. Haywood, Carolyn. *Here Comes the Bus!* (2–4). Illus. by author. 1963, Morrow $6.96. A first-grader's wonderfully funny adventures on the school bus. Also use the Penny stories, such as: *Here's a Penny* (1944, Harcourt, paper $1.75), and *Penny and Peter* (1946, Harcourt $6.95).

1991. Hentoff, Nat. *This School Is Driving Me Crazy* (6–8). 1975, Delacorte $6.95; Dell paper $1.25. Sam objects to attending the school where his father is headmaster, particularly after he is accused of bullying a younger student.

1992. Hodges, Margaret. *The Making of Joshua Cobb* (4–7). Illus. by W. T. Mars. 1971, Farrar $4.50. Many changes take place in 12-year-old Josh when he must adjust to life in a boarding school.

1993. Kerr, M. E. *Is That You, Miss Blue?* (6–9). 1975, Harper $6.50; LB $7.89; Dell paper $1.25. The chronicle of Flanders Brown's first year in a private prep school during which she meets an amazing group of students and teachers, almost gets expelled, and solves some personal problems.

1994. Kingman, Lee. *The Meeting Post: A Story of Lapland* (3–5). Illus. by Des Asmussen. 1972, Crowell $3.95; LB $5.79. An 8-year-old boy, growing up with his grandmother in Finnish Lapland, must leave his comfortable environment to live in a dormitory and attend school.

1995.   Langton, Jane. *The Boyhood of Grace Jones* (4–6). Illus. by Emily McCully. 1972, Harper $8.79; paper $1.50. Grace successfully weathers the perils and pitfalls of adolescence while coping with junior high school. A sequel to *Her Majesty, Grace Jones* (1974, $6.89; paper $2.95).

1996.   Levitin, Sonia. *The Mark of Conte* (6–9). Illus. by Bill Negron. 1976, Atheneum $7.95; paper $1.95. When Conte receives 2 high school program cards because of a complex error, he decides to become 2 students and complete high school in half the time.

1997.   Lovelace, Maud H. *Betsy-Tacy* (3–4). Illus. by Lois Lenski. 1940, Crowell $7.89; Har-Row paper $1.95. Two 5-year-olds are inseparable at school and at play. One of a popular series.

1998.   McNeill, Janet. *Wait for It and Other Stories* (6–9). 1979, Faber paper $2.95. British school life as seen through the eyes of 12 students.

1999.   Merrill, Jean. *Maria's House* (3–5). Illus. by Frances Gruse Scott. 1974, Atheneum $4.95. An art class assignment to draw one's own home causes Maria problems because she lives in a tenement.

2000.   Miles, Betty. *Maudie and Me and the Dirty Book* (5–7). 1980, Random $6.95; LB $6.99. Kate, a sixth-grader, becomes involved in a censorship case involving a first-grade book about birth.

2001.   Murray, Michele. *Nellie Cameron* (4–6). Illus. by Leonore E. Prince. 1971, Seabury $6.95. Nine-year-old Nellie feels out of place in her big black family and has trouble learning to read. With the help of a sympathetic teacher, she makes progress.

2002.   Nordstrom, Ursula. *The Secret Language* (3–5). Illus. by Mary Chalmers. 1960, Harper $7.89; paper $1.95. Boarding school problems begin to look smaller to shy, homesick Vicky when she and her rebelliously outspoken roommate confound the school with their secret language.

2003.   Peck, Robert Newton. *Mr. Little* (4–6). Illus. by Ben Stahl. 1979, Doubleday $6.95; LB $7.90. A new teacher takes over from beloved Miss Kelogg.

2004.   Perl, Lila. *That Crazy April* (5–7). 1974, Seabury $6.95. Scholastic paper $.95. An identity crisis occurs when Chris is torn between a liberated mother and a traditional male teacher.

2005.   Pevsner, Stella. *Cute Is a Four-Letter Word* (6–8). 1980, Houghton $7.95. Clara thinks she is in for a great year—but events prove otherwise.

2006.   Pevsner, Stella. *A Smart Kid like You* (5–7). 1975, Seabury $7.50; Scholastic paper $1.25. Nina's adjustment to a new junior high school becomes more complicated when she discovers that her math teacher is her new stepmother.

2007.   Sachs, Marilyn. *Amy and Laura* (4–6). Illus. by Tracy Sugaman. 1966, Doubleday $4.95. Two sisters face problems at school and at home.

2008.   Sachs, Marilyn. *The Bears' House* (4–7). Illus. by Louis Glanzman. 1971, Doubleday $5.95. A poor girl escapes from reality by living in a fantasy in her classroom.

2009.   Sachs, Marilyn. *Marv* (4–6). Illus. by Louis Glanzman. 1970, Doubleday $4.95; Dell paper $.75. The schemes of Peter and Veronica's daydreaming classmate are endless and impractical.

2010.   Sachs, Marilyn. *Veronica Ganz* (4–6). Illus. by Louis Glanzman. 1968, Doubleday $6.95; paper $1.25. Set in pre–World War II Massachusetts, the contemporary issues faced by this 11-year-old anti-heroine girl bully will appeal to younger girls, as will the sequel (same prices): *Peter and Veronica* (1969).

2011.   Simon, Norma. *We Remember Philip* (2–4). Illus. by Ruth Sanderson. 1979, Whitman $5.25; LB $3.94. Sam and his classmates sympathize when the son of a favorite teacher is killed.

2012.   Sharmat, Marjorie W. *Maggie Marmelstein for President* (4–6). Illus. by Ben Shecter. 1975, Harper $5.95; LB $6.89; paper $1.95. The world of sixth-grade politics is explored in this good-natured novel.

2013.   Tennant, Veronica. *On Stage, Please* (5–7). Illus. by Rita Briansky. 1979, Holt $7.95. A day-by-day account of the training of a ballet student.

2014.   Williams, Ursula. *No Ponies for Miss Pobjoy* (6–9). 1975, Nelson $6.50. At Canterdown School for Girls, the new headmistress is uncomfortable with the "horsey" background

2015.   Windsor, Patricia. *Mad Martin* (5–6). 1976, Harper $5.95; LB $6.89; paper $1.95. Martin, considered mad by his London schoolmates, is actually only lonely and confused.

2016.   Woolley, Catherine. *Ginnie and Geneva* (3–5). Illus. by Iris Beatty Johnson. 1948, Morrow $7.25. Ginnie has problems in her new school, but friend Geneva helps. Also use: *Ginnie and Her Juniors* (1963, $7.25) and *Ginnie and the Cooking Contest* (1966, $6.96).

Adventure and Mystery

2017. Adkins, Jan. *Luther Tarbox* (5–7). 1977, Scribner $5.95. In this rollicking sea tale, a sailor helps a number of assorted vessels back to port in a fog.

2018. Adler, David A. *Cam Jansen and the Mystery of the Stolen Diamonds* (2–4). 1980, Viking $4.95. Cam is captured by diamond thieves but still manages to keep in charge.

2019. Adrian, Mary. *The Fireball Mystery* (3–5). Illus. by Reisie Lonette. 1977, Hastings $5.95. Two youngsters uncover a UFO hoax. Also use: *The Mystery of the Dinosaur Bones* (1965, Hastings $3.84).

2020. Agle, Nan H., and Wilson, Ellen. *Three Boys and a Lighthouse* (2–4). Illus. by Marian Honigman. 1951, Scribner LB $6.95; paper $.95. Triplets assist their father, a lighthouse keeper; with factual information on lighthouses woven into the plot.

2021. Aiken, Joan. *Black Hearts in Battersea* (6–8). 1964, Doubleday $4.50; Dell paper $.95. Simon, a 14-year-old orphan, becomes entangled in uncovering a Hanoverian plot against King James.

2022. Aiken, Joan. *Go Saddle the Sea* (4–6). 1977, Doubleday $7.95. A 12-year-old orphan has many adventures while seeking his inheritance in early nineteenth-century England.

2023. Aiken, Joan. *Midnight Is a Place* (6–8). 1974, Viking $6.95. The sweatshops of industrial-age England form the backdrop of a story about a young boy fighting for his rightful inheritance.

2024. Aiken, Joan. *Nightbirds on Nantucket* (5–7). Illus. by Robin Jacques. 1966, Dell paper $1.25. An intrepid English heroine awakens aboard a Nantucket whaler and is drawn into a series of dramatic and comic adventures.

2025. Aiken, Joan. *Not What You Expected* (5–9). 1974, Doubleday $5.95. A collection of short stories told with the usual style and imagination that have long characterized this author's writing.

2026. Aiken, Joan. *The Wolves of Willoughby Chase* (4–6). Illus. by Pat Marriott. 1963, Doubleday $5.95. Dell paper $1.25. A Victorian melodrama about 2 little girls who outwit their wicked governess-guardian and the wolves who rampage about the English country manor.

2027. Allan, Mabel Esther. *Catrin in Wales* (6–8). 1961, Vanguard $5.95. A charming heroine finds mystery, disaster, and romance in Gwenfron.

2028. Allan, Mabel Esther. *The Rising Tide* (6–9). 1978, Walker $6.95. A teenager inherits 3 small islands near Wales and a mysterious cache of explosives.

2029. Allen, Linda. *Lionel and the Spy Next Door* (3–5). Illus. by Margot Apple. 1980, Morrow $6.95; LB $6.67. Lionel is convinced that his new neighbor named Mark Shakespeare is really a spy.

2030. Allen, Sybil, and Tomelty, Roma. *Lisamor's Child* (6–9). 1975, Nelson $5.95. Kate tries to lift the curse from her family home in this Gothic mystery.

2031. Anckarsvard, Karin. *The Mysterious Schoolmaster* (4–6). Illus. by Paul Galdone. 1959, Harcourt $6.50; paper $1.35. A fast-moving mystery story about spies in a Swedish coastal town. Also use: *The Robber Ghost* (1961, Harcourt $6.50; paper $1.50).

2032. Anderson, Mary. *Matilda Investigates* (4–6). Illus. by Carl Anderson. 1973, Atheneum $5.95. Matty and her brother Jonathan do some sleuthing on New York's upper West Side. Also use: *Just the Two of Them* (1974, Atheneum $6.95).

2033. Anderson, Lonzo. *Ponies of Mykillengi* (3–5). 1966, Harcourt $5.95. Two Icelandic youngsters weather a volcano eruption while their pony is giving birth.

2034. Arden, William. *Alfred Hitchcock and the Three Investigators in the Secret of Shark Reef* (4–8). 1979, Random $1.50. Offshore oil drilling, sharks, and a hurricane are elements in this exciting story.

2035. Arthur, Ruth. *After Candlemas* (5–7). Illus. by Margery Gill. 1974, Atheneum $5.25. Harriet tries to help a teenage boy in this English story of witchcraft.

2036. Ashley, Bernard. *A Kind of Wild Justice* (6–9). Illus. by Charles Keeping. 1979, Phillips $8.95. An English story about underworld life set in present-day London.

2037. Asimov, Isaac. *The Key Words and Other Mysteries* (4–6). Illus. by Rod Burke. 1978, Walker $5.95; LB $5.85. Five short stories about young Larry, an ingenious amateur sleuth.

2038. Association for Childhood Education International. *And Everywhere, Children!* (4–6). 1979, Greenwillow $8.95. An anthology of excerpts from books set in different lands.

2039. Babbitt, Natalie. *Goody Hall* (4–6). Illus. by author. 1971, Farrar $6.95. Gothic mystery told with suspense and humor, centering around the magnificent home of the Goody family.

2040. Babbitt, Natalie. *Kneeknock Rise* (4–7). 1970, Farrar $5.95. Avon paper $1.50. Young Egan sets out to see the people-eating Megrimum.

2041. Bannon, Laura. *When the Moon Is New* (3–5). Illus. by author. 1953, Whitman $5.95. A mystery, a journey, and a great surprise give action and suspense to this colorful story of a Seminole child in the Everglades.

2042. Bawden, Nina. *Devil by the Sea* (5–6). 1976, Lippincott $6.95. No one believes Hilary when she claims to know the identity of a child murderer in this suspenseful English story.

2043. Bawden, Nina. *Rebel on a Rock* (5–7). 1978, Lippincott $7.95. Twelve-year-old Jo becomes involved in foreign intrigue and a possible rebellion.

2044. Bawden, Nina. *The Witch's Daughter* (4–6). 1966, Lippincott $6.95. A blind girl, her brother, and an outcast called the witch's daughter find jewels hidden by smugglers.

2045. Benary-Isbert, Margot. *Blue Mystery* (4–6). Illus. by Enrico Arno. 1957, Harcourt $5.95; paper $1.75. A beautiful new flower is developed by the heroine's father, and when it is stolen, suspicion falls on an apprentice, in this tale set in Germany.

2046. Benary-Isbert, Margot. *The Long Way Home* (6–9). 1959, Harcourt $5.95. A 13-year-old boy escapes from East Germany and comes to the United States.

2047. Bernheim, Marc, and Bernheim, Evelyne. *The Drums Speak: The Story of Kofi, a Boy of West Africa* (3–6). Illustrated. 1972, Harcourt $6.50. Kofi conquers his fear of heights and gains a respected place in his tribe.

2048. Blades, Ann. *A Boy of Tache* (3–5). Illustrated. 1977, Scribner $5.95; paper $2.95. A novel of life in Tache, an Indian reservation in northwest Canada, which focuses on a young boy and a trapping expedition.

2049. Beatty, Patricia. *I Want My Sunday Stranger!* (6–8). 1977, Morrow $8.25; LB $7.92. Andrew Lancy's quest to retrieve his horse, stolen by a Confederate soldier, ends at the Battle of Gettysburg.

2050. Beckett, Hilary. *Rafael and the Raiders* (4–6). Illus. by Leonard Shortall. 1972, Dodd $3.95. A Mexican boy on a visit to New York becomes involved in a robbery at the Metropolitan Museum of Art.

2051. Bellairs, John. *The Treasure of Alpheus Winterborn* (5–7). Illus. by Judith Gwyn Brown.

1978, Harcourt $6.95. A boy's family problems encourage him to seek a buried treasure.

2052. Bodelson, Anders. *Operation Cobra* (5–7). Trans. by Joan Tate. 1979, Nelson $6.95. Three classmates in Copenhagen try to foil a terrorist's plot.

2053. Bodker, Cecil. *The Leopard* (4–6). 1975, Antheneum $7.95. A Danish novel of adventure and suspense set in Ethiopia.

2054. Bodker, Cecil. *Silas and Ben-Godik* (5–7). Trans. from the Danish by Sheila LaFarge. 1978, Delacorte $7.95. Two boys share adventures in this sequel to *Silas the Black Mare* by the Hans Christian Anderson award winner.

2055. Bodker, Cecil. *Silas and the Black Mare* (5–7). Trans. from the Danish by Sheila LaFarge. 1978, Delacorte $6.95; LB $6.46. An adventure story in which a clever boy retains possession of his horse.

2056. Bodker, Cecil. *Silas and the Runaway Coach* (5–7). Trans. from the Danish by Sheila LaFarge. 1978, Delacorte $7.95. In the third book about him, Silas settles down with a wealthy family.

2057. Bond, Ann Sharpless. *Saturdays in the City* (3–5). Illus. by Leonard Shortall. 1979, HM $7.95. A pair of enterprising young boys spends adventurous times in the big city.

2058. Bonham, Frank. *Mystery of the Fat Cat* (5–7). Illus. by Alvin Smith. 1968, Dutton $7.95; Dell paper $1.25. Four Oak Street Boys Club members set out to prove foul play in the death of a cat so the slum neighborhood club can have a half-million-dollar legacy an eccentric originally left to the pet. The sequel: *The Nitty Gritty* (1968, Dutton $6.96).

2059. Bosworth, J. Allan. *White Water, Still Water* (5–7). Illus. by Charles Walker. 1966, Archway paper $1.50. Exciting adventure story of a 13-year-old boy's fight for survival when he is swept 100 miles downriver on a raft.

2060. Bradbury, Bianca. *Two on an Island* (4–6). Illus. by Robert MacLean. 1965, Houghton $6.95. Two children are marooned on a tiny island just offshore from a large city.

2061. Branscum, Robbie. *Three Buckets of Daylight* (3–4). 1978, Lothrop $5.95; LB $5.49. When he steals some apples, Jackie is cursed by a witch.

2062. Brontë, Charlotte. *Jane Eyre* (6–9). Illus. by Ati Forberg. 1962, Macmillan $6.95. The immortal love story of Jane and Mr. Rochester in a fine edition.

2063. Brontë, Emily. *Wuthering Heights* (6–9). Illus. by Bernarda Bryson. 1963, Macmillan $4.95. Heathcliff, Kathy, and their tragic love story in one of many available editions.

2064. Brookins, Dana. *Alone in Wolf Hollow* (5–7). 1978, Seabury $6.95. Two orphans move in with an alcoholic uncle and encounter murder.

2065. Brown, Michael, ed. *A Cavalcade of Sea Legends* (5–8). Illus. by Krystyna Turska. 1972, Walck $9.50. Sinbad, the Flying Dutchman, plus some less familiar characters, makes this a treasure trove of sea tales.

2066. Brown, Roy. *The Viaduct* (5–7). 1968, Macmillan $4.50. An eerie mystery set in contemporary England. Orphaned Phil Benson inherits a trunk of papers, and with the help of Mr. Felix and his knowledge of early railroading, Phil deciphers and discovers the revolutionary locomotive built by the engineering genius.

2067. Brown, Roy. *The White Sparrow* (6–8). 1975, Seabury $6.95. Two young boys continue their shiftless roaming life as outcasts in London, begun in *Flight of Sparrows* (1973, Macmillan $4.95).

2068. Budbill, David. *Bones on Black Spruce Mountain* (5–8). 1978, Dial $6.95; LB $6.46. In a sequel to *Snowshoe Trek to Otter River*, Seth and Daniel again encounter adventure on a camping trip.

2069. Budbill, David. *Snowshoe Trek to Otter River* (5–9). Illustrated. 1976, Dial $5.95; LB $5.47. Three complete short stories of 2 boys who camp in the wilderness at different times of the year.

2070. Bulla, Clyde Robert. *Down the Mississippi* (4–6). Illus. by Peter Burchard. 1954, Crowell $7.95; paper $.95. Various exciting escapades of a farm boy on the Mississippi River.

2071. Bulla, Clyde Robert. *Riding the Pony Express* (2–4). Illus. by Grace Paull. 1948, Crowell $6.89. Adventures of 2 boys, one a city dude, the other a Pony Express rider's son. Also use: *Surprise for a Cowboy* (1950, Crowell $8.95).

2072. Bulla, Clyde Robert. *Viking Adventure* (3–5). Illus. by Douglas Gorsline. 1963, Crowell $6.49. Young Sigurd's endurance is put to the test on a long, dangerous voyage.

2073. Bunting, Eve. *The Ghost of Summer* (6–8). 1977, Warne $4.69. Kevin tries to find the booty of a hanged highwayman.

2074. Burnham, Sophy. *The Dogwalker* (6–9). 1979, Warne $7.95. Two friends must find a dog with a bomb attached to her collar.

2075. Butterworth, Oliver. *The Narrow Passage* (4–6). Illus. by Erik Blegvad. 1973, Atlantic/Little $6.95. Nate Twitchell of *The Enormous Egg* returns as part of an expedition exploring caves in southern France.

2076. Cameron, Eleanor. *The Terrible Churnadryne* (4–6). Illus. by Beth Krush and Joe Krush. 1959, Atlantic/Little $6.95; Archway paper $.75. Two children think that a shape in the fog is a prehistoric monster.

2077. Campbell, Hope. *A Peak beneath the Moon* (4–6). 1979, Four Winds $6.95. Maggie discovers why a large tower in the center of a square lot was never completed.

2078. Carey, M. V. *Alfred Hitchcock and the Three Investigators in the Mystery of the Sinister Scarecrow* (4–7). 1979, Random $4.99. A living scarecrow and killer ants are 2 of the obstacles encountered by 3 heroes in this fast-paced adventure.

2079. Carlson, Natalie Savage. *Sailors' Choice* (4–6). Illus. by George Loh. 1966, Harper $7.89. An orphan stows away on a seal hunting ship and is befriended by the captain and an appealing Newfoundland dog.

2080. Carroll, Ruth, and Carroll, Latrobe. *Beanie* (3–5). Illus. by Ruth Carroll. 1953, Walck $5.95. A small boy in the Great Smoky Mountains and his new puppy run into bear trouble. Sequel: *Runaway Dog* (1963, Walck $5.25).

2081. Catherall, Arthur. *Prisoners in the Snow* (4–6). 1967, Lothrop $6.00. An avalanche tale set in the Austrian Alps.

2082. Christopher, Matt. *Stranded* (3–5). Illus. by Gail Owens. 1974, Little $5.95. After a shipwreck, Andy and his guide dog, Max, are stranded on a small island.

2083. Church, Richard. *Five Boys in a Cave* (4–6). 1951, John Day $6.95. The Tomahawk Club explores a cave.

2084. Clark, Mavis Thorpe. *Wild Fire* (5–7). 1974, Macmillan $5.95. Five youngsters caught in a raging fire in Australia.

2085. Cleaver, Vera, and Cleaver, Bill. *A Little Destiny* (6–9). 1979, Morrow $6.95; LB $6.48. A spunky heroine tries to avenge her father's death.

2086. Clewes, Dorothy. *Missing from Home* (6–9). 1978, Harcourt $6.95. Two English girls hatch a kidnapping plot to bring their parents back together again.

2087. Clifford, Eth. *The Curse of the Moonraker: A Tale of Survival* (5–8). 1977, Houghton $6.95. Cat, a young cabin boy, tells of the shipwreck of the square-rigger *Moonraker*.

2088. Clifford, Eth. *Help! I'm a Prisoner in the Library* (3–5). Illus. by George Hughes. 1979, Houghton $7.95. Two youngsters are locked in a library after it closes.

2089. Clymer, Eleanor. *Santiago's Silver Mine* (3–5). Illus. by Ingrid Fetz. 1973, Atheneum $4.50. In this first-person narrative set in a Mexican village, Santiago hopes to find a treasure for his poor family in an abandoned silver mine.

2090. Clymer, Eleanor. *Take Tarts as Tarts as Passing* (2–4). Illus. by Roy Doty. 1974, Dutton $5.50. Two very different brothers seek their fortunes.

2091. Coatsworth, Elizabeth. *The Princess and the Lion* (4–6). Illus. by Evaline Ness. 1963, Pantheon $5.99. Adventure and suspense in ancient Abyssinia; a young princess strives to reach her imprisoned brother who is to be the new king.

2092. Cobalt, Martin. *Pool of Swallows* (6–9). 1974, Nelson $6.95. An adventure-mystery that explores happenings involving 3 pools of water situated by a house, supposedly haunted, in a rural English community.

2093. Cohen, Peter Z. *Fool Creek* (6–9). Illus. by Alan Mayler. 1972, Atheneum $5.95. By going on a camping trip, a boy unwillingly helps his brother bring back a cache of marijuana.

2094. Collier, James Lincoln. *The Teddy Bear Habit or How I Became a Winner* (6–8). Illus. by Lee Lorenz. 1967, Dell paper $.95. High comic adventure of a boy who clings to his old teddy bear throughout a chase-crime-adventure set in New York City.

2095. Colum, Padraic. *Children's Homer: The Adventures of Odysseus and the Tale of Troy* (6–9). Illustrated. 1962, Macmillan $5.50. A brilliant retelling by the Irish poet.

2096. Conn, Martha Orr. *Crazy to Fly* (6–9). Illus. by Richard Cuffari. 1978, Atheneum $7.95. Tommy's desire to fly conflicts with his farm work in this story of the early days of aircraft.

2097. Corbett, Scott. *Captain Butcher's Body* (4–6). Illus. by Geff Gerlach. 1976, Atlantic/Little $5.95. Two cousins are brought together by a story they read of piracy, buried treasures, and the ghost of Captain Butcher.

2098. Corbett, Scott. *The Great McGonigle Rides Shotgun* (2–4). Illus. by Bill Ogden. 1977, Atlantic/Little $5.95. McGoniggle and friend Ken foil a robbery but in turn receive their due.

2099. Corbett, Scott. *The Red Room Riddle* (4–6). Illus. by Geff Gerlach. 1972, Atlantic/Little $5.95. A scary story of 2 boys in a haunted house in the 1920s.

2100. Corbett, Scott. *Tree House Island* (6–9). 1959, Atlantic/Little $6 95. Two boys in New England discover mystery and adventure when 2 suspicious visitors come to their seaside village.

2101. Corcoran, Barbara. *The Clown* (5–8). 1975, Atheneum $6.95. Lisa uses her American uncle's passport and clothes to smuggle from Russia a clown who is in danger for political reasons. Also use: *Meet Me at Tamerlane's Tomb* (1975, Atheneum $6.95).

2102. Corcoran, Barbara. *The Long Journey* (5–7). Illus. by Charles Robinson. 1970, Atheneum LB $5.50 paper $1.25. Laurie rides alone across Montana to get help for her grandfather.

2103. Corcoran, Barbara, and Angier, Bradford. *A Star to the North* (6–9). 1970, Nelson $4.95. A teenage brother and sister make a perilous journey together across the Canadian wilderness.

2104. Crayder, Dorothy. *The Riddles of Mermaid House* (4–6). 1977, Atheneum $7.95. A young girl, having recently moved to a New England seacoast town, tries to discover why the community hates an elderly recluse.

2105. Crayder, Dorothy. *She, the Adventuress* (4–6). Illus. by Velma Ilsley. 1973, Atheneum $5.95; paper $1.95. Maggie finds fun, adventure, and mystery on her sea trip to visit an aunt in Italy. Also use: *She and the Dubious Three* (1974, Atheneum $6.95).

2106. Cresswell, Helen. *The Beachcombers* (4–6). 1972, Macmillan $5.95. A missing treasure, a boy held by a group of thieves, and a family of beachcombers are elements combined in this suspenseful adventure.

2107. Cumberlege, Vera. *Shipwreck* (3–5). Illus. by Charles Mikolaycak. 1974, Follett $4.95; LB $4.98. A young boy witnesses a disaster at sea and the efforts to effect a rescue.

2108. Curry, Jane Louise. *The Bassumtyte Treasure* (5–7). 1978, Atheneum $6.95. The discovery of hidden treasure enables Tommy to continue to stay with his grandmother.

2109. Curry, Jane Louise. *Ghost Lane* (5–7). 1979, Atheneum $7.95. An English story about a young boy's involvement with a series of art thefts.

2110. Curry, Jane Louise. *The Ice Ghosts Mystery* (4–6). 1972, Atheneum $7.25; paper $1.95. The

Bird family members set out to find their lost father.

2111.   Davies, Andrew. *Conrad's War* (4–6). 1980, Crown $7.95. An English boy's fascination with war games leads to exciting, often hilarious situations.

2112.   Davis, Burke. *Runaway Balloon: The Last Flight of Confederate Air Force One* (4–6). Illus. by Sal. Murdocca. 1976, Coward $5.95. A humorous fictionalized account of an actual Civil War incident involving 2 flights in a balloon by Confederate John Randolph Bryan.

2113.   Day, Veronique. *Landslide!* (5–7). Illus. by Margot Tomes. 1963, Dell paper $1.25. Five youngsters are caught in a landslide and buried in a lonely cottage.

2114.   Degens, T. *The Game on Thatcher Island* (4–6). 1977, Viking $6.95. On a small island, 3 youngsters narrowly escape serious injury at the hands of sadistic boys.

2115.   DeJong, Meindert. *A Horse Came Running* (5–7). Illus. by Paul Sagsoorian. 1970, Macmillan $5.95; paper $1.25. A boy tries to cope with a tornado's effects on his parents, neighbors, and animals.

2116.   Dickinson, Peter. *Annerton Pit* (6–8). 1977, Little $6.95. Blind, 13-year-old Jake helps free his grandfather and brother from revolutionists.

2117.   Dickinson, Peter. *Emma Tupper's Diary* (6–9). Illus. by David Omar White. 1971, Little $5.95. Emma and her 2 male cousins hatch a scheme to trick the news media in this novel set in the Scottish Highlands.

2118.   Dickinson, Peter. *The Gift* (6–9). 1974, Little $6.95. Davy's telepathic gift leads him into a murderous plot in which his father is the scapegoat.

2119.   Dicks, Terrance. *The Baker Street Irregulars in the Case of the Missing Masterpiece* (5–6). 1979, Elsevier $6.95. A group of youngsters solves a crime, catches the villain, and prevents a murder.

2120.   Dixon, Paige. *The Loner: A Story of the Wolverine* (5–7). Illus. by Grambs Miller. 1978, Atheneum $6.95. A struggle for survival by a hunter and a wolverine.

2121.   Dixon, Paige. *Search for Charlie* (5–7). 1976, Atheneum $6.95. In the Montana mountains, Jane participates in a search for her missing younger brother. Also use: *Lion on the Mountain* (1972, Atheneum $6.95).

2122.   Dodd, Wayne. *A Time of Hunting* (6–9). 1975, Seabury $6.95. Several events in young

Jess's life change his attitude toward hunting from enthusiasm to abhorrence.

2123.   Doty, Jean Slaughter. *The Crumb* (5–7). 1976, Greenwillow $6.00; Scholastic paper $.95. Cindy finds mystery and adventure when she takes a part-time job at the Ashford stables to help with the expenses caused by her pony, Crumb.

2124.   Doyle, Arthur Conan. *The Boy's Sherlock Holmes* (6–9). 1961, Harper $8.95; LB $8.79. An excellent collection of the most famous cases.

2125.   Duncan, Lois. *I Know What You Did Last Summer* (6–9). 1973, Little $6.95. The mysterious avenger torments 4 teenagers who have tried to hide their involvement in a hit-and-run death.

2126.   Dunlop, Eileen. *The House on Mayferry Street* (6–8). Illus. by Phillida Gili. 1977, Holt $6.50. An old letter, a missing trunk, and strange flute music are ingredients in this mystery set in Edinburgh.

2127.   Dunnahoo, Terry. *This Is Espie Sanchez* (5–7). 1976, Dutton $6.95. In this second book about Espie, she continues her work with an auxiliary law enforcement group in Los Angeles. Also use: *Who Cares about Espie Sanchez?* (1975, $6.95) and *Who Needs Espie Sanchez?* (1977, $7.95).

2128.   Duran, Cheli. *Kindling* (6–9). 1979, Greenwillow $6.95; LB $6.67. In Crete in 1970, some boys are unjustly held prisoner.

2129.   Ecke, Wolfgang. *The Face at the Window* (5–9). Trans. from German by Stella and Vernon Humphries. Illus. by Rolf Rettich. 1979, Prentice-Hall $7.95. Various European settings are used in these short, solve-it-yourself mysteries.

2130.   Ellis, Ella Thorp. *Roam the Wild Country* (6–8). Illus. by Bret Schlesinger. 1967, Atheneum paper $.95. Top-form action and adventure as men, boys, and horses desperately outrace the herd's almost sure death on Argentina's drought-stricken pampas.

2131.   Ellis, Melvin R. *Caribou Crossing: A Novel* (6–9). 1971, Holt $4.95. Eighteen-year-old Danny and his Indian friend Johnny attempt to establish a fishing resort in the northern Canadian wilderness.

2132.   Enright, Elizabeth. *Gone-Away Lake* (4–6). Illus. by Beth Krush and Joe Krush. 1957, Harcourt $6.50; paper $1.95. An abandoned summer colony bordering a swamp leads to a vacation of glorious exploration for Julian and Portia.

2133.   Estes, Eleanor. *The Lost Umbrella of Kim Chu* (3–4). Illus. by Jacqueline Ayer. 1978, Atheneum $7.95. Kim and her friend MaeLee solve the mystery of a valuable lost umbrella.

2134. Estes, Eleanor. *The Tunnel of Hugsy Goode* (4–6). Illus. by Edward Ardizzone. 1972, Harcourt $5.95. Two boys investigate reports that an underground tunnel runs beneath a familiar alleyway. A warm and humorous sequel to *The Alley*.

2135. Farjeon, Annabel. *The Siege of Trapp's Mill* (5–8). 1974, Atheneum $4.95. Four boys fight off would-be invaders of their deserted mill in this novel set in northern England.

2136. Farley, Carol. *Ms. Isabelle Cornell, Herself* (5–7). 1980, Atheneum $7.95. Ibby must go to live with her new stepfather at an army base in Korea.

2137. Fecher, Constance. *The Leopard Dagger* (6–9). 1973, Farrar $4.95. An orphan sets out to find his identity with a dagger as his only clue, in this adventure story set in Elizabethan London.

2138. Fenner, Phyllis, ed. *The Endless Dark* (5–8). Illus. by Steve Marchesi. 1977, Morrow $7.25; LB $6.96. A theme of total isolation runs through these stories.

2139. Field, Rachel. *Calico Bush* (4–7). 1931, Macmillan $8.95; Dell paper $1.25. Maggie, a little French girl, was "loaned" to a family of American pioneers living in Maine during the days of the French and Indian Wars. A very exciting adventure tale.

2140. Fife, Dale. *Follow That Ghost!* (2–4). Illus. by Joan Drescher. 1979, Dutton $6.95. Two amateur sleuths discover that a tapping, troublesome ghost is really a woodpecker.

2141. Fife, Dale. *Who Goes There, Lincoln?* (3–5). Illus. by Paul Galdone. 1975, Coward $4.86. Lincoln Farnum's gang finds a new clubhouse and a mystery. Also use: *Who'll Vote for Lincoln?* (1977, Coward $4.97).

2142. Fisher, Leonard Everett. *Across the Sea from Galway* (4–6). Illus. by author. 1975, Four Winds $6.95. Young Patric Donavan survives a shipwreck after he is sent from Ireland to find a new life in America in 1849.

2143. Fleischman, Paul. *The Half-a-Moon Inn* (5–7). Illus. by Kathy Jacobi. 1980, Harper $7.95. A young mute boy sets out to find his mother lost in a violent snowstorm.

2144. Flora, James. *Grandpa's Ghost Stories* (2–4). Illus. by author. 1978, Atheneum $6.95. Three grisly short stories told by an old man to his grandson.

2145. Fort, John. *June the Tiger* (4–6). Illus. by Bernice Loewenstein. 1975, Little $5.95. A historical novel set in the rural South about the struggle Mrs. Pinckney and her mongrel dog have with a big black bear.

2146. Fox, Paula. *How Many Miles to Babylon?* (4–6). Illus. by Paul Giovanopoulos. 1967, David White $5.95. Tension and suspense when 10-year-old James Douglas is kidnapped by teenage dog thieves and held captive in an abandoned Coney Island fun house.

2147. Garfield, Leon. *Mister Corbett's Ghost* (5–8). Illus. by Alan E. Cober. 1968, Pantheon $5.69. Horror tale with eerie black-and-white drawings about an apothecary's apprentice in eighteenth-century London.

2148. Garfield, Leon. *Smith* (5–8). Illus. by Anthony Maitland. 1967, Pantheon $5.69. A 12-year-old pickpocket pursued by other thieves leads a swift-paced descent into eighteenth-century London's underground.

2149. Garrigue, Sheila. *All the Children Were Sent Away* (3–5). 1976, Bradbury $6.95. A based-on-fact account of an English girl's evacuation from London to Vancouver, Canada, during World War II.

2150. Gathorne-Hardy, Jonathan. *Operation Peeg* (4–6). Illus. by Glo Coalson. 1974, Lippincott $8.95. A high-spirited adventure story about classmates trapped on a remote Scottish island and a madman trying to take over the world.

2151. George, Jean Craighead. *My Side of the Mountain* (5–7). Illus. by author. 1959, Dutton $6.95; paper $1.95. Sam Gribley spends a winter alone in the Catskill Mountains and learns how to survive and be self-sufficient, although he ultimately realizes that he needs human companionship.

2152. George, Jean Craighead. *River Rats, Inc.* (4–7). 1979, Dutton $7.95. A run down the Colorado River turns into a story of survival.

2153. Gipson, Fred. *Curly and the Wild Boar* (4–6). Illus. by Ronald Himler. 1979, Harper $5.95; LB $6.49. Curly's encounter with a wild boar produces a ripsnorting adventure.

2154. Godden, Rumer. *The Rocking-Horse Secret* (4–6). Illus. by Juliet Stanwell Smith. 1978, Viking $6.95. Tibby solves many problems when she finds a will hidden in a rocking horse.

2155. Gottschalk, Elin Toona. *In Search of Coffee Mountain* (4–6). 1977, Nelson $6.95. After World War II, a young Estonian girl, her brave grandmother, and a great-uncle live in various camps for displaced persons while hoping to get to England.

2156. Gray, Nigel. *The Deserter* (4–6). Illus. by Ted Levin. 1977, Harper $7.95; LB $7.49. Four English children care for an army deserter and help him escape the police.

2157. Griese, Arnold A. *The Way of Our People* (4–6). Illus. by Haru Wells. 1975, Crowell $6.95; LB $8.79. Set in 1838, this story of an adolescent boy's growth to maturity is an accurate picture of life within the Alaska Anvik community.

2158. Hale, Nancy. *The Night of the Hurricane* (5–7). 1978, Coward $6.95. Gene isn't happy staying with his grandmother in New England until she proves her strength the night the hurricane strikes.

2159. Hall, Lynn. *The Mystery of the Schoolhouse Dog* (3–5). Illus. by William Hutchinson. 1979, Garrard $4.40. Is the white dog in the abandoned schoolhouse real or a ghost?

2160. Hallstead, William F. *The Man Downstairs* (6–9). 1979, Nelson $7.95. Political corruption is explored in this fast-moving novel for better readers.

2161. Hamilton, Virginia. *The House of Dies Drear* (5–8). Illus. by Eros Keith. 1968, Macmillan $7.95; paper $1.25. First-rate suspense as history professor Small and his young son Thomas investigate their rented house, formerly a station on the Underground Railroad, unlocking the secrets and dangers from attitudes dating back to the Civil War.

2162. Hamre, Leif. *Operation Arctic* (6–7). 1973, Atheneum $4.95. Trying to find their father, 3 children are isolated on a remote Arctic island.

2163. Harris, Christie. *Mystery at the Edge of Two Worlds* (5–7). Illus. by Lou Crockett. 1978, Atheneum $7.95. A shy girl comes almost out of her shell in a mystery set on the northwest coast of Canada.

2164. Harris, Rosemary. *The Bright and Morning Star* (5–8). 1972, Macmillan $4.95. The concluding volume of the prizewinning trilogy that includes *The Shadow on the Sun* (1970, Macmillan $5.95). Set in Kemi (ancient Egypt), this volume tells how innocent people become involved in a power struggle over who should rule the land.

2165. Harrison, Ted. *Children of the Yukon* (2–4). Illus. by author. 1977, Tundra $7.95. Life in present-day Yukon with a little historical material.

2166. Hayes, Geoffrey. *The Alligator and His Uncle Tooth: A Novel of the Sea* (3–5). Illus. by author. 1977, Harper $6.95; LB $6.89. Corduroy, an alligator, is fascinated by the sea yarns his old Uncle Tooth tells him.

2167. Healey, Larry. *The Claw of the Bear* (5–8). 1978, Watts $6.90. A young boy is stalked by a murderer of four campers in this outdoors story.

2168. Heide, Florence Parry, and Heide, Roxanne. *The Body in the Brillstone Garage* (5–7). 1980, Whitman $6.50. A familiar shirt and a missing cadaver are 2 elements in this exciting story.

2169. Heide, Florence Parry, and Heide, Roxanne. *Mystery of the Mummy's Mask* (3–6). Illus. by Seymour Fleishman. 1979, Whitman $5.95; LB $4.46. A nicely fashioned mystery in easily read language.

2170. Hicks, Clifford B. *Alvin's Swap Shop* (4–6). Illus. by Bill Sokol. 1976, Scholastic paper $1.25. A casual summer activity suddenly becomes the setting of a real detective activity when Alvin the Magnificent Brain takes over. Also use: *Alvin's Secret Code* (1963, Holt $6.50; Scholastic paper $.95) and *Alvin Fernald, Superweasel* (1974, Holt $5.95).

2171. Hightower, Florence C. *The Secret of the Crazy Quilt* (5–8). Illus. by Beth Krush and Joe Krush. 1972, Houghton $6.95. A novel that involves a retrospective retelling of events that took place during Prohibition.

2172. Hildick, E. W. *The Case of the Secret Scribbler* (3–5). Illus. by Lisl Weil. 1978, Macmillan $6.95. Jack McGurk, investigator, foils a robbery.

2173. Hildick, E. W. *The Case of the Treetop Treasure* (4–6). Illus. by Lisl Weil. 1980, Macmillan $7.95. A McGurk mystery that begins with the discovery of a hidden cache of unusual articles.

2174. Hildick, E. W. *Louie's Ransom* (4–6). 1978, Knopf $6.99. Milman Louis comes to New York and is kidnapped.

2175. Hildick, E. W. *The Top-Flight Fully-Automated Junior High School Girl Detective* (6–8). 1977, Archway paper $1.50. Allison, heroine of *The Active-Enzyme Lemon-Freshened Junior High School Witch* (1973, Doubleday $4.95), now sets out to solve the mystery of the theft of an important credit card.

2176. Hitchcock, Alfred, ed. *Alfred Hitchcock's Daring Detectives* (6–8). Illus. by Arthur Shilstone. 1969, Random $5.95; LB $5.99. Eleven thrillers from popular writers such as Agatha Christie and Ellery Queen. Also use: *Alfred Hitchcock's Supernatural Tales* (1973, Random $5.95; LB $5.99).

2177. Hobson, Sam B., and Cary, George. *The Lion of the Kalahari* (5–8). 1976, Greenwillow $7.25; LB $6.96. In this tale from southern Africa, a young boy sets out to avenge his father's murder.

2178. Hoke, Helen, ed. *Creepies, Creepies, Creepies: A Covey of Quiver and Quaver Tales* (6–9). Illus. by Bill Prosser. 1977, Watts $6.90. A spine-tingling collection of short stories and scenes taken chiefly from adult sources. Also use: *Devils, Devils,*

Devils (1975, Watts $6.90) and *Ghostly, Grim and Gruesome* (1977, Nelson $6.95).

2179. Hoke, Helen, ed. *Ghosts and Ghastlies* (6–8). Illus. by Bill Prosser. 1976, Watts $6.90. Stories and poems from well-known writers that should be appealing to better readers. Also use (both 1966, Watts $5.90): *Spooks, Spooks, Spooks* and *Haunts, Haunts, Haunts*.

2180. Hoke, Helen, selected by. *Terrors, Terrors, Terrors* (6–9). Illus. by Bill Prosser. 1979, Watts $5.90. Eleven goose-bump-producing stories chosen by the well-known anthologist.

2181. Holman, Felice. *Slake's Limbo* (5–7). 1974, Scribner $7.95; Dell paper $1.25. Thirteen-year-old Aremis Slake finds an ideal hideaway for 4 months in the labyrinth of the New York subway.

2182. Honness, Elizabeth. *Mystery of the Maya Jade* (5–7). Illus. by Paul Frame. 1971, Lippincott $7.95. Pam becomes involved with thieves who rob archaeological sites in this story set in modern Guatemala.

2183. Hooks, William H. *Maria's Cave* (2–4). Illus. by Victor Juhasz. 1977, Coward $6.95. Maria accompanied her father, an archaeologist, on his exploration of the Altamira Caves and was the first to see the striking Stone Age animal murals on the walls.

2184. Hopkins, Lee Bennett, comp. *Witching Time* (4–6). 1977, Whitman $7.75. A suitably scary collection with many humorous situations.

2185. Household, Geoffrey. *Escape into Daylight* (6–9). Little $5.95. Carrie, daughter of a famous film star, and young Mike are held prisoner by kidnappers in this English suspense story.

2186. Houston, James. *Frozen Fire* (6–8). Illus. by author. 1977, Atheneum $7.95. Two boys—one white and one Eskimo—set out on a rescue mission in the Far North.

2187. Hunter, Mollie. *The Third Eye* (6–9). 1979, Harper $7.95; LB $7.89. A young Scottish girl becomes involved in the investigation of the death of an old earl.

2188. Hutchins, Pat. *Follow That Bus!* (2–5). Illus. by Laurence Hutchins. 1977, Greenwillow $6.96. A school picnic becomes a cops-and-robbers chase involving 2 holdup men in this fast-moving English story.

2189. Ipcar, Dahlov. *Queen of Spells* (6–9). 1973, Viking $5.95. Janet must prove her love for a boy by courageous acts.

2190. Ireson, Barbara. *Haunting Tales* (4–6). Illus. by Freda Woolf. 1974, Dutton $6.95. A collection of hauntingly interesting stories about all kinds of ghosts.

2191. Jeffries, Roderic. *Against Time!* (5–8). Illus. by Robert Winsor. 1964, Harper paper $1.95. Scotland Yard Inspector Dunn has 24 hours to find his kidnapped son.

2192. Jeffries, Roderic. *Police Dog* (6–8). 1965, Harper $7.89; paper $1.50. Combination dog and detective story written in the police procedural vein, based on the methods used in England for training police dogs.

2193. Jeffries, Roderic. *Trapped* (5–8). 1972, Harper paper $1.25. Two boys are lost on the mud flats of a river in southeast England during a violent storm.

2194. Jennings, Gary. *The Rope in the Jungle* (6–8). 1976, Lippincott $7.95. An exciting tale about a boy and a man journeying through the jungle of southern Mexico.

2195. Johnson, Annabel and Johnson, Edgar. *The Grizzly* (5–7). 1964, Harper $7.89; Scholastic paper $1.95. A perceptive story of a father-son relationship in which David, on a camping trip, saves his father's life when a grizzly bear attacks.

2196. Judson, Clara Ingram. *Green Ginger Jar* (4–6). Illus. by Paul Parl. 1949, Houghton $6.95. A mystery involving a family in Chicago's Chinatown.

2197. Kahn, Joan, ed. *Some Things Weird and Wicked: Twelve Stories to Chill Your Bones* (6–9). 1976, Pantheon $5.95. A batch of varied, excellent thrillers, chiefly from well-known writers.

2198. Kastner, Erich. *Emil and the Detectives* (4–6). Illus. by Walter Trier. 1930, Doubleday $5.95. A thoroughly believable and highly amusing story of a boy who turns detective after being robbed while he slept.

2199. Kay, Mara. *In Face of Danger* (5–8). 1977, Crown $6.95. An English girl in pre–World War II Germany tries to help 2 Jewish girls who are in hiding.

2200. Keele, Luqman, and Pinkwater, Daniel. *Java Jack* (4–8). 1980, Crowell $7.95. A mystical journey in Indonesia by a 14-year-old boy searching for his parents.

2201. Kherdian, David. *It Started with Old Man Bean* (6–8). 1980, Greenwillow $7.95. A secret camping trip turns into an ordeal for 2 youngsters.

2202. Konigsburg, E. L. *Father's Arcane Daughter* (5–9). 1976, Atheneum $7.95; paper $1.95. When Caroline reappears after an absence of 17 years, everyone wonders if she is really an imposter in this complex suspense tale.

2203. Konigsburg, E. L. *From the Mixed-Up Files of Mrs. Basil E. Frankweiler* (5–7). Illus. by author. 1967, Atheneum $6.95; paper $1.95. Adventure, suspense, detection, and humor are involved when 12-year-old Claudia and her younger brother elude the security guards and live for a week in New York's Metropolitan Museum of Art. Newbery Award, 1968.

2204. Kusan, Ivan. *The Mystery of the Stolen Painting* (5–7). Illus. by Charles Robenson. 1975, Harcourt $7.95. Two young boys on a visit to Paris become involved with the disappearance of the *Mona Lisa*.

2205. Lasker, Joe. *The Strange Voyage of Neptune's Car* (2–4). Illus. by author. 1977, Viking $5.95. A fictional re-creation of a clipper ship race from New York around Cape Horn to San Francisco.

2206. Lawrence, Mildred. *Touchmark* (6–8). Illus. by Deanne Hollinger. 1975, Harcourt $7.50. A young girl hopes to become a pewterer's apprentice in pre-Revolutionary Boston.

2207. Leeson, Robert. *Silver's Revenge* (6–9). 1979, Collins $7.95. A suspenseful sequel to *Treasure Island*.

2208. Leigh, Bill. *The Far Side of Fear* (4–6). 1978, Viking $7.95. A survival story of four youngsters trapped in an underground network.

2209. L'Engle, Madeleine. *The Young Unicorns* (6–9). 1968, Farrar $6.95. Suspense builds as the invention of Dr. Austin's microlaser enmeshes his family in a bizarre plot to use it to control human minds. Also use 2 stories about the O'Keefes: *Dragons in the Water* (1976, Farrar $7.95) and *The Arm of the Starfish* (1965, Farrar $8.95).

2210. Levy, Elizabeth. *Frankenstein Moved in on the Fourth Floor* (2–4). 1979, Harper $7.95; LB $7.89. Is the strange Mr. Frank really Frankenstein?

2211. Levy, Elizabeth. *Something Queer at the Library: A Mystery* (2–4). Illus. by Mordecai Gerstein. 1977, Delacorte $6.95; LB $6.46; paper $2.75. Jill and Gwen try to track down the person who is mutilating books in the library. Also use: *Something Queer Is Going On* (1973, Delacorte $6.95; LB $6.46; paper $2.75) and *Lizzie Lies a Lot* (1976, Delacorte $6.95; LB $6.46; Dell paper $1.25).

2212. Lingard, Joan. *Snake among the Sunflowers* (6–8). 1977, Elsevier Nelson $6.95. While vacationing in France, the 3 Grant children become intrigued with their strange new neighbors.

2213. Lindquist, Willis. *Haji of the Elephants* (5–7). Illus. by Don Miller. 1976, McGraw $5.72. A young boy is determined that he will become an elephant handler for the great Majda Koom.

2214. Lively, Penelope. *A Stitch in Time* (4–6). 1976, Dutton $6.95. Eleven-year-old Maria is certain that she is gaining a direct connection with the past in this suspenseful English novel.

2215. McHargue, Georgess. *The Talking Table Mystery* (4–6). Illus. by Emanuel Schongut. 1977, Doubleday $5.95. Two youngsters find mystery and excitement when they discover some belongings of a medium in an attic.

2216. Macken, Walter. *The Flight of the Doves* (5–7). 1968, Macmillan $5.95; paper $.95. Two children flee a cruel stepfather in England to find their mother's home in Ireland.

2217. Macken, Walter. *Island of the Great Yellow Ox* (5–8). 1966, Macmillan $4.95. Four boys are swept onto an island off the Irish coast by a storm and become involved with a mad woman and her husband who are searching for ancient treasure.

2218. MacMillan, Bruce. *Finest Kind O'Day: Lobstering in Maine* (2–4). Illustrated. 1977, Lippincott $5.95. Young Brett spends a day as a helper aboard a lobster boat, the *Ruth M*.

2219. Manley, Seon. *The Ghost in the Far Garden and Other Stories* (6–9). Illus. by Emanuel Schongut. 1977, Lothrop $7.25; LB $6.96. Eleven original stories, each of which achieves a fairly high spine-tingle quotient.

2220. Masterman-Smith, Virginia. *The Treasure Trap* (5–8). Illus. by Roseanne Litzinger. 1979, Scholastic $7.95. An old man's disappearance sets off a mad treasure hunt.

2221. Mayne, William. *Royal Harry* (4–7). 1972, Dutton $6.25. Young Harriet inherits a house, a lake, a mountain, and a group of unusual inhabitants.

2222. Mayne, William. *The Yellow Airplane* (3–5). Illus. by Trevor Stubley. 1974, Nelson $6.95. Strange roaring sounds heard in the woods intrigue Rodney, a hostile girl Maureen, and a group known as the Bad Eggs.

2223. Mazer, Harry. *Snow Bound* (6–8). 1973, Delacorte $5.95; Dell paper $1.25. Two teenagers are caught in a blizzard in an isolated area.

2224. Mazer, Norma Fox, and Mazer, Harry. *The Solid Gold Kid* (5–9). 1977, Delacorte $6.95. Five adolescents are kidnapped, and each reacts differently to their harrowing situation.

2225. Melwood, Mary. *Nettlewood* (6–8). 1975, Seabury $8.95. In this English novel, the young heroine Lacie explores Nettlewood, a rundown manor house, and uncovers some interesting secrets.

2226. Miles, Miska. *Hoagie's Rifle Gun* (2–4). Illus. by John Schoenherr. 1970, Atlantic/Little $5.95. Hoagie, a boy in Appalachia, and his little brother go hunting for food, but when Hoagie misses his shot at Old Bob, a mountain cat, he discovers "you can't shoot a thing when you know it by name"—no matter how hungry you are.

2227. Miller, Ruth. *The City Rose* (4–7). 1977, McGraw $6.95. Mystery and danger are combined in this story of an orphaned black girl's stay with a hostile uncle in a southern rural area.

2228. Milton, Hilary. *Emergency! 10-33 on Channel* (5–7). 1977, Watts $5.90. A family gets lost in a storm and is saved through the use of their CB radio.

2229. Milton, Hilary. *Mayday! Mayday!* (5–8). 1979, Watts $6.90. Two boys make their way to safety after a plane wreck.

2230. Moore, S. E. *Secret Island* (5–7). Illus. by Judith Gwyn Brown. 1977, Four Winds $7.95. An exciting yarn about 2 boys and their attempts to catch a gang of renegade Confederate soldiers who have stolen an army payroll.

2231. Morey, Walt. *Canyon Winter* (5–7). 1972, Dutton $7.95. A hermit helps a young surviver of a plane crash.

2232. Morey, Walt. *Deep Trouble* (5–9). 1971, Dutton $6.95. Joe assumes family responsibilities at his father's death in this adventure story set in Alaska.

2233. Mowat, Farley. *The Black Joke* (6–9). Illus. by Victor Mays. 1963, Little $6.95. The *Black Joke's* reputation as a fast fishing schooner leads it into rumrunner's intrigue.

2234. Newman, Robert. *The Case of the Baker Street Irregular: A Sherlock Holmes Story* (4–6). 1978, Atheneum $7.95. Young Andrew unexpectedly finds himself teamed up with Sherlock Holmes.

2235. Newman, Robert. *The Case of the Vanishing Corpse* (5–7). 1980, Atheneum $8.95. Andrew and Sara help London police officer Inspector Wyatt solve a puzzling murder mystery.

2236. Newman, Robert. *Night Spell* (5–7). Illus. by Peter Buchard. 1977, Atheneum $7.95. After the death of his parents, Tad moves to a New England coastal town for a summer and encounters an unsolved mystery.

2237. Norton, Browning. *Wreck of the Blue Plane* (6–9). 1978, Coward $6.95. Mark searches for his kidnapped brother in the Alaskan wilderness.

2238. O'Dell, Scott. *The Black Pearl* (6–9). Illus. by Milton Johnson. 1967, Houghton $5.95. A haunting story of Mexican pearl divers and of Manta Diablo, the monster of the sea and owner of the magnificent black pearl.

2239. O'Dell, Scott. *Island of the Blue Dolphins* (5–8). 1960, Houghton $6.95. An Indian girl spends 18 years alone on an island off the coast of California in the 1800s. Newbery Award, 1961.

2240. O'Dell, Scott. *The 290* (6–8). 1976, Houghton $7.95; Dell paper $1.50. Kim, an American working in a British shipyard during the American Civil War, is approached by his Yankee brother to gather information about *The 290*, a ship destined for the Confederacy.

2241. O'Dell, Scott. *Zia* (5–8). 1976, Houghton $7.95. In this sequel to *Island of the Blue Dolphins*, Zia, niece of Karana, finds her aunt and brings her to the mainland.

2242. Otis, James. *Toby Tyler: Or Ten Weeks with a Circus* (4–6). 1923, Grosset $2.95. A perennial favorite about a subject popular with most children.

2243. Parker, Richard. *Quarter Boy* (6–9). 1976, Nelson $6.95. Charlie, who has been hired to refurbish the town clock, finds himself involved in a research project and a mystery.

2244. Parker, Richard. *Three by Mistake* (5–6). 1974, Nelson $6.95. Three young boys are kidnapped by political terrorists who are trying to secure the freedom of 3 imprisoned hijackers.

2245. Peck, Richard. *Through a Brief Darkness* (6–9). 1973, Viking $5.95; Avon paper $1.50. A suspenseful adventure story in which a young girl is held prisoner by her father's enemies.

2246. Peyton, K. M. *Marion's Angels* (6–8). Illus. by Robert Micklewright. 1979, Oxford $9.95. A young girl sets out to save a crumbling church in this English novel in which Patrick Pennington, hero of earlier Peyton novels, is featured.

2247. Peyton, K. M. *Prove Yourself a Hero* (6–9). 1978, Collins $6.95. Jonathan is obsessed with his own inadequacy as an aftermath of his kidnapping.

2248. Phipson, Joan. *The Cats* (6–9). 1976, Atheneum $6.95. After their parents win a lottery, Jim and Willy are kidnapped in this exciting story with an Australian setting.

2249. Phipson, Joan. *Fly into Danger* (6–8). 1977, Atheneum $6.95. A spunky 13-year-old girl tries to foil a scheme to illegally export exotic birds from Australia.

2250. Phipson, Joan. *When the City Stopped* (5–8). 1978, Atheneum $6.95. A group of children cope with a general strike in an Australian city.

2251. Place, Marian T. *The Boy Who Saw Bigfoot* (3–5). 1979, Dodd $5.95. When a young fourth-grader sights Bigfoot, his adventures begin.

2252. Platt, Kin. *Dracula, Go Home!* (6–9). 1979, Watts $6.90. A hi-lo book that tells an exciting tale with tongue in cheek.

2253. Poignant, Axel. *Bush Walkabout* (3–5). Illustrated. 1974, Addison $7.95. A tale retold in text and photos about 2 lost children who must spend the night in the woods. Winner of Australia's children's book of the year prize.

2254. Politzer, Anie. *My Journals and Sketchbooks by Robinson Crusoe* (5–8). Illustrated. 1974, Harcourt $6.95. The "true" story of Robinson Crusoe —an amazing survival tale.

2255. Poole, Josephine. *Catch as Catch Can* (5–7). Illus. by Kiyo Komoda. 1970, Harper paper $1.95. An adventure set in rural England about 2 boys trying to unravel the mystery of a man jumping off a train and a coded message they find. Also use: *Touch and Go* (1973, Harper, paper $1.95).

2256. Poole, Josephine. *The Visitor* (6–9). 1972, Harper $6.89. Harry is suspicious of his mysterious new tutor, a gaunt, strange man who seems to possess powers over the nearby village.

2257. Press, Hans Jurgen. *The Adventures of the Black Hand Gang* (3–5). 1977, Prentice-Hall $5.95. Four exciting mysteries are solved by a group of 4 children who call themselves the Black Hand Gang.

2258. Raskin, Ellen. *The Westing Game* (5–8). 1978, Dutton $7.95. A convoluted mystery that involves deciphering a will. Newbery Award.

2259. Renner, Beverly Hollett. *The Hideaway Summer* (5–7). 1978, Harper $6.95. A survival story of two youngsters who spend a summer in the woods.

2260. Rettich, Margret. *The Tightwad's Curse and Other Pleasantly Chilling Stories* (4–6). Trans. by Elizabeth D. Crawford. Illus. by Rolf Rettich. 1979, Morrow $6.95; LB $6.67. A collection of innocent mystery stories translated from the German.

2261. Rice, Eve. *The Remarkable Return of Winston Potter Crisply* (5–7). 1978, Greenwillow $6.95; LB $6.43. Becky and Max trail their brother who, although supposedly at Harvard, is mysteriously on the streets of New York City.

2262. Roach, Marilynne K. *Encounters with the Invisible World* (5–7). Illus. by author. 1977, Crowell $6.95. For this reworking of traditional stories, the subtitle is *Being Ten Tales of Ghosts, Witches and the Devil Himself in New England*.

2263. Roberts, Willo Davis. *The Minden Curse* (5–7). Illus. by Sherry Streeter. 1978, Atheneum $7.95. Two youngsters solve a case of petnapping.

2264. Roberts, Willo Davis. *More Minden Curses* (4–6). 1980, Atheneum $9.95. Danny Minden helps 2 elderly sisters escape the ghosts that are driving them from their home in the sequel to *The Minden Curse*.

2265. Roberts, Willo Davis. *The View from the Cherry Tree* (5–9). 1975, Atheneum $6.95; paper $1.95. An exciting story of a boy who witnesses a murder but can't find anyone who will believe him.

2266. Robinson, Joan G. *The Dark House of the Sea Witch* (5–7). 1979, Coward $7.50. Meg and Maxie are left alone for a short period by their parents in this English story.

2267. Rosenbloom, Joseph. *Maximilian, You're the Greatest* (4–6). Illustrated. 1979, Grosset paper $1.50. In each chapter, Maximilian Augustus Adams cracks a new case.

2268. Roth, Arthur. *The Iceberg Hermit* (6–8). 1974, Four Winds $7.95; paper $1.25. Around 1850, a 17-year-old Scottish lad endures incredible hardships in his struggle for survival when his whaling ship sinks.

2269. Roth, Arthur. *Two for Survival* (6–9). 1976, Scribner $7.95. Two young boys, one black and one white, set out to get help for survivors of a plane crash.

2270. Rumsey, Marian. *Lost in the Desert* (5–7). Illus. by Lydia Rosier. 1971, Morrow $6.75; LB $6.48. While trying to save a dog, Jason is swept downstream to a remote area in Nevada. Also use: *Lion on the Run* (1973, Morrow $6.75; LB $6.48).

2271. Rutherford, Douglas. *The Gunshot Grand Prix* (6–8). 1974, Bradbury $6.95. Politics and danger mix in this adventure story with more than just a race at stake for the young hero.

2272. St. George, Judith. *Mystery at St. Martin's* (5–7). 1979, Putnam $7.95. An exciting mystery of a girl's search to uncover the identity of a counterfeiter who has been traced to her father's church.

2273. St. John, Wylly Folk. *Mystery of the Gingerbread House* (5–7). Illus. by Frank Aloise. 1969, Avon paper $1.50. Two boys solve a mystery involving an abandoned body and missing jewels in modern Atlanta.

2274. Sefton, Catherine. *The Haunting of Ellen* (5–7). 1975, Harper paper $1.50. Ghostly doings occur when Ellen and Bella move to a decrepit cottage on the Irish coast. Also use: *In a Blue Velvet Dress* (1973, Harper $4.95; LB $4.79; paper $1.25).

2275. Showell, Ellen Harvey. *The Ghost of Tillie Jean Cassaway* (4–6). Illus. by Stephen Gammell. 1978, Four Winds $6.95. What appear to be ghostly happenings have a logical explanation in this adventure story set in present-day Appalachia.

2276. Shura, Mary Francis. *The Gray Ghosts of Taylor Ridge* (5–7). Illus. by Michael Hampshire. 1978, Dodd $5.95. A boy and his sister find a lost treasure.

2277. Silverthorne, Elizabeth. *Ghost of Padre Island* (4–6). Illus. by Dennis Anderson. 1975, Abingdon $4.95. Three children solve a mystery while on an archaeological dig near Corpus Christi, Texas.

2278. Sivers, Brenda. *The Snailman* (4–6). Illus. by Shirley Hughes. 1978, Little $6.95. Bullies terrorize a young English boy and his friend who raises snails.

2279. Smith, Harry W. *Michael and the Mary Day* (5–7). Illus. by author. 1979, Down East $9.95; paper $6.95. Michael learns about ships and seafaring aboard a windjammer named *Mary Day*.

2280. Smith, Emma. *No Way of Telling* (6–8). 1972, Atheneum $5.50. Amy and her grandmother, marooned by a blizzard, are visited by a strange intruder.

2281. Smith, Nancy, and Bijur, Hilda. *Jason the Lobsterman* (4–5). Illustrated. 1978, Tashmoo Press paper $4.50. Jason takes over when his older brother, a lobsterman, becomes ill.

2282. Sneve, Virginia. *High Elk's Treasure* (4–7). Illus. by Oren Lyons. 1972, Holiday $5.95. Joe discovers a cave and a treasure left there by his great-grandfather, the Sioux warrior High Elk. Also use: *When Thunder Spoke* (1974, Holiday $4.95).

2283. Snyder, Zilpha Keatley. *The Changeling* (5–7). Illus. by Alton Raible. 1970, Atheneum $7.95; paper $.95. A dramatic novel of a talented girl wrongly accused of vandalism and her strange belief that she was a changeling.

2284. Snyder, Zilpha Keatley. *The Famous Stanley Kidnapping Case* (4–7). 1979, Atheneum $8.95. Amanda, young heroine of *The Headless Corpse*, is visiting Italy and becomes involved in a kidnapping.

2285. Snyder, Zilpha Keatley. *The Truth about Stone Hollow* (5–7). Illus. by Alton Raible. 1974, Atheneum $8.95; paper $1.95. Although the ravine's past remains shrouded in mystery, Amy's and Jason's trips to the haunted hollow make a compelling excursion into the semisupernatural.

2286. Sobol, Donald J. *Encyclopedia Brown, Boy Detective* (3–5). Illustrated. 1963, Nelson $5.95; Bantam paper $1.25. Ten-year-old Leroy Brown opens his own detective agency and solves 10 crimes.

2287. Sobol, Donald J. *Encyclopedia Brown Carries On* (3–5). 1980, Four Winds $6.95. In this collection of 10 cases, Encyclopedia solves cases that involve situations like chickens that lay square eggs.

2288. Sobol, Donald J. *Encyclopedia Brown Saves the Day* (3–5). Illus. by Leonard Shortall. 1970, Nelson $5.95; Bantam paper $1.25. As do other titles in this popular series, this consists of a series of short stories told with wit and suspense.

2289. Sorensen, Virginia. *Friends of the Road* (4–6). 1978, Atheneum $5.95. Two daughters of diplomats help make life in Morocco an exciting adventure.

2290. Southall, Ivan. *Ash Road* (5–7). 1978, Greenwillow $6.95; LB $6.67. A group of children are alone and in the path of a devastating fire.

2291. Southall, Ivan. *Hills End* (6–9). 1974, Macmillan $5.95. Seven children caught in a flash flood in an isolated Australian mining town have to fend for themselves.

2292. Southall, Ivan. *King of the Sticks* (6–8). 1979, Greenwillow $6.95; LB $6.67. A young boy named Custard is kidnapped because he supposedly has psychic powers.

2293. Speare, Elizabeth. *The Bronze Bow* (6–9). 1961, Houghton $7.95; paper $2.45. A Jewish boy seeks revenge against the Romans who killed his parents, but he finally loses his hatred after he hears the messages and teachings of Jesus. Newbery Award.

2294. Sperry, Armstrong. *Call It Courage* (5–8). Illus. by author. 1940, Macmillan $4.95; paper $.95. The "Crusoe" theme is interwoven with this story of a Polynesian boy's courage in facing the sea he feared. Newbery Award, 1941.

2295. Spier, Peter. *Tin Lizzie* (4–6). Illus. by author. 1975, Doubleday $7.95; paper $1.95. The life and adventures of a single Model-T Ford made in 1909 and now a showpiece of an antique-car collector.

2296. Stevenson, Robert Louis. *Treasure Island* (6–9). Illus. by N. C. Wyeth. 1972, Western LB $4.92; Pendulum paper $1.45. The classic and famous pirate story.

2297. Stevenson, William. *The Bushbabies* (5–7). Illus. by Victor G. Ambrus. 1965, Houghton $8.95. Apartheid in South Africa underlies the increase in the normal tension attendant on the search for a lost white girl last seen with an old native man.

2298. Stewart, A. C. *Silas and Con* (4–7). 1977, Atheneum $5.95. An abused, pathetic young boy wanders through the Scottish countryside and meets a motley group of strangers.

2299. Storey, Margaret. *Ask Me No Questions* (5–7). 1975, Dutton $6.95. In this English suspense story, a young girl named Imogen is kidnapped by a quiet man whom she later grows to like.

2300. Storr, Catherine. *Kate and the Island* (4–5). Illus. by Gareth Floyd. 1978, Faber $3.95. This recounts the adventures of a young English girl and her attempt at amateur archaeology on a Greek island.

2301. Suhl, Yuri. *Uncle Misha's Partisans* (5–8). 1973, Four Winds $6.95. When his family is killed by the Nazis, Matele joins a group of Jewish refugees hiding in a Ukranian forest.

2302. Swahn, Sven Christer. *The Island through the Gate* (5–8). 1974, Macmillan $4.95. An 11-year-old English boy drifts on an air mattress to a strange island.

2303. Talbot, Charlene Joy. *The Great Rat Island Adventure* (5–6). Illus. by Ruth Sanderson. 1977, Atheneum $7.95. Joel, a child of divorced parents, spends a summer with his father on a lonely island.

2304. Tapley, Caroline. *John Come Down the Backstay* (4–6). Illus. by Richard Cuffari. 1974, Atheneum $6.25. A rescue mission into the Arctic in the mid-1850s, as described by a young member of the crew.

2305. Taylor, Theodore. *The Odyssey of Ben O'Neal* (6–8). Illus. by Richard Cuffari. 1977, Doubleday $5.95; Avon paper $1.50. Action and humor are skillfully combined in this story of a trip by Ben and his friend Tee to England at the turn of the century. Sequel to: *Teetoncey* (1974, Double-

day $4.95; Avon paper $1.25) and *Teetoncey and Ben O'Neal* (1975, Doubleday $5.95).

2306. Terris, Susan. *The Pencil Families* (4–6). 1975, Greenwillow $7.25; LB $6.96. In this humorous adventure story, 2 youngsters discover a corpse in a lagoon at low tide.

2307. Thiele, Colin. *Blue Fin* (6–9). Illus. by Roger Haldane. 1974, Harper $7.89; paper $1.50. A 14-year-old's courage and love are put to the test when his father's tuna ship founders off the coast of Australia.

2308. Thiele, Colin. *Fire in the Stone* (6–9). 1974, Harper LB $6.79. Ernie and his aboriginal friend track down an opal thief in this exciting adventure set in Australia.

2309. Thiele, Colin. *The Hammerhead Light* (5–7). 1977, Harper $6.95; LB $6.89. A young girl Tess and a 70-year-old man operate an abandoned lighthouse and help save Tess's father from drowning, in this exciting Australian novel.

2310. Townsend, John R. *The Intruder* (5–8). Illus. by Joseph A. Phelan. 1970, Lippincott $8.95; Dell paper $1.50. Story of suspense and mystery set on the west coast of England.

2311. Townsend, John R. *Top of the World* (5–8). Illus. by John Wallner. 1977, Lippincott $6.95. Two young apartment dwellers court disaster when, unsupervised, they begin walking catwalks in the penthouse garden.

2312. Ullman, James. *Banner in the Sky* (6–9). 1954, Lippincott $8.95; Archway paper $1.50. Rudi wants more than anything else to follow in his father's footsteps as an alpine guide and conquer the unclimbed Citadel Mountain.

2313. Van Der Loef, A. Rutgers. *Avalanche* (6–9). Illus. by Gustav Schrotter. 1958, Morrow $6.75. An avalanche strikes a Swiss village in the night, killing the schoolmaster and his wife. Their son has to learn to accept their loss and face the future with courage.

2314. Van Iterson, Siny Rose. *The Spirits of Chocamata* (6–8). 1977, Morrow $6.25; LB $6.00. In this suspenseful novel, 2 boys help capture an escaped prisoner on the island of Curacao.

2315. Verne, Jules. *Twenty Thousand Leagues under the Sea* (6–9). Illus. by W. J. Aylward. 1925; 1976, Dent $5.95. The fantastic adventures of Captain Nemo with a submarine in the 1860s. Also use: *Around the World in Eighty Days* (1956, Dodd $8.95).

2316. Verney, John. *Friday's Tunnel* (6–9). Illus. by author. 1966, Holt paper $.60. February and her brother Friday are plunged into the middle of an international mystery. Also use another story about the Challendar family: *February's Road* (1966, paper 60¢).

2317. Viereck, Philip. *The Summer I Was Lost* (5–7). 1965, Crowell $7.50. A boy survives a harrowing ordeal when he is lost on a mountain.

2318. Waldron, Ann. *The French Detection* (4–6). 1979, Dutton $7.95. Bessie copes during her month living in a French village.

2319. Walton, Bryce. *Cave of Danger* (6–8). 1967, Archway paper $.75. Tense suspense as teenager Matt Wilde, so intent on discovering a cave that he disregards the spelunker's rules of safety, is trapped underground for 6 harrowing days.

2320. Warner, Margery. *The Secret of the Disappearing Sultan* (4–6). Illus. by Charles Robinson. 1975, Houghton $5.95. An adventure story in which an American girl, visiting in Paris, tries to help a 12-year-old sultan slated for kidnapping.

2321. Warren, Mary. *Ghost Town for Sale* (3–5). Illus. by Beth Krush and Joe Krush. 1973, Westminster $5.50. An outdoor adventure in an arid Oregon area in which 2 boys get lost in the hill country.

2322. Waters, John F. *Summer of the Seals* (5–7). Illus. by Mike Eagle. 1978, Warne $6.95. Two 11-year-olds discover who is killing the seals in the Maine village.

2323. Westall, Robert. *The Watch House* (6–8). 1978, Greenwillow $6.95. Anne witnesses one ghost haunting another in this tale of stolen gold and revenge.

2324. White, Robb. *Deathwatch* (6–9). 1972, Doubleday $5.95. A young man is hunted by a madman in a desert wilderness.

2325. White, Robb. *Fire Storm* (6–8). 1979, Doubleday $6.95; LB $7.90. A forest ranger and a 14-year-old boy are trapped by a forest fire.

2326. Whitney, Phyllis A. *Mystery of the Haunted Pool* (5–7). 1960, Westminster $7.50; Scholastic paper $.85. An exciting mystery from a master storyteller. Also use: *Secret of the Tiger's Eye* (1961, NAL paper $1.50).

2327. Whitney, Phyllis A. *Secret of the Emerald Star* (5–7). n.d., Grosset paper $.95. A blind girl, an emerald star, an unwelcome stranger, and an unyielding grandmother present a baffling puzzle to the new girl on Catalpa Court. Also use: *Secret of the Spotted Shell* (1967, Westminster $6.95; NAL, paper $1.25).

2328. Whitney, Phyllis A. *Secret of the Stone Face* (5–7). 1977, Westminster $7.75; NAL paper

$1.25. While trying to discredit the reputation of her mother's fiancé, Jo encounters a mystery.

2329. Wibberley, Leonard. *Flint's Island* (6–9). 1972, Farrar $4.95. A continuation of *Treasure Island* with Long John Silver up to his old tricks and Flint's treasure again causing havoc.

2330. Wibberley, Leonard. *Perilous Gold* (6–9). 1978, Farrar $7.95. An action story involving the exploration of a sunken ship in a 2-person submarine.

2331. Willard, Barbara. *The Gardener's Grandchildren* (6–9). Illus. by Gordon King. 1979, McGraw $7.95. Two youngsters find a boy hiding in a cave on a Scottish island.

2332. Willard, Barbara. *The Richleighs of Tantamount* (4–7). Illus. by C. W. Hodges. 1966, Harcourt $5.50. Mystery and suspense surround the 4 Richleigh children on a visit to their sinister ancestral castle in Cornwall.

2333. Woolley, Catherine. *Cathy Uncovers a Secret* (4–6). Illus. by Don Almquist. 1972, Morrow $6.96. Through clever detection, Cathy discovers that a letter from Abraham Lincoln is the "something special" about her house. Other books about Cathy are: *Cathy Leonard Calling* (1961, $7.25) and *Cathy's Little Sister* (1964, $8.16).

2334. Wyss, Johann D. *Swiss Family Robinson* (5–8). Illus. by Lynn Ward and Lee Gregori. n.d., Grosset LB $2.95; deluxe $7.95; Airmont paper $1.25. A family is shipwrecked in this classic story.

2335. York, Carol Beach. *Nothing Ever Happens Here* (6–9). 1970, NAL paper $1.25. Elizabeth's quiet, monotonous life is shattered when new tenants move into the apartment upstairs.

2336. York, Carol Beach. *Takers and Returners: A Novel of Suspense* (6–8). 1973, Elsevier/Nelson $6.95. A group of bored youngsters, led by 15-year-old Julian, try to enliven their summer by stealing and then returning items.

2337. York, Carol Beach. *The Witch Lady Mystery* (4–6). 1976, Nelson $4.95. A young boy wonders if the old lady he works for is really a witch.

2338. Young, Miriam. *A Witch's Garden* (5–7). Illus. by Charles Robinson. 1973, Atheneum $6.95. A novel that explores facets of prejudice in a community after a witchlike woman moves in.

Sports Stories

2339. Altman, Millys N. *Racing in Her Blood* (6–8). 1980, Lippincott $7.89. Jane Barton attempts to break into the male-dominated world of auto racing.

2340. Bishop, Curtis. *Little League Victory* (4–7). 1967, Lippincott $5.50. An exciting baseball story with plenty of sports action.

2341. Bonham, Frank. *The Rascals from Haskell's Gym* (5–7). 1977, Dutton $7.95. Sissy's gymnastic team is challenged by a rival group that doesn't play fair.

2342. Christopher, Matt. *Baseball Flyhawk* (4–5). Illus. by Foster Cadell. 1963, Little $5.95. Chico moves from Puerto Rico to New York City and believes he can make new friends through baseball. Also use: *The Kid Who Only Hit Homers* (1972, Little $5.95) and *Jinx Glove* (1974, Little $5.95).

2343. Christopher, Matt. *Dirt Bike Racer* (3–5). Illus. by Barry Bomzer. 1979, Brown $6.95. Ron finds a bike at the bottom of a lake and begins dirt bike racing.

2344. Christopher, Matt. *The Dog That Stole Football Plays* (2–4). 1980, Little $6.95. Mike is able to communicate with his dog by telepathy in this amusing sports story.

2345. Christopher, Matt. *The Fox Steals Home* (4–6). Illus. by Larry Johnson. 1978, Little $6.95. Baseball and his parents' divorce are the 2 preoccupations of young Billy Canfield.

2346. Christopher, Matt. *No Arm in Left Field* (4–6). Illus. by Byron Goteo. 1974, Little $6.95. Terry is a black newcomer on the baseball team and, as a third strike, has a weak throwing arm.

2347. Christopher, Matt. *Shortstop from Tokyo* (3–5). Illus. by Harvey Kidder. 1970, Little $5.95. Stogie feels resentment when a Japanese boy takes his place on the baseball team.

2348. Christopher, Matt. *The Year Mom Won the Pennant* (3–5). Illus. by Foster Caddell. 1968, Little $5.95; Archway paper $1.25. The Thunderballs gain an unusual distinction—a female coach —and the Little League pennant in this easy-to-read baseball comedy.

2349. Cohen, Barbara. *Thank You, Jackie Robinson* (4–6). Illus. by Richard Cuffari. 1974, Lothrop $6.00. A memoir written by Sam about his friendship with an old man and his devotion as a boy to the Brooklyn Dodgers and Ebbets Field.

2350. Corbett, Scott. *The Hockey Girls* (4–6). 1976, Dutton $6.50. Irma reluctantly joins the field hockey team coached by an old English teacher Miss Tingery in this humorous and different sports story.

2351. Decker, Duane. *Fast Man on a Pivot* (7–9). 1951, Morrow $6.25. Rivalry for "second base" provides excitement on the Blue Socks team. Also use: *Rebel in Right Field* (1961, Morrow $6.25).

2352. Fenner, Phyllis, ed. *Crack of the Bat* (4–8). 1952, Knopf $5.69. Baseball stories and biographical sketches.

2353. Fenner, Phyllis, ed. *Quick Pivot: Stories of Basketball* (6–9). 1965, Knopf $7.95. Stories of this fast-moving sport.

2354. Fenner, Carol. *The Skates of Uncle Richard* (3–4). Illus. by Ati Forberg. 1978, Random $4.95; LB $5.99. Nine-year-old Marsha tries to ice-skate on hand-me-down skates from Uncle Richard.

2355. Foley, Louise M. *Tackle 22* (3–5). Illus. by John Heily. 1978, Delacorte $6.95. Herbie wins the day as a substitute player on the football team.

2356. Gault, William Campbell. *Showboat in the Backcourt* (5–7). 1976, Dutton $7.95. The careers of 2 basketball players from high school to the big leagues. Also use: *The Big Stick* (1975, Dutton $6.95).

2357. Ilowite, Sheldon A. *Centerman from Quebec* (4–6). Illus. by Ned Butterfield. 1972, Hastings $4.95. A move from Quebec to Long Island brings difficulties for Jean Nicol's acceptance onto a new hockey team. Also use: *Penalty Killer* (1973, Hastings $4.95).

2358. Kalb, Jonah. *The Goof That Won the Pennant* (3–6). Illus. by Sandy Kossin. 1976, Houghton $5.95. Losers become winners in this humorous baseball story.

2359. Levy, Elizabeth. *The Tryouts* (4–6). Illus. by Jacquie Hann. 1979, Four Winds $6.95. The boys' basketball team finds that it must accept 2 girls.

2360. Lord, Beman. *Guards for Matt* (3–5). 1961, Walck $5.95; paper $1.50. An easy baseball story with good sports action. Also use: *Bats and Balls* (1967, Walck $5.95).

2361. Lord, Beman. *Rough Ice* (2–4). 1963, Walck $5.95. An exciting hockey story.

2362. Renick, Marion. *Take a Long Jump* (4–6). Illus. by Charles Robinson. 1971, Scribner $5.95. Jay competes with his older brother's athletic prowess by becoming involved with track.

2363. Renick, Marion. *Watch Those Red Wheels Roll* (2–4). Illus. by Leonard Shortall. 1965, Scribner $5.95. Vic's ups and downs as step by step he makes a racer for the junior soapbox derby. Also by the author: *Pete's Home Run* (1967, Scribner $5.95; paper $.95).

2364. Robison, Nancy. *On the Balance Beam* (4–6). Illus. by Rondi Anderson. 1978, Whitman $4.95. Andrea's dream of becoming a gymnast comes true.

2365. Scholz, Jackson. *Dugout Tycoon* (6–9). 1963, Morrow $6.75. Action-filled baseball story. Also use: *Backfield Blues* (1971, Morrow $6.00).

2366. Schulman, Janet. *Jenny and the Tennis Nut* (2–4). Illus. by Marylin Hafner. 1978, Greenwillow $5.95; LB $5.49. Jenny really wants to be a gymnast in spite of her father's love for tennis.

2367. Slote, Alfred. *The Hotshot* (4–6). Photos by William LaCrosse. 1977, Watts $5.90; Dell paper $1.25. A fast-moving, easy-to-read book about a hockey player who slowly learns how to play as part of a team.

2368. Slote, Alfred. *Matt Gargan's Boy* (4–6). 1975, Lippincott $6.95; Avon paper $1.25. A baseball story with substance involving Danny, the team's excellent pitcher, his divorced parents, and a young girl who wants to make the team.

2369. Slote, Alfred. *My Father, the Coach* (4–6). 1972, Avon paper $1.25. The underdogs, managed by a rookie coach, successfully take on the league champions in this refreshingly cheerful baseball story.

2370. Slote, Alfred. *Stranger on the Ball Club* (4–6). 1970, Dell paper $.95. Tim's efforts to make friends at his new school and on the Little League are filled with difficulties.

2371. Slote, Alfred. *Tony and Me* (4–6). 1974, Lippincott $6.95; Avon paper $1.25. Bill's new friend Tony is a whiz at baseball, but unfortunately he is also a thief, and this knowledge forces Bill to make a difficult moral decision.

2372. Taves, Isabella. *Not Bad for a Girl* (4–6). 1972, Evans $4.50. A young girl tries to replace a vacationing boy in the lineup of the town's Little League team. Based on a true occurrence.

2373. Tolle, Jean Bahor. *The Great Pete Penney* (4–6). 1979, Atheneum $7.95. A leprechaun helps a girl move into major league baseball.

2374. Towne, Mary. *First Serve* (5–8). Illus. by Ruth Sanderson. 1976, Atheneum $6.95. Secretly Dulin practices tennis, although her older sister Pat is really the acknowledged court star of the family.

2375. Tunis, John R. *The Kid from Tomkinsville* (5–8). 1940, Harcourt $4.95. One of the author's many sports stories.

2376. Winthrop, Elizabeth. *Marathon Miranda* (4–6). 1979, Holiday $6.95. In spite of her asthma, Miranda joins her friend Phoebe in the big marathon.

Humorous Stories

2377. Ahlberg, Janet, and Ahlberg, Allan. *Burglar Bill* (3–5). Illustrated. 1977, Greenwillow $7.25; LB $6.96; Penguin paper $2.25. The arrival of a baby reforms the rambunctious Burglar Bill.

2378. Ahlberg, Janet, and Ahlberg, Allan. *The Little Worm Book* (3–8). Illustrated. 1980, Viking $2.95. A clever satire on nature study books that purport to give detailed information on "Wormus wormus."

2379. Anderson, Mary. *F*T*C and Company* (5–7). Illus. by Don Sibley. 1979, Atheneum $8.95. The cat and pigeon of *F*T*C Superstar* (1976, Atheneum $7.95) return to help Rosetta Robin with her career in show business.

2380. Annett, Cora. *How the Sitch Got Alf* (3–4). Illus. by Steven Kellogg. 1954, Watts $4.90. A lighthearted story about a donkey who tries to be loved by his master like the other pets around his house.

2381. Atwater, Richard, and Atwater, Florence. *Mr. Popper's Penguins* (4–6). Illus. by Robert Lawson. 1938, Little $6.95; Dell paper $1.25. Mr. Popper has to get a penguin from the zoo to keep his homesick penguin company; soon there are 12.

2382. Baughman, Dorothy. *Piney's Summer* (3–5). Illus. by Tom Allen. 1976, Coward $5.95. A series of everyday adventures of a young boy one summer in a small southern town.

2383. Beatty, Jerome. *Sheriff Stonehead and the Teenage Termites* (5–7). Illus. by Gene Holtan. 1970, Young Scott $5.95. A nonsense novel in which a young boy turns a town on its ears, yet emerges a hero. Also use: *Matthew Looney and the Space Pirates* (1972, Young Scott $5.95; Avon paper $1.25).

2384. Beatty, Patricia. *That's One Ornery Orphan* (6–8). 1980, Morrow $7.95; LB $7.63. An unconventional orphan is adopted 3 times in this story set in nineteenth-century Texas.

2385. Blume, Judy. *Freckle Juice* (2–5). Illus. by Sonia O. Lisker. 1971, Four Winds $5.95. A gullible second-grader pays 50¢ for a recipe to grow freckles.

2386. Bodger, Joan. *Clever-Lazy: The Girl Who Invented Herself* (4–6). 1979, Atheneum $8.95. A folklike story about a liberated girl who became the official inventor at the court of the king.

2387. Bond, Michael. *A Bear Called Paddington* (3–6). Illus. by Peggy Fortnum. 1960, Houghton $6.95; Dell paper $1.25. An endearing bear with a talent for getting into trouble. Sequels (all same publishers): *Paddington Helps Out* (1961, $6.95; paper $1.25), *More about Paddington* (1962, $7.95; paper $1.25), *Paddington at Work* (1967, $6.95; paper $1.25), *Paddington Goes to Town* (1968, $5.95; paper $1.25), *Paddington Abroad* (1972, $6.95; paper $1.25), *Paddington Takes to TV* (1974, $6.95; paper $1.25), and *Paddington on Top* (1975, $5.95; paper $1.25).

2388. Bond, Michael. *Olga Carries On* (3–5). Illus. by Hans Helweg. 1977, Hastings $5.95. Another series of adventures and anecdotes recounted by the engaging guinea pig.

2389. Bond, Michael. *The Tales of Olga de Polga* (4–5). Illus. by Hans Helweg. 1973, Macmillan $4.95; Penguin paper $.95. Olga, another superb creation by the author of Paddington, is a witty imaginative guinea pig who holds other animals spellbound by her stories. Also use: *Olga Meets her Match* (1975, Hastings $6.95; Penguin paper $1.50).

2390. Bontemps, Arna, and Conroy, Jack. *The Fast Sooner Hound* (2–4). Illus. by Virginia L. Burton. 1942, Houghton $7.95. A long-legged, lop-eared hound dog outruns the Cannon Ball Express.

2391. Brooks, Walter R. *Freddy, the Detective* (3–5). Illus. by Kurt Wiese. 1932, Knopf $6.39; Dell paper $1.75. Freddy, the pig, turns into a supersleuth after reading Sherlock Holmes. One of a long and popular series.

2392. Bunting, Eve. *The Big Cheese* (2–5). Illus. by Sal Murdocca. 1977, Macmillan $5.95. Two sisters acquire a huge cheese and must devise methods of protecting it in this amusing story.

2393. Butterworth, Oliver. *The Enormous Egg* (3–6). Illus. by Louis Darling. 1956, Little $7.95; Dell paper $1.50. Story of a boy whose hen lays a large egg, which hatches out a triceratops!

2394. Butterworth, Oliver. *The Trouble with Jenny's Ear* (4–6). 1960, Little $6.95. A humorous story about 2 ingenious boys who capitalize on their sister's sensitive ear—one that can hear thoughts—to earn money.

2395. Byfield, Barbara. *The Haunted Ghost* (3–5). Illus. by author. 1973, Doubleday $4.95. Sir Roger de Rudisill, a ghost, is himself haunted in this amusing spoof.

2396. Carrick, Malcolm. *The Wise Men of Gotham* (4–6). Illus. by author. 1975, Viking $6.95. A collection of English humorous stories dating back several centuries, about the misadventures of a group of dunderheads.

2397. Callen, Larry. *The Deadly Mandrake* (5–7). Illus. by Larry Johnson. 1978, Little $6.95. This second Four Corner story humorously explores superstition and folksiness in backwoods America.

2398. Chew, Ruth. *Wednesday Witch* (3–5). 1972, Holiday $3.95. A witch who travels by vacuum cleaner is featured in this humorous tale. Also use: *The Witch's Gardens* (1979, Hastings $5.95).

2399. Chukovsky, Kornei. *The Telephone* (2–4). Illus. by Blair Lent. 1977, Delacorte $7.95; LB $7.45. A series of requests is made by various animals on the telephone, in this zany story.

2400. Cleary, Beverly. *Ellen Tebbits* (3–5). Illus. by Louis Darling. 1951, Morrow $6.75; LB $6.48; Dell paper $1.75. Eight-year-old Ellen has braces on her teeth, takes ballet lessons, and, worst of all, wears long woolen underwear. A wonderfully humorous, appealing story of an average third-grader.

2401. Cleary, Beverly. *Emily's Runaway Imagination* (3–6). Illus. by Beth Krush and Joe Krush. 1961, Morrow $7.25; LB $6.96. Emily's imagination helps get a library for Pitchfork, Oregon, in the 1920s.

2402. Cleary, Beverly. *Henry Huggins* (3–5). Illus. by Louis Darling. 1950, Morrow $6.75; LB $6.48; Dell paper $1.75. Henry is a small boy with a knack for creating hilarious situations. Other Henry stories (all Morrow) are: *Henry and Beezus* (1952, $7.25; LB $6.96), *Henry and the Paper Route* (1957, $7.25; LB $6.96; also Dell paper $1.75), and *Henry and the Clubhouse* (1962, $6.75; LB $6.48).

2403. Cleary, Beverly. *The Mouse and the Motorcycle* (3–5). Illus. by Louis Darling. 1965, Morrow $6.75; LB $6.48. Whisker-curling exploits of 2 young mice.

2404. Cleary, Beverly. *Otis Spofford* (3–6). Illus. by Louis Darling. 1953, Morrow $6.75; LB $6.48; paper $1.50. This story of Otis stirring up a little excitement at school is full of humor.

2405. Cleary, Beverly. *Runaway Ralph* (3–5). Illus. by Louis Darling. 1970, Morrow $7.25; LB $6.96; Archway paper $1.25. A motorcyclist mouse finds family life too stifling, so he takes to his wheels, only to find that freedom is an evasive thing.

2406. Cleaver, Vera, and Cleaver, Bill. *Delpha Green and Company* (5–7). 1972, Lippincott $8.79;

paper $2.95. Delpha, an astrologist, and her father, a minister of the Church of Blessed Hope, attract an unusual assortment of people needing help.

2407.   Clements, Bruce. *I Tell a Lie Every So Often* (5–8). 1974, Farrar $6.95. The adventures of the 14-year-old narrator, an imaginative bender of the truth, and his older brother on a trip up the Missouri River in 1848.

2408.   Collier, James Lincoln. *Rich and Famous: The Further Adventures of George Stable* (6–9). 1975, Four Winds $6.95. Show business is spoofed in this story, set in New York, about 14-year-old George's attempt to break into TV.

2409.   Conford, Ellen. *Felecia the Critic* (5–7). Illus. by Arvis Stewart. 1973, Little $6.95; Archway paper $1.25. Felicia's habit of being bluntly honest gets her into trouble.

2410.   Corbett, Scott. *The Baseball Trick* (3–5). Illus. by Paul Galdone. 1965, Little $4.95. Kirby and his wonderful chemistry set help Fenton hit a home run. Other popular "Trick" books (all Little) are: *The Lemonade Trick* (1960, $6.95), *The Mailbox Trick* (1961, $5.95), *The Disappearing Dog Trick* (1963, $5.95), *The Hairy Horror Trick* (1967, $5.95), and *The Turnabout Trick* (1967, $5.95).

2411.   Corbett, Scott. *The Case of the Gone Goose* (3–5). Illus. by Paul Galdone. 1966, Little $5.95. Twelve-year-old Inspector Roger Tearle, his twin sister, and his best friend solve the murder of 3 prize geese in a delightfully funny detective story neatly plotted and refreshingly different. Sequels (both 1969, Little): *The Case of the Fugitive Firebug* ($6.95) and *The Case of the Ticklish Tooth* ($4.95).

2412.   Corbett, Scott. *Steady, Freddie!* (3–5). Illus. by Lawrence Beall Smith. 1970, Dutton $6.50. After a trip to the zoo, Donna finds Freddie, a small green frog, in her handbag.

2413.   Coren, Alan. *Arthur's Last Stand* (3–5). Illus. by John Astrop. 1979, Little $6.95. Arthur saves Fort Moccasin from an Indian attack.

2414.   Coren, Alan. *Arthur the Kid* (4–6). Illus. by John Astrop. 1978, Little $5.95. A wild spoof of a shoot-em-up Western adventure.

2415.   Coren, Alan. *Buffalo Arthur* (4–6). Illus. by John Astrop. 1978, Little $5.95. Intrepid Arthur, hero of *Arthur the Kid*, captures a gang of cattle rustlers.

2416.   Coren, Alan. *Klondike Arthur* (4–6). Illus. by John Astrop. 1979, Little $6.95. The hero of *Arthur the Kid* and *Railroad Arthur* beguiles a group of Klondike rough-and-ready characters.

2417.   Coren, Alan. *The Lone Arthur* (4–6). Illus. by John Astrop. 1978, Little $5.95. Ten-year-old Arthur solves a robbery mystery in a tale set in Dodge City.

2418.   Coren, Alan. *Railroad Arthur* (3–5). Illus. by John Astrop. 1978, Little $5.95. Arthur continues to battle bandits and gunslingers in these 2 humorous stories.

2419.   Cresswell, Helen. *Bagthorpes Unlimited* (5–7). 1978, Macmillan $6.95. The Bagthorpe children sabotage a family gathering in this sequel to *Ordinary Jack* (1977) and *Absolute Zero* (1978), both Macmillan $6.95.

2420.   Cresswell, Helen. *Bagthorpes Unlimited: Being the Fourth Part of the Bagthorpe Saga* (5–7). 1979, Macmillan $6.95. A computer error in a bank statement changes a family's life-style in this fourth novel about the Bagthorpe family.

2421.   Cresswell, Helen. *Ordinary Jack: Being the First Part of the Bagthorpe Saga* (5–7). 1977, Macmillan $6.95; Avon paper $1.50. Everyone in the English Bagthorpe's family is precociously accomplished—except Jack.

2422.   Cresswell, Helen. *The Winter of the Birds* (6–9). 1976, Macmillan $8.95. A novel, told from 3 different points of view, about the effects on the residents of an English town when unconventional, delightful Patrick Finn comes to visit.

2423.   Dahl, Roald. *Danny: The Champion of the World* (3–5). Illus. by Jill Bennett. 1975, Knopf $5.95; LB $6.69. Nine-year-old Danny helps his father on a poaching expedition to wealthy Mr. Hazell's woods.

2424.   De Angeli, Marguerite. *Yonie Wondernose* (2–4). 1944, Doubleday $5.95. A Pennsylvania Amish boy earns his funny name from insatiable curiosity.

2425.   DeWeese, Gene. *Major Colby and the Unidentified Flapping Object* (5–7). 1979, Doubleday $5.95. When 14-year-old Russ agrees to help a UFO, a whole town gets involved.

2426.   du Bois, William Pene. *The Alligator Case* (3–6). Illus. by author. 1965, Harper $6.89. A young boy assumes many identities as he tracks down the villains who disguise themselves as alligators.

2427.   du Bois, William Pene. *Call Me Bandicoot* (4–6). Illus. by author. 1970, Harper $4.95; LB $6.89. A freeloading teller of fantastic tales takes his victims on a Staten Island ferry ride, but it costs them more than 25¢.

2428.   du Bois, William Pene. *Lazy Tommy Pumpkinhead* (2–4). Illus. by author. 1966, Harper

$6.89. The eccentric performance of gadgets in an all-electric house provides high-voltage hilarity.

2429. du Bois, William Pene. *Porko von Popbutton* (3–5). Illus. by author. 1969, Harper $5.79. At boarding school, 274-pound Pat O'Sullivan Pinkerton proves himself on the ice hockey rink.

2430. du Bois, William Pene. *The 3 Policemen: Or, Young Bottsford of Farbe Island* (3–5). 1960, Viking $5.95. A humorous and intriguing detective story of 3 policemen and young Bottsford, who solve the mystery of the stolen fishing nets on Farbe Island.

2431. du Bois, William Pene. *Twenty-One Balloons* (4–6). Illus. by author. 1947, Viking $6.95; Dell paper $1.25. Truth and fiction are combined in the adventures of a professor who sails around the world in a balloon. Newbery Award, 1948. Also use (both Viking $5.95): *The Great Geppy* (1940) and *The Giant* (1954).

2432. Durrell, Ann, ed. *Just for Fun* (4–6). 1977, Dutton $5.95. Seven humorous stories by such popular writers as Lloyd Alexander, Scott Corbett, and Marilyn Sachs.

2433. Ellentuck, Shan. *Yankel the Fool* (4–7). Illus. by author. 1973, Doubleday $4.95. A rabbi manages to persuade townspeople that Yankel, whom they had dismissed as the town knucklehead, is really a scholar.

2434. Farley, Carol. *Loosen Your Ears* (4–6). Illus. by Mila Lararevich. 1977, Atheneum $7.95. Narrator Josh Hemmer tells humorous anecdotes about his comical farm family. He also stars in *Settle Your Fidgets* (1977, Atheneum $6.95).

2435. Fenner, Phyllis, ed. *Time to Laugh* (4–6). Illus. by Henry C. Pitz. 1942, Knopf $5.39. Amusing stories from yesterday.

2436. Fife, Dale. *What's the Prize, Lincoln?* (3–5). Illus. by Paul Galdone. 1971, Coward $5.49. Lincoln, the young black hero of many other books by the author (e.g., *Who's in Charge of Lincoln?* 1965, Coward $4.99), wins so much junk in contests that he decides to open a flea market, with predictable humorous results.

2437. Fitzgerald, John D. *The Great Brain* (4–7). Illus. by Mercer Mayer. 1967, Dial $6.95; LB $6.46; Dell paper $1.25. A witty and tender novel in which narrator John recalls the escapades of older brother Tom whose perceptive and crafty schemes set him apart. A sequel: *More Adventures of the Great Brain* (1969, $6.95; LB $6.46).

2438. Fitzgerald, John D. *Me and My Little Brain* (4–6). Illus. by Mercer Mayer. 1971, Dial $6.95; LB $6.46; Dell paper $1.25. In the humorous

books in this series, such as *The Great Brain Reforms* (1973, Dial $6.95; LB $6.46; Dell paper $1.25), John tells about his brother's wheeling and dealing, but in this novel John proves that he also can show his intelligence.

2439. Fitzhugh, Louise. *Sport* (4–6). 1979, Delacourt $7.95. When an 11-year-old boy is left a sizable fortune, his mother tries to regain his custody.

2440. Fleischman, Sid. *By the Great Horn Spoon* (4–6). Illus. by Eric Von Schmidt. 1963, Little $5.95. Accompanied by Praiseworthy, the butler, an orphan boy named Jack Fogg runs away and becomes involved in the California gold rush of 1849 in this hilarious adventure story.

2441. Fleischman, Sid. *Chancy and the Grand Rascal* (5–7). Illus. by Eric Von Schmidt. 1966, Little $7.95. The boy and his uncle, the grand rascal, combine hard work and quick wits to outsmart a scoundrel, hoodwink a miser, and capture a band of outlaws.

2442. Fleischman, Sid. *The Ghost in the Noonday Sun* (5–7). Illus. by Warren Chappell. 1965, Little $6.95; Dell paper $1.25. Pirate story with all the standard ingredients of shanghaied boy, villainous captain, and buried treasure.

2443. Fleischman, Sid. *The Ghost on Saturday Night* (3–5). Illus. by Eric Von Schmidt. 1974, Little $5.95. Ten-year-old Opie's efforts to raise money for a saddle involve him in a ghost-raising session and the recovery of money stolen from a bank.

2444. Fleischman, Sid. *The Hey Hey Man* (4–6). Illus. by Nadine Westcott. 1979, Little $7.95. A tree sprite bests an ornery gold thief. Also use: *Jim Bridger's Alarm Clock and Other Tall Tales* (1978, Dutton $6.95).

2445. Fleischman, Sid. *Humbug Mountain* (4–6). Illus. by Eric Von Schmidt. 1978, Little $7.95. A madcap tall tale adventure in the wild West.

2446. Fleischman, Sid. *Jingo Django* (4–6). Illus. by Eric Von Schmidt. 1971, Little $6.95. A humorous adventure story about a young boy who lives in an orphanage in Boston and, after many escapades, finds his real father.

2447. Fleischman, Sid. *McBroom and the Beanstalk* (3–5). Illus. by Walter Lorraine. 1978, Little $5.95. A tall tale in which McBroom enters the World Champion Liar's Competition.

2448. Fleischman, Sid. *McBroom Tells a Lie* (3–5). Illus. by Walter Lorraine. 1976, Little $4.95. More whoppers and tall tales from a character noted for his fabrication of the truth.

2449. Fleischman, Sid. *Me and the Man on the Moon-Eyed Horse* (3–6). Illus. by Eric Von Schmidt. 1977, Little $5.95. A tall tale about a young boy's humorous involvement with the capture of train wreckers in the West of frontier days.

2450. Fleischman, Sid. *Mr. Mysterious & Company* (3–5). Illus. by Eric Von Schmidt. 1962, Little $6.95; Dell paper $1.25. A traveling magic show during the 1880s makes for an entertaining family story that is also an excellent historical novel.

2451. Gannett, Ruth. *My Father's Dragon* (4–6). Illus. by author. 1948, Random $4.99. Hilarious adventures of Elmer Elevator. Also use: *Elmer and the Dragon* (1950, Random $4.99).

2452. Gilson, Jamie. *Dial Leroi Rupert* (5–7). Illus. by John Wallner. 1979, Lothrop $5.95; LB $5.71. Mitch's imitation of a local disc jockey gets him into trouble.

2453. Gilson, Jamie. *Harvey, the Beer Can King* (4–7). Illus. by John Wallner. 1978, Lothrop $5.95; LB $5.49. Harvey is certain that his collection of beer cans will insure his victory in the Superkid Contest.

2454. Gray, Genevieve. *Ghost Story* (3–5). Illus. by Greta Matus. 1975, Lothrop $5.52. A ghost family, first unhappy with the invasion of their house by a group of hippies, also must face the discomfort of being studied by graduate students.

2455. Greene, Constance C. *I Know You Al* (5–7). Illus. by Byron Barton. 1975, Viking $6.95. Twelve-year-old Al is waist deep in calorie counting and in preparations for her father's second marriage. A delightful sequel to *A Girl Called Al*.

2456. Greene, Constance C. *Isabelle the Itch* (4–6). Illus. by Emily McCully. 1973, Viking $6.95; Dell paper $.95. Isabelle is a hyperactive fifth-grader who expends her energies in many directions, not getting much of anywhere.

2457. Greene, Constance C. *Your Old Pal Al* (6–9). 1979, Viking $7.95. Al, now 14, is as vulnerable but intrepid as ever in a new series of adventures.

2458. Greenwald, Sheila. *It All Began with Jane Eyre: Or the Secret Life of Franny Dilman* (6–9). 1980, Atlantic/Little $7.95. A spoof on current adolescent novels about a girl who really enjoys the classics.

2459. Greenwald, Sheila. *The Mariah Delany Lending Library Disaster* (4–6). 1977, Houghton $6.95. To make extra money, Mariah converts her parents' collection of books into a lending library, but her patrons neglect to return them.

2460. Hale, Lucretia P. *The Complete Peterkin Papers* (5–7). 1960, Houghton $5.95. A series of amusing anecdotes about the Peterkin family, including 4 new stories out of print since 1886.

2461. Haywood, Carolyn. *Annie Pat and Eddie* (2–4). Illus. by author. 1960, Morrow $7.25; LB $6.96. All about Eddie, Annie Pat, and their hilarious times. Others in the series (all Morrow, same prices): *Little Eddie* (1947), *Eddie and the Fire Engine* (1949), *Eddie's Green Thumb* (1964), and *Eddie's Valuable Property* (1975).

2462. Haywood, Carolyn. *Eddie's Menagerie* (3–5). Illus. by Ingrid Fetz. 1978, Morrow $6.95; LB $6.67. Eddie Wilson becomes a volunteer detective for a pet store.

2463. Heide, Florence Parry. *Banana Twist* (4–6). 1978, Holiday $6.95. Jonah tries a flimflam job to get into a prep school and succeeds in spite of his friend Goober.

2464. Hicks, Clifford B. *Alvin Fernald, Foreign Trader* (4–6). Illus. by Bill Sokol. 1966, Holt $6.50; Archway paper $1.50. Alvin wins a trip to Europe for a prizewinning candy recipe and gets involved with industrial spies in a series of humorous incidents.

2465. Hildick, E. W. *The Case of the Condemned Cat* (4–6). Illus. by Lisl Weil. 1975, Macmillan $6.95; Archway paper $1.50. Who killed the white dove? The McGurk Organization solves another crime. Also use: *Deadline for McGurk: A McGurk Mystery* (1975, Archway paper $1.25) and *The Case of the Invisible Dog* (1977, Archway paper $1.50).

2466. Hildick, E. W. *The Case of the Phantom Frog* (4–6). 1979, Macmillan $7.95. Since her young nephew arrived, a phantom frog has been plaguing Mrs. Krantz.

2467. Hildick, E. W. *Louie's Snowstorm* (5–7). Illus. by Iris Schweitzer. 1974, Doubleday $5.95. Louie, the English milkman—hero of other novels—is upset when his new helper turns out to be an American girl.

2468. Hildick, E. W. *Manhattan Is Missing* (4–6). Illus. by Jan Palmer. 1969, Doubleday $4.95; Avon paper $1.25. Operation Catnet is initiated by Peter Clarke, his brother Benjie, and friend Hugh, in an effort to recover Manhattan, the prized Siamese.

2469. Hildick, E. W. *The Nose Knows: A McGurk Mystery* (3–6). Illus. by Unada Glieve. 1972, Grosset paper $1.25. Jack McGurk and Joey Rockaway humorously solve the mystery of the missing catcher's mitt.

2470. Hoban, Russell. *The Twenty-Elephant Restaurant* (2–4). Illus. by Emily McCully. 1978, Atheneum $8.95. The buying of a table ends in opening a restaurant.

2471. Holland, Isabelle. *Journey for Three* (4–6). Illus. by Charles Robinson. 1975, Houghton $4.95. Three orphans, led by 11-year-old Alison, win over the heart of a recluse.

2472. Howe, Deborah, and Howe, James. *Bunnicula: A Rabbit-Tale of Mystery* (4–6). Illus. by Alan Daniel. 1979, Atheneum $7.95. A dog named Harold tells the story of a rabbit many believe to be a vampire.

2473. Hunter, Norman. *The Incredible Adventures of Professor Branestawm* (5–8). Illus. by W. Heath Robinson. 1979, Merrimack $6.96. Fourteen absurd stories about a madcap inventor and his loony inventions.

2474. Hurwitz, Johanna. *Aldo Applesauce* (3–4). Illus. by John Wallner. 1979, Morrow $7.50; LB $7.20. Aldo moves to New York City, acquires a new nickname and a strange friend.

2475. Hurwitz, Johanna. *Much Ado about Aldo* (3–5). Illus. by John Wallner. 1978, Morrow $6.95; LB $6.67. When 8-year-old Aldo learns that animals feed on each other, he becomes a vegetarian.

2476. Hutchins, Pat. *The House That Sailed Away* (3–5). Illus. by Laurence Hutchins. 1975, Greenwillow $6.96. A nonsense novel about an English family's adventures at sea in their uprooted house.

2477. Keller, Beverly. *The Beetle Bush* (2–4). Illus. by Marc Simont. 1976, Coward $5.99; Dell paper $1.50. Nothing went right for Arabelle and she felt she was a born loser until her garden pests were admired by the landlord.

2478. Kennedy, Richard. *The Rise and Fall of Ben Gizzard* (2–4). Illus. by Marcia Sewall. 1978, Little $5.95. A villainous coward meets his match when a young artist comes to town.

2479. Kibbe, Pat. *The Hocus-Pocus Dilemma* (4–6). 1979, Knopf $5.95; LB $5.99. B.J. tries to prove her powers of ESP on an unsuspecting family.

2480. King, Clive. *Me and My Million* (4–6). 1979, Crowell $7.95; LB $7.89. Ringo, a London street urchin, has some amazing and amusing adventures resulting from a learning disability.

2481. Konigsburg, E. L. *About the B'Nai Bagels* (3–6). Illus. by author. 1969, Atheneum $7.95; paper $1.95. Poor Mark—his mother is the manager of the Little League Baseball team on which he plays and his older brother is the coach. A hilarious story.

2482. Krantz, Hazel. *100 Pounds of Popcorn* (5–7). Illus. by Charles Geer. 1961, Vanguard $4.95. Andy and his friends go into business when they receive 100 pounds of popcorn, and learn about business techniques.

2483. Krensky, Stephen. *The Perils of Putney* (5–7). Illus. by Jurg Obrist. 1978, Atheneum $7.95. A spoof of tales of chivalry that involves a peaceful giant and the quest of the Fair Damsel.

2484. Lawson, Robert. *Ben and Me* (5–8). Illus. by author. 1939, Little $6.95; Dell paper $.95. The events of Benjamin Franklin's life, as told by his good mouse Amos, who lived in his old fur cap.

2485. Lawson, Robert. *Mr. Revere and I* (5–8). Illus. by author. 1953, Little $6.95; Dell paper $.95. A delightful account of certain episodes in Revere's life, as revealed by his horse Scheherazade.

2486. Lindgren, Astrid. *Emil and Piggy Beast* (3–4). Illus. by Bjorn Berg. 1973, Follett $5.95. Emil is a precocious 5-year-old whose tricks and schemes are alternately a source of pride and embarrassment for his parents.

2487. Lindgren, Astrid. *Emil's Pranks* (3–5). Illus. by Bjorn Berg. 1971, Follett $5.97. A mischief maker continues the exploits first introduced in *Emil in the Soup Tureen* (1970, $5.95).

2488. Lindgren, Astrid. *Pippi Longstocking* (4–6). Illus. by Louis Glanzman. 1950, Viking $4.95; paper $1.50. A little Swedish tomboy who has a monkey and a horse for companions. Also use (same publisher and prices): *Pippi Goes on Board* (1957) and *Pippi in the South Seas* (1959).

2489. Lowry, Lois. *Anastasia Krupnik* (4–6). 1979, Houghton $6.95. A lively romp with an intelligent and articulate 10-year-old girl leading the way.

2490. Macaulay, David. *Motel of the Mysteries* (6–9). Illus. by author. 1979, Houghton $8.90; paper $4.95. An archaeologist in the year 4022 explores the site of our contemporary motels.

2491. McCloskey, Robert. *Homer Price* (3–6). Illus. by author. 1943, Viking $6.95. Popular and preposterous adventures of a midwestern boy are continued in: *Centerburg Tales* (1977, Viking $7.95; paper $1.95).

2492. Merrill, Jean. *The Pushcart War* (5–7). Illus. by Ronni Solbert. 1964, Young Scott $7.95; paper $.75. Mack, driving a Mighty Mammoth, runs down a pushcart belonging to Morris the Florist, and a most unusual war is on!

2493. Merrill, Jean. *The Toothpaste Millionaire* (4–6). Illustrated. 1974, Houghton $6.95. Kate tells the delightful story of a black boy, Rufus, who challenges the entire business community by marketing a product called simply "toothpaste."

2494. Mian, Mary. *Take Three Witches* (3–5). Illus. by Eric Von Schmidt. 1971, Houghton $4.95. A hilarious tale of a strange cast of characters including a stuffy mayor, 2 girl scouts, and 3 modern witches. Sequel: *Net to Catch War* (1975, $6.95).

2495. Myers, Walter Dean. *Mojo and the Russians* (6–8). 1977, Viking $6.95. A group of friends tries to save one of them from a voodoo spell.

2496. Newton, Suzanne. *What Are You Up to William Thomas?* (6–9). 1977, Westminster $7.95. William is unable to stop meddling with other's affairs in this very funny story.

2497. Peck, Robert Newton. *Hub* (5–7). Illus. by Ted Lewin. 1979, Knopf $5.95; LB $5.99. Hub and friend Spooner back their teacher Miss Guppy in the Overland Obstacle Bicycle Race.

2498. Pinkwater, D. Manus. *Fat Men from Space* (3–6). Illus. by author. 1977, Dodd $5.50. Among other adventures, William encounters raiders of junk food from outer space in this nutrition-conscious farce.

2499. Pinkwater, D. Manus. *The Hoboken Chicken Emergency* (3–7). 1977, Prentice-Hall $6.95; Scholastic paper $.95. A young boy buys a 6-foot, 260-pound chicken in this humorous story.

2500. Pinkwater, D. Manus. *The Last Guru* (4–6). Illus. by author. 1974, Dodd $6.95. Twelve-year-old Harold goes from rags to great riches.

2501. Pinkwater, D. Manus. *Return of the Moose* (4–6). Illus. by author. 1979, Dodd $6.95. In a sequel to *Blue Moose*, our hero writes a novel based on his exploits and goes to Hollywood to supervise its filming.

2502. Pinkwater, D. Manus. *Yobgorgle: Mystery Monster of Lake Ontario* (5–7). 1979, Seabury $7.95. A nonsense novel that provides a clear twist to the Flying Dutchman legend.

2503. Pomerantz, Charlotte. *The Mango Tooth* (3–5). Illus. by Marylin Hofner. 1977, Greenwillow $6.96. In a series of misadventures, Posy loses one tooth after another.

2504. Raskin, Ellen. *The Mysterious Disappearance of Leon (I Mean Noel)* (4–6). Illus. by author. 1971, Dutton $8.95; paper $1.95. Humorous saga of Mrs. Carillon's search for her husband Leon (or Noel), who is the joint heir to a soup fortune.

2505. Raskin, Ellen. *The Tattooed Potato and Other Clues* (5–7). 1975, Dutton $7.50. This zany spoof on detective stories introduces the reader to part-time mystery solver Garson and his assistant, Dickdry Dock.

2506. Ritchie, Barbara. *Ramon Makes a Trade* (3–5). 1959, Parnassus $6.95. Ramon turns out to be a most ingenious trader, as explained in English and Spanish.

2507. Robertson, Keith. *Henry Reed, Inc.* (5–7). Illus. by Robert McCloskey. 1958, Viking $6.96; paper $1.50. Told deadpan in diary form, this story of Henry's enterprising summer in New Jersey presents one of the most amusing boys since Tom and Huck. More about Henry from Viking: *Henry Reed's Journey* (1963, $7.95; paper $1.50). *Henry Reed's Babysitting Service* (1966, $7.95; Dell paper $1.50), and *Henry Reed's Big Show* (1970, $5.50; paper .95).

2508. Robinson, Jean. *The Mystery of Lincoln Detweiler and the Dog Who Barked Spanish* (4–6). Illus. by Giola Fiammenghi. 1977, Follett $5.95; LB $5.97. Farcical adventures involving a newly orphaned boy and a dog smuggled into America from Mexico.

2509. Rockwell, Thomas. *How to Eat Fried Worms* (4–6). Illus. by Emily McCully. 1973, Watts $5.88; Dell paper $1.25. In this very humorous story, Billy takes on a bet—he will eat 15 worms a day. His family and friends help devise ways to cook them.

2510. Rodgers, Mary. *A Billion for Boris* (4–6). 1974, Harper $4.95; LB $5.79; paper $1.95. Anabel, the heroine of *Freaky Friday*, narrates a humorous story about her neighbor Boris and his problems with an eccentric mother.

2511. Rounds, Glen. *The Day the Circus Came to Lone Tree* (3–6). Illus. by author. 1973, Holiday $5.95. The circus's first and last visit to Lone Tree is a disaster when all the animals break loose.

2512. Schellie, Don. *Kidnapping Mr. Tubbs* (6–9). 1978, Four Winds $5.95. Two teenagers abduct an old cowboy, with humorous results.

2513. Selden, George. *Harry Cat's Pet Puppy* (3–6). Illus. by Garth Williams. 1974, Farrar $5.95; Dell paper $1.25. The denizens of a drainpipe in the Times Square subway station in New York City—Harry Cat and Tucker Mouse—are back in a good form taking care of a lost puppy.

2514. Sharmat, Marjorie W. *Getting Something on Maggie Marmelstein* (3–5). Illus. by Ben Shecter. 1971, Harper $6.89; paper $1.95. When Thad's mortal enemy, Maggie, sees him cooking and begins teasing him, Thad must find some way of blackmailing her into silence.

2515. Shura, Mary Francis. *Chester* (4–6). 1980, Dodd $6.95. A group of likable kids are outshone by a newcomer named Chester.

2516. Spykman, E. C. *A Lemon and a Star* (4–6). 1955, Harcourt $5.95. The amusing, often hair-raising antics of 4 children trying to outwit each other and their widowed father's attempts at strict discipline in turn-of-the-century New England. Also use (both Harcourt): *Terrible, Horrible Edie* (1960, $6.50; paper $1.50) and *Edie on the Warpath* (1966, paper $1.45).

2517. Stephens, Mary Jo. *Zoe Zodiac* (3–6). Illus. by Leonard Shortall. 1971, Houghton paper $.95. Zoe's life becomes complicated when she wins first prize in a contest and receives a pet a month.

2518. Stevenson, James. *Here Comes Herb's Hurricane!* (3–5). Illustrated. 1973, Harper paper $1.50. Under Herb's leadership, an animal community prepares for a hurricane in this amusing story.

2519. Stolz, Mary. *Belling the Tiger* (1–5). Illus. by Beni Montresor. 1961, Harper $6.89. Adventures of 2 gentle mice, Asa and Rambo.

2520. Supraner, Robyn. *Think about It, You Might Learn Something* (3–7). Illus. by Sandy Kossin. 1973, Houghton $7.95. A fourth-grader writes down some of his experiences in this hilarious series of vignettes.

2521. Travers, P. L. *Mary Poppins* (4–7). Illus. by Mary Shepard. 1934, Harcourt $6.95. Delightful and humorous things happen when Mary Poppins blows in with the east wind to be nurse for the Banks children. Also use: *Mary Poppins Comes Back* (1955, Harcourt $5.95) and *Mary Poppins in the Park* (1952, Harcourt $5.95).

2522. Tripp, Wallace. *Sir Toby Jingle's Beastly Journey* (3–5). Illus. by author. 1976, Coward $7.95. The beasts set out to trap Sir Toby, but it happens the other way around.

2523. Twain, Mark. *Adventures of Huckleberry Finn* (6–8). Illus. by Donald McKay and Jo Pelseno. n.d., Grossett $4.95. One of many editions.

2524. Twain, Mark. *Adventures of Tom Sawyer* (5–8). Illus. by C. Walter Hodges. 1977, Golden $3.50. One of many fine editions of this American classic.

2525. Udry, Janice May. *Angie* (3–5). Illus. by Hilary Knight. 1971, Harper $7.89. Angie is a refreshingly honest young person with, of all things, a pet goose named Sally.

2526. Unnerstad, Edith. *Little O* (2–5). Illus. by Louis Slobodkin. 1957, Macmillan $4.50. Before she goes to school, Little O has all sorts of amusing adventures in her Swedish home.

2527. Waber, Bernard. *Mice on My Mind* (3–5). Illus. by author. 1977, Houghton $5.95. A cat becomes obsessed with the idea of finding mice in a house where there obviously aren't any.

2528. Wahl, Jan. *Screeching Door: Or What Happened at the Elephant Hotel* (5–7). Illus. by J. Winslow Higginbottom. 1975, Four Winds $6.95. Preposterous doings at the Elephant Hotel are solved by Ephram Effingham Runkle, Jr., and Sister Myrtle Flossie.

2529. Wayne, Jenifer. *Sprout and the Magician* (3–5). Illus. by Gail Owens. 1977, McGraw $6.95. Sprout tries to solve the disappearance of his sister's pet rabbit. Other Sprout books (McGraw $6.95): *Sprout and the Dogsitter* (1977) and *Sprout's Window Cleaner* (1976).

2530. Willard, Nancy. *The Highest Hit* (3–5). Illus. by Emily McCully. 1978, Harcourt $6.95. A young girl tries to make the *Guinness Book of World Records*.

2531. Williams, Jay. *The Burglar Next Door* (4–7). Illus. by Deanne Hollinger. 1976, Four Winds $6.95. In an amusing series of misadventures, Penny tries to exonerate her friend Amos from a charge of burglary.

Fantasy

2532. Adams, Richard. *Watership Down* (6–9). 1977, Macmillan $10.95; Avon paper $1.95. A group of rabbits sets out to find a new home in this English fantasy.

2533. Aiken, Joan. *The Faithless Lollybird* (6–8). Illus. by Eros Keith. 1978, Doubleday $6.95; LB $7.90. A collection of fantasies and a single poem.

2534. Aiken, Joan. *The Kingdom and the Cave* (4–6). Illus. by Victor G. Ambrus. 1974, Doubleday $4.95. A humorous adventure story about the efforts of a young prince and his cat to foil an invasion plot. Also use: *Arabel's Raven* (1974, Doubleday $5.95; Dell paper 95¢).

2535. Ainsworth, Ruth. *The Phantom Carousel and Other Ghostly Tales* (4–5). Illus. by Shirley Hughes. 1978, Follett $7.98. A series of stories in which young people encounter ghosts.

2536. Ainsworth, Ruth. *The Talking Rock* (4–6). Illus. by Joanna Stubbs. 1979, Andre Deutch

$6.95. Jakes encounters a fantasy world at the seashore.

2537. Alexander, Lloyd. *The Book of Three* (5–8). 1964, Holt $5.95. Welsh legend and universal mythology are blended in the tale of an assistant pig keeper who becomes a hero. Others in the Prydain cycle: *Black Cauldron* (1965, Holt $5.95; Dell paper $1.50), *The Castle of Llyr* (1966, Holt $5.95; Dell, paper $1.50), *Taran Wanderer* (1967, Hold $6.95; Dell, paper $1.50), and *The High King* (1968, Holt $6.95), Newbery Award winner.

2538. Alexander, Lloyd. *The Cat Who Wished to Be a Man* (5–6). 1973, Dutton $5.95; paper $1.95. A cat named Lionel, turned into a man by a magician, begins combating the corrupt mayor of the town.

2539. Alexander, Lloyd. *The First Two Lives of Lukas-Kasha* (5–7). 1978, Dutton $8.50. Lukas awakens to find himself in a strange land.

2540. Alexander, Lloyd. *The Marvelous Misadventures of Sebastian* (4–7). 1970, Dutton $9.95; paper $1.95. Fourth fiddler Sebastian meets many trials while crossing a Graustarkian kingdom to reach the arms of his princess.

2541. Alexander, Lloyd. *Time Cat: The Remarkable Journeys of Jason and Gareth* (4–6). 1963, Holt $3.29. Jason's cat takes him to various times and places.

2542. Alexander, Lloyd. *The Truthful Harp* (2–5). Illus. by Evaline Ness. 1967, Holt $3.27. Endearing King Fflewddur Fflam, the would-be bard of the longer Prydain chronicles, learns to sing the ungilded truth about his brave deeds through a magic harp. Another storybook of a Prydain stalwart: *Coll and His White Pig* (1965, Holt $5.95).

2543. Alexander, Lloyd. *The Wizard in the Tree* (4–6). Illus. by Laszlo Kubinyi. 1975, Dutton $7.50. A delightful fantasy of a good-versus-evil struggle involving an orphan, Mallory, his wizard, and their battle against Mrs. Parsel and Squire Scrupnor.

2544. Allan, Mabel Esther. *Romansgrove* (6–8). Illus. by Gail Qwens. 1975, Atheneum $6.95. Two modern-day children find a magic pendant that transports them through time back to 1902.

2545. Allan, Ted. *Willie the Squowse* (3–5). Illus. by Quentin Blake. 1978, Hastings $5.95. Willie, part mouse, part squirrel, lives in walls between the houses of 2 very different families.

2546. Ames, Mildred. *Is There Life on a Plastic Planet?* (5–6). 1975, Dutton $7.50. Hollis is intrigued when Mrs. Eudora, owner of a doll shop, makes a lifelike doll substitute of Hollis, but soon her replacement begins taking over her life. Also use: *Without Hats, Who Can Tell the Good Guys?* (1976, Dutton $6.95).

2547. Amoss, Berthe. *The Chalk Cross* (5–7). 1976, Seabury $6.96. A story involving voodoo in New Orleans.

2548. Anastasio, Dina. *A Question of Time* (4–6). Illus. by Dale Payson. 1978, Dutton $7.50. In this fantasy, a young girl finds a connection between a doll collection, a town tragedy, and her own family.

2549. Anderson, Margaret J. *To Nowhere and Back* (5–7). 1975, Knopf $5.99. In this English novel, a young girl travels back in history when she discovers she is one with a girl who lived long ago.

2550. Arkin, Alan. *The Lemming Condition* (4–7). Illus. by Joan Sandin. 1976, Harper $4.95; LB $6.87; Bantam paper $1.50. Bubber opposes the mass suicide of his companions in this interesting fable.

2551. Arthur, Ruth. *Candle in Her Room* (5–7). Illus. by Margery Gill. 1966, Atheneum paper $1.95. An evil wooden doll influences 3 generations of a Welsh family until one girl courageously destroys it.

2552. Arthur, Ruth. *On the Wasteland* (4–7). Illus. by Margery Gill. 1975, Atheneum $5.95. A young English girl moves from the present into a life with the ancient Vikings.

2553. Babbitt, Natalie. *The Devil's Storybook* (4–6). Illus. by author. 1974, Farrar $5.95. Ten stories about outwitting the devil, in this case personified as a middle-aged, vain, but crafty adversary.

2554. Babbitt, Natalie. *The Search for Delicious* (4–7). Illus. by author. 1969, Farrar $6.95; Avon paper $1.50. The innocent task of polling the kingdom's subjects for personal food preferences, to secure a definition of the word *delicious* for the official dictionary, provokes civil war in a zestful spoof of taste and society.

2555. Babbitt, Natalie. *Tuck Everlasting* (4–6). 1975, Farrar $5.95; Bantam paper $1.95. Violence erupts when the Tuck family members discover that their secret about a spring that brings immortality has been discovered.

2556. Bacon, Martha. *Moth Manor: A Gothic Tale* (4–6). Illus. by Gail Burroughs. 1978, Little $6.95. The story of a dollhouse and 3 generations of its owners.

2557. Bacon, Peggy. *The Ghost of Opalina* (5–7). 1967, Little $5.95. The ghost of a cat tells about her 9 lives.

2558. Bailey, Carolyn Sherwin. *Miss Hickory* (4–6). Illus. by Ruth Gannett. 1946, Viking $7.95; Penguin paper $1.50. The adventures of a doll made from an apple branch with a hickory nut head. Newbery Award, 1947.

2559. Baker, Betty. *Save Sirrushany! (Also Agotha, Princess Gwyn and All the Fearsome Beasts* (5–6). Map by Erick Ingrahm. 1978, Macmillan $7.95. A modern fairy tale involving a young girl, a dragon, and a seedy royal family.

2560. Ballard, Mignon Franklin. *Aunt Matilda's Ghost* (5–7). 1978, Aurora $5.95; paper $3.95. A ghost tries to clear the name of a man wrongfully accused of embezzlement.

2561. Barber, Antonia. *The Ghosts* (4–6). 1969, Farrar $4.95. Two youngsters meet ghosts from another country in their garden.

2562. Barrie, Sir James M. *Peter Pan* (4–6). 1970, Grosset $1.95. The Darling family, Tinker Bell, and the whole beloved cast of characters in a recommended edition.

2563. Beachcroft, Nina. *Well Met by Witchcraft* (4–6). 1972, Atheneum $5.95. Children help an old lady overcome the powers of black witchcraft.

2564. Beckman, Thea. *Crusade in Jeans* (4–6). 1975, Scribner $8.95. By time machine, a boy is transported back to the days of the Children's Crusade.

2565. Bellairs, John. *The Figure in the Shadows* (5–7). Illus. by Mercer Mayer. 1975, Dial $6.95; LB $6.46; Dell paper $1.25. Excitement, magic, and suspense are combined in this story of a boy whose new-found ancient coin is actually an evil talisman. Sequel: *The House with a Clock in Its Walls* (1973, Dial $6.95; LB $6.46; Dell paper $1.25).

2566. Bellairs, John. *Letter, the Witch and the Ring* (4–6). Illus. by Richard Egielski. 1976, Dial $6.95; LB $6.46; Dell paper $1.25. Rosa Rita and neighbor Mrs. Zimmerman encounter the evil powers of a witch. A sequel to *The Figure in the Shadows*

2567. Benary-Isbert, Margot. *The Wicked Enchantment* (5–7). Trans. by Richard and Clara Winston. Illus. by Enrico Arno. 1955, Harcourt $5.50. An excellent fantasy in which present-day life in a German town is interwoven with a medieval legend that comes alive and threatens the people.

2568. Bennett, Anna Elizabeth. *Little Witch* (3–5). Illus. by Helen Stone. 1953, Lippincott $7.95; Scholastic paper $.95. Minx, the little witch, does not like being a witch's child and wants most of all to go to school.

2569. Berestord, Elizabeth. *Invisible Magic* (4–6). Illus. by Judith Valpy. 1977, Beekman $6.95. Kate and young brother Marcus on summer vacation meet a visitor from ancient Britain.

2570. Bethancourt, T. Ernesto. *The Dog Days of Arthur Cane* (6–9). 1976, Holiday $7.95. Arthur, a Long Island, New York, schoolboy, discovers that he has been turned into a dog.

2571. Bond, Nancy. *A String in the Harp* (6–9). 1976, Atheneum $9.95. A young boy discovers a key that allows him to look into the past, in this fantasy about an American family spending a year in Wales.

2572. Bonham, Frank. *The Friends of the Loony Lake Monster* (4–6). 1972, Dutton $6.95. Gussie protects her pet dinosaur in this fanciful story that combines a resourceful heroine and a lesson about conservation.

2573. Boston, L. M. *The Children of Green Knowe* (4–7). Illus. by Peter Boston. 1955, Harcourt $5.95; paper $1.50. A small, lonely boy comes to live in an old English country house where the children who played there generations ago sometimes reappear. Sequels: *Treasure of Green Knowe* (1958, $6.50; paper $1.95), *The River at Green Knowe* (1959, $5.50; paper $1.45), *A Stranger at Green Knowe* (1961, $5.75; paper $1.95), and *An Enemy at Green Knowe* (1964, $5.95; paper $1.95).

2574. Boston, L. M. *The Fossil Snake* (3–6). Illus. by Peter Boston. 1976, Atheneum $4.95. A fossilized snake comes alive and becomes a young boy's constant companion.

2575. Boston, L. M. *The Guardians of the House* (3–7). 1975, Atheneum $5.95. A Green Knowe story in which a young boy, newly moved from Wales, has adventures in the ancient house.

2576. Boston, L. M. *The Sea Egg* (3–5). Illus. by Peter Boston. 1967, Harcourt $4.95. A brief episode of magic perfectly captured in this seaside adventure of 2 brothers whose egg-shaped rock hatches into a baby merman.

2577. Boston, L. M. *The Stones of Green Knowe* (4–6). Illus. by Peter Boston. 1976, Atheneum $6.95. In this installment of the well-known series, a mature country boy moves in time to see future inhabitants of his home.

2578. Bowen, Irene. *Suddenly—a Witch* (4–6). 1970, Lippincott $3.50. Susan mounts a broomstick and suddenly becomes invisible.

2579. Briggs, Katharine. *Hobberdy Dick* (5–7). 1977, Greenwillow $7.25; LB $6.96; Penguin paper $1.50. Set in midseventeenth-century England, this is a fantasy about a hobgoblin who guards a country house.

2580. Brock, Betty. *The Shades* (3–5). Illus. by Victoria de Larrea. 1971, Avon paper $1.25. By using the magic waters of a dolphin fountain, young Hollis is able to see shadows from the past.

2581. Brown, Palmer. *Hickory* (2–4). Illus. by author. 1978, Harper $6.95; LB $7.49. Hickory, a field mouse, is lonely on his own until he makes friends with a grasshopper.

2582. Buchwald, Emilie. *Gildaen: The Heroic Adventures of a Most Unusual Rabbit* (4–6). Illus. by Barbara Flynn. 1973, Harcourt $5.50. Gildaen, an adventure-loving rabbit, joins 2 humans in a mission to save a beleaguered king.

2583. Bunyan, John. *Pilgrim's Progress* (4–6). Ed. by Mary Godolphin. Illus. by Robert Lawson. 1939, Lippincott paper $2.95. A shortened, simplified edition of the classic.

2584. Burnett, Frances Hodgson. *A Little Princess* (4–6). Illus. by Tasha Tudor. 1962, Lippincott $10.00; LB $9.79; Dell paper $1.50. Sad story of the penniless orphan whose fortune is finally restored.

2585. Burnett, Frances Hodgson. *The Secret Garden* (4–6). Illus. by Tasha Tudor. 1962, Lippincott deluxe $10.00; Dell paper $1.50. Three children find a secret garden and make it bloom again; the garden, in turn, changes the children.

2586. Byars, Betsy. *The Winged Colt of Casa Mia* (4–6). Illus. by Richard Cuffari. 1973, Viking $6.95. In this fantasy, a young boy visits the Texas ranch of his uncle, an ex-stunt man, and encounters a colt with supernatural powers.

2587. Byfield, Barbara. *Andrew and the Alchemist* (4–6). Illus. by Deanne Hollinger. 1977, Doubleday $5.95. The amusing fantasy, set in the Middle Ages, about an orphan who becomes an apprentice alchemist.

2588. Byfield, Barbara. *The Haunted Tower* (3–5). Illus. by author. 1976, Doubleday $6.95; LB $4.95. In this installment in the series about the retired detective Hannibal Stern and a 400-year-old ghost, Sir Roger de Rudisill, Hannibal solves the mystery of a missing prince and his crown.

2589. Calhoun, Mary. *Ownself* (5–8). 1975, Harper $7.95; LB $7.89; paper $1.50. Set in horse-and-buggy days, exorcism and fairy spells figure in this story about an imaginative young girl.

2590. Cameron, Eleanor. *The Court of the Stone Children* (5–7). 1973, Dutton $7.95. Avon paper $1.25. Nina's move with her family to San Francisco is a disaster until she encounters a young ghost in a small museum.

2591. Carew, Jan. *Children of the Sun* (3–5). Illus. by Leo Dillon and Diane Dillon. 1980, Little $9.95. The fate of the 2 children born of the Sun and the earth mother is told in this mythlike epic.

2592. Campbell, Hope. *Peter's Angel* (3–5). Illus. by Ralph Pinto. 1976, Four Winds $6.95. Monsters drawn on wall posters frighten Peter until 2 mice intervene.

2593. Carroll, Lewis. *Alice's Adventures in Wonderland and Through the Looking Glass* (4–7). Illus. by John Tenniel. 1963, Macmillan $6.95; paper $1.50. One of many recommended editions.

2594. Catling, Patrick Skene. *The Chocolate Touch* (3–5). Illus. by Margot Apple. 1979, Morrow $5.95; LB $5.91. A Midas-story variation in which a boy turns his mother to chocolate.

2595. Chew, Ruth. *Witch's Buttons* (2–4). Illus. by author. 1974, Hastings $5.95. The strange button that Sandy and her friend find actually belongs to a witch.

2596. Chew, Ruth. *The Would-Be Witch* (3–5). Illus. by author. 1977, Hastings $5.95. Robin and Andy take midnight rides on a flying dustpan. Also use: *Witch's Broom* (1977, Dodd $5.25; Scholastic paper $1.25).

2597. Clapp, Patricia. *Jane-Emily* (5–7). 1969, Lothrop $6.00. After seeing the image of a dead girl in a crystal ball, Jane becomes possessed by the ghost.

2598. Clarke, Pauline. *The Return of the Twelves* (5–7). Illus. by Bernarda Bryson. 1963, Coward $7.95. An original fantasy based on Branwell Brontë's imaginary adventures of a set of wooden soldiers.

2599. Clarke, Pauline. *The Two Faces of Silenus* (5–7). 1972, Coward $5.95. Two English children and an Italian boy become involved in danger and adventure in Italy when the Silenus, the god carved in a fountain, comes alive.

2600. Coatsworth, Elizabeth. *Marra's World* (4–6). Illus. by Krystyna Turska. 1975, Greenwillow $6.00. A Scottish tale transferred to the Maine coast about a waif cared for by a harsh grandmother.

2601. Coblentz, Catherine C. *The Blue Cat of Castle Town* (3–5). Illus. by Janice Holland. 1949, Countryman paper $4.95. A fantasy, set in Vermont in the 1800s, that tells of a little cat's wanderings and how he changed the course of the town's early history.

2602. Coombs, Patricia. *Dorrie and the Dreamyard Monsters* (2–4). Illustrated. 1977, Lothrop $6.25; LB $6.00. Dorrie helps convert fierce monsters into lovable friends in this adventure story for Dorrie fans.

2603. Coombs, Patricia. *Molly Mullett* (3–5). Illustrated. 1975, Lothrop $5.52. An enterprising young heroine overcomes an ogre that has been terrorizing a village.

2604. Cooper, Susan. *Jethro and the Jumbie* (3–4). Illus. by Ashley Bryan. 1979, Atheneum $6.95. On a Caribbean island, a young boy has a humorous encounter with a jumbie, the ghost of a dead person.

2605. Cooper, Susan. *Silver on the Tree* (5–7). 1977, Atheneum $7.95. The fifth and last volume of the series that tells of the final struggle waged by Will Stanton and his friends against the Dark, the powers of evil. Others in the series: *Over Sea, Under Stone* (1966, Harcourt $6.25); *The Dark Is Rising* (1973, Atheneum $7.95; paper $1.95); *Greenwitch* (1974, Atheneum $5.95; paper $1.95), and the Newbery Award winner, *The Grey King* (1975, Atheneum $7.95; paper $1.95).

2606. Corbett, Scott. *The Discontented Ghost* (6–8). 1978, Dutton $7.95. Corbett retells Oscar Wilde's *The Canterville Ghost* in an amusing way.

2607. Corbett, Scott. *The Mysterious Zetabet* (2–4). Illus. by Jon McIntosh. 1979, Little $6.95. In a dream, Zachary Zwicker enters a land with a topsy-turvy alphabet.

2608. Cresswell, Helen. *A Game of Catch* (3–5). Illus. by Ati Forberg. 1977, Macmillan $5.95. A time-warp fantasy in which 2 eighteenth-century children play with their contemporary counterparts.

2609. Cresswell, Helen. *Up the Pier* (5–6). Illus. by Gareth Floyd. 1972, Macmillan $4.95. Carrie meets a boy at a Welsh seaside resort who is trapped in a time warp and wants to leave the present and return to 1921.

2610. Cunningham, Julia. *Macaroon* (4–6). Illus. by Evaline Ness. 1962, Pantheon $5.39; Dell paper $1.50. Fantasy of a raccoon who deliberately sets out to adopt an "impossible" child.

2611. Cunningham, Julia. *Maybe, a Mole* (3–5). Illus. by Cyndy Szekeres. 1974, Pantheon $5.69; Dell paper $.95. Five stories of survival involving a mole who is ostracized by his own kind because he is able to see.

2612. Curry, Jane Louise. *The Birdstones* (6–8). 1977, Atheneum $6.95. A complex fantasy about a brave sixth-grader who removes a sacred carved bird from its rightful home. Also use: *The Daybreakers* (1970, Harcourt $5.95).

2613. Curry, Jane Louise. *Mindy's Mysterious Miniature* (4–6). Illus. by Charles Robinson. 1970, Harcourt $5.95. Mindy is kidnapped by a strange man who controls the power of miniaturizing people and things. Also use: *Parsley, Sage, Rosemary and Time* (1975, Atheneum $5.95).

2614. Curry, Jane Louise. *The Lost Farm* (3–7). Illus. by Charles Robinson. 1974, Atheneum $5.95. Professor Lilliput and his reducing machine are at it again in this charming sequel to *Mindy's Mysterious Miniature.*

2615. Curry, Jane Louise. *The Magical Cupboard* (5–8). Illus. by Charles Robinson. 1976, Atheneum $6.95. The period of witchcraft in New England is recreated through a modern family's search for an old cupboard.

2616. Curry, Jane Louise. *Poor Tom's Ghost* (5–7). 1977, Atheneum $8.95. An actor and his 2 children buy an old country home haunted by the ghost of another Shakespearean actor.

2617. Curry, Jane Louise. *The Sleepers* (4–6). 1968, Harcourt $5.50. Four young people find themselves back in the days of King Arthur.

2618. Curry, Jane Louise. *The Watchers* (5–7). 1975, Atheneum $6.95. Thirteen-year-old Ray stays with a West Virginia family that has difficulty making a living from the land in this unusual novel with fantasy elements.

2619. Cusack, Isabel Langis. *Ivan the Great* (2–4). Illus. by Carol Nicklaus. 1978, Crowell $5.95; LB $5.79. Robby maintains he can hear his parrot Ivan speak when no one else can.

2620. Cutt, W. Towrie. *Seven for the Sea* (4–6). Illustrated. 1974, Follett $4.95; LB $4.98. In a time warp, 2 Scottish children visit days past.

2621. Dahl, Roald. *Charlie and the Chocolate Factory* (4–6). Illus. by Joseph Schindelman. 1964, Knopf $4.95; LB $5.99; Bantam paper $1.95. A rather morbid tale of Charlie and 4 of his nasty friends who tour Willy Wonka's extraordinary chocolate factory. They all meet disaster except Charlie, for he has obeyed orders.

2622. Dahl, Roald. *Charlie and the Great Glass Elevator* (4–6). Illus. by Joseph Schindelman. 1972, Knopf $4.95; LB $5.99; Bantam paper $1.95. Willie Wonka is back with a new impressive list of accomplishments, including changing an elevator into a spacecraft.

2623. Dahl, Roald. *James and the Giant Peach* (4–6). Illus. by Nancy E. Burkert. 1961, Knopf $5.95; LB $5.99. James is unhappy living with his mean aunts until a magic potion produces an enormous peach, which becomes a home for him.

2624. Dahl, Roald. *Magic Finger* (3–5). Illus. by William Pene du Bois. 1966, Harper $5.95; LB $6.89. An 8-year-old girl mysteriously has the power to punish people for wrongdoing by pointing her finger at them.

2625. DeCamp, Lyon Sprague, and Cook, Catherine., eds. *Tales beyond Time* (5–7). Illus. by Ati Forberg. 1973, Lothrop $6.96. Ten imaginative episodes from writers that include L. Frank Baum and Lloyd Alexander.

2626. Dickinson, Peter. *The Weathermonger* (5–7). 1969, Little $5.95; DAW paper $.95. A boy and his sister, along with the people of Britain, are taken back to the Middle Ages. Also use: *Blue Hawk* (1976, Little $8.95; Ballantine paper $1.95).

2627. Donovan, John. *Family* (6–9). 1976, Harper $5.95; LB $6.89. An unusual novel about the flight of 3 apes from the laboratory where they are being held for experiments.

2628. Doty, Jean Slaughter. *Can I Get There by Candlelight?* (5–7). Illus. by Ted Lewin. 1980, Macmillan $7.95. A time-lapse story about a girl who magically enters the world of the nineteenth century.

2629. Drury, Robert W. *The Champion of Merimack County* (4–7). Illus. by Fritz Wegner. 1976, Little $6.95. The Buryfield's house is invaded by mice, including a daredevil bicycle rider who uses the bathtub as a track.

2630. du Bois, William Pene. *The Forbidden Forest* (3–5). Illus. by author. 1978, Harper $7.95; LB $7.89. A marvelous flight of fancy involving 3 unusual protagonists during World War I.

2631. Duncan, Jane. *Janet Reachfar and the Kelpie* (4–5). Illus. by Mairi Hedderwick. 1976, Seabury $7.50. A story about young Janet living on a Scottish farm and her belief that a kelpie lives in her well.

2632. Dunlop, Eileen. *Elizabeth Elizabeth* (5–7). Illus. by Peter Farmer. 1977, Holt $6.95. In this time-shift story, 12-year-old Elizabeth finds a mirror that takes her back to the eighteenth century.

2633. Durrell, Gerald. *The Talking Parcel* (4–7). Illus. by Pamela Johnson. 1975, Lippincott $7.95. Three children journey to Mythologia to recover stolen books of magic.

2634. Eager, Edward. *Knight's Castle* (4–6). Illus. by N. M. Bodecker. 1956, Harcourt $6.75; paper $1.65. Several children are introduced by an old lead soldier into the fantastic world peopled by characters in Scott's *Ivanhoe* and have many lively adventures before returning to their own land.

2635. Eager, Edward. *Seven-Day Magic* (5–6). Illus. by N. M. Bodecker. 1962, Harcourt $5.95; LB $4.95. Magic enters the lives of 5 children through a magic wishing book from the library. Also use: *Half Magic* (1954, Harcourt $6.50; paper $1.95).

2636. Eager, Edward. *The Well-Wishers* (4–6). Illus. by N. M. Bodecker. 1960, Harcourt $6.50. The 6 children of *Magic or Not?* (1959, Harcourt $5.95) return for further fun and adventures.

2637. Enright, Elizabeth. *Tatsinda* (4–5). Illus. by Irene Haas. 1963, Harcourt $6.95. Tatsinda is the object of pity in a wondorous mountain kingdom, for she is the only one with golden hair and brown eyes.

2638. Estes, Eleanor. *The Witch Family* (3–6). Illus. by Edward Ardizzone. 1960, Harcourt $7.50; paper $1.75. Amusing tale of 2 little girls, some fanciful witches, and a bumblebee.

2639. Farber, Norma. *Six Impossible Things before Breakfast* (3–5). Illustrated. 1977, Addison $6.95. Six stories and poems that are at times amusing and exciting, and always imaginative.

2640. Farmer, Penelope. *A Castle of Bone* (5–7). 1972, Atheneum $4.95. A group of children discover a magical cupboard that is able to return objects to their natural state, for instance, a wallet becomes a pig. Real problems begin when one of the children emerges as an infant.

2641. Farmer, Penelope. *Charlotte Sometimes* (4–6). 1969, Harcourt $5.50. A girl awakens at boarding school and finds herself in 1918.

2642. Farmer, Penelope. *Emma in Winter* (4–6). Illus. by James J. Spanfeller. 1955, Harcourt $5.75. Two lonely children travel through time into the past, in this sequel to *The Summer Birds*.

2643. Farmer, Penelope. *The Summer Birds* (4–6). Illus. by James J. Spanfeller. 1962, Harcourt $4.95. A fantasy in which 2 sisters meet a strange boy who teaches them to fly. One by one all the children in school are taught and spend the summer enjoying their flights.

2644. Farmer, Penelope. *William and Mary: A Story* (4–6). 1974, Atheneum $5.95. Two youngsters are transported through time to other places.

2645. Feydy, Anne Lingbergh. *Osprey Island* (3–7). Illus. by Maggie Kaufman Smith. 1974, Houghton $5.95. Three children enter paintings to spend their Sundays together.

2646. Field, Rachel. *Hitty: Her First Hundred Years* (4–6). Illus. by Dorothy P. Lathrop. 1937, Macmillan $7.95. America 100 years ago seen through the adventures of a wooden doll. Newbery Award, 1930.

2647. Fisher, Leonard. *Sweeney's Ghost* (5–7). 1975, Doubleday $4.50. A family discovers that their vacation home is haunted.

2648. Fleischman, Paul. *The Birthday Tree* (3–4). Illus. by Marcia Sewall. 1979, Harper $6.95; LB $7.49. An apple tree mirrors the experiences of a couple's absent son.

2649. Fleming, Ian. *Chitty-Chitty-Bang-Bang* (4–6). Illus. by John Burningham. 1964, Random $4.95. Chitty-Chitty-Bang-Bang, a magical racing car, flies, floats, and has a real talent for getting the Pott family in and out of trouble.

2650. Flora, James. *Wanda and the Bumbly Wizard* (2–4). Illus. by author. 1980, Atheneum $8.95. Wanda joins forces with an inept wizard to outwit a wicked giant.

2651. Foote, Timothy. *The Great Ringtail Garbage Caper* (4–6). Illus. by Normand Chartier. 1980, Houghton $5.95. The raccoons revolt when garbage collection at a summer resort becomes too efficient.

2652. Freeman, Barbara. *A Haunting Air* (5–7). Illus. by author. 1977, Dutton $7.50. Two girls unravel a mystery concerning a Victorian hatbox and a ghost named Hannah that appears in the garden.

2653. Freeman, Barbara. *The Other Face* (6–9). 1976, Dutton $6.95. By time lapse, a young girl helps a romance occurring 150 years ago.

2654. Freeman, Barbara. *A Pocket of Silence* (5–7). Illus. by author. 1978, Dutton $7.50. In a small English town, a young girl encounters the ghost of a proud girl who had disappeared mysteriously many years before.

2655. Fry, Rosalie K. *Mungo* (4–6). Illus. by Velma Ilsley. 1972, Farrar $4.95. On a remote piece of Scottish coastline, young Richie finds Mungo, one of the last sea monsters.

2656. Gage, Wilson. *Down in the Boondocks* (2–4). Illus. by Glen Rounds. 1977, Greenwillow $5.95; LB $5.71. An easy-to-read rhyming text conveys the story of a near-deaf farmer who is impervious to noise and a robot who isn't.

2657. Gage, Wilson. *The Ghost of Five Owl Farm* (4–6). Illus. by Paul Galdone. 1966, Collins $5.91; Archway paper $1.25. Ted finds his vacation on an old farm ruined by his younger twin cousins, and so he creates a ghost to keep them busy— then a REAL ghost furnishes suspense.

2658. Gage, Wilson. *Miss Osborne—the—Mop* (4–6). Illus. by Paul Galdone. 1963, Collins $6.91; Archway paper $1.50. The fun and adventures that result from a girl's finding she has the power to change people and objects into something else and back again.

2659. Gardner, John. *Dragon, Dragon and Other Tales* (4–6). Illus. by Charles Shields. 1975, Knopf $4.95; LB $5.99. Four tales that show many folklore derivations as well as the author's originality and inventiveness.

2660. Garner, Alan. *The Aimer Gate* (4–6). Illus. by Michael Foreman. 1979, Collins $6.95. The fourth in the English family saga begun in *The Stone Book*.

2661. Garner, Alan. *Elidor* (6–8). 1979, Collins $7.95. A fantasy for better readers written by a contemporary master.

2662. Garner, Alan. *Granny Reardun* (4–6). Illus. by Michael Foreman. 1978, Collins $6.95. Joseph decides not to be a stonecutter like his grandfather in this sequel to *The Stone Book*.

2663. Garner, Alan. *The Moon of Gomrath* (6–8). 1979, Collins $7.95. For better readers, a conclusion to the complex tale about 2 youngsters and a struggle between good and evil begun in *The Weirstone of Brisingamen*.

2664. Garner, Alan. *The Weirstone of Brisingamen* (5–7). 1979, Collins $7.95. Colin and Susan find that their 6-month stay in Alderly means encounters with witches and supernatural forces.

2665. Goble, Paul, and Goble, Dorothy. *The Friendly Wolf* (3–5). Illustrated. 1975, Bradbury $7.95. A fantasy in which 2 lost Plains Indian children are helped back home by a wolf. Paul Goble's illustrations are outstanding.

2666. Grahame, Kenneth. *Wind in the Willows* (5 up). Illus. by Ernest H. Shepard. 1953, Scribner $7.95; LB $12.50; paper $3.95. The classic that introduced Mole, Ratty, and Mr. Toad to the world.

2667. Greaves, Margaret. *The Dagger and the Bird: A Story of Suspense* (4–6). Illus. by Laszlo Kubinyi. 1975, Harper $6.89. Two children set out to find their brother, who has been replaced by a fairy changeling.

2668. Greaves, Margaret. *A Net to Catch the Wind* (2–4). Illus. by Stephen Gammell. 1979, Harper $6.95; LB $6.89. A king uses his daughter to trap a unicorn.

2669. Greene, Graham. *The Little Fire Engine* (3–5). Illus. by Edward Ardizzone. 1974, Doubleday $5.95. An old-fashioned fire engine is decreed obsolete, yet emerges the hero. Also use: *The Little Train* (1974, Doubleday $5.95).

2670. Gregorian, Joyce Ballou. *The Broken Citadel* (4–7). 1975, Atheneum $8.95. A complex fantasy about a young girl, her prince, and their quests.

2671. Gripe, Maria. *The Glassblower's Children* (4–6). Illus. by Harold Gripe. 1973, Delacorte $6.46; Dell paper $.95. The story of 2 kidnapped children, their wicked governess, and 2 witches representing good and evil.

2672. Haas, Dorothy. *The Bears Upstairs* (4–6). Illustrated. 1978, Greenwillow $6.95. A young girl hides 2 bears who are awaiting relocation to another planet.

2673. Hamilton, Virginia. *Time-Ago Lost: More Tales of Jahdu* (3–5). Illus. by Ray Prather. 1973, Macmillan $4.95. Each day while his parents go to work, Lee Edward goes to Mama Luka's where she tells him a story about the hero, Jahdu. Sequel to *Time-Ago Tales of Jahdu* (1969, $5.95).

2674. Harris, Rosemary. *Sea Magic: And Other Stories of Enchantment* (6–8). 1974, Macmillan $5.95. Ten legends retold in an exciting colorful way, but in a style that might be difficult for all but the better reader.

2675. Harris, Rosemary. *The Seal-Singing* (7–9). 1971, Macmillan $4.95; paper $1.25. On the wild Scottish island of Carrigona, Miranda discovers that she possesses mysterious powers over the seals.

2676. Haynes, Betsy. *The Ghost of Gravestone Hearth* (4–6). 1977, Nelson $6.95. A 16-year-old ghost comes back to life to recover a buried treasure.

2677. Hearne, Betsy Gould. *Home* (4–6). Illus. by Trina Schart Hyman. 1979, Atheneum $7.95. The young giant Megan goes out questing in this adventure-filled sequel to *South Star*.

2678. Hearne, Betsy Gould. *South Star* (3–7). Illus. by Trina Schart Hyman. 1977, Atheneum $7.95. An odyssey in which a young girl and a resourceful boy accomplish an arduous quest.

2679. Holman, Felice. *The Cricket Winter* (3–5). Illus. by Ralph Pinto. 1967, Dell paper $.75. A boy communicates with a cricket, and together they outwit an evil cat.

2680. Holman, Felice. *The Escape of the Giant Hogstalk* (3–6). Illus. by Ben Shecter. 1974, British Bk. Ctr. $5.50; paper $2.50. An English fantasy in which the seeds of a hogstalk grow out of control at Kew Gardens.

2681. Hopkins, Lee Bennett, comp. *Monsters, Ghoulies and Creepy Creatures* (4–6). Illus. by Vera Rosenberry. 1977, Whitman $7.75. Traditional and modern writers and tales are represented in this appealing collection.

2682. Hughes, Richard. *The Wonder-Dog* (4–6). Illus. by Antony Maitland. 1977, Greenwillow $8.25; LB $7.29. A collection of short stories first published from 1932 to 1966.

2683. Hunter, Mollie. *A Furl of Fairy Wind* (3–6). Illus. by Stephen Gammell. 1977, Harper $7.95; LB $7.89. Four new stories that rely heavily on the creatures and situations associated with traditional Scottish folklore.

2684. Hunter, Mollie. *The Haunted Mountain* (5–7). Illus. by Laszlo Kubinyi. 1972, Harper $6.89; paper $1.95. MacAllister, with the help of a courageous son and an old dog, overcomes the supernatural forces that control a mountain.

2685. Hunter, Mollie. *The Kelpie's Pearls* (4–6). Illus. by Stephen Gammell. 1976, Harper $5.95; LB $6.89. A spellbinding fantasy, set in the Scottish Highlands, concerning a water sprite. Excellent for reading aloud.

2686. Hunter, Mollie. *A Stranger Came Ashore* (6–8). 1975, Harper $5.95; LB $6.89; paper $1.50. A fantasy in which the great Selkie, a bull seal of the Shetland Islands, takes human form and lures a young girl to his underwater palace.

2687. Hunter, Mollie. *The Walking Stones* (5–7). Illus. by Trina S. Hyman. 1970, Harper paper $1.25. A fantasy set in the present time, involving the use of magical powers to prevent the flooding of a glen in Highland Scotland.

2688. Hunter, Mollie. *The Wicked One* (5–7). 1977, Harper $6.95; LB $6.89. A fantasy set in the Scottish Highlands in which a forester invokes the ire of a supernatural power.

2689. Ibbotson, Eva. *The Great Ghost Rescue* (4–7). Illus. by Giulio Maestro. 1975, Walck $7.95. A group of English ghosts seek sanctuary after their stately homes have been destroyed by real estate developers.

2690. Irving, Washington. *Rip Van Winkle and the Legend of Sleepy Hollow* (5–8). Illus. by David Levine. n.d., Macmillan $4.95. A handsome edition of 2 classics.

2691. Jansson, Tove. *Moominvalley in November* (4–6). Illus. by author. 1971, Avon paper $1.25. A sextet of Moomin family friends comes to visit Moominvalley in this wintry time of year. One of the many funny and imaginative fantasies involving the same characters and locales. Also use others in series, including: *Finn Family Moomintroll* (1965, paper $1.25).

2692. Jarrell, Randall. *The Animal Family* (5–7). Illus. by Maurice Sendak. 1965, Pantheon $6.95; paper $1.25. Tale of a lonely hunter and how he acquires a family consisting of a mermaid, a bear, a lynx, and, finally, a boy. Also use: *Fly by Night* (1976, Farrar $5.95).

2693. Jarrell, Randall. *The Bat-Poet* (2–4). Illus. by Maurice Sendak. 1964, Macmillan $3.95; paper $1.95. A little-known bat makes up poems during the day to recite to his fellows.

2694. Johnson, Elizabeth. *Break a Magic Circle* (3–5). 1971, Little $4.50. Two youngsters help an invisible boy become visible again.

2695. Jones, Diana Wynne. *Cart and Cwidder* (4–6). 1977, Atheneum $6.95. The conflict between good and evil is played out in an imaginary land with a medieval flavor.

2696. Jones, Diana Wynne. *Charmed Life* (4–6). 1978, Greenwillow $6.95; LB $6.43. Gwendole tries to obtain supernatural powers from her mysterious guardian.

2697. Jones, Diana Wynne. *The Ogre Downstairs* (5–6). 1975, Dutton $6.95. Two families adjust to one another, although one has particular problems with the new stepfather, nicknamed the Ogre, in this amusing blend of realism and fantasy. Also use: *Power of Three* (1977, Greenwillow $6.96; LB $7.25).

2698. Jones, Diana Wynne. *The Spellcoats* (4–6). 1979, Atheneum $7.95. A young girl tries to control an evil magician by weaving spells.

2699. Jones, Elizabeth Orton. *Twig* (3–5). Illus. by author. 1942, Macmillan $5.95. Four floors below Twig's apartment, there is a tiny backyard, and there Twig meets an elf, a fairy queen, and a family of sparrows, with whom she has magical adventures.

2700. Juster, Norton. *Phantom Tollbooth* (4–6). Illus. by Jules Feiffer. 1961, Random $6.95; paper $1.75. When Milo receives a tollbooth as a gift, he finds that it admits him to a land where many adventures take place. A favorite fantasy.

2701. Karl, Jean. *Beloved Benjamin Is Waiting* (4–6). 1978, Dutton $7.95. Lucinda finds comfort from her loneliness in conversations with the spirit of a long-dead young boy.

2702. Kastner, Erich. *The Little Man* (4–6). Trans. by James Kirkup. Illus. by Rick Schreiter. 1966, Knopf $5.69. A 2-inch-high orphan with the help of his guardian, a circus magician, eventually becomes the greatest *artiste* in the world.

2703. Kendall, Carol. *The Gammage Cup* (4–7). Illus. by Erik Blegvad. 1959, Harcourt $6.50; paper $1.95. Fantasy of the Minnipins, a small people of the "land between the mountains." Sequel: *The Whisper of Glocken* (1965, $5.95).

2704. Kennedy, Richard. *The Blue Stone* (3–5). Illus. by Ronald Himler. 1976, Holiday $6.95. Set in the Middle Ages, this fantasy tells what happens to 2 youngsters after one discovers a stone with magical powers.

2705. Kennedy, Richard. *Inside My Feet: The Story of a Giant* (4–6). Illus. by Ronald Himler. 1979, Harper $7.95; LB $6.89. Two enormous boots carry off a boy's parents in this thriller.

2706. Kooiker, Leonie. *The Magic Stone* (3–7). Trans. from the Dutch by Richard and Clara Winsto. Illus. by Carl Hollander. 1978, Morrow $6.95; LB $6.43. A young boy finds a powerful magic stone owned by a group of witches.

2707. Korner, Wolfgang. *The Green Frontier* (6–9). 1979, Morrow LB $6.96. A 14-year-old boy, living in East Germany, and his escape to the West.

2708. Krensky, Stephen. *The Dragon Circle* (4–6). Illus. by A. Delaney. 1977, Atheneum $6.95. The Wynd children are kidnapped by a circle of 5 ancient dragons.

2709. Kroeber, Theodora. *Carrousel* (2–5). Illus. by Douglas Tait. 1977, Atheneum $5.95. Eight wooden horses on a carousel come to life evenings and have astounding adventures.

2710. Kruss, James. *My Great-Grandfather, the Heroes and I* (4–6). Illus. by Jochen Bartsch. 1973, Atheneum $6.95. A boy and his great-grandfather explore the subject of heroism together in this German story that recounts many tales of brave men.

2711. Kumin, Maxine, and Sexton, Anne. *The Wizard's Tears* (3–5). Illus. by Evaline Ness. 1975, McGraw $6.95; LB $7.95. A recently graduated young wizard has no trouble ending droughts, but he does have trouble correcting the results of his own carelessness.

2712. Lampman, Evelyn Sibley. *The Shy Stegosaurus of Cricket Creek* (3–5). 1955, Doubleday $4.95. Two youngsters meet a talking dinosaur.

2713. Langton, Jane. *The Astonishing Stereoscope* (6–8). Illus. by Erik Blegvad. 1971, Harper $8.79. A terrible accident reveals to a young boy and girl some of the secret of life. An earlier book: *The Diamond in the Window* (1962, Harper, LB $8.79; paper $1.95).

2714. Langton, Jane. *The Fledgling* (5–7). 1980, Harper $7.95; LB $7.89. A young girl learns to fly with her Goose Prince.

2715. Lawson, Robert. *Rabbit Hill* (4–7). Illus. by author. 1944, Viking $6.50; Penguin paper $1.25. The small creatures of a Connecticut countryside —each with a distinct personality—create a warm and humorous story. Newbery Award, 1945. Sequel: *The Tough Winter* (1954, Viking $6.95; Penguin paper $1.95).

2716. Lazarus, Keo Felker. *The Shark in the Window* (3–5). Illus. by Laurel Schindelman. 1972, Morrow $5.71. A delightful fantasy involving Shelly and an egg that hatches into a shark that can live out of water.

2717. Leach, Maria. *The Thing at the Foot of the Bed and Other Scary Tales* (4–6). Illus. by Kurt Werth. 1959, Collins $5.91; Dell paper $1.25. Spine-chilling stories about ghosts.

2718. Lee, Tanith. *The Dragon Hoard* (4–6). Illus. by Graham Oakley. 1971, Farrar $4.50. A struggle between good and evil represented by Prince Jasleth and the witch Maligna is humorously told.

2719. Levitin, Sonia. *Beyond Another Door* (5–8). 1977, Atheneum $8.95. A girl encounters an apparition of her dead grandmother in this novel that explores a mother-daughter relationship.

2720. Lewis, Clive S. *The Lion, the Witch and the Wardrobe: A Story for Children* (4–7). Illus. by Pauline Baynes. 1950, Macmillan $7.95; paper $1.25. A beautifully written modern tale of the adventures of 4 children who go through the back of a huge wardrobe into the magical land of Narnia.

2721. Lifton, Betty Jean. *Jaguar, My Twin* (4–6). Illus. by Ann Leggett. 1976, Atheneum $6.50. Legend and reality are mixed in this story of a Mexican Indian boy and his twin animal spirit, the jaguar.

2722. Lindgren, Astrid. *The Brothers Lionheart* (4–6). Illus. by J. K. Lambert. 1975, Viking $7.50. Two brothers are reunited after death in the magical land of Nangiyala.

2723. Lively, Penelope. *The Ghost of Thomas Kempe* (4–6). Illus. by Antony Maitland. 1973, Dutton $7.95. When his family moves into an old house in an English village, James is blamed when the resident ghost begins to act up.

2724. Lively, Penelope. *The Voyage of QV 66* (4–6). Illus. by Howard Jones. 1979, Dutton $7.95. After a flood has destroyed human life on earth, a group of animals, lead by Stanley, a monkey, march to the London Zoo to free the animals.

2725. Lively, Penelope. *The Whispering Knights* (4–6). Illus. by Gareth Floyd. 1976, Dutton $6.95. Three children accidentally evoke the spirit of the wicked Morgan le Fay.

2726. Lofting, Hugh. *Doctor Dolittle: A Treasury* (3–6). Illustrated. 1967, Lippincott $8.95. A new edition with excerpts from 8 of the Dr. Dolittle books.

2727. Lovejoy, Jack. *The Rebel Witch* (4–6). Illus. by Judith Gwyn Brown. 1978, Lothrop $5.95; LB $5.71. Suzie, with a magic wand, tries to foil evil Professor Sinistrari.

2728. Lutters, Valerie A. *The Haunting of Julie Unger* (5–7). 1977, Atheneum $7.95. Through visits from her dead father, Julie is able to adjust to his death.

2729. Mace, Elizabeth. *The Ghost Diviners* (5–7). 1977, Elsevier/Nelson $6.95. Martin discovers a magical stick that transports him and his sister back in time.

2730. Mace, Elizabeth. *The Rushton Inheritance* (5–7). 1978, Elsevier/Nelson $6.95. A nineteenth-century English boy is visited by a relative from the present.

2731. McGraw, Eloise. *Joel and the Great Merlini* (3–5). Illus. by Jim Arnosky. 1979, Pantheon $5.95; LB $5.99. Joel gains new magical powers from a magician named Merlini.

2732. McGraw, Eloise. *A Really Weird Summer* (5–7). Illustrated. 1977, Atheneum $7.95. While visiting a great-aunt and great-uncle, Nels befriends a strange boy, Alan, who lived in another time.

2733. Maguire, Gregory. *The Lightning Time* (6–8). 1978, Farrar $7.95. Through the help of a ghostly spirit, David saves a mountain from developers.

2734. McHargue, Georgess. *Stoneflight* (5–7). 1975, Viking $6.95. Jane escapes reality on the back of a griffin.

2735. MacKellar, William. *Kenny and the Highland Ghost* (5–7). Illus. by W. T. Mars. 1980, Dodd $6.95. A young boy tries to remove a curse from a friendly Scottish ghost.

2736. MacKellar, William. *The Witch of Glen Gowrie* (5–7). Illus. by Ted Lewin. 1978, Dodd $5.95. Gavin saves a witch's dog and forms a strange friendship.

2737. McKinley, Robin. *Beauty: A Retelling of the Story of Beauty and the Beast* (6–9). 1978, Harper $7.95; LB $7.79. A winning retelling of the familiar story.

2738. McKillip, Patricia A. *The House on Parchment Street* (5–7). Illus. by Charles Robinson. 1973, Atheneum paper $1.95. Two teenagers—one English, one American—unite to discover the secret behind the basement ghosts.

2739. McKillip, Patricia A. *The Riddle-Master of Hed* (5–8). 1976, Atheneum $7.95. A somewhat complex fantasy of a questing lad who sets out to answer the riddle of the 3 stars on his forehead. Sequel: *Heir of Sea and Fire* (1977, $7.95).

2740. Manley, Seon, and Lewis, Gogo., eds. *Baleful Beasts: Great Supernatural Stories of the Animal Kingdom* (6–9). Illus. by Emanuel Schongut. 1974, Lothrop $6.96. These short stories, mostly adult in tone, will intrigue better readers. Includes background information on the animals and biographical sketches of the authors.

2741. Massie, Diane Redfield. *Chameleon Was a Spy* (3–6). Illus. by author. 1979, Crowell $6.95. Chameleon uses his talents in spy work.

2742. Mayne, William. *Earthfasts* (5–8). 1967, Dutton $7.95. A highly original gripping tale of the supernatural, in which the past becomes confused with the present, setting off a series of fantastic events.

2743. Mayne, William. *A Game of Dark* (5–8). 1971, Dutton $6.95. Donald is lonely and unhappily at odds with his family in this engrossing English novel that shifts back and forth from reality to fantasy.

2744. Mayne, William. *A Year and a Day* (4–6). 1976, Dutton $6.95. A family takes in a changeling boy and names this strange child Adam.

2745. Mazer, Norma Fox. *Saturday, the Twelfth of October* (6–8). 1975, Delacorte $7.95; Dell paper $1.25. In a time shift, the heroine leaves behind her contemporary problems involving adolescence and lives with a group of prehistoric cave dwellers.

2746. Miles, Patricia. *The Gods in Winter* (5–7). 1978, Dutton $7.50. The Bramble family is visited by goddess Demeter in disguise.

2747. Milne, A. A. *Winnie-the-Pooh* (K–5). Colored by Hilda Scott. Illus. by Ernest H. Shepard. 1974, Dutton $5.95. The world-famous book that has become a classic. Also use: *The World of Pooh* (1957, Dutton $9.95), *The House at Pooh Corner* (1961, Dutton $5.95; Dell paper $1.25), and *The Christopher Robin Story Book* (1966, Dutton $6.95).

2748. Murphy, Shirley. *The Pig Who Could Conjure the Wind* (2–4). Illus. by Mark Lefkowitz. 1978, Atheneum $6.95. Miss Folly, a flying pig, gets grounded.

2749. Murphy, Shirley. *Silver Woven in My Hair* (4–6). Illus. by Alan Tiegreen. 1977, Atheneum $6.95. In this variation on the Cinderella story, the mistreated heroine triumphs without a fairy godmother. Also use: *The Ring of Fire* (1977, Atheneum $7.95).

2750. Naylor, Phyllis Reynolds. *Witch's Sister* (4–6). Illus. by Gail Owens. 1975, Atheneum $7.95. Lynn is convinced that her sister Judith is becoming a witch.

2751. Naylor, Phyllis Reynolds. *The Witch Herself* (5–7). Illus. by Gail Owens. 1978, Atheneum $7.95. The struggle of Lynn with Mrs. Tuggle begun in *Witch's Sister* and *Witch Water* is continued.

2752. Naylor, Phyllis Reynolds. *Witch Water* (4–6). Illus. by Gail Owens. 1977, Atheneum $7.95. Lynn and her friend Mouse believe their elderly neighbor is a witch.

2753. Nesbit, Edith. *Five Children and It* (4–6). Illus. by H. R. Miller. 1959, British Bk. Ctr. $12.50; Penguin paper $1.50. An enchanting story about a group of children who discover a Psammead, a sand fairy, who both enlivens and confuses their lives. Two more stories about the children: *The Story of the Amulet* (1960, British Bk. Ctr. $11.95; Penguin paper $1.95) and *The Phoenix and the Carpet* (1960, British Book Ctr. $11.95; Penguin paper $1.50).

2754. Newman, Robert. *The Shattered Stone* (4–7). Illus. by John Gretzer. 1975, Atheneum $6.95. Two youngsters attempt to bring peace to 2 warring kingdoms.

2755. Nichols, Ruth. *A Walk Out of the World* (4–6). Illus. by Trina Schart. 1969, Harcourt $6.95. Judith and Tobit enter a world of 500 years ago after a strange walk in the woods. Also use: *The Marrow of the World* (1972, Atheneum $6.95).

2756. Norton, Andre. *Dragon Magic* (5–8). Illus. by Robin Jacques. 1972, Crowell $8.95. While exploring an empty old house, 4 boys experience different adventures by being transported through time and scope.

2757. Norton, Andre. *Lavender-Green Magic* (4–7). Illus. by Judith Gwyn Brown. 1974, Crowell $8.95. A family of black children living north of Boston is drawn into the mysterious colonial past.

2758. Norton, Andre. *The Opal-Eyed Fan* (6–8). 1972, Dutton $7.95. A ghost from a shipwreck haunts a young girl.

2759. Norton, Andre. *Red Hart Magic* (4–7). Illus. by Donna Diamond. 1976, Crowell $8.95. Two misfits see their counterparts at 3 periods in English history in this time-warp fantasy.

2760. Nostlinger, Christine. *Konrad* (4–6). Trans. by Anthea Bell. Illus. by Carol Nicklaus. 1977, Watts $6.90. A daffy fantasy about a woman adopting a boy who has been made perfectly in a factory.

2761. O'Brien, Robert C. *Mrs. Frisby and the Rats of Nimh* (5–7). Illus. by Zena Bernstein. 1971, Atheneum $7.95. Saga of a group of rats made literate and given human intelligence by a series of experiments, who escape from their laboratory to found their own community. Newbery Award.

2762. O'Connell, Jean S. *The Dollhouse Caper* (3–5). Illus. by Erik Blegvad. 1976, Crowell $6.95; Scholastic paper $.95. A convincing adventure-fantasy about a family of dolls that comes to life when no human is about.

2763. Offit, Sidney. *Soupbone* (4–6). 1963, Archway paper $1.25. Light fantasy is added to baseball as 2 boys try to pep up aging and worn-out pitcher Soupbone McDexter with their magic elixir. Also use: *What Kind of a Guy Do You Think I Am?* (1977, Lippincott $6.95).

2764. O'Hanlon, Jacklyn. *The Door* (4–6). 1978, Dial $6.95; LB $6.46. A young girl walks through a door to a place where there are only kidnapped children.

2765. Oppenheim, Shulamith. *The Selchie's Seed* (4–6). Illus. by Diane Goode. 1975, Bradbury $6.95; Avon paper $1.25. Based on a Scottish legend, this tells the story of a young girl who is bewitched by a white whale.

2766. Ormondroyd, Edward. *All in Good Time* (5–7). Illus. by Ruth Robbins. 1975, Parnassus $6.95. As in the earlier *Time at the Top*, Susan travels back in time to the 1880s to visit with the Walker family and help them with their problems.

2767. Ormondroyd, Edward. *Castaways on Long Ago* (4–6). Illus. by Ruth Robbins. 1973, Parnassus $4.95. Three youngsters have an unexpectedly exciting time visiting a farm when they encounter a strange boy from Long Ago Island.

2768. Ormondroyd, Edward. *Time at the Top* (5–7). Illus. by Peggie Bach. 1963, Parnassus $6.50. Susan rides an apartment elevator to a floor that is not there and finds herself in the year 1881.

2769. Owen, Dilys. *Leo Possessed* (4–6). Illus. by Stephen Gammell. 1979, Harcourt $7.95. A family moves into the city and discovers a ghost in the attic of their new house.

2770. Parish, Peggy. *Haunted House* (4–6). 1971, Macmillan $5.95. The Roberts family believes a ghost is loose and nearby.

2771. Parker, Richard. *The Old Powder Line* (6–9). 1971, Elsevier/Nelson $6.95. By means of an old steam train, a young boy is transported back in time to his babyhood.

2772. Pascal, Francine. *Hangin' Out with Cici* (6–8). 1977, Viking $6.95; Archway paper $1.50. Victoria realizes that the girl she meets in Penn Station is really her mother as she was in 1944.

2773. Patten, Brian. *Mr. Moon's Last Case* (4–6). Illus. by Mary Moore. 1976, Scribner $5.95. An ex-police officer and a young boy track down Nameon, one of the few dwarfs ever to visit the world of humans.

2774. Pearce, Ann Philippa. *The Shadow Cage, and Other Tales of the Supernatural* (6–8). Illus. by Ted Lewin. 1977, Crowell $8.95. Ten original tales, each set in Britain, that involve various mysterious and exciting elements of the supernatural.

2775. Pearce, Ann Philippa. *Tom's Midnight Garden* (4–7). Illus. by Susan Einzig. 1959, Dell paper $1.50. When the clock strikes 13, Tom visits his garden and meets Hatty, a strange mid-Victorian girl.

2776. Peck, Richard. *The Ghost Belonged to Me* (6–8). 1975, Viking $6.95. Richard unwillingly receives the aid of his nemesis Blossom Culp in trying to solve the mystery behind the ghost of a young girl who is haunting a barn.

2777. Peck, Richard. *Ghosts I Have Been* (6–8). 1977, Viking $7.95; Dell paper $1.50. Blossom Culp, first introduced in *The Ghost Belonged to Me*, returns with her gift of second sight and ability to create mayhem.

2778. Peretz, I. L. *The Case against the Wind and Other Stories* (5–7). 1975, Macmillan $6.95. Ten wonderful tales by the man considered to be the father of Yiddish literature.

2779. Peyton, K. M. *A Pattern of Roses* (6–9). Illus. by author. 1973, Crowell $7.95. In a fantasy set in contemporary England, Tom gains independence from his father while exploring his strange affinity with 2 children from Victorian times.

2780. Phipson, Joan. *Polly's Tiger* (3–4). Illus. by Erik Blegvad. 1974, Dutton $5.95. To counter her unfriendly welcome in the settlement where her family has moved, Polly invents a tiger companion.

2781. Phipson, Joan. *The Way Home* (5–9). 1973, Atheneum $5.50. Three cousins, stranded in a remote area of Australia, travel back in time.

2782. Pinkwater, D. Manus. *Alan Mendelsohn, the Boy from Mars* (5–7). 1979, Dutton $8.95. Thought control and time warps are humorous elements in this story of misfits at the Bat Masterson Junior High.

2783. Pinkwater, D. Manus. *Lizard Music* (4–7). Illus. by author. 1976, Dodd $4.95; Dell paper $1.25. In this fantasy, a young boy is taken by an old man to a land inhabited and governed by lizards.

2784. Pomerantz, Charlotte. *The Downtown Fairy Godmother* (3–5). Illus. by Susanna Natti. 1978, Addison $5.95. Olivia discovers that her fairy godmother is a rank amateur at her trade.

2785. Poole, Josephine. *Moon Eyes* (5–7). 1967, Little $6.95. A battle against the witchcraft of evil Aunt Rhoda.

2786. Pope, Elizabeth Marie. *The Perilous Gard* (6–9). Illus. by Richard Cuffari. 1974, Houghton $5.95. A fantasy about a girl who challenges the power of the fairy folk in sixteenth-century England.

2787. Pope, Elizabeth Marie. *The Sherwood Ring* (6–9). Illus. by Evaline Ness. 1958, Harcourt $7.95. An adventure story that deftly interweaves a twentieth-century mystery with eighteenth-century intrigue.

2788. Postma, Lidia. *The Stolen Mirror* (3–4). Illustrated. 1976, McGraw $6.96; LB $7.95. A delicate fantasy in which a boy helps a group of people regain their identity, the mirror of the title.

2789. Preussler, Otfried. *The Satanic Mill* (6–9). 1973, Macmillan $5.95. A young apprentice outwits a strange magician in this fantasy that won the German Children's Book prize in 1972.

2790. Price, Susan. *The Devils' Piper* (5–9). 1976, Greenwillow $7.25; LB $6.96. Townspeople try to rescue 4 slum children after they have been spirited away by a crafty leprechaun.

2791. Randall, Florence. *Almost Year* (6–8). 1971, Atheneum $5.95; paper $1.25. Is it because a black girl is visiting the Mallorys that a hateful ghost is released in the household?

2792. Raskin, Ellen. *Figgs and Phantoms* (4–6). Illustrated. 1974, Dutton $7.50; paper $1.95. The family of Figg-Newton have always dreamed of going to Capri, and in this fantasy, heroine Mona Lisa fulfills the wish.

2793. Rawlings, Marjorie K. *The Secret River* (3–5). Illus. by Leonard Weisgard. 1955, Scribner paper $.95. A little girl in Florida, seeking to help her fisherman father, finds a river full of fish.

2794. Robertson, Mary Elsie. *Jemimalle* (3–5). Illus. by Judith Gwyn Brown. 1977, McGraw $6.95; LB $7.95. A cat-poet tries to keep a giant rat out of the house.

2795. Rodgers, Mary. *Freaky Friday* (4–7). 1972, Harper $6.89; paper $1.50. Thirteen-year-old Annabel learns some valuable lessons during the day she becomes her mother.

2796. Rounds, Glen. *Mr. Yowder and the Giant Bull Snake* (3–6). Illus. by author. 1978, Holiday $5.95. Yowder trains a bull snake so that it soon can encircle a heard of buffalo.

2797. Ruskin, John. *King of the Golden River* (5–8). Illus. by Richard Doyle. 1974, Dover paper $1.50. Two mean brothers incur the wrath of the South-West Wind, Esquire.

2798. Ruskin, John. *The King of the Golden River* (1–3). Illus. by Krystyna Turska. 1978, Morrow $8.95. Dramatic, masterful full-color illustrations add to this fine edition of the classic tale.

2799. Saint-Exupery, Antone de. *The Little Prince* (4–7). Trans. by Katherine Woods. Illus. by author. 1967, Harcourt $5.95; paper $1.50. An original fantasy of a little prince who leaves his planet to discover great wisdom.

2800. St. John, Wylly Folk. *The Ghost Next Door* (4–7). Illus. by Trina Schart Hyman. 1971, Harper $6.79. A family accepts the reality of a beloved member's death in this unusual story.

2801. Sauer, Jules L. *Fog Magic* (4–6). Illus. by Lynd Ward. 1943, Viking $5.95; Archway paper $1.25. One day Greta wanders away from home in a heavy fog and discovers a secret hidden village. Lovely haunting tale.

2802. Scism, Carol K. *The Wizard of Walnut Street* (3–5). Illus. by Martha Alexander. 1973, Dial $4.95; LB $4.58. Nine-year-old John begins to believe that wishing on a wishing well will bring results.

2803. Sechrist, Elizabeth, ed. *Thirteen Ghostly Yarns* (6–9). Illus. by Guy Fry. 1963, Macrae $7.97. Excerpts from Mark Twain, Washington Irving, Edgar Allan Poe, and others.

2804. Selden, George. *The Cricket in Times Square* (3–6). Illus. by Garth Williams. 1960, Farrar $5.95; Dell paper $1.25. A Connecticut cricket is transported in a picnic basket to New York's Times Square. Sequel: *Tucker's Countryside* (1969, Farrar $6.95; Avon, paper $1.50).

2805. Selden, George. *The Genie of Sutton Place* (5–6). 1973, Farrar $5.95. The summer Tim lives with his Aunt Lucy in Sutton Place, New York City, he evokes his own magical genie who works not only miracles but mishaps.

2806. Sendak, Maurice. *Higglety Pigglety Pop! or There Must Be More to Life* (2–4). Illus. by author. 1967, Harper $6.95; LB $6.89. Jennie, a Sealyham terrier, has everything but wants more, leaves home in search of experience, and winds up the star of the World Mother Goose Theatre.

2807. Serraillier, Ian. *Suppose You Met a Witch* (2–4). 1973, Little $4.95. Two children are kidnapped by a witch.

2808. Sharma, Partap. *The Surangini Tales* (4–7). Illus. by Demi Hitz. 1973, Harcourt $5.75. Seventeen short stories, each devised to bring back the beautiful Indian girl Surangini, who has disappeared into the pattern of a carpet.

2809. Sharp, Margery. *Bernard into Battle: A Miss Bianca Story* (6–9). Illus. by Leslie Morrill. 1979, Little $7.95. The Mouse Prisoners' Aid Society must rid the premises of a rat invasion.

2810. Sharp, Margery. *Miss Bianca* (4–7). Illus. by Garth Williams. 1962, Little $6.95; Dell paper $1.25. Exciting adventures of Miss Bianca, a clever white mouse, and her friend Bernard of the Mouse Prisoners' Aid Society. Also by the same author and illustrator (Little $6.95): *Miss Bianca in the Salt Mines* (1966) and *Miss Bianca and the Bridesmaid* (1972).

2811. Sharp, Margery. *The Rescuers* (3–6). Illus. by Garth Williams. 1959, Little $7.95. A beguiling fantasy depicting the adventures of 3 courageous, resourceful mice. Also use: *The Turret* (1963, Little $6.95; Dell paper $1.25).

2812. Shecter, Ben. *The River Witches* (3–5). 1979, Row $7.95. Andrew learns about witches firsthand when he visits his aunt.

2813. Shecter, Ben. *The Whistling Whirligig* (5–7). Illus. by author. 1974, Harper $5.50. A lonely boy encounters the ghost of an escaped slave in this novel set in New York State.

2814. Singer, Isaac Bashevis. *Alone in the Wild Forest* (4–6). Illus. by Margot Zemach. 1971, Farrar $4.50. A magical tale about Joseph, who, with the help of an angel's amulet, wins the hand of a princess, is banished by a jealous rival, and returns to change his enemy to stone for his evildoing.

2815. Singer, Isaac Bashevis. *The Fearsome Inn* (4–7). Illus. by Nonny Hogrogian. 1967, Scribner $5.95. Evil is overcome by magic and common sense in a story written in an Eastern European folk manner and superbly illustrated in full color.

2816. Skurzynski, Gloria. *The Poltergeist of Jason Morey* (6–9). 1975, Dodd $4.95. Gradually Jason's family begins to think that the mysterious break-

ings of household objects have been caused by a poltergeist that must be exposed.

2817. Sleator, William. *Among the Dolls* (3–5). Illus. by Trina Schart Hyman. 1975, Dutton $6.95. Vicky is shrunken to doll size and forced to live in her dollhouse with the malicious dolls whose personalities she has created.

2818. Sleator, William. *Blackbriar* (5–8). Illus. by Blair Lent. 1972, Dutton $7.25. Danny and his stepmother move to a mysterious house by the sea in England and encounter many unanswered questions about the place.

2819. Sleator, William. *Into the Dream* (5–7). Illus. by Ruth Sanderson. 1979, Dutton $7.50. Two young children discover that they can read each other's minds.

2820. Snyder, Zilpha Keatley. *And All Between* (5–7). Illus. by Alton Raible. 1976, Atheneum $8.95. In this fantasy, a young girl leaves her underground civilization and mingles with the people of the planet Green Sky.

2821. Snyder, Zilpha Keatley. *Black and Blue Magic* (5–7). Illus. by Gene Holtan. 1966, Atheneum $5.95; paper $.95. A mysterious old man grants a pair of wings to an awkward teenage boy, who embarks on a hilarious series of flights over San Francisco.

2822. Snyder, Zilpha Keatley. *The Headless Cupid* (5–7). Illus. by Alton Raible. 1971, Atheneum $7.95; paper $1.95. Amanda tries to convert David and her other new stepbrothers and stepsisters to a belief in the supernatural. A suspenseful novel of complex human relationships.

2823. Stearns, Pamela. *The Fool and the Dancing Bear* (5–7). Illus. by Ann Strugnell. 1979, Little $8.95. A fool, a bear, and a king embark on a mission to save a kingdom.

2824. Stearns, Pamela. *Into the Painted Bear Lair* (3–7). Illus. by Ann Strugnell. 1976, Hougton $6.95. Gregory enters a new world inhabited by a female knight and a hungry bear when he walks into a playhouse in a toy store.

2825. Steele, Mary Q. *Journey Outside* (5–8). Illus. by Rocco Negri. 1969, Penguin paper $1.95. Young Dilar, believing that his Raft People, seeking a "Better Place," have been circling endlessly, sets out to discover the origin and fate of his kind.

2826. Steele, Mary Q. *The True Men* (5–8). 1976, Greenwillow $7.25; LB $6.96. An allegory in which a boy is banished from his tribe when they discover he glows in the dark.

2827. Steele, Mary Q. *Wish, Come True* (4–6). Illus. by Muriel Batherman. 1979, Greenwillow

$7.95; LB $7.63. A magic ring allows a brother and sister, Joe and Meg, to have unexpected adventures.

2828. Steig, William. *Abel's Island* (4–6). Illustrated. 1976, Farrar $5.95; Bantam paper $1.95. A tale of a pampered mouse who must fend for himself after being marooned on an isolated island.

2829. Steig, William. *Dominic* (4–6). Illus. by author. 1972, Farrar $6.96. A resourceful and engaging hound dog helps a group of animals overcome the wicked Doomsday Gang.

2830. Steig, William. *The Real Thief* (4–5). Illus. by author. 1973, Farrar $4.95; Dell paper $.95. Gawain, a goose, is disgraced when gold and jewels begin disappearing from the Royal Treasury where he is the guard.

2831. Stephens, Mary Jo. *Witch of the Cumberlands* (4–7). Illus. by Arvis Stewart. 1974, Houghton $7.95. Mountain folklore, seances, and charms are interwoven in this story of 3 children who come to live in a rural mining area of Kentucky.

2832. Stewart, Mary. *The Little Broomstick* (4–6). Illus. by Shirley Hughes. 1972, Morrow $6.01; Dell paper $1.25. The prolific author of Gothics has written a fantasy involving a young girl's attempts to free animals held prisoner by a witch.

2833. Stolz, Mary. *Cat in the Mirror* (5–8). 1975, Harper $6.95; LB $7.89. A time-warp story in which a young girl leaves the New York of today, but faces similar problems in a wealthy household in ancient Egypt.

2834. Swift, Jonathan. *Gulliver's Travels* (5–8). Illus. by Willy Pogany. 1962, Macmillan $5.25. The many adventures of the fearless Gulliver.

2835. Syfret, Anne, and Syfret, Edward. *Bella* (4–7). 1978, Farrar $7.95. Two girls fall under the spell of a devil doll.

2836. Terlouw, Jan. *How to Become King* (6–8). 1977, Hastings $6.95. A 17-year-old undergoes several tests to become king in this satirical fantasy.

2837. Thurber, James. *Thirteen Clocks* (3–5). Illustrated. 1950, Simon & Schuster $6.95. A cruel duke and a beautiful princess are enclosed in frozen time.

2838. Titus, Eve. *Basil and the Pigmy Cats* (3–5). Illus. by Paul Galdone. 1971, Archway paper $1.25. In search of the home of pygmy cats, the intrepid mouse detective Basil encounters his enemy Ratigan plus numerous adventures, one involving a monster from Loch Ness.

2839. Titus, Eve. *Basil in Mexico* (3–5). Illus. by Paul Galdone. 1976, McGraw $5.95; LB $6.95. The famous mouse detective travels to solve the mystery of the missing art treasure, the Mousa Lisa.

2840. Tolkien, John R. *The Hobbit* (5–7). Illus. by author. 1938, Houghton $6.95. A popular saga of dwarfs and elves, goblins and trolls, in a far-off, long-ago land.

2841. Tomalin, Ruth. *Gone Away* (5–6). 1979, Faber $8.95. In this English fantasy, a young girl befriends a ghost living in her boarding house.

2842. Towne, Mary. *Goldenrod* (5–7). 1977, Atheneum $6.95. A baby-sitter possesses unusual powers.

2843. Turnbull, Ann. *The Frightened Forest* (4–6). Illus. by Gillian Gaze. 1975, Seabury $6.95. Three children discover the horrible truth behind a freak summer snowstorm.

2844. Walsh, Jill Paton. *A Chance Child* (6–8). 1978, Farrar $7.95. A time-shift story that reveals the horror of child labor practices after the Industrial Revolution.

2845. Wangerin, Walter, Jr. *The Book of the Dun Cow* (6–9). 1978, Harper $6.95. A mature fable of duty, love, and death.

2846. Weldrick, Valerie. *Time Sweep* (5–7). Illus. by Ron Brooks. 1978, Lothrop $6.95; LB $6.67. A young Australian boy travels to London in 1862.

2847. Westall, Robert. *The Devil on the Road* (6–9). 1979, Greenwillow $7.95. An English novel in which a motorcycle vacation becomes a journey back to the seventeenth century.

2848. Westall, Robert. *The Wind Eye* (5–8). 1977, Greenwillow $7.25; LB $6.96. In a time-warp story, 3 children travel to the Middle Ages in this exciting fantasy that also explores complex family relationships.

2849. White, E. B. *Charlotte's Web* (PS–3). Illus. by Garth Williams. 1952, Harper $5.95; LB $6.49; paper $1.95. Classic, whimsical barnyard fable about a spider who saves the life of Wilbur the pig. An ever-engaging mouse is *Stuart Little* (1945, Harper $5.95; LB $6.49; paper $1.50).

2850. White, E. B. *The Trumpet of the Swan* (3–6). Illus. by Edward Frascino. 1970, Harper $6.95; LB $6.89; paper $1.95. Louis, a voiceless trumpeter swan, is befriended by Sam, learns to play a trumpet, and finds fame, fortune, and fatherhood.

2851. Wibberley, Leonard. *The Crime of Martin Coverly* (6–9). 1980, Farrar $8.95. Nicholas

Ormsby is visited one evening by a pirate from the past and suddenly he is transported to the early 1700s.

2852. Wibberley, Leonard. *The Mouse on the Moon* (5–9). 1962, Morrow $6.95. A lively and humorous account of a race to the moon.

2853. Willard, Nancy. *The Island of the Grass King: The Further Adventures of Anatole* (4–6). Illus. by David McPhail. 1979, Harcourt $7.95. Anatole goes to the island of the Grass King to find a cure for Grandmother's asthma.

2854. Williams, Margery. *The Velveteen Rabbit: Or How Toys Become Real* (2–4). Illus. by William Nicholson. n.d., Doubleday $3.95; deluxe $5.95; Avon paper $1.95. Love brings a toy rabbit to life —"When a child loves you for a long time, really loves you, then you become real."

2855. Williams, Ursula. *Bogwoppit* (5–6). 1978, Nelson $6.95. An English story involving a girl, her eccentric aunt, and furry animals named bogwoppits.

2856. Yolen, Jane. *The Mermaid's Three Wisdoms* (4–6). Illus. by Laura Rader. 1978, Collins $6.95. Melusina, a mermaid, is forced to live on land and is befriended by a deaf girl.

2857. Young, Miriam. *A Witch's Garden* (5–7). 1973, Atheneum $6.95. Jenny puts a curse on a club membership committee.

2858. Zhitkov, Boris. *How I Hunted the Little Fellows* (2–4). Illus. by Paul O. Zelinsky. 1979, Dodd $5.95. Boris believes that little people are living on a miniature steamship.

Science Fiction

2859. Asimov, Isaac. *The Heavenly Host* (3–5). Illus. by Bernard Colonna. 1975, Walker $5.95; Penguin paper $1.95. A science fantasy involving strange creatures called Wheels, a planet named Anderson Two, and the message of Christmas.

2860. Bethancourt, T. Ernesto. *The Mortal Instruments* (6–9). 1977, Holiday $6.95. An adolescent with supernatural powers assumes several guises when he becomes the tool of a sadistic computer installation.

2861. Bova, Benjamin. *End of Exile* (5–8). 1975, Dutton $7.95. The final volume of the "Exiled" trilogy, in which Linc leads his friends to safety and a new life.

2862. Bulychev, Kirill. *Alice* (3–5). Trans. by Mirra Ginsburg. Illus. by Igor Galanin. 1977,

Macmillan $6.95. Subtitle: *Some Incidents in the Life of a Little Girl of the Twenty-First Century, Recorded by Her Father on the Eve of Her First Day in School.*

2863. Cameron, Eleanor. *The Wonderful Flight to the Mushroom Planet* (4–6). Illus. by Robert Henneberger. 1954, Little $6.95. Science fiction combined with magic in the story of 2 boys who take off on a spaceship with a magical man named Tyco Bass. More magic and adventure in the sequel: *Time and Mr. Bass* (1967, $7.95).

2864. Christopher, John. *Beyond the Burning Lands* (6–9). 1971, Macmillan $7.95; paper $1.25. In this adventure, Luke fulfills a prophecy and becomes prince in an English city-state that has reverted to a feudal organization. This is the second volume of a trilogy that began with *The Prince Is Waiting* (1970, $4.95; paper 95¢) and ended with *The Sword of the Spirits* (1972, $4.95; paper $1.95).

2865. Christopher, John. *Empty World* (6–8). 1978, Dutton $7.50. A boy struggles for survival in a world depopulated by a plague.

2866. Christopher, John. *The White Mountains* (6–9). 1967, Macmillan $6.95; paper $1.95. The first volume of a trilogy in which a young boy escapes from a futuristically mechanized tyranny. The rest of the trilogy is: *City of Gold and Lead* (1967, $6.95; paper $1.95) and *Pool of Fire* (1968, $7.95; paper $1.95).

2867. Christopher, John. *Wild Jack* (6–9). 1974, Macmillan $7.95; paper $1.95. The first volume of a trilogy set in England during the twenty-third century in which Clive, a fugitive from his society, is befriended by a latter-day Robin Hood, Wild Jack.

2868. Clarke, Arthur C. *Dolphin Island: A Story of the People of the Sea* (6–9). 1963, Holt $4.95. Johnny Clinton, in the twenty-first century, is shipwrecked and rescued by dolphins and soon joins in a research project involving communication with them.

2869. Clark, Margaret Goff. *Barney and the UFO* (5–7). Illus. by Ted Lewin. 1979, Dodd $6.95. An orphan meets a lonely space boy from a UFO.

2870. Corbett, Scott. *The Donkey Planet* (4–6). Illus. by Troy Howell. 1979, Dutton $6.95. Two young scientists must bring back samples of a metal from another planet.

2871. de Camp, Catherine Crook. *Creatures of the Cosmos* (4–6). Illus. by J. Krush. 1977, Westminster $7.95. A collection of 8 stories, each about a strange unearthly animal.

2872. Dodson, Fitzhugh, and Reuben, Paula. *The Carnival Kidnap Caper* (5–7). 1980, Oak Tree

$7.95. Five young geniuses try to make the world a better place in this futuristic romp.

2873. Doyle, Arthur Conan. *The Lost World* (6–8). 1959, Random $4.39; Berkley paper $.95. The classic about a trip to a land in which prehistoric animals still live.

2874. Eldridge, Roger. *The Shadow of the Gloom-World* (5–8). 1978, Dutton $7.95. A postatomic world where people live underground.

2875. Engdahl, Sylvia Louise. *Enchantress from the Stars* (6–9). Illus. by Rodney Shackell. 1970, Atheneum $8.19; paper $.95. A novel that explores 3 worlds at different stages of development.

2876. Engdahl, Sylvia Louise. *This Star Shall Abide* (6–9). Illus. by Richard Cuffari. 1972, Atheneum $6.95; paper $2.50. A young boy learns the innermost secrets of his planetary civilization in this novel that takes place in the future. Sequel: *Beyond the Tomorrow Mountains* (1973, $7.95).

2877. Fisher, Leonard Everett. *Noonan: A Novel about Baseball, ESP and Time Warps* (6–9). 1978, Doubleday $5.95; LB $6.90. A baseball fantasy in which a pitcher is transported in time from 1896 to 1996.

2878. Fisk, Nicholas. *Escape from Splattersbang* (4–6). 1979, Macmillan $6.95. Myki and his talking computer are left behind on a hostile planet.

2879. Fisk, Nicholas. *Grinny* (5–7). 1974, Elsevier/Nelson $6.95. Beth and Tim outwit a visitor from outer space who has adopted the guise of a constantly grinning great-aunt.

2880. Ginsburg, Mirra, ed. *Air of Mars, and Other Stories of Time and Space* (5–8). 1976, Macmillan $6.95. Nine science fiction stories from the best Soviet writers in this genre.

2881. Golberger, Judith M. *The Looking Glass Factor* (5–8). 1979, Dutton $7.95. Life in the twenty-eighth century and a startling scientific discovery.

2882. Harris, Christie. *Sky Man on the Totem Pole?* (5–7). Illus. by Douglas Tait. 1975, Atheneum $7.95. A reworking of the Indian legend in which science fiction and fantasy are used to explain why crops are grown.

2883. Harrison, Harry. *The Men from P.I.G. and R.O.B.O.T.* (4–6). 1978, Atheneum $5.95. Two sci-fi stories about galactic use of computers and specially trained pigs.

2884. Henrick, Paula. *The Girl Who Slipped through Time* (5–7). 1978, Lothrop $5.95. A girl from the twenty-first century is transported to Kansas in the 1930s.

2885. Hoover, H. M. *The Delikon* (6–8). 1977, Viking $6.95. Varina, her faithful guard, and 2 children become involved in a revolution to rid the earth of its rulers, the Delikon.

2886. Hoover, H. M. *The Rains of Eridan* (6–8). 1977, Viking $7.95. In this novel, Theo tries to solve the mystery of a strange fear that grips people on an Earth-type planet.

2887. Hoover, H. M. *Treasures of Morrow* (5–7). 1976, Four Winds $6.95. The 2 youngsters of *Children of Morrow* settle down in the friendly civilization known as Morrow away from their harsh former home.

2888. Jones, Diana Wynne. *Dogsbody* (6–9). 1977, Greenwillow $7.25; LB $6.96; Dell paper $1.50. Sirius, the Dog Star, is banished to earth in the form of a dog in this suspenseful novel.

2889. Karl, Jean. *The Turning Place: Stories of a Future Past* (6–9). 1976, Dutton $8.95. Nine stories that deal with the results of an invasion from a planet called Ciord.

2890. Kesteven, G. R. *The Awakening Water* (6–9). 1979, Hastings $6.95. After humans have destroyed their civilization, the survivors are tranquilized into submission, but some known as the Lost Ones try to assert themselves.

2891. Key, Alexander. *Escape to Witch Mountain* (5–7). Illus. by Leon B. Wisdom. 1968, Westminster $7.50; Archway paper $1.50. Tony and Tina flee to the Smokies searching for their true home and identities while desperately eluding determined sinister pursuers in this superior sci-fi fantasy.

2892. Key, Alexander. *The Forgotten Door* (5–7). 1965, Westminster $7.95; Scholastic paper $1.25. When little Jon falls to earth from another planet, he encounters suspicion and hostility as well as sympathy.

2893. Key, Alexander. *The Preposterous Adventures of Swimmer* (5–7). 1973, Westminster $4.75. A talking otter escapes from his laboratory and has a series of amazing adventures. Also use: *Jagger, the Dog From Elsewhere* (1976, Westminster $6.95).

2894. Lawrence, Louise. *Star Lord* (6–9). 1978, Harper $6.95; LB $6.79. A fantasy set in Wales in which a boy hides a stranger from a distant star.

2895. LeGuin, Ursula. *The Farthest Shore* (6–9). Illus. by Gail Garraty. 1972, Atheneum $9.95. Arren travels with Ged to find and vanquish the power of an evil spirit, in this final part of the trilogy that includes *The Wizard of Earth-Sea* (1968,

Parnassus ($7.50) and *The Tombs of Atuan* (1971, Atheneum $8.95).

2896. L'Engle, Madeleine. *A Swiftly Tilting Planet* (6–8). 1978, Farrar $6.95. Charles Wallace Murrey of *A Wrinkle in Time* is now 15 and fighting an evil power that threatens the world with nuclear destruction.

2897. L'Engle, Madeleine. *A Wrinkle in Time* (6–9). 1962, Farrar $6.95; Dell paper $1.25. A provocative fantasy-science fiction tale of a brother and sister in search of their father, who is lost in the fifth dimension. Newbery Award, 1963. Also use: *Wind in the Door* (1974, Farrar $6.95; Dell, paper $1.25).

2898. Levin, Betty. *The Forespoken* (6–9). 1976, Macmillan $8.95. A girl travels through space and time in this third book in a trilogy, also composed of *The Sword of Culann* (1973, $5.95) and *A Griffon's Nest* (1975, $9.95).

2899. Lightner, A. M. *Star Circus* (6–8). 1977, Dutton $7.95. Gratia finds an unusual animal to add to the menagerie of an interstellar circus company. Also use: *Star Dog* (1973, McGraw $5.72).

2900. Mace, Elizabeth. *Out There* (6–8). 1978, Greenwillow $6.95; LB $6.43. Three young people are survivors of a disaster that has almost wiped out the world's population.

2901. McCaffrey, Anne. *Dragondrums* (6–9). 1979, Atheneum $8.95. Menolly's apprentice Piemier becomes a scout for the Masterharper and has many exciting adventures.

2902. McCaffrey, Anne. *Dragonsinger* (6–8). 1977, Atheneum $7.95. Menolly's gifts as a musician are at last recognized, and she enters school at Harperball with her 9 fire lizards in this sequel to *Dragonsong*.

2903. McCaffrey, Anne. *Dragonsong* (6–8). 1976, Atheneum $8.95. Fifteen-year-old Menolly acquires a band of fire lizards and uses them to achieve her career goal in this superior, although complex, science fiction.

2904. McGowen, Tom. *Odyssey from River Bend* (4–6). 1975, Little $6.95. In this futuristic story, a group of animals set out to visit the land of Long Ago.

2905. MacGregor, Ellen. *Miss Pickerell Goes to Mars* (4–6). Illus. by Paul Galdone. 1951, McGraw $6.95. A sprightly old lady and her fantastic escapades. Also use (McGraw $6.95): *Miss Pickerell Goes Undersea* (1953), *Miss Pickerell and the Geiger Counter* (1953), and *Miss Pickerell Goes to the Arctic* (1954).

2906. MacGregor, Ellen, and Pantell, Dora. *Miss Pickerell to the Earthquake Rescue* (3–5). Illus. by Charles Geer. 1977, McGraw $6.95. The trusty adventurer sets out to solve the mystery behind a rash of unexplained earthquakes. Also use (McGraw $6.95): *Miss Pickerell Harvests the Sea* (1969) and *Miss Pickerell and the Weather Satellite* (1971).

2907. Morressy, John. *The Drought on Ziax* (2–4). Illus. by Stanley Skardinski. 1978, Walker $5.95; LB $5.89. The water supply of the planet Ziax is endangered.

2908. Pesek, Ludek. *The Earth Is Near* (5–8). 1974, Bradbury $6.95. Man's first trip to Mars is described with gripping realism.

2909. Slobodkin, Louis. *Space Ship Under the Apple Tree* (3–5). 1952, Macmillan $6.95; paper $1.95. Eddie discovers small men in his grandmother's apple tree. Also use: *The Round Trip Space Ship* (1968, Macmillan $4.95).

2910. Slote, Alfred. *My Trip to Alpha I* (4–7). Illus. by Harold Berson. 1978, Lippincott $5.95. Jack solves the mystery of a missing aunt lost in an interplanetary travel system.

2911. Snyder, Zilpha Keatley. *Below the Root* (5–7). Illus. by Alton Raible. 1975, Atheneum $8.95. In a society that has survived the almost total destruction encompassing the world, 13-year-old Raamo sets out to explore a civilization that reportedly lives underground.

2912. Stone, Josephine Rector. *Those Who Fall from the Sun* (6–8). 1978, Atheneum $6.95. Alanna and her family are deported to another planet for their crime of independent thinking.

2913. Todd, Ruthven. *Space Cat* (3–5). Illustrated. 1952, Scribner paper $.95. Flyball the cat goes along with the pilot on a rocket ship to outer space. Also use: *Space Cat Meets Mars* (1957, Scribner $5.95).

2914. Townsend, John R. *The Visitors* (6–9). 1977, Lippincott $7.95. A family journey from the future to England of the present has upset the quiet comfortable lives of a Cambridge adolescent and his friends.

2915. Walters, Hugh. *The Blue Aura* (6–9). 1979, Faber $10.50. A group of angels from a friendly civilization visit Earth.

2916. Watson, Simon. *No Man's Land* (6–9). 1976, Greenwillow $7.25; LB $6.96. A boy tries to rebel against the overly mechanized and regulated existence in the next century.

2917. Wilder, Cherry. *The Luck of Brin's Five* (6–8). 1977, Atheneum $7.95. A stranded astronaut becomes the pet of a race of humanlike marsupials.

2918. Williams, Jay. *The Magic Grandfather* (4–6). Illus. by Gail Owens. 1979, Four Winds $7.95. When his grandfather's sorcery misfires, young Sam must undo the damage.

2919. Williams, Jay, and Abrashkin, Raymond. *Danny Dunn and the Homework Machine* (3–5). Illus. by Ezra Jack Keats. 1958, McGraw $6.95. Adventures of Danny and his friends with a miniature automatic computer. Also use: *Danny Dunn and the Anti-Gravity Paint* (1956, McGraw $6.95; Archway, paper $1.50), *Danny Dunn and the Voice from Space* (1967, McGraw $6.95), and *Danny Dunn and the Smallifying Machine* (1969, McGraw $6.95).

2920. Williams, Jay, and Abrashkin, Raymond. *Danny Dunn, Invisible Boy* (4–6). Illus. by Paul Sagsoorian. 1974, McGraw $5.95; LB $6.95; Archway paper $1.50. One of the popular series that blends science, fantasy, and humor in an unbeatable mixture. In this story, Danny projects himself outside the laboratory and discovers a classmate cheating. Also use others in the series: *Danny Dunn on the Ocean Floor* (1970, McGraw $6.95) and *Danny Dunn and the Universal Glue* (1977, McGraw $6.95; Archway, paper $1.50).

2921. Yep, Laurence. *Sweetwater* (6–8). Illus. by Julia Noonan. 1973, Harper $8.95; Avon paper $1.25. A novel in which the narrator and his friends are threatened by a group that wants to modernize and change their planet, Harmony.

Ethnic Groups

2922. Bales, Carol Ann. *Kevin Cloud: Chippewa Boy in the City* (3–5). Illustrated. 1972, Contemporary $5.95. Poverty and prejudice mingle with pride and dignity in this story of a boy growing up in a section of Chicago heavily populated with American Indians.

2923. Barnouw, Victor. *Dream of the Blue Heron* (4–7). Illus. by Lynd Ward. 1966, Delacorte $4.50. A Chippewa boy tries to reconcile the ways of his traditional grandparents with those of a modern father.

2924. Bonham, Frank. *Chief* (6–9). 1971, Dutton $7.95. Teenaged Henry Crowfoot, chief of his small Indian tribe, fights for the territorial rights of his people in this fast-moving, well-plotted novel.

2925. Borland, Hal. *When the Legends Die* (6–8). 1972, Bantam paper $1.50. A Ute Indian boy faces many problems growing in Colorado.

2926. Brandon, Brumsic. *Luther Raps* (2–4). 1971, Eriksson paper $1.95. As he wanders the streets of a big city, young Luther talks about being black. Part of a large series that includes: *Luther's Got Class* (1976, paper $3.95) and *Outta Sight Luther* (1976, paper $1.95).

2927. Brodie, Deborah, ed. *Stories My Grandfather Should Have Told Me* (3–6). Illus. by Carmela Tal-Baron. 1977, Hebrew $6.95. Twelve stories from a variety of authors that explore many aspects of twentieth-century Jewish life.

2928. Bulla, Clyde Robert. *Indian Hill* (3–4). Illus. by James J. Spanfeller. 1963, Crowell $6.95. A young Navajo and his family must adjust to new ways when they move from the reservation to the city.

2929. Burstein, Chaya M. *Rifka Grows Up* (5–7). Illus. by author. 1976, Hebrew $5.95. In this sequel to *Rifka Bangs the Teakettle* (1970, Harcourt $4.95), the young heroine encounters religious prejudice in czarist Russia.

2930. Cavanna, Betty. *Jenny Kimura* (6–9). 1964, Morrow LB $6.96. Jenny, a Japanese-American, travels from Japan to visit her grandmother and finds it hard going.

2931. Chadwick, Roxanne. *Don't Shoot* (5–8). Illus. by Edwin H. Ryan. 1978, Lerner $5.95. A young Inuit (Eskimo) boy must decide on saving a polar bear or a cruel hunter.

2932. Chandler, Edna Walker. *Indian Paintbrush* (4–6). Illus. by Lee Fitzgerald-Smith. 1975, Whitman $5.95. Maria Lopez must adjust to life on an American Indian reservation.

2933. Cohen, Barbara. *Bitter Herbs and Honey* (6–9). 1976, Lothrop $6.00. Difficulties and differences are explored in this story of an orthodox Jewish girl growing up in a New Jersey gentile community in 1916.

2934. Coles, Robert. *Dead-End School* (4–6). Illus. by Norman Rockwell. 1968, Little $4.95. Jim's mother and other adults protest and succeed in getting their children bused to a good white school.

2935. Cone, Molly. *Number Four* (6–9). 1972, Houghton $6.95. After his brother's death, Benjamin begins to establish his native American identity, as his brother did. Tragedy results in this sensitive and convincing novel.

2936. Deveaux, Alexis. *Na-Ni* (3–5). Illus. by author. 1973, Harper $3.50. Na-ni, a young black girl, awaits the welfare check so she can buy a new bicycle.

2937. Distad, Audree. *Dakota Sons* (4–6). Illus. by Tony Chen. 1972, Harper $6.89; paper $1.25. Bobby's friendship with a young Sioux from the American Indian school reveals hidden prejudices within his family.

2938. Dyer, T. A. *The Whipman Is Watching* (5–8). 1979, Houghton $7.95. Children living on an American Indian reservation try to retain their identity in an all-white school.

2939. Forman, James D. *People of the Dream* (6–8). 1972, Farrar $4.95. A novel concerning the flight of Chief Joseph and his Nez Percé people and the gross injustice inflicted on them.

2940. Gardiner, John Reynolds. *Stone Fox* (3–6). Illus. by Marcia Sewall. 1980, Crowell $7.95. Little Willy competes against the Indian Stone Face in the National Dogsled Races.

2941. Graham, Lorenz. *Return to South Town* (6–9). 1976, Crowell $6.95. In this fourth volume of a celebrated series, David Williams, now a doctor, returns to the southern town from which his black family fled years ago.

2942. Hanson, Harvey. *Game Time* (6–9). Illus. by Terry Fehr. 1975, Watts $5.88. A 13-year-old black boy growing up in Chicago of the 1950s.

2943. Heffron, Dorris. *A Nice Fire and Some Moonpennies* (6–9). 1972, Atheneum $4.50. Sixteen-year-old Maizie leaves her Mohawk reservation to try life in Toronto.

2944. Herman, Charlotte. *The Difference of Ari Stein* (5–7). Illus. by Ben Shecter. 1976, Harper $5.79. It is difficult for Ari to remain an orthodox Jew while growing up in the Brooklyn of 1944.

2945. Heyman, Anita. *Exit from Home* (6–9). 1977, Crown $7.50. A Jewish boy's life in prerevolutionary Russia, leading to his decision to immigrate to America.

2946. Hunter, Kristin. *The Soul Brothers and Sister Lou* (6–9). 1968, Scribner $8.95. Louretta Hawkens, a 14-year-old girl, and her friends grow up in an urban ghetto and, in spite of frustration, succeed in creating soul music. Also use: *Guests in the Promised Land* (1973, Scribner $5.95; Avon, paper $1.50).

2947. Jones, Toeckey. *Go Well, Stay Well* (5–7). 1980, Harper $8.95; LB $8.79. A white girl in South Africa meets a black girl her own age and a friendship begins in spite of social pressures.

2948. Karp, Naomi J. *Turning Point* (5–8). 1976, Harcourt $6.95. Hannah and brother Zach encounter anti-Semitism when their Bronx family moves to the suburbs.

2949. Lester, Julius. *Long Journey Home* (6–8). 1972, Dial $7.95; Dell paper $.95. Six (based-on-fact) stories concerning slaves, and ex-slaves, and their lives in a hostile America.

2950. Madison, Winifred. *Maria Luisa* (4–6). 1971, Lippincott $7.89. Maria Luisa encounters prejudice against Chicanos when she and her younger brother move to San Francisco to live with an aunt.

2951. Martel, Cruz. *Yagua Days* (K–2). Illus. by Jerry Pinkney. 1976, Dial $5.95; LB $5.47. Adam Rure visits for the first time his parents' homeland, Puerto Rico.

2952. Miles, Betty. *All It Takes Is Practice* (4–6). 1976, Knopf $5.95; LB $5.99. The arrival of an interracial family in town upsets the quiet lives of Stuart and his fellow fifth-graders.

2953. Mohr, Nicholasa. *Felita* (6–8). Illus. by Ray Cruz. 1979, Dial $6.95; LB $6.46. A Puerto Rican family moves from a friendly neighborhood to one where Spanish is not spoken.

2954. Mohr, Nicholasa. *Nilda* (6–9). Illus. by author. 1973, Harper $5.99; Bantam paper $1.25. Growing up Puerto Rican in New York's Spanish Harlem of the 1940s, as seen through the eyes of a young girl.

2955. Molarsky, Osmond. *A Different Ball Game* (3–4). Illus. by James Zingarelli. 1979, Coward $5.95. An 11-year-old Chilean boy adjusts to his new life in California.

2956. Moskin, Marietta D. *Waiting for Mama* (3–5). Illus. by Richard Lebenson. 1975, Coward $6.95. The story of a Russian-Jewish immigrant family and their adjustments to America while awaiting the arrival of their mother.

2957. Myers, Walter Dean. *It Ain't All for Nothin'* (6–8). 1978, Viking $8.95. A 12-year-old boy is cast adrift in Harlem.

2958. Myers, Walter Dean. *The Young Landlords* (6–9). 1979, Viking $8.95. The gang from *Majo and the Russians* (1977, Viking $6.95) plus the narrator Paul acquire a slum building.

2959. Neufeld, John. *Edgar Allan* (5–8). 1968, Phillips $7.95. The adoption of a 3-year-old black boy by the Reverend Fickett sparks an uprising in a conservative California community.

2960. Pinkwater, D. Manus. *Wingman* (4–6). Illus. by author. 1975, Dodd $5.50. A poor Chinese-American boy living in New York escapes through fantasies involving a superhero.

2961. Shepard, Ray Anthony. *Sneakers* (4–6). n.d., Dutton $6.50. An eighth-grade black student gets into trouble acquiring his new sneakers.

2962. Sterling, Dorothy. *Mary Jane* (5–8). Illus. by Ernest Crichlow. 1959, Scholastic paper $.95. A realistic story about school integration.

2963. Uchida, Yoshiko. *Journey Home* (4–6). Illus. by Charles Robinson. 1978, Atheneum $7.95. Life of a Japanese-American family after their release from a World War II internment camp. A sequel to *Journey to Topaz.*

2964. Uchida, Yoshiko. *Journey to Topaz: A Story of the Japanese-American Evacuation* (5–7). Illus. by Donald Carrick. 1971, Scribner paper $1.49. Based on the author's own experiences, this novel tells of the shameful treatment endured by 11-year-old Uuki and her Japanese-American family after Pearl Harbor.

2965. Waldron, Ann. *The Integration of Mary-Larkin Thornhill* (5–8). 1975, Dutton $7.95. Because her parents insist, a white northern girl must attend a black junior high school.

2966. Wilkinson, Brenda. *Ludell* (5–7). 1975, Harper $5.95; LB $6.89. A tender story of a girl's years in the fifth grade in a southern segregated school during the mid-1950s.

2967. Wilkinson, Brenda. *Ludell and Willie* (6–9). 1977, Harper $5.95; LB $6.89. The further adventures of a black adolescent begun in *Ludell*, the heroine is forced to leave her beloved Willie and her friends after her grandmother dies. Sequel: *Ludell's New York Time* (1980, $6.89).

2968. Yep, Laurence. *Sea Glass* (6–8). 1979, Harper $7.95; LB $7.89. An awkward Chinese-American boy moves to a new junior high school and has trouble adjusting.

Growing into Maturity

Family Problems

2969. Aaron, Chester. *Better Than Laughter* (5–7). 1972, Harcourt $5.75. Allan and Sam run away from a father they fear, but the consequences are tragic.

2970. Adler, Carole S. *In Our House Scott Is My Brother* (5–8). 1980, Macmillan $7.95. The effects of an unsuccessful divorce are explored in this story from the viewpoint of a 13-year-old boy.

2971. Alcock, Gudren. *Run, Westy, Run* (4–6). Illus. by W. T. Mars. 1966, Lothrop $6.01; Archway paper $.60. A realistic and sympathetic story of a runaway boy.

2972. Alexander, Anne. *To Live a Lie* (4–6). Illus. by Velma Ilsley. 1975, Atheneum $8.95. When Noel's mother leaves home, she blames herself and tells her classmates that her mother is dead.

2973. Ames, Mildred. *What Are Friends For?* (5–7). 1978, Scribner $7.95. Amy and Michele share a common bond—they are children of divorce.

2974. Arundel, Honor. *A Family Failing* (6–9). Nelson $6.95. A story set in contemporary Britain involving a family that is drifting apart because of each member's need for dignity and independence.

2975. Association for Childhood Education International, ed. *Told under the City Umbrella* (4–6). Illus. by Lisl Weil. 1972, Macmillan $6.95. Excerpts from various books that explore (usually in a realistic fashion) aspects of urban living.

2976. Bauer, Marion Dane. *Foster Child* (5–7). 1977, Seabury $6.95. Rennie is unable to adjust to a foster home and runs away, in this touching story.

2977. Bawden, Nina. *The Robbers* (4–6). 1979, Lothrop $6.95; LB $6.67. Nine-year-old Philip joins his divorced father in London and faces identity problems.

2978. Blue, Rose. *Grandma Didn't Wave Back* (3–5). Illus. by Ted Lewin. 1972, Watts $4.90; Dell paper $.95. Debbie witnesses the degeneration into senility of her beloved grandma and finally accepts the idea of a nursing home.

2979. Blue, Rose. *A Month of Sundays* (3–4). Illus. by Ted Lewin. 1972, Watts $4.90. Jeffrey's painful adjustment to his parents' divorce, seeing his father only on Sundays, and a move to New York City.

2980. Blume, Judy. *It's Not the End of the World* (4–7). 1972, Bradbury $6.95; Bantam paper $1.75. Twelve-year-old Karen's world seems to end when her parents are divorced and her older brother runs away.

2981. Bond, Nancy. *Country of Broken Stone* (6–9). 1980, Atheneum $10.95. Penelope, her brother, and her father accompany her new stepmother on an archaeological dig in the north of England.

2982. Buchan, Stuart. *When We Live with Pets* (6–8). 1978, Scribner $7.95. A young boy is responsible for bringing his mother and former boyfriend together.

2983. Carrick, Malcom. *I'll Get You!* (5–7). 1979, Harper $7.95; LB $7.89. An English story of a boy who tries to transcend his snobbish parents.

2984. Chaffin, Lillie D. *John Henry McCoy* (4–6). Illus. by Emanuel Schongut. 1971, Macmillan $4.95. John Henry and his granny try to find a place where their family can settle permanently, in this touching story of poverty in Appalachia.

2985. Clifford, Mary Louise. *Salah of Sierra Leone* (6–8). Illus. by Elzia Moon. 1975, Crowell $7.95. Tribal loyalties conflict with today's culture in this story of a boy in Sierra Leone.

2986. Colman, Hila. *Tell Me No Lies* (4–6). 1978, Crown $6.95. Angela discovers the identity of her real father.

2987. Culin, Charlotte. *Cages of Glass, Flowers of Time* (6–8). 1979, Bradbury $8.95. Two friends help Clara adjust to her parent's abuse and alcoholism.

2988. Danziger, Paula. *Can You Sue Your Parents for Malpractice?* (6–9). 1979, Delacorte $6.95. Quarreling parents and a strong-willed father are only 2 of 14-year-old Lauren's problems.

2989. Danziger, Paula. *The Pistachio Prescription* (6–9). 1978, Delacorte $6.95. A thirteen-year-old talks about her school problem and possible divorce in the family.

2990. Dixon, Paige. *Walk My Way* (6–9). 1980, Atheneum $7.95. Kilty, a 14-year-old, flees from an alcoholic father.

2991. Duncan, Lois. *A Gift of Magic* (5–8). Illus. by Arvis Stewart. 1971, Little $6.95. A young girl, gifted with extrasensory perception, adjusts to her parents' divorce.

2992. Ewing, Kathryn. *A Private Matter* (4–5). Illus. by Joan Sandin. 1975, Harcourt $5.95. Although Marcy has completely accepted her parents' divorce, she has difficulty adjusting to the reappearance of her father.

2993. Francis, Dorothy B. *Run of the Sea Witch* (4–6). Illus. by Monroe Eisenberg. 1978, Abingdon $5.95. A young boy gains new respect for his father when he goes to work on his shrimp boat.

2994. Greenberg, Jan. *A Season In-Between* (6–8). 1979, Farrar $8.95. Carrie's life changes dramatically when it is discovered that her father has cancer.

2995. Greenwald, Sheila. *All the Way to Wit's End* (5–7). 1979, Little $6.95. An old-fashioned family moves to a modern housing development, and 11-year-old Drucilla must readjust.

2996. Harris, Mark Jonathan. *With a Wave of the Wand* (5–7). 1980, Lothrop $7.95; LB $7.63. Magic and reality are intertwined in this novel of a girl's adjustment to her parents' divorce.

2997. Hayes, Sheila. *The Carousel Horse* (5–7). 1978, Nelson $6.95. A young girl feels the difference of class when her mother becomes the cook for a wealthy family.

2998. Heide, Florence Parry. *When the Sad One Comes to Stay* (5–6). 1975, Lippincott $6.95; Bantam paper $.95. Sara must choose between 2 value systems—her mother's calculating, opportunistic exploitation of others and the warm, loving idealism represented by her dead father and her friend Maisie.

2999. Holland, Isabelle. *Now Is Not Too Late* (5–7). 1980, Lothrop $6.95; LB $6.67. Cathy discovers the identity of her real mother during a summer at her grandmother's.

3000. Irwin, Hadley. *Bring to a Boil and Separate* (5–8). 1980, Atheneum $7.95. Katie's traumatic thirteenth summer involves her parents' divorce and an uneasy friendship.

3001. Ish-Kishor, Sulamith. *Our Eddie* (6–9). 1969, Pantheon $4.95; LB $5.99; Random paper $.75. A powerful story dealing with the effect of an egotistical, fanatical Jewish father on his family and particularly his son, Eddie.

3002. Klein, Norma. *Taking Sides* (5–7). 1974, Pantheon $5.99; Avon paper $.95. Nur and her young brother adjust to their parents' divorce; then their father's heart attack further upsets their lives.

3003. Kropp, Paul. *Wilted: A Novel* (6–8). 1980, Coward $7.95. Danny's life is a series of ups and downs after his parents separate.

3004. Little, Jean. *Home from Far* (4–6). Illus. by Jerry Lazare. 1965, Little $6.95. After Jenny's twin brother was killed in an auto accident, her mother brought 2 foster children into their home, one a boy just her age. Her adjustment and courage in the face of emotional problems make a moving story.

3005. Little, Jean. *Kate* (5–8). 1971, Harper $7.89; paper $1.95. In this sequel to *Look through My Window*, Kate tries to find solutions to her problems in self-identification caused by being the child of a Jewish/Christian marriage.

3006. Lowry, Lois. *Find a Stranger, Say Goodbye* (6–9). 1978, Houghton $6.95. An adopted girl sets out to find her real mother.

3007. Mann, Peggy. *My Dad Lives in a Downtown Hotel* (4–6). Illus. by Richard Cuffari. 1973, Doubleday $6.95; Avon paper $1.25. Joey tells the story of his adjustment to his parents' separation and their impending divorce.

3008. Mathis, Sharon Bell. *Sidewalk Story* (3–5). Illus. by Leo Carty. 1971, Avon paper $1.25. Littor Etta tries everything possible to help friend Tanya and her family with the problem of eviction.

3009. Mathis, Sharon Bell. *Teacup Full of Roses* (6–9). 1972, Viking LB $5.95. The devastating effect of drugs on a black inner-city family and how addiction causes the death of the youngest son.

3010. Mazer, Harry. *The War on Villa Street* (6–9). 1978, Delacorte $7.50. A drunken father and a gang of bullies are only two of Willis's problems.

3011. Newfield, Marcia. *A Book for Jodan* (3–4). Illus. by Diane deGroat. 1975, Atheneum $8.95. Nine-year-old Jodan must adjust to the gradual breakup of her parents' marriage and their eventual divorce.

3012. Okimoto, Jean Davies. *My Mother Is Not Married to My Father* (5–7). 1979, Putnam $7.95. A story of divorce as seen through the eyes of a sixth-grade girl.

3013. Perl, Lila. *Dumb Like Me, Olivia Potts* (4–6). 1976, Seabury $7.95; Dell paper $1.25. Olivia, following in the wake of her superbright brother and sister, doubts her own intelligence.

3014. Perl, Lila. *The Telltale Summer of Tina C.* (4–6). 1975, Seabury $6.95; Scholastic paper $.95. Tina gains self-confidence and tolerance during her visit to her mother and new stepfather.

3015. Pfeffer, Susan Beth. *The Beauty Queen* (6–9). 1974, Doubleday $4.50; Dell paper $1.25. Prodded by her ambitious mother, Kit unwillingly enters beauty contests. Also use the excellent sequel: *Marly the Kid* (1975, $5.95).

3016. Platt, Kin. *Chloris and the Creeps* (6–8). 1973, Dell paper $1.25. Eleven-year-old Chloris gradually adjusts to the "creep" that has married her mother in this story told by her younger sister Jenny. Sequel: *Chloris and the Freaks* (1975, Bradbury $6.95; Bantam, paper $1.75).

3017. Rabe, Berniece. *Rass* (5–7). 1973, Nelson $6.95. Rass at first hates, then pities, his moody and unstable father, crushed by the responsibilities of bringing up a family in Missouri during the Depression.

3018. Sachs, Marilyn. *A Secret Friend* (4–6). 1978, Doubleday $6.95; LB $7.90. A broken friendship

and overdependence on a parent are two themes explored in this novel.

3019. Seabrooke, Brenda. *Home Is Where They Take You In* (5–7). 1980, Morrow $6.95; LB $6.67. A young girl named Benicia is abandoned by her alcoholic mother.

3020. Sechrist, Elizabeth H., and Woolsey, Janette. *It's Time for Brotherhood* (6–9). Illus. by Clifford Schule. 1962, Macrae $7.95. Stories of individuals and groups that have put the principle of brotherhood into action.

3021. Seidler, Tor. *The Dulcimer Boy* (5–6). Illus. by David Hockney. 1979, Viking $8.95. An historical romp set in New York City involving twins and their father.

3022. Smith, Doris. *Kick a Stone Home* (6–9). 1974, Crowell $6.95. Fifteen-year-old Sara already has problems adjusting to her parents' divorce when troubles with dating and boys also begin to plague her.

3023. Snyder, Anne. *First Step* (5–8). 1975, Holt $5.95. Being saddled with a divorced, alcoholic mother is almost too much for Cindy until she discovers Alateen.

3024. Sobol, Harriet Langsam. *My Other-Mother, My Other-Father* (2–4). Illustrated. 1979, Macmillan $6.95. Children struggle through the problems of their parents' divorces and remarriages.

3025. Stolz, Mary. *The Edge of Next Year* (5–8). 1974, Harper $7.89; Dell paper $1.50. The painful adjustment by the Woodwards—father and 2 sons—to the tragic death of the mother in their once tightly knit family.

3026. Stolz, Mary. *Leap Before You Look* (6–9). 1972, Harper $7.89. Jimmie, the 14-year-old heroine of this perceptive novel, reviews the problems of living through the first year of her parents' divorce.

3027. Sykes, Pamela. *Phoebe's Family* (3–5). 1974, Nelson $6.95. Phoebe tolerates her family's idiosyncrasies while undergoing a traumatic crush on an older man.

3028. Teibl, Margaret. *Davey Come Home* (3–5). Illus. by Jacqueline Bardner Smith. 1979, Harper $6.95; LB $7.89. A young boy adjusts to life with his divorced father and a new housekeeper.

3029. Townsend, John R. *Good-Bye to the Jungle* (6–9). 1967, Lippincott $5.53; Dell paper $1.25. In this realistic novel about modern English slum life, problems and some answers are intelligently explored. Other titles in this series: *Pirate's Island* (1968, Lippincott, LB $5.53; Dell, paper $1.25), and *Trouble in the Jungle* (1969, Lippincott $8.95; LB $8.39; Dell, paper $1.25).

Personal Problems

3030. Aleksin, Anatolii. *My Brother Plays the Clarinet: Two Stories* (5–8). Illus. by Judith Gwyn Brown. 1975, Walck $6.95. Two Russian stories about the pangs and problems of adolescence.

3031. Almedingen, E. M. *Young Mark: The Study of a Venture* (6–9). 1968, Farrar $3.75. Against his father's wishes, Mark runs away from home to become a singer in this compelling story set in czarist Russia.

3032. Anderson, Mary. *Step on a Crack* (6–9). 1978, Atheneum $7.95. Family secrets produce childhood trauma and subsequent maturity in young Sarah.

3033. Arthur, Ruth. *Miss Ghost* (4–6). 1979, Atheneum $6.95. Elphie, after suffering a number of rejections, finds solace in talking to Miss Ghost.

3034. Arundel, Honor. *The Terrible Temptation* (6–9). 1971, Nelson $6.95. The story of Jan, a self-seeking, callous young student at Edinburgh University and how her selfishness eventually brings her unhappiness.

3035. Ashley, Bernard. *All My Men* (6–8). 1978, Phillips $8.95. Gradually Paul adjusts to life in a small town far from his native London.

3036. Baker, Betty. *The Spirit Is Willing* (4–7). 1974, Macmillan $6.95. Carrie, a young precursor of the women's rights movement, performs audacious acts in an Arizona town at the end of the eighteenth century.

3037. Bauer, Marion Dane. *Shelter from the Wind* (5–9). 1976, Seabury $6.95. Twelve-year-old Stacy runs away from home and is taken in by gruff old Ella who teaches her about life.

3038. Bickham, Jack M. *Dinah, Blow Your Horn* (5–8). 1979, Doubleday $8.95. Labor and management clash in the novel of railroading.

3039. Blades, Ann. *Mary of Mile 18* (2–4). Illus. by author. 1978, Tundra $7.95; paper $2.95. Mile 18 is in reality a Mennonite community in Canada, and Mary was a student in the school where the author taught. The picture of the frigid country and the hardworking people who endure the hardships of this isolated community is well portrayed.

3040. Blegvad, Lenore. *Moon-Watch Summer* (3–5). Illus. by Erik Blegvad. 1972, Harcourt $4.75. Adam discovers that the importance of watching the moon landing can be dwarfed by other considerations and values.

3041. Blume, Judy. *Are You There God? It's Me, Margaret* (4–6). 1970, Bradbury $6.95; Dell paper $1.50. Eleven-year-old Margaret is the daughter of a Jewish father and a Catholic mother. The discussions of her problems with God, including her adjustment to a new school, deciding on which church she wants to attend, and her agonized wait for the hoped-for signs of physical maturity, make this a very funny story, especially popular with preteen girls.

3042. Blume, Judy. *Tales of a Fourth Grade Nothing* (3–4). Illus. by Roy Doty. 1972, Dutton $5.95; Dell paper $.95. Peter Hatcher's trials and tribulations, most of which are caused by his 2-year-old pesky brother, Fudge.

3043. Blume, Judy. *Then Again, Maybe I Won't* (5–7). 1971, Bradbury $6.95; Dell paper $1.25. Thirteen-year-old Tony adjusts with difficulty to his family's move to a home in the affluent suburbs of Long Island, New York.

3044. Bond, Nancy. *The Best of Enemies* (5–7). 1978, Atheneum $8.95. In Concord, Massachusetts, a lonely girl becomes involved in the Patriot's Day pageant.

3045. Bonham, Frank. *Durango Street* (6–9). 1965, Dutton $7.50; Dell paper $1.50. A novel of gang warfare in the "jungle" of a big city.

3046. Bonsall, Crosby N. *The Goodbye Summer* (4–6). 1978, Greenwillow $6.95; LB $6.67. An exciting summer of making and losing friends is experienced by Allie, the lively spirited heroine of this humorous story.

3047. Bradbury, Bianca. *The Loner* (5–7). Illus. by John Gretzer. 1970, Houghton $6.95. Rivalry between 2 brothers is lessened during a summer when they gain respect for each other.

3048. Branscum, Robbie. *The Saving of P.S.* (5–6). Illus. by Glen Rounds. 1977, Doubleday $5.95. The narrator, Priscilla Sue, is a preacher's daughter who must adjust to her father's courting of a pretty widow.

3049. Brenner, Barbara. *A Year in the Life of Rosie Bernard* (4–6). Illus. by Joan Sandin. 1971, Harper $6.89; Avon paper $1.50. Set in Brooklyn during the Great Depression, this is the story of Rosie's adjustment to living with her dead mother's family, attending a new school, and accepting her father's girl friend.

3050. Buck, Pearl. *The Big Wave* (4–8). 1973, Scholastic paper $.95. The loss of family and home in a tidal wave reveals the courage of a little Japanese boy.

3051. Bulla, Clyde Robert. *Shoeshine Girl* (3–5). Illus. by Leigh Grant. 1975, Crowell $7.95. A somewhat indolent 10-year-old girl matures during a summer working for Al at his shoeshine stand.

3052. Burch, Robert. *D. J.'s Worst Enemy* (4–6). Illus. by Emil Weiss. 1965, Viking $6.50. D.J., growing up in the Depression-poor rural South, discovers by his thoughtless actions that he is his own worst enemy.

3053. Burch, Robert. *Doodle and the Go-Cart* (4–6). Illus. by Alan Tiegreen. 1972, Viking $4.75. A sixth-grade Georgia farm boy tries various methods to earn $200 for a go-cart.

3054. Burch, Robert. *Queenie Peavy* (4–7). Illus. by Jerry Lazare. 1966, Viking $6.95. A defiant 13-year-old rescues her future from reform school in a Georgia town of the 1930s.

3055. Byars, Betsy. *After the Goat Man* (5–7). Illus. by Ronald Himler. 1974, Viking $6.95; Avon paper $1.25. The effects on a number of people of an old man's vehement refusal to sell his home for the building of a superhighway are explored in this convincing novel.

3056. Byars, Betsy. *The Cartoonist* (4–6). Illus. by Richard Cuffari. 1978, Viking $6.95. Alfie's refuge in his attic room with his cartoons is disrupted by his brother's return.

3057. Byars, Betsy. *Goodbye, Chicken Little* (4–6). 1979, Harper $5.95; LB $5.79. Jennie learns to accept the senseless death of a beloved uncle.

3058. Byars, Betsy. *The House of Wings* (4–6). Illus. by Daniel Schwartz. 1972, Viking $6.95; Dell paper $.95. Sammy is distraught when he is left alone with his grandfather, but things get better when a wounded crane is found and must be taken care of.

3059. Byars, Betsy. *The Night Swimmers* (5–6). Illus. by Troy Howell. 1980, Delacorte $7.59; LB $7.45. An enterprising girl tries to be a housekeeper and to take care of her 2 brothers.

3060. Calhoun, Mary. *The Horse Comes First* (4–6). Illus. by John Gretzer. 1974, Atheneum $6.95. City-raised Randa has trouble adjusting to a summer on grandfather's Iowa farm.

3061. Cameron, Eleanor. *Julia and the Hand of God* (4–6). Illus. by Gail Owens. 1977, Dutton $6.95. Eleven-year-old Julia, a fledgling writer, is growing up in grandma's crowded apartment in the Berkeley of 1923. Continued in *A Room Made of Windows*.

3062. Cameron, Eleanor. *A Room Made of Windows* (5–7). Illus. by Trina Schart Hyman. 1971, Little $7.95. Preteen Julia finds her room a sanctuary that gives her a shield and security from her loneliness.

3063. Cameron, Eleanor. *To the Green Mountains* (5–8). 1975, Dutton $7.95. Thirteen-year-old Kath views a number of adult problems with amazing understanding as she grows up in a small midwestern town where her mother runs a hotel.

3064. Cavanna, Betty. *Ballet Fever* (5–7). 1978, Westminster $7.50. Teddi finds many diversions can interrupt her ballet studies.

3065. Cavanna, Betty. *Going on Sixteen* (6–9). 1946, Westminster $5.75. The problems of a motherless girl's adolescence. Also use: *Accent on April* (1960, Morrow $7.75).

3066. Child Study Association, comp. *Courage to Adventure: Stories of Boys and Girls Growing Up in America* (4–6). Illus. by Reisie Lonette. 1976, Crowell $8.95. This anthology, culled chiefly from full-length novels, covers growing up in America from the Revolution to the present.

3067. Childress, Alice. *A Hero Ain't Nothin' But a Sandwich* (6–9). 1973, Coward $6.95; Avon paper $1.50. Told by various narratives, this is the story of a young Harlem boy, Benjie, and his encounter with drugs. Mature language.

3068. Clark, Ann Nolan. *To Stand against the Wind* (5–7). 1978, Viking $7.95. A young Vietnamese boy changes his outlook when he leaves his war-torn country for the United States.

3069. Clark, Mavis Thorpe. *If the Earth Falls In* (6–8). 1975, Seabury $6.95. A young girl's search for independence is the theme of this novel set in a former gold-mining area of Australia.

3070. Clark, Mavis Thorpe. *The Min-Min* (5–7). 1969, Macmillan $7.95; paper $1.95. An Australian girl and her brother run away deep into the outback and find a sympathetic ear to their problems in Mrs. Tucker, who lives at a sheep station.

3071. Clark, Mavis Thorpe. *The Sky Is Free* (6–9). 1976, Macmillan $6.95. Runaway boys learn to sacrifice their own futures to help each other in this thoughtful, sometimes touching novel set in opal fields in Australia.

3072. Clarke, Joan. *Early Rising* (5–8). 1976, Lippincott $7.95. Adoring Erica discovers the imperfections in her older half-sister, in this novel set in an English vicarage of the 1880s.

3073. Cleaver, Vera, and Cleaver, Bill. *Ellen Grae* (6–8). Illus. by Ellen Raskin. 1967, Lippincott $8.95. Eleven-year-old Ellen, locally noted for her very amusing tall tales, tries one dramatically painful venture into straight reporting and learns that the truth can be rejected when it is something that adults don't want to believe.

3074. Cleaver, Vera, and Cleaver, Bill. *Dust of the Earth* (6–9). 1975, Lippincott $8.95. A first-person novel about a 14-year-old growing up in a large, poor family eking out a living as sheep ranchers in the Badlands of South Dakota.

3075. Cleaver, Vera, and Cleaver, Bill. *Grover* (4–7). Illus. by Frederic Marvin. 1970, Lippincott $8.95. After his mother's suicide and his father's resultant breakdown, 10-year-old Grover must face the hard reality of death and trouble alone and eventually reaches a level of understanding of himself and others.

3076. Clifford, Eth. *The Rocking Chair Rebellion* (5–7). 1978, Houghton $6.95. Opie, age fourteen, helps some oldsters in an old people's home.

3077. Clifford, Mary Louise. *Bisha of Burundi* (5–8). Illus. by Trevor Stubley. 1973, Crowell $7.95. The changing roles of women are explored in this story of a 15-year-old Watusi girl growing up in Burundi.

3078. Clymer, Eleanor. *Luke Was There* (4–7). Illus. by Diane deGroat. 1973, Holt LB $5.95. When Julius's only bit of security—his friendship with a social worker—is denied him, he runs away from the children's home.

3079. Clymer, Eleanor. *My Brother Stevie* (4–6). 1967, Holt $4.95. A story true to inner-city conditions, movingly told in the first person about an older sister's problems with her near-delinquent small brother.

3080. Colman, Hila. *Diary of a Frantic Kid Sister* (4–6). 1973, Archway paper $1.25. Sarah has trouble communicating with her family, so she pours out her soul to her diary.

3081. Cone, Molly. *Dance Around the Fire* (4–6). Illus. by Marvin Friedman. 1974, Houghton $5.95. Joanne faces problems concerning her commitment to her Jewish religion. Also use: *A Promise Is a Promise* (1964, Houghton $8.95).

3082. Corcoran, Barbara. *Cabin in the Sky* (6–9). 1976, Atheneum $7.95. New York show biz of the 1950s is the background for this story of a young man from Maine who comes to the big city for a life in the theater.

3083. Corcoran, Barbara. *The Faraway Island* (5–7). 1977, Atheneum $6.95. Lynn spends a difficult year with her grandmother on Nantucket.

3084. Corcoran, Barbara. *Make No Sound* (5–7). 1977, Atheneum $6.95. Melody must overcome guilt when, after wishing her older brother harm, he has a serious accident.

3085. Corcoran, Barbara. *A Trick of Light* (5–8). Illus. by Lydia Dabcovich. 1972, Atheneum $5.50. A series of short stories that deal primarily with everyday problems faced by young adolescents.

3086. Conford, Ellen. *Anything for a Friend* (5–7). 1979, Little $7.95. A young girl tries various schemes to make new friends.

3087. Conford, Ellen. *Dreams of Victory* (4–6). Illus. by Gail Rockwell. 1973, Little $6.95; Dell paper $.95. Although Vicky is a shy social misfit, in her fantasies she conquers all.

3088. Conford, Ellen. *Hail, Hail Camp Timberwood* (5–7). Illus. by Gail Owens. 1978, Little $6.95. Thirteen-year-old Melanie's first summer at camp.

3089. Craig, John. *Zach* (5–7). 1972, Coward $6.95. When an American Indian boy, Zach, is orphaned in a fire, he sets out to find his roots.

3090. Crawford, Deborah. *Somebody Will Miss Me* (6–9). 1971, Crown $4.95. A harrowing account of a girl growing up with inhospitable relatives in a New Jersey coastal town during the Great Depression.

3091. Cunningham, Julia. *Come to the Edge* (5–7). 1977, Pantheon $4.95; LB $5.99. An unwanted and cruelly treated young boy eventually finds a home with a kindly sign painter.

3092. Cunningham, Julia. *Dorp Dead* (6–8). Illus. by James J. Spanfeller. 1965, Pantheon $3.95; LB $5.99; Avon paper $1.25. An orphan is sent away to live with a fanatically meticulous and psychotic carpenter.

3093. Dahstedt, Marden. *Terrible Wave* (4–6). Illus. by Charles Robinson. 1972, Coward $5.95. A selfish, spoiled young girl finds her life changing as a result of the Johnstown Flood of 1889. Also use: *Stopping Place* (1976, Putnam $6.95).

3094. Dalgliesh, Alice. *The Bears on Hemlock Mountain* (1–4). Illus. by Helen Sewell. 1952, Scribner $7.95; paper $2.95. Jonathan ventured over the mountain by himself after dark and discovered the reality of bear existence!

3095. Donovan, John. *Wild in the World* (6–9). 1971, Harper $6.89; Avon paper $1.25. After the death of the rest of his family, John Gridley befriends a wolf-dog who remains faithful even after John's death. A stark but moving story.

3096. Farley, Carol. *The Garden Is Doing Fine* (5–7). Illus. by Lynn Sweat. 1975, Atheneum $7.95. Fourteen-year-old Carrie faces the death of her beloved father in this novel set in a Michigan town in 1945.

3097. Farmer, Penelope. *August the Fourth* (3–6). Illus. by Jael Jordan. 1976, Parnassus $5.95; LB $4.77. The effects of World War I on a teenage English girl are described well.

3098. Faulkner, G., and Becker, J. *Melindy's Medal* (3–5). Illus. by Elton C. Fax. 1945, Messner $3.50; LB $4.79. Melindy, a little black girl, moves from a basement apartment to a housing project.

3099. Fox, Paula. *Blowfish Live in the Sea* (6–9). 1970, Bradbury $6.95. A touching novel about a boy's reconciliation with his father.

3100. Fox, Paula. *Portrait of Ivan* (5–7). Illus. by Saul Lambert. 1969, Bradbury $6.95. Ivan's world, heretofore austere and numbed, expands while his portrait is painted, to one with the promise of wholeness and hope; a compelling story.

3101. Freuchen, Pipaluk. *Eskimo Boy* (4–6). Illus. by Ingrid Vang Nyman. 1951, Lothrop $5.25. When his father is killed by a walrus, Ivik must become the family's provider in this story of Greenlanders.

3102. Gardam, Jane. *The Summer After the Funeral* (6–9). 1973, Macmillan $4.95. After her father's death, Athene spends a puzzling summer sorting out her life.

3103. George, Jean Craighead. *Julie of the Wolves* (5–8). Illus. by John Schoenherr. 1972, Harper $6.95; LB $6.89; paper $1.50. Julie (Eskimo name, Miyax) begins a trek across frozen Alaska and is saved only by the friendship of a pack of wolves. Newbery Award.

3104. George, Jean Craighead. *The Summer of the Falcon* (5–8). 1962, Crowell $6.95; paper $1.95. June learns to take responsibility and discipline when she trains her own falcons.

3105. Gessner, Lynne. *Malcolm Yucca Seed* (3–4). Illus. by William Sauts Bock. 1977, Harvey House $6.39. Malcolm gains a real name after he tries to save the family farm by getting some yucca seeds to plant.

3106. Gipson, Fred. *Little Arliss* (4–5). Illus. by Ronald Himler. 1978, Harper $5.95; LB $5.79. Arliss of *Old Yeller* proves his worth even though he is small.

3107. Glaser, Dianne. *The Diary of Trilby Frost* (6–8). 1976, Holiday $6.95. Two turbulent and frequently tragic years in the life of a teenager growing up in turn-of-the-century rural America.

3108. Green, Phyllis. *Nantucket Summer* (5–8). 1974, Elsevier/Nelson $6.95; Scholastic paper $.95. A young girl spends an eventful summer on Nantucket employed as a baby-sitter for Mrs. Cramer, an unhappy, insecure woman.

3109. Greene, Bette. *Summer of My German Soldier* (6–9). 1973, Dial $7.95; Bantam paper $1.95. In a small southern town during World War II, Patty's life gains meaning when she harbors an escaped German soldier. Also use the sequel: *Morning Is a Long Time Coming* (1978, $7.95).

3110. Greene, Constance C. *Beat the Turtle Drum* (4–6). Illus. by Donna Diamond. 1976, Viking $5.95; Dell paper $1.50. A young girl must adjust to the accidental death of her beloved younger sister.

3111. Greene, Constance C. *Leo, the Lioness* (5–7). 1970, Viking $6.95; Dell paper $.95. During Tibb's thirteenth summer, she suffers disillusionment and growing pains but reaches a new level of maturity.

3112. Greenwald, Sheila. *The Atrocious Two* (4–6). 1978, Houghton $6.95. Aunt Tessie takes 2 misbehaving children for a summer.

3113. Greenwald, Sheila. *The Secret in Miranda's Closet* (3–5). Illus. by author. 1977, Houghton $6.95; Scholastic paper $.95. Young Miranda hides the fact from her divorced mother, a feminist, that her favorite toy is a doll.

3114. Hall, Lynn. *Flowers of Anger* (5–7). Illus. by Joseph Cellini. 1976, Follett $5.95; LB $5.97. In spite of protests, Ann plans an act of revenge after a neighbor shoots her horse for trespassing on his land.

3115. Hall, Lynn. *The Siege of Silent Henry* (6–9). 1972, Follett $4.95. Wheeler-dealer Robert Short meets his match when he tries to hoodwink Henry Leffert, an elderly recluse.

3116. Hamilton, Virginia. *Arilla Sun Down* (5–7). 1976, Morrow $8.25; LB $7.92. A girl with a dual inheritance—part Black, part American Indian—faces problems in maturing.

3117. Hamilton, Virginia. *Zeely* (4–6). Illus. by Symeon Shimin. 1967, Macmillan $5.95; paper $1.25. An 11-year-old black city girl is lightly guided from her daydreams to reality by Zeely, who is as kind as she is tall and beautiful, during a summer visit to her uncle's farm.

3118. Hassler, Jon. *Four Miles to Pinecone* (6–9). 1977, Warne $6.95. Tom faces the dilemma of reporting to the police 2 people—one a good friend—who are guilty of theft.

3119. Heide, Florence Parry. *The Key* (5–7). Illus. by Ati Forberg. 1971, Atheneum $4.50.

Three stories, each dealing with a child in a difficult situation and his or her ability to cope with it.

3120. Hentoff, Nat. *Jazz Country* (6–9). 1965, Harper $6.89; paper $1.25. A portrayal of the black jazz world, as seen through the eyes of a teenage white boy whose deepest desire is to be a great trumpet player.

3121. Hickman, Janet. *The Stones* (4–6). Illus. by Richard Cuffari. 1976, Macmillan $7.95. In a small midwestern town during World War II, a group of boys unjustly persecute an old German-American man.

3122. Hinton, Nigel. *Collision Course* (6–9). 1977, Elsevier Nelson $6.95; Dell paper $1.50. Ray's joyride on a stolen motorcycle ends in the death of an old woman.

3123. Holland, Isabelle. *The Man Without a Face* (6–9). 1972, Lippincott $8.95. Charles seeks Justin McLeod to be his tutor and becomes involved in a close and disturbing relationship.

3124. Hooks, William H. *Doug Meets the Nutcracker* (4–6). Illus. by James J. Spanfeller. 1977, Warne $5.95. One boy's problems with his peers after he decides to become a ballet dancer.

3125. Hunt, Irene. *Lottery Rose* (6–8). 1976, Scribner $7.95. Georgie is beaten and cruelly treated by his mother until finally the police rescue him.

3126. Hunt, Irene. *Up a Road Slowly* (6–9). 1966, Follett $4.95; LB $4.98; Grosset paper $.95. Julie goes to live with Aunt Cordelia after her mother's death and finds the adjustment very difficult. Newbery Award.

3127. Hurwitz, Johanna. *Once I Was a Plum Tree* (4–5). Illus. by Ingrid Fetz. 1980, Morrow $7.50. In spite of her parents' indifference, Geraldine becomes aware of her Jewish inheritance.

3128. Irwin, Hadley. *The Lilith Summer* (6–8). 1979, Feminist Press $7.95. Twelve-year-old Ellen learns about old age when she "lady sits" with 77-year-old Lilith Adams.

3129. Kalnay, Francis. *It Happened in Chichipica* (4–6). Illus. by Charles Robinson. 1971, Harcourt $4.95. In his small Mexican village, young Chucho is falsely accused of a crime and almost loses his chance at a scholarship.

3130. Kennedy, Richard. *Come Again in the Spring* (3–5). Illus. by Marcia Sewall. 1976, Harper $6.89. An old man outwits death and retains his life until the spring in this moving story.

3131. Kennedy, Richard. *Oliver Hyde's Dishcloth Concert* (2–5). Illus. by Robert Andrew Parker.

1977, Little $4.95. A recluse rejoins society after an unusual experience, in this homespun American tale.

3132. Kingman, Lee. *Break a Leg, Betsy Maybe!* (6–9). 1976, Houghton $7.95. Betsy's seventeenth year, in which she falls in love, becomes an actress, and adjusts to a new home.

3133. Kirk, Barbara. *Grandpa, Me and Our House in the Tree* (3–5). Illustrated. 1978, Macmillan $7.95. The friendship of a boy and his grandfather during the old man's last illness.

3134. Klein, Norma. *Tomboy* (4–6). 1978, Four Winds $5.95. In this sequel to *Confessions of an Only Child*, Toe is denied admission to the Tomboy Club because she has too many female traits.

3135. Konigsburg, E. L. *Altogether, One at a Time* (4–6). Illus. by Gail E. Haley. 1971, Atheneum $7.95; paper $1.25. Four short stories by the Newbery Award-winning writer, each of which explores the theme that compromise is often necessary to appreciate life fully.

3136. Konigsburg, E. L. *Throwing Shadows* (6–9). 1979, Atheneum $8.95. Five stories that explore the inner character of some interesting young people.

3137. Krumgold, Joseph. *Henry III* (6–9). Illus. by Alvin Smith. 1967, Atheneum $5.95; Archway paper $.75. Suburbia, as seen through the eyes of keenly intelligent, 13-year-old Henry, who decides never to compromise himself. Others in the trilogy about boys on the threshold of young manhood, both Newbery winners, are: *And Now Miguel* (1953, Crowell $8.95; Apollo, paper $1.95) and *Onion John* (1959, Crowell $8.95; Apollo, paper $2.95).

3138. Lee, Mildred. *The Rock and the Willow* (6–9). 1963, Lothrop $6.75; Archway paper $.75. A realistic portrayal of a teenager growing up in rural Alabama in 1930, the oldest of a large family, who dreams of becoming a teacher and writer.

3139. Lee, Mildred. *Sycamore Year* (6–8). 1974, Lothrop $7.25; LB $6.96; NAL paper $1.25. Fourteen-year-old Wren must make many adjustments during her first year in Sycamore, including coping with her sister's pregnancy.

3140. Levoy, Myron. *Alan and Naomi* (6–9). 1977, Harper $6.95; LB $6.79; Dell paper $1.50. A young boy in New York City helps a girl traumatized by Nazi brutality.

3141. Lowry, Lois. *A Summer to Die* (6–8). Illus. by Jenni Oliver. 1977, Houghton $6.95. Meg's hostility toward her sister Molly turns to guilt and bewilderment when she learns Molly has a fatal disease.

3142. McCord, Jean. *Turkeylegs Thompson* (6–8). 1979, Atheneum $8.95. A young girl begins life again after a tragic summer.

3143. Major, Kevin. *Hold Fast* (6–8). 1980, Delacorte $8.95. An orphaned 14-year-old boy in Newfoundland flees from an overbearing uncle.

3144. Mann, Peggy. *The Street of the Flower Boxes* (4–6). Illus. by Peter Burchard. 1966, Coward $4.49; Archway paper $.60. New York City toughs uproot the plantings in window boxes but admit to their vandalism.

3145. Mann, Peggy. *There Are Two Kinds of Terrible* (5–7). 1977, Doubleday $5.95; Avon paper $1.50. Rob lives through his mother's illness and the anguish of her death from cancer.

3146. Mark, Jan. *Under the Autumn Garden* (5–6). Illus. by Judith Gwyn Brown. 1979, Crowell $8.95; LB $8.79. A quiet boy tries to complete a school assignment by looking for the ruins of an old priory in this slow-paced, introspective English story.

3147. Mazer, Norma Fox. *A Figure of Speech* (6–9). 1973, Delacorte $7.95; Dell paper $1.25. The rejection and death of a beloved grandfather are seen through the sensitive eyes of Jenny.

3148. Miles, Betty. *Looking On* (6–8). 1978, Knopf $6.95. A lonely young girl is befriended by a young couple who move into a nearby trailer.

3149. Miles, Betty. *The Real Me* (4–6). 1974, Knopf $5.99; Avon paper $1.25. Barbara decides to fight injustice when a company refuses to let her take over her brother's newspaper delivery route.

3150. Miles, Betty. *The Trouble with Thirteen* (5–8). 1979, Knopf $6.95; LB $6.99. Annie's life is disrupted by many changes, including a move to New York City.

3151. Miles, Miska. *Annie and the Old One* (2–5). Illus. by Peter Parnall. 1971, Little $6.95. Annie, a young Navajo girl, realizes her wonderful grandmother is dying, and tries to put off the inevitable.

✓**3152.** Morgan, Alison. *All Kinds of Pickles* (6–8). 1979, Nelson $7.95. Davy's pet goat is killed by his guardians, and this complicates an adjustment to life without his beloved grandfather.

3153. Morgan, Alison. *A Boy Called Fish* (6–9). 1973, Harper LB $6.79; paper $1.25. A lonely boy takes in a stray dog in this story set in Wales.

3154. Naylor, Phyllis Reynolds. *Eddie, Incorporated* (4–6). Illus. by Blanche Sims. 1980, Atheneum $8.95. After many tries, a sixth-grader finally finds a way to make money.

3155. Norris, Gunilla B. *Friendship Hedge* (3–5). 1973, Dutton $5.50. A misunderstanding between 2 friends causes the death of a pet guinea pig.

3156. Orgel, Doris. *The Mulberry Music* (4–6). Illus. by Dale Payson. 1971, Harper $7.89. A moving story of a young girl's difficult adjustment to the death of her beloved grandma.

3157. Owen, Dodson. *Boy at the Window* (6–8). 1977, Farrar $7.95. A grim story about a 9-year-old black boy and his reactions to his beloved mother's illness and death. Original title: *When Trees Are Green*.

3158. Pascal, Francine. *My First Love and Other Disasters* (6–8). 1979, Viking $7.95. First love is encountered in Victoria's summer at the beach.

3159. Paterson, Katherine. *The Great Gilly Hopkins* (4–6). 1978, Crowell $6.95. Precocious Gilly bounces from one foster home to another.

3160. Peck, Richard. *Representing Super Doll* (6–9). 1974, Viking $6.95; Avon paper $.95. Verna accompanies her friend Darlene to New York for the Teen Super Doll contest in this novel about adolescent concerns.

3161. Perl, Lila. *Don't Ask Miranda* (5–7). 1979, Seabury $7.50. Miranda faces many adjustment problems when she moves to a new neighborhood.

3162. Pfeffer, Susan Beth. *Just Morgan* (5–9) Archway paper $.75. Fourteen-year-old Morgan is orphaned and must adjust to life with her suave, sophisticated guardian, Uncle Tom.

3163. Platt, Kin. *Chloris and the Weirdos* (6–8). 1978, Bradbury $7.95. Jenny continues the saga of her sister, Chloris. This time Jenny has a boyfriend, Harold, to help her.

3164. Pollowitz, Melinda. *Cinnamon Cane* (5–7). 1977, Harper $6.95; LB $6.79. Cassie must sort out her emotions after the death of a grandfather she had once loved but also neglected.

3165. Rabe, Berniece. *Naomi* (6–9). 1975, Nelson $6.95; Bantam paper $1.25. A disarmingly honest portrait of a girl's adolescence amid the poverty and ignorance of rural life in Missouri in the 1930s.

3166. Rabe, Berniece. *The Girl Who Had No Name* (6–8). 1977, Dutton $6.95. Girlie is shunted from one home to another because of her father's guilt, in this touching novel set in Depression-time Missouri.

3167. Rabe, Berniece. *The Orphans* (5–7). 1978, Dutton $7.95. Orphaned twins scheme and connive to insure adoption together.

3168. Rinkoff, Barbara. *Member of the Gang* (4–7). Illus. by Harold James. 1968, Crown $4.95. Woodie learns that being a member of a slum gang can mean only trouble.

3169. Roberts, Willo Davis. *Don't Hurt Laurie!* (4–6). Illus. by Ruth Sanderson. 1977, Atheneum $7.95. Seen from the viewpoint of 11-year-old Laurie, this is a harrowing story of child abuse.

3170. Russ, Lavinia. *The April Age* (6–9). 1975, Atheneum $5.25. Peakie, the young heroine of the author's earlier *Over the Hills and Far Away* and now almost 18, sails for Europe in 1925 with 5 other girls.

3171. Russ, Lavinia. *Over the Hills and Far Away* (6–9). 1968, Harcourt $5.50. In the Midwest of 1917, Peakie Maston, a spirited, independent-minded adolescent, finds the process of growing up painful.

3172. Sachs, Marilyn. *A December Tale* (5–7). 1976, Doubleday $5.95. Myra decides to save herself and her younger brother from the constant abuse they receive in their foster homes.

3173. Sachs, Marilyn. *A Summer's Lease* (6–9). 1979, Dutton $7.95. A strong-willed egocentric girl learns to pity and love during a summer when she works at the home of her English teacher.

3174. Seed, David. *Stream Runner* (5–7). 1979, Four Winds $7.95. A 14-year-old boy recalls important memories of his four years in a small town in northern California.

3175. Shecter, Ben. *Someplace Else* (4–6). 1971, Harper $6.89. Eleven-year-old Arnie has to cope with such problems of growing up as preparing for a bar mitzvah, the loss of a pet, and unwanted attentions from a female admirer. Also use: *Game for Demons* (1972, Harper $6.89).

3176. Shotwell, Louisa R. *Adam Bookout* (4–6). Illus. by W. T. Mars. 1967, Viking $3.95. After his parents' death, Adam runs away from Oklahoma to his cousin in Brooklyn and learns a great deal about tolerance and how to face his own problems.

3177. Shreve, Susan. *Family Secrets: Five Very Important Stories* (3–4). Illus. by Richard Cuffari. 1979, Knopf $5.95; LB $5.99. Five essaylike ruminations on serious subjects by a young boy named Sammy.

3178. Shura, Mary Francis. *The Season of Silence* (5–9). Illus. by Ruth Sanderson. 1976, Atheneum $6.95. A sensitive story of a young girl's adolescence and of the many trials and conflicts it brings.

3179. Shyer, Marlene Fanta. *My Brother, The Thief* (5–7). 1980, Scribner $8.95. A young girl is caught up in her brother's habit of stealing.

3180. Simon, Marcia L. *A Special Gift* (5–7). 1978, Harcourt $5.95. Peter keeps his ballet classes a secret.

3181. Slepian, Jan. *The Alfred Summer* (6–9). 1980, Macmillan $7.95. Four youngsters with various problems construct a boat to use at Coney Island.

3182. Smith, Doris. *A Taste of Blackberries* (4–6). Illus. by Charles Robinson. 1973, Crowell $7.95; LB $7.89; Scholastic paper $1.25. Young Jamie dies unexpectedly of a bee sting, and his friends adjust to this loss.

3183. Sorensen, Virginia. *Plain Girl* (4–6). Illus. by Charles Geer. 1955, Harcourt $6.50; paper $1.45. An Amish girl finds it difficult to accept both her cultural heritage and the world around her.

3184. Southall, Ivan. *Benson Boy* (5–7). Illus. by Ingrid Fetz. 1973, Macmillan $4.95. One night in a young boy's life in which he must muster all his inner resources to help in a family emergency.

3185. Southall, Ivan. *What about Tomorrow?* (6–9). 1977, Macmillan $6.95. After Sam loses his source of livelihood, he begins wandering aimlessly in the countryside around his Australian home.

3186. Stefansson, Thorsteinn. *The Golden Future* (6–8). 1977, Nelson $6.95. This autobiographical novel tells of a young writer's boyhood in Iceland.

3187. Stewart, A. C. *Dark Dove* (6–9). 1974, Phillips $8.95. Roddy's constant quarreling with his father leads to his leaving his Scottish home to become a sailor.

3188. Stewart, A. C. *Ossian House* (6–8). 1976, Phillips $8.95. Eleven-year-old John Murray inherits the ancestral home in Scotland and must live there 8 weeks of each year.

3189. Stolz, Mary. *By the Highway Home* (6–9). 1971, Harper $6.95; LB $7.89; paper $1.95. Cathy's family moves to Vermont, and there she finds a new life and is able to adjust to her brother's death in Vietnam.

3190. Stolz, Mary. *Ferris Wheel* (4–7). 1977, Harper $6.95; LB $6.79. Polly suffers the pangs of preadolescent worries and concerns in this realistic novel set in a small Vermont town.

3191. Stoutenburg, Adrien. *Where to Now, Blue?* (5–7). 1978, Four Winds $6.95. Blue sets out with a cat, a parrot, and a 6-year-old orphan to find her uncle.

3192. Stuart, Jesse. *Penny's Worth of Character* (3–5). Illus. by Robert Henneberger. 1954, McGraw $7.95. A lesson of honesty is learned through a simple errand.

3193. Terris, Susan. *Whirling Rainbows* (5–7). 1974, Doubleday $4.95. Leah, raised in a Jewish household, tries to recapture her American-Indian roots while attending a summer camp.

3194. Uchida, Yoshiko. *The Promised Year* (4–6). Illus. by William Hutchinson. 1959, Harcourt $6.50. Keiko, in America from Japan for a year's visit, grows to love and understand her new country.

3195. Valencak, Hannelore. *A Tangled Web* (5–7). Trans. from the German by Patricia Crampton. 1978, Morrow $6.95; LB $6.67. Annie's lies get her into trouble, particularly with an overbearing schoolmate.

3196. Van Stockum, Hilda. *The Borrowed House* (5–6). 1975, Farrar $6.95. Only after she leaves Germany does 12-year-old Janna realize how evil is the Nazi regime she once supported.

3197. Vogel, Ilse-Margaret. *My Twin Sister Erika* (5–7). Illus. by author. 1976, Harper $6.89. Inge's relations with her identical twin reach a tragic conclusion when Erika dies.

3198. Wagner, Jane. *J.T.* (4–6). Photos by Gordon Par 1969, Dell paper $.95. J. T. Gamble lives in Harlem, and his most prized possessions are a tiny portable radio and a stray cat, for whom he has made a home. When the cat is killed by a car, he receives support and understanding from the adults in his life.

3199. Waldron, Ann. *The Luckie Star* (5–7). 1977, Dutton $7.50. A summer in Florida helps the misfit in the Luckie family, young Quincy, to come to terms with herself.

3200. Walsh, Jill Paton. *Toolmaker* (3–6). Illus. by Jeroo Roy. 1974, Seabury $6.95. Ra, a member of a Stone Age tribe, is left behind to hunt for himself.

3201. Wier, Esther. *The Loner* (6–8). Illus. by Christine Price. 1963, McKay $5.95. A woman sheepherder gives shelter to a starving young immigrant orphan, who, in turn, learns why people can't always go their way alone.

3202. Wojciechowska, Maia. *Shadow of a Bull* (5–7). Illus. by Alvin Smith. 1964, Atheneum $6.95; paper $1.95. Manolo, surviving son of a great bullfighter, has his own "moment of truth"

when he faces his first bull. Newbery Award, 1965.

3203. Wolitzer, Hilma. *Toby Lived Here* (5–7). 1978, Farrar $6.95. Two sisters adjust in different ways to a foster home.

3204. Woodford, Peggy. *Please Don't Go* (6–9). 1973, Dutton $4.95. A girl falls in love with a much older man.

3205. Wrightson, Patricia. *The Feather Star* (6–8). Illus. by Noela Young. 1963, Harcourt $4.95. During a summer in a coastal fishing village, a 14-year-old Australian girl experiences the change from childhood to adolescence.

3206. Young, Miriam. *Truth and Consequences* (4–6). Illus. by Diane deGroat. 1975, Four Winds $6.50; Scholastic paper $.95. Kim Jones faces unexpected consequences when she makes a vow always to tell the truth.

3207. Zolotow, Charlotte, comp. *An Overpraised Season: 10 Stories of Youth* (6–9). 1973, Harper $6.95; LB $7.89. Problems of adolescents, particularly relating to adults, are explored in 10 short stories by such authors as Updike, Vonnegut, and Lessing.

Physical and Emotional Problems

3208. Albert, Louise. *But I'm Ready to Go* (6–9). 1976, Bradbury $7.95; Dell paper $1.50. In spite of a learning disability, Judy gallantly strikes out on her own to find fame in New York City.

3209. Allan, Mabel Esther. *The View Beyond My Father* (6–9). 1978, Dodd $5.95. A girl regains her eyesight in this English novel set in the 1930s.

3210. Armer, Alberta. *Screwball* (5–7). Illus. by W. T. Mars. 1963, Grosset paper $.95. A former polio victim gains strength and security when he prepares for competition in a Soap Box Derby.

3211. Baldwin, Anne Norris. *A Little Time* (4–6). 1978, Viking $6.95. Ten-year-old Sarah tells about her 4-year-old brother who has Down's syndrome.

3212. Blue, Rose. *Me and Einstein: Breaking through the Reading Barrier* (4–6). Illus. by Peggy Luks. 1979, Human Sciences $6.95. Bobby, a dyslexic youngster, tries to hide the fact that he can't read.

3213. Blume, Judy. *Blubber* (4–6). 1974, Bradbury $6.95. Jill finds out what it's like to be an outsider when she defends Linda, a classmate who is teased because of her fatness.

3214. Blume, Judy. *Deenie* (5–7). 1974, Bradbury $7.95; Dell paper $1.50. Instead of becoming a model, as her mother wishes, Deenie must cope with sclerosis and wearing a spinal brace.

3215. Bottner, Barbara. *Dumb Old Casey Is a Fat Tree* (2–4). Illus. by author. 1979, Harper $6.95; LB $6.89. In spite of her weight, Casey still hopes to be a ballet dancer.

3216. Branscum, Robbie. *For Love of Jody* (6–8). Illus. by Allen Davis. 1979, Lothrop $6.95; LB $6.67. Francie, growing up in a poor family, finds it difficult to accept her mentally retarded sister.

3217. Bridgers, Sue Ellen. *All Together Now* (5–7). 1979, Knopf $7.95; LB $7.99. Twelve-year-old Casey forms a strong friendship with a 30-year-old retarded man.

3218. Brown, Roy. *Escape the River* (6–9). 1972, Seabury $6.95. Twelve-year-old Paul tries to find a new life for himself and his brain-damaged brother in this English novel.

3219. Byars, Betsy. *The Summer of the Swans* (5–7). Illus. by Ted Coconis. 1970, Viking $6.95; Avon paper $1.50. The story of a 14-year-old girl named Sara—moody, unpredictable, and on the brink of womanhood—and how her life changes when her younger, mentally retarded brother disappears. Newbery Award, 1971.

3220. Byars, Betsy. *The TV Kid* (3–4). Illus. by Richard Cuffari. 1976, Viking $6.95. In his loneliness, a young boy escapes into the world of television watching and soon has difficulty distinguishing fact from fancy.

3221. Carpelan, Bo. *Bow Island: The Story of a Summer That Was Different* (5–7). 1971, Delacorte $4.95; LB $4.58. Eleven-year-old Johan develops a fascination for the sea and an attachment with a mentally retarded youth during a summer vacation.

3222. Carpelan, Bo. *Dolphins in the City* (6–9). 1976, Delacorte $5.95. A retarded young man and his mother face hardships when they move from their island home to Helsinki.

3223. Cleaver, Vera, and Cleaver, Bill. *Me Too* (5–7). 1973, Lippincott $8.95. Lydia secretly decides to help her twin sister, Lorna, who is retarded.

3224. Cohen, Barbara. *My Name Is Rosie* (4–6). 1978, Lothrop $6.95. Rosie Gold escapes her unhappy life through fantasy.

3225. Corcoran, Barbara. *Axe-Time, Sword-Time* (6–9). 1976, Atheneum $6.95. A girl copes with both a learning disability and family disunity in this novel of an 18-year-old's search for independence.

3226. Corcoran, Barbara. *A Dance to Still Music* (6–9). Illus. by Charles Robinson. 1974, Atheneum $8.95. Threatened by her mother with attending a special school for the deaf, Margaret runs away and finds unexpected help.

3227. Ellis, Ella Thorp. *Celebrate the Morning* (5–9). 1972, Atheneum $7.95. A story of a touching relationship between a young girl and her mentally ill mother.

3228. Fassler, Joan. *Howie Helps Himself* (2–4). Illus. by Joe Lasker. 1975, Whitman $5.75. Howie adjusts to cerebral palsy and the use of his wheelchair.

3229. Fox, Paula. *The Stone-Faced Boy* (4–7). Illus. by Donald MacKay. 1968, Bradbury $6.95. Gus, a sensitive and timid middle child in a family of 5, learns to mask his feelings and present a "stone face" to the world.

3230. Friis-Baastad, Babbis. *Kristy's Courage* (4–6). Trans. by Lise Somme McKinnon. Illus. by Charles Geer. 1965, Harcourt $5.95. Seven-year-old Kristy is handicapped by a speech defect and finds the world unsympathetic to her problems.

3231. Garrigue, Sheila. *Between Friends* (5–7). 1978, Bradbury $6.95. Through her friendship with Dedi, Jill learns about retardation and the value of friendship.

3232. Greene, Constance C. *The Ears of Louis* (3–5). Illus. by Nola Langner. 1974, Viking LB $6.95; Dell paper $.95. Louis at last finds a solution to the social problems caused by having such large ears that people call his "Sugar Bowl."

3233. Ter Haar, Jaap. *The World of Ben Lighthart* (6–8). Trans. by Martha Mearns. 1977, Delacorte $5.95. A boy adjusts to blindness in this novel set in Europe.

3234. Hamilton, Virginia. *The Planet of Junior Brown* (6–9). 1971, Macmillan $7.95; paper $.95. Buddy helps his fellow eighth-grade dropout Junior Brown by taking him to his hangout (his planet) and trying to retain Junior's tentative grip on reality. A complex novel.

3235. Heide, Florence Parry. *Growing Anyway Up* (5–7). 1976, Lippincott $7.95. A seriously disturbed girl is alienated from her mother and finds difficulty adjusting to her new private school.

3236. Heide, Florence Parry. *Secret Dreamer, Secret Dreams* (6–8). 1978, Lippincott $6.95. A mentally handicapped girl tells her own secret story.

3237. Hermes, Patricia. *What If They Knew?* (4–6). 1980, Harcourt $6.95. Jeremy has epilepsy and must adjust to living with her grandparents.

3238. Holland, Isabelle. *Dinah and the Green Fat Kingdom* (5–7). 1978, Lippincott $7.95. Twelve-year-old Dinah agonizes over her weight problem.

3239. Kelley, Sally. *Trouble with Explosives* (5–7). 1976, Bradbury $6.95. With the help of many people, Polly overcomes her stuttering.

3240. Kent, Deborah. *Belonging* (6–8). Illus. by Gary Watson. 1978, Dial $7.50. A blind teenager finds that being different has its compensations.

3241. Konigsburg, E. L. *George* (6–9). Illus. by author. 1970, Atheneum $5.95; paper $1.25. George lives inside Ben and in times of mental stress emerges as the dark side of Ben's personality.

3242. Lasker, Joe. *He's My Brother* (2–4). Illus. by author. 1974, Whitman $5.95. Family attitudes and their wonderful treatment of their retarded family member, Jamie, is told by his older brother.

3243. Levine, Edna S. *Lisa and Her Soundless World* (3–5). Illus. by Gloria Kamen. 1974, Behavioral $6.95. The plight of a deaf girl is explored in this gripping, realistic story of Lisa and her problems.

3244. Little, Jean. *From Anna* (4–6). Illus. by Joan Sandin. 1972, Harper $7.89; paper $1.95. Anna's family immigrates to Canada to escape Nazi persecution, and this opens up a new world and a wonderful change for the partially sighted girl.

3245. Little, Jean. *Listen for the Singing* (5–7). 1977, Dutton $6.95. Visually handicapped Anna helps her brother adjust to blindness caused by an accident.

3246. Little, Jean. *Mine for Keeps* (4–6). Illus. by Lewis Parker. 1962, Little $6.95. The exceptionally well-handled story of Sal, a cerebral palsy victim, who must adjust to her family after being in a special school. The sequel, with Sal's younger sister Meg as the heroine, is: *Spring Begins in March* (1966, $6.95).

3247. Little, Jean. *Take Wing* (5–7). Illustrated. 1968, Little $6.95. Laurel loves her brother James, who is mentally retarded, but it is not until after her mother's absence that his retardation comes to light and his situation is acknowledged by the family.

3248. Parker, Richard. *He Is Your Brother* (5–6). 1976, Nelson $6.95; Scholastic paper $.95. Eleven-year-old Mike gradually learns to accept and help his autistic brother, Orry.

3249. Potter, Marian. *The Shared Room* (4–5). 1979, Morrow $6.95; LB $6.67. Ali copes with the fact that her mother is in a hospital suffering from mental illness.

3250. Robinson, Veronica. *David in Silence* (5–7). 1966, Lippincott $8.95. A deaf boy encounters varying reactions when he first shares the usual activities of children who can hear; a realistic, revealing story about this disability.

3251. Rodowsky, Colby F. *What about Me?* (6–9). 1976, Watts $5.90; Dell paper $1.50. Only after his death does Dorrie realize how much she loved her brother Fred, who had Down's syndrome.

3252. Rodowsky, Colby F. *P.S. Write Soon: A Novel* (5–6). 1978, Watts $6.90. A handicapped girl tells of her life to a pen pal.

3253. Sallis, Susan. *An Open Mind* (6–9). 1978, Harper $7.95; LB $7.49. David learns to get along with a variety of people, including youngsters in a school for special children.

3254. Shyer, Marlene Fanta. *Welcome Home, Jellybean* (5–7). 1978, Scribner $6.95. Twelve-year-old Neil encounters a near-tragic situation when his older retarded sister comes home to stay.

3255. Singer, Marilyn. *It Can't Hurt Forever* (5–7). Illus. by Leigh Grant. 1978, Harper $7.95; LB $7.49. Ellie survives a harrowing experience as a heart patient in a hospital.

3256. Slote, Alfred. *Hang Tough, Paul Mather* (4–7). 1973, Lippincott $7.95; Avon paper $1.25. Paul recollects from his hospital bed the details of his struggle with leukemia. Told candidly and without sentimentality.

3257. Smith, Doris. *Kelly's Creek* (4–6). Illus. by Alan Tiegreen. 1975, Crowell $7.95. Through the help of an older boy, Kelly gains confidence and partially overcomes the effects of the physical handicap that has produced his lack of coordination.

3258. Snyder, Zilpha Keatley. *The Witches of Worm* (5–8). Illus. by Alton Raible. 1972, Atheneum $6.95; paper $1.95. A deeply disturbed girl believes that her selfish and destructive acts are caused by bewitchment.

3259. Sobol, Harriet Langsam. *My Brother Steven Is Retarded* (2–4). Photos by Patricia Agre. 1977, Macmillan $5.95. Eleven-year-old Beth describes candidly and unflinchingly her conflicting emotions about her retarded older brother.

3260.   Spence, Eleanor. *The Devil Hole* (6–9). 1977, Lothrop $6.75; LB $6.48. The effect of having an autistic younger brother is told in this family story set in contemporary Australia.

3261.   Spence, Eleanor. *The Nothing Place* (5–7). Illus. by Geraldine Spence. 1973, Harper $7.89. Glen, a deaf boy, is insulted when his friends collect money to buy him a hearing aid, in this Australian novel.

3262.   Spencer, Zane, and Leech, Jay. *Cry of the Wolf* (5–8). 1977, Westminster $7.95. Jim slips into self-pity after an accident that kills his father and leaves him unable to walk.

3263.   Vogel, Ilse-Margaret. *Farewell, Aunt Isabell* (5–7). Illus. by author. 1979, Harper $6.95; LB $6.89. The twins, Erika and Inge, form a friendship with their mentally ill Aunt Isabell.

3264.   Waldorf, Mary. *Jake McGee and His Feet* (3–5). Illus. by Leonard Shortall. 1980, Houghton $5.95. A believable story about a boy who has trouble reading and whose feet always get him into trouble.

3265.   Weik, Mary Hays. *The Jazz Man* (4–6). Illus. by Ann Grifalconi. 1966, Atheneum $6.95; paper $1.95. The heartrending story of crippled Zeke, who never leaves his Harlem apartment and whose only delight is in watching the jazz man play his piano in a nearby apartment.

3266.   Wrightson, Patricia. *A Race Course for Andy* (4–6). Illus. by Margaret Horder. 1968, Harcourt $5.95. The poignant, touching story of a mentally retarded boy who is convinced that he owns the local race track that he "bought" from a ragpicker for $3.

Historical Fiction

Africa

3267.   Burchard, Peter. *Chinwe* (6–9). Illus. by author. 1979, Putnam $6.95. Chinwe, an Ibo girl, is sold into slavery in the Africa of 1838.

3268.   Christopher, John. *Dom and Va* (6–8). 1973, Macmillan $5.95. A power struggle between fierce hunters and peaceful farmers, set in the Africa of 5,000 years ago.

3269.   Gilroy, Tom. *In Bikole* (4–5). Illus. by Monica Vachula. 1978, Knopf $5.95; LB $5.99. Subtitle: *Eight Modern Stories of Life in a West African Village.*

3270.   Mirsky, Reba P. *Thirty-One Brothers and Sisters* (4–8). Illustrated. 1952, Dell paper $1.25. Life on the South African veld and of Nomusa, daughter of a Zulu chieftain.

3271.   Mitchison, Naomi. *The Family of Ditlabeng* (4–6). Illus. by Joanna Stubbs. 1970, Farrar $3.95. A fictional account of a family in the African state of Botswana. Also use: *Sunrise Tomorrow* (1973, Farrar $4.50).

3272.   O'Neill, Mary. *Ali* (4–6). Illus. by Juan C. Barberis. 1968, Atheneum $3.95. Ali faces problems growing up in his Bedouin settlement in Tunisia.

3273.   Seed, Jenny. *The Great Thirst* (5–8). 1974, Bradbury $5.95. A story of tribal life and a young boy's search for vengeance in a historical novel about southwest Africa during the first part of the nineteenth century.

Asia

3274.   Bunting, Eve. *Magic and the Night River* (2–4). Illus. by Allen Say. 1978, Harper $5.95; LB $5.79. A boy and his grandfather fish with cormorants on the coast of Japan.

3275.   Chrisman, Arthur B. *Shen of the Sea* (4–6). Illus. by Else Hasselriis. 1925; 1968 Dutton $7.95. These engaging short stories of Chinese life received the Newbery Award, 1926.

3276.   Larsen, Peter, and Larsen, Elaine. *Boy of Nepal* (3–5). Illustrated. 1970, Dodd $4.50. Photographs abound in this account by Vishnu, his family, their way of life, and his mountainous homeland.

3277.   Lattimore, Eleanor Frances. *More about Little Pear* (3–4). Illus. by author. 1971, Morrow $6.25. An episodic story about a young boy growing up in a small Chinese town in the 1920s. Other titles in the series include: *Little Pear* (1931, Harcourt $7.50; paper $1.75) and *Little Pear and the Rabbits* (1956, Morrow $6.25).

3278.   Lewis, Elizabeth Forman. *Young Fu of the Upper Yangtze* (5–8). Illus. by Ed Young. 1973, Holt $6.95; Dell paper $1.50. Young Fu must pay back a debt of $5 or face public shame. Newbery Award.

3279.   Merrill, Jean. *The Superlative Horse* (4–7). Illus. by Ronni Solbert. 1961, Young Scott $5.95. Because of his superior ability, a lowly son of a fuel seller becomes the head groom in the royal stables.

3280. Paterson, Katherine. *The Master Puppeteer* (6–9). Illus. by Haru Wells. 1976, Crowell $8.95. Feudal Japan is the setting for this story about a young apprentice puppeteer and his search for a mysterious bandit.

3281. Paterson, Katherine. *Of Nightingales That Weep* (6–9). Illus. by Haru Wells. 1974, Crowell $8.95. A story set in feudal Japan tells of Takiko, a samurai's daughter who is sent to the royal court when her mother remarries.

3282. Paterson, Katherine. *The Sign of the Chrysanthemum* (5–7). Illus. by Peter Landa. 1973, Crowell $8.95. At the death of his mother, a young boy sets out to find his samurai father in twelfth-century Japan.

3283. Rankin, Louise. *Daughter of the Mountains* (4–7). Illus. by Kurt Wiese. 1948, Archway paper $1.25. A Tibetan girl's pilgrimage to Calcutta to claim her dog.

3284. Say, Allen. *The Ink-Keeper's Apprentice* (6–8). 1979, Harper $7.95. A post–World War II glimpse of Tokyo by a boy set to immigrate to the United States.

3285. Wartski, Maureen Crane. *A Boat to Nowhere* (4–5). 1980, Westminster $9.95. An adventure story about the Vietnamese "boat people."

Europe

3286. Barringer, D. Moreau. *And the Waters Prevailed* (4–7). Illus. by P. A. Hutchinson. 1956, Dutton $6.95. A Stone Age boy realizes that some day his tribal land will be covered with water.

3287. Benchley, Nathaniel. *Beyond the Mists* (6–9). 1975, Harper $7.95; LB $7.89. The story of an eleventh-century Norseman, Gunnar Egilsen; and his involvement with the explorations of Leif Ericson.

3288. Blaine, Marge. *Dvora's Journey* (3–5). Illus. by Gabriel Lisowski. 1979, Holt $6.95. In an effort to escape the anti-Semitism of prerevolutionary Russia, a Jewish family decides to immigrate to America.

3289. Bloch, Marie. *Aunt America* (4–7). Illus. by Joan Berg. 1963, Atheneum paper $.95. Lenya, growing up in a Ukrainian town, is visited by her aunt from America.

3290. Buff, Mary, and Buff, Conrad. *The Apple and the Arrow* (3–6). Illus. by author. 1951, Houghton $6.95; paper $1.25. A retelling of the William Tell story.

3291. Carlson, Natalie Savage. *The Happy Orpheline* (3–5). Illus. by Garth Williams. 1957, Harper LB $8.79. Brigitte, happy in a French orphanage, tries to avoid being adopted. Sequels (all Harper $8.79): *A Brother for the Orphelines* (1959), *A Pet for the Orphelines* (1962), and *The Orphelines in the Enchanted Castle* (1964).

3292. Clark, Margery. *Poppy Seed Cakes* (2–4). Illus. by Maud Petersham and Miska Petersham. 1924, Doubleday $6.95. A great favorite with young children, this is the story of small Andrewshek and his Auntie Katushka, who journey to America and find themselves neighbors in New York.

3293. DeJong, Meindert. *Journey from Peppermint Street* (3–5). Illus. by Emily McCully. 1968, Harper $7.95; paper $2.95. A small boy's first journey away from his Dutch village by the sea is recounted with warmth and understanding.

3294. De Jong, Meindert. *Shadrach* (2–4). Illus. by Maurice Sendak. 1953, Harper $7.89. Based on the author's own childhood in the Netherlands, this tells of Davie's great joy when his grandfather promises him a real rabbit for his very own pet and the anxious days until it finally arrives.

3295. DeJong, Meindert. *Wheel on the School* (4–7). Illus. by Maurice Sendak. 1954, Harper $8.95; LB $8.79; paper $2.95. The storks are brought back to their island by the schoolchildren in a Dutch village. Also use: *Far Out the Long Canal* (1964, Harper, LB $8.79).

3296. Dickinson, Peter. *The Dancing Bear* (6–9). Illus. by David Smee. 1973, Little $6.95. The slave Silvester and his trained bear, survive the sacking of Byzantium by the Huns in A.D. 558.

3297. Dillon, Ellis. *The Shadow of Vesuvius* (6–8). 1977, Nelson $6.95. A young Greek slave's adventure in Pompeii before its destruction.

3298. Dodge, Mary Mapes. *Hans Brinker: Or the Silver Skates* (5–8). Illus. by G. W. Edwards. 1915, Scribner $5.95; Airmont paper $1.25. Hans hopes to enter the racing contest and win the silver skates; one of several fine editions of this story set in the Netherlands.

3299. Gray, Elizabeth Janet. *Adam of the Road* (6–9). Illus. by Robert Lawson. 1942, Viking $7.50. Adventure of a thirteenth-century minstrel boy. Newbery Award, 1943.

3300. Griffiths, Helen. *The Last Summer: Spain 1936* (5–7). Illus. by Victor G. Ambrus. 1979, Holiday $7.95. A boy and his horse are swept up in the Spanish Civil War.

3301. Griffiths, Helen. *The Mysterious Appearance of Agnes* (6–8). Illus. by Victor G. Ambrus. 1975, Holiday $5.95. A young girl is accused of witchcraft in this powerful novel set in sixteenth-century Germany.

3302. Hall, Lynn. *Dog of the Bondi Castle* (6–9). 1979, Follett $6.95; LB $6.99. A staghound and an ill-fated couple are the central characters in the story set in medieval France.

3303. Hamori, Laszlo. *Dangerous Journey* (6–9). 1962, Harcourt $5.95; paper $1.75. A dramatic escape story of 2 Hungarian boys who jump the iron curtain to Austria.

3304. Haugaard, Erik C. *Chase Me, Catch Nobody* (5–9). 1980, Houghton $7.95. A young Danish boy takes an adventure-filled trip into Nazi Germany in 1937.

3305. Haugaard, Erik C. *Hakon of Rogen's Sage* (6–8). Illus. by Leo Dillon and Diane Dillon. 1963, Houghton $6.95; paper $.95. Through his uncle's treachery, orphaned Hakon is temporarily deprived of his birthright to Rogen Island in Norway during the time of the Vikings. Sequel: *A Slave's Tale* (1965, $7.95).

3306. Hirsh, Marilyn. *Deborah the Dybbuk: A Ghost Story* (2–4). Illus. by author. 1978, Holiday $5.95. A mischievous dybbuk inhabits Hannah's body in a nineteenth-century Jewish village in Hungary.

3307. Hoover, H. M. *The Lion's Cub* (6–9). 1974, Four Winds $6.95. In this historical novel set in the early nineteenth century, an Arab boy is forced to live at the court of his hated enemy Nicholas I.

3308. Ish-Kishor, Sulamith. *A Boy of Old Prague* (5–8). Illus. by Ben Shahn. 1963, Pantheon $5.99. First-person story of a peasant boy, born in 1540, and how he is affected by life in the ghetto of Prague.

3309. Ish-Kishor, Sulamith. *The Master of Miracle; A New Novel of the Golem* (5–7). Illus. by Arnold Lobel. 1971, Harper LB $7.89. In sixteenth-century Prague, a lonely orphan helps to save the ghetto population from a pogram.

3310. Jensen, Niels. *Days of Courage: A Medieval Adventure* (5–7). 1973, Harcourt $5.75. The story of 2 young survivors of the Black Death and their courage in trying to plan for the future. A Danish children's book prize winner.

3311. Kelly, Eric P. *The Trumpeter of Krakow* (5–8). revised edition. Illus. by Janina Domanska. 1928, Macmillan $7.95; 1966, paper $1.95. Mystery surrounds a precious jewel and the youthful patriot who stands watch over it in a church tower

in this novel of fifteenth-century Poland. Newbery Award, 1929.

3312. Konigsburg, E. L. *A Proud Taste for Scarlet and Miniver* (6–9). Illus. by author. 1973, Atheneum $8.95; paper $1.95. The life of Eleanor of Aquitaine as told by different members of her entourage; written with wit and style.

3313. Konigsburg, E. L. *The Second Mrs. Giaconda* (6–9). 1975, Atheneum $6.95; paper $1.95. A fictional series of episodes involving Leonardo da Vinci, his enterprising apprentice, and the story behind the Mona Lisa.

3314. Marcuse, Katherine. *The Devil's Workshop* (5–7). Illus. by Paul Zelinsky. 1979, Abingdon $6.50. A boy becomes an apprentice to printer Johann Gutenberg in fifteenth-century Mainz.

3315. Millstead, Thomas. *Cave of the Moving Shadows* (6–8). 1979, Dial $7.95; LB $7.45. A boy grows to maturity in prehistoric times.

3316. Monjo, F. N. *The House on Stink Alley* (3–5). Illus. by Robert Quackenbush. 1977, Holt $6.95. Mr. Brewster plans to move his family to America on the *Mayflower*.

3317. Monjo, F. N. *Letters to Horseface* (5–7). Illustrated. 1975, Viking $7.95. The subtitle tells all —*Being the Story of Wolfgang Amadeus Mozart's Journey to Italy 1769–1770, When He Was a Boy of Fourteen.*

3318. Monjo, F. N. *The Sea Beggar's Son* (4–6). Illus. by C. Walter Hodges. 1975, Coward $5.95. The story of audacious Dutch seadogs, father and son, in the time of William of Orange.

3319. Ofek, Uriel. *Smoke over Golan* (6–8). Illus. by Lloyd Bloom. 1979, Harper $7.95; LB $7.89. The battle on Golan Heights as seen through the eyes of a young Israeli.

3320. Pyle, Howard. *Otto of the Silver Hand* (6–9). Illus. by author. 1916, Scribner $4.95; Dover paper $2.75. Life in feudal Germany, the turbulence and cruelty of robber barons, and the peaceful, scholarly pursuits of the monks are presented in the story of the kidnapped son of a robber baron.

3321. Robbins, Ruth. *The Emperor and the Drummer Boy* (3–6). Illus. by Nicholas Sidjakov. 1962, Parnassus $4.95; LB $5.38. A young drummer boy waits at Napoleon's side for the safe return of his friend, who floats ashore clinging to his drum.

3322. Seredy, Kate. *The Good Master* (4–6). Illus. by author. 1935, Viking $4.00; Dell paper $1.25. Warm and humorous story of a city girl on her uncle's farm in prewar Hungary. Also use: *The Singing Tree* (1939, Dell, paper 95¢).

3323. Skurzynski, Gloria. *What Happened in Hamelin* (5–7). 1979, Four Winds $7.95. A retelling of the Pied Piper story as narrated by one of the survivors.

3324. Steele, William O. *The Magic Amulet* (4–6). 1979, Harcourt $6.95. A story, set in prehistoric times, features a resourceful hero and such animals as saber-toothed tigers and mammoths.

3325. Trevino, Elizabeth de. *I, Juan de Pareja* (6–9). 1965, Farrar $5.95. Through the eyes of his devoted black slave, Juan de Pareja, the character of the artist Velasquez is revealed. Newbery Award.

3326. Walsh, Jill Paton. *Children of the Fox* (5–8). Illus. by Robin Eaton. 1978, Farrar $7.95. Three short stories set in Greece during the Persian Wars.

3327. Winterfeld, Henry. *Detectives in Togas* (5–7). Illus. by Charlotte Kleinert. 1956, Harcourt paper $1.45. A jolly mystery story set in ancient Rome, involving a group of schoolboys unjustly accused of defacing a temple.

3328. Winterfeld, Henry. *Mystery of the Roman Ransom* (5–8). Illus. by Fritz Biermann. 1971, Harcourt $5.95; paper $1.75. The intrepid young heroes of the author's earlier *Detectives in Togas* attempt to save the life of a Roman senator threatened with murder.

3329. Zei, Alki. *The Sound of the Dragon's Feet* (4–6). 1979, Dutton $8.50. A ten-year-old encounters hardships and inequality in prerevolutionary Russia.

Great Britain and Ireland

3330. Andrews, J. S. *Cargo for a King* (4–7). 1973, Dutton $5.95. A struggle against pirates highlights this story set around the Irish Sea during the thirteenth century.

3331. Avery, Gillian. *Ellen and the Queen* (3–5). Illus. by Krystyna Turska. 1975, Nelson $4.95. A slight but amusing story of wish fulfillment in which a young girl is able to see Queen Victoria.

3332. Branson, Karen. *The Potato Eaters* (5–8). Illus. by Jane Sterrett. 1979, Putnam $8.95. A moving story of the O'Connors and their plight during the famine of 1846.

3333. Bibby, Violet. *Many Waters Cannot Quench Love* (6–8). 1975, Morrow $5.95. In this story set in seventeenth-century England, a girl loves someone other than her betrothed.

3334. Briggs, Katharine. *Kate Crackernuts* (6–8). 1980, Greenwillow $9.95. Two Kates—one wild, one mild—are involved in witchcraft and intrigue in seventeenth-century Scotland.

3335. Bulla, Clyde Robert. *The Beast of Lor* (4–6). Illus. by Ruth Sanderson. 1977, Crowell $6.50. The story of the friendship between a boy and an elephant brought to England during the Roman conquest.

3336. Bulla, Clyde Robert. *The Sword in the Tree* (2–5). Illus. by Paul Galdone. 1956, Crowell $6.95. A simply written account of knighthood at the time of King Arthur.

3337. Bunting, Eve. *The Haunting of Kildoran Abbey* (6–8). 1978, Warne $6.95. Twins join a gang of waifs to survive in famine-stricken Ireland of 1847.

3338. Burton, Hester. *Beyond the Weir Bridge* (6–9). Illus. by Victor G. Ambrus. 1970, Crowell $4.95. Story of 3 young people deeply committed to the battle for religious and political freedom in the days of England's Cromwell.

3339. Burton, Hester. *Time of Trial* (6–9). Illus. by Victor G. Ambrus. 1964, World $5.91; Dell paper $1.50. An outspoken bookseller and his daughter are caught up in the crusade for freedom of speech in early nineteenth-century London.

3340. Chute, Marchette. *The Wonderful Winter* (6–9). 1954, Dutton $5.95. A young boy's exciting time as a bit actor in Shakespeare's theater. The author writes of Chaucer's England in *The Innocent Wayfaring* (1955, Dutton $7.95).

3341. Clarke, Pauline. *Torolov the Fatherless* (6–9). Illus. by Cecil Leslie. 1978, Faber $5.95. An English historical novel set during the reign of Ethelred the Unready.

3342. Clements, Bruce. *Prison Window, Jerusalem Blue* (6–8). 1977, Farrar $7.95. In the year 1031, a brother and sister from the south shore of England become slaves of the Vikings.

3343. Darke, Marjorie. *A Question of Courage* (6–9). 1975, Crowell $5.95. A realistic novel of the sacrifices and hardships faced by women involved in the suffragist movement in England.

3344. De Angeli, Marguerite. *The Door in the Wall* (5–7). Illus. by author. 1949, Doubleday $6.95; paper $1.95. Crippled Robin proves his courage in plague-ridden fourteenth-century London. Newbery Award, 1950.

3345. Farber, Norma. *Three Wanderers from Wapping* (4–6). Illus. by Charles Mikolaycak. 1978,

Addison $6.95. Three friends flee from a plague-ridden town in England during 1665.

3346. Garfield, Leon. *The Night of the Comet: A Courtship Featuring Bostock and Harris* (6–8). 1979, Delacorte $7.95; LB $7.45. Three unusual love stories culminate on the night a comet is due.

3347. Garfield, Leon. *The Strange Affair of Adelaide Harris* (6–9). Illus. by Fritz Wegner. 1971, Pantheon $5.69. Another rollicking historical adventure by the English novelist, filled with the usual mistaken or unknown identities, amazing coincidences, and wit.

3348. Godden, Rumer. *The Kitchen Madonna* (4–6). Illus. by Carol Barker. 1967, Viking $5.95. A little boy in a London household helps Marta, the maid, get an icon of Our Lady—a Kitchen Madonna—such as she had in her Ukrainian home years ago.

3349. Haugaard, Erik C. *Cromwell's Boy* (6–8). 1978, Houghton $7.95. Thirteen-year-old Oliver fights with Cromwell against King Charles in this sequel to *A Messenger for Parliament* (1976, $6.95).

3350. Hodges, C. Walter. *The Namesake* (6–9). Illus. by author. 1964, Coward $6.95. Alfred the One Legged, scribe and namesake of Alfred the Great, tells how Aflred became king and drove the Danes from the country.

3351. Hunter, Mollie. *The Stronghold* (6–9). 1974, Harper $6.95; LB $7.89. In this historical novel set in northern Scotland, a young crippled boy discovers a way to withstand the devastating raids by the Romans.

3352. Lingard, Joan. *Across the Barricades* (6–9). 1973, Elsevier/Nelson $6.95. A girl and boy—one Catholic, the other Protestant—fall in love in contemporary Belfast. A sequel to *The Twelfth Day of July* (1972, $6.95).

3353. Lingard, Joan. *A Proper Place* (6–9). 1975, Elsevier/Nelson $6.95. Religious prejudice and bigotry follow a young married couple—one Catholic, the other Protestant—when they escape Ireland to find a new home in Liverpool.

3354. McGraw, Eloise. *Master Cornhill* (6–9). Illustrated. 1973, Atheneum $6.25. A young boy is left without family or funds when the plague hits, in this historical novel set in London.

3355. Pyle, Howard. *Men of Iron* (5–8). 1891; 1930 Harper $8.95; LB $8.79; Airmont paper $.75. Brave deeds and knightly adventure in England—an old favorite.

3356. Roach, Marilynne K. *Presto; Or the Adventures of a Turnspit Dog* (5–7). Illus. by author. 1979, Houghton $7.95. The adventures of a runaway dog and his master, a puppeteer in eighteenth-century London.

3357. Schlee, Ann. *The Consul's Daughter* (5–8). 1972, Atheneum $4.50. A 14-year-old girl becomes involved with the British fleet's bombardment of Algiers in 1816.

3358. Streatfeild, Noel. *Thursday's Child* (5–8). Illus. by Peggy Fortnum. 1971, Atheneum $4.50. A lively little girl escapes a cruel orphanage to seek adventure among the eccentrics and nobility of Victorian England.

3359. Sutcliff, Rosemary. *Blood Feud* (6–8). 1977, Dutton $7.50. Two young men, Jestyn and Thormod, set out to avenge the murder of Thormod's father in tenth-century Europe. Also use: *The Shield Ring* (1972, Walck $6.95).

3360. Sutcliff, Rosemary. *Dawn Wind* (6–9). Illus. by Charles Keeping. 1973, Walck $7.95; paper $1.95. Enslaved by the Saxons during the invasion of sixth-century Britain, Owain and Regina overcome the difficulties in their lives and are reunited in this exciting tale.

3361. Sutcliff, Rosemary. *Heather, Oak and Olive* (5–8). Illus. by Victor G. Ambrus. 1972, Dutton $6.50. Bravery, friendship, and devotion are recurring themes in these 3 tales set in ancient times.

3362. Sutcliff, Rosemary. *Song for a Dark Queen* (6–9). 1979, Crowell $6.95. A novel for mature readers about Queen Boadicea and her revolt against the Roman conquerors.

3363. Sutcliff, Rosemary. *Sun Horse, Moon Horse* (6–8). Illus. by Shirley Felts. 1978, Dutton $7.95. A boy sacrifices himself for his people in pre-Roman Britain.

3364. Sutcliff, Rosemary. *The Witch's Brat* (6–9). Illus. by Richard Lebenson. 1970, Walck $6.95. A small crippled boy learns about the power of herbs and medicinal roots in this story set in Norman England.

3365. Symons, Geraldine. *Miss Rivers and Miss Bridges* (6–8). Illus. by Alexy Pendle. 1972, Macmillan $4.95. Two young girls in pre–World War I London decide to help the suffragist movement. Sequel to *The Workhouse Child* (1971, $4.95).

3366. Trease, Geoffrey. *The Baron's Hostage* (5–8). 1975, Elsevier/Nelson $6.50. Two young people face danger and capture in this yarn of thirteenth-century England.

3367. Walsh, Jill Paton. *The Huffler* (5–7). Illus. by Juliette Palmer. 1975, Farrar $5.95. A proper Victorian miss poses as a servant to prove a point in this delightful story that reveals a great deal about life on English canals of the period.

3368. Willard, Barbara. *The Iron Lily* (6–9). 1974, Dutton $5.95. Tudor England is the setting for this fourth novel about Mantlemass, the home of the Medley family.

Latin America

3369. Baker, Betty. *Walk the World's Rim* (6–8). 1965, Harper $7.89; paper $1.25. Colonial Mexico and the Indian life are the background for this engrossing story of Cabeza de Vaca and his black slave's trek from eastern Texas to Mexico.

3370. Bulla, Clyde Robert. *The Poppy Seeds* (2–4). Illus. by Jean Charlot. 1955, Crowell $7.50. A young Indian boy in Mexico plants poppy seeds throughout the village.

3371. Clark, Ann Nolan. *Secret of the Andes* (4–8). Illus. by Jean Charlot. 1952, Viking $7.95; Penguin paper $1.25. Cusi, a young Inca boy, tends a precious llama herd high in the Peruvian mountains and ponders his future. Newbery Award, 1953.

3372. Mangurian, David. *Children of the Incas* (3–6). Illustrated. 1979, Four Winds $8.95. The story of a poor boy growing up in a little town in Peru.

3373. O'Dell, Scott. *The King's Fifth* (6–9). Illus. by Samuel Bryant. 1966, Houghton $5.95; Dell paper $1.50. A powerful story of the young mapmaker, Esteban, whose search for knowledge was clouded by his lust for gold.

3374. O'Dell, Scott. *The Treasure of Topo-el-Bampo* (K–4). Illus. by Lynd Ward. 1972, Houghton $4.95. Two donkeys make a very poor Mexican village rich.

3375. Stuart, Morna. *Marassa and Midnight* (5–7). Illus. by Alvin Smith. 1967, Dell paper $1.25. An arresting novel of Haiti's first revolutionary stirrings in the early 1790s.

United States

Indians of North America

3376. Armer, Laura A. *Waterless Mountain* (5–7). Illus. by author. 1931; 1959 McKay $8.95. Story of a young Navaho boy who feels keenly the beauty and power of his heritage, although he

lives on the fringe of white civilization. Newbery Award, 1932.

3377. Baker, Betty. *And One Was a Wooden Indian* (6–9). 1970, Macmillan $4.95. A young Apache's first encounter with whites in this perceptive novel set in the Southwest of the midnineteenth century. Also use: *Shaman's Last Raid* (1973, Harper, LB $7.89).

3378. Baker, Betty. *A Stranger and Afraid* (6–9). 1972, Macmillan $5.95. A Wichita youth serves as a guide for the ruthless Spaniards in their search for gold in the Southwest during Coronado's time.

3379. Buff, Mary. *Hah-Nee of the Cliff Dwellers* (3–6). Illus. by Conrad Buff. 1956, Houghton $5.95. The culture and history of the primitive cliff dwellers is revealed in this story of an American Indian boy, who, because of tribal superstition, is forced to leave his much-loved home.

3380. Bulla, Clyde Robert, and Syson, Michael. *Conquista!* (3–5). Illus. by Ronald Himler. 1978, Crowell $6.95; LB $7.49. A young Indian boy encounters his first horse, a refugee from the Coronado expedition.

3381. Carlson, Natalie Savage. *Alphonse, That Bearded One* (3–5). Illus. by Nicolas Mordvinoff. 1954, Harcourt $6.95. A bear makes peace with the Iroquois.

3382. Gessner, Lynne. *To See a Witch* (6–8). 1978, Nelson $6.95. A novel set within a group of cliff-dwelling Indians in a time before Columbus.

3383. Griese, Arnold A. *At the Mouth of the Luckiest River* (4–6). Illus. by Glo Coalson. 1973, Crowell $8.95; LB $8.79. A young Indian boy, growing up around Lake Athalasea in the late 1800s, makes enemies with the tribe's powerful medicine man.

3384. Jones, Weyman. *Edge of Two Worlds* (5–8). Illus. by J. K. Kocsis. 1968, Dell paper $.95. Sequoyah, an aging Cherokee leader, and 14-year-old Clavin, lone survivor of a Comanche raid, journey across the Texas wilderness.

3385. Lampman, Evelyn Sibley. *The Potlatch Family* (5–8). 1976, Atheneum $6.95. A young girl becomes aware and proud of her Indian heritage through her older brother. Also use: *Cayuse Courage* (1970, Harcourt $5.50).

3386. Lampman, Evelyn Sibley. *Rattlesnake Cave* (4–6). Illus. by Pamela Johnson. 1974, Atheneum $7.95. While visiting an aunt in Montana, Jamie learns about Indian life and culture from an old Cheyenne and his grandson.

3387. Lampman, Evelyn Sibley. *Squaw Man's Son* (5–8). 1978, Atheneum $6.95. In the 1880s, a young boy—half white, half Indian—seeks his identity.

3388. Lampman, Evelyn Sibley. *White Captives* (5–6). 1975, Atheneum $6.95. The fictional story of Olive Oatman's 5 years as a captive, first of the Apaches and later the Mohaves.

3389. Lauritzen, Jonreed. *The Ordeal of the Young Hunter* (4–6). Illus. by Hoke Denetsosie. 1954, Little $4.95. An Indian boy and his increasing understanding of his own culture's values in relation to those of white people. Dramatic and penetrating.

3390. Richter, Conrad. *Light in the Forest* (6–8). Illus. by Warren Chappell. 1966, Knopf $5.99; Bantam paper $1.75. A young white boy is captured by Indians and, after becoming a true tribe member, is suddenly returned to his parents.

3391. Rockwood, Joyce. *Groundhog's Horse* (4–6). Illus. by Victor Kalin. 1978, Holt $6.95. An eleven-year-old Cherokee decides to rescue his horse when it is stolen by the Crus.

3392. Rockwood, Joyce. *Long Man's Song* (6–9). 1975, Holt $6.95. Much Indian lore fills this story of a young Cherokee growing up in his tribe before the time of Columbus.

3393. Rockwood, Joyce. *To Spoil the Sun* (6–9). 1976, Holt $6.95; Dell paper $1.50. Historical recreation of Cherokee life and the arrival of the first white people, as seen through the eyes of a sixteenth-century Indian girl.

3394. Simpson, Ben E. *Start with the Sun* (6–9). 1975, Farrar $5.95. A young warrior wants to prove his manhood by a feat of great daring.

3395. Sneve, Virginia. *Jimmy Yellow Hawk* (3–5). Illus. by Oren Lyons. 1972, Holiday $5.95. A good picture of contemporary Indian life and of Little Jim's success in trapping a mink and earning his father's approval. Received the Council on Interracial Books award for the best book by an Indian author.

3396. Steele, William O. *The War Party* (4–6). Illus. by Lorinda Bryan. 1978, Harcourt $4.95. A young Indian brave understands the cruelty of war when he is wounded during his first war party.

3397. Thompson, Jean. *Brother of the Wolves* (6–8). Illus. by Steve Marchesi. 1978, Morrow $6.95. A young Indian boy raised by wolves returns to his tribe.

3398. Wolf, Bernard. *Tinker and the Medicine Man: The Story of a Navajo Boy of Monument Valley*

(4–6). 1973, Random $4.95; LB $6.39. A young Navajo boy wants to become like his father, the tribe's medicine man, and learns about the duties and responsibilities of this position.

Colonial Period

3399. Avi. *Encounter at Easton* (5–7). 1980, Pantheon $6.95; LB $6.99. The fate of 2 runaway indentured servants in eighteenth-century America is told in this sequel to *Night Journeys*.

3400. Avi. *Night Journeys* (4–7). 1979, Pantheon $6.95; LB $4.99. Peter and his stepfather help 2 runaway indentured servants in colonial Pennsylvania.

3401. Bulla, Clyde Robert. *John Billington, Friend of Squanto* (2–4). Illus. by Peter Burchard. 1956, Crowell $6.95. The story of the early days of the Plymouth colony. John is captured but released when Squanto intercedes.

3402. Clapp, Patricia. *Constance: A Story of Early Plymouth* (6–9). 1968, Lothrop $6.48. Historical novel based on a journal that records a girl's journey from London at the age of 15 and the hardships and stern pleasures of colonial life in Massachusetts.

3403. Dalgliesh, Alice. *Courage of Sarah Noble* (3–5). Illus. by Leonard Weisgard. 1954, Scribner LB $6.95; paper $2.95. The true story of a brave little girl who, in 1707, went with her father into the wilds of Connecticut.

3404. Edmonds, Walter. *The Matchlock Gun* (5–7). Illus. by Paul Lantz. 1941, Dodd $5.95. Exciting, true story of a courageous boy who protected his mother and sister from the Indians of the Hudson Valley. Newbery Award, 1942.

3405. Finlayson, Ann. *Greenhorn on the Frontiers* (5–8). Illus. by W. T. Mars. 1974, Warne $5.95. A frontier story about a brother and sister setting up a homestead on the Pennsylvania-Virginia border before the Revolution.

3406. Fisher, Leonard Everett. *The Warlock of Westfall* (5–7). Illus. by author. 1974, Doubleday $5.95. A witch hunt in colonial times that ends in the death of an innocent old man is told in text and pictures by a master.

3407. Gackenbach, Dick. *The Leatherman* (2–4). Illus. by author. 1977, Seabury $6.95. Ben becomes fascinated with a strange man who periodically visits his village in colonial Connecticut.

3408. Levitin, Sonia. *Roanoke: A Novel of the Lost Colony* (6–9). Illustrated. 1973, Atheneum $7.95.

A lively novel centering on a boy and his vain efforts to save the colony of Roanoke.

3409. Monjo, F. N. *The Secret of the Sachem's Tree* (2–4). Illus. by Margot Tomes. 1972, Coward $4.69; Dell paper $.95. Mysterious events occur one Halloween eve in 1687 when King James orders his agent to seize the Connecticut Charter, hidden in the hollow of an oak tree.

3410. Moskin, Marietta D. *Lysbet and the Fire Kittens* (2–4). Illus. by Margot Tomes. 1974, Coward $4.49. In this tale set in New Amsterdam, 9-year-old Lysbet is left alone to prepare pa's dinner and care for their pregnant cat.

3411. Petry, Ann. *Tituba of Salem Village* (6–9). 1964, Crowell $8.95. The story of the slave Tituba and her husband, John Indian, from the day they were sold in the Barbados until the tragic Salem witchcraft trials.

3412. Speare, Elizabeth. *The Witch of Blackbird Pond* (6–9). 1958, Houghton $8.95; Dell paper $1.25. Historical romance set in Puritan Connecticut with the theme of witchcraft. Newbery Award. Also use: *Calico Captive* (1957, Houghton $7.95).

The Revolution

3413. Beatty, John, and Beatty, Patricia. *Who Comes to King's Mountain?* (6–9). 1975, Morrow LB $6.48. The divided loyalties of the Scottish pioneer in South Carolina in 1780 are explored through the experiences of young Alec MacLord, who eventually joins the Swamp Fox, Francis Marion.

3414. Burchard, Peter. *Whaleboat Raid* (5–7). 1977, Coward $6.95. A novel with a 16-year-old hero that explores the actual attack by Americans on the British at Sag Harbor, in Long Island, New York, during the Revolutionary War.

3415. Collier, James, and Collier, Christopher. *The Bloody Country* (6–9). 1976, Four Winds $7.95. Ben Buck narrates this story of the hardships endured by his Connecticut family after their resettlement in Pennsylvania at the time of the Revolution.

3416. Collier, James, and Collier, Christopher. *My Brother Sam Is Dead* (6–9). 1974, Four Winds $7.95; paper $1.50. The story, based partially on fact, of a Connecticut family divided in loyalties during the Revolutionary War.

3417. Collier, James, and Collier, Christopher. *The Winter Hero* (6–9). 1978, Four Winds $5.95. A fictionalized account of Shays's Rebellion set in the Massachusetts of 1787.

3418. Finlayson, Ann. *Rebecca's War* (5–8). Illus. by Sherry Streeter. 1972, Warne $5.95. Philadelphia during the Revolutionary War, where 14-year-old Rebecca tries to hide military secrets from British soldiers billeted in her home.

3419. Forbes, Esther. *Johnny Tremain: A Novel for Old and Young* (6–9). Illus. by Lynd Ward. 1943, Houghton $6.95; Dell paper $1.50. Story of a young silversmith's apprentice, who plays an important part in the American Revolution. Newbery Award, 1944.

3420. Fritz, Jean. *The Cabin Faced West* (3–6). Illus. by Feodor Rojankovsky. 1958, Coward $7.95. The western Pennsylvania territory of 1784 is a very lonely place for Ann until General Washington comes to visit.

3421. Fritz, Jean. *Early Thunder* (6–9). Illus. by Lynd Ward. 1967, Coward $7.95. In 1775, the early thunder of the Revolution was heard in Massachusetts, and the town of Salem was divided into contradictory factions. Daniel West had to make up his mind on which side he was going to fight.

3422. Fritz, Jean. *George Washington's Breakfast* (3–5). Illus. by Paul Galdone. 1969, Coward $5.49. George W. Allen knows all there is to know about our first president—except what he had for breakfast.

3423. Gauch, Patricia Lee. *This Time, Tempe Wick?* (2–5). Illus. by Margot Tomes. 1974, Coward $5.95. Tempe (Temperance) Wick helped the Revolutionary soldiers who camped on her farm in New Jersey in 1780, until they tried to steal her horse, and then she got mad. Also use: *Aaron and the Green Mountain Boys* (1972, Coward $4.69).

3424. Monjo, F. N. *King George's Head Was Made of Lead* (2–4). Illus. by Margot Tomes. 1974, Coward $5.95. The events leading up to the American Revolution, as told by a statue of George III. A different approach to the story of colonial protest.

3425. Monjo, F. N. *A Namesake for Nathan: Being an Account of Captain Nathan Hale by His Twelve-Year-Old Sister, Joanna* (5–8). Illus. by Eros Keith. 1977, Coward $6.95. The impact of the Revolution on a colonial family, the Hales, is described through the reactions of a young girl when her brothers, including Nathan, go to war.

3426. Monjo, F. N. *Poor Richard in France* (2–4). Illus. by Brinton Turkle. 1973, Holt $5.95; Dell paper $.95. An easy-to-read book that recounts the trip made to France by Benjamin Franklin and his grandson to ask for help for the American Revolution.

3427. Monjo, F. N. *Zenas and the Shaving Mill* (4–7). Illus. by Richard Cuffari. 1976, Coward $5.95. The misadventures of a group of Quakers during the American Revolution, as seen by Zenas, a 17-year-old boy.

3428. O'Dell, Scott. *Sarah Bishop* (5–8). 1980, Houghton $8.95. A first-person narrative of a girl who lived through the American Revolution and its toll of suffering and misery.

3429. Peck, Robert Newton. *Rabbits and Redcoats* (4–6). Illus. by Laura Lydecker. 1976, Walker $6.95; LB $6.85. In 1775, 2 teenage boys participate in the capture of Fort Ticonderoga by Ethan Allen and his Green Mountain Boys.

3430. Schick, Alice, and Allen, Margorie N. *The Remarkable Ride of Israel Bissell* (3–4). Illus. by Joel Schick. 1976, Lippincott $5.95. This Revolutionary War tale has the subtitle: *Being the True Account of an Extraordinary Post Rider Who Persevered.*

3431. Steele, William O. *The Man with the Silver Eyes* (5–7). 1976, Harcourt $5.95. A young American Indian boy gradually develops a respect for a peace-loving white man in this story set in Tennessee during the Revolutionary War.

3432. Wibberley, Leonard. *John Treegate's Musket* (6–9). 1959, Farrar $6.95. Story of a young apprentice to a maker of barrel staves in Boston in 1769, and his adventures in the Revolutionary War. Another in the series: *Sea Captain from Salem* (1961, $4.50).

The Young Nation: 1789–1861

3433. Avi. *Emily Upham's Revenge* (4–6). Illus. by Paul O. Zelinsky. 1978, Pantheon $6.99. Subtitle: *How Deadwood Dick Saved the Banker's Niece; A Massachusetts Adventure.*

3434. Bacon, Margaret Hope. *Rebellion at Christiana* (6–9). 1975, Crown $5.95. An 1851 slave rebellion and ensuing treason trial are reconstructed through contemporary sources, including the account of William Parker, fugitive slave leader.

3435. Blair, Ruth. *Mary's Monster* (4–5). Illus. by Richard Cuffari. 1975, Coward $5.95. A fictional account of Mary Anning and her lifelong interest in fossils during the 1800s.

3436. Blos, Joan W. *A Gathering of Days: A New England Girl's Journal, 1830–32* (6–9). 1979, Scribner $7.95. A fictional diary kept by 13-year-old Catherine Cabot who is growing up in the town of Meredith, New Hampshire. Newbery Award, 1979.

3437. Brady, Esther W. *The Toad on Capital Hill* (4–6). 1978, Crown $6.95. A young boy and his stepbrother are in the line of advancing British troops in 1814.

3438. Burchard, Peter. *Bimby* (4–6). Illus. by author. 1968, Coward $5.95. The knowledge of an impending slave auction in Georgia, just before the Civil War, forces Bimby's decision to seek freedom from slavery and brings him abruptly to the beginnings of manhood.

3439. Chesnutt, Charles W. *Conjure Tales* (5–9). Retold by Ray Anthony Shephard. Illus. by John Ross and Clare Romano. 1973, Dutton $6.95. A selection of stories by a black author that deal with slavery, originally published in 1899.

3440. Coatsworth, Elizabeth. *Away Goes Sally* (4–6). Illus. by Helen Sewell. 1934, Macmillan $6.95. A little girl travels through New England in a house drawn by oxen, in this pioneer tale.

3441. Fall, Thomas. *Canalboat to Freedom* (6–9). Illus. by Joseph Cellini. 1966, Dell paper $1.25. A boy on a canalboat learns courage through his friendship with a freed black slave.

3442. Fisher, Leonard Everett. *The Death of "Evening Star": The Diary of a Young New England Whaler* (5–9). Illus. by author. 1972, Doubleday $4.95. When a young whaler's diary is uncovered, the reader is transported back to the adventures and mystique of the struggle between man and whale.

3443. Fox, Paula. *The Slave Dancer* (6–9). Illus. by Eros Keith. 1973, Bradbury $8.95. Fourteen-year-old Jessie is kidnapped and press-ganged aboard an American slave ship bound for Africa. Newbery Award.

3444. Fritz, Jean. *Brady* (4–7). Illus. by Lynd Ward. 1960, Coward $6.95. When Brady discovers his father is an Underground Railroad agent, he learns to control his tongue and form his own opinion about slavery.

3445. Hoff, Carol. *Johnny Texas* (4–6). Illus. by Bob Myers. 1967, Dell paper $1.25. A family from Germany settles in Texas.

3446. Howard, Elizabeth. *Out of Step with the Dancers* (6–8). 1978, Morrow $7.95; LB $7.35. A young girl moves to a Shaker community in New York State in 1853.

3447. Jacob, Helen Pierce. *The Diary of the Strawbridge Place* (5–7). 1978, Atheneum $6.95. A gripping novel about helping runaway slaves in the days of the Underground Railroad. A companion volume to *The Secret of the Strawbridge Place* (1976, $7.95).

3448. Loeper, John J. *The Golden Dragon* (5–6). 1978, Atheneum $5.95. A fictional account of a clipper ship's voyage from New York to San Francisco in the midnineteenth century.

3449. Meader, Stephen. *Who Rides in the Dark?* (6–8). Illus. by James MacDonald. 1966, Harcourt paper $.75. A highwayman causes havoc in postcolonial Connecticut in this fast-paced adventure story. Also use: *Whaler Round the Horn* (1950, Harcourt $5.95).

3450. Meltzer, Milton. *Underground Man: A Novel* (5–8). 1972, Bradbury $6.95; Dell paper $.95. In this novel about a young boy who joins the abolitionist movement, the reader learns a great deal about slavery.

3451. Monjo, F. N. *The Drinking Gourd* (2–4). Illus. by Fred Brenner. 1970, Harper $5.95; LB $6.89. A New England white boy helps a black family escape on the Underground Railway.

3452. Monjo, F. N. *Grand Papa and Ellen Aroon* (2–4). Illus. by Richard Cuffari. 1974, Holt $5.50; Dell paper $.95. Times spent together by Thomas Jefferson and his favorite granddaughter. As in *The One Bad Thing about Father* (1970, Harper $5.95; LB $6.89), the author portrays a major historical figure from a child's point of view.

3453. Monjo, F. N. *Prisoners of the Scrambling Dragon* (4–6). Illus. by Arthur Geisert. 1980, Holt $8.95. A 13-year-old cabin boy describes his first voyage aboard a Yankee sailing vessel.

3454. O'Daniel, Janet. *A Part for Addie* (5–8). 1974, Houghton $7.95. Two orphans decide to win over their estranged grandfather and find themselves a home, in this novel set in the 1820s.

3455. Smucker, Barbara. *Runaway to Freedom* (3–5). Illus. by Charles Lilly. 1978, Harper $6.95; LB $6.89. Two slave girls try to reach Canada and freedom.

3456. Steele, William O. *The Lone Hunt* (5–7). Illus. by Paul Galdone. 1956, Harcourt $6.75; paper $1.75. Story of early Tennessee and an 11-year-old boy's hunt for the last buffalo in the Cumberland Mountains. More pioneer stories by the author (all Harcourt): *The Buffalo Knife* (1952, paper $1.75), *Winter Danger* (1954, $6.75), and *The Far Frontier* (1959, $5.50).

3457. Stowe, Harriet Beecher. *Uncle Tom's Cabin* (4–6). Adapt. by Anne Terry White. 1966, Braziller $7.95. An adaptation of the classic story of southern slavery.

3458. Turkle, Brinton. *Rachel and Obadiah* (3–4). Illus. by author. 1978, Dutton $7.95. Obadiah and his sister, Rachel, vie to be first with the news of a ship's arrival in port.

3459. Underwood, Betty. *The Forge and the Forest* (6–9). 1975, Houghton $6.95. In this sequel to *The Tamarack Tree*, an orphaned French girl encounters oppression in the Connecticut of the 1830s.

3460. Underwood, Betty. *The Tamarack Tree* (6–9). Illus. by Bea Holmes. 1971, Houghton $5.95. The consequences of having black students attend Prudence Crandell's academy in nineteenth-century Connecticut, and one girl's involvement with this cause.

3461. Vining, Elizabeth. *The Taken Girl* (5–9). 1972, Viking $5.95. The abolitionist movement, John Greenleaf Whittier, and a young orphan girl sent to live with a Quaker family all figure in this adventure in pre–Civil War Philadelphia.

3462. Wibberley, Leonard. *The Last Battle* (6–9). 1976, Farrar $6.95. The last volume of the series about the participation of the Treegate family and the War of 1812. Others are: *The Leopard's Prey* (1971, $4.50) and *Red Pawns* (1973, $5.95).

Westward Expansion and Pioneer Life

3463. Beatty, Patricia. *The Bad Bell of San Salvador* (5–8). 1973, Morrow $7.25; LB $6.96. Early California is re-created in this story of Jacinto, who wants to recover his true Comanche birthright.

3464. Beatty, Patricia. *Hail Columbia* (5–8). Illus. by Liz Dauber. 1970, Morrow $7.44. The Oregon of the 1890s is the unlikely setting for a visit from Aunt Columbia, a spirited, liberated suffragist, but nieces Louisa and Rowena are delighted.

3465. Beatty, Patricia. *How Many Miles to Sundown?* (5–7). 1974, Morrow $6.96. Youngsters on a quest travel through the Southwest of the 1880s in this humorous adventure, a companion to *A Long Way to Whiskey Creek* (1971, $6.96).

3466. Beatty, Patricia. *Something to Shout About* (5–8). 1976, Morrow $6.96. Set in the Montana territory of the 1870s, this story tells how a group of townswomen fight to have a decent schoolhouse built.

3467. Beatty, Patricia. *Wait for Me, Watch for Me, Eula Bee* (6–8). 1978, Morrow $7.95; LB $7.63. Two children are taken captive by Comanche Indians in Texas in 1861.

3468. Brenner, Barbara. *On the Frontier with Mr. Audubon* (5–8). Illustrated. 1977, Coward $6.95. A thoroughly researched account of a frontier journey, described by a 13-year-old apprentice to Audubon, the great nature artist.

3469. Brock, Emma L. *Drusilla* (4–6). Illus. by author. 1937, Macmillan $3.95. The journey of a family to Minnesota by covered wagon is told by a cornhusk doll.

3470. Bulla, Clyde Robert. *White Bird* (3–5). Illus. by Leonard Weisgard. 1966, Crowell $6.50. Set in pioneer days in Tennessee, John Thomas, an orphan, learns that there is good in people, particularly in Luke, the harsh man who brings him up.

3471. Carr, Mary Jane. *Children of the Covered Wagon* (4–6). Illus. by Bob Kuhn. 1957, Crowell $9.95. Wagon trains westward and the courageous pioneers who made the perilous trek.

3472. Clark, Ann Nolan. *All This Wild Land* (5–7). 1976, Viking $6.95. The central character is 11-year-old Maija, in this story of Finnish pioneers in the Minnesota of 1876.

3473. Coerr, Eleanor. *Waza Wins a Windy Gulch* (2–3). Illus. by Janet McCaffery. 1977, Putnam $4.99. Breezy, humorous anecdotes about one of the camels brought to Texas in the midnineteenth century to be used as pack animals on the trail to California.

3474. Coatsworth, Elizabeth. *The Sod House* (2–4). Illus. by Manning de V. Lee. 1954, Macmillan $5.95. A family of new Americans braves the rigors of frontier life.

3475. Clifford, Eth. *The Year of the Three-Legged Deer* (5–7). Illus. by Richard Cuffari. 1972, Dell paper $.95. Prejudice and hatred against Indians and blacks destroy a family, in this tragic story set in Indiana.

3476. Constant, A. W. *Miss Charity Comes to Stay* (6–8). 1959, Crowell $8.95. Twelve-year-old Betsy tells the story of her family's homesteading in the Oklahoma Territory of 1893.

3477. Ericson, Stig. *Dan Henry in the Wild West* (6–9). 1976, Delacorte $5.95. The first volume of an award-winning Swedish trilogy that tells of the adventures of young Daniel Gustafsson, renamed Dan Henry, when he immigrates to the United States in the 1870s.

3478. Flory, Jane. *The Golden Venture* (4–6). 1976, Houghton $6.95. San Francisco during the gold rush is the setting for this novel about a young girl and her father who move west to improve their fortune.

3479. Hancock, Sibyl. *The Blazing Hills* (3–5). Illus. by Richard Cuffari. 1975, Putnam $5.49. The story of how some settlers in Texas in 1846 try to make peace with the Indians.

3480. Holling, Holling C. *Tree in the Trail* (4–7). Illus. by author. 1942, Houghton $8.95. The history of the Santa Fe Trail, described through the life of a cottonwood tree, a 200-year-old landmark to travelers and a symbol of peace to the Indians.

3481. Keith, Harold. *The Obstinate Land* (6–8). 1977, Crowell $8.50. A realistic portrait of the Romberg family's struggle to gain a livelihood from the hostile land of the Cherokee Strip.

3482. Levitin, Sonia. *The No Return Trail* (5–7). 1978, Harcourt $6.95. Seventeen-year-old Nancy Kelsey, a wife and mother, accompanies a wagon train to California in 1841.

3483. Mason, Miriam E. *Caroline and Her Kettle Named Maud* (3–4). Illus. by Kathleen Voute. 1951, Macmillan $3.95. A pioneer story of a little girl who wanted a gun for her birthday and received a kettle.

3484. Masson, Miriam E. *Middle Sister* (4–6). Illus. by Grace Paull. 1947, Macmillan $3.95. A pioneer story about Sarah and her family's move to Minnesota.

3485. Meadowcroft, Enid. *By Wagon and Flatboat* (5–7). Illus. by Ninon MacKnight. 1938, Crowell $7.95. The Burd family travels from Pennsylvania to Ohio by flatboat.

3486. Monjo, F. N. *Indian Summer* (1–2). Illus. by Anita Lobel. 1968, Harper $6.89. Matt and Toby, in charge of protecting the family while pa is away fighting the British, suspect their cabin will soon be a target for Kentucky's Indians.

3487. Moore, Ruth Nulton. *Wilderness Journey* (4–6). Illus. by Allan Eitzen. 1979, Herald $5.95; paper $3.95. Two Irish boys travel over a mountainous wilderness from Philadelphia to Pittsburgh to join their mother.

3488. O'Dell, Scott. *Carlota* (6–9). 1977, Houghton $7.95. After the Mexican-American War, a brave group of Californians, including the enterprising heroine Carlota, who wishes independence, do battle with the U.S. Army.

3489. St. George, Judith. *The Halo Wind* (5–7). 1978, Putnam $7.95. Hardship on a wagon train to Oregon, as experienced by Ella Jane, a 13-year-old pioneer.

3490. Schaefer, Jack. *Mavericks* (6–8). Illus. by Lorence Bjorklund. 1967, Houghton $6.95. Expert writing in this story of a stalwart of the romantic Old West, Jake Hanlon. The novel shifts between his recollections and the contrasting present.

3491. Snedeker, Caroline. *Downright Dencey* (4–6). Illus. by Maginel Wright Barney. 1927, Doubleday $3.95. A perennial favorite about a Quaker girl and her promise to teach a young waif to read.

3492. Steele, William O. *Flaming Arrows* (4–6). Illus. by Paul Galdone. 1957, Harcourt $5.95; paper $1.15. Story of a group of Tennessee settlers sheltered in a fort against raiding Indians. Also use: *The Year of the Bloody Sevens* (1963, Harcourt $6.75).

3493. Stevens, Carla. *Trouble for Lucy* (4–6). Illus. by Ronald Himler. 1979, Houghton $7.95. Lucy's pup Finn causes trouble during a wagon train trip to the Oregon territory.

3494. Terris, Susan. *Tucker and the Horse Thief* (6–9). 1979, Four Winds $7.95. In the California gold rush of 1856, Sol Weil doesn't realize his buddy is really a girl.

3495. Wormser, Richard. *The Black Mustanger* (5–9). Illus. by Don Bolognese. 1971, Morrow $6.00. After the Civil War, Dan's family moves to Texas, and there, after the father is injured, only Will, part black and part Apache, comes to their aid.

3496. Yates, Elizabeth. *Carolina's Courage* (3–5). Illus. by Nora S. Unwin. 1964, Dutton $7.50. Carolina and her china doll brave the transition from New Hampshire to her new home in Nevada, in pioneer days.

Civil War

3497. Archer, Myrtle. *The Young Boys Gone* (6–9). 1978, Walker $7.95. A gripping tale of a boy's divided loyalties during the Civil War.

3498. Cummings, Betty Sue. *Hew Against the Grain* (6–9). 1977, Atheneum $6.95. The story of the ravages of the Civil War on a divided Virginia family, as expressed by the youngest daughter.

3499. Davis, Burke. *Mr. Lincoln's Whiskers* (4–5). Illus. by Douglas Gorsline. 1979, Coward $6.95. Based on fact, a story of a girl who suggests that Lincoln let his whiskers grow.

3500. Gauch, Patricia Lee. *Thunder at Gettysburg* (3–5). Illus. by Stephen Gammell. 1975, Coward $6.95. Young Tillie Pierce, a resident of Gettysburg, is swept along with the battle when it arises.

3501. Haynes, Betsy. *Cowslip* (6–8). 1973, Elsevier/Nelson $6.95. In 1861, a 12-year-old slave named Cowslip realizes her own worth.

3502. Hickman, Janet. *Zoar Blue* (6–9). 1978, Macmillan $7.95. A pacifist community and the effects of the Civil War on it as experienced by a young girl.

3503. Hunt, Irene. *Across Five Aprils* (6–8). 1964, Follett $4.95; LB $4.95; Grosset paper $1.25. A young boy's experiences during the Civil War in the backwoods of southern Illinois. One brother joins the Union forces, the other the Confederacy, and the family is divided.

3504. Keith, Harold. *Rifles for Watie* (6–9). 1957, Crowell $8.95. Life of a Union soldier and spy fighting the Civil War in the West. Newbery Award, 1958.

3505. Monjo, F. N. *Me and Willie and Pa: The Story of Abraham Lincoln and His Son Tad* (3–5). Illus. by Douglas Gorsline. 1973, Simon $6.95. In fictional form, an accurate retelling of Abraham Lincoln's White House years, as seen by his son Tad.

3506. Monjo, F. N. *The Vicksburg Veteran* (2–4). Illus. by Douglas Gorsline. 1971, Simon & Schuster $4.70. A first-person account of 13-year-old Fred Grant and his participation with his famous father in a Civil War campaign.

3507. O'Dell, Scott. *Sing Down the Moon* (5–8). 1970, Houghton $7.95; Dell paper $.95. The tragic forced march of the Indians to Fort Sumner in 1864, told by a young Navajo girl.

3508. Sneve, Virginia. *Betrayed* (5–7). 1974, Holiday $5.95. This bitter, graphic account of Indian-white conflicts during the Civil War is based on fact.

3509. Steele, William O. *The Perilous Road* (5–7). Illus. by Paul Galdone. 1954, Harcourt $6.25; paper $1.95. Chris, a Yankee-hating Tennessee mountain boy, learns by experience the futility of war, in this fast-paced Civil War story.

Reconstruction to World War II: 1865–1941

3510. Beatty, Patricia. *Lacy Makes a Match* (5–7). 1979, Morrow $7.95; LB $7.63. California of 1893 is the setting of this story of a girl trying to marry off her older brothers.

3511. Beatty, Patricia. *Just Some Weeds from the Wilderness* (5–7). 1978, Morrow $7.95; LB $7.35. A resourceful young girl helps her aunt produce patent medicines in Oregon of the late nineteenth century.

3512. Bolton, Carole. *Never Jam Today* (6–9). 1971, Atheneum paper $.95. Young Maddy works for the suffragettes in this novel set in America during 1917.

3513. Branscum, Robbie. *The Ugliest Boy* (5–7). Illus. by Mike Eagle. 1978, Lothrop $5.95. Reb struggles through growing-up pangs during the Great Depression in rural Arkansas.

3514. Burch, Robert. *Wilkin's Ghost* (5–7). Illus. by Lloyd Bloom. 1978, Viking $7.95. Wilkin, of *Tyler, Wilkin and Skee* (Dell, paper $1.25), befriends an older boy who was once accused of theft, in a story set in Georgia during 1935.

3515. Caroselli, Remus F. *The Mystery Cottage in Loft Field* (6–8). 1979, Putnam $7.95. Set in the gangster era of the 1920s, this is a gripping mystery.

3516. Colver, Anne, and Graff, Stewart. *The Wayfarer's Tree* (3–6). 1973, Dutton $5.95. A young boy spends a year in nineteenth-century Concord, in this novel that also introduces such notable townsfolk as Thoreau, Emerson, and the Alcotts.

3517. Constant, A. Wilson. *Does Anybody Care about Lou Emma Miller?* (5–7). 1979, Crowell $7.95; LB $7.87. A family novel set in Kansas prior to World War I that also highlights a girl's growing pains.

3518. Cummings, Betty Sue. *Now, Ameriky* (5–8). 1979, Atheneum $8.95. Brigid Ni Cleary comes to America from Ireland to raise passage money for the rest of the family.

3519. Curley, Daniel. *Hilarion* (3–5). Illus. by Judith Gwyn Brown. 1979, Houghton $6.95. The adventures of a group of immigrants in a large American city at the turn of the century.

3520. De Angeli, Marguerite. *Copper-Toed Boots* (3–6). Illus. by author. 1938, Doubleday $5.95. American family life in the early twentieth century.

3521. De Angeli, Marguerite. *Henner's Lydia* (3–5). Illus. by author. 1963, Doubleday $5.95. A little Amish girl and her family on a farm in Pennsylvania.

3522. Ellison, Lucile Watkins. *Butter on Both Sides* (4–6). Illus. by Judith Gwyn Brown. 1979, Scribner $7.95. A family story set in rural Alabama during the early 1900s.

3523. Flory, Jane. *It Was a Pretty Good Year* (3–5). 1977, Houghton $6.95. A memoir about the everyday happenings in the life of a 10-year-old growing up in Philadelphia at the turn of the century.

3524. Flory, Jane. *The Liberation of Clementine Tipton* (4–6). Illus. by author. 1974, Houghton $5.95. Set in Philadelphia in 1876, this novel's 10-year-old heroine Clementine, is a fighter for women's rights.

3525. Gessner, Lynne. *Navajo Slave* (5–7). 1976, Harvey LB $7.44. The story of a Navajo boy after the Civil War and his escape from slavery in New Mexico.

3526. Holman, Felice. *The Murderer* (5–7). 1978, Scribner $7.95. A young Jewish boy growing up in the days of the Great Depression is bullied by local boys and accused of murdering Christ.

3527. Hooks, William H. *Crossing the Line* (5–7). 1978, Knopf $6.95. Remembrance of an adventure in the rural South of the 1930s.

3528. Jacobs, William Jay. *Mother, Aunt Susan and Me: The First Fight for Women's Rights* (5–7). Illustrated. 1979, Coward $7.50. The accomplishments of Susan B. Anthony and Elizabeth Cady Stanton as seen through the eyes of Stanton's daughter Harriet.

3529. Kirkpatrick, Doris. *Honey in the Rock* (5–8). 1979, Nelson $8.95. Lenny and her family face relocation in this novel set in rural Vermont in 1936.

3530. Lehmann, Linda. *Better Than a Princess* (5–7). 1978, Nelson $6.95. Seventy years after she arrived, an old lady tells her daughter about coming to the United States at the turn of the century.

3531. Lenski, Lois. *Strawberry Girl* (4–6). Illus. by author. 1945, Lippincott $8.95; Dell paper $1.50. Lively adventures of a little girl, full of the flavor of the Florida lake country. Other regional stories in this series: *Judy's Journey* (1947, Lippincott $8.95; Dell, paper $1.25), and *Prairie School* (1941, Dell, paper $1.25).

3532. Mays, Lucinda. *The Other Shore* (6–9). 1979, Atheneum $8.95. An immigrant Italian girl arrives in the United States with her family in 1911.

3533. Moskin, Marietta D. *Day of the Blizzard* (3–4). Illus. by Stephen Gammell. 1978, Coward $6.95. A 12-year-old girl's experiences in New York City during the blizzard of 1888.

3534. Naylor, Phyllis Reynolds. *Walking Through the Dark* (6–9). 1976, Atheneum $6.95. The effects of poverty caused by the Great Depression, as seen through the eyes of an adolescent girl.

3535. Sawyer, Ruth. *Roller Skates* (4–6). Illus. by Valenti Angelo. 1936, Dell paper $1.25. A little girl explores New York City on roller skates in the 1890s. Newbery Award, 1937.

3536. Sebestyen, Ouida. *Words by Heart* (5–7). 1979, Little $7.95. Race relations are explored when a black family moves to an all-white community during the Reconstruction Era.

3537. Snyder, Carol. *Ike and Mama and the Once-a-Year Suit* (2–4). Illus. by Charles Robinson. 1978, Coward $5.95. New York City in 1918 is the setting for this humorous story about bargain hunting on the lower East Side.

3538. Sypher, Lucy Johnston. *The Edge of Nowhere* (4–6). Illus. by Ray Abel. 1972, Atheneum $6.95. A pioneer story set in a small town in North Dakota during 1916.

3539. Talbot, Charlene Joy. *An Orphan for Nebraska* (4–6). 1979, Atheneum $7.95. An orphaned Irish immigrant boy is sent west in the 1870s.

3540. Waldron, Ann. *Scaredy Cat* (4–5). 1975, Dutton $7.50. A youngster's fears are explored in this story set in Alabama during the Great Depression.

3541. Weik, Mary Hays. *A House on Liberty Street* (5–8). Illus. by Ann Grifalconi. 1973, Atheneum $4.50. An inspiring story based on fact about an immigrant's contributions to America.

3542. Yep, Laurence. *Dragonwings* (5–9). 1977, Harper paper $1.95. A young Chinese boy adjusts to life in San Francisco during the time of the earthquake.

World War II

3543. Anderson, Margaret J. *Searching for Shona* (4–6). 1978, Knopf $6.95; LB $6.99. In England during World War II, two girls exchange places; one goes to Scotland, the other to Canada.

3544. Bawden, Nina. *Carrie's War* (4–6). 1973, Lippincott $8.95; Penguin paper $1.95. Twelve-year-old Carrie and her younger brother are evacuated from London to a small Welsh town.

3545. Benary-Isbert, Margot. *The Ark* (5–9). 1952, Harcourt $6.50; paper $1.95. A family's struggles in a bombed-out, postwar German city.

3546. Bishop, Claire Huchet. *Twenty and Ten* (4–6). Illus. by William Pene du Bois. 1952, Viking $6.50; Penguin paper $1.95. A nun and 20 French children hide 10 young refugees from the Nazis.

3547. Bloch, Marie. *Displaced Person* (6–9). Illus. by Allen Davis. 1978, Morrow $6.95; LB $6.67. A Ukranian boy flees a German refugee camp in the final days of World War II.

3548. Burnford, Sheila. *Bel Ria* (6–9). 1978, Little $7.95. A performing dog is rescued by a British soldier during the evacuation at Dunkirk.

3549. Degens, T. *Transport 7-41-R* (6–9). 1974, Viking $5.95. A nightmarish trip through post–World War II Germany by a young refugee girl.

3550. DeJong, Meindert. *The House of Sixty Fathers* (6–9). Illus. by Maurice Sendak. 1956, Harper LB $7.89. Tien Pao and his pig, Glory-of-the-Republic, journey to find his parents in Japanese-occupied China.

3551. Evenhuis, Gertie. *What about Me?* (3–5). Illus. by Ron Stenberg. 1976, Nelson $6.95. The rivalry between 2 brothers is set against the framework of German-occupied Holland in 1943.

3552. Fife, Dale. *North of Danger* (5–7). Illus. by Haakon Saether. 1978, Dutton $6.95. A boy's adventures in Norway during World War II.

3553. Gardam, Jane. *A Long Way from Verona* (6–8). 1972, Macmillan $4.95; paper $1.25. A first-person narrative set in England during World War II, in which a sensitive young girl tries her hand at writing.

3554. Griese, Arnold A. *The Wind Is Not a River* (4–6). Illus. by Glo Coalson. 1978, Crowell $6.95; LB $6.79. A World War II story about 2 children who help a wounded Japanese soldier in the Aleutian Islands.

3555. Haugaard, Erik C. *The Little Fishes* (6–8). Illus. by Milton Johnson. 1967, Houghton $6.95. The starvation, filth, and death apparent in Italy during World War II surround the story of Guido, whose mother's exhortation to be strong and kind keeps his spirit alive, enabling him to survive and to help other orphans.

3556. Holm, Anne. *North to Freedom* (6–8). 1965, Harcourt $5.95; paper $1.25. A boy who has never known anything except life in a concentration camp makes his way across Europe alone, and escapes to freedom.

3557. Kerr, Judith. *The Other Way Round* (6–8). 1975, Coward $7.95. The life of Jewish refugees in England during World War II is described with sensitivity in this sequel to *When Hitler Stole Pink Rabbit*.

3558. Kerr, Judith. *When Hitler Stole Pink Rabbit* (4–7). Illus. by author. 1972, Coward $6.95; Dell paper $1.25. Based on incidents in the author's life, this is an exciting story of a German-Jewish family and their escape from Nazi Germany.

3559. Levitin, Sonia. *Journey to America* (5–8). Illus. by Charles Robinson. 1970, Atheneum paper

$.95. A Jewish mother and her 3 daughters flee Nazi Germany in 1938 for a long and difficult journey to join their father in America.

3560. Lowry, Lois. *Autumn Street* (6–9). 1980, Houghton $6.95. Six-year-old Elizabeth, her sister, and mother go to live with grandmother in Pennsylvania during World War II.

3561. McSwigan, Marie. *Snow Treasure* (4–7). Illus. by Mary Reardon. 1942, Dutton $8.95; Scholastic paper $1.25. Children smuggle gold out of occupied Norway on their sleds.

3562. Nostlinger, Christine. *Fly Away Home* (6–9). 1975, Watts $5.88. How a family coped during the German and Russian occupations of Vienna during and after World War II, as seen through the eyes of Christel, a young girl.

3563. Orgel, Doris. *The Devil in Vienna* (6–8). 1978, Dial $7.95. A novel based on fact that centers around the Nazi occupation of Austria.

3564. Reiss, Johanna. *The Journey Back* (5–8). 1976, Crowell $8.95. A continuation of *The Upstairs Room*, recounting the experiences of the De-Leeuw family when they are reunited after World War II.

3565. Reiss, Johanna. *The Upstairs Room* (5–8). 1972, Crowell $8.95. Two young Jewish girls are hidden for over 2 years in the home of a simple Dutch peasant during the German occupation.

3566. Richter, Hans Peter. *Friedrich* (6–9). 1970, Holt $5.95. Two boys, one Jewish, the other Gentile, growing up in the tragedy that was Nazi Germany.

3567. Richter, Hans Peter. *I Was There* (6–9). 1972, Holt $5.95. A first-person story of a boy who joins the Hitler Youth movement in pre–World War II Germany.

3568. Rydberg, Lou, and Rydberg, Ernie. *The Shadow Army* (6–8). 1976, Elsevier/Nelson $6.95. Three years in the life of young Demetrios, when Crete, his island home, is occupied by German soldiers during World War II.

3569. Sachs, Marilyn. *A Pocket Full of Seeds* (5–7). Illus. by Ben Stahl. 1973, Doubleday $5.95. A family of French Jews suffer the heartache of persecution during World War II.

3570. Serraillier, Ian. *The Silver Sword* (6–8). Illus. by C. Walter Hodges. 1959, Phillips $8.95. A World War II story of Polish children who are separated from their parents and finally reunited.

3571. Streatfeild, Noel. *When the Sirens Wailed* (4–6). Illus. by Judith Gwyn Brown. 1976, Random $5.95; LB $6.99. The story of a cockney family separated during the London blitz.

3572. Terlouw, Jan. *Winter in Wartime* (6–9). 1976, McGraw $6.95. Young Michiel takes care of a wounded British airman in the Netherlands during World War II.

3573. Tunis, John R. *Silence over Dunkerque* (6–9). Illustrated. 1962, Morrow $6.96. Drama of an English sergeant and his twin sons during the famous battle.

3574. Van Stockum, Hilda. *The Winged Watchman* (4–6). 1962, Farrar $6.95. Fast-paced, realistic story of a Dutch family during the Nazi occupation.

3575. Walsh, Jill Paton. *Fireweed* (6–9). 1969, Farrar $3.95; Avon paper $1.50. A story of 2 young people in London during the World War II blitz, who fall in love but must part since Bill will not be accepted by Julie's wealthy family.

3576. Wuorio, Eva-Lis. *To Fight in Silence* (5–8). 1973, Holt $5.95. The fortunes and misfortunes of a Scandinavian family during World War II, which culminate in the operation to save Danish Jews by sending them to Sweden.

3577. Zei, Alki. *Petros' War* (5–7). Tr. by Edward Fenton. 1972, Dutton $7.50. A Greek boy changes his ideas about war, and his family suffers great hardships during the German occupation.

3578. Zei, Alki. *Wildcat under Glass* (5–7). Trans. from the Greek by Edward Fenton. 1968, Holt $4.50. Vivid characterizations reveal the interfamily personal crises traceable to the international threat of fascism; set in Greece just prior to World War II.

Mysteries, Monsters, and Curiosities

3579. Arnold, Oren. *What's in a Name: Famous Brand Names* (5–8). 1979, Messner $7.29. Stories behind such names as Coca Cola and Ivory Soap.

3580. Aylesworth, Thomas G. *The Alchemists: Magic into Science* (5–8). Illustrated. 1973, Addison $6.95. From ancient Egypt to the present, a history of those who tried to turn metals into gold.

3581. Aylesworth, Thomas G. *The Story of Werewolves* (5–7). Illustrated. 1978, McGraw $6.95. A chilling account that begins in Greek and Roman times and ends in the modern period. Also use: *The Story of Vampires* (1977, McGraw $6.95).

3582. Aylesworth, Thomas G. *The Story of Witches* (5–7). Illustrated. 1979, McGraw $7.95. An account of the history of witchcraft and its practices throughout the world.

3583. Aylward, Jim. *You're Dumber in the Summer* (2–5). Illus. by Jan Chambless-Rigie. 1980, Rinehart $6.95. A collection of most unusual facts.

3584. Baumann, Elwood D. *Bigfoot: America's Abominable Snowman* (5–7). 1975, Watts $5.90. An exploration of the evidence that proves or disproves the existence of Bigfoot.

3585. Baumann, Elwood D. *The Devil's Triangle* (6–7). Illustrated. 1976, Watts $6.90. An account of the mysterious disappearances and tragedies associated with this area in the Atlantic Ocean.

3586. Baumann, Elwood D. *Monsters of North America* (6–9). Illustrated. 1978, Watts $6.90. Tales of six lesser-known monsters with black and white sketches.

3587. Berger, Melvin. *The Supernatural: From ESP to UFO's* (6–9). Illustrated. 1977, John Day $6.95. Basic material is well presented on an intriguing subject.

3588. Blakely, Pat, ed. *The Second Rainbow Book* (2–6). Illustrated. 1979, Meadowbrook paper $2.95. This second edition of a 1976 publication contains 250 free items youngsters can send for.

3589. Blumberg, Rhoda. *Witches* (5–8). Illustrated. 1979, Watts $5.90. A history of witchcraft and the horrendous witch hunts in Europe and America.

3590. Branley, Franklyn M. *Age of Aquarius: You and Astrology* (4–6). Illus. by Leonard Kessler. 1979, Crowell $6.95; LB $6.89. An explanation of the 12 zodiac signs and a world history of astrology are included in this account.

3591. Branley, Franklyn M. *A Book of Flying Saucers for You* (3–4). Illus. by Leonard Kessler. 1973, Crowell $8.79. A report on the phenomena considered as flying saucers and details on probable explanations.

3592. Brooks, Daniel Fitzgerald. *Numerology* (5–9). Illustrated. 1978, Watts $4.90. Background history plus information on how to work out your own numerology chart are included.

3593. Calhoun, Mary. *Medicine Show: Conning People and Making Them Like It* (6–9). Illustrated. 1976, Harper $6.95; LB $7.89. An entertaining survey of the confidence games as practiced in medicine shows from the midnineteenth century to the 1940s.

3594. Campbell, Hannah. *Why Did They Name It?* (3–6). Illustrated. 1964, Fleet $7.50. The stories behind such brand names as Sanka and Kodak.

3595. Clyne, Patricia Edwards. *Strange and Supernatural Animals* (5–8). Illus. by Ted Lewin. 1979, Dodd $6.95. Fifteen tales about common animals that have returned to haunt sites where they have lived.

3596. Cohen, Daniel. *The Body Snatchers* (6–8). Illustrated. 1975, Lippincott $7.95; paper $2.95. The spine-tingling, fascinating subject of the history of grave robbing, handled with taste.

3597. Cohen, Daniel. *Creatures from UFO's* (6–8). Illustrated. 1978, Dodd $5.95. A collection of stories of encounters with aliens, often in the exact words of the original observers.

3598. Cohen, Daniel. *Curses, Hexes and Spells* (5–7). Illustrated. 1974, Lippincott $7.95; paper $2.50. A lively discussion of all sorts of creepy phenomena and evil magic.

3599. Cohen, Daniel. *Famous Curses* (4–6). Illustrated. 1979, Dodd $5.95. Stories that range from King Tut to the Ingoldsby Indians.

3600. Cohen, Daniel. *Frauds, Hoaxes and Swindles* (4–7). Illustrated. 1979, Watts $6.90. A book that tells about the people behind some of our great hoaxes, including the Clifford Irving/Howard Hughes biography scandal.

3601. Cohen, Daniel. *Mysteries of the World* (6–9). Illustrated. 1979, Doubleday $7.95. Ten unsolved mysteries such as the strange explosion in Siberia in 1908 are presented.

3602. Cohen, Daniel. *Real Ghosts* (5–7). Illustrated. 1977, Dutton $5.95. A nonfiction study of encounters with ghosts, complete with photographs supposedly taken of spirits. Also use: *In Search of Ghosts* (1972, Dodd $5.95).

3603. Cohen, Daniel. *The World's Most Famous Ghosts* (6–9). 1978, Dodd $5.95. A report in 10 short chapters of better-known incidents accredited to ghosts.

3604. Cohen, Daniel. *Young Ghosts* (6–9). Illustrated. 1978, Dutton $7.95. An eerie but fascinating collection of material about ghosts of children.

3605. Cornell, James C. *Nature at Its Strangest* (5–9). Illustrated. 1974, Sterling $4.05; LB $4.98. A wonderful browsing book on strange, short-lived natural phenomena, such as stones suddenly pushing out of the ground in an Oklahoma pasture.

3606. Distad, Audree. *Come to the Fair* (5–8). Illustrated. 1977, Harper $5.95; LB $5.79. A glimpse of the activities, many involving 4-H groups, that involve youngsters and the South Dakota State Fair.

3607. Feinman, Jeffrey. *Freebies for Kids* (4–9). 1979, Simon & Schuster paper $2.50. All kinds of free materials are listed here under such subject headings as careers, pets, and health.

3608. Haislip, Barabra. *Stars, Spells, Secrets and Sorcery: A Do-It-Yourself Book of the Occult* (6–7), Illustrated. 1976, Little $7.95; Dell paper $1.50. Many types of Asian occult phenomena, including I Ching and Tarot cards, are explored.

3609. Hayman, LeRoy. *Thirteen Who Vanished* (4–6). 1979, Messner $7.29. True stories about such famous people as Amelia Earhart and Judge Crater who disappeared mysteriously.

3610. Hazen, Barbara S. *Last, First, Middle and Nick: All about Names* (3–6). Illus. by Sam Weissman. 1979, Prentice-Hall $7.95. A book about how names originated, their meanings, trends in naming, and how names can be changed.

3611. Hilton, Suzanne. *Here Today and Gone Tomorrow: The Story of World's Fairs and Expositions* (5–8). Illustrated. 1978, Westminster $8.95. An entertaining and interesting account of fairs in America from 1853 to 1965.

3612. Jennings, Gary. *Black Magic, White Magic* (6–9). Illus. by Barbara Begg. 1965, Dial $5.95. Account of magic in history, modern superstitions, and attempts to alter nature with the aid of the supernatural; witchcraft and witch hunts, alchemy, magic in medicine, and ritual magic. Also use: *Devils and Demons* by Nancy Garden (1976, Lippincott $7.95; Dell, paper 95¢).

3613. Keller, Charles. *The Best of Rube Goldberg* (6–8). Illustrated. 1979, Prentice-Hall $9.95; paper $7.95. Ninety-four wacky inventions are pictured with accompanying directions.

3614. Kettelkamp, Larry. *Astrology* (5–7). 1973, Morrow $6.01. A concise guide to astrology, the zodiac, and horoscopes.

3615. Kettelkamp, Larry. *Haunted Houses* (4–6). Illus. by author. 1969, Morrow $6.25; LB $6.00. The author documents 10 case histories where ghosts or poltergeists have made their presence known, and speculates on the reasons for these supernatural occurrences.

3616. Kettelkamp, Larry. *Investigating Psychics: Five Life Histories* (5–9). Illustrated. 1977, Morrow $6.25; LB $6.00. Parapsychology is examined through the lives of several psychics who have worked with scientists to explain this phenomenon.

3617. Kettelkamp, Larry. *Sixth Sense* (5–9). 1970, Morrow $6.00. A guide to extrasensory perception.

3618. Klein, Aaron E. *Science and the Supernatural: A Scientific View of the Occult* (6–9). 1979, Doubleday $7.95. A discussion of the various explanations given for a belief in the supernatural.

3619. Knight, David C. *Those Mysterious UFO's* (4–6). Illustrated. 1975, Parents $5.95; LB $5.41. A history of various mysterious objects that people have seen in the sky. Also use: *Investigating UFO's* by Larry Kettelkamp (1971, Morrow $6.00).

3620. Kohn, Bernice. *Out of the Cauldron: A Short History of Witchcraft* (5–7). Illustrated. 1972, Holt $5.95. A fascinating history of the origins of witchcraft with emphasis on western Europe and Massachusetts.

3621. Lambert, Eloise, and Pei, Mario. *Our Names: Where They Come from and What They Mean* (5–8). 1960, Lothrop $6.95. A fascinating collection of personal names, including brand names.

3622. Landau, Elaine. *Occult Visions* (5–9). Illustrated. 1979, Messner $7.79. An overview of the various forms of fortune-telling and methods of predicting the future.

3623. Lauber, Patricia. *Mystery Monsters of Loch Ness* (3–5). Illustrated. 1978, Garrard $4.74. A report by an author who obviously believes that such creatures exist.

3624. McHargue, Georgess. *Facts, Frauds, and Phantasms: A Survey of the Spiritualists Movement* (6–9). Illustrated. 1972, Doubleday $4.95. An engrossing listing of a fascinating subject told with objectivity and humor.

3625. McHargue, Georgess. *Meet the Vampire* (5–8). Illustrated. 1979, Lippincott $7.95; LB $7.89. A compilation of facts and fallacies about vampires, including the story of the original Dracula.

3626. McHargue, Georgess. *Meet the Werewolf* (2–5). Illus. by Stephen Gammell. 1976, Lippincott $7.95; paper $2.95. Stories, legends, and other material are entertainingly presented.

3627. McHargue, Georgess. *Mummies* (5–8). Illustrated. 1972, Lippincott $7.95; paper $1.95. All aspects of mummification are explored, including the freezing of Siberian mammoths as well as extensive treatment of Egyptian embalming.

3628. Madison, Arnold. *Lost Treasures of America: Searching Out Hidden Riches* (6–9). Illus. by Dick Wahl. 1977, Rand $5.95; LB $5.97. Nine accounts of buried treasure, including Montezuma's gold and Jesse James's cache.

3629. Maynard, Christopher. *All about Ghosts* (4–7). Illustrated. 1978, EMC $4.95. An introduction to this fascinating subject; great for browsing.

3630. Mooser, Stephen. *Into the Unknown: Nine Astounding Stories* (3–6). Illustrated. 1980, Lippincott $7.95; LB $7.89. Nine accounts, somewhat fictionized, of unexplained occurrences involving ESP, reincarnation, and so forth.

3631. Murphy, Jim. *Weird and Wacky Inventions* (4–6). Illustrated. 1978, Crown $7.95. Unusual and bizarre gizmos from the Patent Office are described.

3632. Newton, Michael. *Monsters, Mysteries and Man* (6–9). Illustrated. 1979, Addison $8.95; paper $5.95. An overview of such tantalizing mysteries as Bigfoot, Nessie, and the Abominable Snowman.

3633. Ostrander, Sheila, and Schroeder, Lynn. *Psychic Experiences: ESP Investigated* (6–9). 1978, Sterling $6.95. Forty cases of psychic phenomenon are cited and analyzed in this fascinating account.

3634. Palmer, Robin. *A Dictionary of Mythical Places* (5–9). Illus. by Richard Cuffari. 1975, Walck $7.95. A fascinating collection of mythical places, stretching from Aalu, ancient Egypt's heaven, to Ys, a Celtic undersea city.

3635. Perl, Lila. *America Goes to the Fair: All about State and County Fairs in the U.S.* (5–8). Illustrated. 1974, Morrow $6.75; LB $6.48. The history, purposes, and hoopla of one of America's grandest institutions.

3636. Pizer, Vernon. *Ink, Art, and All That: How American Places Got Their Names* (6–8). Illus. by Tom Huffman. 1976, Putman $6.95. In roughly chronological fashion, the author tells the intriguing stories behind many placenames.

3637. Place, Marian T. *Bigfoot All over the Country* (5–9). 1978, Dodd $6.95. A detailed, often fascinating account of the search for Sasquatch.

3638. Place, Marian T. *On the Track of Bigfoot* (5–7). Illustrated. 1974, Archway paper $1.75. An investigation of the Pacific Northwest monster also known as Sasquatch.

3639. Quinn, John R. *Nature's World Records* (3–6). Illus. by author. 1977, Walker $5.95; LB $5.85; Scholastic paper $.95. Nature's slowest, fastest, and so forth, are listed in this chronicle of the unusual.

3640. Rabinowich, Ellen. *The Loch Ness Monster* (3–5). Illus. by Sally Law. 1979, Watts $5.90. Fact and theory are divided equally in this well-illustrated account.

3641. Ripley, Robert LeRoy. *Ripley's Believe It or Not!* (4–6). 1979, Golden $2.65. Hundreds of unusual facts from all over the world.

3642. Rudley, Stephen. *The Abominable Snowcreature* (6–9). Illustrated. 1978, Watts $5.90. An account of the sightings and existing evidence involving the mysterious creature of the Himalayas.

3643. Sarnoff, Jane, and Ruffins, Reynold. *Take Warning! A Book of Superstititions* (4–6). 1978, Scribner $8.95. A dictionary of the origins and practices surrounding major superstitions.

3644. Schwartz, Alvin. *Cross Your Fingers, Spit in Your Hat: Superstitions and Other Beliefs* (4–6). Illus. by Glen Rounds. 1974, Lippincott $7.95; paper $2.95. An amazing collection of information on a variety of superstitions. Also use: *Superstitions* by Daniel Cohen (1972, Dodd $7.50).

3645. Seuling, Barbara. *You Can't Eat Peanuts in Church and Other Little-Known Laws* (4–7). Illus. by author. 1975, Doubleday $4.95; paper $1.75. A collection of unusual laws gathered from all parts of the United States.

3646. Simon, Seymour. *Creatures from Lost Worlds* (6–9). Illustrated. 1979, Lippincott $7.89. Surveys worlds created in movies, books, and television and tells about the strange beings found there.

3647. Snyder, Gerald S. *Is There a Loch Ness Monster? The Search for a Legend* (6–9). Illustrated. 1977, Messner $7.79. An objective account that, as expected, leaves the reader with many questions unanswered.

3648. Sobol, Donald J. *Disaster* (5–8). 1979, Archway paper $1.50. Events from the Black Death to a 1970 cyclone in East Pakistan are chronicled.

3649. Suid, Murray, and Harris, Ron. *Made in America: Eight Great All-American Creations* (4–6). Illustrated. 1978, Addison $10.95; paper $5.95. Creations highlighted include Coca Cola, McDonald's, and Superman.

3650. Taves, Isabella. *True Ghost Stories* (5–7). Illus. by Michael Deas. 1978, Watts $5.90. Six supposedly true supernatural tales.

3651. Wilding-White, Ted. *All about UFO's* (4–7). Illustrated. 1978, EMC $4.95. An entertaining account of UFO's—probable cause and how to make one.

3652. Wilkins, Frances. *Wizards and Witches* (3–6). Illus. by Fritz Wegner. 1966, Walck $5.95. Lively profiles of sorcerers from different times and countries.

3653. Wise, William. *Monsters from Outer Space* (3–4). Illus. by Richard Cuffari. 1979, Putnam $5.29. UFO's and other phenomena are discussed objectively and with candor.

3654. Yolen, Jane. *The Wizard Islands* (6–8). Illus. by Robert Quackenbush. 1973, Crowell $8.95. An account of many of the world's islands, such as the Galapagos, Atlantis, and Easter Island, which evoke mystery and legend.

Mythology

General and Miscellaneous

3655. Baker, Betty. *At the Center of the World: Based on Papago and Pima Myths* (4–6). Illus. by Murray Tinkelman. 1973, Macmillan $4.95. The myths are primarily involved with creation of the earth and its various inhabitants.

3656. Bernstein, Margery, and Kobrin, Janet. *The First Morning: An African Myth Retold* (2–3). Illus. by Enid Warner Romanek. 1976, Scribner $7.95. Stark, dramatic illustrations accompany this simple retelling of an African myth that recounts how light came to the world.

3657. Bernstein, Margery, and Kobrin, Janet. *The Summer Maker: An Ojibway Indian Myth* (2–3). Illus. by Ann Burgess. 1977, Scribner $5.95. Ojug, the fisher, sets out with several friends in search of summer.

3658. Chafex, Henry. *Thunderbird and Other Stories* (4–6). Illus. by Ronni Solbert. 1964, Pantheon $5.99. An explanation of how thunder and lightning originated is the theme of these 3 American Indian myths.

3659. Farmer, Penelope, comp. *Beginnings: Creation Myths of the World* (6–8). Illus. by Antonio Frasconi. 1979, Atheneum $8.95. Many retellings of stories dealing with the creation of life drawn from several cultures.

3660. Hamilton, Edith. *Mythology* (6–9). Illus. by Steele Savage. 1942, Little $7.95. A book of Greek, Roman, and Norse myths, modern in language, sound in scholarship.

3661. Hodges, Margaret. *The Other World: Myths of the Celts* (4–7). Illus. by Eros Keith. 1973, Farrar $5.95. After an introduction on mythology in general and Celtic mythology in particular, 10 myths are splendidly retold.

3662. Lum, Peter. *The Stars in Our Heavens: Myths and Fables* (5–8). Illus. by Anne Marie Jauss. 1948, Pantheon $5.99. The beliefs of Greeks, Romans, Babylonians, Norse, Chinese, and Indians concerning the stars.

3663. Marriott, Alice Lee, and Rachlin, Carol K. *American Indian Mythology* (5–7). 1968, Crowell $12.50; paper $3.95. Folktales and myths representing 7 tribes are presented in an easily read anthology.

3664. McDermott, Beverly Brodsky. *Sedna: An Eskimo Myth* (K–3). Illus. by author. 1975, Viking $5.95. Food is denied starving Eskimos until they pay proper homage to the sea spirit, Sedna.

3665. McDermott, Gerald. *Arrow to the Sun: A Pueblo Indian Tale* (K–3). Illus. by author. 1974, Viking $8.95; Penguin paper $2.50. Brilliant colors effectively highlight this adaptation of a Pueblo myth—the search by a young Indian boy for his father, the Sun.

3666. McDermott, Gerald. *The Voyage of Osiris: A Myth of Ancient Egypt* (K–3). Illus. by author. 1977, Dutton $8.95. After death, Osiris becomes ruler of the underworld in this brilliantly illustrated retelling of an unusual story.

3667. Rose, Anne. *Spider in the Sky* (1–3). Illus. by Gail Owens. 1978, Harper $5.95; LB $5.79. An American Indian myth on how Grandmother Spider brought fire and light to the animals.

3668. Roy, Cal. *The Serpent and the Sun* (4–7). Illus. by author. 1972, Farrar $5.95. Twelve myths, chiefly of Aztec origins, speak about the beginnings of the earth and elements that control its destiny.

3669. Synge, Ursula. *Land of Heroes: A Retelling of the Kalovala* (6–9). 1978, Atheneum $6.95. A spellbinding but complex retelling of the Finnish national epic.

Classical

3670. Anderson, John Lonzo. *Arion and the Dolphins, Based on an Ancient Greek Legend* (1–3). Illus. by Adrienne Adams. 1978, Scribner $7.95. An excellent retelling of an ancient sea story impressively depicted by lovely watercolors.

3671.   Barth, Edna. *Cupid and Psyche: A Love Story* (4–6). Illus. by Ati Forberg. 1976, Seabury $7.95. The Greek myth adroitly retold and highlighted by tasteful wash drawings.

3672.   Benson, Sally. *Stories of the Gods and Heroes* (4–6). Illus. by Steele Savage. 1940, Dial $7.95; Dell paper $1.50. A selection of tales of the Trojan War based on *The Age of Fable* by Bulfinch.

3673.   Church, A. J. *The Iliad and the Odyssey* (6–9). 1964, Macmillan $5.95. An interesting rendering of the classic epics.

3674.   Colum, Padraic. *The Golden Fleece and the Heroes Who Lived Before Achilles* (5–7). Illus. by Willy Pogany. 1962, Macmillan $5.50. Jason's search for the Golden Fleece incorporates some of the best-known myths and legends of ancient Greece.

3675.   Coolidge, Olivia. *Greek Myths* (4–7). Illus. by Eduard Sandoz. 1949, Houghton $7.95. Twenty-seven well-known myths dramatically retold with accompanying illustrations.

3676.   D'Aulaire, Ingri, and D'Aulaire, Edgar. *D'Aulaires' Book of Greek Myths* (3–6). Illus. by author. 1962, Doubleday $9.95. Full-color pictures highlight these brief stories, which are excellent for first readers in mythology.

3677.   Farmer, Penelope. *The Story of Persephone* (4–6). Illus. by Graham McCallum. 1973, Morrow $6.75; LB $6.75. Seasonal changes are explained in this restrained retelling of the story of goddess Demeter and her lovely lost daughter.

3678.   Gates, Doris. *A Fair Wind for Troy* (5–8). 1976, Viking $6.95. A retelling of legends connected with the Trojan War.

3679.   Gates, Doris. *Lord of the Sky: Zeus* (3–6). Illus. by Robert Handville. 1972, Viking $5.95. In the first of a series, the author has retold simply and directly myths in which Zeus plays a central part. Also use: *The Golden God: Apollo* (1973, Viking $7.95).

3680.   Gates, Doris. *Mightiest of Mortals: Heracles* (4–6). Illus. by Richard Cuffari. 1975, Viking $6.95. All of the tales of Heracles are presented in logical order and with a breezy, informal writing style.

3681.   Gates, Doris. *The Warrior Goddess: Athena* (4–6). Illus. by Don Bolognese. 1972, Viking $5.95. A spirited retelling of the myths associated with Athena. Also use: *Two Queens of Heaven: Aphrodite and Demeter* (1974, Viking $5.95).

3682.   Guerber, H. A. *The Myths of Greece and Rome* (4–6). Illustrated. 1963, British Bk. Ctr. $12.00. A thorough collection of Greek myths,

well illustrated from famous pictures that also include genealogies and a map.

3683.   Hawthorne, Nathaniel. *Wonderbook and Tanglewood Tales* (5–7). 1853; 1972 Houghton $6.95. This is a highly original retelling of the Greek myths.

3684.   Hodges, Margaret. *Persephone and the Springtime* (K–3). Illus. by Arvis Stewart. 1973, Little $5.95. A gentle retelling of the origins of springtime that occurred when Persephone was released from Hades.

3685.   McLean, Mollie, and Wiseman, Ann. *Adventures of the Greek Heroes* (4–6). Illus. by W. T. Mars. 1961, Houghton $7.95; paper $2.95. Easily read version of myths involving such heroes as Jason, Hercules, and Theseus.

3686.   Proddow, Penelope. *Art Tells a Story: Greek and Roman Myths* (4–9). Illustrated. 1979, Doubleday $6.95; LB $7.90. The work of various artists are used to illustrate classic myths.

3687.   Sellew, Catharine F. *Adventures with the Gods* (5–7). Illus. by George Hauman and Doris Hauman. 1945, Little $6.95. Sixteen popular Greek myths retold simply and vividly.

3688.   Serraillier, Ian. *Fall from the Sky: The Story of Daedalus* (4–6). Illus. by William Stobbs. 1966, Walck $4.95. Strong, vigorous illustrations and a direct style make this retelling of a favorite Greek myth very popular with young readers.

Norse

3689.   Colum, Padraic. *Children of Odin* (4–6). 1930; 1962 Macmillan $6.95. Collection of Norse sagas.

3690.   Coolidge, Olivia. *Legends of the North* (5–7). Illus. by Eduard Sandoz. 1951, Houghton $7.95. This is a fine collection of Norse myths that includes those about Thor.

3691.   D'Aulaire, Ingri, and D'Aulaire, Edgar. *Norse Gods and Giants* (4–6). Illus. by author. 1967, Doubleday $8.95. A vigorous retelling of many of the Norse myths, illustrated with bold, colorful lithographs.

3692.   Feagles, Anita. *Thor and the Giants* (4–6). Illus. by Gertrude Barter Russell. 1968, Young Scott $5.95. The old Norse legend about Thor's struggles against the Giants is well retold.

3693.   Hodges, Margaret. *Baldur and the Mistletoe: A Myth of the Vikings* (4–6). Illus. by Gerry Hoover. 1973, Little $6.95. The fall of the gods is caused by the death of the hero Baldur from poisonous mistletoe.

3694. Hosford, Dorothy G. *Thunder of the Gods* (5–7). Illus. by Claire Louden and George Louden. 1952, Holt $5.95. A beautiful collection of 15 Norse myths, told simply and dramatically. Also use: *Adventures with the Giants* by Catharine F. Sellew (1950, Little $6.95).

Religion

General and Miscellaneous

3695. Asimov, Isaac. *Animals of the Bible* (3–7). Illustrated. 1978, Doubleday $6.95. The kinds and uses of animals mentioned in the Bible.

3696. Daves, Michael. *Young Reader's Book of Christian Symbolism* (5–8). Illus. by Gordon Laite. 1967, Abingdon $7.95. The "history and description of symbolism in the Protestant church."

3697. Edmonds, I. G. *Buddhism* (5–8). Illustrated. 1978, Watts $4.90. As well as background information, this simple survey discusses the role of Buddhism in the world today.

3698. Edmonds, I. G. *Hinduism* (3–6). Illustrated. 1979, Watts $5.90. A basic introduction to the world's third largest religion.

3699. Edmonds, I. G. *Other Lives: The Story of Reincarnation* (6–9). 1979, McGraw $7.95. An examination of reincarnation, particularly as found in Buddhism and Hinduism.

3700. Elgin, Kathleen. *The Mormons: The Church of Jesus Christ of Latter-Day Saints* (4–7). 1969, McKay $5.95. A fine addition to "The Freedom to Worship" series.

3701. Faber, Doris. *The Perfect Life: The Shakers in America* (6–9). Illustrated. 1974, Farrar $6.95. The author astutely appraises this communal movement that anticipated the concerns of modern back-to-nature advocates.

3702. Farb, Peter. *The Land, Wildlife and People of the Bible* (6–9). Illus. by Harry McNaught. 1967, Harper $6.95; LB $7.89. Ancient events in the Holy Land are linked to modern scientific knowledge.

3703. Fellows, Lawrence. *A Gentle War: The Story of the Salvation Army* (5–8). Illustrated. 1979, Macmillan $7.95. A narrative that traces the history and present status of the Salvation Army.

3704. Fitch, Florence Mary. *A Book about God* (K–3). Illus. by Leonard Weisgard. 1953, Lothrop $6.96. A beautiful book, acceptable to all faiths, showing manifestations of God's work in the wonders of nature.

3705. Fitch, Florence Mary. *One God: The Ways We Worship Him* (5 up). Illustrated. 1944, Lothrop $5.52. Religious ceremonies displayed by text and photographs and endorsed by national Catholic, Jewish, and Protestant organizations. Also use: *Their Search for God* (1947, Lothrop $6.96).

3706. Freeman, Grace R., and Sugarman, Joan G. *Inside the Synagogue* (3–5). Illustrated. 1965, American Hebrew Cong $4.00. The present and past significance of various parts and areas of the synagogue.

3707. Gaer, Joseph. *How the Great Religions Began* (6–9). 1956, Dodd $6.00. A mature narrative that deals with the origins of the world's important religions.

3708. Greene, Laura. *I Am an Orthodox Jew* (2–4). Illus. by Lisa C. Wesson. 1979, Holt $5.95. What it means to be an Orthodox Jew is well described in this beautifully illustrated book.

3709. Haskins, James. *Religions* (6–9). 1973, Lippincott $7.95. The history, founders, and practices of 5 religions—Buddhism, Christianity, Hinduism, Islam and Judaism—are described in this introductory survey.

3710. Lathrop, Dorothy P., ed. *Animals of the Bible* (1–3). Illus. by Editor. 1969, Lippincott $8.95. A picture book with suitable accompanying text from the King James version. Caldecott Medal, 1938.

3711. Moskin, Marietta D. *In Search of God: The Story of Religion* (6–9). Illustrated. 1979, Atheneum $10.95. An account that explores the many ways men and women have searched for a meaning to life.

3712. Naylor, Phyllis Reynolds. *An Amish Family* (6–9). Illus. by George Armstrong. 1975, O'Hara $5.95; LB $5.97. In a story concentrating on 3 generations of an Amish family, the author tells about the beliefs, problems, and way of life of this religious sect.

3713. Rice, Edward. *The Five Great Religions* (6–9). Illus. by author. 1973, Four Winds $9.95. A mature account of the origins and practices of the 5 major world religions.

3714. Rice, Edward. *Ten Religions of the East* (6–9). Illustrated. 1978, Four Winds $7.95. The history and principal teachers of 10 Eastern faiths, including some, such as Cao Dai and Bon, rarely written about.

3715. Rossel, Seymour. *The First Book of Judaism* (5–7). Illustrated. 1976, Watts $4.90. A clear introduction to various aspects of Judaism and its many subdivisions.

3716. Seeger, Elizabeth. *Eastern Religions* (6–8). Illustrated. 1973, Crowell $10.00. The lives and teachings of Buddha, Confucius, and Lao-tse are highlighted in this well-organized valuable account.

3717. Serage, Nancy. *The Prince Who Gave Up a Throne* (4–6). Illus. by Kazue Mizumura. 1966, Crowell $7.95. The life of Buddha and the meanings of his teachings.

3718. Synge, Ursula. *The Giant at the Ford* (6–8). Illus. by Shirley Felts. 1980, Atheneum $8.95. A retelling of several legends associated with the lives of the saints.

3719. Terrien, Samuel. *The Golden Bible Atlas* (4–7). Illustrated. 1957, Golden $7.95; LB $10.69. Colorful maps of the Holy Land, faithfully reproduced.

3720. Van de Wetering, Janwillem. *Little Owl: An Eightfold Buddhist Admonition* (5–7). Illus. by Marc Brown. 1978, Houghton $6.95. Each of the 8 basic Buddhist rules of life are examined in this simple introduction to this major religion.

3721. Yolen, Jane. *Simple Gifts: The Story of the Shakers* (5–7). Illus. by Betty Fraser. 1976, Viking $6.95. A brief account of the Shaker way of life.

Bible Stories

3722. Asimov, Isaac. *The Story of Ruth* (5–7). Illustrated. 1972, Doubleday $5.95. A detailed account that gives much background information about the customs of the time.

3723. Banks, Lynne Reid. *Sarah and After: Five Women Who Founded a Nation* (6–8). 1977, Doubleday $6.95. Five Biblical women spanning the generations from Abraham to Joseph are portrayed convincingly.

3724. Bishop, Claire Huchet. *Yeshu Called Jesus* (4–6). Illus. by Don Bolognese. 1966, Farrar $3.95. A simple account of Jesus's life with material on his childhood.

3725. Bollinger, Max. *Joseph* (4–7). 1969, Delacorte $4.95. The story of the Biblical leader who brought his people to Egypt.

3726. Bollinger, Max, ed. *Noah and the Rainbow: An Ancient Story* (K–3). Trans. by Clyde Robert Bulla. Illus. by Helga Aichinger. 1972, Crowell $7.95; paper $2.95. Handsome illustrations and rhythmic text are used most effectively in this interpretation of the Bible story of the Flood.

3727. Brodsky, Beverly. *Jonah: An Old Testament Story* (K–3). Illus. by author. 1977, Lippincott $8.95. A first-person narrative stunningly illustrated.

3728. Bulla, Clyde Robert. *Jonah and the Great Fish* (2–5). Illus. by Helga Aichinger. 1970, Crowell $7.95. A beautiful version of this ageless biblical favorite.

3729. Cohen, Barbara. *The Binding of Isaac* (2–4). Illus. by Charles Mikolaycak. 1978, Lothrop $6.95. Isaac, as an old man, tells the story of himself and Abraham.

3730. Cohen, Barbara. *I Am Joseph* (3–4). Illus. by Charles Mikolaycak. 1980, Lothrop $9.95; LB $9.55. The story of the biblical Joseph in simple, dignified text and color pencil drawings.

3731. De La Mare, Walter, ed. *Stories from the Bible* (5–8). Illus. by Edward Ardizzone. 1961, Knopf $8.99. This is based on the first 9 books of the Old Testament, King James version.

3732. Doane, Pelagie, ed. *A Small Child's Bible* (K–4). Illus. by Editor. 1946, Walck $6.95. Seventy Bible stories retold in color.

3733. Farber, Norma. *A Ship in a Storm on the Way to Tarshish* (1–3). Illus. by Victoria Chess. 1977, Greenwillow $7.25; LB $6.96. A brilliant adaptation of 2 chapters from the Book of Jonah.

3734. Farber, Norma. *Where's Gomer?* (K–3). Illus. by William Pene du Bois. 1974, Dutton $8.50. Gomer, son of Japheth, son of Noah, is missing when it is time to board the ark.

3735. Graham, Lorenz. *David He No Fear* (K–3). Illus. by Ann Grifalconi. 1971, Crowell $6.89. A humorous, colloquial version of the story of David and Goliath, told with great charm by an African storyteller.

3736. Graham, Lorenz. *God Wash the World and Start Again* (2–5). Illus. by Clare Ross. 1971, Crowell $6.95; LB $6.89. The familiar Bible story of Noah told in the African idiom.

3737. Haley, Gail E. *Noah's Ark* (K–1). Illus. by author. 1971, Atheneum $8.95. A modern Noah collects 2 of all animals for his ark, but leaves out the ostrich.

3738. Hutton, Warwick. *Noah and the Great Flood* (1–3). Illus. by author. 1977, Atheneum $7.95. The version of the Flood from the King James Bible is excellently illustrated by a master artist.

3739. Jones, Jessie O., ed. *Small Rain: Verses from the Bible* (4–7). Illus. by Elizabeth Orton Jones. 1943, Penguin paper $.95. Some of the most moving passages from the King James version, selected for young children and beautifully illustrated.

3740. L'Engle, Madeleine. *Ladder of Angels: Scenes from the Bible* (5–8). Illustrated. 1979, Seabury $17.50. Sixty-five Old Testament stories are retold with illustrations by children from 26 countries.

3741. Maury, Jean W., ed. *First Bible* (4–7). Illus. by Helen Sewell. 1934, Walck $8.95. The words of King James version are used in telling these favorite stories.

3742. Nash, Ogden. *The Cruise of the Aardvark* (3–5). Illus. by Wendy Watson. 1967, Evans $3.95. The sea cruise taken by the aardvark turns out to be the voyage with Noah in this rhyming story.

3743. Petersham, Maud, and Petersham, Miska. *David: From the Story Told in the First Book of Samuel and the First Book of Kings* (3–5). Illus. by author. 1967, Macmillan $4.95. A lovely retelling of the story of the boy who slew Goliath.

3744. Petersham, Maud, and Petersham, Miska. *Joseph and His Brothers* (4–6). Illus. by author. 1958, Macmillan $4.95. Colorful illustrations enhance this story from the Old Testament.

3745. Proddow, Penelope. *Art Tells a Story: The Bible* (4–9). Illustrated. 1979, Doubleday $6.95; LB $7.90. Bible stories are represented through the work of famous artists.

3746. Reed, Gwendolyn E. *Adam and Eve* (1–3). Illus. by Helen Siegl. 1968, Lothrop $6.96. The creation story and life in the Garden of Eden are recreated with dignity.

3747. Singer, Isaac Bashevis. *The Wicked City* (4–8). Illus. by Leonard Everett Fisher. 1972, Farrar $6.95. An unusual retelling of the story of Lot in Sodom from the book of Genesis.

3748. Spier, Peter, illus. *Noah's Ark* (PS–K). 1977, Doubleday $6.95. Vital, humorous detailed pictures present a panorama of the animals and their voyage in the Ark. Caldecott Medal, 1977.

3749. Turner, Philip. *Brian Wildsmith's Bible Stories* (2–6). Illus. by Brian Wildsmith. 1969, Watts $8.90; paper $5.95. Beautiful illustrations and a text that gives a consecutive narrative of the Old and New Testament Bible stories make this an outstanding book.

3750. Wahl, Jan. *Runaway Jonah and Other Tales* (1–4). Illus. by Uri Shulevitz. 1968, Macmillan $3.95. Jonah, Daniel, Noah's Ark, David and Goliath, and Joseph and His Brothers—each story has been abridged and adapted for the youngest children.

3751. Weil, Lisl. *The Very First Story Ever Told* (PS–2). Illus. by author. 1976, Atheneum $7.95. The Genesis account of creation retold in simple text and pictures.

Nativity

3752. Aichinger, Helga. *The Shepherd* (K–3). Illus. by author. 1967, Crowell $7.95. A Nativity story with strong, primitive illustrations to match the compelling force and purity of the reverence that illuminates the simple text.

3753. Baker, Laura N. *Friendly Beasts* (PS–2). Illus. by Nicolas Sidjakov. 1957, Parnassus $4.95. The story of the animals that waited in wonder in the Bethlehem stable for the Christ Child's birth.

3754. Brown, Margaret Wise. *Christmas in the Barn* (PS–1). Illus. by Barbara Cooney. 1952, Crowell $7.95; LB $7.89. A beautiful retelling of the Nativity story with effective illustrations.

3755. de Paola, Thomas, ed. *The Christmas Pageant* (K–2). Illus. by author. 1978, Winston $5.95. A simple introduction to the Nativity story.

3756. Graham, Lorenz. *Every Man Heart Lay Down* (2–5). Illus. by Colleen Browning. 1970, Crowell $6.95. The story of the Nativity as told in an African folk idiom.

3757. Gregorowski, Christopher. *Why a Donkey Was Chosen* (1–3). Illus. by Caroline Browne. 1976, Doubleday $5.95. A Christmas story about a donkey who thinks he is unworthy of carrying people until he is chosen to bear Mary, the mother of Jesus.

3758. Hoffmann, Felix. *The Story of Christmas: A Picture Book* (K–3). Illus. by author. 1975, Atheneum $6.95. Beautiful lithographic illustrations portraying the story of the Nativity.

3759. Hurd, Edith Thacher. *Christmas Eve* (PS–2). Illus. by Clement Hurd. 1962, Harper $6.95; LB $6.89. Picture story of the traditional animals' Christmas Eve.

3760. Kurelek, William. *A Northern Nativity: Christmas Dreams of a Prairie Boy* (1–3). Illustrated. 1976, Tundra $7.95. Twenty paintings of the Holy Family transferred to various locales, accompanied by a lyrical text.

3761. Miyoshi, Sekiya. *The Christmas Lamb* (PS–3). Illustrated. 1979, Dawne-Leigh $8.95; paper $5.95. A timid lamb is coaxed into visiting the manger by a cherub.

3762. Petersham, Maud, and Petersham, Miska. *The Christ Child: As Told by Matthew and Luke* (K–3). Illustrated. 1931, Doubleday $7.95. With outstanding illustrations, this story uses direct quotations from the Bible.

3763. Slaughter, Jean, comp. *And It Came to Pass: Bible Verse and Carols* (K–4). Illus. by Leonard Weisgard. 1971, Macmillan $4.95. Story of the Nativity told in Bible verses and appropriate carols.

Prayers

3764. Field, Rachel. *Prayer for a Child* (1–3). Illus. by Elizabeth Orton Jones. 1944, Macmillan $5.95. A prayer bespeaking the faith, hope, and love of little children. Caldecott Medal, 1945.

3765. Ingzel, Marjorie, ed. *Table Graces for the Family* (4–6). 1964, Nelson paper $1.95. A small book of graces from various Protestant sources.

3766. Tudor, Tasha. *First Prayers* (K–3). Illus. by author. 1952, Walck $2.95. A small-sized, simple book with prayers for different times of the day. Also use: *First Graces* (1955, Walck $2.95).

3767. Vipont, Elfrida, ed. *Bless This Day: A Book of Prayer for Children* (2–5). Illus. by Harold Jones. 1958, Harcourt $5.95. A varied and rich collection of brief prayers divided into 4 categories—prayers for working, for bedtime, for thanksgiving, and of praise.

3768. Yates, Elizabeth. *Your Prayers and Mine* (6–9). Illus. by Nora S. Unwin. 1954, Houghton $3.95. A collection of prayers from many different religions and periods of history.

Holidays and Holy Days

General and Miscellaneous

3769. Barth, Edna. *Shamrocks, Harps and Shillelaghs: The Story of St. Patrick's Day Symbols* (3–5). Illus. by Ursula Arndt. 1977, Seabury $8.95. Customs and symbols associated with St. Patrick's Day, with the origin of each explained.

3770. Bulla, Clyde Robert. *Washington's Birthday* (1–4). Illus. by Don Bolognese. 1967, Crowell $6.89. In addition to a brief biography, this book tells of the many ways Washington's birthday is celebrated.

3771. Bunting, Eve. *St. Patrick's Day in the Morning* (PS–2). Illus. by Jan Brett. 1980, Houghton $7.95. A story about how a young boy celebrates St. Patrick's Day.

3772. Burnett, Bernice. *The First Book of Holidays* (4–7). 1974, Watts $4.90. Brief backgrounds on many holidays, foreign and domestic.

3773. Cantwell, Mary. *St. Patrick's Day* (1–3). Illus. by Ursula Arndt. 1967, Crowell $6.89. The life of St. Patrick and how his day is celebrated around the world.

3774. Cavanah, Frances, and Pannell, Lucille., eds. *Holiday Round Up* (4–8). Illus. by Elsie J. McCorkell. 1968, Macrae $6.97. Fifty-two stories covering 27 holidays for children of every denomination.

3775. Cheng, Hou-tien. *The Chinese New Year* (K–3). 1976, Holt $5.50. Various facets and meanings of the cycle of animal signs and the festivities surrounding the celebration of the Chinese New Year.

3776. Cole, Ann, et al. *A Pumpkin in a Pear Tree: Creative Ideas for Twelve Months of Holiday Fun* (4–7). Illus. by Debby Young. 1976, Little $7.95; paper $4.95. Games and other activities for various holidays.

3777. Dobler, Lavinia. *Customs and Holidays around the World* (5–8). Illus. by Josephine Little. 1962, Fleet $6.50. Survey of holidays arranged by season, with a detailed index for specific holidays.

3778. Eisner, Vivienne. *Quick and Easy Holiday Costumes* (3–6). Illus. by Carolyn Bentley. 1977, Lothrop $6.96. Plans for over 60 costumes are given representing 23 holidays.

3779. Epstein, Sam, and Epstein, Beryl. *Spring Holidays* (4–6). Illus. by Ted Schroeder. 1964, Garrard $4.90. A simple description of various spring holidays, such as April Fool's Day and Groundhog Day.

3780. Fenner, Phyllis, ed. *Feasts and Frolics* (5–8). Illus. by Helen R. Durney. 1964, Knopf $5.69. A fine collection of stories that deal with a variety of holidays.

3781. Fisher, Aileen. *Holiday Programs for Boys and Girls* (4–7). 1970, Plays $9.95. A collection of plays, poetry, and prose useful for holiday celebrations. Also use: *Creative Plays and Programs for Holidays* by Rowena Bennett (1966, Plays $9.95).

3782. Fisher, Aileen, and Rabe, Olive. *Human Rights Day* (1–3). Illus. by Lisl Weil. 1966, Crowell $6.89. Many milestones in the human fight for freedom—from the Magna Carta to the U.N. Declaration of Human Rights.

3783. Gaer, Joseph. *Holidays around the World* (6–9). Illus. by Anne Marie Jauss. 1953, Little $5.95. An account of the origin and observance of holidays in the Buddhist, Jewish, Hindu, Christian, and Muslim religions. Last chapter concerns United Nations Day. Also use: *The Book of Holidays* (1940, 1958, Crowell $8.95).

3784. Graves, Charles P. *Fourth of July* (2–5). Illus. by Ken Wagner. 1963, Garrard $4.90. Interesting descriptions of the many patriotic symbols associated with this day.

3785. Groh, Lynn. *New Year's Day* (1–3). Illus. by Leonard Shortall. 1964, Garrard $4.90. How and why New Year's Day is celebrated all over the world.

3786. Janice. *Little Bear's New Year's Party* (PS–K). Illus. by Mariana. 1973, Lothrop $6.00. Little Bear and his friends have never been invited to a New Year's party and decide to have one of their own. It's a great success, even though many more guests arrive than were invited.

3787. Larrick, Nancy. *Poetry for Holidays* (4–6). Illus. by Kelly Oechsli. 1966, Garrard $4.20. A variety of poems describing 10 well-known holidays, including a birthday.

3788. Livingston, Myra Cohn, ed. *Callooh! Callay! Holiday Poems for Young Readers* (4–6). Illus. by Janet Stevens. 1978, Atheneum $7.95. A lovely collection of poems about holidays and anniversaries.

3789. Livingston, Myra Cohn, ed. *O Frabjous Day! Poetry for Holidays and Special Occasions* (5–8). 1977, Atheneum $7.95. A splendid anthology arranged by headings "To Honor," "To Celebrate," and "To Remember" rather than the conventional chronological approach.

3790. Manning-Sanders, Ruth, ed. *Festivals* (3–6). Illus. by Raymond Briggs. 1973, Dutton $7.25. An anthology of prose and poetry arranged chronologically by monthly holidays. A month-by-month account of the world's most famous holidays as seen through the eyes of famous writers.

3791. Parish, Peggy. *Let's Celebrate: Holiday Decorations You Can Make* (2–4). Illus. by Lynn Sweat. 1976, Greenwillow $5.71. Simple instructions for making holiday decorations, many from paper.

3792. Parlin, John. *Patriots' Days* (5–7). Illus. by Robert Doremus. 1964, Garrard $4.90. The lives of 6 famous Americans from Washington to Kennedy.

3793. Phelan, Mary Kay. *Election Day* (1–3). Illus. by Robert Quackenbush. 1967, Crowell $6.95; LB $6.89. An account of the voting process in America and how it culminates in Election Day.

3794. Phelan, Mary Kay. *The Fourth of July* (1–3). Illus. by Symeon Shimin. 1966, Crowell $6.89. The origins of the Declaration of Independence and information on its signers.

3795. Phelan, Mary Kay. *Mother's Day* (1–3). Illus. by Aliki. 1965, Crowell $6.89. A brief history of this holiday from its origins to its spread around the world.

3796. Quackenbush, Robert, ed. *The Holiday Song Book* (3–7). Illus. by Editor. 1977, Lothrop $9.95; LB $9.55. Over 100 songs arranged under various holidays.

3797. Rabe, Olive. *United Nations Day* (1–3). Illus. by Aliki. 1965, Crowell $5.95; LB $6.89. The significance of this day is explained through a description of the United Nations and its work.

3798. Sechrist, Elizabeth H., and Woolsey, Janette. *Red Letter Days: A Book of Holiday Customs* (5–8). 1940; 1965, Macrae $6.67; LB $6.47. An in-

teresting account of the origins of important holidays and how they are celebrated. Also use: *Poems for Red Letter Days* (1951, Macrae $5.97).

3799. Showers, Paul. *Columbus Day* (1–3). 1965, Crowell $6.89. The beginnings of this national holiday and how it is celebrated today.

3800. Tudor, Tasha. *Tasha Tudor's Sampler: A Tale for Easter/Pumpkin Moonshine/The Dolls' Christmas* (PS–3). 1977, McKay $7.95. Three holiday stories originally published separately in 1938, 1941, and 1950.

3801. Tudor, Tasha. *A Time to Keep* (PS–3). Illus. by author. 1977, Rand $6.95; LB $6.97. Subtitled The Tasha Tudor Book of Holidays; the author reminisces about her family's New England festivities.

Christmas

3802. Barth, Edna. *Holly, Reindeer and Colored Lights: The Story of the Christmas Symbols* (3–6). Illus. by Ursula Arndt. 1971, Seabury $7.95. Christmas and its symbols from around the world.

3803. Cooney, Barbara. *Christmas* (2–4). Illus. by author. 1967, Crowell LB $6.39. A serene and joyful book about Christmas, its background, and significance.

3804. Foley, Daniel J. *Christmas the World Over* (4–6). Illus. by Charlotte Edmands Bowden. 1963, Chilton $10.00. How Christmas is celebrated in North and South America, Europe, and Asia.

3805. Patterson, Lillie. *Christmas Feasts and Festivals* (3–4). Illus. by Cliff Schule. 1968, Garrard $4.90. A simple account of many ways in which Christmas is celebrated and how these customs originated.

3806. Sawyer, Ruth. *Joy to the World: Christmas Legends* (3–6). Illus. by Trina Schart Hyman. 1966, Little $5.95. Legends from Arabia, Serbia, Ireland, and Spain, accompanied by a Christmas carol for each of the 6 stories.

3807. Sechrist, Elizabeth H. *Christmas Everywhere* (3–6). 1962, Macrae $6.75; LB $6.71. Tales of Christmas celebrations and activities in some 40 countries.

3808. Sechrist, Elizabeth H., and Woolsey, Janette. *It's Time for Christmas* (4–8). 1959, Macrae $6.50; LB $5.97. Traditional Christmas tales, history of carols, various customs, and more.

3809. Spicer, Dorothy Gladys. *Forty-Six Days of Christmas* (4–7). Illus. by Anne Marie Jauss. 1960,

Coward $4.99. In a chronological arrangement, the author describes Christmas celebrations in Europe and Asia from December 4 to January 18.

3810. Stevens, Patricia Bunning. *Merry Christmas! A History of the Holiday* (6–9). Illustrated. 1979, Macmillan $8.95. An examination of both historical and contemporary customs associated with this holiday in various countries.

3811. Tudor, Tasha, ed. *Take Joy: The Tasha Tudor Christmas Book* (1–6). Illus. by Editor. 1966, Collins $9.95; LB $9.91. An anthology of Christmas stories, poems, carols, lore, and legend carefully selected and lovingly illustrated.

3812. Wernecke, H. H., ed. *Celebrating Christmas around the World* (4–6). 1962, Westminster $5.95. A collection of the origins of the most important ways of celebrating Christmas.

Fiction

3813. Adams, Adrienne. *The Christmas Party* (1–3). Illus. by author. 1978, Scribner $7.95. An Easter egg bunny helps prepare for a Christmas party.

3814. Adshead, Gladys L. *Brownies—It's Christmas* (K–3). Illus. by Velma Ilsley. 1955, Walck $5.50; paper $1.95. How the playful brownies are rewarded for their kindness and receive their own Christmas tree.

3815. Alden, Raymond. *Why the Chimes Rang* (4–7). Illus. by Rafaello Busoni. 1954, Bobbs-Merrill $6.95. An anthology of 11 tales, some about Christmas.

3816. Andersen, Hans Christian. *The Fir Tree* (2–4). Illus. by Nancy E. Burkert. 1970, Harper $8.95; LB $8.79. Exquisitely detailed color pictures add distinction to this favorite Christmas story.

3817. Association for Childhood Education, eds. *Told under the Christmas Tree* (4–7). Illus. by Maud Petersham and Miska Petersham. 1948, Macmillan $6.95. An anthology of Christmas stories and verse, including 14 Hanukkah stories.

3818. Bach, Alice. *The Day after Christmas* (K–2). Illus. by Mary Chalmers. 1975, Harper $6.89. The day after Christmas is a letdown for 7-year-old Emily—just an ordinary day, with no more presents.

3819. Bladow, Suzanne. *The Midnight Flight of Moose, Mops and Marvin* (2–4). Illus. by Joseph Mathieu. 1975, McGraw $5.95. Three mice are accidental stowaways on Santa's Christmas ride.

3820. Bolognese, Don. *A New Day* (PS–2). 1970, Delacorte $4.95; LB $4.58. A migrant worker's family becomes the Holy Family in this reworking of the Nativity.

3821. Bonsall, Crosby N. *Twelve Bells for Santa* (1–3). Illustrated. 1977, Harper $5.95; LB $6.89. When Santa disappears, 3 children start out for the North Pole to find him, in this easily read book.

3822. Briggs, Raymond. *Father Christmas* (K–3). 1973, Coward $4.95; Penguin paper $1.50. Christmas Eve, as Santa sees it, is pictured by the author-artist (winner of the Kate Greenaway Medal) in full-color, comic-strip style. Also use: *Father Christmas Goes on a Holiday* (1975, Coward $6.95; 1977, Penguin, paper $1.50).

3823. Bright, Robert. *Georgie's Christmas Carol* (K–2). 1975, Doubleday $6.95. Georgie, the friendly ghost, organizes an unusual Christmas surprise for 2 children and their uncle, gloomy Mr. Glooms, who has never celebrated Christmas before.

3824. Carroll, Ruth. *Christmas Kitten* (K–3). Illustrated. 1970, Walck $5.95. A home-seeking kitten finally finds acceptance.

3825. Caudill, Rebecca. *A Certain Small Shepherd* (3–6). Illus. by William Pene du Bois. 1965, Holt $6.95; paper $1.95. A little mute boy gets an opportunity to play one of the shepherds in a Christmas pageant. Also use: *A Pocketful of Cricket* (1964, Holt $5.95; paper $1.95).

3826. Chalmers, Mary. *Merry Christmas, Harry* (PS–2). Illus. by author. 1977, Harper $3.95; LB $4.79. Harry, a small cat, asks Santa for a kitten.

3827. Dalgliesh, Alice. *Christmas: A Book of Stories Old and New* (4–7). Illus. by Hildegard Woodward. 1962, Scribner $6.95. A standard collection of stories and poems that have delighted children for years.

3828. De Angeli, Marguerite. *The Lion in the Box* (4–6). Illus. by author. 1975, Doubleday $5.95. The 5 children in the poor, fatherless Scher family prepare for Christmas in this novel set in turn-of-the-century New York.

3829. De Bosschere, Jean, and Morris, M. C. *Christmas Tales of Flanders* (2–5). Illustrated. 1972, Peter Smith $5.00. A good presentation of holiday stories.

3830. de Paola, Tomie, ed. *The Clown of God* (K–3). Illus. by author. 1978, Harcourt $8.95. On Christmas Eve, a juggler gives to a statue of Christ his only possession, the gift of his art.

3831. Duvoisin, Roger. *Petunia's Christmas* (K–3). Illus. by author. 1952, Knopf $5.99. Petunia, the beloved goose, decides to rescue Charles, a gander, destined for a Christmas dinner table.

3832. Eaton, Ann Thaxter, ed. *The Animals' Christmas* (2–5). Illus. by Valenti Angelo. 1944, Viking $5.95. Poems and stories relating the Christmas legend to animals.

3833. Erickson, Russell E. *Warton's Christmas Eve Adventure* (2–4). Illus. by Lawrence Di Fiori. 1977, Lothrop $6.25; LB $6.00. Warton's attempts to fill the hours until he can open his Christmas presents lead to some exciting adventures.

3834. Estes, Eleanor. *The Coat-Hanger Christmas Tree* (4–6). Illus. by author. 1973, Atheneum $7.95. Marianna and her brother decide on a substitute when their mother forbids them to have a Christmas tree.

3835. Ets, Marie Hall, and Labastida, Aurora. *Nine Days to Christmas* (K–2). Illustrated. 1959, Viking $6.95. Kindergartner Ceci is old enough to have her first posado—one of the 9 special parties held in Mexico, one a day preceding the day of Christmas. Caldecott Medal.

3836. Foreman, Michael. *Winter's Tales* (1–3). Illus. by Friere Wright. 1979, Doubleday $7.95; LB $8.90. Six stories involving the celebration of Christmas.

3837. Francoise. *Noel for Jeanne-Marie* (PS). Illus. by author. 1953, Scribner $7.95. Charming picture story involving a little pet sheep and a pair of wooden shoes.

3838. Goodall, John S., illus. *An Edwardian Christmas* (K–3). 1978, Atheneum $7.95. A wordless book about celebrating Christmas during Edwardian times.

3839. Hall, Rosalys Haskall. *The Three Begger Kings* (K–3). Illus. by Kurt Werth. 1974, Random $4.95; LB $5.99. An old German setting is used in this story of a young boy's participation in the celebration of Epiphany.

3840. Harper, Wilhelmina. *Merry Christmas to You: Stories for Christmas* (4–7). Illus. by Fermin Rocker. 1965, Dutton $7.95. Many old favorites are included in this wonderful collection of stories and poems.

3841. Hays, Wilma Pitchford. *Christmas on the Mayflower* (3–5). Illus. by Roger Duvoisin. 1956, Coward $4.99. Giles, a young boy on the *Mayflower*, is about to go ashore and gather presents for Christmas.

3842. Haywood, Carolyn. *Merry Christmas from Betsy* (3–4). Illus. by author. 1970, Morrow $6.96.

Chiefly excerpts from other Betsy books that deal with Christmas.

3843. Henry, O. *The Gift of the Magi* (6–8). Illus. by Shelley Freshman. 1978, Bobbs-Merrill $5.95. The familiar story of marital sacrifice with unusual illustrations.

3844. Hoban, Lillian. *Arthur's Christmas Cookies* (1–2). Illus. by author. 1972, Harper $5.95; LB $6.89. What can Arthur give his parents for Christmas? Christmas cookies such as he learned to bake in Cub Scouts are the answer, but a hilarious mixup occurs when salt is used instead of sugar.

3845. Hoban, Russell. *Emmet Otter's Jug-Band Christmas* (K–3). Illus. by Lillian Hoban. 1971, Parents $3.95; LB $3.99. Emmet Otter and his ma just manage to scrape along—by taking in laundry and doing odd jobs—but still manage to have the "best Christmas ever."

3846. Hoban, Russell. *The Mole Family's Christmas* (K–3). Illus. by Lillian Hoban. 1969, Parents $5.95; LB $5.41. A mole family receives a telescope for Christmas with amazing and amusing results.

3847. Hodges, Cyril Walter. *Plain Lane Christmas* (4–7). Illus. by author. 1978, Coward $7.95. An unusual Christmas pageant helps save the buildings on Plain Lane from demolition.

3848. Hoff, Syd. *Santa's Moose* (K–3). Illus. by author. 1979, Harper $6.89. Milton, a big clumsy moose, helps Santa one Christmas.

3849. Holm, Maylin Mack. *A Forest Christmas* (PS–K). Illus. by author. 1977, Harper $5.95; LB $5.79. A group of forest rodents gather at Mrs. Rabbit's house to celebrate Christmas.

3850. Hutchins, Pat. *The Silver Christmas Tree* (PS–K). 1974, Macmillan $6.95. Squirrel decorates his tree as a gift for his friends at Christmas.

3851. Irion, Ruth Hershey. *The Christmas Cookie Tree* (3–5). Illus. by author. 1976, Westminster $6.95. A slight but tender story of a young girl's experiences in a new home in Pennsylvania Dutch country immediately before Christmas.

3852. Janice. *Little Bear's Christmas* (PS–K). Illus. by Mariana. 1964, Lothrop $6.00. Little Bear's Christmas Eve trip with Santa and the surprise party that awaits his homecoming.

3853. Johnson, Lois S. *Christmas Stories Round the World* (3–5). Illus. by David K. Stone. 1970, Rand paper $2.95. Twelve enchanting stories from different countries, each prefaced by a description of how Christmas is celebrated there.

3854. Johnston, Tony. *Little Mouse Nibbling* (PS–K). Illus. by Diane Stanley. 1979, Putnam $7.95. A shy mouse, a cricket, and 3 carolers share a Christmas together.

3855. Joslin, Sesyle. *Baby Elephant and the Secret Wishes* (3–6). 1962, Harcourt $6.50. Baby elephant makes Christmas presents for the family that they really want.

3856. Kahl, Virginia. *Plum Pudding for Chirstmas* (K–3). Illus. by author. 1956, Scribner $8.95. The king accepts an invitation to Christmas dinner "if you serve a pudding and that pudding is plum."

3857. Kent, Jack. *Jack Kent's Twelve Days of Christmas* (K–3). Illustrated. 1973, Parents $5.95; LB $5.41. A small boy showers a little girl with a partridge in a pear tree and all the ensuing gifts mentioned in the traditional carol, much to her delight at first and then to her frantic consternation.

3858. Kraus, Robert. *How Spider Saved Christmas* (K–3). Illustrated. 1970, Dutton paper $1.25. Spider spends Christmas with Fly and Ladybug and helps out in a most unusual way.

3859. Kroeber, Theodora. *A Green Christmas* (K–3). Illus. by John Larrecq. 1967, Parnassus $5.95; LB $4.98. Children new to California discover that Santa Claus will visit places without snow.

3860. Kroll, Steven. *Santa's Crash-Bang Christmas* (K–3). Illus. by Tomie de Paola. 1977, Holiday $6.95. Santa's blunderings are graciously repaired by his faithful elf Gerald.

3861. Lindgren, Astrid. *Christmas in Noisy Village* (K–2). Illus. by Ilon Wikland. 1964, Viking $6.50. Children of 3 neighboring farms share the joys of Christmas in a Swedish setting.

3862. Lindgren, Astrid. *Christmas in the Stable* (PS–2). Illus. by Harald Wiberg. 1962, Coward $5.89; LB $2.50; Putnam paper $2.50. A mother tells her child the story of the birth of Jesus, and the child projects the tale into her own present-day farm-life setting.

3863. Low, Joseph. *The Christmas Grump* (PS–3). Illus. by author. 1977, Atheneum $6.95. A Scrooge-like mouse is transformed by the kindness of Santa Claus.

3864. MacKellar, William. *The Silent Bells* (4–6). Illus. by Ted Lewin. 1978, Dodd $5.95. A charming Christmas story set in Switzerland.

3865. Menotti, Gian-Carlo. *Amahl and the Night Visitors* (4–6). Illus. by Roger Duvoisin. 1952, McGraw $6.95. The story of a crippled boy who entertained the Wise Men on their way to Bethlehem.

3866. Miller, Edna. *Mousekin's Christmas Eve* (K–3). Illus. by author. 1965, Prentice-Hall $5.95; paper $1.50. Mousekin finds a new home and visits a stable where a baby sleeps in a manger.

3867. Moeri, Louise. *Star Mother's Youngest Child* (PS–2). Illus. by Trina Schart. 1975, Houghton $3.95. An old woman and a star child celebrate Christmas.

3868. Paterson, Katherine. *Angels and Other Strangers: Family Christmas Stories* (5–8). 1979, Crowell $7.95. Nine stories that explore various meanings of Christmas and what it should represent to people.

3869. Raskin, Ellen. *Twenty-Two, Twenty-Three* (K–3). Illus. by author. 1976, Atheneum $7.95. The author concocts a holiday message "Merry Christmas," with nonsensically dressed animals.

3870. Rettich, Margret. *The Silver Touch and Other Family Christmas Stories* (4–6). Trans. from the German by Elizabeth D. Crawford. Illus. by Rolf Rettich. 1978, Morrow $6.95; LB $6.67. Several short stories about the joys and excitement of Christmas.

3871. Robinson, Barbara. *The Best Christmas Pageant Ever* (4–6). Illus. by Judith Gwyn Brown. 1972, Avon $5.95; LB $5.79; paper $1.50. When a family of unrestrained children take over the church Christmas pageant, the results are hilarious.

3872. Rock, Gail. *The House without a Christmas Tree* (4–6). Illus. by Charles C. Gehm. 1974, Knopf $4.95; LB $5.99; Bantam paper $1.75. A conflict between a father and daughter about having a Christmas tree.

3873. Rockwell, Anne. *Befana: A Christmas Story* (1–4). Illus. by author. 1974, Atheneum $6.95. The legend of Befana, a lonely old woman who sets out on Christmas night to see the newborn Christ in Bethlehem.

3874. Rollins, Charlemae, comp. *Christmas Gif* (4–6). Illus. by Tom O'Sullivan. 1963, Follett $7.95. Anthology of Christmas poems, songs, and stories, written by and about blacks.

3875. Sawyer, Ruth. *The Christmas Anna Angel* (2–5). Illus. by Kate Seredy. 1944, Viking $5.95. Christmas on a Hungarian farm with a little girl. Also use: *Maggie Rose: Her Birthday Christmas* (1952, Harper, LB $6.89).

3876. Seuss, Dr. *How the Grinch Stole Christmas* (K–3). Illus. by author. 1957, Random $4.95; LB

$5.99. A rhyming book about a queer creature, the Grinch, who plans to do away with Christmas.

3877. Thayer, Jane. *The Puppy Who Wanted a Boy* (K–3). Illus. by Seymour Fleishman. 1958, Morrow $6.48. A lonely puppy wanted a boy for Christmas more than anything else in the world and got 50 when he reached the orphan home.

3878. Theroux, Paul. *A Christmas Card* (5–8). Illus. by John Lawrence. 1978, Houghton $6.95. A magical Christmas card adds charm to this story of a family lost in a snowstorm.

3879. Tudor, Tasha. *Becky's Christmas* (1–4). Illus. by author. 1961, Viking $5.95. All the fun of preparing for Christmas—baking cookies, wrapping gifts, trimming the tree—and, at the end, a surprise for Becky. Also use: *The Doll's Christmas* (1950, Walck $5.95; paper $2.25).

3880. Uttley, Alison. *Stories for Christmas* (4–6). Illus. by Gavin Rowe. 1977, Merrimack $7.95. A selection of 12 stories about old-fashioned Christmas celebrations, culled from the anthologies of this prolific English author.

3881. Van Leeuwen, Jean. *The Great Christmas Kidnapping Caper* (3–5). Illus. by Steven Kellogg. 1975, Dial $7.95; LB $7.47. A group of mice who live in a dollhouse at Macy's solve the mystery of the disappearance of Santa Claus.

3882. Wells, Rosemary. *Morris's Disappearing Bag: A Christmas Story* (PS–K). Illustrated. 1975, Dial $5.95; LB $5.47; paper $1.95. Morris, a rabbit, finds one more present under the Christmas tree—a bag that makes him invisible, and then he becomes the envy of his brothers and sisters.

3883. Wenning, Elizabeth. *The Christmas Mouse* (PS–3). Illus. by Barbara Remington. 1959, Holt $5.95. Kaspar, the church mouse, plays a part in the first singing of "Silent Night" in a little Austrian village.

3884. Wiggin, Kate Douglas. *The Birds' Christmas Carol* (3–5). Illus. by Jessie Gillespie. 1941, Houghton $6.95; memorial ed. $9.95; Scholastic paper $.95. A beautiful edition of the story first published in 1888.

3885. Zakhoder, Boris. *How a Piglet Crashed the Christmas Party* (K–3). Illus. by Kurt Werth. 1971, Lothrop $6.96. Oinky, a clever, overly confident pig, goes to a school Christmas party disguised as a boy.

Crafts

3886. Coskey, Evelyn. *Christmas Crafts for Everyone* (6–9). Illus. by Roy Wallace. 1976, Abingdon $8.95. The projects, complete with explicit, step-by-step directions, are based on Christmas customs from various parts of the world.

3887. Cutler, Katherine N., and Bogle, Kate Cutler. *Crafts for Christmas* (3–7). Illus. by Jacqueline Aciato. 1974, Lothrop $6.48. All sorts of craft projects, including many gifts associated with Christmas.

3888. Glovach, Linda. *The Little Witch's Christmas Book* (3–5). Illustrated. 1974, Prentice-Hall $5.95. A pleasant, breezy presentation of simple projects, games, and recipes for the holiday season.

3889. Krahn, Fernando. *The Biggest Christmas Tree on Earth* (1–3). Illustrated. 1978, Little $5.95. A wordless picture book about decorating a Christmas tree.

3890. Meyer, Carolyn. *Christmas Crafts: Things to Make the 24 Days before Christmas* (5–8). Illus. by Anita Lobel. 1974, Harper $5.95; LB $6.89. Beginning with December 1, this attractive "how to" book gives instructions for each day, until the making of a chocolate Yule log on Christmas Eve.

3891. Pettit, Florence H. *Christmas All around the House: Traditional Decorations You Can Make* (6–9). Illus. by Wendy Watson. 1976, Crowell $12.95. Detailed illustrations help demonstrate these interesting simple projects from around the world. Also use: *December Decorations* by Peggy Parish (1975, Macmillan $6.95).

3892. Purdy, Susan. *Christmas Cookbook* (5–7). Illus. by author. 1976, Watts $6.90; paper $2.95. Although some of these recipes are intricate, the directions and allied material are clearly explained in a logical fashion.

3893. Purdy, Susan. *Christmas Decorations for You to Make* (4–7). 1965, Lippincott $8.95. Instructions are simple, materials readily available, and finished products look appropriately festive. Also use: *Christmas Gifts You Can Make* (1976, Lippincott $7.95; paper $4.95).

3894. Shoemaker, Kathryn E. *Creative Christmas; Simple Crafts from Many Lands* (4–6). Illustrated. 1978, Winston $5.59. Ideas for decorations, gifts, cards, and wrapping paper.

3895. Tichenor, Tom. *Christmas Tree Crafts* (6–7). Illustrated. 1975, Lippincott $7.95; paper $3.95. Easy-to-make ornaments that can be produced from readily available materials.

Music

3896. Davis, Katherine, and others. *The Little Drummer Boy* (K–2). Illus. by Ezra Jack Keats. 1968, Macmillan $7.95; paper $1.95. The lyrics of a modern Christmas song are enhanced by richly colored pictures.

3897. Domanska, Janina. *Din Dan Don, It's Christmas* (PS–3). Illus. by author. 1975, Greenwillow $7.25. The story of the first Christmas as told in this traditional Polish carol, stunningly illustrated with paintings that resemble a medieval illuminated manuscript.

3898. Horder, Mervyn. *On Christmas Day: First Carols to Play and Sing* (3–7). 1969, Macmillan $5.95. A fine collection of the most famous and beloved carols.

3899. Langstaff, John, comp. *The Season for Singing: American Christmas Songs and Carols* (all ages) Musical settings by Seymour Barak. 1974, Doubleday $7.95. Piano and guitar arrangements accompany this collection of American Christmas carols, which reflect the country's cultural diversity and heritage. Also use: *On Christmas Day in the Morning* (1959, Harcourt $5.95).

3900. Lobel, Adrianne. *A Small Sheep in a Pear Tree* (K–3). Illus. by author. 1977, Harper $6.95; LB $6.89. When the word sheep is substituted for the names of each of the gifts in "The Twelve Days of Christmas," an amusing new twist results.

3901. Seeger, Ruth C. *American Folk Songs for Christmas* (4–7). Illus. by Barbara Cooney. 1953, Doubleday $6.95; LB $5.95. More than 30 American folk songs that explore various facets of Christmas.

3902. Simon, Henry W. *A Treasury of Christmas Songs and Carols* (5–9). 1973, Houghton $9.95; paper $6.95. An excellent collection that spans many countries.

3903. Tudor, Tasha. *Tasha Tudor's Favorite Christmas Carols* (3–7). Illus. by Tasha Tudor and Linda Allen. 1978, McKay $7.95. Seventeen carols are included along with background stories and piano and guitar arrangements.

3904. Wildsmith, Brian. *Brian Wildsmith's The Twelve Days of Christmas* (2–5). Illus. by author. 1972, Watts $3.95; LB $4.90. With his usual dazzling color, Wildsmith pictures all the strange presents "my true love gave to me."

Plays

3905. Kamerman, Sylvia E., ed. *On Stage for Christmas* (3–7). 1978, Plays $10.95. Subtitle: *A Collection of Royalty Free One-Act Christmas Plays for Young People.*

3906. Preston, Carol. *A Trilogy of Christmas Plays for Children* (5–7). Illustrated. 1967, Harcourt $5.95. Three plays with music selected by John Langstaff that deal with different aspects of the Nativity.

3907. Langstaff, John. *Saint George and the Dragon: A Mummer's Play* (4–8). Illus. by David Gentleman. 1973, Atheneum $4.95. The text in play form plus advice on producing it are accompanied by striking illustrations.

Poetry

3908. Barth, Edna, ed. *A Christmas Feast: An Anthology of Poems, Sayings, Greetings and Wishes* (4–6). Illus. by Ursula Arndt. 1979, Houghton $9.95. A collection of Christmas poetry divided into 20 sections like "Christmas Is Coming" and "The Three Kings."

3909. Brewton, Sara, and Brewton, John E. *Christmas Bells Are Ringing* (4–7). Illus. by Decie Merwin. 1951, Macmillan $4.95. An old and well-respected treasury of poems.

3910. Clifton, Lucille. *Everett Anderson's Christmas Coming* (K–3). Illus. by Evaline Ness. 1971, Hall $3.95. A little black boy reveals his thoughts and feelings about Christmas in nice brief poems.

3911. Frost, Frances Mary. *Christmas in the Woods* (K–3). Illus. by Aldren Watson. 1976, Harper $3.50; LB $4.89. Reissue of a lovely poem, beautifully illustrated, about the animals in the woods on Christmas night.

3912. Hopkins, Lee Bennett. *Sing Hey for Christmas Day* (K–3). Illus. by Laura Jean Allen. 1975, Harcourt $4.75. A selection of short poems in celebration of the Christmas season.

3913. McGinley, Phyllis. *A Wreath of Christmas Legends* (5–8). Illus. by Leonard Weisgard. 1967, Macmillan $5.95; paper $.95. Some of the legendary miracles associated with the birth of Christ form the inspiration for excellent poetry displaying the grace and conveying the wonder of Christmas.

3914. McGinley, Phyllis. *The Year without a Santa Claus* (K–3). Illus. by Kurt Werth. 1947, Lippincott $8.95. A pleasant story-poem that tells what happens when Santa Claus declares he is too tired for Christmas.

3915. Moore, Clement. *The Night before Christmas* (PS–3). Illus. by Arthur Rackham. 1977, Doubleday $5.95. A lovely edition of this popular and loved Christmas poem.

3916. Moore, Clement. *A Visit from St. Nicholas: A Facsimile of the 1848 Edition* (K–6). Illus. by T. C. Boyd. 1971, Simon & Schuster $3.95. The classic edition of a perennial favorite.

3917. Thomas, Dylan. *A Child's Christmas in Wales* (5–9). Illus. by Fritz Eichenberg. 1959, New Directions $7.00; paper $2.95. A prose poem about the poet's childhood in a small Welsh village.

Easter

3918. Barth, Edna. *Lilies, Rabbits and Painted Eggs: The Story of the Easter Symbols* (3–6). Illus. by Ursula Arndt. 1970, Seabury $7.95. The pagan and Christian origins of many of the celebrations associated with Easter.

3919. Cole, Marion, and Cole, Olivia H. *Things to Make and Do for Easter* (3–4). 1979, Watts $6.90. Stories and projects about Easter.

3920. Coskey, Evelyn. *Easter Eggs for Everyone* (5–8). Illustrated. 1973, Abingdon $8.95. Directions for making and decorating Easter eggs, plus a description of the customs and games associated with them.

3921. Fisher, Aileen. *Easter* (3–5). Illus. by Ati Forberg. 1968, Crowell $6.89. Easter customs in the Christian faith, some secular, some religious.

3922. Hopkins, Lee Bennett, ed. *Easter Buds Are Springing* (2–4). Illus. by Tomie de Paola. 1979, Harcourt $5.95. A collection of 19 poems about various facets of Easter.

3923. Milhous, Katherine. *The Egg Tree* (PS–3). Illus. by author. 1950, Scribner $8.95. Winner of the Caldecott Medal, this picture book tells how to make a delightful Easter egg tree.

3924. Patterson, Lillie. *Easter* (3–5). Illus. by Kelly Oechsli. 1966, Garrard LB $4.90. A retelling of the Easter story, plus a description of how Easter is celebrated in various parts of the world.

3925. Sechrist, Elizabeth H., and Woolsey, Janette. *It's Time for Easter* (4–7). Illustrated. 1961, Macrae $8.50. Anthology of scriptural accounts, customs, legends, and stories of Easter music and poetry.

3926. Sockman, Ralph W. *The Easter Story for Children* (2–4). Illus. by Gordon Laite. 1966, Abingdon $4.95. A simple account of the events described in the Bible that are associated with Easter.

Fiction

3927. Adams, Adrienne. *The Easter Egg Artists* (PS–2). 1976, Scribner $7.95. A rabbit family paints 100 dozen eggs for Easter, helped greatly by the son's flair for comic design.

3928. Friedrich, Priscilla, and Friedrich, Otto. *The Easter Bunny That Overslept* (PS–1). Illus. by Adrienne Adams. 1957, Lothrop $7.25; LB $6.96. Santa Claus helps a tardy Easter bunny who has trouble getting up on time.

3929. Gackenbach, Dick. *Hattie, Tom and the Chicken Witch* (1–3). 1980, Harper $5.95; LB $6.89. A book that proves both chickens and rabbits are important to Easter.

3930. Harper, Wilhelmina. *Easter Chimes: Stories for Easter and the Spring Season* (3–5). Illus. by Hoot von Zitzewitz. 1965, Dutton $7.95. The celebration of Easter in many countries.

3931. Hazeltine, Alice I., and Smith, Elva. *The Easter Book of Legends and Stories* (4–6). Illus. by Pamela Bianco. 1947, Lothrop $7.44. Stories, poems, and a play for Easter.

3932. Heyward, DuBose. *The Country Bunny and the Little Gold Shoes* (K–3). Illus. by Marjorie Flack. 1939, Houghton $7.95; paper $2.45. Cottontail, the mother of 21 bunnies, finally realizes her great ambition to be an Easter bunny.

3933. Hoban, Lillian. *The Sugar Snow Spring* (PS–3). Illus. by author. 1973, Harper $5.95; LB $6.89. The Easter Bunny saves a mouse family hard pressed by an ever-watchful barn cat.

3934. Roser, Wiltrud. *Everything about Easter Rabbits* (K–3). Illus. by author. 1973, Crowell $7.95; LB $7.84. A nonsense book about all kinds of Easter rabbits, including the "Genuine, Original Easter Rabbit."

Halloween

3935. Barth, Edna. *Witches, Pumpkins and Grinning Ghosts: The Story of the Halloween Symbols* (3–6).

Illus. by Ursula Arndt. 1972, Seabury $7.95. The origins of Halloween and how it is celebrated in many countries.

3936. Borten, Helen. *Halloween* (1–3). Illus. by author. 1965, Crowell LB $6.89. The origins of the holiday and of various Halloween customs.

3937. Dobrin, Arnold. *Make a Witch, Make a Goblin: A Book of Halloween Crafts* (3–5). Illustrated. 1977, Four Winds $6.95. Costumes, masks, party favors, food, and puppets are only a few of the creative projects for the young hobbiest.

✓**3938.** Glovach, Linda. *Little Witch's Halloween Book* (3–5). Illustrated. 1975, Prentice-Hall $5.95. Simple directions for variety of Halloween activities, including games, favors, and costumes.

3939. Hopkins, Lee Bennett, comp. *Hey-How for Halloween* (3–6). Illus. by Janet McCaffery. 1974, Harcourt $4.75. A varied and appealing selection of poems about happenings and creatures associated with Halloween.

3940. McGovern, Ann. *Squeals and Squiggles and Ghostly Giggles* (2–5). Illus. by Jeffrey Higginbottom. 1973, Four Winds $6.95. A charming compendium of tricks, ghost stories, games, and more.

3941. Moore, Lilian. *See My Lovely Poison Ivy and Other Verses about Witches, Ghosts and Things* (1–5). Illus. by Diane Dawson. 1975, Atheneum $7.95. An amusing collection for and about Halloween and creatures associated with it.

3942. Patterson, Lillie. *Halloween* (2–5). Illustrated. 1965, Garrard $4.90. Well-selected facts about the historical background of the holiday.

3943. Prelutsky, Jack. *It's Halloween* (1–3). Illus. by Marylin Hofner. 1977, Greenwillow $5.95; LB $5.71. Thirteen brief and easily read poems explore various aspects of this scary holiday.

3944. Sechrist, Elizabeth H. *Heigh-Ho for Halloween* (5–8). 1948, Macrae LB $6.71. A charming anthology of material.

Fiction

3945. Adams, Adrienne. *A Woggle of Witches* (PS–3). Illus. by author. 1971, Scribner $8.95; paper $2.95. The activities of a group of witches on Halloween night as they go about their business of dining on bat stew and riding on a broom.

3946. Anderson, Lonzo. *The Halloween Party* (PS–2). Illus. by Adrienne Adams. 1974, Scribner $8.95; paper $2.95. Faraday Folson almost becomes part of 2 witches' stew in this Halloween story.

3947. Asch, Frank. *Popcorn: A Frank Asch Bear Story* (PS–K). Illustrated. 1979, Parents $4.95; LB $4.99. Sam Bear decides to pop everyone's popcorn at a Halloween party.

3948. Avi. *No More Magic* (4–6). 1975, Pantheon $6.99. Chris encounters many mysterious events one Halloween night.

3949. Barton, Byron. *Hester* (PS–1). Illus. by author. 1975, Greenwillow $6.96; Penguin paper $1.95. A crocodile goes out spooking on Halloween.

3950. Battles, Edith. *The Terrible Trick or Treat* (1–3). Illustrated. 1970, Addison LB $5.95. Chris starts to trick or treat one day early.

3951. Bradbury, Ray. *The Halloween Tree* (5–7). 1972, Doubleday $4.95. Boys visit a deserted house and find a pumpkin tree.

3952. Bright, Robert. *Georgie's Halloween* (PS–2). Illus. by author. 1958, Doubleday $4.95. A shy ghost gets a surprise from his friends.

3953. Carlson, Natalie Savage. *The Night the Scarecrow Walked* (3–4). Illus. by Charles Robinson. 1979, Scribner $6.95. On Halloween night before the eyes of 2 disbelieving youngsters, a scarecrow moves from its post.

3954. Coombs, Patricia. *Dorrie and the Halloween Plot* (2–4). Illustrated. 1976, Lothrop LB $6.00. Dorrie foils a plot to kidnap the Great Sorceress.

3955. Embry, Margaret. *The Blue-Nosed Witch* (2–4). 1956, Holiday $4.95. A witch meets a group of children out on Halloween.

3956. Foster, Doris Van Liew. *Tell Me, Mr. Owl* (PS–K). Illus. by Helen Stone. 1957, Lothrop LB $6.96. An owl reassures a boy about the strange occurrences on Halloween.

3957. Godden, Rumer. *Mr. McFadden's Halloween* (4–6). 1975, Viking $6.95. A young girl befriends a grumpy old man.

3958. Harper, Wilhelmina. *Ghosts and Goblins* (2–5). Illus. by William Wiesner. 1965, Dutton $6.95. A standby for Halloween, these stories of strange and mysterious happenings are fun to tell or read aloud at any time of the year.

3959. Jasner, W. K. *Which is the Witch?* (1–3). Illus. by Victoria Chess. 1979, Random $3.95; LB $4.99. Jenny trades places with a real witch on Halloween night in this easily read account.

3960. Kahl, Virginia. *Gunhilde and the Halloween Spell* (K–3). Illus. by author. 1975, Scribner $6.95. Gunhilde's unraveled scarf is used to effect a rescue after she and her sisters have been turned into toads by a wicked witch.

3961. Keats, Ezra Jack. *The Trip* (1–3). Illus. by author. 1978, Greenwillow $7.95. Halloween proves to be a time when Louis isn't lonely anymore.

3962. Kraus, Robert. *How Spider Saved Halloween* (K–3). Illus. by author. 1973, Parents $5.95; LB $5.41; Dutton paper $.95. Spider saves the fun of Halloween by creating an ingenious disguise.

3963. Lystad, Mary. *The Halloween Parade* (PS–1). Illus. by Cyndy Szekeres. 1973, Putnam $4.95. Deciding on a costume for Halloween is a problem.

3964. Massey, Jeanne. *The Littlest Witch* (K–2). Illus. by Adrienne Adams. 1959, Knopf $4.99. A small witch's disobedience loses her a chance to fly to the moon.

3965. Mooser, Stephen. *The Ghost with the Halloween Hiccups* (1–3). Illus. by Tomie de Paola. 1977, Watts $3.95; LB $4.90. Penny's hiccups are cured only by being frightened by 2 costumed kids.

3966. Parker, Nancy W. *The Party of the Old Farm: A Halloween Story* (4–6). 1971, Macmillan $5.95. Everything goes wrong for Plumber Bear one Halloween night.

3967. Rockwell, Anne. *A Bear, a Bobcat and Three Ghosts* (1–2). Illustrated. 1977, Macmillan $6.95. Halloween tricks abound in this tale of children frightening those who should frighten them.

3968. Schulman, Janet. *Jack the Bum and the Halloween Handout* (2–4). Illus. by James Stevenson. 1977, Greenwillow $5.95; LB $5.71; UNICEF paper $3.00. On Halloween night, a hobo learns the meaning of UNICEF.

3969. Von Hippel, Ursula. *The Craziest Halloween* (K–2). Illus. by author. 1957, Coward LB $4.49. A rebellious young witch causes an uproar.

3970. Watson, Jane W. *Which is the Witch?* (1–3). Illus. by Victoria Chess. 1979, Pantheon $4.99. A real witch trades places with Jenny on Halloween.

3971. Wiseman, Bernard. *Halloween with Morris and Boris* (PS–K). Illus. by author. 1975, Dodd $4.95; paper $.25. Two friends enjoy Halloween together in this easily read story.

3972. Zolotow, Charlotte. *A Tiger Called Thomas* (1–3). Illus. by Kurt Werth. 1963, Lothrop $6.00.

A new boy in the neighborhood ventures out on Halloween in his tiger suit and discovers new friends.

Thanksgiving

3973. Barth, Edna. *Turkeys, Pilgrims and Indian Corn: The Story of the Thanksgiving Symbols* (3–6). 1975, Seabury $7.95. Historical details about the origin of this festival and how we celebrate it today.

3974. Bartlett, Robert Merrill. *Thanksgiving Day* (1–3). Illus. by W. T. Mars. 1965, Crowell $6.89. An introduction to the harvest festival and, in particular, Thanksgiving in America.

3975. Behrens, June. *Feast of Thanksgiving* (1–3). Illus. by Anne Siberell. 1974, Childrens Press $7.35. A 2-act play about the first Thanksgiving dinner.

3976. Child, Lydia Maria. *Over the River and Through the Wood* (1–3). Illus. by Brinton Turkle. 1974, Coward $6.95; Scholastic paper $1.50. A favorite song of a family's Thanksgiving visit to grandparents.

3977. Hopkins, Lee Bennett, comp. *Merrily Comes Our Harvest In: Poems for Thanksgiving* (2–4). Illus. by Ben Shecter. 1978, Harcourt $4.95. A gentle collection of 20 poems dealing with Thanksgiving.

3978. Luckhardt, Mildred Corell. *Thanksgiving, Feast and Festival* (4–7). Illus. by Ralph McDonald. 1966, Abingdon $12.95. An anthology of prose and verse about the origins of Thanksgiving and how it is celebrated.

3979. Sechrist, Elizabeth H., and Woolsey, Janette. *It's Time for Thanksgiving* (4–7). Illus. by Guy Fry. 1957, Macrae $5.97. An anthology of Thanksgiving material including stories, plays, recipes, and games.

3980. Weisgard, Leonard. *The Plymouth Thanksgiving* (K–3). Illus. by author. 1967, Doubleday $5.95. Account of the first Thanksgiving, documented from the diary of William Bradford.

3981. Wyndham, Lee. *Thanksgiving* (2–5). 1963, Garrard $4.66. The story of the first Thanksgiving—its origins in other harvest festivals and how it is celebrated today.

Fiction

3982. Barksdale, Lena. *The First Thanksgiving* (2–5). Illus. by Lois Lenski. 1942, Knopf $4.99. The story of a little girl who comes from England to Massachusetts to celebrate the new holiday with her grandmother.

3983. Dalgliesh, Alice. *The Thanksgiving Story* (PS–4). Illus. by Helen Sewell. 1954, Scribner $8.95; paper $2.95. The Hopkins family's experiences on the *Mayflower* to the first Thanksgiving.

3984. Janice. *Little Bear's Thanksgiving* (K–2). Illus. by Mariana. 1967, Lothrop $6.00. Little Bear is taught the meaning of Thanksgiving from many of his forest friends.

3985. Harper, Wilhelmina. *Harvest Feast: Stories of Thanksgiving, Yesterday and Today* (4–8). Illustrated. 1938; 1965, Dutton $7.95. An updated selection and format for this standard collection.

3986. Rock, Gail. *The Thanksgiving Treasure* (4–6). Illus. by Charles C. Gehm. 1974, Knopf $4.95; LB $5.69; Bantam paper $1.50. Addie's desire to rekindle the spirit of friendship at Thanksgiving produces an unexpected reward.

3987. Williams, Barbara. *Chester Chipmunk's Thanksgiving* (4–6). 1978, Dutton $5.95. Chester's invitation to share his Thanksgiving pecan pie is turned down by everyone except Oswald Opossum.

Valentine's Day

3988. Barth, Edna. *Hearts, Cupids and Red Roses: The Story of the Valentine Symbols* (4–6). Illus. by Ursula Arndt. 1974, Seabury $8.95. A fascinating compilation of facts and lore about St. Valentine's Day.

3989. Bulla, Clyde Robert. *St. Valentine's Day* (1–3). Illus. by Valenti Angelo. 1965, Crowell $6.89. An explanation of the legends and celebrations associated with this holiday.

3990. de Paola, Tomie. *Things to Make and Do for Valentine's Day* (1–3). Illustrated. 1976, Watts $4.90. Games, crafts, and recipes dealing with this day are included with easily followed instructions.

3991. Guilfoile, Elizabeth. *Valentine's Day* (2–5). 1965, Garrard $4.90. The beginnings of and ways to celebrate Valentine's Day, in an easily read book.

3992. Hopkins, Lee Bennett, ed. *Good Morning to You, Valentine* (2–5). Illus. by Tomie de Paola.

1976, Harcourt $4.79. Poems, jingles, and couplets gaily illustrated on subjects related to this holiday.

3993. Yaroslava, ed. *I Like You, and Other Poems for Valentine's Day* (3–5). Illus. by author. 1976, Scribner $6.95. Poems for children and adults on the vagaries of love, handsomely anthologized.

Fiction

3994. Balian, Lorna. *A Sweetheart for Valentine* (K–3). Illus. by author. 1979, Abingdon $8.95. An original, highly imaginative explanation for the origins of Valentine's Day.

3995. Bulla, Clyde Robert. *The Valentine Cat* (PS–3). Illus. by Leonard Weisgard. 1959, Crowell $8.95. A valentine fantasy of a homeless kitten who was all black, except for a white heart on his forehead.

3996. Cohen, Miriam. *Be My Valentine!* (1–3). Illus. by Lillian Hoban. 1978, Greenwillow $6.95; LB $6.67. George is dismayed when he doesn't receive as many valentines as his friends.

3997. Nixon, Joan Lowery. *The Valentine Mystery* (1–3). Illus. by Jim Cummins. 1979, Whitman $3.71. Susan, with the help of her brothers, finds out who has sent her an anonymous valentine.

3998. Schultz, Owen. *The Blue Valentine* (1–3). Illus. by Elizabeth Coberly. 1979, Morrow $5.95; LB $5.71. Cindy is disappointed at the initial reception her teacher gives to receiving her blue valentine.

Jewish Holy Days

3999. Becker, Joyce. *Hanukkah Crafts* (4–8). Illustrated. 1978, Hebrew $9.95; paper $6.95. Directions for creating more than 200 different objects.

4000. Becker, Joyce. *Jewish Holiday Crafts* (5–8). Illus. by author. 1977, Hebrew $9.95; paper $6.95. Simple craft projects—mainly, but not always, directly related to Jewish religious holidays—are clearly described in words and pictures. Also use: *The Jewish Holiday Book* by Wendy Lazar (1977, Doubleday $7.95).

4001. Cedarbaum, Sophia N. *Passover: The Festival of Freedom* (2–4). Illus. by Clare Ross and John Ross. 1965, American Hebrew Cong $2.00. One of a series that includes many Jewish holidays.

4002. Cone, Molly. *The Jewish New Year* (1–3). Illus. by Jerome Snyder. 1966, Crowell $6.89. An interesting and enlightening account of the meaning and customs associated with this holiday.

4003. Cone, Molly. *Purim* (1–3). Illus. by Helen Borten. 1967, Crowell $6.89. A simple retelling of how Queen Esther saved her people and how this event is commemorated.

4004. Cuyler, Margery. *Jewish Holidays* (3–5). Illustrated. 1978, Holt $5.95. The history and significance of nine important Jewish holidays are described.

4005. Epstein, Morris. *All about Jewish Holidays and Customs* (4–6). Illus. by Arnold Lobel. 1970, Ktav $4.50. A history and presentation of the customs involved with all of the major Jewish holidays.

4006. Gilbert, Arthur, and Tarcor, Oscar. *Your Neighbor Celebrates* (4–6). Illustrated. 1957, Friendly-Ktav $5.00. How and why American Jews celebrate various religious holidays and how children participate in them.

4007. Greenfeld, Howard. *Passover* (4–6). Illus. by Elaine Grove. 1978, Holt $5.95. The history, traditions, and meaning of this important holiday. Also use: *Chanukah* (1976, Holt $5.95).

4008. Greenfeld, Howard. *Rosh Hashanah and Yom Kippur* (5–7). Illus. by Elaine Grove. 1979, Holt $5.95. The origin, significance, and ways of observing these two important Jewish holy days are well presented.

4009. Hirsh, Marilyn. *The Hanukkah Story* (K–2). Illus. by author. 1977, Bonim $7.95. A simple narrative with full-page illustrations explains the origins of Hanukkah.

4010. Hirsh, Marilyn. *One Little Goat: A Passover Song* (1–3). Illus. by author. 1979, Holiday $6.95. A traditional holiday song is presented with illustrations and the music.

4011. Purdy, Susan. *Jewish Holiday Cookbook* (5–9). Illustrated. 1979, Watts $6.90; paper $2.95. Eleven Jewish holidays are briefly described and accompanied by easily followed recipes.

4012. Simon, Norma. *Hanukkah* (1–3). Illus. by Symeon Shimin. 1966, Crowell $6.89. An informative and dignified account of the story of Hannukkah; the Festival of Lights and the rituals and customs observed on this holy holiday. Also use: *The Complete Book of Hanukkah* by Kinneret Chiel (1959, Friendly-Ktav $4.00).

4013. Simon, Norma. *Passover* (1–3). Illus. by Symeon Shimin. 1965, Crowell $6.89. The origin of Passover in Egypt and how it is celebrated by Jews today.

Fiction

4014. Adler, David A. *The House on the Roof: A Sukkoth Story* (K–4). 1976, Bonim $5.95. An old man hauls all sorts of material into his apartment and builds a Sukkah to celebrate the holiday of Sukkoth.

4015. Aleichem, Sholem. *Hanukkah Money* (K–3). Illus. by Uri Shulevitz. 1978, Morrow $6.95. A young boy and his brother participate in the celebration of Hanukkah in this charming story.

4016. Aleichem, Sholem. *Holiday Tales of Sholom Aleichem* (4–6). 1979, Scribner $8.95. Seven diverse tales that deal with joyous holidays.

4017. Hirsh, Marilyn. *Potato Pancakes All Around: A Hanukkah Tale* (1–3). 1978, Hebrew $6.95. A humorous story about making pancakes for Hanukkah.

4018. Levitin, Sonia. *A Sound to Remember* (1–3). Illustrated. 1979, Harcourt $6.95. A young Jewish boy is chosen to blow the shofar during the High Holidays.

4019. Shulevitz, Uri. *The Magician* (K–2). Adapt. from the Yiddish of I. L. Peretz. Illustrated. 1973, Macmillan $7.95; paper $1.95. A Passover story based on a Yiddish folk legend about Elijah disguised as a magician who comes to the home of a poor couple and produces a fine feast for the ceremonial meal.

Jokes, Riddles, Puzzles

Jokes and Riddles

4020. Bernstein, Joanne E. *Fiddle with a Riddle* (3–6). Illus. by Giulio Maestro. 1979, Dutton $7.95. A simple guide on how to write your own riddles with many examples.

4021. Blake, Quentin, and Yeoman, John. *The Improbable Book of Records* (2–6). Illus. by Quentin Blake. 1976, Atheneum $6.95. An engaging spoof on Guinness that will delight all.

4022. Cerf, Bennett. *Bennett Cerf's Book of Animal Riddles* (K–2). Illus. by Roy McKie. 1964, Random $3.50; LB $4.39. Easily read riddles that are very popular with young children. Also use: *Bennett Cerf's Book of Riddles* (1960, $3.50; LB $4.39).

4023. Chrystie, Frances N. *Riddle Me This* (2–5). Illus. by Elizabeth B. Ripley. 1940, Walck $4.25; paper $1.25. A collection, amusingly illustrated, of riddles for and by young people.

4024. Churchill, Elmer Richard, and Churchill, Linda R. *The Bionic Banana* (4–6). Illus. by Carol Nicklaus. 1979, Watts $5.90. Nonsensical riddles about fruits and vegetables.

4025. Clark, David Allen. *Jokes, Puns, and Riddles* (3–7). Illus. by Lionel Kalish. 1968, Doubleday $4.95. A collection that will "tickle the funny bones" of young children.

4026. Cole, William. *Give Up? Cartoon Riddle Rhymers* (3–6). Illus. by Mike C. Thaler. 1978, Watts $4.90. A collection of riddles with rhyming answers.

4027. Cole, William. *Knock Knocks: The Most Ever* (4–6). Illus. by Mike C. Thaler. 1976, Watts $4.90. Almost 150 zany knock-knock jokes complemented by cartoonlike illustrations.

4028. Corbett, Scott. *Jokes to Read in the Dark* (4–6). Illus. by Annie Gusman. 1980, Dutton $7.95; paper $2.95. A fine collection of sure-fire jokes.

4029. Cunningham, Bronnie. *The Best Book of Riddles, Puns & Jokes* (3–7). Illus. by Amy Aitken. 1979, Doubleday $6.95; LB $7.90. More than 1,000 jokes, etc., are crammed into this collection.

4030. De Regniers, Beatrice S. *The Abraham Lincoln Joke Book* (4–6). Illustrated. 1965, Random LB $4.69. All sorts of funny stories, jokes, and riddles about Mr. Lincoln.

4031. Doty, Roy. *Q's Are Weird O's: More Puns, Gags, Quips and Riddles* (5–7). Illus. by author. 1975, Doubleday $4.95. "When was the Iron Age?" "Just before the Drip Dry Era!" is a sample of the outrageous jokes in this collection. Also use: *Puns, Gags, Quips and Riddles* (1974, Doubleday $4.95; Archway, paper $1.50).

4032. Emrich, Duncan, comp. *The Hodge-Podge Book* (2–6). Illus. by Ib Ohlsson. 1972, Four Winds $8.95. A bit of everything—games, jokes, tongue twisters, even medical advice—is included in this charming nonsense book.

4033. Emrich, Duncan. *The Nonsense Book of Riddles, Rhymes, Tongue Twisters, Puzzles and Jokes from American Folklore* (2–6). Illus. by Ib Ohlsson. 1970, Four Winds $8.95. A sure-fire popular favorite.

4034. Emrich, Duncan. *The Whim-Wham Book* (3–5). Illus. by Ib Ohlsson. 1975, Four Winds $8.95. A miscellany of jokes, superstitions, camp songs, riddles, and more.

4035. Fox, Sonny. *Jokes and How to Tell Them* (4–6). Illus. by B. Grey. 1965, Putnam $4.99. A how-to book for the would-be comedian.

4036. Gerler, William R. *Pack of Riddles* (1–3). Illus. by Giulio Maestro. 1975, Dutton $6.95. A refreshingly hilarious collection of riddles about animal life.

4037. Gilbreath, Alice. *Beginning-to-Read Riddles and Jokes* (2–4). Illus. by Susan Perl. 1967, Follett $2.97; paper $1.50. This collection is simple to read, but still lots of fun.

4038. Gomez, Victoria. *Scream Cheese and Jelly: Jokes, Riddles and Puns* (2–3). Illus. by Joel Schick. 1979, Lothrop $5.71. All sorts of jokes about words and puns.

4039. Hample, Stuart E. *Stoo Hample's Silly Joke Book* (3–7). Illustrated. 1978, Delacorte $5.47. Lots of fun complete with amusing drawings.

4040. Hoff, Syd. *Syd Hoff's Joke Book* (2–4). Illus. by author. 1972, Putnam $4.89. Riddles and other kinds of jokes, many of them old standbys, illustrated with great style and humor. Also use: *Jokes to Enjoy, Draw and Tell* (1974, Putnam $5.29).

4041. Hoke, Helen, ed. *Jokes, Jokes, Jokes* (5–7). Illus. by Richard Erdoes. 1954, Watts $6.90. A collection divided into subjects. Also use from Watts: *Jokes and Fun* (1973, $3.90) and *Hoke's Jokes* (1975, $4.90).

4042. Keller, Charles. *More Ballpoint Bananas* (2–6). Illus. by Leonard Shortall. 1977, Prentice-Hall $4.95. Screwball humor with riddles, jokes, and rhymes that will please a large audience. Also use: *Ballpoint Bananas* (1974, $4.95; paper $1.25).

4043. Keller, Charles. *Llama Beans* (2–6). Illus. by Dennis Nolan. 1979, Prentice-Hall $5.95. Thirty-one clever riddles about animals.

4044. Keller, Charles. *The Nutty Joke Book* (2–6). Illus. by Jean Claude Swares. 1978, Prentice-Hall $4.95. A collection of jokes about nuts.

4045. Keller, Charles. *School Daze* (2–6). Illus. by Sam Q. Quissman. 1979, Prentice-Hall $5.95. Zany jokes and cartoons about school.

4046. Keller, Charles, and Baker, Richard. *The Star-Spangled Banana and Other Revolutionary Riddles* (3–6). Illus. by Tomie de Paola. 1974, Prentice-Hall $3.95. Outrageous puns and jokes that celebrate the Spirit of '76. Also use: *Glory, Glory, How Peculiar* (1976, Prentice-Hall $4.95).

4047. Kohl, Marguerite, and Young, Frederica. *Jokes for Children* (4–8). Illus. by Bob Patterson. 1963, Hill & Wang $4.95. Over 650 rhymes, riddles, puns, and jokes. Also use: *More Jokes for Children* (1966, $4.95).

4048. Leach, Maria. *Riddle Me, Riddle Me, Ree* (3–6). Illus. by William Wiesner. 1970, Viking $4.95; 1977, Penguin paper $1.50. Over 200 riddles originating in folklore with a selection of jokes appended.

4049. Leeming, Joseph. *Riddles, Riddles, Riddles* (4–6). Illus. by S. Lane Miller. 1953, Watts $6.90. Contains enigmas, anagrams, puns, puzzles, quizzes, conundrums.

4050. Leonard, Marcia. *Cricket's Jokes, Riddles and Other Stuff* (2–6). Illustrated. 1977, Random $2.95; LB $3.99. Lots of knock-knocks, elephant jokes, and tongue twisters in this funny, funny book.

4051. Levine, Caroline Anne. *Knockout Knock Knocks* (2–4). Illus. by Giulio Maestro. 1978, Dutton $6.95; paper $1.95. A very funny collection of 61 knock-knock jokes.

4052. Low, Joseph. *Five Men under One Umbrella and Other Ready-to-Read Riddles* (1–3). Illus. by author. 1975, Macmillan $5.95. Lots of fun in this collection of jokes humorously illustrated.

4053. Low, Joseph. *A Mad Wet Hen and Other Riddles* (2–4). Illus. by author. 1977, Greenwillow $5.71. Witty riddles accompanied by equally amusing drawings.

4054. Low, Joseph. *What If . . . ?* (2–5). Illus. by author. 1976, Atheneum $6.95. An exploration of 14 fanciful encounters, such as how to behave if a shark invites you for a swim.

4055. Morrison, Lillian. *Black Within and Red Without* (4–6). Illus. by Jo Spier. 1953, Crowell $7.95. Riddles from all over, for all ages.

4056. Rees, Ennis. *Pun Fun* (3–7). Illus. by Quentin Blake. 1965, Abelard LB $5.79. A fine collection humorously illustrated.

4057. Rockwell, Thomas. *The Portmanteau Book* (5–7). Illus. by Gail Rockwell. 1974, Little $6.95. A charming sampling of puzzles, humorous recipes, and other amusements.

4058. Rosenbloom, Joseph. *Biggest Riddle Book in the World* (3–6). Illus. by Joyce Behr. 1976, Sterling $5.95; LB $6.69; paper $2.95. About 2,000 old and new riddles arranged under various subjects and amusingly illustrated.

4059. Sarnoff, Jane. *Giants! A Riddle Book and Mr. Bigperson's Side: A Story Book* (1–3). Illus. by Reynold Ruffins. 1977, Scribner $7.95. A combination storybook (on the right-hand side of pages) and riddle book (on the left).

4060. Sarnoff, Jane, and Ruffins, Reynold. *I Know! A Riddle Book* (1–4). Illus. by Reynold Ruffins. 1976, Scribner $7.95. A joyful collection of old and new riddles arranged by general subjects.

4061. Sarnoff, Jane. *The Monster Riddle Book* (1–4). Illus. by Reynold Ruffins. 1975, Scribner $7.95. A collection of riddles along with a glossary of mythical monsters.

4062. Sarnoff, Jane. *What? A Riddle Book* (2–4). Illus. by Reynold Ruffins. 1974, Scribner $9.95; LB $3.95. A delightful collection of daffy riddles grouped by various subjects.

4063. Schwartz, Alvin, comp. *Witcracks: Jokes and Jests from American Folklore* (3–6). Illus. by Glen Rounds. 1973, Lippincott $6.95; paper $2.50. All sorts of humor associated with America's past, from old riddles to knock-knock jokes.

4064. Steig, William. *C D B!* (3–6). Illus. by author. 1968, Simon $3.95; LB $3.07; Dutton paper $1.50. When each set of letters and/or numbers is repeated aloud and riddle buffs apply a bit of imagination, the amusing caption accompanying each cartoon becomes apparent.

4065. Sterne, Noelle. *Tyrannosaurus Wrecks: A Book of Dinosaur Riddles* (2–6). Illustrated. 1979, Crowell $6.95; LB $6.89. Many short riddles, all dealing amusingly with prehistoric animals.

4066. Stine, Jovial Bob. *The Pigs' Book of World Records* (2–3). Illus. by Peter Lippman. 1980, Random $3.95. Ninety-four pages of pig jokes.

4067. Thaler, Mike. *The Yellow Brick Toad* (3–5). 1978, Doubleday $5.95; LB $6.90. Subtitle: *Funny Frog Cartoons, Riddles and Silly Stories.*

4068. Thorndike, Susan. *The Electric Radish and Other Jokes* (2–3). Illus. by Ray Cruz. 1973, Doubleday $4.95; paper $2.95. A wacky collection of jokes accompanied by suitably flamboyant illustrations.

4069. Underwood, Ralph, ed. *Ask Me Another Riddle* (K–3). Illus. by Crosby N. Bonsall. 1964, Grosset $4.95. A fine collection for the beginning reader.

4070. Watson, Clyde. *Quips and Quirks* (3–6). Illus. by Wendy Watson. 1975, Crowell $6.95. A collection of epithets from such standbys as "Smartalack" to the more esoteric "Grizzleguts."

4071. White, Laurence B., and Broekel, Ray. *The Trick Book* (3–5). Illus. by Will Winslow. 1979, Doubleday $6.95. A fine selection of practical jokes and word games.

4072. Wiesner, William. *The Riddle Pot* (K–3). Illus. by author. 1973, Dutton $4.95; paper $1.50. Outlandish riddles, jokes, and puzzles designed to delight all. Also use: *A Pocketful of Riddles* (1966, Dutton $4.50; paper $1.50).

4073. Withers, Carl, and Benet, Sula., eds. *The American Riddle Book* (4–9). Illus. by Marc Simont. 1954, Abelard $7.89. Approximately 1,000 riddles from many lands representing different times. Also use: *Riddles of Many Lands* (1956, Abelard $7.89).

Puzzles

4074. Adler, Irving. *The Adler Book of Puzzles and Riddles* (1–3). Illus. by Peggy Adler. 1962, Day LB $6.89. A simple collection of entertaining puzzles for very young readers.

4075. Adler, Peggy. *Geography Puzzles* (4–7). Illus. by author. 1979, Watts $5.90. A fine collec-

tion of puzzles, most of which involve geographical concepts.

4076. Brandreth, Gyles. *Brain-Teasers and Mind-Benders* (4–6). Illus. by Ann Axworthy. 1979, Sterling $4.99. All sorts of puzzles with answers.

4077. Burns, Marilyn. *The Book of Thing (or How to Solve a Problem Twice Your Size)* (5–7). Illus. by Martha Weston. 1976, Little $6.95; paper $4.95. A stimulating collection of puzzles to make children think; informally and entertainingly presented.

4078. Fixx, James F. *Solve It! A Perplexing Profusion of Puzzles* (5–7). Illustrated. 1978, Doubleday $5.95; LB $6.90. An array of puzzles that seldom require more than a simple knowledge of arithmetic.

4079. Fletcher, Helen Jill. *Put on Your Thinking Cap* (4–8). Illus. by Quentin Blake. 1968, Abelard $5.95; LB $5.79. A collection of 108 brain-teasers, including mazes, perceptual and verbal problems, scrambled words, and riddles. Also use: *Puzzles and Quizzles* (1971, Abelard $4.50).

4080. Hitz, Demi. *Where Is It?* (2–4). Illustrated. 1980, Doubleday $7.95; LB $8.90. A simple puzzle book on identifying hidden objects.

4081. Lamb, Geoffrey. *Pencil and Paper Tricks* (5–7). 1979, Nelson $5.50. All kind of ways to amuse oneself or friends with only a pencil and paper.

4082. Leeming, Joseph. *Fun with Pencil and Paper* (4–6). Illus. by Jessie Robinson. 1975, Lippincott $8.95. A variety of pencil and paper games, with quizzes and puzzles.

4083. Ruben, Patricia. *What is New? What Is Missing? What Is Different?* (PS–1). Illus. by author. 1978, Lippincott $6.95. Puzzles involving careful observations are contained in carefully arranged photographs.

Word Games

4084. Brandreth, Gyles. *The Biggest Tongue Twister Book in the World* (4–6). Illus. by Alex Chin. 1978, Sterling $4.99. Hundreds of twisters (mostly one-liners) plus cartoonlike drawings make this a most enjoyable book.

4085. Rosenbloom, Joseph. *Twist These on Your Tongue* (4–7). Illus. by Joyce Behr. 1978, Nelson $5.95. An extensive collection that will delight all.

4086. Schwartz, Alvin, comp. *A Twister of Twists, a Tangler of Tales* (4–7). Illus. by Glen Rounds.

1972, Lippincott $6.95; paper $1.95. A browsing book of tongue twisters in different languages. Also use: *Tomfoolery: Trickery and Foolery with Words* (1973, Lippincott $7.95; paper $2.50; Bantam, paper $1.75).

4087. Tremain, Ruthven. *Teapot, Switcheroo, and Other Silly Word Games* (2–4). Illustrated. 1979, Greenwillow $5.95. Riddles, knock-knocks, and interesting word origins are included in this enjoyable collection.

Hobbies

General and Miscellaneous

4088. Hussey, Lois J., and Pessino, Catherine. *Collecting for the City Naturalist* (4–6). Illus. by Barbara Neill. 1975, Crowell $6.95. This survey stresses techniques of collecting and preserving a wide variety of nature specimens.

4089. Keen, Martin L. *Be a Rockhound* (4–7). Illus. by author. 1979, Messner $6.97. An informative and concise introduction to the hobby of rock collecting.

4090. Kettelkamp, Larry. *Song, Speech and Ventriloquism* (5–8). 1967, Morrow $5.95; LB $5.49. The structure and function of the speech organs and the formation of speech sounds with explicit instructions in ventriloquism.

4091. McLoone, Margo, and Siegel, Alice. *Sports Cards: Collecting, Trading and Playing* (4–6). Illustrated. 1979, Holt $8.95; LB $4.95. An introduction to this hobby illustrated with many examples.

4092. Math, Irwin. *Morse, Marconi and You* (1–9). 1979, Scribner $8.95. A handbook for the young radio amateur.

4093. Salny, Roslyn W. *Hobby Collections A-Z* (5–9). Illus. by Robert Galster. 1965, Crowell $6.95. Necessary information is given for each specific hobby, together with suggestions for additional hobbies.

4094. Shedenhelm, W. R. C. *The Young Rockhound's Handbook* (6–9). Illustrated. 1978, Putnam $6.95. A practical guide to many aspects of the growing hobby.

4095. Waltner, Willard, and Waltner, Elma. *The New Hobbycraft Book* (4–6). Illustrated. 1963, Lantern $6.70. A basic introduction to various hobbies and projects involving each.

4096. Wels, Byron G. *Here Is Your Hobby: Amateur Radio* (6–9). 1968, Putnam $5.29. A complex hobby introduced with clarity and completeness.

4097. Zubrowski, Bernie. *A Children's Museum Activity Book: Bubbles* (4–6). Illus. by Joan Drescher. 1979, Little $6.95; paper $3.95. Bubble blowing is used to create many activities.

Cooking

4098. Adkins, Jan. *The Bakery* (5–9). Illus. by author. 1976, Scribner $5.95. An informal jaunty guide to bread making and a history of the art.

4099. Ault, Roz. *Kids Are Natural Cooks* (4–8). Illus. by Lady McCrady. 1974, Houghton $6.95. Interesting, simple recipes arranged by season and informally presented.

4100. Barkin, Carol, and James, Elizabeth. *Slapdash Cooking* (5–9). Illus. by Rita Floden Leydon. 1976, Lothrop $5.75; LB $5.52. Time-saving devices and recipes are stressed in this fine cookbook.

4101. Barta, Ginevera. *Metric Cooking for Beginners* (6–8). Illustrated. 1978, Ridley Enslow $6.95. Some fine recipes are presented using only metric measurements.

4102. Better Homes and Gardens. *New Junior Cook Book* (3–6). 1979, Meredith $3.95. A total of 75 field-tested, simple recipes are included.

4103. Blanchard, Marjorie Page. *The Outdoor Cookbook* (4–7). 1977, Watts $5.90. All one needs to know about barbecuing and other forms of outdoor cooking.

4104. Blanchard, Marjorie Page. *The Vegetarian Menu Cookbook* (6–9). Illustrated. 1979, Watts $6.90. A health-oriented cookbook filled with pleasing recipes and expert directions.

4105. Borghese, Anita. *The International Cookie Jar Cookbook* (5–8). Illus. by Yaroslava Mills. 1975, Scribner $3.95. Seventy cookie recipes with accompanying background notes from 5 major global areas.

4106. Cobb, Vicki. *Arts and Crafts You Can Eat* (6–8). Illus. by Peter Lippman. 1974, Lippincott $7.95; paper $2.75. Pasta mobiles are only one of the projects in this fascinating book.

4107. Cobb, Vicki. *More Science Experiments You Can Eat* (5–8). 1979, Lippincott $7.89. Important scientific principles are demonstrated with edible results. A companion to the author's *Science Experiments You Can Eat.*

4108. Cooper, Terry Touff, and Ratner, Marilyn. *Many Hands Cooking: An International Cookbook for Girls and Boys* (4–7). Illus. by Tony Chen. 1974, Crowell $4.00. Produced with the co-operation of the U.S. Committee for UNICEF, this is an interesting collection of recipes from all over the world.

4109. Getzoff, Carole. *The Natural Cook's First Book: A Natural Foods Cookbook for Beginners* (4–6). Illus. by Jill Pinkwater. 1973, Dodd $4.95. A clever selection of recipes, each accompanied by lists of utensils, ingredients, and helpful illustrations. Also use: *The Down to Earth Cookbook* by Anita Borghese (1973, Scribner $6.95).

4110. Girl Scouts of the United States of America. *Girl Scout Cookbook* (6–9). 1971, Cowles $6.95. For the beginning and intermediate cook with a series of practical recipes finely detailed and arranged by type of food.

4111. Gretz, Susanna, and Sage, Alison. *The Teddybears Cookbook* (K–3). 1978, Doubleday $5.95. Five teddy bears make dishes for breakfast, lunch, and dinner and share their recipes.

4112. Janice. *Little Bear Learns to Read the Cookbook* (K–3). Illus. by Mariana. 1969, Lothrop $6.25; LB $6.00. A humorous introduction to cooking for very young readers.

4113. Johnson, Hannah Lyons. *Let's Bake Bread* (3–5). Illustrated. 1973, Lothrop $6.48. A step-by-step description for the amateur of the utensils, ingredients, and processes involved in bread making.

4114. Kohn, Bernice. *Easy Gourmet Cooking for Young People and Beginners* (5–8). Illus. by Tony Apilado. 1973, Bobbs-Merrill $6.95. Simple but impressive foods that should be interesting and easy for the novice cook.

4115. Lerman, Ann. *The Big Green Salad Book* (4–8). Illus. by Teresa Anderko. 1977, Running $9.80; paper $3.95. A basic handbook on how to make a variety of salads and dressings.

4116. MacGregor, Carol. *The Storybook Cookbook* (3–6). Illus. by Roy Cruz. 1967, Doubleday $4.95. Prentice-Hall paper $1.95. Twenty-two recipes inspired by literary characters, such as "Captain Hook's poison cake." Also use: *The Pooh Cookbook* by Virginia H. Ellison (1969, Dutton $5.95; Dell, paper $1.25).

4117. McCleary, Julia G. *Cooking Metric Is Fun* (5–8). Illus. by Jan Pyk. 1979, Harcourt $8.95. Recipes from breakfast to dinner desserts presented in metric measurements with many cooking hints.

4118. Meyer, Carolyn. *The Bread Book: All about Bread and How To Make It* (4–7). Illus. by Tricia Schart Hyman. 1971, Harcourt $6.95; paper $1.95. The importance of bread from early times, its place in religious ceremonies, and the many forms in which it has been made. Recipes included.

4119. Moore, Eva. *The Cookie Book* (3–5). Illus. by Talivaldis Stubis. 1973, Seabury $6.95; Scholastic paper $1.25. A simple book giving clear instructions for 12 cookie recipes for special holidays.

4120. Moore, Eva. *The Seabury Cook Book for Boys and Girls* (1–3). Illus. by Talivaldis Stubis. 1971, Seabury $5.95. A fine first cookbook with 9 easy recipes.

4121. Newman, Nanette. *The Fun Food Factory* (4–6). Illus. by Alan Cracknell. 1977, Crown $4.95. A refreshingly amusing introduction to cooking with emphasis on sound nutrition.

4122. Noad, Susan Strand. *Recipes for Science Fun* (4–6). Illus. by Arnold Dobrin. 1979, Watts $5.90. Recipes that are not only representative of sound nutrition, but also demonstrate basic scientific principles.

4123. Paul, Aileen. *Kids Cooking Complete Meals: Menus, Recipes, Instructions* (3–6). Illus. by John Delulio. 1975, Doubleday $4.95. Complete menus for special occasions are handled thoroughly and logically. A companion to the somewhat easier *Kids Cooking*.

4124. Paul, Aileen, and Hawkins, Arthur. *Candies, Cookies, Cakes* (4–7). Illustrated. 1974, Doubleday $4.95. General information on utensils, ingredients, and techniques precedes the recipes.

4125. Paul, Aileen, and Hawkins, Arthur. *Kids Cooking: The Aileen Paul Cooking School Cookbook* (3–6). 1970, Doubleday $5.95. A lively, well-organized introduction to cooking with easily followed recipes and plenty of background information.

4126. Penner, Lucille Recht. *The Colonial Cookbook* (4–7). Illustrated. 1976, Hastings $7.95. Interspersed with several easily followed recipes is interesting material on how colonists lived and ate. Also use: *Slumps, Grunts and Snickerdoodles: What Colonial America Ate and Why* by Lila Perl (1975, Seabury $7.95).

4127. Perkins, Wilma L. *The Fannie Farmer Junior Cookbook* (6–9). Illus. by Martha P. Setchell. 1942; 1957, Little $6.95. A cookbook based on the famous Boston Cooking School Cook Book.

4128. Perl, Lila. *The Hamburger Book: All about Hamburgers and Hamburger Cookery* (5–9). Illus. by

Ragna Tischler Goddard. 1974, Seabury $6.95. Information on national dishes around the world and various schools of cooking are included with many ground beef recipes and material on the history, present status, and storage of the hamburger.

4129. Perl, Lila. *Hunter's Stew and Hangtown Fry: What Pioneer America Ate and Why* (5–8). Illus. by Richard Cuffari. 1977, Seabury $8.95. The eating habits and preferences, cooking techniques, and 20 recipes are included in this volume.

4130. Rombauer, Irma S. *A Cookbook for Girls and Boys* (4–7). 1952, Bobbs-Merrill $6.95. A beginning cookbook by the original author of *The Joy of Cooking*. Also use: *Betty Crocker's Cookbook for Boys and Girls* (1975, Golden, spiral $5.95; LB $9.15; paper $2.95).

4131. Schwartz, Paula Dunaway. *You Can Cook: How to Make Good Food for Your Family and Friends* (5–8). Illus. by Byron Barton. 1976, Atheneum $7.95. Basic recipes, including complete menus, are given simply and logically.

4132. Shapiro, Rebecca. *A Whole World of Cooking* (5–9). Illus. by author. 1972, Little $5.95. One or 2 recipes from each part of the world are included in this geographical cook's tour. Although not for the beginning chef, the explanations are quite simple.

4133. Solomon, Hannah. *Bake Bread!* (5–7). Illustrated. 1976, Lippincott $7.95; paper $3.95. Procedures used in bread making are clearly explained along with basic recipes.

4134. Van der Linde, Polly, and Van der Linde, Tasha. *Around the World in Eighty Dishes* (3–7). Illus. by Horst Lemke. 1971, Scroll $5.95. The compilers and testers of these recipes from many continents are 2 little girls, 8 and 10 years old.

4135. Walker, Barbara M. *The Little House Cookbook* (5–7). Illus. by Garth Williams. 1979, Harper $8.95; LB $8.95. Frontier food, such as green pumpkin pie from the Little House books, served up in tasty, easily used recipes.

4136. Williams, Barbara, and Williams, Rosemary. *Cookie Craft* (4–7). Illustrated. 1977, Holt $6.95. Subtitle: *No-Bake Designs for Edible Party Favors and Decorations.*

4137. Williams, Vera B. *It's a Gingerbread House; Bake It, Build It, Eat It!* (2–4). 1978, Greenwillow $5.95. How to build a gingerbread house from simple materials.

4138. Zweifel, Frances. *Pickle in the Middle and Other Easy Snacks* (1–3). Illus. by author. 1979, Harper $5.95. A simple how-to cookbook on the preparation of easily prepared treats.

Gardening

4139. Davis, Burke. *Newer and Better Organic Gardening* (6–9). Illus. by Honi Werner. 1976, Putnam $5.95; LB $4.46. A fine book for the beginning gardener plus an eloquent plea for natural gardening.

4140. Fenten, D. X. *Gardening . . . Naturally* (5–9). Illus. by Howard Berelson. 1973, Watts $5.88; paper $2.95. An introduction to organic gardening with good coverage on composting, mulching, and pest control without insecticides.

4141. Fenten, D. X. *Indoor Gardening* (4–7). Illus. by Howard Berelson. 1974, Watts $4.90. A good introduction to the factors that affect successful cultivation of house plants, and a fine listing of suitable varieties.

4142. Elbert, Virginia Fowler. *Grow a Plant Pet* (2–4). 1977, Doubleday $6.95. The care and feeding of healthy, happy plants, simply and graphically presented.

4143. Herda, D. J. *Making a Native Plant Terrarium* (4–6). Illus. by author. 1977, Messner $7.29. A logical step-by-step presentation of various facets of stocking and nurturing the contents of a terrarium.

4144. Herda, D. J. *Vegetables in a Pot* (4–7). Illus. by Kathy Fritz McBride. 1979, Messner $7.29. A thorough, clear explanation of growing plants in containers.

4145. Hudlow, Jean. *Eric Plants a Garden* (2–4). Illustrated. 1971, Whitman $5.95. The first steps in gardening told in a clear, direct style with excellent photographs.

4146. Jobb, Jamie. *My Garden Companion* (4–7). Illus. by Martha Weston. 1977, Scribner $9.95; paper $4.95. Subtitle: *A Complete Guide for the Beginner with a Special Emphasis on Useful Plants and Instructive Planting in the Wayside, Dooryard, Patio, Rooftop and Vacant Lot.*

4147. Johnsen, Jan. *Gardening without Soil* (5–7). Illustrated. 1979, Lippincott $7.95; LB $7.89. An introduction to hydroponics including a number of projects that can be carried out at home.

4148. Johnson, Hannah Lyons. *From Seed to Salad* (2–4). Illustrated. 1978, Lothrop $6.95. A beginning do-it-yourself guide to gardening. Companion to *From Seed to Jack-O'-Lantern* (1974, $6.00).

4149. Kramer, Jack. *Queen's Tears and Elephant's Ears: A Guide to Growing Unusual House Plants* (4–7). Illus. by Michael Valdiz and Robert Johnson. 1977, Collins $5.95. The care and feeding of unusual, exotic plants told simply and with spirit and imagination.

4150. Kramer, Jack. *Plant Sculptures: Making Miniature Indoor Topiaries* (4–6). Illus. by Tom Adams. 1978, Morrow $5.95; LB $5.71. Ten simple projects are included on how to train indoor house plants into designs.

4151. Lavine, Sigmund A. *Wonders of Terrariums* (5–8). Illus. by Jane O'Regan. 1978, Dodd $5.95. A beginner's guide to creating miniature habitats for plants and small animals.

4152. Mandry, Kathy. *How to Grow a Jelly Glass Farm* (K–3). Illus. by Joe Toto. 1974, Pantheon $4.99. Fourteen simple indoor garden projects are described.

4153. Millard, Adele. *Plants for Kids to Grow Indoors* (5–8). Illustrated. 1975, Sterling $6.95; LB $6.69. A comprehensive guide to all types of indoor plant growing, including regular potted plants, terrariums, and window boxes.

4154. Mintz, Lorelie. *Vegetables in Patches and Pots: A Child's Guide to Organic Vegetable G* (4–7). Illustrated. 1976, Farrar $6.95. A basic introductory guide to gardening, written with wit and enthusiasm.

4155. Paul, Aileen. *Kids Outdoor Gardening* (3–6). Illustrated. 1978, Doubleday $5.95. The hows and whys of simple outdoor gardening are well covered.

4156. Riedman, Sarah R. *Gardening without Soil* (5–7). Illus. by Rod Slater. 1979, Watts $5.45. A simple, well-organized guide to hydroponic gardening for the beginner.

4157. Rockwell, Harlow. *The Compost Heap* (1–3). Illus. by author. 1974, Doubleday $4.95. How a leaf pile changes into garden riches is described in text and drawings.

4158. Selsam, Millicent E. *How to Grow House Plants* (4–7). Illus. by Kathleen Elgin. 1960, Morrow $6.96. After a discussion of the structure of plants, the author gives basic instructions on their care and feeding.

4159. Soucie, Anita Holmes. *Plant Fun: Ten Easy Plants to Grow Indoors* (5–9). Illus. by Grambs Miller. 1974, Four Winds $7.95. All the important topics involved in indoor gardens, from soil and light to propagation and pruning, are handled in this excellent guide.

4160. Walsh, Anne Batterberry. *A Gardening Book: Indoors and Outdoors* (4–7). Illustrated. 1976, Atheneum $6.95. A fine introduction to the subject with easily followed directions for many and varied projects.

4161. Wanhala, Julie M. *You Can Grow Tomatoes* (4–6). Illus. by Cathy Pavia. 1979, Childrens Press $5.96. Easy-to-follow instructions on growing tomatoes in pots and gardens.

4162. Wickers, David, and Tuey, John. *How to Make Things Grow* (4–7). 1972, Van Nostrand $4.95; Scholastic paper $.95. After introductory sections on how plants live, there are chapters on planting and cultivating for both indoor and outdoor gardeners.

4163. Wong, Herbert H., and Vessel, Matthew F. *Our Terrariums* (K–3). Illus. by Aldren A. Watson. 1969, Addison $5.95. A beginning guide for a modest terrarium. Also use: *Terrariums* by John Hoke (1972, Watts, LB $4.90).

4164. Zim, Herbert S. *Plants* (6–9). Illus. by John W. Brainerd. 1947, Harcourt $8.50. A survey of garden hobbies for the amateur, including identification and classification of plants and other useful information.

Magic

4165. Arnold, Ned, and Arnold, Lois. *The Great Science Magic Show* (3–7). Illustrated. 1979, Watts $6.90. Scientific principles are demonstrated in 20 tricks.

4166. Brown, Bob. *How to Fool Your Friends* (3–6). Illustrated. 1978, Golden $7.62; paper $1.95. Amateur magicians will delight in the 46 different tricks and puzzles presented in this book.

4167. Broekel, Ray, and White, Laurence B. *Now You See It; Easy Magic for Beginners* (3–5). Illus. by Bill Morrison. 1979, Little $6.95. Forty proven magic tricks good for amateur shows.

4168. Kettelkamp, Larry. *Magic Made Easy* (4–7). Illus. by author. 1954, Morrow $5.52. An introduction to magic including a number of simple tricks. Also use: *Spooky Magic* (1955, Morrow $5.09; Scholastic, paper 95¢).

4169. Kraske, Robert. *Magicians Do Amazing Things* (2–4). Illus. by Richard Bennett. 1979, Random $2.95; LB $3.99. Kraske reveals the secrets behind 6 great tricks, including one of Houdini's most famous.

4170. Lamb, Geoffrey. *Mental Magic Tricks* (6–8). Illustrated. 1973, Elsevier/Nelson $6.95. A series of interesting tricks that appear to result from clairvoyance.

4171. Michalski, Martin. *Magic Made Easy* (6–9). Illustrated. 1978, Nelson $6.95. More than 70 different tricks are presented, plus details on how to prepare for a show.

4172. Permin, Ib. *Hokus Pokus: With Wands, Water and Glasses* (5–8). Illustrated. 1978, Sterling $3.95. Over 25 tricks for the beginning magician, plus hints for their artful execution.

4173. Rigney, Francis. *A Beginner's Book of Magic* (4–6). Illustrated. 1963, Devin $4.95. Subtitle: *The Do-It-Yourself Book of Tricks, Magic and Stunts.*

4174. Seuling, Barbara. *Abracadabra* (4–6). Illus. by author. 1975, Messner $7.29. Archway paper $1.25. Subtitle: *Creating Your Own Magic Show from Beginning to End.*

4175. Severn, Bill. *Bill Severn's Big Book of Magic* (6–9). Illus. by Katherine Wood. 1973, McKay $8.95. An excellent collection of standard tricks with simple instructions and historical backgrounds. Also use: *Magic across the Table* (1972, McKay $6.95; Bantam, paper $1.75).

4176. Severn, Bill. *Magic in Your Pockets* (4–6). 1964, McKay $2.50. A guide book from a master magician.

4177. Stoddard, Edward. *The First Book of Magic* (5–8). Illus. by Robin King. 1953, Watts $4.90. The best and simplest tricks, each one a real mystery.

4178. Wels, Byron G. *Here Is Your Hobby: Magic* (4–6). Illustrated. 1967, Putnam $5.29. An entertaining book on a popular hobby.

Model Making

4179. Curry, Barbara A. *Model Aircraft* (4–6). Illustrated. 1979, Watts $5.45. A variety of simple models are included, including some folded paper planes.

4180. Gilmore, H. H. *Model Planes for Beginners* (6–9). Illustrated. 1957, Harper $5.95; LB $6.89. Plans for building simplified model planes.

4181. Gilmore, H. H. *Model Rockets for Beginners* (4–8). 1961, Harper $6.89. History of rockets, with plans for building simplified models of American and Soviet types.

4182. Kettelkamp, Larry. *Gliders* (3–5). 1961, Morrow $6.96. Guide to building and flying model gliders with a brief history of powerless flight.

4183. Lopshire, Robert. *Beginner's Guide to Building and Flying Model Airplanes* (4–8). Illustrated. 1967, Harper $7.89. Step-by-step instructions for building many types of model airplanes are most clearly described and illustrated for younger hobbyists, together with an outline of the principles of aerodynamics and helpful hints about tools and techniques.

4184. Maginley, C. J. *Models of America's Past and How to Make Them* (5–8). Illus. by Elizabeth D. McKee. 1969, Harcourt $6.25. Simple directions on how to make such objects from the past as articles of furniture, utensils, and several buildings. Also use: *Historic Models of Early America: And How to Make Them* (1947, Harcourt $5.95; paper 60¢).

4185. Olney, Ross R. *Out to Launch: Modern Rockets* (5–9). Illustrated. 1979, Lothrop $6.95; LB $6.67. This clear introduction to a growing hobby covers the subject from construction information to recovery problems.

4186. Ross, Frank. *Antique Car Models: Their Stories and How to Make Them* (5–8). Illustrated. 1978, Lothrop $7.95. Four antique cars are introduced and plans are supplied to make models of them.

4187. Ross, Frank. *Flying Paper Airplane Models* (5–8). Illustrated. 1975, Lothrop $6.48. Step-by-step directions for making models, plus information on the real aircraft on which the models are based.

4188. Simon, Seymour. *The Paper Airplane Book* (3–6). Illus. by Byron Barton. 1971, Viking $6.50; Penguin paper $1.95. Using how to make paper airplanes as the take-off point, the author explains why planes fly and how changes in their construction can cause variations in flight.

4189. Weiss, Harvey. *How to Run a Railroad: Everything You Need to Know about Model Trains* (5–9). Illustrated. 1977, Crowell $8.95. A thorough description of this popular hobby from purchasing or building the components to various aspects of assembling and operating the system.

4190. Weiss, Harvey. *Model Airplanes and How to Build Them* (5–8). 1975, Crowell $8.95. A well-organized, easily used presentation.

4191. Weiss, Harvey. *Model Buildings and How to Make Them* (5–8). Illus. by author. 1979, Crowell $7.95. Plans and techniques for constructing a variety of buildings.

4192. Weiss, Harvey. *Model Cars and Trucks and How to Build Them* (4–7). Illustrated. 1974, Crowell $8.95. A beginner's book that gives exact and clear directions and advice concerning tools, techniques, and projects to the novice in the model car hobby.

4193. Weiss, Harvey. *Ship Models and How to Build Them* (5–9). Illustrated. 1973, Crowell $8.95. After background information on tools and materials, projects are introduced with clear, step-by-step directions.

4194. Yates, Raymond F. *The Boys' Book of Model Railroading* (5–9). Illustrated. 1951, Harper $6.89. A basic title that has become a standard.

4195. Zarchy, Harry. *Model Railroading* (5–9). Illus. by author. 1955, Knopf $6.39. A complete guide for the fan.

Photography and Filmmaking

4196. Andersen, Yvonne. *Make Your Own Animated Movies* (5–8). Illustrated. 1970, Little $7.95. A thorough survey of the preparation techniques and the actual filming of animated films.

4197. Bendick, Jeanne, and Bendick, Robert. *Filming Works Like This* (6–9). Illustrated. 1970, McGraw $6.95. Step-by-step approach for making a first film.

4198. Czaja, Paul Clement. *Writing with Light: A Simple Workshop in Basic Photography* (6–9). Illustrated. 1973, Viking $5.95. Along with the basics of photography, this work tells how to make images with light.

4199. Davis, Edward E. *Into the Dark* (6–9). 1979, Atheneum $9.95. Subtitle: *A Beginner's Guide to Developing and Printing Black and White Negatives.*

4200. Forbes, Robin. *Click: A First Camera Book* (3–5). Illustrated. 1979, Macmillan $6.95; paper $2.95. An interesting guide for would-be shutterbugs.

4201. Herda, D. J. *Photography: Take a Look* (4–6). Illustrated. 1977, Raintree $5.21. The parts of a camera and a simple guide to taking good pictures.

4202. Holland, Viki. *How to Photograph Your World* (3–5). Illus. by author. 1974, Scribner $6.95. An introductory guide to the hobby, using a simple camera.

4203. Horvath, Joan. *Filmmaking for Beginners* (6–9). Illustrated. 1974, Elsevier/Nelson $6.95; Cornerstone paper $2.95. An awardwinning filmmaker explains simply and directly the various facets of this timely subject in a very well-organized book.

4204. Noren, Catherine. *Photography: How to Improve Your Technique* (5–7). 1973, Watts $4.90. A

how-to manual that gives the beginner many useful pointers.

4205. Sandler, Martin W. *The Story of American Photography* (6–9). Illustrated. 1979, Little $16.95. A fascinating account for the better reader.

4206. Webster, David. *Photo Fun* (6–8). Illustrated. 1973, Watts $5.90. Subtitle: *An Idea Book for Shutterbugs.*

4207. Weiss, Harvey. *How to Make Your Own Movies* (5–7). Illustrated. 1973, Young Scott $7.95. A simple and lucid introduction to the art of movie making. Also use: *Young Filmmakers* by Roger Larsen (1969, Avon, paper 95¢).

4208. Weiss, Harvey. *Lens and Shutter: An Introduction to Photography* (5–8). Illustrated. 1971, Young Scott $7.95. An excellent beginner's book that uses examples by well-known photographers.

Stamp and Coin Collecting

4209. Cetin, Frank. *Here Is Your Hobby: Stamp Collecting* (5–8). Illustrated. 1962, Putnam $5.29. A book for both novice and experienced stamp collectors, including interesting information on the history of stamp collecting.

4210. Hobson, Burton. *Getting Started in Stamp Collecting* (5–8). Illustrated. 1963, Sterling $5.95; LB $5.89. An excellent beginner's guide. Also use: *Collecting Stamps* by Paul Villiard (1974, Doubleday $6.95).

4211. Olcheski, Bill. *Beginning Stamp Collecting* (5–7). 1976, Walck $8.95. This well-written account provides an excellent review of the basics involved with this hobby.

4212. Patrick, Douglas, and Patrick, Mary. *The Stamp Bug: An Illustrated Introduction to Stamp Collecting* (6–8). 1979, McGraw $8.95. A beginner's guide to the fascinating world of stamp collecting.

4213. Reinfeld, Fred, and Hobson, Burton. *How to Build a Coin Collection* (4–8). Illustrated. 1977, Sterling $5.95; LB $5.89. A basic comprehensive guide for the beginner. Also use: *Coin Collecting as a Hobby* by Burton Hobson (1977, Sterling $5.95; LB $5.89).

4214. Rosenfeld, Sam. *The Story of Coins* (5–8). 1968, Harvey House paper $5.39. The interesting stories behind some of the world's most famous coins.

4215. Tower, Samuel A. *Makers of America; Stamps That Honor Them* (4–6). 1978, Messner $7.29. Profile of distinguished Americans as they have been portrayed on postage stamps.

4216. Zarchy, Harry. *Stamp Collector's Guide* (6–9). Illus. by author. 1956, Knopf $6.99. An excellent beginner's guide to stamp collecting. Also use: *Standard Handbook of Stamp Collecting* by Richard Cabeen (1979, Crowell, $13.95).

Crafts

General and Miscellaneous

4217. Allison, Linda. *The Sierra Club Summer Book* (4–6). Illus. by author. 1977, Sierra $7.95; paper $4.95. Projects, activities, and games with one connecting theme—they are all summer pursuits.

4218. Arnold, Susan. *Eggshells to Objects: A New Approach to Egg Craft* (5–8). Illus. by author. 1979, Holt $7.95. A craft book that gives about 30 different projects using egg shells.

4219. Arnold, Wesley F., and Cardy, Wayne C. *Fun with Next to Nothing* (4–6). Illus. by author. 1962, Harper $7.89. Subtitle: *Handicraft Projects for Boys and Girls.*

4220. Beaney, Jan. *Adventures with Collage* (5–7). Illustrated. 1970, Warne $5.95. Encourages individual observation and inventiveness; discusses textures, patterns, and materials.

4221. Brock, Virginia. *Pinatas* (4–7). Illus. by Anne Marie Jauss. 1966, Abingdon $6.50. A history of this Mexican custom, plus instructions on how to make 11 piñatas.

4222. Caney, Steven. *Kids' America* (4–6). Illustrated. 1978, Workman $12.50; paper $6.95. A potpourri of crafts, puzzles, facts, and fun about the United States.

4223. Caney, Steven. *Steven Caney's Play Book* (3–5). Illustrated. 1975, Workman $9.95; paper $4.95. All sorts of activities involving discarded or inexpensive materials, thoroughly and clearly presented.

4224. Cattlidge, Michelle. *The Bears' Bazaar* (1–3). Illustrated. 1980, Lothrop $6.95; LB $6.67. A school bazaar is the occasion for presenting some simple craft projects.

4225. Cole, Ann, and others. *Children Are Children Are Children* (4–7). Illus. by Lois Axeman. 1978, Little $9.95; paper $6.95. Subtitle: *An Activity Approach to Exploring Brazil, France, Iran, Japan, Nigeria and the U.S.S.R. A book of games, crafts, and projects.*

4226. Comins, Jeremy. *Eskimo Crafts and Their Cultural Background* (4–6). Illustrated. 1975, Lothrop LB $6.00. An explanation of Eskimo crafts plus step-by-step directions for do-it-yourself projects.

4227. Conaway, Judith. *City Crafts from Secret Cities* (4–6). Illustrated. 1978, Follett $8.95. Crafts projects that originated in such places as Ur and Timbuktu.

4228. Conaway, Judith. *Manos: South American Crafts for Children* (4–8). Illustrated. 1979, Follett $8.97. The making of everyday objects plus models of people and villages are clearly presented.

4229. Cooper, Michael. *Things to Make and Do for George Washington's Birthday* (4–8). 1978, Watts $6.90. Facts about Washington, plus a number of appropriate projects.

4230. Cramblit, Joella, and Loebel, Jo Ann. *Flowers Are for Keeping* (5–7). Illustrated. 1979, Messner $7.79. Subtitle: *How to Dry Flowers and Make Gifts and Decorations.*

4231. Crook, Beverly Courtney. *Invite a Bird to Dinner: Simple Feeders You Can Make* (4–6). Illustrated. 1978, Morrow $5.71. A variety of projects are described involving construction of many bird feeders from everyday materials.

4232. Cutler, Katherine N. *Creative Shell Craft* (4–6). Illus. by Giulio Maestro. 1971, Lothrop $6.48; paper $2.95. A background book that includes instructions for making shell jewelry and other ornaments. Also use: *Fun with Shells* by Joseph Leeming (1958, Lippincott $4.82)

4233. Cyril, Marshall. *Foilcraft* (5–8). Illustrated. 1977, Stackpole $12.95. A variety of projects using metal foils are described clearly and logically.

4234. Deyrup, Astrith. *Tie Dyeing and Batik* (4–6). Illus. by Nancy Lou Gahen. 1974, Doubleday $6.95. Directions for projects involving 2 interesting crafts that are easily mastered.

4235. Donna, Natalie. *Peanut Craft* (4–6). Illus. by author. 1974, Lothrop $6.75; LB $6.48. A delightful project book using peanut shells.

4236. Ellison, Virginia H. *The Pooh Get-Well Book* (2–5). Illus. by Ernest H. Shepard. 1973, Dutton $5.95; Dell paper $1.25. Subtitle: *Recipes and Activities to Help You Recover from Wheezles and Sneezles.*

4237. Fiarotta, Phyllis, and Fiarotta, Noel. *Confetti: The Kids' Make It Yourself, Do-It-Yourself Party Book* (4–7). Illustrated. 1978, Workman $10.95; paper $5.95. Hundreds of ideas for throwing 22 different kinds of parties.

4238. Foster, Laura Louise. *Keeping the Plants You Pick* (4–7). Illus. by author. 1970, Crowell $8.50. Good material on how to preserve plants, with emphasis on pressing and drying flowers. Also use: *Flower Pressing* by Marge Eaton (1973, Lerner $3.95).

4239. Gibbons, Gail. *Things to Make and Do for Your Birthday* (1–3). Illus. by author. 1978, Watts $3.95; LB $6.90. Craft projects such as making a piñata and special foods are included with simple explanations.

4240. Graham, Ada. *Foxtails, Ferns and Fish Scales: A Handbook of Art and Nature Projects* (3–7). Illus. by Dorethea Stoke. 1976, Four Winds $8.95. Projects involving forms found in nature are described in easy-to-follow instructions utilizing inexpensive art materials.

4241. Hautzig, Esther. *Let's Make More Presents: Easy and Inexpensive Gifts for Every Occasion* (4–7). Illus. by Ray Skibinski. 1973, Macmillan $5.95. All sorts of presents from food to home gifts are presented in this fine sequel to *Let's Make Presents* (1962, Crowell $8.95).

4242. Hogrogian, Nonny. *Handmade Secret Hiding Places* (3–5). Illus. by author. 1975, Viking $4.95. The construction of 6 hiding places from a mud hut to a hideaway made from blankets over chairs is described in words and pictures.

4243. Holz, Loretta. *Mobiles You Can Make* (5–9). Illustrated. 1975, Lothrop $6.75; LB $6.48. Excellent diagrams and logical explanations make this a fine introduction for the novice.

4244. Kerina, Jane. *African Crafts* (5–8). Illus. by Tom Feelings and Marylyn Katzman. 1970, Lion $6.39. Many projects arranged geographically by the region in Africa where they originated. Also use: *African Crafts for You to Make* by Janet D'Amato and Alex D'Amato (1969, Messner $7.79).

4245. Lopshire, Robert. *How to Make Snop Snappers and Other Fine Things* (2–4). Illus. by author. 1977, Greenwillow $5.71. Simple projects and games that can be made with readily available materials.

4246. Marks, Mickey Klar. *Op-Tricks: Creating Kinetic Art* (5–9). Illustrated. 1972, Lippincott $7.95. A group of projects that create fascinating optical effects, most using material found around the house. Also use: *Creating Things That Move: Fun with Kinetic Art* by Harry Helfman (1975, Morrow $5.04).

4247. Miller, Donna, and Dunne, Robert L. *Egg Carton Critters* (2–5). Illustrated. 1979, Walker $5.95. How to make all sorts of weird and wonderful model animals from egg cartons.

4248. Parish, Peggy. *Beginning Mobiles* (2–4). Illus. by Lynn Sweat. 1979, Macmillan $6.95. A simple book of projects involving easily found materials presented in an easy-to-follow format.

4249. Rahn, Joan Elma. *Seven Ways to Collect Plants* (5–7). Illustrated. 1978, Atheneum $5.95. A fine introduction to this hobby with special hints on collecting, drying, and pressing of specimens.

4250. Razzi, James. *Bag of Tricks! Fun Things to Make and Do with the Groceries* (K–5). Illustrated. 1971, Parents $5.95; LB $5.41. Projects to do from materials found in the kitchen—for home, school, or scouts.

4251. Rockwell, Harlow. *I Did It* (1–3). Illustrated. 1973, Macmillan $4.95. Very simple projects for the beginning crafter.

4252. Rockwell, Harlow. *Look at This* (1–3). Illus. by author. 1978, Macmillan $6.95. Three stories, each containing a simple project for a child.

4253. St. Tamara. *Asian Crafts* (4–6). Illus. by author. 1970, Lion $5.98. A collection of such crafts as jewelry and mask making from various Asian countries.

4254. Schwartz, Alvin. *The Rainy Day Book* (1–6). 1973, Simon & Schuster paper $2.95. Many games, activities, and craft ideas as well as dramatics, music, and science experiments make up this helpful book for harassed parents and children.

4255. Shaw, Ray. *Candle Art* (4–7). Illus. by author. 1973, Morrow $9.95. Subtitle: *A Gallery of Candle Designs and How to Make Them.* Also use: *Candles for Beginners to Make* by Alice Gilbreath (1975, Morrow $6.25; LB $6.00).

4256. Simons, Robin. *Recyclopedia: Games, Science Equipment and Crafts from Recycled Materials* (5–9). Illus. by author. 1976, Houghton $7.95; paper $3.95. Clear directions complemented by good illustrations characterize this book of interesting projects using waste materials.

4257. Stokes, Jack. *Let's Make a Tent* (4–6). Illustrated. 1980, McKay $6.95. A simple step-by-step account that, nevertheless, will probably need the help of an adult.

4258. Stranks, Susan. *Family Fun: Things to Make, Do and Play* (6–9). Illustrated. 1980, Barron's $11.95; to schools $9.56. Crafts, such as producing paper flowers and rag dolls, which will interest both youngsters and parents are well presented.

4259. Temko, Florence. *Felt Craft* (4–6). Illus. by Steve Madison. 1973, Doubleday $4.95. Twenty-two projects that range from finger puppets to a poncho for a doll. Also use: *Make It with Felt* by Arden J. Newsome (1972, Lothrop $6.00).

4261. Trivett, Daphne, and Trivett, John. *Time for Clocks* (6–8). Illustrated. 1979, Crowell $6.89. Plans are included for several easy-to-make clocks.

4262. Tudor, Tasha, and Allen, Linda. *Tasha Tudor's Old-Fashioned Gifts* (5–9). 1979, McKay $10.95. Over 30 craft and gift projects are outlined, including several recipes.

4263. Weiss, Harvey. *Collage and Construction* (4–7). Illustrated. 1970, Young Scott $7.95. A step-by-step guide to creating such forms as box pictures, wire sculpture, and string pictures.

4264. Weiss, Harvey. *The Gadget Book* (4–7). Illustrated. 1971, Crowell $6.50. Many interesting projects including water clocks and wind chimes are introduced in an entertaining way.

4265. Weiss, Harvey. *How to Make Your Own Books* (5–9). Illus. by author. 1974, Crowell $8.95. Details on how to make various types and parts of books.

4266. Williams, Barbara, and Arnold, Susan. *Pins, Picks, and Popsicle Sticks* (4–6). Illustrated. 1977, Holt $7.95. Directions for creating a number of toys, decorations, and gifts from common, often-discarded materials. Also use: *Sticks, Spools and Feathers* by Harvey Weiss (1962, Young Scott $7.95).

4267. Wiseman, Ann. *Making Things Book 2: Handbook of Creative Discovery* (4–7). Illustrated. 1975, Little $8.95; paper $4.95. Clear directions for making such articles as Tiffany lamp shades and string bikinis from materials found around the house. Also use: *Making Things* (1973, Little $6.95; paper $4.95).

American Historical Crafts

4268. Hofsinde, Robert. *Indian Games and Crafts* (5–7). 1957, Morrow $5.71. Instructions on how to make a variety of Indian artifacts. Also use: *Indian Beadwork* (1958, Morrow $5.52).

4269. Hoople, Cheryl G. *The Heritage Sampler: A Book of Colonial Arts and Crafts* (5–7). Illus. by Richard Cuffari. 1975, Dial $6.95; LB $6.46. Each chapter deals with a different colonial craft, followed by simple instructions on projects that can be done today. Also use: *Colonial Crafts for You to Make* by Janet D'Amato and Alex D'Amato (1975, Messner $7.29).

4270. Kinney, Jean, and Kinney, Cle. *Twenty-One Kinds of American Folk Art and How to Make Each One* (4–6). Illustrated. 1972, Atheneum $6.95. A quick overview of such American folk activities as pottery making, wood carving, and tap dancing.

4271. Pettit, Florence H. *How to Make Whirligigs and Whimmy Diddles and Other American Folkcraft Objects* (5–8). Illus. by Laura Louise Foster. 1972, Crowell $16.95. A fascinating collection of projects that young people can make if supervised by adults.

4272. Parish, Peggy. *Let's Be Early Settlers with Daniel Boone* (2–4). Illus. by Arnold Lobel. 1976, Harper $7.89. Easy-to-follow directions for making many items associated with pioneer days. Also use: *Let's Be Indians* (1962, Harper $5.79).

4273. Simon, Nancy, and Wolfson, Evelyn. *American Indian Habitats: How to Make Dwellings and Shelters with Natural Materials* (6–9). Illus. by Nancy Poydar. 1978, McKay $7.95. How to build a wigwam, tepee, and other Native American dwellings.

Clay and Other Modeling Crafts

4274. Brockway, Maureen. *Clay Projects* (2–4). Illus. by George Overlie. 1973, Lerner $3.95. Simple projects for the beginner that involve constructing such objects as a wall plaque and bird feeder. For an older audience use: *Modeling in Clay, Plaster and Papier-Mache* by Richard Slade (1968, Lothrop, paper $2.95).

4275. Chernoff, Goldie Taub. *Clay-Dough, Play-Dough* (2–4). Illus. by Margaret A. Hartelius. 1974, Walker $3.95; Scholastic paper $1.25. Simple directions for making many articles from a mixture of flour, water, and salt.

4276. Elbert, Virginia Fowler. *Potterymaking* (4–7). Illustrated. 1974, Doubleday $4.95. A beginner's book with explicit practical directions for simple projects that can be fired in the kitchen oven.

4277. Gilbreath, Alice. *Slab, Coil and Pinch: A Beginner's Pottery Book* (3–5). Illus. by Barbara Fiore. 1977, Morrow $5.75; LB $5.52. Very simple projects for the beginner potter using self-hardening clay or terra cotta.

4278. Leeming, Joseph. *Fun with Clay* (4–6). Illustrated. 1944, Lippincott $8.95. Beginner's instructions with minimum materials. Also use: *Creating with Clay* by James E. Seidelman (1967, Macmillan $5.95).

4279. Sommer, Elyse. *The Bread Dough Craft Book* (3–7). Illus. by Giulio Maestro. 1972, Lothrop $6.48; paper $2.50. With a few bread slices, glue, and liquid detergent, the novice can create almost 60 different projects.

4280. Weiss, Harvey. *Ceramics from Clay to Kiln* (5–7). Illustrated. 1964, Young Scott $7.95. An excellent beginning book that stresses creativity.

4281. Lidstone, John. *Building with Wire* (4–7). 1972, Van Nostrand $8.95. An introduction to wire sculpture with simple projects.

Costume Making

4282. Barwell, Eve. *Disguises You Can Make* (4–6). Illus. by Richard Rosenblum. 1977, Lothrop $6.96. With simple materials and instructions, youngsters can transform themselves into such creatures as Martians, monsters, or witches.

4283. Bruun-Rasmussen, Ole, and Petersen, Grete. *Make-Up, Costumes and Masks for the Stage* (5–9). Illustrated. 1976, Sterling $6.95; LB $6.69. A useful compilation of material on backstage skills for putting on plays.

4284. Chernoff, Goldie Taub. *Easy Costumes You Don't Have to Sew* (3–6). Illus. by Margaret A. Hartelius. 1977, Four Winds $6.95; paper $1.25. Paper bags, cartons, and old cloth are only 3 of the materials used in making these simple costumes.

4285. Haley, Gail E. *Costumes for Plays and Playing* (4–6). Illus. by author. 1979, Methuen $7.95. Colorful illustrations highlight this introduction to costume making.

4286. Mooser, Stephen. *Monster Fun* (4–6). Illus. by Dana Herkelrath. 1979, Messner $7.29. An activity book that tells youngsters how to become monsters.

4287. Parish, Peggy. *Costumes to Make* (3–6). Illus. by Lynn Sweat. 1970, Macmillan $6.95. Simple patterns that can be turned into a wide array of masquerades and disguises.

4288. Purdy, Susan. *Costumes for You to Make* (4–9). Illus. by author. 1971, Lippincott $8.95. Simple, easily followed directions with coverage on costumes, makeup, and masks.

4289. Schnurnberger, Lynn. *Kings, Queens, Knights and Jesters: Making Medieval Costumes* (4–8). Illustrated. 1978, Harper $7.95. This book presents an introduction to the clothing of the Middle Ages and how to make several examples.

4290. Whitney, Alex. *American Indian Clothes and How to Make Them* (5–8). Illus. by Marie Ostberg and Nils Ostberg. 1979, McKay $7.95. A description of many kinds of American Indian dress with do-it-yourself techniques.

Drawing and Painting

4291. Ames, Lee J. *Draw, Draw, Draw* (4–6). 1962, Doubleday $5.95. Easy-to-follow instructions on how to draw common objects. For the very young also use: *Start to Draw* by Ann Campbell (1968, Watts $4.90).

4292. Ames, Lee J. *Draw 50 Famous Cartoons* (4–6). 1979, Doubleday $3.99. How to draw such characters as Dick Tracy and the Flintstones.

4293. Ames, Lee J. *Draw Fifty Airplanes, Aircraft and Spacecraft* (3–7). Illustrated. 1977, Doubleday $6.95. Simple directions for drawing various airborne articles, from the Wright brothers' plane to the Saturn V rocket. Also use from Doubleday ($6.95): *Draw Fifty Animals* (1974) and *Draw Fifty Boats, Ships, Trucks and Trains* (1976).

4294. Emberley, Ed. *Ed Emberley's Drawing Book: Make a World* (2–4). Illus. by author. 1972, Little $4.95. Illustrations and examples on how to draw objects from flags to faces. A companion to the author's *Drawing Book of Animals* (1970, Little $4.95). Also use from Little: *Trains* (1973, paper $1.00), *Birds* (1973, paper $1.00), *Farms* (1973, paper $1.00), and *Faces* (1975, $4.95).

4295. Emberley, Ed. *Dinosaurs!* (PS–K). Illustrated. 1980, Little $5.95. Step-by-step lessons on how to draw 10 different dinosaurs.

4296. Emberley, Ed. *Ed Emberley's Big Green Drawing Book* (2–4). Illus. by author. 1979, Little $6.95; paper $3.95. A do-it-yourself drawing book using basic shapes, explained by a master.

4297. Frame, Paul. *Drawing Cats and Kittens* (6–8). Illustrated. 1979, Watts $6.90. A detailed explanation of how to draw cats that emphasizes the need to practice.

4298. Hawkinson, John. *Collect, Print and Paint from Nature* (2–4). Illus. by author. 1963, Whitman $5.95. Basic instructions for leaf printing, spatter painting, and elementary brush techniques. Also by the author and publisher: *Pastels Are Great* (1968, $6.25).

4299. Hawkinson, John. *Pat, Swish, Twist and the Story of Patty Swish* (1–2). Illus. by author. 1978, Whitman $6.95. The basics on how to mix colors and paint in watercolors, simply given.

4300. Rauch, Hans-Georg. *The Lines Are Coming: A Book about Drawing* (2–6). Illustrated. 1978, Scribner $7.95. A description of various kinds of lines and how each can be used in the art of drawing.

4301. Seidelman, James E., and Mintonye, Grace. *Creating with Paint* (5–7). Illus. by Peter Landa. 1967, Crowell $4.95. Beginner information to encourage experimentation with paints.

4302. Spilka, Arnold. *Paint All Kinds of Pictures* (K–3). Illustrated. 1963, Walck $6.25. A beautiful picture book that leads young children into self-expression through painting. For an older audience use: *How to Paint with Water Colors* by Arthur Zaidenberg (1968, Vanguard $4.95).

4303. Weiss, Harvey. *Pencil, Pen and Brush: Drawings for Beginners* (5–7). 1961, Young Scott $7.95; Scholastic paper $.95. Basic techniques and step-by-step directions on drawing from photographs as models. Also use: *Paint, Brush and Palette* (1966, Young Scott $7.95).

4304. Zaidenberg, Arthur. *How to Draw People: A Book for Beginners* (7–9). 1952, Vanguard $4.95. Two other books by this master teacher are: *How to Draw Cartoons: A Book for Beginners* (1959, Vanguard $4.95; Scholastic, paper 95¢) and *How to Draw Heads and Faces* (1966, Abelard $6.79).

4305. Zaidenberg, Arthur. *How to Draw with Pen and Brush: A Book for Beginners* (4–7). 1965, Vanguard $4.95. An explanation with examples on various effects that can be created with pens and paintbrushes. Also use: *The First Book of Drawing* by Louis Slobodkin (1958, Watts $4.90).

Masks and Mask Making

4306. Alkema, Chester Jay. *Masks* (5–9). Illustrated. 1971, Sterling $3.95; LB $4.59. Basic material on mask making is given in sections organized by the type of material used, such as paper, cardboard, papier-mâché.

4307. Hunt, Kari, and Carlson, Bernice W. *Masks and Mask Makers* (5–7). 1961, Abingdon $5.95. Stories behind the masks used in primitive and modern societies, with instructions for making some of them.

4308. Meyer, Carolyn. *Mask Magic* (4–6). Illustrated. 1978, Harcourt $7.95. A simple guide to mask making and the relation of masks to many of our celebrations.

4309. Price, Christine. *The Mystery of Masks* (6–8). Illustrated. 1978, Scribner $7.95. A description of masks and their relation to the cultures that made and used them.

4310. Ross, Laura. *Mask Making with Pantomine and Stories from American History* (4–6). Illustrated. 1975, Lothrop $6.00. Simple, clear instructions on how to make masks are given along with their place in history and several short plays utilizing masks.

Paper Crafts

4311. Amidon, Eva V. *Easy Quillery: Projects with Paper Coils and Scrolls* (3–5). Illus. by Charles H. Amidon, Jr. 1977, Morrow $6.25; LB $6.00. The handicraft of quilling, or simulating metal filigree with coils of paper, is carefully and logically introduced in several child-tested projects.

4312. Anderson, Mildred. *Papier Mache Crafts* (6–8). 1975, Sterling $8.95. A fine introduction that gives directions for making many objects.

4313. Araki, Chiyo. *Origami in the Classroom* (4–7). Illustrated. 1965, Tuttle $4.75. In 2 volumes, each deals with paper crafts for 2 of the seasons. Also use: *The ABC's of Origami* by Claude Sarasas (1964, Tuttle $4.50).

4314. Cheng, Hou-tien. *Scissor Cutting for Beginners* (1–3). Illustrated. 1978, Holt $6.50. Little text and many pictures show youngsters how to cut out numbers and letters and make posters.

4315. Dieringer, Beverly, and Morton, Marjorie. *The Paper Bead Box* (5–7). Illustrated. 1977, McKay $9.95; paper $4.95. A useful hobby that will produce attractive jewelry.

4316. Gilbreath, Alice. *Simple Decoupage: Having Fun with Cutouts* (4–6). Illustrated. 1978, Morrow $5.50. Thirteen inexpensive projects are described in detail and with simple instructions.

4317. Granit, Inga. *Cardboard Crafting* (4–7). 1965, Sterling $6.95; LB $6.69. A number of interesting projects carefully and explicitly explained.

4318. Johnson, Lillian. *Papier-Mâché* (5–8). Illustrated. 1958, McKay $6.95. A guide to creating unlimited varieties of displays, dolls, figures, and masks.

4319. Linsley, Leslie. *Decoupage for Young Crafters* (3–6). Illustrated. 1977, Dutton $7.95. Nine projects ranging from simple to more difficult are thoroughly presented and well illustrated. Also use: *Designing with Cutouts: The Art of Decoupage* by Elyse Sommer (1973, Lothrop $6.48) and *Decoupage Crafts* by Florence Temko (1976, Doubleday $5.95).

4320. Norvell, Flo Ann Hedley. *The Great Big Box Book* (4–6). Illustrated. 1979, Crowell $8.95; LB $8.79. Over 15 projects are described that turn boxes into such objects as castles and spaceships.

4321. Pflug, Betsy. *Funny Bags* (1–3). Illustrated. 1968, Van Nostrand $8.95. Masks, puppets, and games are a few of the things that can be made from paper bags.

4322. Seidelman, James E., and Mintonye, Grace. *Creating with Papier-Mâché* (3–6). Illus. by Christine Randall. 1971, Crowell $4.95. A clear, well-organized craft book with details on many projects.

4323. Soong, Maying. *The Art of Chinese Paper Folding* (4–7). Illus. by author. 1948, Harcourt $6.50. A square of paper is all that is necessary to make a variety of objects.

4324. Temko, Florence. *Paper Cutting* (3–6). Illus. by Steve Madison. 1973, Doubleday $4.95. Clear, easily followed directions for making a number of objects from paper.

4325. Temko, Florence, and Takahama, Toshie. *The Magic of Kirigami: Happenings with Paper and Scissors* (4–7). Illustrated. 1978, Japan Pubs. $9.95. Many interesting projects are outlined, using Japanese paper cutting.

4326. Weiss, Harvey. *Working with Cardboard and Paper* (5–7). Illustrated. 1978, Addison $7.95. Such project ideas as model houses and castles, as well as mobiles and paper mosaics, are detailed.

Printmaking

4327. Cross, Jeanne. *Simple Printing Methods* (6–9). Illustrated. 1972, Phillips $8.95. An introduction to printmaking techniques, mainly using materials found around the house. Well illustrated with many examples in color.

4328. Pettit, Florence H. *The Stamp-Pad Printing Book* (4–6). Illus. by author. 1979, Crowell $7.95; LB $7.89. How to make a variety of objects, for example, posters and bookmarks, from stamps cut from erasers.

4329. MacStravic, Suellen. *Print Making* (3–5). Illus. by George Overlie. 1973, Lerner $3.95. The techniques used in making various kinds of prints and an introduction in clear, simple text with informative illustrations.

4330. Rockwell, Harlow. *Printmaking* (6–8). Illus. by author. 1974, Doubleday $4.95. Easy-to-follow directions for making 12 different kinds of prints.

4331. Weiss, Harvey. *Paper, Ink and Roller* (4–7). 1958, Addison $7.95. An excellent, clear introduction to printmaking for beginners, including techniques for press, transfer, potato, stencil, cardboard, and linoleum printing.

4332. Weiss, Peter. *Simple Printmaking* (5–8). Illus. by Sally Gralla. 1976, Lothrop $5.52. Techniques for producing prints of many types and the necessary equipment are described in a clear, authoritative manner.

Sewing and Needle Crafts

4333. Allison, Linda, and Allison, Stella. *Rags: Making a Little Something Out of Almost Nothing* (6–9). Illustrated. 1979, Crown $14.95; paper $6.95. A wonderful collection of projects using only scraps.

4334. Barkin, Carol, and James, Elizabeth. *Slapdash Alterations: How to Recycle Your Wardrobe* (5–7). Illustrated. 1977, Lothrop $5.75; LB $5.52. A simple, do-it-yourself guide to remodeling girl's clothes. Also use: *Slapdash Sewing* (1975, Lothrop $5.04).

4335. Bradley, Duane. *Design It, Sew It and Wear It* (5–8). Illus. by Judith Hoffman. 1979, Crowell $8.79. Subtitle: *How to Make Yourself a Super Wardrobe without Commercial Patterns*.

4336. Cone, Ferne Geller. *Knutty Knitting for Kids* (3–6). Illustrated. 1977, Follett $6.95; LB $6.99. Unusual projects are used to introduce youngsters to the basic knitting stitches.

4337. Corrigan, Barbara. *I Love to Sew* (4–7). Illustrated. 1974, Doubleday $5.95. Hand and machine sewing and a variety of projects are introduced in this informative introduction. Also use: *Of Course You Can Sew!* (1971, Doubleday $4.95).

4338. Harayda, Marel. *Needlework Magic with Two Basic Stitches* (5–9). Illustrated. 1978, McKay

$6.95. A variety of projects are introduced using the Gobelin and Continental stitches.

4339. Hodgson, Mary Anne, and Paine, Josephine Ruth. *Fast and Easy Needlepoint* (4–7). Illustrated. 1979, Doubleday $5.95. A basic introduction that includes directions for 10 different stitches.

4340. Kelly, Karin. *Weaving* (4–6). Illus. by George Overlie. 1973, Lerner $3.95. Directions for making a cardboard loom and simple weaving projects using it. Also use: *Fun with Weaving* by Alice Gilbreath (1976, Morrow $5.75; LB $5.52)

4341. Lightbody, Donna M. *Easy Weaving* (4–6). Illustrated. 1974, Lothrop $6.75; LB $6.48. A simple, easily followed book of attractive projects for the beginner.

4342. Lightbody, Donna M. *Let's Knot: A Macrame Book* (5–9). Illustrated. 1972, Lothrop $6.48; paper $2.95. A beginner's book with simple descriptions of individual knots and clear instructions for basic projects.

4343. Meyer, Carolyn. *Yarn—The Things It Makes and How to Make Them* (4–7). Illus. by Jennifer Perrott. 1972, Harcourt $5.95. The history of all forms of needlework plus simple projects.

4344. Miller, Irene P., and Lubell, Winnifred. *The Stitchery Book: Embroidery for Beginners* (5–8). Illustrated. 1965, Doubleday $4.95. After a chapter on the history, the basic materials, and all the classic stitches, the emphasis turns to creative stitchery, and the reader is encouraged to experiment and to vary the basic stitches. Also use: *Stitchery for Children* by Jacqueline Enthoven (1968, Reinhold, paper $7.95).

4345. Parker, Xenia Ley. *A Beginner's Book of Knitting and Crocheting* (5–8). Illustrated. 1974, Dodd $5.95. Detailed and explicit directions highlight this easily used book.

4346. Parker, Xenia Ley. *A Beginner's Book of Needlepoint and Embroidery* (4–6). Illustrated. 1975, Dodd $5.95. A clearly presented account, well illustrated.

4347. Phillips, Mary Walker. *Knitting* (4–6). 1977, Watts $5.90. A beginning account that explains the basics clearly.

4348. Ratner, Marilyn. *Plenty of Patches* (5–9). Illustrated. 1978, Crowell $7.95. An introduction to patchwork, quilting, and appliqué.

4349. Rubenstone, Jessie. *Knitting for Beginners* (5–8). Illustrated. 1973, Lippincott $7.95; paper $2.95. Beginning with the most simple procedures, the author builds to more complicated stitches and projects. Good use of photographs.

Also use: *Crochet for Beginners* (1974, Lippincott $7.95; paper $2.95).

4350. Sommer, Elyse, and Sommer, Joellen. *Patchwork, Applique, and Quilting Primer* (4–8). Illus. by Giulio Maestro. 1975, Lothrop $6.00. These historic crafts are introduced through a series of useful projects.

4351. Von Wartburg, Ursula. *The Workshop Book of Knitting* (4–7). Illustrated. 1978, Atheneum $9.95. An easily understood book of patterns that includes toys and animals and articles of clothing.

4352. Wilson, Erica. *Fun with Crewel Embroidery* (3–7). Illustrated. 1965, Scribner $5.95. The craft of stitching with wool on fabric is explained to youngsters with clear word-and-photograph instructions covering over 24 of the most popular, frequently used stitches.

4353. Wiseman, Ann. *Cuts of Cloth: Quick Classics to Sew and Wear* (6–8). Illustrated. 1978, Little $7.95; paper $4.95. A compendium of 23 simply made designs.

Toys and Dolls

4354. Ackley, Edith F. *Dolls to Make for Fun and Profit* (5–8). Illus. by Telka Ackley. 1951, Lippincott $9.95. A practical craft book. Also use: *Make Your Own Dolls* by Eleanor B. Heady (1974, Lothrop $6.00).

4355. Beisner, Monika. *Fantastic Toys* (4–6). Illus. by author. 1974, Follett $5.94; LB $6.99. How to make strange and wonderful toys from simple instructions and ordinary materials.

4356. Benbow, Mary, and others. *Dolls Traditional and Topical and How to Make Them* (5–7). Illustrated. 1970, Plays $8.95. Descriptions and directions for making dolls from other lands and other times.

4357. Gilbreath, Alice. *Making Toys That Crawl and Slide* (4–6). Illustrated. 1978, Follett $5.97; paper $2.95. Simple instructions and suitable drawings enhance information on 14 projects. Also use: *Making Toys That Swim and Float* (1978, Follett $5.97; paper 2.95).

4358. Glubok, Shirley. *Dolls, Dolls, Dolls* (3–6). Illustrated. 1975, Follett $5.95; LB $5.97. Dolls old and new from various areas of the world are pictured and given a brief explanation.

4359. Huff, Vivian. *Let's Make Paper Dolls* (2–3). Illustrated. 1978, Harper $4.79. Simple instructions and clear photographs help youngsters make paper dolls of various sizes.

4360. Joseph, Joan. *Folk Toys around the World and How to Make Them* (6–8). Illustrated. 1972, Parents $5.95; LB $5.41; U.S. Comm. UNICEF $3.50. Detailed plans for making 18 toys from different countries. For a younger audience use: *Toy Book* by Steven Caney (1972, Workman $8.95; paper $3.95).

4361. Kraska, Edie. *Toys and Tales from Grandmother's Attic* (4–8). Illus. by author. 1979, Houghton $12.95; paper $6.95. Historical information and projects are given for 15 toys and crafts.

4362. Morton, Brenda. *Do-It-Yourself Dinosaurs: Imaginative Toy Craft for Beginners* (4–6). Illus. by author. 1974, Taplinger $6.95. This book on stuffed toys describes how to make a dozen dinosaurs and other prehistoric creatures.

4363. Roche, P. K. *Dollhouse Magic: How to Make and Find Simple Dollhouse Furniture* (3–5). Illus. by Richard Cuffari. 1977, Dial $7.95; LB $7.45. Clear instructions and step-by-step sketches introduce this fascinating craft to the novice. Also use: *Boxed-in-Doll Houses* by Betsy Pflug (1971, Lippincott $7.95).

4364. Waltner, Willard, and Waltner, Elma. *Hobbycraft Toys and Games* (4–6). Illustrated. n.d. Lantern $6.70. A basic book for the beginning craftsperson.

Woodworking

4365. Adkins, Jan. *Toolchest* (5–9). Illus. by author. 1973, Walker $6.95; LB $6.85. An excellent book for the beginning carpenter that describes each basic tool, its care and uses.

4366. Lasson, Robert, and Shupak, Sidney. *Glue It Yourself: Woodworking without Nails* (6–9). Illustrated. 1978, Dutton $8.95. Making wastebaskets and sewing boxes are just two of the many projects described in this well-illustrated book.

4367. Lasson, Robert. *If I Had a Hammer: Woodworking with Seven Basic Tools* (5–8). Illustrated. 1974, Dutton $7.95. Basic tools, how to use them, and several simple projects are given in this useful introduction to the craft.

4368. Lidstone, John. *Building with Balsa Wood* (4–7). 1965, Reinhold $8.95. Photographs and brief text show basic techniques of creating abstract "constructions, mobiles, screens, masks, and other designs."

4369. Meyer, Carolyn. *Saw, Hammer and Paint: Woodworking and Finishing for Beginners* (6–9). Illus. by Toni Martignori. 1973, Morrow $6.75; LB $6.48. So straightforward, well organized, and uncondescending that it could be used by adults. Interesting projects clearly described.

4370. Rockwell, Anne. *The Toolbox* (1–2). Illus. by Harlow Rockwell. 1971, Macmillan $4.95; paper $1.25. A description of each tool in the toolbox and what it does, told in simple language and illustrated with exact pictures.

4371. Torre, Frank D. *Woodworking for Kids* (6–9). Illustrated. 1978, Doubleday $6.95. Photographs help amplify this introduction to basic tools and a few interesting projects.

4372. Walker, Les. *Housebuilding for Children* (4–7). Illustrated. 1977, Viking $10.00. The construction of 6 different kinds of houses, including a tree house, are clearly described in text and pictures.

4373. Weiss, Peter. *Balsa Wood Craft* (4–7). Illus. by author. 1972, Lothrop paper $2.50. A fine range of projects is detailed with clear illustrations and supportive background material.

4374. Weiss, Harvey. *Carving: How to Carve Wood and Soap* (6–9). 1976, Addison $7.95. Working from simple projects to the more complex, this manual is well organized and clearly written.

4375. Yates, Raymond F. *The Boys' Book of Tools* (4–6). Illustrated. 1957, Harper $6.89. An explanation of the types and uses of many household tools.

Sports and Games

General and Miscellaneous

4376. Bancroft, Jessie H. *Games* (5–8). Illustrated. 1937, Macmillan $9.00. A collection of 600 games "for the playground, home, school, and gymnasium."

4377. Barr, George. *Young Scientist and Sports: Featuring Baseball—Football—Basketball* (4–7). Illus. by Mildred Waltrip. 1962, McGraw $6.50. The scientific principles fundamental in 3 sports are well explained.

4378. Benson, Rolf. *Skydiving* (6–9). Illustrated. 1979, Lerner $5.95. Free-fall forms, equipment, and jumping techniques.

4379. Boccaccio, Tony. *Racquetball Basics* (5–8). Illustrated. 1979, Prentice-Hall $6.95. The history of this increasingly popular sport, as well as rules and the types of equipment needed.

4380. Boston Children's Medical Center. *What to Do When There's Nothing to Do* (5–8). 1968, Delacorte $5.95; Dell paper $1.50. A fine collection of games for young people.

4381. Colby, C. B. *First Rifle* (4–6). Illustrated. 1954, Coward $4.79. A heavily illustrated title with a minimum of text.

4382. Ferretti, Fred. *The Great American Book of Sidewalk, Stoop, Dirt, Curb and Alley Games* (3–6). Illustrated. 1975, Workman $3.95. Sixty American street games described by a clear text as well as photographs and diagrams. Also use: *The Great American Marble Book* (n.d., Workman $2.95).

4383. Fichter, George S. *Racquetball* (4–7). Illustrated. 1979, Watts $5.90. A lucid presentation of the history and fundamentals of this growing sport.

4384. Flanagan, Henry E., and Gardner, Robert. *Basic Lacrosse Strategy* (6–9). Illus. by John Lane. 1979, Doubleday $7.95. An introduction to the fundamental rules and techniques of the game.

4385. Freeman, Tony. *An Introduction to Radio-Controlled Sailplanes* (3–6). Illustrated. 1979, Children's Press $5.95. A brief introduction that includes material on equipment and techniques.

4386. Gemme, Leila Boyle. *T-Ball Is Our Game* (1–3). Illustrated. 1978, Children's Press $5.50. T-ball introduced in a simple less-than-100 word text.

4387. Golf Digest editors. *Better Golf for Boys* (4–6). Illustrated. 1965, Dodd $4.50. A fine introduction to this sport.

4388. Gould, Marilyn. *Playground Sports: A Book of Ball Games* (2–4). Illustrated. 1978, Morrow $6.95. Rules and techniques are given for a variety of games, including tetherball and beanbag games.

4389. Halacy, Dan. *Soaring* (3–6). Illus. by James Tallon. 1972, Lippincott $7.95. This brief survey of gliding is enhanced by clear color photographs. Also use: *Hot Air Ballooning* by Peter B. Mohn (1975, Crestwood $4.95).

4390. Herda, D. J. *Roller Skating* (4–6). Illustrated. 1979, Watts $5.45. An excellent introduction to this sport, stressing safety.

4391. Hunt, Sarah E. *Games and Sports the World Around* (4–9). 1964, Ronald $10.95. All kinds of play activities are outlined in this comprehensive volume.

4392. Ice Skating Institute, and United States Olympic Committee. *Olympic Bobsledding* (5–8). Illustrated. 1979, Childrens Press $5.95. The history, present status, and techniques associated with the sport highlight this narrative.

4393. Kamm, Herbert. *The New Junior Illustrated Encyclopedia of Sports* (5–8). Illus. by Willard Mullin. 1975, Bobbs-Merrill $8.95. Statistics, rules, and biographies of important players are given for 13 major sports. Also use: *The Concise Encyclopedia of Sports* by Gerald Newman (1979, Watts $8.95).

4394. Kay, Eleanor. *Skydiving* (4–6). Illustrated. 1971, Watts $4.89. An intriguing survey of the history and basics of this daredevil sport. Also use: *Hang Gliding* by Otto Penzler (1976, Troll $5.89; paper $2.50).

4395. Keith, Harold. *Sports and Games* (5–8). 1976, Crowell $9.95. A basic guide to a variety of recreational activities.

4396. Knight, Richard Alden. *The Boy's Book of Gun Handling* (6–9). Illus. by Pody. 1964, Putnam $5.49. An entertaining account that stresses caution and safety.

4397. McCoy, Elin. *The Incredible Year-Round Playbook* (4–7). Illus. by Irene Trivas. 1979, Random $5.99; paper $3.95. All kinds of interesting activities—games, recipes, tricks, and experiments—are outlined for play indoors and out.

4398. McWhirter, Norris, and McWhirter, Ross., eds. *Guinness Sports Record Book* (4–7). Illustrated. 1978, Sterling $5.95; LB $5.89. A compilation of the "longest," "fastest" world records. Also use: *Great Moments in American Sports* by Jerry Bronfields (1974, Random $4.95; LB $5.99).

4399. Olney, Ross R., and Bush, Chan. *Roller Skating* (6–9). Illustrated. 1979, Lothrop $6.50; LB $6.24. An impressive guide book to an increasingly popular sport.

4400. Olney, Ross R. *Tricky Discs* (4–6). 1979, Lothrop $6.95. The origin, use, and care of the Frisbee and other flying discs.

4401. Ravielli, Anthony. *What Is Golf?* (3–6). Illus. by author. 1976, Atheneum $6.95. An interesting introduction to the sport, which includes a history and description of techniques. Also use: *Golf Techniques: How to Improve Your Game* by Parker Smith (1973, Watts $4.90).

4402. Rockwell, Anne. *Games (and How to Play Them)* (2–4). Illus. by author. 1973, Crowell $9.95; LB $9.79. Forty-three popular children's indoor and outdoor games are described, and clear, simple illustrations given for their execution.

4403. Roth, Arnold. *A Comick Book of Sports* (4–7). Illus. by author. 1974, Scribner $6.95. A zany pseudohistory of sports, illustrated with 2-color cartoons.

4404. Sabin, Louis. *100 Great Moments in Sports* (4–8). Illustrated. 1979, Putnam $5.96. An entertaining sampling of some red-letter days in sports.

4405. Savitz, Harriet May. *Wheelchair Champions* (5–7). 1978, Crowell $7.95; LB $7.79. Subtitle: *A History of Wheelchair Sports.*

4406. Sullivan, George. *Better Archery for Boys and Girls* (5–7). Illustrated. 1970, Dodd $4.95. Excellent information for the beginning archer, plus helpful hints on correcting faults, caring for equipment, and safety measures.

4407. Sullivan, George. *Better Table Tennis for Boys and Girls* (5–7). Illustrated. 1972, Dodd $4.95. A history and guide to basic strategies in this well-illustrated manual.

4408. Sullivan, George. *Better Volleyball for Girls* (6–9). Illustrated. 1979, Dodd $5.95. Basic volley ball strategies are described in this useful guide.

4409. Sullivan, George. *Sports Superstitions* (4–9). Illustrated. 1978, Coward $7.50. An entertaining compendium of talismans, jinxes, and unfounded beliefs associated with important sports figures and teams.

4410. Williams, Lee Ann. *Basic Field Hockey Strategy: An Introduction for Young People* (5–8). Illustrated. 1978, Doubleday $5.95. A well-illustrated beginning account.

4411. Wright, Graeme. *Rand McNally Illustrated Dictionary of Sports* (4–9). 1979, Rand $14.95. An introduction to the most important sports and their specialized terminology.

4412. Wulffson, Don L. *How Sports Came to Be* (3–5). 1980, Lothrop $5.95; LB $5.71. Short accounts that trace the history of such sports as bowling and badminton.

Automobile Racing

4413. Coombs, Charles. *Drag Racing* (6–9). 1970, Morrow $6.00. An excellent introduction that covers such aspects as drag racing history, types of cars, and a sample race. Also use: *Drag Racing Pix Dix: A Picture Dictionary* by Edward Radlauer (1970, Bowmar $4.50; paper $3.50).

4414. Jackson, Robert B. *Road Race Round the World: New York to Paris* (4–7). Illustrated. 1977, Walck $6.95. The 1908 event to publicize the automobile—when cars from France, Germany, Italy, and the United States ran a 17,000-mile race from New York to Seattle, Washington, by boat to Japan, and by road again to Paris.

4415. Jackson, Robert B. *Swift Sport: Car Racing Up Close* (4–7). Illustrated. 1978, Walck $6.85. An informative book about grand prix racing.

4416. McFarland, Kenton, and Sparks, James C., Jr. *Midget Motoring and Karting* (6–9). Illus. by Denys McMains. 1961, Dutton $7.95. An old but still interesting book on this sport.

4417. Olney, Ross R. *Illustrated Auto Dictionary for Young People* (4–8). Illus. by David Ross. 1978, Hale $5.89. A helpful compendium of auto racing terms.

4418. Olney, Ross R. *Modern Racing Cars* (6–9). Illustrated. 1978, Dutton $8.95. A variety of racing cars are described in text and pictured in excellent black and white photos.

4419. Olney, Ross R. *Drama on the Speedway* (5–9). Illustrated. 1978, Morrow $5.95. An exciting recreation of some important automobile races.

4420. Olney, Ross R. *How to Understand Auto Racing* (5–9). Illustrated. 1979, Lothrop $6.95; LB $6.67. This often-confusing sport is introduced in a concise manner.

4421. Radlauer, Edward. *Soap Box Racing* (1–4). 1973, Childrens Press $7.95; paper $1.95. Instructions on how to build a racer and enter derbies.

4422. Stevenson, Peter, and Stevenson, Mike. *The Buffy-Porson: A Car You Can Build and Drive* (4–8). Illustrated. 1973, Scribner $6.95. Directions on how to make a small racer with the help of an adult.

Baseball

4423. Brewster, Benjamin. *Baseball* (3–5). Illustrated. 1970, Watts $5.90. An elementary introduction to the rules of the game and baseball jargon.

4424. Cebulash, Mel. *Baseball Players Do Amazing Things* (2–4). Illustrated. 1973, Random $3.95; LB $3.99. A fascinating book of records involving various aspects of the sport.

4425. Coombs, Charles. *Be a Winner in Baseball* (5–7). Illustrated. 1973, Morrow $6.48. After introductory material on the history and rules of the game, there are separate chapters on such skills as pitching and hitting.

4426. Dickmeyer, Lowell A. *Baseball Is for Me* (2–3). Illustrated. 1978, Lerner $5.95. A simple introduction to the sport told in the first person.

4427. Dyer, Mike. *Getting into Pro Baseball* (6–9). Illustrated. 1979, Watts $5.90. A realistic account that stresses the college route.

4428. Epstein, Sam, and Epstein, Beryl. *The Game of Baseball* (3–6). 1965, Garrard $4.48. A basic introduction to the sport, its origin, rules, and history.

4429. Freeman, S. H. *Basic Baseball Strategy* (4–6). 1965, Doubleday $5.95. A fine guide aimed at improving the young player's technique.

4430. Jackson, C. Paul. *How to Play Better Baseball* (3–6). Illus. by Leonard Kessler. 1962, Crowell $8.95. Illustrated manual of fundamental rules.

4431. Jaspersohn, William. *The Ballpark* (4–7). Illustrated. 1980, Brown $8.95; paper $4.95. Subtitle: *One Day Behind the Scenes at a Major League Game.*

4432. Kalb, Jonah. *The Easy Baseball Book* (1–3). Illus. by Sandy Kossin. 1976, Houghton $5.95. A beginner's guide with easy-to-read directions in short, simple sentences. For older readers use: *How to Play Baseball Better Than You Did Last Season* (1974, Macmillan $5.95; paper $1.50).

4433. Liss, Howard. *Winning Baseball* (6–9). Illus. by Marie Ostberg and Nils Ostberg. 1979, McKay $6.95. Subtitle: *Fundamentals of Offensive and Defensive Strategy.*

4434. May, Julian. *World Series* (5–8). Illustrated. 1975, Creative Education $8.95. Game highlights and brief biographies of famous players are included in this overview. Also use: *Greatest World Series Thrillers* by Ray Robinson (1965, Random $2.50; LB $3.69).

4435. Robinson, Jackie. *Jackie Robinson's Little League Baseball Book* (4–7). Illustrated. 1972, Prentice-Hall $5.95. A chatty guide that combines good advice with personal reminiscences.

4436. Walker, Henry. *Illustrated Baseball Dictionary for Young People* (4–8). Illustrated. 1970, Harvey House $6.29; Prentice-Hall paper $1.95. Terms clearly defined for fans and young players. Also use: *Baseball Talk for Beginners* by Joe Archibald (1969, Messner $5.79).

Basketball

4437. Antonacci, Robert J., and Barr, Jene. *Basketball for Young Champions* (4–7). 1979, McGraw $7.95. An excellent overview of the game for boys and girls with a section on wheelchair basketball. Also use: *Basketball Talk for Beginners* by Howard Liss (1970, Messner $5.79).

4438. Clark, Steve. *Illustrated Basketball Dictionary for Young People* (4–6). Illus. by Frank Baginski. 1977, Harvey House $5.95. Engaging, often humorous drawings add a light touch to this introduction to plays and terms essential in basketball.

4439. Cook, Joseph J. *Famous Firsts in Basketball* (4–6). Illustrated. 1976, Putnam $4.97. Historical highlights are listed with interesting background information.

4440. Coombs, Charles. *Be a Winner in Basketball* (5–7). 1975, Morrow $6.48; paper $2.45. The rudiments of the game are explained with clarity and precision.

4441. Devaney, John. *The Story of Basketball* (5–9). Illustrated. 1976, Random $4.95; LB $5.99. An excellent, well-illustrated overview that covers highlights of the history, important players, and important games since the sport's beginning in 1891.

4442. Gault, Clare, and Gault, Frank. *The Harlem Globetrotters and Basketball's Funniest Games* (3–6). Illus. by Charles McGill. 1977, Walker $5.95. A history of the Globetrotters, including many amusing anecdotes.

4443. Jackson, C. Paul. *How to Play Better Basketball* (4–6). Illus. by Leonard Kessler. 1968, Crowell $8.95. A fine how-to account that concentrates on basics.

4444. Lyttle, Richard B. *Getting into Pro Basketball* (6–9). Illustrated. 1979, Watts $5.90. A useful book that gives good encouragement plus cautionary advice.

4445. Masin, Herman L. *How to Star in Basketball* (4–6). Illustrated. 1966, Four Winds $3.95; Scholastic paper $.95. Practical tips on every aspect of playing a winning game. Also use: *Basketball: How to Improve Your Technique* by Arthur Kaplan (1974, Watts $4.90).

4446. May, Julian. *N.B.A. Playoffs: Basketball's Classic* (4–6). 1975, Creative Education $8.95. A brief but interesting history of basketball's most important play-offs. Also use for older readers: *The Winners: National Basketball Association Championship Playoffs* by Howard Liss (1968, Delacorte $4.95).

4447. Schiffer, Don. *The First Book of Basketball* (4–7). Illustrated. 1959, Watts $4.90. Readable guide for spectators and players. Also use: *Basic Basketball Strategy* by Harley Knosher (1972, Doubleday $5.95).

4448. Sullivan, George. *Better Basketball for Girls* (5–7). Illustrated. 1978, Dodd $5.95. A clear exposition along with material that will encourage the female athlete.

Bicycles

4449. Coombs, Charles. *Bicycling* (5–8). Illustrated. 1972, Morrow $6.75; LB $6.48. This exhaustive book on the bicycle includes its history, construction, varieties, and care, as well as tips on safety and competitive aspects of bike riding. Also use: *Better Bicycling for Boys and Girls* by George Sullivan (1974, Dodd $4.95).

4450. Dahnsen, Alan. *Bicycles* (3–5). Illustrated. 1978, Watts $4.90. The coverage on the parts of a bicycle is particularly strong in this easily read account.

4451. Fichter, George S. *Bicycles and Bicycling* (4–6). Illustrated. 1978, Watts $4.90. Bicycles—their history, parts, and operation—are nicely presented.

4452. Frankel, Lillian, and Frankel, Godfrey. *Bike-Ways (101 Things to Do with a Bike)* (4–6). Illustrated. 1972, Sterling $4.95; LB $5.89. An up-to-date source on all aspects of bicycles and bicycling. Also use: *Bicycle Racing* by Robert B. Jackson (1976, Walck $6.95).

4453. Kleeberg, Irene. *Bicycle Repair* (5–8). Illus. by Meryl Joseph. 1973, Watts $4.90. A simple how-to volume that gives basic instructions on repair.

4454. Lindblom, Steven. *The Fantastic Bicycles Book* (5–8). Illus. by author. 1979, Houghton $8.95; paper $3.95. How to salvage parts from old bicycles and create new ones.

4455. Monroe, Lynn Lee. *The Old-Time Bicycle Book* (2–4). Illus. by George Overlie. 1979, Carolrhoda $4.95. A beginner's history of the bicycle, carefully and imaginatively illustrated.

4456. Radlauer, Edward. *Some Basics about Bicycles* (4–8). Illustrated. 1978, Childrens Press $5.50. An easily read account with many color photographs.

4457. Sarnoff, Jane, and Ruffins, Reynold. *A Great Bicycle Book* (4–7). Illustrated. 1973, Scribner $8.95; paper $2.95. A lucid introduction to many aspects of the subject with good coverage on maintenance and repair.

4458. Thomas, Art. *Bicycling Is for Me* (3–5). Illustrated. 1979, Lerner $5.95. A young narrator describes the basics of this sport.

Bowling

4459. Dolan, Edward F. *The Complete Beginner's Guide to Bowling* (5–7). Illustrated. 1974, Doubleday $6.95. A good book for beginners and for those who wish to get rid of bad bowling habits. Also use: *Better Bowling for Boys* by David C. Cooke (1963, Dodd $4.95).

4460. Ravielli, Anthony. *What Is Bowling?* (4–6). Illus. by author. 1975, Atheneum $6.95. Along with the history and rules of the game, the author gives many tips, often illustrated with drawings, for good bowling. Also use: *Bowling Talk for Beginners* by Howard Liss (1973, Archway, paper 75¢).

4461. Schuon, Karl. *The First Book of Bowling* (4–6). 1966, Watts $4.90. A simple but thorough introduction.

Camping and Backpacking

4462. Boy Scouts of America. *Boy Scout Fieldbook* (5–9). Illustrated. 1978, Workman $4.95. A practical guide to camping that has become a standard text thoughout the years.

4463. Janes, Edward C. *The First Book of Camping* (4–6). Illus. by Julio Granda. 1977, Watts $5.45. Basic techniques and needed equipment for campers.

4464. Kenealy, James P. *Better Camping for Boys* (5–8). Illustrated. 1974, Dodd $4.95. Equipment, skills, camp lore, and cooking are only a few of the areas covered in this well-organized introduction.

4465. Kleeberg, Irene. *Going to Camp* (4–6). Illustrated. 1978, Watts $4.90. All you have to know on preparing yourself—even psychologically—for camp.

4466. Lyttle, Richard B. *The Complete Beginner's Guide to Backpacking* (5–7). Illustrated. 1975, Doubleday $4.95. Planning trips and purchasing equipment are among the many topics covered.

4467. McManus, Patrick F. *Kid Camping from Aaaaiii! to Zip* (5–7). Illus. by Roy Doty. 1979, Lothrop $6.95. A practical camping guide presented in an amusing way.

4468. Ormond, Clyde. *Complete Book of Outdoor Lore* (5–8). Illustrated. 1964, Harper $9.95. A thorough manual on how to live off the land. Also use: *Handbook for Emergencies: Coming Out Alive* by Anthony Greenback (1976, Doubleday $6.95; paper $3.95).

4469. Paul, Aileen. *Kids Camping* (4–6). Illus. by John Delulio. 1973, Doubleday $4.95; Archway paper $.75. For the novice camper, instructions are given for selection of a tent, sleeping bags, and camp equipment, as well as safety precautions.

4470. Pausen, Gary, and Morris, John. *Hiking and Backpacking* (6–9). Illus. by Ruth Wright.

1978, Messner $7.29. A mature but straightforward how-to-do-it guide.

Chess

4471. Carroll, David. *Make Your Own Chess Set* (5–8). Illustrated. 1975, Prentice-Hall $8.95. History and description of each chess piece, plus directions for making 30 different chess sets from such materials as screws, paper, and gumdrops.

4472. Fenton, Robert S. *Chess for You* (4–6). Illustrated. 1975, Grosset paper $.99. A simple, straightforward presentation of chess basics with a glossary of terms. Also use: *The Royal Game* by Edith L. Weart (1948, Vanguard $4.95).

4473. Kidder, Harvey. *Illustrated Chess for Children* (4–6). Illus. by author. 1970, Doubleday $7.95. Origin and rudiments for young players.

4474. Langfield, Paul. *A Picture Guide to Chess* (3–7). Illustrated. 1977, Lippincott $5.95; paper $2.95. Basic principles and strategies are described with the beginner in mind.

4475. Leeming, Joseph. *The First Book of Chess* (5–7). Illus. by Doris Stolberg. 1953, Watts $4.90. Diagrams and practice games to help make chess easy to learn.

4476. Lombardy, William, and Marshall, Bette. *Chess for Children: Step by Step* (5–8). Illustrated. 1977, Little $8.95; paper $4.95. A clear introduction that makes the rudiments of this complex game extremely clear.

4477. Rosenberg, Arthur D. *Chess for Children and the Young at Heart* (4–8). Illustrated. 1977, Atheneum $9.95. The author, a tournament player, gives easy step-by-step instructions amplified by photographs.

4478. Sarnoff, Jane. *The Chess Book* (3–5). Illus. by Reynold Ruffins. 1973, Scribner $6.95. The basic elements of chess and vignettes from its history are told in this entertaining account.

Fishing

4479. Bartram, Robert. *Fishing for Sunfish* (3–5). Illustrated. 1978, Lippincott $6.95. A beginner's guide from selecting equipment to cleaning and eating the catch.

4480. Liss, Howard. *Fishing Talk for Beginners* (3–6). Illustrated. 1978, Messner $7.29. A variety of terms associated with fishing are defined in dictionary form.

4481. Stokes, Bill. *You Can Catch Fish* (2–3). 1976, Raintree $7.33. A basic guide to the techniques, problems, and pleasures of catching fish.

4482. Waters, John F. *Fishing* (3–6). Illustrated. 1978, Watts $4.90. A general and highly readable introduction to both fresh and saltwater fishing.

Football

4483. Antonacci, Robert J., and Barr, Jene. *Football for Young Champions* (4–7). Illus. by Rus Anderson. 1976, McGraw $7.95. Formations, positions, and basic skills are interestingly presented.

4484. Coombs, Charles. *Be a Winner in Football* (5–7). Illustrated. 1974, Morrow $6.48; paper $2.45. A useful guide to football basics. Also use: *How to Play Better Football* by C. Paul Jackson (1972, Crowell $8.95).

4485. Dickmeyer, Lowell A. *Football Is for Me* (3–5). Illustrated. 1979, Lerner $5.95. A first-person account that enthusiastically introduces the sport.

4486. Hodge, Ben. *The First Book of Football* (3–6). Illustrated. 1977, Watts $4.90. A useful primer that provides a serviceable introduction to the sport.

4487. Hollander, Zander, ed. *Great Moments in Pro Football* (4–6). Illustrated. 1969, Random $2.50; LB $3.69. Fourteen memorable games are described by key sportswriters. Also use: *More Strange but True Football Stories* (1973, Random $4.39).

4488. Liss, Howard. *Football Talk for Beginners* (4–7). Illus. by Frank Robbins. 1970, Messner $7.29. Football jargon, plays, signals, and more are briefly defined in an alphabetical arrangement. Also use: *Illustrated Football Dictionary for Young People* by Joseph Olgin (1975, Harvey House $6.29; Prentice-Hall, paper $1.95).

4489. McCallum, John Dennis. *Getting into Pro Football* (6–9). Illustrated. 1979, Watts $5.90. A complete rundown, including physical preparedness and game strategies.

4490. Sullivan, George. *Pro Football's Kicking Game* (6–9). Illustrated. 1973, Dodd $4.50. Various aspects of kicking are thoroughly discussed in this author's sequel to *Pro Football's Passing Game* (1972, Dodd $4.50). Also use: *This Is Pro Football* (1975, Dodd $5.95).

Gymnastics

4491. Boulogne, Jean. *The Making of a Gymnast* (5–9). Illustrated. 1978, Hawthorn $8.95. The story of the Canadian gymnast who, at 13, was a member of an Olympic team.

4492. Krementz, Jill. *A Very Young Gymnast* (4–6). Illus. by author. 1978, Knopf $8.95. Ten-year-old Torrance York tells of her training that led to a place in the Junior Olympics.

4493. Olney, Ross R. *Gymnastics* (4–6). Illus. by Mary Ann Duganne. 1976, Watts $4.90. An introduction that includes types of events, equipment, and necessary training.

4494. Radlauer, Edward, and Radlauer, Ruth. *Gymnastics School* (4–7). ¬Illustrated. 1976, Watts $6.90. Training and techniques are stressed in this account of what happens at a summer gymnast camp.

4495. Sullivan, George. *Better Gymnastics for Girls* (4–9). Illustrated. 1977, Dodd $5.95. Fundamentals of the sport are well presented through text and many photographs. Also use: *Better Gymnastics for Boys* by Marshall Claus (1970, Dodd $5.95).

4496. Traetta, John, and Traetta, Mary Jean. *Gymnastics Basics* (4–7). Illus. by Bill Gow. 1979, Prentice-Hall $6.95. Maneuvers and techniques are included in this well-written introduction to the sport.

Horsemanship

4497. Anderson, Clarence W. *Heads Up—Heels Down* (5–8). Illus. by author. 1944, Macmillan $5.95. The selection, care, and handling of horses. Also use: *Complete Book of Horses and Horsemanship* by C. W. Anderson (1963, Macmillan $6.95).

4498. Haney, Lynn. *Ride 'Em Cowgirl!* (5–9). Illus. by Peter Burchard. 1975, Putnam $6.95. Female rodeo participants, their training, and problems.

4499. Krementz, Jill. *A Very Young Rider* (3–6). Illus. by author. 1977, Knopf $8.95. The story of a 10-year-old girl passionately caught up in the world of horses.

4500. Radlauer, Edward. *Rodeo School* (5–9). Illustrated. 1976, Watts $6.90. Many action photographs illustrate this account of the experiences of fledgling riders at a rodeo school.

4501. Sullivan, George. *Better Horseback Riding for Boys and Girls* (5–7). Illustrated. 1969, Dodd $4.95. An elementary introduction that presents material on mounting, jumping, trail riding, and other basics. Also use: *The First Book of Horseback Riding* by Frederick Devereux (1976, Watts $4.90).

4502. Winter, Ginny L. *The Riding Book* (K–3). Illus. by author. 1963, Astor-Honor $4.50. An introductory account for the very young rider.

Ice Hockey

4503. Coombs, Charles. *Be a Winner in Ice Hockey* (5–8). Illustrated. 1974, Morrow $6.48; paper $2.45. A do-it-yourself sports book with many fine tips on how to improve one's game, along with a history of the sport, its rules, and regulations.

4504. Dickmeyer, Lowell A. *Hockey Is for Me* (2–3). Illustrated. 1978, Lerner $5.95. A young boy, Ryan, introduces the reader to this growing, popular sport.

4505. Gemme, Leila Boyle. *Hockey Is Our Game* (1–3). Illustrated. 1979, Childrens Press $5.50. A picture book format is used to introduce this sport in easily read text.

4506. Ice Skating Institute, and United States Olympic Committee. *Olympic Ice Hockey* (5–8). Illustrated. 1979, Childrens Press $5.95. A short account that discusses such topics as the history of the sport, as well as its place in the Olympic games.

4507. Kalb, Jonah. *The Easy Hockey Book* (3–5). Illus. by Bill Morrison. 1977, Houghton $6.95. A collection of sound advice on various aspects of the game.

4508. Orr, Frank. *The Story of Hockey* (5–9). Illustrated. 1971, Random $2.50; LB $3.69. The history and development of hockey are included along with record-breaking games and anecdotes about important players of the past and present.

4509. Scharff, Robert. *Ice Hockey Rules in Pictures* (5–9). Illus. by John McDermott. 1974, Grosset paper $2.95. The rink, various players, and basic rules are introduced and explained in this profusely illustrated work.

4510. Sullivan, George. *Better Ice Hockey for Boys* (6–9). Illustrated. 1965, Dodd $4.95. Ice hockey's offense and defense, selection of skates, stick skating techniques, general strategy, rules, and official signals are included.

4511. Sullivan, George. *This Is Pro Hockey* (5–9). Illustrated. 1976, Dodd $4.95. Excellent coverage is given to all important aspects of this sport in a clear, solid, well-organized text.

Ice Skating

4512. Dickmeyer, Lowell A., and Rolens, Lin. *Ice Skating Is for Me* (2–3). Illustrated. 1980, Lerner $5.95. A first-person narrative about learning the basics of ice skating.

4513. Faulkner, Margaret. *I Skate!* (5–8). Illus. by author. 1979, Little $8.95. Competitive skating as seen through the eyes of an 11-year-old girl and many photographs.

4514. Ice Skating Institute. *Olympic Figure Skating* (3–8). Illustrated. 1979, Childrens Press $5.95. An interesting historical look at this sport.

4515. Ice Skating Institute. *Olympic Speed Skating* (3–8). Illustrated. 1979, Childrens Press $5.95. An introduction to this event in the Olympics, its rules and regulations, and world's records.

4516. Krementz, Jill. *A Very Young Skater* (4–7). Illus. by author. 1979, Knopf $9.95. Family support is stressed in this account of 10-year-old Katherine Healy, an amateur figure skater.

4517. Winter, Ginny L. *The Skating Book* (K–3). Illus. by author. 1963, Astor-Honor $4.50. A beginning account for the young skater.

Indoor Games

4518. Astrop, John, illus. *The Jumbo Book of Board Games* (5–7). 1979, Nelson $11.95. All kinds of board games like backgammon and checkers are introduced in this book best suited for home purchase and use.

4519. Belton, John, and Cramblit, Joella. *Solitare Games* (4–7). Illustrated. 1975, Raintree $7.38; LB $6.60. Simple, step-by-step directions for 9 forms of solitaire.

4520. Cassell, Sylvia. *Indoor Games and Activities* (2–5). Illus. by author. 1960, Harper $4.95. Easy-to-do experiments, cooking, puzzles, painting, and many other homecrafts.

4521. Frame, Jean, and Frame, Paul. *How to Give a Party* (4–6). Illus. by Paul Frame. 1972, Watts $4.90. A complete guide to giving various kinds of parties, including many party games.

4522. Grayson, Marion F. *Let's Do Fingerplays* (PS–2). Illus. by Nancy Weyl. 1962, Luce $6.95. Comprehensive collection of finger plays under such headings as "Things That Go," "Animal Antics," and "Holidays."

4523. Helfman, Harry C. *Tricks with Your Fingers* (4–6). 1967, Morrow $5.04. Explicit instructions for do-it-yourself amusements. Also use: *Strings on Your Fingers* (1965, Morrow $5.52).

4524. Marran, Ray J. *Table Games: How to Make and Play Them* (5–7). 1976, Barnes $7.95. Simple directions for making and playing various interesting games.

4525. Reisberg, Ken. *Card Games* (4–8). Illustrated. 1979, Watts $5.45. The rules and necessary tactics for 13 card games. Also use: *Card Games* by John Belton and Joella Cramblit (1976, Raintree $6.60; LB $7.33).

4526. Sivulich, Sandra Stroner. *I'm Going on a Bear Hunt* (PS–K). Illus. by Glen Rounds. 1973, Dutton $5.50. A participation game that is very useful for storytellers since the boys and girls can share in the story by performing the proper motions.

4527. Sullivan, George. *The Complete Beginner's Guide to Pool and Other Billiard Games* (4–6). 1979, Doubleday $7.95. Discusses the equipment, techniques, and game strategy of a variety of billiard games.

4528. Tashjian, Virginia A. *A Juba This and Juba That* (PS–4). Illus. by Victoria de Larrea. 1969, Little $6.95. A package of "story-hour stretchers," delightful group activity entertainment in this silly, superb assemblage of chants, rhymes, poetry, stories, songs, riddles, finger plays, and tongue twisters.

4529. Tashjian, Virginia A., ed. *With a Deep Sea Smile: Story Hour Stretches for Large or Small Groups* (4–6). Illus. by Rosemary Wells. 1974, Little $6.95. Particularly useful to storytellers since it includes finger plays, riddles, chants, poems, and songs for use with groups of children.

Kite Making and Flying

4530. Bahadur, Dinesh. *Come Fight a Kite* (3–5). Illustrated. 1978, Harvey House $3.95. An introduction to kite construction and the Indian sport of kite fighting.

4531. Downer, Marion. *Kites: How to Make and Fly Them* (4–7). Illustrated. 1959, Lothrop $6.48. An excellent introduction to kite making, which

includes coverage of tools, materials, and plans for 11 kites. Also use: *Let's Make a Kite* by Jack Stokes (1975, Walck $6.95).

4532. Fowler, H. Waller. *Kites: A Practical Guide to Kite Making and Flying* (4–7). Illustrated. 1953, Ronald $9.95. Material includes simple directions for construction of a variety of kites. Also use: *Kites* by Larry Kettelkamp (1959, Morrow $6.48).

4533. Yolen, Jane. *World on a String: The Story of Kites* (4–7). Illustrated. 1975, Collins $5.95; LB $5.91. A thoroughly engaging account of kites throughout history—in transportation, aviation, sport and war, as religious symbols and art objects.

Motorcycles and Motor Bikes

4534. Alth, Max. *Motorcycles and Motorcycling* (5–6). Illustrated. 1979, Watts $5.90. The history, uses, and parts of the motorcycles are covered, as well as a run-down on the many variations available today.

4535. Bygrave, Mike, and Dowdall, Mike. *Motorcycle* (5–7). 1978, Glouster $3.95. Sparse text and ample photos make this an interesting volume.

4536. Coombs, Charles. *Mopeding* (6–8). Illustrated. 1978, Morrow $5.95. The construction, operating, and maintenance of these little vehicles are described.

4537. Mundale, Susan. *Mopeds: The Go-Everywhere Bikes* (5–7). Illustrated. 1979, Lerner $5.95. An introduction to the vehicle that has gained widespread popularity in America. Also use: *Mo-Ped: The Wonder Vehicle* by Jerry Murray (1976, Putnam $6.95).

4538. Navarra, John Gabriel. *Wheels for Kids* (3–6). Illustrated. 1973, Doubleday $5.95. A beginner's book on the use of motor bikes that stresses safety.

4539. Puleo, Nicole. *Motorcycle Racing* (6–8). Illustrated. 1973, Lerner $5.95. The events associated with various types of motorcycle races are fully described.

4540. Radlauer, Edward. *Some Basics about Motorcycles* (4–8). Illustrated. 1978, Childrens Press $5.50. A lightweight account profusely illustrated.

4541. Yaw, John, and Rae, Rusty. *Grand National Championship Races* (5–9). Illustrated. 1978, Lerner $5.95. A history of various important motorcycle races.

4542. Yaw, John. *Motocross Motorcycle Racing* (5–9). Illustrated. 1978, Lerner $5.95. An introduction to motocross competitions, the equipment needed, and present-day luminaries in the sport.

Olympic Games

4543. Durant, John. *Highlights of the Olympics from Ancient Times to the Present* (5–9). Illustrated. 1977, Hastings $9.35; paper $5.95. A standard work that includes material on the 1976 games at Innesbruck and Montreal.

4544. Glubok, Shirley, and Tamarin, Alfred. *Olympic Games in Ancient Greece* (5–8). Illustrated. 1976, Harper $7.89. Using a fictitious Olympiad set in the fifth century B.C., the author offers a great deal of background information in an imaginative, satisfying way.

4545. Litsky, Frank. *The Winter Olympics* (4–7). Illustrated. 1979, Watts $5.90. A history of the highlights of the Winter Olympics from their beginning in 1924.

4546. Walsh, John. *The First Book of the Olympic Games* (4–7). Illustrated. 1971, Watts $4.90. The history of the Olympic games from the beginning to the present, and something about the greatest participants.

Running and Jogging

4547. Asch, Frank, and Asch, Jan. *Running with Rachel* (3–5). Illustrated. 1979, Dial $7.29; paper $3.95. A young girl's introduction to techniques and equipment involved in the sport of running.

4548. Benjamin, Carol Lee. *Running Basics* (5–8). Illus. by author. 1979, Prentice-Hall $6.95. A well-organized account on basics, which does not include jogging.

4549. Gruber, Elisa. *The Kids' Running Book* (4–8). 1979, Tempo paper $1.50. A fine introduction that is filled with good advice on the rapidly growing sport.

4550. Syttle, Richard B. *Jogging and Running* (5–8). Illustrated. 1979, Watts $5.90. A basic guide from what to wear to how to treat blisters.

4551. Olney, Ross R. *The Young Runner* (6–9). Illustrated. 1978, Morrow $5.95. An effective, sensible introduction to this subject for both boys and girls.

Sailing and Boating

4552. Adkins, Jan. *The Craft of Sail* (6–9). Illus. by author. 1973, Walker $6.95. An introduction to sailing that covers topics such as principles of air pressure, sailing terms, ship structures, and the techniques of sailing.

4553. Burchard, Peter. *Ocean Race: A Sea Venture* (6–9). Illus. by author. 1978, Putnam $7.95. A mature account of the 1976 Newport-to-Bermuda race.

4554. Gibbs, Tony. *Sailing* (4–6). Illus. by Gary L. Falkenstern. 1974, Watts $4.90. A fine introduction to terms, techniques, and skills involved in this sport.

4555. Zarchy, Harry. *Let's Go Boating* (4–6). Illus. by author. 1952, Knopf $5.69. Includes information on canoeing, rowboating, and sailing. Also use: *Safe Motorboating for Kids* by John Gabriel Navarra (1974, Doubleday $4.95).

Self-Defense

4556. Kozuki, Russell. *Junior Karate* (5–7). Illustrated. 1971, Sterling $4.95; LB $4.99. An easily understood beginning book with information on such aspects as stances, blocks, and kicks. Also use: *Karate for Young People* (1974, Sterling $4.95; LB $4.99) and for younger groups: *Billy Learns Karate* by Bernard Wiseman (1976, Holt $5.95).

4557. Ribner, Susan, and Chin, Richard. *The Martial Arts* (5–8). Illustrated. 1978, Harper $7.95. The principles and history of such activities as judo and karate.

4558. Silks, Donald K. *Boxing for Boys* (4–6). Illus. by author. 1953, Knopf $4.99. Fundamentals of the art for youngsters. Also use: George Sullivan's *Better Boxing for Boys* (1966, Dodd $4.95).

4559. Thomas, Art. *Wrestling Is for Me* (3–5). Illustrated. 1979, Lerner $5.95. A young enthusiast describes the basics of this sport.

Skateboarding

4560. Bunting, Glenn, and Bunting, Eve. *Skateboards: How to Make Them, How to Ride Them* (5–7). Illustrated. 1977, Scholastic paper $1.50. The first half is on the construction of skateboards and how variations cause differing performances; the rest is on instruction and safety. Many photographs.

4561. Dickmeyer, Lowell A. *Skateboarding Is for Me* (2–3). Illustrated. 1978, Lerner $5.95. Many fine black-and-white photographs introduce this sport.

4562. Olney, Ross R., and Bush, Chan. *Better Skateboarding for Boys and Girls* (5–7). Illustrated. 1977, Dodd $4.95. Tips on riding, repair, and competitions, with emphasis on safety.

4563. Radlauer, Edward. *Some Basics about Skateboards* (4–6). Illustrated. 1978, Childrens Press $5.50. A heavily illustrated book aimed at the reluctant reader.

4564. Reiser, Howard. *Skateboarding* (5–8). Illustrated. 1979, Watts $4.90. This relatively new sport is given a good introductory treatment that stresses safety.

Skiing

4565. Chappell, Annette Jo. *Skiing Is for Me* (2–3). Illustrated. 1978, Lerner $5.95. A first-person account that introduces this sport.

4566. Coombs, Charles. *Be a Winner in Skiing* (4–8). Illustrated. 1977, Morrow $6.25; LB $6.00. An absorbing, enthusiastic account that covers most aspects of the sport, such as history, maneuvers, equipment, and varieties of skiing.

4567. Ice Skating Institute, and United States Olympic Committee. *Olympic Alpine Skiing* (5–8). Illustrated. 1979, Childrens Press $5.95. A slim book that is a good introduction.

4568. Ice Skating Institute, and United States Olympic Committee. *Olympic Nordic Skiing* (5–8). Illustrated. 1979, Childrens Press $5.95. An exciting account that supplies basic information from the standpoint of Olympic competition.

4569. Tinker, Gene. *Let's Learn Ski Touring: Your Guide to Cross-Country Fun* (6–8). Illustrated. 1971, Walker $4.95; LB $4.85. An introduction to all aspects of cross-country skiing.

Soccer

4570. Antonacci, Robert J., and Puglisi, Anthony J. *Soccer for Young Champions* (4–6). Illus. by Patti Boyd. 1978, McGraw $7.95. A guide with rules for boys and girls plus good coverage on skills and drills.

4571. Coombs, Charles. *Be a Winner in Soccer* (5–8). Illustrated. 1977, Morrow $6.25; LB $6.00.

Soccer basics explained in a simple, relaxed style for boys and girls; illustrated with fine black-and-white photos. Also use: *How to Star in Soccer* by Hubert Vogelsinger (1967, Four Winds $4.95).

4572. Dickmeyer, Lowell A. *Soccer Is for Me* (2–3). Illustrated. 1978, Lerner $5.95. Basic rules and techniques simply presented.

4573. Fichler, Stanley I., and Friedman, Richard. *Getting into Pro Soccer* (6–9). Illustrated. 1979, Watts $5.90. Nutritional requirements, safety precautions, and game strategies are only 3 of the many topics covered.

4574. Gardner, James. *Illustrated Soccer Dictionary for Young People* (5–8). Illus. by David Ross. 1976, Harvey House $6.29. Basic, clear, and helpful.

4575. Jackson, C. Paul. *How to Play Better Soccer* (3–7). Illustrated. 1978, Crowell $6.95. A thorough account that is enlivened by fine illustrations.

4576. Laitin, Ken, and Laitin, Steve. *The World's #1 Best Selling Soccer Book* (6–9). Illustrated. 1979, Soccer for Americans $5.95. The authors—both teenagers—give enthusiastic advice to the novice.

4577. Liss, Howard. *The Great Game of Soccer* (6–8). Illustrated. 1979, Putnam $8.95. An attractive book that supplies history, rules, and contemporary statistics of this sport.

4578. Sullivan, George. *Better Soccer for Boys and Girls* (4–7). Illustrated. 1978, Dodd $5.95. A fine introduction to the sport and basic playing techniques.

4579. Toye, Clive. *Soccer* (4–7). 1969, Watts $5.45; LB $4.90. A brief but useful introduction to the sport.

Surfing and Water Skiing

4580. Cook, Joseph J., and Romeika, William J. *Better Surfing for Boys* (4–6). Illustrated. 1967, Dodd $4.50. An account that gives details of maneuvers and special techniques. Also use: *Surf-Riding* by H. Arthur Klein (1972, Lippincott $4.95; LB $4.82).

4581. Halacy, D. S., Jr. *Surfer!* (6–8). Illustrated. 1965, Macmillan $5.50. A basic introduction to a still-growing sport.

4582. Joseph, James. *Better Water Skiing for Boys* (5–7). Illustrated. 1964, Dodd $4.50. A detailed introduction, including clear instructions, to an increasingly popular sport.

4583. Klein, H. Arthur, and Klein, M. C., eds. *Surf's Up!* (6–9). Illustrated. 1966, Bobbs-Merrill $5.95. A fine account for the surfing enthusiast.

4584. Madison, Arnold. *Surfing: Basic Techniques* (4–9). Illustrated. 1979, McKay $6.95. Guidelines and strategies are conveyed through text and amusing drawings.

Swimming and Diving

4585. Counsilman, James E. *The Complete Book of Swimming* (6–9). Illustrated. 1977, Atheneum $9.95. Beginners to advanced swimmers will gain from this clear, concise, and well-illustrated manual.

4586. Frey, Shaney. *The Complete Beginner's Guide to Skin Diving* (6–9). 1965, Doubleday $5.95. Introduction to all aspects of the sport by an experienced diver.

4587. Kramp, Harry, and Sullivan, George. *Swimming* (4–6). 1971, Follett $3.95; LB $5.97. A good account that gives basics plus many safety tips.

4588. Mohn, Peter B. *Scuba Diving and Snorkeling* (5–7). Illustrated. 1975, Crestwood $4.95. Photographs enliven this introduction to 2 underwater sports.

4589. Sullivan, George. *Better Swimming and Diving for Boys and Girls* (5–7). 1967, Dodd $4.95. Clear photographs illustrate the explanations for basic strokes and springboard dives.

Tennis

4590. Ashe, Arthur, and Robinson, Louie. *Getting Started in Tennis* (5–9). Illustrated. 1977, Atheneum $6.95. A full introduction, including equipment, serving, and other court strategies.

4591. Cook, Joseph J. *Famous Firsts in Tennis* (5–9). Illustrated. 1978, Putnam $4.99. Tennis history from its inception to today's trailblazers.

4592. Coombs, Charles. *Be a Winner in Tennis* (4–6). 1975, Morrow $6.01. The history, equipment, and techniques associated with the sport are well presented. Also use: *Better Tennis for Boys and Girls* by Harry Hopman (1972, Dodd $4.95).

4593. Dickmeyer, Lowell A. *Tennis Is for Me* (2–3). Illustrated. 1978, Lerner $5.95. Through a first-person narration, introductory material is presented on this sport.

4594. Duroska, Lud. *Tennis for Beginners* (3–7). Illustrated. 1975, Grosset $4.95. Various aspects of tennis, including rules, grips, and strokes, are presented through photographs and simple text.

4595. Ravielli, Anthony. *What Is Tennis?* (4–6). Illus. by author. 1977, Atheneum $6.95. An excellent introduction, including a fascinating history. Also use: *Tennis: A Basic Guide* by Clare Riessen (1969, Lothrop $6.00).

4596. Sweeney, Karen O'Connor. *Illustrated Tennis Dictionary for Young People* (4–8). Illus. by David Ross. 1979, Harvey House $6.96. All important tennis terms are defined with amusing illustrations.

Track and Field

4597. Antonacci, Robert J. *Track and Field for Young Champions* (4–7). Illus. by Frank Mullins. 1974, McGraw $7.95. The history and rules of many track events, such as relays, hurdles, and vaulting. Also use: *Track and Field* by Earl "Bud" Myers (1959, Creative Education $7.95).

4598. Coombs, Charles. *Be a Winner in Track and Field* (4–8). 1976, Morrow $7.25; LB $6.48. After introductory material on the history of the sport, there is coverage on various events and the required skills.

4599. Dickmeyer, Lowell A. *Track Is for Me* (3–5). Illustrated. 1979, Lerner Pubns $5.95. A first-person account of a track meet that can serve as a good introduction to this sport.

4600. Sullivan, George. *Better Track and Field Events for Boys* (4–6). 1967, Dodd $4.95; LB $4.50. An old but still valuable introduction to the basic track and field events.

The Arts and Language

Art and Architecture

General and Miscellaneous

4601. Baron, Nancy. *Getting Started in Calligraphy* (4–7). Illus. by author. 1979, Sterling $12.95; LB $11.69; paper $7.95. A well-organized text from an experienced teacher of lettering.

4602. Chase, Alice Elizabeth. *Looking at Art* (6–9). Illustrated. 1966, Crowell $8.95. A simple, thoughtful discussion of the various ways in which an artist views and creates a picture.

4603. Downer, Marion. *Discovering Design* (6–9). Illustrated. 1947, Lothrop $7.25. An exploration of the patterns that occur in nature and of designs in everyday things.

4604. Fine, Joan. *I Carve Stone* (5–9). Illustrated. 1979, Crowell $7.95; LB $7.89. A 300-pound marble block becomes a work of art in this excellently illustrated account.

4605. Fisher, Leonard Everett. *Alphabet Art: Thirteen ABCs from Around the World* (5–9). Illustrated. 1978, Four Winds $8.95. Thirteen alphabets—from Arabic to Tibetan—are pictured with their English equivalents.

4606. Glubok, Shirley. *The Art of Photography* (5–8). Illustrated. 1977, Macmillan $7.95. Primarily an account of great photographers and their work, beginning with Daguerre and ending with many modern masters.

4607. Glubok, Shirley. *The Art of Ancient Mexico* (4–6). Illustrated. 1968, Harper $7.89. Coverage of Indian culture from the Aztecs to the Zapotecs in text and pictures.

4608. Glubok, Shirley. *The Art of Ancient Peru* (4–6). Illustrated. 1966, Harper $7.89. Text and pictures detail the art treasures of this ancient land.

4609. Glubok, Shirley. *The Art of the Eskimo* (4–7). Illustrated. 1964, Harper $7.89. Eskimo culture and art history are revealed through masks and carvings.

4610. Grigson, Geoffrey, and Grigson, Jane. *Shapes and Stories: A Book about Pictures* (5–7). Illustrated. 1965, Vanguard $7.95. The contents of specific pictures are analyzed in this unusual book.

4611. Janson, Horst Woldemar, and Janson, Dora Jane. *The Story of Painting from Cave Painting to Modern Times* (6–9). 1977, Abrams, rev. ed. paper $7.95. This basic history has a larger, more attractive format than the 1962 edition and also contains updated material.

4612. Kennet, Frances, and Measham, Terry. *Looking at Paintings* (4–6). Illus. by Malcolm Livingstone. 1979, Van Nostrand $7.95. Art appreciation taught through close examination of a few paintings.

4613. King, Marian. *Adventures in Art: National Gallery of Art, Washington, D.C.* (6–9). Illustrated. 1978, Abrams $14.95. A profusely illustrated tour of the wonders of our National Gallery.

4614. MacAgy, Douglas, and MacAgy, Elizabeth. *Going for a Walk with a Line* (PS–3). Illustrated. 1959, Doubleday $1.95. A tour of art for younger children—Rousseau to Klee.

4615. Moore, Janet. *The Many Ways of Seeing: An Introduction to the Pleasures of Art* (6–9). Illustrated. 1969, World $9.95; LB $9.91. A stimulating discussion of art and artists for beginning viewers, accompanied by a fine selection of reproductions.

4616. Paine, Roberta M. *Looking at Architecture* (5–9). Illustrated. 1974, Lothrop $6.96. Using an interesting selection of famous buildings as a framework, the author introduces architecture and its various modern manifestations.

4617. Pratson, Frederick J. *The Special World of the Artisan* (6–8). Illustrated. 1974, Houghton $5.95. Important aspects of the work of 5 craftsmen—potter, woodcarver, glassblower, instrument maker, and weaver.

4618. Price, Christine. *Arts of Clay* (5–8). Illus. by author. 1977, Scribner $6.95. A worldwide introduction to the art of pottery making from prehistoric times to the present.

4619. Price, Christine. *Arts of Wood* (4–7). Illus. by author. 1976, Scribner $6.95. From all over the world, examples of the wood carver's art have been collected and described in detailed drawings and concise text.

4620. Price, Christine. *Made in the South Pacific: Arts of the Sea People* (6–9). Illus. by author. 1979, Dutton $11.95. An overview of the weaving masks, canoes, pottery, and other arts from the Pacific.

4621. Ruskin, Ariane. *History in Art* (6–9). 1974, Watts $14.90. A basic introduction on how history has been reflected in art.

4622. Scheffer, Victor B. *The Seeing Eye* (5–7). Illus. by author. 1971, Scribner $5.95. Science and aesthetics meet in a beautiful photographic picture book.

4623. Sullivan, George. *Understanding Architecture* (5–9). Illustrated. 1971, Warne $6.95. The science of building from ancient structures to prefabricated houses is explained in simple language accompanied by diagrams and photographs.

4624. Weisgard, Leonard. *Treasures to See: A Museum Picture Book* (1–4). Illus. by author. 1956, Harcourt $6.95. An excellent introduction to the fine arts museums and what young readers may expect to find there.

4625. Williams, Diane. *Demons and Beasts in Art* (4–6). Illustrated. 1970, Lerner $4.95. Fantastic creatures are portrayed as they exist in various art forms. Also use: *Sports and Games in Art* by Barbara Shissler (1966, Lerner $4.95).

The Ancient World

4626. Leacroft, Helen, and Leacroft, Richard. *The Buildings of Ancient Greece* (5–7). Illus. by author. 1966, Young Scott $7.95. The architecture of Greece from prehistory to 800 B.C.

4627. Glubok, Shirley. *The Art of Ancient Rome* (4–7). Illustrated. 1965, Harper $7.89. A variety of forms introduce Roman art, including statutes, mosaics, and monuments. Also use: *The Art of the Etruscans* (1967, Harper $7.89).

4628. Leacroft, Helen, and Leacroft, Richard. *The Buildings of Ancient Egypt* (5–8). Illus. by author. 1963, Young Scott $7.95. Drawings and diagrams of homes, temples, and pyramids from the Early Kingdom to about 1300 B.C. Also use: *The Buildings of Ancient Man* (1973, Young Scott $7.95).

4629. Macaulay, David. *City: A Story of Roman Planning and Construction* (6–9). Illus. by author. 1974, Houghton $9.95. The imaginary Roman city of Verbonia is constructed through accurate and finely detailed drawings. Also use: *The Buildings of Ancient Rome* by Helen Leacroft and Richard Leacroft (1969, Young Scott, $7.95).

4630. Macaulay, David. *Pyramid* (5–9). Illus. by author. 1975, Houghton $9.95. The engineering and architectural feats of the Egyptians are explored with detailed drawings.

4631. Rockwell, Anne. *Temple on a Hill: The Building of the Parthenon* (6–9). 1969, Atheneum $5.95. An account of the building of the temple complex that was one of the glories of ancient Greece.

Middle Ages and Renaissance

4632. Berenstain, Michael. *The Castle Book* (K–3). Illus. by author. 1977, McKay $6.95. Various types of castles and their uses are outlined in this simple introduction.

4633. Boardman, Fon W. *Castles* (6–8). Illustrated. 1957, Walck $7.95. The historical importance of castles of many countries; photographs and line drawings.

4634. Downer, Marion. *Long Ago in Florence: The Story of Della Robbia Sculpture* (4–6). Illus. by Mamoru Funai. 1968, Lothrop $5.50; LB $5.28. A history of this art form, fascinatingly told.

4635. Glubok, Shirley. *The Art of the Vikings* (5–7). Illustrated. 1978, Macmillan $8.95. Some of the objects included are ships, swords, jewelry, and carved stones.

4636. Macaulay, David. *Castle* (5–9). Illus. by author. 1977, Houghton $9.95. Another of the author's brilliant, detailed works, this one on the planning and building of a Welsh castle.

4637. Macaulay, David. *Cathedral: The Story of Its Construction* (6–9). Illus. by author. 1973, Houghton $9.95. Gothic architecture as seen through a detailed examination of the construction of an imaginary cathedral. Also use: *Cathedrals* by Neil Grant (1972, Watts $4.90).

4638. McLanathan, Richard. *The Pageant of Medieval Art and Life* (6–9). Illustrated. 1966, Westminster $6.95. A mature introduction to the Middle Ages and the various art forms that flourished then.

4639. Price, Christine. *Made in the Renaissance* (5–8). Illus. by author. 1963, Dutton $6.95. About the craftspeople who created the armor, furniture, and jewelry of the Renaissance.

4640. Watson, Percy. *Building the Medieval Cathedrals* (6–9). Illustrated. 1979, Lerner $4.95. The materials and methods of construction are thoroughly presented.

4641. Unstead, R. J., ed. *See Inside a Castle* (5–7). Illus. by Dan Escott, Brian Lewis, and Richard Hook. 1979, Warwick $6.90. A profusely illustrated glimpse into the architecture and activities associated with a medieval castle.

Asia

4642. Alden, Carella. *Sunrise Island: A Story of Japan and Its Arts* (5–8). Illustrated. 1971, Parents $5.95; LB $5.41. An outstanding survey of Japanese art, with many rich details on the history of Japan.

4643. Glubok, Shirley. *The Art of India* (4–7). Illustrated. 1969, Macmillan $5.95. The arts of ancient India as seen through its principal religions.

4644. Glubok, Shirley. *The Art of China* (4–6). Illus. by Gerard Nook. 1973, Macmillan $6.95. A brief but informative survey of the history of Chinese arts, with important periods and styles highlighted in text and illustration.

4645. Spencer, Cornelia. *Made in Japan* (6–9). with photos. Illus. by Richard M. Powers. 1963, Knopf $5.99. An introduction to the arts and crafts of Japan through the centuries, with emphasis on the Japanese love of beauty in all facets of living. For a younger group use: *The Art of Japan* by Shirley Glubok (1970, Macmillan $5.95).

Africa

4646. D'Amato, Janet, and D'Amato, Alex. *African Animals through African Eyes* (5–8). Illus. by author. 1971, Messner $4.95; LB $4.79. The animals of Africa, their history, and their representation in various art forms.

4647. Glubok, Shirley. *The Art of Africa* (4–6). Illus. by Alfred Tamarin. 1965, Harper $6.95; LB $7.89. A well-illustrated introduction to this subject.

4648. Price, Christine. *Dancing Masks of Africa* (2–4). Illus. by author. 1975, Scribner $6.95. A picture book about the types and functions of masks in African culture.

4649. Price, Christine. *Made in West Africa* (6–9). Illustrated. 1975, Dutton $9.95. A handsome addition to the author's many books on the arts and crafts of various regions of the world. Also use: *Black Images: The Art of West Africa* by Penelope Naylor (1973, Doubleday $6.95).

Indian Arts and Crafts

4650. Baylor, Byrd. *They Put on Masks* (3–5). Illus. by Jerry Ingram. 1974, Scribner $7.95. Describes the masks of many American Indian tribes, their uses, and the ceremonies in which they were worn.

4651. Baylor, Byrd. *When Clay Sings* (2–5). Illus. by Tom Bahti. 1972, Scribner $8.95. An exploration of the designs that originally appeared on the pottery of the Indians of the Southwest.

4652. Brindze, Ruth. *The Story of the Totem Pole* (5–7). Illus. by Yeffe Kimball. 1951, Vanguard $5.95. History and symbolism of the totem pole are woven into stories. Also use: *Talking Totem Poles* by Glenn Holder (1973, Dodd $4.95).

4653. Glubok, Shirley. *The Art of the North American Indian* (4–7). Illustrated. 1964, Harper $7.89. A general survey of the arts and artifacts of the North American Indian, illustrated with striking photographs.

4654. Glubok, Shirley. *The Art of the Plains Indians* (4–7). Illustrated. 1975, Macmillan $7.95. The author has clearly and simply recaptured the many artistic aspects of Great Plains tribes.

4655. Glubok, Shirley. *The Art of the Southeastern Indians* (4–7). Illustrated. 1978, Macmillan $7.95. Artifacts and accompanying information are introduced by text and striking black-and-white photographs.

4656. Glubok, Shirley. *The Art of the Southwest Indians* (4–7). Illus. by Alfred Tamarin. 1971, Macmillan $5.95. This useful book contains information and illustrations of the artwork and incidental tribal customs of the Apache, Navajo, and Pueblo peoples. Also use: *The Art of the Northwest Coast Indians* (1975, Macmillan $7.95).

4657. Glubok, Shirley. *The Art of the Woodland Indians* (4–6). Illus. by Alfred Tamarin. 1976, Macmillan $7.95. Part of Glubok's useful, low-keyed series on the arts and crafts of American Indians.

4658. Hofsinde, Robert. *Indian Arts* (4–7). Illus. by author. 1971, Morrow $5.52. A survey of North American Indian arts beginning with early rock painting and ending with the status of the arts today. Includes information and illustrations on such special areas as ceremonial masks and southwestern Katchina dolls.

4659. Highwater, Jamake. *Many Smokes, Many Moons* (5–8). Illustrated. 1978, Lippincott $8.95. Subtitle: *A Chronology of Indian History through Indian Art.*

United States

4660. Alden, Carella. *From Early American Paintbrushes* (4–7). Illustrated. 1971, Parents $5.95; LB $5.41. A charming history of American art during the colonial period.

4661. Batterberry, Ariane, and Batterberry, Michael. *The Pantheon Story of American Art for Young People* (6–9). Illustrated. 1976, Pantheon $12.95. A basic history chronologically arranged, beginning with Indian art and ending with the twentieth century. Well illustrated, but without an index.

4662. Coen, Rena Neumann. *American History in Art* (5–7). Illustrated. 1966, Lerner $4.95. American history is revealed through various artworks.

4663. Gladstone, M. J. *A Carrot for a Nose: The Form of Folk Sculpture on America's City Streets and Country Roads* (5–8). Illustrated. 1974, Scribner $1.99. Folk sculpture found out-of-doors, from weathervanes and snowmen to gravestones and scarecrows, described in text and copious illustrations.

4664. Glubok, Shirley. *The Art of America in the Gilded Age* (4–7). Illustrated. 1974, Macmillan $6.95. A history of American art from the Civil War to the twentieth century. This volume is followed by: *The Art of America in the Early Twentieth Century* (1974, $6.95) and *The Art of America Since World War II* (1976, $7.95).

4665. Glubok, Shirley. *The Art of Colonial America* (4–7). Illustrated. 1970, Macmillan $5.95. A history of fine and decorative arts in the early days of the colonies. This is the first of the series on American art and is followed by (both $6.95): *The Art of the New American Nation* (1972) and *The Art of America from Jackson to Lincoln* (1973).

4666. Glubok, Shirley. *The Art of the Comic Strip* (4–7). Illustrated. 1979, Macmillan $8.95. The history of the newspaper comic strip in America arranged in chronological order.

4667. Glubok, Shirley. *The Art of the Old West* (4–7). Illustrated. 1971, Macmillan $5.95. Paint-ing, sculpture, and photographs that tell the story of the development of the West.

4668. Glubok, Shirley. *The Art of the Spanish in the United States and Puerto Rico* (4–7). Illustrated. 1972, Macmillan $7.95. Three centuries of Spanish domination in colonial America as reflected in art objects—principally religious artifacts—described through photographs and an illuminating text.

4669. Hiller, Carl E. *From Tepees to Towers* (4–7). Illustrated. 1967, Little $6.95. Subtitle: *A Photographic History of American Architecture.*

4670. Hoag, Edwin. *American Houses: Colonial, Classic and Contemporary* (5–8). Illustrated. 1964, Lippincott $10.00. A useful, beautifully illustrated history of houses in America.

4671. Horwitz, Elinor. *Mountain People, Mountain Crafts* (7–9). Illus. by Joshua Horwitz and Anthony Horwitz. 1974, Lippincott $8.95; paper $3.95. Folk artists' own words and vivid photographs portray traditional Appalachian crafts.

4672. Madian, Jon. *Beautiful Junk* (4–6). Illus. by Barbara Jacobs and Lou Jacobs, Jr. 1968, Little $4.95. The curiosity of a hostile boy is aroused by an old man who religiously collects junk—and creates The Watts Towers of Los Angeles.

4673. Mendelson, Lee, and Schulz, Charles. *Happy Birthday, Charlie Brown* (4–7). 1979, Random $14.95. A narrative that traces the origins and history of Charlie Brown and the Peanuts group.

4674. Meyer, Carolyn. *People Who Make Things: How American Craftsmen Live and Work* (6–9). Illustrated. 1975, Atheneum $6.50. The history and present status of 8 different crafts are discussed, including quilting, woodworking, and bookbinding.

4675. Myron, Robert, and Sundell, Abner. *Modern Art in America* (7–9). Illustrated. 1971, Macmillan $5.95. A chronologically arranged survey of the many forms of art as they developed in twentieth-century America; also a discussion of theories, trends, and movements, as well as individual artists.

Communication

4676. Colby, C. B. *Communications: How Man Talks to Man Across Land, Sea, and Space* (4–7). Illustrated. 1964, Coward $5.19. A brief description of 30 forms of communications.

4677.   Neal, Harry Edward. *Communication: From Stone Age to Space Age* (6–9). Illustrated. 1974, Messner, rev. ed. $7.29. A history of communication with special coverage on the development and functions of language.

4678.   Stewig, John Warren. *Sending Messages* (1–4). Illustrated. 1978, Houghton $6.95. A simple introduction to all forms of communication from body language to the Morse code.

4679.   Wood, Barbara Sundene. *Messages Without Words* (2–4). Illustrated. 1978, Raintree $5.49. A simple but amazingly thorough introduction to the world of communication.

Signs and Symbols

4680.   Adkins, Jan. *Symbols: A Silent Language* (4–6). Illustrated. 1979, Walker $7.95. Road signs, blueprints, and military insignias are three of the many areas explored in this book.

4681.   Amon, Aline. *Talking Hands: Indian Sign Language* (3–6). Illus. by author. 1968, Doubleday $4.95. A simple explanation of how to use Indian sign language.

4682.   Aylesworth, Thomas G. *Understanding Body Talk* (5–9). Illustrated. 1979, Watts $5.45. Body talk is the subject of this book on nonverbal communication.

4683.   Charlip, Remy; Ancona, Mary Beth; and Ancona, George. *Handtalk: An ABC of Finger Spelling and Sign Language* (3–6). 1974, Parents $5.95; LB $5.41. This work gives the letter signs in photographs and words in handtalk.

4684.   Fronval, George, and Dubois, Daniel. *Indian Signs and Signals* (5–9). Illustrated. 1979, Sterling $12.95; LB $11.69. An explanation of over 800 signs grouped under subjects.

4685.   Gay, Kathlyn. *Body Talk* (5–8). Illustrated. 1974, Scribner $8.95. Explains how an observant person can learn about people from their physical movements. Also use: *Face Talk, Hand Talk and Body Talk* by Sue Castle (1977, Doubleday $7.95).

4686.   Helfman, Elizabeth. *Signs and Symbols Around the World* (6–9). Illustrated. 1967, Lothrop $6.67. Traces the development of written communication from cave painting to alphabets and numerals and the special language of magic, science, industry, and religion to more recent proposals for an international language.

4687.   Hofsinde, Robert. *Indian Picture Writing* (4–7). Illustrated. 1959, Morrow $5.52. A brief history of Indian picture writing, with almost 250 symbols. Also use: *Indian Sign Language* (1956, Morrow $5.52).

4688.   Lubell, Winifred, and Lubell, Cecil. *Picture Signs and Symbols* (2–5). 1972, Parents LB $5.41. An entertaining introduction to such symbols as are found in road signs, maps, or are associated with holidays, festivals, and religions.

4689.   Myller, Rolf. *Symbols and Their Meanings* (4–7). 1978, Atheneum $9.95. An explanation of symbols and their part in communication.

Codes and Ciphers

4690.   Albert, Burton. *More Codes for Kids* (3–5). Illus. by Jerry Warshaw. 1979, Whitman $5.50; LB $4.13. A total of 25 new codes based on such bases and maps, letters, and numbers.

4691.   Babson, Walt. *All Kinds of Codes* (4–6). 1976, Four Winds $8.95. A fascinating collection of material on a variety of codes.

4692.   Bennet, Gari. *Fargo North's Decoder Game Book* (2–3). 1978, Grosset $2.95. A code board allows readers to decode messages left by Paul the Gorilla.

4693.   Gardner, Martin. *Codes, Ciphers and Secret Writing* (6–9). Illustrated. 1972, Simon & Schuster $5.95. All sorts of puzzles and codes from the simple to the highly complex. Chapters are devoted to such topics as invisible writing and code machines.

4694.   James, Elizabeth, and Barkin, Carol. *How to Keep a Secret: Writing and Talking in Code* (6–8). Illustrated. 1978, Lothrop $5.95. Both well-known and obscure codes are described with decoding information given in an appendix.

4695.   Kohn, Bernice. *Secret Codes and Ciphers* (4–7). Illus. by Frank Aloise. 1968, Prentice-Hall $4.95; paper $1.50. The difference between codes and ciphers is explained with many examples of each. Also use: *Secrets with Ciphers and Codes* by Joel Rothman (1969, Macmillan $4.95; paper $1.25).

4696.   Lamb, Geoffrey. *Secret Writing Tricks* (6–8). 1975, Elsevier/Nelson $6.95. Various techniques for writing secret messages, such as using numbers or pinpricks, are described with famous codes of the past. Also use: *Codes and Ciphers: Secret Writing Through the Ages* by John Laffin (1964, Abelard $6.50).

4697.   Peterson, John. *How to Write Codes and Send Secret Messages* (2–4). Illus. by Bernice Myers. 1970, Four Winds $5.95; paper $.95. An easily read book on coding and decoding secret messages. Also use: *Codes for Kids* by Burton Albert (1976, Whitman $5.50).

4698. Zim, Herbert S. *Codes and Secret Writing* (5–8). Illustrated. 1948, Morrow $5.52. Children love this fun book, which shows them how to encode and decode messages, how to write and read secret languages, and how to use invisible writing to send messages. Also use: *First Book of Codes and Ciphers* by Sam and Beryl Epstein (1956, Watts $4.90).

Flags

4699. Crouthers, David D. *Flags of American History* (3–6). 1973, Hammond $4.50; LB $4.39. The story of 89 flags associated with our history. Also use: *Flags of the U.S.A.* by David Eggenberger (1964, Crowell $8.95).

4700. Freeman, Mae. *Stars and Stripes: The Story of the American Flag* (2–5). Illus. by Lorence Bjorklund. 1964, Random $4.99. The story of the American flag and how it has changed through the years. With an older group, use: *The American Flag* by Thomas Parrish (1973, Simon & Schuster $5.95).

4701. Pedersen, Christian. *The International Flag Book in Color* (5–8). Illustrated. 1971, Morrow $6.95. A beautifully illustrated guide to almost 900 flags and coats of arms.

4702. Thompson, Brenda, and Giesen, Rosemary. *Flags* (2–3). Illus. by David Brogan and Rosemary Giesen. 1977, Lerner $3.95. A selection of national sports flags and other flags and their meanings.

Language and Languages

4703. Adler, Irving, and Adler, Joyce. *Language and Man* (3–5). Illus. by Laurie Jo Lambie. 1970, John Day $6.89. An interesting introduction to the importance of language, the various groups, and the history of the English language. Also use: *The Magic of Words* by Arthur Alexander (1962, Prentice-Hall $4.95).

4704. Cooper, Lee, and McIntosh, Clifton. *Fun with French* (4–7). Illus. by Ann Atene. 1963, Little $6.95. French words are introduced by pictures, stories, and songs. Others in the series (from Little, same price) are: *Fun with Spanish* (1960) and *Fun with German* (1965).

4705. Frasconi, Antonio. *See and Say: A Picture Book in Four Languages* (1–3). 1955, Harcourt $6.95; paper $1.35. Colored woodcuts of familiar objects identified in French, Spanish, Italian, and English, with pronounciation guide.

4706. Greenfeld, Howard. *Sumer Is Icumen in: Our Ever-Changing Language* (6–9). 1978, Crown $5.95. A basic history of our language, plus a discussion of the human influences that have caused it to change.

4707. Hautzig, Esther. *In School: Learning In Four Languages* (1–4). Illus. by Nonny Hogrogian. 1969, Macmillan $4.95. A simple phrase book, in English, Spanish, French, and Russian, showing that schools and learning are much the same no matter where children live.

4708. Hautzig, Esther. *In the Park: An Excursion in Four Languages* (1–4). Illus. by Ezra Jack Keats. 1968, Macmillan $4.95. The fun of a park in New York City, Paris, Moscow, or Madrid is simply expressed in the languages native to each. Also use: *At Home: A Visit In Four Languages* (1968, Macmillan $4.95).

4709. Joslin, Sesyle. *There Is a Bull on My Balcony and Other Useful Phrases in Spanish and English* (1–4). 1966, Harcourt $5.95. Also use: *There Is a Dragon in My Bed and Other Useful Phrases in French and English* (1966, $4.95).

4710. Kohn, Bernice. *What a Funny Thing to Say!* (4–7). Illus. by R. O. Blechman. 1974, Dial $5.95; LB $5.47. A book about our language, its origin, changing uses, and games that young people will enjoy.

4711. Ludovici, Laurence J. *The Origins of Language* (6–8). Illus. by Raymonde Ludovici. 1965, Putnam $4.89. Explains the anatomical structure of the speech organs and outlines the history and changing character of language.

4712. Ogg, Oscar. *The 26 Letters* (4–6). Illustrated. 1971, Crowell $11.95. The story behind our alphabet, fascinatingly told.

4713. Pei, Mario. *All about Language* (6–9). Illus. by Donat Ivanovsky. 1954, Lippincott $8.95. A narrative on the origin and development of human language.

4714. Wolff, Diane. *Chinese Writing: An Introduction* (4–6). Calligraphy by Jeanette Chien. 1975, Holt $5.95. An explanation of Chinese characters, their formation, and meaning. Also use: *You Can Write Chinese* by Kurt Wiese (1945, Penguin, paper 95¢).

Words

4715. Adelson, Leone. *Dandelions Don't Bite: The Story of Words* (3–5). Illus. by Lou Myers. 1972, Pantheon $5.99. In 9 chapters, humorously illustrated, this is an introduction to the origin of words and their meaning.

4716. Asimov, Isaac. *Words from the Myths* (5–9). Illus. by William Barss. 1961, Houghton $8.95. Excellent essays on modern words derived from classical myths, with emphasis on scientific vocabulary.

4717. Barrol, Grady. *The Little Book of Anagrams* (2–5). Illustrated. 1978, Harvey House $3.49. An explanation of what are anagrams, plus 60 entertaining examples.

4718. Basil, Cynthia. *Breakfast in the Afternoon: Another Beginning Word Book* (K–2). Illustrated. 1979, Morrow $6.95. An easy-to-read introduction to the origins of several familiar words.

4719. Basil, Cynthia. *How Ships Play Cards: A Beginning Book of Homonyms* (1–3). Illus. by Janet McCaffery. 1980, Morrow $7.95; LB $7.63. The author uses riddles to introduce words that look and sound alike.

4720. Basil, Cynthia. *Nailheads and Potato Eyes: A Beginning Word Book* (3–5). Illus. by Janet McCaffery. 1976, Morrow $6.96. A quiz book that teaches meanings of words while entertaining the reader.

4721. Bossom, Naomi. *A Scale Full of Fish and Other Turnabouts* (PS–2). Illus. by author. 1979, Greenwillow $6.95; LB $6.67. Word play using homonyms done with imaginative text and woodcuts.

4722. Carle, Eric. *My Very First Book of Words* (PS–1). Illus. by author. 1974, Crowell $2.95. A nicely illustrated beginning word book.

4723. Carothers, Gibson, and Lacey, James. *Slanguage* (4–6). 1979, Sterling $5.89. The origins of such slang expressions as hunky-dory and top dog.

4724. Dantzie, Cynthia Maris. *Sounds of Silents* (1–2). 1976, Prentice-Hall $5.21. Words that contain silent letters are introduced.

4725. Fitzgerald, Cathleen. *Let's Find Out about Words* (2–5). Illus. by Georgia Froom. 1971, Watts $4.47. The origin of many words commonly used in our language.

4726. Greet, W. Cabell et al. *Junior Thesaurus: In Other Words II* (5–9). Illustrated. 1970, Lothrop $9.36. Synonyms, antonyms, and material illustrating meanings and usage are given in this useful work for students unable to use an adult thesaurus.

4727. Greet, W. Cabell; Jenkins, William; and Schiller, Andrew. *In Other Words: A Beginning Thesaurus* (3–6). Illustrated. 1969, Lothrop $8.50; LB $8.16. A beginning reference—a treasury of words for children in the middle grades in 3 sections: (1) how to use the book, (2) synonyms and antonyms, (3) sets of related words clearly illustrated.

4728. Halsey, William D., and Morris, Christopher. *The Magic World of Words; A Very First Dictionary* (1–3). Illustrated. 1977, Macmillan $6.95. Definitions of 1,500 words are included as well as examples of their uses in sentences.

4729. Hanson, Joan. *More Similes: Roar Like a Lion, as Loud as Thunder . . .* (1–2). 1979, Lerner $3.95. A simple introduction to similes.

4730. Hefter, Richard. *Yes and No: A Book of Opposites* (1–3). Illustrated. 1975, Strawberry $3.50. Contrasts for the young reader.

4731. Kraske, Robert. *The Story of the Dictionary* (5–9). Illustrated. 1975, Harcourt $6.50. An enthralling book about the great lexicographers and their works, from the *Oxford English Dictionary* to dictionaries for children.

4732. Maestro, Betsy, and Maestro, Giulio. *Busy Day; A Book of Action Words* (K–2). Illus. by author. 1978, Crown $5.95. Action words are used to depict a day's activities at the circus.

4733. Maestro, Betsy, and Maestro, Giulio. *On the Go: A Book of Adjectives* (PS–K). Illustrated. 1979, Crown $5.95. Through the activities of a clown and an elephant, several basic adjectives are introduced.

4734. Nevins, Ann. *From the Horse's Mouth* (4–6). 1977, Prentice-Hall $5.21. The origin of about 150 expressions are explained.

4735. Russell, Yvonne. *Words in My World* (PS–1). Illus. by Dennis Hockerman. 1979, Rand $5.95. About 300 words are described and illustrated in this beginning word identification book.

4736. Schwartz, Alvin, ed. *Chin Music: Tall Talk and Other Talk Collected from American Folklore* (4–6). Illus. by John O'Brian. 1979, Lippincott $7.95; LB $7.89. An alphabetical glossary of our slang and dialect from 1815 to 1950.

4737. Steckler, Arthur. *101 Words and How They Began* (4–6). Illus. by James Flora. 1979, Doubleday $6.95. Interesting word origins about names of food, animals, etc.

4738. Thayer, Jane. *Try Your Hand* (1–3). Illus. by Joel Schick. 1980, Morrow $6.95; LB $6.67. This work uses riddles and phrases to show several meanings for the word *hand*.

4739. Wilbur, Richard. *Opposites* (5–7). Illus. by author. 1973, Harcourt $4.95. Through verses and cartoonlike illustrations, a series of antonyms are given for words.

4740. Wittels, Harriet, and Wittels, Greisman. *Perfect Speller* (4–6). 1973, Grosset $5.95. An alphabet of 3,000 commonly misspelled words.

Books and Printing

4741. Berger, Melvin. *Printing Plant* (4–6). Illustrated. 1978, Watts $4.90. An up-to-date account of various printing processes, including material on the use of the computer and laser beams.

4742. Epstein, Sam, and Epstein, Beryl. *First Book of Printing* (4–6). Illus. by Laszlo Roth. 1974, Watts $4.90. The history of printing from its invention to the present.

4743. Greenfeld, Howard. *Books: From Writer to Reader* (5–8). Illustrated. 1976, Crown $8.95. A beautifully illustrated, comprehensive account of how books are made. For a younger group use: *Books: A Book to Begin On* by Susan Bartlett (1968, Holt $3.27).

4744. Nickel, Mildred L. *Let's Find Out about a Book* (3–5). Illus. by Tad Krumeich. 1971, Watts $4.47. An easy introduction to the parts of a book and a brief history of the printed book. Also use: *Pencil to Press: How this Book Came to Be* by Marjorie Spector (1975, Lothrop $6.00).

4745. Simon, Irving B. *The Story of Printing: From Wood Blocks to Electronics* (6–9). Illustrated. 1965, Harvey House $6.29. A history of printing for the more mature reader.

Writing and Speaking

4746. Brandt, Sue R. *The First Book of How to Write a Report* (4–6). Illus. by Peter P. Plasencia. 1968, Watts $4.90; paper $.95. Clear instructions on how to gather facts, organize time, and write a finished report.

4747. Cassedy, Sylvia. *In Your Own Words: A Beginner's Guide to Writing* (6–9). 1979, Doubleday $7.95; LB $8.90. A thorough but basic guide to creative writing.

4748. Cosman, Anna. *How to Read and Write Poetry* (4–7). Illustrated. 1979, Watts $5.45. A simple introduction to the writing of poetry.

4749. Hardendorff, Jeanne B. *Libraries and How to Use Them* (4–6). Illustrated. 1979, Watts $5.45. A logically organized guide to such areas as classification systems, the card catalog, and basic reference books.

4750. Hughes, Ted. *Poetry Is* (6–9). 1970, Doubleday $5.95. A discussion of the elements of poetry based on a BBC series by this eminent poet.

4751. Joslin, Sesyle. *Dear Dragon* (1–4). Illustrated. 1962, Harcourt $4.50. Subtitle: *And Other Useful Letter Forms for Young Ladies and Gentlemen Engaged in Everyday Correspondence.* Also use for older readers: *The First Book of Letter Writing* by Helen Jacobson (1957, Watts $4.90; paper $1.25).

4752. Kalina, Sigmund. *How to Sharpen Your Study Skills* (6–9). Illus. by Richard Rosenblum. 1975, Lothrop $5.52. A practical and useful handbook that covers such topics as budgeting time, note taking, skimming materials, and test taking. Also use: *The First Book of Facts and How to Find Them* by David C. Whitney (1966, Watts $4.90).

4753. Lyman, Nanci A. *The School Newspaper: How It Works: How to Write for It* (6–8). Illustrated. 1973, Watts $4.47; LB $4.90. The functions of the school newspaper are well presented, plus material on writing, editing, proofreading.

4754. Plagemann, Bentz. *How to Write a Story* (4–9). 1971, Lothrop $5.09; LB $5.52. The author describes the techniques (e.g., character building, dialogue writing) and the mechanics of story writing.

4755. Powers, David C. *First Book of How to Run Meetings* (4–6). 1967, Watts $4.90. An introduction to parliamentary procedure.

4756. Powers, David C. *The First Book of How to Make a Speech* (4–7). Illus. by Peter Plasencia. 1963, Watts $4.90; paper $1.25. A guide to public speaking with sections on how to collect and organize material, as well as hints on good delivery.

4757. Weiss, Ann E. *News or Not? Facts and Feelings on the News Media* (6–9). Illustrated. 1977, Dutton $8.95. News gathering today and its accompanying problems are interestingly analyzed.

4758. Wikler, Janet. *How to Study and Learn* (4–6). Illustrated. 1978, Watts $4.90. After some theory about learning, the author covers study techniques.

Music

General

4759. Bierhorst, John. *A Cry from the Earth: Music of the North American Indians* (6–8). 1979, Four Winds $8.95. An informative account of the part played by music in the lives of American Indians interspersed with many examples.

4760. Broldo, Arnold, and Davis, Marilyn. *Music Dictionary* (6–9). Illus. by Winifred Greene. 1956, Doubleday $5.95. More than 800 brief definitions of musical terms, names of instruments, etc.

4761. Bulla, Clyde Robert. *More Stories of Favorite Operas* (4–7). Illus. by Joseph Low. 1965, Crowell $8.95. A condensation of 22 operas together with cast analyses.

4762. Bulla, Clyde Robert. *Stories of Gilbert and Sullivan Operas* (4–7). Illus. by Ruth McCrea and James McCrea. 1968, Crowell $8.95. Summaries of 11 of their popular operettas charmingly retold.

4763. Clymer, Theodore. *Four Corners of the Sky: Poems, Chants and Oratory* (K–3). Illus. by Marc Brown. 1975, Little $6.95. Songs, chants, and sayings from various tribes of American Indians are presented.

4764. Fichter, George S. *American Indian Music and Musical Instruments* (4–8). Illustrated. 1978, McKay $7.95. Includes material not only on the music, but even directions on how to make and decorate some musical instruments.

4765. Hill, Thomas A. *Country Music* (5–8). Illustrated. 1978, Watts $4.90. An account that concentrates on personalities.

4766. Hofmann, Charles. *American Indians Sing* (3–6). Illus. by Nicholas Amrostia. 1967, John Day $12.49. A beautifully illustrated book that explains how and why the American Indian made music. Also use: *Indian Music Makers* by Robert Hofsinde (1967, Morrow $5.52).

4767. Hughes, Langston. *The First Book of Jazz* (5–7). Illus. by Cliff Roberts. 1976, Watts $4.90. A basic history of jazz from African origins to modern forms built around the career of Louis Armstrong. Also use: *Jazz* by Arlo Blocher (1976, Troll $5.89; paper $2.50).

4768. Hurd, Michael. *The Oxford Junior Companion to Music* (5–9). Illustrated. 1979, Oxford $25.00. A useful dictionary on people, places, compositions, terms, and instruments.

4769. Krishef, Robert K. *The Grand Ole Opry* (5–9). Illustrated. 1978, Lerner $5.95. An introduction to the national shrine of country and western music.

4770. Krishef, Robert K. *Introducing Country Music* (5–9). Illustrated. 1979, Country Music Library $5.95. The growth and development of country music from the 1920s through the 1970s.

4771. Scholes, Percy A. *Oxford Junior Companion to Music* (6–9). 1954, Oxford $25.00. A collection of articles on composers, various types of music, and musical instruments.

4772. Siegmeister, Elie. *Invitation to Music* (6–9). Illustrated. 1961, Harvey House $6.69. History of music and the development of various forms; includes sketches of composers.

4773. Van Der Horst, Brian. *Rock Music* (5–7). 1973, Watts $4.90. An inside history of rock music; still fairly up-to-date.

4774. Warren, Fred, and Warren, Lee. *The Music of Africa* (6–8). Illustrated. 1970, Prentice-Hall $5.95. An excellent overview of African music, past and present, and the part it has played in the people's lives.

Folk Songs and Ballads

4775. Aliki. *Go Tell Aunt Rhody* (1–3). Illus. by author. 1974, Macmillan $5.95. The ever-popular folksong about the death of the famous gray goose. Also use: *Go Tell Aunt Rhody* by Robert Quackenbush (1973, Lippincott $8.95).

4776. Aliki. *Hush Little Baby* (1–3). Illus. by author. 1968, Prentice-Hall $5.95; paper $1.50. This old English folksong is reprinted with colorful drawings and the original music. Also use: *Hush*

Little Baby by Margot Zemach (1975, Dutton $6.95).

4777. Berger, Melvin. *The Story of Folk Music* (6–9). 1976, Phillips $8.95. How and why American folk music evolved, with biographical information on singers from Woody Guthrie to John Denver. Also use: *Folk Music in America* by Brian Van Der Horst (1972, Watts $4.90).

4778. Bookbinder, David. *What Folk Music Is All About* (5–7). Illustrated. 1979, Messner $9.29. A history of American folk music from its beginnings to the present.

4779. Boni, Margaret B. *Fireside Book of Folk Songs* (5–8). Illustrated. 1966, Simon & Schuster $17.50. An excellent collection now complete with guitar chords.

4780. Engvick, William. *Lullabies and Night Songs* (K–3). Illus. by Maurice Sendak. 1965, Harper $15.00; LB $12.89. A collection of the poet's verses and those of others set to music by Alec Wilder.

4781. Gauch, Patricia Lee. *On to Widecombe Fair* (K–3). Illus. by Trina Schart Hyman. 1978, Putnam $7.95. A rollicking version of the familiar folksong.

4782. Glazer, Tom. *Eye Winker, Tom Tinker, Chin Chopper* (1–3). Illus. by Ronald Himler. 1973, Doubleday $6.95; paper $1.95. Fifty wonderful songs complete with fingerplays.

4783. Graboff, Abner. *Old MacDonald Had a Farm* (K–3). Illus. by author. 1973, Scholastic paper $.95. The ever-popular cumulative song about farm animals and implements.

4784. Ipcar, Dahlov. *The Cat Came Back* (K–3). Illus. by author. 1971, Knopf $5.99. An amusing story of a cat that is able to overcome all odds.

4785. Langstaff, John. *Frog Went A-Courtin'* (K–3). Illus. by Feodor Rojankovsky. 1955, Harcourt $6.50; paper $1.95. A rollicking folksong with matching illustrations.

4786. Langstaff, John. *Hi! Ho! The Rattlin' Bog and Other Folk Songs for Group Singing* (4–7). Illus. by Robin Jacques. 1969, Harcourt $5.50. Fifty excellent folk songs printed with guitar chords and simple piano accompaniments.

4787. Langstaff, Nancy, and Langstaff, John. *Jim Along, Josie* (K–4). Illus. by Jan Pienkowski. 1970, Harcourt $7.50. Subtitled: *A Collection of Folk Songs and Singing Games for Young Children.*

4788. Langstaff, John. *Oh, A-Hunting We Will Go* (K–3). Illus. by Nancy W. Parker. 1974, Atheneum $7.95. Old and new verses have been com-

bined to make this the definitive version of the folksong.

4789. Langstaff, John. *Swapping Boy* (K–3). Illus. by Joe Krush and Beth Krush. 1960, Harcourt $6.50. The story of a foolish boy and his swappings, told in song and pictures.

4790. Langstaff, John. *Sweetly Sings the Donkey* (K–3). Illus. by Nancy W. Parker. 1976, Atheneum $6.95. Subtitled: *Animal Rounds for Children to Sing or Play on Recorders.*

4791. Lomax, Allen, and Lomax, John A. *American Ballads and Folk Songs* (6–9). 1934, Macmillan $10.00. An excellent collection by two leading collectors of folk music.

4792. Lomax, Allen, and Lomax, John A. *Cowboy Songs and Other Frontier Ballads* (6–9). 1966, Macmillan $8.95. Aspects of frontier life are explored in these songs.

4793. Nic Leodhas, Sorche. *Always Room for One More* (K–3). Illus. by Nonny Hogrogian. 1965, Holt $5.95; paper $1.65. The generosity of Lachie MacLachlan leads to a very crowded home in this Scottish folksong.

4794. Quackenbush, Robert. *Skip to My Lou* (1–3). Illus. by author. 1975, Lippincott $8.95. A disastrous engagement party is portrayed in this classic folksong. Also use: *Clementine* (1974, Lippincott $8.95).

4795. Quackenbush, Robert. *There'll Be a Hot Time in the Old Town Tonight* (K–3). 1974, Lippincott $6.95. The old standard, complete with bold, colorful illustrations.

4796. Rounds, Glen, illus. *Sweet Betsy from Pike* (2–4). 1973, Childrens Press $6.60. The beloved folksong charmingly illustrated.

4797. Sackett, S. J. *Cowboys and the Songs They Sang* (4–7). Illustrated. 1967, W. R. Scott $5.95. Music, lyrics, and background information on each song.

4798. Seeger, Pete, and Seeger, Charles. *The Foolish Frog* (K–3). Illus. by Miloslav Jagor. 1973, Macmillan $4.95. The story of a farmer and his amazing song about a hopping frog.

4799. Seeger, Ruth C. *American Folk Songs for Children* (2–6). Illus. by Barbara Cooney. 1948, Doubleday $8.95. All kinds of songs, including chants and ballads, that will delight and amuse children.

4800. Spier, Peter. *The Erie Canal* (K–3). Illus. by author. 1970, Doubleday $6.95; paper $1.95. A folksong describing life on the Erie Canal in the 1850s.

4801. Spier, Peter. *The Fox Went Out on a Chilly Night* (K–3). Illus. by author. 1961, Doubleday $6.95; paper $1.49. The old folksong about a fox's journey to catch the famous plump geese.

4802. Spier, Peter. *London Bridge Is Falling Down* (K–3). Illus. by author. 1967, Doubleday $6.95; paper $1.49. The Mother Goose rhyme set to music with accompanying historical sketch.

4803. Taylor, Mark. *Jennie Jenkins* (K–3). Illus. by Glen Rounds. 1974, Little $4.95; Scholastic paper $.95. A humorous old folk tune about Jennie and her antics at the Nettle Bottom Ball.

4804. Westcott, Nadine. *I Know an Old Lady Who Swallowed a Fly* (2–4). Illus. by author. 1980, Little $8.95; paper $4.95. A newly illustrated edition of this outrageously funny song.

4805. Yurchenco, Henrietta. *Fiesta of Folk Songs of Spain and Latin America* (2–6). Illus. by Jules Maidoff. 1967, Putnam $5.97. A good collection of Spanish tunes.

4806. Zemach, Harve. *Mommy, Buy Me a China Doll* (K–2). Illus. by Margot Zemach. 1975, Farrar $5.95. Little Eliza Lou thinks up all sorts of ways in which she can get a China doll.

Musical Instruments

4807. Bailey, Bernadine. *Bells, Bells, Bells* (5–8). Illustrated. 1978, Dodd $5.95. A history of bells beginning with the Chinese in 4000 B.C.

4808. Berger, Melvin. *The Clarinet and Saxophone Book* (3–7). Illustrated. 1975, Lothrop $6.48. A well-organized account that covers such topics as history, how the instruments are made, and famous musicians who played them.

4809. Berger, Melvin. *The Flute Book* (4–7). 1973, Lothrop $6.25; LB $6.00. The author discusses the history, construction, and place of the flute in the orchestra.

4810. Berger, Melvin. *The Trumpet Book* (5–9). Illustrated. 1978, Lothrop $6.50. The author discusses such topics as the instrument's history and construction, as well as important music for it.

4811. Dietz, Betty W. *Musical Instruments of Africa* (6–8). Illustrated. 1965, John Day $9.95. Subtitle: *Their Nature, Use and Place in the Life of a Deeply Musical People.*

4812. Etkin, Ruth. *Playing and Composing on the Recorder* (6–9). 1975, Sterling $5.95; LB $5.89. Even a beginner can compose music at once on this easily played instrument.

4813. Etkin, Ruth. *The Rhythm Band Book* (3–5). Illustrated. 1979, Sterling $6.95. Many hints on organizing and playing in a rhythm band, plus a collection of 27 songs.

4814. Gilmore, Lee. *Folk Instruments* (4–6). Illus. by George Overlie. 1962, Lerner $3.95. Fascinating information on the history, construction, and playing of such instruments as harmonica, guitar, and fiddle.

4815. Hill, Thomas A. *The Guitar: An Introduction to the Instrument* (5–7). 1973, Watts $4.90. The history of the guitar and its music, as well as its construction and famous guitarists. Also use: *The Drum: An Introduction to the Instrument* (1975, Watts $4.90).

4816. Kupferberg, Herbert. *Rainbow of Sound: The Instruments of the Orchestra and Their Music* (4–6). Illus. by Morris Warman. 1973, Scribner $5.95. An explanation of the role played by the various instruments in the symphony orchestra. Also use: *Meet the Orchestra* by William W. Suggs (1966, Macmillan $4.95).

4817. Kettelkamp, Larry. *Singing Strings* (4–7). Illus. by author. 1958, Morrow $6.00. The 4 groups of stringed instruments are briefly discussed and pictured.

4818. Kettelkamp, Larry. *Drums, Rattles and Bells* (4–7). Illus. by author. 1960, Morrow $6.48. The history and design of percussion instruments presented in simple text and informative illustrations.

4819. Lacey, Marion. *Picture Book of Musical Instruments* (4–6). Illus. by Leonard Weisgard. 1942, Lothrop $6.48. The history and present state of 24 instruments included in text and pictures.

4820. Luttrell, Guy. *The Instruments of Music* (6–9). Illustrated. 1978, Nelson $6.95. A history and description of the major musical instruments.

4821. Mandell, Muriel, and Woods, Robert E. *Make Your Own Musical Instruments* (4–6). Illustrated. 1959, Sterling $4.95; LB $5.89. Easy-to-follow directions highlight this simple account.

4822. Price, Christine. *Talking Drums of Africa* (2–5). Illustrated. 1953, Scribner $5.95. The various kinds and uses of African drums from different locations.

4823. Posell, Elsa Z. *This Is an Orchestra* (4–7). Illustrated. 1973, Houghton $6.95. In addition to describing and showing the instruments of the orchestra, this book contains important information on choosing and buying an instrument and building a home record collection.

4824. Segovia, Andres, and Mendoza, Andres Segovia. *My Book of the Guitar; Guidance for the Beginner* (5–9). Illustrated. 1979, Collins $9.95. An instructional book that teaches the basics of reading music and supplies a few simple studies to perform.

4825. Wiseman, Ann. *Making Musical Things* (3–6). Illustrated. 1979, Scribner $8.95. A step-by-step manual in making musical instruments from such objects as milk cartons.

4826. Yolen, Jane. *Ring-Out: A Book of Bells* (5–9). Illus. by Richard Cuffari. 1974, Seabury $6.95. A wonderful work that gives varied information about bells, including legends and history.

National Anthems and Patriotic Songs

4827. Bangs, Edward. *Yankee Doodle* (1–4). Illus. by Steven Kellogg. 1976, Parents $5.95; LB $5.41. Music and text of the famous song, with colorful illustrations. Also use: *Yankee Doodle* by Richard Schackburg (1965, Prentice-Hall, paper $1.50).

4828. Browne, C. A. *The Story of Our National Ballads* (5–8). 1960, Crowell $9.95. The songs, plus biographical and historical information.

4829. Lyons, John Henry. *Stories of Our American Patriotic Songs* (4–7). Illus. by Jacob Landau. n.d., Vanguard $5.95. Material behind 10 of America's favorite songs, plus the words and music.

4830. Shaw, Martin, and others. *National Anthems of the World* (4–7). 1976, Arco $24.95. Approximately 165 anthems included with words in the original language and translation.

4831. Spier, Peter. *The Star Spangled Banner* (K–6). Illustrated. 1973, Doubleday $7.95. Many of the pictures show the battle scenes that inspired Francis Scott Key's immortal verses.

Songs and Singing Games

4832. Bierhorst, John. *Songs of the Chippewa* (4–8). Illus. by Joe Servello. 1974, Farrar $6.95. Seventeen songs of various types, such as lullabys and love songs, are included in this handsomely illustrated book.

4833. Bley, Edgar S. *The Best Singing Games for Children of All Ages* (1–5). Illus. by Patt Willen. 1959, Sterling $6.95; LB $6.69. Presents 50 children's songs that can be acted out as games.

4834. Boni, Margaret B. *The Fireside Book of Favorite American Songs* (4–9). Illus. by Aurelius Battaglia. 1952, Simon & Schuster $9.95. A wonderful cross section of American popular music of yesterday.

4835. Bryan, Ashley. *Walk Together Children* (2–5). Illus. by author. 1974, Atheneum $7.95. A collection of 24 Black American spirituals with background historical information.

4836. Carroll, Lewis. *Songs from Alice: Alice in Wonderland and Through the Looking Glass* (4–6). Music by Don Harper. Illus. by Charles Folkard. 1979, Holiday $8.95. Nineteen newly composed songs for Lewis Carroll's classics.

4837. Conover, Chris. *Six Little Ducks* (1–3). Illus. by author. 1976, Crowell $5.95; LB $6.95. A little duck leads his friends to market in this simple song.

4838. Emberley, Barbara. *Drummer Hoff* (K–3). Illus. by Ed Emberley. 1967, Prentice-Hall $6.95; paper $1.95. The classic song about the assembling of a canon. Caldecott Medal.

4839. Fowke, Edith. *Sally Go Round the Sun: Three Hundred Children's Songs, Rhymes and Games* (K–6). Illus. by Carlos Marchiori. 1970, Doubleday $9.95. Many types of simple songs are presented with chords and piano accompaniments.

4840. Garson, Eugenia, ed. *The Laura Ingalls Wilder Songbook* (4–6). Illus. by Garth Williams. 1968, Harper $8.95; LB $8.79. Sixty-two songs from the Little House books.

4841. John, Timothy, ed. *The Great Song Book* (1–6). Illus. by Tomi Ungerer. 1978, Doubleday $12.50. A collection of 68 favorite songs in simple arrangements with guitar chords.

4842. Kapp, Paul. *Cock-A-Doodle-Doo! Cock-A-Doodle Dandy* (2–4). Illus. by Anita Lobel. 1966, Harper $6.89. Sixty-six charming songs from such sources as authors Lewis Carroll, John Bunyan, and Edward Lear.

4843. Langstaff, John, comp. *Hot Cross Buns and Other Old Street Cries* (1–4). Illus. by Nancy W. Parker. 1978, Atheneum $7.95. Thirty street cries from Old England arranged as songs.

4844. Langstaff, John, and Langstaff, Carol. *Shimmy Shimmy Coke-Ca-Pop!* (2–5). Illustrated. 1973, Doubleday $4.95. Subtitled: *A Collection of City Children's Street Games and Rhymes.*

4845. Miller, Carl. *Sing Children Sing* (2–5). Illustrated. 1972, UNICEF $3.50; Times paper $3.50. Subtitled: *Songs, Dances and Singing Games of Many Lands and Peoples.* Also use: *Rockabye Baby; Lulla-*

bies from Many Nations and Peoples (1975, UNICEF, paper $3.50).

4846.   Mitchell, Cynthia. *Halloweena Hecatee, and Other Rhymes* (1–3). Illus. by Eileen Browne. 1979, Crowell $6.95; LB $6.79. A book of jump rope rhymes from 10 to 112 jumps in length.

4847.   Nelson, Esther L. *Singing and Dancing Games for the Very Young* (K–3). Illus. by Minn Matsuda. 1977, Sterling $5.95; LB $5.89. Over 40 songs with accompanying activities.

4848.   Wessells, Katharine Tyler. *The Golden Song Book* (3–6). Illus. by Gertrude Elliott. 1945, Golden $9.15. Words and music for 56 favorite songs for children, with suggestions for singing games.

4849.   Winn, Marie. *The Fireside Book of Children's Songs* (K–5). Illus. by John Alcorn. 1966, Simon &

Schuster $9.95. More than 100 songs in this collection, including nursery songs and games.

4850.   Winn, Marie. *The Fireside Book of Fun and Game Songs* (2–6). Illus. by Whitney Darrow, Jr. 1974, Simon & Schuster $12.50. All sorts of playful songs are included, such as question-and-answer songs and riddles. Also use: *What Shall We Do and Allee Galloo: Playsongs and Singing Games for Young Children* (1971, Harper $7.89).

4851.   Worstell, Emma V. *Jump the Rope Jingles* (1–4). Illus. by Sheila Greenwald. 1961, Macmillan $4.95; paper $.95. A compilation of calls and jingles used in jumping rope.

4852.   Zuromskis, Diane S., illus. *The Farmer in the Dell* (PS–1). 1978, Little $6.95. The familiar singing game presented with fresh drawings.

Performing Arts

Circus

4853. Adler, David A. *You Think It's Fun to Be a Clown* (PS–1). Illus. by Ray Cruz. 1980, Doubleday $8.95; LB $9.90. A clown's life is not a happy one according to this rhyming picture book.

4854. American Heritage, eds. *Great Days of the Circus* (5–7). 1962, American Heritage $5.95; LB $6.89. A comprehensive, attractive, and nostalgic book.

4855. Klayer, Connie, and Kuhn, Joanna. *Circus Time! How to Put On Your Show* (4–6). Illus. by Carol Nicklaus. 1979, Lothrop $6.95; LB $6.67. A fascinating account that covers all topics from publicity to the opening performance.

4856. Krementz, Jill. *A Very Young Circus Flyer* (4–6). Illustrated. 1979, Knopf $9.95. The first-person narrative of nine-year-old Tato Farfan, an aerialist.

4857. McGovern, Ann. *If You Lived in the Circus* (2–4). Illus. by Ati Forberg. 1972, Four Winds 1976; Scholastic paper $.95. Through questions and answers, a picture of the daily life of circus performers is given, including information on training, safety and other pertinent matters. Also use: *What Happens at the Circus* by Arthur Shay (1972, Regnery $5.95).

4858. Meggendorfer, Lothar. *International Circus* (2–6). 1980, Viking $7.95. A pop-up book first published in Germany in 1887.

4859. Powledge, Fred. *Born on the Circus* (5–6). Illustrated. 1976, Harcourt $7.95. The world of the circus as seen through the eyes of the young-est member of the famous Cristiani family.

4860. Prelutsky, Jack. *Circus* (K–3). Illus. by Arnold Lobel. 1974, Macmillan $5.95; paper $2.50. Vivid, loud illustrations and swinging verses capture the vitality of the circus. Also use: *Circus* by Beatrice S. De Regniers (1966, Viking $5.95).

4861. Swortzell, Lowell. *Here Come the Clowns* (4–7). Illus. by C. Walter Hodges. 1978, Viking $10.00. Subtitle: *A Cavalcade of Comedy from Anti-quity to the Present.*

4862. Wildsmith, Brian. *Brian Wildsmith's Circus* (PS–3). Illus. by author. 1970, Watts $4.95. Bold and brilliant colors create a wonderful world of an imaginary circus.

Dance

4863. Baylor, Byrd. *Sometimes I Dance Mountains* (K–3). Illustrated. 1973, Scribner $5.95. Emotions and objects are expressed by a dancer's move-ments.

4864. Berger, Melvin. *The World of Dance* (6–9). Illustrated. 1978, Phillips $8.95. An overview of the subject that begins in prehistoric times and ends with today's social dancing and ballet.

4865. Bullard, Brian, and Charlsen, David. *I Can Dance* (4–8). Illustrated. 1979, Putnam $10.95. A how-to book that explains the basics of dance.

4866. Chappell, Warren. *The Nutcracker* (2–5). Illustrated. 1958, Knopf $5.69. Beautifully de-signed picture book with the principal musical themes and story.

4867. Cosi, Liliana. *The Young Ballet Dancer* (5–8). Illustrated. 1979, Stein & Day $10.95. De-tails of training are given for both male and fe-male dancers as well as a history and the stories of some famous ballets.

4868. Diamond, Donna. *Swan Lake* (3–6). Illus. by author. 1980, Holiday $8.95. The story of one of the world's most famous ballets.

4869. Goulden, Shirley. *The Royal Book of Ballet* (5–8). Illus. by Maraja. 1964, Follett $6.95. The stories of 6 well-known ballets, beautifully illus-trated.

4870. Gross, Ruth Belov. *If You Were a Ballet Dancer* (3–5). Illustrated. 1980, Dial $6.95; LB $6.46. Basic questions are answered about ballet, with accompanying photographs.

4871. Isadora, Rachel. *My Ballet Class* (1–3). Il-lus. by author. 1980, Greenwillow $6.95; LB

$6.67. The first-person account that traces a young girl's actions during a ballet class.

4872. Jessel, Camilla. *Life at the Royal Ballet School* (6–9). Illus. by author. 1979, Methuen $10.95. An account of the trials and tribulations involved in becoming a ballet dancer.

4873. Krementz, Jill. *A Very Young Dancer* (4–8). Illustrated. 1976, Knopf $9.95. Excellent photographs enhance this story of a young girl's preparation to appear in a production of "The Nutcracker."

4874. Lawson, Joan. *Ballet Stories* (5–9). Illustrated. 1979, Mayflower $6.95. Stories of 14 favorite ballets are retold, including Giselle and the major ones of Tchaikovsky.

4875. Maiorano, Robert, and Isadora, Rachel. *Backstage* (PS). Illustrated. 1978, Greenwillow $5.95. A girl goes backstage at a ballet theater.

4876. Price, Christine. *Dance on the Dusty Earth* (4–7). Illus. by author. 1979, Scribner $8.95. The origins and history of primitive dance.

4877. Swope, Martha. *The Nutcracker: The Story of the New York City Ballet's Production Told In Pictures* (3–6). Illustrated. 1975, Dodd $6.95. A simple text together with black-and-white photos describe the action of this world-famous ballet production.

4878. Streatfeild, Noel. *A Young Person's Guide to Ballet* (4–7). Illus. by Georgette Bordier. 1975, Warne $8.95. An excellent introduction to this art form, organized around the experiences of a young boy and girl who enter ballet school. Also use: Thalia Mara's *First Steps in Ballet* (1955, Doubleday $5.95; Dance Horizon, paper $3.25).

4879. Walker, Katherine Sorley, and Butler, Joan. *Ballet for Boys and Girls* (4–7). Illustrated. 1980, Prentice-Hall $8.95. An entertaining and enlightening introduction to the world of ballet.

4880. Woodward, Ian. *Ballet and the Dance* (5–7). Illus. by Peter Revitt. 1979, Chatto $2.95. An overview of the world of dance, its history, components, and how to appreciate it.

Motion Pictures and Television

4881. Beal, George. *See Inside a Television Studio* (3–5). Illustrated. 1978, Watts $5.90. Topics such as satellite broadcasting and special effects are covered in this simple account.

4882. Burr, Lonnie. *Two for the Show: Great Comedy Teams* (6–9). Illustrated. 1979, Messner $8.29. Famous show biz teams such as Burns and Allen

and the Marx Brothers are covered in this informative account.

4883. Edelson, Edward. *Great Monsters of the Movies* (6–9). Illustrated. 1973, Doubleday $5.95; Pocket Books paper $1.25; Archway paper $1.50. Vampires and zombies share space with Frankenstein and King Kong in this popular work. Also use: *Funny Men of the Movies* (1976, Doubleday $5.95).

4884. Edelson, Edward. *Tough Guys and Gals of the Movies* (6–9). Illustrated. 1978, Doubleday $5.95. A history that covers the field from von Stroheim to Clint Eastwood and Harlow to Jane Fonda.

4885. Jones, Eurfron Gwynne. *Television Magic* (2–7). Illustrated. 1978, Viking $5.95. Many illustrations and simple text highlight this account of how various television shows are produced.

4886. Thurman, Judith, and David, Jonathan. *The Magic Lantern: How Movies Got to Move* (4–6). Illustrated. 1978, Atheneum $8.95. A history of early movie making that begins with the Chinese 1,000 years ago.

Play Production

4887. Berger, Melvin. *Putting on a Show* (5–7). Illustrated. 1980, Watts $5.90. A good introduction to play production and theater life.

4888. Carlson Bernice W. *Act It Out* (4–6). Illus. by Laszlo Matulay. 1956, Abingdon $5.75. Material for simple dramatics for both live and puppet performances. Also use: *The Right Play for You* (1960, Abingdon $3.75).

4889. Carlson, Bernice W. *Let's Pretend It Happened to You: A Real-People and Storybook-People Approach to Creative Dramatics* (2–4). Illus. by Ralph McDonald. 1973, Abingdon $5.95. An introduction to the many forms of improvisational theatrics.

4890. Howard, Vernon. *The Complete Book of Children's Theater* (5–9). Illus. by Doug Anderson. 1969, Doubleday $9.95. Over 350 nonroyalty productions are included in this comprehensive volume, which gives basic information on staging and theater techniques.

4891. Jacobs, Susan. *On Stage: The Making of a Broadway Play* (5–8). 1972, Knopf $4.95. The step-by-step story of a Broadway production.

4892. McCaslin, Nellie. *Shows on a Shoestring: An Easy Guide to Amateur Productions* (5–9). Illustrated. 1979, McKay $7.95. How to put on inexpensive amateur productions from rehearsals to program distribution.

4893. Stolzenberg, Mark. *Exploring Mime* (5–9). Illus. by Jim Moore. 1980, Sterling $9.95; LB $9.29. An unusually complete introduction that includes many famous routines and illustrations.

Puppets and Marionettes

4894. Ackley, Edith F. *Marionettes: Easy to Make! Fun to Use!* (5–9). Illus. by Marjorie Flack. 1939, Lippincott $8.79. Guide includes full-size patterns and 5 marionette plays.

4895. Cochrane, Louise. *Shadow Puppets in Color* (2–5). Illus. by Kate Simunek. 1972, Plays $5.95. An introduction to shadow puppetry for younger children, including some adaptations of traditional plays. Also use: *Shadowplay* by George Mendoza (1974, Winston $5.95).

4896. Cochrane, Louise. *Tabletop Theatres and Plays* (5–8). Illus. by Kate Simunek. 1974, Plays $5.95. Directions for building small stages, puppets, costumes, and the scripts of 4 plays are included.

4897. Currell, David. *The Complete Book of Puppetry* (6–9). Illustrated. 1975, Plays $14.95. A comprehensive guide that includes material on the history and uses of puppetry, plus how to stage puppet shows.

4898. Emberley, Ed. *Punch & Judy: A Play for Puppets* (3–6). Illus. by author. 1965, Little $5.95. A brief history of Punch introduces this centuries-old play to young puppeteers.

4899. Engler, Larry. *Making Puppets Come Alive* (4–6). 1973, Taplinger $9.95. Directions on making puppets and how to perform with them.

4900. Lynch-Watson, Janet. *The Shadow Puppet Book* (4–7). Illustrated. 1980, Sterling $8.95; LB $8.29. A thorough and fascinating introduction to the world of shadow puppetry.

4901. Pels, Gertrude. *Easy Puppets: Making and Using Hand Puppets* (3–6). Illus. by Albert Pels. 1951, Crowell $8.95. Easy and simple directions.

4902. Politi, Leo. *Mr. Fong's Toy Shop* (1–3). Illus. by author. 1978, Scribner $6.95. In preparing children to celebrate the Moon Festival, Mr. Fong shows them how to make puppets.

4903. Ross, Laura. *Hand Puppets: How to Make and Use Them* (4–6). 1969, Lothrop $6.67; paper $2.95. Materials, sources, and instructions for making paper bag puppets, rod puppets for a shadow play, and papier-mâché puppets.

4904. Ross, Laura. *Scrap Puppets: How to Make and Move Them* (4–6). Illustrated. 1978, Holt $7.95. Leftover materials are used to construct 4 different types of puppets.

4905. Young, Ed, and Beckett, Hilary. *The Rooster's Horns: A Chinese Puppet Play To Make and Perform* (1–3). Illus. by Ed Young. 1978, Collins $5.95; LB $5.91. First the story, then step-by-step directions to perform it as a puppet play.

Shakespeare

4906. Chute, Marchette. *An Introduction to Shakespeare* (6–9). 1957, Dutton $9.95. An exciting and informative presentation of the way in which Shakespeare's plays were written, costumed, and staged.

4907. Chute, Marchette. *Stories from Shakespeare* (6–9). 1956, Collins $9.95; NAL paper $1.75. An illuminating guide for the young person reading Shakespeare for the first time.

4908. Hodges, C. Walter. *Shakespeare's Theatre* (6–9). Illus. by author. 1964, Coward $7.50. The development of English drama from its origins in medieval religious observance to mystery and morality plays to Shakespeare's Globe Theatre. Includes reconstruction of a production of *Julius Caesar*.

4909. Lamb, Charles, and Lamb, Mary. *Tales from Shakespeare* (4–8). Illus. by Elinore Blaisdell. 1807; 1942; 1960, Dutton $6.00; paper $2.95; 1963, Macmillan $4.95. The classic retelling of several of Shakespeare's most popular plays.

4910. Miles, Bernard. *Favorite Tales from Shakespeare* (5–8). Illus. by Victor G. Ambrus. 1977, Rand $8.95. Five popular plays rewritten in prose by an English actor.

Plays

4911. Aiken, Joan. *The Mooncusser's Daughter* (5–7). Illus. by Arvis Stewart. 1974, Viking $5.95. A supernatural drama with songs about the remorse of a shipwrecker.

4912. Aiken, Joan. *Street: A Play* (6–8). Music by John Sebastian Brown. Illus. by Arvis Stewart. 1978, Viking $7.95. A two-act musical play that mingles fantasy and reality in a story of lovers divided by a busy superhighway.

4913. Alexander, Sue. *Small Plays for You and a Friend* (1–3). Illus. by Olivia H. Cole. 1974, Seabury $5.95. Five simple skits, each involving only 2 characters, are presented in easily read language.

4914. Bradley, Alfred, and Bond, Michael. *Paddington on Stage* (3–5). Illus. by Peggy Fortnum. 1977, Houghton $5.95; Dell paper $1.25. Seven short plays about the adventures of the bear who always gets in and out of trouble.

4915. Carlson, Bernice W. *Funny-Bone Dramatics* (K–3). Illus. by Charles Cox. 1974, Abingdon $4.95. A series of skits, plays, and jokes for younger children.

4916. Childress, Alice. *Let's Hear It for the Queen* (4–5). Illus. by Loring Eutemey. 1976, Coward $6.95. A play about a girl who tries to dramatize the rhyme that begins "The Queen of Hearts, She Made Some Tarts."

4917. Childress, Alice. *When the Rattlesnake Sounds* (5–9). Illustrated. 1975, Coward $5.95. A one-act play based on Harriet Tubman's experience one summer as a laundress in a New Jersey resort hotel.

4918. Davis, Ossie. *Escape to Freedom: A Play about Young Frederick Douglass* (6–9). 1978, Viking $7.95. A drama with music based on the life of the famous slave and his struggle for freedom.

4919. Hughes, Ted. *The Tiger's Bones and Other Plays for Children* (5–8). Illus. by Alan E. Cober. 1974, Viking $5.95. Five plays based chiefly on such traditional stories as "Orpheus" and "Beauty and the Beast."

4920. Korty, Carol. *Silly Soup* (4–6). Illustrated. 1977, Scribner $8.95. Subtitled: *Ten Zany Plays with Songs and Ideas for Making Them Your Own.*

4921. Korty, Carol. *Plays from African Folktales* (3–6). Illus. by Sandra Cain. 1975, Scribner $7.95. Four fast-moving, humorous plays with hints on scenery, costumes, and other aspects of their production.

4922. Miller, Helen L. *First Plays for Children* (3–7). 1971, Plays $8.95. A useful collection of nonroyalty plays. Also use: *Short Plays for Children* (1969, Plays $8.95).

4923. Thane, Adele. *Plays from Famous Stories and Fairy Tales* (4–6). 1967, Plays $9.95. Twenty-eight, royalty-free one-act plays adapted from favorite children's stories. Also use: *Dramatized Folk Tales of the World* by Sylvia E. Kamerman (1971, Plays $9.95).

4924. Winter, Barbara. *Plays from Folktales of Africa and Asia* (3–5). 1976, Plays $9.95. A collection of very short, easy-to-produce plays, most of them humorous.

Poetry

General

4925. Abercombie, Barbara Mattes. *The Other Side of a Poem* (3–6). Illustrated. 1977, Harper $5.95; LB $6.89. Such headings as "mysteries or puzzles," "ordinary things," and "poems make pictures" are used.

4926. Adoff, Arnold. *Eats* (4–6). Illus. by Susan Russo. 1979, Lothrop $6.95; LB $6.67. A joyous collection that praises such morsels as apple pie and newly baked bread.

4927. Adoff, Arnold, ed. *It Is the Poem Singing into Your Eyes: Anthology of New Young Poets* (7–9). 1971, Harper $6.89. A collection of the work of young poets, reflecting such contemporary concerns as pollution, alienation, and war.

4928. Adoff, Arnold. *Under the Early Morning Trees* (4–6). Illus. by Ronald Himler. 1978, Dutton $7.50. A girl's early morning walk told in poetry.

4929. Adshead, Gladys L., and Duff, Annis, eds. *An Inheritance of Poetry* (5–7). Illus. by Nora S. Unwin. 1948, Houghton $7.95. An excellent anthology on a wide variety of subjects.

4930. Agree, Rose H., ed. *How to Eat a Poem and Other Morsels* (3–5). Illus. by Peggy Wilson. 1967, Pantheon $4.99. A wonderful collection of mouth-watering poems about food.

4931. Aldis, Dorothy. *All Together: A Child's Treasury of Verse* (1–3). Illus. by Marjorie Flack, Margaret Freeman, and Helen D. Jameson. 1952, Putnam $6.45. The author's personal choice of her poems.

4932. Arbuthnot, May Hill, and Root, Shelton L., Jr., eds. *Time for Poetry* (4–8). Illus. by Arthur Paul. 1967, Scott $11.95. A comprehensive collection that has become a standard in the field.

4933. Asch, Frank. *City Sandwich* (1–3). Illustrated. 1978, Greenwillow $5.95; LB $5.71. A book of poems and sketches to inspire and amuse city lovers.

4934. Association for Childhood Education, International, eds. *Sung Under the Silver Umbrella* (1–3). Illus. by Dorothy P. Lathrop. 1935, Macmillan $4.95. A collection of 200 tried-and-true favorites.

4935. Behn, Harry. *The Little Hill* (2–4). Illus. by author. 1949, Harcourt $4.50. A little book by a poet who has a magic way of interweaving verse and the fantasy of elves, goblins, and fairies. Also use: *The Wizard in the Well* (1956, Harcourt $4.95).

4936. Benet, Rosemary, and Benet, Steven Vincent. *A Book of Americans* (5–7). Illus. by Charles Child. 1933, Holt $5.95. Fifty-six poems about famous Americans from Christopher Columbus to Woodrow Wilson, entwined by freshly humorous drawings.

4937. Blishen, Edward, ed. *Oxford Book of Poetry for Children* (4–7). Illus. by Brian Wildsmith. 1963, Watts $7.90. An exuberant collection for children to listen to or read themselves. Bold, bright illustrations.

4938. Bogan, Louise, and Smith, William J., eds. *The Golden Journey: Poems for Young People* (3–8). Illus. by Fritz Kredel. 1976, Contemporary paper $3.95. A rich and inviting collection chosen by 2 poets.

4939. Browning, Robert. *The Pied Piper of Hamelin* (4–6). Illus. by C. Walter Hodges. 1971, Coward $5.29. The piper's revenge on the town of Hamelin in text and richly dramatic, full-colored illustrations.

4940. Carmer, Carl. *The Boy Drummer of Vincennes* (3–5). Illus. by Seymour Fleishman. 1972, Harvey $5.39. A first-person poem tells the story of a young drummer boy in 1779 during an American Revolution campaign in Illinois.

4941. Causley, Charles. *Figgie Hobbin* (3–4). Illus. by Trina Schart Hyman. 1974, Walker $4.95; LB $4.85. A grabbag of various kinds of poems from nonsense to narrative.

4942. Clithero, Sally, ed. *Beginning to Read Poetry* (PS–3). Illus. by Erik Blegvad. 1967, Follett $2.50; LB $2.97. An excellent introductory selection of 25 poems by Christina Rossetti, Rachel Field, Robert Louis Stevenson, and others for young readers and listeners.

243

4943. Cole, William, ed. *I'm Mad at You* (2–4). Illus. by George MacClain. 1978, Collins $6.95. A collection of poems on various facets of anger and its aftermath.

4944. Cole, William, ed. *Poems of Magic and Spells* (5–9). Illus. by Peggy Bacon. 1971, Collins $6.91. Ninety poems about enchantments and magical events.

4945. Cole, William, ed. *Rough Men, Tough Men: Poems of Action and Adventure* (5–7). 1969, Viking $5.95. Narrative poems filled with movement and suspense.

4946. Colum, Padraic, ed. *Roofs of Gold: Poems to Read Aloud* (6–8). 1964, Macmillan $5.95. An anthology of more than 80 poems chosen by the noted Irish storyteller for reading aloud.

4947. Cooney, Barbara, adapt. *Chanticleer and the Fox* (1–4). Illustrated. 1958, Crowell $6.95; LB $6.79. Chaucer's *Nun's Priest Tale* adapted by the illustrator. Caldecott Medal 1959.

4948. deGerez, Toni, ed. *2-Rabbit, 7-Wind: Poems from Ancient Mexico* (5–9). Illustrated. 1971, Viking $4.75. A collection of touching and impressive fragments of Nahuatl texts. The preface supplies interesting background information.

4949. De La Mare, Walter, ed. *Come Hither* (4–8). Illus. by Warren Chappell. 1957, Knopf $18.95. A collection of over 500 "rhymes and poems for the young of all ages."

4950. De La Mare, Walter. *Peacock Pie* (3–6). Illus. by Barbara Cooney. 1961, Knopf $8.95. Merrimack paper $2.95. Dancing rhymes of fairies, witches, and farmers.

4951. Dickinson, Emily. *Poems for Youth* (5–7). Illus. by George Hauman and Doris Hauman. 1934, Little $7.95. A wonderful introduction to the simpler poems of this master.

4952. Downie, Mary Alice, and Robertson, Barbara., eds. *The Wind Has Wings* (5–7). Illus. by Elizabeth Cleaver. 1968, Oxford paper $7.95. An interesting anthology of Canadian verse, some translated from the French.

4953. Dunning, Stephen; Lueders, Edward; and Smith, Hugh, eds. *Reflections on a Gift of Watermelon Pickle . . . and Other Modern Verse* (6–9). Illustrated. 1966, Lothrop $6.95; LB $6.67. An attractive volume of 114 expressive poems by recognized modern poets, illustrated with striking photographs.

4954. Dunning, Stephen; Lueders, Edward; and Smith, Hugh, eds. *Some Haystacks Don't Even Have Any Needle and Other Complete Modern Poems* (6–9). Illustrated. 1969, Lothrop $8.95. For the "now

generation"—an anthology of more than 125 poems by such masters as Roethke, Yevtushenko, Updike, and McKuen.

4955. Emrich, Duncan, ed. *American Folk Poetry* (4–7). 1974, Little $25.00. A thorough, scholarly collection arranged under broad subjects.

4956. Farber, Norma. *There Goes Feathertop!* (4–6). Illus. by Marc Brown. 1979, Dutton $6.95. A version in verse of Hawthorne's "moralized legend" *Feathertop*, about a scarecrow.

4957. Farjeon, Eleanor. *Eleanor Farjeon's Poems for Children* (4–6). Illus. by Lucinda Wakefield. 1951, Lippincott $4.95. The author's earlier works and 24 new poems in one attractive volume.

4958. Ferris, Helen, ed. *Favorite Poems Old and New* (4–6). Illus. by Leonard Weisgard. 1957, Doubleday $9.95. A book brimming with all kinds of poetry—lyrics, rhymes, doggerel, songs.

4959. Field, Eugene. *Wynken, Blynken and Nod* (K–2). Illus. by Barbara Cooney. 1970, Hastings $4.95. The famous poem illustrated in simple white-on-black.

4960. Fleming, Alice, ed. *America Is Not All Traffic Lights: Poems of the Midwest* (5–8). Illustrated. 1976, Little $6.95. Poets from the more rural areas, such as Carl Sandburg and Sherwood Anderson, are represented in this unique collection.

4961. Foster, John. *A First Poetry Book* (4–6). Illustrated. 1980, Oxford $10.95; paper $5.95. A fine selection of English poetry.

4962. Fox, Siv Cedering. *The Blue Horse and Other Night Poems* (K–2). Illus. by Donald Carrick. 1979, Seabury $8.95. A series of simple poems that evoke the night.

4963. Fowke, Edith, ed. *Ring around the Moon* (3–5). Illus. by Judith Gwyn Brown. 1977, Prentice-Hall $6.95. A concoction of old riddles, songs, and rhymes compiled by an eminent folklorist.

4964. Frost, Robert. *Stopping by Woods on a Snowy Evening* (K–4). Illus. by Susan Jeffers. 1978, Dutton $7.95. A richly illustrated version of Frost's most famous poem.

4965. Frost, Robert. *You Come Too: Favorite Poems for Young Readers* (5–7). Illus. by Thomas W. Nason. 1959, Holt $5.95. A collection of some of the best-loved Frost poems, illustrated with wood engravings. Also use: *The Road Not Taken* (1951, Holt $8.95).

4966. Geismer, Barbara, and Suter, Antoinette B. *Very Young Verses* (PS–1). Illus. by Mildred Bronson. 1945, Houghton $7.95. A pleasant collection for the very young, arranged by such subjects as seasons, bugs, weather.

4967. Greenfield, Eloise. *Honey, I Love, and Other Love Poems* (2–4). Illus. by Diane Dillon and Leo Dillon. 1978, Crowell $4.95; LB $4.79. Sixteen poems on family love and friendship as experienced by a black girl.

4968. Hannum, Sara, and Chase, John Terry, eds. *To Play Man Number One* (6–9). Illus. by Erwin Sahachner. 1969, Atheneum $5.95. A selection about modern people and society, strikingly illustrated with woodcuts.

4969. Hill, Helen, and others, eds. *Straight on Till Morning: Poems of the Imaginary World* (5–7). Illus. by Ted Lewin. 1977, Crowell $9.95. Mystery and marvel in selections chiefly from modern writers.

4970. Hine, Al, ed. *This Land Is Mine: An Anthology of American Verse* (6–7). Illus. by Leonard Vosburgh. 1965, Lippincott $8.95. More than 100 poems arranged chronologically that trace the history of America.

4971. Holman, Felice. *At the Top of My Voice: And Other Poems* (2–4). Illus. by Edward Gorey. 1970, Norton $5.95. A pleasant collection of short poems entwined by Gorey's elegant illustrations.

4972. Hopkins, Lee Bennett, ed. *City Talk* (2–3). Illus. by Roy Arenella. 1970, Knopf $5.99. Mood poems about urban life, written by children and illustrated with photographs.

4973. Hopkins, Lee Bennett, ed. *Elves, Fairies and Gnomes* (3–5). Illus. by Rosekrans Hoffman. 1980, Random $5.95; LB $5.99. A generous selection of lighthearted verses.

4974. Hopkins, Lee Bennett, ed. *Go to Bed! A Selection of Bedtime Poems* (K–3). Illustrated. 1979, Knopf $5.95. A reassuring book of 20 poems to fit all moods at bedtime.

4975. Hopkins, Lee Bennett, ed. *Me! A Book of Poems* (K–2). Illus. by Talivaldis Stubis. 1970, Seabury $5.95. Simple poems chiefly by contemporaries on subjects familiar to youngsters.

4976. Hopkins, Lee Bennett. *Morning, Noon and Nighttime, Too* (2–5). Illus. by Nancy Hannans. 1980, Harper $7.95. Poetry that tracks children through a normal school day.

4977. Hopkins, Lee Bennett, ed. *To Look at Anything* (5–8). Illustrated. 1978, Harcourt $6.95. Thoughtful photographs illustrate a fine collection of lyric verse.

4978. Huffard, Grace Thompson, and Carlisle, Laura Mae, eds. *My Poetry Book: An Anthology of Modern Verse for Boys and Girls* (5–7). Illus. by Willy Pogany. 1956, Holt $7.95. An extensive anthology of more than 500 poems arranged by subjects familiar to young readers.

4979. Hughes, Ted. *Moon-Whales and Other Moon Poems* (6–9). Illus. by Leonard Baskin. 1976, Viking $7.95. In an exuberant burst of imagination, the famous British poet invents a series of strange, sometimes grotesque moon creatures.

4980. Janeczko, Paul B., ed. *Postcard Poems: A Collection of Poetry for Sharing* (6–8). 1979, Bradbury $8.95. Very short poems (104) chosen to attract nonpoetry readers.

4981. Kuskin, Karla. *Near the Window Tree* (3–4). Illustrated. 1975, Harper $6.89. A small collection of light verse with each poem prefaced by notes on its origin and background. Also use: *Any Me I Want to Be* (1972, Harper $8.79).

4982. Langstaff, John. *The Two Magicians* (K–3). Illus. by Fritz Eichenberg. 1973, Atheneum $4.95. A witch transforms a young magician in this adaptation of an early English ballad.

4983. Larrick, Nancy, ed. *Bring Me All of Your Dreams* (6–9). Illustrated. 1980, Dutton $7.95. A beautiful collection of dream poems from a variety of times and cultures.

4984. Larrick, Nancy, ed. *Crazy to Be Alive in Such a Strange World: Poems about People* (5–9). Illustrated. 1977, Evans $6.95. The complexity of human beings is explored in this anthology of chiefly contemporary poetry.

4985. Larrick, Nancy, ed. *I Heard a Scream in the Street: Poems by Young People in the City* (5–8). Illustrated. 1970, Evans $5.95. Almost 80 poems by young people in 23 different cities are presented from a variety of sources. Also use: *On City Streets* (1968, Evans $6.95).

4986. Larrick, Nancy, ed. *Piper, Pipe That Song Again! Poems for Boys and Girls* (1–5). Illus. by Kelly Oechsli. 1965, Random $4.69. Animals, children, the city, and the seasons are represented in this collection of 62 verses from sources as familiar as the Bible and as contemporary as John Ciardi. Also use: *Piping Down the Valleys Wild* (1968, Delacorte $4.95; LB $4.95).

4987. Lee, Dennis. *Alligator Pie* (1–3). Illus. by Frank Newfeld. 1975, Houghton $6.95. Some 40 engaging and imaginative poems by an original and distinctive Canadian poet.

4988. Lee, Dennis. *Nicholas Knock and Other People* (3–6). Illus. by Frank Newfeld. 1977, Houghton $7.95. An engaging collection by the Canadian poet that ranges from the outrageously daffy to the quietly lyrical.

4989. Lenski, Lois. *City Poems* (2–3). Illus. by author. 1971, Walck $7.95. Poems for the urban child that realistically describe life in a big city.

4990. Lewis, Claudia Louise. *Up and Down the River: Boat Poems* (4–6). Illus. by Bruce Degen. 1979, Harper $7.95; LB $7.89. Thirteen poems about boats, with pencil drawings.

4991. Lewis, Richard, ed. *Miracles: Poems by Children of the English-Speaking World* (4–9). Illustrated. 1966, Simon & Schuster $8.95. Poems on a variety of subjects by children from 4 to 13.

4992. Livingston, Myra Cohn. *4-Way Stop and Other Poems* (5–9). Illus. by James J. Spanfeller. 1976, Atheneum $4.95. A collection of many moods and on many subjects by an eminent writer of children's poems.

4993. Livingston, Myra Cohn, ed. *Listen, Children, Listen: An Anthology of Poems for the Very Young* (K–4). 1972, Harcourt $5.50. A collection from 46 poets, from Shakespeare to Harry Behn, intended to be read aloud to children.

4994. Livingston, Myra Cohn, ed. *A Time beyond Us: A Collection of Poetry* (6–9). Illus. by James J. Spanfeller. 1968, Harcourt $7.50. An excellent anthology, worldwide in scope and with selections varied in form and subject matter.

4995. Livingston, Myra Cohn. *The Way Things Are and Other Poems* (5–7). Illus. by Jenni Oliver. 1974, Atheneum $4.95. Everyday things in a preadolescent's life are evoked in these simple verses.

4996. Longfellow, Henry Wadsworth. *The Children's Own Longfellow* (5–8). Illustrated. 1920, Houghton $7.95. Eight selections from the best-known and loved of Longfellow's poems.

4997. McCord, David. *Away and Ago: Rhymes of the Never Was and Always Is* (4–7). Illus. by Leslie Morrill. 1975, Little $5.95. Fifty poems on a variety of subjects important in childhood, from kings to baseball.

4998. McCord, David. *Everytime I Climb a Tree* (2–4). Illus. by Marc Simont. 1967, Little $7.95. An irresistible collection, illustrated with lovely, gay illustrations.

4999. McCord, David. *Far and Few: Rhymes of the Never Was and Always Is* (3–6). Illus. by Henry B. Kane. 1952, Little $6.95; Dell paper $.75. A collection that ranges from nonsense verse to thoughtful quiet poetry.

5000. McCord, David. *For Me to Say: Rhymes of the Never Was and Always Is* (4–6). Illus. by Henry B. Kane. 1970, Little $5.95. A witty collection of various kinds of poetry with an emphasis on young people writing their own.

5001. McCord, David. *One at a Time: His Collected Poems for the Young* (3–8). Illus. by Henry B. Kane. 1977, Little $10.95. All 7 of the poet's anthologies in one handsome volume.

5002. McCord, David. *The Star in the Pail* (K–3). Illus. by Marc Simont. 1975, Little $6.95. A beautifully illustrated collection suitable for very young children.

5003. McCullough, Frances M., ed. *Earth, Air, Fire and Water* (6–9). 1971, Coward $5.95. A selection of 125 mostly contemporary poems that deal with such topics as war, baseball, love, death, and politics.

5004. McFarland, Wilma, ed. *For a Child: Great Poems, Old and New* (K–3). Illus. by Ninon. 1947, Westminster $4.50. A collection to please younger children; includes simple verse and many illustrations in color.

5005. MacKay, David, ed. *A Flock of Words: An Anthology of Poetry for Children and Others* (6–9). Illus. by Margery Gill. 1970, Harcourt $8.50. A wide-ranging general selection of poetry with proven appeal to a young audience.

5006. Mayer, Mercer, ed. *A Poison Tree and Other Poems* (5–8). Illus. by editor. 1977, Scribner $7.95. Poems involving such emotions as love, loneliness, and fear, chiefly by contemporary poets, beautifully illustrated in subdued tones.

5007. Merriam, Eve. *It Doesn't Always Have to Rhyme* (4–6). Illus. by Malcolm Spooner. 1964, Atheneum $5.95. Poems expressing the fun of poetry and its possibilities.

5008. Merriam, Eve. *Rainbow Writing* (4–8). 1976, Atheneum $6.95. A fine collection of poems, many dealing with contemporary concerns.

5009. Millay, Edna St. Vincent. *Edna St. Vincent Millay's Poems Selected for Young People* (6–9). Illus. by Ronald Keller. 1979, Harper $8.79. An excellent selection of poems in a beautifully designed book.

5010. Moore, Lilian. *I Feel the Same Way* (1–4). Illus. by Robert Quackenbush. 1967, Atheneum paper $1.95. Poems of city and suburb, nature and human nature recapture universal childhood experiences, and sensitive illustrations reveal the beauty to be discerned in even the most unlikely surroundings.

5011. Moore, Lilian, comp. *Go with the Poem* (4–8). 1979, McGraw $7.95. A choice collection of poems mostly by moderns, on such subjects as sports and the seasons.

5012. Moore, Lilian, and Thurman, Judith, eds. *To See the World Afresh* (5–8). 1974, Atheneum $5.95. A collection of honest, straightforward poems that explore nature, emotions, and human relationships.

5013. Morton, Miriam, ed. *The Moon Is Like a Silver Sickle: A Celebration of Poetry by Russian Children* (5–9). Illus. by Eros Keith. 1972, Simon & Schuster $4.95. Ninety-two poems that cover a wide range of moods and emotions.

5014. O'Hare, Colette. *What Do You Feed Your Donkey On? Rhymes from a Belfast Childhood* (4–7). Illus. by Jenny Rodwell. 1978, Collins $6.95. A charming collection of traditional rhymes with atmospheric illustrations.

5015. O'Neill, Mary. *Hailstones and Halibut Bones* (PS–3). Illus. by Leonard Weisgard. 1961, Doubleday $5.95; paper $1.95. Imaginative poems about color.

5016. Opie, Iona, and Opie, Peter, eds. *The Oxford Book of Children's Verse* (K–8). 1973, Oxford $13.95. The best of 500 years of poetry for children, from Chaucer to Ogden Nash, has been chosen and arranged in chronological groupings.

5017. Peck, Richard, ed. *Mindscapes: Poems for the Real World* (6–9). 1971, Delacorte $5.95. The preface states that *Mindscapes* is a "collection of poems, mostly modern, that deal in encounters with a real, hectic, unpretty and recognizable world."

5018. Plotz, Helen, ed. *As I Walked Out One Evening: A Book of Ballads* (6–9). 1976, Greenwillow $8.25; LB $7.92. An imaginative anthology of many kinds of ballads together with an impressive introduction that gives background information to this art form.

5019. Plotz, Helen, ed. *The Gift Outright: America to Her Poets* (6–9). 1977, Greenwillow $8.25; LB $7.92. An anthology of 88 American writers that supplies an excellent introduction from colonial times to the present.

5020. Plotz, Helen, ed. *Imagination's Other Place: Poems of Science and Mathematics* (6–9). 1955, Crowell $10.00. A useful collection on subjects usually not considered poetic fare.

5021. Plotz, Helen, comp. *Life Hungers to Abound: Poems of the Family* (6–9). 1978, Greenwillow $7.95; LB $7.63. A fine, quite mature collection of poems on familial relationships.

5022. Plotz, Helen. *This Powerful Rhyme: A Book of Sonnets* (6–9). 1979, Greenwillow $7.95; LB $7.63. About 130 sonnets are presented from a variety of authors ranging from Shakespeare to Edmund Wilson.

5023. Pomerantz, Charlotte. *The Tamarindo Puppy, and Other Poems* (K–2). Illus. by Byron Barton. 1980, Greenwillow $7.95; LB $7.63. A bilingual poetry book that intersperses Spanish words with English.

5024. Prelutsky, Jack. *The Headless Horseman Rides Tonight: More Poems to Trouble Your Sleep* (2–5). Illus. by Arnold Lobel. 1980, Greenwillow $7.95; LB $7.63. Twelve scarey poems by a master of the art.

5025. Prelutsky, Jack. *Nightmares: Poems to Trouble Your Sleep* (5–9). Illus. by Arnold Lobel. 1976, Greenwillow $7.25; LB $6.96. Shuddery, macabre poems that will frighten but amuse a young audience.

5026. Prelutsky, Jack. *The Snopp on the Sidewalk and Other Poems* (3–6). Illus. by Byron Barton. 1977, Greenwillow $6.00. Twelve wildly imaginative poems about strange imaginary beasts that bring to mind the Jabberwocky.

5027. Read, Herbert, ed. *This Way, Delight* (3–7). Illus. by Juliet Kepes. 1956, Pantheon $5.69. Introduces young readers to poetry whose inspiration is within the realm of their experience.

5028. Reit, Ann, ed. *Alone Amid All This Noise: A Collection of Women's Poetry* (6–9). 1976, Four Winds $6.95. A universal collection in relation to time and place of origin that reflects the concerns of women.

5029. Rossetti, Christina. *Sing-Song* (K–3). Illus. by Marguerite Davis. 1952, Macmillan $3.50. Many of the poems are about small creatures and familiar objects and have a singing quality that young children enjoy.

5030. Russo, Susan, comp. *The Moon's the North Wind's Cooky: Night Poems* (K–3). Illus. by author. 1979, Lothrop $5.95; LB $5.71. Fourteen poems about the night and its charm.

5031. Sandburg, Carl. *Wind Song* (4–7). Illus. by William A. Smith. 1960, Harcourt $5.95; paper $1.50. Carl Sandburg selects his own poetry for children.

5032. Saunders, Dennis, comp. *Magic Lights and Streets of Shining Jet* (4–7). Illustrated. 1978, Greenwillow $7.95; LB $7.35. A varied, entertaining collection of poems from such masters as Longfellow, Wordsworth, and Yeats.

5033. Schick, Eleanor. *City Green* (K–2). Illustrated. 1974, Macmillan $4.95. Short, unrhymed poems that depict two children's thoughts about the city.

5034. Schwartz, Delmore. *"I Am Cherry Alive," The Little Girl Sang* (PS–2). Illus. by Barbara Cooney. 1979, Harper $7.95; LB $7.79. A poem that celebrates the joys of being alive.

5035. Schweninger, Ann. *The Man in the Moon as He Sails the Sky and Other Moon Verses* (PS–1). Illus. by author. 1979, Dodd $7.95. Twenty-one poems about night and the moon from various authors.

5036. Sechrist, Elizabeth H., ed. *One Thousand Poems for Children* (K–8). Illus. by Henry C. Pitz. 1946, Macrae $9.75. A large anthology divided into poetry for the young and for the advanced reader.

5037. Silverstein, Shel. *Where the Sidewalk Ends* (3–6). Illus. by author. 1974, Harper $8.95; LB $8.79. The author explores various facets and interests of children, with appropriate cartoonlike drawings.

5038. Starbird, Kaye. *The Covered Bridge House* (4–6). Illus. by Jim Arnosky. 1979, Four Winds $6.95. A lively collection of both lyric and narrative poems.

5039. Stevenson, Burton Egbert, ed. *The Home Book of Verse for Young Folks* (6–9). Illus. by Willy Pogany. 1915, Holt $8.95. A standard anthology grouped by theme with index to first lines, authors, and titles.

5040. Stevenson, Robert Louis. *A Child's Garden of Verses: A Selection of 24 Poems* (4–6). Illus. by Erik Blegvad. 1978, Random paper $.95. Beautiful watercolor illustrations add to the charm of this work.

5041. Stevenson, Robert Louis. *A Child's Garden of Verses* (K–4). Illus. by Gyo Fujikawa. 1957, Grosset $4.95. Verses known and loved by generations of young people, brilliantly illustrated.

5042. Teasdale, Sara. *Stars To-Night* (4–6). Illus. by Dorothy P. Lathrop. 1930, Macmillan $3.95. The poet's verses about the stars have a special appeal to children.

5043. Thompson, Blanche Jennings, ed. *All the Silver Pennies* (3–6). Illustrated. 1967, Macmillan $7.95. Collections to delight boys or girls, suitable for reading aloud.

5044. Thurman, Judith. *Flashlight and Other Poems* (1–5). Illus. by Reina Rubel. 1976, Atheneum $6.95. A fine little collection that explores many aspects of growing up in the city.

5045. Townsend, John R., ed. *Modern Poetry* (6–9). Illustrated. 1974, Lippincott $9.95. A well-balanced discriminating collection of important poems and poets from the 1940s through the 1960s.

5046. Tudor, Tasha, ed. *Wings from the Wind* (3–6). Illus. by editor. 1964, Lippincott $7.79. From Mother Goose to Shakespeare in an enchanting collection of 65 poems.

5047. Untemeyer, Louis, ed. *A Galaxy of Verse* (2–6). 1978, Evans $6.95. A varied collection of English and American verse.

5048. Untemeyer, Louis, ed. *Rainbow in the Sky* (2–6). Illus. by R. Birch. 1935, Harcourt $9.50. An anthology especially suitable for younger children.

5049. Untemeyer, Louis, ed. *This Singing World* (5–9). Illustrated. 1923, Harcourt $9.50. An anthology by the editor of: *The Magic Circle* (1952, Harcourt $7.95) and *The Golden Treasury of Poetry* (1959, Golden $8.95; LB $16.85).

5050. Wallace, Daisy, ed. *Fairy Poems* (3–5). Illus. by Trina Schart Hyman. 1980, Holiday $6.95. A collection that includes poems by such writers as Tolkien, Farjeon, and de la Mare.

5051. Wallace, Daisy, comp. *Ghost Poems* (4–7). Illus. by Tomie de Paola. 1979, Holiday $5.95. New and old poems to delight and frighten young readers.

5052. Wallace, Daisy, ed. *Giant Poems* (K–3). Illus. by Margot Tomes. 1978, Holiday $5.95. A collection of poems about giants and ogres.

5053. Wallace, Daisy, ed. *Witch Poems* (3–6). Illus. by Trina Schart Hyman. 1976, Holiday $5.95. Eighteen poems chosen from several different sources on a wide variety of witches.

5054. Whitman, Walt. *Overhead the Sun: Lines from Walt Whitman* (PS–3). Illus. by Antonio Frasconi. 1969, Farrar $4.95. Striking colored woodcuts illustrate brief excerpts from the poet's *Leaves of Grass*.

5055. Wilner, Isabel, ed. *The Poetry Troupe: An Anthology of Poems to Read Aloud* (1–6). Illus. by editor. 1977, Scribner $9.95. An excellent collection very much in tune with children's needs and interests, organized under intriguing subject headings.

5056. Worth, Valerie. *More Small Poems* (4–7). Illus. by Natalie Babbitt. 1976, Farrar $5.95. Simple poems about everyday things that reveal the poet's skill and fertile imagination.

5057. Worth, Valerie. *Small Poems* (4–7). Illus. by Natalie Babbitt. 1972, Farrar $4.95. Twenty-four short poems about such topics as grasses, jewels, and cows.

5058. Worth, Valerie. *Still More Small Poems* (4–7). Illus. by Natalie Babbitt. 1978, Farrar $5.95. Short poems about familiar objects.

Animals

5059. Aiken, Conrad. *Cats and Bats and Things with Wings: Poems* (1–4). Illus. by Milton Glaser. 1965, Atheneum $6.95. These poems about strange and familiar animals are excellent for reading aloud.

5060. Armour, Richard. *Strange Monsters of the Sea* (2–4). Illus. by Paul Galdone. 1979, McGraw $7.95. Lighthearted verses about real and imaginary sea creatures.

5061. Blegvad, Lenore, ed. *Hark! Hark! The Dogs Do Bark and Other Rhymes about Dogs* (K–3). Illus. by Erik Blegvad. 1976, Atheneum $5.95. Familiar and less-well-known poems are included in this charming anthology.

5062. Blegvad, Lenore, ed. *Mittens for Kittens and Other Rhymes about Cats* (K–3). Illus. by Erik Blegvad. 1974, Atheneum $5.95. Twenty-five charming poems about cats in a nicely illustrated volume.

5063. Brewton, John E., ed. *Under the Tent of the Sky* (4–6). Illus. by Robert Lawson. 1937, Macmillan $5.95. All kinds of animals parade through this anthology. Also use: *Gaily We Parade* (1940, Macmillan $4.95).

5064. Chen, Tony. *Run, Zebra, Run* (3–5). Illus. by author. 1972, Lothrop $6.96. Animal verses that point out lessons of conservation because most are about endangered species.

5065. Cole, William, comp. *An Arkful of Animals: Poems for the Very Young* (3–5). Illus. by Lynn Munsinger. 1978, Houghton $5.95. A fine collection of the most humorous poems about animals.

5066. Cole, William, ed. *The Birds and the Beasts Were There: Animal Poems* (5–7). Illus. by Helen Siegl. 1963, Collins $7.91. This collection about all kinds of animals, from farmyard to mythical creatures, will delight animal lovers.

5067. Cole, William, ed. *Dinosaurs and Beasts of Yore* (3–6). Illus. by Susanna Natti. 1979, Collins $8.95. Poems, mostly lighthearted, about the strange creatures that once roamed the earth.

5068. Cole, William, ed. *The Poetry of Horses* (5–8). Illus. by Ruth Sanderson. 1979, Scribner $8.95. A superb collection of horse poems divided into 9 subject groups.

5069. De Regniers, Beatrice S. *It Does Not Say Meow: And Other Animal Riddle Rhymes* (PS–K). Illus. by Paul Galdone. 1972, Seabury $5.95. Simple rhymes give the clue to the familiar animals pictured on the following pages. The game-playing format will please young children.

5070. Farber, Norma. *Never Say Ugh to a Bug* (4–7). Illus. by Jose Aruego. 1979, Greenwillow $6.95. Humorous verses about a species that interests young people.

5071. Fisher, Aileen. *Do Bears Have Mothers, Too?* (K–2). Illus. by Eric Carle. 1973, Crowell $8.29. An anthology of short poems, built around the theme of mother-child relationships among animals, and brilliantly illustrated in collage.

5072. Fisher, Aileen. *Feathered Ones and Furry* (1–3). Illus. by Eric Carle. 1971, Crowell $6.89. Compelling illustrations enhance this collection of simple poems about animals. Good for reading aloud to a younger audience.

5073. Fisher, Aileen. *My Cat Has Eyes of Sapphire Blue* (2–5). Illus. by Marie Angel. 1973, Crowell $7.95; LB $7.49. A poet and an illustrator—both obvious cat lovers—have created a gem of a book.

5074. Gardner, John. *A Child's Bestiary* (1–3). Illustrated. 1977, Knopf $4.95; LB $5.99. Sixty humorous and sophisticated poems about animals illustrated by the author and several members of his family.

5075. Hoberman, Mary Ann. *The Raucous Auk: A Menagerie of Poems* (K–3). Illus. by Joseph Low. 1973, Viking $4.95. This engaging collection about animals, with raffish drawings, is a welcome addition to the poetry shelves.

5076. Hopkins, Lee Bennett, ed. *My Mane Catches the Wind* (4–6). Illus. by Sam Savitt. 1979, Harcourt $8.95. Twenty-two poems about horses.

5077. Kherdian, David. *Country Cat, City Cat* (K–4). Illus. by Nonny Hogrogian. 1978, Four Winds $5.95. Twenty-one poems about various animals in a variety of settings.

5078. Kherdian, David. *The Dog Writes on the Window with His Nose* (2–3). Illus. by Nonny Hogrogian. 1977, Four Winds $4.46. A number of animals are highlighted in these 22 poems.

5079. Norris, Leslie. *Merlin and the Snake's Egg* (5–8). Illus. by Ted Lewin. 1978, Viking $6.95. A fine collection of original poems principally about animals.

5080. Prelutsky, Jack. *The Pack Rat's Day and Other Poems* (2–4). Illus. by Margaret Bloy Graham. 1974, Macmillan $5.95. Fifteen humorous poems about animals.

5081. Steele, Mary Q. *The Fifth Day* (4–7). Illus. by Janina Domanska. 1978, Greenwillow $6.95; LB $6.43. A collection of poems about all the creatures on the earth after the fifth day of creation.

5082. Yolen, Jane. *How Beastly!* (2–4). Illus. by James Marshall. 1980, Collins $7.95. This book of imaginative poetry introduces a menagerie through clever rhymes.

Black Poetry

5083. Abdul, Raoul, ed. *The Magic of Black Poetry* (6–9). Illus. by Dane Burr. 1972, Dodd $4.95. This varied collection includes poetry from the United States, Africa, Latin America, and Arab countries, with notes on each poet.

5084. Adoff, Arnold, ed. *Black Out Loud: An Anthology of Modern Poems by Black Americans* (6–9). Illus. by Alvin Hollingsworth. 1970, Macmillan $5.95. A simple anthology of modern poems. Also use: *I Am the Darker Brother: An Anthology of Modern Poems by Negro Americans* (1968, Macmillan $7.95; text ed. $2.12; paper $1.95).

5085. Adoff, Arnold, ed. *My Black Me: A Beginning Book of Black Poetry* (3–6). 1974, Dutton $6.50. An anthology by black writers, stressing the positive aspects of blackness, pride, and joy.

5086. Adoff, Arnold. *Big Sister Tells Me That I'm Black* (3–5). Illus. by Lorenzo Lynch. 1976, Holt $4.95. Sister tells her younger brother in poem form that he should feel strength and pride in his blackness.

5087. Bontemps, Arna, ed. *Golden Slippers: An Anthology of Negro Poetry for Young Readers* (5–8). Illus. by Henrietta Bruce Sharon. 1941, Harper $10.00; LB $8.97. The significant contributions of many black poets are included in this anthology.

5088. Brooks, Gwendolyn. *Bronzeville Boys and Girls* (2–5). Illus. by Ronni Solbert. 1956, Harper $5.95; LB $6.89. Everyday experiences of black children growing up in Chicago are revealed in these simple poems.

5089. Clifton, Lucille. *Everett Anderson's Friend* (K–2). Illus. by Ann Grifalconi. 1976, Holt $5.95. Everett Anderson, a small black boy, is dismayed when the children in the new family moving in across the hall turn out to be girls.

5090. Clifton, Lucille. *Everett Anderson's 1-2-3* (K–2). Illus. by Ann Grifalconi. 1977, Holt $5.95. A story in verse of Everett Anderson's adjustment to a stepfather coming into the family. One is lonely, Two is what he is used to, but Three can be just right.

5091. Clifton, Lucille. *Everett Anderson's Year* (K–2). Illus. by Ann Grifalconi. 1974, Holt $4.95. Twelve poems describe the events of the seventh year in Everett's life.

5092. Dunbar, Paul Laurence. *I Greet the Dawn* (5–8). Illus. by Ashley Bryan. 1978, Atheneum $7.95. A fine introduction to the nondialect verse of the turn-of-the-century black poet.

5093. Fufuka, Karama. *My Daddy Is a Cool Dude* (2–5). Illus. by Mahiri Fufuka. 1975, Dial $6.95; LB $6.47. A collection of 27 poems that explore life in an urban black neighborhood.

5094. Giovanni, Nikki. *Ego-Tripping and Other Poems for Young People* (6–9). Illus. by George Ford. 1974, Lawrence Hill $5.95; paper $3.95. A selection of poems from the author's works, which she thinks are particularly relevant to young people today. Also use: *Spin a Soft Black Song* (1971, Lawrence Hill $7.95).

5095. Grimes, Nikki. *Something on My Mind* (3–5). Illus. by Tom Feelings. 1978, Dial $7.50; LB $7.28. A collection of poems about the black experience.

5096. Hopkins, Lee Bennett, ed. *On Our Way: Poems of Pride and Love* (4–8). Illustrated. 1974, Knopf $5.99. Pride and happiness are the major themes in this anthology by black poets.

5097. Hughes, Langston. *Don't You Turn Back: Poems Selected by Lee Bennet Hopkins* (4–6). Illus. by Ann Grifalconi. 1969, Knopf $5.69. Dramatic woodcuts add to the expressiveness of these poems by an outstanding black poet. Also use: *The Dream Keeper* (1932, Knopf $5.69).

5098. Jordan, June, and Bush, Terri, eds. *The Voice of the Children* (5–8). 1970, Holt paper $1.95. Poems and poetic prose selected from the writings of black and Puerto Rican children.

5099. Jordan, June. *Who Look at Me* (4–7). Illustrated with 27 paintings. 1969, Crowell $9.95. A young black poet takes pride in her race.

Haiku

5100. Atwood, Ann. *Haiku: Vision in Poetry and Photography* (4–7). Illus. by author. 1977, Scribner

$7.95. A lyrical book that tries to elicit responses to the beauty and wonder of nature.

5101. Atwood, Ann. *Haiku: The Mood of the Earth* (5–8). Illus. by author. 1971, Scribner $9.95; paper $4.95. Beautiful color photographs give a visual interpretation to each poem.

5102. Behn, Harry, trans. *Cricket Songs: Japanese Haiku* (4–6). Illustrated. 1964, Harcourt $4.95. The unrhymed 17-syllable verse, accompanied by many Japanese paintings.

5103. Behn, Harry. *The Golden Hive: Poems and Pictures* (4–6). Illus. by author. 1966, Harcourt $4.50. Poems that reflect nature and the poet's joy of childhood.

5104. Behn, Harry, trans. *More Cricket Songs: Japanese Haiku* (5–9). Illustrated. 1971, Harcourt $4.50. Haiku from 29 poets, sensitively and simply translated.

5105. Caudill, Rebecca. *Wind, Sand and Sky* (3–6). Illus. by Donald Carrick. 1976, Dutton $6.95. An enchanting collection of Haiku poetry.

5106. Lewis, Richard, ed. *In a Spring Garden* (K–4). Illus. by Ezra Jack Keats. 1965, Dial $6.95; LB $6.46. A beautifully illustrated collection of Haiku in which the verses follow a day of spring.

5107. Livingston, Myra Cohn. *O Sliver of Liver: Together with Other Triolets, Cinquains, Haiku, Verses and a Dash of Poems* (4–6). Illus. by Van Rynbach. 1979, Atheneum $7.95. Personal reactions in poetry to everyday events and objects.

5108. Mizumura, Kazue. *Flower Moon Snow: A Book of Haiku* (2–5). Illus. by author. 1977, Crowell $7.95; LB $7.89. Thirty Haiku written by the brilliant Japanese-born American author and artist.

5109. Mizumura, Kazue. *If I Were a Cricket* (K–3). 1973, Crowell $7.95; LB $7.89. A lovely collection of Haiku poetry.

Humorous Poetry

5110. Belloc, Hilaire. *The Bad Child's Book of Beasts* (K–3). Illustrated. 1965, Dover paper $2.00. A reissue of an old favorite.

5111. Bodecker, N. M. *Hurry, Hurry, Mary Dear! And Other Nonsense Poems* (2–5). Illus. by author. 1976, Atheneum $6.95. The rhythm and humor of the poetry, together with the droll illustrations, make this collection immediately appealing to children.

5112. Bodecker, N. M. *Let's Marry Said the Cherry and Other Nonsense Poems* (4–6). Illus. by author.

1974, Atheneum $5.95. An excellent book for browsing, filled with daffy nonsense verses humorously illustrated with line drawings.

5113. Brewton, John E., and Blackburn, Lorraine A. *They've Discovered a Head in the Box for the Bread and Other Laughable* (3–5). Illustrated. 1978, Harper $6.79. A sure-fire hit for introducing limericks to children.

5114. Brewton, Sara; Brewton, John E.; and Blackburn, Meredith G., III., eds. *My Tang's Tungled and Other Ridiculous Situations* (4–6). Illus. by Graham Booth. 1973, Crowell $7.95. Nonsense verse, tongue twisters, and other humorous poems brought together in an irresistible collection. Also use: *Laughable Limericks* (1965, Crowell $7.95).

5115. Brewton, Sara; Brewton, John E.; and Blackburn, Meredith G., III., eds. *Of Quarks, Quasers and Other Quirks: Quizzical Poems of the Supersonic Age* (5–8). Illus. by Quentin Blake. 1977, Crowell $7.95. Contemporary poems that poke fun at such modern innovations as transplants and water beds. Also use: *Shrieks at Midnight* (1969, Crowell $7.95).

5116. Cameron, Polly. *"I Can't" Said the Ant* (PS–2). Illus. by author. 1961, Coward $4.49. Delightful nonsense poem of an ant's attempts to solve a kitchen crisis. Also use: *The Green Machine* (1969, Coward $5.39).

5117. Carroll, Lewis. *The Hunting of the Snark* (4–6). Illus. by Helen Oxenbury. 1970, Merrimack $3.95. Carroll's nonsense poem is imaginatively illustrated in this oversize book.

5118. Carroll, Lewis. *Jabberwocky* (K–3). Illus. by Jane Breskin. 1977, Warne $8.95. Carroll poems and extracts from the Alice books delicately illustrated.

5119. Carroll, Lewis. *Poems of Lewis Carroll* (5–8). Illustrated. 1973, Crowell $6.95. A wonderful collection with original illustrations and fine explanatory notes for each poem, plus a biographical sketch of the author.

5120. Ciardi, John. *Fast and Slow: Poems for Advanced Children and Beginning Parents* (1–4). Illus. by Becky Gaver. 1975, Houghton $6.95; paper $1.95. Humorous, often witty poems for children by a master.

5121. Ciardi, John. *I Met a Man* (K–1). Illus. by Robert Osborn. 1961, Houghton $8.95; paper $2.95. Lighthearted nonsense poems for the beginning reader. Also use: *The Man Who Sang the Sillies* (1961, Lippincott $7.95).

5122. Cole, William, ed. *Beastly Boys and Ghastly Girls* (3–6). Illus. by Tomi Ungerer. 1964, Collins

$6.41; Dell paper $.95. Poems and line drawings depict a crew of naughty yet appealing children.

5123. Cole, William, ed. *Humorous Poetry for Children* (5–7). Illus. by Ervine Metzl. 1955, Collins $6.91. A master anthologist has compiled a most interesting anthology that covers many tastes and levels of sophistication.

5124. Cole, William, ed. *Oh, Such Foolishness* (4–6). Illus. by Tomie de Paola. 1978, Lippincott $5.95. Humorous poems with illustrations to match.

5125. Cole, William, ed. *Oh, What Nonsense!* (3–6). Illus. by Tomi Ungerer. 1966, Viking $6.95; Penguin paper $.75. A bouncy collection of 50 traditional and contemporary jump-rope chants, nonsense rhymes, and rib-ticklers. Also use from Viking: *Oh That's Ridiculous* (1972, $5.95) and *Oh, How Silly* (1970, $3.95).

5126. Dugan, Michael, ed. *Stuff and Nonsense* (3–8). Illus. by Deborah Niland. 1977, Collins $5.95. More than 60 nonsense rhymes from Australia, with similarly zany line drawings.

5127. Kennedy, X. J. *One Winter Night in August and Other Nonsense Jingles* (3–6). Illus. by David McPhail. 1975, Atheneum $5.95. More than 50 charmingly humorous poems written for youngsters.

5128. Kennedy, X. J. *The Phantom Ice Cream Man: More Nonsense Verse* (3–5). Illus. by David McPhail. 1979, Atheneum $5.95. Contemporary nonsense verse on a variety of subjects.

5129. Lear, Edward. *Complete Nonsense Book* (4–6). Illus. by author. 1943, Dodd $6.95. Verse, prose, drawings, alphabets, and other amusing absurdities.

5130. Lear, Edward. *The Owl and the Pussycat* (PS–3). Illus. by Gwen Fulton. 1977, Atheneum $6.95. Elegant full-page illustrations enliven this well-loved poem. Another recommended edition is illustrated by Owen Wood (1979, Viking $8.95).

5131. Lear, Edward. *The Pelican Chorus* (PS–2). Illus. by Harold Berson. 1967, Parents $4.95. A picture-book version of Lear's rollicking nonsense poem with 4-color drawings of the birds in all their finery along their beloved Nile, complete with a pelican-headed sphinx.

5132. Lear, Edward. *The Pobble Who Has No Toes* (K–3). Illus. by Kevin W. Maddison. 1978, Viking $5.95. Supernonsense from the old master.

5133. Lear, Edward. *The Scroobious Pip* (2–5). Completed by Ogden Nash. Illus. by Nancy Ekholm Burkert. 1968, Harper $8.95; LB $8.79. Animals of the world are attracted to the strange,

inscrutable creature in one of Lear's most engaging nonsense poems, with alluring pastel paintings and drawings.

5134. Lee, Dennis. *Garbage Delight* (K–4). Illus. by Frank Newfeld. 1978, Houghton $6.95. Nonsense poems from a fine Canadian writer.

5135. Livingston, Myra Cohn. *A Lollygag of Limericks* (5–7). Illus. by Joseph Low. 1978, Atheneum $4.95. A lively collection humorously illustrated.

5136. Livingston, Myra Cohn, ed. *Speak Roughly to Your Little Boy* (6–9). Illus. by Joseph Low. 1971, Harcourt $8.50. The subtitle is *A Collection of Parodies and Burlesques, Together with the Original Poems, Chosen and Annotated for Young People.*

5137. Livingston, Myra Cohn, ed. *What a Wonderful Bird the Frog Are: An Assortment of Humorous Poetry a* (4–7). 1973, Harcourt $5.25. A delightful anthology on a variety of subjects and from sources as differing as Haiku and nonsense jingles.

5138. Love, Katherine, ed. *A Little Laughter* (3–7). Illus. by Walter Lorraine. 1957, Crowell $6.95. A collection that represents the lighter works of distinguished poets.

5139. Lyfick, Warren, ed. *The Little Book of Limericks* (3–5). Illus. by Chris Cummings. 1978, Harvey House $3.49. A happy book that contains over 70 limericks and many cartoonlike drawings.

5140. Merriam, Eve. *The Birthday Cow* (2–3). Illus. by Guy Michel. 1978, Knopf $5.95; LB $5.99. Fifteen humorous poems that use nonsense situations and sounds.

5141. Milne, A. A. *When We Were Very Young* (PS–3). Illus. by Ernest H. Shepard. 1961, Dutton $5.95; Dell paper $1.25. Whimsical nonsense verses that have enchanted 3 generations. Also use: The combined volume, *The World of Christopher Robin* (1958, Dutton $9.95), boxed with *World of Pooh* ($18.50), and *Now We Are Six* (1961, Dutton $5.95; Dell, paper $1.25).

5142. Morrison, Lillian, ed. *Best Wishes Amen: A New Collection of Autograph Verses* (4–8). Illus. by Loretta Lustig. 1974, Crowell $6.95. A beguiling collection of jokes, jibes, and verses that is a wrothy companion to the author's *Yours Till Niagara Falls* (1950, Crowell $6.95).

5143. Morrison, Lillian, ed. *A Diller, A Dollar: Rhymes and Sayings for the Ten O'Clock Scholar* (5–8). 1955, Crowell $7.95. All kinds of humorous schoolroom rhymes and folk sayings. Also use: *Remember Me When This You See* (1961, Crowell $6.95).

5144. Morrison, Lillian. *Who Would Marry a Mineral? Riddles, Runes and Love Tunes* (4–7). 1978, Lothrop $5.95. Nonsense verses filled with word play and fun.

5145. Nash, Ogden. *Custard and Company* (4–7). Illus. by Quentin Blake. 1980, Brown $8.95. A gathering of 128 pages of child-pleasing poems by Ogden Nash.

5146. Nash, Ogden. *Parents Keep Out: Elderly Poems for Youngerly Readers* (6–9). Illus. by Barbara Corrigan. 1951, Little $7.95. A lively collection of humorous poetry.

5147. Ness, Evaline, ed. *Amelia Mixed the Mustard, and Other Poems* (3–5). Illustrated. 1975, Scribner $7.95. Twenty poems about independent and outrageous girls.

5148. Nolan, Dennis. *Wizard McBean and His Flying Machine* (1–3). Illus. by author. 1977, Prentice-Hall $6.95. Through nonsense rhymes, this cumulative tale tells how a man rids himself of one pest after another.

5149. Orgel, Doris. *Merry, Merry FIBruary* (K–3). Illus. by Arnold Lobel. 1977, Parents $6.25; LB $5.71. Twenty-eight nonsense verses like "Toothday," "Wind's Day"—one for each day in the month of February.

5150. Petersham, Maud, and Petersham, Miska, eds. *The Rooster Crows: A Book of American Rhymes and Jingles* (K–2). 1945, Macmillan $5.95; paper $.95. This Caldecott Medal winner is a diverting book for browsing.

5151. Prelutsky, Jack. *The Queen of Eene* (K–3). Illus. by Victoria Chess. 1978, Greenwillow $6.95; LB $6.43. Humorous imaginative poems cleverly illustrated.

5152. Prelutsky, Jack. *Rolling Garvey Down the Hill* (1–3). Illus. by Victoria Chess. 1980, Greenwillow $7.95; LB $7.63. Humorous verses about everyday mischief, illustrated with black-and-white drawings.

5153. Richards, Laura E. *Tirra Lirra* (K–4). Illus. by Marguerite Davis. 1932; 1955, Little $5.95. These familiar rhymes and nonsense verses are a great favorite with young children.

5154. Rose, Anne. *How Does a Czar Eat Potatoes?* (2–4). Illus. by Janosch. 1973, Lothrop $6.00. A poor little girl imagines how a czar would live as contrasted with her peasant way of life.

5155. Silvis, Craig. *Rat Stew* (3–6). Illus. by Annie Gusman. 1979, Houghton $6.95. Unusual love poems served up in a delicious concoction.

5156. Tripp, Wallace, ed. *A Great Big Ugly Man Came Up and Tied His Horse to Me: A Book of Nonsense Verse* (K–3). Illus. by editor. 1973, Little $6.95; paper $2.95. The hilarious drawings that accompany this selection of nonsense verses make this an especially entertaining book.

5157. Watson, Clyde. *Catch Me and Kiss Me and Say It Again* (K–2). Illus. by Wendy Watson. 1978, Collins $7.95. A collection of rhymes to accompany such activities as brushing teeth or clipping fingernails.

5158. Watson, Clyde. *Father Fox's Penny-Rhymes* (PS–2). Illus. by Wendy Watson. 1971, Crowell $7.95; LB $7.89; Scholastic paper $1.50. Foot-stomping, clap-along nonsense rhymes, with witty watercolor and pen-and-ink illustrations that feature snatches of conversation in cartoon-like balloons. Also use: *Tom Fox and the Apple Pie* (1972, Crowell $3.95; LB $4.79).

5159. Withers, Carl, ed. *A Rocket in My Pocket* (4–6). Illus. by Susanne Suba. 1948, Holt $5.95. Rhymes and chants of young Americans. Also use: *I Saw a Rocket Walk a Mile: Nonsense Tales, Chants, and Songs from Many Lands* (1965, Holt $5.95).

Indians of North America and Eskimo Poetry

5160. Allen, Terry, ed. *The Whispering Wind: Poetry by Young American Indians* (5–8). 1972, Doubleday $4.95; paper $1.95. Fourteen students from Eskimo, Aleut, and American Indian tribes have contributed to this thoughtful, satisfying anthology.

5161. Belting, Natalia M., ed. *Our Fathers Had Powerful Songs* (4–7). Illus. by Laszlo Kubinyi. 1974, Dutton $7.50. Nine poems from North American Indian tribes that reveal great reverence for nature and the gods.

5162. Belting, Natalia M., ed. *Whirlwind Is a Ghost Dancing* (4–8). Illus. by Leo Dillon and Diane Dillon. 1974, Dutton $7.50. A number of North American Indian poems, many involving creation myths, delicately illustrated in muted tones by 2 award-winning artists.

5163. Bierhorst, John, ed. *In the Trail of the Wind: American Indian Poems and Ritual Orations* (5–9). 1971, Farrar $6.95; paper $4.95. From a large number of North and South American Indian tribes comes this collection of chants, songs, prayers, plus explanations and other relevant background material.

5164. Clark, Ann Nolan. *Along Sandy Trails* (2–4). Illus. by Alfred A. Cohen. 1969, Viking $5.95. A little Papago Indian girl and her grandmother walk the Arizona desert and describe the fauna and flora in poetic terms.

5165. Field, Edward, ed. *Eskimo Songs and Stories* (4–7). Illus. by Kiakshuk and Pudlo. 1973, Delacorte $6.95. The illustrations by Eskimo artists add atmosphere and authenticity to this collection of poems that reveal the beliefs and cultural patterns of the Eskimos.

5166. Houston, James, ed. *Songs of the Dream People* (4–8). Illus. by editor. 1972, Atheneum $5.95. Songs and chants from the Eskimos and Indians of North America arranged by geographical location, for example, the Central Plains, the Northwest Coast.

5167. Jones, Hettie, ed. *The Trees Stand Shining: The Poetry of the North American Indians* (3–6). Illus. by Andrew Parker. 1971, Dial $7.95; LB $7.45. Full-color paintings accompany these short poems from 15 North American tribes.

5168. Maher, Ramona. *Alice Yazzie's Year: Poems* (3–6). Illustrated. 1977, Coward $7.95. A year in the life of a 12-year-old Navajo girl at her grandfather's, told through a poem for each month.

5169. Rasmussen, Knud, ed. *Beyond the High Hills: A Book of Eskimo Poems* (4–7). Illus. by Guy Mary-Rousseliere. 1961, Collins $6.96. A distinctive and beautiful selection of chants and songs, from those collected by the Danish explorer from among the Eskimos of the Hudson Bay area.

5170. Wood, Nancy, ed. *Many Winters: Prose and Poetry of the Pueblos* (5–9). Illus. by Frank Howell. 1974, Doubleday $6.95; LB $7.70; limited ed. $25.00. Sayings by the elders of the Taos Indians presented with accompanying realistic portraits.

Nature and the Seasons

5171. Adams, Adrienne, ed. *Poetry of Earth* (3–5). Illustrated. 1972, Scribner $6.95. A fine choice of poetry, mostly by established authors, about the beauties of earth, its creatures, and the sky. Stylized illustrations in soft colors.

5172. Adoff, Arnold. *Tornado!* (3–5). Illus. by Ronald Himler. 1977, Delacorte $6.95; LB $6.46. Simple poems, spoken by a child, explore a family's encounter with a tornado.

5173. Asch, Frank. *Country Pie* (2–4). Illus. by author. 1979, Morrow $6.95. Fourteen poems about nature, a companion to the author's *City Sandwich: Poems.*

5174. Baylor, Byrd. *The Way to Start a Day* (3–5). Illus. by Peter Parnall. 1978, Scribner $7.95. A poetic tribute to the many ways people have greeted a new day.

5175. Binzen, William. *Year After Year* (K–5). Illus. by author. 1976, Coward $6.95. With color photographs and brief quotes from Emily Dickinson, the author explores the seasons of the year.

5176. Brewton, Sara, and Brewton, John E. *Birthday Candles, Burning Bright* (4–7). Illus. by Vera Bock. 1960, Macmillan $4.95. A collection from a wide group of poets celebrating various aspects of birthdays. Also use: *Sing a Song of Seasons* (1955, Macmillan $5.95).

5177. Cole, William, ed. *Poems for Seasons and Celebrations* (5–8). Illus. by Johannes Troyer. 1961, Collins $7.91. Selections from the Bible, Shakespeare, contemporary poets, and some original work written especially for this anthology.

5178. Farber, Norma. *Small Wonders* (2–4). Illus. by Kazue Mizumura. 1979, Coward $6.50. Twenty-six poems on the wonders of nature.

5179. Fisher, Aileen. *Cricket in a Thicket* (1–3). Illus. by Feodor Rojankovsky. 1963, Scribner $4.95; paper $.95. Sprightly poems about nature and the out-of-doors.

5180. Greenaway, Kate. *Marigold Garden* (PS–K). Illus. by author. 1910, Warne $6.95. Flower verses written in simple rhyme for young children, beautifully illustrated. Also use: *Under the Window* (n.d, Warne $6.95).

5181. Hannum, Sara, and Chase, John Terry, eds. *The Wind Is Round* (5–9). Illus. by Ron Bowen. 1970, Atheneum $4.75. A fine compilation of nature poems arranged by the seasons.

5182. Hazeltine, Alice I, and Smith, Elva, eds. *The Year Around: Poems for Children* (4–6). Illus. by Paula Hutchinson. 1956, Arno $13.25. A collection of seasonal poems.

5183. Hughes, Ted. *Season Songs* (6–9). Illus. by Leonard Baskin. 1975, Viking $10.00. A collection by a leading British poet, arranged by season and illustrated by simple mood pictures.

5184. Ichikawa, Satomi. *A Child's Book of Seasons* (K–3). Illus. by author. 1976, Parents $5.95; LB $5.41. A group of pictures accompanied by rhyming couplets explores the differences in the seasons.

5185. Ichikawa, Satomi. *Sun through Small Leaves* (1–3). Illus. by author. 1980, Collins $8.95. Poetry about spring, brilliantly illustrated.

5186.   Ichikawa, Satomi. *Susan and Nicholas in the Garden* (K–3). Illus. by author. 1978, Watts $6.90. A nature book for the young set.

5187.   Larrick, Nancy, ed. *Room for Me and a Mountain Lion: Poetry of Open Space* (5–8). Illustrated. 1974, Evans $6.95. A collection of nature poems arranged under such headings as woods and mountains.

5188.   Moss, Elaine, ed. *From Morn to Midnight* (PS–3). Illus. by Satomi Ichikawa. 1977, Crowell $6.95. Twenty-one brief verses by well-known poets, each dealing with a particular time of day and illustrated with watercolor paintings.

5189.   Moss, Howard. *Tigers and Other Lilies* (4–6). Illus. by Frederick Henry Belli. 1977, Atheneum $5.95. Some 25 whimsical poems about plants that have animal names, such as spiderwort and dandelion.

5190.   Parker, Elinor, ed. *Echoes from the Sea* (5–7). Illus. by Jean Vallario. 1977, Scribner $6.95. A far-ranging, rich collection about the sea.

Sports

5191.   Adoff, Arnold. *I Am the Running Girl* (3–5). Illus. by Ronald Himler. 1979, Harper $6.95; LB $6.89. A series of poems that celebrate the joy and wonder of running.

5192.   Fleming, Alice, ed. *Hosannah the Home Run! Poems about Sports* (5–9). Illustrated. 1972, Little $6.95. About 20 sports are represented in this collection that reveals various attitudes toward the subject; notes on authors included.

5193.   Morrison, Lillian, ed. *The Sidewalk Racer and Other Poems of Sports and Motion* (5–9). Illustrated. 1977, Lothrop $6.00. Excellent collection of action poems that vary from the standpoint of the participant to that of the audience.

5194.   Morrison, Lillian, ed. *Sprints and Distances: Sports in Poetry and the Poetry of Sport* (5–8). Illus. by Clare Ross and John Ross. 1965, Crowell $9.95. A very popular anthology including a wide range of moods and sources, with emphasis on sports popular in the United States.

5195.   Thayer, Ernest Lawrence. *Casey at the Bat* (4–7). Illus. by Paul Frame. 1964, Prentice-Hall $4.95; paper $1.50. Joyless Mudville recreated in a picture book format. Another recommended edition is illustrated by Wallace Tripp (1978, Coward $7.95).

Fairy Tales

5196. Alexander, Lloyd. *The Four Donkeys* (2–4). Illus. by Lester Abrams. 1972, Holt paper $3.88. Good for reading aloud, this story, in folk tradition, tells of the comic misadventures of a tailor, a baker, and a shoemaker.

5197. Alexander, Lloyd. *The King's Fountain* (K–4). Illus. by Ezra Jack Keats. 1971, Dutton $6.95. Wise men and scholars fail to convince a king that he should not build a fountain that will deprive the city people of water. A quiet peasant finally convinces the king with his simple, basic wisdom.

5198. Alexander, Lloyd. *The Town Cats and Other Tales* (4–6). Illus. by Laszlo Kubinyi. 1977, Dutton $7.50. Eight original tales involving several very wise cats.

5199. Andersen, Hans Christian. *Ardizzone's Hans Andersen: Fourteen Classic Tales* (3–5). Illus. by Edward Ardizzone. 1979, Atheneum $10.95. A highly recommended edition.

5200. Andersen, Hans Christian. *The Complete Fairy Tales and Stories* (4–6). Trans. by Erik Haugaard. 1974, Doubleday $16.95. A real joy to have all of these tales admirably translated in one volume.

5201. Andersen, Hans Christian. *Dulac's . . . The Snow Queen and Other Stories from Hans Andersen* (2–4). Illus. by Edmund Dulac. 1976, Doubleday $7.95. A handsome edition of this standard classic.

5202. Andersen, Hans Christian. *The Emperor's New Clothes* (2–4). Trans. by Erik Blegvad. Illus. by Erik Blegvad. 1959, Harcourt $5.95; LB $5.79. This time-honored tale appears in the three other recommended editions: Illus. by Virginia Burton (1962, Houghton $5.95); Illus. by Jack Delano and Irene Delano (1971, Random $4.95; LB $5.99), and retold by Ruth B. Gross and illus. by Jack Kent (1977, Four Winds $4.95; paper $1.25).

5203. Andersen, Hans Christian. *Hans Andersen: His Classic Fairy Tales* (3–5). Illus. by Michael Foreman. 1978, Doubleday $8.95. Eighteen tales retold from a new translation by Erik Haugaard.

5204. Andersen, Hans Christian. *Hans Christian Andersen's Favorite Fairy Tales* (4–6). Illus. by Paul Durand. 1974, Western $6.95; LB $12.23. A handsome edition of these all-time favorites.

5205. Andersen, Hans Christian. *Hans Clodhopper* (K–3). Illus. by Leon Shtainmets. 1975, Lippincott $6.95. The youngest and least likely of 3 sons wins the princess in this classic fairy tale.

5206. Andersen, Hans Christian. *It's Perfectly True: And Other Stories* (5–8). Foreword by Hugh Walpole. Illus. by Richard Bennett. 1938, Harcourt $7.50. Twenty-eight of Andersen's best stories.

5207. Andersen, Hans Christian. *The Little Match Girl* (4–6). Illus. by Blair Lent. 1968, Houghton $7.95. The touching story of the lonely, shivering little match girl who sees visions in the flames of the matches she cannot sell.

5208. Andersen, Hans Christian. *The Nightingale* (K–4). Tr. by Eva Le Gallienne. Illus. by Nancy E. Burkert. 1965, Harper $7.95; LB $7.89. The mood of the story is supported by 8 magnificent, full-page paintings.

5209. Andersen, Hans Christian. *The Princess and the Pea* (K–3). Illus. by Paul Galdone. 1978, Seabury $7.95. A story of the supersensitive princess given a new look.

5210. Andersen, Hans Christian. *Seven Tales* (2–5). Trans. by Eva Le Gallienne. Illus. by Maurice Sendak. 1959, Harper $8.79. An excellent edition for reading aloud.

5211. Andersen, Hans Christian. *The Snow Queen* (4–6). Adapted by Naomi Lewis. Illus. by Errol LeCain. 1979, Viking $10.00. A new version of this tale, accompanied by enchanting illustrations.

5212. Andersen, Hans Christian. *The Steadfast Tin Soldier* (6–8). Illus. by Paul Galdone. 1979, Houghton $8.95. Courage and tragedy are mingled in this classic tale newly illustrated.

5213. Andersen, Hans Christian. *Thumbelina* (K–2). Retold by Amy Ehrlich. Illus. by Susan Jeffers. 1979, Dial $8.95; LB $8.44. A lavishly illustrated edition of this ever-popular tale.

5214. Andersen, Hans Christian. *The Ugly Duckling* (K–3). Retold by Lorinda Bryan Cauley. 1979, Harcourt $8.95; paper $3.50. The classic story illustrated with bold full-color pictures.

5215. Andersen, Hans Christian. *The Snow Queen* (3–5). Trans. by R. P. Keigwin. Illus. by Marcia Brown. 1972, Scribner $6.95. Two outstanding editions of the wintry tale about Gerda's enchanted search for her beloved Kay. Impressionistic paintings in rich hues warm the Scribner edition; pen-and-ink drawings enhance the Scroll edition.

5216. Andersen, Hans Christian. *The Steadfast Tin Soldier* (K–4). Illus. by Marcia Brown. 1953, Scribner $8.95. The adventures of a little tin soldier and his love for a toy dancer is a favorite Andersen tale.

5217. Andersen, Hans Christian. *Thumbelina* (PS–2). Illus. by Adrienne Adams. 1961, Scribner $6.95. The tale of the tiniest of favorite heroines is illustrated with soft watercolor paintings.

5218. Andersen, Hans Christian. *The Ugly Duckling* (K–3). Trans. by R. P. Keigwin. Illus. by Adrienne Adams. 1965, Scribner $8.95; paper $1.25. A lovely edition of this standard classic.

5219. Andersen, Hans Christian. *The Wild Swans* (4–6). Illus. by Marcia Brown. 1963, Scribner $6.95. The purity of heart of a gentle princess triumphs over evil.

5220. Association for Childhood Education, eds. *Told Under the Magic Umbrella* (1–3). 1967, Macmillan $5.95. Collection of well-known tales and stories selected for their realistic approach and imagination. Also use (Macmillan $4.95): *Told Under the Green Umbrella* (1930) and *Told Under the Blue Umbrella* (1933, 1962).

5221. Banks, Lynne Reid. *The Farthest-Away Mountain* (4–6). Illus. by Victor G. Ambrus. 1977, Doubleday $5.95. A modern fairy tale about a young girl's encounter with an assortment of trolls, ogres, witches, and an enchanted frog.

5222. Baum, L. Frank. *The Wizard of Oz* (3–6). Illus. by W. W. Denslow. 1970, Macmillan $5.95. An edition with the original illustrations.

5223. Bomans, Godfried. *The Wily Witch and All the Other Tales and Fables* (4–7). Trans. by Patricia Crampton. Illus. by Wouter Hoogendijk. 1977, Stemmer $9.95. Works of the popular Dutch author, brilliantly translated.

5224. Coatsworth, Elizabeth. *The Cat Who Went to Heaven* (4–6). Illus. by Lynd Ward. 1930; 1958 Macmillan $6.95; paper $.95. A charming legend of a Japanese artist, his cat, and a Buddhist miracle. Newbery Award, 1930.

5225. Collodi, Carlo. *The Adventures of Pinocchio* (3–6). Illus. by Fritz Kredel. 1946, Grosset deluxe ed. $7.95; LB $5.95; paper $2.95. One of many recommended editions.

5226. Coombs, Patricia. *The Magic Pot* (K–3). Illus. by author. 1977, Lothrop $6.25; LB $6.00. After an old man finds a magic pot by the side of a road, unexpected events occur.

5227. Dickens, Charles. *The Magic Fishbone* (2–5). Illus. by Louis Slobodkin. 1953, Vanguard $4.95. A young princess is given a magic fishbone by a fairy.

5228. Flory, Jane. *The Lost and Found Princess* (2–4). Illus. by author. 1979, Houghton $5.95. A woman, a dragon, and a cat form a team and set out to find a lost princess.

5229. Fox, Paula. *The Little Swineherd and Other Tales* (4–7). Illus. by Leonard Lubin. 1978, Dutton $7.95. A collection of 5 original fable-fairy tales impressively told.

5230. Grahame, Kenneth. *The Reluctant Dragon* (2–4). Illus. by Ernest H. Shepard. 1938; 1953 Holiday $4.95. Tongue-in-cheek story of a boy who makes friends with a peace-loving dragon.

5231. Gray, Nicholas Stuart. *A Wind from Nowhere* (4–6). 1979, Faber $8.95. A delightful collection of fairy tales from various sources.

5232. Haviland, Virginia, ed. *The Fairy Tale Treasury* (4–6). Illus. by Raymond Briggs. 1972, Coward $8.49. A handsome collection of 32 mostly familiar stories (many appeared previously in the compiler's well-known "Favorite Fairy Tales" series), illustrated by a distinguished artist.

5233. Hauff, Wilhelm. *The Adventures of Little Mouk* (4–5). Illus. by Monika Laimgruber. 1975, Macmillan $6.95. An old German tale about a dwarf who goes into the world to seek his fortune.

5234. Housman, Laurence. *The Rat-Catcher's Daughter: A Collection of Stories* (4–7). Illus. by Julia Noonan. 1974, Atheneum $6.95. Twelve charming tales selected by Ellin Greene from 4 out-of-print collections.

5235. Jeffers, Susan. *Wild Robin* (2–4). Illus. by author. 1976, Dutton $8.95. A young boy captured by fairies is rescued by his sister.

5236. Johnson, Sally P., ed. *The Princesses: Sixteen Stories about Princesses* (3–6). Illus. by Beni Montresor. 1962, Harper $7.89. Tales of young royalty.

5237. Kennedy, Richard. *The Dark Princess* (4–6). Illus. by Donna Diamond. 1978, Holiday $7.95. A fool sacrifices his life to help a blind princess.

5238. Lang, Andrew, comp. *Blue Fairy Book* (4–6). Ed. by Brian Alderson. 1978, Kestrel/Viking $12.95. A new edition of this classic collection. Also reissued in this format (1978, Viking $18.95) are: *Red Fairy Book* and *Green Fairy Book*.

5239. Lang, Andrew, ed. *Blue Fairy Book* (2–5). Illus. by H. J. Ford and G. P. Hood. 1965, Viking $12.95. One of the many favorite "rainbow" fairy books reprinted in facsimile editions by Dover.

5240. Lawrence, Ann. *The Half-Brothers* (6–9). 1973, Walck $6.50. A fairy tale in which 3 half-brothers pay court to the same young duchess.

5241. MacDonald, George. *The Complete Fairy Tales of George MacDonald* (4–7). Illus. by Arthur Hughes. 1979, Schocken $8.95. A classic work reprinted with the original illustrations.

5242. MacDonald, George. *The Light Princess* (3–6). Illus. by William Pene du Bois. 1962, Crowell $7.89. Classic story of the princess who lost her gravity. Also use the edition illustrated by Maurice Sendak (1977, Farrar $5.95; Dell, paper $1.25).

5243. McGinley, Phyllis. *The Plain Princess* (1–3). Illus. by Helen Stone. 1945, Lippincott $8.95. A modern, endearing tale in which plain Esmeralda is transformed into a beauty.

5244. Nesbit, Edith. *The Complete Book of Dragons* (4–6). Illus. by Erik Blegvad. 1973, Macmillan $5.95. Although well-grounded in the spirit and language of Victorian England, these 9 stories are diverting, particularly for Nesbit fans.

5245. Norton, Mary. *Bed-Knob and Broom-Stick* (4–6). Illus. by Erik Blegvad. 1957, Harcourt $5.95; paper $1.65. Charles, Carey, and Paul meet a woman who is studying to become a witch, and she takes them on many exciting but gruesome adventures.

5246. Norton, Mary. *The Borrowers* (4–6). Illus. by Beth Krush and Joe Krush. 1953, Harcourt $5.50; paper $1.50. A group of little people, no taller than a pencil, live in old houses and borrow what they need from humans. Sequels are: *The Borrowers Afield* (1955, $5.95; paper $1.50), *The Borrowers Afloat* (1959, $5.50; paper $1.50), and *The Borrowers Aloft* (1961, $5.50; paper $1.50).

5247. Norton, Mary. *Poor Stainless* (3–5). Illus. by Beth Krush and Joe Krush. 1971, Harcourt $4.95. Further adventures of the Borrowers; this time Homily recounts the story of the search for her lost neighbor Stainless.

5248. Provensen, Alice, and Provensen, Martin, eds. *The Provensen Book of Fairy Tales* (4–6). Illus. by author. 1971, Random $6.99. Twelve modern tales by such masters as Arthur Rackham, Howard Pyle, and Hans Christian Andersen, reprinted with delightful drawings.

5249. Pyle, Howard. *King Stork* (K–3). Illus. by Trina Schart Hyman. 1973, Little $6.95. New illustrations highlight this story from *The Wonder Clock*.

5250. Pyle, Howard. *Pepper and Salt* (4–6). Illus. by author. 1885; 1941 Harper $8.79; Dover paper $2.50. Clever and delightful stories based on old tales, a popular favorite.

5251. Pyle, Howard. *The Wonder Clock: Or Four and Twenty Marvelous Tales* (4–6). Illus. by author. 1887; 1915 Harper $8.79; Dover paper $4.50. Tales for each hour in the day, told by figures on a clock.

5252. Rackham, Arthur, ed. *The Arthur Rackham Fairy Book* (2–5). Illus. by editor. 1933; 1950 Lippincott $10.00. Twenty-three favorite fairy and folktales.

5253. Ritchie, Alice. *The Treasure Of Li-Po* (4–7). Illus. by T. Ritchie. 1949, Harcourt $4.50. Six original tales set in China.

5254. Robb, Brian, ed. *Twelve Adventures of the Celebrated Baron Munchausen* (4–6). Illus. by author. 1979, Deutsch $5.95. Twelve Baron Munchausen stories, retold simply.

5255. Ross, Eulalie S., ed. *The Lost Half Hour: A Collection of Stories* (4–6). Illus. by Enrico Arno. 1963, Harcourt $5.95. A good selection of stories, particularly useful for storytellers.

5256. Sandburg, Carl. *Rootabaga Stories* (4–6). Illus. by Maud Petersham and Miska Petersham. 1922; 1951 Harcourt $10.95; paper $1.95. collection of modern tales from Rootabaga country.

5257. Selfridge, Oliver G. *Trouble with Dragons* (4–6). Illus. by Shirley Hughes. 1978, Addison $7.95. Celia traps a dragon and wins a prince.

5258. Stearns, Pamela. *The Mechanical Doll* (4–6). Illus. by Trina Schart Hyman. 1979, Houghton $6.95. A modern fairy tale of a young musician's love for a mechanical doll.

5259. Stockton, Frank R. *The Bee-Man of Orn* (3–5). Illus. by Maurice Sendak. 1964, Holt $3.27; paper $1.65. A favorite tale by this fine author.

5260. Thurber, James. *Many Moons* (4–5). Illus. by Louis Slobodkin. 1944, Harcourt $5.95; paper $2.25. A little princess who wanted the moon and how her wish came true. Also use: *The Great Quillow* (1944, Harcourt, paper $1.95).

5261. Thurber, James. *The White Deer* (6–7). Illus. by author and Don Freeman. 1945, Harcourt paper $2.25. Three princes, a princess, and magic occurrences in this modern fairy tale.

5262. Tregarthen, Enys. *The Doll Who Came Alive* (1–4). Illus. by Nora S. Unwin. 1972, John Day $4.95. A kindly sailor gives an orphan girl a doll that comes alive in this Cornish tale.

5263. Wilde, Oscar. *The Birthday of the Infanta* (4–6). Illus. by Leonard Lubin. 1979, Viking $7.95. For better readers, a tale of a dwarf and his sad realization that the Infanta considers him ugly.

5264. Wilde, Oscar. *The Selfish Giant* (4–6). Illus. by Michael Foreman and Friere Wright. 1978, Methuen $7.95. Many full-color illustrations enliven this classic story.

5265. Wilde, Oscar. *The Star Child: A Fairy Tale* (2–3). Illus. by Fiona French. 1979, Scholastic $9.95. An abandoned child searches for his mother.

5266. Williams, Jay. *The Practical Princess and Other Liberating Fairy Tales* (2–4). Illus. by Rick Schreiter. 1978, Parents $8.50; LB $7.61. Six modern tales told with gusto.

5267. Yolen, Jane. *Dream Weaver* (6–8). Illus. by Michael Hague. 1979, Collins $10.95. Seven modern fairy tales, each told by an old woman for a penny each.

5268. Yolen, Jane. *The Girl Who Cried Flowers, and Other Tales* (5–6). Illus. by David Paladini. 1974, Crowell $7.50; LB $7.89. New wine in old bottles describes these 5 original tales that rely on plot elements and situations loved by all. Seven more tales are in *The Hundredth Dove and Other Tales* (1977, Crowell, $7.50).

5269. Yolen, Jane. *The Magic Three of Solatia* (5–7). Illus. by Julia Noonan. 1974, Crowell $6.95. Wizard's spells, the struggle between good and evil, and the magic of the guest are familiar elements in this 4-part fantasy.

Folklore

General

5270. Arbuthnot, May Hill, and Taylor, Mark, eds. *Time for Old Magic* (5–8). Illus. by John Averill. 1970, Scott, Foresman $11.50. An excellent cross section of the folktales of the world.

5271. Bang, Molly, ed. *The Buried Moon and Other Stories* (4–6). Illus. by editor. 1977, Scribner $5.95. Five stories of magic from various sources, told with style and suspense.

5272. Baumann, Hans, ed. *The Stolen Fire: Legends of Heroes and Rebels from around the World* (4–6). Illus. by Herbert Holzing. 1974, Pantheon $6.39. Courage and perseverance dominate these tales from such diverse areas as Africa, America, and Siberia.

5273. Colwell, Eileen, ed. *The Magic Umbrella and Other Stories for Telling* (4–7). Illus. by Shirley Felts. 1977, McKay $6.95. This fine collection stretches from Greek and Norse legends to more modern tales.

5274. Fenner, Phyllis, ed. *Giants and Witches and a Dragon or Two* (4–6). Illus. by Henry C. Pitz. 1943, Knopf $5.99. Seventeen tested stories, many from out-of-print collections.

5275. Greene, Ellin, ed. *Midsummer Magic: A Garland of Stories, Charms and Recipes* (5–8). Illus. by Barbara Cooney. 1976, Lothrop $7.25; LB $6.96. Folktales and accompanying material from Europe that deal with the rites and ceremonies connected with Midsummer Eve.

5276. Hazeltine, Alice I, ed. *Hero Tales from Many Lands* (5–7). Illus. by Gordon Laite. 1961, Abingdon $9.95. Samplings from 30 excellent collections.

5277. Holme, Brian, ed. *Tales from Times Past* (4–6). Illustrated. 1977, Viking $10.00. A handsome collection of classic tales and fables with illustrations by such masters as Greenaway, Crane, and Rackham.

5278. Hutchinson, Veronica S., ed. *Chimney Corner Stories* (PS–2). Illus. by Lois Lenski. 1925, Putnam $7.69. A collection of 16 familiar short tales

popular with younger children. Also use: *Candlelight Stories* (1928, Putnam $6.86).

5279. Jagendorf, M. A., ed. *Noodlehead Stories from around the World* (4–8). Illus. by Shane Miller. 1957, Vanguard $6.95. Sixty-five funny stories from 36 countries.

5280. Leach, Maria, ed. *The Lion Sneezed: Folktales and Myths of the Cat* (4–6). Illus. by Helen Siegl. 1977, Crowell $7.95. Twenty short stories, plus riddles and proverbs, are illustrated with unusual woodcuts in this endearing tribute to the cat.

5281. Leach, Maria, ed. *Noodles, Nitwits and Numskulls* (5–7). Illus. by Kurt Werth. 1961, Collins $6.91; paper $1.25. A collection of stories and riddles from many countries.

5282. Leach, Maria, ed. *Whistle in the Graveyard: Folktales to Chill Your Bones* (4–6). Illus. by Ken Rinciari. 1974, Viking $6.95. A collection about ghosts that will satisfy young readers intent on getting a good scare from their reading.

5283. Lefevre, Felicite. *The Cock, the Mouse and the Little Red Hen* (1–3). 1947, Macrae $6.47. A repetitive tale of the wise hen who saves her friends from the fox.

5284. Lurie, Alison. *Clever Gretchen, and Other Forgotten Folk Tales* (4–6). Illus. by Margot Tomes. 1980, Crowell $7.95; LB $7.89. Fourteen folk tales, each with active forceful heroines.

5285. McDowell, Robert Eugene, and Lavitt, Edward, eds. *Third World Voices for Children* (4–7). Illus. by Barbara Kohn Isaac. 1971, Odaki $5.95. A geographically arranged collection of folktales, poems, and songs from Africa, Black America, and New Guinea.

5286. McHargue, Georgess. *The Impossible People* (4–6). Illus. by Frank Bozzo. 1972, Holt $6.95. A history natural and unnatural of beings terrible and wonderful.

5287. Manning-Sanders, Ruth, ed. *A Book of Charms and Changelings* (4–6). Illus. by Robin Jacques. 1972, Dutton $6.95. Fairy changelings and the complications they produce are the subject of 15 charmingly illustrated tales.

5288. Manning-Sanders, Ruth, ed. *A Book of Dragons* (4–6). Illus. by Robin Jacques. 1965, Dutton $6.95. Fourteen tales from many countries about friendly and evil beasts. Also use: *A Book of Devils and Demons* (1970, Dutton $6.95).

5289. Manning-Sanders, Ruth, ed. *A Book of Enchantments and Curses* (5–6). Illus. by Robin Jacques. 1977, Dutton $6.95. A collection of 13 folktales from various sources, each dealing with magic spells.

5290. Manning-Sanders, Ruth. *A Book of Kings and Queens* (3–6). Illus. by Robin Jacques. 1978, Dutton $7.95. A variety of members of royalty—wise to foolish—are represented in this 10-story collection.

5291. Manning-Sanders, Ruth, ed. *A Book of Magic Animals* (4–6). Illus. by Robin Jacques. 1975, Dutton $8.50. A collection of 11 folktales dealing with animals who use their magic powers to intervene in the affairs of humans.

5292. Manning-Sanders, Ruth. *A Book of Spooks and Spectres* (5–7). Illus. by Robin Jacques. 1980, Dutton $7.95. Twenty-three entertaining ghost stories from around the world. Also use: *A Book of Ghosts and Goblins* (1969, Dutton, paper $1.25).

5293. Manning-Sanders, Ruth, ed. *A Book of Witches* (4–5). Illus. by Robin Jacques. 1966, Dutton $6.95. Twelve stories about various types of witches. Also use: *A Book of Ogres and Trolls* (1973, Dutton $6.95).

5294. Manning-Sanders, Ruth, ed. *A Choice of Magic* (4–6). Illus. by Robin Jacques. 1971, Dutton $7.50. This master anthologist has chosen 32 of her favorite folk and fairy tales chiefly from her previously published collections.

5295. Manning-Sanders, Ruth, ed. *Tortoise Tales* (1–3). Illus. by Donald Chaffin. 1974, Elsevier/-Nelson $5.95. A very useful collection of short folktales about animals, good for reading aloud.

5296. Mayo, Margaret, ed. *The Book of Magical Horses* (4–6). Illus. by Victor G. Ambrus. 1977, Hastings $6.95. Thirteen tales from various sources, all dealing with enchanted horses.

5297. Minard, Rosemary, ed. *Womenfolk and Fairy Tales* (4–6). Illus. by Suzanna Klein. 1975, Houghton $6.95. In each of these 18 stories, the female characters triumph because of wit, spunk, and courage.

5298. Palmer, Robin. *Dragons, Unicorns and Other Magical Beasts* (3–5). Illustrated. 1966, Walck $6.95. A dictionary of strange and imaginary beasts.

5299. Phelps, Ethel Johnston. *Tatterhood and Other Tales* (3–6). Illus. by Pamela Baldwin Ford. 1978, Feminist Press $10.95. Tales in which women play a vital and decisive role.

5300. Rackham, Arthur, ed. *Fairy Tales from Many Lands* (3–6). Illus. by editor. 1974, Penguin paper $5.95. Nineteen folktales from several sources in different countries.

5301. Rockwell, Anne, ed. *The Three Bears and 15 Other Stories* (1–4). Illus. by editor. 1975, Crowell $9.95; LB $10.95. Folktales from England and stories from the Grimm collections are the sources of these charmingly illustrated stories.

5302. Rojankovsky, Feodor, ed. *The Tall Book of Nursery Tales* (K–2). Illus. by editor. 1944, Harper $4.95; LB $5.49. Twenty-four traditional tales in an unusual format.

5303. Tarrant, Margaret Winifred. *Fairy Tales* (PS–2). Illus. by author. 1978, Crowell $6.95; LB $7.49. Such favorites as "The Three Bears," "Tom Thumb," and "Puss in Boots" are included in this fine collection.

5304. Tudor, Tasha. *Tasha Tudor's Bedtime Book* (K–2). Ed. by Kate Klimo. 1978, Platt $4.95. Fourteen classic tales, including "Snow White," "The Sorcerer's Apprentice," and "The Babes in the Woods."

5305. Wolkstein, Diane, ed. *Lazy Stories* (4–5). Illus. by James Marshall. 1976, Seabury $6.95; Dell paper $.95. Tales from Japan, Laos, and Mexico that tell of what befalls various lazy people.

Africa

5306. Aardema, Verna, ed. *Behind the Back of the Mountain: Black Folktales from Southern Africa* (4–6). Illus. by Leo Dillon and Diane Dillon. 1973, Dial $5.95; LB $5.47. Illustrated in black and white by award-winning artists. The stories, which vary in merit, represent 6 language groups in South Africa.

5307. Aardema, Verna. *Half-a-Ball-of-Kenki: An Ashanti Tale* (K–2). Illus. by Diane S. Zuromskis. 1979, Warne $8.95. How leopards gained their spots and why flies sit on leaves are explained in this Ashanti folktale.

5308. Aardema, Verna, ed. *Who's in Rabbit's House? A Masai Tale* (K–3). Illus. by Leo Dillon and Diane Dillon. 1977, Dial $7.95; LB $7.45; paper $2.50. Rabbit's friends try to evict a mysterious Long One who has moved into her house.

5309. Aardema, Verna, ed. *Why Mosquitoes Buzz in Peoples' Ears: A West African Folktale, Retold* (K–3). Illus. by Leo Dillon and Diane Dillon. 1975, Dial $7.95; LB $7.45; paper $2.50. Bold, stylized paintings illustrate this tale of a mosquito who tells a whopping lie, thus setting off a chain of events. Caldecott Medal, 1976.

5310. Appiah, Peggy, ed. *Ananse the Spider: Tales from an Ashanti Village* (4–7). Illus. by editor. 1966, Pantheon $5.99. Thirteen tales about the clever spider who outwits those around him.

5311. Arkhurst, Joyce Cooper. *The Adventures of Spider: West African Folktales* (4–7). Illus. by Jerry Pinkney. 1964, Little $6.95. Six humorous stories featuring the crafty spider.

5312. Arnott, Kathleen, comp. *African Myths and Legends* (4–6). Illus. by Joan Kiddell-Monroe. 1978, Oxford $9.95. An effective retelling of several myths from various parts of Africa.

5313. Berson, Harold. *Kassim's Shoes* (K–3). Illus. by author. 1977, Crown $5.95. In this adaptation of a Moroccan folktale, Kassim finds it impossible to part with his old shoes.

5314. Bible, Charles. *Hamdaani: A Traditional Tale from Zanzibar* (1–3). Illus. by author. 1977, Holt $6.50. A moral tale in which an ungrateful man gets his just desserts.

5315. Bryan, Ashley, ed. *The Adventures of Aku* (4–6). Illus. by author. 1976, Atheneum $7.95. This collection of African tales has as a subtitle, *How It Came about That We Shall Always See Okra The Cat Lying on a Velvet Cushion, While Okraman the Dog Sleeps among the Ashes.*

5316. Bryan, Ashley. *The Ox of the Wonderful Horns and Other African Folktales* (1–5). Illus. by author. 1971, Atheneum $6.95. Four amusing short stories about animals trying to outwit one another.

5317. Carew, Jan. *The Third Gift* (3–5). Illus. by Leo Dillon and Diane Dillon. 1974, Little $7.95. An African folktale about the valuable gifts a tribe receives from the young men who climb to the peak of Nameless Mountain.

5318. Courlander, Harold, and Herzog, George. *The Cow-Tail Switch: And Other West African Stories* (4–6). Illus. by Madye Lee Chastain. 1947, Holt $5.95. Appealing stories for middle readers. Also use: *Olode the Hunter and Other Tales from Nigeria* (1968, Harcourt $4.50).

5319. Courlander, Harold, and Prempeh, Albert K. *The Hat-Shaking Dance and Other Ashanti Tales from Ghana* (3–6). Illus. by Enrico Arno. 1957, Harcourt $5.75. Twenty-one folktales about the wiley spider Anansi, the folk hero of the Ashantis.

5320. Courlander, Harold. *The King's Drum and Other African Stories* (4–6). Illus. by Enrico Arno. 1962, Harcourt $6.50; paper $.75. Humorous tales of wise and foolish people and animals.

5321. Dayrell, Elphinstone. *Why the Sun and the Moon Live in the Sky* (K–2). Illus. by Blair Lent. 1968, Houghton paper $1.95. Stylized illustrations add to the distinction of this simply told adaptation of a Nigerian folktale.

5322. Domanska, Janina. *The Tortoise and the Tree* (PS–2). Illus. by author. 1978, Morrow $7.95; LB $7.63. A Bantee tale about a tortoise who punishes animals who have abused him.

5323. Elkin, Benjamin. *Such Is the Way of the World* (K–2). Illus. by Yoko Mitsuhashi. 1968, Parents $5.95; LB $5.41. A dog frightens away Desta's pet monkey, which begins a series of adventures in this whimsical Ethiopian folktale.

5324. Fuja, Abayomi, ed. *Fourteen Hundred Cowries, and Other African Tales* (4–7). Illus. by Ademola Olugebefola. 1971, Lothrop paper $1.25. This collection of Yoruba fables, "why" stories, and animal tales was made by the author during the 1930s and 1940s.

5325. Gerson, Mary-Joan. *Why the Sky's Far Away: A Folktale from Nigeria* (1–3). Illus. by Hope Meryman. 1974, Harcourt $4.95. When people begin misusing the generosity of the sky, it moves away.

5326. Guirma, Frederic. *Princess of the Full Moon* (4–6). Illus. by author. 1970, Macmillan $4.95. Many of the standard elements of the fairy tale—beautiful princess, evil prince, and trusting, simple shepherd—are found in this African story.

5327. Haley, Gail E. *A Story, a Story* (1–4). Illus. by author. 1970, Atheneum $7.89; paper $1.95. How African "spider stories" began is traced back to the time when Ananse, the Spider Man, made a bargain with the Sky God. Caldecott Medal, 1971.

5328. Heady, Eleanor B. *Safri the Singer: East African Tales* (3–5). Illus. by Harold James. 1972, Follett $5.95; LB $5.97. A collection of 17 tales, mostly about talking animals.

5329. McDermott, Gerald. *Anansi, the Spider: A Tale from the Ashanti* (K–3). Illus. by author. 1972, Holt $6.95. Because Anansi and his sons quarrel, the moon remains in the sky.

5330. McDermott, Gerald. *The Magic Tree: A Tale from the Congo* (K–3). Illus. by author. 1973, Holt $5.95; Penguin paper $1.95. A young boy discovers a magic tree, but loses its riches when he tells its secrets; adapted from the author's film.

5331. Prather, Ray. *The Ostrich Girl* (1–3). Illus. by author. 1978, Scribner $8.95. A girl has fantastic adventures in the East African legend.

5332. Robinson, Adjai. *Femi and Old Grandaddie* (K–3). Illus. by Jerry Pinkney. 1972, Coward $4.69. A charming folktale that the author first heard as a child in Sierra Leone.

5333. Robinson, Adjai. *Singing Tales of Africa* (4–6). Illus. by Christine Price. 1974, Scribner $5.95. Seven enchanting stories compiled and retold.

5334. Robinson, Adjai. *Three African Tales* (3–5). Illus. by Carole Byard. 1979, Putnam $6.95. Tales with humans as central characters from Sierra Leone and Kenya.

5335. Rose, Anne, ed. *Akima and the Magic Cow: A Folktale from Africa* (1–3). Illus. by Hope Meryman. 1979, Four Winds $5.95. A poor man saves his magically acquired worth from a greedy man.

5336. Seed, Jenny. *The Bushman's Dream: African Tales of the Creation* (4–6). Illus. by Bernard Bratt. 1975, Bradbury $5.95. Twelve tales retold with a connecting narration.

5337. Serwadda, W. Moses. *Songs and Stories from Uganda* (3–5). Illus. by Leo Dillon and Diane Dillon. 1974, Crowell $6.50; LB $7.39. A mixture of folk materials from Uganda, including songs in the native language (with translations) and a description of accompanying dance steps.

5338. Smith, Bob, ed. *Old African Tales Told Again* (4–5). Illus. by Dorothy Jungels. 1978, Academy $4.95. A cross section of short tales from many African regions.

5339. Walker, Barbara K. *The Dancing Palm Tree, and Other Nigerian Folktales* (4–6). Illus. by Helen Siegl. 1968, Parents $5.95; LB $5.41. Eleven tales of uncommon people and animals.

Asia

5340. Asian Cultural Centre of Unesco, eds. *Folk Tales from Asia for Children Everywhere: Book Three* (2–5). Illustrated. 1975, Weatherhill $6.50. Nine tales with a wide range of folk themes in a fine companion to Books One and Two.

5341. Courlander, Harold. *The Tiger's Whisker, and Other Tales and Legends from Asia and the Pacific* (3–6). Illus. by Enrico Arno. 1959, Harcourt $5.25. Thirty-one tales from various Asian countries.

5342. Kirkup, James. *The Magic Drum* (3–5). Illus. by Vo-Dinh. 1973, Knopf $5.69; LB $4.50. This drama about a boy's spirit living in a drum is retold with grace and beauty.

China

5343. Carpenter, F. R. *Tales of a Chinese Grandmother* (5–7). Illus. by Malthe Hasselrus. 1973, Tuttle paper $3.95. A boy and a girl listen to 30 classic Chinese tales.

5344. Cheng Hou-tien, ed. *Six Chinese Brothers: An Ancient Tale* (K–3). Illus. by editor. 1979, Holt $5.95. Another retelling of the folktale immortalized in *Five Chinese Brothers* by Claire Huchet Bishop.

5345. Demi, ed. *Under the Shade of the Mulberry Tree* (K–2). Illus. by author. 1979, Prentice-Hall $8.95. A Chinese tale in which a beggar outwits a greedy rich man.

5346. Hume, Lotta Carswell. *Favorite Children's Stories from China and Tibet* (3–6). Illus. by Lo Koon-Chiu. 1962, Tuttle $7.50. An enjoyable retelling of 19 tales from the East, many with an uncanny resemblance to Western counterparts.

5347. Kendall, Carol, and Li Yao-wen. *Sweet and Sour: Tales from China* (5–7). Illustrated. 1979, Seabury $7.95. A choice collection of some enchanting Chinese folktales.

5348. Manton, Jo, and Gittings, Robert, eds. *The Flying Horses: Tales from China* (5–6). Illus. by Derek Collard. 1977, Holt $6.95. Stories and legends that range from centuries past to contemporary times.

5349. Merrill, Jean. *The Superlative Horse* (4–7). Illus. by Ronni Solbert. 1961, Young Scott $5.95. A Taoist legend inspired this story of a peasant boy who becomes chief groom in the finest stable in ancient China.

5350. Mosel, Arlene. *Tikki Tikki Tembo* (K–2). Illus. by Blair Lent. 1968, Holt $6.95. Explains why the Chinese no longer honor their firstborn with an unusually long name.

5351. Wolkstein, Diane. *White Wave: A Chinese Tale* (3–7). Illus. by Ed Young. 1979, Crowell $7.95; LB $7.89. A subdued story of a young boy's encounter with the goddess who promised him supernatural help.

5352. Wriggins, Sally Hovey, ed. *White Monkey King: A Chinese Fable* (4–6). Illus. by Ronni Solbert. 1977, Pantheon $5.95; LB $6.99. The monkey king conquers many enemies until he meets his match at the throne of the Buddha.

5353. Wyndham, Robert. *Tales the People Tell in China* (4–6). Illus. by Jay Yank. 1971, Messner $7.29. An anthology that contains a rich cross section of many forms of writing—folktales, sayings, and some legends based on historical fact.

5354. Yolen, Jane. *The Emperor and the Kite* (K–3). Illus. by Ed Young. 1967, Collins $6.91. Unusual, vibrant illustrations using an ancient, intricate Oriental papercut technique enhance this version of the Chinese legend about the unshakable loyalty of the Emperor's smallest daughter.

5355. Young, Ed. *The Terrible Nung Gwama: A Chinese Folktale* (1–3). Illus. by author. 1978, Collins $5.95. A horrible monster is overcome by a tearful heroine in this Chinese tale.

5356. Ziner, Feenie. *Cricket Boy: A Chinese Tale* (PS–3). Illus. by Ed Young. 1977, Doubleday $6.95. A father hopes that his son, through his interest in crickets, will overcome their poverty and gain the approval of the emperor.

Japan

5357. Bang, Garrett. *Men from the Village Deep in the Mountains and Other Japanese Folktales* (3–6). Illus. by author. 1973, Macmillan $4.95. Twelve deftly told tales, handsomely illustrated.

5358. Bartoli, Jennifer. *The Story of the Grateful Crane: A Japanese Folktale* (K–2). 1977, Whitman $7.50. A crane expresses its gratitude to its savior by becoming a girl and assuming the role of his daughter.

5359. Brenner, Barbara. *Little One Inch* (1–3). Illus. by Fred Brenner. 1977, Coward $6.95. A retelling of several folktales about the "Japanese Tom Thumb."

5360. Garrison, Christian. *The Dream Eater* (K–2). Illus. by Diane Goode. 1978, Bradbury $8.95. Yukio meets a creature who eats bad dreams in this Japanese folktale.

5361. Haviland, Virginia, ed. *Favorite Fairy Tales Told in Japan* (3–5). Illus. by George Suyeoka. 1967, Little $7.95. An excellent collection about animals and people, nicely illustrated.

5362. Hodges, Margaret. *The Wave* (2–5). Illus. by Blair Lent. 1964, Houghton $3.25. A Japanese folktale about a man who burns his own rice fields to warn the villagers of an approaching tidal wave.

5363. McDermott, Gerald. *The Stone Cutter: A Japanese Folktale* (K–3). Illus. by author. 1975, Viking $7.50; Penguin paper $2.50. The familiar tale of the stone cutter who kept demanding greater power is brilliantly illustrated with colorful, stylized collage paintings.

5364. Mosel, Arlene. *The Funny Little Woman* (PS–4). Illus. by Blair Lent. 1972, Dutton $7.95; paper $1.95. A Japanese folktale about a little woman whose pursuit of a rice dumpling that falls from her table leads to her capture by wicked people.

5365. Skade, Florence. *Japanese Children's Favorite Stories* (2–4). Illus. by Yoshisuke Kurosaki. 1958, Tuttle $9.50. Twenty charming tales with proven appeal to children.

5366. Say, Allen. *Once Under the Cherry Blossom Tree* (1–3). Illus. by author. 1974, Harper $6.89. Through various changes, a mean old man becomes a pond for all to enjoy in this Japanese tale.

5367. Stamm, Claus. *Three Strong Women: A Tall Tale from Japan* (3–5). Illus. by Kazue Mizumura. 1962, Penguin paper $.95. A conceited wrestler meets his match in 3 women.

5368. Uchida, Yoshiko. *The Dancing Kettle, and Other Japanese Folk Tales* (3–5). Illus. by Richard C. Jones. 1949, Harcourt $6.50. Twelve dramatic and often humorous tales. Also use: *The Magic Listening Cap: More Folktales from Japan* (1955, Harcourt $6.75; paper $1.65).

5369. Yashima, Taro. *Seashore Story* (K–2). Illus. by author. 1967, Viking $4.95. An ancient Japanese legend of Urashima, a fisherman whose kindness to a turtle is repaid by the sea people. Misty, delicate paintings accompany the story.

5370. Winthrop, Elizabeth. *Journey to the Bright Kingdom* (3–5). Illus. by Charles Mikolaycak. 1979, Holiday $7.95. A blind woman is granted a look at her daughter in this retelling of a Japanese folk tale.

5371. Zemach, Kaethe. *The Beautiful Rat* (K–2). Illus. by author. 1979, Four Winds $7.95. A mother rat prods her husband into finding a suitable son-in-law for her daughter.

India

5372. Bang, Betsy. *The Cucumber Stem* (K–2). Illus. by Tony Chen. 1980, Greenwillow $5.95; LB

$5.71. A magical boy must marry the raja's daughter in this Bengali folktale.

5373. Bang, Betsy. *The Old Woman and the Red Pumpkin: A Bengali Folktale* (K–3). Illus. by Molly Bang. 1975, Macmillan $6.95. An old woman's adventures with animals on her way to and from her granddaughter's home.

5374. Bang, Betsy, ed. *The Old Woman and the Rice Thief* (K–3). Illus. by Molly Bang. 1978, Greenwillow $6.95; LB $6.43. An old woman sets out to catch the thief who has stolen her rice in this Bengali tale.

5375. Bang, Betsy. *Tuntuni, the Tailor Bird* (1–3). Illus. by Molly Bang. 1978, Greenwillow $5.95; LB $5.71. Two animal stories based on a Bengali folktale.

5376. Brown, Marcia. *The Blue Jackal* (1–3). Illus. by author. 1977, Scribner $6.95. After falling into a vat of indigo dye, a jackal is regarded as king, in this retelling of an East Indian tale.

5377. Brown, Marcia. *Once a Mouse . . . A Fable Cut in Wood* (PS–3). 1961, Scribner $8.95. An Indian tale retold: A hermit, gifted with magical powers, ponders the idea of big vs. little and changes a mouse into a royal tiger, only to change it back again when the tiger reacts ungratefully. Caldecott Medal 1962.

5378. Duff, Maggie. *Rum Pum Pum: A Folktale from India* (K–2). Illus. by Jose Aruego and Ariane Dewey. 1978, Macmillan $7.95. Blackbird beats his drum and outwits a greedy king.

5379. Gaer, Joseph. *The Fables of India* (5–7). Illus. by Randy Monk. 1955, Little $6.95. A selection of Indian animal tales, excellent for storytelling.

5380. Jatakas. *Jataka Tales* (1–3). Ed. by Ellen C. Babbit. Illus. by Ellsworth Young. 1940, Prentice-Hall $4.95. Also ed. by Nancy Deroin. Illus. by Ellen Lanyon (3–5). (1975, Houghton $5.95; Dell, paper 95¢). Two fine editions of fables about ancient Buddhist legends.

5381. Jatakas. *The Monkey and the Crocodile: A Jataka Tale from India* (K–3). Ed. by Paul Galdone. Illus. by Paul Galdone. 1969, Seabury $7.50. A retelling of one of the Jataka tales from India in which a crocodile decides he will catch a monkey, but the monkey has other ideas.

5382. Price, Christine. *The Valiant Chattee-Maker* (K–3). Illus. by author. 1965, Warne $4.95. Indian folktale about a village potter.

5383. Quigley, Lillian F. *The Blind Men and the Elephant* (1–3). Illus. by Janice Holland. 1959, Scribner $6.95; paper $.95. An East Indian tale

about 6 blind men who try to describe an elephant.

5384. Shivkumar, K. *The King's Choice* (K–3). Illus. by Yoko Mitsuhashi. 1971, Parents $5.95; LB $5.41. A simple retelling of an Indian folktale with stylized illustrations, excellent for storytelling or reading aloud.

5385. Spellman, John W. *The Beautiful Blue Jay and Other Tales of India* (4–6). Illus. by Jerry Pinkney. 1967, Little $4.50. Twenty-five traditional folktales in print for the first time with this edition. Black-and-white drawings reflect a distinctive Eastern quality.

5386. Towle, Faith M. *The Magic Cooking Pot* (K–3). Illus. by author. 1975, Houghton $6.95. An Indian folktale about a cooking pot that fills itself with rice.

Southeast Asia

5387. Aung, Maung Htin, and Trager, Helen G. *A Kingdom Lost for a Drop of Honey* (4–7). Illus. by Paw Oo Thet. 1968, Parents $5.95; LB $5.41. Princell Learned-in-the-Law, possessor of a Solomonlike wisdom and a dominant figure of Burmese folklore, appears throughout this collection.

5388. Ginsburg, Mirra, ed. *Little Rystu* (4–6). Illus. by Tony Chen. 1978, Greenwillow $6.95. A Central Asian tale about an evil Khan who has enslaved some animals.

5389. Graham, Gail B. *The Beggar in the Blanket, and Other Vietnamese Tales* (4–7). Illus. by Brigitte Bryan. 1970, Dial $4.58. Eight favorites of the author, enhanced with drawings in the Chinese style.

5390. Kha, Dang Manh, and Clark, Ann Nolan. *In the Land of Small Dragon: A Vietnamese Folktale* (1–3). Illus. by Tony Chen. 1979, Viking $8.95. A fascinating tale that bears a certain resemblance to the Cinderella story.

5391. Kim, So-un. *The Story Bag: A Collection of Korean Folk Tales* (4–7). Illus. by Kim Eurhwan. 1955, Tuttle paper $3.25. Thirty tales with a variety of lessons to learn from each.

5392. Robertson, Dorothy Lewis. *Fairy Tales from Vietnam* (4–6). Illus. by W. T. Mars. 1968, Dodd $4.50. Tales based on versions told to the author by her foster son.

Australia and the Pacific Islands

5393. Aruego, Jose, and Dewey, Ariane. *A Crocodile's Tale: A Philippine Folk Story* (K–2). 1972, Scribner $7.95; paper $1.50. A clever humorous story tells how a small boy saves himself from a wily crocodile, whose life he has just saved.

5394. Bunter, Bill, and others. *Djugurba: Tales from the Spirit Time* (6–9). Illustrated. 1976, Indiana U. P. $6.95. An enchanting, often exciting collection of folktales of the aborigine people.

5395. Gittins, Anne. *Tales from the South Pacific Islands* (4–6). Illus. by Frank Rocca. 1977, Stemmer $4.95. Twenty-two folktales from such places as Fiji and Samoa in which the sea and its creatures play prominent roles.

5396. Roughsey, Dick. *The Giant Devil-Dingo* (1–3). Illus. by author. 1975, Macmillan $6.95. An Australian aboriginal legend about a fierce dog and a medicine man.

5397. Sechrist, Elizabeth H. *Once in the First Times* (4–6). Illus. by John Sheppard. 1969, Macrae $6.50; LB $5.97. Fifty-one varied tales that reflect the diverse cultures of the Philippines.

5398. Thompson, Vivian L. *Hawaiian Legends of Tricksters and Riddlers* (4–6). Illus. by Sylvie Selig. 1969, Holiday $6.95. Twelve of the oldest and best-known Hawaiian tales. Introductory factual background is given for each story with a glossary of Hawaiian words.

5399. Thompson, Vivian L. *Hawaiian Tales of Heroes and Champions* (4–6). Illus. by Herbert Kawainui Kane. 1971, Holiday $6.95. Twelve tales of magical powers that help conquer evil enemies. Also use: *Hawaiian Myths of Earth, Sea and Sky* (1966, Holiday $6.95).

5400. Williams, Jay. *The Surprising Things Maui Did* (K–3). Illus. by Charles Mikolaycak. 1979, Four Winds $8.95. A retelling of the fantastic exploits of Maui, a god in Hawaiian folklore.

Europe

Great Britain and Ireland

5401. Briggs, Katharine. *Abbey Lubbers, Banshees and Boggarts: An Illustrated Encyclopedia of Fairies* (5–8). Illus. by Yvonne Gilbert. 1979, Pantheon $10.00. Reference book on all kinds of supernatural beings in the British Isles.

5402. Briggs, Katharine. *British Folktales* (6–8). 1977, Pantheon $10.00. A varied and useful collection.

5403. Brooke, L. Leonard. *Golden Goose Book* (1–3). 1977, Warne $7.95. Four favorite folktales are included in this volume.

5404. Brown, Marcia. *Dick Whittington and His Cat* (K–4). Illustrated. 1950, Scribner $7.95. The familiar story of the boy who went to London to seek his fortune.

5405. Calhoun, Mary. *Jack the Wise and the Cornish Cuckoos* (1–3). 1978, Morrow $6.95; LB $6.43. A series of nonsensical adventures make Jack the most respected man in town.

5406. Colum, Padraic, ed. *A Treasury of Irish Folklore* (6–9). 1969, Crown $9.95. A marvelous collection of traditional Irish tales.

5407. Colwell, Eileen. *Round about and Long Ago: Tales from the English Countries* (4–6). Illus. by Anthony Colbert. 1974, Houghton $4.95. Twenty-eight short narratives about all kinds of witches, fairies, and goblins.

5408. Crossley-Holland, Kevin. *The Pedlar of Swaffham* (4–6). Illus. by Margaret Gordon. 1971, Seabury $6.95. The English folktale of a man who discovers gold under his own hawthorn tree, told with vitality and local color.

5409. Curley, Daniel. *Billy Beg and the Bull* (4–6). Illus. by Frank Bozzo. 1978, Crowell $6.95; LB $6.79. Billy Beg performs good works as he wanders the globe in this Irish folktale.

5410. Cutt, Nancy, and Towrie, W. *The Hogboon of Hell and Other Strange Orkney Tales* (4–7). Illus. by Richard Kennedy. 1979, Deutsch $7.95. A group of folktales, chiefly unfamiliar, from the Orkney Islands.

5411. Danaher, Kevin. *Folktales of the Irish Countryside* (5–7). Illus. by Harold Berson. 1970, David White $4.95; LB $4.76. Fourteen delightful tales collected by the author from 6 different storytellers.

5412. Domanska, Janina. *Little Red Hen* (PS–K). Illus. by author. 1973, Macmillan $7.95. Stylized, bold, geometrically designed illustrations give vitality and humor to this terse retelling of the old familiar tale.

5413. Du Bois, William Pene. *The Three Little Pigs* (PS–1). Illus. by author. 1962, Viking $5.95. The old folktale told in verse.

5414. Erslin, Bernard. *The Green Hero: Early Adventures of Finn McCool* (6–9). Illus. by Barbara Bascove. 1975, Four Winds $8.95. A witty and adroit retelling of the legends of Finn McCool, principally those involving his struggles with Gall McMorna.

5415. Finlay, Winifred. *Tattercoats and Other Folk Tales* (4–6). Illus. by Shirley Hughes. 1977, Harvey House $5.39. A fine collection of familiar and obscure folktales from Scotland and Northern England.

5416. Galdone, Paul. *The Gingerbread Boy* (PS–1). Illus. by author. 1975, Seabury $7.95. Humorous and vigorous illustrations enhance this favorite folktale of the adventures of a runaway gingerbread boy.

5417. Galdone, Paul. *Henny Penny* (K–2). Illus. by author. 1968, Seabury $6.95. A retelling of the favorite cumulative folktale of the hen who thought the sky was falling.

5418. Galdone, Paul. *The History of Mother Twaddle and the Marvelous Achievements of Her Son Jack* (PS–2). Illus. by author. 1974, Seabury $6.95. A charming retelling of an old version of "Jack and the Beanstalk."

5419. Galdone, Paul. *King of the Cats: A Ghost Story by Joseph Jacobs* (K–2). Illus. by author. 1980, Houghton $8.95. A gravedigger relates a strange story to his wife and pet cat, Tom.

5420. Galdone, Paul. *The Little Red Hen* (K–2). Illus. by author. 1973, Seabury $5.95; Scholastic paper $1.25. A little hen works for her lazy housemates in this reworking of the old tale.

5421. Galdone, Paul. *The Three Bears* (K–2). Illus. by author. 1972, Seabury $7.95. The illustrations for this familiar story are large, colorful, and humorous; excellent to use with a group.

5422. Galdone, Paul. *The Three Little Pigs* (K–2). Illus. by author. 1972, Seabury $6.95. The classic folktale about the pigs who built houses hoping to protect themselves from the wolf.

5423. Godden, Rumer. *The Old Woman Who Lived in a Vinegar Bottle* (K–3). Illus. by Mairi Hedderwick. 1972, Viking $4.95. The old familiar folktale told with style and elegant simplicity.

5424. Green, Kathleen. *Leprechaun Tales* (3–6). Illus. by Victoria de Larrea. 1968, Lippincott $4.50. The spell of Irish folklore is created through an inventive retelling of these magical stories.

5425. Guard, David. *Dierdre: A Celtic Legend* (5–8). Illus. by Gretchen Guard. 1977, Celestial Arts $4.95. A Druid correctly foretold at Dierdre's birth that her beauty would bring only death and destruction.

5426. Haviland, Virginia, ed. *Favorite Fairy Tales Told in Ireland* (3–5). Illus. by Arthur Marokvia. 1961, Little $6.95. Six tales of animals, humans, and a leprechaun. Also use (Little $6.95): *Favorite Fairy Tales Told in England* (1959) and *Favorite Fairy Tales Told in Scotland* (1963).

5427. Harper, Wilhelmina. *The Gunniwolf* (K–2). Illus. by William Wiesner. 1967, Dutton $7.95. A variation on an old folktale of the little girl who wandered into the jungle searching for flowers, when suddenly up rose the fierce gunniwolf.

5428. Hieatt, Constance, ed. *The Castle of Ladies* (5–7). Illus. by Norman Laliberte. 1973, Crowell $8.95. Various sections of the King Arthur legend are woven together in this colorful account of one of Sir Gawain's quests.

5429. Hieatt, Constance, ed. *The Knight of the Cart* (5–6). Illus. by John Gretzer. 1969, Crowell $8.79. A retelling of a King Arthur legend about Sir Lancelot.

5430. Hieatt, Constance, ed. *The Sword and the Grail* (5–7). Illus. by David Palladini. 1972, Crowell $8.95; LB $6.49. The part of the King Arthur legend in which a callow youth becomes Percival the Red Knight and savior of the King of the Grail is retold with simplicity and vigor.

5431. Jacobs, Joseph. *Johnny Cake* (K–3). Illus. by Emma L. Brock. 1967, Putnam $4.29. A charming retelling of the folktale of a runaway pancake. Also use: *Jack the Giant Killer* (1971, Walck $5.95).

5432. Jacobs, Joseph. *The Stars in the Sky: A Scottish Tale* (1–3). Illus. by Airdrie Antmann. 1979, Farrar $6.95. An old tale about a young girl who wanted the stars for playthings.

5433. Lobel, Anita. *The Pancake* (2–3). Illus. by author. 1978, Greenwillow $5.95; LB $5.49. The familiar tale of how a pancake escapes being eaten.

5434. Lockhead, Marion. *The Other Country: Legends and Fairy Tales of Scotland* (4–6). Illustrated. 1978, Hamish $9.95. Twenty-two selections that contain the standard magical ingredients—fairies, princesses, heroes—found in this art form.

5435. McLeish, Kenneth. *Chicken Licken* (PS–1). Illus. by Jutta Ash. 1974, Bradbury $6.95. The cumulative story given a refreshing retelling with excellent illustrations.

5436. MacManus, Seumas. *Hibernian Nights* (4–6). Illus. by Paul Kennedy. 1963, Macmillan $5.95. Twenty-two folktales from Ireland.

5437. Miles, Bernard. *Robin Hood: His Life and Legend* (5–7). Illus. by Victor G. Ambrus. 1979,

Rand $8.95. A birth-to-death retelling of the legends about Robin Hood.

5438. Nic-Leodhas, Sorche. *All in the Morning Early* (K–3). Illus. by Evaline Ness. 1963, Holt $3.50; paper $1.65. A little boy journeys to the mill one morning, picking up unusual companions on the way—Scottish folktale.

5439. Nic-Leodhas, Sorche. *Heather and Broom: Tales of the Scottish Highlands* (4–6). Illus. by Consuelo Joerns. 1960, Holt $3.07. Pleasurable reading from the Highlands.

5440. Nic-Leodhas, Sorche. *Twelve Great Black Cats and Other Eerie Scottish Tales* (4–7). Illus. by Vera Bock. 1971, Dutton $6.95. Ghosts, hauntings, and other supernatural tales from Scotland.

5441. Peppe, Rodney, retel. *Three Little Pigs* (PS–2). Illus. by author. 1980, Lothrop $7.95; LB $7.63. An action-filled retelling of this familiar tale.

5442. Pugh, Ellen. *More Tales from the Welsh Hills* (4–6). Illus. by Joan Sandin. 1971, Dodd $4.50. A further collection of stories based on those told to the author by her Welsh grandparents. Sequel to: *Tales from the Welsh Hills* (1968, $4.50).

5443. Pyle, Howard. *Some Merry Adventures of Robin Hood* (5–8). Illus. by author. 1967, Watts $7.95. Stories about Robin Hood and the inhabitants of Sherwood Forest.

5444. Pyle, Howard, ed. *The Story of King Arthur and His Knights* (6–9). Illus. by author. 1903, Scribner $17.50. One of the most famous editions of these classic stories.

5445. Reeves, James. *English Fables and Fairy Stories* (3–6). 1954, Walck $10.95. Nineteen beautiful retellings of such standard English tales as "Jack and the Beanstalk."

5446. Reeves, James. *The Shadow of the Hawk and Other Stories by Marie de France* (3–6). Illus. by A. Dalton. 1977, Seabury $7.95. Six dramatic stories of romance and enchantment originally told at the court of Henry II of England.

5447. Robbins, Ruth, ed. *Taliesin and King Arthur* (3–6). Illustrated. 1970, Parnassus $4.75; LB $4.59. How Taliesin, a poet of Welsh legend, delighted King Arthur with his songs and stories.

5448. Seuling, Barbara. *The Teeny Tiny Woman: An Old English Ghost Tale* (K–3). Illus. by author. 1976, Viking $5.95; Penguin paper $1.75. A picture-book version of the classic story about the little woman and her soup bone.

5449. Sewall, Marcia, ed. *The Little Wee Tyke: An English Folktale* (K–3). Illus. by author. 1979, Atheneum $7.95. A story of a dog so small, nobody wanted him.

5450. Steel, Flora Annie. *Tattercoats: An Old English Tale* (K–3). Illus. by Diane Goode. 1976, Bradbury $8.95. An English folktale reminiscent of the Cinderella theme, beautifully illustrated in full-color paintings.

5451. Sutcliff, Rosemary. *The High Deeds of Finn McCool* (1–4). Illus. by Michael Charlton. 1976, Penguin paper $1.25. Fourteen tales featuring the exploits of Finn, the legendary Irish hero.

5452. Sutcliff, Rosemary. *Tristan and Iseult* (6–8). 1971, Dutton $6.95; Penguin paper $1.50. The classic love tragedy retold with poignancy, drama, and authenticity.

5453. Wahl, Jan. *Needle and Noodle and Other Silly Stories* (PS–1). Illus. by Stan Mack. 1979, Random $5.95. Six nonsense stories based on old English folktales.

5454. Wetterer, Margaret K. *Patrick and the Fairy Thief* (1–3). Illus. by Enrico Arno. 1980, Atheneum $6.95. Patrick breaks the spell that has kept his mother a prisoner of the leprechauns.

5455. Wilkinson, Barry. *The Diverting Adventures of Tom Thumb* (PS–2). Illus. by author. 1969, Harcourt $4.95. The perils of the diminutive boy are reinterpreted in picture book format with striking, modernistic illustrations in brilliant hues.

5456. Williams-Ellis, Amabel. *Fairy Tales from the British Isles* (5–7). Illus. by Pauline Baynes. 1964, British Bk. Ctr. $15.00. A wide, varied collection of 48 wondrous tales, chiefly from England.

5457. Yolen, Jane. *Greyling: A Picture Story from the Islands of Shetland* (2–5). Illus. by William Stobbs. 1968, Collins $4.91. Scottish legend of a gentle boy who is revealed to be one of the selchies (seals who take human form on land).

5458. Zemach, Harve. *Duffy and the Devil: A Cornish Tale Retold* (1–3). Illus. by Margot Zemach. 1973, Farrar $6.95. A variant of "Rumpelstiltskin," this folktale is told with humor and verve, and boldly illustrated. Caldecott Medal 1974.

Low Countries

5459. Spicer, Dorothy Gladys. *The Owl's Nest* (4–6). Illus. by Alice Wadowski-Bak. 1968, Coward $4.99. Seven interesting and simple folktales from northern Holland.

5460. Williams, Jay. *The Wicked Tricks of Tyl Uilenspiegel* (4–6). Illus. by Friso Henstra. 1978,

Four Winds $8.95. Four adventures of the mischievous folk hero.

Spain and Portugal

5461. Davis, Robert. *Padre Porko: The Gentlemanly Pig* (4–6). Illus. by Fritz Eichenberg. 1948, Holiday $4.95. Eleven Spanish stories about a surprisingly wise pig who helps many creatures in trouble.

5462. Haviland, Virginia. *Favorite Fairy Tales Told in Spain* (4–6). Illus. by Barbara Cooney. 1963, Little $6.95. A lighthearted collection of stories involving many unusual characters.

France

5463. Baldwin, James. *Story of Roland* (6–8). Illus. by Peter Hurd. 1930, Scribner $12.50. The exploits of one of the greatest heroes of the Middle Ages retold in a classic edition.

5464. Berson, Harold. *Balarin's Goat* (K–3). Illus. by author. 1972, Crown $3.95. In this humorous retelling of an old French folktale, Balarin's goat is treated better than his wife. When his wife rebels and will only respond to his overtures with a "baa," Balarin changes his ways.

5465. Berson, Harold. *How the Devil Gets His Due* (4–5). Illus. by author. 1972, Crown $4.95. This adaptation of a French folktale tells how the devil was paid back for misusing a young servant boy.

5466. Brown, Marcia. *Stone Soup* (1–4). Illus. by author. 1947, Scribner $7.95; paper $1.25. An old French tale about 3 soldiers who make soup of stones.

5467. D'Aulnoy, La Comtesse. *The White Cat and Other Old French Tales* (3–6). Illus. by E. MacKinstry. 1967, Macmillan $4.95. A reissue of the 1928 edition with the original outstanding illustrations.

5468. Evans, C. S. *Sleeping Beauty* (2–4). Illus. by Arthur Rackham. 1972, Viking $5.95. A reissue of the classic tale first published in 1920, with distinguished illustrations.

5469. Harris, Rosemary, retel. *Beauty and the Beast* (3–5). Illus. by Errol LeCain. 1980, Doubleday $7.95. A concise retelling made memorable by dazzling pictures.

5470. Haviland, Virginia, ed. *Favorite Fairy Tales Told in France* (4–6). Illus. by Roger Duvoisin. 1959, Little $6.95. A fascinating collection that captures the Gallic spirit.

5471. Holman, Felice, and Valen, Nanine. *The Drac: French Tales of Dragons and Demons* (4–6). Illus. by Stephen Walker. 1975, Scribner $6.95. Five fearsome, fanciful fables from French folklore.

5472. LePrince de Beaumont, Marie. *Beauty and the Beast* (3–6). Illus. by Diane Goode. 1978, Bradbury $7.95. A faithful translation of the French tale.

5473. Mayer, Marianna. *Beauty and the Beast* (K–3). Illus. by Mercer Mayer. 1978, Four Winds $9.95. In text and elaborate illustrations, the Mayers have produced an outstanding version of this fairy tale.

5474. Perrault, Charles. *Cinderella* (PS–2). Illus. by Paul Galdone. 1978, McGraw $7.95. An action-filled, lighthearted retelling of this classic.

5475. Perrault, Charles. *Cinderella* (1–3). Illus. by Otto S. Svend. 1978, Larousse $6.95. A translation of Perrault's version is used as the text in this handsome edition.

5476. Perrault, Charles. *Perrault's Complete Fairy Tales* (4–6). Illus. by Heath Robinson. 1971, Dodd $5.95. Fourteen tales in an excellent translation from the French.

5477. Perrault, Charles. *Puss in Boots* (K–3). Ed. by Marcia Brown. Illus. by Marcia Brown. 1952, Scribner $8.95. Also illus. by Paul Galdone, 1976, Seabury $6.95. Two handsome editions of a favorite French folktale.

5478. Perrault, Charles. *The Little Red Riding Hood* (2–4). Illus. by William Stobbs. 1973, Walck $6.95. The original tale, unhappy ending and all, with superb illustrations.

5479. Rockwell, Anne. *Poor Goose: A French Folktale* (K–3). Illus. by author. 1976, Crowell $7.95; LB $7.89. A cumulative story about a goose's travels in search of peppermint tea to relieve her headache.

5480. Scribner, Charles, Jr. *The Devil's Bridge* (2–4). Illus. by Evaline Ness. 1978, Scribner $7.95. A French folktale about a bridge where one must forfeit one's soul to cross.

5481. Valen, Nanine. *The Devil's Tail: Based on an Old French Legend* (3–5). Illus. by David McPhail. 1978, Scribner $7.95. Why the devil flattened the nose of everyone in a town in Burgundy is told in this French folktale.

5482. Wahl, Jan. *Drakestail* (1–3). Illus. by Byron Barton. 1978, Greenwillow $5.95; LB $5.71. A duck sets out to see a king in this classic French folktale.

Germany

5483. Gauch, Patricia Lee. *Once upon a Dinkelsbuhl* (K–3). Illus. by Tomie de Paola. 1977, Putnam $6.95. A group of children decide to save their city when a band of marauding warriors attacks.

5484. Grimm Brothers. *About Wise Men and Simpletons: Twelve Tales from Grimm* (4–6). Trans. by Elizabeth Shub. Illus. by Nonny Hogrogian. 1971, Macmillan $5.95. Such old favorites as "Hansel and Gretel" and "Rumpelstiltskin" are translated in simple, direct prose.

5485. Grimm Brothers. *The Bear and the Kingbird; A Tale from the Brothers Grimm* (K–3). Trans. by Lore Segal. Illus. by Chris Conover. 1979, Farrar $8.95. Animals of the sky vs. those of the earth and sea, in a battle with amazing consequences.

5486. Grimm Brothers. *The Bearskinner* (K–3). Illus. by Felix Hoffman. 1978, Atheneum $8.95. A soldier makes a bargain with the devil in this traditional tale.

5487. Grimm Brothers. *The Best of Grimm's Fairy Tales* (K–3). Trans. by Anthea Bell and Anne Rogers. Illus. by Otto S. Svend. 1979, Larousse $9.95; LB $10.95. A collection made noteworthy by its full-color illustrations.

5488. Grimm Brothers. *The Brave Little Tailor* (1–3). Trans. by Anthea Bell. Illus. by Otto S. Svend. 1979, Larousse $6.95. The boastful tailor is reborn in intriguingly original illustrations.

5489. Grimm Brothers. *The Bremen Town Musicians* (K–3). Illus. by Paul Galdone. 1968, McGraw $7.95. Four animals frighten away robbers in this charming retelling of the old folktale.

5490. Grimm Brothers. *The Brothers Grimm Popular Folk Tales* (4–6). Trans. by Brian Alderson. Illus. by Michael Foreman. 1978, Doubleday $8.95. An impressive version of these classic tales.

5491. Grimm Brothers. *The Complete Grimm's Fairy Tales* (4–6). Illus. by Josef Scharl. 1974, Pantheon $12.95. Based on Margaret Hunt's translation, this has become the standard edition of these perennial favorites.

5492. Grimm Brothers. *Clever Kate* (1–4). Ed. by Elizabeth Shub. Illus. by Anita Lobel. 1973, Macmillan $4.95. Married only one week, Kate makes a succession of mistakes in this familiar tale.

5493. Grimm Brothers. *The Donkey Prince* (2–3). Adapted by M. Jean Craig. Illus. by Barbara Cooney. 1977, Doubleday $6.95. A charming adaptation of a familiar Grimm tale, illustrated with paintings in full color.

5494. Grimm Brothers. *The Fisherman and His Wife* (2–3). Trans. by Randall Jarrell. Illus. by Margot Zemach. 1980, Farrar $10.95. This classic story of the effects of greed on 2 people is superbly told.

5495. Grimm Brothers. *The Fisherman and His Wife* (2–3). Trans. by Elizabeth Shub. Illus. by Monika Laimgruber. 1979, Greenwillow $8.95. A new version of the German tale, which adds dialogue to the story.

5496. Grimm Brothers. *The Four Clever Brothers* (K–3). Illus. by Felix Hoffmann. 1967, Harcourt $6.95. Vivid, full-page illustrations highlight the tale of 4 brothers—a hunter, a thief, a stargazer, and a tailor—who combine their talents to rescue a princess held captive by a dragon. Also use from Harcourt: *The Seven Ravens* (1963, $6.95), and *Rapunzel* (1961, $7.95).

5497. Grimm Brothers. *Grimm's Fairy Tales: Twenty Stories* (4–6). Illus. by Arthur Rackham. 1973, Viking $6.95; Penguin paper $5.95. A generous selection from the classic edition that includes most of the standard treasures.

5498. Grimm Brothers. *Grimm's Tales for Young and Old* (4–6). Trans. by Ralph Manheim. 1977, Doubleday $12.50. Ten legends and 200 tales clearly and straightforwardly presented in simple prose without illustrations.

5499. Grimm Brothers. *Hans in Luck* (PS–1). Illus. by Paul Galdone. 1980, Parents $5.95. A retelling of the well-loved story.

5500. Grimm Brothers. *Hansel and Gretel* (3–5). Trans. by Charles Scribner. Illus. by Adrienne Adams. 1975, Scribner $6.95; paper $2.95. Handsomely complemented by atmospheric paintings. Also use: *Hansel and Gretel* by Arnold Lobel (1971, Delacorte $6.95; LB $6.46).

5501. Grimm Brothers. *Hansel and Gretel* (K–4). Trans. from the German by Elizabeth D. Crawford. Illus. by Lisbeth Zwerger. 1980, Morrow $7.95; LB $7.63. A fresh translation with ink-and-wash illustrations of this classic.

5502. Grimm Brothers. *Jorinda and Joringel* (2–5). Trans. by Elizabeth Shub. Illus. by Adrienne Adams. 1968, Scribner $5.95. The traditional tale of Jorinda, transformed into a nightingale by a wicked witch, and Joringel, who rescues her.

5503. Grimm Brothers. *The Juniper Tree and Other Tales from Grimm* (4–8). Selected and trans. by Lore Segal. Illus. by Maurice Sendak. 1973, Farrar $15.00; paper $4.95. A 2-volume cornucopia of stories—popular and lesser known—with 4 additional stories translated by Randall Jarrell.

5504. Grimm Brothers. *King Grisly-Beard* (K–3). Illus. by Maurice Sendak. 1973, Farrar $3.95. Lovely humorous pictures make this a delightful picture book version of the folktale about the disdainful princess who is taught humility by her husband.

5505. Grimm Brothers. *Red Riding Hood* (PS–3). Ed. by Beatrice S. De Regniers. Illus. by Edward Gorey. 1972, Atheneum $5.95. Droll illustrations for a book whose subtitle is *Retold in Verse for Boys and Girls to Read Themselves.*

5506. Grimm Brothers. *Little Red Riding Hood* (K–2). Illus. by Paul Galdone. 1974, McGraw $6.95; LB $7.95. A retelling of the favorite tale about a little girl and her encounter with a wolf.

5507. Grimm Brothers. *Rumpelstiltskin* (K–3). Illus. by Jacqueline Ayer. 1967, Harcourt $7.50. A miller's daughter must pay dearly for the help she receives from a clever little man.

5508. Grimm Brothers. *The Seven Ravens: A Grimm's Fairy Tale* (1–3). Illus. by Donna Diamond. 1979, Viking $6.95. A young girl sets out to free her brother in this faithful retelling of a favorite.

5509. Grimm Brothers. *The Shoemaker and the Elves* (K–2). Illus. by Adrienne Adams. 1960, Scribner $5.95; paper $.95. A favorite German tale illustrated with soft watercolors.

5510. Grimm Brothers. *The Sleeping Beauty* (K–2). Illus. by Warwick Hutton. 1979, Atheneum $9.95. A handsome understated version of this story.

5511. Grimm Brothers. *The Sleeping Beauty: From the Brothers Grimm* (4–6). Illus. by Trina Schart Hyman. 1977, Little $7.95. A graceful retelling of the classic tale with lavish illustrations.

5512. Grimm Brothers. *Snow White* (4–6). Trans. by Paul Heim. Illus. by Trina Schart Hyman. 1974, Little $6.95. A handsome addition to a folklore collection.

5513. Grimm Brothers. *Snow White and Rose Red* (K–3). Illus. by Barbara Cooney. 1966, Delacorte $4.95; LB $4.58. Also illus. by Adrienne Adams. (1964, Scribner $5.95). Two fine editions of a favorite story.

5514. Grimm Brothers. *Snow White and the Seven Dwarfs* (1–4). Trans. by Wanda Gag. Illus. by Wanda Gag. 1938, Coward $5.49. Also trans. by Randall Jarrell. Illus. by Nancy Ekholm Burkert. 1972, Farrar $7.95. Two editions of this classic.

5515. Grimm Brothers. *The Sorcerer's Apprentice* (3–5). Ed. by Wanda Gag. Illus. by Margot Tomes. 1979, Coward $6.95. A newly illustrated version of the classic story from the Grimm Brothers.

5516. Grimm Brothers. *Tales from Grimm* (3–5). Ed. by Wanda Gag. Illus. by Wanda Gag. 1936, Coward $7.95. Sixteen familiar and lesser-known Grimm tales, simply retold. Also use: *More Tales from Grimm* (1947, Coward $6.95).

5517. Grimm Brothers. *Thorn Rose or the Sleeping Beauty* (K–3). Illus. by Errol Le Cain. 1977, Bradbury $7.95. Illustrations that resemble medieval tapestries enhance this classic tale.

5518. Grimm Brothers. *Tom Thumb* (K–3). Illus. by Felix Hoffmann. 1973, Atheneum $7.95. A delightfully illustrated picture book version of this favorite folktale, which brings out the sturdy peasant quality of the story. Also use by the same illustrator: *King Thrushbeard* (1970, Harcourt $5.95).

5519. Grimm Brothers. *The Twelve Dancing Princesses* (4–6). Illus. by Errol Le Cain. 1978, Viking $8.95. A handsomely illustrated and richly told version of this classic tale.

5520. Grimm Brothers. *The Twelve Dancing Princesses* (K–3). Ed. by Janet Louise Swoboda Lunn. Illus. by Lazlo Gal. 1980, Methuen $10.95. A farm boy discovers the secret of the princesses and wins a bride and a fortune.

5521. Grimm Brothers. *Wanda Gag's Jorinda and Joringel* (2–3). Illus. by Margot Tomes. 1978, Coward $6.95. A maid is changed into a nightingale in this classic retelling of the familiar folktale.

5522. Grimm Brothers. *The Wolf and the Seven Little Kids* (K–2). Trans. by Anne Rogers. Illus. by Otto S. Svend. 1977, Larousse $6.95. The classic story of 7 goats and their encounter with a big, bad wolf.

5523. Hoffman, E. T. A. *The Nutcracker* (5–6). Adapt. by Alexandre Dumas. Trans. by Douglas Munro. Illus. by Phillida Gili. 1978, Oxford $10.95. The retelling of the Hoffman story that Tchaikovsky used in his ballet.

5524. Hoffman, E. T. A. *The Nutcracker* (3–5). Adapt. by Janet Schulman. Illus. by Kay Chorao. 1979, Dutton $6.95. An excellent adaptation of the original German tale.

5525. Koenig, Alma Johanna. *Gudrun* (6–9). 1979, Lothrop $7.95; LB $7.63. A thirteenth-century German epic of medieval daring-do.

5526. Jagendorf, M. A. *Tyll Ulenspiegel's Merry Pranks* (4–6). Illus. by Fritz Eichenberg. 1938, Vanguard $6.95. Thirty-seven stories of the irrepressible hero of German folklore.

5527. Rockwell, Anne. *The Old Woman and Her Pig and Ten Other Stories* (PS–1). Illus. by author. 1979, Crowell $10.95; LB $10.79. A collection of some favorite folktales.

Scandinavia

5528. Asbjornsen, Peter C., and Moe, Jorgen. *The Cat on the Dovrefell: A Christmas Tale* (1–3). Illus. by Tomie de Paola. 1979, Putnam $8.95; LB $3.95. A band of hostile trolls victimize a Norwegian householder.

5529. Asbjornsen, Peter C., and Moe, Jorgen. *East of the Sun and West of the Moon: Twenty-One Norwegian Folk Tales* (3–6). Ed. by Ingri d'Aulaire and Edgar d'Aulaire. Illus. by Ingri d'Aulaire and Edgar d'Aulaire. 1969, Viking $3.95. A beautifully and forcefully illustrated collection of 21 Norwegian folktales telling of trolls, giants, talking cats, and mountains made of glass.

5530. Asbjornsen, Peter C., and Moe, Jorgen. *Norwegian Folk Tales* (3–6). Illus. by Erik Werenskiold and Theodor Kittelsen. 1845; 1961 Vanous $20.00. The later edition retains the original illustrations.

5531. Asbjornsen, Peter C., and Moe, Jorgen. *The Squire's Bride* (3–5). Illus. by Marcia Sewall. 1975, Atheneum $6.95. A wily peasant girl outwits a squire intent on marrying her in this retelling of a classic Norwegian folktale.

5532. Asbjornsen, Peter C., and Moe, Jorgen. *The Three Billy Goats Gruff* (PS–1). Illus. by Marcia Brown. 1957, Harcourt $6.50; paper $2.25. A troll meets his match.

5533. Barth, Edna. *Balder and the Mistletoe: A Story for the Winter Holidays* (4–6). Illus. by Richard Cuffari. 1979, Seabury $7.95. A masterful retelling of the Norse legend of the death of Balder by the cunning of Loki.

5534. Bason, Lillian. *Those Foolish Molboes!* (2–4). Illus. by Margot Tomes. 1977, Coward $4.99. Like the fools of Chelm, the Molboes, noodleheads of Denmark, are cheerful and stupid in these humorous stories. Good for reading aloud.

5535. Bowman, James C., and Bianco, Margery. *Tales from a Finnish Tupa* (4–6). Illus. by Laura Bannon. 1936, Whitman $5.95. Fables of magic and drollery.

5536. Dasent, Sir George Webbe, trans. *The Cat on the Dovrefell* (PS–3). Illus. by Tomie de Paola. 1979, Putnam $8.95. On Christmas Eve, mischievous trolls mistake a sleeping bear for a harmless cat.

5537. D'Aulaire, Ingri, and D'Aulaire, Edgar. *D'Aulaires' Trolls* (3–5). Illus. by author. 1972, Doubleday $5.95. The many types and activities of trolls are described along with several troll stories—served up by 2 master artists.

5538. D'Aulaire, Ingri, and D'Aulaire, Edgar. *The Terrible Troll Bird* (K–3). Illus. by author. 1976, Doubleday $7.95. A new edition of the 1933 picture book.

5539. Ginsburg, Mirra. *How Wilka Went to Sea* (4–6). Illus. by Charles Mikolaycak. 1975, Crown $7.95. Nine Finnish and Turkish folktales.

5540. Hatch, Mary C. *13 Danish Tales* (3–5). Illus. by Edgun. 1947, Harcourt $4.50. An engaging and humorous collection, homely, witty, and reflecting peasant life.

5541. Haviland, Virginia, ed. *Favorite Fairy Tales Told in Denmark* (3–5). Illus. by Margot Zemach. 1971, Little $7.95. Six interesting tales masterfully retold. Similar collections for other Scandinavian countries (Little $6.95) are: *Favorite Fairy Tales Told in Norway* (1961) and *Favorite Fairy Tales Told in Sweden* (1966).

5542. Lobel, Anita. *King Rooster, Queen Hen* (K–3). Illus. by author. 1975, Greenwillow $5.71. An adaptation of a Danish folktale in which King Rooster and Queen Hen and their entourage set out to see the city, but encounter a fox who has other plans for them.

5543. Lundbergh, Holder, trans. *Great Swedish Fairy Tales* (4–6). Illus. by John Bauer. 1973, Delacorte $10.00. A collection of enchanting stories in which various sorts of trolls play important roles.

5544. McGovern, Ann. *Half a Kingdom: An Icelandic Folktale* (K–3). Illus. by Nola Langner. 1977, Warne $6.95; Scholastic paper $.95. A poor peasant girl rescues a noble prince in this unusual folktale.

5545. Olenius, Elsa. *Great Swedish Fairy Tales* (4–7). Illus. by John Bauer. 1973, Delacorte paper $6.95. Twenty-one enchantingly fresh tales that have both appeal and vigor.

5546. Stalder, Valerie. *Even the Devil Is Afraid of a Shrew: A Folktale of Lapland* (K–3). Illus. by Richard Brown. 1972, Addison $6.95. How quiet, little Pava Jal Vi frees himself from his nagging, shrewish wife is humorously told in this old Lapp tale. Good for storytelling.

Greece and Italy

5547. Aesop. *The Caldecott Aesop. A Facsimile of the 1883 Edition* (6–9). Intro. by Michael Patrick Hearn. Illus. by Randolph Caldecott. 1978, Doubleday $11.95; LB $12.90. A classic edition worthy of rescuing through facsimile printing.

5548. Aesop. *Fables of Aesop* (4–6). Ed. by Joseph Jacobs. Illus. by David Levine. 1964, Macmillan $4.95. One of many recommended editions of this classic.

5549. Aesop. *The Hare and the Tortoise* (K–3). Illus. by Paul Galdone. 1962, McGraw $7.95. A picture book retelling of one of the classic races of all time—between the hare and the tortoise—with an outcome that surprised even the hare. Also use: *Three Aesop Fox Fables* (1971, Seabury $6.95) and *The Town Mouse and the Country Mouse* (1971, McGraw $6.95).

5550. Aesop. *The Lion and the Mouse* (K–3). Illus. by Ed Young. 1980, Doubleday $7.95; LB $8.90. The age-old story of the mouse that saves a lion from the hunter's net.

5551. Aesop. *Once in a Wood* (1–3). Illus. by Eve Rice. 1979, Greenwillow $5.95. Ten tales from Aesop cleverly retold for beginning readers.

5552. Aesop. *A Wise Monkey Tale* (K–2). Ed. by Betsy and Giulio Maestro. Illus. by Giulio Maestro. 1975, Crown $6.95. A variant of one of Aesop's fables, this is a picture book version of the monkey who fell in a hole and then cleverly persuaded other animals to join him, so he could climb on their backs and get out.

5553. Aesop. *Borrowed Feathers and Other Fables* (K–3). Ed. by Byrna Stevens. Illustrated. 1978, Random $3.95; LB $4.99. Seven fables from Aesop retold for young children.

5554. Aliki. *The Twelve Months: A Greek Folktale* (K–3). Illustrated. 1978, Greenwillow $6.95. Twelve gifts suitably humble a greedy woman.

5555. de Paola, Tomie. *Big Anthony and the Magic Ring* (1–3). Illus. by author. 1979, Harcourt $7.95; paper $3.95. Once again Big Anthony meddles with his employer's magic in this sequel to *Strega Nona*.

5556. de Paola, Tomie. *The Prince of the Dolomites* (5–8). Illus. by author. 1980, Harcourt $8.95; paper $4.50. An Italian folktale about the winning of a moon princess.

5557. de Paola, Tomie. *Strega Nona: An Old Tale, Retold* (K–3). Illus. by author. 1975, Prentice-Hall $6.95. In this beautifully illustrated picture book version of an Italian folktale, Strega Nona (grandmother witch) produces pasta from her magical pot.

5558. Haviland, Virginia, ed. *Favorite Fairytales Told in Greece* (3–6). Illus. by Nonny Hogrogian. 1970, Little $6.95. A delightful collection with most unusual characters.

5559. Haviland, Virginia. *Favorite Fairytales Told in Italy* (4–6). Illus. by Evaline Ness. 1965, Little $6.95. A varied collection, charmingly illustrated.

5560. Horace. *Two Roman Mice* (K–3). Retold by Marilynne K. Roach. Illus. by Marilynne K. Roach. 1975, Crowell $5.50. The familiar tale of the country mouse and the city mouse told simply and directly; illustrated with authentic pictures of Roman architecture and life.

5561. Jagendorf, M. A. *The Priceless Cats and Other Italian Folk Stories* (4–6). Illus. by Gioia Fiammenghi. 1956, Vanguard $6.95. Retellings of old Italian lore.

5562. Zemach, Harve. *Awake and Dreaming* (PS–3). Illus. by Margot Zemach. 1970, Farrar $4.95. A Tuscan legend of a man who has nightmares and makes a bargain with the King of the Land of Pleasant Dreams.

Central and Eastern Europe

5563. Ambrus, Victor G. *The Three Poor Tailors* (K–2). Illustrated. 1966, Harcourt $6.50. The tailors, tired of sewing, explore the town in this funny Hungarian folktale.

5564. Domanska, Janina. *The Best of the Bargain* (1–3). Illus. by author. 1977, Greenwillow $7.95; LB $7.63. In this adaptation of a Polish folktale, a fox and a hedgehog decide to work together.

5565. Domanska, Janina. *King Krakus and the Dragon* (K–3). Illus. by author. 1979, Greenwillow $8.95; LB $8.59. A Polish folktale that tells how a young apprentice slays a fierce dragon.

5566. Duvoisin, Roger. *The Three Sneezes and Other Swiss Tales* (2–4). Illus. by author. 1941, Knopf $5.99. Thirty-seven peasant tales divided by the 2 chief regions of Switzerland.

5567. Gag, Wanda. *Gone Is Gone: Or, the Story of a Man Who Wanted to Do Housework* (K–3). Illus. by author. 1935, Coward $4.49. An old Bohemian tale about the problems that confront a bumbling man when he is overconfident about his abilities as a housewife.

5568. Ginsburg, Mirra. *How the Sun Was Brought Back to the Sky* (K–2). Adapt. from a Slovenian folktale. Illus. by Jose Aruego and Ariane Dewey. 1975, Macmillan $6.95. Colorful, vigorous illustrations enliven this cumulative folktale about 5 chicks who set out to find the sun, coax it out of its house, and help it shine again.

5569. Kimmel, Eric A. *Mishka, Pishka and Fishka and Other Galician Tales* (3–7). Illus. by Christopher J. Spollen. 1976, Coward $5.95. Five humorous tales from the area now partly in Poland, partly in Russia.

5570. Quinn, Zdenka, and Paul, John. *The Water Sprite of the Golden Town: Folktales of Bohemia* (4–8). 1971, Macrae $6.25. Kings, princes, and peasant boys figure in these 9 tales from classic czar sources.

5571. Reid, Barbara, and Reid, Eva. *The Cobbler's Reward* (K–3). Illus. by Charles Mikolaycak. 1978, Macmillan $6.95. Janek, a cobbler, tries to rescue a maiden held prisoner by a witch in this Polish folktale.

5572. Seredy, Kate. *The White Stag* (5–9). Illus. by author. 1937, Viking $6.95. Penguin paper $1.95. A legendary account of the westward migration of the Hungarians to new lands. Newbery Medal 1938.

5573. Turska, Krystyna. *The Magician of Cracow* (2–4). Illus. by author. 1975, Greenwillow $8.25. A magician makes a pact with the devil to gain power, in this ornately illustrated version of the popular legend.

5574. Turska, Krystyna. *The Woodcutter's Duck* (K–2). 1973, Macmillan $5.95. A brilliantly illustrated retelling of a Polish folktale about a poor woodcutter and his pet duck.

5575. Van Woerkom, Dorothy O., ed. *Alexandra the Rock-Eater* (K–3). Illus. by Rosekrans Hoffman. 1978, Knopf $6.95; LB $6.99. Alexandra outwits a dragon to feed her hungry children in this Rumanian folktale.

Russia

5576. Afanasyev, Alexander. *Marko the Rich and Vasily the Unlucky* (1–4). Trans. by Thomas Whitney. Illus. by Igor Galanin. 1974, Macmillan $5.95. Vasily triumphs over Marko in this retelling of the Russian tale.

5577. Afanasyev, Alexander, ed. *Russian Fairy Tales* (4–7). Illus. by Alexander Alexeieff. 1975, Pantheon $12.95. The definitive collection of folktales reissued in the 1945 edition.

5578. Afanasyev, Alexander. *Soldier and Tsar in the Forest: A Russian Tale* (K–3). Trans. by Richard Lourie. Illus. by Uri Shulevitz. 1972, Farrar $5.95. Handsome, brilliant illustrations accompany this story of a soldier who saves the tsar's life and is rewarded by being made a general.

5579. Afanasyev, Alexander. *Vasilisa the Beautiful* (2–5). Trans. by Thomas P. Whitney. Illus. by Nonny Hogrogian. 1970, Macmillan $4.95. A Russian version of the Cinderella story, which, in spite of several differences, ends in a royal wedding.

5580. Aiken, Joan. *The Kingdom under the Sea and Other Stories* (5–7). Illus. by Jan Pienkowski. 1979, Cape $7.95. A retelling of 11 magical folktales from Eastern Europe.

5581. Artzybasheff, Boris. *Seven Simeons: A Russian Tale* (4–6). Illus. by author. 1937; 1961 Viking $3.95. The ironic story of how 7 peasant boys outwit the wise King Douda.

5582. Black, Algernon D. *The Woman of the Wood: A Tale from Old Russia* (K–3). Illus. by Evaline Ness. 1973, Holt $5.95. Three men quarrel over the possessions of the woman they have created.

5583. Brown, Marcia. *The Bun: A Tale from Russia* (K–2). 1972, Harcourt $6.95. This folktale, also known as *The Pancake*, tells how a bun outwits many animals, but not the fox!

5584. Carey, Bonnie, trans. *Grasshopper to the Rescue: A Georgian Story* (1–3). Illus. by Lady McCrady. 1979, Morrow $6.95; LB $6.67. An ant falls in the water and the grasshopper sets up a rescue operation in this Russian tale.

5585. Daniels, Guy. *The Peasant's Pea Patch: A Russian Folktale* (K–3). Illus. by Robert Quackenbush. 1971, Delacorte $5.47. Gay, colorful illustrations enhance this humorous tale of a silly peasant's misadventures.

5586. De Regniers, Beatrice S. *Little Sister and the Month Brothers* (K–3). Illus. by Margot Tomes. 1976, Seabury $8.00. In this delightful retelling of an old Slavic tale reminiscent of the Cinderella theme, Little Sister is befriended by the 12 Month brothers when her cruel stepmother sends her out in the snow to gather violets and strawberries.

5587. Domanska, Janina. *The Turnip* (K–2). Illus. by author. 1969, Macmillan $5.95. Russian tale of a turnip that grew so large, it took grandfather, grandmother, grandchild, and various animals to pull it out of the ground.

5588. Eastwick, Ivy O. *Seven Little Popovers* (K–2). Illus. by Gabriel Lisowski. 1979, Follett

$6.95. A poor widow bakes magical popovers in this tale set in old Russia.

5589. Franko, Ivan. *Fox Mykyta* (4–6). Illus. by William Kurelek. 1978, Tundra $12.95. A Ukrainian folktale about a cunning fox.

5590. Galdone, Paul. *A Strange Servant: A Russian Fable* (PS–2). Trans. by Blanch Ross. Illus. by author. 1977, Knopf $6.95; LB $6.99. A folktale about wily Nassir-Yeddin and how he outwits 3 wealthy merchants.

5591. Ginsburg, Mirra, ed. *The Fisherman's Son: Adapted from a Georgian Folktale* (1–3). Illus. by Tony Chen. 1979, Greenwillow $7.95. A fisherman's son wins the hand of his love by avoiding her magical mirror in this Georgian tale.

5592. Ginsburg, Mirra, trans. *The Lazies: Tales of the Peoples of Russia* (3–5). Illus. by Marian Parry. 1973, Macmillan $4.95. How various lazy protagonists—some people, some animals—learn their lesson, is told in 15 delightful tales.

5593. Ginsburg, Mirra. *The Night It Rained Pancakes* (K–2). Illus. by Douglas Florian. 1980, Greenwillow $5.95; LB $5.71. Brother Ivan tries to make his brother look like a fool in order to retain a pot of gold.

5594. Ginsburg, Mirra. *One Trick Too Many: Fox Stories from Russia* (3–5). Illus. by Helen Siegl. 1973, Dial $5.95; LB $5.47. A collection of 9 Russian folktales; in each a cunning fox outwits its enemies.

5595. Ginsburg, Mirra, ed. *Striding Slippers: An Udmurt Tale* (K–3). Illus. by Sal Murdocca. 1978, Macmillan $7.95. A retelling of a Russian morality tale about crime, punishment, and magical slippers.

5596. Ginsburg, Mirra. *The Strongest One of All* (K–3). Illus. by Jose Aruego and Ariane Dewey. 1977, Greenwillow $7.25; LB $6.96. A little lamb sets out to find "the strongest one of all" in this story based on a Caucasian folktale.

5597. Ginsburg, Mirra. *Three Rolls and One Doughnut: Fables from Russia* (3–6). Illus. by Anita Lobel. 1970, Dial $5.47. Collection of fables and riddles from the many and varied cultures of the Soviet Union.

5598. Ginsburg, Mirra. *The Twelve Clever Brothers and Other Fools* (3–5). Illus. by Charles Mikolaycak. 1979, Lippincott $8.95; LB $8.79. Russian tales of absurd, nonsensical situations and characters.

5599. Heller, Linda. *Alexis and the Golden Ring* (1–3). Illus. by author. 1980, Macmillan $8.95. A Russian folktale about a peasant's magical adventures to reach his bride.

5600. Hogrogian, Nonny. *The Contest* (3–5). Illus. by author. 1976, Greenwillow $7.95. Adaptation of the folktale about 2 robbers who discover that they are engaged to the same girl.

5601. Hogrogian, Nonny. *One Fine Day* (K–3). Illus. by author. 1971, Macmillan $7.95; LB $7.63. Based on an Armenian folktale, this cumulative story is ideal for reading aloud. Caldecott winner.

5602. Hogrogian, Nonny. *Rooster Brother* (K–2). Illus. by author. 1974, Macmillan $5.95. A boy outwits 3 robbers in this retelling of an Armenian tale.

5603. Jameson, Cynthia. *Clay Pot Boy: Adapted from a Russian Tale by Cynthia Jameson* (K–2). Illus. by Arnold Lobel. 1973, Coward $4.99; Dell paper $.95. An old man and an old woman who are childless make a clay pot in the shape of a boy, who demands food and becomes so voracious that he eats the old couple and everything in sight.

5604. Jameson, Cynthia. *The House of Five Bears* (1–2). Illus. by Lorinda Bryan Cauley. 1978, Putnam $5.29. A couple move into a house inhabited by bears in this Russian folktale.

5605. Jameson, Cynthia. *Tales from the Steppes* (3–6). Illus. by Christopher J. Spollen. 1975, Coward $5.95. Four trickster tales amusingly told.

5606. McDermott, Beverly Brodsky. *The Crystal Apple: A Russian Tale* (K–3). Illus. by author. 1974, Viking $6.95. A girl loses a magic apple that allows her to see far-off places.

5607. McDermott, Gerald. *The Knight of the Lion* (4–6). Illus. by author. 1979, Four Winds $8.95. The story of the questing of a medieval knight, Yvain.

5608. Onassis, Jacqueline, ed. *The Firebird and Other Russian Fairy Tales* (4–7). Illus. by Boris Zvorykin. 1978, Viking $12.95. A lavishly illustrated edition of these classic fairy tales.

5609. Polushkin, Maria. *Bubba and Babba: Based on a Russian Folktale* (K–3). Illus. by Diane deGroat. 1976, Crown $5.95. Two lazy bears quarrel over who should clean up after dinner.

5610. Pushkin, Alexander. *The Tale of the Golden Cockerel* (3–5). Illus. by J. Bilibin. 1975, Crowell $5.95. In this retelling of an old Russian folktale, Czar Dadon refuses to acknowledge his promise to a sorcerer, with tragic results.

5611. Ransome, Arthur. *The Fool of the World and the Flying Ship* (1–4). Illus. by Uri Shulevitz. 1968, Farrar $7.95. Colorful, panoramic scenes extend this retelling of a popular Russian folktale about a simple peasant boy who acquires a flying ship. Caldecott winner. Also use: *Peter's Russian Tales* (1976, Elsevier/Nelson $5.95).

5612. Reyher, Becky. *My Mother Is the Most Beautiful Woman in the World* (2–5). Illus. by Ruth Gannett. 1945, Lothrop $6.48. A small girl tries to find her mother in this Russian setting.

5613. Riordan, James, ed. *Tales from Central Russia: Russian Tales: Volume One* (5–8). Illus. by Anthony Colbert. 1979, Viking $12.50. A selection from Afanasyev's stories. Also use: *Tales from Tartary: Russian Tales: Volume Two* (1979, Viking $12.50).

5614. Robbins, Ruth. *Baboushka and the Three Kings* (2 up). Illus. by Nicolas Sidjakov. 1960, Parnassus $4.95; LB $4.23. The Russian legend of the old woman who refused to follow the 3 kings in search of the Holy Child. Caldecott Medal 1961.

5615. Small, Ernest. *Baba Yaga* (1–3). Illus. by Blair Lent. 1966, Houghton $7.95. A simplified version of the tale of the evil Russian witch who flies in a mortar and pestle and lives in a hut supported by chicken legs.

5616. Titiev, Estelle, and Pargment, Lila. *How the Moolah Was Taught a Lesson and Other Tales from Russia* (3–5). Illus. by Ray Cruz. 1976, Dial $5.95; LB $5.47. Four stories, each with a simple moral, such as the rewards of being kind to others.

5617. Tresselt, Alvin, ed. *The Mitten* (K–2). Illus. by Yaroslava. 1964, Lothrop $6.95. An old Ukrainian folktale about a little boy and his lost mitten.

5618. Whitney, Thomas P., trans. *In a Certain Kingdom: Twelve Russian Fairy Tales* (3–6). Illus. by Dieter Lange. 1972, Macmillan $5.95. Chosen from the collection of Afanasyev, Russia's "Brothers Grimm."

5619. Wyndham, Lee, ed. *Tales the People Tell in Russia* (3–5). Illus. by Andrew Antal. 1970, Messner $4.64. A collection of folktales, fables, and proverbs retold with force and charm.

5620. Zemach, Harve. *Salt: A Russian Tale* (1–3). Illus. by Margot Zemach. 1965, Follett $7.95. A picture book version of a Russian folktale that tells how Ivan the Fool introduces salt to the King and wins the hand of the princess.

Jewish Folklore

5621. Adler, David A. *The Children of Chelm* (K–3). Illus. by Arthur Friedman. 1980, Bonim $5.95; paper $1.95. Three easy-to-read stories from Jewish folklore.

5622. Aronin, Ben. *The Secret of the Sabbath Fish* (1–3). Illus. by Shay Rieger. 1979, Jewish Pub. Co. $5.95. The preparation of gefilte fish reminds a Jewish woman of the sorrows of her people in this eastern European tale.

5623. Gershator, Phillis. *Honi and His Magic Circle* (K–3). Illus. by Shay Rieger. 1980, Jewish Pub. Soc. $6.95. A Talmudic story about Honi who sowed seeds throughout Israel.

5624. Gross, Michael. *The Fable of the Fig Tree* (K–3). Illus. by Mila Lazarevich. 1975, Walck $6.95. Rooted in Hebrew tradition, this is a story of generosity rewarded and greed punished.

5625. Hirsh, Marilyn. *Could Anything Be Worse? A Yiddish Tale* (K–3). Illus. by author. 1974, Holiday $6.95. A man dissatisfied with all the noise and confusion in his household asks the rabbi for advice, with humorous results.

5626. Hirsh, Marilyn. *The Rabbi and the Twenty-Nine Witches: A Talmudic Legend* (K–3). Illus. by author. 1976, Holiday $6.95; Scholastic paper $1.25. Through the efforts of a wise rabbi, village people are able to rid themselves of 29 witches.

5627. Ish-Kishor, Sulamith. *The Carpet of Solomon: A Hebrew Legend* (4–6). Illus. by Uri Shulevitz. 1966, Pantheon $4.99. A dramatic retelling of the Hebrew legend in which the proud King Solomon learns the wisdom of humility.

5628. Rose, Anne, ed. *The Triumph of Fuzzy Fogtop* (1–3). Illus. by Tomie de Paola. 1979, Dial $8.95; LB $8.44. Three simple, humorous stories set in Eastern Europe derived from Jewish folklore.

5629. Singer, Isaac Bashevis. *Elijah the Slave* (PS–3). Illus. by Antonio Frasconi. 1970, Farrar $6.95. Retelling of a Hebrew legend.

5630. Singer, Isaac Bashevis. *The Fools of Chelm and Their History* (5–6). Illus. by Uri Shulevitz. 1973, Farrar $4.95. Nonsense stories about the village that is the setting of other Singer tales.

5631. Singer, Isaac Bashevis. *Mazel and Shlimazel: Or the Milk of a Lioness* (3–5). Illus. by Margot Zemach. 1967, Farrar $6.95. The fate of a peasant and a princess depend on a battle between good and evil spirits.

5632. Singer, Isaac Bashevis. *Naftali the Storyteller and His Horse, Sus, and Other Stories* (5–8). Illus. by Margot Zemach. 1976, Farar $6.95. Singer's favorite town, Chelm, where fools reign supreme, is the setting for many of these stories.

5633. Singer, Isaac Bashevis. *When Shlemiel Went to Warsaw and Other Stories* (4–7). Illus. by Margot Zemach. 1968, Farrar $7.95; Dell paper $1.25. Illustrations and the 8 stories retold here delightfully reveal the distinctive people of Chelm and their extraordinary, universally exportable wisdom.

5634. Singer, Isaac Bashevis. *Zlateh the Goat and Other Stories* (4–6). Illus. by Maurice Sendak. 1966, Harper $10.00; LB $9.89. Warm, humorous, and ironical stories based on middle European Jewish folklore and on the author's childhood memories.

5635. Soyer, Abraham. *The Adventures of Yemina and Other Stories* (4–8). Illus. by Raphael Soyer. 1979, Viking $8.95. Six stories translated from the Hebrew that reveal the hardness but hope in life.

5636. Zemach, Margot. *It Could Always Be Worse: A Yiddish Folktale* (K–3). Illus. by author. 1976, Farrar $7.95. A Yiddish version of an old tale with colorful, humorous illustrations.

Middle East

5637. Dawood, N. J, adapt. *Tales from the Arabian Nights* (5–8). Adapted from the Arabic. Illus. by Ed Young. 1978, Doubleday $12.95; LB $13.90. Exciting version of these classic tales, several not previously included in anthologies for children.

5638. Green, Roger Lancelyn. *Tales of Ancient Egypt* (6–9). Illus. by Elaine Raphael. 1968, Penguin paper $1.50. Some of the oldest stories known.

5639. Manniche, Lise, trans. *How Djadja-Emankh Saved the Day: A Tale from Ancient Egypt* (4–6). Illus. by author. 1977, Crowell $6.95; deluxe ed. $8.95. An ancient Egyptian fantasy resembling the original in format and paper.

5640. Mehdevi, Anne Sinclair. *Persian Folk and Fairy Tales* (4–6). Illus. by Paul Kennedy. 1965, Knopf $5.99. Eleven tales, told originally by an old woman named Nana Roosie to the nieces and nephews of the author.

5641. Skurzynski, Gloria. *Two Fools and a Faker: Three Lebanese Folktales* (1–3). Illus. by William Papas. 1977, Lothrop $8.25; LB $7.92. Three rollicking stories about buffoonish characters in humorous situations.

5642. Van Woerkom, Dorothy O., ed. *Abu Ali: Three Tales of the Middle East* (2–3). Illus. by Harold Berson. 1976, Macmillan $6.95. Three stories, based on the Turkish Hodja tales, recount the humorous adventures of a wise fool, Abu Ali, and his friends.

5643. Van Woerkom, Dorothy O. *The Friends of Abu Ali* (K–3). Illus. by Harold Berson. 1978, Macmillan $6.95. Subtitle: *Three More Tales of the Middle East.*

5644. Walker, Barbara K. *The Round Sultan and the Straight Answer* (K–3). Illus. by Friso Henstra. 1970, Parents $5.95. "Once there was and twice there wasn't a Turkish sultan who loved to eat"— this folktale is told with gusto and humor, and illustrated in an exaggerated style that suits the subject nicely. Excellent for reading aloud.

5645. Wiggin, Kate Douglas, and Smith, Nora A., eds. *Arabian Nights: Their Best Known Tales* (4–6). Illus. by Maxfield Parrish. 1974, Scribner paper $3.95. A collection of 10 tales first published in 1909 with stylized illustrations.

5646. Wolkstein, Diane. *The Red Lion: A Tale of Ancient Persia* (PS–3). Illus. by Ed Young. 1977, Crowell $7.50; LB $8.39. Azgid must conquer his fears and prove himself a worthy candidate to become king by fighting a lion.

Middle America

Mexico

5647. Aardema, Verna. *The Riddle of the Drum: A Tale from Tizapan, Mexico* (K–3). Illus. by Tony Chen. 1979, Four Winds $7.95. A handsome prince solves a thorny problem to win the hand of a princess.

5648. Titus, Eve. *Why the Wind God Wept* (4–6). Illus. by James Barkley. 1972, Doubleday $5.95. Although others failed, a simple poet uncovers the secret of the Wind God in this Mexican folktale.

Central America

5649. Baker, Betty. *No Help at All* (1–2). Illus. by Emily McCully. 1978, Greenwillow $5.95; LB $5.71. The West Wind of Maya has trouble finding a suitable helper.

5650. Carter, Dorothy Sharp, ed. *The Enchanted Orchard, and Other Folktales of Central America* (5–7). Illus. by W. T. Mars. 1973, Harcourt $5.95. A varied collection of relatively brief tales that include "why" stories and legends of the supernatural.

Puerto Rico and Other Caribbean Islands

5651. Alegria, Ricardo E. *The Three Wishes: A Collection of Puerto Rican Folktales* (4–6). Illus. by Lorenzo Homar. 1969, Harcourt $6.75. Twenty-three tales that reflect the mixing of the island's cultures.

5652. Belpre, Pura. *Once in Puerto Rico* (3–6). Illus. by Christine Price. 1973, Warne $4.95. Sixteen short tales gathered by a master storyteller who was educated in Puerto Rico. Also use: *Dance of the Animals* (1972, Warne $4.95).

5653. Belpre, Pura. *Perez and Martina* (2–3). Illus. by Carlos Sanchez. 1932; 1961 Warne $5.95. A charming Puerto Rican folktale that has been handed down orally. Also use: *Ote: A Puerto Rican Tale* (1969, Pantheon $5.39).

5654. Belpre, Pura. *The Rainbow-Colored Horse* (4–6). Illus. by Antonia Martorell. 1978, Warne $8.95. A favorite story from Puerto Rico about a man who wins a bride with the help of an enchanted horse.

5655. Bryan, Ashley, ed. *The Dancing Granny* (K–3). Illus. by editor. 1977, Atheneum $6.95. Granny Anika, who loves to dance, beats the traditional character, Spider Ananse, pictured in this adaptation as a tall, vigorous man.

5656. Carter, Dorothy Sharp, ed. *Greedy Mariani, and Other Folktales of the Antilles* (4–6). Illus. by Trina Schart Hyman. 1974, Atheneum $5.50. Excellent retelling of several stories.

5657. Chardiet, Bernice. *Juan Bobo and the Pig: A Puerto Rican Folktale Retold* (1–3). Illus. by Hope Meryman. 1973, Walker $5.95; LB $5.85. Juan Bobo plays a trick on the family pig.

5658. Courlander, Harold. *The Piece of Fire and Other Haitian Tales* (4–6). Illus. by Beth Krush and Joe Krush. 1964, Harcourt $4.95. Twenty-six stories—humor, trickster tales, a ghost story, and several tall tales.

5659. Sherlock, Philip M. *Anansi, the Spider Man: Jamaican Folktale* (4–6). Illus. by Marcia Brown. 1954, Crowell $8.95. Tales of a famous Caribbean folk hero. Also use: *West Indian Folk Tales* (1960, Oxford $10.95).

5660. Wolkstein, Diane, comp. *The Magic Orange Tree and Other Haitian Folktales* (5–8). Illus. by Elsa Hanriquez. 1978, Knopf $6.95; LB $6.99. A magical collection of outstanding folktales.

South America

5661. Llerena, Carlos Antonio. *Sticks, Stones* (1–3). 1977, Holt $5.95. A Peruvian tale about a mischievous puma, told with spirit and humor.

5662. Finger, Charles J. *Tales from Silver Lands* (4–6). Illus. by Paul Honore. 1924, Doubleday $7.95. Folklore from South America. Newbery Medal winner 1925.

5663. Jagendorf, M. A., and Boggs, R. S. *The King of the Mountains* (4–6). Illus. by Carybe. 1960, Vanguard $6.95. Favorite tales of Latin American peoples.

5664. Maestro, Giulio, adapt. *The Tortoise's Tug of War* (K–3). Illustrated. 1971, Bradbury $6.95. Based on a South American folktale, this is a variant on the familiar theme of smaller animals tricking larger ones.

North America

Canada

5665. Carlson, Natalie Savage. *The Talking Cat: And Other Stories of French Canada* (4–6). Illus. by Roger Duvoisin. 1952, Harper $7.89. Seven delightful stories from early pioneer life in Quebec.

5666. Coatsworth, Elizabeth. *Pure Magic* (3–6). Illus. by Ingrid Fetz. 1973, Macmillan $4.95. Young Giles has the ability to transform himself into a fox, in this retelling of an old legend now set in French Canada.

Eskimo

5667. Clymer, Theodore. *The Travels of Atunga* (1–3). Illus. by John Schoenherr. 1973, Little $6.95. An Eskimo tale of a young hero's search for food for his tribe.

5668. Gillham, Charles E. *Beyond the Clapping Mountains: Eskimo Stories from Alaska* (4–5). Illus. by Chanimun. 1943, Macmillan $4.95. Thirteen animal folktales that originated with the Eskimos.

5669. Houston, James. *Tikta'liktak: An Eskimo Legend* (4–6). Illus. by author. 1965, Harcourt $6.25. Legend of a young Eskimo hunter who is carried out to sea on a drifting ice floe with only his bow and arrows and a harpoon. Also use from Harcourt: *The White Archer: An Eskimo Legend* (1967, $6.50) and *Akavak: An Eskimo Journey* (1968, $5.95; LB $4.95).

5670. Houston, James. *Kiviok's Magic Journey: An Eskimo Legend* (3–5). Illus. by author. 1973, Atheneum $5.25. A retelling of the ancient legend of a bird girl who renounces her animal form for the love of a man.

Indians of North America

5671. Baylor, Byrd. *And It Is Still That Way: Legends Told by Arizona Indian Children* (2–4). 1976, Scribner $7.95. These legends and folktales were told to the compiler.

5672. Brown, Dee. *Tepee Tales of the American Indian* (6–8). Illus. by Louis Mofsie. 1979, Holt $7.95. A cross section of Indian tales from various tribes and periods.

5673. Bruchac, Joseph. *Stone Giants and Flying Heads: Adventure Stories of the Iroquois* (3–6). Illustrated. 1979, Crossing Press $6.95; paper $3.95. Eight selections in prose and free verse that serve as a companion to *Turkey Brothers and Other Tales* (1975, $6.95; paper $3.95).

5674. Compton, Margaret. *American Indian Fairy Tales* (4–6). Illus. by Lorence Bjorklund. 1971, Dodd $4.50. Authentic legends told by Pacific Coast, Midwest, and New England tribesmen.

5675. Courlander, Joseph. *People of the Short Blue Corn: Tales and Legends of the Hopi Indians* (5–7). Illus. by Enrico Arno. 1970, Harcourt $6.95. Seventeen legends that explore various facets, including the hardships of desert life with the Hopi Indians.

5676. Crompton, Anne Eliot. *The Winter Wife: An Abenaki Folktale* (2–4). Illus. by Robert Andrew Parker. 1975, Little $6.95. An Indian trapper gains a companion for the winter when a strange, quiet woman appears at his wigwam.

5677. Curtis, Edward. *The Girl Who Married a Ghost and Other Tales from the North American Indian* (6–8). Illustrated. 1977, Four Winds $9.95. Mature retellings of 9 tales that do not avoid the ghoulish or stark elements of the texts.

5678. DeWit, Dorothy, ed. *The Talking Stone* (6–8). 1979, Greenwillow $8.95; LB $8.59. Subtitle: *An Anthology of Native American Tales and Legends.*

5679. Erdoes, Richard. *The Sound of Flutes and Other Indian Legends* (5–7). Illus. by Paul Goble. 1976, Pantheon $6.99. A collection of tales, some based on fact, gathered from the Plains Indians.

5680. Gustafson, Anita, retel. *Monster Rolling Skull and Other Native American Tales* (3–8). Illus. by John Stadler. 1980, Crowell $6.95; LB $6.89. Coyote is both narrator and character in these nine American Indian folktales.

5681. Harris, Christie. *Mouse Woman and the Muddleheads* (4–6). Illus. by Douglas Tait. 1979, Atheneum $7.95. Another collection of seven tales of the tiny creatures that live in the Northwest wilderness.

5682. Harris, Christie. *Mouse Woman and the Mischief-Makers* (4–6). Illus. by Douglas Tait. 1977, Atheneum $7.95. Seven titles about this grandmotherly spirit who always tries to set things straight.

5683. Harris, Christie. *Mouse Woman and the Vanished Princesses* (4–6). Illus. by Douglas Tait. 1976, Atheneum $6.95. Six legends from the Indians of the Northwest about the rescue of princesses by a small supernatural creature who often assumes the shape of a mouse.

5684. Harris, Christie. *Once More upon a Totem* (4–7). Illus. by Douglas Tait. 1973, Atheneum $5.95. West Coast Indian legends retold with excitement and a sense of wonder.

5685. Highwater, Jamake. *Anpao: An American Indian Odyssey* (5–8). Illus. by Fritz Scholder. 1977, Lippincott $8.95. A young hero encounters great danger on his way to meet his father, the Sun, in this dramatic American Indian folktale.

5686. Hillerman, Tony, ed. *The Boy Who Made Dragonfly: A Zuni Myth* (5–7). Illus. by Laszlo Kubinyi. 1972, Harper $5.79. A Zuni boy and his little sister are left behind by their tribe and survive hunger and deprivation through the intervention of the Cornstalk Being.

5687. Hodges, Margaret, ed. *The Fire Bringer: A Paiute Indian Legend* (3–5). Illus. by Peter Parnall. 1972, Little $6.95. The coyote helps a Paiute boy withstand the cold of winter by stealing a brand from the Fire Spirits.

5688. Houston, James. *Ghost Paddle: A Northwest Coast Indian Tale* (4–6). Illus. by author. 1972, Harcourt $5.50. A young prince, tired of war, aids his father in attempts to bring peace to his tribe.

5689. Jones, Hettie. *Longhouse Winter: Iroquois Transformation Tales* (3–7). Illus. by Nicholas Gaetano. 1972, Holt $5.95. Four tales of magic and imagination in which humans are transformed into various animal forms as punishment or reward. Also use: *Coyote Tales* (1974, Holt $4.95).

5690. Martin, Frances Gardiner. *Raven-Who-Sets-Things-Right: Indian Tales of the Northwest Coast* (5–7). Illus. by Dorothy McEntee. 1975, Harper $5.50; LB $6.89. Nine tales retold with handsome illustrations and preparatory material on the origin of each story.

5691. Mobley, Jane. *The Star Husband* (5–7). Illus. by Anna Vojtech. 1979, Doubleday $6.95; LB $7.90. An Indian legend of a girl who leaves earth to fulfill a desire for a star husband.

5692. Parker, Arthur C. *Skunny Wundy: Seneca Indian Tales* (4–6). Illus. by George Armstrong. 1970, Whitman $5.95. Skunny Wundy tricks Fox into telling a series of animal stories, many of them "why" tales. This collection, written by the grandson of a Seneca chief, first appeared in 1926.

5693. Pugh, Ellen. *The Adventures of Yoo-Lah-Teen: A Legend of the Salish Coastal Indians* (4–6). Illus. by Laszlo Kubinyi. 1975, Dial $6.95; LB $6.46. A legendary hero outwits a child-eating witch and her ogre lover.

5694. Sleator, William. *The Angry Moon* (K–3). Illus. by Blair Lent. 1970, Little $6.95. Tlingit Indian legend in which a little boy, with the aid of his grandmother's magic, rescues a girl held captive by the angry moon.

5695. San Souci, Robert. *The Legend of Scarface: A Blackfeet Indian Tale* (2–4). Illus. by Daniel San Souci. 1978, Doubleday $7.95. A young brave travels to the land of the Sun to seek permission to marry the maiden he loves.

5696. Toye, William. *The Fire Stealer* (1–3). Illus. by Elizabeth Cleaver. 1980, Oxford $6.95. An Ojibwa legend of how Nanabozho brought fire to his people.

5697. Toye, William. *The Loon's Necklace* (K–3). Illus. by Elizabeth Cleaver. 1977, Oxford $5.95. In this familiar Indian legend, an old man rewards a loon with a necklace for helping him regain his sight. Also use: *How Summer Came to Canada* (1969, Oxford, paper $4.95).

5698. Yellow Robe, Rosebud. *Tonweya and the Eagles and Other Lakota Indian Tales* (4–7). Illus. by Jerry Pinkney. 1979, Dial $7.95; LB $7.45. A famous storyteller recalls stories she heard from her father.

United States

5699. Anderson, Jean. *The Haunting of America: Ghost Stories from Our Past* (6–7). Illus. by Eric von Schmidt. 1973, Houghton $6.95. All sorts of supernatural beings are recalled in these exciting folktales.

5700. Bang, Molly. *Wiley and the Hairy Man* (2–4). Adapted from an American folktale. 1976, Macmillan $7.95. In this story from Alabama, Wiley's mother helps him outwit the Hairy Man, a terrible swamp creature.

5701. Barth, Edna. *Jack-O-Lantern* (3–5). Illus. by Paul Galdone. 1974, Seabury $6.95. A retelling of the old legend about Mean Jack and what happens when he is refused admittance to both heaven and hell.

5702. Blassingame, Wyatt. *Pecos Bill and the Wonderful Clothesline Snake* (1–3). Illus. by Herman Vestal. 1978, Garrard $4.20. Make-believe snakes are introduced by the legendary cowboy.

5703. Calhoun, Mary. *Old Man Whickutt's Donkey* (K–3). Illus. by Tomie de Paola. 1975, Parents $5.95; LB $5.41. La Fontaine's fable is retold in the language and setting of an American rural mountain folktale.

5704. Chase, Richard. *Grandfather Tales* (4–6). Illus. by Berkeley Williams. 1948, Houghton $8.95. Folktales gathered from the South. Also use: *The Jack Tales* (1943, Houghton $7.95).

5705. Credle, Ellis. *Tall Tales from the High Hills* (5–7). Illus. by R. Bennett. 1957, Nelson $6.95. Twenty folktales from the Blue Ridge Mountains reflect the tall tale and witty quality of American folklore.

5706. Crompton, Anne Eliot. *The Lifting Stone* (1–3). 1978, Holiday $6.95. Mandy Jane will marry whoever can lift a massive stone.

5707. Davis, Hubert, ed. *A January Fog Will Freeze a Hog and Other Weather Folklore* (2–4). Illus. by John Wallner. 1977, Crown $6.95. Weather sayings that are part of the folklore of the United States, handsomely illustrated with stylized drawings. A fascinating book.

5708. Faulkner, William J. *The Days When the Animals Talked: Black American Folktales and How They Came to Be* (4–7). Illus. by Troy Howell. 1977, Follett $7.95; LB $7.98. Excellent folktales that deal either with the life of southern black slaves or the exploits of Brer Rabbit.

5709. Felton, Harold W. *John Henry and His Hammer* (5–7). Illus. by Aldren A. Watson. 1950, Knopf $5.99. A spirited retelling of tales about

John Henry, his hammer that helped build a railroad, and his eventual fatal duel with a steam drill.

5710. Galdone, Joanna. *Amber Day: A Very Tall Tale* (K–3). Illus. by Paul Galdone. 1978, McGraw $7.95. A husband and wife are changed into half-human/half-mules because of their quarreling.

5711. Galdone, Joanna. *The Tailypo: A Ghost Story* (1–3). Illus. by Paul Galdone. 1977, Seabury $7.50. In this ghostly story, a mysterious creature returns to retrieve his tail, cut off by an old man.

5712. Harris, Joel Chandler. *Brer Rabbit* (3–5). Ed. by Margaret Wise Brown. Illustrated. 1941, Harper $6.89. A retelling and simplifying of 23 of Uncle Remus's most famous stories.

5713. Haviland, Virginia, ed. *North American Legends* (4–6). Illus. by Ann Strugnell. 1979, Collins $7.95. A rich collection representing Indian, black, immigrant, and tall tales.

5714. Jagendorf, M. A. *Folk Stories of the South* (4–7). Illus. by Michael Parks. 1973, Vanguard $6.95. A satisfying collection of folklore—including tall tales, Indian legends, and old ghost stories—arranged by states. Also use: *New England Bean Pot* (1948, Vanguard $6.95).

5715. Jagendorf, M. A. *The Ghost of Peg-Leg Peter and Other Stories of Old New York* (4–6). Illus. by Lino Lipinsky. 1965, Vanguard $6.95. A wonderful collection of stories, some dating back to the original Dutch settlers.

5716. Keats, Ezra Jack. *John Henry: An American Legend* (1–3). Illus. by author. 1965, Pantheon $5.39. Large, bold figures capture the spirit of the hero who was born with a hammer in his hand.

5717. Lent, Blair. *John Tabor's Ride* (1–3). Illus. by author. 1966, Little $6.95. A tall tale based on a New England legend in which a shipwrecked old man is given a wild ride home on the back of a whale.

5718. Lester, Julius. *The Knee-High Man and Other Tales* (K–2). Illus. by Ralph Pinto. 1972, Dial $5.95; LB $5.47. Six black American folktales concerned with animals make this an appealing selection for reading aloud or storytelling to younger readers.

5719. McCormick, Dell J. *Paul Bunyan Swings His Axe* (4–6). Illus. by author. 1936, Caxton $4.95. The stories of the giant woodsman and his great blue ox named Babe are favorites among American folktales.

5720. Maher, Ramona. *When Windwagon Smith Came to Westport* (3–5). Illus. by Tom Allen. 1977, Coward $5.95. A tall tale about a wagon propelled by sails and its owner's plan to build a fleet of them.

5721. Maitland, Antony. *Idle Jack* (1–3). Illus. by author. 1979, Farrar $8.95. A ne'er-do-well finds unexpected fame in this old folktale.

5722. Malcolmson, Anne. *Yankee Doodle's Cousins* (5–9). Illus. by Robert McCloskey. 1941, Houghton $7.95. Thirty heroes of American folklore.

5723. Peck, Leigh. *Pecos Bill and Lightning* (4–6). Illus. by Kurt Wiese. 1940, Houghton $6.95. A collection of tall tales about the deeds of the legendary hero.

5724. Roberts, Nancy. *Appalachian Ghosts* (5–7). Illustrated. 1978, Doubleday $6.90. Twelve tales, mostly quite brief, evoke the atmosphere of the Appalachian region.

5725. Rounds, Glen. *Mr. Yowder and the Steamboat* (3–6). Illus. by author. 1977, Holiday $5.95. A tall tale that involves the winning of an ocean liner at cards and the subsequent adventures trying to dock it. Also use: *Mr. Yowder and the Lion Roar Capsules* (1976, $4.95).

5726. Rounds, Glen. *Ol' Paul, the Mighty Logger* (3–6). Illus. by author. 1936, Holiday $6.95. Subtitled: *A True Account of the Seemingly Incredible Exploits and Inventions of the Great Paul Bunyan, Properly Illustrated by Drawings Made at the Scene by the Author.*

5727. Sawyer, Ruth. *Journey Cake, Ho!* (K–3). Illus. by Robert McCloskey. 1953, Viking $5.95; Penguin paper $1.95. Retelling of the old folktale of Johnny and his chase after a journey cake that rolls away singing a taunting verse.

5728. Schwartz, Alvin, ed. *Kickle Snifters and Other Fearsome Critters Collected from American Folklore* (3–5). Illus. by Glen Rounds. 1976, Lippincott $7.95. Bantam paper $1.25. A dictionary of beasts found chiefly in American tall tales with descriptions and amusing illustrations.

5729. Schwartz, Alvin, ed. *Whoppers: Tall Tales and Other Lies Collected from American Folklore* (3–5). 1975, Lippincott $7.95; paper $2.95. A collection of long and short humorous tales from a number of sources.

5730. Shapiro, Irwin. *Heroes in American Folklore* (4–7). Illus. by Donald McKay and James Daugherty. 1962, Messner $6.29. Tales of 5 heroes of American folklore have been collected in this book that has a special appeal for young people.

5731. Shapiro, Irwin. *Joe Magarac and His U.S.A. Citizen Papers* (4–6). Illus. by James Daugherty. 1979, Univ. of Pittsburgh paper $2.50. A tall tale in which a steel giant gets his U.S. citizenship.

5732. Shephard, Esther. *Paul Bunyan* (5–7). Illus. by Rockwell Kent. 1941, Harcourt $6.50. Classic legends about the gigantic lumberman.

5733. Still, James. *Jack and the Wonder Beans* (K–3). Illus. by Margot Tomes. 1977, Putnam $6.95. The beanstalk story in different form and set in Appalachia.

5734. Wolkstein, Diane. *The Cool Ride in the Sky* (K–2). Illus. by Paul Galdone. 1973, Knopf $5.69. A vulture meets his match in a clever monkey.

History and Geography

General

5735. Foster, Genevieve. *Birthdays of Freedom: From Early Egypt to July 4, 1776* (6–9). Illus. by author. 1974, Scribner $6.95. Great historical events from prehistoric times to July 4, 1776.

5736. Fox, Lilla Margaret. *Folk Costume of Eastern Europe* (5–8). Illus. by author. 1977, Plays $4.95. Excellent illustrations highlight this overview. Also use from Plays ($4.95): *Folk Costume of Western Europe* (1971) and *Folk Costume of Southern Europe* (1973).

5737. Morgan, Edmund S. *So What about History?* (4–6). 1969, Atheneum $5.95. A fine introduction with emphasis on the historical method and the significance of history in our lives.

5738. Ogilvie, Bruce, and Waitley, Douglas. *Picture Atlas of the World* (3–5). 1979, Rand $7.95; LB $7.97. A useful atlas that contains comprehensive textual material as well as excellent maps.

5739. Van Loon, Hendrik W. *The Story of Mankind* (6–9). 1972, W. S. P. paper $1.45. This famous history of the development of civilization won the first Newbery Medal in 1922.

5740. Windrow, Martin. *The Invaders* (5–7). Illustrated. 1980, Arco $6.95. Accounts of major attacks and battles in European history.

Maps and Mapmaking

5741. Brown, Lloyd. *Map Making: The Art That Became a Science* (5–7). Illustrated. 1960, Little $6.95. The history of map making from early times to the present, including an explanation of the methods and instruments used by the cartographer. Also use: *Maps Mean Adventure* by Christie McFall (1973, Dodd $5.95).

5742. Cartwright, Sally. *What's in a Map?* (K–2). Illus. by Dick Gackenbach. 1976, Coward $5.92. An excellent book for beginning map work with young children, written by a science teacher.

5743. Epstein, Sam, and Epstein, Beryl. *The First Book of Maps and Globes* (4–6). Illustrated. 1959, Watts $4.90. An easily read survey of various kinds of maps and how to read them.

5744. Freeman, Dorothy R. *How to Read a Highway Map* (1–4). Illus. by Harry Garo. 1970, Grove $7.35. An easy introduction to all facets of reading highway maps, including their various symbols.

5745. Madden, James F. *The Wonderful World of Maps* (3–5). Illustrated. 1977, Hammond $3.95. An atlas plus an introductory section on how to read maps.

5746. Oliver, John E. *What We Find When We Look at Maps* (2–4). Illus. by Robert Galster. 1970, McGraw $6.95. An introductory survey of the purposes and uses of maps, as well as a clear explanation of their parts, such as grids, scale markings, standard symbols.

5747. Tannenbaum, Beulah, and Stillman, Myra. *Understanding Maps: Charting the Land, Sea, and Sky* (6–8). Illus. by Adolph E. Brotman. 1969, McGraw $5.72. An introduction to cartography, its history and uses.

Paleontology

5748. Aliki. *Fossils Tell of Long Ago* (2–3). Illus. by author. 1972, Crowell $6.89. A good introduction to fossils, how they are formed, what they can reveal about the past, and where they might be found, written simply enough for the beginning reader.

5749. Aliki. *My Visit to the Dinosaurs* (2–3). Illus. by author. 1969, Crowell $6.95; LB $6.89; paper $1.45. A beginning science book that serves as an introduction to the subject. Also use: *The Dinosaur Story* by Joanna Cole (1976, Morrow $5.52; Scholastic, paper 95¢).

5750. Aliki. *Wild and Woolly Mammoths* (2–3). Illus. by author. 1977, Crowell $6.89. A clear, succinct text describes the woolly mammoth's structure, habits, and the way in which it was hunted by early peoples.

5751. Ames, Gerald, and Wyler, Rose. *The Story of the Ice Age* (5–8). Illus. by Thomas W. Voter. 1956, Harper $6.89. An introduction to this fascinating geological period told in text and pictures.

5752. Andrews, Roy Chapman. *All about Strange Beasts of the Past* (4–6). Illustrated. 1956, Random $4.39. A description of many unusual beasts chiefly from the Ice Age. Also use: *In the Days of the Dinosaur* (1959, Random $3.50; LB $4.69).

5753. Bloch, Marie. *Dinosaurs* (4–6). Illustrated. 1955, Coward $4.89. A fine introduction to these prehistoric animals and why they disappeared.

5754. Carrick, Carol. *The Crocodiles Still Wait* (2–4). Illus. by Donald Carrick. 1980, Houghton $8.95. A prehistoric giant crocodile and her life in a swamp.

5755. Clark, Mary Lou. *The True Book of Dinosaurs* (2–4). Illus. by Chauncy Maltman. 1955, Childrens Press $7.95. An elementary view of the appearance and living habits of dinosaurs.

5756. Cohen, Daniel. *What Really Happened to the Dinosaurs?* (4–6). Illus. by Haru Wells. 1977, Dutton $7.50. Founded on solid research, this is a readable account of why the dinosaurs became extinct.

5757. Cole, Joanna. *Saber-Toothed Tiger and Other Ice Age Mammals* (2–4). Illustrated. 1977, Morrow $7.25; LB $6.96. A description in words and pictures of the giant mammals that roamed the earth during the Ice Age.

5758. Cosgrove, Margaret. *Plants in Time: Their History and Mystery* (4–6). Illus. by author. 1967, Dodd $4.50. A presentation of the process of plant evolution as revealed by fossils.

5759. Darling, Lois, and Darling, Louis. *Before and After Dinosaurs* (5–7). Illustrated. 1959, Morrow $5.52. Pictures and text trace the evolution of vertebrates.

5760. Dickinson, Alice. *The First Book of Prehistoric Animals* (4–6). 1954, Watts $4.90. A valuable introduction that supplies basic information.

5761. Ensign, Georgianne. *The Hunt for the Mastodon* (5–8). Illustrated. 1971, Watts $4.90. An account of the 1962 discovery of mastodon teeth by 2 schoolboys in New Jersey and the scientific work by paleontologists that followed.

5762. Greene, Carla. *Before the Dinosaurs* (5–7). 1970, Bobbs-Merrill $4.95. A clear reconstruction through fossils of early life on the North American continent.

5763. Halstead, Beverly. *A Closer Look at Prehistoric Reptiles* (3–6). Illustrated. 1978, Glouster $5.90. A well-designed, readable account that gives a concise introduction to the subject.

5764. Halstead, L. B. *The Evolution and Ecology of the Dinosaurs* (6–8). Illus. by Giovanni Caselli. 1978, Peter Lowe $7.95. Various species are described according to the time period in which they lived.

5765. Hussey, Lois J, and Pessino, Catherine. *Collecting Small Fossils* (3–6). Illus. by Anne Marie Jauss. 1971, Crowell $6.95. A brief do-it-yourself manual on collecting and organizing fossils, with data on their formation. Also use: *The Fossil Book* by Carroll Lane Fenton (1959, Doubleday $19.95).

5766. Kaufmann, John. *Flying Reptiles in the Age of Dinosaurs* (4–6). 1976, Morrow $5.25; LB $5.04. A fascinating account of the tremendous variety of flying reptiles that lived more than 100 million years ago.

5767. Kaufmann, John. *Little Dinosaurs and Early Birds* (K–2). Illus. by author. 1977, Crowell $6.89. In simple text and accurate drawings, the author explores the evolution of the earliest birds from prehistoric reptiles. Also use: *Dinosaur Time* by Peggy Parish (1974, Harper $5.95).

5768. Lambert, David. *The Age of Dinosaurs* (4–6). Illustrated. 1978, Warwick $2.95. A good introduction to prehistoric animals.

5769. McGowen, Tom. *Album of Dinosaurs* (3–5). Illus. by Rod Ruth. 1972, Rand $5.95; LB $5.75. Twelve genus of dinosaurs are highlighted in illustrations and text.

5770. McGowen, Tom. *Dinosaurs and Other Prehistoric Animals* (4–6). Illus. by Rod Ruth. 1978, Rand $6.95. A combination of the previously published *Album of Dinosaurs* and *Album of Prehistoric Animals*.

5771. May, Julian. *Dodos and Dinosaurs Are Extinct* (5–7). Illustrated. 1970, Creative Education $6.95. In an interesting format, the author discusses the concept of extinction through the case studies of dinosaurs and dodo birds.

5772. Ostrom, John H. *The Strange World of Dinosaurs* (5–8). Illus. by Joseph Sibal. 1964, Putnam $6.69. Dinosaur hunting and descriptions of the families and species of dinosaurs.

5773. Pluckrose, Henry. *Dinosaurs* (2–4). Illus. by Richard Orr and Stephen Bennett. 1979, Watts $2.95; LB $4.90. Habits, behavior, and reasons for extinction are covered in this simple introductory account of dinosaurs.

5774. Pringle, Laurence. *Dinosaurs and People: Fossils, Facts and Fantasies* (4–7). Illustrated. 1978, Harcourt $6.95. The work and finding of paleontologists is reviewed. Also use: *Dinosaurs and Their World* (1976, Harcourt $4.95).

5775. Rhodes, Frank H. T. *Fossils: A Guide to Prehistoric Life* (6–9). Illus. by Raymond Perlman. 1962, Western $9.15; paper $1.95. A survey of ancient life and fossil formation, as well as information on fossil collections. Also use: *From Bones to Bodies: A Story of Paleontology* by William Fox (1959, Walck $5.95).

5776. Ricciuti, Edward R. *Older than the Dinosaurs: The Origin and Rise of the Mammals* (6–8). Illus. by Edward Malsberg. 1980, Crowell $7.95; LB $7.89. An account of the early days of mammals that draws parallels between extinction then and problems of animal survival today.

5777. Scheele, William E. *The First Mammals* (4–6). Illustrated. 1955, World $6.91. An introduction to the ancestors of many present-day mammals.

5778. Selsam, Millicent E. *Sea Monsters of Long Ago* (2–4). Illus. by John Hamberger. 1978, Four Winds $5.95; paper $1.50. Many strange animals that lived during the age of dinosaurs are presented.

5779. Selsam, Millicent E. *Tyrannosaurus Rex* (3–5). Illustrated. 1978, Harper $5.95. A review of our knowledge of this huge meat-eating dinosaur and how we have been able to gather this information.

5780. Shuttlesworth, Dorothy E. *To Find a Dinosaur* (4–7). Illustrated. 1973, Doubleday $5.95. Describes the search for fossils and what happens when they are found. Also use: *Dodos and Dinosaurs* (1968, Hastings $3.99).

5781. Whitaker, George O., and Meyers, Joan. *Dinosaur Hunt* (5–8). 1965, Harcourt $5.95. Account of scientists from the American Museum of Natural History who spent a field season in 1947 collecting animal fossil remains in New Mexico.

5782. Wise, William. *Monsters of the Ancient Seas* (4–7). 1968, Putnam $4.49. An early history of the seas and the denizens that inhabited them.

5783. Zallinger, Peter. *Dinosaurs* (2–4). Illustrated. 1977, Random $3.99; paper $.95. About 25 types of dinosaurs are pictured in words and pictures.

5784. Zim, Herbert S. *Dinosaurs* (4–7). Illus. by James G. Irving. 1954, Morrow $5.09. A basic introduction to these prehistoric animals. Also use: *All about Dinosaurs* by Roy Chapman Andrew (1953, Random $3.50; LB $4.99).

Anthropology

5785. Asimov, Isaac. *How Did We Find Out about Our Human Roots?* (5–8). Illus. by David Wool. 1979, Walker $6.95. An overview of human evolution in theory and fossil finds.

5786. Baity, Elizabeth Chesley. *Americans before Columbus* (6–9). Illus. by C. B. Falls. 1951, Viking $7.95. The civilizations of inhabitants of the North American continent from the last Ice Age to Columbus. Also use: *Man Comes to America* by Harold Coy (1973, Little $7.95).

5787. Baumann, Hans. *The Caves of the Great Hunters* (5–8). Illustrated. 1954, Pantheon $6.69. A true story of the discovery of an Ice Age cave by 4 boys and their dog. Illustrated with photographs of prehistoric art. For a younger group, use: *Lets Find Out about Cavemen* by Martha Shapp and Charles Shapp (1972, Watts $4.47).

5788. Chapham, Frances M. *Our Human Ancestors* (6–8). Illustrated. 1977, Watts $6.90; Warwick $5.95. An overview of humankind from hunter to urban dweller.

5789. Goode, Ruth. *People of the Ice Age* (5–7). Illus. by David Palladini. 1973, Macmillan $5.95. A discussion of the first people and their evolution into farmers.

5790. Edel, May. *The Story of People: Anthropology for Young People* (6–8). Illus. by Herbert Danska. 1953, Little $5.95. An interesting introduction to this science. Also use: *The Adventure of Man* by Arthur Gregor (1966, Macmillan $4.94).

5791. Freed, Stanley A., and Freed, Ruth. *Man from the Beginning* (4–6). Illustrated. 1967, Creative Education $6.95. The story of how humans and society have developed.

5792. Gregor, Arthur S. *Life Styles: An Introduction to Cultural Anthropology.* (6–9). 1978, Scribner $9.95. An introductory account to such topics as family structures, mores, and religion.

5793. McGowen, Tom. *Album of Prehistoric Man* (4–6). Illustrated. 1975, Rand $5.95. An introduction to human progress from the cave to the first civilizations.

5794. May, Julian. *Before the Indians* (2–4). Illus. by Symeon Shimin. 1969, Holiday $6.95. Simple introduction to the culture of the prehistoric American Paleo-Indian.

5795. Maynard, Christopher. *Prehistoric Life* (4–6). Illustrated. 1976, Watts $3.95; LB $5.90. An overview that details the speculations concerning the beginning of life and the emergence of humans.

5796. Marcus, Rebecca B. *Survivors of the Stone Age* (5–7). Illustrated. 1975, Hastings $6.95. A description of 9 primitive tribes in the world today.

5797. Reynolds, Peter John. *Life in the Iron Age* (6–9). Illustrated. 1979, Lerner $4.95. A recreation of life as it was experienced during the Iron Age.

5798. Walsh, Jill Paton. *The Island Sunrise: Prehistoric Cultures in the British Isles* (6–9). 1976, Seabury $8.95. The beginning volume in a series that will explore the entire spectrum of British history.

5799. Weisgard, Leonard. *The First Farmers in the New Stone Age* (4–7). Illus. by author. 1966, Coward $5.49. Clear explanation of life in the Neolithic Age, based on archaeological studies, stressing the influence of human discovery of agriculture upon primitive society development; includes glossary and reading list.

5800. White, Anne Terry. *Prehistoric America* (5–7). Illus. by Aldren Watson. 1951, Random $4.99. The story of America before the Indians.

5801. Wood, Bernard. *The Evolution of Early Man* (6–8). Illus. by Giovani Caselli. 1978, Two Continents $8.95. An overview of the early history of humans as discovered by paleontologists.

Archaeology

5802. Aylesworth, Thomas G. *Mysteries from the Past* (6–8). Illustrated. 1971, Nat. Hist. Press $4.95. Unraveling such mysteries as those of Atlantis and Easter Island, subtitled *Stories of Scientific Detections from Nature and Science.*

5803. Freeman, Mae Bleeker. *Finding Out About the Past* (3–5). Illustrated. 1967, Random $2.95; LB $4.39. The work of the archaeologist is viewed through such explorations as those in Pompeii and Machu Picchu. Also use: *The First Book of Archeology* by Nora B. Kubie (1957, Watts $4.90).

5804. Gemming, Elizabeth. *Lost City in the Clouds: The Discovery of Machu Picchu* (4–6). Illus. by Mike Eagle. 1980, Coward $5.99. A vivid and exciting account of this spectacular discovery and of background information of the Incan civilization.

5805. Glubok, Shirley. *Art and Archeology* (5–7). Illus. by Gerard Nook. 1966, Harper $6.95; LB $6.79. A very brief discussion of the who and what in archaeology, with photographs of sites throughout the world.

5806. Hall, Jennie. *Buried Cities* (5–7). Illustrated. 1964, Macmillan $4.95. Daily life in 4 buried cities—Pompeii, Herculaneum, Olympia, and Mycenae—is depicted using photographs.

5807. Harker, Ronald. *Digging Up the Bible Lands* (6–9). Illus. by Martin Simmons. 1973, Walck $9.59. Extensive treatment of the archaeology of the Holy Lands, well illustrated and clearly written.

5808. Kirk, Ruth, and Daugherty, Richard. *Hunters of the Whale: An Adventure in Northwest Coast Archeology* (6–9). Illustrated. 1974, Morrow $6.95; LB $5.94. An account of excavating an Indian site in the Pacific Coast region, with incidental information of anthropologists and their concerns.

5809. LeSueur, Meridel. *The Mound Builders* (4–7). 1974, Watts $4.90. The life of the Hopewell Indians.

5810. Magnusson, Magnus. *Introducing Archaeology* (6–9). Illus. by Martin Simmons. 1973, Walck $9.95; paper $4.95. An excellent overview, well organized, lucidly written, and handsomely illustrated.

5811. Porell, Bruce. *Digging the Past: Archaeology in Your Own Backyard* (5–7). Illustrated. 1979, Addison $8.95; paper $5.95. A sound introduction to the science of archaeology and the methods of investigation it employs.

5812. Steele, William O. *Talking Bones: Secrets of Indian Burial Mounds* (4–6). Illustrated. 1978, Harper $6.95. An introduction to the findings that archaeologists have made by studying prehistoric burial grounds.

Ancient History

General

5813. Gregor, Arthur S. *How the World's Cities Began* (6–8). 1967, Dutton $6.50. A history of the beginnings of cities in ancient history.

5814. Unstead, R. J. *Looking at Ancient History* (5–8). Illustrated. 1966, Macmillan $8.95. A well-illustrated overview of the ancient world and history.

Egypt and Mesopotamia

5815. Asimov, Isaac. *The Egyptians* (6–9). Illustrated. 1967, Houghton $9.95. The history of ancient Egypt from its rise to greatness to its downfall.

5816. Asimov, Isaac. *The Near East 10,000 Years of History* (6–9). Illustrated. 1968, Houghton $4.95. A well-organized, brief history of the Fertile Crescent from ancient times to the present. Also use: *Tents to City Sidewalks* by Doreen Ingrams (1974, EMC $4.95; paper $2.95).

5817. Aliki. *Mummies Made in Egypt* (3–5). Illus. by author. 1979, Crowell $8.95; LB $8.89. The burial practices and beliefs of the ancient Egyptians are explored in text and handsome illustrations.

5818. Baumann, Hans. *In the Land of Ur: The Discovery of Ancient Mesopotamia* (6–8). Illustrated. 1969, Pantheon $6.39. Through archaeological finds, the author reconstructs the history of the land between the Tigris and Euphrates. Also use: *They Lived Like This In Ancient Mesopotomia* by Marie Neurath (1965, Watts $3.90).

5819. Boase, Wendy. *Ancient Egypt* (4–8). Illustrated. 1978, Watts $5.90. An introductory overview that concentrates on history.

5820. Cottrell, Leonard. *Land of the Pharoahs* (6–8). Illus. by Richard M. Powers. 1960, World $6.91. A fascinating study of this important period in Egyptian history, with concentration on Tutankhamen's reign. Also use: *The Pharoahs of Ancient Egypt* by Elizabeth Payne (1964, Random $4.99).

5821. Glubok, Shirley. *Discovering Tut-Ankhamen's Tomb* (5–8). Illustrated. 1968, Macmillan $12.95; paper $5.95. A fascinating account of the unearthing of the rich treasures of a pharoah's tomb.

5822. Glubok, Shirley, and Tamarin, Alfred. *The Mummy of Ramose: The Life and Death of an Ancient Egyptian Nobleman* (6–9). 1978, Harper $6.95; LB $6.79. Funeral practices in ancient Egypt are highlighted in this thorough and fascinating book.

5823. James, T. G. H. *The Archaeology of Ancient Egypt* (6–9). Illus. by Rosemonde Nairae. 1973, Walck $9.95. Excellent format and organization characterize this well-balanced account. Also use: *Builder on the Desert* by Janet Van Duyn (1974, Messner $6.64).

5824. Millard, Anne. *Ancient Egypt* (5–7). Illustrated. 1979, Warwick $6.90. An overview of how people lived in Ancient Egypt.

5825. Pace, Mildred. *Wrapped for Eternity: The Story of the Egyptian Mummies* (6–9). Illustrated. 1974, McGraw $6.95. Not only coverage on various aspects of mummification as practiced by the ancient Egyptians, but also material on their religion, tombs, and burial practices.

5826. Paterson, James Hamilton. *Mummies: Death and Life in Ancient Egypt* (7–9). Illustrated. 1979, Viking $9.95. The process of mummification and the beliefs of the ancient Egyptians that produced this practice.

5827. Robinson, Charles A., Jr. *The First Book of Ancient Egypt* (5–7). Illustrated. 1961, Watts $4.90. A brief outline of Egyptian history to its fall in 1085 B.C.

5828. Swinburne, Irene, and Swinburne, Laurence. *Behind the Sealed Door: The Discovery of the Tomb and Treasure of Tutankhamen* (6–9). Illustrated. 1977, Sniffen Court $12.95. Published in cooperation with the Metropolitan Museum of Art, this beautifully designed book tells the history and discovery of Tutankhamen's tomb.

5829. White, Jon Manchip. *Everyday Life in Ancient Egypt* (6–9). Illus. by Helen Nixon Fairfield. 1964, Putnam $6.00. An account of the day-to-day life and activities of the various strata of ancient Egyptian society.

Greece

5830. Connolly, Peter. *The Greek Armies* (6–8). Illus. by author. 1980, Silver Burdett $6.99. Detailed information plus pictures on Greek warriers from Troy to Alexander the Great.

5831. Coolidge, Olivia. *The Golden Days of Greece* (5–8). Illus. by Enrico Arno. 1968, Crowell $8.95. The culture and everyday life of Athens and Sparta. Also use: *The Trojan War* (1952, Houghton $6.95).

5832. Fagg, Christopher. *Ancient Greece* (5–7). Illustrated. 1979, Warwick $6.90. A fine overview of life in ancient Greece from the government to the Olympic Games.

5833. Quennell, Marjorie, and Quennell, C. H. B. *Everyday Things in Ancient Greece* (6–9). Illus. by author. 1954, Putnam $4.90. Life and thoughts in Greece, from earliest times to 404 B.C.

5834. Renault, Mary. *The Lion in the Gateway* (6–9). Illus. by C. Walter Hodges. 1964, Harper $7.89. How the Greeks defied the Persians at Marathon, Salamis, and Thermopylae, and pulled victory out of defeat.

5835. Robinson, Charles A. Jr. *The First Book of Ancient Greece* (2–4). 1960, Watts $4.47. An introduction to the history and culture of the ancient Greeks.

5836. Rutland, Jonathan. *See Inside an Ancient Greek Town* (5–7). Ed. by R. J. Unstead. Illustrated. 1979, Watts $6.90. A description of city life with illustrations of their principal buildings.

Rome

5837. Asimov, Isaac. *The Roman Republic* (6–8). 1966, Houghton $9.95. An interesting account of ancient Rome and its culture. Also use: *Imperial Rome* by H. E. L. Mellersh (1964, John Day $7.89).

5838. Brooks, Polly Schoyer, and Walworth, Nancy. *When the World Was Rome: 753 B.C. to A.D. 476* (6–9). Illustrated. 1972, Lippincott $9.95. A solidly researched history of Rome with emphasis on political and cultural aspects, but slight coverage on social conditions.

5839. Connolly, Peter. *Hannibal and the Enemies of Rome* (6–8). Illus. by author. 1980, Silver Burdett $6.99. An account of ancient Rome's struggle with foreign invaders.

5840. Connolly, Peter. *The Roman Army* (6–8). Illus. by author. 1980, Silver Burdett $6.99. The days of ancient Rome's expansion in the early days of the empire.

5841. Cunliffe, Barry. *Rome and the Barbarians* (6–9). Illustrated. 1975, Walck $9.95. A ·fascinating description of Rome's expansion from Scotland to Romania.

5842. Dillon, Ellis. *Rome Under the Emperors* (6–9). Illustrated. 1975, Nelson $6.95. A description of a day in the life of 4 different families at the time of Emperor Trajan, A.D. 110.

5843. Fagg, Christopher. *Ancient Rome* (4–6). Illus. by Nigel Chamberlain, Brian Lewis, and Constance Dear. 1979, Watts $6.90. A brief but informative overview of the ancient civilization.

5844. Liversidge, Joan. *Everyday Life in the Roman Empire* (6–8). Illus. by Eva Wilson. 1977, Putnam $7.50. Social and financial conditions are stressed in the cultural history of Rome during the first and second centuries.

5845. Mills, Dorothy. *The Book of the Ancient Romans: An Introduction to the History and Civilization of Rome from The Traditional Date of The Founding of The City to Its Fall in 476 A.D.* (6–8). Illustrated. 1937, Putnam $7.95. An introduction to Roman civilization.

5846. Robinson, Charles A., Jr. *The First Book of Ancient Rome* (5–7). Illustrated. 1965, Watts $4.90. In addition to a brief history of Rome, this survey covers its culture and contributions. Also use: *A Picture History of Ancient Rome* by Richard Erdoes (1967, Macmillan $4.95).

5847. Rutland, Jonathan. *See Inside a Roman Town* (3–6). Illustrated. 1978, Watts $5.90. A description of several kinds of buildings is given in text and illustrations.

5848. Unstead, R. J. *See Inside a Roman Town* (4–6). Illustrated. 1978, Warwick $5.90. All sorts of buildings from shops and town houses to the baths and amphitheater are depicted.

Middle Ages

5849. Buehr, Walter. *The Crusaders* (4–6). Illustrated. 1959, Putnam $5.79. Realistic presentation of those who fought in the religious wars. Also use: *Knights, Castles and Feudal Life* (1957, Putnam $5.29) and *Chivalry and the Mailed Knight* (1963, Putnam $5.29).

5850. Gibson, Michael. *The Knights* (5–7). Illustrated. 1980, Arco $6.95. A brief account that covers armor, castles, and tournaments.

5851. Glubok, Shirley. *Knights to Armor* (4–6). Illus. by Gerald Nook. 1969, Harper $7.89. A narrative on knighthood, armor, and weapons.

5852. Goodenough, Simon. *The Renaissance* (5–7). Illustrated. 1980, Arco $6.95. An account that covers the great breakthrough in science and art, and also supplies a basic history.

5853. Lasker, Joe. *Merry Ever After: The Story of Two Medieval Weddings* (3–5). Illus. by author. 1976, Viking $7.95. Intricate details of medieval life are revealed through verbal descriptions and many paintings of 2 weddings from different social classes. For an older group, use: *Medieval and Tudor Costume* by Phillis Cunningham (1968, Plays $4.95).

5854. Uden, Grant. *A Dictionary of Chivalry* (6–8). Illus. by Pauline Baynes. 1969, Crowell $25.00. An illustrated treasury of knighthood.

5855. Unstead, R. J. *Living in a Crusader Land* (5–6). Illustrated. 1973, Addison $5.95. A graphic depiction of life during the Crusades.

5856. Unstead, R. J. *Living in a Medieval City* (5–6). Illus. by Ron Stenberg. 1973, Addison $5.95. The author describes everyday life in Benfield, a small town. Companion volumes (both 1973, Addison $5.95) are: *Living in a Castle* and *Living in a Medieval Village*.

World War I

5857. Castor, Henry. *America's First World War: General Pershing and the Yanks* (5–8). 1957, Random $4.99. The story of America's contribution in World War I and of the great U.S. general.

5858. Colby, C. B. *Fighting Gear of World War I* (4–6). Illustrated. 1961, Coward $5.79. A pictorial presentation of the equipment and weapons used in World War I.

5859. Cowley, Robert. *1918: Gamble for Victory: The Greatest Attack of World War I* (6–8). 1964, Macmillan $4.50. The story of a decisive battle of World War I.

5860. Gurney, Gene. *Flying Aces of World War I* (5–7). Illustrated. 1965, Random $4.99. An action-filled account of the daring exploits of World War I pilots.

5861. Hoobler, Dorothy, and Hoobler, Thomas. *The Trenches: Fighting on the Western Front in World War I* (6–9). 1978, Putnam $8.95. A realistic picture of the horrors of war.

5862. Snyder, Louis L. *The First Book of World War I* (5–7). 1958, Watts $4.90. An interesting overview of the causes, campaigns, and results of this war that changed world history. Also use: *Album of World War I* by Dorothy Hoobler (1976, Watts $5.90).

World War II

5863. Bliven, Bruce. *From Casablanca to Berlin: The War in North Africa and Europe, 1942–1945* (6–8). Illustrated. 1965, Random $4.99. This concise account traces Allied advances in North Africa and Europe to the conclusion of the war. Also use: *The Battle of the Bulge* by Stephen Sears (1969, American Heritage $5.95; LB $6.89).

5864. Bliven, Bruce. *From Pearl Harbor to Okinawa: The War in the Pacific, 1941–1945* (6–8). Illustrated. 1960, Random $4.39. A graphic description of the course of the Pacific War from tragedy and defeat to eventual triumph.

5865. Bliven, Bruce. *The Story of D–Day* (5–8). 1956, Random $2.95; LB $4.39. The story of June 6, 1944 and its consequences on the outcome of World War II.

5866. Carter, Hodding. *The Commandos of World War II* (5–7). 1966, Random $2.95; LB $4.39. An exciting recreation of the activities of these hit-and-run fighters who played such an important part in the war.

5867. Considine, Bob, and Lawson, Ted. *Thirty Seconds over Tokyo* (5–9). 1953, Random $4.39. The story of Doolittle's daring bombing raid over Japanese territory in 1942.

5868. Colby, C. B. *The Fighting Gear of World War II* (4–6). Illustrated. 1961, Coward $5.79. Subtitle: *Equipment and Weapons of the American G.I.*

5869. Frank, Anne. *The Diary of a Young Girl* (6–9). Trans. 1952, Doubleday $8.95. A moving diary of a young Jewish girl hiding from the Nazis in World War II Amsterdam.

5870. Graff, Stewart. *The Story of World War II* (4–6). Illustrated. 1978, Dutton $7.95. A brief account that contains many photographs.

5871. Hautzig, Esther. *The Endless Steppe: Growing Up in Siberia* (6–9). 1968, Crowell $8.95. In this warm, personal narrative, 11-year-old Esther describes life, hardships, and the undaunted spirit of her family after they are shipped from Poland to Siberia in 1941.

5872. Hoobler, Dorothy, and Hoobler, Thomas. *An Album of World War II* (5–7). Illustrated. 1977, Watts $5.90. An overview of the war, concentrating on the military; black-and-white photographs frequently used.

5873. Hough, Richard. *The Battle of Midway: Victory in the Pacific* (5–8). Illustrated. 1970, Macmillan $4.50. The incredible story of how a small U.S. force defeated the Japanese during this 1942 sea battle.

5874. Hoyt, Edwin Palmer. *War in the Deep: Pacific Submarine Action in World War II* (6–9). Illustrated. 1978, Putnam $7.95. A realistic account arranged geographically and illustrated by Navy photographs.

5875. Janssen, Pierre. *A Moment of Silence* (5–9). Illustrated. 1970, Atheneum $4.25. A historical overview of the involvement and courage of the Dutch during World War II as seen through many of their monuments.

5876. Kluger, Ruth, and Mann, Peggy. *The Secret Ship* (4–7). 1978, Doubleday $5.95. A true story based on an escape mission during World War II.

5877. Lawson, Don. *The Secret World War II* (6–9). Illustrated. 1978, Watts $6.90. A mature account of several espionage activities during World War II.

5878. Leckie, Robert. *The Story of World War II* (5–7). Illustrated. 1964, Random $4.95; LB $5.99. A competent general account that emphasizes the war in the Pacific.

5879. Loomis, Robert D. *Great American Fighter Pilots of World War II* (5–8). Illustrated. 1961, Random $4.39. A moving tribute to the gallant pilots of World War II. Also use: *Air War against Hitler's Germany* by Stephen Sears (1969, American Heritage $5.95; LB $6.89).

5880. Meltzer, Milton. *Never to Forget: The Jews of the Holocaust* (6–9). Illustrated. 1976, Harper $8.95; LB $8.79; Dell paper $1.50. Quoting the victims themselves, Meltzer clarifies why and how the Holocaust happened.

5881. Reynolds, Quentin. *The Battle of Britain* (6–8). Illus. by Clayton Knight. 1953, Random $4.99. A distinguished war correspondent's account of the defeat of the German Luftwaffe. Also use: *The Battle of Britain: The Triumph of R.A.F. Fighter Pilots* by Richard Hough (1971, Macmillan $5.95).

5882. Shirer, William L. *The Sinking of the Bismarck* (5–8). Illus. with photos. 1962, Random $5.39. A suspenseful, true story of World War II, involving the sinking of the great German battleship in 1941.

5883. Snyder, Louis L. *The First Book of World War II* (5–7). Illus. with photos. 1958, Watts $4.90; paper $1.25. A brief account of the events leading to World War II and the conflict that ensued.

5884. Stein, R. Conrad. *The Story of D-Day* (4–6). Illus. by Tom Dinnington. 1977, Childrens Press $4.50. Events surrounding the landing in Normandy, June 6, 1944.

5885. Stein, R. Conrad. *The Story of the Battle for Iwo Jima* (4–6). Illus. by Len W. Meents. 1977, Childrens Press $4.50. The heartbreaking story of the battle that cost thousands of American lives.

5886. Stein, R. Conrad. *The Story of the Battle of the Bulge* (4–6). Illus. by Lou Aronson. 1977, Childrens Press $4.50. The story of the Germans' final attempt to stop an Allied victory.

5887. Takashima, Shizuye. *A Child in Prison Camp* (5–9). Illustrated. 1974, Morrow $8.25; LB $7.35. A harrowing and moving account of a Japanese-Canadian family's experience during World War II in an internment camp.

5888. Taylor, Theodore. *Air-Raid—Pearl Harbor! The Story of December 7, 1941* (6–9). Illus. by W. T. Mars. 1971, Crowell $7.95. A detailed, well-documented account of the events preceding the tragedy of Pearl Harbor.

5889. Taylor, Theodore. *Battle in the Arctic Seas: The Story of Convoy PQ 17* (6–9). Illus. by Robert Andrew Parker. 1976, Crowell $7.91. An exciting account, for better readers, of a World War II naval disaster involving an ill-fated convoy.

5890. Tregaskis, Richard. *Guadalcanal Diary* (5–9). 1955, Random $4.39; paper $2.95. An agonizing account of the battles in the Solomon Islands during World War II. Also use: *Battle of Bataan: America's Greatest Defeat* by Robert Conroy (1969, Macmillan $4.95).

Polar Regions

5891. Adrian, Mary. *Day and Night in the Arctic* (4–6). Illus. by Genevieve Vaughan-Jackson. 1970, Hastings $3.84. A study of Arctic wildlife and how it adjusts to the climate.

5892. Adrian, Mary. *Wildlife in the Antarctic* (5–8). Illus. by Bette J. Davis. 1978, Messner $6.97. Little-known animals of the Antarctic and their present ecological problems are described.

5893. Asimov, Isaac. *How Did We Find Out about Antarctica?* (5–7). Illus. by David Wool. 1979, Walker $6.95; LB $6.85. Ideas, people, and occupations that have influenced our knowledge of the Antarctica.

5894. Bringle, Mary. *Eskimos* (5–7). Illustrated. 1973, Watts $3.90. An introductory volume that explores many aspects of Eskimo life. Also use: *The Eskimo: Arctic Hunters and Trappers* by Sonia Bleeker (1959, Morrow $5.71).

5895. Cheney, Cora, and Partridge, Ben. *Crown of the World: A View of the Inner Arctic* (5–7). Illustrated. 1979, Dodd $7.95. An overview of the complex and varied environment that is usually considered inhospitable.

5896. Cheney, T. A. *Land of the Hibernating Rivers: Life in the Arctic* (4–6). 1968, Harcourt $4.50. A book that describes many aspects of life in the Far North.

5897. Dukert, Joseph M. *This Is Antarctica* (6–8). 1965; 1972 Coward $5.49. Scientific information blended with anecodotes on the history, present, and future of Antarctica. Also use: *Antarctic: Bottom of the World* by Julian May (1972, Creative Education $5.95).

5898. Elliott, Paul Michael. *Eskimos of the World* (4–6). 1976, Messner $7.29. An introduction to the history and culture of the Eskimo through several Eskimo children.

5899. Goetz, Delia. *The Arctic Tundra* (3–5). Illus. by Louis Darling. 1958, Morrow $5.52. A handsomely illustrated book that emphasizes Arctic flora and fauna. Also use: *The First Book of the Arctic* by Douglas Liversidge (1967, Watts $4.90).

5900. Hagbrink, Bodil. *Children of Lapland* (3–5). Trans. by George Simpson. Illus. by author. 1979, Tundra $12.95. The day-to-day activities of 2 Lapp children are recounted in text and bold full-color illustrations.

5901. Harrington, Lyn. *The Polar Regions: Earth's Frontiers* (5–7). Illustrated. 1973, Elsevier/-Nelson $6.95. A well-organized, nicely illustrated report on the geography and history of these regions.

5902. Horizon Magazine, eds. *Heroes of Polar Exploration* (6–8). Illustrated. 1962, American Heritage $5.95. The story of the gallant men who explored the tips of the earth. Also use: *The First Book of Arctic Exploration* by Douglas Liversidge (1970, Watts $4.90).

5903. Huntington, Lee Pennock. *The Arctic and the Antarctic, What Lives There* (2–4). Illus. by Murray Tinkelman. 1975, Coward $5.95. Plants and animals and how they survive this hostile environment.

5904. Icenhower, J. B. *The First Book of the Antarctic* (4–6). Illustrated. 1971, Watts $4.90. A simple account that concentrates on the climate, animal life, and uses of this polar region.

5905. Jenness, Aylette. *Dwellers of the Tundra: Life in an Alaskan Eskimo Village* (5–8). Illus. with photos. 1970, Macmillan $7.95. Everyday life of the people who live in the tiny village of Makumiut.

5906. Johnson, Sylvia A. *Animals of the Polar Regions* (4–6). Illus. by Alcuin C. Dornisch. 1976, Lerner $4.95. In addition to a description of the environment, the author highlights 10 animals from these regions.

5907. Laycock, George. *Beyond the Arctic Circle* (5–7). Illustrated. 1978, Four Winds $7.95. The history and contemporary conditions in the Arctic.

5908. Meyer, Carolyn. *Eskimos: Growing Up in a Changing Culture* (6–8). 1977, Atheneum $7.95. An account that stresses present-day problems of the Eskimos. Also use for younger readers: *Children of the North Pole* by Ralph Heirmann (1963, Harcourt $5.50).

5909. Pine, Tillie S., and Levine, Joseph. *The Eskimos Knew* (2–4). Illus. by Ezra Jack Keats. 1962, McGraw $7.95. How Eskimos have solved many of their problems and how those solutions are applied to today's world. Also use: *Let's Find Out about Eskimos* by Eleanor Wiesenthal and Ted Wiesenthal (1969, Watts $4.47).

5910. Pitseolak, Peter. *Peter Pitseolak's Escape from Death* (3–5). Illus. by author. 1978, Delacorte $7.95; LB $7.45. A true account of an Eskimo's brush with death on an ice floe.

5911. Scarf, Maggie. *Antarctica: Exploring the Frozen Continent* (3–6). Illustrated. 1970, Random $4.39. An account of the exploration of this area and its present-day uses, including weather forecasting. Also use: *Antarctica: The Worst Place in the World* by Allyn Baum (1966, Macmillan $4.95).

5912. Schlein, Miriam. *Antarctica: The Great White Continent* (4–6). Illustrated. 1980, Hastings $7.95. An overview of the history, wildlife, and importance of Antarctica.

5913. Sperry, Armstrong. *All about the Arctic and Antarctic* (4–6). Illus. by author. 1957, Random $4.39. A treasury of information about the polar regions, including a history of exploration.

5914. Sutton, George Miksch. *High Arctic: An Expedition to the Unspoiled North* (6–8). Illustrated. 1971, Eriksson $14.95; paper $10.00. A report on the amazing birds and animals encountered during a Canadian Arctic expedition in 1968.

Africa

General

5915. Aardema, Verna. *Ji-Nongo Means Riddles* (4–5). Illus. by Jerry Pinkney. 1978, Four Winds $6.95. Riddles from Africa about everyday life.

5916. Bernheim, Marc, and Bernheim, Evelyne. *In Africa* (2–4). Illustrated. 1973, Atheneum $8.95. Beautiful photographs effectively portray a variety of life-styles in Africa, from the desert to the city.

5917. *The Encyclopedia of Africa* (4–7). Illustrated. 1976, Watts $14.90. Through alphabetical listings, plus chapters arranged by subject, this book supplies excellent reference materials.

5918. Hughes, Langston. *The First Book of Africa* (4–6). 1965, Watts $4.90. A somewhat dated overview, but still valuable background material.

5919. Joseph, Joan. *Black African Empires* (5–7). 1974, Watts $4.90. A fascinating and unusual overview of the great African empires from ancient Kush to the Zimbabwe civilizations of the nineteenth century. Also use: *A Glorious Age in Africa* by Daniel Chu (1965, Doubleday $4.95; paper $2.50).

5920. Lacy, Leslie Alexander. *The First Book of Black Africa on the Move* (4–7). Illustrated. 1969, Watts $4.90. A history of the great African kingdoms and their status today. Also use: *Colonial Conquest of Africa* by Robin McKown (1971, Watts $4.90).

5921. Murphy, E. Jefferson. *Understanding Africa* (6–9). Illus. by Louise E. Jefferson. 1978, Crowell $8.95; LB $8.79. A survey brimming with information about the past, present, and future of Africa by an author well qualified to explode popularly held misconceptions about the Dark Continent.

5922. Musgrove, Margaret. *Ashanti to Zulu: African Traditions* (3–5). Illus. by Leo Dillon and Diane Dillon. 1976, Dial $8.95; LB $8.44. A Caldecott Medal winner that describes distinctive life-styles of 26 African tribes in text and stunning pictures.

5923. Pine, Tillie S., and Levine, Joseph. *The Africans Knew* (2–4). Illus. by Ann Grifalconi. 1967, McGraw $7.95. A survey of knowledge possessed by the ancient Africans that we use today.

5924. Sutherland, Efua. *Playtime in Africa* (2–5). Illustrated. 1962, Atheneum $6.95. Collection of verses and photographs of children at play in Africa.

North Africa

5925. Carpenter, Allan, and Balow, Tom. *Algeria* (4–7). Illustrated. 1978, Childrens Press $5.95. A useful addition to this series.

5926. Carpenter, Allan, and Chourou, Bechir. *Enchantment of Africa—Tunisia* (4–6). Illustrated. 1973, Childrens Press $5.75. A well-organized, useful introduction. Other North African nations in this series—same authors, publisher, and price —are: *Enchantment of Africa—Morocco* (1975), *Enchantment of Africa—Sudan* (1976), *Enchantment of Africa—Libya* (1977), and *Enchantment of Africa —Algeria* (1978).

5927. Edmonds, I. G. *Ethiopia: Land of the Conquering Lion of Judah* (6–8). Illustrated. 1975, Holt $6.95. A history that begins in Biblical times and stresses the life of Haile Selassie. Also use: *Ethiopia* by Barbara Nolen (1971, Watts $4.90).

5928. Englebert, Victor. *Camera on the Sahara: The World of Three Young Nomads* (3–5). Illustrated. 1971, Harcourt $5.50. The life of nomadic herdsmen of the Sahara is depicted primarily through the activities of 3 young people. Excellent photographs are also found in the author's *Camera on*

Africa: The World of an Ethiopian Boy (1970, Harcourt $5.50).

5929. Joy, Charles R. *Getting to Know the Sahara* (3–5). Illus. by Haris Petie. 1963, Coward $4.49. An elementary survey of the geography and life-styles of the inhabitants of the Sahara.

5930. Kula, Edna Mason. *The Land and People of Ethiopia* (6–8). 1972, Lippincott $8.95. Fine background material on the history and geography of this country.

5931. Lawson, Don. *Morocco, Algeria, Tunisia and Libya* (4–6). Illustrated. 1978, Watts $4.90. Current life-styles and relationships with other African countries are covered along with history and geography.

5932. Perl, Lila. *Ethiopia, Land of the Lion* (5–7). Illustrated. 1972, Morrow $6.96. An excellent survey that covers all the basic topics. Also use for a younger group: *Gennet Lives in Ethiopia* by Anna Riwkin-Brick (1968, Macmillan $3.95).

5933. Spencer, William. *The Land and People of Morocco* (1–3). 1973, Lippincott $8.95. Wide coverage is given on the past and present conditions in Morocco.

Central and East Africa

5934. Bleeker, Sonia. *The Masai: Herders of East Africa* (4–7). Illus. by Kisa N. Sasaki. 1963, Morrow $5.71. An intriguing picture of the life of a nomadic tribe. Also use: *The Pygmies: Africans of the Congo Forest* (1968, Morrow $5.71).

5935. Carpenter, Allan, and Hughes, James. *Enchantment of Africa—Uganda* (4–6). Illustrated. 1973, Childrens Press $5.75. This account gives interesting background material, but does not include current information on the political situation. Also in this series—same authors, publisher, and price—are: *Enchantment of Africa—Kenya* (1973), *Enchantment of Africa—Rwanda* (1973), and *Enchantment of Africa—Tanzania* (1974).

5936. Carpenter, Allan, and Maginnis, Matthew. *Enchantment of Africa—Zaire* (4–6). Illustrated. 1974, Childrens Press $5.75. A simple account that covers history, geography, major cities, and resources of the land once known as the Congo. Also covered in this series—same authors, publisher, and price—are: *Enchantment of Africa— Burundi* (1973), *Enchantment of Africa—Central African Republic* (1977), *Enchantment of Africa—Congo* (1977), and *Enchantment of Africa—Gabon* (1977).

5937. Elting, Mary, and McKown, Robin. *A Congo Homecoming* (3–5). Illus. by M. Barnett.

1969, Evans $3.95. Congolese life is explored through a young girl's trip from a large city to a rural village.

5938. Jacobs, Francine. *Africa's Flamingo Lake* (4–6). Illustrated. 1979, Morrow $5.95; LB $5.71. An interesting description of the ecology of Lake Nakuru in Kenya.

5939. Kaula, Edna M. *The Land and People of Kenya* (6–8). Illustrated. 1973, Lippincott $8.95. This account covers the history, geography, subjects related to the country, and its flora and fauna. For a younger group use: *First Book of Kenya* by F. Blanche Foster (1969, Watts $4.90).

5940. Kittler, Glenn D. *Central Africa: The New World of Tomorrow* (5–8). Illustrated. 1971, Nelson $6.95. A basic history of 9 African nations and their development since independence.

5941. Lauber, Patricia. *The Congo: River into Central Africa* (4–6). Illus. by Ted Schroeder. 1964, Garrard $3.68. A simple account of the explorations of the Congo and the countries and people along this waterway.

5942. McKown, Robin. *The Republic of Zaire* (4–6). Illustrated. 1972, Watts $4.47. Historical survey of the former Belgian Congo, which includes good material on the struggle after independence.

5943. Perl, Lila. *East Africa: Kenya, Tanzania, Uganda* (4–7). Illustrated. 1973, Morrow $6.49. Backround on geography, history, and social conditions. Also use: *The Land and People of Tanzania* by Edna M. Kaula (1972, Lippincott $8.95).

West Africa

5944. Barker, Carol. *Worlds of Yesterday: An Oba of Benin* (4–6). Illus. by author. 1977, Addison $6.95. The history of this ancient African nation, including the changes made by the Belgians.

5945. Bernheim, Marc, and Bernheim, Evelyne. *African Success Story: The Ivory Coast* (6–9). Illustrated. 1970, Harcourt $6.95. A history of the Ivory Coast before and after gaining independence in 1960 and a good picture of how the inhabitants live.

5946. Bleeker, Sonia. *The Ashanti of Ghana* (4–6). 1966, Morrow $5.52. Their history, customs, and unique society ranging from slave to noble.

5947. Carpenter, Allan, and Baker, Janice. *Enchantment of Africa—Niger* (4–6). Illustrated. 1976, Childrens Press $5.75. This book traces the history of Niger, its geography, government, and

economic life. Neighbors of Niger covered in this series—same authors, publisher, and price—are: *Enchantment of Africa—Upper Volta* (1974), *Enchantment of Africa—Mali* (1975), *Enchantment of Africa—Chad* (1976), and *Enchantment of Africa—Mauritania* (1977).

5948. Carpenter, Allan, and Hughes, James. *Enchantment of Africa—Cameroon* (4–6). Illustrated. 1977, Childrens Press $5.75. This interesting overview covers such topics as education, population, principal cities, and attractions, as well as history and geography. Other West African titles in this series—same authors, publisher, and price—are: *Enchantment of Africa—Ghana* (1977), *Enchantment of Africa—Ivory Coast* (1977), *Enchantment of Africa—Togo* (1977), *Enchantment of Africa—Benin* (1978).

5949. Carpenter, Allan. *Enchantment of Africa—Nigeria* (4–7). 1978, Childrens Press $5.95. A basic introduction that covers history, geography, and present-day conditions.

5950. Carpenter, Allan, and Owen, Harrison. *The Enchantment of Africa—Liberia* (4–6). Illustrated. 1974, Childrens Press $5.75. A survey of geography, social institutions, and famous landmarks. Neighbors of Liberia dealt with in this series—same authors, publisher, and price—are: *Enchantment of Africa—Sierra Leone* (1974), *Enchantment of Africa—Guinea* (1976), *Enchantment of Africa—Gambia* (1977), and *Enchantment of Africa—Senegal* (1977).

5951. Clifford, Mary Louise. *The Land and People of Sierra Leone* (5–7). Illustrated. 1974, Lippincott $8.95. Geography, history, economy, and present-day conditions are covered in this survey volume. Another West African nation covered in this series (Lippincott $8.95) is: *The Land and People of Liberia* (1971).

5952. Dunbar, Ernest. *Nigeria* (5–7). Illustrated. 1974, Watts $4.90. This African nation comes to life in this well-organized account. Also use for a younger group: *Getting to Know Nigeria* by Sam Olden (1960, Coward $3.97).

5953. Jenness, Aylette. *Along the Niger River: An African Way of Life* (5–9). Illus. by author. 1974, Crowell $8.95. The author, who lived in Africa for many years, describes in this photographic documentary the history and way of life of the people who live along the banks of the Niger River. For a younger group, use: *The Niger: Africa's River of Mystery* by Jane W. Watson (1971, Garrard $3.68).

5954. Latchem, Colin. *Looking at Nigeria* (4–6). Illustrated. 1976, Lippincott $8.95. A highly readable introduction to various aspects, chiefly geographical, about this country. For an older group use: *The Land and People of Nigeria* by Brenda-Lu Forman and Harrison Forman (1972, Lippincott $8.95).

5955.　Sale, J. Kirk. *The Land and People of Ghana* (6–9). 1972, Lippincott $8.95. An account that covers many aspects of life in Ghana, including economics and culture.

South Africa

5956.　Bleeker, Sonia. *The Zulu of South Africa: Cattlemen, Farmers and Warriors* (4–7). Illus. by Kisa N. Sasaki. 1970, Morrow $5.71. Life and history of the Zulu in this fine addition to an excellent series.

5957.　Carpenter, Allan, and Maginnis, Matthew. *Enchantment of Africa—Swaziland* (4–6). Illustrated. 1975, Childrens Press $5.75. An interesting overview including tourist attractions of this tiny South African country. Other books in this series that deals with several South African countries—same authors, publisher, and price—are: *Enchantment of Africa—Lesotho* (1975) and *Enchantment of Africa—Malawi* (1977).

5958.　Carpenter, Allan, and Ragin, Lynn. *Enchantment of Africa—Zambia* (4–6). Illustrated. 1973, Childrens Press $5.75. A survey of the country formerly known as Northern Rhodesia. Neighbors of Zambia covered in this series—same authors, publisher, and price—are: *Enchantment of Africa—Malagasy Republic* (1972), *Enchantment of Africa—Botswana* (1973), and *Enchantment of Africa—Rhodesia* (1974).

5959.　Kaula, Edna M. *The Land and People of Rhodesia* (6–9). 1967, Lippincott $8.95. Outdated, but still a useful account for background information. Also use: *The Land and People of Zambia* by Eliza T. Dresang (1975, Lippincott $7.95).

5960.　Newlon, Clarke. *Southern Africa: The Critical Land* (6–9). Illustrated. 1978, Dodd $6.95. In addition to history, this account gives good coverage to present-day problems.

5961.　Paton, Alan. *The Land and People of South Africa* (5–9). Illustrated. 1972, Lippincott $8.95. An excellent introduction to this land, which includes background material on racial tensions.

5962.　Perkins, Carol, and Perkins, Marlin. *I Saw You from Afar: A Visit to the Bushmen of the Kalahari Desert* (4–6). Illustrated. 1965, Atheneum $6.95. Simple text and photographs tell of the daily life and traditions of the Kalahari Desert Bushmen.

Asia

China

5963.　Caldwell, John C. *Let's Visit China Today* (4–6). Illustrated. 1973, John Day $7.89. A heavily illustrated simple account that gives basic background material.

5964.　Carpenter, F. R. *The Old China Trade: Americans in Canton 1784–1843* (6–9). Illus. by Demi Hitz. 1976, Coward $7.95. A thorough, straightforward account of the opening of Chinese-American trade that does not gloss over details of exploitation and ruthlessness.

5965.　Gray, Noel. *Looking at China* (4–6). Illustrated. 1974, Lippincott $8.95. A well-illustrated account of how people live in today's China. Also use: *People's Republic of China: Red Star of the East* by Jane W. Watson (1976, Garrard $4.96).

5966.　Knox, Robert. *Ancient China* (4–6). 1978, Warwick $6.90. An account of many aspects of the history and culture of ancient China.

5967.　Pine, Tillie S., and Levine, Joseph. *The Chinese Knew* (2–4). Illus. by Ezra Jack Keats. 1958, McGraw $7.95. A description of the things the Chinese knew how to do long ago that are still in use today.

5968.　Rau, Margaret. *The People of the New China* (4–6). Illustrated. 1978, Messner $7.79. A cursory view, augmented by the author's own photographs. Also use: *The China Challenge* by Albert Axelbank (1978, Watts $5.90).

5969.　Rau, Margaret. *Our World: The People's Republic of China* (5–7). Illustrated. 1978, Messner $7.29. As well as history and government, the author discusses at length internal conditions and concerns in this fine survey. Also use: *The First Book of Communist China* by William Kimmond (1972, Watts $4.90).

5970.　Rau, Margaret. *The Yangtze River* (4–6). Illustrated. 1970, Messner $3.64. The fascinating story of the river that serves one-tenth of the human race. Also use: *The Yellow River* (1969, Messner $3.64).

5971.　Sidel, Ruth. *Revolutionary China: People, Politics and Ping-Pong* (6–7). Illustrated. 1974, Delacorte $6.95. An account of a trip to China in 1971, together with interesting historical information. Also use: *The Land and People of China* by Cornelia Spencer (1972, Lippincott $8.95).

5972.　Tamarin, Alfred, and Glubok, Shirley. *Voyaging to Cathay: Americans in the China Trade*

(4–6). Illustrated. 1976, Viking $10.00. A history of America's Chinese trade until the Opium Wars, as well as its effect on U.S. history.

Japan

5973. Gidal, Sonia, and Gidal, Tim. *My Village in Japan* (4–6). Illustrated. 1966, Pantheon $5.69. A glimpse of Japanese life and culture as seen through the eyes of a youngster. Also use: *Japan: A Week in Daisuke's World* by Martha Sternberg (1973, Macmillan $4.95).

5974. Jakeman, Alan. *Getting to Know Japan* (3–5). Illus. by Don Lambo. 1971, Coward $3.97. An easily read introduction to Japan and its culture.

5975. Vaughan, Josephine B. *The Land and People of Japan* (6–8). Illustrated. 1972, Lippincott $8.95. A well-rounded account of many aspects of past and present Japanese life. Also use: *The Industrialization of Japan* by John Roberts (1971, Watts $4.90).

India

5976. Barker, Carol. *Arjun and His Village in India* (4–5). Illus. by author. 1979, Oxford $9.95. An introduction to village life in northwest India.

5977. Bothwell, Jean. *The First Book of India* (5–7). Illustrated. 1978, Watts $4.90. An introduction to India that includes material on geography, history, government, and the economy.

5978. Chandavarkar, Sumana. *Children of India* (1–3). Illustrated. 1971, Lothrop $6.75; LB $6.48. A simple text accompanies these photographs of Indian children. Also use: *Salima Lives in Kashmir* by Anna Riwkin-Brick (1971, Macmillan $4.50).

5979. Shaw, Ray, and Zolotow, Charlotte. *A Week in Lateef's World: India* (1–3). Illus. by Ray Shaw. 1970, Macmillan $4.95; text ed. $1.36. Lateef lives in a small boat in Kashmir.

5980. Sucksdorff, Astrid B. *Chendru: The Boy and the Tiger* (4–6). English version by William Sansom. Illus. by author. 1960, Harcourt $6.50. The friendship of a boy and a tiger in a jungle village is portrayed through excellent color photographs. Also use: *Tooni, the Elephant Boy* (1971, Harcourt $5.95).

5981. Watson, Jane W. *Indus: South Asia's Highway of History* (4–7). Illustrated. 1970, Garrard $3.68. Historical and geographical introduction to the land and people involved in the course of this river.

Other Asian Countries

5982. Buell, Hal. *Viet Nam: Land of Many Dragons* (5–7). Illustrated. 1968, Dodd $4.50. A brief, accurate history of Viet Nam. Also use: *The Children of Vietnam* by Betty Jean Lifton (1972, Atheneum $5.95).

5983. Clifford, Mary Louise. *The Land and People of Afghanistan* (5–7). Illustrated. 1973, Lippincott $8.95. An introduction to past and present life in this central Asian country.

5984. Cooke, David C. *Taiwan, Island China* (5–8). Illustrated. 1975, Dodd $4.95. Background material in addition to an account of the authors trip to Taiwan.

5985. Gurney, Gene. *North and South Korea* (5–7). Illustrated. 1973, Watts $4.47. A concise history of the two Koreas with information on the economic and social life of these countries. For an older group, use: *The Land and People of Korea* by S. E. Solberg (1973, Lippincott $8.95).

5986. Johnston, Richard J. H. *Getting to Know the Two Koreas* (4–6). Illustrated. 1965, Coward $3.97. An interesting background book, somewhat dated. Also use: *My Village in Korea* by Sonia Gidal and Tim Gidal (1968, Pantheon $5.69).

5987. Lang, Robert. *The Land and People of Pakistan* (6–9). 1974, Lippincott $8.95. Includes material on the civil war and separation of Bangladesh.

5988. Laure, Jason, and Laure, Ettagale. *Joi Bangla! The Children of Bangladesh* (4–6). Illustrated. 1974, Farrar $7.95. Interviews with children from various social strata give material on their lives, customs, and problems.

5989. Lefroy, C. Maxwell. *The Land and People of Burma* (6–9). 1965, Macmillan $3.95. An introduction to the history, geography, and culture.

5990. Poole, Frederick King. *The First Book of Indonesia* (4–7). Illustrated. 1971, Watts $4.90. A brief history of this small country with incidental material on its geography and culture. For an older group use: *The Land and People of Indonesia* by Datus C. Smith (1972, Lippincott $8.95).

5991. Poole, Frederick King. *Malaysia and Singapore* (5–7). Illustrated. 1975, Watts $3.90. An interesting, basic introduction to these adjacent countries. Also use: *Living in Singapore* by Gwenn R. Boardman (1971, Elsevier/Nelson $5.95).

5992. Poole, Frederick King. *Southeast Asia* (5–8). Illustrated. 1973, Watts $4.90. A firsthand report on the 10 Southeast Asian nations in a candid text describing the political situation, ways of life, and histories of each country, with photos and maps. For additional information use: *The Land and People of Cambodia* (1972, Lippincott $8.95).

5993. Poole, Frederick King. *Thailand* (5–7). Illustrated. 1973, Watts $4.90. A good survey that gives basic information. For an older group use: *The Land and People of Thailand* by Eunice I. Matthew (1964, Lippincott $5.95).

5994. Redford, Lora. *Getting to Know the Central Himalayas: Nepal, Sikkim, Bhutan* (5–8). Illustrated. 1964, Coward $3.97. A fascinating account of this small region.

5995. Sasek, M. *This Is Hong Kong* (3–5). Illustrated. 1965, Macmillan $5.95. In brilliant colors and brief text, the author takes the reader on a tour of the colony. Also use: *Children of Hong Kong* by Terry Shannon (1975, Childrens Press $7.95).

5996. Wilber, Donald N. *The Land and People of Ceylon* (6–8). 1972, Lippincott $8.95. A thorough introduction for better readers.

Australia and the Pacific Islands

5997. Bergamini, David. *The Land and Wildlife of Australia* (6–9). Illustrated. 1964, Time-Life $8.97. An introduction to diverse and unique flora and fauna. Also use: *The Wildlife of Australia and New Zealand* by Dorothy E. Shuttlesworth (1967, Hastings $5.95).

5998. Blunden, Godfrey. *The Land and People of Australia* (6–9). Illustrated. 1972, Lippincott $8.95. In addition to the geography and native people, the author describes the government and social life of the modern nation.

5999. Harrington, Lyn. *Australia and New Zealand: Pacific Community* (6–8). Illustrated. 1969, Nelson $6.80. A well-illustrated introduction. Also use: *Australia: Wonderland Down Under* by Barbara K. Wilson (1969, Dodd $4.50).

6000. Horizon Magazine, eds. *Captain Cook and the South Pacific* (6–8). Illustrated. 1963, Harper $5.95; LB $6.89. The 3 major voyages of James Cook, with general history of Pacific exploration.

6001. Hoyt, Olga. *Aborigines of Australia* (6–8). Illustrated. 1969, Lothrop $6.48. A reconstruction of the way in which aborigines lived when white settlers arrived in Australia. Also use for a younger group: *Ngari, The Hunter* by Ronald Rose (1968, Harcourt $5.95).

6002. Kaula, Edna M. *The Land and People of New Zealand* (6–8). Illustrated. 1972, Lippincott $8.95. After a short history, this introductory account tells about present-day New Zealand. Also use: *New Zealand* by Ngaio Marsh (1964, Macmillan $3.95).

6003. MacDougall, Trudie. *Beyond Dreamtime: The Life and Lore of the Aboriginal Australian* (4–6). Illus. by Pat Cummings. 1978, Coward $5.64. A history of the aboriginals who settled about 30,000 years ago in Australia.

6004. May, Charles Paul. *Oceania: Polynesia, Melanesia, Micronesia* (5–7). Illustrated. 1973, Elsevier/Nelson $6.95. A survey of various aspects of the Pacific Islands, including history and geography.

6005. Nance, John. *The Land and People of the Philippines* (5–8). Illustrated. 1977, Lippincott $8.95. A description of the varied peoples and cultures that comprise these islands.

6006. Perkins, Carol. *The Sound of Boomerangs* (4–6). Illustrated. 1972, Atheneum $6.25. A description of the nomadic people and the strange wildlife that exists along the northern seacoast of Australia.

6007. Pine, Tillie S., and Levine, Joseph. *The Polynesians Knew* (4–6). Illus. by Marilyn Hirsh. 1974, McGraw $7.95. Modern-day applications of scientific discoveries from the Polynesians.

6008. Piognant, Axel. *Bush Walkabout* (4–6). Illustrated. 1974, Addison $7.95. Various aspects of aboriginal life in Australia are told in this simple account.

6009. Ritchie, Paul. *Australia* (6–8). Illustrated. 1968, Macmillan $3.95. This work covers history, government, education, and social life. Also use for a younger group: *Looking at Australia* by W. F. Henderson (1977, Lippincott $8.95).

6010. Sterling Publishing Co, eds. *New Zealand in Pictures* (4–6). n.d, Sterling paper $2.50. A brief introduction, chiefly through pictures.

Europe

Great Britain and Ireland

6011. Asimov, Isaac. *The Shaping of England* (6–8). Illustrated. 1969, Houghton $4.50. An excellent introduction to English history and culture.

6012. Barber, Richard. *A Strong Land and a Sturdy* (6–8). Illustrated. 1976, Seabury $8.95. The Norman period in British history is brilliantly recreated.

6013. Branley, Franklyn M. *The Mystery of Stonehenge* (4–6). Illus. by Victor G. Ambrus. 1969, Crowell $8.79. Mysteries about this ancient spot fall under scientific scrutiny.

6014. Crossley-Holland, Kevin. *Green Blades Rising: The Anglo-Saxons* (6–9). Illustrated. 1976, Seabury $8.95. A comprehensive survey of the history, living habits, and religion of the Anglo-Saxons to the Norman Conquest.

6015. Dobrin, Arnold. *Ireland: The Edge of Europe* (6–8). Illustrated. 1971, Elsevier/Nelson $6.96; LB $6.80. This interesting addition to the *World Neighbors* series gives valuable background on the history and culture of Ireland. Also use: *Ireland* by Lillian F. Quigley (1964, Macmillan $2.95).

6016. Drabble, Margaret. *For Queen and Country: Britain in the Victorian Age* (6–9). Illustrated. 1980, Houghton $8.95. A mature account of the Victorian age, its paradoxes, and glories.

6017. Duggan, Alfred. *Growing Up in 13th Century England* (6–8). Illus. by C. Walter Hodges. 1962, Pantheon $5.99. Everyday life in the homes of an earl, a country knight, a peasant, a rich merchant, and a craftsman, described and contrasted.

6018. Goodall, John S. *The Story of an English Village* (2–6). Illustrated. 1979, Atheneum $7.95. Five hundred years in the history of an English village, in text and pictures.

6019. Hinds, Lorna. *Looking at Great Britain* (5–7). 1973, Lippincott $8.95. A brief overview of the history and geography of the British Isles.

6020. Hodges, C. Walter. *The Norman Conquest* (4–7). Illus. by author. 1966, Coward $4.99. This beautifully illustrated account is particularly strong in background information on the Conquest.

6021. O'Brien, Elinor. *The Land and People of Ireland* (5–7). Illustrated. 1972, Lippincott $8.95. A basic introduction to life, history and culture. Also use in the series: *The Land and People of Scotland* by Freda M. Buchanan (1962, $7.95) and *The Land and People of England* by Elinor O'Brien (1969, $8.95).

6022. Pittinger, W. Norman. *Early Britain: The Celts, Romans and Anglo-Saxons* (5–7). Illus. by Errol LeCain. 1972, Watts $4.90. The history and

salient differences of the 3 early cultures in ancient Britain.

6023. Sasek, M. *This Is Historic Britain* (3–6). Illustrated. 1974, Macmillan $6.95. Through text and finely detailed pictures, the reader is introduced to historic buildings in Great Britain.

6024. Sasek, M. *This Is London* (3–5). Illus. by author. 1969, Macmillan $4.95. An engagingly illustrated introduction to the major city sights. Also use in this series: *This Is Edinburgh* (1968, $5.95) and *This is Ireland* (1969, $4.95).

6025. Campbell, Donald Grant, and Nach, Irving. *Scotland in Pictures* (4–6). 1979, Sterling $4.59. A photographic study of life in Scotland by Campbell, Nach, and other Sterling editors.

6026. Snodin, David. *A Mighty Ferment* (6–9). Illustrated. 1978, Seabury $8.95. Subtitled: *England in the Age of Revolution 1750–1850*.

6027. Streatfeild, Noel. *The Thames: London's River* (4–6). Illus. by Kurt Wiese. 1964, Garrard $3.68. The geography and history of England's famous river.

6028. Villiers, Alan. *The Battle of Trafalgar: Lord Nelson Sweeps the Seas* (6–8). 1965, Macmillan $4.50. The story of the decisive sea battle during the Napoleonic Wars.

6029. Wilkins, Frances. *Growing Up in the Age of Chivalry* (6–8). Illustrated. 1978, Putnam $6.95. Everyday life in Tudor England is described in text and many pictures.

Low Countries

6030. Cohn, Angelo. *The First Book of the Netherlands* (4–6). Illustrated. 1971, Watts $4.90. An explanation of how Holland has saved its land from the sea is followed by information about its people and way of life. Also use: *Looking at Holland* by Anna Loman (1966, Lippincott $8.95) and, for an older group, *Land and People of Holland* by Adriaan J. Barnouw (1972, Lippincott $8.95).

6031. Horizon Magazine, eds. *The Battle of Waterloo* (6–8). 1967, American Heritage $5.95; LB $6.89. A well-illustrated account of the battle that changed the destiny of Europe. Also use: *The Battle of Waterloo: The End of an Empire* by Manuel Komroff (1964, Macmillan $4.50).

6032. Wolseley, Roland. *Low Countries: Gateways to Europe* (6–8). Illustrated. 1969, Elsevier/Nelson $6.95. A fine addition to the *World Neighbors* series.

Spain and Portugal

6033. Gidal, Sonia. *My Village in Portugal* (4–6). Illustrated. 1972, Pantheon $5.69. Carlos Verissumo tells of his life in the small fishing village of Nazare.

6034. Goldston, Robert. *Spain* (4–6). Illustrated. 1972, Watts $4.90. A basic guide to Spanish geography and the social life and customs of the people. Also use: *My Village in Spain* by Sonia Gidal and Tim Gidal (1962, Pantheon $5.69) and, for an older group, *Spain* by Robert Goldston (1967, Macmillan $4.95).

6035. Loder, Dorothy H. *The Land and People of Spain* (5–8). Illustrated. 1972, Lippincott $8.95. An introduction to the history and civilization of Spain, with emphasis on famous Spaniards and their contributions to world culture. For a younger group use: *Looking at Spain* by Rupert Martin (1970, Lippincott $7.95).

6036. Wohlrabe, Raymond A., and Krusch, Werner E. *The Land and People of Portugal* (5–8). Illustrated. 1963, Lippincott $8.79. An interesting addition to this popular series. Also use: *Spain and Portugal: Iberian Portrait* by Daniel Madden (1969, Elsevier/Nelson $6.95; LB $6.80).

France

6037. Edwards, Harvey. *France and the French* (6–8). Illustrated. 1972, Elsevier/Nelson $6.95. An excellent presentation of many facets of French life and customs. Also use: *The Land and People of France* by Lillian J. Bragdon (1972, Lippincott $8.95) and, for a younger group, *A Week in Daniel's World: France* by Hugh Weiss (1969, Macmillan $4.95).

6038. Lloyd, Ronald. *France* (4–6). 1975, Watts $3.90. An interesting, informative survey of life and customs.

6039. Sasek, M. *This Is Paris* (3–5). Illus. by author. 1959, Macmillan $3.95. Parisian landmarks are well presented in bold, colorful illustrations.

Germany

6040. Fles, Barthold. *East Germany* (5–7). Illustrated. 1973, Watts $4.90. A history that begins with World War II and includes social and cultural as well as political history.

6041. Forman, James D. *Nazism* (6–9). Illustrated. 1978, Watts $5.90. An informative brief history with a biography of Hitler.

6042. Goldston, Robert. *The Life and Death of Nazi Germany* (6–9). Illustrated. 1967, Bobbs-Merrill $7.95; Fawcett paper $1.75. A fascinating account of German history that concentrates on the life of Adolf Hitler.

6043. Hoover, John P. *East Germany in Pictures* (6–8). Illustrated. 1978, Sterling $3.99. Information on the land, history, government, people, and economy.

6044. Singer, Julia. *Impressions: A Trip to the German Democratic Republic* (5–8). Illustrated. 1979, Atheneum $8.95. Subjective, but telling impressions of a country behind the Iron Curtain.

6045. Switzer, Ellen. *How Democracy Failed* (5–7). Illustrated. 1975, Atheneum $7.95. A unique history of the Nazi period in Germany, illustrated with photographs.

6046. Wohlrabe, Raymond A., and Krusch, Werner E. *The Land and People of Germany* (5–7). Illustrated. 1972, Lippincott $8.95. A basic introduction to the past and present of the 2 Germanys.

Scandinavia

6047. Bader, Barbara. *Trademark Scandinavia* (4–6). Illustrated. 1976, Greenwillow $7.25; LB $6.96. The crafts and industries of the 4 Scandinavian countries are examined with excellent accompanying photographs.

6048. Berry, Erick. *The Land and People of Finland* (6–8). Illustrated. 1972, Lippincott $8.95. A basic introduction covering many facets of Finnish life, past and present.

6049. Berry, Erick. *The Land and People of Iceland* (5–8). Illustrated. 1972, Lippincott $8.95. An introduction to this island republic.

6050. Franzen, Greta. *The Great Ship Vasa* (6–8). Illustrated. 1971, Hastings $6.95. An account of the 1628 sinking of the warship *Vasa*, now on display in a special museum in Stockholm, and of its salvaging in the twentieth century.

6051. Hall, Elvajean. *The Land and People of Norway* (6–8). 1973, Lippincott $8.95. Norway, its land, history, and people are covered clearly in this comprehensive text.

6052. Merrick, Helen H. *Sweden* (4–6). Illustrated. 1971, Watts $4.90. An account that covers such topics as the way in which Swedes live and work today. Also use: *Looking at Sweden* by Maj Arbman (1971, Lippincott $7.95).

6053. Rudstrom, Lennart. *A Family* (3–6). Illus. by Carl Larsson. 1980, Putnam $7.95. A reconstruction of Swedish family life at the turn of the century.

6054. Rudstrom, Lennart. *A Home* (2–4). Illus. by Carl Larsson. 1974, Putnam $7.95. A beautifully illustrated picture book from Sweden. Also use: *A Farm* (1976, Putnam $7.95).

6055. Sterling Publishing Co, eds. *Finland in Pictures* (4–6). Illustrated. 1968, Sterling $4.59; paper $2.50. An account well illustrated with photographs.

6056. Wohlrabe, Raymond A. *The Land and People of Denmark* (4–6). 1972, Lippincott $8.95. Geography and history of Denmark.

Greece and Italy

6057. Johnson, Dorothy M. *Greece: Wonderland of the Past and Present* (6–7). Illus. by author. 1964, Dodd $3.95. Plants, animals, and places are linked with names of gods and legendary heroes in this history of the country. Also use: *Land and People of Greece* by Theodore Gianckoulis (1972, Lippincott $8.95).

6058. Martin, Rupert. *Looking at Italy* (4–6). Illustrated. 1967, Lippincott $8.95. An overview that discusses the country, people, geography, and culture. Also use: *The First Book of Italy* by Sam Epstein and Beryl Epstein (1972, Watts $4.90).

6059. Sasek, M. *This Is Greece* (4–6). 1966, Macmillan $3.95. A colorful introduction that presents the major sights in bold drawings.

6060. Sasek, M. *This Is Rome* (3–6). Illus. by author. 1960, Macmillan $5.95. A fascinating volume with paintings about Rome and its inhabitants. Also use: *This Is Venice* (1967, Macmillan $4.95).

6061. Warren, Ruth. *Modern Greece* (4–6). Illustrated. 1979, Watts $5.90. An excellent introduction to politics and social life in present-day Greece.

6062. Winwar, Frances. *The Land and People of Italy* (6–9). 1972, Lippincott $8.95. A thorough account for mature readers.

6063. Zolotow, Charlotte, and Getsug, Donald. *A Week in Yone's World: Greece* (1–3). 1969, Macmillan $4.50; text ed. $1.36. A description of the everyday life of a young boy in Greece.

Central and Eastern Europe

6064. Epstein, Sam, and Epstein, Beryl. *The First Book of Switzerland* (4–6). 1964, Watts $4.90. Geographical features, along with social and political history, are covered in this introductory account. Also use: *My Village in Switzerland* by Sonia Gidal and Tim Gidal (1961, Pantheon $5.69) and *Austria and Switzerland: Alpine Countries* by Bernadine Bailey (1968, Elsevier/Nelson $6.80).

6065. Gidal, Sonia. *My Village in Hungary* (4–6). Illustrated. 1974, Pantheon $5.69. As in other books in this series, a youngster describes, in text and through pictures, family life in a typical village. For a slightly older group use: *The Land and People of Hungary* by Emil Lengyel (1972, Lippincott $8.95).

6066. Hall, Elvajean. *The Land and People of Czechoslovakia* (6–9). Illustrated. 1972, Lippincott $8.95. An account that concentrates on present-day conditions.

6067. Kelly, Eric P., and Kostich, Dragos. *The Land and People of Poland* (6–9). Illustrated. 1972, Lippincott $7.95. An introductory survey of Polish history and georgraphy.

6068. Kostich, Dragos. *The Land and People of the Balkans: Albania, Bulgaria and Yugoslavia* (6–8). Illustrated. 1973, Lippincott $8.95. An introduction to varied background material. Also use: *Yugoslavia, Romania, Bulgaria: New Era in the Balkans* by Lila Perl (1970, Elsevier/Nelson $6.95) and *The Land and People of Romania* by Julian Hale (1972, Lippincott $8.95).

6069. Sterling Publishing Co, eds. *Austria in Pictures* (4–6). 1964, Sterling $4.59; paper $2.50. A slight volume that introduces Austria, chiefly through photographs.

6070. Tillyard, Angela. *The Land and People of Yugoslavia* (6–9). Illustrated. 1963, Macmillan $3.95. Somewhat dated and in need of revision, this book is still valuable for background material.

6071. Wohlrabe, Raymond A., and Krusch, Werner E. *The Land and People of Austria* (6–9). 1972, Lippincott $8.95. The people, history, geography, and culture of Austria are well treated in this survey volume. Also use: *Austria* by Carol Z. Rothkopf (1976, Watts $4.90).

Russia

6072. Almedingen, E.M. *Land of Muscovy: The History of Early Russia* (6–8). Illus. by Michael Charlton. 1972, Farrar $4.95. A fascinating account of Russia's early history.

6073. Arsenyev, Vladimir. *With Dersu the Hunter: Adventures in the Taiga* (6–8). Adapt. by Anne Terry White. n.d, Braziller $3.95. An account of expeditions into the Taiga of Siberia.

6074. Hewitt, Phillip. *Looking at Russia* (4–6). Illustrated. 1977, Lippincott $8.95. A brief introduction to the land and its people. Also use: *Soviet Union: Land of Many Peoples* by Jane W. Watson (1973, Garrard $5.20).

6075. Lengyel, Emil. *Siberia* (4–6). Illustrated. 1974, Watts $4.90. An intriguing look at this forbidding part of the U.S.S.R.

6076. Levin, Deana. *Nikolai Lives in Moscow* (2–4). Illus. by Dimitri Baetermants. 1968, Hastings $3.84. A glimpse of everyday life in Russia.

6077. Morton, Miriam. *Pleasures and Palaces: The After-School Activities of Russian Children* (4–6). 1972, Atheneum $5.25. A humanizing view of the recreational activities of Russian youngsters.

6078. Nazaroff, Alexander. *The Land and People of Russia* (5–8). 1972, Lippincott $8.95. This is primarily an overview of Russian history from early times to today. Also use: *The Soviet Union: The View from Within* by Franklin Folsom (1965, Elsevier/Nelson $6.95; LB $6.80) and *The First Book of the Soviet Union* by Louis L. Snyder (1972, Watts $4.90).

Middle East

6079. Berger, Gilda. *Kuwait and the Rim of Arabia* (4–6). Illustrated. 1978, Watts $4.90. A well-researched, up-to-date guide to the Persian Gulf states.

6080. Clifford, Mary Louise. *The Land and People of the Arabian Peninsula* (6–8). Illustrated. 1977, Lippincott $8.95. An overview that deals with the many cultural, historical, and geographical ties that bring these people together. Other titles in this Lippincott ($8.95) series dealing with Middle East countries, include: *The Land and People of Syria* by Paul W. Copeland (1972) and *The Land and People of Lebanon* by Viola H. Winder (1973).

6081. Fakhro, Bahia, and Walko, Ann. *Customs of the Arabian Gulf* (2–4). Illus. by the students of Kortoba, Kornata, and Khuds primary schools. 1979, Arab Customs $5.95. Subtitle: *Arab Children Portray Their Daily Life and Holiday Customs.*

6082. Fichter, George S. *Iraq* (4–6). Illustrated. 1978, Watts $4.90. History, geography, and culture are highlighted in this basic account.

6083. Henderson, Larry. *The Arab Middle East: Lebanon, Syria, Jordan, Arabia* (5–7). Illustrated. 1970, Elsevier/Nelson $6.95. An interesting overview and guide to these 4 important countries. Also use from Watts ($4.90): *The First Book of the Arab World* by Ruth Warren (1963) and *The Oil Countries of The Middle East* by Emil Lengyel (1973).

6084. Hinckley, Helen. *The Land and People of Iran* (6–8). Illustrated. 1973, Lippincott $8.95. A basic introduction that concentrates on contemporary conditions.

6085. Hoyt, Olga. *The Bedouins* (4–6). Illustrated. 1969, Lothrop $6.48. A fascinating history of these nomads of the desert from thousands of years ago to the present.

6086. Jacobs, David, and Mango, Cyril. *Constantinople: City of the Golden Horn* (6–8). Illustrated. 1969, American Heritage $5.95; LB $6.89. A lavishly illustrated history of Constantinople from ancient times to the 1920s.

6087. Lancaster, Fidelity. *The Bedouin* (4–6). Illus. by Maurice Wilson. 1978, Watts $5.90. An overview of the life, history, and customs of these nomads.

6088. Lengyel, Emil. *The First Book of Turkey* (4–6). 1979, Watts $4.90. Some of the topics discussed are history and geography. For an older group use: *The Land and People of Turkey* by William Spencer (1972, Lippincott $8.95).

6089. Lengyel, Emil. *Iran* (4–6). Illustrated. 1978, Watts $4.90. Good background information on the land, its people, and its economy.

6090. Newman, Gerald. *Lebanon* (4–6). Illustrated. 1978, Watts $4.90. Current political and economic problems are well handled in this basic account.

6091. Pine, Tillie, and Levine, Joseph. *The Arabs Knew* (3–5). 1976, McGraw $6.95. An exploration of the discoveries, inventions, and other contributions made to civilization by the Arabs.

6092. Poole, Frederick K. *Jordan* (5–7). Illustrated. 1978, Watts $4.90. An introductory survey that simplifies without distorting the complex history of this divided land. With an older group use: *The Land and People of Jordan* by Paul W. Copeland (1972, Lippincott $8.95).

6093. Woods, Geraldine. *Saudi Arabia* (4–6). Illustrated. 1978, Watts $4.90. Material on the culture, history, and geography of Saudi Arabia as well as a description of how oil has changed life in this country.

Egypt

6094. Burchell, S. C. *Getting to Know the Suez Canal* (3–5). Illustrated. 1971, Coward $3.97. An excellently illustrated history that chronicles the history of the canal.

6095. Jacobs, Francine. *The Red Sea* (4–6). Illustrated. 1978, Morrow $5.71. A thorough study that includes history and geography as well as biology.

6096. Lengyel, Emil. *Modern Egypt* (5–7). Illustrated. 1978, Watts $4.90. In addition to standard background material, this book includes material on Egyptian-Israeli relations.

6097. Mahmoud, Zaki N. *The Land and People of Egypt* (6–8). Illustrated. 1972, Lippincott $8.95. Although there is some material on ancient history, this account concentrates on contemporary conditions.

6098. Weingarten, Violet. *Nile, Lifeline of Egypt* (4–6). Illustrated. 1964, Garrard $3.68. An introduction to one of the world's great waterways.

Israel

6099. Comay, Joan, and Pearlman, Moshe. *Israel* (5–9). Illustrated. 1964, Macmillan $3.95. History, geography, information on the country today, people, education, language, government, and external affairs.

6100. Ellis, Harry B. *Israel: One Land, Two Peoples* (6–9). Illustrated. 1972, Crowell $7.95. An objective, comprehensive account that spares none of the complexities of the present situation, but still gives an excellent background of the conflict.

6101. Kubie, Nora B. *Israel* (4–6). Illustrated. 1978, Watts $8.95. An introduction to the history and the political and social life of the modern state. For an older group use: *The Land and People of Israel* by Gail Hoffman (1972, Lippincott $8.95).

6102. Rutland, Jonathan. *Looking at Israel* (4–6). Illustrated. 1970, Lippincott $6.95. An interesting overview that begins with the establishment of the state of Israel in 1948. Also use: *My Village in Israel* by Sonia Gidal and Tim Gidal (1959, Pantheon $5.69).

6103. Sasek, M. *This Is Israel* (3–5). Illustrated. 1962, Macmillan $4.95. Colorful illustrations and lively text capture the vitality of this country.

Middle America

Mexico

6104. Bleeker, Sonia. *The Aztec Indians of Mexico* (4–7). 1963, Morrow $5.71. A history of the Aztecs and their civilization. Also use: *The First Book of the Aztecs* by Barbara L. Beck (1966, Watts $4.90).

6105. Bray, Warwick. *Everyday Life of the Aztecs* (6–9). Illus. by Eva Wilson. 1969, Putnam $6.75. A discussion of Aztec ways. For a younger group use: *One Day in Aztec Mexico* by G. R. Kirtland (1963, Harcourt $4.50).

6106. Epstein, Sam, and Epstein, Beryl. *The First Book of Mexico* (4–7). Illustrated. 1967, Watts $4.90. A tour of various towns and cities and highlights from Mexican civilization.

6107. Karen, Ruth. *Feathered Serpent: The Rise and Fall of the Aztecs* (6–9). Illustrated. 1979, Four Winds $8.95. A survey of the Aztec civilization enriched by frequent quotations from primary sources.

6108. Larralde, Elsa. *The Land and People of Mexico* (3–5). 1968, Lippincott $8.95. The history and geography of Mexico is given in this mature account.

6109. LeSueur, Meridel. *The Conquistadores* (5–7). Illus. by Richard Cuffari. 1973, Watts $4.90. The history of these Spanish adventurers and how they plundered the New World.

6110. Lewis, Thomas P. *Hill of Fire* (1–3). Illus. by Joan Sandin. 1971, Harper $5.95; LB $6.89. The eruption of the volcano Paricutin and its affect on the lives of the people.

6111. Nevins, Albert J. *Away to Mexico* (6–8). 1966, Dodd $3.95. Highpoints in Mexican history from the Mayan and Aztec civilizations to modern times.

6112. Perl, Lila. *Mexico, Crucible of the Americas* (6–8). Illustrated. 1978, Morrow $7.95; LB $7.63. A background book that surveys both the history and present-day conditions in Mexico.

Central America

6113. Bleeker, Sonia. *The Maya: Indians of Central America* (4–7). 1961, Morrow $5.71. A thorough account of the history and culture of the Mayan civilization. Also use: *Maya: Land of the Turkey and the Deer* by Victor W. Von Hagen (1960, Collins $5.91).

6114. Carpenter, Allan. *Enchantment of Central America: Costa Rica* (4–6). Illustrated. 1971, Childrens Press $9.25. A survey of life, past and present.

6115. Carpenter, Allan, and Baker, Eloise. *Enchantment of Central America: El Salvador* (4–6). Illustrated. 1971, Childrens Press $7.70. An examination of the geography, government, history, and people. Other titles in this series, by the same authors and publisher (all 1971, $7.70), are: *Enchantment of Central America: British Honduras, Enchantment of Central America: Honduras,* and *Enchantment of Central America: Nicaragua.*

6116. Chirinos, Lito. *Lito the Shoeshine Boy* (3–5). Trans. by David Mangurian. Illus. by David Mangurian. 1975, Four Winds $6.95. A heart-wrenching account of a poor 9-year-old boy living in Honduras.

6117. Halsell, Grace. *Getting to Know Guatemala and the Two Honduras* (3–5). 1964, Coward $3.97. An introductory survey. Also use: *Getting to Know Panama* by Dee Day (1958, Coward $3.97).

6118. Karen, Ruth. *The Land and People of Central America* (5–7). 1972, Lippincott $8.95. A general introduction to life in each of the Central American countries.

6119. Markun, Patricia Maloney. *The Panama Canal* (5–7). Illustrated. 1979, Watts $5.90. Includes the 1978 treaty and its implications.

6120. Pine, Tillie S., and Levine, Joseph. *The Mayans Knew* (2–4). Illus. by Ezra Jack Keats. 1971, McGraw $7.95. A discussion of Mayan contributions to civilization and their present-day applications. For an older group use: *The First Book of the Ancient Maya* by Barbara L. Beck (1965, Watts $4.90).

6121. Price, Christine. *Heirs of the Ancient Maya: A Portrait of the Lacandon Indians* (6–9). Illustrated. 1972, Scribner $5.95. A description through words and photographs of the present life-style of a tribe that has shunned civilization, and of their extraordinary Mayan ruins.

Puerto Rico and Other Caribbean Islands

6122. Colorado, Antonio. *The First Book of Puerto Rico* (4–7). Illustrated. 1978, Watts $4.47. A background account that concentrates on the capital city of San Juan.

6123. Kurtis, Arlen H. *Puerto Ricans from Island to Main Land* (6–8). 1969, Messner $3.64. The story of a people, their island, and their migrations.

6124. Maiorano, Robert. *Francisco* (K–3). Illus. by Rachel Isadora. 1978, Macmillan $7.95. An affectional picture of a Dominican Republic family.

6125. Manning, Jack. *Young Puerto Rico* (4–6). 1962, Dodd $3.95. A narrative of the young people of Puerto Rico.

6126. Marshall, Anthony D. *Trinidad/Tobago* (4–7). Illustrated. 1975, Watts $4.47. A survey of the history and geography of these 2 islands.

6127. Masters, Robert V. *Puerto Rico in Pictures* (4–6). 1977, Sterling $3.39. A photographic tour of this fascinating island.

6128. Matthews, Herbert L. *Cuba* (6–8). Illustrated. 1964, Macmillan $4.95. Although dated, this account gives some good background information.

6129. Ortiz, Victoria. *The Land and People of Cuba* (6–8). Illustrated. 1973, Lippincott $8.95. A sympathetic account that concentrates on modern Cuban history and Castro's regime.

6130. Sherlock, Philip M. *The Land and People of the West Indies* (5–8). Illustrated. 1967, Lippincott $7.95. A background account of the history, social life, and customs of the area.

6131. Singer, Julia. *We All Come from Puerto Rico, Too* (3–5). Illus. by author. 1977, Atheneum $6.95. Life in Puerto Rico as seen through the eyes of several children of varying interests and backgrounds.

6132. Singer, Julia. *We All Come from Someplace: Children of Puerto Rico* (4–6). Illus. by author. 1976, Atheneum $6.95. The various kinds of life-styles found in Puerto Rico are explained in photographs and simple text.

South America

6133. Bates, Marston. *The Land and Wildlife of South America* (6–9). Illustrated. 1968, Time-Life

$8.97. A well-illustrated report on the great diversity of climate, vegetation, and wildlife in various areas of the continent.

6134. Baumann, Hans. *Gold and Gods of Peru* (6–8). Illustrated. 1963, Pantheon $6.39. An overview of the history of many early cultures in Peru, ending with the Incas.

6135. Beals, Carleton. *The Incredible Incas: Yesterday and Today* (5–7). Illustrated. 1974, Abelard $6.95. A history that concentrates on everyday life. Also use: *The Incas: People of the Sun* by Victor W. Von Hagen (1961, Collins $5.91).

6136. Beck, Barbara L. *The First Book of the Incas* (6–9). 1966, Watts $4.90. A thorough and enthralling picture of the Incas.

6137. Bowen, J. David. *The Land and People of Chile* (6–8). Illustrated. 1976, Lippincott $8.95. An up-to-date account that covers the contemporary situation as well as background material. Also use: *Land and People of Chile* by George Pendle (1960, Macmillan $3.95)

6138. Brown, Rose, and Warren, Leslie F. *The Land and People of Brazil* (6–8). Illustrated. 1972, Lippincott $8.95. A picture of Brazil and the lifestyle of its people.

6139. Caldwell, John C. *Let's Visit Peru* (3–5). Illustrated. 1962, John Day $7.89. A somewhat dated account, but still of value for background material. Also use: *Enchantment of South America: Peru* by Allan Carpenter (1970, Childrens Press $9.25).

6140. Carpenter, Allan. *Enchantment of South America: Brazil* (3–5). 1968, Childrens Press $5.75. An easily read general introduction to Brazil.

6141. Carpenter, Allan. *Enchantment of South America: Chile* (4–6). Illustrated. 1969, Childrens Press $9.25. A simple account that concentrates on geography and economics.

6142. Carpenter, Allan, and Lyon, Jean C. *Enchantment of South America: Colombia* (4–6). Illustrated. 1969, Childrens Press $5.75; LB $7.70. The land, its resources, and how the people live are covered in this overview.

6143. Carpenter, Allan, and Balow, Tom. *Enchantment of South America: Paraguay* (4–6). Illustrated. 1970, Childrens Press $9.25. An easily read overview. Also use: *The Land and Peoples of Paraguay and Uruguay* by George Pendle (1968, Macmillan $3.95).

6144. Carpenter, Allan. *Enchantment of South America: Venezuela* (4–6). Illustrated. 1970, Childrens Press $9.25. A good overview of the country.

6145. Carter, William E. *The First Book of Bolivia* (4–7). Illustrated. 1963, Watts $4.90. An overview of the history and geography of this mountainous country. Also use: *Enchantment of South America: Bolivia* by Allan Carpenter (1970, Childrens Press $9.25).

6146. Carter, William E. *The First Book of South America* (4–7). Illustrated. 1972, Watts $4.90. History, folklore, and religion.

6147. Comins, Jeremy. *Latin American Crafts and Their Cultural Backgrounds* (6–8). Illustrated. 1974, Lothrop $6.00. An introduction to the many crafts of this continent.

6148. Crosby, Alexander L. *The Rimac, River of Peru* (4–6). Illustrated. 1966, Garrard $3.68. The story of the river that has played a major role in the history of Peru.

6149. Dobler, Lavinia. *The Land and People of Uruguay* (6–8). Illustrated. 1972, Lippincott $8.95. This account includes materials on past and present facets of life in Uruguay. For a younger group use: *Enchantment of South America: Uruguay* by Allan Carpenter (1969, Childrens Press $9.25).

6150. Fletcher, Alan M. *The Land and People of the Guianas* (6–8). Illustrated. 1972, Lippincott $8.95. Life and times in the Guianas. For a slightly younger group use: *The Enchantment of South America: French Guiana, The Enchantment of South America: Guyana,* and *The Enchantment of South America: Surinam* by Allan Carpenter (all 1970, Childrens Press $5.75; LB $7.70).

6151. Glubok, Shirley. *The Fall of the Incas* (4–6). 1967, Macmillan $5.95. The last days of the Inca Empire are well reconstructed.

6152. Hall, Elvajean. *The Land and People of Argentina* (6–8). Illustrated. 1972, Lippincott $8.95. An introductory volume on the history and people. For a younger group use: *Enchantment of South America: Argentina* by Allan Carpenter (1969, Childrens Press $5.75; LB $7.70).

6153. Hornos, Axel. *Argentina, Paraguay and Uruguay* (5–7). Illustrated. 1969, Elsevier/Nelson $6.80. An attractive, well-illustrated introduction. Also use: *Getting to Know Argentina* by Sam Olden (1961, Coward $3.97).

6154. Jenness, Aylette. *A Life of Their Own: An Indian Family in Latin America* (4–7). Illustrated. 1975, Crowell $8.95. A documentary told in words and many photographs of the Hernandez family.

6155. Joy, Charles R. *Getting to Know the River Amazon* (4–6). Illustrated. 1963, Coward $3.97. The 3,900-mile course of the Amazon is described together with life on its banks.

6156. May, Charles Paul. *Peru, Bolivia, Ecuador: The Indian Andes* (5–7). Illustrated. 1969, Elsevier/Nelson $6.95. An introduction to past and present life. Also use: *Boy of Bolivia* by Peter Larsen (1971, Dodd $4.50).

6157. Pendle, George. *The Land and People of Peru* (6–8). Illustrated. 1968, Macmillan $3.95. A survey of history, geography, and economics.

6158. Mann, Peggy. *Easter Island: Land of Mysteries* (6–8). Illustrated. 1976, Holt $6.95. The history and geography of the island whose stone carvings have intrigued visitors for centuries.

6159. Pine, Tillie S., and Levine, Joseph. *The Incas Knew* (2–4). Illus. by Ann Grifalconi. 1968, McGraw $7.95. The accomplishments of the ancient Incas are related to today's technology.

6160. Reit, Seymour. *A Week in Bico's World: Brazil* (1–3). Illus. by Claudia Andujar. 1970, Macmillan $4.95. A simple story of life with a Sao Paulo family.

6161. Selsam, Millicent E. *Land of the Giant Tortoise: The Story of the Galapagos* (3–5). Illustrated. 1977, Four Winds $7.95. Photographs and text introduce the reader to these volcanic islands.

6162. Sheppard, Sally. *The First Book of Brazil* (4–7). Illustrated. 1972, Watts $4.90. An interesting overview of the history and economic and cultural life of Brazil and its people. Also use: *Looking at Brazil* by Sarita Kendall (1975, Lippincott $6.95).

6163. Shuttlesworth, Dorothy E. *The Wildlife of South America* (6–9). Illus. by George F. Mason. 1974, Hastings $6.95. An overview of South American wildlife, how it has been used in the past, and the need for present-day conservation.

6164. Sterling Publishing Co, eds. *Ecuador in Pictures* (4–6). Illustrated. 1969, Sterling $4.59; paper $2.50. An account well illustrated with photographs.

6165. Warren, Leslie F. *The Land and People of Bolivia* (6–8). Illustrated. 1974, Lippincott $8.95. An excellent overview of life in this republic.

6166. Wohlrabe, Raymond A., and Krusch, Werner E. *The Land and People of Venezuela* (6–9). Illustrated. 1959, Lippincott $8.79. A survey of the history, geography, and living conditions in this oil-rich nation. Also use: *Away to Venezuela* by Albert J. Nevins (1970, Dodd $4.50).

North America

Canada

6167. Ferguson, Linda W. *Canada* (5–8). Illustrated. 1979, Scribner $9.95. Canadian history, geography, and current concerns are nicely traced in this account.

6168. Peck, Anne M. *The Pageant of Canadian History* (6–8). 1963, McKay $7.95. An account of Canadian history that would benefit from updating.

6169. Rollins, Frances. *Getting to Know Canada* (3–5). Illustrated. 1966, Coward $3.97. A simple introduction to the history and society of Canada.

6170. Ross, Frances Aileen. *The Land and People of Canada* (5–7). Illustrated. 1964, Lippincott $8.95. This account traces the political and social history and geography of Canada. For a younger group use: *Canada* by Theo L. Hill (1974, Fideler $6.96; paper $4.94).

6171. Schull, Joseph. *Battle for the Rock: The Story of Wolfe and Montcalm* (4–6). 1961, St. Martins $4.95. The story of the battle for Quebec that determined France's role in North America.

6172. Watson, Jane W. *Canada: Giant Nation of the North* (4–6). Illustrated. 1968, Garrard $5.20. A summary overview of history and geography.

6173. White, Anne Terry. *The St. Lawrence: Seaway of North America* (4–7). Illustrated. 1961, Garrard $3.68. The history of the St. Lawrence River from the early explorers to the building of the seaway. Also use: *The Mackenzie: River to the Top of the World* by Beatrice R. Lambie (1967, Garrard $3.68).

United States

General

6174. Arnold, Pauline, and White, Percival. *How We Named Our States* (5–7). Illustrated. 1966, Abelard $7.95. The origins of the names of the 50 states and their capitals interestingly told.

6175. Berg, Annemarie. *Great State Seals of the United States* (4–7). Illustrated. 1979, Dodd $6.95. In pictures and descriptive text, each of the states' seals are covered.

6176. Brandt, Sue R. *Facts about the Fifty States* (5–7). Illustrated. 1970, Watts $5.90. A rundown of information and salient facts about each of the 50 states. Also use: *Stories of the States* by Frank Ross (1969, Crowell $10.05).

6177. Carpenter, Allan. *Far-Flung America* (5–7). Illustrated. 1979, Childrens Press $6.95. A brief, attractive introduction to the geography of America.

6178. Colby, C. B. *Historic American Landmarks: From the Old North Church to The Santa Fe* (4–6). Illustrated. 1968, Coward $5.19. A very brief introduction to 25 important American landmarks.

6179. Craz, Albert G. *Getting to Know the Mississippi River* (3–5). Illus. by N. Goldstein. 1965, Coward $3.97. A somewhat dated introduction to America's greatest river system.

6180. Dowden, Anne. *State Flowers* (5–9). Illustrated. 1978, Crowell $7.95. Background information is given along with detailed drawings of each flower by the author.

6181. Earle, Olive L. *State Trees* (4–7). Illus. by author. 1973, Morrow $5.52. Through text and detailed illustrations, information on each of the state trees is interestingly presented. Also use: *State Birds and Flowers* (1961, Morrow $5.52).

6182. Farb, Peter, and The Editors of *Life*. *The Land and Wildlife of North America* (4–6). Illustrated. 1964, Time $8.97. An introduction to the topography and natural history of North America.

6183. Goetz, Delia. *State Capital Cities* (4–6). Illustrated. 1971, Morrow $6.96. A brief history of the national capital and each of the state capitals.

6184. Holling, Holling C. *Paddle-to-the-Sea* (3–6). Illus. by author. 1941, Houghton $9.95. From Ontario to the Atlantic in a toy canoe, in this standard juvenile tale.

6185. Naden, Corinne J. *The Mississippi: America's Great River System* (5–7). Illustrated. 1974, Watts $4.90. An introduction to the history and geography of this great waterway. Also use: *The Mississippi: Giant at Work* by Patricia Lauber (1961, Garrard $3.68).

6186. National Geographic Society. *National Geographic Picture Atlas of Our Fifty States* (4–6). Illustrated. 1978, National Geographic $16.95. A beautifully illustrated book in which the text is divided into 10 geographical areas.

6187. Ronan, Margaret. *All about Our 50 States* (4–6). Illus. by William Meyerriecks. 1978, Random $4.99. Useful information plus maps and photographs are included in this account.

6188. Sedeen, Margaret, ed. *Picture Atlas of our Fifty States* (4–6). 1978, National Geographic $16.95. An atlas plus hundreds of photos, charts, and other illustrations.

6189. Simon, Hilda. *Bird and Other Flower Emblems of the United States* (4–8). Illustrated. 1978, Dodd $7.95. Alphabetically by state, the author gives details on each one's flower and bird emblems.

Northeast

6190. Bailey, Bernadine. *Picture Book of Connecticut* (2–4). Illus. by Kurt Wiese. 1974, Whitman $4.75. A very simple account; part of a well-known series. Also use (all $4.95): *Picture Book of Maine* (1967), *Picture Book of New Jersey* (1968), *Picture Book of New York* (1968), *Picture Book of Massachusetts* (1969), *Picture Book of New Hampshire* (1971), *Picture Book of Rhode Island* (1971) and *Picture Book of Pennsylvania* (1972).

6191. Carmer, Elizabeth, and Carmer, Carl. *The Susquehanna: From New York to Chesapeake* (4–6). Illustrated. 1964, Garrard $3.68. The 400-mile course of this river is chronicled with historical information.

6192. Carmer, Carl. *The Hudson River* (4–7). Illus. by Rafaello Busoni. 1962, Holt $4.95. The geography and history of this important waterway. Also use: *The Hudson: River of History* by May McNeer (1962, Garrard $3.68).

6193. Carpenter, Allan. *Connecticut* (4–6). Illustrated. 1979, Childrens Press $9.25. A basic introduction; part of *The New Enchantment of America* series. Also include (all $9.25): *Massachusetts* (1978), *New York* (1978), *Pennsylvania* (1978), *Maine* (1979), *New Hampshire* (1979), *New Jersey* (1979), *Rhode Island* (1979), and *Vermont* (1979).

6194. Cavallo, Dinan. *Lower East Side* (3–6). Illustrated. 1970, Macmillan $6.95. The story of the area in New York City that was a melting pot for newly arrived immigrants.

6195. Ellis, David M. *New York: The Empire State* (4–7). Illustrated. 1969, Prentice-Hall $10.40. Geography and history from prehistoric times to the present. Also use: *Getting to Know New York State* by William B. Fink (1971, Coward $3.97).

6196. Gemming, Elizabeth. *Getting to Know the Connecticut River* (3–5). Illustrated. 1974, Coward $3.97. Highlights history and life along this New England waterway.

6197. Kaufmen, Michael. *Rooftops and Alleys: Adventures with a City Kid* (4–6). Illustrated. 1973,

Knopf $4.95; LB $5.99. The author and photographer accompany Michael, the city kid, around his immediate neighborhood and his town, Manhattan.

6198. McCabe, Inger. *A Week in Henry's World: El Barrio* (3–5). Illus. by author. 1971, Macmillan $4.95; paper $1.36. A well-illustrated account of the daily activities of a Puerto Rican family in New York City.

6199. Mercer, Charles. *Statue of Liberty* (5–9). Illustrated. 1979, Putnam $8.95. The history of Miss Liberty from inception to the 1976 Operation Sail in New York harbor.

6200. Miller, Natalie. *The Story of the Statue of Liberty* (4–6). Illus. by John Hawkenson and Lucy Hawkenson. 1965, Childrens Press $7.35. The story of Miss Liberty from France to the New World.

6201. *The New York Kid's Book* (4–7). 1979, Doubleday $8.95. A delightful guide book that is subtitled: *167 Children's Writers and Artists Celebrate New York City.*

6202. Patterson, Lillie. *Meet Miss Liberty* (4–6). Illustrated. 1962, Macmillan $4.50. A complete, fascinating history of the concept of the Statue of Liberty, its execution, and the people behind it. Also use: *Statue of Liberty Comes to America* by Robert Kraske (1972, Garrard $4.88).

6203. Radlauer, Ruth. *Acadia National Park* (3–5). Illustrated. 1978, Childrens Press $7.35. An introduction and visitor's guide to this park in Maine.

6204. Sasek, M. *This Is New York* (3–5). Illus. by author. 1960, Macmillan $5.95; paper $.95. An impressionistic view of this city's past and present.

South

6205. Bailey, Bernadine. *Our Nation's Capital, Washington, D.C.* (1–3). Illus. by Kurt Wiese. 1967, Whitman $4.75. A simple introduction to our capital.

6206. Bailey, Bernadine. *Picture Book of Alabama* (2–4). Illus. by Kurt Wiese. 1975, Whitman $4.75. Part of a series. Also use (all $4.75): *Picture Book of Georgia* (1966), *Picture Book of Arkansas* (1967), *Picture Book of Kentucky* (1967), *Picture Book of Louisiana* (1967), *Picture Book of Maryland* (1970), *Picture Book of Florida* (1972), and *Picture Book of Delaware* (1977).

6207. Bailey, Bernadine. *Picture Book of Mississippi* (2–4). Illus. by Kurt Wiese. 1972, Whitman $4.75. Part of a series. Also use (all $4.75): *Picture Book of North Carolina* (1970), *Picture Book of Virginia* (1970), *Picture Book of West Virginia* (1970), *Picture Book of Tennessee* (1974), and *Picture Book of South Carolina* (1975).

6208. Bell, Thelma, and Bell, Corydon. *North Carolina* (6–8). 1971, Coward $5.99. An interesting introduction to the history, economics, and social life in this state.

6209. Blassingame, Wyatt. *The Everglades: From Yesterday to Tomorrow* (4–6). Illustrated. 1974, Putnam $5.29. The Everglades story from Indian days to the present.

6210. Carpenter, Allan. *Alabama* (4–6). Illustrated. 1978, Childrens Press $9.25. Part of the *New Enchantment of America* series. Also use ($9.25 each): *Arkansas* (1978), *Georgia* (1978), *Delaware* (1979), *District of Columbia* (1979), *Florida* (1979), *Louisiana* (1979), and *Maryland* (1979).

6211. Carpenter, Allan. *Mississippi* (4–6). Illustrated. 1978, Childrens Press $9.25. Part of *The New Enchantment of America* series. Also use ($9.25 each): *Virginia* (1978), *North Carolina* (1979), *South Carolina* (1979), *Tennessee* (1979) and *West Virginia* (1979).

6212. Fichter, George S. *Florida in Pictures* (5–7). Illustrated. 1979, Sterling $4.59; paper $2.50. A useful but superficial overview, also suitable for browsing.

6213. Prolman, Marilyn. *The Story of the Capitol* (3–5). Illus. by Darrell Wiskur. 1969, Childrens Press $7.35. The history and architecture of the nation's capitol building.

6214. Radlauer, Ruth. *Mammoth Cave National Park* (3–5). Illustrated. 1978, Childrens Press $7.35. Interesting material about this Kentucky park.

6215. Roberts, Bruce, and Roberts, Nancy. *Where Time Stood Still: A Portrait of Appalachia* (6–9). Illustrated. 1970, Crowell $6.95. Text and photographs capture the poverty, disease, unemployment, and strength of the people of Appalachia. Also use: *Appalachia: The Mountains, the Place and the People* by Betty L. Toone (1972, Watts $4.90).

6216. Rogers, Jan Faulk. *Georgia: Home of President Jimmy Carter* (4–6). Illustrated. 1978, Childrens Press $5.50. A brief introduction to the land and people of the "Empire State of the South."

6217. Sasek, M. *This Is Washington* (2–4). Illustrated. 1969, Macmillan $4.95; paper $2.25. An introduction to the U.S. capital in picture-book format.

6218. Shaw, Ray. *Washington for Children* (4–8). Illustrated. 1975, Scribner paper $3.95. Subtitle: *A Comprehensive Guide to the Unusual, Offbeat, and Exciting in and Around Washington for Young People, Families and Teachers.*

6219. Shull, Peg. *The Children of Appalachia* (4–6). Illustrated. 1969, Messner $3.64. An account of 3 very different families and how they live in this isolated area.

6220. Tveten, John L. *Exploring the Bayous* (4–7). Illus. by author. 1979, McKay $7.95. The beauty and mystery of the bayous are captured in this account.

Midwest

6221. Ault, Phil. *These Are the Great Lakes* (5–7). Illustrated. 1972, Dodd $5.95. A description of the lakes and their place in U.S. history and geography. Also use: *The Great Lakes* by James P. Barry (1976, Watts $4.90).

6222. Bailey, Bernadine. *Picture Book of Illinois* (2–4). Illus. by Kurt Wiese. 1967, Whitman $4.75. Part of a series. Also use ($4.75): *Picture Book of Michigan* (1967), *Picture Book of Minnesota* (1967), *Picture Book of Iowa* (1969), *Picture Book of Kansas* (1969), and *Picture Book of Indiana* (1974).

6223. Bailey, Bernadine. *Picture Book of Missouri* (2–4). Illus. by Kurt Wiese. 1974, Whitman $4.75. Part of a series. Also use ($4.75): *Picture Book of Nebraska* (1966), *Picture Book of South Dakota* (1966), *Picture Book of Ohio* (1967), *Picture Book of North Dakota* (1971) and *Picture Book of Wisconsin* (1975).

6224. Carpenter, Allan. *Illinois* (4–6). Illustrated. 1979, Childrens Press $9.25. Part of the *New Enchantment of America* series. Also use ($9.25 each): *Michigan* (1978), *Minnesota* (1978), *Indiana* (1979), *Iowa* (1979), and *Kansas* (1979).

6225. Carpenter, Allan. *Missouri* (4–6). Illustrated. 1978, Childrens Press $9.25. Part of the *New Enchantment of America* series. Also use ($9.25 each): *South Dakota* (1978), *Wisconsin* (1978), *Nebraska* (1979), *North Dakota* (1979), and *Ohio* (1979).

6226. Fradin, Dennis B. *Wisconsin in Words and Pictures* (2–5). Illustrated. 1977, Childrens Press $4.95. Interesting background information is interspersed with essential historical and geographical facts.

6227. Frazier, Carl, and Frazier, Rosalie. *The Lincoln Country in Pictures* (4–6). Illustrated. 1963, Hastings $4.95. An introduction to the land where Lincoln was born.

6228. Renick, Marion. *Ohio* (6–8). Illustrated. 1970, Coward $5.99. Many facets of this important state, including recreation and social activities, are covered in this well-organized account. For a younger group use: *The Ohio River* by Jeannette C. Nolan (1974, Coward $3.97).

6229. Veglahn, Nancy. *Getting to Know the Missouri River* (3–5). Illus. by William K. Plummer. 1972, Coward $3.97. An introduction to the history and geography surrounding this important waterway.

Mountain States

6230. Bailey, Bernadine. *Picture Book of Colorado* (2–4). Illus. by Kurt Wiese. 1971, Whitman $4.75. Part of a series. Also use ($4.75): *Picture Book of Idaho* (1967), *Picture Book of Utah* (1967), *Picture Book of Montana* (1969), *Picture Book of Wyoming* (1972), *Picture Book of Nevada* (1974).

6231. Carpenter, Allan. *Colorado* (4–6). Illustrated. 1978, Childrens Press $9.95. Part of the *New Enchantment of America* series. Also use ($9.25): *Idaho* (1979), *Montana* (1979), *Nevada* (1979), *Utah* (1979) and *Wyoming* (1979).

6232. Crosby, Alexander L. *The Colorado: Mover of Mountains* (4–6). Illustrated. 1961, Garrard $3.68. The story of the river that carved out the Grand Canyon.

6233. Johnson, Dorothy M. *Montana* (6–8). 1971, Coward $5.99. An overview of past and present conditions in this western state.

6234. Kirk, Ruth. *Yellowstone: The First National Park* (5–7). Illustrated. 1974, Atheneum $6.25. Famous landmarks in the park are described as well as its plant and animal life.

6235. Radlauer, Ruth. *Bryce Canyon National Park* (3–5). Illustrated. 1980, Childrens Press $6.50. An overview of the extraordinary park in southwest Utah.

6236. Radlauer, Ruth. *Zion National Park* (3–5). Illustrated. 1978, Childrens Press $7.35. The Utah park introduced in text and many color photographs.

Southwest

6237. Bailey, Bernadine. *Picture Book of Arizona* (2–4). Illus. by Kurt Wiese. 1967, Whitman $4.25. Part of a series. Also use (same price): *Picture Book* *of New Mexico* (1966), *Picture Book of Oklahoma* (1967), and *Picture Book of Texas* (1967).

6238. Carpenter, Allan. *Arizona* (4–6). Illustrated. 1979, Childrens Press $9.25. Part of the *New Enchantment of America* series. Also use ($9.25): *New Mexico* (1978), *Oklahoma* (1979), and *Texas* (1979).

6239. Fradin, Dennis B. *Arizona in Words and Pictures* (2–4). Illustrated. 1980, Children's Press $6.50. One in an extensive, useful series.

6240. Radlauer, Ruth. *Grand Canyon National Park* (3–4). Illustrated. 1977, Children's Press $3.95; LB $7.95. A simple treatment of the physical characteristics and the plant and animal life of this scenic park; part of the series, *Parks for People*, which deals with major American national parks.

6241. Sasek, M. *This Is Texas* (1–3). Illus. by author. 1967, Macmillan $5.95. A simple, heavily illustrated account in picture-book format.

6242. Sperry, Armstrong. *Great River, Wide Land, the Rio Grande through History* (5–7). Illus. by author. 1967, Macmillan $4.50. The part this mighty river has played in U.S. history. For a younger group use: *The Rio Grande* by Alexander L. Crosby (1966, Garrard $3.68).

6243. Wakeman, Norman Hammond. *Southwest Desert Wonderland* (6–8). Illustrated. 1965, Dodd $3.25. The climate, geography, and vegetation are highlighted.

Pacific States

6244. Bailey, Bernadine. *Picture Book of California* (2–4). Illus. by Kurt Wiese. 1968, Whitman $4.75. Part of a series. Also use ($4.75): *Picture Book of Washington* (1966), *Picture Book of Oregon* (1967), *Picture Book of Hawaii* (1967), and *Picture Book of Alaska* (1968).

6245. Carpenter, Allan. *California* (4–6). Illustrated. 1978, Childrens Press $9.25. Part of the *New Enchantment of America* series. Also use ($9.25): *Alaska* (1979), *Hawaii* (1979), *Oregon* (1979), and *Washington* (1979).

6246. Epstein, Sam, and Epstein, Beryl. *The Sacramento: Golden River of California* (6–9). Illustrated. 1968, Garrard $3.68. An introduction to the geography and history surrounding this river.

6247. Fradin, Dennis B. *Alaska in Words and Pictures* (2–5). Illustrated. 1977, Childrens Press paper $4.95. Historical and geographical information are supplied, along with interesting sidelights.

6248. Fradin, Dennis B. *California in Words and Pictures* (2–3). Illus. by Robert Ulm. 1977, Childrens Press $7.95. A simple picture tour that highlights history and physical characteristics.

6249. Frank, Phil, and Frank, Susan. *Subee Lives on a Houseboat* (4–6). Illustrated. 1980, Messner $6.97. Subee lives in a very special community—the houseboat area in Sausalito, California.

6250. Latham, Jean Lee. *The Columbia: Powerhouse of North America* (4–7). Illustrated. 1967, Garrard $3.68. History and geography are combined in this account of a great river.

6251. Laschever, Barnett D. *Getting to Know Hawaii* (4–7). Illustrated. 1959, Coward $3.97. The islands, their development, and geography are included.

6252. Laycock, George. *Death Valley* (4–7). Illustrated. 1976, Four Winds $6.95. A general introduction to the geography and history of this interesting but barren region.

6253. Lewin, Ted. *World within a World—Baja* (5–7). Illus. by author. 1978, Dodd $5.95. An impressionistic view of the flora and fauna of Baja, California.

6254. McDonald, Cawley. *California in Pictures* (4–6). Illustrated. 1979, Sterling $4.59; paper $2.50. The land, people, and economy of this state. •

6255. Pratt, Helen Jay. *The Hawaiians: An Island People* (6–8). Illustrated. 1963, Tuttle $8.95. An account of early Hawaii and its inhabitants, with emphasis on folk customs.

6256. Radlauer, Ruth. *Haleakala National Park* (3–5). Illustrated. 1979, Childrens Press $5.95. Maui's national park in Hawaii comes alive in photographs and text.

6257. Radlauer, Ruth. *Olympic National Park* (3–5). Illustrated. 1978, Childrens Press $7.35. A visit to the Washington park that is one of the most interesting.

6258. Sasek, M. *This Is San Francisco* (3–5). Illus. by author. 1962, Macmillan $5.95; paper $.95. Colorful pictures introduce the readers to important landmarks and way of life in the Golden Gate city.

6259. Stefansson, Evelyn Baird. *Here Is Alaska* (5–8). Illustrated. 1973, Scribner $6.95. All aspects of Alaskan life are explored in this well-organized, nicely illustrated guide.

History—General

6260. Asimov, Isaac. *The Birth of the United States 1763–1816* (6–9). Illustrated. 1974, Houghton $6.95. An informal overview of U.S. history from the Treaty of Paris to the end of the War of 1812. Sequel to: *The Shaping of North America* (1973, Houghton $5.95).

6261. Commager, Henry Steele. *The First Book of American History* (4–6). Illus. by Leonard Everett Fisher. 1957, Watts $4.90; paper $1.25. A very brief but readable account that tends to oversimplify the material.

6262. Faber, Harold. *From Sea to Sea: The Growth of the United States* (3–6). 1967, Farrar $5.95. The story of how our country took shape state by state.

6263. Gardner, Joseph L., and Weisberger, Bernard. *Labor on the March: The Story of America's Unions* (6–8). Illustrated. 1969, American Heritage $6.89. An advanced account of how labor organized in America.

6264. Johnson, Gerald W. *America: A History for Peter* (5–8). Illus. by Leonard Everett Fisher. 1960, Morrow $7.50. A trilogy of American history clearly written for children in the following volumes (all Morrow $7.75): *America Is Born* (1959), *America Grows Up* (1960), and *America Moves Forward* (1960).

6265. McNeer, May. *Profile of American History* (5–7). Illustrated. 1965, Hammond $4.50; LB $4.39. Growth of the United States shown in 64 color maps.

6266. Warren, Ruth. *A Pictorial History of Women in America* (4–6). 1975, Crown $7.95. An interesting overview on the contribution of women to U.S. history. Also use: *An Album of Women in American History* by Leonard Ingraham and Claire Ingraham (1972, Watts $5.90).

Indians of North America

6267. American Heritage, eds. *Indians of the Plains* (6–9). Illustrated. 1960, American Heritage/Harper $5.95; LB $6.89. History, customs, warfare, and ceremonies supplemented with distinguished illustrations.

6268. Baker, Betty. *Settlers and Strangers: Native Americans of the Desert Southwest and History as They Saw It* (3–6). Illustrated. 1977, Macmillan $7.95. A concise history of Southwest Indians, including the Pueblos and Hopi, from their arrival via the land bridge from Siberia to the present.

6269. Baldwin, Gordon C. *The Apache Indians: Raiders of the Southwest* (6–8). Illustrated. 1978, Four Winds $9.95. A carefully researched, accurate description of the Apache history and culture.

6270. Baylor, Byrd. *Before You Came This Way* (2–4). Illus. by Tom Bahti. 1969, Dutton $6.50. The illustrations are based on prehistoric Indian rock drawings found in the southwestern United States; an introduction to the way of life of these people.

6271. Baylor, Byrd. *The Desert Is Theirs* (2–4). Illus. by Peter Parnall. 1975, Scribner $6.95. Through colorful strong pictures and a lyric text, the life of the Papago Indians and their reverence for the desert are revealed.

6272. Bealer, Alex W. *Only the Names Remain: The Cherokees and the Trail of Tears* (4–6). Illus. by William Sauts Bock. 1972, Little $5.95. A history of the Cherokees with emphasis on their tragic exile west of the Mississippi in 1839.

6273. Benchley, Nathaniel. *Small Wolf* (1–3). Illus. by Joan Sandin. 1972, Harper $6.89. The relationship between Indians and whites on Manhattan Island in pre-Revolutionary days.

6274. Bleeker, Sonia. *The Chippewa Indians: Rice Gatherers of the Great Lakes* (5–6). Illustrated. 1955, Morrow $5.71. Life and social organization are highlighted. Also use: *The Sioux Indians: Hunters and Warriors of the Plains* (1962, $5.71).

6275. Bleeker, Sonia. *Indians of the Longhouse: The Story of the Iroquois* (4–6). Illustrated. 1950, Morrow $5.71. An excellent account of the village life of the Iroquois through the 4 seasons. Other Eastern tribes described in this series (all Morrow $5.71) are: *The Cherokee: Indians of the Mountains* (1952), *The Delaware Indians: Eastern Fishermen and Farmers* (1953), and *The Seminole Indians* (1954).

6276. Bleeker, Sonia. *The Navajo: Herder, Weavers and Silversmiths* (4–6). Illus. by Patricia Boodell. 1958, Morrow $5.71. This account includes material on history, customs, and present-day life. Other Indian tribes of the Southwest in this series (Morrow) are: *The Apache Indians: Raiders of the Southwest* (1951, $5.52), and *The Pueblo Indians: Farmers of the Rio Grande* (1955, $5.71).

6277. Bleeker, Sonia. *The Sea Hunters: Indians of the Northwest Coast* (4–7). Illus. by Althea Karr. 1951, Morrow $5.71. A description of the life, customs, and arts of Pacific Northwest tribes. Other Indians of the West described in this series are: *Horsemen of the Western Plateaus: The Nez Perce Indians* (1957, $5.71).

6278.   Clark, Ann Nolan. *Circle of Seasons* (5–8). Illus. by W. T. Mars. 1970, Farrar $4.95. The Pueblo year along with the appropriate ceremonies are poetically described.

6279.   Davis, Christopher. *Plains Indians* (6–8). Illustrated. 1978, Watts $5.90. A well-illustrated overview of the culture of the Plains Indians.

6280.   Dickinson, Alice. *Taken by the Indians: True Tales of Captivity* (6–9). 1976, Watts $6.90. Six true stories based on diaries and other accounts that tell of capture and captivity.

6281.   Ehrlich, Amy. *Wounded Knee: An Indian History of the American West* (6–8). Illustrated. 1974, Holt $6.95. An adaptation for young readers of Dee Brown's *Bury My Heart at Wounded Knee.*

6282.   Erdoes, Richard. *The Native Americans: Navajos* (4–6). Illustrated. 1979, Sterling $12.95; LB $11.69. A fully realized treatment of the history, traditions, life-styles of the Navajos.

6283.   Erdoes, Richard. *The Rain Dance People* (6–8). Illustrated. 1976, Knopf $7.95. A history of the Pueblo Indians from prehistory to the U.S. Bureau of Indian Affairs. Also use: *Red Power on the Rio Grande: The Native American Revolution of 1680* by Franklin Folsom (1973, Follett $5.95; LB $5.97).

6284.   Goble, Paul, and Goble, Dorothy. *Brave Eagle's Account of the Fetterman Fight: 21 December 1866* (5–7). Illus. by Paul Goble. 1972, Pantheon $4.95; LB $5.99. The true story of the defeat of soldiers led by Captain Fetterman, who tried to invade Sioux territory.

6285.   Goble, Paul, and Goble, Dorothy. *Lone Bull's Horse Raid* (5–8). Illus. by Paul Goble. 1973, Bradbury $8.95. Lone Bull, a 14-year-old Sioux, longs to capture a horse from his tribe's enemies, the Crows.

6286.   Gorsline, Marie, and Gorsline, Douglas. *North American Indians* (6–8). Illustrated. 1978, Random $3.95; paper $.95. Major tribes are identified and described briefly.

6287.   Gridley, Marion E. *Story of the Seminole* (5–8). Illus. by Robert Glaubke. 1973, Putnam $5.97. The origin and history of the Florida tribe from their beginnings to today.

6288.   Hofsinde, Robert. *The Indian Medicine Man* (4–6). Illus. by author. 1966, Morrow $5.52. Sioux, Iroquois, Apache, Navaho, Ojibwa, and Northwest coast medicine men from past to present.

6289.   Hofsinde, Robert. *Indian Warriors and Their Weapons* (4–6). Illustrated. 1965, Morrow $5.52. An overview of weapons and battle tactics used by several tribes.

6290.   Hofsinde, Robert. *Indians at Home* (4–7). Illus. by author. 1964, Morrow $5.52. A description of the homes of various Indian tribes. Also use: *Indian Hunting* (1962, $5.52).

6291.   Hofsinde, Robert. *Indians on the Move* (4–6). Illus. by author. 1970, Morrow $5.52. All about Indian migration, causes, destinations, and equipment. Also use: *Indian Fishing and Camping* (1963, Morrow $5.52).

6292.   Jacobson, Daniel. *Hunters* (5–8). Illus. by Richard Cuffari. 1974, Watts $4.90. The life and customs of 3 central North American tribes are explored in this interesting account. Also use: *Indians of the Northern Plains* by William K. Powers (1969, Putnam $6.75).

6293.   Johnson, Dorothy M. *All the Buffalo Returning* (7–9). 1979, Dodd $6.95. An account of Sioux history from Little Big Horn to Wounded Knee from the standpoint of one Indian family.

6294.   Jones, Kenneth M. *War with the Seminoles: 1835–1842* (4–7). Illustrated. 1975, Watts $4.47. Subtitle: *The Florida Indians Fight for Their Freedom and Homeland.*

6295.   Kirk, Ruth. *David, Young Chief of the Quileutes: An American Indian Today* (4–6). Illus. by author. 1967, Harcourt $5.95. A description of the present-day life of a Washington State tribe of Indians as seen through the experiences of an 11-year-old boy.

6296.   Lavine, Sigmund A. *The Games the Indians Played* (5–7). Illustrated. 1974, Dodd $4.95. Fascinating descriptions of recreational pastimes of American Indians and Eskimos; origins, rules, and how the games differed from tribe to tribe.

6297.   Luling, Virginia. *Indians of the North American Plains* (5–8). Illustrated. 1979, Silver Burdett $6.99. A well-illustrated narrative that gives a rounded picture of the life of the Plains Indians.

6298.   Lyons, Grant. *The Creek Indians* (6–8). Illustrated. 1978, Messner $7.29. The sad story of the history of an Indian tribe and its destruction by whites.

6299.   McGovern, Ann. *If You Lived with the Sioux Indians* (2–4). Illus. by Robert Levering. 1974, Four Winds $5.95. Using a question-and-answer technique, the author gives a great deal of information about the daily life of the Sioux and their relationship with white people.

6300.   Martin, Patricia Miles. *Indians, the First Americans* (4–6). 1970, Parents $5.41. Customs of Indians are given.

6301. Marriott, Alice Lee. *Indians on Horseback* (4–6). Illus. by Margaret Lefranc. 1968, Crowell $8.95. Life and customs of the Plains Indians, including a cookbook. Also use: *The Sun Dance People: The Plains Indians, Their Past and Present* by Richard Erdoes (1972, Knopf $5.95; LB $6.99).

6302. Nabokov, Peter, ed. *Native American Testimony* (6–9). Illustrated. 1978, Crowell $8.95; LB $8.79. A mature book of readings subtitled: *An Anthology of Indian and White Relations—First Encounter to Dispossession.*

6303. Payne, Elizabeth. *Meet the North American Indians* (1–3). Illustrated. 1965, Random $3.95; LB $3.99. A narrative that introduces many tribes, their locations, and life-styles.

6304. Pine, Tillie S., and Levine, Joseph. *The Indians Knew* (2–4). Illus. by Ezra Jack Keats. 1957, McGraw $7.95. The many ways earlier peoples dealt with problems of everyday living.

6305. Reit, Seymour. *Child of the Navajos* (2–4). Photos by Paul Conklin. 1971, Dodd $4.95. Everyday activities of a contemporary Navaho boy living on a reservation in Arizona are highlighted by excellent, well-chosen photographs.

6306. Rounds, Glen. *Buffalo Harvest* (4–6). Illus. by author. 1952, Holiday $4.95. An account of the Plains Indians and their massive buffalo hunts conducted in the autumn.

6307. Sandoz, Mari. *The Battle of the Little Bighorn* (6–8). Illustrated. 1966, Lippincott $6.95. A stirring account of this bloody battle.

6308. Siegel, Beatrice. *Indians of the Woodland, Before and After the Pilgrims* (4–6). Illus. by Baptiste Shunatona. 1972, Walker $5.85. A look at how the Indians lived before the white settlers came, and how their civilization was destroyed.

6309. Supree, Burton, and Ross, Ann. *Bear's Heart: Scenes from the Life of a Cheyenne Artist of One Hundred Years Ago with Pictures by Himself* (5–9). 1977, Lippincott $8.95. The harrowing story of the flight of several Plains Indians from their reservations in 1874, their capture, and later imprisonment told through text and pictures.

6310. Tamarin, Alfred, and Glubok, Shirley. *Ancient Indians of the Southwest* (4–6). Illustrated. 1975, Doubleday $5.95. Traces the history and accomplishments of these people from the Ice Age through the period of Spanish domination.

6311. Tamarin, Alfred. *We Have Not Vanished: Eastern Indians of the United States* (4–6). Illustrated. 1974, Follett $5.97. Identifies and describes over 60 tribes and gives material about their life-styles.

6312. Tunis, Edwin. *Indians* (5–9). Illus. by author. 1979, Crowell $12.95; LB $12.79. Superlative text and illustrations enliven this revision of this classic, originally published in 1959.

6313. Witt, Shirely Hill. *The Tuscaroras* (4–6). 1972, Macmillan $4.95. An introduction to the sixth tribe to enter the Iroquois Confederacy.

6314. Wood, Nancy. *Hollerin Sun* (5–9). Illustrated. 1972, Simon & Schuster $4.95. A history and presentation of Indian philosophy as revealed in poems, legends, and sayings of the Taos people.

6315. Yellow Robe, Rosebud. *An Album of the American Indian* (4–6). Illustrated. 1969, Watts $5.90. Through excellent illustrations and a brief text, the culture of the American Indian is explored.

Discovery and Exploration

6316. American Heritage, eds. *Discoverers of the New World* (6–9). 1960, American Heritage/Harper $5.95. Three hundred years of exploration by people of many countries.

6317. Benchley, Nathaniel. *Snorri and the Strangers* (1–2). Illus. by Don Bolognese. 1976, Harper $5.95; LB $6.89. Snorri was the first white child born in America, and this Viking boy's adventures make a fascinating story for beginning readers.

6318. Buehr, Walter. *The French Explorers in America* (3–6). Illus. by author. 1961, Putnam $5.25. A lively account of such explorers as Cartier, LaSalle, and Champlain. Also use: *The Spanish Conquistadores in North America* (1962, Putnam $5.29).

6319. Buehr, Walter. *The Portuguese Explorers* (4–6). Illustrated. 1966, Putnam $5.29. An account that concentrates on Portugal's domination of the seas in the fifteenth century.

6320. Carter, Samuel. *Vikings Bold: Their Voyages and Adventures* (5–7). Illus. by Ted Burwell. 1972, Crowell $8.95. The life and times of the Vikings and their voyages from 800 to 1000 A.D., told with many quotes from ancient poems and sagas. For an older group use: *The Vikings* by Frank P. Donovan (1964, Horizon $9.89).

6321. Dalgliesh, Alice. *America Begins: The Story of the Finding of the New World* (4–7). Illus. by Lois Maloy. 1959, Scribner $6.95. Brief narratives of explorers from Leif the Lucky to Champlain.

6322. Foster, Genevieve. *Year of Columbus, 1492* (4–7). Illustrated. 1959, Scribner $5.95. An account that includes material on Columbus and others who lived at that time. Also use for a slightly older group: *The World of Columbus and Sons* (1965, Scribner $7.95).

6323. Golding, Morton J. *The Mystery of the Vikings in America* (6–8). Illustrated. 1973, Lippincott $8.95. An explanation of the Viking way of life and the controversies surrounding their contributions.

6324. Grant, Neil. *The Discoverers* (5–7). Illustrated. 1980, Arco $6.95. An elementary introduction to both sea voyages and land explorations.

6325. Holbrook, Sabra. *The French Founders of North America and Their Heritage* (6–9). Illustrated. 1976, Atheneum $7.95. A full account of the many contributions to North American history made by the French, with concluding chapters on the contemporary situation in Quebec.

6326. Johnston, Johanna. *Who Found America?* (3–5). Illus. by Anne Siberell. 1973, Childrens Press $7.35. A discussion of various explorers, each of whom could be considered a discoverer of America.

6327. Irwin, Constance. *Strange Footprints on the Land* (6–9). 1980, Harper $8.95. An investigation of the exploits of the Vikings in America.

6328. Rich, Louise Dickinson. *The First Book of the Vikings* (4–7). 1962, Watts $4.90. An excellent introduction to the life and accomplishments of these bold seafarers. Also use: *The Viking Explorers* by Walter Buehr (1967, Putnam $5.29).

6329. Rich, Louise Dickinson. *The First Book of the Fur Trade* (5–7). Illus. by Claudine Nankivel. 1965, Watts $4.90. The story of the search for fur and the resulting exploration of the North American continent.

6330. Rich, Louise Dickinson. *The First Book of New World Explorers* (4–6). Illus. by Page Cary. 1960, Watts $4.90; paper $1.25. A brief narrative highlighting major explorers and their voyages.

Colonial Period

6331. Alderman, Clifford L. *The Story of the Thirteen Colonies* (5–7). Illus. by Leonard Everett Fisher. 1966, Random $4.39. How the colonies were founded and who were their leaders.

6332. Alderman, Clifford L. *The Devil's Shadow* (4–6). Illustrated. 1967, Messner $4.79. Subtitle: *The Story of Witchcraft in Massachusetts.*

6333. Alderman, Clifford L. *Witchcraft in America* (5–8). 1974, Messner $7.29. A useful and intriguing history of many forms of witchcraft as they existed in various parts of the United States.

6334. American Heritage, eds. *The French and Indian War* (5–8). Illustrated. 1962, Harper $6.95. A well-illustrated survey of the 4 wars that determined British control of North America. Also use: *The First Book of the Indian Wars* by Richard B. Morris (1959, Watts $4.90).

6335. Behrens, June, and Brower, Pauline. *Colonial Farm* (2–4). Illustrated. 1975, Childrens Press $7.95. A look at a colonial farm in Virginia, illustrated with color photographs.

6336. Borreson, Mary Jo. *Let's Go to Colonial Williamsburg* (4–6). Illus. by M. Barnett. 1962, Putnam $4.29. A visit to Williamsburg reveals how people lived in the colonies.

6337. Brown, Ira L. *The Georgia Colony* (5–7). Illustrated. 1970, Macmillan $5.95. Georgia's history from the early explorers through the Revolution. Also use: *The Colony of Georgia* by Harold Cecil Vaughan (1974, Watts $4.90) and, for an older group, *Colonial Georgia* by Clifford S. Capp (1972, Nelson $6.95).

6338. Burney, Eugenia. *Colonial South Carolina* (6–9). Illustrated. 1970, Nelson $6.95. A detailed history that concludes with the role of South Carolina in the Revolution. For a younger group use: *The Colony of South Carolina* by Nanci A. Lyman (1975, Watts $4.90) and *The South Carolina Colony* by Marguerite C. Steedman (1970, Macmillan $5.95).

6339. Campbell, Elizabeth A. *The Carving on the Tree* (3–6). Illus. by William Bock. 1968, Little $6.95. An account of the lost colony of Roanoke. Also use: *The Lost Colony* by Dan Lacy (1972, Watts $4.47).

6340. Christensen, Gardell D., and Burney, Eugenia. *Colonial Delaware* (6–9). Illustrated. 1975, Nelson $6.95. A detailed history of colonial Delaware and its role in the Revolution. For a younger group use: *The Colony of Delaware* by Nanci A. Lyman (1975, Watts $4.90) and *The Delaware Colony* by H. Clay Reed (1970, Macmillan $5.95).

6341. Daugherty, James. *The Landing of the Pilgrims* (5–7). Illus. by author. 1950, Random $4.99. Based on his own writings, this is the story of the Pilgrims from the standpoint of William Bradford. Also use: *The Pilgrims of Plymouth* by Barbara L. Beck (1972, Watts, paper $1.25).

6342. Davis, Burke. *Getting to Know Jamestown* (4–6). Illus. by Tran Mawicke. 1971, Coward $3.97. A history of the English colony from its founding to its destruction in 1698. Also use:

Jamestown: The Beginning by Elizabeth A. Campbell (1974, Little $5.95).

6343. Davis, Burke. *Getting to Know Thomas Jefferson's Virginia* (4–6). Illus. by Haris Petie. 1971, Coward $3.97. A reconstruction of life and social activities in the colony.

6344. Dickinson, Alice. *The Colony of Massachusetts* (5–7). Illustrated. 1975, Watts $4.90. From the Plymouth Pilgrims to the Revolution. Also use: *The Massachusetts Colony* by Robert Smith (1969, Macmillan $5.95) and, for an older group, *Colonial Massachusetts* by James P. Wood (1969, Nelson $6.75).

6345. Earle, Alice M. *Home and Child Life in Colonial Days* (5–8). Illus. with photos by Alfred Tamarin. 1969, Macmillan $7.95. A consolidation and abridgement of Earle's fine books, *Home Life in Colonial Days* and *Child Life in Colonial Days.*

6346. Fisher, Leonard Everett. *The Architects* (5–7). Illus. by author. 1970, Watts $4.90. A beautifully illustrated introduction to this colonial profession. Other books in this series on colonial craftspeople, by the same author/artist and publisher, include (each $4.47 unless noted otherwise): *The Glassmakers* (5–7, 1964), *The Hatters* (5–7, 1965), *The Papermakers* (4–6, 1965), *The Printers* (4–6, 1965), *The Silversmiths* (5–7, 1965), *The Wigmakers* (5–7, 1965), *The Cabinetmakers* (5–7, 1966, $3.90), *The Tanners* (5–7, 1966), *The Weavers* (5–7, 1966), *The Schoolmasters* (5–7, 1967), *The Shipbuilders* (5–7, 1967), *The Shoemakers* (5–7, 1967), *The Doctors* (5–7, 1968), *The Peddlers* (5–7, 1968), *The Potters* (5–7, 1969), *The Homemakers* (4–6, 1973), and *The Blacksmiths* (5–7, 1976, $3.90).

6347. Foster, Genevieve. *The World of Captain John Smith* (5–7). Illus. by author. 1959, Scribner $20.00. A comparative history of the world during John Smith's time.

6348. Foster, Genevieve. *The World of William Penn* (4–7). Illus. by author. 1973, Scribner $15.00. Using the main events in Penn's life as a framework, the author supplies details on contemporary happenings in other areas of the world and relates U.S. history to that of other lands.

6349. Fritz, Jean. *Who's That Stepping on Plymouth Rock?* (3–5). Illus. by J. B. Handelsman. 1975, Coward $6.95. Another entertaining, lively, and accurate romp through history by this prolific author.

6350. Giffen, Daniel H. *New Hampshire Colony* (4–6). Illustrated. 1970, Macmillan $5.95. The colony's story told from the first exploration by a white man in the seventeenth century to the American Revolution. Also use: *Colony of New Hampshire* by Emil Lengyel (1975, Watts $4.90) and, for an older group, *Colonial New Hampshire* by James P. Wood (1973, Nelson $6.95).

6351. Gurney, Gene, and Gurney, Clare. *The Colony of Maryland* (4–6). Illustrated. 1972, Watts $4.90. A history from the colony's beginnings through the Revolution. Also use: *The Maryland Colony* by F. Van Wyck Mason (1969, Macmillan $5.95) and, for an older group, *Colonial Maryland* by Ann Finlayson (1974, Nelson $6.95).

6352. Hall, Elvajean, and Criner, Beatrice. *Today in Old Philadelphia* (4–6). Illus. by Lois Axeman. 1975, Childrens Press $6.60. Through surviving landmarks, the authors recreate major events in the Colonial and Revolutionary periods. Also use: *Philadelphia* by Susan Lee and John Lee (1975, Childrens Press $6.60).

6353. Hults, Dorothy Niebrugge. *New Amsterdam Days and Ways* (4–7). Illustrated. 1963, Harcourt $5.95. An account of the Dutch settlers in the New World and how their capital became New York.

6354. Johnston, Johanna. *The Connecticut Colony* (5–7). Illustrated. 1969, Macmillan $5.95. A well-organized and detailed account of the colony from its beginning until the signing of the Declaration. Also use: *The Colony of Connecticut* by Clifford L. Alderman (1975, Watts $4.90).

6355. Lacy, Dan. *The Colony of North Carolina* (4–6). Illustrated. 1975, Watts $4.90. A history from the Lost Colony on Roanoke Island through the Revolution. Also use: *North Carolina Colony* by William S. Powell (1969, Macmillan $5.95) and, for an older group, *Colonial North Carolina* by Eugenia Burney (1975, Nelson $6.95).

6356. Lacy, Dan. *The Colony of Virginia* (5–6). Illustrated. 1973, Watts $4.90. A brief history that traces the colony from its beginnings at Jamestown to the adoption of the Constitution in 1788. Also use: *The Virginia Colony* by Elswyth Thane (1969, Macmillan $5.95).

6357. Lee, Susan, and Lee, John. *New York* (4–6). 1975, Childrens Press $6.60. A history of New York City from its beginnings to the Revolutionary War.

6358. Loeb, Robert H., Jr. *Meet the Real Pilgrims: Everyday Life on Plymouth Plantation in 1627* (4–6). Illustrated. 1979, Doubleday $6.95. The lives and living conditions of the Pilgrims in early New England. Also use: *Meet the Pilgrim Fathers* by Elizabeth Payne (1966, Random $3.95).

6359. Lobel, Arnold. *On the Day Peter Stuyvesant Sailed into Town* (K–3). Illus. by author. 1971, Harper $8.79. How Peter Stuyvesant, the new governor of the Dutch Colony, put the citizens to work cleaning up their town, told in humorous verse and pictures.

6360. Loeper, John J. *Flying Machine: A Stagecoach Journey in 1774* (4–7). Illustrated. 1976, Atheneum $4.95. Based on fact, an account of the fun and discomforts of a stagecoach trip from Philadelphia to New York City.

6361. Loeper, John J. *Going to School in 1776* (3–6). Illustrated. 1973, Atheneum $6.95. An interesting account of education and childhood activities in Colonial America. Also use: Ann McGovern's *If You Lived in Colonial Times* (1966, Four Winds $4.95).

6362. Loeper, John J. *The Shop on High Street: The Toys and Games of Early America* (5–8). Illustrated. 1978, Atheneum $6.95. A history of leisure pursuits of children in America from 1750 to 1850.

6363. McGovern, Ann. *If You Sailed on the Mayflower* (3–4). Illus. by J. B. Handelsman. 1970, Scholastic paper $9.54. In a question-and-answer format, information is given on the historic voyage and the settlement in New England. For a slightly older group use: *The Story of the Mayflower Compact* by Norman Richards (1967, Childrens Press $7.35).

6364. Naden, Corinne J. *The Colony of New Jersey* (4–6). Illustrated. 1974, Watts $4.90. Carries the history of New Jersey through its role in the Constitutional Convention. Also use: *The New Jersey Colony* by Fred J. Cook (1969, Macmillan $5.95) and, for an older group, *Colonial New Jersey* by John T. Cunningham (1971, Nelson $6.95).

6365. Nurenberg, Thelma. *The New York Colony* (5–7). Illustrated. 1969, Macmillan $5.95. An account that stresses the exploration, settlement, and growth of the colony. Also use: *The Colony of New York* by David Goodnough (1973, Watts $4.90) and, for an older group, *Colonial New York* by Gardell D. Christensen (1969, Nelson $6.95).

6366. Petersham, Maud, and Petersham, Miska. *The Silver Mace: A Story of Williamsburg* (4–6). Illus. by author. 1964, Macmillan $4.75. The history of Williamsburg, which includes some material on its recent restoration. Also use: *Williamsburg* by Susan Lee and John Lee (1975, Childrens Press $6.60).

6367. Raskin, Joseph. *Newcomers: Ten Tales of American Immigrants* (4–7). Illus. by Kurt Werth. 1974, Lothrop $7.25; LB $6.96. Ten true stories of colonial immigrants, taken from primary sources.

6368. Raskin, Joseph, and Raskin, Edith. *Tales of Indentured Servants* (5–7). Illus. by William Sauts Bock. 1978, Lothrop $6.50; LB $6.24. Eight stories based on fact about indentured servants during the Colonial Period.

6369. Rich, Louise Dickinson. *The First Book of the Early Settlers* (3–6). Illustrated. 1959, Watts $4.90; paper $1.25. Short accounts of Jamestown, Plymouth, New Amsterdam, and Fort Christina.

6370. Rich, Louise Dickinson. *King Philip's War, 1675–76* (5–7). Illustrated. 1972, Watts $4.47. Subtitle: *The New England Indians Fight The Colonists.*

6371. Siegel, Beatrice. *A New Look at the Pilgrims: Why They Came to America* (5–7). Illus. by Douglas Morris. 1977, Walker $5.95; LB $5.85. Extensive background information on Puritans and Separatists and the true nature of those who came over on the Mayflower.

6372. Sloane, Eric. *ABC Book of Early Americana* (4–7). Illus. by author. 1963, Doubleday $4.95. Subtitle: *A Sketchbook of Antiquities and American Firsts.*

6373. Smith, E. Brooks, and Meridith, Robert. *Pilgrim Courage* (5–7). Illus. by Leonard Everett Fisher. 1962, Little $5.95. Subtitle: *Selected Episodes from 'Of Plimoth Plantation' and Passages from the Journals of William Bradford and Edward Winslow.* For a younger group use: *The Coming of the Pilgrims: Told from Governor Bradford's Firsthand Account* (1964, Little $5.95).

6374. Soderlind, Arthur E. *Colonial Connecticut* (6–9). 1976, Nelson $6.95. A well-organized history reconstructed from such original documents as letters and diaries.

6375. Spier, Peter. *The Legend of New Amsterdam* (2–4). Illus. by author. 1979, Doubleday $6.95. The town of New Amsterdam in paintings and text that ends with an unexpected glimpse into the future.

6376. Starkey, Marion L. *Tall Men from Boston* (3–5). Illustrated. 1975, Crown $5.95. An account of the witch-hunting hysteria that hit Salem Village in 1692. Also use for slightly older readers: *The Witchcraft of Salem Village* by Shirley Jackson (1956, Random $2.95).

6377. Stearns, Monroe. *The Story of New England* (5–7). Illustrated. 1967, Random $4.95. A history of New England with emphasis on its earliest days.

6378. Stevens, S. K. *The Pennsylvania Colony* (5–7). Illustrated. 1970, Macmillan $5.95. A well-organized, compact history. Also use: *The Colony of Pennsylvania* by Emil Lengyel (1974, Watts

$4.90) and, for an older group *Colonial Pennsylvania* by Lucille Wallower (1969, Nelson $6.95).

6379. Szekeres, Cyndy. *Long, Long Ago* (3–4). Illustrated. 1977, McGraw $7.95. Costumed animals recreate the social life and customs of the colonial period.

6380. Tunis, Edwin. *Colonial Living* (5–9). Illus. by author. 1976, Crowell $10.95. A beautifully illustrated account of everyday life in Colonial America. Also use: *Colonial Craftsmen: And the Beginnings of American Industry* (1976, Crowell $12.95).

6381. Tunis, Edwin. *Shaw's Fortune: The Picture Story of a Colonial Plantation* (4–7). Illus. by author. 1976, Crowell $8.95. Recreation of everyday life on a Virginia tobacco plantation.

6382. Tunis, Edwin. *The Tavern at the Ferry* (4–7). Illus. by author. 1973, Crowell $9.95. Through outstanding illustrations and accompanying text, focusing principally on a New Jersey ferry and tavern owned by Quakers, the author gives a great amount of information about the Colonial Period.

6383. Webb, Robert N. *The Colony of Rhode Island* (5–7). Illustrated. 1972, Watts $4.90. From discovery to statehood is outlined in this interesting overview. Also use: *The Rhode Island Colony* by Clifford L. Alderman (1969, Macmillan $6.95) and, for an older group, *Colonial Rhode Island* by Carleton Beals (1970, Nelson $6.75).

6384. Williams, Selma R. *Kings, Commoners and Colonists: Politics in Old and New England 1603–1660* (6–9). 1974, Atheneum $7.95. An excellent history of the life, politics, leaders, and problems of the Massachusetts Bay Colony.

6385. Wright, Louis Booker. *Everyday Life in Colonial America* (5–9). Illustrated. 1966, Putnam $6.75. An account of how the colonists worked and played.

Revolutionary Period

6386. Alderman, Clifford L. *The War We Could Have Lost: The American Revolution* (5–8). Illustrated. 1974, Four Winds $6.00. An account emphasizing that the outcome of the war was always in doubt. Also use: *The Revolutionary War* by Bart McDowell (1967, National Geographic $5.75).

6387. Benchley, Nathaniel. *George, The Drummer Boy* (1–2). Illus. by Don Bolognese. 1977, Harper $5.95; LB $6.89. The beginning of the American Revolution from the viewpoint of a young British soldier, told simply and dramatically.

6388. Benchley, Nathaniel. *Sam the Minuteman* (2–4). Illus. by Arnold Lobel. 1969, Harper $5.95; LB $6.89. An easy-to-read book that gives information on the way of life at the beginning of the Revolution.

6389. Bliven, Bruce. *The American Revolution 1760–1783* (5–7). Illustrated. 1958, Random $2.95; LB $4.39. The causes, principal events, and results of the war are given in this basic overview.

6390. Colby, Jean P. *Lexington and Concord 1775; What Really Happened* (5–7). Illus. by Barbara Cooney. 1975, Hastings $7.95. The 2 early battles in the Revolutionary War, along with a summary of background events and famous people of the time.

6391. Colby, C.B. *Revolutionary War Weapons* (6–9). Illustrated. 1963, Coward $5.19. Subtitle: *Pole Arms, Hand Guns, Shoulder Arms and Artillery.*

6392. Commager, Henry Steele. *The Great Declaration: A Book for Young Americans* (6–7). Illus. by Don Bolognese. 1958, Bobbs-Merrill $6.95. The story of the Declaration of Independence, how it came into being, and something about the men who drafted, discussed, and debated it.

6393. Dalgliesh, Alice. *The Fourth of July Story* (3–5). 1956, Scribner $8.95; paper $.95. The history behind the writing of the Declaration of Independence, readably retold.

6394. Foster, Genevieve. *Year of Independence 1776* (3–5). Illus. by author. 1970, Scribner $5.95. The relations between England and the Colonies that led to the outbreak of the Revolution and the writing of the Declaration of Independence are included in this excellent history book.

6395. Haley, Gail E. *Jack Jouett's Ride* (3–4). Illus. by author. 1973, Viking $5.95. Penguin paper $1.75. Based on a true incident in the Revolutionary War, the story of a 40-mile midnight ride to warn the southern revolutionaries of the coming of the British dragoons.

6396. Lomask, Milton. *The First American Revolution* (6–8). Illustrated. 1974, Farrar $7.95. This book covers the years 1763 to 1784, from various viewpoints—military, political, economic, and social. For a slightly younger group use: *The First Book of the American Revolution* by Richard B. Morris (1956, Watts $4.90; paper $1.25).

6397. Lowrey, Janette Sebring. *Six Silver Spoons* (1–3). Illus. by Robert Quackenbush. 1971, Harper $6.87. Tim and Debbie ride to Lexington to bring mother a birthday present of 6 silver spoons during the American Revolution.

6398. Milhous, Katherine. *Through These Arches* (4–6). Illus. by author. 1964, Lippincott $6.50. A tour through Independence Hall in Philadelphia with stories about Colonial events associated with it. Also use: *The Story of the Liberty Bell* by Natalie Miller (1965, Childrens Press $7.35).

6399. Munves, James. *Thomas Jefferson and the Declaration of Independence* (6–8). Illustrated. 1978, Scribner $12.50. Subtitled: *The Writing and Editing of the Document That Marked the Birth of the United States of America.*

6400. Pearson, Michael. *Those Yankee Rebels* (5–8). 1974, Putnam $6.95. Subtitle: *Being the True and Amasing History of the Audacious American Revolution as Seen through British Eyes and Being a Young People's Version of Those Doomed Rebels.*

6401. Phelan, Mary Kay. *Four Days in Philadelphia 1776* (4–6). Illus. by Charles Walker. 1967, Crowell $7.95. The story behind the shaping of the Declaration of Independence.

6402. Phelan, Mary Kay. *Midnight Alarm: The Story of Paul Revere's Ride* (4–6). Illustrated. 1968, Crowell $7.95. An exciting recreation of the famous midnight ride.

6403. Phelan, Mary Kay. *The Story of the Boston Massacre* (5–9). Illus. by Allan Eitzen. 1976, Crowell $7.95. A present-day narrative adds immediacy to this well-presented account. Also use: *The Story of the Boston Tea Party* (1974, Crowell $7.95).

6404. Taylor, Theodore. *Rebellion Town, Williamsburg 1776* (6–9). Illus. by Richard Cuffari. 1973, Crowell $7.95. The surge to independence as seen through the activities of the inhabitants of Williamsburg as they band together to oppose British rule.

The Young Nation: 1789–1861

6405. Alderman, Clifford L. *Rum, Slaves and Molasses: The Story of New England's Triangular Trade* (5–8). Illustrated. 1972, Macmillan $4.95. A description of the 3-way trade cycle, with emphasis on the capture and treatment of slaves.

6406. Baker, Betty. *The Pig War* (K–2). Illus. by Robert Lopshire. 1961, Harper $6.89. A humorous confrontation in 1858 between the United States and Canada over an island that each side insists belongs to them. When a British pig runs into an American garden, war is declared—fortunately short-lived.

6407. Bernheim, Marc, and Bernheim, Evelyne. *Growing Up in Old New England* (4–6). Illustrated. 1971, Macmillan $7.95. A well-illustrated account of everyday life in rural New England during the 1820s.

6408. Boardman, Fon W. *America and the Jacksonian Era, 1825–1850* (5–7). 1976, Walck $8.95. A readable, well-organized introduction.

6409. Bowen, Gary. *My Village, Sturbridge* (4–6). Illus. by author. 1977, Farrar $6.95. A series of pictures with commentary depicting everyday life in an 1827 New England village. Also use: *New England Village: Everyday Life in 1810* by Robert H. Loeb (1976, Doubleday $5.95).

6410. Castor, Henry. *The First Book of the War with Mexico* (4–6). Illus. by Albert Micale. 1964, Watts $4.90. An account of the war that gave the U.S. much of the Southwest.

6411. Crouse, Anna Erskine, and Crouse, Russell. *Alexander Hamilton and Aaron Burr* (4–7). Illus. by Walter Buehr. 1958, Random $4.99. The background and inner story of the duel that changed U.S. history.

6412. Fisher, Leonard Everett. *The Factories* (5–7). Illus. by author. 1979, Holiday $6.95. Part of a series *Nineteenth Century America*, this account describes the origins and development of manufacturing in America.

6413. Fisher, Leonard Everett. *The Hospitals* (5–8). Illus. by author. 1980, Holiday $7.95. An account of the growth and expansion of hospitals in nineteenth-century America.

6414. Gemming, Elizabeth. *Blow Ye Winds Westerly: The Seaports and Sailing Ships of Old New England* (6–9). Illustrated. 1972, Crowell $7.95. A fantastic compendium of information about many aspects of life in the age of sailing ships. There is coverage on the people who sailed them, life in seaports, and the seaports, and the fishing and shipping industries.

6415. Johnson, William. *The Birth of Texas* (5–8). Illus. by Herb Mott. 1960, Houghton $2.95. Background history and events involved with the siege of the Alamo in 1836. Also use: *The Valiant Few: Crisis at the Alamo* by Lon Tinkle (1964, Macmillan $4.50).

6416. Kohn, Bernice. *The Amistad Mutiny* (5–8). Illustrated. 1971, McCall $6.95. The saga of the *Amistad*, its crew of mutinous black slaves, and their reception when they land on Long Island.

6417. Mason, F. Van Wyck. *The Battle of Lake Erie* (4–7). Illus. by Victor Mays. 1960, Houghton $2.95. The story of Perry's victory in 1813, which gave the United States control of the Great Lakes.

6418. Mitchell, Barbara. *Cornstalks and Cannonballs* (1–3). Illus. by Karen Ritz. 1980, Carolrhoda $4.95. The town of Lewis, Delaware, defeats the British Navy during the War of 1812.

6419. Morris, Richard B. *The First Book of the Founding of the Republic* (4–6). Illus. by Leonard Everett Fisher. 1968, Watts $4.90; paper $1.25. A simple history of the first days of the republic. Also use: *The Young United States 1783 to 1830* by Edwin Tunis (1976, Crowell $9.95).

6420. Morris, Richard B. *The First Book of the War of 1812* (4–6). 1961, Watts $4.90. An account of the war from which came the National Anthem. For an older group use: *The War of 1812* by Don Lawson (1966, Abelard $6.95).

6421. Phelan, Mary Kay. *The Story of the Louisiana Purchase* (6–8). 1979, Crowell $7.95; LB $7.89. An exciting, suspenseful account of this event, well illustrated from original documents.

6422. St. George, Judith. *The Amazing Voyage of the New Orleans* (3–5). Illus. by Glen Rounds. 1980, Putnam $6.95. An amazing account of the 1811 voyage of a steamboat down the Mississippi.

6423. Sterling, Dorothy, comp. *Speak Out in Thunder Tones: Letters and Other Writings by Black Northerners 1787–1867* (6–9). 1974, Doubleday $5.95. A collection of sources that gives an interesting picture of life in northern black communities from the Revolution to the Civil War.

6424. Tallant, Robert. *The Louisiana Purchase* (5–7). Illus. by Warren Chapell. 1952, Random $4.99. The negotiations and results of one of the most interesting and significant land sales in world history.

Westward Expansion and Pioneer Life

6425. Adams, Samuel H. *Pony Express* (5–9). Illustrated. 1950, Random $4.99. The story of the men who carried the mail westward, told in a lovely style. Also use: *Riders of the Pony Express* by Ralph Moody (1958, Houghton $2.95).

6426. Adams, Samuel H. *The Santa Fe Trail* (5–9). Illustrated. 1951, Random $4.99. A history of the men who developed the trail that opened up the Southwest.

6427. American Heritage. *The California Gold Rush* (5–8). Illustrated. 1961, American Heritage $6.89. Varied aspects of this part of history, with paintings, prints, and maps for an effective presentation.

6428. Daugherty, James. *Of Courage Undaunted* (5–8). Illus. by author. 1951, Viking $5.00. The Lewis and Clark expedition told through text and powerful illustrations.

6429. Dines, Glen. *Overland Stage* (4–6). Illus. by author. 1961, Macmillan $3.95. Subtitle: *The Story of the Famous Overland Stagecoaches of the 1860s.*

6430. Fletcher, Sydney E. *The Big Book of Cowboys* (5–6). Illustrated. 1950, Grosset $1.50. A colorful picture book of cowboy lore with a glossary of riding and working gear. For a slightly older group use: *Album of the American Cowboy* by John Malone (1971, Watts $5.90).

6431. Gorsline, Marie, and Gorsline, Douglas. *Cowboys* (3–4). Illustrated. 1980, Random $3.99; paper $1.25. An amazing amount of information is included in this slim text.

6432. Grant, Bruce. *The Cowboy Encyclopedia: The Old and the New West from the Open Ranges* (3–6). Illus. by Jackie Mastri and Fiore Mastri. 1951, Rand paper $1.50. A short-entry dictionary of about 600 listings.

6433. Grant, Bruce. *Famous American Trails* (5–7). Illus. by Lorence Bjorklund. 1971, Rand $4.79. An account of 12 important trails used by Indians, explorers, and frontierspeople.

6434. Jones, Evan, and Morgan, Dale L., and Editors of American Heritage. *Trappers and Mountain Men* (6–8). 1961, American Heritage/Harper $6.89. A colorful volume filled with many illustrations and mature text.

6435. Levenson, Dorothy. *Homesteaders and Indians* (4–6). Illustrated. 1971, Watts $4.90; paper $1.25. The opening of the West after the passing of the Homestead Act of 1862.

6436. Neuberger, Richard L. *The Lewis and Clark Expedition* (4–7). Illustrated. 1951, Random $4.99. A suspenseful retelling of the expedition that explored the Louisiana Territory. Also use: *The Lewis and Clark Expedition, 1804–06* by Dan Lacy (1974, Watts $4.47).

6437. Poynter, Margaret. *Gold Rush! The Yukon Stampede of 1898* (6–9). Illustrated. 1979, Atheneum $6.95. An anecdotal account that stresses human values.

6438. Rounds, Glen. *The Cowboy Trade* (5–8). 1972, Holiday $6.95. The authentic life of the cowboy is introduced.

6439. Rounds, Glen. *The Prairie Schooners* (4–6). Illustrated. 1968, Holiday $6.95. A report of life on a wagon train in 1843 during a trip from Missouri to the Oregon Territory.

6440. Seidman, Laurence I. *The Fools of '49: The California Gold Rush 1848–1856* (6–8). Illustrated.

1976, Knopf $7.95. This fascinating text is enlivened with such primary materials as maps, songs, and old prints. Also use: *The California Gold Rush* by May McNeer (1950, Random $4.99).

6441.   Steele, William O. *Westward Adventure: The True Stories of Six Pioneers* (5–6). Illustrated. 1962, Harcourt $5.95. Five very different men and one woman who moved from the 13 colonies to the West. For older readers use: *The Old Wilderness Road: An American Journey* (1968, Harcourt $5.95).

6442.   Stein, R. Conrad. *The Story of the Homestead Act* (3–6). Illustrated. 1978, Childrens Press $4.95. The events around this important piece of legislation in 1804.

6443.   Strait, Treva Adams. *The Price of Free Land* (5–7). Illustrated. 1979, Lippincott $8.95; LB $8.79. A true account of a family of Nebraskan homesteaders who settled there in 1914.

6444.   Tunis, Edwin. *Frontier Living* (5–9). Illus. by author. 1976, Crowell $10.95. Excellent large illustrations and accompanying text convey the flavor of life on the frontier.

6445.   Wellman, Paul I. *The Greatest Cattle Drive* (5–8). Illus. by Lorence Bjorklund. 1964, Houghton $2.95. Cowboys on a drive from Texas to Montana.

The Civil War

6446.   Commager, Henry Steele. *The Great Proclamation* (5–8). 1960, Bobbs-Merrill $5.95. A dramatic presentation of the events leading up to the Proclamation.

6447.   Davis, Burke. *Appomattox: Closing Struggle of the Civil War* (5–7). Illustrated. 1963, Harper $8.79. Documentary account of Lee's surrender, with maps and photographs.

6448.   Foster, Genevieve. *Sunday in Centerville: The Battle of Bull Run, 1861* (6–9). Illus. by Harold Berson. 1971, White $5.76. A recreation for the better reader of the bloody Civil War battle.

6449.   Foster, Genevieve. *Year of Lincoln, 1861* (3–6). Illustrated. 1970, Scribner $5.95. Coverage of the war and other world events are included in this brief survey. For an older group use: *Abraham Lincoln's World* (1944, Scribner $15.00).

6450.   Kantor, MacKinlay. *Gettysburg* (5–9). Illustrated. 1952, Random $4.99. This explains how Gettysburg became the site of the bloodiest Civil War battle; a vivid recreation of the struggle.

6451.   Kantor, MacKinlay. *Lee and Grant at Appomattox* (5–7). Illus. by Donald McKay. 1950,

Random $4.39. The confrontation that ended the Civil War told in sympathetic detail.

6452.   Latham, Frank B. *Lincoln and the Emancipation Proclamation, January 1, 1863* (4–7). Illustrated. 1969, Watts $4.90; paper $1.25. Subtitle: *The Document that Turned the Civil War into a Fight for Freedom.*

6453.   Levenson, Dorothy. *The First Book of the Civil War* (5–7). Illus. by Leonard Everett Fisher. 1968, Watts $4.90; paper $1.25. A basic introduction to the War between the States. Also use: *Album of the Civil War* by William Katz (1974, Watts $5.90).

6454.   McCarthy, Agnes, and Reddick, Lawrence. *Worth Fighting For* (4–6). Illus. by Colleen Browning. 1955, Doubleday $4.95; paper $2.50. Subtitle: *A History of the Negro in the United States During the Civil War and Reconstruction.* Also use: *Marching Toward Freedom: The Negro in the Civil War* by James M. McPherson (1967, Knopf $5.99).

6455.   Pratt, Fletcher. *The Civil War* (5–7). Illus. by Lee J. Ames. 1955, Doubleday $6.95. A readable account that gives interesting details. Also use: Irving Werstein's *The Many Faces of the Civil War* (1961, Messner $4.79).

Reconstruction to the Korean War: 1865–1950s

6456.   Brown, Fern, and Grabe, Andree Vilas. *When Grandpa Wore Knickers: Life in the Early Thirties* (4–6). Illus. by Joe Lasker. 1966, Whitman $5.95. An account of everyday life in the early 1930s from a city dweller's point of view.

6457.   Castor, Henry. *Teddy Roosevelt and the Rough Riders* (4–6). Illus. by William Reusswig. 1954, Random $4.39. The Spanish-American War and how the United States became a world power as a result of it. Also use: *The Battle of Manila Bay: The Spanish American War in the Philippines* by Robert Conroy (1968, Macmillan $3.50).

6458.   Dodds, John W. *Everyday Life in Twentieth-Century America* (6–8). 1966, Putnam $6.75. An introduction to how people have lived during this century.

6459.   Hilton, Suzanne. *The Way It Was—1876* (6–9). Illustrated. 1975, Westminster $6.95. All aspects of everyday life long ago in the United States discussed in a lively, often amusing style.

6460.   Hoffman, Edwin, D. *Fighting Mountaineers: The Struggle for Justice in the Appalachians* (6–9). 1979, Houghton $8.95. The struggle against oppression throughout history of the mountain people of Appalachia.

6461.   Katz, William Loren. *An Album of the Great Depression* (5–8). Illustrated. 1978, Watts $5.90. A book of photographs and running commentary that reconstructs the 1930s in the United States

6462.   Lawson, Don. *FDR's New Deal* (6–8). Illustrated. 1979, Crowell $6.95. A fine recreation of the period without overdue emotion or sentiment.

6463.   Levenson, Dorothy. *The First Book of Reconstruction* (5–7). Illustrated. 1970, Watts $4.90. A well-organized overview of this disturbing period in U.S. history.

6464.   Lindop, Edmund. *Modern America: The Dazzling Twenties* (6–9). Illustrated. 1970, Watts $4.33. From the 1918 Armistice to the 1929 Stock Market Crash, told in a pungent, interesting narrative. Sequel: *Modern America: The Turbulent Thirties* (1970, Watts $3.90).

6465.   Meltzer, Milton. *Bread and Roses: The Struggle of American Labor, 1865–1915* (6–9). Illustrated. 1967, Knopf $5.99; Random paper $2.95. An engrossing history of the fight for rights and improvement of working conditions by American laborers.

6466.   Meltzer, Milton. *Brother, Can You Spare a Dime? The Great Depression 1929–1933* (6–9). Illustrated. 1969, Knopf $5.99; Random paper $1.95. The human side of the Depression years is effec-tively recreated. Also use: *The Hungry Years* by Adrian A. Paradis (1967, Chilton $4.95).

6467.   Meltzer, Milton, and Meier, August. *Time of Trial, Time of Hope* (4–6). Illus. by M. Barnett. 1966, Doubleday $4.95; paper $2.50. This easily read book covers the history of blacks in the United States from 1919 to 1941. Also use: *The Unfinished March: The Negro in the United States, Reconstruction to World War I* by Carol E. Drisko (1967, Doubleday $4.95).

6468.   Meltzer, Milton. *Violins and Shovels: The WPA Arts Projects, A New Deal for America's Hungry Artists of the 1930s* (6–9). Illustrated. 1976, Delacorte $6.95. The author explores those hopeful but poverty stricken days when writers and artists were aided by the New Deal.

6469.   Schwartz, Alvin, ed. *When I Grew Up Long Ago* (5–8). 1978, Lippincott $8.95. Oral histories that cover America in the years of 1890–1914.

6470.   Sterling, Dorothy, ed. *The Trouble They Seen: Black People Tell the Story of Reconstruction* (6–8). Illustrated. 1976, Doubleday $8.95. A dramatic retelling of the post–Civil War period as seen by free blacks.

6471.   Trelease, Allen W. *Reconstruction: The Great Experiment* (6–9). 1971, Harper $8.79. A brilliant recreation of the flavor and facts associated with this period filled with contradictions and conflicts.

6472.   Marshall, S. L. A. *A Military History of the Korean War* (6–8). 1963, Watts $4.50. A simple, well-balanced account of the war.

Biography

Historical and Contemporary Americans

Collective

6473. Beard, Charles A. *The Presidents in American History* (5–7). Illustrated. 1977, Messner $7.79. Brief, but revealing sketches of the men and their times. Also use: *Presidents of the United States* by Cornel A. Lengyel (1964, Golden $5.95; LB $12.23).

6474. Burt, Olive W. *Black Women of Valor* (4–7). Illus. by Paul Frame. 1974, Messner $6.29. A vivid presentation of the lives of 4 courageous black women who succeeded in twentieth-century America.

6475. Chittenden, Elizabeth F. *Profiles in Black and White: Stories of Men and Women Who Fought Again* (5–7). Illustrated. 1973, Scribner $6.95. The lives of 12 people who helped blacks before the Civil War are recounted with sympathy.

6476. Coit, Margaret. *The Fight for Union* (5–9). Illustrated. 1961, Houghton $3.95. Pulitzer Prize author's vivid story of the heroes who tried to avert the Civil War.

6477. Conta, Marcia Maher. *Women for Human Rights* (5–8). Illus. by Jane Palecek. 1975, Raintree $7.49. A profile of several prominent women in the struggle for human rights.

6478. Coy, Harold. *The First Book of Presidents* (5–7). Illustrated. 1977, Watts $4.90; paper $1.25. Thumbnail sketches of the presidents, their elections, and terms of office. Also use: *The Vice-Presidents of the United States* by John Feerick and Amalie Feerick (1977, Watts $4.90).

6479. Davis, Burke. *Black Heroes of the American Revolution* (4–6). 1976, Harcourt $6.95. A look at American blacks who performed key roles in the American Revolution.

6480. Davis, Burke. *Three for Revolution* (4–6). 1975, Harcourt $4.19. The early careers of Patrick Henry, Thomas Jefferson, and George Washington.

6481. Eiseman, Alberta. *Rebels and Reformers: Biographies of Four Jewish Americans* (5–8). Illus. by Herb Steinberg. 1976, Zenith $5.95. The story of 4 Jewish humanitarians and civic-minded individuals.

6482. Dobler, Lavinia, and Toppin, Edgar A. *Pioneers and Patriots* (4–6). 1965, Doubleday $4.95; paper $2.50. The lives of six blacks of the Revolutionary Era.

6483. Franklin, Folsom. *Famous Pioneers* (4–6). Illustrated. 1964, Harvey House $6.19. Interesting heroes of important early settlers.

6484. Foley, Rae. *Famous American Spies* (4–6). Illustrated. 1962, Dodd $3.95. Exciting biographies that span our history.

6485. Hoople, Cheryl G., ed. *As I Saw It: Women Who Lived the American Adventure* (6–9). Illustrated. 1978, Dial $8.95. Firsthand accounts from a number of women depict a wide diversity of experiences from U.S. history.

6486. Hughes, Langston. *Famous American Negroes* (5–7). Illustrated. 1954, Denison $3.50; paper $1.75. From Phillis Wheatley to Jackie Robinson, the lives of 17 noted black Americans. Also use: *Famous Negro Heroes of America* (1958, Dodd $3.95).

6487. Johnston, Johanna. *A Special Bravery* (3–5). Illus. by Ann Grifalconi. 1967, Dodd $4.50. Mood-evoking illustrations and brief sketches of bravery performed by 15 black Americans from Crispus Attucks to Martin Luther King, Jr, make an excellent, visual introduction to black history.

6488. Keating, Bern. *Famous American Cowboys* (5–7). Illus. by Lorence Bjorklund. 1977, Rand $5.95. An account of some of our most famous cowboys.

6489. Kennedy, John F. *Profiles in Courage* (5–8). 1964, Harper $12.50; paper $1.95. Sketches of Americans who took courageous stands on important issues.

6490. Lawson, Robert. *They Were Strong and Good* (4–6). Illus. by author. 1940, Viking $6.50. The author has drawn word-and-pen portraits of his grandparents, typical Americans of their time —proud, hard-working families of integrity. Caldecott award 1941.

6491. Newlon, Clarke. *Famous Mexican Americans* (6–9). Illustrated. 1972, Dodd $4.50. Biographies of 20 Chicanos who have achieved distinction in a variety of fields.

6492. Prindiville, Kathleen. *First Ladies* (4–6). 1964, Macmillan $4.95. The lives of the wives of American presidents.

6493. Roland, Albert. *Great Indian Chiefs* (6–8). Illustrated. 1968, Macmillan $5.95. Biographies of some of the most famous Indians associated with our history.

6494. Rollins, Charlemae. *They Showed The Way: Forty American Negro Leaders* (5–7). 1964, Crowell $7.95. Brief stories of blacks who were pioneers in their particular field or occupation.

6495. Ross, Pat. *Young and Female* (5–8). Illustrated. 1972, Random $3.95; LB $4.99; paper $2.95. Personal accounts of important moments in the lives of 8 contemporary women.

6496. Stoddard, Hope. *Famous American Women* (6–9). Illustrated. 1970, Crowell $10.00. A biographical encyclopedia of 42 modern women who triumphed in various fields and had a major impact on the American scene.

6497. Ulyatt, Kenneth. *Outlaws* (6–8). Illustrated. 1978, Lippincott $7.95. A fascinating collection of tales about the Daltons, Billy the Kid, and other miscreants.

6498. Williams, Barbara. *Breakthrough: Women in Politics* (5–8). Illustrated. 1979, Walker $9.95. A profile of 7 American women who have become important in politics.

6499. Wilson, Beth P. *Giants for Justice: Bethune, Randolph, and King* (5–6). Illustrated. 1978, Harcourt $6.95. Lively profiles of 3 important black crusaders.

Historical Figures

Adams, Samuel

6500. Fritz, Jean. *Why Don't You Get a Horse Sam Adams?* (3–5). Illus. by Trina Hyman. 1974, Coward $6.95. How Sam Adams was finally per-

suaded into riding a horse is told in this humorous recreation of Revolutionary times.

Carnegie, Andrew

6501. Shippen, Katherine B. *Andrew Carnegie and the Age of Steel* (5–8). 1964, Random $4.39. Story of a poor Scottish boy who became a millionaire-philanthropist.

Davis, Jefferson

6502. Lee, Susan. *Jefferson Davis* (2–4). Illustrated. 1978, Childrens Press $4.95. An elementary, straightforward account of the life of this controversial figure.

Douglas, Stephen

6503. Nolan, Jeannette C. *The Little Giant: Stephen A. Douglas* (6–9). 1964, Messner $3.34. A biography of the very popular orator and political leader.

Farragut, David

6504. Latham, Jean Lee. *Anchor's Aweigh: The Story of David Glasgow Farragut* (5–9). Illus. by Eros Keith. 1968, Harper $7.87. The biography of the American Naval officer who gained fame during the Civil War.

Franklin, Benjamin

6505. Aliki. *The Many Lives of Benjamin Franklin* (1–3). Illus. by author. 1977, Prentice-Hall $6.95. Franklin's life is described through captioned cartoons.

6506. American Heritage. *The Many Worlds of Benjamin Franklin* (5–8). Illustrated. 1964, Harper $5.95; LB $6.89. An account of the life and times of one of the most versatile of our founding fathers.

6507. Daugherty, James. *Poor Richard* (6–7). Illus. by author. 1941, Viking $6.50. An excellent biography that concentrates on the political aspects of Ben Franklin's life. Also use: *The Kite That Won the Revolution* by Isaac Asimov (1973, Houghton, paper 95¢).

6508. d'Aulaire, Ingri, and d'Aulaire, Edgar. *Benjamin Franklin* (3–5). Illus. by author. 1950, Doubleday $8.95. A story biography enriched with full-page color lithographs. Also use: *Meet Benjamin Franklin* by Maggie Scarf (1968, Random $2.95).

6509. Fritz, Jean. *What's The Big Idea, Ben Franklin?* (3–5). Illus. by Margot Tomes. 1976, Coward $6.95. Franklin's life told in the usual clever, lively manner associated with this author.

Hale, Nathan

6510. Brown, Marion. *Young Nathan* (5–8). Illus. by Don McDonough. 1949, Westminster $4.75. The youth of the Revolutionary War hero.

Hancock, John

6511. Fritz, Jean. *Will You Sign Here, John Hancock?* (3–5). Illus. by Trina Schart Hyman. 1976, Coward $6.95. Under the sprightly title is a delightful, well-researched biography of the signer of the Declaration of Independence.

Henry, Patrick

6512. Compion, Nardi R. *Patrick Henry: Firebrand of the Revolution* (6–9). 1961, Little $6.95. Henry and his political background, with interesting details of life in colonial Virginia and especially of his colorful family.

6513. Fritz, Jean. *Where Was Patrick Henry on the 29th of May?* (3–5). Illus. by Margot Tomes. 1975, Coward $6.95. A biography that is fun to read.

Hickok, Wild Bill

6514. Holbrook, Stewart. *Wild Bill Hickok Tames the West* (4–6). Illus. by Ernest Richardson. 1952, Random $4.99. The life story of a remarkable man best known for bringing law and order to a wild, wild West.

Houston, Samuel

6515. Latham, Jean Lee. *Retreat to Glory: The Story of Sam Houston* (6–9). 1965, Harper $7.89. The biography of the man who helped Texas gain its independence from Mexico.

Holmes, Oliver Wendell

6516. Peterson, Helen Stone. *Oliver Wendell Holmes: Soldier, Lawyer, Supreme Court Justice* (6–9). Illustrated. 1979, Fox Hills $7.95. A biography of this great Supreme Court Judge.

Jackson, Stonewall

6517. Fritz, Jean. *Stonewall* (6–9). Illus. by Stephen Gammell. 1979, Putnam $7.95; paper $3.95. A realistic, honest portrayal of the complex Stonewall Jackson.

Jones, John Paul

6518. Grant, Matthew. *John Paul Jones* (2–3). Illustrated. 1974, Children Press $4.95. The U. S. Naval hero is introduced in an account that does not ignore either his strengths or his weaknesses.

Lee, Robert E.

6519. Commager, Henry Steele. *America's Robert E. Lee* (6–9). Illus. by Lynd Ward. 1951, Houghton $8.95. Written with sympathy, dignity, and respect for great leadership by a noted historian.

6520. Graves, Charles P. *Robert E. Lee: Hero of the South* (4–6). 1964, Garrard $3.40. The story of the great general who commanded the Confederate Army.

Paine, Thomas

6521. Coolidge, Olivia. *Tom Paine, Revolutionary* (6–8). 1969, Scribner $10.00. The story of the pamphleteer who influenced the leaders of the Revolution.

Penn, William

6522. Aliki. *The Story of William Penn* (K–2). Illus. by author. 1964, Prentice-Hall $5.95; paper $.95. A refreshingly straightforward account in easy-to-read picture-book format.

Revere, Paul

6523. Forbes, Esther. *America's Paul Revere* (5–9). Illus. by Lynd Ward. 1946, Houghton $8.95; paper $2.95. Includes informative background of the Revolutionary period. Also use: *Paul Revere and the Minute Men* by Dorothy C. Fisher (1950, Child's World $4.95).

6524. Fritz, Jean. *And Then What Happened, Paul Revere?* (3–5). Illus. by Margot Tomes. 1973, Coward $6.95. An amusing, exciting account of Revere's ride, its causes, and effects.

Williams, Roger

6525. Jacobs, William Jay. *Roger Williams* (5–6). Illustrated. 1975, Watts $4.90. A partial biography that concentrates on Williams's banishment from Massachusetts and his establishment of Providence. For an older group use: *Lone Journey: The Life of Roger Williams* by Jeanette Eaton (1944, Harcourt $5.95).

Presidents

Carter, Jimmy

6526. Poynter, Margaret. *The Jimmy Carter Story* (4–6). Illustrated. 1978, Messner $7.29. The author traces Jimmy Carter's life to the point where he becomes the 39th President.

6527. Walker, Barbara J. *The Picture Life of Jimmy Carter* (4–6). 1977, Watts $4.47. A brief, simple account that ends with Carter's election to the presidency. For a younger group use: *My Name Is Jimmy Carter* by June Behrens (1978, Childrens Press $4.95).

Hoover, Herbert

6528. Peare, Catherine O. *The Herbert Hoover Story* (4–6). 1965, Crowell $8.95. The 31st president portrayed sympathetically.

Jackson, Andrew

6529. Coit, Margaret. *Andrew Jackson* (6–9). Illus. by Milton Johnson. 1965, Houghton $3.50. Description and explanation of Jackson's administrations, including domestic and foreign affairs, and

the men and women around the president. For younger readers use: *Andrew Jackson* by Patricia Miles Martin (1966, Putnam $4.49).

6530. Remini, Robert V. *The Revolutionary Age of Andrew Jackson* (6–8). 1976, Harper $7.89. The story of the 7th president. For a younger group use: *Meet Andrew Jackson* by Ormonde deKay (1967, Random $2.95; LB $2.99).

Jefferson, Thomas

6531. Barrett, Marvin. *Meet Thomas Jefferson* (2–4). Illus. by Angelo Torres. 1967, Random $3.95; LB $3.99. A simple, informal story of the 3rd president.

6532. Eichner, James A. *Thomas Jefferson: The Complete Man* (6–8). 1966, Watts $4.90. A spirited biography that tries to cover the many facets of this amazing man.

Johnson, Lyndon Baines

6533. Lynch, Dudley M. *The President from Texas: Lyndon Baines Johnson* (4–6). Illustrated. 1975, Crowell $8.95. A balanced account on this controversial president. Also use: *Lyndon B. Johnson* by Helen D. Olds (1965, Putnam $4.49).

Kennedy, John F.

6534. Martin, Patricia Miles. *John Fitzgerald Kennedy* (2–4). Illus. by Paul Frame. 1964, Putnam $4.49. Emphasis in this simple book is on Kennedy's heroism in World War II. For older readers use: *The Life and Words of John F. Kennedy* by James Playsted Wood (1964, Country Beautiful $9.95).

6535. Schoor, Gene. *Young John Kennedy* (6–8). Illustrated. 1963, Harcourt $6.95. The boyhood of the 35th president.

Lincoln, Abraham

6536. American Heritage. *Abraham Lincoln in Peace and War* (6–9). Illustrated. 1964, Harper $5.95; LB $6.89. The many-sided Lincoln—humorous, shrewd, introspective, war leader, and family man—analyzed in relation to his times and contemporaries. For a younger group use: *If You Grew Up with Abraham Lincoln* by Ann McGovern (1969, Scholastic 95¢).

6537. Coolidge, Olivia. *The Statesmanship of Abraham Lincoln* (6–9). Illustrated. 1977, Scribner $7.95. Lincoln's presidency is the focus of this excellent book that continues *The Apprenticeship of Abraham Lincoln* (1974, Scribner $6.95).

6538. d'Aulaire, Ingri, and d'Aulaire, Edgar. *Abraham Lincoln* (2–5). Illus. by author. 1957, Doubleday $7.95. Lincoln's life from boyhood to a tired war-president. Caldecott Medal 1970.

6539. Phelan, Mary Kay. *Mr. Lincoln's Inaugural Journey* (5–6). Illus. by Richard Cuffari. 1972, Crowell $7.95. A detailed, factual account of Lincoln's trip from Springfield to Washington, enlivened by the discovery of a plot to assassinate the new president. Also use: *America's Abraham Lincoln* by May McNeer (1957, Houghton $3.57).

6540. Sandburg, Carl. *Abe Lincoln Grows Up* (6–9). Illus. by James Daugherty. 1931, Harcourt $6.95; 1975, paper $1.95. Classic account of Lincoln's boyhood based on Volume I of *The Prairie Years*.

Roosevelt, Franklin D.

6541. American Heritage. *Franklin Delano Roosevelt* (6–9). Illustrated. 1970, American Heritage $5.95; LB $6.89. A sumptuously illustrated work with an excellent text.

6542. Quackenbush, Robert. *Franklin D. Roosevelt: Four Times President* (4–6). 1966, Garrard $4.20. An interesting account of this amazing president's life.

6543. Peare, Catherine O. *The FDR Story* (5–8). Illustrated. 1962, Crowell $8.95. An excellent picture of a president, which explains the many forces that helped to mold Roosevelt's life and personality. Also use: *Franklin D. Roosevelt, Portrait of a Great Man* by Gerald W. Johnson (1967, Morrow $7.25; LB $6.96).

Roosevelt, Theodore

6544. American Heritage. *Theodore Roosevelt: The Strenuous Life* (6–9). Illustrated. 1967, Harper $5.95; LB $6.89. An objective view of the life and times of the 26th president, profusely illustrated with photographs, paintings, drawings, and political cartoons of the time. Also, for slightly younger readers use: *Theodore Roosevelt: An Initial Biography* by Genevieve Foster (1954, Scribner $5.95).

6545. Hancock, Sibyl. *Theodore Roosevelt* (4–6). Illustrated. 1978, Putnam $4.49. An easy-to-read but informative biography.

Truman, Harry S.

6546. Martin, Ralph G. *President from Missouri: Harry S. Truman* (6–8). 1973, Messner $4.79. The story of this unusual and surprisingly competent President.

Washington, George

6547. d'Aulaire, Ingri, and d'Aulaire, Edgar P. *George Washington* (2–3). Illus. by author. 1936, Doubleday $7.95. A simple recounting of the life of the first president.

6548. Eaton, Jeanette. *Leader by Destiny* (6–9). Illus. by Jack Manley Rose. 1938, Harcourt $6.95. The development of George Washington's character from boyhood to maturity.

6549. Griffin, Judith Berry. *Phoebe and the General* (3–6). Illus. by Margot Tomes. 1976, Coward $7.95. The girl who becomes General Washington's housekeeper and helps save him from an assassination plot.

Wilson, Woodrow

6550. Steinberg, Alfred. *Woodrow Wilson* (4–6). Illus. by Paul Galdone. 1961, Putnam $4.97. The story of the president who led us through World War I.

Black Americans

Bethune, Mary McLeod

6551. Greenfield, Eloise. *Mary McLeod Bethune* (2–4). Illus. by Jerry Pinkney. 1977, Crowell $6.49. Bethune was the only one of 17 children in her family to go to school. Through courage and hard work, she became an educator of national importance.

6552. Radford, Ruby L. *Mary McLeod Bethune* (2–4). Illus. by Lydia Rosier. 1973, Putnam $4.49. The inspiring story of the black woman who founded a school and hospital for black people in Florida. Also use for an older group: *She Wanted to Read: The Story of Mary McLeod Bethune* by Ella Kaiser Carruth (1966, Abingdon $3.50; Archway, paper $1.25).

6553. Sterne, Emma G. *Mary McLeod Bethune* (6–9). Illus. by Raymond Lufkin. 1957, Knopf

$5.39. A warm, sympathetic biography of the great black educator.

Brown, William Wells

6554. Warner, Lucille. *From Slave to Abolitionist: The Life of William Wells Brown* (6–9). 1976, Dial $7.95. Adapted from an autobiography published in 1847, this is the story of an escaped slave who founded the Abolitionist movement.

Chisholm, Shirley

6555. Brownmiller, Susan. *Shirley Chisholm* (5–9). 1970, Doubleday $5.95; Archway paper $.85. Story of the first black woman to be elected to the U. S. Congress.

Douglass, Frederick

6556. Bontemps, Arna. *Frederick Douglass: Slave-Fighter-Freeman* (5–7). Illus. by Harper Johnson. 1960, Knopf $4.99. A man, born a slave, escapes and becomes a leader in the Abolitionist movement. Also use: *Frederick Douglass* by Charles P. Graves (1970, Putnam $4.49).

6557. Patterson, Lillie. *Frederick Douglass: Freedom Fighter* (2–5). Illustrated. 1965, Garrard $4.20. The biography of a onetime slave who, as a free man, became a noted author and speaker.

6558. Ritchie, Barbara. *Life and Times of Frederick Douglass* (6–9). 1966, Crowell $6.95. An adaptation of Douglass's own autobiography, which describes the full impact of the early struggle for freedom by blacks. The companion volume: *The Mind and Heart of Frederick Douglass: Excerpts from Speeches of the Great Negro Orator* (1968, Crowell $6.95).

DuBois, W. E. B.

6559. Hamilton, Virginia. *W. E. B. DuBois: A Biography* (5–9). Illustrated. 1972, Crowell $8.95. Chronicles the successes and failures of this fighter for black rights.

Fortune, Amos

6560. Yates, Elizabeth. *Amos Fortune: Free Man* (6–9). Illus. by Nora S. Unwin. 1967, Dutton

$6.95. The simplicity and dignity of the human spirit and its triumph over degradation are movingly portrayed in this portrait of a slave who bought his freedom. Newbery Medal winner.

Freeman, Elizabeth

6561. Felton, Harold W. *Mumbet: The Story of Elizabeth Freeman* (4–6). Illus. by Donn Albright. 1970, Dodd $4.50. A black slave who gained her freedom in 1781 by fighting her case through the Massachusetts courts.

Hamer, Fannie Lou

6562. Jordan, June. *Fannie Lou Hamer* (3–5). Illus. by Albert Williams. 1972, Crowell $6.95; LB $6.89; paper $1.45. The story of a gallant black woman who worked for voter registration in Mississippi in 1962 and helped found the Freedom Farm Cooperative.

King, Martin Luther, Jr.

6563. Clayton, Edward T. *Martin Luther King: The Peaceful Warrior* (4–6). Illus. by David Hodges. 1968, Prentice-Hall $5.95; paper $1.50. The life of the great civil rights leader.

6564. Faber, Doris, and Faber, Harold. *The Assassination of Martin Luther King, Jr.* (6–8). Illustrated. 1978, Watts $4.90. A biography that centers around the events involved in the death of this black leader.

6565. Haskins, James. *The Life and Death of Martin Luther King, Jr.* (5–8). Illustrated. 1977, Lothrop $6.25; LB $6.00. A simple, easily read account that is straight forward and honest. For younger readers use: *The Picture Life of Martin Luther King, Jr.* by Margaret B. Young (1968, Watts $4.90) and *Martin Luther King, Jr.* by Beth P. Wilson (1971, Putnam $4.49).

6566. Miklowitz, Gloria D. *Dr. Martin Luther King, Jr.* (4–6). Illustrated. 1978, Grosset $4.99; paper $1.50. A readable, basic account of King's life and death.

6567. Preston, Edward. *Martin Luther King: Fighter for Freedom* (4–7). Illustrated. 1970, Doubleday $5.95. A short, objective portrait of the late civil rights leader and the ideals for which he stood.

Malcolm X

6568. Adoff, Arnold. *Malcolm X* (3–5). Illus. by John Wilson. 1970, Crowell $6.95; paper $1.95. A realistic portrayal of this spokesman for the black cause in the United States until his assassination in 1965.

6569. Curtis, Richard. *The Life of Malcolm X* (4–6). Illustrated. 1971, Macrae $6.25. The story of the civil rights leader and his untimely death.

Parks, Rosa

6570. Greenfield, Eloise. *Rosa Parks* (2–4). Illus. by Eric Marlow. 1973, Crowell $6.95; LB $6.89. A convincing sketch of the woman whose brave stand precipitated the Montgomery bus strike, and her ensuing involvement with the civil rights struggle.

6571. Meriwether, Louise. *Don't Ride the Bus on Monday: The Rosa Parks Story* (3–5). Illus. by David Scott Brown. 1973, Prentice-Hall $5.95. A dramatic and sympathetic account of the Montgomery bus boycott and the woman most closely associated with it.

Smalls, Robert

6572. Meriwether, Louise. *The Freedom Ship of Robert Smalls* (3–5). Illus. by Lee Morton. 1971, Prentice-Hall $5.95. The saga of a black slave and his courageous voyage that delivered *The Planter* to the Union forces during the Civil War.

Still, Peter

6573. Mann, Peggy, and Siegal, Vivian W. *The Man Who Bought Himself: The Story of Peter Still* (6–9). 1975, Macmillan $7.95. A freed slave attempts to be reunited with his family.

Truth, Sojourner

6574. Pauli, Hertha. *Her Name Was Sojourner Truth* (6–9). 1976, Avon paper $1.50. The life of the American black abolitionist and fighter for women's rights.

Tubman, Harriet

6575. Lawrence, Jacob. *Harriet and the Promised Land* (2–5). Illus. by author. 1968, Simon & Schuster $6.75. Bold, stylized illustrations and free verse recreate the story of Harriet Tubman, who escaped from slavery in Maryland and then returned to lead many of her people to the "Promised Land".

6576. Petry, Ann. *Harriet Tubman: Conductor on the Underground Railroad* (6–9). 1955, Crowell $8.95; Archway paper $1.25. A dramatic and stirring biography of an indomitable woman.

6577. Sterling, Dorothy. *Freedom Train: The Story of Harriet Tubman* (4–8). Illus. by Ernest Crichlow. 1954, Doubleday $5.95. Story of the courageous ex-slave who devoted her life to helping others to freedom.

Turner, Nat

6578. Griffin, Judith Berry. *Nat Turner* (3–5). Illus. by Leo Carty. 1970, Coward $3.99. A simple but effective story of the slave who led an unsuccessful rebellion.

Washington, Booker T.

6579. Graham, Shirley. *Booker T. Washington: Education of Hand, Head and Heart* (5–7). 1955, Messner $5.29. The amazing story of a slave who founded a college.

Wheatley, Phillis

6580. Graham, Shirley. *The Story of Phillis Wheatley* (6–9). 1949, Archway paper $1.25. The tragic life of one of America's first black poets, a slave during the Colonial Period. Also use: *Phillis Wheatley: America's First Black Poetess* by Miriam Morris Fuller (1971, Garrard $4.48).

Young, Andrew

6581. Haskins, James. *Andrew Young: Man with a Mission* (5–8). 1979, Lothrop $7.50. The life of the famous black American statesman is well recreated in this account.

Indians of North America

Black Hawk

6582. Anderson, LaVere. *Black Hawk-Indian Patriot* (2–3). Illus. by Lois F. Cary. 1972, Garrard $4.20. The plight of the American Indian is highlighted in this simple biography.

6583. Cunningham, Margaret. *Black Hawk* (5–7). Illustrated. 1979, Dillon $5.95. The tragic story of the Sauk Indian leader.

Chief Joseph

6584. Davis, Russell, and Ashabranner, Brent. *Chief Joseph: War Chief of the Nez Perce* (5–7). 1962, McGraw $7.95. A touching portrait of the Indian leader who longed for peace, but was forced to fight for the rights of his people.

Cochise

6585. Carlson, Vada F. *Cochise, Chief of the Chiricahuas* (4–6). 1973, Harvey House $5.39. The American Indian who was beloved by his people and respected by the white settlers.

Crazy Horse

6586. Meadowcroft, Enid. *Crazy Horse: Sioux Warrior* (4–6). Illustrated. 1965, Garrard $4.20. The life of this valiant chief of the Oglala tribe of the Sioux.

Eastman, Charles

6587. Lee, Betsy. *Charles Eastman* (6–8). Illustrated. 1979, Dillon $5.95. The story of the Santee Sioux who helped keep his people's culture alive in the early twentieth century.

Geronimo

6588. Moody, Ralph. *Geronimo: Wolf of the Warpath* (5–8). 1958, Random $4.39. The story of the last great war leader of the Apaches. Also use: *Geronimo* by Charles Morrow Wilson (1973, Dillon $5.95).

Ishi

6589. Kroeber, Theodora. *Ishi, Last of His Tribe* (5–7). Illus. by Ruth Robbins. 1964, Parnassus $7.50; Bantam paper $1.95. A California Yahe Indian, the last of his tribe, leaves his primitive life and enters the modern world.

Little Turtle

6590. Cunningham, Maggi. *Little Turtle* (6–8). Illustrated. 1978, Dillon $5.95. Little Turtle was a chief of the Miami Indian tribe.

Lonesome Star

6591. Sobol, Rose. *Woman Chief* (6–8). 1976, Dial $6.95; Dell paper $1.25. The story of the famous Crow warrior.

Pocahontas

6592. D'Aulaire, Ingri, and D'Aulaire, Edgar. *Pocahontas* (2–4). Illus. by author. 1949, Doubleday $4.95. The story of the Indian girl who saved the life of John Smith. Also use: *Pocahontas* by Patricia Miles Martin (1964, Putnam $4.49).

Ross, John

6593. Harrell, Sara Gordon. *John Ross* (5–7). Illustrated. 1979, Dillon $5.95. The story of Cherokee Indian leader and his fight to save his people's land.

Sacajawea

6594. Burt, Olive W. *Sacajawea* (5–7). Illustrated. 1978, Watts $4.90. An honest account of this brave woman, illustrated with historical prints and photographs. Also use: *Sacajawea, Indian Guide* by Wyatt Blassingame (1965, Garrard $4.20).

6595. Voight, Virginia F. *Sacajawea* (1–3). 1967, Putnam $4.49. The tale of the Shoshone princess who helped to guide Lewis and Clark on their expedition to the Pacific.

Sealth (Indian Chief)

6596. Boring, Mel. *Sealth, The Story of an American Indian* (5–8). Illustrated. 1978, Dillon $5.95. The story of the Indian chief for whom Seattle was named.

Sequoyah

6597. Marriott, Alice Lee. *Sequoyah: Leader of the Cherokees* (4–6). Illustrated. 1956, Random $4.39. The story of the great Cherokee leader who invented a system of writing.

Sitting Bull

6598. Anderson, Lavere. *Sitting Bull: Great Sioux Chief* (3–5). Illus. by Cary. 1970, Garrard $3.96. A simple account of the man and his struggle to save his people. Also use: *Sitting Bull: War Chief of the Sioux* by Richard O'Connor (1969, Farrar $5.75).

Squanto

6599. Bulla, Clyde Robert. *Squanto, Friend of the Pilgrims* (3–6). Illus. by Peter Burchard. 1954, Crowell $7.95. The first American Indian to reach Europe.

Tecumseh

6600. Fleischer, Jane. *Tecumseh: Shawnee War Chief* (3–4). Illus. by Hal Frenck. 1979, Troll $4.89. A basic account of this Indian chief and his fight to prevent a territorial takeover by the white settlers.

6601. Schraff, Anne E. *Tecumseh* (5–7). Illustrated. 1979, Dillon $5.95. The moving story of the Shawnee Indian chief and his losing battle to save the land of his people. Also use: *Tecumseh: Destiny's Warrior* by David C. Cooke (1959, Messner $4.29).

Hispanic Americans

Chavez, Cesar

6602. Franchere, Ruth. *Cesar Chavez* (2–5). Illus. by Earl Thollander. 1970, Crowell $6.89; paper $2.95. An inspiring story of the man who rose from poverty to become the union organizer of his people.

Famous American Women

Anthony, Susan B.

6603. Noble, Iris. *Susan B. Anthony* (5–7). 1975, Messner $5.29. A sympathetic account of the life of America's pioneer fighter for women's rights.

Barton, Clara

6604. Boylston, Helen D. *Clara Barton, Founder of the American Red Cross* (5–8). Illus. by Paula Hutchison. 1955, Random $4.99. The story of the courageous woman who devoted her life to others. For a younger group use: *Clara Barton: Soldier of Mercy* by Mary Catherine Rose (1960, Garrard $4.20).

Crandall, Prudence

6605. Yates, Elizabeth. *Prudence Crandall, Woman of Courage* (4–6). Illus. by Nora S. Unwin. 1955, Dutton $8.50. Biography of a Quaker teacher who fought intolerance.

Duniway, Abigail Scott

6606. Morrison, Dorothy Nafus. *Ladies Were Not Expected: Abigail Scott Duniway and Woman's Rights* (5–7). Illustrated. 1977, Atheneum $6.95. A lively tale of a courageous Oregon crusader for women's rights around the turn of the century.

Jemison, Mary

6607. Lenski, Lois. *Indian Captive: The Story of Mary Jemison* (6–9). Illus. by author. 1941, Lippincott $7.95. True story of a 22-year-old girl as an Indian captive of the Senecas. Also use: *Mary Jemison: Senaca Captive* by Jeanne LeMonnier Gardner (1966, Harcourt $5.50).

Jones, Mary Harris

6608. Atkinson, Linda. *Mother Jones, the Most Dangerous Woman in America* (6–8). 1978, Crown $7.95. A graphic biography of the woman who devoted her life to secure justice for coal miners.

Keller, Helen

6609. Peare, Catherine O. *The Helen Keller Story* (5–7). 1959, Crowell $8.95. A stirring tale of the blind and deaf girl who learned to communicate with others and who became an outstanding force as writer and lecturer. Also use: *Helen Keller* by Eileen Bigland (1967, Phillips $8.95) and, for younger readers, *Helen Keller: Toward the Light* by Stewart Graff and Polly Graff (1965, Garrard $4.20).

6610. Waite, Helen E. *Valiant Companions: Helen Keller and Anne Sullivan Macy* (6–8). 1959, Macrae $6.25. The story of a wonderful friendship and of overcoming a handicap.

Kemble, Fanny

6611. Scott, John A. *Fanny Kemble's America* (6–9). Illustrated. 1973, Crowell $6.95; Dell paper $.95. An adroit biography of the woman who contributed to the antislavery crusade and the feminist movement.

Liliuokalani

6612. Malone, Mary. *Liliuokalani, Queen of Hawaii* (4–6). 1975, Garrard $4.20. The story of a most unusual woman and splendid queen.

Nation, Carry

6613. Madison, Arnold. *Carry Nation* (5–8). 1977, Nelson $6.95. The most famous prohibitionist in U.S. history.

Roosevelt, Eleanor

6614. Goodsell, Jane. *Eleanor Roosevelt* (2–4). Illus. by Wendell Minor. 1970, Crowell $6.49; 1973, paper $1.45. Concentrates on the transformation from ugly duckling to renowned world figure.

6615. Graves, Charles P. *Eleanor Roosevelt: First Lady of the World* (4–6). 1966, Garrard $4.20. Fictionalized biography.

Ross, Betsy

6616. Mayer, Jane. *Betsy Ross and the Flag* (4–6). Illustrated. 1952, Random $4.39. A simple biography of the seamstress who made the first American flag that had stars and stripes.

Sampson, Deborah

6617. Clapp, Patricia. *I'm Deborah Sampson: A Soldier in the War of the Revolution* (5–8). 1977, Lothrop $6.48. A first-person retelling of the amazing woman who, disguised as a man, served in the Continental Army during the Revolution.

6618. McGovern, Ann. *The Secret Soldier: The Story of Deborah Sampson* (3–5). Illus. by Ann Grifalconi. 1975, Four Winds $5.95; paper $1.25. The story of the woman who, disguised as a man, served in the Continental Army.

Stanton, Elizabeth Cady

6619. Faber, Doris. *Oh, Lizzie: The Life of Elizabeth Cady Stanton* (6–9). Illustrated. 1972, Lothrop $6.48; Archway paper $.75. The amazing career of the fighter for women's rights.

Sullivan, Anne

6620. Malone, Mary. *Annie Sullivan* (2–4). Illus. by Lydia Rosier. 1971, Putnam $4.96. Over half of this book deals with Sullivan's association with Helen Keller. For an older audience use: *The Silent Storm* by Marion Brown (1963, Abingdon $7.95; Archway, paper 75¢).

World Figures

Collective

6621. Coolidge, Olivia. *Lives of Famous Romans* (6–8). 1965, Houghton $3.50. Includes such famous names as Augustus, Cicero, Constantine, and Hadrian.

6622. Davar, Ashok. *The Wheel of King Asoka* (2–4). Illus. by author. 1977, Follett $6.95; LB $6.99. The story of the ancient ruler whose wheel is at the center of the flag of India.

6623. Gross, David C. *Pride of Our People: The Stories of One Hundred Outstanding Jewish Men* (5–8). Illus. by William D. Bramhall, Jr. 1979, Doubleday $14.95. A collection of useful biographies, including 15 Jewish women, of those who have made contributions to their people and to the world.

6624. McNeer, May, and Ward, Lynd. *Armed with Courage* (4–6). Illus. by Lynd Ward. 1957, Abingdon $6.95. Biographies of 7 men and women who have shown great physical and spiritual courage—Florence Nightingale, Father Damien, George Washington Carver, Jane Addams, Wilfred Grenfell, Mahatma Gandhi, and Albert Schweitzer.

6625. Meyer, Edith Patterson. *In Search of Peace: The Winners of the Nobel Peace Prize, 1901–1975* (6–9). Illustrated. 1978, Abingdon $7.95. A useful reference work on the prize recipients, their lives, and accomplishments.

6626. Ojigbo, A. Okion, ed. *Young and Black in Africa* (6–9). Illustrated. 1971, Random $3.95; paper $1.50. Autobiographical accounts of 7 young people growing up in today's Africa (plus one historical document of a boy sold into slavery in 1756).

Individual

Bolivar, Simon

6627. Webb, Robert N. *Simon Bolivar: The Liberator* (4–6). 1966, Watts $5.90. The life of the South American hero told effectively. Also use: *Simon Bolivar: The Great Liberator* by Arnold Whitridge (1954, Random $4.39).

Braille, Louis

6628. DeGering, Etta. *Seeing Fingers: The Story of Louis Braille* (5–7). Illus. by Emil Weiss. 1977, McKay $5.95. Not only the story of Braille's raised dot code, but a history of the beginning of education for the blind. For a younger audience use: *Louis Braille: The Boy Who Invented Books for the Blind* by Margaret Davidson (1972, Hastings $5.95).

Caesar, Julius

6629. Komroff, Manuel. *Julius Caesar* (6–8). 1955, Messner $4.79. The story of the famous emperor and his exploits.

Chukovsky, Kornei

6630. Chukovsky, Kornei. *The Silver Crest: My Russian Boyhood* (6–9). 1976, Holt $6.95. An autobiographical account of a boy's futile attempt to remain in school.

de Medici, Lorenzo

6631. Mee, Charles L., and The Editors of Horizon Magazine. *Lorenzo de Medici and the Renaissance* (6–8). Illustrated. 1969, American Heritage $5.95. The world of the Renaissance as seen through the life of a powerful man.

George III

6632. Fritz, Jean. *Can't You Make Them Behave, King George?* (3–5). Illus. by Tomie de Paola. 1977, Coward $6.95. A charming, amiable biography of George III, which includes an approach to the American Revolution not usually found in children's books.

Gandhi, Mohandas

6633. Coolidge, Olivia. *Gandhi* (6–8). 1971, Houghton $5.95. The story of the pacifist who effectively fought against British rule in India.

Hannam, Charles

6634. Hannam, Charles. *A Boy in That Situation* (6–8). Illustrated. 1978, Harper $7.95. An autobiographical account of a young Jew growing up in Nazi Germany.

Hitler, Adolf

6635. Devaney, John. *Hitler, Mad Dictator of World War II* (6–8). Illustrated. 1978, Putnam $7.95. A clear, detailed, lucid account.

6636. Shirer, William L. *The Rise and Fall of Adolf Hitler* (5–8). Illustrated. 1967, Random $4.99. A simple but accurate account of Germany's dictator.

Hsiao, Ellen

6637. Hsiao, Ellen. *A Chinese Year* (4–6). Illus. by author. 1970, Evans $3.95. An autobiographical incident from childhood when the author spent a year in a small Chinese town with her grandfather.

Joan of Arc

6638. Ross, Nancy Wilson. *Joan of Arc* (4–6). 1953, Random $4.39. The story of the French heroine who fought against the English. For an older group use: Albert Paine's *The Girl in White Armor* (1967, Macmillan $4.50).

Juarez, Benito

6639. Syme, Ronald. *Juarez: The Founder of Modern Mexico* (6–9). Illus. by Richard Cuffari. 1972, Morrow $5.95. A biography of the man most responsible for bringing Mexico into the modern world, plus a history of Mexico in the nineteenth century. Also use: James D. Atwater's *Out from Under: Benito Juarez and the Struggle for Mexican Independence* (1969, Doubleday, paper $2.50).

Kherdian, David

6640. Kherdian, David. *The Road from Home: The Story of an Armenian Childhood* (6–9). 1979, Greenwillow $8.95. A memoir of a survivor of the Turkish destruction of Armenians.

Lawrence of Arabia

6641. MacLean, Alistair. *Lawrence of Arabia* (6–8). Illus. by Gil Walker. 1962, Random $4.39. A simply written biography that concentrates on Lawrence's exploits with the Arabs.

Lim, Sing

6642. Lim, Sing. *West Coast Chinese Boy* (5–7). Illus. by author. 1979, Tundra $12.95. The childhood and youth of a boy growing up in Vancouver's Chinatown.

Meir, Golda

6643. Davidson, Margaret. *The Golda Meir Story* (5–7). 1976, Scribner $6.95. A heavily fictionized account of this important world leader. Also use: *Life for Israel: The Story of Golda Meir* by Arnold Dobrin (1974, Dial $4.95; LB $4.58).

Nelson, Horatio

6644. Warner, Oliver, and Nimitz, Chester W. and the Editors of Horizon Magazine. *Nelson and the Age of Fighting Sail* (6–8). Illustrated. 1963, Harper $5.95. Distributed by Har-Row, LB $6.89. The story of England's famous naval hero.

Nightingale, Florence

6645. Hume, Ruth Fox. *Florence Nightingale* (4–6). Illus. by Robert Frankenberg. 1960, Random $4.99. The life of the great humanitarian and founder of the modern nursing movement.

Nehru, Jawaharlal

6646. Apsler, Alfred. *Fighter for Independence: Jawaharlal Nehru* (6–8). 1963, Messner $3.34. The story of the man who carried out Gandhi's dreams in India.

Pankhurst, Emmeline

6647. Noble, Iris. *Emmeline and Her Daughters: The Pankhurst Suffragettes* (6–9). 1971, Messner $5.29. The enthralling story of a proper Victorian lady who left her comfortable surroundings to engage in a 30-year struggle to obtain the vote for women in England.

Royale, Madame

6648. Powers, Elizabeth. *The Journal of Madame Royale* (5–8). Illustrated. 1976, Walker $7.50; LB $7.39. The French Revolution as seen through the eyes of Marie Antoinette's daughter.

Sadako

6649. Coerr, Eleanor. *Sadako and the Thousand Paper Cranes* (3–5). Illus. by Ronald Himler. 1977, Putnam $7.95. The moving biography of a young Japanese girl who dies of leukemia that developed as a result of radiation sickness from the bombing of Hiroshima.

Schweitzer, Albert

6650. Daniel, Anita. *The Story of Albert Schweitzer* (4–6). Illustrated. 1957, Random $4.39. The great doctor and the humanitarian comes to life in this biography.

Singer, Isaac B.

6651. Singer, Isaac Bashevis. *A Day of Pleasure: Stories of a Boy Growing up in Warsaw* (6–9). 1969, Farrar $6.95; paper $4.95. A famous author's fond remembrances of the world in which he grew up.

Toussaint

6652. Syme, Ronald. *Toussaint the Black Liberator* (5–9). Illus. by William Stobbs. 1971, Morrow $5.95; LB $5.71. An interesting biography of the man who was born a slave, yet became a leader in the struggle to free his people on the island of Haiti from domination by whites.

Tutankhamen

6653. Reig, June. *Diary of the Boy King Tut-Ankh-Amen* (6–8). 1978, Scribner $7.95. A fictionized account that will intrigue young readers.

Wesley, John

6654. McNeer, May, and Ward, Lynd. *John Wesley* (4–6). Illustrated. 1951, Abingdon $4.50; paper $2.95. The life of a great reformer in the Christian religion.

Wiesenthal, Simon

6655. Noble, Iris. *Nazi Hunter, Simon Wiesenthal* (5–9). 1979, Messner $7.29. A biography of the man responsible for bringing Eichmann to trial in 1960.

Explorers and Adventurers

Collective

6656. Cochran, Hamilton, and Nesmith, Robert I. and the Editors of American Heritage. *Pirates of the Spanish Main* (6–9). 1961, Harper $5.95; LB $6.89. A well-illustrated account for the better readers.

6657. Duvoisin, Roger. *They Put Out to Sea: The Story of the Map* (5–7). Illus. by author. 1944, Knopf $5.99. The story of early explorers— Darius, Marco Polo, Magellan, and others.

6658. Schoder, Judith. *Brotherhood of Pirates* (3–5). Illus. by Paul Frame. 1979, Messner $7.29. An account of 7 famous pirates who plundered the Caribbean during the seventeenth and eighteenth centuries.

6659. Whipple, Addison. *Famous Pirates of the New World* (5–7). Illus. by Robert Pioers. 1958, Random $4.39. An amazing array and variety of pirates are introduced. Also use: *Buccaneers and Pirates of Our Coasts* by Frank R. Stockton (1967, Macmillan $6.95; paper 95¢).

6660. Sobol, Donald J. *True Sea Adventures* (4–7). 1975, Elsevier/Nelson $6.95. Twenty-two stories of the sea retold briefly and with great gusto.

Individual

Allen, Ethan

6661. Holbrook, Stewart. *America's Ethan Allen* (5–7). Illus. by Lynd Ward. 1949, Houghton $8.95; paper $3.95. The story of the Green Mountain boys and of their fearless leader, the hero of Fort Ticonderoga. Also use: *Ethan Allen and the Green Mountain Boys* by Slater Brown (1956, Random $4.99).

Appleseed, Johnny

6662. Aliki. *The Story of Johnny Appleseed* (K–3). Illus. by author. 1963, Prentice $5.95; paper $1.25. A picture story of the man who wandered through the Midwest spreading love and apple seeds.

Balboa

6663. Mirsky, Jeanette. *Balboa: Discoverer of the Pacific* (5–8). Illus. by Hans Guggenheim. 1964, Harper $7.89. An interesting account of this famous explorer's life.

Beckwourth, Jim

6664. Place, Marian T. *Mountain Man: The Life of Jim Beckwourth* (6–8). Illus. by Paul Williams. 1970, Macmillan $3.95. Based on Beckwourth's personal reminiscences, this is an amazing account of one of the West's colorful characters.

Boone, Daniel

6665. Averill, Esther. *Daniel Boone* (4–6). 1945, Harper $9.89. A readable account about the famous wilderness scout. For slightly older readers use: *Daniel Boone* by John Mason Brown (1952, Random $4.39).

6666. Shapp, Martha, and Shapp, Charles. *Let's Find Out about Daniel Boone* (2–4). Illus. by Vic Donahue. 1967, Watts $4.47. A simple account of an exciting adventurer.

Bowditch, Nathaniel

6667. Latham, Jean Lee. *Carry On, Mr. Bowditch* (6–9). Illus. by John O'Hara Cosgrave. 1955, Houghton $7.95. This fictionalized biography of the great American navigator is enlivened by fascinating material on sailing ships and the romance of old Salem. Newbery Medal winner.

Burningham, John

6668. Burningham, John. *Around the World in Eighty Days* (3–7). Illustrated. 1979, Merrimack $10.95. The author describes a memorable trip he took on the same route as Phileas Fogg.

Cabot, John and Sebastian

6669. Kurtz, Henry Ira. *John and Sebastian Cabot* (2–4). Illustrated. 1973, Watts $5.90. The story of the father and son who explored Canadian Atlantic waters. Also use: *John Cabot and His Son Sebastian* by Ronald Syme (1972, Morrow $6.00).

Cartier, Jacques

6670. Averill, Esther. *Cartier Sails the St. Lawrence* (3–6). Illus. by Feodor Rojankovsky. 1956, Harper $9.89. A beautifully designed book describing the Frenchman's North American exploration. Also use: *Cartier: Finder of the St. Lawrence* by Ronald Syme (1958, Morrow $5.28).

Champlain, Samuel de

6671. Jacob, W. J. *Samuel de Champlain* (6–9). 1974, Watts $4.90. Champlain's discoveries and efforts to colonize New France.

Cody, Buffalo Bill

6672. D'Aulaire, Ingri, and D'Aulaire, Edgar. *Buffalo Bill* (2–4). Illus. by author. 1952, Doubleday $8.95. A truthful retelling of this adventurer's life in picture-book format.

Columbus, Christopher

6673. Ceserani, Gian Paolo. *Christopher Columbus* (3–4). Illus. by Piero Ventura. 1979, Random $3.95. A familiar story told brightly and with good humor.

6674. Dalgliesh, Alice. *The Columbus Story* (1–4). Illus. by Leo Politi. 1955, Scribner $7.95. Picture biography. Also use: *Columbus* by Ingri D'Aulaire and Edgar P. D'Aulaire (1955, Doubleday $6.95).

6675. Sperry, Armstrong. *Voyages of Christopher Columbus* (6–8). 1950, Random $4.99. An account of the explorer's 4 voyages. Also use: *Columbus: Finder of the New World* by Ronald Syme (1952, Morrow $5.71).

6676. Ventura, Piero. *Christopher Columbus* (4–6). Illus. by author. 1978, Random $3.95. An interesting biography of the world's most famous explorer.

Crockett, Davy

6677. Holbrook, Stewart. *Davy Crockett* (5–7). 1955, Random $2.95; LB $4.39. All sorts of stories about Davy Crockett, one of the most interesting frontier scouts.

Da Gama, Vasco

6678. Sanderlin, George. *Eastward to India: Vasco da Gama's Voyage* (6–9). Illus. by Alan E. Cober. 1965, Harper $8.79. Portugal's century of glory, from Prince Henry the Navigator's expeditions along the African coast to the sea battle of Diu in 1509. Also use: *Vasco da Gama: Sailor toward the Sunrise* by Ronald Syme (1959, Morrow $6.00).

Earhart, Amelia

6679. Mann, Peggy. *Amelia Earhart: First Lady of Flight* (3–5). Illus. by Kiyo Komoda. 1970, Coward $4.99. A fictionized biography that stresses this amazing woman's courage and endurance. Also use: *Amelia Earhart* by Burke Davis (1972, Putnam $5.49).

Earp, Wyatt

6680. Holbrook, Stewart. *Wyatt Earp: U.S. Marshal* (5–7). 1956, Random $4.99. The story of the colorful lawman of Dodge City.

Ericson, Leif

6681. Jensen, Malcolm C. *Leif Ericson the Lucky* (6–8). Illustrated. 1979, Watts $5.45. The text is brought to life with many authentic prints and documents.

6682. Shippen, Katherine, B. *Leif Ericson: First Voyager to America* (6–9). 1951, Harper $6.89. The story of the discoverer of Greenland and America.

Graham, Robin

6683. Graham, Robin Lee. *The Boy Who Sailed around the World Alone* (5–7). Illustrated. 1973, Golden $6.95; LB $12.23. The 5-year saga of Robin Graham, who circled the globe in a 24-foot sloop.

Heyerdahl, Thor

6684. Blassingame, Wyatt. *Thor Heyerdahl: Viking Scientist* (5–7). Illustrated. 1979, Nelson $7.95. Both the scientist and the man of adventure are revealed in this lively biography.

6685. Heyerdahl, Thor. *Kon-Tiki* (4–7). Illustrated. 1960, Rand $10.00; Pocket Books paper $1.95. This special edition for young readers tells of the hazardous crossing of the Pacific by raft. Also use: *Thor Heyerdahl and the Reed Boat Ra* by Barbara Murphy (1974, Lippincott $7.95).

LaFitte, Pierre

6686. Tallant, Robert. *The Pirate LaFitte and the Battle of New Orleans* (5–7). 1951, Random $4.39. The story of the smuggler and pirateer who helped the Americans in the Battle of New Orleans.

LaSalle, Robert de

6687. Jacobs, William Jay. *Robert Cavelier De La Salle* (6–8). Illustrated. 1975, Watts $4.90. An effective biography of the explorer of the Mississippi.

MacKenzie, Alexander

6688. Syme, Ronald. *Alexander Mackenzie: Canadian Explorer* (3–7). 1964, Morrow $6.00. A biography of the man who explored Canada's Northwest.

McLoughlin, John

6689. Morrison, Dorothy Nafus. *The Eagle and the Fort: The Story of John McLoughlin* (6–8). Illustrated. 1979, Atheneum $7.95. A biography of the man who established a number of fur-trading forts in the Oregon territory.

Magellan, Ferdinand

6690. Israel, Charles E. *Five Ships West: The Story of Magellan* (4–6). Illustrated. 1966, Macmillan $5.95. The first voyage around the world highlights this vivid life story of the Portuguese navigator. Also use: *Magellan: First around the World* by Ronald Syme (1953, Morrow $5.71).

Marquette, Pere

6691. Kjelgaard, James A. *Explorations of Pere Marquette* (4–6). Illus. by Stephen J. Voorhies. 1951, Random $4.39. A simple account of the famous French priest who, with Joliet, opened up the Mississippi area. Also use: *Marquette and Joliet: Voyagers on the Mississippi* by Ronald Syme (1974, Morrow $6.25).

Ortiz, Juan

6692. Steele, William O. *The Wilderness Tatoo: A Narrative of Juan Ortiz* (5–9). Illustrated. 1972, Harcourt $5.95. The story of the sixteenth-century Conquistadores and of a young Spaniard who spent 11 years with an Indian tribe in Florida.

Richthofen, Freiherr von

6693. Wright, Nicolas. *The Red Baron* (5–9). Illustrated. 1977, McGraw $6.95. The first biography for a young audience on Freiherr von Richthofen, the audacious German air ace of World War I.

Raleigh, Sir Walter

6694. Syme, Ronald. *Walter Raleigh* (4–6). Illus. by William Stobbs. 1962, Morrow $5.32. The life of the romantic adventurer and explorer, dramatically told.

Rogers, Robert

6695. Gauch, Patricia Lee. *The Impossible Major Rogers* (4–6). Illus. by Robert Andrew Parker. 1977, Putnam $5.95. An immensely readable life of the controversial frontiersman Robert Rogers.

St. Brendan

6696. Fritz, Jean. *Brendan the Navigator: A History Mystery about the Discovery of America* (3–5). Illustrated. 1979, Coward $6.95. An imaginative re-

creation of what could have been the discovery of America by St. Brendan.

Smith, John

6697. Syme, Ronald. *John Smith of Virginia* (4–7). 1954, Morrow $5.95. An excellent account of the explorer's career and friendship with Pocahontas.

Verrazano, Giovanni da

6698. Syme, Ronald. *Verrazano: Explorer of the Atlantic Coast* (4–6). Illus. by William Stobbs. 1973, Morrow $5.95; LB $5.49. A clear, succinct account of the Florentine explorer who traveled up the coast of North America and entered New York harbor.

Vespucci, Amerigo

6699. Baker, Nina B. *Amerigo Vespucci* (5–7). Illus. by Paul Valentino. 1956, Knopf $4.99. A lively account of the explorer whose name was given to the New World.

Scientists and Inventors

Collective

6700. Bowman, Kathleen. *New Women in Medicine* (5–7). Illustrated. 1976, Childrens Press $5.95. Part of the fine *New Women In* series, this book supplies 7 short biographies of women who have succeeded in medicine.

6701. Emberlin, Diane. *Contributions of Women: Science* (5–7). Illustrated. 1977, Dillon $6.95. Short biographies of women who have excelled in science.

6702. Facklam, Margery. *Wild Animals, Gentle Women* (6–9). Illustrated. 1978, Harcourt $5.95. Biographies of 11 women who have studied various wild animals.

6703. Haber, Louis. *Women Pioneers of Science* (6–9). 1979, Harcourt $7.95. An introduction to some of the lesser-known women scientists and their contributions.

6704. Hirsch, S. Carl. *Guardian of Tomorrow: Pioneers in Ecology* (6–8). Illus. by William Steinel. 1971, Viking $4.95. Eight people, including Thoreau and Rachel Carson, who were the forerunners of today's conservation program.

6705. Manchester, Harland F. *New Trail Blazers of Technology* (6–9). Illustrated. 1976, Scribner $7.95. The Xerox process, cable TV, and the wankel engine are some of the modern advances explored in these 10 biographies.

6706. Pizer, Vernon. *Shortchanged by History: America's Neglected Innovators* (6–8). Illus. by Catherine Stock. 1979, Putnam $8.95. After an historic survey, 8 cases are highlighted.

Individual

Banneker, Benjamin

6707. Patterson, Lillie. *Benjamin Banneker: Genius of Early America* (3–6). Illustrated. 1978, Abingdon $5.95. A biography of the famous black mathematician.

Beaumont, William

6708. Epstein, Sam, and Epstein, Beryl. *Dr. Beaumont and the Man with a Hole in His Stomach* (6–8). 1978, Coward $5.49. The story of the doctor and his patient who helped us to learn about the human stomach.

Bell, Alexander Graham

6709. Montgomery, Elizabeth Rider. *Alexander Graham Bell: Man of Sound* (3–6). Illustrated. 1963, Garrard $4.20. The life of the inventor of the telephone, told simply with many drawings.

Blackwell, Elizabeth

6710. Clapp, Patricia. *Dr. Elizabeth: The Story of the First Woman Doctor* (6–9). 1974, Lothrop $6.00. A first-person biography of the first woman to earn a medical degree in the United States. Also use: *First Woman Doctor: The Story of Elizabeth Blackwell, M.D.* by Rachel Baker (1944, Messner $6.64).

Burbank, Luther

6711. Faber, Doris. *Luther Burbank* (4–6). Illustrated. 1963, Garrard $5.95. The life of the famous American plant breeder.

Carson, Rachel

6712. Sterling, Philip. *Sea and Earth: The life of Rachel Carson* (6–8). Illustrated. 1970, Crowell $7.95. A woman who used her scientific knowledge to alert people to the dangers of pollution.

Carver, George Washington

6713. Aliki. *A Weed Is a Flower: The Life of George Washington Carver* (K–3). Illus. by author. 1965, Prentice-Hall $5.95; paper $1.50. Born a slave, Carver became a great scientist and teacher. Also, for slightly older groups, use: *George Washington Carver* by Peter Towne (1975, Crowell $6.79).

6714. Graham, Shirley, and Lipscomb, George. *Dr. George Washington Carver: Scientist* (6–9). Illus. by Elton C. Fox. 1944, Messner $8.29; paper $1.25. A moving account of this scientist and his tremendous accomplishments.

Clark, Eugenie

6715. McGovern, Ann. *Shark Lady: True Adventures of Eugenie Clark* (3–5). Illus. by Ruth Chew. 1979, Four Winds $6.95. A biography of the work and accomplishments of this scientist and director of a marine laboratory.

Copernicus

6716. Veglahn, Nancy. *Dance of the Planets: The Universe of Nicolaus Copernicus* (3–5). Illus. by George Ulrich. 1979, Coward $5.49. An easily read biography that makes Copernicus and his theories accessible to young readers.

Cousteau, Jacques

6717. Iverson, Genie. *Jacques Cousteau* (3–5). Illus. by Hal Ashmead. 1976, Putnam $4.49. A simple-to-read biography of the underwater explorer and fighter for sea life.

Curie, Marie

6718. Veglahn, Nancy. *The Mysterious Rays: Marie Curie's World* (3–5). Illus. by Victor Juhasz. 1977, Coward $4.99. An appealing, suspenseful account that emphasizes the many years of trial and error before success.

Darwin, Charles

6719. Shapiro, Irwin. *Darwin and the Enchanted Isles* (4–6). Illus. by Christopher J. Spollen. 1977, Coward $4.99. This account concentrates on Darwin's voyages on the *Beagle* and ends with the debate over his theories by British scientists in 1860.

Leonardo da Vinci

6720. Cooper, Margaret. *The Inventions of Leonardo da Vinci* (6–9). Illustrated. 1968, Macmillan $6.95. An account of the scientific aspects of da Vinci's life.

Drew, Charles

6721. Bertol, Roland. *Charles Drew* (3–5). Illus. by Jo Polseno. 1970, Crowell $7.89. The fascinating story of the black doctor who pioneered work with blood preservation and transfusions.

Einstein, Albert

6722. Freeman, Mae. *The Story of Albert Einstein: The Scientist Who Searched Out the Secrets of the Universe* (4–7). Illustrated. 1958, Random $5.39. Einstein's many accomplishments and his personal life are covered.

Ericsson, John

6723. Burnett, Constance Buel. *Captain John Ericsson: Father of the Monitor* (6–9). 1960, Vanguard $5.95. A story of the American engineer and inventor who designed and built the *Monitor*.

6724. Latham, Jean Lee. *Man of the Monitor: Story of John Ericsson* (6–8). Illus. by Leonard Everett Fisher. 1962, Harper $7.89. Swedish engineer who built the ironclad *Monitor* of Civil War fame.

Field, Cyrus

6725. Latham, Jean Lee. *Young Man in a Hurry: The Story of Cyrus Field* (6–8). Illus. by Victor Mays. 1958, Harper $7.89. The life of the man associated with the first telegraph cable across the Atlantic.

Ford, Henry

6726. Paradis, Adrian A. *Henry Ford* (1–2). Illustrated. 1968, Putnam $4.49. A simple text with many illustrations of the automobile pioneer.

6727. Quackenbush, Robert. *Along Came the Model T: How Henry Ford Put the World on Wheels* (2–5). Illustrated. 1978, Parents $6.50. A simple account of the life of the father of the horseless carriage.

Fuller, R. Buckminster

6728. Lord, Athena V. *Pilot for Spaceship Earth: R. Buckminster Fuller, Architect, Inventor* (6–8). 1978, Macmillan $7.95. A biography of one of the most influential designers and thinkers in history.

Fulton, Robert

6729. Judson, Clara Ingram. *Boat Builder: The Story of Robert Fulton* (4–6). Illus. by Armstrong Sperry. 1940, Scribner $5.95. The life of the father of the steamboat, told simply but with interesting detail, particularly of his boyhood. Also use: *Robert Fulton* by Ruby L. Radford (1970, Putnam $4.59).

Galileo

6730. Cobb, Vicki. *Truth on Trial: The Story of Galileo Galilei* (4–5). Illus. by George Ulich. 1979, Coward $5.49. An inspiring biography that deals more with Galileo's ideas and the inner conflicts they produced than with the details of his life.

6731. Rosen, Sidney. *Galileo and the Magic Numbers* (6–9). Illus. by Harve Stein. 1958, Little $6.95. The Italian astronomer who was persecuted for his beliefs concerning the earth's relationship to the sun.

Goddard, Robert H.

6732. Quackenbush, Robert. *The Boy Who Dreamed of Rockets: How Robert H. Goddard Became the Father of the Space Age* (3–5). Illustrated. 1979, Parents $6.50; LB $5.99. A well-researched account of the wizard of rocketry, plus directions on how to build a model space suit.

Goodall, Jane

6733. Coerr, Eleanor. *Jane Goodall* (2–4). Illus. by Kees de Kiette. 1976, Putnam $4.29. The amazing story of the young woman who went to Tanzania to study chimpanzees.

Harvey, William

6734. Marcus, Rebecca B. *William Harvey: Trailblazer of Scientific Medicine* (6–9). 1962, Watts $5.90. The biography of the Englishman who investigated the circulation system of the blood.

Jenner, Edward

6735. Levine, I. E. *Conqueror of Smallpox: Dr. Edward Jenner* (6–9). 1960, Messner $3.34. The story of a great doctor and his amazing accomplishments.

Koch, Robert

6736. Knight, David C. *Robert Koch: Father of Bacteriology* (6–9). Illus. by Gustav Schrotter. 1961, Watts $5.90. The life of the scientist who opened up a new world of living things.

Leakey, Louis

6737. Malatesta, Ann, and Friedland, Ronald. *The White Kikuyu* (6–8). Illustrated. 1978, McGraw $7.95. The fascinating story of Dr. Louis Leakey, the anthropologist who discovered remains of primitive peoples in Africa.

Lu Pan

6738. Hitz, Demi. *Lu Pan, the Carpenter's Apprentice* (3–4). 1978, Prentice-Hall $5.95. A bi-

ography of a famous architect and engineer in ancient China who is credited with inventing the first kite.

Mayo, William and Charles

6739. Goodsell, Jane. *The Mayo Brothers* (2–4). Illus. by Louis Glanzman. 1972, Crowell $6.49; paper $1.45. Will and Charles Mayo learned medicine from their father and established the famous clinic in 1914.

Mead, Margaret

6740. Epstein, Sam, and Epstein, Beryl. *She Never Looked Back: Margaret Mead in Samoa* (4–6). Illus. by Victor Juhasz. 1980, Coward $5.99. A narrative that concentrates on Margaret Mead's study of Samoan youth in the 1920s.

Mitchell, Maria

6741. Morgan, Helen L. *Maria Mitchell: First Lady of American Astronomy* (5–8). 1977, Westminster $7.95. The story of the astronomer and her career at Vassar.

Newton, Isaac

6742. Knight, David C. *Isaac Newton Mastermind of Modern Science* (6–9). Illus. by John Griffin. 1961, Watts $5.90. The life of the famous astronomer.

Ramon y Cajal, Santiago

6743. Clifford, Eth. *The Wild One* (6–9). Illus. by Arvis Stewart. 1974, Houghton $5.95. A biography in the first person about the youth of Santiago Ramon y Cajal, who won the 1906 Nobel prize for medicine.

Roebling, Washington

6744. Veglahn, Nancy. *The Spider of Brooklyn Heights* (5–7). Illustrated. 1967, Scribner paper $1.99. The difficulties and sacrifices made by Washington Roebling and his son in the completion of the Brooklyn Bridge in 1883, after years of delay, are dramatized in this biographical novel, illustrated with contemporary prints and photographs.

Schliemann, Heinrich

6745. Selden, George. *Heinrich Schliemann: Discoverer of Buried Treasure* (1–3). Illus. by Lorence Bjorklund. 1964, Macmillan $3.50. The story of the man who explored Troy.

Spallanzani, Lazzaro

6746. Epstein, Sam, and Epstein,Beryl. *Secret in a Sealed Bottle: Lazzaro Spallanzani's Work with Microbes* (5–6). Illus. by Jane Sterrett. 1979, Coward $5.49. An informative biography of Lazzaro Spallanzani, the 18th-century pioneer in microbiology.

Wright, Orville and Wilbur

6747. Graves, Charles P. *The Wright Brothers* (1–3). Illus. by Fermin Rocker. 1973, Putnam $4.49. A beginning reader will easily master this life story of the conquerers of the air.

6748. Reynolds, Quentin. *The Wright Brothers* (4–7). 1950, Random $4.99; paper $2.95. The lives of 2 mechanical geniuses.

Artists, Writers, Composers, and Performers

Collective

6749. Abdul, Raoul. *Famous Black Entertainers of Today* (6–9). Illustrated. 1974, Dodd $4.95. Eighteen sketches in dialogue form cover people in a variety of artistic areas; sample subjects—Alvin Ailey, Martina Arroyo, Aretha Franklin, Flip Wilson.

6750. Bakeless, Katherine. *Story Lives of Great Composers* (6–9). 1962, Lippincott $10.00. Biographies of 13 renowned men of music.

6751. Chandler, Anna C. *Story-Lives of Master Artists* (6–8). Illustrated. 1953, Lippincott $5.50. Brief biographies of some of the world's great artists.

6752. Harris, Stacy. *Comedians of Country Music* (5–8). 1978, Lerner $5.95. An introduction to well-known country music comics.

6753. Horwitz, Elinor. *Contemporary American Folk Artists* (6–9). Illustrated. 1975, Lippincott $8.50; paper $3.95. After a general introduction to folk art, the author devotes single chapters to such individual artists as Simon Rodie, the builder of Watts Towers.

6754. Jones, Hettie. *Big Star Fallin' Mama! Five Women in Black Music* (6–8). 1974, Viking $5.95; Dell paper $.95. The lives of Ma Rainey, Bessie Smith, Mahalia Jackson, Billie Holiday, and Aretha Franklin sensitively presented.

6755. Krishef, Robert K. *More New Breed Stars* (5–9). Illustrated. 1979, Country Music Library $5.95. Ten short biographies of country-pop stars such as Kris Kristofferson, Linda Ronstadt, and Charley Pride.

6756. Krishef, Robert K. *Western Stars of Country Music* (5–9). 1978, Lerner $5.95. Brief profiles of some of the very popular stars in country music.

6757. Manchel, Frank. *The Talking Clowns: From Laurel and Hardy to the Marx Brothers* (6–9). Illustrated. 1976, Watts $6.90. A history of one aspect of the motion picture industry in the 1930s and 1940s, as seen through the lives of some great comedians.

6758. Polsky, Milton E. *Today's Young Stars of Stage and Screen* (5–8). Illustrated. 1979, Watts $6.90. Twelve short biographies of such stars as Gary Coleman, Melissa Gilbert, and Brooke Shields.

6759. Posell, Elsa Z. *American Composers* (5–7). Illustrated. 1963, Houghton $3.95. Twenty-nine important composers beginning with Stephen Foster and ending with Norman Dello Joio, with emphasis on their personal lives.

6760. Rollins, Charlemae. *Famous American Negro Poets* (5–7). Illustrated. 1965, Dodd $3.95. Brief sketches on the lives and works of 12 black poets. Also use: *Famous Negro Entertainers of Stage, Screen, and TV* (1967, Dodd $3.95).

Artists

Blegvad, Erik

6761. Blegvad, Erik. *Self-Portrait: Erik Blegvad* (5–8). Illus. by author. 1979, Wesley $7.95. A candid, lively autobiography of the well-known picture-book illustrator.

Brady, Mathew

6762. Hoobler, Dorothy, and Hoobler, Thomas. *Photographing History: The Career of Mathew Brady* (5–8). Illustrated. 1977, Putnam $8.95. The man who graphically recorded the Civil War with his photographs.

Cassatt, Mary

6763. Wilson, Ellen. *American Painter in Paris: A Life of Mary Cassatt* (6–9). Illustrated. 1971, Farrar $4.95. A well-rounded portrait of the artist and the influences that helped to shape her career; illustrated with reproductions and photographs.

Curtis, Edward S.

6764. Boesen, Victor, and Graybill, Florence Curtis. *Edward S. Curtis: Photographer of the North American Indian* (5–8). Illustrated. 1977, Dodd $6.95. The highlight of this work is the excellent photographs by Curtis.

Des Jarlait, Patrick

6765. Des Jarlait, Patrick. *Patrick Des Jarlait: The Story of an American Indian Artist* (6–9). Illustrated. 1975, Lerner $5.95. Transcribed from taped interviews; the artist describes his life as a Chippewa Indian. Accompanying pictures supply atmosphere.

Disney, Walt

6766. Montgomery, Elizabeth Rider. *Walt Disney: Master of Make-Believe* (3–5). Illus. by Victor Mays. 1971, Garrard $4.48. A simple account of the life of a master cartoonist, with emphasis on his rise to fame.

Feelings, Tom

6767. Feelings, Tom. *Black Pilgrimage* (5–8). Illus. by author. 1972, Lothrop $6.96. This black artist describes why he decided to move to Africa and the consequences of that decision.

Giotto

6768. Rockwell, Anne. *The Boy Who Drew Sheep* (4–6). Illustrated. 1973, Atheneum $4.50. The fourteenth-century Italian painter Giotto illustrated with 8 reproductions of his works.

Homer, Winslow

6769. Hyman, Linda. *Winslow Homer: America's Old Master* (6–7). Illustrated. 1973, Doubleday $4.95. All aspects of this famous painter's life, including his work as a Civil War illustrator, are well depicted.

Kurelek, William

6770. Kurelek, William. *A Prairie Boy's Summer* (3–5). Illus. by author. 1975, Houghton $7.95. Each of this Canadian artist's paintings depicts a farm activity, which the accompanying text describes in this companion piece to the author's earlier *A Prairie Boy's Winter* (1973, $7.95).

Noguchi, Isamu

6771. Tobias, Tobi. *Isamu Noguchi: The Life of a Sculptor* (4–6). Illustrated. 1974, Crowell $6.89. The inner struggles and artistic success are well chronicled in this story of a man unable to identify fully with either his Japanese or his American background.

Peale, Charles Willson

6772. Epstein, Sam, and Epstein, Beryl. *Mister Peale's Mammoth* (3–5). Illus. by Martin Avillex. 1977, Coward $5.95. A life of Charles Willson Peale, famed portrait painter of the Revolution and amateur paleontologist.

Potter, Beatrix

6773. Aldis, Dorothy. *Nothing Is Impossible: The Story of Beatrix Potter* (3–6). Illus. by Richard Cuffari. 1969, Atheneum $6.95. A remarkable woman whose lonely childhood in London was relieved only by her pets, her reading, and her drawings.

Remington, Frederic

6774. Baker, Donna. *Frederic Remington* (4–6). 1977, Childrens Press $6.94. The famous artist of the American West in a brief biography.

Sharon, Mary Bruce

6775. Sharon, Mary Bruce. *Scenes from Childhood* (6–8). Illustrated. 1978, Dutton $7.95. The privileged, pampered life of an American painter, accompanied by many paintings.

Tudor, Tasha

6776. Tudor, Bethany. *Drawn from New England: Tasha Tudor* (4–8). Illustrated. 1979, Collins $10.95. Tasha Tudor's daughter tells about her mother's illustrious life as an illustrator.

Van Der Zee, James

6777. Haskins, Jim. *James Van Der Zee, the Picture Takin' Man* (6–9). 1979, Dodd $8.95. The portrait of the man who spent his life photographing his world.

Van Gogh, Vincent

6778. Dobrin, Arnold. *I Am a Stranger on the Earth: The Story of Vincent Van Gogh* (5–7). Illustrated. 1975, Warne $7.95. A direct and solid account, well illustrated with reproductions of Van Gogh's paintings, some in color.

West, Benjamin

6779. Henry, Marguerite. *Benjamin West and His Cat Grimalkin* (4–6). Illus. by Wesley Dennis. 1947, Bobbs-Merrill $6.95. West's struggle to study painting against the wishes of his Quaker parents, and the cat who was his friend and ally.

Zemach, Margot

6780. Zemach, Margot. *Self-Portrait: Margot Zemach* (4–7). Illus. by author. 1978, Addison $7.95. An autographical portrait in words and pictures of the famous picture-book artist.

Writers

Alcott, Louisa May

6781. Meigs, Cornelia L. *Invincible Louisa* (6–8). Illustrated. 1968, Little $7.95. The Newbery award-winning biography of Louisa May Alcott.

Buck, Pearl

6782. Westervelt, Virginia. *Pearl Buck: A Biographical Novel* (6–9). 1979, Nelson $8.95. An absorbing account that presents the strengths and weaknesses of this complex woman.

Dickinson, Emily

6783. Barth, Edna. *I'm Nobody! Who Are You? The Story of Emily Dickinson* (5–8). Illus. by Richard Cuffari. 1971, Seabury $6.95. A well-researched but informal tale that begins when Emily is 9 years old; numerous quotations from her writing, plus a selection of poems at the end of the biographical material.

Hansberry, Lorraine

6784. Scheader, Catherine. *Lorraine Hansberry* (6–9). Illustrated. 1978, Childrens Press $5.95. A brief, readable biography of the tragically short life of the brilliant black American writer.

Hughes, Langston

6785. Meltzer, Milton. *Langston Hughes: A Biography* (6–9). 1968, Crowell $8.95. An excellent portrayal of the noted black poet.

6786. Walker, Alice. *Langston Hughes: American Poet* (2–4). Illus. by Don Miller. 1974, Crowell $6.79. An easy-to-read biography that emphasizes Hughes's early life.

Johnson, Pauline

6787. Harley, Lucie. *Pauline Johnson* (5–8). Illustrated. 1978, Dillon $5.95. The poignant story of Canada's Indian poet.

Peck, Robert Newton

6788. Peck, Robert Newton. *Bee Tree and Other Stuff* (4–6). Illus. by Laura Lydecker. 1975, Walker $6.95; LB $6.85. A tender recollection of the writer's boyhood on a Vermont farm, as told in prose and verse.

Sandburg, Carl

6789. Sandburg, Carl. *Prairie-Town Boy* (6–8). Illus. by Joe Krush. 1955, Harcourt $6.95; paper $1.75. The boyhood of the famous poet and biographer of Lincoln.

Steffens, Lincoln

6790. Steffens, Lincoln. *Boy on Horseback* (6–9). Illus. by Sanford Tousey. 1935, Harcourt $5.50. The author's childhood in the California of the 1870s.

Stowe, Harriet Beecher

6791. Johnston, Johanna. *Harriet and the Runaway Book: The Story of Harriet Beecher Stowe and Uncle Tom's Cabin* (3–5). Illus. by Ronald Himler. 1977, Harper $5.79. A fictionalized account that focuses on the writing of *Uncle Tom's Cabin*.

6792. Scott, John A. *Woman against Slavery: The Story of Harriet Beecher Stowe* (6–9). Illustrated. 1978, Crowell $7.95; LB $7.79. A well-documented, mature account of the life of the abolitionist and feminist.

Twain, Mark

6793. McNeer, May. *America's Mark Twain* (5–7). Illus. by Lynd Ward. 1962, Houghton $6.95. An account of America's most famous humorist.

6794. Sanderlin, George. *Mark Twain: As Others Saw Him* (6–8). 1978, Coward $5.89. A biography of excerpts from primary sources.

Composers

Bach, Johann Sebastian

6795. Holst, Imogen. *Bach* (5–7). 1965, Crowell $8.79. Insights into the life and work of the great composer.

Bernstein, Leonard

6796. Cone, Molly. *Leonard Bernstein* (1–3). Illus. by Robert Galster. 1970, Crowell paper $1.45. A simple account of this multitalented musician and composer.

Ellington, Duke

6797. Gutman, Bill. *Duke: The Musical Life of Duke Ellington* (5–8). Illustrated. 1977, Random $6.95. Includes a great deal of material on the history of jazz.

Guarneri del Gesee

6798. Wibberley, Leonard. *Guarneri: Story of a Genius* (6–9). 1974, Farrar $5.95. A biography told through the eyes of a young apprentice of Guarneri del Gesee and the other master violin makers of Cremona.

Handy, William C.

6799. Montgomery, Elizabeth Rider. *William C. Handy: Father of the Blues* (3–4). Illus. by David Hodges. 1968, Garrard $4.48. An authentic, candid life history.

Ives, Charles

6800. Sive, Helen R. *Music's Connecticut Yankee* (6–9). Illustrated. 1976, Atheneum $6.95. Subtitled: *An Introduction to the Life and Music of Charles Ives.*

Johnson, James Weldon

6801. Egypt, Ophelia Settle. *James Weldon Johnson* (2–4). Illus. by M. Barnett. 1974, Crowell

$4.50; LB $6.89. The great black songwriter who was also a teacher, lawyer, diplomat, and the originator of the first black newspaper in the United States.

MacDowell, Edward

6802. Wheeler, Opal, and Deucher, Sybil. *Edward MacDowell and His Cabin in the Pines* (4–6). Illus. by Mary Greenwalt. 1940, Dutton $5.50. A simple account of the man and his music.

Schubert, Franz

6803. Goffstein, M. B. *A Little Schubert* (K–4). Illus. by author. 1972, Harper $5.95. A story about poverty-stricken composer Franz Schubert and how he wrote his music; recording of 5 waltzes included.

Entertainers

Alonso, Alicia

6804. Siegel, Beatrice. *Alicia Alonso: The Story of a Ballerina* (4–6). Illustrated. 1979, Warne $8.95. In spite of being almost blind, Alicia Alonso has become one of the world's greatest ballerinas.

Anderson, Marian

6805. Tobias, Tobi. *Marian Anderson* (2–4). Illus. by Symeon Shimin. 1972, Crowell $6.89. A simply written, sympathetic portrait of the great black concert and operatic singer, beautifully illustrated. For a slightly older audience use: *Marian Anderson: Lady from Philadelphia* by Shirlee P. Newman (1966, Westminster $5.50).

Armstrong, Louis

6806. Iverson, Genie. *Louis Armstrong* (3–5). Illus. by Kevin Brooks. 1976, Crowell $6.89. A well-rounded account of a jazz great and a remarkable human being. Also use: *Louis Armstrong: Ambassador Satchmo* by Jean Gay Cornell (1972, Garrard $4.48; 1975, Dell, paper 95¢).

Bailey, Hachaliah

6807. Cross, Helen Reeder. *A Curiosity for the Curious* (3–5). Illus. by Margot Tomes. 1978, Coward $7.95. A fictionized biography of the originator of the circus.

Barnum, P. T.

6808. Edwards, Anne. *P. T. Barnum* (2–4). Illus. by Marylin Hafner. 1977, Putnam $4.29. A humorous, easily read introduction.

Baryshnikov, Mikhail

6809. Goodman, Saul. *Baryshnikov* (5–8). Illustrated. 1979, Harvey House $5.39. An introduction to the private and professional life of this ballet superstar.

Carter Family

6810. Krishef, Robert K, and Harris, Stacy. *The Carter Family: Country Music's First Family* (5–9). Illustrated. 1978, Lerner $5.95. A readable biography of the three members of the Carter family.

Cassidy, Shaun

6811. Berman, Connie. *Shaun Cassidy* (4–6). Ed. by Barbara Williams. 1979, Grosset $6.34. The family, life, and hopes of this teenage star.

Chaplin, Charlie

6812. Jacobs, David. *Chaplin, The Movies and Charlie* (5–8). Illustrated. 1975, Harper $6.95; LB $7.89. Concentrates on the early days of films and the evolution of the tramp character.

Charles, Ray

6813. Mathis, Sharon Bell. *Ray Charles* (2–5). Illus. by George Ford. 1973, Crowell $6.95; LB $6.89. A simple story of the highly popular black singer.

Couffer, Jack

6814. Couffer, Jack, and Couffer, Mike. *African Summer* (6–9). Illustrated. 1976, Putnam $6.95. A father and son alternate in telling the story of a summer spent on an island in East Africa filming a television series.

Graham, Martha

6815. Terry, Walter. *Frontiers of Dance: The Life of Martha Graham* (6–9). Illustrated. 1975, Crowell $8.95. A well-rounded portrait of one of the greatest influences on modern American dance.

Gordy, Pop

6816. Gordy, Berry, Sr. *Movin' Up: Pop Gordy Tells His Story* (5–8). Illustrated. 1979, Harper $7.95. The autobiography of the founder of Motown Records.

Houdini, Harry

6817. Edwards, Anne. *The Great Houdini* (2–4). Illus. by Joseph Ciardiello. 1977, Putnam $4.29. A very easy biography of the escape artist and magician. For older readers use: *Houdini: Master of Escape* by Lace Kendall (1960, Macrae $6.50).

6818. White, Florence Meiman. *Escape: The Life of Harry Houdini* (4–6). 1979, Messner $7.79. The life of the greatest conjurer and magician of his time.

Jackson, Mahalia

6819. Jackson, Jesse. *Make a Joyful Noise unto the Lord! The Life of Mahalia Jackson, Queen of Gospel Singers* (6–9). Illustrated. 1974, Crowell $8.95; Dell paper $.95. The inspiring story of a woman who overcame prejudice and poverty to pursue her art as she wished without abandoning her principles. For younger readers use: *Mahalia Jackson: Queen of Gospel Song* by Jean Gay Cornell (1974, Garrard $4.48).

McNichol, Kristy and Jimmy

6820. Katz, Susan. *Kristy and Jimmy McNichol* (4–6). Ed. by Barbara Williams Prabhu. 1979, Grosset $4.66. The lives of this popular brother and sister team.

Mitchell, Arthur

6821. Tobias, Tobi. *Arthur Mitchell* (3–5). Illus. by Carole Byard. 1975, Crowell $6.79. An affectionate portrait of the black dancer who founded the Dance Theater of Harlem.

Oakley, Annie

6822. Alderman, Clifford L. *Annie Oakley and the World of Her Time* (6–8). 1979, Macmillan $8.95. A straightforward account of Annie Oakley, her career, and her life with Frank Butler. For a younger group use: *Annie Oakley, The Shooting Star* by Charles P. Graves (1961, Garrard $4.20).

Ringling Brothers

6823. Cone, Molly. *The Ringling Brothers* (2–4). Illus. by James McCrea and Ruth McCrea. 1971, Crowell $6.95; LB $6.89. By hard and persistent work, the 6 Ringling boys developed their show into the largest circus in the world.

Robeson, Paul

6824. Hamilton, Virginia. *Paul Robeson: The Life and Times of a Free Black Man* (6–9). 1974, Harper $7.95; LB $7.89 Dell paper $1.50. The complex life of the black entertainer who was persecuted because of his political beliefs. For younger readers use: *Paul Robeson* by Eloise Greenfield (1975, Crowell $6.89).

Rodgers, Jimmie

6825. Krishef, Robert K. *Jimmie Rodgers* (4–6). Illustrated. 1978, Lerner $5.95. An entertaining biography of the father of country and western music. Also use: *Loretta Lynn* (1978, Lerner $5.95).

Rogers, Will

6826. Campbell, Chester W. *Will Rogers* (6–8). 1979, Dillon $5.95. A portrait of the American humorist, who was part Cherokee, who became a beloved entertainer.

Sullivan, Tom

6827. Gill, Derek L. T. *Tom Sullivan's Adventures in Darkness* (5–9). 1976, McKay $7.95; NAL paper $1.50. Blind from infancy, Sullivan conquered this handicap and became successful in many fields, including singing.

Tallchief, Maria

6828. Tobias, Tobi. *Maria Tallchief* (2–3). Illus. by Michael Hampshire. 1970, Crowell $6.89. An easily read biography of the American Indian who became a world-famous ballerina.

Williams, Hank

6829. Krishef, Robert K. *Hank Williams* (5–9). Illustrated. 1978, Lerner $5.95. The tragic life of one of the great stars of western music.

Wonder, Stevie

6830. Haskins, James. *The Story of Stevie Wonder* (6–9). Illustrated. 1976, Lothrop $5.75; LB $5.52; Dell paper $1.25. A relaxed, candid biography of this phenomenal blind musician and his career.

6831. Wilson, Beth P. *Stevie Wonder* (3–5). Illustrated. 1979, Putnam $4.49. An easily read biography of this popular singer and writer of songs.

Sports Figures

Collective

6832. Borstein, Larry. *After Olympic Glory: The Lives of Ten Outstanding Medalists* (6–9). Illustrated. 1978, Warne $7.95. The lives of 10 Olympic winners, including Dr. Benjamin Spock, who continued to achieve throughout their lives.

6833. Clary, Jack. *The Captains* (6–8). Illustrated. 1978, Atheneum $7.95. The stories of the men who lead their teams to victory.

6834. Corson, Richard. *Champions at Speed* (6–9). Illus. by author. 1979, Dodd $5.95. The stories of 8 historic Grand Prix racing champions.

6835. Gleasner, Diana C. *Women in Sports: Track and Field* (5–9). Illustrated. 1977, Harvey House $5.69. Six female track stars are introduced through their accomplishments and personal reminiscences.

6836. Glickman, William G. *Winners on the Tennis Court* (4–7). Illustrated. 1978, Watts $4.90. Simple, short introductions to some major athletes in tennis.

6837. Golden, Flora. *Women in Sports: Horseback Riding* (4–7). Illustrated. 1978, Harvey House $5.29. After basic background information, this book focuses on the careers of 5 women.

6838. Gutman, Bill. *Superstars of the Sports World* (5–8). Illustrated. 1978, Messner $7.29. Five outstanding athletes are profiled in an account that stresses the obstacles that each overcame.

6839. Hirshberg, Al. *The Greatest American Leaguers* (6–9). 1970, Putnam $5.29. A master at sports biographies covers, with imaginative writing, the careers of 20 all-star players.

6840. Klein, Dave. *On the Way Up: What It's Like in the Minor Leagues* (5–9). Illustrated. 1977, Messner $6.64. Ten major league stars tell of the trials and troubles of life in the minor leagues.

6841. Lawrence, Andrew. *Tennis: Great Stars, Great Moments* (5–7). 1976, Putnam $5.49. Biographies of 12 tennis stars from Bill Tilden to Jimmy Conners and Chris Evert.

6842. Libby, Bill. *Baseball's Greatest Sluggers* (5–7). Illustrated. 1973, Random $2.50; LB $3.69. From Babe Ruth to Hank Aaron in lively, human portraits.

6843. Litsky, Frank. *Winners in Gymnastics* (4–7). Illustrated. 1978, Watts $4.90. Easily read, brief accounts of important present-day athletes.

6844. Murray, Tom, ed. *Sport Magazine's All-Time All Stars* (6–9). 1977, NAL $2.25. Twenty-two articles that appeared in *Sport Magazine* from 1948 through 1974 on the greatest baseball players.

6845. Sabin, Francene. *Women Who Win* (6–9). Illustrated. 1975, Random $3.95; LB $4.99; Dell paper $1.25. Biographies of 14 women athletes from a variety of sports.

6846. Shapiro, Milton J. *The Pro Quarterbacks* (6–9). Illustrated. 1971, Messner $4.64. Great moments in the lives of football superstars—Namath, Unitas, Dawson, Jurgenson, and others.

6847. Shoemaker, Robert H. *The Best in Baseball* (5–9). 1974, Crowell $6.95. Sketches of many of the most important baseball players from Ty Cobb and Babe Ruth to the present.

6848. Smith, Robert. *Pioneers of Baseball* (6–9). Illustrated. 1978, Little $7.95. Short sketches of outstanding baseball players, many now relatively unknown.

6849. Stambler, Irwin. *Women in Sports* (6–8). Illustrated. 1975, Doubleday $4.95. Many sports, including speed skating and drag racing, are represented in this collection.

6850. Sullivan, George. *Modern Olympic Superstars* (3–6). Illustrated. 1979, Dodd $5.94. The story of 6 champions, such as Bruce Jenner, who won gold medals.

6851. Sullivan, George. *Queens of the Court* (6–9). Illustrated. 1974, Dodd $5.95. Biographical sketches of 6 important women tennis players, plus an overview of changes in women's tennis.

Baseball

Aaron, Hank

6852. Young, B. E. *The Picture Story of Hank Aaron* (3–5). Illustrated. 1974, Messner $5.79. The life and career of this quiet black baseball player who broke Babe Ruth's home-run record, told in easy-to-read style, accompanied by excellent photographs.

Carew, Rod

6853. Burchard, Marshall. *Sports Hero: Rod Carew* (2–4). Illustrated. 1978, Putnam $5.49. A lively introduction to the popular Panamanian baseball star.

6854. Libby, Bill. *Rod Carew: Master Hitter* (5–7). 1976, Putnam $5.29. Rod Carew's life from a childhood of poverty to his baseball career with the Minnesota Twins.

Clemente, Roberto

6855. Rudeen, Kenneth. *Roberto Clemente* (2–4). Illus. by Frank Mullins. 1974, Crowell $6.89. A simply written account of the great black athlete, star of the Pittsburgh Pirates baseball team. For older readers use: *Roberto Clemente: Batting King* by Arnold Hano (1973, Putnam $5.29) and *Roberto Clemente: Pride of the Pirates* by Jerry Brandfield (1976, Garrard $4.48).

DiMaggio, Joe

6856. Schoor, Gene. *Joe DiMaggio: A Biography* (6–9). Illustrated. 1980, Doubleday $8.95; LB $9.80. An introspective biography of the legendary Yankee Clipper.

Foster, George

6857. Drucker, Malka, and Foster, George. *The George Foster Story* (5–9). Illustrated. 1979, Holiday $6.95. The life of the Cincinnati Reds' mighty hitter.

Garvey, Steve

6858. Vass, George. *Steve Garvey: The Bat Boy Who Became a Star* (5–8). Illustrated. 1979, Childrens Press $4.50. An easily read basic biography.

Gehrig, Lou

6859. Luce, Willard. *Lou Gehrig: Iron Man of Baseball* (3–5). Illus. by Dom Lupo. 1970, Garrard $4.48. A touching portrait of a man whose life and career became an inspiration.

6860. Rubin, Robert. *Lou Gehrig: Courageous Star* (5–8). Illustrated. 1979, Putnam $5.96. The legendary life of the New York Yankee player that has been a model of courage and endurance.

Hunter, Jim "Catfish"

6861. Burchard, Sue. *Sports Star: Jim "Catfish" Hunter* (3–5). Illus. by Paul Frame. 1976, Harcourt $4.95; paper $1.95. An easily read biography of the major league pitcher.

Jackson, Reggie

6862. Gutman, Bill. *The Picture Life of Reggie Jackson* (3–4). Illustrated. 1978, Watts $4.90. An acceptable biography of baseball's famous outfielder.

6863. Jackson, Reggie. *Reggie Jackson's Scrapbook* (4–7). Illustrated. 1978, Windmill $9.95. Many photographs make this an easily read biography of one of baseball's superstars.

6864. Sullivan, George. *The Picture Story of Reggie Jackson* (4–7). Illustrated. 1977, Messner $6.97. A simple account of the life of the superstar.

6865. Vass, George. *Reggie Jackson: From Superstar to Candy Bar* (5–8). Illustrated. 1979, Childrens Press $4.50. Plenty of interesting biographical details in this easy-to-read biography. Also use: *The Reggie Jackson Story* by Bill Libby (1979, Lothrop $6.95).

LeFlore, Ron

6866. Burchard, Marshall. *Sports Hero, Ron LeFlore* (4–6). Illustrated. 1979, Putnam $6.29. A stirring biography of the amazing black centerfielder of the Detroit Tigers.

Mays, Willie

6867. Sullivan, George. *Willie Mays* (1–3). Illus. by David Brown. 1973, Putnam $4.49. The life story of the star player who made baseball history. Also use: *Willie Mays: Baseball Superstar* by Sam Epstein (1975, Garrard $4.48).

Morgan, Joe

6868. Burchard, Marshall. *Sports Hero, Joe Morgan* (4–7). Illustrated. 1978, Putnam $5.49. Action text and photographs highlight this biography of a famous batter and base-stealer.

Paige, Satchel

6869. Rubin, Robert. *Satchel Paige: All-Time Baseball Great* (5–8). 1974, Putnam $5.29. A well-rounded biography of one of baseball's most renowned figures.

Robinson, Jackie

6870. Robinson, Jackie, and Duckett, Alfred. *Breakthrough to the Big League: The Story of Jackie Robinson* (5–8). Illustrated. 1965, Harper $7.89. The first black big-league baseball player talks about himself and the game.

6871. Rudeen, Kenneth. *Jackie Robinson* (2–4). Illus. by Richard Cuffari. 1971, Crowell $6.89; paper $2.95. The life story of the first black man to play in the major leagues.

Rose, Pete

6872. Rose, Pete. *Pete Rose: My Life in Baseball* (4–7). Illustrated. 1979, Doubleday $6.95; LB $7.90. A candid account of this baseball star's phenomenal career, told in conversational style.

6873. Rubin, Bob. *Pete Rose* (5–7). 1975, Random $3.69. The story of "Charlie Hustle" will be especially popular with young readers.

Sanguillen, Manny

6874. Cohen, Joel H. *Manny Sanguillen: Jolly Pirate* (5–7). 1975, Putnam $5.29. This biography outlines Sanguillen's life from Panama to Pittsburgh and fame in the baseball world.

Seaver, Tom

6875. Belsky, Dick. *Tom Seaver: Baseball's Superstar* (4–7). Illustrated. 1977, Walck $5.95. An engaging biography that offers insights into the personality of "Tom Terrific."

6876. Drucker, Malka, and Seaver, Tom. *Tom Seaver: Portrait of a Pitcher* (6–8). Illustrated. 1978, Holiday $7.95. A realistic but sympathetic portrait of this extraordinary athlete.

Stengel, Casey

6877. Verral, Charles. *Casey Stengel, Baseball's Great Manager* (4–7). Illustrated. 1978, Garrard $4.48. The breezy, informal writing style matches the life-style of this colorful man.

Football

Bradshaw, Terry

6878. Denaney, John. *The Picture Story of Terry Bradshaw* (4–8). Illustrated. 1977, Messner $6.97. A slim but inviting biography of the quarterback for the Pittsburgh Steelers.

Campbell, Earl

6879. Phillips, Betty Lou. *Earl Campbell, Houston Oiler Superstar* (5–9). Illustrated. 1979, McKay

$7.95. A spectacular football career interestingly presented.

Dorsett, Tony

6880. Burchard, Sue. *Sports Hero: Tony Dorsett* (2–4). Illustrated. 1979, Harcourt $6.00. A simple account that traces Dorsett's career from high school football to the Dallas Cowboys.

6881. Conrad, Dick. *Tony Dorsett: From Heisman to Super Bowl in One Year* (5–8). Illustrated. 1979, Childrens Press $4.50. The life of the gifted black football player told in text and pictures.

Griffin, Archie

6882. Dolan, Edward F., and Lyttle, Richard B. *Archie Griffin* (5–8). Illustrated. 1977, Doubleday $5.95; Archway paper $1.25. A well-balanced account of the personal and professional life of this inspiring football player. Also use: *Bobby Clarke* (1977, Doubleday $5.95).

Harris, Franco

6883. Hahn, James, and Hahn, Lynn. *Franco Harris* (4–6). 1979, EMC $4.46. A biography of the Pittsburgh Steelers star running back. Also use: *Franco Harris* by Thomas Braun (1975, Creative Education $4.95).

Payton, Walter

6884. Conrad, Dick. *Walter Payton: The Running Machine* (5–8). Illustrated. 1979, Childrens Press $4.50. An interesting biography of the famous black football player.

Simpson, O. J.

6885. Burchard, Marshall, and Burchard, Sue. *Sports Hero: O. J. Simpson* (4–6). Illustrated. 1975, Putnam $5.49. An interesting account of this amazing football player's childhood and professional career.

Tarkenton, Fran

6886. Burchard, Marshall. *Sports Hero: Fran Tarkenton* (3–8). Illustrated. 1977, Putnam $5.49. A well-rounded picture of this star quarterback.

Tennis

Austin, Tracy

6887. Hahn, James, and Hahn, Lynn. *Tracy Austin* (4–6). 1978, EMC $4.46. The career of the teenage tennis powerhouse.

6888. Robison, Nancy. *Tracy Austin* (3–5). Illustrated. 1978, Harvey House $5.39. A simple biography of this amazing tennis star, with many quotations from people who know her.

Connors, Jimmy

6889. Burchard, Marshall. *Sports Hero: Jimmy Connors* (4–6). 1976, Putnam $5.49. The well-presented life story of the controversial tennis player.

Evert, Chris

6890. Burchard, Sue. *Sports Star: Chris Evert* (2–4). Illustrated. 1976, Harcourt $4.95; paper $1.95. This brief, simply written biography of the popular tennis player will be enjoyed by young children. Also use: *Sports Hero: Billie Jean King* (1975, Putnam $5.49).

McEnroe, John

6891. Burchard, Sue. *Sports Star: John McEnroe* (3–6). Illustrated. 1979, $5.95; paper $2.25. A standard biography that includes coverage through victory in the 1979 U.S. Open.

Track and Field

Jenner, Bruce

6892. Asseng, Nathan. *Bruce Jenner: Decathalon Winner* (3–5). Illustrated. 1979, Lerner $5.95.

This is not only an interesting biography, but also an introduction to the decathlon.

Owens, Jesse

6893. Owens, Jesse. *The Jesse Owens Story* (4–6). 1970, Putnam $5.29. The story of the legendary track star who became the hero of the 1936 Olympics.

Paul, Wesley

6894. Fogel, Julianna A. *Wesley Paul, Marathon Runner* (4–6). Illustrated. 1979, Lippincott $7.95; LB $7.89. A profile of a 9-year-old marathon runner and his training.

Thorpe, Jim

6895. Fall, Thomas. *Jim Thorpe* (2–5). Illus. by John Gretzer. 1970, Crowell paper $1.95. A well-rounded biography of the Indian athlete who won the Olympic decathlon in 1912.

Basketball

Abdul-Jabbar, Kareem

6896. Haskins, James. *From Lew Alcindor to Kareem Abdul-Jabbar* (5–9). Illustrated. 1978, Morrow $5.95. A newer edition of the popular biography that tells of an astounding basketball career.

Chamberlain, Wilt

6897. Rudeen, Kenneth. *Wilt Chamberlain* (2–5). Illus. by Frank Mullins. 1970, Crowell $5.95; LB $6.89. An easily read biography of the basketball superstar.

Erving, Julius

6898. Braun, Thomas. *Julius Erving* (4–6). Illus. by John Keely. 1976, Creative Education $4.95. A profile of this great basketball player. For younger readers use: *Sports Hero: Dr. J.* by Marshall Burchard (1976, Putnam $5.29).

Frazier, Walt

6899. Batson, Larry. *Walt Frazier* (4–7). Illus. by Harold Henriksen. 1974, Creative Education $5.50; paper $2.50. A fine retelling of the amazing sports career of the former New York Knicks star. Also use: *Picture Story of Walt Frazier* by Howard Liss (1976, Messner $5.79).

6900. Burchard, Sue. *Sports Star: Walt Frazier* (3–5). Illus. by Paul Frame. 1975, Harcourt $4.95. An easily read biography of this great black athlete.

McAdoo, Bob

6901. Haskins, James. *Bob McAdoo, Superstar* (5–9). Illustrated. 1978, Morrow $6.95. A chatty biography of this superstar of basketball, including his fight for civil rights.

Walton, Bill

6902. Hahn, James, and Hahn, Lynn. *Bill Walton: Maverick Cager* (3–6). 1978, EMC $5.95. The life of the controversial basketball star interestingly told.

Boxing

Corbett, James

6903. Hoff, Syd. *Gentleman Jim and the Great John L* (1–4). Illus. by author. 1977, Coward $4.69. The rise and fall of one of the greatest boxing stars, simply told.

Muhammad Ali

6904. Burchard, Marshall. *Sports Hero: Muhammad Ali* (3–5). Illustrated. 1975, Putnam $4.49. A simple biography of Ali's career from Olympic gold medal winner to more recent accomplishments.

6905. Edwards, Audrey, and Wohl, Gary. *Muhammad Ali, The People's Champ* (6–9). Illustrated. 1977, Little $7.95. An absorbing record that contains much personal information, although it tends to idealize.

6906. Lipsyte, Robert. *Free to Be Muhammad Ali* (6–9). 1978, Harper $5.95. A well-rounded biograhy by the veteran sports writer.

Young, Jimmy

6907. Dolan, Edward F., and Lyttle, Richard B. *Jimmy Young: Heavyweight Challenger* (6–8). 1979, Doubleday $5.95. An easily read life of the prominent black boxer.

Automobile Racing

Andretti, Mario

6908. Burchard, Marshall. *Sports Hero: Mario Andretti* (3–6). Illustrated. 1977, Putnam $5.49. A brief introduction to the famous racer.

Foyt, A. J.

6909. Olney, Ross R. *A. J. Foyt: The Only Four Time Winner* (4–6). 1978, Walck $6.85. The phenomenal career of the race car driver.

Guthrie, Janet

6910. Olney, Ross R. *Janet Guthrie: First Woman at Indy* (4–9). Illustrated. 1979, Harvey House $4.99. The incredible career of the race car driver.

6911. Robison, Nancy. *Janet Guthrie: Race Car Driver* (5–8). Illustrated. 1979, Childrens Press $4.50. An unusual life told in simple text with many photographs.

Rutherford, Johnny

6912. Higdon, Hal. *Johnny Rutherford* (5–8). 1980, Putnam $6.29. A biography of the two-time winner of the Indy 500.

Other Sports

Beckenbauer, Franz

6913. Hahn, James, and Hahn, Lynn. *Franz Beckenbauer* (4–6). 1978, EMC $4.46. The career of the German soccer superstar.

Cauthen, Steve

6914. Miklowitz, Gloria D. *Steve Cauthen* (4–7). Illustrated. 1979, Grosset $4.99. Tempo paper $1.50. A simple-to-read biography of the popular jockey.

6915. Mueser, Anne Marie. *The Picture Story of Jockey Steve Cauthen* (3–6). Illustrated. 1979, Messner $6.97. A well-researched, informative biography of "the kid."

6916. Tuttle, Anthony. *Steve Cauthen: Boy Jockey* (4–6). Illustrated. 1978, Putnam $7.95. An easily read biography of the jockey who began his career at age 16.

Comaneci, Nadia

6917. Braun, Thomas. *Nadia Comaneci* (4–6). Illustrated. 1977, Creative Education $5.50; paper $2.50. The story in text and pictures of the phenomenal young star of the 1976 Olympics.

Dunn, Natalie

6918. Miklowitz, Gloria D. *Natalie Dunn: World Roller Skating Champion* (3–5). Illustrated. 1979, Harcourt $2.95. A believable portrait of this shy, unassuming champion.

Esposito, Phil

6919. Burchard, Marshall, and Burchard, Sue. *Sports Hero: Phil Esposito* (3–4). Illustrated. 1975, Putnam $5.49. A simple, well-illustrated account of one of hockey's great players, with emphasis on his tenure with the Boston Bruins. Also use: *Phil Esposito: Hockey's Greatest Scorer* by Bill Libby (1975, Putnam $5.95).

Hamill, Dorothy

6920. Phillips, Betty Lou. *The Picture Story of Dorothy Hamill* (4–6). Illustrated. 1978, Messner $6.95. Excellent photographs complement the text of this readable biography of the famous figure skater.

Lopez, Nancy

6921. Robison, Nancy. *Nancy Lopez: Wonder Woman of Golf* (5–8). Illustrated. 1979, Childrens Press $4.50. A well-illustrated basic biography about a dedicated Mexican-American athlete.

Orr, Bobby

6922. Jackson, Robert B. *Here Comes Bobby Orr* (4–6). Illustrated. 1971, Walck $5.95; paper $1.25. The career and accomplishments of hockey's best all-around and most popular player, who led the Boston Bruins to their first Stanley Cup in 29 years. Also use: *Picture Life of Bobby Orr* by Audrey Edwards (1976, Watts $4.90).

Pickett, Bill

6923. Hancock, Sibyl. *Bill Pickett: First Black Rodeo Star* (4–6). Illus. by Lorinda Bryan Cauley. 1977, Harcourt $5.95; paper $1.95. An exciting story of a brave young black man's rise to fame.

Rote, Kyle, Jr.

6924. Dolan, Edward F., and Lyttle, Richard B. *Kyle Rote Jr.: American-Born Soccer Star* (6–8). Illustrated. 1979, Doubleday $5.95. The life story of one of soccer's superstars in an easily read format.

Russo, Leslie

6925. Haney, Lynn. *Perfect Balance: The Story of an Elite Gymnast* (5–7). Illustrated. 1979, $8.95. The story of Leslie Russo and her struggle to become an Olympic-caliber gymnast.

The Individual and Society

Ecology and the Environment

General

6926. Bendick, Jeanne. *Ecology* (2–4). Illus. by author. 1975, Watts $4.90. Although this is a simple account, such concepts as the water cycle, ecosystems, and food chains are introduced. Also use: *Place to Live* (1970, Parents $5.41).

6927. Billington, Elizabeth. *Understanding Ecology* (5–7). Illus. by Robert Galster. 1971, Warne $6.95. Such concepts as food chains and ecosystems are introduced in this fascinating account that includes some projects. Also use: *Ecology: The Circle of Life* by Harold R. Hungerford (1971, Childrens Press $7.95).

6928. Chester, Michael. *Let's Go to Fight a Forest Fire* (3–5). Illustrated. 1978, Putnam $4.29. An introductory account seen through the eyes of a young boy. Also use: *Historical Catastrophes: Fires* by Walter R. Brown and Norman D. Anderson (1976, Addison $7.95).

6929. Hirsch, S. Carl. *The Living Community: A Venture into Ecology* (6–9). Illus. by William Steinel. 1966, Viking $5.95. A study of the interrelationships among plants and animals.

6930. Hoke, John. *Man's Effects on His Environment and Its Mechanisms* (4–6). Illus. by Richard Cuffari. 1977, Watts $5.45. A concise introduction to the study of ecology with emphasis on basic concepts and the way people have changed their environment. Also use: *Save the Earth! An Ecology Handbook for Kids* by Betty Miles (1974, Knopf $5.95; paper $2.50).

6931. Hopf, Alice L. *Misplaced Animals, Plants and Other Creatures* (6–9). Illustrated. 1976, McGraw $6.95. A description of the problems caused when a stable ecology is set off-balance by artificially introducing a new element.

6932. Milgrom, Harry. *ABC of Ecology* (1–3). Illus. by Donald Crews. 1972, Macmillan paper $1.95. An alphabet book that discusses urban pol-lution. Also use: *Who Cares? I Do* by Munro Leaf (1971, Lippincott $4.95; paper $2.25).

6933. Perl, Lila. *The Global Food Shortage: Food Scarcity on Our Planet and What We Can Do about It* (6–9). Illustrated. 1976, Morrow $6.00. A useful and informative discussion of a growing problem. Also use: *New World of Food* (1968, Dodd $4.50).

6934. Pringle, Laurence. *Ecology: Science of Survival* (5–8). 1971, Macmillan $6.95. The relationships between living things and their environment are discussed with emphasis on our present ecological situation.

6935. Pringle, Laurence. *Natural Fire: Its Ecology in Forests* (4–6). Illustrated. 1979, Morrow $5.95; LB $5.71. How fire plays a natural and necessary part in our environment.

6936. Pringle, Laurence. *Our Hungry Earth: The World Food Crisis* (5–7). Illustrated. 1976, Macmillan $6.95. A beginning discussion of the many factors, such as food production and population, that have created our present food crisis. Also use: *This Hungry World* by Elizabeth S. Helfman (1970, Lothrop $6.01).

6937. Pringle, Laurence. *Pests and People* (5–7). Illustrated. 1972, Macmillan $5.95. Subtitle: *The Search for Sensible Pest Control*. Also use: *Insect Pests* by George S. Fichter (1966, Golden, paper $1.95).

6938. Roth, Charles E. *The Most Dangerous Animal in the World* (5–7). Illus. by Salvatore Raciti. 1971, Addison $5.95. A discussion and history of people and their treatment of the environment.

6939. Silverstein, Alvin, and Silverstein, Virginia B. *Animal Invaders: The Story of Imported Wildlife* (4–7). Illustrated. 1974, Atheneum $6.95. How animals that have been artificially introduced to an environment change its ecology.

6940. Smith, Frances. *The First Book of Conservation* (4–7). Illus. by Mary DeBall Kwitz. 1972, Watts $4.90. A well-organized informative introduction. Also use: *Conservation of Nature* by Eric Duffey (1971, McGraw $5.72).

Cities

6941. Gregor, Arthur S. *Man's Mark on the Land* (4–7). Illustrated. 1974, Scribner $5.95. Subtitle: *The Changing Environment from the Stone Age to the Age of Smog, Sewage and Tar on Your Feet.*

6942. Muller, Jorg. *The Changing City and The Changing Countryside* (4–8). Illustrated. 1977, Atheneum $11.95. Two folios of loose pictures without text. The first shows the history of a city from 1953 to 1976; the second depicts the gradual destruction of a natural environment by the encroachment of industrialized society.

6943. Pringle, Laurence. *City and Suburb: Exploring an Ecosystem* (4–7). Illustrated. 1975, Macmillan $5.95. A study of all forms of life—human, animal, vegetable—in a metropolitan area.

6944. Ross, Pat. *What Ever Happened to the Baxter Place?* (2–4). Illus. by Roger Duvoisin. 1976, Pantheon $5.99. A thriving Maryland farm is sold off piece by piece, and what was once a rural landmark becomes part of an urban sprawl.

6945. Schwartz, Alvin. *Central City Spread City: The Metropolitan Regions Where More and More of Us Spend Our Lives* (5–7). Illustrated. 1973, Macmillan $4.95. A cry for the necessity of urban planning is explored in this study of interrelationship between city and suburb.

Endangered Species

6946. Gordon, Esther S., and Gordon, Bernard L. *Once There Was a Passenger Pigeon* (4–7). Illus. by Lawrence Di Fiori. 1976, Walck $5.95. A history of this once-populous bird and of how humans caused its extinction.

6947. Harris, John, and Pahl, Aleta. *Endangered Predators* (4–7). Illustrated. 1976, Doubleday $5.95. Five stories based on fact that feature the wolf, fox, cougar, and bobcat.

6948. Hogner, Dorothy Childs. *Endangered Plants* (4–6). Illus. by Arabelle Wheatley. 1977, Crowell $6.95. The ways in which plants can become endangered (strip mining, zealous pickers, and the like) and ways they can be preserved are described in this well-illustrated volume.

6949. McClung, Robert M. *America's Endangered Birds* (6–8). Illus. by George Founds. 1979, Morrow $7.95; LB $7.63. Subtitle: *Programs and People Working to Save Them.*

6950. McClung, Robert M. *Hunted Mammals of the Sea* (6–8). Illus. by William Downey. 1978, Morrow $7.95; LB $7.35. A discussion of various sea mammals from whales to polar bears that are objects of current conservation efforts.

6951. McClung, Robert M. *Lost Wild America: The Story of Our Extinct and Vanishing Wild Life* (6–9). Illus. by Bob Hines. 1969, Morrow $7.75. A comprehensive survey of an important area of ecology. Also use: *Wildlife for America* by William R. Van Dersal (1970, Walck $7.50).

6952. McCoy, Joseph J. *In Defense of Animals* (5–7). Illustrated. 1978, Seabury $8.95. The past and present ways humans have helped to protect animals.

6953. Roth, Charles E. *Then There Were None* (5–8). Illustrated. 1978, Addison $5.21. An account of extinct American cultures and of extinct or near-extinct animals.

6954. Silverberg, Robert. *The Auk, the Dodo and the Oryx: Vanished and Vanishing Creatures* (5–7). Illus. by Jacques Hnizdovsky. 1967, Crowell $8.95. A plea for conservation through this account of extinction and near-extinction of the world's wildlife.

6955. Wegen, Ron. *Where Can the Animals Go?* (4–7). Illustrated. 1978, Greenwillow $6.95. An account of the effect people have had on African wildlife.

6956. Wise, William. *Animal Rescue: Saving Our Endangered Wildlife* (5–7). Illustrated. 1978, Putnam $5.89. How some animals have been saved from extinction. Also use: *Our Threatened Wildlife: An Ecological Study* by Bill Perry (1970, Coward $4.99).

Garbage

6957. Black, Hallie. *Dirt Cheap: The Evolution of Renewable Resource Management* (6–8). Illustrated. 1979, Morrow $7.95; LB $7.63. This account stresses methods by which we can conserve our natural resources.

6958. Hahn, James, and Hahn, Lynn. *Recycling: Re-Using Our World's Solid Wastes* (4–7). Illustrated. 1973, Watts $4.90. A survey of the ways in which usable waste can be collected, sorted, and reprocessed for extended use. Also use: *Recycling Resources* by Laurence Pringle (1974, Macmillan $5.95).

6959. Lauber, Patricia. *Too Much Garbage* (5–7). 1974, Garrard $4.48. A discussion of the problems of disposing of solid waste.

6960. Olney, Ross R. *Keeping Our Cities Clean* (4–5). Illustrated. 1979, Messner $6.97. Many photographs enliven this account of such municipal services as garbage collection and snow removal.

6961. Shanks, Ann Zane. *About Garbage and Stuff* (K–2). Illus. by author. 1973, Viking $5.95. An introduction to recycling waste materials, told in terms young children can readily understand, and what they can do to help with the problem. For an older group use: *What Happens to Garbage?* by Rona Beame (1975, Messner $6.95; LB $6.29).

6962. Showers, Paul. *Where Does the Garbage Go?* (2–3). Illus. by Loretta Lustig. 1974, Crowell $6.95; LB $6.89. A discussion of the problems of sanitation, conservation, and recycling of garbage as seen from a child's point of view. Also use: *Let's Go to the Sanitation Department* by Joanna Harris (1972, Putnam $3.86).

6963. Shuttlesworth, Dorothy E., and Cervasio, Thomas. *Litter—The Ugly Enemy: An Ecology Story* (3–5). 1973, Doubleday $5.95. Two children encounter the garbage problem when they start a campaign to clean up their city. For a younger group use: *Sparrows Don't Drop Candy Wrappers* by Margaret Gabel (1971, Dodd $3.95).

Pollution

6964. Adamson, Wendy. *Saving Lake Superior: A Story of Environmental Action* (6–9). 1974, Dillon $5.95. A vivid description of Lake Superior before and after pollution, and, in particular, the case against many industrial concerns.

6965. Aylesworth, Thomas G. *This Vital Air, This Vital Water: Man's Environmental Crisis* (5–8). Illustrated. 1968, Rand $5.95; LB $5.79. The causes and effects of pollution throughout the world are well described.

6966. Bartlett, Margaret F. *The Clean Brook* (1–3). Illus. by Aldren A. Watson. 1960, Crowell $6.89. The process of dirtying and purifying a brook is told through the activities of plants and animals.

6967. Berger, Melvin. *The New Water Book* (4–6). Illus. by Leonard Kessler. 1973, Crowell $6.95. The properties and uses of water are discussed clearly, as well as present problems related to supply and pollution. Also use: *Our Dirty Water* by Sarah M. Elliott (1973, Messner $5.29).

6968. Breiter, Herta S. *Pollution* (2–4). Illustrated. 1978, Raintree $5.49. A clear overview of this topical subject.

6969. Brown, Joseph E. *Oil Spills: Danger in the Sea* (6–9). Illustrated. 1978, Dodd $5.95. The sources and effects of a growing pollution problem.

6970. Elliott, Sarah M. *Our Dirty Land* (4–7). Illustrated. 1976, Messner $6.29. Garbage disposal, strip mining, and use of pesticides are only 3 polluting factors discussed.

6971. Gilfond, Henry. *Water: A Scarce Resource* (5–9). Illustrated. 1978, Watts $4.90. Information on how we use water and the threat of a real water crisis.

6972. Jennings, Gary. *The Shrinking Outdoors* (6–9). 1972, Lippincott $6.95. A chilling indictment of America's role in pollution, with particular emphasis on the part played by the automobile.

6973. Kalina, Sigmund. *Three Drops of Water* (3–5). Illus. by Charles Robinson. 1974, Lothrop $5.22. The water cycle from melting snow to streams and rivers, with material on pollution and the animal food chain. Also use with a younger group: *At Last to the Ocean* by Joel Rothman (1971, Macmillan $4.95).

6974. Kavaler, Lucy. *Dangerous Air* (6–8). Illus. by Carl Smith. 1967, John Day $7.95. The part that various agencies play in the production and reduction of air pollution.

6975. Kavaler, Lucy. *The Dangers of Noise* (5–8). Illus. by Richard Cuffari. 1978, Crowell $7.95. Noise pollution, its effects, and what to do about it are the major topics covered in this book. Also use: *Our Noisy World* by John Gabriel Navarra (1969, Doubleday $4.95).

6976. McCoy, Joseph J. *A Sea of Troubles* (6–8). Illus. by Richard Cuffari. 1975, Seabury $7.95. Upsetting material on the many human-caused problems, such as pollution, that have been inflicted on the oceans.

6977. Millard, Reed. *Clean Air–Clean Water for Tomorrow's World* (6–9). Illustrated. 1971, Messner $7.29. Prepared and written with the help of the editors of Science Book Associates, this is one of the most thorough treatments available on this subject.

6978. Orlowsky, Wallace, and Perera, Thomas B. *Who Will Wash the River?* (4–6). Illus. by Richard Cuffari. 1970, Coward $4.49. Two children discover the cause and cure of water pollution.

6979. Perera, Thomas B. *Who Will Clean the Air?* (1–3). 1971, Coward $4.49. An introduction to air pollution. For an older audience use: Michael Chester's *Let's Go to Stop Air Pollution* (1968, Putnam $4.29).

6980. Sootin, Harry. *Easy Experiments with Water Pollution* (5–7). Illus. by Lucy Bitner. 1974, Four Winds $6.95. Clever, easily performed experiments that illustrate aspects of pollution and how they can be alleviated.

6981. Tannenbaum, Beulah, and Stillman, Myra. *Clean Air* (4–6). Illustrated. 1974, McGraw $6.95. How we pollute the air and how we can clean it up and keep it clean. Also use: *Ecology and Pollution—Air* by Martin J. Gutnick (1973, Childrens Press $7.95).

Population

6982. Drummond, A. H. *Population Puzzle* (5–7). Illustrated. 1973, Addison $6.95. Subtitle: *Overcrowding and Stress among Animals and Men.* Also use: *Population* by Robert J. Lowenherz (1970, Creative Education $5.95).

6983. McClung, Robert M. *Mice, Moose and Men: How Their Populations Rise and Fall* (4–7). 1973, Morrow $6.25; LB $6.00. Natural life cycles are described and human interference with the natural flow of life is discussed, followed by material on human population growth.

6984. Pringle, Laurence. *One Earth, Many People: The Challenge of Human Population Growth* (6–9). Illustrated. 1971, Macmillan $4.95. A variety of viewpoints from interested groups are explored on the effects of population growth. Also use: *Earth: Our Crowded Spaceship* by Isaac Asimov (1974, John Day, paper $2.50).

Economics and Business

General

6985. Axon, Gordon V. *Let's Go to a Stock Exchange* (5–7). Illus. by Frank Aloise. 1973, Putnam $4.29. A stockbroker explains the rudiments of how the stock market works.

6986. Cavin, Ruth. *A Matter of Money: What You Can Do with a Dollar* (5–7). Illustrated. 1978, Phillips $8.95. Such concepts as inflation, interest, and taxes are explained in simple terms.

6987. Cooke, David C. *How Money Is Made* (4–6). Illustrated. 1972, Dodd $4.95. A clear description of how money is made by the U.S. Mint.

6988. Corcos, Lucille. *City Book* (1–3). Illus. by author. 1972, Golden $10.69. A description of a working day's activities in a large city.

6989. Crane, Robert. *Understanding Today's Economics* (6–9). Illustrated. 1979, Watts $5.45. A well-organized account for better readers. Also use: *Money Isn't Everything: The Story of Economics at Work* by Kathlyn Gay (1967, Delacorte $4.58).

6990. Faber, Doris. *Wall Street, A Story of Fortunes and Finance* (6–8). 1979, Harper $8.95. A history of Wall Street and its impact on national and world affairs.

6991. Fodor, R. V. *Nickels, Dimes and Dollars: How Currency Works* (4–6). Illustrated. 1980, Morrow $6.95; LB $6.67. A discussion of the U.S. money system and such topics as inflation, international exchange, and money management.

6992. Maher, John E. *Ideas about Money* (4–6). 1970, Watts $4.33. A simple introduction to the place of money in our lives.

6993. Molloy, Anne. *Wampum* (6–8). Illustrated. 1977, Hastings $6.95. A richly historical account of the origins and meanings behind the beads used by North American Indians for currency.

6994. Morgan, Tom. *Money, Money, Money: How to Get It and Keep It* (5–9). Illustrated. 1978, Putnam $7.95. Using common childhood experiences, the author discusses basic concepts in business.

6995. O'Toole, Edward T. *The New World of Banking* (4–6). Illustrated. 1965, Dodd $4.50. A description of banks and their functions. For a younger audience use: Laura Sootin's *Let's Go to a Bank* (1957, Putnam $4.29).

6996. Tarshis, Barry. *Barter, Bills and Banks* (4–6). Illustrated. 1970, Messner $3.95; LB $3.64. A look at the workings of the money system.

6997. Winn, Marie. *The Fisherman Who Needed a Knife: A Story about Why People Use Money* (1–3). Illustrated. 1970, Simon & Schuster $3.50; LB $3.39. The origin of the money concept is explained in story form.

Consumerism

6998. Berger, Melvin. *Consumer Protection Labs* (6–8). Illustrated. 1975, John Day $8.79. How various governmental and private testing labs work to protect the consumer.

6999. Gay, Kathlyn. *Be a Smart Shopper* (4–6). Illustrated. 1974, Messner $6.64. Consumer education plus tips on sources of income for children are surveyed in this timely overview.

7000. Hilton, Suzanne. *Beat It, Burn It and Drown It* (6–8). Illustrated. 1974, Westminster $5.95. An account of the thorough and often outlandish methods used to test products before they are released for sale to the public.

7001. Pompian, Richard O. *Advertising* (6–8). Illustrated. 1970, Watts $6.90. In addition to a brief history, this discusses types of advertising outlets.

7002. Saunders, Rubie. *Smart Shopping and Consumerism* (6–9). Illus. by Gail Owens. 1973, Watts $4.90. Practical advice for young buyers, including tips on budgeting, bargain hunting, and shopping for gifts.

7003. Sullivan, George. *How Do They Package It?* (5–7). 1976, Westminster $7.50. The history and contemporary use of packaging, which also touches on allied facets of conservation and pollution.

7004. Thypin, Marilyn, and Glasner, Lynne. *Try It On* (4–6). Illustrated. 1979, EMC $3.33. Consumerism and practical pointers are revealed in this story about a girl buying a dress.

Retail Stores

7005. Chapman, Victoria. *Let's Go to a Supermarket* (1–3). Illus. by Frank Aloise. 1971, Putnam $4.29. An introduction told through a visit to the supermarket by 2 children, who learn the value of money.

7006. Lubell, Winifred, and Lubell, Cecil. *Street Markets around the World* (2–5). 1974, Parents $5.41. An informative and intriguing introduction to different street markets. The authors suggest that modern supermarkets might be brightened by adding some street market features.

7007. Schwartz, Alvin. *Stores* (3–5). Illustrated. 1977, Macmillan $7.95. Different stores and their workers are described in the town of Princeton, New Jersey.

Money-making Ideas

7008. James, Elizabeth, and Barkin, Carol. *How to Grow a Hundred Dollars* (5–7). Illus. by Joel Schick. 1979, Lothrop $5.95. Simple budgetry and financial concepts are explained through a story of a girl who sets out to earn some money.

7009. Sattler, Helen R. *Dollars from Dandelions: 101 Ways to Earn Money* (6–9). Illus. by Rita Floden. 1979, Lothrop $7.95; LB $7.63. All kinds of ways for young people to earn, from farm work to helping in the kitchen.

7010. Saunders, Rubie. *Franklin Watts Concise Guide to Baby-Sitting* (6–9). Illus. by Tomie de Paola. 1972, Watts $4.90. A useful manual, particularly for the beginner, because it gives special material on preparing for the first job.

7011. Sweeney, Karen O'Connor. *How to Make Money* (4–6). Illus. by Carolyn Bentley. 1977, Watts $5.90. Information on various ways to make money. Also use: *How Kids Can Really Make Money* by Shari Lewis (1979, Holt $3.32).

7012. Young, Jim, and Young, Jean. *Kids' Money-Making Book* (4–7). Illus. by Michael Young. 1976, Doubleday $5.95. A description of 32 projects by which children can earn money. Also use: *Good Cents* (1974, Houghton $3.95) from the Amazing Life Games Company.

Politics and Government

United Nations

7013. Larsen, Peter. *The United Nations at Work throughout the World* (4–6). Illustrated. 1971, Lothrop $6.00. A well-organized account of the various agencies of the United Nations, and their activities and projects. Also use: *The United Nations* by Edna Epstein (1973, Watts $4.90).

7014. Sasek, M. *This Is the United Nations* (3–5). Illus. by author. 1968, Macmillan $5.95. A slim volume that gives the reader a guided tour of the U.N. while supplying incidental background information.

7015. Shippen, Katherine B. *The Pool of Knowledge* (6–8). 1965, Harper $5.79. The history, functions, and problems of the U.N.

Courts and the Law

7016. Brindze, Ruth. *All about Courts and the Law* (5–8). Illus. by Leonard Slonevsky. 1964, Random $4.99. Explanations of how the various courts operate, using some fictional cases—the traffic court, the state supreme court, criminal courts, and the United States Supreme Court, with special emphasis on the Warren Court's activities in school integration cases. For a younger group use: *Shiver, Gobble and Snore* by Marie Winn (1971, Simon & Schuster $4.95).

7017. Fincher, E. B. *The American Legal System* (6–8). 1980, Watts $5.90. An introduction to the U.S. legal system that concentrates on juvenile problems.

7018. Forte, David F. *The Supreme Court* (4–6). 1979, Watts $5.90. The history and duties of the Supreme Court are examined through landmark cases.

7019. Johnson, Gerald W. *The Supreme Court* (5–7). Illus. by Leonard Everett Fisher. 1962, Morrow $6.48. An excellent introduction to the history and functions of the Supreme Court.

7020. Levy, Elizabeth. *Lawyers for the People: A New Breed of Defenders and Their Work* (6–9). 1974, Knopf $5.99. Biographical sketches and material on their cases are given for 9 dedicated lawyers who have worked to provide justice for the defenseless. Also use: *You Be the Judge* by Sidney B. Carroll (1971, Lothrop $5.32).

7021. Lewis, Anthony. *The Supreme Court and How It Works* (5–8). Illustrated. 1966, Random paper $2.45. The functions of the Supreme Court are revealed in this account of the case of Clarence Gideon, a convict who claimed that he was denied his civil liberties. Also use for a younger group: *The First Book of the Supreme Court* by Harold Coy (1958, Watts $4.90).

7022. McKown, Robin. *Seven Famous Trials in History* (6–8). 1913, Vanguard $5.95. Aspects of our legal system are explored through famous cases.

7023. Sgroi, Peter. *Blue Jeans and Black Robes: Teenagers and the Supreme Court* (6–9). 1979, Messner $7.79. A book that explores the legal rights, and lack of them, of young people.

7024. Stevens, Leonard. *Death Penalty: The Case of Life vs. Death in the United States* (6–9). 1978, Coward $6.29. An in depth look at the 1972 Furman vs. Georgia court case and its consequences.

United States Government

Constitution

7025. Lawson, Don. *The Changing Face of the Constitution: Prohibition, Universal Sufferage and Women's Civil Rights and Religious Freedom* (6–9). 1979, Watts $6.90. A useful look at prohibition and women's rights.

7026. Morris, Richard B. *The First Book of the Constitution* (5–7). Illus. by Leonard Everett Fisher. 1958, Watts $4.90. Simple account of the formation of the U.S. Constitution, its strengths and weaknesses, and how it has been interpreted. Also use: *The First Book of the Constitutional Amendments* by William Loren Katz (1974, Watts $4.90).

7027. Peterson, Helen Stone. *The Making of the United States Constitution* (4–7). 1974, Garrard $2.48. A useful survey of the U.S. Constitution and how it came into being.

Federal

7028. Acheson, Patricia C. *Our Federal Government: How It Works, An Introduction to the United States* (6–9). Illustrated. 1978, Dodd $8.95. An updated version of a standard guide for better readers.

7029. Burt, Olive W. *I Am an American* (4–6). Illustrated. 1968, John Day $5.79. An explanation of what good citizenship means.

7030. Gray, Lee Learner. *How We Choose a President: The Election Year* (5–7). 1972, St. Martins $6.50. A step-by-step description of a presidential year, beginning with a search for candidates. Also use: *We Elect a President* by David E. Weingast (1977, Messner $8.29).

7031. Hoopes, Roy. *What a United States Senator Does* (5–8). 1975, John Day $4.50. A basic guide to the Senate and the activities of its members. Also use: *What Does a Senator Do?* by David Lavine (1967, Dodd $4.50).

7032. Johnson, Gerald W. *The Cabinet* (5–7). Illus. by Leonard Everett Fisher. 1966, Morrow $6.48. In addition to a description of the history and role of the U.S. cabinet, this survey highlights important past cabinets.

7033. Johnson, Gerald W. *The Congress* (5–7). Illus. by Leonard Everett Fisher. 1963, Morrow $6.48. The history, powers, and operating procedures of the Congress of the United States are discussed in this basic guide.

7034. Lavine, David. *What Does a Congressman Do?* (4–6). Illustrated. 1965, Dodd $4.50. A basic guide to the activities of a member of the Congress, including interesting material on the legislative process.

7035. Myers, Walter Dean. *Social Welfare* (6–9). Illustrated. 1976, Watts $4.90. A detailed examination of the many components of the social welfare system, such as Social Security, as they exist in the United States today.

7036. Parker, Nancy Winslow. *The President's Cabinet and How It Grew* (4–6). 1978, Parents $6.50. An introduction to the history, structure, and functions of the cabinet.

7037. Seuling, Barbara. *The Last Cow on the White House Lawn* (4–7). Illus. by author. 1978, Doubleday $4.95; LB $5.90. A collection of little-known, often amusing facts about the presidency.

7038. Stevens, Leonard. *How a Law Is Made: The Story of a Bill against Pollution* (6–9). Illus. by Robert Galster. 1970, Crowell $6.95. An explanation of the process by which the average citizen helps to make the laws that affect our lives. Also use: *Save the Mustangs! How a Federal Law Is Passed* by Ann E. Weiss (1974, Messner $6.92).

7039. Weiss, Ann E. *The American Congress* (6–8). Illustrated. 1977, Messner $7.29. After a general discussion of the history and functions of Congress, this work covers the basic duties and responsibilities of Congress members.

7040. Weiss, Ann E. *American Presidency* (5–7). Illustrated. 1976, Messner $7.29. A history of the presidency from Washington through Ford, emphasizing how various presidents have affected the office. Also use: *The Presidency* by Gerald W. Johnson (1962, Morrow $6.50).

7041. Winn, Marie. *The Thief-Catcher: A Story about Why People Pay Taxes* (1–3). Illus. by Whitney Darrow, Jr. 1972, Simon & Schuster $4.95. An explanation of why taxes are levied, told in simple enough terms for young children to grasp the concept.

Elections and Political Parties

7042. Cook, Fred J. *The First Book of the Rise of American Political Parties* (5–7). Illustrated. 1971, Watts $4.90. A simple introduction to the history and evolution of the 2-party system of government.

7043. Hoopes, Roy. *Primaries and Conventions* (4–6). Illustrated. 1978, Watts $4.90. The processes by which political candidates are chosen.

7044. Lindop, Edmund. *The First Book of Elections* (4–6). Illus. by Gustave E. Nebel. 1972, Watts $4.90. An analysis of the American election process; also tells about various kinds of elections.

7045. Markun, Patricia Maloney. *A First Book of Politics* (4–6). Illus. by Ted Schroeder. 1970, Watts $4.90. A basic introduction to the political process in the United States.

Municipal Government

7046. Eichner, James A. *The First Book of Local Government* (4–7). Illus. by Bruce Bacon. 1976, Watts $4.90. The various forms of organization, main functions, and the complex problems of local political units.

7047. Williams, Barbara. *I Know a Mayor* (3–5). Illustrated. 1967, Putnam $4.29. A simple introduction to a mayor's duties and the election process.

Civil Rights

7048. Agostinelli, Maria Enrica, illus. *On Wings of Love: The United Nations Declaration of the Rights of the Child* (2–4). 1979, World $6.95; LB $6.91. A simplified version of the declaration, illustrated by muted watercolors.

7049. Bullard, Pamela, and Stoia, Judith. *The Hardest Lesson: Personal Accounts of a Desegregation Crisis* (6–9). 1980, Little $8.95. Fourteen narratives that explore the Boston 1974 school desegregation crisis.

7050. Burns, Marilyn. *I Am Not a Short Adult: Getting Good at Being a Kid* (5–7). Illus. by Martha Weston. 1977, Little $7.95; paper $4.95. Many facets of childhood are discussed, including children's legal status and institutions that affect them.

7051. Carlson, Dale Bick. *Girls Are Equal Too: The Women's Movement for Teenagers* (6–9). Illus. by Carol Nicklaus. 1973, Atheneum $6.95. A discussion with many examples of sexism as it exists in society.

7052. Chute, Marchette. *The Green Tree of Democracy* (6–9). 1971, Dutton $8.50. A history of suffrage in America from its limited application during colonial days to the extension of voting privileges to 18-year-olds in 1970.

7053. Collier, Zena. *Seven for the People: Public Interest Groups at Work* (6–9). 1979, Messner $7.79. Better readers will learn about such groups as the American Civil Liberties Union, Common Cause, and NOW from this book.

7054. Dorman, Michael. *Under 21: A Young People's Guide to Legal Rights* (7–9). 1970, Delacorte $5.95. A straightforward and objective treatment of the difficulties and court rulings pertaining to the social, legal, and cultural rights of young people.

7055. Englebardt, Leland S. *You Have a Right* (6–8). 1979, Lothrop $7.50; LB $7.20. The legal rights of young people and sources of help are discussed.

7056. Fincher, E. B. *The Bill of Rights* (6–9). Illustrated. 1978, Watts $4.90. An examination of our basic civil rights and how they are protected.

7057. Komisar, Lucy. *The New Feminism* (4–6). Illustrated. 1971, Watts LB $6.89. A history of the women's movement and its causes.

7058. Loescher, Gil, and Loescher, Ann. *Human Rights: A Global Crisis* (5–8). Illustrated. 1979, Dutton $8.95. Human rights as they are protected and violated in many countries are explored in this narrative.

7059. Sterling, Dorothy. *Tear Down the Walls: A History of the American Civil Rights Movement* (6–9). 1968, Doubleday $6.95. The dramatic account of the struggle of black people to gain equality in America. Also use: *Black Struggle* by Bryan Fulk (1969, Delacorte $6.95) and *I Have a Dream* by Emma G. Sterne(1965, Knopf $5.99).

7060. Stevenson, Janet. *The Montgomery Bus Boycott, December 1955: American Blacks Demand an End to Segregation* (6–9). Illustrated. 1971, Watts $4.90. A detailed account of the trailblazing crusade for black rights that began with Rosa Parks's refusal to give up her seat on a bus.

7061. Stevenson, Janet. *The School Segregation Cases: Brown v. Board of Education of Topeka and Others* (5–9). Illustrated. 1973, Watts $4.90. A crisis-by-crisis history of the fight for desegregation, culminating in the Supreme Court decisions of 1954 and 1955.

7062. Stevenson, Janet. *Women's Rights* (5–7). Illustrated. 1972, Watts $4.90; paper $1.25. A history of this movement, told chiefly through biographies of important suffragettes. Also use: *Woman's Rights: The Suffrage Movement in America 1848–1920* by Olivia Coolidge (1966, Dutton $6.95).

7063. Weiss, Ann E. *We Will Be Heard: Dissent in the United States* (4–7). 1972, Messner $4.79. A historical survey of kinds of dissent and their consequences on American life. Also use: *Civil Rights* by Peter Goldman (1965, Coward $4.00).

7064. Wise, William. *American Freedom and the Bill of Rights* (2–4). Illus. by Roland Rodegast. 1975, Parents $5.41. A discussion of the 25 amendments to the Constitution, with a special section on the Equal Rights Amendment. Also use: *The Spirit and the Letter: The Struggle for Rights in America* by Bernice Kohn (1974, Viking $6.95).

Crime and Criminals

7065. Blassingame, Wyatt. *Science Catches the Criminal* (5–7). Illustrated. 1975, Dodd $5.50. Actual cases are used to describe the importance of such devices as fingerprinting in crime detection. Also use: *Fingerprint Detective* by Robert H. Millimaki (1973, Lippincott $5.95).

7066. Colby, C. B. *FBI: How the G-Men Use Science as Well as Weapons to Combat Crime* (4–7). 1970, rev. ed. Coward $5.19. How criminals are apprehended by the FBI through applying modern science.

7067. David, Andrew. *Famous Criminal Trials* (5–9). 1979, Lerner $6.95. Scopes, Leopold and Loeb, Sacco and Vanzetti, and Sirhan Sirhan are ony a few of the many covered in this book.

7068. Healey, Tim. *Spies* (6–8). Illustrated. 1979, Silver Burdett $6.99. A fascinating glimpse at spying through the ages.

7069. Madison, Arnold. *Arson!* (5–8). Illustrated. 1978, Watts $5.90. An introduction to the causes and results of this fast-growing crime.

7070. Madison, Arnold. *Don't Be a Victim! Protect Yourself and Your Belongings* (6–8). Illustrated. 1978, Messner $6.97. Do's and don'ts in the fight against crime involving young people.

7071. Taylor, L. B. *Shoplifting* (6–9). 1979, Watts $6.90. An explanation of teenage shoplifting and its consequences.

7072. Waters, John F. *Crime Labs: The Science of Forensic Medicine* (6–9). 1979, Watts $5.45. An interesting account of how crime is investigated through medical procedures.

Communism

7073. Forman, James D. *Communism* (6–9). 1979, Watts $6.90; paper $4.95. An account for mature readers.

7074. Johnson, Gerald W. *Communism: An American's View* (6–9). Illus. by Leonard Everett Fisher. 1964, Morrow $6.75. The ideas, personalities, and events connected with the history of Russian Communism.

Ethnic Groups

Immigration

7075. Bales, Carol Ann. *Tales of the Elders: A Memory Book of Men and Women Who Came to America as Immigrants 1900–1930* (6–9). Illustrated. 1977, Follett $6.95; LB $6.99. Twelve accounts based on interviews with immigrants involving the reasons for their coming to America, their journeys, and their adjustments.

7076. Hartmann, Edward George. *American Immigration* (5–8). Illustrated. 1979, Lerner $5.95. The people who came to America and why, from the Colonial Period to the present.

7077. Katz, William Loren. *Early America, 1492–1812* (5–7). Illustrated. 1974, Watts $4.90. The first volume of the excellent 6-volume series by the author that traces minorities in American history to the present.

7078. Tripp, Eleanor B. *To America* (6–9). 1969, Harcourt $5.95. An account of immigration from 1630 to 1920, with a description of the causes that forced various groups to come to the United States. Also use: *We Came to America* by Frances Cavanneh (1954, McCrea $6.47).

Blacks

7079. Bontemps, Arna. *Story of the Negro* (5–8). Illus. by Raymond Lufkin. 1969, Knopf $5.69. From the African past to the American present. Also use: the 6-volume work *The Black Man in America* by Florence Jackson (1970–1975, Watts $4.90 each).

7080. Buckmaster, Henrietta. *Flight to Freedom: The Story of the Underground Railroad* (5–7). 1958, Crowell $8.95. In addition to the history of the railroad, the author traces the growth of the abolition movement and its leaders.

7081. Goodman, Walter. *Black Bondage: The Life of Slaves in the South* (6–7). 1969, Farrar $3.95. Firsthand reports of former slaves make up this telling account of slavery.

7082. Greenfield, Eloise, and Little, Lessie Jones. *Childtimes: A Three Generation Memoir* (5–8). Illustrated. 1979, Crowell $8.95; LB $8.79. The childhood of 3 generations of black women.

7083. Johnston, Johanna. *Together in America: The Story of Two Races and One Nation* (5–7). Illus. by Morton Kunstler. 1965, Dodd $3.90; paper $.95. An exploration of the contributions of people of European and African backgrounds.

7084. Lester, Julius. *To Be a Slave* (5–8). Illus. by Tom Feelings. 1968, Dial $7.95; Dell paper $1.25. Through the words of the victims themselves, the reader is helped to realize what it was like to be a slave in America. Also use: *Slavery in the United States* by Leonard Ingraham (1968, Watts $4.90).

7085. Meltzer, Milton, ed. *In Their Own Words: A History of the American Negro* (6–9). Illustrated. Crowell. In 3 volumes, a social history of black Americans dramatically told in their own words and illustrated with many reproductions. Vol. 1, 1619–1865 (1964, $8.95; paper $1.65), Vol. II, 1865–1916 (1965, $8.95; paper $1.65), Vol. III, 1916–1966 (1967, $8.95; paper $1.45).

7086. Meltzer, Milton. *Slavery: From the Rise of Western Civilization to the Renaissance* (6–9). 1971, Contemporary paper $1.75. The historic, economic, and political bases of slavery are explored and related to today's problems. Also use: *Slavery: From the Rise of Western Civilization to Today* (1977, Dell, paper $1.75).

7087. Swift, Hildegarde. *North Star Shining* (5–9). Illus. by Lynd Ward. 1947, Morrow $6.95. Vivid account of the important role played by blacks in U.S. history.

7088. Thum, Marcella. *Exploring Black America: A History and Guide* (6–9). Illustrated. 1975, Atheneum $10.95. Each chapter is devoted to a single important topic in black history, such as slavery, the Underground Railway. In addition to an informational overview, material is given on such sources as museums and historic sites.

7089. Young, Margaret B. *The First Book of American Negroes* (4–6). Illustrated. 1966, Watts $4.90. Concise, factual account of the struggles and accomplishments of American blacks from 1619 to the present.

Other Groups

7090. Avakian, Arra S. *The Armenians in America* (4–6). 1977, Lerner $4.95. A history of the Armenian immigration to America and of the contributions of these people.

7091. Bales, Carol Ann. *Chinatown Sunday: The Story of Lillian Der* (3–5). Illustrated. 1973, Contemporary $5.95. Based on tapes made by a 10-year-old Chinese-American girl from Chicago, this is a candid, honest portrait of a family in a Chinese-American community.

7092. Engle, Eloise. *The Finns in America* (5–7). 1977, Lerner $4.95. An account of Finnish migration, their settlements in and contributions to America.

7093. Jones, Jayne Clark. *The Greeks in America* (5–7). Illustrated. 1969, Lerner $5.95. One of the many interesting titles in the In America series, which includes (each $4.95): *The French in America* by Virginia B. Kunz (1966), *The Norwegians in America* by Percie V. Hillbrand (1967), and *The Russians in America* by Nancy Eubank (1973).

7094. LaGumina, Salvatore J. *An Album of the Italian-American* (4–7). Illustrated. 1972, Watts $5.90. The experiences, problems, and contributions of Italian-Americans from the early explorers to the present.

7095. Meltzer, Milton. *Taking Root: Jewish Immigrants in America* (6–8). 1976, Farrar $7.95. A well-researched history of the trials and problems of Jewish immigrants. Also use *World of Our Fathers: The Jews of Eastern Europe* (1974, Farrar $7.95).

7096. Molnar, Joe, ed. *Elizabeth: A Puerto Rican-American Child Tells Her Story* (4–6). Illustrated. 1975, Watts $4.90. From a taped interview, this first-person narrative depicts the life and activities of a young girl growing up in a loving family in Spanish Harlem.

7097. Molnar, Joe, ed. *Gaciela: A Mexican-American Child Tells Her Story* (4–6). Illustrated. 1972, Watts $4.90. Based on taped interviews, this is the story of a 12-year-old daughter, one of 10 children, of migrant Chicano workers.

7098. Suhl, Yuri. *Album of the Jews in America* (5–7). 1972, Watts $5.90. A history of Jews in America and of their contribution to American life.

7099. Sung, Betty Lee. *Chinese in America* (4–6). Illustrated. 1972, Macmillan $6.95. A report on the history and role of the Chinese in the United States from 1848 to the present. Also use: *Passage to the Golden Gate* by Daniel Chu (1967, Doubleday, paper $2.50).

7100. Weiner, Sandra. *Small Hands, Big Hands: Seven Profiles of Chicano Migrant Workers and Their Families* (4–7). Illustrated. 1970, Pantheon $5.69. From taped interviews, the author recreates the life of Chicano farm workers. Also use: *Forgotten Minority* by Ruth Holland (1970, Macmillan $5.95).

7101. Wolf, Bernard. *In This Proud Land: The Story of a Mexican American Family* (6–9). Illustrated. 1978, Lippincott $8.95. An inspiring, affectionate picture of the Hermandez family in Texas.

Youth Groups

7102. Blassingame, Wyatt. *Story of the Boy Scouts* (4–7). Illus. by David Hodges. 1968, Garrard $4.48. An interesting account of the history and worldwide activities of the scouting movement.

7103. Boy Scouts of America. *Boy Scout Handbook* (5–7). 1972, Boy Scouts of America $3.50. The standard handbook. Other BSA handbooks are: *Field Book* (1967, $3.35), *Bear Cub Scoutbook* (1973, $1.50), *Webelos Scoutbook* (1973, $1.50), and *Wolf Cub Scout Book* (1973, $1.25).

7104. Boy Scouts of America. *Official Boy Scout Handbook* (5–9). Illustrated. 1979, Simon & Schuster $9.95; paper $3.00. The 9th edition of this standard handbook has some illustrations by Norman Rockwell.

7105. de Leeuw, Adele. *The Girl Scout Story* (2–5). Illus. by Robert Doremus. 1965, Garrard $4.28. Girl scouting from its beginning to the present worldwide organization.

7106. Girl Scouts of the United States of America. *Junior Girl Scout Handbook* (4–7). 1963, Girl Scouts of the United States of America $3.50. A handbook for 9-to-11-year-olds on the activities of Girl Scouts. For a younger group, this organization also publishes: *The Brownie Girl Scout Handbook* (1963, $3.50).

7107. James, Laurie. *Adventure* (4–6). Illus. by Beth Charney. 1973, Camp Fire Girls $1.35. The basic handbook of the Camp Fire Girls, which outlines the aims and activities of the organization. Also use: *The Blue Bird Wish* (1970, Camp Fire Girls $1.25) and *Discovery* (1971, Camp Fire Girls $1.35).

7108. Walz, Lila Phillips. *Camp Fire Blue Bird Series* (1–3). Illus. by Margaret A. Hartelius. 1973, Camp Fire Girls $1.00 per volume. Three booklets that describe activities and projects for younger Camp Fire Girls.

Personal Development

Behavior

General

7109. Berger, Terry. *I Have Feelings* (K–5). Illus. by I. Howard Spivack. 1971, Behavioral $6.95. Text and photos show children that their feelings and emotions—good and bad—are natural. Also use: *Feelings between Friends* by Marcia Maher Conta (1974, Childrens Press $6.60).

7110. Black, Algernon D. *The First Book of Ethics* (5–7). Illus. by Rick Schreiter. 1965, Watts $4.90. An introduction to the study of how people behave toward each other. Also use: *What Every Kid Should Know* by Jonah Kalb (1976, Houghton $5.95).

7111. Fleming, Alice. *Something for Nothing: A History of Gambling* (6–8). Illustrated. 1978, Delacorte paper $.95. The history and present status of various forms of gambling, including dice, horses, and lotteries.

7112. Gersten, Irene Fandel. *Ecidujerp, Prejudice: Either Way It Doesn't Make Sense* (5–7). Illus. by Richard Rosenblum. 1974, Watts $3.90. A discussion of the origins and effects of prejudice and what to do when one encounters it. Also use: *Look at Prejudice and Understanding* by Rebecca Anders (1976, Lerner $4.95).

7113. Griffin, John Howard. *A Time to Be Human* (5–7). Illustrated. 1977, Macmillan $6.95. Writer of the adult book *Black Like Me* retells its central thesis—the dehumanizing effects of prejudice—for younger readers.

7114. Hall, Elizabeth. *From Pigeons to People: A Look at Behavior Shaping* (6–9). 1975, Houghton $6.95. Opinion and facts concerning reinforcement theory and behavior modification are well explored.

7115. Hall, Elizabeth. *Why We Do What We Do: A Look at Psychology* (6–9). 1973, Houghton $6.95. A fine overview of the main concerns of psychologists, with separate chapters on learning, memory, motivation, and other major areas.

7116. Haskins, James. *Gambling—Who Really Wins?* (6–9). Illustrated. 1979, Watts $5.90. A description of types of gambling plus a discussion of the causes and treatment of compulsive gambling.

7117. Laiken, Deidre S., and Schneider, Alan J. *Listen To Me, I'm Angry* (6–9). Illus. by Bernice Myers. 1980, Lothrop $6.95; LB $6.67. A narrative on causes and types of anger and how young people can cope with it.

7118. Madison, Arnold. *Runaway Teens: An American Tragedy* (6–9). 1979, Nelson $6.95. A book for young people and adults that details the hardships of running away and sources of help.

7119. Miles, Betty. *Around and Around—Love* (3–5). Illustrated. 1975, Knopf $4.99. All kinds of love, as expressed by various ethnic groups.

7120. Naylor, Phyllis Reynolds. *Getting Along with Your Friends* (4–6). Illus. by Rick Cooley. 1980, Abingdon $6.95. A commonsense manual on how to make and keep friends.

7121. Weiss, Ann E. *Polls and Surveys* (4–6). 1979, Watts $5.90. The history and present-day uses of public opinion research.

Etiquette

7122. Hoke, Helen. *Etiquette: Your Ticket to Good Times* (3–5). Illus. by Carol Wilde. 1970, Watts $4.90. An easily read introduction to the basics of good manners and behavior. For an older group use: *What to Do When and Why* by Marjabelle Young Stewart (1975, McKay $7.95).

7123. Joslin, Sesyle. *What Do You Say, Dear?* (1–3). Illus. by Maurice Sendak. 1958, Young Scott $5.95. Humorous handbook on manners for young ladies and gentlemen of 6 to 8. Also use: *What Do You Do, Dear?* (1961, Young Scott $5.95).

7124. Leaf, Munro. *Manners Can Be Fun* (3–4). Illus. by author. 1955, Lippincott $6.95. Includes material on television manners.

7125. Lee, Tina. *Manners to Grow On* (3–6). Illus. by Manning de Lee. 1955, Doubleday $4.95. Interesting and lively presentation of basic principles of manners for youngsters. Also use: *Let's Find Out about Manners* by Valerie Pitt (1972, Watts $4.47).

7126. Maschler, Fay. *A Child's Book of Manners* (1–3). Illus. by Helen Oxenbury. 1979, Atheneum $8.95. Through clever verses and colored paintings, good and bad manners are distinguished.

7127. Parish, Peggy. *Mind Your Manners* (6–9). Illustrated. 1979, Greenwillow $5.95. A useful guide to basic etiquette.

7128. Post, Elizabeth L. *The Emily Post Book of Etiquette for Young People* (5–7). Illustrated. 1967, Funk $9.95. A basic etiquette book that stresses unselfishness and consideration for others. Also use: *What to Do: Everyday Guides for Everyone* by Jeanne Bendick and Marian Warren (1967, McGraw $5.72).

7129. Slobodkin, Louis. *Thank You—You're Welcome* (PS–2). Illus. by author. 1957, Vanguard $4.95. Simple, clever verse and artistic illustrations teach good manners in a humorous manner. Also use: *Excuse Me! Certainly* (1959, Vanguard $4.95).

Family Relationships

7130. Berger, Terry. *How Does It Feel When Your Parents Get Divorced?* (3–4). Illustrated. 1977, Messner $6.64. Guidance, help, and understanding are given to young people undergoing the effects of divorce.

7131. Boeckman, Charles. *Surviving Your Parents' Divorce* (6–9). 1980, Watts $5.90. A straightforward self-help book to aid youngsters through the conflicts of a divorce.

7132. Forrai, Maria S., and Pursell, Margaret S. *A Look at Adoption* (K–3). 1978, Lerner $4.95. A simple description of the process of adoption, including reasons for parents' giving up their children.

7133. Gilfond, Henry. *Genealogy: How to Find Your Roots* (6–9). Illustrated. 1978, Watts $4.90. A basic handbook on how to do research on your family tree.

7134. Henriod, Lorraine. *Ancestor Hunting* (4–6). Illus. by Janet D'Amato. 1979, Messner $6.97. An interesting introduction to genealogy, with tips on how to organize the information collected.

7135. LeShan, Eda. *Learning to Say Good-by: When a Parent Dies* (5–7). Illus. by Paul Giovanopoulos. 1976, Macmillan $6.95; paper $2.95. A sympathetic explanation of the many reactions children have to death.

7136. LeShan, Eda. *What's Going to Happen to Me? When Parents Separate or Divorce* (4–7). Illus. by Richard Cuffari. 1978, Four Winds $6.95. The various steps involved in getting a divorce and adjusting to it are examined as they affect a young person.

7137. Naylor, Phyllis Reynolds. *Getting Along in Your Family* (6–8). Illus. by Rick Cooley. 1976, Abingdon $5.50. Explores family problems and how to cope with them. Also use: *All Kinds of Families* by Norma Simon (1976, Whitman $4.75).

7138. Perry, Patricia, and Lynch, Marietta. *Mommy and Daddy Are Divorced* (PS–2). Illustrated. 1978, Dial $6.95. A first-person account in fictional terms, but with realistic photographs.

7139. Richards, Arlene, and Willis, Irene. *How to Get It Together When Your Parents Are Coming Apart* (6–9). 1976, McKay $7.95. A self-help book written for adolescents trying to cope with parental marriage problems. Also use: *Boys and Girls Book about Divorce* by Richard Gardner (1970, Aronsen $10.00).

7140. Seixas, Judith S. *Living with a Parent that Drinks Too Much* (4–7). 1979, Greenwillow $6.95. Common behavior patterns of alcoholics are cited, and ways to cope with them.

7141. Showers, Paul. *Me and My Family Tree* (2–3). Illus. by Don Madden. 1978, Crowell $6.95; LB $6.89. An elementary lesson in genealogy, taught by a master.

7142. Sinberg, Janet. *Divorce Is a Grown Up Problem: A Book about Divorce for Young Children* (PS–2). Illustrated. 1978, Avon paper $2.95. A book to be shared by parent and child.

7143. Spilke, Francine Susan. *The Family That Changed* (2–3). 1979, Crown $3.99. The reasons for divorce are discussed and adjustments to the separation of parents. Also use: *Where Is Daddy? The Story of a Divorce* by Beth Goff (1969, Beacon, $5.95).

7144. Stein, Sara B. *On Divorce* (2–4). Illustrated. 1979, Walker $6.95. Photographs and text cover this subject in an elementary fashion.

7145. Wasson, Valentina P. *The Chosen Baby* (PS–K). Illus. by Glo Coalson. 1977, Lippincott $6.95. A new edition of an excellent book on adoption.

7146. White, Ann S. *Divorce* (3–6). Illustrated. 1979, Watts $5.45. Factual questions involving financial settlements are discussed as well as custodial considerations.

Careers

General

7147. Ancona, George. *And What Do You Do? A Book about People and Their Work* (2–5). Illustrated. 1975, Dutton $7.95. A description of more than 20 careers that do not require a college degree.

7148. Anders, Rebecca. *Careers in a Library* (2–4). Illustrated. 1978, Lerner $3.95. An introductory look at many types of jobs involving libraries. Also use: *I Want to Be a Librarian* by Donna Baker (1978, Childrens Press $7.35).

7149. Berger, Melvin. *Jobs That Save Our Environment* (6–8). Illustrated. 1973, Lothrop $6.25. A guide to occupations involved with improving our physical environment.

7150. Colby, C. B. *Night People: Workers From Dusk to Dawn* (3–5). Illustrated. 1971, Coward $5.19. Various occupations of people who work at night, such as taxi drivers and bakers.

7151. Colby, C. B. *Park Ranger: Equipment, Training and Work of the National Park Rangers* (3–6). Illustrated. 1971, Coward $5.19. A well-illustrated description of the training and duties of various kinds of park rangers. Also use: *Guarding the Treasured Lands: The Story of the National Park Service* by Ann Sutton (1965, Lippincott $4.95) and *Park Rangers and Game Wardens the World Over* by Floyd James Torbert (1968, Hastings $4.95).

7152. Colby, C. B. *West Point: Cadets, Training and Equipment* (4–7). Illustrated. 1963, Coward $5.19. An account of the schooling and military training of cadets at the U.S. Military Academy.

7153. Criner, Beatrice, and Criner, Calvin. *Jobs In Personal Services* (3–5). Illustrated. 1974, Lothrop $6.25. Such jobs as plumber, travel agent, and veterinarian are described, along with qualifications. Also use: *Jobs in Public Service* (1974, Lothrop $5.95).

7154. English, Betty Lou. *Women at Their Work* (K–3). Illustrated. 1977, Dial $6.96; LB $6.46. Short accounts of 21 different women with diverse jobs such as carpenters, judges, and airline pilots.

7155. Fodor, R. V. *What Does a Geologist Do?* (5–7). Illustrated. 1978, Dodd $5.25. Such usual topics as necessary educational background are handled along with a fine breakdown of the fields of specialization. Also use: *What Can She Be? A Geologist* by Gloria Goldreich (1976, Lothrop $4.95; LB $4.59).

7156. Goldreich, Gloria, and Goldreich, Esther. *What Can She Be? A Computer Scientist* (3–5). Illustrated. 1979, Lothrop $5.95. An introduction to this occupation as seen through the eyes of computer scientist Linda Wong.

7157. Goldreich, Gloria, and Goldreich, Esther. *What Can She Be? A Legislator* (4–6). 1978, Lothrop $5.50. An account that centers around the career of Carol Bellamy, state senator and president of the New York City Council. Also use: *What Can She Be? A Lawyer* (1974, Lothrop $5.04).

7158. Graham, Ada, and Graham, Frank. *Careers in Conservation* (6–9). Illustrated. 1980, Sierra $9.95. This book shows the great variety of jobs available in the exciting field.

7159. Gurney, Gene, and Gurney, Clare. *Agriculture Careers* (6–9). Illustrated. 1978, Watts $4.90. An overview of the many career opportunities in agriculture, with emphasis on those particularly related to the farm.

7160. Houlehen, Robert J. *Jobs in Agribusiness* (4–6). Illustrated. 1974, Lothrop $6.95. An introduction to the various and varied career opportunities in agriculture and allied industries.

7161. Kurelek, William. *Lumberjack* (5–9). Illus. by author. 1974, Houghton $6.95. Using his own experience as a basis, a Canadian painter describes, through text and pictures, life and work in a lumber camp.

7162. Noble, Iris. *Life on the Line: Alternate Approaches to Work* (6–9). Illustrated. 1977, Coward $5.49. Experiments to lessen worker on-the-job discontent are described, as well as background coverage on how we use human resources.

7163. Paige, David. *A Day in the Life of a Forest Ranger* (3–4). Illustrated. 1979, Troll $5.89; paper $2.25. A narrative of an average day spent in this challenging career.

7164. Palladian, Arthur. *Careers in the Air Force* (2–4). Illustrated. 1978, Lerner $3.95. A brief overview of jobs in the air force, from navigator to recruiter.

7165. Palladian, Arthur. *Careers in the Army* (2–4). Illustrated. 1978, Lerner $3.95. A simple guide to a variety of jobs involved with the army.

7166. Pelta, Kathy. *There's a Job for You in Food Service* (7–9). Illustrated. 1979, Dodd $7.95. A description of the many kinds of jobs available in food service and management.

7167. Ross, Frank. *Jobs in Marine Science* (5–7). Illustrated. 1974, Lothrop $6.25. Describes the work of oceanographers and fishermen, as well as those involved in marine salvage and construction.

7168. Saul, Wendy. *Butcher, Baker, Cabinetmaker: Photographs of Women at Work* (K–2). Illustrated. 1978, Crowell $7.95; LB $7.89. The lives of women in a variety of jobs, told in text and photographs.

7169. Sobol, Harriet Langsam. *Cosmo's Restaurant* (2–4). Illustrated. 1978, Macmillan $7.95. A young boy learns about restaurants when he helps out in the one owned by his parents.

7170. Torbert, Floyd James. *Postmen the World Over* (4–6). Illus. by author. 1966, Hastings $4.95. An overview of careers in the mail service.

Business

7171. Hall, Elvajean. *Jobs in Marketing and Distribution* (5–7). Illustrated. 1974, Lothrop $8.95. The functions, skills, and training for 37 different kinds of work in marketing.

7172. Haskins, James. *Real Estate Careers* (6–8). Illustrated. 1978, Watts $4.90. A fine orientation to the field with quotes from practitioners.

7173. Houlehen, Robert J. *Jobs in Manufacturing* (6–8). Illustrated. 1973, Lothrop $6.15. A thorough discussion of jobs in production, marketing, repairing, and administering aspects of manufacturing.

7174. Solomon, Marc, and Wiener, Norman. *Marketing and Advertising Careers* (6–9). Illustrated. 1977, Watts $4.47. Necessary educational background, the nature of the work, and job opportunities are 3 of the topics in this broad overview.

7175. Van Gelder, Patricia. *Careers in the Insurance Industry* (6–8). Illustrated. 1978, Watts $4.90. Basic information plus material on licensing and exams are well covered in this introductory work.

7176. Whatley, Jo Ann. *Banking and Finance Careers* (6–8). Illustrated. 1978, Watts $4.90. A useful introduction that touches on many aspects of these fields, including the commodities market.

7177. Williams, Barbara. *I Know a Salesperson* (2–3). 1978, Putnam $4.29. Jill's younger brother describes her job in the sports department of a retail store.

Engineering and Technology

7178. Harrison, C. William. *Here Is Your Career, the Building Trades* (6–9). Illustrated. 1979, Putnam $7.95. Various labor activities such as plumbing, bricklaying, and carpentry are described, along with the kinds of jobs in each area.

7179. Liebers, Arthur. *Jobs in Construction* (5–8). 1973, Lothrop $6.25. Many jobs are discussed, along with the apprenticeship program and the role of unions today.

7180. Liebers, Arthur. *You Can Be a Welder* (6–8). Illustrated. 1977, Lothrop $5.95; LB $6.25. An introduction to the trade, types of jobs, and future occupational prospects. Also by the same author and publisher (each $6.25) are: *You Can Be a Carpenter* (1973), *You Can Be an Electrician* (1974), *You Can Be a Plumber* (1974), *You Can Be a Machinist* (1975), and *You Can Be a Mechanic* (1975).

7181. McHugh, Mary. *Careers in Engineering and Engineering Technology* (6–8). Illustrated. 1978, Watts $4.90. Eleven major engineering specialities are described, plus the educational training needed for each.

7182. Zim, Herbert S., and Skelly, James R. *Telephone Systems* (4–6). Illustrated. 1971, Morrow paper $1.25. A description of various jobs in the telephone field.

Fine Arts

7183. Berger, Melvin. *Jobs in Fine Arts and Humanities* (5–8). Illustrated. 1974, Lothrop $6.25. Career opportunities in music, theater, literature, and allied fields.

7184. Blumenfeld, Milton J. *Careers in Photography* (3–4). Illus. by author. 1979, Lerner $3.95. An easy career book that introduces various kinds of jobs in this field.

7185. Doyle, Robert V. *Your Career in Interior Design* (4–6). 1975, Messner $7.79. Interior decoration and design are discussed as career possibilities.

7186. Goldreich, Gloria, and Goldreich, Esther. *What Can She Be? A Film Producer* (4–6). Illustrated. 1977, Lothrop $5.04. Like others in this series, an interesting and thorough woman's-eye view of an occupation.

7187. Goldreich, Gloria, and Goldreich, Esther. *What Can She Be? An Architect* (2–4). 1974, Lothrop

$5.04. An introduction to architects and the jobs they do, from a woman's point of view.

7188. Haeberlie, Billi. *Looking Forward to a Career: Radio and Television* (6–9). 1979, Dillon $6.95. A variety of jobs at various levels are described. For a younger group use: *Finding Out about Jobs: TV Reporting* by Jeanne Bendick (1976, Parents $5.41).

7189. Klever, Anita. *Women in Television* (6–8). Illustrated. 1975, Westminster $5.95. An overview of various careers for women in TV.

7190. Liebers, Arthur. *You Can Be a Professional Photographer* (6–8). Illustrated. 1979, Lothrop $5.95; LB $6.67. An overview of the various occupations and fields of specialization open to the professional photographer.

7191. May, Charles Paul. *Publishing Careers: Magazines and Books* (6–8). Illustrated. 1978, Watts $4.90. A well-organized, thorough account of these careers and opportunities in them.

7192. Meyer, Charles Robert. *How to Be a Clown* (5–8). Illustrated. 1977, McKay $5.95. Information on routines, makeup, and costumes is interwoven with fascinating glimpses of life under the Big Top. Also use: *How to Be a Juggler* (1977, McKay $5.95).

7193. Paige, David. *A Day in the Life of a Rock Musician* (3–4). Illustrated. 1979, Troll $5.89; paper $2.25. A somewhat idealized account of a typical day in a songwriter-musician's life.

7194. Seed, Suzanne. *Fine Trades* (6–8). Illustrated. 1979, Follett $7.95; LB $7.98. A tribute to such artisans as a bookbinder, a violin maker, and a chef.

7195. Trainer, David. *A Day in the Life of a TV News Reporter* (3–4). Illustrated. 1979, Troll $5.89; paper $2.25. An exciting career explained through a typical day technique. Also use: *What Can She Be? A Newscaster* by Gloria Goldreich and Esther Goldreich (1973, Parents $5.41).

Medicine and Health

7196. Berger, Melvin. *Cancer Lab* (4–6). 1975, John Day $8.79. Careers in cancer prevention and treatment are discussed.

7197. Dodge, Bertha S. *The Story of Nursing* (6–8). 1965, Little $6.95. An overview of the profession.

7198. Englebardt, Stanley L. *Jobs in Health Care* (5–7). Illustrated. 1973, Lothrop $6.25. Sixty-six careers in health care are described, such as lab technician, nurse's aide, and medical secretary.

7199. Greene, Carla. *Doctors and Nurses: What Do They Do?* (1–3). 1963, Harper $4.95; LB $4.79. A very simple introduction to these professions. For an older group use: *What It's Like to Be a Doctor* by Arthur Shay (1963, Harper $5.95).

7200. Kane, Betty. *Looking Forward to a Career: Dentistry* (4–6). Illus. by Dick Sutphen. 1972, Dillon $5.95. A description of dental careers and how to prepare for them.

7201. Taylor, L. B. *Emergency Squads* (5–7). Illus. by Mal Luber. 1980, Watts $6.90. A discussion of all kinds of emergency squads—from bomb squads to ambulance personnel, to crews that specialize in hostage negotiations.

7202. Witty, Margot. *A Day in the Life of an Emergency Room Nurse* (3–4). Illustrated. 1979, Troll $5.89; paper $2.25. A realistic account of a day's experience in this exciting profession.

Police and Firefighters

7203. Baker, Donna. *I Want to Be a Police Officer* (1–2). Illus. by Richard Wahl. 1978, Childrens Press $7.35. Betty, Bill, and Ramon visit a police school and learn about this career.

7204. Beame, Rona. *Calling Car 24 Frank: A Day with the Police* (1–3). Illustrated. 1972, Messner $4.29. The reader accompanies 2 police officers on a busy tour of duty in New York City. Also use: *Police: Skill and Science Combat Crime* by C. B. Colby (1971, Coward $4.69).

7205. Beame, Rona. *Ladder Company 108* (3–5). Illustrated. 1973, Messner $5.29. The activities of a firefighting unit serving a section of Brooklyn, New York, with emphasis on what happens when a fire alarm is answered.

7206. Feldman, Anne. *Firefighters* (6–8). Illustrated. 1979, McKay $6.95. Lengthy and authoritative information on firefighters and their equipment. For a younger group use: *Let's Find Out about Firemen* by Martha Shapp and Charles Shapp (1962, Watts $4.47).

7207. Ray, Jo Anne. *Careers with a Police Department* (4–6). Illustrated. 1973, Lerner $3.95. A rundown on various careers available in law enforcement. Also use: *What Can She Be? A Police Officer* by Gloria Goldreich and Esther Goldreich (1975, Lothrop $5.04).

7208. Robinson, Nancy. *Firefighters* (1–3). Illustrated. 1979, Scholastic $1.50. A simple treatment of what firefighting involves, complete with a 2-page summary of terms.

7209. Slobodkin, Louis. *Read about the Policeman* (1–3). Illus. by author. 1966, Watts $4.47. What a policeman does, simply introduced. Also use: *Let's Find Out about Policemen* by Martha Shapp and Charles Shapp (1962, Watts $4.47).

Transportation

7210. Dean, Jennifer Brooks. *Careers with an Airline* (3–5). Illustrated. 1973, Lerner $3.95. Discusses 18 careers involving a variety of talents and qualifications.

7211. Gray, Genevieve. *Jobs in Transportation* (4–7). Illustrated. 1973, Lothrop $6.25. Qualifications, working conditions, and job opportunities are described for several occupations involving vehicles.

7212. Greene, Carla. *Truck Drivers: What Do They Do?* (1–3). Illus. by Leonard Kessler. 1967, Harper $6.89. An introduction to various kinds of truck drivers and how they help the community. Also use: *I Know a Bus Driver* by Genevieve Gray (1972, Putnam $4.29).

7213. Lerner, Mark. *Careers in Trucking* (3–4). Illus. by Milton J. Blumenfeld. 1976, Lerner $3.95. A simple account that supplies only basic information. For an older group use: *You Can Be a Professional Driver* by Arthur Liebers (1976, Lothrop $5.50; LB $5.09).

7214. Meade, Chris. *Careers with a Railroad* (4–6). Illustrated. 1975, Lerner $3.95. Fifteen different jobs on railroads are discussed. For an older group use: *Your Future in Railroading* by Thomas M. Goodfellow (1970, Rosen $4.80).

7215. Stilley, Frank. *Here Is Your Career: Airline Pilot* (5–8). Illustrated. 1978, Putnam $7.95. Stresses qualifications, training, and the nature of the work of an airline pilot.

Veterinarians

7216. Berger, Melvin. *Animal Hospital* (4–7). Illustrated. 1973, John Day $8.79. The roles of veterinarians and their assistants.

7217. Buchenholz, Bruce. *A Way with Animals* (5–8). Illustrated. 1978, Viking $12.95. A description of all sorts of people who work with animals. Also use: *What Does a Veterinarian Do?* by Grant Compton (1964, Dodd $4.95).

7218. Curtis, Patricia. *Animal Doctors: What It Is Like to Be a Veterinarian* (5–8). 1977, Delacorte $7.95. The training and work of vets are discussed through fictitious accounts based on real-life interviews.

7219. Gillum, Helen L. *Looking Forward to a Career: Veterinary Medicine* (5–7). Illustrated. 1976, Dillon $5.95. A discussion of obvious and lesser-known careers in working with animals.

7220. Hall, Lynn. *Careers for Dog Lovers* (5–9). Illustrated. 1978, Follett $7.95. A description of various dog-related jobs, qualifications, and work conditions.

7221. Jaspersohn, William. *A Day in the Life of a Veterinarian* (3–6). Illus. by author. 1978, Little $7.95. A description of the activities during one day of a vet in rural Vermont.

7222. Strong, Arline. *Veterinarian: Doctor for Your Pet* (3–6). Illustrated. 1977, Atheneum $7.95. The many roles of an animal doctor are explored in this work that emphasizes the love that veterinarians have for their patients. Also use: *What Can She Be? A Veterinarian* by Gloria Goldreich (1972, Lothrop $4.95; LB $5.04).

The Human Body and Health

The Human Body

7223. Asimov, Isaac. *The Human Body: Its Structure and Operation* (6–9). Illustrated. 1963, Houghton $10.95. A mature introduction to the systems and parts of the human body. For a younger group use: *The Human Body and How It Works* by Mitchell A. Wilson (1959, Golden $13.77).

7224. Berry, James R. *Why You Feel Hot, Why You Feel Cold: Your Body's Temperature* (2–4). Illus. by William Ogden. 1973, Little $4.95. This book tells how body temperature is maintained and why abnormal cold and heat can be a sign of illness.

7225. Brenner, Barbara. *Bodies* (K–3). Illus. by George Ancona. 1973, Dutton $6.95. The qualities that make the animal world different from plants and inanimate objects are pointed out, and the uniqueness of each individual is stressed. Also use: *Faces* (1970, Dutton $6.95).

7226. Gilbert, Sara. *Feeling Good: A Book about You and Your Body* (6–9). 1978, Four Winds $6.95. A book about the body changes that occur during adolescence.

7227. Glemser, Bernard. *All about the Human Body* (5–8). Illustrated. 1958, Random $4.45; LB $5.39. A good basic introduction to the various parts of the human body. Also use: *Anatomy for Children* by Ilse Goldsmith (1974, Sterling $5.45; LB $5.89).

7228. Kavaler, Lucy. *Life Battles Cold* (6–9). Illus. by Leslie Morrill. 1973, John Day $7.95. A description of how all forms of life—including human—have adjusted to cold.

7229. Kettelkamp, Larry. *A Partnership of Mind and Body: Biofeedback* (5–9). Illustrated. 1976, Morrow $6.25; LB $6.00. A direct and clear explanation of theories, experiments, conclusions, and the present status of this topical but often controversial subject.

7230. Klein, Aaron E. *You and Your Body* (3–6). Illus. by John Love. 1977, Doubleday $5.95. A manual that emphasizes activities that can help the young reader to learn about his/her body. Also use: *Your Body and How It Works* by Patricia Lauber (1962, Random $2.95; LB $4.99).

7231. Krishef, Robert K. *Our Wonderful Hands* (4–6). Illus. by Allan R. Smith. 1967, Lerner $3.95. The structure and uses of our hands are presented together with how the brain controls hand movements. For a younger group use: *My Hands* by Aliki (1962, Crowell $6.89).

7232. Rothman, Joel, and Palacios, Argentina. *This Can Lick a Lollipop: Body Riddles for Kids/Esto Goza Chupando un Caramelo* (4–6). Illustrated. 1979, Doubleday $6.95. Pictures and short poems illustrate the parts of the body in this bilingual book.

7233. Rutland, Jonathan. *Human Body* (4–7). Illustrated. 1977, Watts $4.90. A simple, well-illustrated overview organized by various body systems.

7234. Showers, Paul. *How You Talk* (1–3). Illus. by Robert Galster. 1966, Crowell $6.89; paper $1.45. Simple introductory explanation about how numerous speech sounds are produced; includes experiments. For an older group use: *How We Talk: The Story of Speech* by Marilyn B. Bennett (1966, Lerner $3.95).

7235. Silverstein, Alvin, and Silverstein, Virginia B. *The Left-Hander's World* (4–6). Illustrated. 1977, Follett $5.95; LB $5.97. The life of this "oppressed minority" is described, as well as how left-handedness occurs. Also use: *Lefty: The Story of Left-Handedness* by Marguerite Rush Lerner (1960, Lerner $3.95).

7236. Wilson, Ron. *How the Body Works* (4–7). Illustrated. 1979, Larousse $7.95. Parts of the body and its systems are covered from the standpoint of how they function.

7237. Zim, Herbert S. *What's Inside Me?* (2–5). Illus. by Herschel Wartik. 1952, Morrow $5.52. An explanation of the functions of the human body—a book for parents and children to read together. Also use: *Blood and Guts: A Working Guide to Your Own Little Insides* by Linda Allison (1976, Little $6.95; paper $3.95).

Circulatory System

7238. Limburg, Peter R. *The Story of Your Heart* (4–6). Illus. by Ellen G. Jacobs. 1979, Coward $6.49. The human heart, its functions, and possible malfunctions are discussed in this basic account.

7239. Schneider, Leo. *Lifeline* (6–9). Illustrated. 1958, Harcourt $5.95. Subtitle: *The Story of Your Circulatory System*. Also use: *Circulatory Systems: The Rivers Within* by Alvin Silverstein (1970, Prentice-Hall $5.95).

7240. Showers, Paul. *Hear Your Heart* (1–3). Illus. by Joseph Low. 1968, Crowell $6.89; paper $1.45. A simple introduction to the heart and how it works. Also use: *A Drop of Blood* (1967, Crowell $6.89; paper $1.45).

7241. Silverstein, Alvin, and Silverstein, Virginia B. *Heart Disease* (6–9). Illustrated. 1976, Follett $5.95; LB $5.97. A solid, well-organized overview of cardiovascular disease, with sections on prevention and treatment.

7242. Simon, Seymour. *About Your Heart* (2–3). Illus. by Angie Culfogienis. 1974, McGraw $6.95. An introduction to the heart and its functions, along with some simple projects.

7243. Weart, Edith L. *The Story of Your Blood* (4–6). Illus. by Z. Onyshkewych. 1960, Coward $5.49. An elementary introduction to the composition and uses of blood.

7244. Zim, Herbert S. *Blood* (4–6). Illus. by Rene Martin. 1968, Morrow $5.52. This work discusses many topics, including the composition of blood, how the body uses it, and the variety of blood types. For a slightly younger group use: *Your Blood and Its Cargo* by Sigmund Kalina (1974, Lothrop $5.09).

7245. Zim, Herbert S. *Your Heart and How It Works* (4–6). Illus. by Gustav Schrotter. 1959, Morrow $5.52. A description of the structure and function of the heart and its role in the circulatory system. Also use: *The Human Body: The Heart* by Kathleen Elgin (1968, Watts $4.90).

Digestive and Excretory Systems

7246. Berger, Melvin. *Enzymes in Action* (6–9). 1971, Crowell $7.95. An interesting view of the uses and functions of enzymes, including a history of research in the area and an explanation of their production through synthetic means.

✓**7247.** Elgin, Kathleen. *The Human Body: The Digestive System* (3–6). Illus. by author. 1973, Watts $4.90. A clear text with simple informative drawings. Also use: *The Digestive System: How Living Creatures Use Food* by Alvin Silverstein (1970, Prentice-Hall $5.95).

7248. Showers, Paul. *What Happens to a Hamburger* (1–3). Illus. by Anne Rockwell. 1970, Crowell $6.95; paper $1.45. A beginning, easily read introduction to the digestive system.

7249. Silverstein, Alvin, and Silverstein, Virginia B. *The Excretory System: How Animals Get Rid of Waste* (4–6). Illus. by Lee J. Ames. 1972, Prentice-Hall $6.95. The roles of skin, lungs, and the digestive system in animals and humans are explored.

7250. Zim, Herbert S. *Your Stomach and Digestive Tract* (4–6). Illus. by Rene Martin. 1973, Morrow $5.50; LB $5.09. A tour through the digestive tract.

Endocrine System

7251. Silverstein, Alvin. *The Endocrine System: Hormones in the Living World* (6–8). 1971, Prentice-Hall $4.95. An introduction to the endocrine system.

7252. Weart, Edith Lucie. *The Story of Your Glands* (4–6). Illus. by Jan Fairservis. 1962, Coward $5.49. The story of the exocrine and endocrine glands and their uses.

Nervous System

7253. Goldenson, Robert M. *All about the Human Mind* (6–9). Illustrated. 1963, Random $4.39. How the brain works and how personality develops. Also use: *The Brains of Animals and Man* by Russell Freedman (1972, Holiday $6.95).

7254. Haines, Gail Kay. *Brain Power: Understanding Human Intelligence* (6–9). Illustrated. 1979, Watts $5.45. An overview of what we know about the human brain and intelligence.

7255. Kalina, Sigmund. *Your Nerves and Their Messages* (3–5). Illus. by Arabelle Wheatley. 1973, Lothrop $5.52. A good introduction to nerve cells, their pathways, and networks. For an older group use: *The Nervous System: The Inner Networks* by Alvin Silverstein (1971, Prentice-Hall $5.95).

7256. Showers, Paul. *Use Your Brain* (2–3). Illus. by Rosalind Fry. 1971, Crowell $6.95. The structure and function of the brain and some information on the other parts of the nervous system are included in this simple text.

7257. Weart, Edith L. *The Story of Your Brain and Nerves* (5–7). Illus. by Alan Tompkins. 1961, Coward $5.49. Simple introduction to the human nervous system and its functions. Also use: *Your Brain: Master Computer* by Margaret O. Hyde (1964, McGraw $6.95).

7258. Zim, Herbert S. *Your Brain and How It Works* (4–6). Illus. by Rene Martin. 1972, Morrow $5.09. The growth and development of the human brain, its parts and functions, and a comparison with the brains of other animals are covered in this fascinating treatment. Also use: *The Human Body: The Brain* by Kathleen Elgin (1967, Watts $4.90).

Respiratory System

7259. Branley, Franklyn M. *Oxygen Keeps You Alive* (2–3). Illus. by Don Madden. 1971, Crowell $6.95; LB $6.89; paper $2.95. A description of how oxygen is carried throughout the body, how plants and fish use it, and how people who can't get enough oxygen must carry a supply with them.

7260. Silverstein, Alvin, and Silverstein, Virginia B. *The Respiratory System: How Living Creatures Breathe* (4–6). Illus. by George Bakacs. 1969, Prentice-Hall $6.95. The breathing of several kinds of animals and plants is outlined, with emphasis on humans. Also use: *Breath of Air and a Breath of Smoke* by John S. Marr (1971, Evans $3.95).

7261. Simon, Seymour. *About Your Lungs* (2–5). Illustrated. 1978, McGraw $6.95. The anatomy and physiology of the human lung and the respiratory system. For an older group use: *The Story of Your Respiratory System* by Edith L. Weart (1964, Crowell $5.49).

Skeletal-Muscular System

7262. Balestrino, Philip. *The Skeleton inside You* (2–4). Illus. by Don Bolognese. 1971, Crowell $6.89. This matter-of-fact, informal discussion of bones of the body describes their shape, structure, and function.

7263. Cosgrove, Margaret. *Your Muscles—And Ways to Exercise Them* (4–6). 1980, Dodd $6.95. A description of the composition and uses of muscles, as well as how to keep them in shape. Also use: *The Muscular System: How Living Creatures Move* by Alvin Silverstein (1972, Prentice-Hall $4.95).

7264. Gross, Ruth Belov. *A Book about Your Skeleton* (2–3). Illus. by Deborah Robison. 1979, Hastings $5.95. A brief, nontechnical introduction to bones, their composition and functions.

7265. Silverstein, Alvin, and Silverstein, Virginia B. *The Skeletal System: Frameworks for Life* (4–6). Illus. by Lee J. Ames. 1972, Prentice-Hall $6.95. The skeletal structures of several animals are pictured and discussed, with concentration on the human body. Also use: *The Human Body: The Skeleton* by Kathleen Elgin (1971, Watts $4.90).

7266. Zim, Herbert S. *Bones* (3–6). Illus. by Rene Martin. 1969, Morrow $5.52. Parts and functions of the human skeleton with explanation of the composition and formation of bones. Also use: *The Story of Your Bones* by Edith L. Weart (1966, Coward $5.49).

Senses

7267. Adler, Irving, and Adler, Ruth. *Your Eyes* (3–5). Illustrated. 1962, John Day $6.89. This account treats the structure of the eye and the nature of sight. Also use: *The Human Body: The Eye* by Kathleen Elgin (1967, Watts $4.90).

7268. Aliki. *My Five Senses* (1–3). Illustrated. 1962, Crowell $6.89; paper $1.95. A very basic introduction to human senses and how they work.

7269. Brindze, Ruth. *Look How Many People Wear Glasses: The Romance of Lenses* (6–9). Illustrated. 1975, Atheneum $7.95. A comprehensive look at eyeglasses—their history, composition, uses, and limits. Also use: *Why Glasses? The Story of Vision* by George Sands (1960, Lerner $3.95).

7270. Kelley, Alberta. *Lenses, Spectacles, Eyeglasses, and Contacts: The Story of Vision Aids* (6–9). 1979, Nelson $6.95. A precise, detailed account of past, present, and possible future aids to human vision.

7271. Liberty, Gene. *The First Book of the Human Senses* (4–7). Illus. by Robert Tidd. 1961, Watts $4.90. Explanation of the 5 basic senses, plus hunger, thirst, muscle sense, and balance. Also use: *The Human Senses* by Jeanne Bendick (1968, Watts $4.90; paper $1.25).

7272. Litchfield, Ada B. *A Button in Her Ear* (1–3). Illus. by Eleanor Mill. 1976, Whitman $5.75. A simple introduction to hearing problems and correctional devices such as the hearing aid.

7273. Scott, John M. *The Senses: Seeing, Hearing, Smelling, Tasting, Touching* (4–6). Illus. by John E. Johnson. 1975, Parents $5.41. A well-organized narrative that gives material on the physiological basis and functions of our senses. Also use: *Taste, Touch and Smell* by Irving Adler (1966, John Day $6.89).

7274. Showers, Paul. *Follow Your Nose* (1–3). Illus. by Paul Galdone. 1963, Crowell $6.89; paper $1.45. An elementary account of the sense of smell and how we use our noses.

7275. Showers, Paul. *Look at Your Eyes* (1–3). Illus. by Paul Galdone. 1962, Crowell $6.95; paper $1.45. Such topics as eye color and the uses of eyelids and eyebrows are discussed in this elementary book.

7276. Simon, Seymour. *Finding Out with Your Senses* (4–6). 1971, McGraw $6.95. An activity book with projects that help explore human senses. Also use: *Wonders of Your Senses* by Margaret Cosgrove (1958, Dodd $4.50).

7277. Stone, A. Harris. *Science Projects That Make Sense* (3–5). Illus. by Mel Furukawa. 1971, McCall $6.95. Simple experiments that explore the strengths and limitations of our 5 senses.

7278. White, Anne Terry, and Lietz, Gerald S. *Windows on the World* (4–6). Illustrated. 1965, Garrard $4.28. A review of the functions of the 5 senses. For a younger group use: *The Senses* by John A. Scott (1975, Parents $5.41).

7279. Zim, Herbert S. *Our Senses and How They Work* (4–6). Illus. by Herschel Wartik. 1956, Morrow $5.52. An introduction to the 5 major senses and the nervous system. Also use: *The Sense Organs: Our Link with the World* by Alvin Silverstein (1971, Prentice-Hall $6.95).

Skin and Hair

7280. Doss, Helen. *Your Skin Holds You In* (3–5). Illustrated. 1978, Messner $6.97. Many aspects of the subject, including basic structure and functions, are well handled.

7281. Flandermeyer, Kenneth L. *Clear Skin: A Step-By-Step Program to Stop Pimples, Blackheads, Acne* (6–9). Illus. by Monique M. Davis. 1979, Little $8.95; paper $5.95. A sensible plan to treat minor skin disorders.

7282. Goldin, Augusta. *Straight Hair, Curly Hair* (1–3). Illus. by Ed Emberley. 1966, Crowell $6.89; paper $1.45. A very simple explanation of the composition and characteristics of human hair.

7283. Showers, Paul. *Your Skin and Mine* (1–3). Illus. by Paul Galdone. 1965, Crowell $6.95; paper $1.45. An explanation of the many functions of our skin and other related information.

7284. Silverstein, Alvin, and Silverstein, Virginia B. *The Skin: Coverings and Linings of Living Things* (4–6). Illus. by Lee J. Ames. 1972, Prentice-Hall $6.95. A discussion of outer coverings of various forms of animals and plants, with emphasis on human skin.

7285. Zim, Herbert S. *Your Skin* (4–6). Illus. by Jean Zallinger. 1979, Morrow $6.50; LB $6.24. The composition, uses, and layers of the body's covering and problems in dysfunction.

Teeth

7286. Barnett, Naomi. *I Know a Dentist* (K–3). Illustrated. 1978, Putnam $3.99. A reassuring tale of a young girl's first trip to the dentist.

7287. Hammond, Winifred G. *Riddle of Teeth* (4–6). Illustrated. 1971, Coward $4.99. This book discusses the formation and composition of teeth, how they function, and how to take care of them. Also use: *All the Better to Bite With* by Helen Doss (1976, Messner $7.29).

7288. Rockwell, Harlow. *My Dentist* (1–2). Illustrated. 1975, Macmillan $6.95; LB $6.67. A matter-of-fact informative book about dentists and the instruments they use.

7289. Showers, Paul. *How Many Teeth?* (1–3). Illustrated. 1962, Crowell $5.95; paper $1.45. An explanation of the types of teeth and their numbers. Also use: *Our Tooth Story* by Edith Kessler (1972, Dodd $4.95).

7290. Silverstein, Alvin, and Silverstein, Virginia B. *So You're Getting Braces: A Guide to Orthodontics* (6–9). Illustrated. 1978, Lippincott $6.95. An excellent introduction to the subject, which should lessen fears and frustrations.

Sleep and Dreams

7291. Kastner, Jonathan, and Kastner, Marianna. *Sleep: The Mysterious Third of Your Life* (4–6). Illus. by Don Madden. 1968, Harcourt $5.75. A discussion of the causes and needs for sleep and what happens to people when asleep.

7292. Litowinsky, Olga, and Willoughby, Bebe. *The Dream Book* (6–9). Illustrated. 1978, Coward $7.95. All kinds of dreams are analyzed, and their relation to everyday experiences is explained.

7293. Shapiro, Irwin. *The Gift of Magic Sleep: Early Experiments in Anesthesia* (4–6). Illus. by Pat Rotondo. 1979, Coward $5.49. A history of the use of ether and its effect on medical procedures.

7294. Showers, Paul. *Sleep Is for Everyone* (1–3). Illus. by Wendy Watson. 1974, Crowell $6.95. A clear explanation of what happens to our bodies and brains during sleep, and the effects of lack of sleep.

7295. Silverstein, Alvin, and Silverstein, Virginia B. *Sleep and Dreams* (6–8). 1974, Lippincott $6.95. A study of the sleeping habits of animals, including humans, and of the importance of dreams. Also use: Larry Kettelkamp's *Dreams* (1968, Morrow $6.00).

Genetics

7296. Bendick, Jeanne. *How Heredity Works: Why Living Things Are as They Are* (3–5). 1975, Parents $5.41. A clear presentation of heredity in plants, animals, and people.

7297. Cohen, Robert. *The Color of Man* (5–8). Illus. by Ken Heyman. 1968, Random $3.95; LB $5.99. An objective study of the biological and sociological aspects of color differences in humans, which does much to dispel the myths of color prejudice. Also use: *The Many Faces of Man* by Sharon S. McKern (1972, Lothrop $6.43).

7298. Dunbar, Robert E. *Heredity* (4–9). Illustrated. 1978, Watts $4.90. An insightful introduction to the subject, which includes interesting historical information.

7299. Engdahl, Sylvia Louise, and Roberson, Rick. *Tool for Tomorrow* (5–8). 1979, Atheneum $3.99. An account of recent studies and knowledge in the field of genetics.

7300. Facklam, Margery, and Facklam, Howard. *From Cell to Clone* (6–8). Illus. by Paul Facklam. 1979, Harcourt $7.95. A simple account, including a discussion of possible human cloning.

7301. May, Julian. *Why People Are Different Colors* (2–4). Illus. by Symeon Shimin. 1971, Holiday $7.95. A description of many kinds of differentiation in people—noses, lips, eyes, hair, size of bodies—making clear that all adaptations are only superficial distinctions.

7302. Pomerantz, Charlotte. *Why You Look Like You, Whereas I Tend to Look Like Me* (4–6). Illustrated. 1969, Young Scott $6.95. A concise and simple presentation of the work of Mendel and the laws of inheritance.

7303. Silverstein, Alvin, and Silverstein, Virginia B. *The Code of Life* (5–8). Illus. by Kenneth Gosner. 1972, Atheneum $6.95. The authors investigate the genetic code, explaining how DNA and RNA work together.

7304. Zappler, Georg. *From One Cell to Many Cells* (3–5). Illus. by Elise Piquet. 1970, Messner $7.29. The cell as a basic unit of life; line drawings and diagrams, suggested projects. For a slightly older group use: *You and Your Cells* by Leo Schneider (1964, Harcourt $5.95).

Bionics and Transplants

7305. Berger, Melvin. *Bionics* (5–7). Illustrated. 1978, Watts $4.90. A simple introduction to the study of the structure and systems of plants and animals.

7306. Freese, Arthur S. *The Bionic People Are Here* (6–9). Illustrated. 1979, McGraw $6.95. The restoration of limbs and organs through artificial parts is discussed.

7307. Nolen, William A. *Spare Parts for the Human Body* (6–9). Illustrated. 1971, Random $3.95; LB $4.99. A thorough discussion of recent developments in organ replacement, with sections on plastic bones, pacemakers, artificial kidneys, and other internal organs.

7308. Silverstein, Alvin, and Silverstein, Virginia B. *The World of Bionics* (5–7). Illustrated. 1979, Methuen $7.95. An overview of the use of artificial organs using TV's "Six Million Dollar Man" as a starting place.

7309. Skurzynski, Gloria. *Bionic Parts for People* (6–8). Illustrated. 1978, Four Winds $7.95. Subtitle: *The Real Story of Artificial Organs and Replacements.*

Hygiene and Physical Fitness

7310. Abrams, Joy. *Look Good, Feel Good, through Yoga, Grooming, Nutrition* (6–9). Illustrated. 1978, Holt $7.95. A book that attempts to develop natural beauty habits.

7311. Carr, Rachel. *Be a Frog, a Bird or a Tree* (1–3). 1973, Doubleday $6.95. A simple introduction to yoga for young children.

7312. Checki, Haney Erene, and Richards, Ruth. *Yoga for Children* (3–5). Illus. by Betty Schilling. 1973, Bobbs-Merrill $7.50. Simple exercises that will not strain children are described with accompanying diagrams.

7313. Fodor, R. V., and Taylor, G. J. *Growing Strong* (6–9). Illustrated. 1980, Sterling $6.95; LB $6.69. All kinds of muscle-building exercises, including weight lifting, are described.

7314. Giles, Frank. *Toughen Up: A Boy's Guide to Better Physical Fitness* (6–8). Illustrated. 1963, Putnam $5.49. A basic introduction that will help youngsters to shape up.

7315. Jacobs, Helen Hull. *Better Physical Fitness for Girls* (6–8). Illustrated. 1964, Dodd $5.95. Exercises and shaping-up activities specially suitable for girls.

7316. Klein, Aaron E., and Klein, Cynthia L. *Mind Trips: The Story of Consciousness Raising Movements* (6–9). 1979, Doubleday $7.95. Yoga, Zen, ESP, and TM are only a few of the movements described in this intriguing introduction.

7317. Kozuszek, Jane Everly. *Hygiene* (3–5). Illustrated. 1978, Watts $4.90. A straightforward guide to cleanliness and its importance.

7318. Lewis, Nancy, and Lewis, Richard. *Keeping in Shape* (4–6). Illustrated. 1976, Watts $4.90. An introduction for those who wish to start a physical fitness program. Also use: *Physical Fitness for Young Champions* by Robert J. Antonacci (1975, McGraw $6.84).

7319. Lyttle, Richard B. *The Complete Beginner's Guide to Physical Fitness* (6–9). Illustrated. 1978, Doubleday $6.95. This account emphasizes the fun and satisfaction of achieving physical fitness.

7320. Marshall, Lyn. *Lyn Marshall's Yoga for Your Children* (K–6). Illustrated. 1979, Schocken $9.95; paper $4.95. Parents and children can use this simple informative guide together.

7321. Petersen, W. P. *Meditation Made Easy* (5–9). Illus. by Terry Fehr. 1979, Watts $5.90. A history of meditation and a step-by-step guide to its practice are included in this overview.

7322. Saunders, Rubie. *Franklin Watts Concise Guide to Good Grooming for Boys* (5–7). Illustrated. 1972, Watts $5.45. Clothes, manners, and diet are just 3 of the many topics handled in this useful guide.

7323. Walsh, John. *The First Book of Physical Fitness* (4–6). 1961, Watts $4.90. Salient facts of keeping fit through planned exercise, diet, and correct habits.

7324. Wise, William. *Fresh as a Daisy, Neat as a Pin* (1–3). Illus. by Dora Leder. 1970, Parents $5.41. The importance of cleanliness in the animal and human worlds.

Diseases and Other Illnesses

7325. Asimov, Isaac. *How Did We Find Out about Germs?* (4–6). Illus. by David Wool. 1974, Walker $5.85. A survey of human knowledge of germs, including historical information and material on viruses and vaccines.

7326. Berger, Melvin. *Disease Detectives* (5–9). Illustrated. 1978, Crowell $6.95. A discussion of the work of the Center for Disease Control that uses the Legionnaires disease as a focal point. Also use: *Epidemic!* by Jules Archer (1977, Harcourt $5.95).

7327. Burnstein, John. *Slim Goodbody: What Can Go Wrong and How to Be Strong* (2–5). Illustrated. 1978, McGraw $6.95. An introduction to common illnesses and injuries and how to combat them.

7328. Cohen, Daniel. *Vaccination and You* (3–6). Illus. by Haris Petie. 1969, Messner $3.79. The history of immunization against disease from Jenner to the present.

7329. Connelly, John P., and Berlow, Leonard. *You're too Sweet: A Guide for the Young Diabetic* (4–6). Illustrated. 1969, Astor-Honor $3.95. The cause and treatment of diabetes from the standpoint of a 9-year-old boy.

7330. Donahue, Parnell, and Capellaro, Helen. *Germs Make Me Sick: A Health Handbook for Kids* (4–6). Illus. by Kelly Oechsli. 1975, Knopf $5.99; paper $2.95. A lively and, at times, amusing guide to the viral illnesses that children may encounter.

7331. Haines, Gail Kay. *Natural and Synthetic Poisons* (6–8). Illustrated. 1978, Morrow $5.95. Animals, plants, and various substances that can harm people.

7332. Hyde, Margaret O. *VD: The Silent Epidemic* (5–9). Illustrated. 1973, McGraw $6.95. In a direct, honest treatment, the author describes the types of VD, symptoms, prevention and treat-

ment, and the alarming growth of this disease. Also use: *VD: Facts You Should Know* by Andre Blanzaco (1970, Lothrop $6.50; LB $6.01).

7333. Johnson, Eric W. *VD* (5–9). Illustrated. 1978, Lippincott $6.95. A clear, concise, nonmoralizing revision of the excellent 1973 title.

7334. Kipnis, Lynne, and Adler, Susan. *You Can't Catch Diabetes from a Friend* (3–5). Illustrated. 1979, Triad Scientific $9.95. The facts of the disease are revealed through the lives of four diabetic children.

7335. Nourse, Alan E. *Fractures, Dislocations and Sprains* (4–8). Illustrated. 1978, Watts $4.90. The nature of these injuries is explained along with some first aid tips.

7336. Nourse, Alan E. *Lumps, Bumps and Rashes: A Look at Kids' Diseases* (5–7). Illustrated. 1976, Watts $4.90. Common childhood diseases and infections are discussed.

7337. Nourse, Alan E. *Viruses* (5–7). Illustrated. 1976, Watts $4.90. An account that begins with the work of Jenner and Pasteur and traces the research on viruses to the present day.

7338. Riedman, Sarah R. *Allergies* (4–6). Illustrated. 1978, Watts $4.90. All kinds of allergies are discussed together with their causes and treatments.

7339. Showers, Paul. *No Measles, No Mumps for Me* (1–3). Illus. by Harriett Barton. 1980, Crowell $7.95; LB $7.89. In story form, an introduction to germs and viruses and to the practice of vaccination.

7340. Silverstein, Alvin, and Silverstein, Virginia B. *Cancer* (5–7). Illus. by Andrew Antal. 1977, John Day $6.95. An excellent introduction to types of cancerous cells, how they function, and the current status of cancer prevention and treatment.

7341. Silverstein, Alvin, and Silverstein, Virginia B. *Cells: The Building Blocks of Life* (3–7). 1969, Prentice-Hall $6.95. A well-presented look at the basic building material of the body.

7342. Silverstein, Alvin, and Silverstein, Virginia B. *Diabetes: The Sugar Disease* (6–8). Illustrated. 1979, Lippincott $6.95. A well-organized, straightforward treatment aimed chiefly at nondiabetics.

7343. Silverstein, Alvin, and Silverstein, Virginia B. *Epilepsy* (6–8). 1975, Lippincott $5.95; paper $1.95. The causes, types, and treatment of epilepsy.

7344. Silverstein, Alvin, and Silverstein, Virginia B. *Itch, Sniffle and Sneeze* (3–5). Illus. by Roy Doty. 1978, Four Winds $6.95. Subtitle: *All about Asthma, Hay Fever and Other Allergies.*

7345. Winn, Marie. *The Sick Book* (4–6). Illustrated. 1976, Four Winds $8.95. Subtitle: *Questions and Answers about the Hiccups and Mumps, Sneezes and Bumps, and Other Things That Go Wrong with Us.*

7346. Wolfe, Louis. *Disease Detectives* (4–6). Illustrated. 1979, Watts $5.90. An explanation of the work of the Center for Disease Control.

Drugs, Alcohol, and Smoking

7347. Curtis, Robert H. *Questions and Answers about Alcoholism* (5–7). Illustrated. 1976, Prentice-Hall $5.95. In question-and-answer form, many facets of alcohol are explained. Also use: *Alcoholism* by Alvin Silverstein (1975, Lippincott $6.50; paper $2.95).

7348. Englebardt, Stanley L. *Kids and Alcohol, the Deadliest Drug* (5–8). 1975, Lothrop $5.25; LB $5.04. An explanation of what alcohol is and how it affects the human body.

7349. Gorodetsky, Charles, and Christian, Samuel T. *What You Should Know about Drugs* (5–7). 1970, Harcourt $5.95. Clear-cut facts that will help children make intelligent decisions when confronted with the drug problem. Use with an older group: *The Drug Epidemic: What It Means and How to Combat It* by Wesley C. Westman (1970, Dial $5.95).

7350. Hyde, Margaret O. *Know about Alcohol* (5–8). Illustrated. 1978, McGraw $6.95. Objective presentations on the effects of alcohol on the body.

7351. Hyde, Margaret O., and Hyde, Bruce G. *Know about Drugs* (4–6). Illus. by Bill Morrison. 1979, McGraw $7.95. Drug use and abuse are covered succinctly in this account.

7352. Madison, Arnold. *Drugs and You* (4–7). Illustrated. 1971, Messner $7.29. The various forms of drugs, their uses, effects, and the legalities involved are discussed in a nonpedantic, yet realistic fashion. Also use: *Mind Drugs* by Margaret O. Hyde (1974, McGraw $6.75).

7353. Marr, John S. *The Good Drug and the Bad Drug* (3–4). Illus. by Lynn Sweat. 1970, Evans $4.95. The courses in the body of a beneficial and a harmful drug and their effects.

7354. Seixas, Judith S. *Alcohol: What It Is, What It Does* (2–4). Illus. by Tom Huffman. 1977, Greenwillow $5.95; LB $4.49. A very simple account of the physical and social effects of alcohol.

7355. Sonnett, Sherry. *First Book of Smoking* (4–6). Illustrated. 1977, Watts $4.90. After a brief history of tobacco and its use, the author concentrates on the harmful effects of smoking as revealed by modern research. Also use: *Smoking and You* by Arnold Madison (1975, Messner $5.79).

7356. Stwertka, Eve, and Stwertka, Albert. *Marijuana* (5–8). Illustrated. 1979, Watts $5.90. The history, production, uses, and effects of marijuana are well presented in this basic account.

7357. Tobias, Ann. *Pot* (3–4). Illus. by Tom Huffman. 1979, Greenwillow $5.71. The basic facts about marijuana, its uses and dangers.

7358. Woods, Geraldine. *Drug Use and Drug Abuse* (5–8). Illustrated. 1979, Watts $5.90. From caffeine to narcotics, the entire drug spectrum is covered, with emphasis on the effects for users.

Safety and Accidents

7359. Bolian, Polly, and Hinds, Shirley. *The First Book of Safety* (4–6). Illustrated. 1970, Watts $4.90. A guide to safety in such activities as biking and swimming. For a younger group use: *Tale of Two Bicycles* by Leonard Kessler (1971, Lothrop $6.00) and *Who Tossed That Bat?* by Leonard Kessler (1973, Lothrop $6.00).

7360. Elgin, Kathleen. *The Fall Down, Break a Bone, Skin Your Knee, Book* (3–5). Illus. by author. 1975, Walker $5.85. The most common injuries, such as broken bones, bruises, and cuts, are discussed, and the healing process is described.

7361. Gore, Harriet M. *What to Do When There's No One but You* (2–5). Illus. by David Lindroth. 1974, Prentice-Hall $4.95. The causes and treatment of 26 common household accidents. Also use: *Try It Again, Sam: Safety When You Walk* by Judith Viorst (1970, Lothrop $6.00).

7362. Shapp, Martha, and Shapp, Charles. *Let's Find Out about Safety* (1–3). Illus. by Carolyn Bentley. 1975, Watts $4.90. Safety at home, at school, and outdoors. Also use: *Safety Can Be Fun* By Munro Leaf (1961, Lippincott $6.95).

7363. Vandenburg, Mary Lou. *Help! Emergencies That Could Happen to You and How to Handle Them* (2–5). Illus. by R. L. Markham. 1975, Lerner $3.95. Emergencies such as fire, lightning, and common accidents are discussed with helpful hints for treatment. Also use: *The Emergency Book* by Jeanne Bendick (1967, Random $4.79; paper $1.50).

Doctors and Medicine

7364. Cobb, Vicki. *How the Doctor Knows You're Fine* (2–4). Illus. by Anthony Ravielli. 1973, Lippincott $7.95. Explains the procedure and reasons for each aspect of the medical examination. Also use: *My Doctor* by Harlow Rockwell (1973, Macmillan $7.95).

7365. Curtis, Robert H. *Medical Talk for Beginners* (4–6). Illus. by William Jaber. 1976, Messner $6.95; LB $7.29. A simple medical dictionary that defines the basic terms young people might encounter. Also use: *Modern Medical Discoveries* by Irmengarde Eberle (1968, Crowell $6.95).

7366. Kavaler, Lucy. *Cold against Disease: The Wonders of Cold* (6–9). Illustrated. 1971, John Day $7.95. A matter-of-fact presentation of the ways in which cold helps in medicine, from space applications to organ transplants.

7367. Kettelkamp, Larry. *The Healing Arts* (6–8). Illustrated. 1978, Morrow $5.95. Healing techniques—conventional and unconventional (like spiritual healing)—are covered.

7368. Zim, Herbert S. *Medicine* (4–6). Illus. by Judith Hoffman Corwin. 1974, Morrow $5.50; LB $5.09. The many uses of medicine and precautions concerning amount of dosage.

Hospitals

7369. Kay, Eleanor. *The Emergency Room* (4–6). Illustrated. 1970, Watts $4.47. An objective, straightforward account that is a companion piece to Kay's *The Operating Room* (1970, Watts $4.47).

7370. Kay, Eleanor. *The First Book of the Clinic* (4–6). Illustrated. 1971, Watts $4.90. The purposes and functions of health clinics are treated along with additional information on such specialized agencies as those operated by the World Health Organization (WHO).

7371. Rothkopf, Carol Z. *The First Book of the Red Cross* (4–6). 1971, Watts $4.90. A brief description of the history, present organization, and current activities of the Red Cross, with additional material on the Junior Red Cross and how young people can participate in its programs.

7372. Sobol, Harriet Langsam. *Jeff's Hospital Book* (K–2). Illus. by Patricia Agre. 1975, Walck $6.95. A photo-documentary account of Jeff's stay in the hospital for an operation to correct his crossed eyes. Also use: James Lincoln Collier's *Danny Goes to the Hospital* (1970, Grosset $3.99).

7373. Weber, Altons. *Elizabeth Gets Well* (3–5). Illus. by Jacqueline Blass. 1970, Crowell $8.79. The realistic and reassuring story of Elizabeth's experience in a hospital. Also use: *Let's Find Out about the Hospital* by Eleanor Kay (1971, Watts $4.90) and *A Visit to the Hospital* by Francine Chase (1977, Grosset, paper $2.95).

Aging and Death

7374. Ancona, George. *Growing Older* (3–5). Illustrated. 1978, Dutton $7.95. Interviews with 13 elderly people explore the process of getting old.

7375. Bernstein, Joanne E., and Gullo, Stephen V. *When People Die* (K–3). Illus. by Rosemarie Hauscher. 1977, Dutton $7.59. Written by a psychologist, this is a sensible, fairly comprehensive, and tender discussion of death, neither somber nor mawkish. One of the best of the more recent books on the subject.

7376. Pringle, Laurence. *Death Is Natural* (4–5). Illustrated. 1977, Four Winds $6.95. An explanation of death as interpreted through the balance of nature concept.

7377. Silverstein, Alvin, and Silverstein, Virginia B. *Aging* (6–9). 1979, Watts $6.90. An account of the aging process, its changes, causes, and problems.

7378. Zim, Herbert S., and Bleeker, Sonia. *Life and Death* (4–7). Illus. by Rene Martin. 1970, Morrow $5.52. An objective, comprehensive account of many aspects of aging, death, and dying.

Physical and Mental Handicaps

7379. Adams, Barbara. *Like It Is: Facts and Feelings about Handicaps from Kids Who Know* (5–8). Illustrated. 1979, Walker $8.95. A group of handicapped kids talk about their problems and adjustments.

7380. Berger, Gilda. *Physical Disabilities* (6–8). Illustrated. 1979, Watts $6.90. The characteristics, causes, and consequences of common physical handicaps are discussed.

7381. Dunbar, Robert E. *Mental Retardation* (4–7). Illustrated. 1978, Watts $4.90. A basic, honest account of the causes of mental retardation and its effects.

7382. Kamien, Janet. *What If You Couldn't? A Book about Special Needs* (5–7). Illus. by Signe Hanson. 1979, Scribner $7.95. A discussion of various physical handicaps and how they are treated.

7383. Stein, Sara B. *About Handicaps* (2–3). Illustrated. 1974, Walker $5.95. A book about learning to accept people who have physical handicaps.

7384. Sullivan, Mary Beth. *Feeling Free* (4–8). 1979, Addison $9.95; paper $5.95. Physical disabilities are explored through the perceptions of young people.

7385. Wolf, Bernard. *Anna's Silent World* (2–4). Photos by author. 1977, Lippincott $8.95. Six-year-old Anna was born deaf. How she learns to talk and is able to attend classes with children who have normal hearing is shown through text and excellent photographs.

7386. Wolf, Bernard. *Don't Feel Sorry for Paul* (3–6). Illus. by author. 1974, Lippincott $8.95. A true story dramatically illustrated with photographs about 7-year-old Paul Jockimo and his adjustments to severe birth defects.

Sex Education and Reproduction

Sex Education

7387. Aho, Jennifer J., and Petras, John J. *Learning about Sex: A Guide for Children and Their Parents* (6–8). Illustrated. 1978, Holt $7.95; paper $3.95. An explicit, thorough treatment with suggestions to parents on its use.

7388. Elgin, Kathleen, and Osterritter, John F. *Twenty-Eight Days* (5–7). Illustrated. 1973, McKay $5.95. A book about the menstrual cycle that includes information on the reproductive organs.

7389. Gardner-Loulan, JoAnn; Lopez, Bonnie; and Quackenbush, Marcia. *Period* (6–8). Illus. by Marcia Quackenbush. 1979, My Mama's Press $5.00. An outstanding book on menstruation.

7390. Gordon, Sol. *Facts about Sex for Today's Youth* (6–8). Illus. by Vivien Cohen. 1973, John Day $4.95; paper $1.90. A brief, straightforward account that covers anatomy and human sexuality.

7391. Johnson, Eric W. *Love and Sex in Plain Language* (6–9). Illus. by Edward C. Smith. 1967, Lippincott $6.95. A discussion of the physical, emotional, and moral aspects of love and sex. Also use: *Love and Sex and Growing Up* (1970, Lippincott $6.50).

7392. Johnson, Eric W. *Sex: Telling It Straight* (5–8). Illustrated. 1979, Lippincott $7.95. An update of the 1970 edition of this highly respected, straightforward account.

7393. Mintz, Thomas, and Miller, Lorelie. *Threshold: Straightforward Answers to Teenagers' Questions about Sex* (5–8). Illustrated. 1978, Walker $7.95. A series of direct questions in brief straightforward terms.

7394. Pomeroy, Wardell B. *Boys and Sex* (6–8). 1968, Delacorte $7.95. Straightforward advice addressed to young teenage boys. The companion book by the author: *Girls and Sex* (1969, Delacorte $7.95).

Human Reproduction

7395. Bendick, Jeanne. *What Made You You?* (3–5). Illus. by author. 1971, McGraw $5.92. In simple language and diagrams, the author describes fertilization, the gestation period, birth, and the role of genes in the human reproductive process.

7396. Day, Beth, and Liley, Margaret. *The Secret World of the Baby* (6–8). Illus. by Lennart Nilsson and others. 1968, Random $5.69. Descriptions of the growth phases and movements of the embryo in its private world.

7397. DeSchweinitz, Karl. *Growing Up: How We Become Alive, Are Born, and Grow* (1–3). Illustrated. 1968, Macmillan paper $1.50. Beginning with a simple but explicit description of animal mating, the author goes on to the facts about human reproduction and growing up.

7398. Dragonwagon, Crescent. *Wind Rose* (K–3). Illus. by Ronald Himler. 1976, Harper $6.95. An authentic and dignified treatment of birth as a mother tells her daughter what her parents did, felt, and planned before she was born.

7399. Forrai, Maria S., and Pursell, Margaret S. *A Look at Birth* (K–3). Illustrated. 1978, Lerner $4.95. A straightforward examination through text and pictures of the birth process.

7400. Gruenberg, Sidonie M. *The Wonderful Story of How You Were Born* (1–4). Illus. by Hildegard Woodward. 1962, Doubleday $6.95. A skillful and understanding presentation of the facts of life for young readers.

7401. Holland, Viki. *We Are Having a Baby* (1–3). Illustrated. 1972, Scribner $6.95. Photographs show 4-year-old Dana and her family as they look forward to the birth of a baby—and then Dana's adjustment to having a new little brother at home.

Also use: *Did the Sun Shine before You were Born?* by Sol Gordon (1974, Third Press $4.95).

7402. Meeks, Esther K, and Bagwell, Elizabeth. *How New Life Begins* (1–3). Illustrated. 1969, Follett $3.48. Animal reproduction is discussed in very simple terms. Also use: *A New Baby Comes* by Julian May (1970, Creative Education $6.95).

7403. Nilsson, Lennart. *How Was I Born?* (3–6). Illustrated. 1975, Delacorte $5.95. An excellent sex education book described as "a photographic story of reproduction and birth for children."

7404. Parker, Stephen, and Bavosi, John. *Life before Birth: The Story of the First Nine Months* (3–6). Illus. by John Bavosi. 1979, Cambridge $6.95; paper $2.50. The human gestation period from fertilization of the egg through birth.

7405. Portal, Colette. *The Beauty of Birth* (3–6). Illustrated. 1972, Crowell $4.99. The development of the baby from conception through the fetal period to birth told through simple text and delicate watercolors.

7406. Power, Jules. *How Life Begins* (4–6). Illus. by Barry Geller. 1968, Simon & Schuster $4.95; paper $1.95. A description of how fish, birds, and mammals are born leads up to the informative discussion on the development and birth of the human baby.

7407. Showers, Paul, and Showers, Kay. *Before You Were a Baby* (1–3). Illus. by Ingrid Fetz. 1968, Crowell $6.89. Simple, succinct, and informative, this promotes understanding of the conception, growth, and birth of a baby. Also use: *A Baby Starts to Grow* (1969, Crowell $6.89; paper $1.45).

7408. Silverstein, Alvin, and Silverstein, Virginia B. *The Reproductive System: How Living Creatures Multiply* (4–6). Illus. by Lee J. Ames. 1971, Prentice-Hall $5.95. Mating habits and reproduction facts are presented about plants and humans.

7409. Strain, Frances B. *Being Born* (4–7). Illustrated. 1970, Hawthorn $4.95. This is a standard handbook of sex instruction illustrated with photographs and diagrams.

Babies

7410. Ancona, George. *It's a Baby* (1–4). Illustrated. 1979, Dutton $7.95. The first 12 months of a baby's life in simple text and many photographs. Also use: *Let's Find Out about Babies* by Martha Shapp and Charles Shapp (1975, Watts $4.90).

7411. Harris, Robie H., and Levy, Elizabeth. *Before You Were Three: How You Began To Walk, Talk, Explore and Have Feelings* (5–8). Illustrated. 1977, Delacorte $7.95; LB $7.45. The first 3 years of life and the accompanying developmental processes as experienced by a boy and a girl.

7412. Samson, Joan. *Watching the New Baby* (3–5). Illustrated. 1974, Atheneum $7.95. After an introduction on the process of birth, the behavior of infants is explained in a way to help older brothers or sisters adjust to having a new member in the family.

7413. Williams, Gurney, III. *Twins* (5–7). Illustrated. 1979, Watts $5.45. A fascinating account of what causes twins and what we know about the phenomenon.

The Sciences

General

7414. Allison, Linda. *The Wild Inside: Sierra Club's Guide to the Great Indoors* (4–7). Illus. by author. 1979, Scribner $9.95; paper $5.95. All kinds of science from household pests and plants to sewage and plumbing—found indoors.

7415. Asimov, Isaac. *Great Ideas of Science* (6–9). Illus. by Lee J. Ames. 1969, Houghton $6.95. A description of the major theories in science and how each has contributed to our body of knowledge.

7416. Asimov, Isaac. *Words of Science and the History behind Them* (5–9). Illus. by William Barss. 1959, Houghton paper $1.50. Both the reader interested in science and the reader interested in language will find this a fascinating book. Also use: *More Words of Science* (1971, Houghton $6.95).

7417. Bova, Benjamin. *Through the Eyes of Wonder: Science Fiction and Science* (6–9). Illustrated. 1975, Addison $6.95. A discussion of the science fiction genre and its gradual acceptance as a genuine literary form.

7418. Knight, David C. *Bees Can't Fly, but They Do: Things That Are Still a Mystery to Science* (3–5). Illus. by Barbara Wolff. 1976, Macmillan $6.95. Some of the several mysteries that are inexplicable to scientists, such as fire walkers, the 6-sided snowflake, and divining rods.

Experiments

7419. Barr, George. *Research Ideas for Young Scientists* (6–8). Illus. by John Teppich. 1958, McGraw $6.50. Well written and chock full of ideas for unusual science projects.

7420. Cobb, Vicki, and Darling, Kathy. *Bet You Can't! Science Impossibilities to Fool You* (5–8). Illus. by Martha Weston. 1980, Lothrop $6.95; LB $6.67. Sixty different tricks and experiments involving such scientific subjects as fluids and energy.

7421. Cobb, Vicki. *Science Experiments You Can Eat* (5–7). Illus. by Peter Lippman. 1972, Lippincott $7.95; paper $4.95. Experiments illustrating principles of chemistry and physics utilize edible ingredients.

7422. Cooper, Elizabeth K. *Science in Your Own Back Yard* (5–8). Illustrated. 1958, Harcourt $5.95; paper $1.35. An invitation to firsthand experimentation for the young naturalist.

7423. Freeman, Mae, and Freeman, Ira. *Fun with Science* (4–6). Illustrated. 1957, Random $4.39. A well-illustrated book of easy home experiments involving the principles of physics. Also use: *Fun with Scientific Experiments* (1960, Random $3.99; LB $4.39).

7424. Gardner, Martin. *Science Puzzlers* (6–8). Illus. by Anthony Ravielli. 1960, Viking $2.50. An array of entertaining experiments using commonplace materials. For a younger group use: *Science Puzzles* by Laurence B. White (1975, Addison $5.95).

7425. Goldstein, K. *Experiments with Everyday Objects: Science Activities for Children, Parents and Teachers* (5–7). Illustrated. 1978, Prentice-Hall $9.95. There are over 75 experiments included, organized by such topics as air, water, and surface tension.

7426. Herbert, Don. *Mr Wizard's Experiments for Young Scientists* (5–9). Illus. by Don Noonan. 1966, Doubleday $4.95. Directions for 13 science experiments that can be done easily with equipment found in the home.

7427. Milgrom, Harry. *Adventures with a Paper Cup* (1–3). Illus. by Leonard Kessler. 1968, Dutton $3.46; LB $4.95. An assortment of simple activities using common household items that entertainingly and ingeniously explain science concepts. Also use (both Dutton $6.50): *Adventures with a Cardboard Tube* (1972) and *Adventures with a Straw* (1967).

7428. Milgrom, Harry. *Paper Science* (2–4). Illus. by Daniel Nevins. 1978, Walker $6.95; LB $6.85. Simple experiments with paper that demonstrate a wide variety of scientific principles.

7429. Moorman, Thomas. *How to Make Your Science Project Scientific* (5–9). Illustrated. 1974, Atheneum $8.95; paper $1.95. A highly readable introduction to the scientific method of research and the various forms (experiments, surveys) of its methodology.

7430. Schneider, Herman, and Schneider, Nina. *Science Fun for You in a Minute or Two: Quick Science Experiments You Can Do* (2–5). Illus. by Leonard Kessler. 1975, McGraw $6.95. Simple, speedy science experiments with little equipment are related to important scientific principles. Also use: *The First Book of Science Experiments* by Rose Wyler (1971, Watts, $4.90).

7431. Selsam, Millicent E. *Is This a Baby Dinosaur? And Other Science Puzzles* (K–3). Illus. with photographs. 1972, Harper $6.89; Scholastic paper $.95. Magnified black-and-white photographs that show part of an animal or plant are frequently deceptive, and on the following page the picture shows the whole life form: the "baby dinosaur" is, when the whole picture is seen, really a baby pelican. A good book to sharpen powers of observation.

7432. Simon, Seymour. *Exploring Fields and Lots: Easy Science Projects* (3–5). Illustrated. 1978, Garrard $4.48. Simple activities involving sunlight, common insects, everyday plant life, and the like are well introduced.

7433. Simon, Seymour. *Science in a Vacant Lot* (2–5). Illus. by Kizo Domoda. 1970, Viking $4.95. A book of projects involving nature study in a typical empty city lot.

7434. Stepp, Anne. *Setting Up a Science Project* (4–6). Illus. by Polly Bolian. 1965, Prentice-Hall $4.95. A "how to" book that gives hints on how to organize and carry out a science project.

7435. Stone, George K. *Science Projects You Can Do* (4–6). Illus. by Stephen R. Peck. 1963, Prentice-Hall $6.95. Some fine ideas for the amateur scientist.

7436. UNESCO. *700 Science Experiments for Everyone* (6–8). 1958, UNESCO $6.95. An excellent collection of experiments noted for its number of entries and breadth of coverage.

7437. Webster, David. *More Brain Boosters* (4–7). 1975, Doubleday $5.95. A collection of puzzles and experiments that will help arouse an interest in science in young readers.

7438. White, Laurence B. *Investigating Science with Nails* (4–7). Illustrated. 1970, Addison $5.95. This book contains many simple experiments using nails to demonstrate principles involving magnetism, heat, and so on. Also use by the same

author and publisher (each $5.95): *Investigating Science with Coins* (1969), *Investigating Science with Rubber Bands* (1969), and *Investigating Science with Paper* (1970).

7439. Williams, Jerome, and Williams, Lelia K. *Science Puzzles* (5–8). Illus. by Myran Grossman. 1979, Watts $5.90. Riddles and puzzles involving many areas of science are given, plus their answers.

7440. Wyler, Rose. *What Happens If—? Science Experiments You Can Do by Yourself* (2–4). Illus. by Daniel Nevins. 1974, Walker $4.87; paper $.85. Experiments with balloons, flashlights, shadow pictures, and ice, using simple materials and with clear, safe instructions. Also use: *Prove It!* (1975, Addison $3.79).

7441. Zubrowski, Bernie. *Ball-Point Pens: A Children's Museum Activity Book* (4–6). Illus. by Linda Bourke. 1979, Little $6.95; paper $3.95. Numerous activities based on scientific principles. Also use: *Milk Carton Blocks* (1979, Little $6.95; paper $3.95).

Mathematics

General

7442. Bendick, Jeanne, and Levin, Marcia. *Mathematics Illustrated Dictionary: Facts, Figures and People Including the New Math* (4–7). Illustrated. 1965, McGraw $6.95; LB $6.84. About 2,000 entries trace the history and present status of terms and famous people involved in the world of mathematics.

7443. Bendick, Jeanne, and Levin, Marcia. *Take Shapes, Lines and Letters: New Horizons in Mathematics* (5–7). Illus. by Jeanne Bendick. 1961, McGraw $6.95. An account that takes the reader beyond the usual topics discussed in books on mathematics. Also use from Prentice-Hall: *New Ways in Math* (1962, $4.95) and *More New Ways in Math* both by Arthur Jonas (1964, $5.95).

7444. Gersting, Judith L., and Kuczkowski, Joseph. *Yes-No; Stop-Go; Some Patterns in Mathematical Logic* (3–5). Illus. by Don Madden. 1977, Crowell $5.95. In solving a king's problems, the reader is introduced to mathematical logic.

Numbers and Number Systems

7445. Adler, David A. *Base 5* (3–5). Illus. by Larry Ross. 1975, Crowell $6.89. Through the use of everyday objects, the author explains number systems with bases of 5 and 10.

7446. Adler, David A. *3D, 2D, ID* (1–3). Illus. by Harvey Weiss. 1975, Crowell $6.95; LB $5.95. The concept of dimension is introduced and explored in simple text and fine illustrations.

7447. Adler, Irving, and Adler, Ruth. *Numerals: New Dresses for Old Numbers* (5–6). 1964, John Day $6.89. Numeral systems other than base 10 are explored. Also use: *Integers: Positive and Negative* (1972, Day $6.89).

7448. Adler, Irving, and Adler, Ruth. *Sets and Numbers for the Very Young* (K–2). Illustrated. 1969, John Day paper $2.40. A very simple introduction to cardinal and ordinal numbers, sets, and counting. For an older group use: *Names, Sets and Numbers* by Jeanne Bendick (1971, Watts $4.90; paper $1.25).

7449. Asimov, Isaac. *How Did We Find Out about Numbers?* (4–6). Illus. by Daniel Nevins. 1973, Walker $4.95; LB $5.85. A lucid account of the history of various numerical systems (e.g, Roman, Arabic) and the problems inherent in their use. For a younger group use: *How Did Numbers Begin?* by Mindel Sitomer (1972, Crowell $5.95).

7450. Asimov, Isaac. *Realm of Numbers* (6–9). Illus. by Robert Belmore. 1959, Houghton $8.95. An explanation of mathematical principles and procedures, beginning with simple arithmetic and moving on to more advanced mathematics.

7451. Barr, Donald. *Arithmetic for Billy Goats* (4–6). Illus. by Don Madden. 1966, Harcourt $4.95. William Gruff, an enterprising young goat, invents a system for counting corncobs, and in the process gives examples of computer arithmetic.

7452. Charosh, Mannis. *Number Ideas through Pictures* (2–4). Illus. by Giulio Maestro. 1974, Crowell $6.89. The concept of odd and even numbers, square and triangular numbers, and how they can be combined and used is clearly explained through simple text and excellent pictures.

7453. Dennis, J. Richard. *Fractions Are Parts of Things* (2–4). Illus. by Donald Crews. 1971, Crowell paper $1.45. An introduction to simple fractions, beginning with one-half, through thirds and fourths. Also use: *Easy Book of Fractions* by David C. Whitney (1970, Watts $4.90).

7454. Froman, Robert. *The Greatest Guessing Game: A Book about Dividing* (2–4). Illus. by Gioia Fiammenghi. 1978, Crowell $5.79. Through real-life situations, the principles of division are introduced and explained.

7455. Froman, Robert. *Less Than Nothing Is Really Something* (2–4). Illus. by Don Madden. 1973, Crowell $6.95. A clear presentation of positive and negative numbers, and how they may be added and subtracted.

7456. Froman, Robert. *Venn Diagrams* (1–3). Illus. by Jan Pyk. 1972, Crowell $4.50; LB $5.95. In a simple text, Venn diagrams are introduced and used to solve various mathematical problems.

7457. O'Brian, Thomas C. *Odds and Evens* (2–4). Illus. by Allan Eitzen. 1971, Crowell paper $1.45. Through examples, puzzles, and other activities, the concept of odd and even numbers is introduced. Also use: *One, Two, Three and Many: A First Look at Numbers* by Solveig P. Russell (1970, Walck, $5.95).

7458. St. John, Glory. *How to Count like a Martian* (4–7). Illustrated. 1975, Walck $7.95. A history of how people have counted during various civilizations and the principles behind these systems.

7459. Sitomer, Mindel, and Sitomer, Harry. *Zero Is Not Nothing* (2–4). Illustrated. 1978, Crowell $5.79. A beginning math book on the value of negative numbers.

7460. Srivastava, Jane Jonas. *Number Families* (1–3). Illustrated. 1979, Crowell $5.89. Such concepts as odd, even, triangle, and square are explained in this picture book.

7461. Watson, Clyde. *Binary Numbers* (2–4). Illus. by Wendy Watson. 1977, Crowell $5.95. One of the simplest descriptions of the binary system published for children, this has a lucid text and helpful illustrations.

7462. Weiss, Malcolm E. *666 Jelly Beans! All That? An Introduction to Algebra* (3–4). Illus. by Judith Hoffman Corwin. 1976, Crowell $5.95. The reader is shown step-by-step how to find unknown numbers from clues given in this introduction for young children.

7463. Whitney, David C. *Easy Book of Numbers and Numerals* (4–6). Illus. by Anne Marie Jauss. 1973, Watts $4.90. A simple explanation that traces historically the growth of numerical systems and the uses of numbers today.

7464. Whitney, David C. *Easy Book of Sets* (3–5). Illus. by Tony Forde. 1972, Watts $4.90. The basic theory behind sets and problems involving their application is simply presented.

7465. Whitney, David C. *Let's Find Out about Subtraction* (1–3). Illus. by Eva Cellini. 1968, Watts $4.90. Easy-to-understand explanation for young readers.

Metric System

7466. Baird, Eva-Lee, and Wyler, Rose. *Going Metric the Fun Way* (3–5). Illus. by Talivaldis Stubis. 1980, Doubleday $7.95; LB $8.90. Puzzles, games, and jokes are used to explain the metric system.

7467. Bitter, Gary G., and Metos, Thomas H. *Exploring with Metrics* (3–5). Illustrated. 1975, Messner $6.29. An explanation and history of the metric system, plus games and puzzles. Also use for an older group: *Metric Is Here!* by William Moore (1974, Putnam $5.95).

7468. Branley, Franklyn M. *Think Metric!* (4–6). Illus. by Graham Booth. 1973, Crowell $6.95; LB $7.95. A simple introduction to the metric system that describes metric measurement, its history and advantages, and methods of conversion from the present U.S. form. Also use: *Measure with Metric* (1975, Crowell $6.95; paper $1.45).

7469. Deming, Richard. *Metric Power: Why and How We Are Going Metric* (6–9). 1974, Nelson $6.95. The advantages of the metric system, as well as the history of its development and the resistance to its adoption in the United States. Also use: *The Metric System: Measures for All Mankind* by Frank Ross (1974, Phillips $8.95).

7470. Hahn, James, and Hahn, Lynn. *The Metric System* (5–6). 1975, Watts $4.90. A history of the metric system from the French Revolution to its status in the United States today. Also use: *Let's Talk about the Metric System* by Joyce Lamm (1974, Jonathan David $5.95).

7471. Morganstern, Steve. *Metric Puzzles, Tricks and Games* (3–6). Illustrated. 1977, Sterling $4.99. Fun with the metric system.

7472. Rahn, Joan Elma. *Metric System* (6–9). 1976, Atheneum $5.95. A discussion of the metric system, particularly as related to the United States.

7473. Segan, Ann. *One Meter Max* (K–2). Illus. by author. 1979, Prentice-Hall $6.95. A rhyming text that introduces measuring with the metric system.

7474. Shimek, William J. *The Metric System* (K–2). Illus. by George Overlie. 1975, Lerner $3.95. A general introduction to this system of measurement. Continuations in the series (all

1975, $3.95 ea.) are: *The Gram, The Liter,* and *The Meter.*

7475. Stover, Allan C. *You and the Metric System* (6–9). Illus. by Charles Jakubowski. 1974, Dodd $4.50. A lucid, basic introduction to the metric system, its logic, and the necessity of U.S. conversion to its use. Also use: *Metric Measure* by Herbert S. Zim (1974, Morrow $5.09).

Weights and Measures

7476. Asimov, Isaac. *The Realm of Measure* (6–8). Illus. by Robert Belmore. 1960, Houghton $5.95. This work contains an explanation of measurement concepts and tools. Also use: *Man the Measurer* by Roy A. Gallant (1972, Doubleday $5.95).

7477. Bendick, Jeanne. *Measuring* (4–6). 1971, Watts $4.90. The English and metric systems are introduced and compared. Also use: *How Much and How Many: The Story of Weights and Measures* (1960, McGraw $4.72).

7478. Branley, Franklyn M. *How Little and How Much: A Book about Scales* (1–3). Illus. by Byron Barton. 1976, Crowell $6.89. A simple history of measuring scales and how they are used today, including Fahrenheit and Celsius. Also use: *Celsius Thermometer* by William J. Shimek (1975, Lerner $3.95).

7479. Froman, Robert. *Bigger and Smaller* (2–4). Illus. by Gioia Fiammenghi. 1971, Crowell paper $1.45. The concepts of relative size are clearly explained in this simply written book.

7480. Gilleo, Alma. *About the Thermometer* (3–4). Illus. by Nancy Inderieden. 1977, Child's World $5.51. Hobo, the clown, learns about the Celsius thermometer.

7481. Pine, Tillie S., and Levine, Joseph. *Measurements and How We Use Them* (2–4). Illus. by Harriet Sherman. 1977, McGraw $5.72. A delightful introduction to measurements and their uses in a variety of situations. Also use: *Weighing and Balancing* by Jane Jonas Srivastava (1970, Crowell $5.95).

7482. Russell, Solveig P. *Size, Distance, Weight: A First Look at Measuring* (3–5). Illus. by Margot Tomes. 1968, Walck $5.95. An examination of the various ways we measure time, height, weight, and such.

7483. Srivastava, Jane Jonas. *Area* (2–3). Illus. by Shelley Freshman. 1974, Crowell $6.89. Various kinds of surface areas are introduced along with methods of measurement and some related do-it-yourself activities.

Computers

7484. Berger, Melvin. *Computers* (5–9). 1972, Coward $4.90. After basic background information, the book concentrates on the uses of the computer.

7485. Bitter, Gary G., and Metos, Thomas H. *Exploring with Pocket Calculators* (4–7). Illustrated. 1977, Messner $6.64. After a brief history of calculating machines, the authors concentrate on problems and tricks using the 4-function pocket calculator.

7486. DeRossi, Claude J. *Computers: Tools for Today* (4–6). 1972, Childrens Press $7.95. A simple but accurate explanation of the history and functions of the computer and of such concepts as the flow chart, programming, and the binary system. Also use: *What Makes a Computer Work?* by D. S. Halacy, Jr. (1973, Little $4.95).

7487. Dilson, Jesse. *The Abacus: A Pocket Computer* (5–7). Illus. by Angela Pozzi. 1968, St. Martins paper $2.95. A history of the abacus, with directions on how to construct and use it.

7488. Goeller, Lee. *How to Make an Adding Machine That Even Adds Roman Numerals* (4–6). Illus. by Kiyo Komoda. 1979, Harcourt $7.95. Through breezy text and drawings, the author tells how to construct an abacus from egg cartons and marbles.

7489. Lewis, Bruce. *Meet the Computer* (3–5). Illus. by Leonard Kessler. 1977, Dodd $5.25. An introductory glimpse at these machines with an emphasis on their usefulness.

7490. Madison, Arnold, and Drotar, David L. *Pocket Calculators: How to Use and Enjoy Them* (5–8). Illustrated. 1978, Nelson $6.95. Four kinds of calculators are featured, with possible uses.

7491. O'Brien, Linda. *Computers* (4–7). Illustrated. 1978, Watts $4.90. This clear presentation includes coverage on the nature and uses of various kinds of computers.

7492. Srivastava, Jane Jonas. *Computers* (2–4). Illus. by James McCrea and Ruth McCrea. 1972, Crowell $6.89. Introduction to the computer as a counting machine, explained simply and accompanied by graphic illustrations.

7493. Wall, Elizabeth S. *Computer Alphabet Book* (3–4). Illus. by Julia E. Cousins. 1979, Bayshore $8.95. The letters of the alphabet are used to introduce computer terms.

Geometry

7494. Barr, Stephen. *Experiments in Topology* (6–9). Illus. by Ava Morgan. 1964, Crowell $8.95. An explanation of sets through various activities geared to the advanced science.

7495. Bendick, Jeanne. *Shapes* (2–4). Illus. by author. 1968, Watts $4.90; paper $1.25. A basic introduction to geometry that begins with simple concepts and ends with a discussion of 3-dimensional figures. Also use: *Finding Out about Shapes* by Mae Freeman (1969, McGraw $3.95).

7496. Charosh, Mannis. *Straight Lines, Parallel Lines, Perpendicular Lines* (3–4). Illus. by Enrico Arno. 1970, Crowell $6.89; paper $1.45. A basic mathematics book that explores the interrelationships of various kinds of lines and cites examples from everyday objects. Also use: *The Ellipse* (1971, Crowell $6.89).

7497. Diggins, Julia E. *String, Straightedge and Shadow: The Story of Geometry* (6–8). Illus. by Corydon Bell. 1965, Viking $7.95. The history of geometry told through the simple tools used by early scientists.

7498. Froman, Robert. *Angles Are Easy as Pie* (3–5). Illus. by Byron Barton. 1976, Crowell $6.89. Activities of several hungry alligators are used to point out characteristics of angles.

7499. Holt, Michael. *Maps, Tracks and the Bridges of Konigsberg* (3–5). Illus. by Wendy Watson. 1975, Crowell $4.50; LB $5.95. An introduction to some concepts in topology through problems involving linking cities together by networks.

7500. Phillips, Jo. *Exploring Triangles: Paper Folding Geometry* (2–4). Illus. by Jim Rolling. 1975, Crowell $6.89. The properties of triangles are explored through paper-folding exercises.

7501. Russell, Solveig P. *Lines and Shapes: A First Look at Geometry* (1–4). Illus. by Arnold Spilka. 1965, Walck $5.95. Lines and shapes of familiar objects are used to explain geometric concepts in the simplest terms.

7502. Sitomer, Mindel, and Sitomer, Harry. *Circles* (2–4). Illus. by George Giusti. 1971, Crowell $6.95. The concepts of radius and circumference are explained in this introduction to the mathematical principles involved in circles.

7503. Sitomer, Mindel, and Sitomer, Harry. *Lines, Segments, Polygons* (2–4). Illus. by Robert

Quackenbush. 1972, Crowell $6.95. A simple, often humorous introduction to geometry.

7504. Sitomer, Mindel, and Sitomer, Harry. *What is Symmetry?* (1–3). Illus. by Ed Emberley. 1970, Crowell $6.95; paper $1.45. Symmetry and its varied forms are presented in simple text and suitable illustrations.

7505. Trivett, Daphne. *Shadow Geometry* (1–3). Illus. by Henry Roth. 1974, Crowell $6.89. With paper, scissors, and a light source, all sorts of geometric figures can be produced.

Statistics

7506. James, Elizabeth, and Barkin, Carol. *What Do You Mean by "Average"?* (5–7). Illus. by Joel Schick. 1978, Lothrop $5.95; LB $5.71. Simple statistical concepts are explained using a classroom situation as a setting. Use for younger groups: *Averages* by Jane Jonas Srivastava (1975, Crowell $6.89).

7507. Linn, Charles F. *Probability* (2–4). Illus. by Wendy Watson. 1972, Crowell $6.29. An introduction to such concepts as data gathering, ratios, and other laws of probability, lucidly explained and illustrated with cartoon-style pictures. Also use: *Estimation* (1970, Crowell $4.50; LB $5.95; paper $1.45).

7508. Lowenstein, Dyno. *Graphs* (5–7). Illus. by author. 1976, Watts $4.90. A well-organized, accurate introduction to various types of graphs and their uses.

7509. Riedel, Manfred G. *Winning with Numbers: A Kid's Guide to Statistics* (5–8). Illus. by Paul Coker, Jr. 1978, Prentice-Hall $6.95. How to lie with statistics is shown in this lively guide.

7510. Srivastava, Jane Jonas. *Statistics* (2–4). Illus. by John J. Reiss. 1973, Crowell $6.89. What statistics are, how they are gathered, and their uses, as well as methods of presentation. Also use: *Sports-Math* by Lee Arthur (1975, Lothrop $5.49).

Mathematical Puzzles

7511. Adler, Peggy, and Adler, Irving. *Math Puzzles* (4–6). Illus. by Peggy Adler. 1978, Watts $4.90. Forty-four story problems involving humans and hedgehogs.

7512. Barr, George. *Entertaining with Number Tricks* (4–6). Illus. by Mildred Waltrip. 1971, McGraw $6.95. An entertaining book of puzzles and pastimes involving simple mathematics.

7513. Burns, Marilyn. *The I Hate Mathematics! Book* (5–8). Illus. by Martha Hairston. 1975, Little $7.95; paper $3.95. A lively collection of puzzles and other mind stretchers that illustrate mathematical concepts.

7514. Gardner, Martin. *Mathematical Puzzles* (6–9). Illus. by Anthony Ravielli. 1961, Coward $6.50. Many different kinds of puzzles provide "stimulating glimpses into the fascinating endless patterns of mathematics." Also use: *A Miscellany of Puzzles: Mathematical and Otherwise* by Stephen Barr (1965, Crowell $8.95).

7515. Gardner, Martin. *Perplexing Puzzles and Tantalizing Teasers* (4–7). Illus. by Laszlo Kubinyi. 1969, Simon & Schuster paper $1.25. An assortment of math problems, visual teasers, and tricky questions to challenge young, alert minds; perky drawings.

7516. Kadesch, Robert M. *Math Menagerie* (6–9). Illus. by Mark A. Binn. 1970, Harper $6.79. Twenty-five ingenious mathematical puzzles, clearly described and illustrated.

7517. Walls, Fred. *Puzzles and Brain Twisters* (4–6). Illustrated. 1970, Watts $4.90; paper $1.25. Enjoyable mathematical puzzles using everyday objects.

7518. Weiss, Malcolm E. *Solomon Grundy, Born on Oneday: A Finite Arithmetic Puzzle* (K–3). Illus. by Tomie de Paola. 1977, Crowell $5.95. Solving the problem of Solomon Grundy is used to introduce an arithmetical system.

7519. Wyler, Rose, and Ames, Gerald. *Funny Number Tricks: Easy Magic with Arithmetic* (1–2). Illus. by Talivaldis Stubis. 1976, Parents $5.95; LB $5.41. Only a basic knowledge of addition and subtraction is necessary to perform these tricks and solve these puzzles.

Time and Clocks

7520. Berger, Melvin. *Time after Time* (2–4). Illus. by Richard Cuffari. 1975, Coward $4.90. An excellent book on time, simply written and well illustrated. For a slightly older group use: *The First Book of Time* by Jeanne Bendick (1963, Watts $4.90).

7521. Breiter, Herta S. *Time and Clocks* (2–4). Illustrated. 1978, Raintree $5.49. A carefully planned, well-organized beginner's book.

7522. Brindze, Ruth. *The Story of Our Calendar* (4–7). Illus. by Helene Carter. 1949, Vanguard $5.95. From Babylonian sky gazers to the present. Also use: *The Calendar* by Irving Adler (1967, Day $5.95).

7523. Burns, Marilyn. *This Book Is about Time* (5–7). Illustrated. 1978, Little $4.95. This work explores many facets of the concept of time, including a history of the calendar.

7524. Gibbons, Gail. *Clocks and How They Go* (2–4). Illus. by author. 1979, Crowell $6.95; LB $6.89. An introductory account that explains how clocks work.

7525. Jespersen, James, and Fitz-Randolph, Jane. *Time and Clocks for the Space Age* (6–9). Illustrated. 1979, Atheneum $10.95. A mature introduction to time and its measurement.

7526. Johnson, Chester. *What Makes a Clock Tick?* (8–9). Illustrated. 1969, Little $4.50. History of clocks and of their inner mechanisms.

7527. Rice, Stanley. *Tell Time* (4–6). Illus. by author. 1963, Harcourt paper $3.50. The concept of time and its measurement is introduced.

Physics

General

7528. Anderson, Norman D. *Investigating Science in the Swimming Pool and Ocean* (5–8). Illustrated. 1978, McGraw $7.95. Such concepts as buoyancy and water displacement are explored. Companion to *Investigating Science Using Your Whole Body* (1975, $6.95).

7529. Aylesworth, Thomas G. *Science at the Ball Game* (5–8). Illustrated. 1977, Walker $5.85. Principles of physics are applied to such aspects of baseball as pitching, catching, and even stealing bases.

7530. Bendick, Jeanne. *Motion and Gravity* (3–5). Illus. by author. 1972, Watts $4.90. The author explores the basic concepts of motion and gravity through a question-and-answer approach. For an older group use: *Forces in the Earth: A Book about Gravity and Magnetism* by R. J. Lefkowitz (1976, Parents $5.41).

7531. Bendick, Jeanne. *Solids, Liquids and Gases* (3–5). Illus. by author. 1974, Watts $4.90. The 3 states of matter and their characteristics are explained in simple text, demonstrations, and other activities. Also use: *Matter All around You: A Book about Solids, Liquids and Gases* by R. J. Lefkowitz (1972, Parents $5.41).

7532. Bendick, Jeanne. *Space and Time* (2–4). Illus. by author. 1968, Watts $4.90; paper $1.25. Different concepts of space and its relationship to time, along with simple experiments, are presented in this easily read book.

7533. Branley, Franklyn M. *Floating and Sinking* (1–3). Illus. by Robert Galster. 1967, Crowell $6.89. A discussion of why things float and sink, with simple text and interesting activities. For an older group use: *What Makes a Boat Float?* by Scott Corbett (1970, Little $5.95).

7534. Branley, Franklyn M. *Gravity Is a Mystery* (1–3). Illus. by Don Madden. 1970, Crowell $6.89. With the use of color illustration, the concept of gravity is explained in a lighthearted, amusing fashion. Also use: *Gravity* by Melvin Berger (1969, Coward $4.49).

7535. Branley, Franklyn M. *Weight and Weightlessness* (1–3). Illus. by Graham Booth. 1972, Crowell $6.89. Gravity, spaceships, and weightlessness are introduced in this elementary explanation.

7536. Brewer, Mary. *What Floats?* (1–3). Illus. by Nancy Inderieden. 1976, Childrens Press $4.95. The idea of floating and sinking is explained in relation to a variety of objects.

7537. Chase, Sara B. *Moving to Win: The Physics of Sports* (5–8). Illustrated. 1977, Messner $6.64. Famous athletes demonstrate the laws of physics in this interesting approach.

7538. Cherrier, Francois. *Fascinating Experiments in Physics* (6–9). 1979, Sterling $8.95; LB $8.39. A project book for the better reader and more mature student.

7539. Cobb, Vicki. *The First Book of Gases* (5–7). Illus. by Ellie Haines. 1970, Watts $4.90. This simple introduction describes the discovery and uses of such gases as oxygen, nitrogen, and hydrogen.

7540. Feravolo, Rocco V. *Easy Physics Projects: Air, Water and Heat* (4–7). Illus. by Lewis Zacks. 1966, Prentice-Hall $5.95. A series of simple experiments, using inexpensive equipment, that illustrate basic concepts in physics. Also use: *More Easy Physics Projects: Magnetism, Electricity, Sound* (1968, Prentice-Hall $5.95).

Energy and Motion

7541. Adler, Irving. *Energy* (3–5). Illus. by Ellen Viereck. 1970, John Day $6.89. A basic book that deals with such concepts as force, friction, heat, and various forms of energy. Also use: *Energy All around Us* by Tillie S. Pine (1975, McGraw $6.95).

7542. Bendick, Jeanne. *Why Things Work: A Book about Energy* (2–5). Illustrated. 1972, Parents $5.41. The various forms of energy and how they are used.

7543. Gardner, Robert, and Webster, David. *Moving Right Along: A Book of Science Experiments and Puzzlers about Motion* (6–9). Illustrated. 1978, Doubleday $6.95. A useful book about science experiments.

7544. Harrison, George R. *The First Book of Energy* (5–7). 1965, Watts $4.90. A simple discussion of the various forms of energy and their sources with simple explanations of terminology. Also use: *How Did We Find Out about Energy?* by Isaac Asimov (1975, Walker $5.85).

7545. Hellman, Hal. *Energy and Inertia* (4–7). 1970, Evans $4.95. Energy and its different forms and uses are discussed.

7546. Lefkowitz, R. J. *Push, Pull, Stop, Go: A Book about Forces and Motion* (4–6). Illus. by June Goldsborough. 1975, Parents $5.41. The properties of force and motion are introduced and explored with several activities and examples.

7547. Rutland, Jonathan. *Exploring the World of Speed* (3–6). Illustrated. 1979, Watts $2.95; LB $4.90. The concept of speed is explored in nature, transportation, sports, and even photography.

7548. Simon, Seymour. *Everything Moves* (2–4). Illustrated. 1975, Nelson $5.85. Principles involving energy and motion are introduced in simple text and pictures.

Heat

7549. Adler, Irving. *Fire in Your Life* (6–9). Illus. by Ruth Adler. 1955, John Day $6.89. The concept of combustion and the chemical changes it produces and its uses.

7550. Adler, Irving, and Adler, Ruth. *Heat and Its Uses* (4–6). Illustrated. 1973, John Day $6.89. An exploration of the concepts behind heat, its causation, measurement, and uses. For a younger group use: *Hot as an Ice Cube* by Philip Balestrino (1971, Crowell $4.50; LB $5.95) and *Heat All Around* by Tillie S. Pine (1963, McGraw $5.72).

7551. Daub, Edward E. *Fire* (2–4). Illustrated. 1978, Raintree $5.49. Attractive color illustrations

accompany this text on characteristics and precautions involving fire.

7552. Feravolo, Rocco V. *Junior Science Book of Heat* (2–4). Illus. by Ernest Kent Barth. 1964, Garrard $3.40. Describes in very simple terms the nature and properties of heat.

7553. Simon, Seymour. *Hot and Cold* (2–4). Illus. by Joel Snyder. 1972, McGraw $5.95. A discussion of heat and cold with simple experiments young children can perform using readily available materials.

Magnetism and Electricity

7554. Asimov, Isaac. *How Did We Find Out about Electricity?* (4–6). Illus. by Matthew Kalmenoff. 1973, Walker $4.95; LB $5.85. The contributions of Volta, Faraday, and Franklin, among others, are discussed in this entertaining history.

7555. Bailey, Mark W. *Electricity* (2–4). Illustrated. 1978, Raintree $5.49. A well-organized introduction.

7556. Branley, Franklyn M. *Mickey's Magnet* (K–3). Illus. by Crockett Johns Scholastic paper $1.25. A simple account of the properties and uses of magnets.

7557. Epstein, Sam, and Epstein, Beryl. *The First Book of Electricity* (5–7). Illus. by Rod Stater. 1978, Watts $4.47. A slim volume that reveals the basics of electricity from the theoretical to practical. Also use: *Let's Find Out What Electricity Does* by Martha Shapp and Charles Shapp (1975, Watts $4.90).

7558. Feravolo, Rocco V. *Junior Science Book of Magnets* (3–5). Illus. by Evelyn Urbanowich. 1960, Garrard $3.40. The author discusses the properties and uses of various magnets and details simple experiments. For a slightly older group use: *The Boys' Book of Magnetism* by Raymond F. Yates (1959, Harper $6.89).

7559. Kirkpatrick, Rena K. *Look at Magnets* (K–2). Illustrated. 1978, Raintree $5.49. A basic introduction, suitable for browsing.

7560. Shapp, Martha. *Let's Find Out about Electricity* (2–4). Illustrated. 1975, Watts $4.90. An elementary account that outlines in simple terms the basic concepts and uses of electricity.

7561. Stone, A. Harris. *Turned On: A Look at Electricity* (5–7). 1970, Prentice-Hall $5.75. An introduction to the properties and uses of electricity. Also use: *Junior Science Book of Electricity* by Rocco V. Feravolo (1960, Garrard $3.40).

7562. Yates, Raymond F. *A Boy and a Battery* (5–7). Illustrated. 1959, Harper $6.89. Diagrams help to explain electricity and how it works.

Light and Color

7563. Adler, Irving. *Color in Your Life* (6–9). Illustrated. 1962, John Day $6.50. Physical and psychological color phenomena.

7564. Anderson, L. W. *Light and Color* (2–4). Illustrated. 1978, Raintree $5.49. Color illustrations enliven this easily read introduction.

7565. Beeler, Nelson F., and Branley, Franklyn M. *Experiments with Light* (4–6). Illus. by Anne Marie Jauss. 1958, Crowell $6.95. A simple experiment book involving light and shadow.

7566. Branley, Franklyn M. *Color: From Rainbows to Lasers* (6–9). Illustrated. 1978, Crowell $8.95. The relationships between color and light waves are clearly explained.

7567. Branley, Franklyn M. *Light and Darkness* (1–3). Illustrated. 1975, Crowell $6.29. A simply read explanation of what light is, its importance, and how it travels.

7568. Freeman, Mae, and Freeman, Ira. *Fun and Experiments with Light* (4–6). Illustrated. 1963, Random $3.95. How to make a periscope, why the pupil of the eye looks black, why the sky looks blue.

7569. Freeman, Ira. *The Science of Light and Radiation* (5–7). Illus. by George T. Resch. 1968, Random $3.50; LB $4.99. A discussion of light, how it travels, and its uses, as well as lasers are covered in this concise introduction.

7570. Gardner, Robert, and Webster, David. *Shadow Science* (3–5). Illustrated. 1976, Doubleday $5.95. A book that explores the ideas of shadows through games, puzzles, and other activities.

7571. Harrison, George R. *Lasers* (5–7). Illus. by Robert Smith. 1972, McGraw $4.47. The construction and use of masers and lasers.

7572. Huber, Frederick C. *Light: Color and Life for the World* (6–9). Illustrated. 1978, McKay $6.95. Light and its relation to life and color.

7573. Kettelkamp, Larry. *Lasers, the Miracle Light* (6–9). Illustrated. 1979, Morrow $6.95; LB $6.67. The laser—its origin and uses—is described in text and photographs.

7574. Lewis, Bruce. *What Is a Laser?* (4–5). Illustrated. 1979, Dodd $5.95. This and other related questions are answered in simple terms with accompanying cartoonlike illustrations.

7575. Mims, Forrest M. *Lasers: Incredible Light Machines* (6–8). Illustrated. 1978, McKay $6.95. The basics of this scientific tool, well presented.

7576. Ridiman, Bob. *What Is a Shadow?* (2–3). Illus. by author. 1973, Parents $5.95; LB $5.41. Simple experiments explain the nature and use of electricity, shadows, mirrors, and gravity.

7577. Ruchlis, Hy. *The Wonder of Light* (5–7). 1960, Harper $6.89. Subtitle: *A Picture Story of How and Why We See.*

7578. Schneider, Herman. *Laser Light* (6–9). Illus. by Radu Vero. 1978, McGraw $7.95. A mature account of this amazing beam of light and its uses.

7579. Schneider, Herman, and Schneider, Nina. *Science Fun with a Flashlight* (1–3). Illus. by Harriet Sherman. 1975, McGraw $6.95. Simple experiments with a flashlight that explore concepts about light, the sun, the moon, and so on.

Optical Illusions

7580. Beeler, Nelson F., and Branley, Franklyn M. *Experiments in Optical Illusion* (5–7). Illus. by Fred H. Lyon. 1951, Crowell $6.95. After explaining the composition of the eye, the author describes many fascinating experiments to prove its fallibility.

7581. Paraquin, Charles H. *Eye Teasers: Optical Illusion Puzzles* (4–6). 1976, Sterling $3.95; LB $4.39. Fun with optical illusions and explanations that are also entertaining.

7582. Simon, Seymour. *The Optical Illusion Book* (4–6). Illus. by Constance Flera. 1976, Four Winds $7.95. In addition to illustrations that show several optical illusions, there are explanations for each and a chapter on illusion in art. Also use: *Tricks of Eye and Mind: The Story of Optical Illusion* by Larry Kettelkamp (1974, Morrow $5.49).

7583. Walter, Marion. *Make a Bigger Puddle: Make a Smaller Worm* (1–3). Illus. by author. 1971, Lippincott $3.95. Activities involving the use of a mirror in ways to change the shape and composition of various illustrations.

Sound

7584. Alexenberg, Melvin L. *Sound Science* (1–3). Illus. by Tomie de Paola. 1968, Prentice-Hall paper $.95. Using everyday materials, the young experimenter can explore the wonders of science.

7585. Branley, Franklyn M. *High Sounds, Low Sounds* (1–2). Illus. by Paul Galdone. 1967, Crowell $6.95; paper $1.45. How sounds are produced and received in the ear is described simply with related activities.

7586. Knight, David C. *The First Book of Sound* (4–6). Illustrated. 1960, Watts $4.90. The nature of sound with 14 simple experiments.

7587. Kohn, Bernice. *Echoes* (2–4). Illus. by Dan Connor. 1979, Dandelion $3.50; paper $1.50. Sound and sound waves are carefully explained for a young audience.

Simple Machines

7588. Hellman, Hal. *The Lever and the Pulley* (3–5). Illus. by Lynn Sweat. 1971, Lippincott $4.95. Through clear, uncluttered diagrams and a simple text, the principles and functions of these machines are explored. Also use: *Simple Machines and How They Work* by Elizabeth Sharp (1959, Random $4.39).

7589. James, Elizabeth, and Barkin, Carol. *The Simple Facts of Simple Machines* (4–6). Illustrated. 1975, Lothrop $5.28. Six machines, including the wedge, the pulley, and the screw, are used to explain basic principles in physics.

7590. Jupo, Frank. *The Story of Things* (3–5). Illustrated. 1972, Prentice-Hall $4.75. The development of such common objects as hammers, brooms, and forks.

7591. Pine, Tillie S., and Levine, Joseph. *Simple Machines and How We Use Them* (3–5). Illustrated. 1965, McGraw $6.84. A basic introduction to such simple machines as the pulley and lever.

7592. Rockwell, Anne, and Rockwell, Harlow. *Machines* (PS–2). Illus. by Anne Rockwell and Harlow Rockwell. 1972, Macmillan $5.95. Simple machines such as levers and wheels are described with a minimum of words and watercolor pictures.

7593. Wade, Harlan. *Gears* (1–2). Illus. by Denis Wrigley. 1979, Raintree $4.49. A simple account of how gears work and their uses.

Chemistry

7594. Cherrier, Francois. *Fascinating Experiments in Chemistry* (6–8). Illustrated. 1978, Sterling $8.95. A very attractive addition to experiment books; contains both simple and advanced projects.

7595. David, Eugene. *Crystal Magic* (K–2). Illus. by Abner Graboff. 1965, Prentice-Hall paper $.95. Simple examples of what a crystal is, with clear directions for making a salt crystal garden and rock candy.

7596. Freeman, Mae, and Freeman, Ira. *Fun with Chemistry* (4–6). Illustrated. 1967, Random $4.39. A series of simple chemical experiments using materials found around the house.

7597. Freeman, Ira, and Patton, A. Rae. *The Science of Chemistry* (5–7). Illustrated. 1968, Random $3.50; LB $4.99. An overview of this field with special attention to careers in chemistry.

7598. Gans, Roma. *Millions and Millions of Crystals* (2–3). Illus. by Giulio Maestro. 1973, Crowell $6.89. The topic of crystalline structure is simply explained to the young reader, describing some familiar crystals and how groupings of atoms produce the regular structure of crystal and the varieties that many ensue.

7599. Gray, Charles. *Explorations in Chemistry* (6–8). 1965, Dutton $7.25. An introduction to the world of chemistry. Also use: *The Story of Chemistry* by Mae Freeman and Ira Freeman (1962, Random $4.99).

7600. Morgan, Alfred P. *First Chemistry Book for Boys and Girls* (5–7). Illustrated. 1977, Scribner $5.95. An introduction to this science with accompanying interesting projects and activities.

7601. Shalit, Nathan. *Cup and Saucer Chemistry* (4–6). Illus. by Charles Waterhouse. 1972, Grosset paper $2.95. A book of clear, simple experiments involving such kitchen items as food and cleaning products.

7602. Stone, Harris. *The Chemistry of a Lemon* (3–6). Illus. by Peter P. Plasencia. 1966, Prentice-Hall $5.95. Each experiment uses a lemon to demonstrate basic chemical reactions.

Astronomy

General

7603. Adler, Irving. *Dust* (5–7). Illustrated. 1958, Day $6.89. Explanations of sunlit specks to cosmic particles.

7604. Asimov, Isaac. *ABC's of Space* (3–6). Illustrated. 1970, Walker $5.95; LB $5.85. In an alphabet book format, the author supplies basic information about astronomy.

7605. Asimov, Isaac. *How Did We Find Out about Black Holes?* (5–7). Illus. by David Wool. 1978, Walker $6.95; LB $5.85. A well-researched and logically organized account.

7606. Asimov, Isaac. *To the Ends of the Universe* (6–9). 1967, Walker $6.50; LB $6.39. A stimulating history of astronomy.

7607. Berger, Melvin. *Planets, Stars and Galaxies* (4–6). Illustrated. 1978, Putnam $5.69. A well balanced, up-to-date introduction to astronomy.

7608. Ciupik, Larry A. *The Universe* (2–4). Illustrated. 1978, Raintree $5.49. Difficult-to-understand concepts are well handled in this simple account.

7609. Engdahl, Sylvia Louise. *Planet-Girded Suns: Man's View of Other Solar Systems* (6–8). Illustrated. 1974, Atheneum $7.50. A history of life in outer space, including present-day views. Also use: *A Book of Outer Space for You* by Franklyn M. Branley (1970, Crowell $8.95).

7610. Freeman, Mae, and Freeman, Ira. *The Sun, the Moon and the Stars* (2–4). Illustrated. 1979, Random $3.99. The easy first look at astronomy in a revised edition.

7611. Gallant, Roy A. *Exploring the Universe* (5–7). Illus. by Lowell Hess. 1968, Doubleday $6.95. Interesting historical information is supplied in this account that also gives up-to-date concepts about the universe. Also use: *The Universe* by Herbert S. Zim (1973, Morrow $5.09; paper $1.25).

7612. Jobb, Jamie. *The Night Sky Book: An Everyday Guide to Every Night* (5–7). Illus. by Linda Bennett. 1977, Little $7.95; paper $4.95. An informal chatty guide to astronomy. Also use: *Look to the Night Sky* by Seymour Simon (1977, Viking $6.95).

7613. Kraske, Robert. *Is There Life in Outer Space?* (5–8). Illustrated. 1976, Harcourt $6.95. A fascinating account that discusses many topics such as the UFO's, radio telescopes, and the new science of exobiology.

7614. Lauber, Patricia. *The Look-It-Up Book of Stars and Planets* (3–5). Illus. by John Polgreen. 1967, Random $4.95; LB $5.99. An alphabetically arranged book on major stars and planets.

7615. McGowen, Tom. *Album of Astronomy* (4–6). Illus. by Rod Ruth. 1979, Rand $6.95; LB $6.97. A basic introduction to the various entities found in space, from stars to black holes.

7616. Mayall, Newton, and et al. *The Sky Observer's Guide: A Handbook for Amateur Astronomers* (6–8). Illus. by John Polgreen. 1965, Western $1.95. A guide to stars and their placement in each of the seasons.

7617. Maynard, Christopher. *The Young Scientist Book of Stars and Planets* (4–7). Illustrated. 1978, EMC $5.95. Attractive illustrations and plentiful experiments and projects add to this book's appeal.

7618. Mitton, Jacqueline, and Mitton, Simon. *Concise Book of Astronomy* (6–8). Illustrated. 1979, Prentice-Hall $12.95. A fine introduction to a basic concept of astronomy with many diagrams.

7619. Rey, H. A. *Find the Constellations* (5–7). Illustrated. 1976, Houghton $7.95; paper $4.95. Through clear text and illustrations, the reader is helped to recognize stars and constellations in the northern United States. Also use: *The Stars: A New Way to See Them* (1967, Houghton $6.99).

7620. Seevers, James A. *Space* (2–4). Illustrated. 1978, Raintree $5.49. Clear descriptions and color illustrations help this simply read introduction.

7621. Simon, Seymour. *The Long View into Space* (3–5). Illustrated. 1979, Crown $7.95. A well-organized introduction to the universe, nicely illustrated with photographs.

7622. Stilley, Frank. *The Search: Our Quest for Intelligent Life in Outer Space* (6–9). 1977, Putnam $6.95. Current research findings and the speculation they produce are well presented.

7623. Wicks, Keith. *Stars and Planets* (5–7). Illustrated. 1977, Watts $5.90. From Babylon to space science, this is a fine history of astronomy.

Stars

7624. Adler, Irving. *The Stars: Decoding Their Messages* (6–8). Illustrated. 1980, Crowell $7.89. This authoritative account discusses the properties and behavior of stars.

7625. Asimov, Isaac. *Galaxies* (1–3). Illustrated. 1968, Follett $2.50; LB $2.97. A well-illustrated simple introduction to the Milky Way galaxy. Also use: *A Book of the Milky Way for You* by Franklyn M. Branley (1965, Crowell $7.95).

7626. Branley, Franklyn M. *The Big Dipper* (K–2). Illus. by Ed Emberley. 1962, Crowell $6.89. An introduction to the composition, mythology, and location of the Big and Little Dippers.

7627. Fisher, David E. *The Creation of Atoms and Stars* (6–9). Illustrated. 1979, Holt $7.95. An up-to-date account of stellar evolution.

7628. Gallant, Roy A. *The Constellations: How They Came to Be* (5–8). Illustrated. 1979, Four Winds $11.95. Mythology and fact are combined in this guide to 44 northern hemisphere constellations. Also use: *What's in the Name of Stars and Constellations* by Peter R. Limburg (1976, Coward $5.49).

7629. Gallant, Roy A. *Fires in the Skies: The Birth and Death of Stars* (5–9). Illustrated. 1978, Four Winds $7.95. A simple account of the history of our knowledge about stars and their life history.

7630. Knight, David C. *Galaxies, Islands in Space* (5–7). Illustrated. 1979, Morrow $5.95. Good information on the formation and functions of galaxies.

7631. Moore, Patrick, and Hardy, David. *New Challenge of the Stars* (6–9). Illustrated. 1978, Rand $9.95. An up-to-date report on recent findings.

7632. Polgreen, John, and Polgreen, Cathleen. *The Stars Tonight* (5–9). 1967, Harper $6.89. Instructions for locating constellations together with legends to aid in remembering them and detailed star charts. Also use: *The Stars by Clock and Fist* by Henry M. Neely (1972, Viking $5.95).

7633. Simon, Seymour. *Look to the Night Sky: An Introduction to Star Watching* (4–6). Illustrated. 1977, Viking $6.95. Directions on how to identify constellations with the naked eye, as well as material on binoculars and simple telescopes.

7634. Zim, Herbert S., and Baker, Robert H. *Stars* (5–8). Illus. by James Gordon Irving. 1956, Golden $5.95; paper $1.95. Subtitle: *A Guide to the Constellations, Sun, Moon, Planets and Other Features of the Heavens.* Also use: *A Book of Stars for You* by Franklyn M. Branley (1967, Crowell $8.95).

Solar System

7635. Asimov, Isaac. *How Did We Find Out about Comets?* (5–7). Illustrated. 1975, Walker $4.95; LB $5.85. The history of comets, their nature, and their effects on people are covered in this overview. Also use: *Comets, Meteoroids and Asteroids: Mavericks of the Solar System* by Franklyn M. Branley (1974, Crowell $7.95).

7636. Asimov, Isaac. *The Solar System* (4–6). Illus. by David Cunningham. 1975, Follett $2.50; LB $2.97. An introduction to the 9 planets with suggested activities to amplify the text. Also use:

Exploring and Understanding Our Solar System by Dan Q. Posin (1968, Benefic $4.20).

7637. Fodor, R. V. *Meteorites: Stones from the Sky* (4–6). Illustrated. 1976, Dodd $4.25. The types, sizes, and shapes of meteorites are discussed, as well as the effects of their fall to earth.

7638. Gardner, Martin. *Space Puzzles* (6–8). Illustrated. 1971, Simon & Schuster $4.95; LB $5.70. Subtitle: *Curious Questions and Answers about the Solar System.*

7639. Knight, David C. *The Thirty-Two Moons: The Natural Satellites of Our Solar System* (5–7). Illustrated. 1974, Morrow $6.00. This account not only supplies information on the moons of the solar system, but also gives details about the planets they circle.

7640. Nourse, Alan E. *The Asteroids* (5–7). Illustrated. 1975, Watts $4.90. An accurate account of the discovery, possible origin, and contemporary beliefs about asteroids and their place in the solar system. Also use: *The Tiny Planets: Asteroids of Our Solar System* by David C. Knight (1973, Morrow $6.00).

7641. Zim, Herbert S. *Comets* (4–6). Illus. by Gustav Schrotter. 1957, Morrow $5.52. Comets—their size, composition, and orbits—are explored in simple text and illustrations.

7642. Zim, Herbert S. *Shooting Stars* (4–7). Illus. by Gustav Schrotter. 1958, Morrow $5.75. The origins, effects, and properties of these celestial phenomena.

Sun

7643. Allison, Linda. *The Reasons for Seasons* (5–7). Illustrated. 1975, Little $7.95; paper $4.95. A project-experiment book that also contains fascinating information about the 4 seasons.

7644. Asimov, Isaac. *What Makes the Sun Shine?* (4–6). Illus. by Marc Brown. 1971, Little $5.95. In addition to an explanation of the sun and the nature of its energy, this book outlines simple experiments to explore the solar system. Also use: *The Sun* by Herbert S. Zim (1975, Morrow $2.50; LB $2.91).

7645. Branley, Franklyn M. *Eclipse: Darkness in Daytime* (2–4). Illus. by Donald Crews. 1973, Crowell $6.89. A clear explanation of the total solar eclipse phenomenon, as well as the effects of the eclipse on animals and people in ancient times.

7646. Branley, Franklyn M. *The Sun: Our Nearest Star* (1–3). Illus. by Helen Borten. 1962, Crowell

$6.89. An easily read book about the sun and its importance in our lives. Also use: *Let's Find Out about the Sun* by Martha Shapp (1975, Watts $4.90).

7647. Branley, Franklyn M. *Sunshine Makes the Seasons* (3–4). Illus. by Shelley Freshman. 1974, Crowell $6.89. A very simple account that explains the seasons by exploring the relationship of the sun to the earth and its orbit. Also use: *Sunlight and Shadow* by John Polgreen (1967, Doubleday $5.95).

7648. Shapp, Martha, and Shapp, Charles. *Let's Find Out about Spring* (1–3). Illus. by Laszlo Roth. 1963, Watts $4.90. A beginning book that explores the reasons for and characteristics of this season. Also use (both 1963, Watts $4.47): *Let's Find Out about Winter* and *Let's Find Out about Fall*. For an older group use: *The Golden Circle: A Book of Months* by Hal Borland (5–8). Illus. by Ophelia Dawson. (1977, Crowell $8.95).

Planets

7649. Asimov, Isaac. *Jupiter: The Largest Planet* (6–8). Illustrated. 1976, Lothrop $7.50. A well-organized account that gives a capsule report on what was once believed, and is now known, about this planet and its satellites.

7650. Asimov, Isaac. *Mars: The Red Planet* (6–9). Illustrated. 1977, Lothrop $8.25. A well-researched account for the better reader.

7651. Asimov, Isaac. *Saturn and Beyond* (6–9). Illustrated. 1979, Lothrop $7.95. A general discussion of the planets and their moons.

7652. Branley, Franklyn M. *A Book of Planets for You* (1–3). 1961, Crowell $8.79. A basic introduction to the 9 planets of the solar system.

7653. Branley, Franklyn M. *A Book of Venus for You* (3–5). Illustrated. 1969, Crowell $8. A fresh look at our neighboring planet.

7654. Branley, Franklyn M. *The Nine Planets* (6–8). Illus. by Helmut K. Wimmer. 1978, Crowell $8.95. A clearly written and well-organized description of the planets in our solar system and the mythology that surrounds them. Also use: *The Giant Planets* by Alan E. Nourse (1974, Watts $4.90).

7655. Gallant, Roy A. *Exploring Mars* (4–8). Illus. by Lowell Hess. 1968, Doubleday $4.95. Lively and colorful accounts of what humans have discovered in the world of space.

7656. Gallant, Roy A. *Exploring the Planets* (4–6). Illustrated. 1967, Doubleday $6.95. A well-illustrated introduction to the planets.

7657. Knight, David C. *The First Book of Mars: An Introduction to the Red Planet* (4–6). Illustrated. 1973, Watts $4.90. Mars, in fact and fiction, including the Mariner flights. For a younger group use: *A Book of Mars for You* by Franklyn M. Branley (1968, Crowell $6.95; LB $7.95).

7658. Moche, Dinah L. *Mars* (3–5). Illustrated. 1978, Watts $4.90. An easily read description of this planet and its relationship to our earth.

7659. Shurkin, Joel N. *Jupiter—the Star That Failed* (6–9). Illustrated. 1979, Westminster $7.95. An historical account that begins in ancient Egypt and ends with the launching of the Voyagers in 1977.

Earth

7660. Branley, Franklyn M. *A Book of Planet Earth for You* (3–5). Illus. by Leonard Kessler. 1975, Crowell $8.79. A description of the size, composition, and motion of the earth as it might be observed from another planet.

7661. Branley, Franklyn M. *The End of the World* (5–9). Illus. by David Palladini. 1974, Crowell $8.79. A revealing account of the causes and the eventual death of our planet billions of years from now.

7662. Branley, Franklyn M. *North, South, East, West* (1–3). Illus. by Robert Galster. 1966, Crowell $6.89. The author gives a basic introduction to directions, the position of the sun, and the compass.

7663. Branley, Franklyn M. *What Makes Day and Night* (K–3). Illus. by Helen Borten. 1961, Crowell $6.89; paper $2.95. A book for beginning readers explains how the earth's rotation causes day and night.

7664. Knight, David C. *Let's Find Out about Earth* (2–4). Illustrated. 1975, Watts $4.90. An introduction to the characteristics of our planet with material on its atmosphere and seasons.

7665. Lambert, David. *The Earth and Space* (5–8). Illustrated. 1979, Watts $7.90. An introduction to the earth, its surface, and to basic concepts of astronomy.

7666. Schwartz, Julius. *Earthwatch: Space-Time Investigations with a Globe* (6–8). Illus. by Radu Vero. 1977, McGraw $6.84. A group of experiments about the earth that can be accomplished by examination of common phenomena.

Moon

7667. Asimov, Isaac. *The Moon* (2–4). Illus. by Alex Ebel. 1966, Follett $3.59. A very simple introduction to the moon.

7668. Bergaust, Erik. *The Next 50 Years on the Moon* (5–7). Illustrated. 1974, Putnam $5.49. The probable development of moon exploration and study.

7669. Branley, Franklyn M. *A Book of Moon Rockets for You* (1–3). Illustrated. 1970, Crowell $8.79. Simple explanation of what moon rockets are and how they were used to help us understand the moon.

7670. Branley, Franklyn M. *The Moon: Earth's Natural Satellite* (6–9). Illus. by Helmut K. Wimmer. 1972, Crowell $6.95. A simple introduction about the composition of the moon. For a younger group use: *What the Moon Is Like* (1963, Crowell $4.50; LB $5.95).

7671. Branley, Franklyn M. *Pieces of Another World: The Story of Moon Rocks* (5–8). Illus. by Herbert Danska. 1972, Crowell $8.79. A description of how the crew of Apollo II gathered soil and rock specimens from the moon and a discussion of their composition and significance. Also use: *Apollo Moon Rocks* by Marcus Langseth (1972, Coward $4.64).

7672. Shuttlesworth, Dorothy E., and Williams, Lee Ann. *Moon: The Steppingstone to Outer Space* (4–7). Illustrated. 1977, Doubleday $5.95. A book that incorporates latest evidence about the moon's composition and value. For a younger group use: *Let's Find Out about the Moon* by Martha Shapp (1975, Watts $4.90).

Earth and Geology

7673. Ames, Gerald, and Wyler, Rose. *The Earth's Story* (5–7). Illus. by Cornelius De Witt. 1967, Creative Education $6.95. An introduction to earth's history with special coverage on its natural and mineral resources. Also use: *Earth through the Ages* by Philip B. Carona (1968, Follett $2.97).

7674. Anderson, Alan H. *The Drifting Continents* (6–9). Illustrated. 1971, Putnam $5.49. A thorough explanation of the theory of continental drift plus a history of those drifts responsible for continent formation and a discussion of future applications.

7675. Asimov, Isaac. *ABC's of the Earth* (3–5). Illustrated. 1971, Walker $5.95; LB $5.85. An introduction to earth science in ABC fashion with 2 terms defined and illustrated by photographs for each letter. Also use: *Your Changing Earth* by Hy Ruchlis (1963, Harvey House $5.09).

7676. Asimov, Isaac. *How Did We Find Out the Earth Is Round?* (4–6). Illus. by Matthew Kalmenoff. 1972, Walker $6.85. Early theories of the shape and structure of the earth are discussed, ending with the proof supplied by the explorations of Columbus and Magellan.

7677. Branley, Franklyn M. *The Beginning of the Earth* (2–4). Illus. by Giulio Maestro. 1972, Crowell $6.95. The evolution of the earth told succinctly and directly.

7678. Branley, Franklyn M. *Shakes, Quakes and Shifts: Earth Tectonics* (5–9). Illus. by Daniel Maffia. 1974, Crowell $8.95. An informative, clear explanation of the theory of plate tectonics, of how earth movements occur, and the theory's status today.

7679. Burton, Virginia L. *Life Story* (3–5). Illus. by author. 1962, Houghton $8.95; paper $2.95. A work about the changes that have taken place on the earth and in its flora and fauna, from the beginning of time until the present.

7680. Fodor, R. V. *Earth in Motion: The Concept of Plate Tectonics* (5–8). Illustrated. 1978, Morrow $5.95. A difficult subject introduced with clarity and accuracy.

7681. Kiefer, Irene. *Global Jigsaw Puzzle: The Story of Continental Drift* (6–8). Illus. by Barbara Levine. 1978, Atheneum $6.95. A basic knowledge of the subject is presupposed in this account that concentrates on theoretical aspects.

7682. Lauber, Patricia. *Tapping Earth's Heat* (3–5). Illustrated. 1978, Garrard $4.74. Present and possible uses for the earth's tremendous internal heat.

7683. McNulty, Faith. *How to Dig a Hole to the Other Side of the World* (2–4). Illus. by Marc Simont. 1979, Harper $6.95; LB $6.89. A journey to the center of the earth.

7684. Matthews, William H. *The Earth's Crust* (5–7). Illustrated. 1971, Watts $4.48. A history of the earth's crust, formation, and resources.

7685. Matthews, William H. *The Story of the Earth* (6–9). 1968, Harvey House $6.29. An introduction to the history of our earth.

7686. Waters, John F. *The Continental Shelves* (6–9). Illustrated. 1975, Abelard $7.95. This well-organized, useful account describes the present position and composition of continental shelves and how they were formed. Also use: *Underwater*

Continent: The Continental Shelves by Christie McFall (1975, Dodd $5.95).

7687. Wyckoff, Jerome. *The Story of Geology: Our Changing Earth through the Ages* (5–7). Illustrated. 1976, Golden $7.95; LB $8.95. The history, composition, and uses of the earth's crust are well presented in this survey volume.

7688. Zim, Herbert S. *What's Inside the Earth?* (4–7). Illus. by Raymond Perlman. 1953, Morrow $6.00. Much information about wells, caves, mines, earthquakes, and mountains.

Space Exploration

7689. Asimov, Isacc. *Environments Out There* (5–7). Illustrated. 1967, Abelard $6.95. A discussion of known facts about planets and the possibility of life on them. Also use: Norman F. Smith's *Space: What's Out There?* (1976, Coward $5.29).

7690. Bendick, Jeanne. *Space Travel* (3–4). Illustrated. 1969, Watts $4.90. An introduction that answers basic questions.

7691. Bergaust, Erik. *Colonizing Space* (6–8). Illustrated. 1978, Putnam $4.95. What space colonies will look like and how people will live in them are discussed.

7692. Bergaust, Erik. *Colonizing the Planets* (6–8). Illustrated. 1975, Putnam $4.96. Subtitle: *The Factual Story of Manned Interplanetary Flight into the 21st Century.*

7693. Branley, Franklyn M. *A Book of Satellites for You* (3–5). Illus. by Leonard Kessler. 1971, Crowell $8.79. Such satellites as Explorer, Sputnik, and Vanguard are introduced. Also use: *Satellites in Outer Space* by Isaac Asimov (1966, Random $4.39).

7694. Branley, Franklyn M. *Columbia and Beyond: The Story of the Space Shuttle* (5–8). Illustrated. 1979, Collins $12.95. The present status of space shuttle projects and possible future developments.

7695. Branley, Franklyn M. *Rockets and Satellites* (1–3). Illus. by Al Nagy. 1970, Crowell $6.95. A very short, simple introduction enhanced by excellent illustrations.

7696. Cipriano, Anthony J. *America's Journeys into Space: The Astronauts of the United States* (6–9). 1979, Messner $8.29. An introduction to the astronauts and their accomplishments.

7697. Ciupik, Larry H., and Seevers, James A. *Space Machines* (2–4). Illustrated. 1979, Raintree $5.99. A simple introduction to all kinds of space vehicles.

7698. Clarke, Arthur C., and Silverberg, Robert. *Into Space: A Young Person's Guide to Space* (5–7). Illustrated. 1971, Harper $3.95; LB $5.79. A step-by-step account from rockets through manned space flight to the landing on the moon.

7699. Collins, Michael. *Flying to the Moon and Other Strange Places* (6–7). Illustrated. 1976, Farrar $6.95. A first-person account of taking part in a manned space flight.

7700. Coombs, Charles. *Passage to Space: The Shuttle Transportation* (4–6). Illustrated. 1979, Morrow $6.95. A glimpse of tomorrow's network for space exploration and use.

7701. Cromie, William J. *Skylab: The Story of Man's First Station in Space* (6–9). Illustrated. 1977, McKay $9.95. An authoritative, direct account of the 3 space missions that involved teams of astronauts living in an orbiting laboratory. Also use: *Spacetrack: Watchdog of the Skies* by Charles Coombs (1969, Morrow $6.01) and *Workshops in Space* by Ben Bova (1974, Dutton $6.01).

7702. Couper, Heather, and Henbest, Nigel. *Space Frontiers* (2–7). Illustrated. 1978, Viking $5.95. Plenty of illustrations and fine background information, simply stated.

7703. Elting, Mary. *Spacecraft at Work* (3–5). Illus. by Ursula Koering. 1966, Harvey House $5.39. Project Apollo, the American and Russian satellites, space probes, and plans for future space stations and moon bases. Also use: *Man in Space to the Moon* by Franklyn M. Branley (1970, Crowell $4.95).

7704. Freeman, Mae. *Space Base* (3–5). 1972, Watts $4.90. An introduction to space stations and the technology they involve.

7705. Fuchs, Erich. *Journey to the Moon* (K–3). Illus. by author. 1970, Delacorte $5.95; LB $5.47. Picture book version of the Apollo II mission. Absence of text makes it possible for young astronauts to supply their own commentary. Also use: *Let's Go to the Moon* by Michael Chester (1974, Putnam $3.86).

7706. Gatland, Kenneth. *The Young Scientist Book of Spacecraft* (4–7). Illustrated. 1978, EMC $5.95. A nicely illustrated introduction with several interesting projects.

7707. Gemme, Leila Boyle. *The True Book of Spinoffs from Space* (2–4). Illustrated. 1977, Childrens Press $7.35. A description of the unusual benefits we have reaped (such as nonflammable clothes) from the space program.

7708. Gemme, Leila Boyle. *The True Book of the Mars Landing* (2–5). Illustrated. 1977, Childrens Press $4.95. A description of the planet and the attempts that culminated in the 1976 landing.

7709. Goodwin, Harold L. *All about Rockets and Space Flight* (6–8). Illus. by John Polgreen. 1970, Random $4.39. The history and technology of rockets, earth and sun satellite mechanics, and space exploration.

7710. Gurney, Gene. *Americans to the Moon: The Story of Project Apollo* (5–6). 1970, Random $4.95; LB $5.99. Project Apollo, from the planning stages to the second moonwalk mission, including the successes and failures along the way.

7711. Gurney, Gene, and Gurney, Clare. *The Launching of Sputnik, October 4, 1957: The Space Age Begins* (5–8). Illustrated. 1975, Watts $4.90. A history of early rockets and their structure precedes this account of the launching that opened up space exploration.

7712. Gurney, Gene. *Walk in Space: The Story of Project Gemini* (6–9). Illustrated. 1967, Random $4.39. A summary of the objectives, activities, and accomplishments of the project and its relation to the Apollo program. Also use: *Gemini: A Personal Account of Man's Venture into Space* by Virgil Grissom (1968, Macmillan $5.95).

7713. Kerrod, Robin. *See Inside a Space Station* (6–8). Illustrated. 1979, Watts $6.90. A slim overview with emphasis on cutaway illustrations.

7714. Kohn, Bernice. *Communications Satellites: Message Centers in Space* (4–6). Illus. by Jerome Kuhl. 1975, Four Winds $5.95. Telstar and other satellites are described and interesting background information is furnished on the past and future of this development.

7715. Moche, Dinah L. *The Astronauts* (1–3). Illustrated. 1979, Random $3.99. A description of various spacecraft and how astronauts are trained to use them.

7716. Moche, Dinah L. *Search for Life Beyond Earth* (6–9). Illustrated. 1978, Watts $4.90. A look at how life started on earth, how it might exist elsewhere, and how we can try to find it.

7717. Moche, Dinah L. *Star Wars Question and Answer Book about Space* (3–6). Illus. by David Kawami. 1979, Random $4.95; LB $5.95. Basic questions about space and space travel are answered in this attractive book.

7718. Rosenfeld, Sam. *Science Experiments for the Space Age* (5–7). Illustrated. 1972, Harvey House $6.72. Clear directions are supplied for experiments dealing with space technology, using inexpensive materials. Also use: *Experiments in the Prin-*

ciples of Space Travel by Franklyn M. Branley (1973, Crowell $6.95).

7719. Ross, Frank. *Model Satellites and Spacecraft: Their Stories and How to Make Them* (6–8). Illus. by author. 1969, Lothrop $6.48. A project book for the outer space enthusiasts.

7720. Ross, Frank. *The Space Shuttle: Its Story and How to Make Flying Paper Models* (6–9). Illustrated. 1979, Lothrop $6.50; LB $6.24. A mature account that is quite technical in approach.

7721. Sasek, M. *This Is Cape Kennedy* (2–5). Illus. by author. 1964, Macmillan $5.95. Pictorial treatment of the space center, its rockets, and equipment.

7722. Simon, Seymour. *Science at Work: Projects in Space Science* (4–7). Illus. by Lynn Sweat. 1971, Watts $4.90. A simple presentation of 30 projects that demonstrate concepts related to space travel.

7723. Stine, George Harry. *Shuttle into Space: A Ride in America's Space Transportation System* (5–9). LB $8.97 1978, Follett paper $4.95. A description of an imaginary ride on a space shuttle in the future.

7724. Taylor, L. B. *Space Shuttle* (5–9). Illustrated. 1979, Crowell $7.95. An account that stresses the construction of space shuttles and the many benefits we will derive from them.

Physical Geography

7725. Atwood, Ann. *The Wild Young Desert* (6–9). Illustrated. 1970, Scribner $5.95. The desert landscape, the effects of weather, and reactions of plants and wildlife, depicted through color photographs and poetic text.

7726. Batten, Mary. *The Tropical Forest* (5–7). Illustrated. 1973, Crowell $9.95. The author describes the characteristics of tropical forests and the relationship between the animals and plants that grow there. Also use: *Tropical Rain Forests* by Delia Goetz (1957, Morrow $5.52).

7727. Berger, Gilda. *Mountain Worlds: What Lives There* (2–4). Illus. by Stefen Bernath. 1978, Coward $5.89. An interesting description of the flora and fauna of mountainous regions.

7728. Borten, Helen. *The Jungle* (3–5). 1968, Harcourt $5.75. A vivid description of the flora and fauna found in a typically tropical land. Also use: *All about the Jungle* by Armstrong Sperry (1959, Random $4.39).

7729. Bronin, Andrew. *The Cave: What Lives There* (2–4). Illus. by Ben Stahl. 1972, Coward $4.99. Black-and-white pictures and a simple text effectively describe the way caves are formed and the animal life that lives there. Also use: *First Book of Caves* by Elizabeth Hamilton (1956, Watts $4.90).

7730. Buck, Margaret Waring. *In Ponds and Streams* (4–6). 1955, Abingdon $3.95. A description of the sights and sounds of a pond and its inhabitants.

7731. Carrick, Carol, and Carrick, Donald. *The Pond* (K–2). Illustrated. 1970, Macmillan $5.95. A simple description of pond wildlife from dawn to dusk. Also use: *The Brook* (1967, Macmillan $4.95).

7732. Coburn, Doris K. *A Spit Is a Piece of Land: Landforms in the U.S.A.* (4–6). Illustrated. 1978, Messner $7.79. Various land forms are discussed with information on their formation and physical characteristics.

7733. Epstein, Sam, and Epstein, Beryl. *All about the Desert* (4–6). Illus. by Fritz Kredel. 1957, Random $4.39. Maps and charts of the world's deserts. Also use: *The First Book of Deserts* by David C. Knight (1964, Watts $4.90).

7734. Freschet, Berniece. *A Year on Muskrat Marsh* (3–5). Illus. by Peter Parnall. 1974, Scribner $6.95. A year in the animal and plant life found in a Minnesota marshland. Also use: *Marshes and Marsh Life* by Arnold Dobrin (1969, Coward $5.99).

7735. Gans, Roma. *Caves* (2–4). Illus. by Giulio Maestro. 1977, Crowell $6.89. How caves are formed, their varying sizes, some of their peculiar features, and the lure of cave exploration are simply and directly explained in a book for the young reader

7736. Goetz, Delia. *Deserts* (3–7). Illus. by Louis Darling. 1956, Morrow $5.52. A simple introduction that discusses the origin of deserts and the life-styles of those who live there.

7737. Goetz, Delia. *Lakes* (3–5). Illus. by Lydia Rosier. 1973, Morrow $5.25. How lakes are formed, how they change, and the kinds of life they support, told in simple, clear prose.

7738. Goetz, Delia. *Valleys* (3–5). Illustrated. 1976, Morrow $5.25. Concepts about the formation and importance of valleys are explored through examples in the United States. Also use for an older audience: *Secrets of Redding Glen: The Natural History of a Wooded Valley* by Jo Polseno (1973, Golden $5.95).

7739. Goetz, Delia. *Mountains* (3–6). Illustrated. 1962, Morrow $5.52. A discussion of the creation of the world's most important mountains and how they have affected the history of the human race.

7740. Jaspersohn, William. *How the Forest Grew* (1–3). Illus. by Chuck Eckart. 1980, Greenwillow $5.95; LB $5.71. A simple account of how a farm field is changed into a dense forest.

7741. Kirkpatrick, Rena K. *Look at Pond Life* (K–2). Illustrated. 1978, Raintree $5.49. An introduction to the subject through brief text and many illustrations. Also use: *Pond Life* by George K. Reid (1967, Golden $5.50; paper $1.95).

7742. Laycock, George. *Exploring the Great Swamp* (4–6). Illustrated. 1978, McKay $6.95. A general discussion of swamps in general and several of America's most famous ones in particular.

7743. Laycock, George. *Caves* (5–7). Illustrated. 1976, Four Winds $6.95. How caves are formed and what life one can expect to find when exploring them is well presented.

7744. Lerner, Carol. *On the Forest Edge* (2–3). Illustrated. 1978, Morrow $5.95. An exploration of both plant and animal life found where forest and field meet.

7745. List, Albert, and List, Ilka. *A Walk in the Forest: The Woodlands of North America* (5–9). Illus. by Albert List and Ilka List. 1977, Crowell $9.95. A survey of life in forests complete with activities, many pictures in question-and-answer format. Also use: *Kingdom of the Forest* by Ann Atwood (1972, Scribner $1.49).

7746. Naden, Corinne J. *Grasslands Around the World* (4–6). 1970, Watts $4.90. A description of various types of grasslands, and their flora and fauna.

7747. Newton, James R. *Forest Log* (4–6). Illus. by Irene Brady. 1980, Crowell $6.95; LB $6.89. A narrative that explains how a dead Douglas fir continues to support life.

7748. Norden, Carroll R. *Deserts* (2–4). Illustrated. 1978, Raintree $5.49. An introduction to the climate, plants, and animals involved with desert life.

7749. Norden, Carroll R. *The Jungle* (2–4). Illustrated. 1978, Raintree $5.49. Tropical rain forests and their inhabitants are presented clearly with good illustrations.

7750. Pope, Joyce. *A Closer Look at Jungles* (4–7). Illustrated. 1978, Watts $5.90. A brief narrative that explores jungle life from forest floor to the skies.

7751. Pringle, Laurence. *Estuaries—Where Rivers Meet the Sea* (3–5). Illustrated. 1973, Macmillan $4.95. A thorough description of the unique nature of the estuary land formation and of the life that thrives in this environment. Also use with a younger group: *Let's Find Out about Rivers* by Eleanor Weisenthal (1971, Watts $4.90).

7752. Pringle, Laurence. *The Gentle Desert* (4–6). Illustrated. 1977, Macmillan $6.95. The flora and fauna of the desert and their adjustments to a hostile environment are introduced in this survey volume. For younger groups, use: *Desert Life* by Ruth Kirk (1976, Nat. Hist. Pr. $4.95).

7753. Pringle, Laurence. *Into the Woods: Exploring the Forest Ecosystem* (4–6). Illustrated. 1973, Macmillan $4.95. From the layers on the forest floor to the highest leaf structures, the author explores the forest, its life and the need for conservation of its resources.

7754. Pringle, Laurence. *This Is a River: Exploring an Ecosystem* (4–6). 1972, Macmillan $4.95. A discussion of the interdependence of humans, animals, and plants around and in a river. Also use: *Rivers* by Delia Goetz (1969, Morrow $5.09).

7755. Samson, John G. *The Pond: The Life of the Aquatic Plants, Insects, Fish, Amphibians, Reptiles, Mammals and Birds That Inhabit the Pond and Its Surf, Hillside and Swamp* (6–9). Illustrated. 1979, Knopf $7.95. The story of all the activities in a pond.

7756. Selsam, Millicent E. *Birth of a Forest* (4–6). Illus. by Barbara Wolff. 1964, Harper $6.89. How a lake changes into a forest over thousands of years. Also use: *See through the Forest* (1956, Harper $3.79).

7757. Selsam, Millicent E. *Birth of an Island* (3–5). 1959, Harper $6.89. The evolution of a rocky mass that emerged from an undersea volcanic eruption to become a productive land.

7758. Smith, Frances. *First Book of Swamps and Marshes* (4–6). Illustrated. 1969, Watts $4.90. An overview of swamps and marshes that concentrate on uses and productivity. Also use: *Swamp Spring* by Carol Carrick (1974, Coward $4.95).

7759. Tresselt, Alvin. *The Beaver Pond* (1–3). Illus. by Roger Duvoisin. 1970, Lothrop $6.95; LB $6.43. The tremendous variety of life in a pond is presented in very simple text and lovely pictures. Also use: *Tale of a Pond* by Henry B. Kane (1960, Knopf $3.50; LB $5.39).

7760. White, Anne Terry. *All about Great Rivers of the World* (4–6). 1957, Random $4.39. An introduction to the most important rivers in the world and the life they sustain.

7761. White, Anne Terry. *All about Mountains* (5–7). Illustrated. 1962, Random $2.95; LB $4.39. Broad coverage of the subject along with techniques of mountaineering and stories of famous climbers. For a slightly older group use: *The Mountains* by Lorus J. Milne (1962, Time-Life $11.56).

7762. Wong, Herbert H., and Vessel, Matthew F. *Pond Life: Watching Animals Find Food* (2–4). Illustrated. 1970, Addison $6.95. Basic ecological concepts in picture book format. Also use: *Pond Life: Watching Animals Grow Up* (1970, Addison $6.95).

7763. Zim, Herbert. *Caves and Life* (3–5). Illus. by Richard Cuffari. 1978, Morrow $5.95; LB $5.71. The formation of caves and the life that they house.

Rocks, Minerals, and Soil

7764. Cartwright, Sally. *Sand* (K–2). Illus. by Don Madden. 1975, Coward $4.97. An explanation of how sand is formed and what it is used for.

7765. Cormack, M. B. *The First Book of Stones* (5–7). Illus. by M. K. Scott. 1950, Watts $4.90. A simple introduction that helps a young collector identify and organize a beginning rock collection. Also use: *The Wonders of Stones* by Christie McFall (1970, Dodd $4.50).

7766. Fenton, Carroll Lane, and Adams, Mildred. *Rocks and Their Stories* (4–6). Illustrated. 1951, Doubleday $5.95. A brief but expert account that, among other information, discusses 40 different minerals.

7767. Gallob, Edward. *City Rocks, City Blocks, and the Moon* (3–5). Photos by author. 1973, Scribner $6.95. Excellent photographs and a clear text show how city blocks can make an inviting treasure hunt for a beginning geologist.

7768. Heady, Eleanor B. *The Soil That Feeds Us* (1–3). Illustrated. 1972, Parents $5.41. A description of the origins and nature of soil and its relation to growing things. Also use: *Soil, A Field Trip Guide* by Helen Ross Russel (1972, Little $4.95).

7769. Keen, Martin L. *The World Beneath Our Feet: The Story of Soil* (4–6). Illustrated. 1974, Messner $6.64. The origin and composition of soil, and an exploration of plant and animal life in the earth.

7770. Kerrod, Robin. *Rocks and Minerals* (6–8). Illustrated. 1978, Watts $5.90. A thin volume, but well packed with useful information of a basic nature.

7771. Pearl, Richard M. *Wonders of Rocks and Minerals* (5–7). Illustrated. 1961, Dodd $4.95. This book highlights unusual rocks such as fossils and meteorites. Also use: *Minerals* by Herbert S. Zim (1943, Harcourt $6.95).

7772. Pough, Frederick H. *A Field Guide to Rocks and Minerals* (5–7). 1960, Houghton $6.95. A guide to the identification of various specimens.

7773. Ruchlis, Hy. *How a Rock Came to Be in a Fence on a Road Near a Town* (2–4). Illus. by Mamoru Funai. 1974, Walker $4.50. A simple explanation of how a rock formed millions of years ago finally landed in a farmer's field.

7774. Shuttlesworth, Dorothy E. *The Story of Rocks* (5–7). Illustrated. 1956, Doubleday $5.95. After discussing how rocks are formed and how to identify them, the author covers some unusual rocks and minerals.

7775. Simon, Seymour. *Beneath Your Feet* (2–4). Illus. by Daniel Nevins. 1977, Walker $5.95; LB $5.85. A description of different types of soil, how rocks and other matter became soil, and the ways in which animals and plants use and improve soil.

7776. Wyler, Rose, and Ames, Gerald. *Secrets in Stones* (2–5). Illustrated. 1971, Four Winds $5.95; LB $5.62; paper $.95. Introduction to stones and rocks, simple experiments for growing crystals and testing stone content.

7777. Zim, Herbert S. *Diamonds* (5–7). Illustrated. 1959, Morrow $5.09. The formation of diamonds, their properties, and uses.

Earthquakes and Volcanoes

7778. Asimov, Isaac. *How Did We Find Out about Earthquakes?* (4–5). Illustrated. 1978, Messner $6.97. An introductory survey that begins with the Lisbon quake of 1755 and ends at the present.

7779. Aylesworth, Thomas G. *Geological Disasters: Earthquakes and Volcanoes* (6–8). Illustrated. 1979, Watts $5.45. Major quakes and volcanoes are discussed, plus plate tectonics and prediction methods.

7780. Brown, Billye, and Brown, Walter B. *Historical Catastrophes: Earthquakes* (5–8). Illustrated. 1974, Childrens Press $7.95. From the Lisbon quake of 1755 to Alaska's 1964 disaster.

7781. Harris, Susan. *Volcanoes* (2–4). Illustrated. 1979, Watts $5.90. A complex subject nicely simplified with accompanying fine color photographs. Also use: *Volcanoes and Earthquakes* by Robert Irving (1962, Knopf $5.37).

7782. Lauber, Patricia. *This Restless Earth* (4–7). Illus. by John Polgreen. 1970, Random $4.99. A review of how the earth changes, through a discussion of such phenomena as earthquakes and volcanoes. Also use: *When Nature Runs Wild* by Thomas P. Johnson (1968, Creative Education $5.95).

7783. Matthews, William H. *The Story of Volcanoes and Earthquakes* (4–6). Illustrated. 1969, Harvey House $5.89. From Pompeii to the Iranian quake of 1968, this work shows the causes and importance of these destructive posers in world history. For a younger group, use: *Why the Earth Quakes* by Julian May (1969, Holiday $4.95).

7784. Miklowitz, Gloria D. *Earthquake* (4–6). Illus. by William Jaber. 1977, Messner $7.29. Causes, prediction, and possible effects are covered in this basic volume. Also use: *Earthquakes* by Patricia Lauber (1974, Random $4.95).

7785. Nixon, Hershell H., and Nixon, Joan Lowery. *Volcanoes: Nature's Fireworks* (3–5). Illustrated. 1978, Dodd $4.95. The history and causes of this destructive force plus a description of the world's major volcanoes.

7786. Pough, Frederick H. *All about Volcanoes and Earthquakes* (4–8). Illus. by Kurt Wiese. 1953, Random $4.39. The causes and effects of these catastrophes are detailed along with historical information. Also use: *The First Book of Volcanoes and Earthquakes* by Rebecca B. Marcus (1972, Watts $4.90).

7787. Simon, Seymour. *Danger from Below: Earthquakes—Past, Present, and Future* (5–7). Illus. by author. 1979, Four Winds $7.95. A history of important earthquakes is included in this account, which concentrates on causes and effects.

Icebergs and Glaciers

7788. Anderson, Madelyn Klein. *Iceberg Alley* (6–8). 1976, Messner $6.97. An overview of what scientists know about icebergs, with references to such events as the sinking of the *Titanic*.

7789. Gans, Roma. *Icebergs* (1–3). Illus. by Vladimir Bobri. 1964, Crowell $6.89. The formation of icebergs, how they reach the ocean, and how they are useful as well as dangerous.

7790. Lauber, Patricia. *Junior Science Book of Icebergs and Glaciers* (3–5). Illus. by Evelyn Urbanowich. 1961, Garrard $3.40. A description of how polar ice formations are created and their effects. For a slightly older group use: *Icebergs and Their*

Voyages by Gwen Schultz (1975, Morrow $5.49).

7791. Nixon, Hershell H., and Nixon, Joan Lowery. *Glaciers: Nature's Frozen Rivers* (3–5). Illustrated. 1980, Dodd $4.95. A brief account that gives information on the causes and effects of glaciers. Also use: *The First Book of Glaciers* by Rebecca B. Marcus (1962, Watts $4.90).

7792. Tallcott, Emogene. *Glacier Tracks* (5–8). Illustrated. 1970, Lothrop $6.67. Identification of various forms of glacier tracks, data on the Ice Age, and the work of scientists in Antarctica. Also use: *The Story of Glaciers and the Ice Age* by William H. Matthews (1974, Harvey House $5.89).

7793. Tangborn, Wendell V. *Glaciers* (1–3). 1965, Crowell $4.50; LB $5.95. A simple account of the origin of glaciers and how they have affected us.

Energy

7794. Breiter, Herta S. *Fuel and Energy* (2–4). Illustrated. 1978, Raintree $5.49. A complex subject treated in a simple but accurate manner.

7795. Dennis, Landt. *Catch the Wind: A Book of Windmills and Windpower* (4–6). Illustrated. 1976, Four Winds $7.95. An absorbing presentation of the ways in which windmills and windpower have been used in the past and could be used in the future.

7796. Doty, Roy, and Maar, Len. *Where Are You Going with That Energy?* (5–8). Illus. by Roy Doty. 1977, Doubleday $5.95. An account of various forms of energy and their future availability and uses.

7797. Kiefer, Irene. *Energy for America* (6–8). Illustrated. 1979, Atheneum $9.95. An advanced discussion of the forms and uses of energy.

7798. Pringle, Laurence. *Energy: Power for People* (6–8). 1975, Macmillan $8.95. A realistic survey of sources of power, their often diminishing supplies, problems of pollution and conservation, and possible future developments. Also use: *Energy for the Twenty-First Century* by Franklyn M. Branley (1975, Crowell $6.50).

7799. Shuttlesworth, Dorothy E., and Williams, Lee Ann. *Disappearing Energy: Can We End the Crisis?* (5–7). 1974, Doubleday $6.95. The use and misuse of various kinds of energy are described in this well-organized account.

7800. Watson, Jane W. *Alternate Energy Sources* (5–8). Illustrated. 1979, Watts $5.45. A discussion of capturing energy from water, wind, and sun.

Coal, Gas, and Oil

7801. Adler, Irving. *Petroleum: Gas, Oil and Asphalt* (3–6). Illustrated. 1975, John Day $6.89. Includes material on the location, uses, and pollution involved with this energy resource.

7802. Chaffin, Lillie D. *Coal: Energy and Crisis* (3–5). Illus. by Ray Abel. 1974, Harvey House $4.29. This book not only gives generous background information on coal, but also presents material on the energy crisis and pollution.

7803. Coombs, Charles. *Pipeline across Alaska* (4–6). Illustrated. 1978, Morrow $5.95. The history, present status, and potential of the world's most expensive construction project.

7804. Gans, Roma. *Oil: The Buried Treasure* (2–3). Illus. by Giulio Maestro. 1975, Crowell $4.50; LB $5.95. An explanation of oil deposits, methods of drilling for oil, and how it is used in many manufactured products.

7805. Harter, Walter L. *Coal: The Rock That Burns* (6–8). Illustrated. 1979, Nelson $6.95. An account of the origins and uses of coal, as well as material on mining techniques.

7806. Kraft, Betsy Harvey. *Oil and Natural Gas* (5–8). Illustrated. 1978, Watts $4.90. Supplies, processing and conservation are highlighted in this account.

7807. Neal, Harry Edward. *The Story of Offshore Oil* (3–5). Illustrated. 1977, Messner $6.97. Using the activities and functions of an actual oil rig as a focus, the book gives a brief but accurate overview.

7808. Reading, Robert H. *The Alaska Pipeline* (3–5). Illustrated. 1980, Childrens Press $6.50. An account that concentrates on the nature of the structure and its construction.

7809. Ridpath, Ian. *Man and Materials: Gas* (4–6). Illustrated. 1975, Addison $4.95. The story of natural gas, its uses, discovery, and how it is transported.

7810. Ridpath, Ian. *Man and Materials: Oil* (4–6). Illustrated. 1975, Addison $4.95. An account of how oil deposits were formed and how they are located, as well as the refining and uses of oil.

7811. Shumaker, Virginia O. *The Alaska Pipeline* (4–6). Illustrated. 1979, Messner $6.97. Both the ecological and the energy-producing aspects of this project are well presented.

Nuclear Energy

7812. Adler, Irving. *Atomic Energy* (5–7). Illus. by Ellen Viereck. 1971, John Day $6.89. The structure of the atom, radiation, and atomic energy are 3 of the topics discussed in this work.

7813. Asimov, Isaac. *How Did We Find Out about Atoms?* (5–7). Illus. by David Wool. 1976, Walker $6.89. This simple account covers the earliest theories on atom structure through the status of our present knowledge. Also use: *How Did We Find Out about Nuclear Power?* (1976, Walker $6.85).

7814. Bronowski, J, and Selsam, Millicent E. *Biography of an Atom* (4–7). Illus. by Weimer Pursell. 1965, Harper $6.79. The evolutionary journey of the carbon atom, and the ever-changing roles it may have played upon the earth.

7815. Chester, Michael. *Particles: An Introduction to Particle Physics* (6–8). Illus. by Erick Ingraham. 1978, Macmillan $8.95. A fresh look at the atom and the gaps in our knowledge about it.

7816. Colby, C. B. *The Atom at Work: How Nuclear Power Can Benefit Man* (4–6). Illustrated. 1968, McCann $5.79. A very simple account of possible uses of atomic energy.

7817. Grey, Vivian. *The Secret of the Mysterious Rays: The Discovery of Nuclear Energy* (6–8). Illus. by Ed Marsberg. 1966, Basic, text ed. $7.95. A clear history of how the power of the atom was explored.

7818. Halacy, D.S, Jr. *Nuclear Energy* (4–6). Illustrated. 1978, Watts $4.90. A brief introduction that covers the major areas, but downplays its dangers.

7819. Pringle, Laurence. *Nuclear Power* (6–9). 1979, Macmillan $7.95. A pro-nuclear power account that, nevertheless, stresses caution.

7820. Rosenfeld, Sam. *Ask Me a Question about the Atom* (5–7). Illus. by James E. Barry. 1969, Harvey House $5.39. A question-and-answer book that explores many aspects involved with atomic theory, energy, and uses.

Solar Energy

7821. Adams, Florence. *Catch a Sunbeam: A Book of Solar Study* (4–6). Illustrated. 1978, Harcourt $7.95. A good source of projects involving solar energy.

7822. Bendick, Jeanne. *Putting the Sun to Work* (3–5). Illustrated. 1979, Garrard $4.74. A beginner's guide to solar energy and the ways we can and do use it.

7823. Berger, Melvin. *Energy from the Sun* (1–3). Illus. by Giulio Maestro. 1976, Crowell $5.95. A simple explanation of how important the sun is in our lives.

7824. Gadler, Steve J, and Adamson, Wendy. *Sun Power: Facts about Solar Energy* (6–8). Illustrated. 1978, Lerner $6.95. An excellent survey of many aspects of the subject, including how this energy can be harnessed.

7825. Hoke, John. *Solar Energy* (6–9). Illustrated. 1978, Watts $4.90. Up-to-date information, including recent trends and a variety of solar projects.

7826. Knight, David C. *Harnessing the Sun: The Story of Solar Energy* (5–7). Illustrated. 1976, Morrow $5.49. The history, theory, and present status of solar energy and its uses. Also use: *Sun Power* by Norman F. Smith (1976, Coward $4.64).

7827. Metos, Thomas H., and Bitter, Gary G. *Exploring with Solar Energy* (5–8). Illustrated. 1978, Messner $6.97. An overview of the subject that also includes several projects.

Weather and Atmosphere

Weather

7828. Bendick, Jeanne. *How to Make a Cloud* (1–3). Illus. by author. 1971, Parents $5.41. A simple explanation of clouds as well as their types, formation, and effects.

7829. Boesen, Victor. *Doing Something about the Weather* (5–7). 1975, Putnam $6.95. This treatment emphasizes our ability to predict weather and our efforts to control it. Also use: *The National Weather Service* by Melvin Berger (1971, John Day $5.95).

7830. Bova, Benjamin. *Man Changes the Weather* (5–8). Illustrated. 1973, Addison $6.95. An overview on how past and present people have, through design or accident, changed the weather and atmosphere, with a final glimpse into the future. A companion volume is: *The Weather Changes Man* (1974, $6.95).

7831. Breiter, Herta S. *Weather* (2–4). Illustrated. 1978, Raintree $5.49. Color illustrations accompany this simple, but surprisingly thorough, treatment.

7832. Courtney, William. *What Does a Barometer Do?* (2–5). Illustrated. 1963, Little $4.50. The weather and how it is interpreted by barometers is described in this interesting work.

7833. Heuer, Kenneth. *Rainbows, Halos and Other Wonders* (5–8). Illustrated. 1978, Dodd $5.95. Various forms of atmospheric optics are described and explained.

7834. May, Julian. *Weather* (2–4). Illus. by Jack White. 1967, Follett $5.97. Air masses, humidity, weather instruments, and forecasting are among the topics introduced.

7835. Milgrom, Harry. *Understanding Weather* (5–7). Illus. by Lloyd Birmingham. 1970, Macmillan $4.95. A background book on the hows and whys of the weather. Also use: *Everyday Weather and How It Works* by Herman Schneider (1961, McGraw $6.95).

7836. Ryan, Martha. *Weather* (2–4). Illus. by Gavin Rowe. 1976, Watts $3.90. An easily read text about weather that includes material on clouds and the work of meteorologists. Also use: *Let's Find Out about Weather* by David C. Knight (1967, Watts $4.90).

7837. Sattler, Helen R. *Nature's Weather Forecasters* (5–7). 1978, Nelson $6.95. How to foretell weather using nature's indicators.

7838. Weiss, Malcolm E. *What's Happening to Our Climate?* (6–8). Illustrated. 1978, Messner $7.29. An explanation of what causes weather and various weather trends of the past.

7839. Wolff, Barbara. *Evening Gray, Morning Red* (2–4). Illus. by author. 1976, Macmillan $6.95. Folk sayings, rhymes about weather predictions, and instructions for making a weather vane are included in this simply written book.

Air

7840. Branley, Franklyn M. *Air Is All around You* (1–3). Illus. by Robert Galster. 1962, Crowell $6.89. An introduction to our atmosphere and its importance.

7841. Brewer, Mary. *The Wind Is Air* (1–3). Illustrated. 1975, Childrens Press $6.60. A very simple introduction to the wind, its force, and usefulness.

7842. Kalina, Sigmund. *Air: The Invisible Ocean* (2–4). 1973, Lothrop $5.09. A simple introduction to the uses and properties of air.

7843. Knight, David C. *The First Book of Air: A Basic Guide to the Earth's Atmosphere* (4–6). Illustrated. 1961, Watts $4.90. A guide to the functions and composition of air.

7844. Simon, Seymour. *Projects with Air: Science At Work* (3–6). 1975, Watts $4.90. A series of simple experiments that explore the properties and uses of air.

Water

7845. Blough, Glenn O. *Not Only for Ducks: The Story of Rain* (1–4). Illus. by Jeanne Bendick. 1954, McGraw $6.95. Simple story of the water cycle and the part rain plays in it.

7846. Gans, Roma. *Water for Dinosaurs and You* (1–3). Illus. by Richard Cuffari. 1972, Crowell $6.89; paper $1.45. An account of the part water has always played in animals' lives and an introduction to the water cycle are included in this account.

7847. Goldin, Augusta. *The Shape of Water* (3–4). Illus. by Demi. 1979, Doubleday $6.95; LB $7.90. A description of the properties of the 3 states of water and simple experiments that can be done at home.

7848. Shapp, Martha, and Shapp, Charles. *Let's Find Out about Water* (1–3). Illus. by Carol Nicklaus. 1975, Watts $4.90. Water, its properties, and uses are explored in this simple text.

7849. Sootin, Harry. *Experiments with Water* (6–8). Illus. by Julio Granda. 1971, Grosset $5.95. Safety is emphasized in these interesting experiments that explore the properties of water.

Storms

7850. Berger, Melvin. *Storms* (2–4). Illus. by Joseph Cellini. 1970, Coward $4.49. An introduction to the cause of storms and what often accompanies them, such as lightning, sleet, and hail. For an older group use: *Storms—from the Inside Out* by Malcolm E. Weiss (1973, Messner $5.79).

7851. Bixby, William. *Hurricanes* (4–7). Illustrated. 1979, McKay $6.95. Causes and effects of hurricanes are explored with reference to many contemporary disasters.

7852. Branley, Franklyn M. *Flash, Crash, Rumble and Roll* (1–3). 1965, Crowell $6.89. A simple explanation of the causes and effects of thunderstorms. Also use: *Rain and Hail* (1963, Crowell $6.95).

7853. Brown, Billye, and Brown, Walter B. *Historical Catastrophes: Floods* (5–7). Illustrated. 1975, Addison $7.95. Describes the destructiveness of water, particularly in relation to disastrous floods since the 1950s.

7854. Buehr, Walter. *Storm Warning: The Story of Hurricanes and Tornadoes* (4–6). Illus. by author. 1972, Morrow $6.00. The origins and characteristics of cyclonic storms are discussed, and in a lengthy section details are given on how these storms are forecast. Also use: *Hurricanes: Monster Storms from the Sea* by Ruth Brindze (1973, Atheneum $5.95).

7855. Busch, Phyllis S. *A Walk in the Snow* (2–4). Photos by Mary M. Thacher. 1971, Lippincott $7.95. Beautiful photographs show winter scenes and enable children to find out many answers to their questions about snow. Also use: *Snow is Falling* by Franklyn M. Branley (1963, Crowell $5.50).

7856. Jennings, Gary. *The Killer Storms: Hurricanes, Typhoons, and Toronadoes* (5–7). Illustrated. 1970, Lippincott $7.95. An account of how these storms are created and forecast, along with their effects on people and land. Also use: *Historical Catastrophes: Hurricanes and Tornadoes* by Billye Brown (1972, Addison $6.95).

7857. Keen, Martin L. *Lightning and Thunder* (4–6). Illus. by Haris Petie. 1969, Messner $8.95. An explanation of the origins and effects of these 2 phenomena and how to protect oneself against lightning storms. Also use: *Lightning and Thunder* by Herbert S. Zim (1952, Morrow $6.00).

7858. Laycock, George. *Tornadoes, Killer Storms* (6–8). 1979, McKay $6.95. An introduction to the origin, history, and characteristics of tornadoes.

7859. Peterson, Hans. *The Big Snowstorm* (2–4). Trans. by Eric Bibb. Illus. by Harald Wiberg. 1976, Coward $5.79. The effects of a rural snowstorm in Sweden, told simply and directly, and illustrated with handsome paintings.

Botany

Seeds

7860. Hutchins, Ross E. *The Amazing Seeds* (5–8). Illustrated. 1965, Dodd $3.75; LB $5.95. The great variations among seeds, how they germinate, travel along the ground and through the air, their ability to sprout after centuries of dormancy, their uses in cooking, and their identification. Also use: *The Wonders Of Seeds* by Alfred Stefferud (1956, Harcourt $4.95).

7861. Jordan, Helene J. *Seeds by Wind and Water* (1–3). Illus. by Nils Hogner. 1962, Crowell $6.95. A very simple account of how seeds travel.

7862. Petie, Haris. *The Seed the Squirrel Dropped* (K–3). 1976, Prentice-Hall $5.95. The growth of a cherry tree from seed to a fruit-producing tree, appealingly told. Also use: *The Tiny Seed* by Eric Carle (1970, Crowell $5.95; LB $6.95).

7863. Selsam, Millicent E. *Play with Seeds* (1–3). Illus. by Helen Ludwig. 1957, Morrow $6.00. A simple activity book that explains the function of seeds.

7864. Selsam, Millicent E. *Seeds and More Seeds* (K–3). Illus. by Tomi Ungerer. 1959, Harper $5.95. An introduction for beginning readers to the world of seeds. Also use: *How a Seed Grows* by Helene J. Jordan (1960, Crowell $6.89; paper $1.95).

7865. Shuttlesworth, Dorothy E. *The Hidden Magic of Seeds* (2–4). 1976, Rodale $5.95. A simple explanation that introduces various seed types and their composition and growth stages.

Plants

7866. Aldrich, Arthur. *Flowers and Flowering Plants* (2–4). Illus. by Lida Brychta. 1976, Watts $3.90. The parts of plants and their families, uses, and propagation are briefly discussed in this simple account.

7867. Branley, Franklyn M. *Roots Are Food Finders* (2–4). Illustrated. 1975, Crowell $4.50; LB $6.89. An explanation of the function and importance of a plant's root system.

7868. Busch, Phyllis S. *Cactus in the Desert* (2–3). Illus. by Harriett Barton. 1979, Crowell $6.95. How cacti grow in the desert and their various uses are highlighted in this easily read account.

7869. Cole, Joanna. *Plants in Winter* (1–3). Illus. by Kazue Mizumura. 1973, Crowell $6.89. An account of how certain plants survive the winter.

7870. Dowden, Anne. *Wild Green Things in the City: A Book of Weeds* (5–9). Illustrated. 1972, Crowell $8.95. A book on weeds—their structure, identifiable characteristics, propagation—as they are found in New York City, Denver, and Los Angeles.

7871. Earle, Olive L. *Pond and Marsh Plants* (3–5). Illus. by author. 1972, Morrow $5.52. Several plants are pictured and discussed along with facts about parts, reproductive processes, and conservation problems. For a younger group use: *Water Plants* by Laurence Pringle (1975, Crowell $4.50; LB $5.95).

7872. Graham, Ada, and Graham, Frank. *The Milkweed and Its World of Animals* (6–9). Illustrated. 1976, Doubleday $5.95. Through text and many photographs, this book gives an informal look at the many living creatures that use various parts of the milkweed.

7873. Guilcher, J. M., and Noailles, R. H. *A Fern Is Born* (5–7). Illustrated. 1971, Sterling $5.89. An introduction through photographs and text to a variety of fern species and to their unusual method of reproduction. Also use: *Plants without Flowers* by Bernice Kohn (1968, Hawthorn $5.95).

7874. Hogan, Paula Z. *The Dandelion* (1–3). Illus. by Yoshi Miyake. 1979, Raintree $5.99. Simple text and large bold illustrations highlight this elementary introduction.

7875. Hogner, Dorothy Childs. *Water Plants* (6–8). Illustrated. 1977, Holiday $6.95. An encyclopedic survey by categories of fresh and saltwater plants with descriptions of each variety.

7876. Lavine, Sigmund A. *Wonders of the Cactus World* (5–7). 1974, Dodd $9.15. In addition to material on the characteristics of cacti and their uses, there is interesting data on how to collect and care for them. Also use: *Cacti* by Frank Venning (1974, Golden $5.95; paper $1.95).

7877. Limburg, Peter R. *Watch Out, It's Poison Ivy!* (4–6). Illustrated. 1973, Messner $5.79. A book that supplies background information on the plant, how to avoid contamination, and how to treat infections.

7878. Rahn, Joan Elma. *How Plants Are Pollinated* (5–7). Illustrated. 1975, Atheneum $5.95. An explanation of the reproduction process in plants.

7879. Rahn, Joan Elma. *How Plants Travel* (4–6). Illus. by Ginny L. Winter. 1973, Atheneum $4.95. A relaxed, informal account about plant dissemi-

nation. For a younger group use: *Travelers All: The Story of How Plants Go Places* by Irma E. Webber (1944, Childrens Press $4.95).

7880. Rahn, Joan Elma. *More about What Plants Do* (3–5). Illus. by Ginny L. Winter. 1975, Atheneum $6.95. Twenty experiments illustrate various ways in which plants grow.

7881. Rahn, Joan Elma. *Seeing What Plants Do* (3–5). Illus. by Ginny Linville. 1972, Atheneum $6.00. An activity book that outlines 21 simple experiments involving parts of plants. Also use for a younger group: *Predicting with Plants* by Illa Podendorf (1971, Childrens Press $5.49).

7882. Rahn, Joan Elma. *Nature in the City: Plants* (3–5). Illustrated. 1977, Raintree $7.33. Eighteen common plants such as clover, dandelion, and thistle are described.

7883. Rahn, Joan Elma. *Watch It Grow, Watch It Change* (6–8). Illustrated. 1978, Atheneum $6.95. Growth patterns of plants are explained through use of a variety of prototypes.

7884. Ricciuti, Edward R. *Plants in Danger* (6–9). Illus. by Ann Zwinger. 1979, Harper $8.95; LB $8.79. A well-researched, advanced treatment of our endangered plant life and how it can be saved.

7885. Rinkoff, Barbara. *Guess What Grasses Do* (K–2). Illus. by Beatrice Darwin. 1972, Lothrop $6.25; LB $6.00. An informative introduction to various types of grasses and their uses. For an older group use: *Grasses* by Irmengarde Eberle (1960, Walck $4.95).

7886. Schaeffer, Elizabeth. *Dandelion, Pokeweed, and Goosefoot* (4–7). Illus. by Grambs Miller. 1972, Childrens Press $5.95. Subtitled: *How the Early Settlers Used Plants for Food and Medicine in the Home.*

7887. Selsam, Millicent E. *The Amazing Dandelion* (2–4). Illus. by Jerome Wexler. 1977, Morrow $6.25; LB $6.00. The life cycle, structure, and reproduction methods of this tenacious weed are fascinatingly described.

7888. Selsam, Millicent E. *Bulbs, Corms, and Such* (3–5). Illustrated. 1974, Morrow $7.25; LB $6.96. An authoritative picture of these many types of roots and their growth patterns.

7889. Selsam, Millicent E., and Hunt, Joyce. *A First Look at the World of Plants* (3–6). Illus. by Harriet Springer. 1978, Walker $5.95. A simple description of the various groups of plants, with proper terminology.

7890. Selsam, Millicent E., and Wexler, Jerome. *Mimosa, the Sensitive Plant* (2–5). Illustrated. 1978,

Morrow $6.95. A useful introduction to this unusual plant, plus a number of experiments that can be performed on it.

7891. Selsam, Millicent E. *Play with Plants* (2–5). Illustrated. 1978, Morrow $6.67. An introduction to the plant world and to simple nature activities.

7892. Stone, A. Harris, and Leskowitz, Irving. *Plants Are Like That* (4–7). Illus. by Peter P. Plasencia. 1968, Prentice-Hall $5.95. A series of activities that demonstrate plant characteristics and growth patterns.

7893. Stonehouse, Bernard. *A Closer Look at Plant Life* (6–8). Illustrated. 1978, Watts $5.90. An overview that touches on plant evolution and basic plant processes.

7894. Waters, John F. *Carnivorous Plants* (4–6). Illustrated. 1974, Watts $4.90. A description of such meat-eaters as the Venus Flytrap. Also use: *Poisonous Plants* by Peter R. Limburg (1976, Messner $7.29).

7895. Webber, Irma E. *Bits That Grow Big: Where Plants Come From* (2–5). Illus. by author. 1949, Childrens Press $4.95. An introduction to the development of plants from seeds, cuttings, and spores.

7896. Webber, Irma E. *Up above and Down Below* (1–3). Illustrated. 1943, Childrens Press $4.95. In text and illustrations, all of the parts of plants are described. Also use: Herbert S. Zim's *What's Inside of Plants* (1952, Morrow $6.00).

7897. Weiner, Michael A. *Man's Useful Plants* (4–7). Illustrated. 1976, Macmillan $7.95. A variety of plants are introduced that benefit humans, from supplying food to providing paper.

7898. Wong, Herbert H., and Vessel, Matthew F. *Plant Communities: Where Can Cattails Grow?* (1–3). Illus. by Mike Eagle. 1970, Addison $6.95. A child's discovery that cattails cannot grow everywhere leads to an elementary discussion on the importance of environment.

7899. Wright, Robert H. *What Good Is a Weed? Ecology in Action* (4–6). Illustrated. 1972, Lothrop $6.01. Fifteen weeds and their life cycles are reported in this account that stresses conservation.

Trees and Leaves

7900. Adler, David A. *Redwoods Are the Tallest Trees in the World* (2–3). Illus. by Kazue Mizumura. 1978, Crowell $5.79. A young boy tells about the giant redwoods he has seen in a California national park.

7901. Allen, Gertrude E. *Everyday Trees* (K–3). Illustrated. 1968, Houghton $5.95. A very simple introuduction to some of the most common American trees. Also use: *Trees* by Francis Donaldson (1976, Watts $3.90).

7902. Bulla, Clyde Robert. *A Tree Is a Plant* (K–2). Illus. by Lois Ligrell. 1960, Crowell $6.89. Several types of trees and their life cycles are introduced and nicely illustrated.

7903. Caulfield, Peggy. *Leaves* (4–6). Illustrated. 1962, Coward $4.29. The life story of leaves from spring to fall, plus a section on how to collect and preserve them. For a younger group use: *I Found a Leaf* by Sharon Lerner (1967, Lerner $3.95).

7904. Collingwood, G. H., and Brush, Warren D. *Knowing Your Trees* (5–8). Illustrated. n.d, American Forestry $3.50. In addition to providing material on tree identification, growing locations are indicated in small maps. Also use: *A Field Guide to Trees and Shrubs* by George A. Petrides (1972, Houghton $7.92; paper $5.95).

7905. Cooper, Elizabeth K, and Cooper, Padraic. *A Tree Is Something Wonderful* (1–3). Illustrated. 1972, Childrens Press $5.50. An interesting book about the wonder of trees and how they grow.

7906. Dowden, Anne. *The Blossom on the Bough: A Book of Trees* (6–9). Illus. by author. 1975, Crowell $8.95. The well-known botanical artist describes trees, their flowers and fruits, and the importance of forests in this beautifully illustrated volume. For a younger group use: *Let's Find Out about Trees* by Martha Shapp and Charles Shapp (1970, Watts $4.90).

7907. Edwards, Joan. *Caring for Trees on City Streets* (4–6). 1975, Scribner $6.95. For urban students, this account tells how to choose and care for trees in the city. Also use: *City Leaves, City Trees* by Edward Gallob (1972, Scribner $6.95).

7908. Fenton, Carroll Lane, and Pallas, Dorothy C. *Trees and Their World* (4–7). Illustrated. 1957, John Day $4.50. A general introduction to the study of trees, how they grow their fruit, and their propagation. Also use: *This is a Tree* by Ross E. Hutchins (1964, Dodd $4.50).

7909. Guilcher, J. M., and Noailles, R. H. *A Tree Is Born* (4–6). Illustrated. 1964, Sterling $5.89. Life cycle of 4 trees, shown in photographs. Also use: *Trees Alive* by Sarah R. Riedman (1974, Lothrop $6.50; LB $6.01).

7910. Hogan, Paula Z. *The Oak Tree* (1–3). Illus. by Kinuko Craft. 1979, Raintree $5.99. An informative, although elementary, introduction to trees, their function and annual changes.

7911. Hutchins, Ross E. *This Is A Leaf* (5–8). Illustrated. 1962, Dodd $5.00. Describes a variety of leaves and how they grow, feed, and protect the plants. Also use: *Biography of a Leaf* by Burke Davis (1972, Putnam $4.97).

7912. Kirkpatrick, Rena K. *Look at Leaves* (K–2). Illustrated. 1978, Raintree $5.49. Brief text and many illustrations provide a basic introduction to the subject.

7913. Kirkpatrick, Rena K. *Look at Trees* (K–2). Illustrated. 1978, Raintree $5.49. A simple introduction to the subject with a few projects. Also use: *Play with Trees* by Millicent E. Selsam (1950, Morrow $6.00).

7914. Nagel, Shirley. *Tree Boy* (5–7). Illustrated. 1978, Sierra $6.95. A boy's personal crusade to plant thousands of trees.

7915. Norris, Louanne, and Smith, Howard E. *An Oak Tree Dies and a Journey Begins* (K–3). Illus. by Allen Davis. 1979, Crown $6.95. The journey of an uprooted oak from stream to ocean to shore.

7916. Patterson, Allen. *The World of the Tree* (2–5). Illustrated. 1978, Grosset $4.99. The story of an oak tree and the life it harbors.

7917. Rich, Louise Dickinson. *The First Book of Lumbering* (4–6). Illus. by Victor Mays. 1967, Watts $4.90. This survey gives historical information as well as material on the uses of wood and modern forest conservation. Also use: *Tree Farms: Harvest for the Future* by Dorothy Dowdell (1965, Bobbs-Merrill $4.00).

7918. Selsam, Millicent E. *Maple Tree* (1–4). Illus. by Jerome Wexler. 1968, Morrow $6.96. Forty outstanding photos, some in color, coordinated with a clear and accurate text, detail the development of a Norway maple from pollination to maturity.

7919. Simon, Seymour. *A Tree on Your Street* (1–3). Illus. by Betty Faser. 1973, Holiday $3.95. The care of trees is highlighted in this simple text, which also tells about tree parts and their importance.

7920. Tresselt, Alvin. *The Dead Tree* (K–2). Illus. by Charles Robinson. 1972, Parents $5.41. When an oak falls and decays, it becomes food and shelter for many creatures and plants.

7921. Wohlrabe, Raymond A. *Exploring the World of Leaves* (6–8). Illustrated. 1976, Crowell $8.95. The structure, functions, and importance of leaves to plant and animal life are discussed, as well as some suggestions for experiments.

7922. Zim, Herbert S. *Trees* (5–8). Illustrated. 1952, Golden $6.95; paper $1.95. A small, handy volume packed with information and colored illustrations that help identify our most important trees.

Flowers

7923. Allen, Gertrude E. *Everyday Wildflowers* (K–2). Illus. by author. 1965, Houghton $5.95. An excellent, simple introduction to such common wildflowers as skunk cabbage and Queen Anne's lace.

7924. Dowden, Anne. *Look at a Flower* (6–8). Illus. by author. 1963, Crowell $8.95. Guide to the study of botany with many drawings of flower parts. Also use: *This Is a Flower* by Ross E. Hutchins (1963, Dodd $5.95; LB $4.50).

7925. Lerner, Carol. *Flowers of a Woodland Spring* (3–5). Illus. by author. 1979, Morrow $7.95; LB $7.63. An exquisite book in which text and drawings combine to give an accurate picture of spring foliage.

7926. Martin, Lynne. *The Orchid Family* (4–6). Illus. by Lydia Rosier. 1974, Morrow $6.25; LB $6.00. An interesting book about the largest of the plant families. Also use: *The Rose Family* by Olive L. Earle (1970, Morrow $5.52).

7927. Milne, Lorus J., and Milne, Margery. *Because of a Flower* (4–6). Illus. by Kenneth Gosner. 1975, Atheneum $6.95. Unusual facts about a variety of plants.

7928. Munari, Bruno. *A Flower with Love* (3–6). Illustrated. 1974, Crowell $7.89. A well-illustrated book on the art of Japanese flower arrangement using simple household items and common flora.

7929. Selsam, Millicent E., and Hunt, Joyce. *A First Look at Flowers* (K–3). Illus. by Harriet Springer. 1977, Walker $5.95; LB $5.85. A succinct, direct introduction to flowers and flower parts, describing differences in shape, number of stamens and pistils, number of petals, and so on.

7930. Zim, Herbert S. *Flowers: A Guide to Familiar American Wildflowers* (5–8). 1950, Golden $9.15; Western paper $1.95. An identification guide that describes many species in words and pictures.

Fungi

7931. Davis, Bette J. *The World of Mosses* (6–9). Illus. by author. 1975, Lothrop $5.50; LB $5.09. A comprehensive presentation of all aspects of mosses and liverworts, including their many uses to humans.

7932. Froman, Robert. *Mushrooms and Molds* (1–3). Illus. by Grambs Miller. 1972, Crowell $6.89. A simple account that defines its subjects and supplies activities to identify their characteristics.

7933. Hutchins, Ross E. *Plants without Leaves* (5–7). Illustrated. 1966, Dodd $5.95. Subtitle: *Lichens, Fungi, Moss, Liverworts, Slimemolds, Algae, Horsetails.* Also use: *Non-Flowering Plants* by Floyd S. Shuttleworth (1967, Golden $5.95; paper $1.95).

7934. Kavaler, Lucy. *The Wonders of Algae* (4–6). Illustrated. 1961, John Day $6.89. A handy volume that classifies and discusses various forms of algae and their life cycles.

7935. Kavaler, Lucy. *The Wonders of Fungi* (5–7). Illus. by Richard Ott. 1964, John Day $6.89. Molds, mushrooms, the fermentation process, medicinal and industrial applications, their uses as food and as a potential staple for space travel.

7936. Kohn, Bernice. *Our Tiny Servants: Molds and Yeasts* (3–5). Illustrated. 1962, Prentice-Hall $6.95. An exploration of the types of molds and yeasts, as well as their usefulness.

Foods, Farming, and Fishing

Foods

7937. Adler, Irving. *Food* (3–5). Illus. by Peggy Adler. 1977, Crowell $5.79. An interesting overview that introduces a variety of subjects—from the uses of food to data and problems on cultivation.

7938. Aliki. *Green Grass and White Milk* (2–4). Illus. by author. 1974, Crowell $5.95. A simple written text, attractively illustrated, explains how cows digest food, the milking process, its pasteurization, and some of the foods made from milk.

7939. Berger, Melvin. *Food Processing* (4–6). 1977, Watts $4.90. An account of what happens in a food processing plant from the gathering of ingredients to packaging and marketing.

7940. Brown, Elizabeth Burton. *Grains* (6–9). Illustrated. 1966, Prentice-Hall $8.95. Subtitle: *An Illustrated History with Recipes.*

7941. Buehr, Walter. *Food from Farm to Home* (4–6). Illus. by author. 1970, Morrow $6.00. An introduction to modern food production amd marketing.

7942. de Paola, Tomie. *The Popcorn Book* (1–3). Illustrated. n.d, Holiday $6.95. While Tony makes a plate of popcorn, Tiny tells interesting facts about this delicious food.

7943. Earle, Olive L., and Kantor, Michael. *Nuts* (3–5). Illustrated. 1975, Morrow $5.50; LB $5.09. Various kinds of nuts.

7944. Fenton, Carroll Lane, and Kitchen, Hermine B. *Plants We Live On* (4–7). Illus. by Carroll L. Fenton. 1971, John Day $6.50. Revised and enlarged edition of the authors' *Plants That Feed Us* (1956, John Day). Also use: *The Plants We Eat* by Millicent E. Selsam (1955, Morrow $6.01).

7945. Floethe, Louise Lee. *Farming around the World* (2–4). Illus. by Richard Floethe. 1970, Scribner $5.95. A global tour that highlights various methods of farming and crops. Also use: *Of Cabbages and Cattle: The Story of America's Farms* by Dirk Gringhuis (1962, Dial $4.58)

7946. Gemming, Elizabeth. *Maple Harvest: The Story of Maple Sugaring* (4–6). 1976, Coward $5.95. A history of the production of maple sugar in the U.S. and an engrossing account of present-day conditions and methods.

7947. Greene, Ellin, ed. *Clever Cooks: A Concoction of Stories, Charms, Recipes and Riddles* (4–6). Illus. by Trina Schart Hyman. 1973, Lothrop $6.96; Scholastic paper $.95. A collection of stories about food by such writers as Walter De La Mare and Andrew Lang, with accompanying appropriate recipes. An enjoyable and delicious idea.

7948. Hammond, Winifred G. *Sugar from Farm to Market* (4–6). 1967, Coward $4.59. Topics discussed are the sugar industry and its history, plus the many uses of sugar and its by-products.

7949. Jonness, Aylette. *The Bakery Factory, Who Puts the Bread on Your Table* (5–8). Illustrated. 1978, Crowell $6.95. A mother and daughter visit a local bakery in text and photographs by the author.

7950. Kenworthy, Leonard Stout. *The Story of Rice* (3–6). Illustrated. 1979, Messner $6.97. A thorough and fascinating account of this food staple and its cultivation around the world.

7951. Lavine, Sigmund A. *Indian Corn and Other Gifts* (4–7). Illustrated. 1974, Dodd $4.95. Such foods as corn, potatoes, and maple syrup are covered in this intriguing history. Also use: *Foods the Indians Gave Us* (1973, Washburn $5.95).

7952. Loeper, John J. *Mr. Marley's Main Street Confectionery* (5–8). Illustrated. 1979, Atheneum $6.95. The history of candy, ice cream, and other sweets and how they came into being in America.

7953. Meyer, Carolyn. *Milk, Butter and Cheese* (4–6). Illus. by Giulio Maestro. 1974, Morrow $5.21. The dairy family of foods from how they are produced to recipes on how to use them.

7954. Pringle, Laurence. *Wild Foods: A Beginner's Guide to Identifying, Harvesting and Cooking Safe and Tasty Plants from the Outdoors* (4–6). Illustrated. 1978, Four Winds $9.95. Also use: *Natural Foods* by Barbara Fenten (1974, Watts $4.49).

7955. Scheib, Ida, and Welker, Carole E. *The First Book of Food* (4–6). Illus. by Robert Byrd. 1974, Watts $4.90. A simple introduction to the world of food.

7956. Selsam, Millicent E. *Peanut* (1–4). Illustrated. 1969, Morrow $6.43. The life cycle and uses of the peanut plant.

7957. Selsam, Millicent E. *Popcorn* (2–5). Illus. by Jerome Wexler. 1976, Morrow $5.95; LB $5.49. Excellent photographs and a clear text explain the difference between popcorn and other corn varieties.

7958. Smaridge, Norah. *The Story of Cake* (5–7). 1979, Abingdon $5.95. A history of these tasty morsels from ancient times, including several recipes.

7959. Smaridge, Norah. *The World of Chocolate* (4–6). Illus. by Don Lambo. 1969, Messner $3.95. A history of chocolate from 1519, when Cortez was first introduced to it, to the present.

7960. Watts, Franklin. *Peanuts* (3–4). Illus. by Gene Sharp. 1978, Childrens Press $5.51. The origin, cultivation, and uses of the peanut plant.

7961. Wise, William. *Fresh, Canned and Frozen: Food from Past to Future* (3–5). Illus. by Shelley Fink. 1971, Parents $5.41. Securing food and processing it are 2 topics discussed in relation to the past, present, and future.

7962. Young, Eleanor R. *Rice* (5–7). 1971, Watts $4.90. The past and present status of rice production around the world.

7963. Zim, Herbert S., and Skelly, James R. *Eating Places* (4–6). Illus. by Frank Schwarz. 1975, Morrow $5.50; LB $5.09. The preparation and storage of food served in public eating places is discussed.

Condiments

7964. Brooks, Anita. *The Picture Book of Salt* (3–6). Illustrated. 1964, John Day $5.50. A well-illustrated book that concentrates on the ways salt is obtained. Also use: George Cecil's *Salt* (1976, Watts $3.90).

7965. Cooper, Elizabeth K. *And Everything Nice: The Story of Sugar, Spice and Flavoring* (3–5). Illus. by Julie Maas. 1966, Harcourt $5.50. A history of the culture, harvesting, and use of these important additives. Also use: *Salt, Sugar and Spice* by Walter Buehr (1969, Morrow $5.49).

7966. Dowden, Anne. *This Noble Harvest: A Chronicle of Herbs* (5–8). Illus. by author. 1979, Collins $10.95. An introduction to a variety of herbs and their uses.

7967. Goldin, Augusta. *Salt* (1–3). 1966, Crowell $5.95. Discusses the sources, composition, and uses of salt.

7968. Lavine, Sigmund A. *Wonders of Herbs* (4–7). Illustrated. 1976, Dodd $4.95. An account of the history, uses, and growth patterns of a variety of herbs.

7969. Siegel, Alice, and McLoone, Margo. *The Herb and Spice Book for Kids* (4–6). 1978, Holt $6.95. Forty-five ideas on how to use herbs and spices for gifts, in recipes and in trade formulas.

Fruit

7970. Fenton, Carroll Lane, and Kitchen, Hermine B. *Fruits We Eat* (4–7). Illustrated. 1971, John Day $5.50. First fruits are classified by types, then information is given on the origins and cultivation of each. Also use: *The First Book of Fruits* by Barbara L. Beck (1967, Watts $4.90).

7971. Hunt, Bernice K. *Apples: A Bushel of Fun and Facts* (3–5). Illus. by Roland Rodegast. 1976, Parents $5.41. This readable book covers cultivation, grafting, and development, as well as varieties of apples and some recipes.

7972. Johnson, Hannah Lyons. *From Apple Seed to Applesauce* (3–5). Illustrated. 1977, Lothrop $6.95; LB $6.43. Apples, from growing them to their uses.

7973. McMillan, Bruce. *Apples, How They Grow* (2–7). Illustrated. 1979, Houghton $6.95. A well-presented work on the life cycle and uses of the apple as revealed in a series of captioned photographs.

7974. Selsam, Millicent E. *The Apple and Other Fruits* (3–5). Illustrated. 1973, Morrow $6.95; LB $5.94. Beginning with a description of the reproductive process of the apple, this book discusses its life cycle and concludes with a description of other fruits.

Vegetables

7975. Aliki. *Corn Is Maize: The Gift of the Indians* (2–4). Illus. by author. 1976, Crowell $5.95. A simply written, comprehensive treatment of corn, its origins, how it is husbanded and harvested, and its many uses.

7976. Beck, Barbara L. *The First Book of Vegetables* (4–6). Illus. by Page Cary. 1970, Watts $4.90. The history and classification of many vegetables are presented with their uses.

7977. Cavagnaro, David, and Cavagnaro, Maggie. *The Pumpkin People* (3–5). 1979, Sierra $8.95. Growing pumpkins, their uses, and the cycle of life are highlighted in this account.

7978. Earle, Olive L. *Peas, Beans and Licorice* (3–5). Illustrated. 1971, Morrow $5.95. A specific vegetable and groups that contain both common and exotic members.

7979. Gambino, Robert. *Easy to Grow Vegetables* (4–6). Illus. by Anne Marie Jauss. 1975, Harvey House $4.69. Information on planting and caring for favorite vegetables.

7980. Rahn, Joan Elma. *Grocery Store Botany* (3–5). 1974, Atheneum $6.95. A book that investigates common vegetables and other edible plants, along with some unusual experiments.

7981. Selsam, Millicent E. *The Carrot and Other Root Vegetables* (2–5). Illus. by Jerome Wexler. 1971, Morrow $6.43. An interesting basic account of the life cycle and uses of several root vegetables.

7982. Selsam, Millicent E. *More Potatoes!* (1–3). Illus. by Ben Shecter. 1972, Harper $4.95; LB $4.79. Sue's class visits the farm and the market to learn more about this popular vegetable and how it is grown and sold.

7983. Selsam, Millicent E. *The Tomato and Other Fruit Vegetables* (2–5). Illustrated. 1970, Morrow $5.49. Using the tomato as a focal point, the author describes a plant's life cycle.

7984. Selsam, Millicent E. *Vegetables from Stems and Leaves* (2–5). Illus. by Jerome Wexler. 1972, Morrow $6.95; LB $5.43. A clear, accurate description of 12 common vegetables and how they propagate.

7985. Silverstein, Alvin, and Silverstein, Virginia B. *Potatoes: All about Them* (4–7). Illus. by Shirley Chan. 1974, Prentice $5.95. Everything of importance about potatoes is reviewed, including sections on history, growing patterns, and nutritive value.

7986. Watts, Franklin. *Tomatoes* (3–4). Illus. by Gene Sharp. 1978, Childrens Press $5.51. The origins, history, growth patterns, and uses of tomatoes.

7987. Watts, Franklin. *Corn* (3–4). Illus. by Tom Dunnington. 1977, Childrens Press $5.51. The history, growth, and uses of corn.

Farms and Farming

7988. Adler, Irving, and Adler, Ruth. *Irrigation: Changing Deserts into Gardens* (1–3). Illustrated. 1964, John Day $5.95. Human efforts to work the desert from ancient Egypt to today are recounted simply. Also use: *Wheels, Scoops, and Buckets: How People Lift Water for Their Fields* by Elizabeth S. Helfman (1968, Lothrop $5.50).

7989. Brown, Joseph E. *The Sea's Harvest: The Story Of Aquaculture* (5–7). Illustrated. 1975, Dodd $4.95. The various types of ocean farms and the many techniques that are, or could be, used.

7990. Cole, Joanna. *A Calf Is Born* (K–2). Photos by Jerome Wexler. 1975, Morrow $5.52. Excellent photographs show the birth of a calf. Many other animals on the farm are also included.

7991. Fenten, D. X. *Harvesting the Sea* (5–6). Illustrated. 1970, Lippincott $5.95. Basic information on how we use the resources of the sea and the direction that future developments may take. Also use: *The Sea: The Story of the Rich Underwater World* by Ruth Brindze (1971, Harcourt $5.95).

7992. Fenton, Carroll Lane, and Kitchen, Herminie B. *Animals That Help Us: The Story of Domestic Animals* (5–6). Illustrated. 1973, John Day $5.95. A history of the domestication of animals through a history of individual groups and species.

7993. Gemming, Elizabeth. *Born in a Barn* (2–4). Illustrated. 1974, Coward $5.95. The development to maturity of several domesticated animals. Also use with a younger group: *Baby Farm Animals* by Garth Williams (1959, Golden $1.50; LB $3.95).

7994. Ipcar, Dahlov. *Ten Big Farms* (K–4). Illus. by author. 1958, Knopf $5.99. The Jordans visit different kinds of farms, such as fruit, horse, tobacco, poultry, dairy, cattle, pig, wheat, sheep, and truck farms.

7995. Miller, Jane. *Lambing Time* (1–3). Illustrated. 1978, Methuen $6.95. The first two weeks in the lives of twin lambs.

7996. Richards, Norman. *Tractors, Plows and Harvesters: A Book about Farm Machines* (1–3). Illustrated. 1978, Doubleday $5.95. A picture book album of large farm machinery.

7997. Russell, Solveig P. *Farm* (1–3). Illus. by Shelley Fink. 1970, Parents $5.41. A brief introduction to the animals and activities associated with farms.

7998. Shuttlesworth, Dorothy E., and Shuttlesworth, Gregory J. *Farms for Today and Tomorrow: The Wonders of Food Production* (6–9). Illustrated. 1979, Doubleday $7.95. An account of how agriculture has progressed to vast modern farms.

7999. Sullivan, George. *How Do They Grow It?* (5–7). Illustrated. 1968, Westminster $5.95. A variety of crops from rubber and tobacco to mushrooms and grapefruit are discussed.

8000. Weaver, Martin, and Weaver, Virginia. *Lambs* (K–3). Illustrated. 1970, Knopf $4.99. A photo essay on lambs, from their first struggles to stand to their spring frolics.

8001. Wykeham, Nicholas. *Farm Machines* (2–4). Illustrated. 1979, Raintree $5.99. Combines, harvesters, and other farm machines are pictured and described in simple text.

Nutrition

8002. Berger, Melvin, and Berger, Gilda. *The New Food Book: Nutrition, Diet, Consumer Tips, and Foods of the Future* (6–8). Illus. by Byron Barton. 1978, Crowell $6.98. An up-to-date account of present food sources, the nature of today's food, and future developments.

8003. Burns, Marilyn. *Good for Me: All about Food in 32 Bites* (6–8). Illus. by Sandy Clifford. 1978, Little $7.95. Nutrition and digestion are the major topics discussed in this book.

8004. Fodor, R. V. *The Science of Nutrition* (4–6). Illustrated. 1979, Morrow $5.95. This work discusses the components of a basic diet and the consequences of poor nutrition. Also use: *Understanding Food: The Chemistry of Nutrition* by Beulah Tannenbaum (1962, McGraw $6.95).

8005. Fodor, R. V. *What to Eat and Why* (4–6). Illustrated. 1979, Morrow $5.71. A thorough introduction to the fundamentals of good nutrition, accompanied by photographs and diagrams.

8006. Gilbert, Sara. *Fat Free: Common Sense for Young Weight Worriers* (6–9). 1975, Macmillan $6.95. A solid, fact-filled book about fat and fat storage in the body, food intake, and types of diets, with wholesome cautionary advice.

8007. Jones, Hettie. *How to Eat Your ABC's: A Book about Vitamins* (4–7). Illus. by Judy Glasser. 1976, Four Winds $7.95. A breezy account of the nature of the various nutrients, chiefly vitamins and their sources in foods.

8008. Nourse, Alan E. *Vitamins* (6–9). Illustrated. 1977, Watts $4.90. The history of vitamin research as well as the nature, effects, and sources of vitamins are interestingly treated.

8009. Riedman, Sarah R. *Food for People* (4–6). 1976, Abelard $6.95. An account of how the world is fed.

8010. Silverstein, Alvin, and Silverstein, Virginia B. *The Chemicals We Eat and Drink* (5–8). 1973, Follett $5.95; LB $5.97. A discussion of the natural and artificial poisons and the helpful chemicals that are found in the food we eat. Also use: *Bugs in the Peanut Butter: Dangers in Everyday Food* by Michael Weiner (1976, Little $5.95).

8011. Simon, Seymour. *About the Foods You Eat* (4–7). Illus. by Dennis Kendrick. 1979, McGraw $6.95. A breezy account that introduces digestion and nutrition and gives simple experiments.

8012. Weiss, Malcolm E., and Weiss, Ann E. *The Vitamin Puzzle* (4–7). Illus. by Pat De Aloe. 1976, Messner $7.29. In addition to such topics as the need for and sources of vitamins, the author supplies a clear, well-organized history of vitamin research. Also use: *How Did We Find Out about Vitamins?* by Isaac Asimov (1974, Walker $5.85).

Commercial Fishing

8013. Dixon, Sarah, and Dixon, Peter. *Lester* (4–6). Illustrated. 1979, Cypress $4.50. Part of a series about families around the world who make their living from the sea. This book takes place in Trinidad; others in the series are: *Marie* (Japan), *Dennis* (Canada), *Gilberto* (Mexico), and *Joel* (U.S.A.).

8014. Matteson, George. *Draggermen: Fishing on Georges Bank* (5–7). Illustrated. 1979, Four Winds $7.95. Fact, philosophy, and character sketches are combined in this story of a typical voyage of a trawler.

8015. Zim, Herbert S., and Krantz, Lucretia. *Commercial Fishing* (3–5). Illus. by Lee J. Ames. 1973, Morrow $5.50; LB $5.09; paper $1.25. An overview of commercial fishing that stresses modern methods of fish detection and catching. Also use: *Fishing around the World* by Louise Lee Floethe (1972, Scribner $5.95).

Textiles and Clothing

8016. Buehr, Walter. *Cloth from Fiber to Fabric* (5–7). Illus. by author. 1965, Morrow $6.00. Many of the processes connected with the making of cloth are described. Also use: *The New World of Fabrics* by Irmengarde Eberle (1964, Dodd $4.50).

8017. Cavanna, Betty, and Harrison, George R. *The First Book of Wool* (4–6). Illustrated. 1966, Watts $4.90. Two of the many topics are the kinds of animals that produce wool and the history of spinning.

8018. Cobb, Vicki. *Supersuits* (4–6). Illus. by Peter Lippman. 1975, Lippincott $6.50; paper $2.95. An explanation of the types of clothing needed in various climates and situations, including under the sea and in outer space.

8019. Eiseman, Alberta, and Eiseman, Nicole. *Gift from a Sheep: The Story of How Wool Is Made* (3–5). 1979, Atheneum $7.95. Jenny raises a lamb, has it sheared, and makes a poncho.

8020. Gemming, Elizabeth. *Wool Gathering: Sheep Raising in old New England* (4–6). Illustrated. 1979, Coward $6.95. How a cotton industry in New England has become a big business.

8021. Hammond, Winifred G. *Cotton: From Farm to Market* (4–7). Illustrated. 1968, Coward $4.59. The story of cotton from the field, through the gin, and to the mill.

8022. Houck, Carter. *Warm as Wool, Cool as Cotton* (3–6). Illus. by Nancy W. Parker. 1975, Seabury $6.94. Subtitle: *Natural Fibers and Fabrics and How to Work with Them.*

8023. Knox, Albert. *Cloth* (2–4). Illustrated. 1976, Watts $3.90. Types of cloth, their sources, and the ways in which they are made.

8024. Lubell, Cecil, and Lubell, Winifred. *Clothes Tell a Story: From Skin to Space Suits* (2–4). Illustrated. 1971, Parents $5.41. An introduction to clothes from animal skins through the many changes that have occurred through the ages.

8025. Petersham, Maud, and Petersham, Miska. *Let's Learn about Silk* (2–4). Illus. by James E. Barry. 1967, Harvey House $5.39. A brief introduction to the history of silk, the use of the silkworm, and substitute fabrics that have been developed today. For an older audience use: *Silkworms and Science: The Story of Silk* by Elizabeth K. Cooper (1961, Harcourt $4.95).

8026. Raben, Marguerite. *Textile Mill* (5–8). Illustrated. 1978, Watts $4.90. This work deals mainly with the process of changing fibers into cloth.

8027. Rosenbloom, Jonathan. *Blue Jeans* (3–5). 1976, Messner $6.64. A narrative that focuses on the manufacture of a pair of blue jeans from cotton farm to retail store.

8028. Shepherd, Walter. *Textiles* (6–8). Illustrated. 1971, John Day $6.89. A generous introduction to the manufacture of textiles with a special section on synthetics.

Biology

8029. Beer, Kathleen C. *What Happens in the Spring* (2–5). Illustrated. 1977, National Geographic $5.50. A description of the changes that occur in nature when spring arrives.

8030. Bendick, Jeanne. *Adaptation* (3–5). Illus. by author. 1971, Watts $4.90. Various forms of plant and animal adaptations (for food, protection, and the like) explored in text and pictures.

8031. Bendick, Jeanne. *Living Things* (3–5). Illus. by author. 1969, Watts $4.90; paper $1.25. A straightforward account that differentiates by properties between living and nonliving things.

8032. Busch, Phyllis S. *Exploring as You Walk in the City* (1–4). Illustrated. 1972, Lippincott $4.95. An account of the world of nature in the city. Also use: *Exploring as You Walk in the Meadow* (1972, Lippincott $4.95).

8033. Busch, Phyllis S. *Living Things That Poison, Itch and Sting* (4–7). Illus. by Harriet Springer. 1976, Walker $6.85. Some of the animals discussed are types of jellyfish, snails, and insects, plus many poisonous plants.

8034. Clement, Roland C. *Hammond Nature Atlas of America* (5–9). Illustrated. 1973, Hammond $19.95. Short entries are given for major forms of plant and animal life as well as rocks and minerals. Maps locate where they can be found. Also use: *The Face of North America* by Peter Farb (1964, Harper, paper $3.95).

8035. Earle, Olive L. *Scavengers* (3–5). Illus. by author. 1973, Morrow $5.50; LB $5.52. Insects, mammals, and birds who perform the valuable role of nature's garbage collectors.

8036. George, Jean C. *All upon a Sidewalk* (3–5). Illus. by Don Bolognese. 1974, Dutton $7.95. An ant's eye view of life on city streets.

8037. Goldstein, Philip. *Animals and Plants That Trap* (4–7). Illus. by Matthew Kalmenoff. 1974, Holiday $5.95. The spider, Venus Flytrap, and pitcher plants are 3 of the many species covered.

8038. Hopf, Alice L. *Animal and Plant Life Spans* (5–8). Illustrated. 1978, Holiday $6.95. Material on comparative lengths of life of both plants and animals, plus recent research.

8039. Horsburgh, Peg. *Living Light: Exploring Bioluminescence* (4–6). Illustrated. 1978, Messner $7.29. After an explanation of this phenomenon, there are examples of where it occurs in nature.

8040. Hutchins, Ross E. *Nature Invented It First* (5–8). Illus. by author. 1980, Dodd $5.95. This wildlife study points out that such phenomena as air conditioning and chemical warfare originated in nature.

8041. Jacker, Corinne. *The Biological Revolution: A Background Book on the Making of a New World* (6–9). 1971, Parents $4.95; LB $4.59. Such frontiers in the world of biology as cloning, transplants, and prolonging life are treated with unusual perception.

8042. Kane, Henry B. *Four Seasons in the Woods* (3–5). Illus. by author. 1968, Knopf $3.50; LB $5.39. Changes that occur to plants and animals are presented in text, drawings, and photographs. Also use: *Fall Is Here* by Dorothy Sterling (1966, Natural Hist. Pr. $4.95).

8043. May, Julian. *First Living Things* (4–6). Illus. by Howard Berelson. 1970, Holiday $4.50. An account of the conditions scientists believe existed to create the first life, and the nature of the first organisms.

8044. May, Julian. *Wildlife in the City* (4–6). Illus. by William Barss. 1970, Creative Education $4.95. The natural world of the city is introduced with such examples as butterflies, houseflies, and rats.

8045. Nayman, Jacqueline. *Atlas of Wildlife* (5–7). Illustrated. 1972, John Day $10.00. A region-by-region treatment that explains the geographical distribution of animals and plants.

8046. Patent, Dorothy. *Animal and Plant Mimicry* (7–9). Illustrated. 1978, Holiday $6.95. An extensive account that gives many examples of how plants and animals fool each other.

8047. Patent, Dorothy. *Plants and Insects Together* (5–7). Illus. by Matthew Kalmenoff. 1976, Holiday $5.95. Both beneficial and harmful relationships between plants and insects are described in this well-organized text.

8048. Pringle, Laurence. *Chains, Webs and Pyramids: The Flow of Energy in Nature* (4–7). Illus. by Joan Adkins. 1975, Crowell $7.95; LB $7.89. Food chains and allied systems are explored, as well as how the world food crisis may be lessened.

8049. Pringle, Laurence. *The Hidden World, Life under a Rock* (3–6). Illustrated. 1977, Macmillan $6.95. Life in cool, dark places is explored, and creatures that live under objects on land an in water are described. For a younger group use: *What We Find When We Look under Rocks* by Frances L. Behnke (1971, McGraw $4.72).

8050. Riedman, Sarah R. *Naming Living Things: The Grouping of Plants and Animals* (4–6). Illus. by Jerome Connolly. 1963, Rand $3.79. The history and nature of classification systems for plants and animals, and the people behind them.

8051. Rounds, Glen. *Wildlife at Your Doorstep* (5–7). Illus. by author. 1974, Holiday $4.95. An illustrated almanac of such commonplace "wildlife" as squirrels, wasps, toads, and ants.

8052. Russell, Solveig P. *Like and Unlike: A First Look at Classification* (3–5). Illus. by Lawrence Di-Fiori. 1973, Walck $5.95. After discussing the need for classification and ways in which it is accomplished, the author details how plants and animals are grouped.

8053. Selsam, Millicent E. *Benny's Animals and How He Put Them in Order* (1–3). Illus. by Illa Podendorf. 1966, Harper $6.89. A small boy with a penchant for tidiness and order decides he wants to arrange his sea shells and animal pictures. With help from a museum zoologist, he learns how to classify. Also use: *Things Are Alike and Different* by Illa Podendorf (1970, Childrens Press $5.25).

8054. Selsam, Millicent E. *How to Be a Nature Detective* (2–4). Illus. by Ezra Jack Keats. 1966, Harper $7.89. Very simple information on identifying the tracks of 2 birds, 6 small animals, and 3 amphibians.

8055. Sheehan, Angela, ed. *The Doubleday Nature Encyclopedia* (3–6). Illustrated. 1974, Doubleday $6.95. A description of the world's major groups of plants and animals and their adaptations to various regions.

8056. Silverstein, Alvin, and Silverstein, Virginia B. *Metamorphosis: The Magic Change* (4–7). Illustrated. 1971, Atheneum $6.25. An interesting introduction to the changes in form that take place with such animals and insects as frogs, salamanders, eels, butterflies, and honeybees.

8057. Simon, Hilda. *Living Lanterns: Luminescence in Animals* (6–9). Illus. by author. 1971, Viking $4.95; LB $4.53. A fascinating introduction to the phenomenon of self-luminescence in early and present day animal forms. For a younger group use: *Nature's Light: The Story of Bioluminescence* by Francine Jacobs (1974, Morrow $5.95; LB $5.49).

8058. Simon, Seymour. *The Secret Clocks: Time Senses of Living Things* (4–6). Illustrated. 1979, Viking $8.95. The time sense of living things presented in a well-organized way.

8059. Wilkins, Marne. *The Long Ago Lake: A Child's Book of Nature Lore and Crafts* (5–7). Illus. by Martha Weston. 1978, Sierra/Scribner $8.95. A poem to nature, as expressed by the author in northern Wisconsin during the 1930s.

Microbiology

8060. Anderson, Lucia. *The Smallest Life Around* (4–6). Illustrated. 1978, Crown $7.95. An overview of the life and structure of one-celled animals and plants.

8061. Beeler, Nelson F., and Branley, Franklyn M. *Experiments with a Microscope* (5–8). Illus. by Anne Marie Jauss. 1957, Crowell $6.95. A series of simple projects that point up the uses of the microscope.

8062. Grillone, Lisa, and Gennaro Joseph. *Small Worlds Close Up* (6–9). Illustrated. 1978, Crown $7.95. Everyday objects as seen through the microscope.

8063. Klein, Aaron E. *The Electron Microscope: A Tool of Discovery* (6–9). Illustrated. 1974, McGraw $6.95. How this amazing machine was developed and its various uses.

8064. Lewis, Lucia Z. *The First Book of Microbes* (5–7). Illus. by Howard Berelson. 1972, Watts $4.47. A fine introduction that describes both plant and animal microbes, their discovery and effects on humans. Also use: *Microbes Are Something Else* by A. Harris Stone (1969, Prentice-Hall $4.95).

8065. Morrison, Sean. *The Amoeba* (4–6). 1971, Coward $4.69. A glimpse at the nature and characteristics of the one-celled animal.

8066. Schwartz, George I. *Life in a Drop of Water* (6–9). Illustrated. 1970, Nat. Hist. Press $4.95. Amoebas, diatoms, and algae are 3 of the many living organisms described in this well-illustrated (with photographs) work. Also use *A World in a Drop of Water* by Alvin Silverstein and Virginia Silverstein (1969, Atheneum $4.95).

8067. Selsam, Millicent E. *Microbes at Work* (5–7). Illus. by Helen Ludwig. 1953, Morrow $6.96. Bacteria, molds, and yeasts, including simple experiments. Also use: *Microbes in Your Life* by Leo Schneider (1966, Harcourt $6.50).

8068. Selsam, Millicent E. *Greg's Microscope* (K–3). Illus. by Arnold Lobel. 1963, Harper $6.89. Greg and his parents observe small household items through a microscope. Also use with an older group: *Exploring with a Microscope* by Seymour Simon (1969, Random $2.95; LB $3.99).

8069. Shostak, Stanley. *The Hydra* (6–9). Illustrated. 1978, Coward $5.96. A description of this amazing tiny freshwater animal, a distant relative of the jellyfish.

8070. Wolberg, Barbara J. *Zooming In: Photographic Discoveries under the Microscope* (5–9). Illustrated. 1974, Harcourt $7.75. The beauties of nature as revealed under the microscope, as well as some information about microscopes and slide making.

Land Invertebrates

8071. Darling, Lois, and Darling, Louis. *Worms* (1–3). Illus. by author. 1972, Morrow $5.09. An informative work that describes the body structure, life history, and uses of the earthworm.

8072. Ford, Barbara. *Can Invertebrates Learn?* (4–6). Illus. by Haris Petie. 1972, Messner $4.79. This question is answered through a presentation of the various kinds of nervous systems of invertebrates and the results of experiments that tested memory and behavioral responses.

8073. Hess, Lilo. *The Amazing Earthworm* (3–5). Illustrated. 1979, Scribner $7.95. The life, structure, and behavior of earthworms are revealed in text and excellent photographs.

8074. Hess, Lilo. *A Snail's Pace* (3–5). Illustrated. 1974, Scribner $4.95. A survey of snails—habits, food, and life cycles.

8075. Holling, Holling C. *Pagoo* (4–6). Illustrated. 1957, Houghton $10.95. Life cycle of the hermit crab.

8076. Kellin, Sally Moffett. *The Book of Snails* (2–5). Illustrated. 1968, Addison $5.95. A simple text on characteristics, life span, reproduction, and types of snails.

8077. Nespojohn, Katherine V. *Worms* (4–6). Illus. by Haris Petie. 1972, Watts $4.90. Worms, their various species and how to study them are topics covered in this survey.

8078. Patent, Dorothy. *The World of Worms* (5–8). Illustrated. 1978, Holiday $6.95. A description of the life and habits of worms of various types.

8079. Pringle, Laurence. *Twist, Wiggle and Squirm: A Book about Earthworms* (2–4). Illus. by Pe-

ter Parnall. 1973, Crowell $4.50; LB $5.95. Detailed illustrations complement a text that describes the life history of the earthworm and such phenomena as locomotion, teeding, and reproduction. Also use: *Earthworms: Underground Farmers* by Patricia Lauber (1976, Garrard $4.48).

8080. Rhine, Richard. *Life in a Bucket of Soil* (5–7). Illus. by Elsie Wrigley. 1972, Lothrop $5.95; LB $5.49. Such organisms as beetles, worms, and snails are discussed.

8081. Ryder, Joanne. *Snail in the Woods* (1–3). Illus. by Jo Polseno. 1979, Harper $5.95; LB $6.89. The life cycle of a snail, from egg to mature adult, is given in this simple account.

8082. Selsam, Millicent E., and Hunt, Joyce. *First Look at Animals without Backbones* (1–4). Illus. by Harriet Springer. 1977, Walker $5.50; LB $5.39. Invertebrates are introduced with drawings that supply a clear elementary overview.

8083. Simon, Hilda. *Snails of Land and Sea* (6–9). Illus. by author. 1976, Vanguard $5.95. A multifaceted account of the varieties, uses, and growth patterns of snails and other gastropods. Also use: *Snails* by Herbert S. Zim (1975, Morrow $5.50; LB $5.09).

8084. Simon, Seymour. *Discovering What Earthworms Do* (3–5). Illus. by Jean Zallinger. 1969, McGraw $6.95. Through various activities, the reader learns about the nature and uses of earthworms.

8085. Stephens, William, and Stephens, Peggy. *Hermit Crab Lives in a Shell* (4–6). Illus. by Christine Sapicha. 1969, Holiday $4.50. The life cycle of this land crab that lives in the tropics is explored, along with habits and characteristics.

Insects

General

8086. Adrian, Mary. *Secret Neighbors: Wildlife in a City Lot* (2–5). 1972, Hastings $4.95. A year in the life of inhabitants of a vacant city lot—ants, spiders, and assorted insects.

8087. Allen, Gertrude E. *Everyday Insects* (K–2). Illus. by author. 1963, Houghton $5.95. Brief life cycle of 6 familiar insects.

8088. Causey, Don. *Killer Insects* (6–9). Illustrated. 1979, Watts $5.90. A full description of insects that bite, sting, and cause death in other ways.

8089. Cole, Joanna, and Wexler, Jerome. *Find the Hidden Insect* (2–3). Illustrated. 1979, Morrow $6.95; LB $6.67. Animal mimicry for camouflage is covered in photos and text.

8090. Conklin, Gladys. *The Bug Club Book: A Handbook for Young Bug Collectors* (3–6). Illus. by Girard Goodenow. 1966, Holiday $4.95. How to start a club, the equipment needed, and how to raise and exhibit bugs. Also use: *You Can Make an Insect Zoo* by Hortense R. Robert (1974, Childrens Press $6.00).

8091. Conklin, Gladys. *How Insects Grow* (3–6). Illustrated. 1969, Holiday $4.95. A description of the life cycle of insects from egg to adult.

8092. Conklin, Gladys. *Insects Build Their Homes* (1–3). Illus. by Jean Zallinger. 1972, Holiday $6.95. A simple introduction to insects and what they construct to use as homes.

8093. Conklin, Gladys. *We Like Bugs* (PS–3). Illus. by Arthur Marokvia. 1962, Holiday $5.95. Beginner's book of insects.

8094. Conklin, Gladys. *When Insects Are Babies* (K–3). Illus. by Arthur Marokvia. 1969, Holiday $5.95. Children will be drawn to these easy-to-read descriptions of the growth cycles of 16 insects.

8095. Graham, Ada, and Graham, Frank. *Bug Hunters* (5–7). Illus. by D. D. Tyler. 1978, Delacorte $6.95; LB $6.45. How biological control rather than pesticides can help combat an insect menace.

8096. Griffen, Elizabeth. *A Dog's Book of Bugs* (1–2). Illus. by Peter Parnall. 1967, Atheneum paper $1.25. A dog with more curiosity than itch undertakes an elementary study of bugs, including ants, stinging bugs, friendly bugs, beetles, and fleas.

8097. Huntington, Harriett E. *Let's Look at Insects* (1–4). Illustrated. 1969, Doubleday $4.95. A beginning book that gives elementary information on the insect world.

8098. Hutchins, Ross E. *The Bug Clan* (5–8). Illustrated. 1973, Dodd $5.50. A survey of the insects we call bugs, with sections on structure, habits, and effects on people. Also use: *Good Bugs and Bad Bugs in Your Garden* by Dorothy Childs Hogner (1974, Crowell $7.50).

8099. Hutchins, Ross E. *Hop, Skim and Fly: An Insect Book* (1–3). 1970, Parents $5.41. Common insects found in the woods, gardens, or the home are introduced in this simple text.

8100. Hutchins, Ross E. *Insects and Their Young* (5–7). Illustrated. 1975, Dodd $6.95. Insects are divided into 4 different groups and thoroughly described.

8101. Patent, Dorothy. *How Insects Communicate* (4–7). 1975, Holiday $5.95. Many examples are cited and explained on how insects use various senses to communicate, with emphasis on the role of certain hormones.

8102. Petie, Haris. *A Book of Big Bugs* (K–3). Illus. by author. 1977, Prentice-Hall $6.95. Informative, accurate, handsome pictures demonstrate many insects. The entries are arranged in order of increasing size, making this a useful book for identification.

8103. Ritchie, Carson I. *Insects, the Creeping Conquerors and Human History* (6–9). 1979, Nelson $7.95. A mature account of the effects of insects on the course of human history.

8104. Selsam, Millicent E., and Hunt, Joyce. *A First Look at Insects* (2–4). Illus. by Harriett Springer. 1975, Walker $5.50. Careful drawings and a lucid text help children learn how animals are classified and how to distinguish various insects.

Also use: *Insects Do the Strangest Things* by Leonora Hornblow (1968, Random $2.95; LB $3.99).

8105. Simon, Hilda. *Exploring the World of Social Insects* (4–6). Illus. by author. 1963, Vanguard $6.95. The activities of honeybees, ants, termites, and wasps. Also use: *Exploring the Insect World* by Margaret J. Anderson (1974, McGraw $5.72).

8106. Sterling, Dorothy. *Insects and the Homes They Build* (3–6). Illustrated. 1954, Doubleday $4.95. The homes and construction techniques used by various insects are described.

8107. Stevens, Carla. *Insect Pets: Catching and Caring for Them* (3–5). Illustrated. 1978, Morrow $5.95. A fascinating how-to approach that reveals important insect lore, including some learning experiments.

8108. Teale, Edwin W. *The Junior Book of Insects* (5–9). Illustrated. 1952, Dutton $9.95. Interesting facts about common insects, with simple instructions for collecting and studying them.

8109. Zim, Herbert S., and Cotton, Clarence. *Insects* (4–7). Illustrated. 1961, Golden $5.95. Western paper $1.95. Subtitle: *A Guide to Familiar American Insects*.

Ants

8110. Bronson, Wilfrid S. *The Wonder World of Ants* (4–6). 1937, Morrow $5.25. A discussion of an ant's daily life, as well as various kinds of ants.

8111. Freschet, Berniece. *The Ants Go Marching* (K–3). Illus. by Stephan Martin. 1973, Scribner $6.95. A nature book that explains why ants march in line. Also use: *If You Were an Ant* by Barbara Brenner (1973, Harper $5.79).

8112. Hopf, Alice L. *Biography of an Ant* (2–4). Illus. by Jean Zallinger. 1974, Putnam $4.97. An excellent, simply written scientific account of the first year in a wood ant's life.

8113. Hutchins, Ross E. *A Look at Ants* (3–6). Illustrated. 1978, Dodd $4.95. An informative, straightforward account supplemented by excellent photographs.

8114. Myrick, Mildred. *Ants Are Fun* (1–3). Illus. by Arnold Lobel. 1968, Harper $4.95; LB $4.79. Three boys try to rebuild an ant colony and learn about the inhabitants in the process.

8115. Selsam, Millicent E. *Questions and Answers about Ants* (2–5). Illus. by Arabelle Wheatley. 1967, Four Winds $6.95. Question-and-answer format about the anatomy and behavior of these fascinat-

ing insects, based on the author's own observations. Also use: *The First Book of Ants* by Helen Hoke (1970, Watts $4.47).

8116. Shuttlesworth, Dorothy E. *The Story of Ants* (5–8). Illus. by SuZan Swain. 1964, Doubleday $4.95. A description of an ant colony and material on the ant's anatomy and life cycle. Also use: *Tales of the Warrior Ants* by Dee Brown (1973, Putnam $4.29).

8117. Simon, Seymour. *Deadly Ants* (4–6). Illus. by William Downey. 1979, Four Winds $7.95. A vivid account of army ants.

Bees and Wasps

8118. Cloudsley-Thompson, J. L. *Bees and Wasps* (3–5). Illus. by Joyce Bee. 1976, McGraw $5.72. A fine, well-organized presentation of the life cycle of various kinds of bees and wasps.

8119. Fox, William. *The Amazing Bee* (K–3). Illustrated. 1977, Walck $6.95. An excellent introduction to bees and their work.

8120. Hawes, Judy. *Bees and Beelines* (K–2). Illus. by Aliki. 1964, Crowell $4.50; paper $1.45. Simple description about beehive activity and why bees always find their way home.

8121. Hoban, Brom. *Jason and the Bees* (1–3). Illus. by author. 1980, Harper $5.95; LB $6.89. A local beekeeper answers Jason's questions about bees in this easily read account.

8122. Hogan, Paula Z. *The Honeybee* (1–3). Illus. by Geri K. Strigenz. 1979, Raintree $5.99. A simple treatment of the life cycle of the bee.

8123. Hopf, Alice L. *Animals That Eat Nectar and Honey* (5–7). Illus. by Matthew Kalmenoff. 1979, Holiday $6.95. Bees, wasps, and other nectar eaters are described in this nicely presented account.

8124. Hutchins, Ross E. *Paper Hornets* (3–5). Illus. by Peter Zallinger. 1973, Addison $5.95. The 4 seasons of the year as seen through the life and activities of a colony of hornets.

8125. Ipsen, D. C. *What Does a Bee See?* (4–6). 1971, Addison $5.95. An account of the senses of a bee and its behavior.

8126. McClung, Robert M. *Bees, Wasps and Hornets: And How They Live* (3–5). Illus. by author. 1971, Morrow $5.95. The differences and similarities of these insects are clearly explained.

8127. Oxford Scientific Films, ed. *Bees and Honey* (3–5). Illustrated. 1977, Putnam $5.95. Lavishly illustrated with captioned color photographs, this overview includes 6 pages of text.

8128. Russell, Franklin. *The Honeybees* (1–3). Illus. by Colette Portal. 1967, Knopf $5.69. A lyrical text describing the yearly cycle of a honeybee colony.

8129. Shebar, Sharon Sigmond. *The Mysterious World of Honeybees* (4–6). Illustrated. 1979, Messner $6.97. Through a visit by 2 children to an apiary, material on bees is presented in text and photographs.

8130. Sheehan, Angela. *The Bumblebee* (3–5). Illus. by Maurice Pledger. 1977, Watts $3.50. The division of labor in a bee colony is highlighted in this well-illustrated nature book.

8131. Shuttlesworth, Dorothy E. *All Kinds of Bees* (3–5). Illus. by SuZan Swain. 1967, Random $4.99. A discussion of various kinds of bees, their anatomy, life cycle, and habits. Also use: *Let's Find Out about Bees* by Cathleen Fitzgerald (1973, Watts $4.47).

Beetles

8132. Bronson, Wilfrid S. *Beetles* (4–6). Illus. by author. 1963, Harcourt $5.50. Different varieties of beetles, including the firefly and the glowworm.

8133. Conklin, Gladys. *I Like Beetles* (K–3). Illus. by Jean Zallinger. 1975, Holiday $6.95. Twenty-nine different types of beetles described in illustrations and brief text.

8134. Hutchins, Ross E. *Insects in Armor: A Beetle Book* (4–6). Illustrated. 1972, Parents $5.41. A good look at beetles.

8135. Patent, Dorothy, and Schroeder, Paul C. *Beetles and How They Live* (6–9). Illustrated. 1978, Holiday $7.95. A well-organized, thorough account of various types of beetles and their living habits.

Butterflies and Moths

8136. Hogan, Paula Z. *The Butterfly* (1–3). Illus. by Geri K. Strigenz. 1979, Raintree $5.99. Large, bright illustrations highlight this introductory account.

8137. McClung, Robert M. *Caterpillars and How They Live* (2–4). Illus. by author. 1965, Morrow $5.49. This informative account discusses the anatomy and life of the caterpillar.

8138. Overbeck, Cynthia. *The Butterfly Book* (2–4). Illustrated. 1978, Lerner $3.95. A colorful introduction to the life of butterflies and to 10 of the most popular varieties.

8139. Patent, Dorothy. *Butterflies and Moths: How They Function* (6–9). 1979, Holiday $7.95. A straightforward, thorough account that explains all aspects of the life and habits of lepidoptera.

8140. Selsam, Millicent E. *Terry and the Caterpillars* (K–3). Illus. by Arnold Lobel. 1962, Harper $4.79. The life cycle of a caterpillar is simply told with charming pictures. Also use: *I Like Caterpillars* by Gladys Conklin (1958, Holiday $5.95).

8141. Sterling, Dorothy. *Caterpillars* (3–6). Illus. by Winifred Lubell. 1961, Doubleday $3.50. Fascinating and humorous book about 50 caterpillars.

8142. Whitlock, Ralph. *A Closer Look at Butterflies and Moths* (4–6). Illustrated. 1978, Watts $5.90. The life cycles, ecological effects and migrating patterns of butterflies and moths are well covered.

Spiders

8143. Conklin, Gladys. *Black Widow Spider—Danger!* (2–4). Illustrated. 1979, Holiday $4.95. An interesting account that includes material on living habits, including food, of the black widow.

8144. Conklin, Gladys. *Tarantula: The Giant Spider* (1–3). Illus. by Glen Rounds. 1972, Holiday $4.50. The life cycle of male and female California tarantulas.

8145. Freschet, Berniece. *The Web in the Grass* (1–2). Illus. by Roger Duvoisin. 1972, Scribner $8.95. Clear, bright, colorful illustrations and a poetic text describe the life cycle of a spider. Also use: *Wolfie* by Janet Chenery (1969, Harper $5.95).

8146. Goldin, Augusta. *Spider Silk* (1–3). Illus. by Joseph Low. 1964, Crowell $4.50; LB $6.95; paper $1.45. The complete story of spiders and the various kinds of webs they weave. Also use: *Spider Web* by Julie Brinckloe (1974, Doubleday $3.95).

8147. Hawes, Judy. *My Daddy Longlegs* (1–3). Illus. by Walter Lorraine. 1972, Crowell $6.95. In a simple text, the reader is given directions on how to study this spider.

8148. Lavine, Sigmund A. *Wonders of the Spider World* (4–6). Illustrated. 1966, Dodd $4.95. Interesting facts, including the varieties of spiders and their habits. Also use: *Spiders* by Dorothy Hogner (1955, Crowell $7.39).

8149. Lexau, Joan M. *The Spider Makes a Web* (2–4). Illus. by Arabelle Wheatley. 1979, Holiday $5.95. A simple introductory account of the life cycle of a spider.

8150. Oxford Scientific Films, ed. *The Spider's Web* (4–8). Illustrated. 1978, Putnam $5.95. The webs of two different spiders are explored in a brief text and many striking photographs.

8151. Shuttlesworth, Dorothy E. *The Story of Spiders* (5–8). Illus. by SuZan Swain. 1959, Doubleday $5.95. The habits and habitats of spiders are discussed along with material on webs. Also use: *Spiders and Scorpions* by J. L. Cloudsley-Thompson (1973, McGraw $5.72).

8152. Victor, Joan Berg. *Tarantulas* (3–5). Illus. by author. 1979, Dodd $5.95. The facts about this spider are much less frightening than the incorrect stories often believed.

8153. Walther, Tom. *A Spider Might* (3–5). Illustrated. 1978, Sierra $7.95. All sorts of things you could do, if you were a spider.

Other Insects

8154. Ault, Philip H. *Wonders of the Mosquito World* (5–7). Illustrated. 1970, Dodd $4.50. Structure, species, habitats, and measures used to control this nuisance. Also use with a younger group: *Mosquitoes* by Charles L. Ripper (1969, Morrow $5.49).

8155. Cole, Joanna. *Cockroaches* (3–6). Illus. by Jean Zallinger. 1971, Morrow $4.84. A concise and interesting nature study that presents little-known facts about the cockroach, the amazing insect that has survived almost unchanged for some 300 million years, and why it is important to scientists today.

8156. Cole, Joanna. *Fleas* (3–5). Illus. by Elsie Wrigley. 1973, Morrow $5.09. A fascinating account of the life cycle and habits of fleas, including their role in flea circuses.

8157. Conklin, Gladys. *I Watch Flies* (1–3). Illus. by Jean Zallinger. 1977, Holiday $6.95. There are 27 species of flies, and the reader learns about each.

8158. Conklin, Gladys. *Praying Mantis; The Garden Dinosaur* (2–3). Illus. by Glen Rounds. 1978, Holiday $4.95. Simple text and forceful drawings are used to tell about the life and habits of a praying mantis.

8159. Earle, Olive L. *Crickets* (K–2). 1956, Morrow $5.09. The world of crickets is interestingly explored.

8160. George, Jean Craighead. *All Upon a Stone* (2–3). Illus. by Don Bolognese. 1971, Crowell $7.50. A male cricket emerges from the earth deep under a stone, explores his environment, encounters other male crickets, and returns.

8161. Hess, Lilo. *The Praying Mantis, Insect Cannibal* (3–6). Illustrated. 1971, Scribner $6.95. Through excellent photographs and a clear text, the praying mantis is discussed. Also use: *Praying Mantis* by Olive L. Earle (1969, Morrow $5.09).

8162. Hogner, Dorothy Childs. *Grasshoppers and Crickets* (2–5). Illus. by Nils Hogner. 1960, Crowell $6.95. A simple account that distinguishes between various species and gives the life history of each. Also use *The Grasshopper Book* by Wilfrid S. Bronson (1943, Harcourt $4.95).

8163. Hutchins, Ross E. *The World of Dragonflies and Damselflies* (5–7). Illustrated. 1969, Dodd $5.50. The author distinguishes between these species, tells about their life cycles, and gives instructions on how to collect and identify them.

8164. McClung, Robert M. *Green Darner* (2–3). Illus. by Carol Lerner. 1980, Morrow $6.95; LB $6.67. The classic account of the life and habits of a dragonfly, originally published in 1956.

8165. McClung, Robert M. *Ladybug* (2–4). Illus. by author. 1966, Morrow $4.81. A lively, scientific account of the life cycle of this familiar beetle. Also use: *Ladybug, Ladybug Fly Away Home* by Judy Hawes (1967, Crowell $4.50; LB $5.95).

8166. Pringle, Laurence. *Cockroaches: Here, There and Everywhere* (K–3). Illus. by James McCrea and Ruth McCrea. 1971, Crowell $4.50; LB $5.95. An easily read science book about the history, intelligence, and habits of the cockroach.

8167. Ryder, Joanne. *Fireflies* (1–3). Illus. by Don Bolognese. 1977, Harper $4.95; LB $4.79. An easily read introduction to the life history of a firefly. Also use: *Fireflies in the Night* by Judy Hawes (1963, Crowell $4.50; paper $1.45).

8168. Simon, Hilda. *Dragonflies* (5–7). Illus. by author. 1972, Viking $4.95. A simple, accurate account of the life of dragonflies and of their various species.

8169. White, William Jr, and White, Sara Jane. *A Mosquito Is Born* (5–7). Illustrated. 1978, Sterling $4.95; LB $4.99. The birth, life cycle, and place in history of the mosquito.

8170. Wong, Herbert H., and Vessel, Matthew F. *My Ladybug* (1–3). Illus. by Marie Nonnast Behlen. 1969, Addison $5.95. Short and simple text and color illustrations introduce the life, habits, and value of ladybugs.

Reptiles and Amphibians

General

8171. Allen, Gertrude E. *Everyday Turtles, Toads and Their Kin* (1–3). 1970, Houghton $5.95. A basic introduction to the world of reptiles and amphibians, with material on the classes such as lizards, snakes, and frogs.

8172. Angell, Madeline. *Snakes and Frogs and Turtles and Such* (4–8). Illustrated. 1978, Bobbs $7.95. A well-organized, clearly presented overview of American reptiles and amphibians.

8173. Cochran, Doris M. *Living Amphibians of the World* (6–8). Illustrated. 1966, Doubleday $19.95. The characteristics and classification of various species of amphibians.

8174. Fenton, Carroll Lane, and Pallas, Dorothy C. *Reptiles and Their World* (4–7). Illustrated. 1961, John Day $4.50. A description of the types, habits, habitats, and usefulness of reptiles. Also use: *The Book of Reptiles and Amphibians* by Michael H. Bevan (1956, Doubleday $5.95).

8175. Harris, Susan. *Reptiles* (1–4). Illustrated. 1978, Watts $4.90. An easily read science book that supplies basic information.

8176. Huntington, Harriet E. *Let's Look at Reptiles* (2–4). Illustrated. 1973, Doubleday $5.95. A description of the major North American reptiles, their structures, and living habits. Also use: *Reptiles Do the Strangest Things* by Leonora Hornblow (1970, Random $2.95; LB $3.99).

8177. McGowen, Tom. *Album of Reptiles* (4–6). Illus. by Rod Ruth. 1978, Rand $5.95. The author makes an extremely clear presentation of material on the reptile and its world.

8178. Patent, Dorothy. *Reptiles and How They Reproduce* (6–9). Illus. by Matthew Kalmenoff. 1977, Holiday $6.95. Introductory material on reptiles, followed by a detailed account of reproduction in various species.

8179. Pope, Clifford H. *Reptiles Round the World* (6–9). Illus. by Helen D. Tee-Van. 1957, Knopf $5.99. A simplified natural history of snakes, lizards, turtles, and crocodilians.

8180. Stonehouse, Bernard. *A Closer Look at Reptiles* (3–5). Illus. by Gary Hincks; Alan Male; and Phil Weare. 1979, Watts $5.90. A discussion of 4 groups of reptiles—snakes, lizards, crocodiles, and tortoises.

8181. Wise, William. *Giant Snakes and Other Amazing Reptiles* (4–6). Illus. by Joseph Sibal. 1970, Putnam $3.96. The cobra, sea snake, iguana, and alligator are among the many unusual reptiles described.

8182. Zim, Herbert S. *Reptiles and Amphibians* (4–6). 1956, Golden West $5.95; paper $1.95. This book contains brief descriptions of 100 common reptiles and amphibians.

Crocodiles and Alligators

8183. Curto, Josephine J. *Biography of an Alligator* (3–5). Illus. by Bill Elliott. 1976, Putnam $4.97. The dramatic life story of an alligator in the Florida Everglades.

8184. Graham, Ada, and Graham, Frank. *Alligators* (6–8). Illus. by D. D. Tyler. 1979, Delacorte $7.95. A life-cycle book that emphasizes human responsibility to keep this species alive.

8185. Gross, Ruth Belov. *Alligators and Other Crocodilians* (3–5). Illustrated. 1978, Four Winds $5.95. The characteristics and behavior of four members of the crocodilian family.

8186. Lauber, Patricia. *Who Needs Alligators?* (2–4). Illustrated. 1974, Garrard $4.48. A very useful book on alligators—their habits, homes in ponds and streams, reproductive cycle, and animals that prey on them.

8187. Ricciuti, Edward R. *The American Alligator: Its Life in the Wild* (5–7). Illustrated. 1972, Harper $7.89. A detailed discussion of the life and habits of the alligator, with additional information on its evolution and future.

8188. Shaw, Evelyn. *Alligator* (1–2). Illus. by Frances Zweifel. 1972, Harper $5.95; LB $6.89. An accurate description of the alligator's life cycle told in simple narrative form.

8189. Zim, Herbert S. *Alligators and Crocodiles* (3–6). Illustrated. 1978, Morrow $5.71. The author differentiates between the two, tells where they can be found, and gives information on their habits.

Frogs and Toads

8190. Billings, Charlene W. *Spring Peepers Are Calling* (4–5). Illustrated. 1979, Dodd $4.95. The life cycle of the tree frog with black-and-white pictures.

8191. Chenery, Janet. *The Toad Hunt* (1–3). Illus. by Ben Shecter. 1967, Harper $5.95. While hunting for a toad, Teddy and Peter find a turtle, salamander, polliwogs, and frogs. Also use: *What I Like about Toads* by Judy Hawes (1969, Crowell $5.95; paper $1.45).

8192. Hawes, Judy. *Spring Peepers* (2–3). Illus. by Graham Booth. 1975, Crowell $6.89. A simply written description of a tree frog's life, with advice on how to observe these common spring peepers.

8193. Hawes, Judy. *Why Frogs Are Wet* (1–3). Illus. by Don Madden. 1968, Crowell paper $2.95. The life of frogs and their history back to prehistoric times. Also use: *Frogs and Polliwogs* by Dorothy C. Hogner (1956, Crowell $4.50).

8194. Hogan, Paula Z. *The Frog* (2–3). Illus. by Geri K. Strigenz. 1979, Raintree $5.99. The growth and development of the frog in a well-illustrated account. Also use: *Bufo: The Story of a Toad* by Robert M. McClung (1954, Morrow $6.45).

8195. Hogeweg, Martin. *The Green Frog* (3–5). Illus. by Ries Moonen. 1979, Barron's $4.95. A life-cycle account notable for its simple text and stunning watercolors.

8196. McClung, Robert M. *Peeper, First Voice of Spring* (2–4). Illus. by Carol Lerner. 1977, Morrow $5.95; LB $5.49. This simple, direct account follows one tiny frog through its life cycle. Also use: *Hyla (Peep) Crucifer* by Carol Cornelius (1978, Child's World $5.51).

8197. McClung, Robert M. *Spotted Salamander* (2–4). Illus. by author. 1964, Morrow $6.01. A year in the life of a salamander from its awakening one spring until the next.

8198. Naden, Corinne J. *Let's Find Out About Frogs* (K–3). Illus. by Jerry Lang. 1972, Watts $4.47. An easily read introduction to the habits and habitats of frogs.

8199. Oxford Scientific Films, ed. *Common Frog* (4–8). Illustrated. 1979, Putnam $6.95. The life cycle of the frog brilliantly conveyed chiefly through photographs.

8200. Patent, Dorothy. *Frogs, Toads, Salamanders and How They Reproduce* (4–7). Illus. by Matthew Kalmenoff. 1975, Holiday $6.95. Fascinating facts about amphibians with excellent material on their many adaptations. Also use: *Frogs, Toads and Newts* by F. D. Ommanney (1975, McGraw $5.72).

8201. Rockwell, Anne, and Rockwell, Harlow. *Toad* (PS–K). Illustrated. 1972, Doubleday $4.95. A matter-of-fact account of a year in a toad's life, written simply and poetically. Also use: *A First Look at Frogs, Toads and Salamanders* by Millicent E. Selsam (1976, Walker $4.47).

8202. Simon, Hilda. *Frogs and Toads of the World* (5–9). Illus. by author. 1975, Lippincott $7.95. Each chapter deals with different varieties of amphibians in this well-illustrated, entertaining account. Also use: *Wonders of Frogs and Toads* by Wyatt Blassingame (1975, Dodd $4.95).

8203. Simon, Seymour. *Discovering What Frogs Do* (2–4). Illus. by Jean Zallinger. 1969, McGraw $6.95. An introduction to the world of frogs and how to collect and take care of them. Also use: *Frogs and Toads* by Herbert S. Zim (1950, Morrow $5.09).

Lizards

8204. Conklin, Gladys. *I Caught A Lizard* (K–3). 1967, Holiday $5.95. A close-up look at a small lizard.

8205. Freschet, Berniece. *Lizard Lying in the Sun* (1–3). Illus. by Glen Rounds. 1975, Scribner $5.95. An easily read account of a lizard's adventure and escape.

8206. Hartman, Jane E. *Looking At Lizards* (6–9). Illustrated. 1978, Holiday $6.95. A well-organized account with separate chapters on important species.

8207. Hess, Lilo. *The Remarkable Chameleon* (2–4). Illus. by author. 1968, Scribner $5.95. Outstanding photographs; many previously held misconceptions about this small lizard are discredited as a result of this close study.

Snakes

8208. Brenner, Barbara. *A Snake-Lover's Diary* (5–9). Illustrated. 1970, Addison $5.95. How to catch and care for reptiles, with many details on habits, appearance, and behavior.

8209. Gross, Ruth Belov. *Snakes* (3–5). Illustrated. 1975, Four Winds $6.95. An easy-to-read introduction, well illustrated with black-and-white and color photographs.

8210. Hecht, Bessie. *All about Snakes* (5–7). Illus. by Rudolf Freund. 1956, Random $4.39. Various types of snakes and how they live and reproduce.

8211. Leen, Nina. *Snakes* (4–8). Illustrated. 1978, Holt $6.95. A brief text on the various life functions of snakes expertly illustrated with fine photographs.

8212. McClung, Robert M. *Snakes: Their Place in the Sun* (3–5). Illustrated. 1979, Garrard $5.10. The structure and life cycle of the snake are covered in this introductory account.

8213. Roever, Joan M. *Snake Secrets* (6–9). Illustrated. 1979, Walker $7.95. This volume entertainingly explores the habits and behavior of snakes and how to raise one as a pet.

8214. Shapp, Martha, and Shapp, Charles. *Let's Find Out about Snakes* (K–3). Illustrated. 1968, Watts $4.90. General characteristics of snakes and specific types.

8215. Simon, Hilda. *Snakes: The Facts and the Folklore* (6–9). Illus. by author. 1973, Viking $6.95. Various aspects of snake lore are explored (with special coverage on venomous and nonvenomous varieties), how to keep snakes as pets, and snakes through the ages.

8216. Simon, Seymour. *Discovering What Garter Snakes Do* (3–5). Illustrated. 1975, McGraw $5.72. A sympathetic informative view of the living habits of garter snakes.

8217. Simon, Seymour. *Meet the Giant Snakes* (3–5). Illus. by Harriet Springer. 1979, Walker $7.95; LB $7.85. A straightforward account of the habits and life cycle of such reptiles as pythons and boas.

8218. Zim, Herbert S. *Snakes* (3–5). Illustrated. 1949, Morrow $5.52. The snake, its structure, and anatomy are simply introduced. Also use: *The First Book of Snakes* by John Hoke (1967, Watts $4.90).

Turtles and Tortoises

8219. Bare, Colleen Stanley. *The Durable Desert Tortoise* (3–5). Illus. by author. 1979, Dodd $4.95. The life cycle of the desert tortoise, including mating and egg-laying habits.

8220. Darling, Lois, and Darling, Louis. *Turtles* (3–5). Illustrated. 1962, Morrow $5.09. This account covers basic information on the structure, habits, and life cycle of turtles.

8221. Freschet, Berniece. *Turtle Pond* (K–3). Illus. by Donald Carrick. 1971, Scribner $6.95. Many facets of pond life, centering on a turtle and her eggs.

8222. Goode, John. *Turtles, Tortoises and Terrapins* (4–6). Illus. by Alec Bailey. 1974, Scribner $4.95. Many species from around the world are introduced along with material on their history, characteristics, and life cycles.

8223. Johnson, Fred. *Turtles and Tortoises* (1–3). Illustrated. 1974, National Wildlife $2.50. Two stories about these amphibians and a plea for conservation. Also use: *Creepy Crawly Things* by the National Geographic Society (1974, $6.95).

8224. Holling, Holling C. *Minn of the Mississippi* (4–6). Illus. by author. 1951, Houghton $4.95. A snapping turtle's trip down the Mississippi.

8225. Scott, Jack. *Loggerhead Turtle: Survivor from the Sea* (5–8). Illustrated. 1974, Putnam $6.95. A fine book about an unusual creature that has remained unchanged for ages.

8226. Waters, John F. *Green Turtle Mysteries* (1–3). Illus. by Mamoru Funai. 1972, Crowell $4.50; LB $5.95. The author poses unanswered questions about the creature's life in the sea. Also use: *Long Voyage: The Life Cycle of a Green Turtle* by Alvin Silverstein (1972, Warne $3.95).

Birds

General

8227. Anderson, John M. *The Changing World of Birds* (6–8). Illustrated. 1973, Holt $5.59. The life cycle of birds, with emphasis on the disastrous effect of humans.

8228. Austin, Elizabeth S. *Birds That Stopped Flying* (4–6). Illustrated. 1969, Random $3.99. A report on flightless birds beginning with the evolution of birds.

8229. Baskin, Tobias. *Hosie's Aviary* (4–8). Illus. by Leonard Baskin. 1979, Viking $10.00. Impressive paintings and lyric text introduce common and exotic birdlife to youngsters.

8230. Blough, Glenn O. *Bird Watchers and Bird Feeders* (1–3). Illus. by Jeanne Bendick. 1963, McGraw $5.72. How to recognize the most common birds; simple instructions for feeders, menus, and such. Also use: *Bird Watching* by Aubrey Burns (1968, Watts $4.47).

8231. Dugdale, Vera. *Album of North American Birds* (5–7). Illus. by Clark Bronson. 1967, Rand $4.95; paper $2.95. The appearance and life cycles of 52 well-known birds, with excellent illustrations, many in color.

8232. Earle, Olive L. *Birds and Their Beaks* (3–6). Illus. by author. 1965, Morrow $5.09. An account that uses examples from 46 birds to show how the bill or beak serves different purposes.

8233. Garelick, May. *It's about Birds* (2–4). Illus. by Tony Chen. 1978, Holt $6.95. A simple presentation of basic facts about the structure and life of birds.

8234. Hogner, Dorothy Childs. *Birds of Prey* (4–6). Illus. by Nils Hogner. 1969, Crowell $4.50. Fifty birds of prey, their nests and habits are described. Also use: *Birds That Hunt* by Willard Luce (1970, Follett $2.97).

8235. Hornblow, Leonora. *Birds Do the Strangest Things* (1–3). Illus. by Michael K. Frith. 1965, Random $2.95; LB $3.99. Simply presented material on many interesting birds such as the hummingbird and the ostrich.

8236. Kieran, John. *An Introduction to Birds* (6–9). Illus. by Don Eckelberry. 1965, Doubleday $5.95. An informal guide to the most commonly seen birds, with accompanying illustrations and basic material. Also use: *Birds: A Guide to the Most Familiar American Birds* by Herbert S. Zim (1956, Golden $5.95; paper $1.95).

8237. Limburg, Peter R. *What's in the Names of Birds* (5–7). Illus. by Tom Huffman. 1975, Coward $5.49. The names and habits of 48 birds of North America.

8238. Pluckrose, Henry. *Birds* (2–4). Illus. by John Rignall and Maurice Wilson. 1979, Watts $2.95; LB $4.90. The habits, behavior, and varieties of birds are briefly introduced in this simple account.

8239. Robbins, Chandler. *Birds of North America: A Guide to Field Identification* (6–9). Illus. by Arthur B. Singer. 1965, Golden $7.95; LB $6.50; paper $4.95. Describes hundreds of birds on the continent.

8240. Selsam, Millicent E., and Hunt, Joyce. *A First Look at Birds* (2–4). Illus. by Harriet Springer. 1973, Walker paper $.95. Through questions and simple text, the authors introduce the salient characteristics of birds and their various environmental adaptations. Also use: *Let's Discover Birds in Our World* by Ada Graham (1974, Golden $5.95).

8241. Shaw, Richard, ed. *The Bird Book* (3–5). Illustrated. 1974, Warne $4.95. An anthology of various kinds of literature, chiefly poems and stories about birds, with 19 attractive illustrations by various artists.

8242. Welty, Susan F. *Birds with Bracelets: The Story of Bird-Banding* (4–7). Illus. by John Kaufmann. 1965, Prentice-Hall $4.95. How scientists learn about birds and their migrations through banding.

8243. Wildsmith, Brian. *Brian Wildsmith's Birds* (K–3). Illus. by author. 1967, Watts $4.95. Brilliant illustrations of common birds.

8244. Williamson, Margaret. *The First Book of Birds* (4–6). Illus. by author. 1951, Watts $4.90. A simple introduction to such topics as how birds fly, gather food, and build their nests. Also use: *The Random House Book of Birds* by Elizabeth S. Austin (1970, Random $4.95).

Habits and Behavior

8245. Conklin, Gladys. *If I Were a Bird* (1–3). Illus. by Arthur Marokvia. 1965, Holiday $5.95. Songs, calls, and characteristics of 27 common birds. Musical notations for easily recognized calls. For an older group use: *How Birds Learn to Sing* by Barbara Ford (1975, Messner $6.25; LB $5.79).

8246. Earle, Olive L. *Birds and Their Nests* (3–6). Illustrated. 1952, Morrow $5.09. The nests of 42 different species are presented with information on how the young are cared for.

8247. Farrar, Richard. *The Bird's Woodland: What Lives There* (3–6). Illus. by William Downey. 1976, Coward $4.99. Through text and drawings, this book explains the way birds live in the woods.

8248. Freedman, Russell. *How Birds Fly* (4–6). Illus. by Lorence Bjorklund. 1977, Holiday $6.95. A logical, lucid explanation of the elements in a bird's structure that contribute to its ability to fly. Also use: *Birds in Flight* by John Kaufmann (1970, Morrow $5.49).

8249. Gans, Roma. *Bird Talk* (1–3). Illus. by Jo Polseno. 1971, Crowell $4.50; LB $5.95. An explanation on how birds make different sounds on different occasions.

8250. Gans, Roma. *Birds at Night* (1–3). Illus. by Aliki. 1968, Crowell $5.95. A discussion of how a bird's structure enables it to exist through the night.

8251. Gans, Roma. *Birds Eat and Eat and Eat* (1–3). Illus. by Ed Emberley. 1963, Crowell $4.50; LB $5.95; 1975, paper $1.45. Basic information on what and how birds eat.

8252. Gans, Roma. *It's Nesting Time* (1–3). Illus. by Kazue Mizumura. 1964, Crowell $5.95; paper $1.45. Simple text and many illustrations convey basic information about nests.

8253. Gans, Roma. *When Birds Change Their Feathers* (1–3). Illus. by Felicia Bond. 1980, Crowell $7.89. An easily read account of the molting habits of birds.

8254. Henry, Marguerite. *Birds at Home* (2–5). Illus. by Jacob B. Abbott. 1972, Hubbard $7.95. A description of over 20 common birds and how they care for their young.

8255. Holden, Raymond. *Ways of Nesting Birds* (4–6). Illus. by Grace DeWitt. 1970, Dodd $4.50. The nesting habits of 49 kinds of birds are discussed.

8256. Hudson, Robert G. *Nature's Nursery: Baby Birds* (4–7). Illustrated. 1971, John Day $4.50. The young of 14 different species are pictured in text and photographs, with additional information on feeding.

8257. Kaufmann, John. *Birds Are Flying* (2–4). Illus. by author. 1979, Crowell $6.95; LB $6.89. Information on how birds fly is given along with various ways of flying.

Reproduction

8258. Cosgrove, Margaret. *Eggs—and What Happens Inside Them* (3–6). Illus. by author. 1966, Dodd $4.95. A valuable introduction to embryology for young readers. Also use: *Window into an Egg* by Geraldine Flanagan (1969, Young Scott $6.95).

8259. Henley, Karyn. *Hatch!* (2–4). Illus. by Susan Kennedy. 1980, Carolrhoda $4.95. A variety of nestmaking, egg-laying, and hatching methods are described.

8260. Lauber, Patricia. *What's Hatching Out of That Egg?* (2–4). Illustrated. 1979, Crown $7.95. Photographs enliven this question-and-answer approach to the birth of various animals.

8261. May, Julian. *Millions of Years of Eggs* (3–5). Illus. by Tom Dolan. 1970, Creative Education $6.95. How eggs have been a method of reproduction throughout world history is presented with eye-catching illustrations.

8262. Milgrom, Harry. *Egg-Ventures* (1–3). Illus. by Giulio Maestro. 1974, Dutton $6.95. Simple experiments and activities are outlined to reveal various properties of eggs. Also use: *Science Projects with Eggs* by David Webster (1976, Watts $4.90).

8263. Oxford Scientific Films. *The Chicken and the Egg* (4–8). Illustrated. 1979, Putnam $6.95. Incredibly detailed photographs outline the life cycles of the chicken from embryo to adult. For a younger group use: *A Chick Hatches* by Joanna Cole (1976, Morrow $6.95; LB $6.43).

8264. Selsam, Millicent E. *All about Eggs and How They Change into Animals* (K–3). Illus. by Helen Ludwig. 1952, Young Scott $5.95. A concise guide to how an egg develops. Also use: *Egg to Chick* (1970, Harper $4.79).

Ducks and Geese

8265. Fegely, Thomas D. *Wonders of Geese and Swans* (4–6). Illustrated. 1976, Dodd $4.95. The swans and geese of North America are introduced through interesting text, photographs, and line drawings.

8266. Fegely, Thomas D. *Wonders of Wild Ducks* (5–9). Illustrated. 1975, Dodd $4.95. A manual about ducks—habits, enemies, flight patterns—with emphasis on conservation.

8267. Ferguson, Dorothy. *Black Duck* (2–4). Illus. by Douglas Morris. 1978, Walker $6.85. Salt marsh life as seen from the viewpoint of a black duck and her seven ducklings.

8268. Goldin, Augusta. *Ducks Don't Get Wet* (K–2). Illus. by Leonard Kessler. 1965, Crowell $5.95; paper $1.45. An easy experiment that enables children to clarify why ducks can shed water. Pictures of various ducks in migration.

8269. Mannheim, Grete. *The Geese Are Back* (2–4). Illustrated. 1969, Parents $5.95; LB $5.41. Photographs tell of the return north of several migratory birds, including geese, ducks and swans.

8270. Scott, Jack. *Canada Geese* (5–9). Illustrated. 1976, Putnam $6.95. The habits and way of life of the Canada goose are explored along with fascinating sections on migration and flight patterns.

8271. Shaw, Evelyn. *A Nest of Wood Ducks* (1–2). Illus. by Cherryl Pape. 1976, Harper $4.95; LB $4.79. The yearly cycle of a wood duck, with a description of the mating, nesting, and brooding of one pair and the hatching of their young.

8272. Sheehan, Angela. *The Duck* (2–3). Illustrated. 1979, Watts $2.50; LB $4.90. Many basic facts are given in this account, such as eating habits, migration and natural enemies.

Eagles and Hawks

8273. Adrian, Mary. *The American Eagle* (3–5). Illus. by Genevieve Vaughan-Jackson. 1947, Hastings $4.95. Six months in the life of 2 eaglets.

8274. Arnosky, Jill. *A Kettle of Hawks and Other Wildlife Groups* (2–4). Illus. by author. 1979, McCann $7.50. A thoughtful book on the characteristics of various types of wildlife and their societies.

8275. Graham, Ada, and Graham, Frank. *Falcon Flight* (6–8). Illustrated. 1978, Delacorte $6.95. A

description of this bird and the reasons for its present declining population.

8276. Kaufmann, John, and Meng, Heinz. *Falcons Return* (5–9). Illustrated. 1975, Morrow $6.43. An introduction to how falcons live and the current methods used to try to save this endangered species.

8277. Kaufmann, John. *Fish Hawk* (4–6). Illus. by author. 1967, Morrow $5.50; LB $5.09. The life cycle of this bird of prey and how humans have endangered its future.

8278. Lavine, Sigmund A. *Wonders of the Eagle World* (4–6). Illustrated. 1974, Dodd $4.50. After a discussion of eagles in mythology and literature, this treatment covers varieties, habitats, and characteristics. Also use: *The Magnificent Bald Eagle: America's National Bird* by John F. Turner (1971, Random $3.50).

8279. Lavine, Sigmund A. *Wonders of the Hawk World* (4–7). Illustrated. 1972, Dodd $4.50. The hawk is revealed in fact and fiction, with emphasis on structure and behavior.

8280. Schick, Alice. *The Peregrine Falcons* (6–9). Illus. by Peter Parnall. 1975, Dial $5.95; LB $5.47. Using 2 actual birds named Zeus and Artemis as her subjects, the author describes the life cycle of this endangered group and efforts to help save them from extinction.

Gulls

8281. Darling, Louis. *The Gull's Way* (5–7). Illus. by author. 1965, Morrow $9.94. Life cycle of a herring gull family observed on an island off the Maine coast. For a younger group use: *Gulls* by Sarel Eimerl (1969, Simon & Schuster $3.79).

8282. Holling, Holling C. *Seabird* (4–6). 1948, Houghton $8.95; 1978, paper $3.95. A gull accompanies a whaling expedition.

8283. Schreiber, Elizabeth Anne, and Schreiber, Ralph. *Wonders of Sea Gulls* (5–8). Illustrated. 1975, Dodd $4.95. A well-illustrated account of the living habits of sea gulls.

8284. Scott, Jack. *The Gulls of Smuttynose Island* (5–8). Illustrated. 1977, Putnam $6.95. Every aspect of the life cycle of gulls is explored in this account of the birds that take over a small Atlantic island each year.

Owls

8285. Catchpole, Clive. *Owls* (3–6). Illustrated. 1978, McKay $5.52. An attractive addition to the literature on one of the most interesting bird families.

8286. Flower, Phyllis. *Barn Owl* (1–3). Illus. by Cheryll Paper. 1978, Harper $4.95. An easily read science book about the first year in an owl's life.

8287. Frewer, Glyn. *Tyto: The Odyssey of an Owl* (6–8). Illus. by Dick Kramer. 1977, Lothrop $6.95. Five years in the life of a barn owl, carefully but dramatically told. Also use: *Wonders of the Owl World* by Sigmund A. Lavine (1971, Dodd $4.50).

8288. Garelick, May. *About Owls* (2–4). Illus. by Tony Chen. 1975, Four Winds $6.95. This beautifully illustrated introduction to the elf, barn, and great-horned owls includes information on their habits and habitats. Also use: *The Mother Owl* by Edith Thacher Hurd (1974, Little $4.95).

8289. George, John, and George, Jean Craighead. *Bubo, The Great Horned Owl* (4–6). Illus. by Jean Craighead George. 1954, Dutton $5.95. The life story of Bubo and his mate in their forest surroundings. For a younger group use: *Owlet, the Great Horned Owl* by Irene Brody (1974, Houghton $4.95).

8290. Hoke, Helen L., and Pitt, Valerie. *Owls* (4–6). Illus. by Robert Jefferson. 1975, Watts $4.47. The structure, homes, and living habits of various kinds of owls are described in brief text and detailed drawings.

8291. Hopf, Alice L. *Biography of a Snowy Owl* (3–5). Illustrated. 1979, Putnam $5.49. Interesting information about the life style, food, and enemies of the snowy owl in a life-story format.

8292. MacArthur-Onslow, Annette. *Uhu* (4–7). Illus. by author. 1970, Knopf $5.99. A visit to the author's house by a baby owl and the temporary upsets caused by its sudden appearance.

Penguins

8293. Austin, Elizabeth S. *Penguins: The Birds with Flippers* (4–6). Illustrated. 1968, Random $4.39. The characteristics of 15 species are detailed in this interesting account.

8294. Hogan, Paula Z. *The Penguin* (1–3). Illus. by Geri K. Strigenz. 1979, Raintree $5.99. For

very young readers, an account that has marvelous illustrations.

8295. Johnston, Johanna. *Penguin's Way* (2–4). Illus. by Leonard Weisgard. 1962, Doubleday $5.95. Factual picture book about Antarctic Emperor penguins. Also use: *Penguins Are Coming* by R. L. Penney (1969, Harper $4.79).

8296. Stonehouse, Bernard. *Penguins* (5–8). Illus. by Trevor Boyer. 1980, McGraw $7.95. A simple introduction to the habits and characteristics of these birds.

8297. Tenaza, Richard. *Penguins* (5–8). Illustrated. 1980, Watts $6.90. The thorough and absorbing narrative of the life and ways of these birds.

8298. Thompson, David H. *The Penguin: Its Life Cycle* (4–7). 1974, Sterling $5.95; LB $5.89. The author spent 3 years in a penguin rookery collecting information for this fascinating chronicle. Also use: *Penguins Live Here* by Irmengarde Eberle (1975, Doubleday $4.95).

Other Birds

8299. Amon, Aline. *Roadrunners and Other Cuckoos* (6–9). Illus. by author. 1978, Atheneum $7.95. Various members of the cuckoo family are described and classified.

8300. Blassingame, Wyatt. *Wonders of Crows* (6–8). Illustrated. 1979, Dodd $5.95. Scientific facts are presented entertainingly, plus the inclusion of several humorous pet crow stories.

8301. Brenner, Barbara. *Baltimore Orioles* (1–2). Illus. by J. Winslow Higginbottom. 1974, Harper $4.95; LB $4.79. The yearly life cycle of one oriole family accurately and simply described for the beginning reader.

8302. Earle, Olive L. *Birds of the Crow Family* (3–4). Illus. by author. 1962, Morrow $5.09. Habits and peculiarities of the common crow, fish crow, raven, magpie, and blue jay.

8303. Farrar, Richard. *The Hungry Snowbird* (2–4). Illus. by Matthew Kalmenoff. 1975, Coward $4.49. The migration and winter feeding patterns of juncos, simply and capably told.

8304. Fisher, Harvey I, and Fisher, Mildred L. *Wonders of the World of the Albatross* (4–7). Illustrated. 1974, Dodd $4.50. The life cycle of the Laysan Albatross told through excellent text and unusual photographs.

8305. Flanagan, Geraldine, and Morris, Sean. *Window into a Nest* (5–9). Illustrated. 1976,

Houghton $7.95. Through an ingenious device, the authors were able to see and record the behavior of a family of chickadees.

8306. Freschet, Berniece. *Biography of a Buzzard* (3–5). Illus. by Bill Elliott. 1977, Putnam $4.97. A straightforward narrative of the life cycle of a turkey buzzard, illustrated with black-and-white drawings.

8307. Galinsky, Ellen. *Catbird* (1–3). Illustrated. 1971, Coward $5.95. Beautiful photographs in this account of the mating and nesting of 2 catbirds.

8308. Hopf, Alice L. *Biography of an Ostrich* (3–5). Illus. by Ben Stahl. 1975, Putnam $4.97. An interesting life story of these flightless birds. Also use: *Ostriches* by Aileen Fisher (1970, Crowell $5.50).

8309. Hogan, Paula Z. *The Black Swan* (1–3). Illus. by Kinuko Craft. 1979, Raintree $5.99. An introductory account about this exotic bird.

8310. Hurd, Edith Thacher. *Sandpipers* (1–3). Illus. by Lucienne Block. 1961, Crowell $4.50; LB $5.95. A year in the life of sandpipers, which includes information on nest building, raising young, and their unusual migration south.

8311. Hyde, Dayton O. *Cranes in My Corral* (4–6). Illustrated. 1971, Dial paper $1.95. Four sandhill cranes are raised by the author on his ranch in Oregon.

8312. Kahl, M. P. *Wonders of Storks* (5–8). Illustrated. 1978, Dodd $5.95. An introduction to the various species and their habits.

8313. Kaufmann, John. *Chimney Swift* (4–6). Illus. by author. 1979, Morrow $5.09. The fascinating behavior of the fastest of all birds.

8314. Kaufmann, John. *Robins Fly North, Robins Fly South* (3–5). Illus. by author. 1970, Crowell $5.95. An introduction to the life and habits of robins, with particular emphasis ŏn annual migrations.

8315. Lubell, Winifred, and Lubell, Cecil. *Birds in the Street: The City Pigeon Book* (3–5). Illus. by Winifred Lubell. 1971, Parents $5.41. The history of the pigeon in relation to humans, its adaptability to city life, and the attitudes of city dwellers toward them.

8316. McClung, Robert M. *Redbird: The Story of a Cardinal* (3–5). Illus. by author. 1968, Morrow $5.61; paper $3.80. The story of a year in the life of a cardinal during which he and his mate raise a family.

8317. Martin, Lynne. *Peacocks* (6–8). Illustrated. 1975, Morrow $5.95; LB $5.49. An overview that tells of the beliefs about and the history of peacocks as well as life-style and habits.

8318. Martin, Lynne. *Puffin: Bird of the Open Seas* (4–6). Illus. by Ted Lewin. 1976, Morrow $5.95; LB $5.49. A description of the life cycle, habits, and habitats of these interesting sea birds.

8319. May, Julian. *Wild Turkeys* (1–3). Illus. by John Hamberger. 1973, Holiday $4.95. A survey of the behavior patterns and struggles for survival of the wild turkey.

8320. Pringle, Laurence. *Listen to the Crows* (4–6). Illus. by Ted Lewin. 1976, Crowell $6.95. Twenty-three different sounds made by crows and their possible meanings.

8321. Schreiber, Elizabeth Anne. *Wonders of Terns* (5–9). Illustrated. 1978, Dodd $5.95. A detailed, thorough description of the life and habits of this sea bird.

8322. Scott, Jack. *Discovering the American Stork* (5–9). Illustrated. 1976, Harcourt $6.50. A satisfying and thorough description of the life-style and habits of the American stork, complemented by excellent photographs. Also use: *Stork* by Iliane Roels (1969, Grosset $6.95).

8323. Scott, Jack. *Discovering the Mysterious Egret* (5–7). Illustrated. 1978, Harcourt $7.98. A photo essay about a mysterious and fascinating bird.

8324. Scott, Jack. *The Submarine Bird* (4–6). Illustrated. 1979, Putnam $8.95. An account of the life and behavior of the cormorant.

8325. Scott, Jack. *That Wonderful Pelican* (5–8). Illustrated. 1975, Putnam $6.95. The types and habits of pelicans are described, as well as places where they can be found, and the poor prospects for their survival. Also use: *Wonders of the Pelican World* by Joseph J. Cook (1974, Dodd $4.50) and *Scoop: The Last of the Brown Pelicans* by Robert M. McClung (1972, Morrow $5.50; LB $5.49).

8326. Simon, Hilda. *Wonders of Hummingbirds* (4–6). Illus. by author. 1964, Dodd $4.50. An introduction to the amazing migration, feeding habits, and other wonders associated with these birds. Also use: *Ruby Throat: The Story of a Hummingbird* by Robert M. McClung (1950, Morrow $5.61; paper $3.80).

8327. Stemple, David. *High Ridge Gobbler: A Story of the American Wild Turkey* (5–7). Illus. by Ted Lewin. 1979, Collins $7.95. A brood of turkeys are examined from hatching to their first mating.

8328. Turner, Ann W. *Vultures* (5–7). Illus. by Marian Gray Warren. 1973, McKay $8.95. These feathered scavengers are presented in a fascinating account that also introduces many related species.

8329. Voight, Virginia F. *Brave Little Hummingbird* (2–4). Illus. by Lydea Rosier. 1971, Putnam $3.49. The phenomenal flight of a ruby-throated hummingbird from a Central American jungle to New England. For a younger group use: *Hummingbirds in the Garden* by Roma Gans (1969, Crowell $5.95).

8330. Zoll, Max Alfred. *A Flamingo Is Born* (1–3). Illustrated. 1978, Putnam $5.95. Through text and large black-and-white photos, the reproductive process of flamingos is depicted.

Land Animals

General

8331. Anderson, Sydney. *The Lives of Animals* (5–7). 1965, Creative Education $6.95. A thorough study including general information in the field of biology.

8332. Barker, Will. *Familiar Animals of America* (6–8). Illus. by Carl Burger. 1956, Harper $9.87. A guide to more than 50 species. Also use: *Parade of the Animal Kingdom* by Robert Hegner (1967, Macmillan $4.95).

8333. Brady, Irene. *Wild Babies: A Canyon Sketchbook* (4–5). Illus. by author. 1979, Houghton $8.95. A sketchbook of such common wildlife as young deer, bobcats, and squirrels.

8334. Caras, Roger. *The Bizarre Animals* (5–8). Illustrated. 1974, Crown $3.95. Brief descriptions and photographs of 60 unusual animals, such as the platypus and chameleon.

8335. Caras, Roger A. *On Safari with Roger Caras* (3–5). Illustrated. 1979, Windmill $7.95. A naturalist and his son share adventures on a Kenya safari.

8336. Clemens, Virginia Phelps. *Super Animals and Their Unusual Careers* (4–6). 1979, Westminster $8.95. Animals that perform unusual tasks are highlighted.

8337. Cober, Alan E. *Cober's Choice* (3–7). Illus. by author. 1979, Dutton $9.95. A series of animal studies drawn by a master.

8338. Cohen, Daniel. *Night Animals* (4–6). Illus. by Haris Petie. 1970, Messner $4.79. How night animals adapt themselves—adjusting their vision, substituting hearing for vision, and their biological "alarm clocks". Also use: *Wonders of the Woods and Desert at Night* by Jacquelyn Berrill (1963, Dodd $4.50).

8339. Cooper, Gale. *Inside Animals* (3–5). Illus. by author. 1978, Little $6.95. The innards of 14 animals from the simple amoeba to the guinea pig.

8340. Dugdale, Vera. *Album of North American Animals* (5–7). Illus. by Clark Bronson. 1966, Rand paper $2.95. The life cycles of the larger animals of North America concisely described, including the grizzly bear, buffalo, cougar, sea lion, and beaver. Also use: *Wild Animals of North America* by the National Geographic Society (1960, $7.75).

8341. Earle, Olive L. *Paws, Hoofs, and Flippers* (4–6). Illus. by author. 1954, Morrow $5.49. A classification of animals by outer appendages.

8342. Epple, Anne Orth. *Lookalikes* (4–6). Illus. by Yoshiko Bright. 1971, St. Martins $4.95. Twenty-nine pairs of similar animals are compared in this lively book.

8343. Gilbreath, Alice. *Creatures of the Night: Nocturnal Animals of North America* (4–7). Illustrated. 1979, McKay $7.95. The habits and ways of life of more than 45 night animals are described.

8344. Hafslund, Per. *Little Wonders of Nature* (4–6). Illustrated. 1964, Stuart $4.00. The hedgehog and titmouse are 2 of the animals highlighted in this book.

8345. Hellman, Hal. *The Right Size* (6–8). Illus. by Sam Salant. 1968, Putnam $4.89. Subtitle: *Why Some Creatures Survive and Others Are Extinct.*

8346. Hopf, Alice L. *Misunderstood Animals* (4–7). Illustrated. 1973, McGraw $5.72. Disliked animals, such as the octopus and hyena, have their reputations restored in this well-researched book. Also use: *Animals That Frighten People: Fact Versus Myths* by Dorothy E. Shuttlesworth (1973, Dutton $6.95).

8347. Johnson, Sylvia A. *Animals of the Deserts* (5–7). Illus. by Alcuin C. Dornisch. 1976, Lerner $4.95. Part of a set of 6 volumes that describe and sample animal life in various climatic regions. Another in the set: *Animals of the Mountain* (1976, $4.95).

8348. Johnson, Sylvia A. *Animals of the Grasslands* (3–5). Illus. by Alcuin C. Dornisch. 1976, Lerner $4.95. One title in a fine series that includes: *Animals of the Temperate Forests* and *Animals of the Tropical Forests* (each 1976, $4.95).

8349. Johnson, Sylvia A. *The Wildlife Atlas* (5–7). Illus. by Alcuin C. Dornisch. 1977, Lerner $10.00.

Sixty animals of various species are presented in relation to the 6 major geographical areas of the world.

8350. Kellner, Esther. *Animals Come to My House: A Story Guide to the Care of Small Wild Animals* (5–7). Illus. by Heidi Palmer. 1976, Putnam $7.95. A collection of stories and nonfiction material on the care of such small animals as squirrels, opossums, and groundhogs.

8351. Laycock, George. *Wild Hunters: North America's Predators* (6–8). Illustrated. 1978, McKay $7.95. An interesting introduction to such wildlife as sharks and cougars, as well as wrens and shrews.

8352. Limburg, Peter R. *What's in the Name of Wild Animals* (5–9). Illus. by Murray Tinkelman. 1977, Coward $5.49. Stories, background information, and out-of-the way facts on 46 animals from different regions of the world.

8353. Merrill, Margaret W. *Skeletons That Fit* (4–6). Illus. by Pamela Carroll. 1979, Coward $5.29. A description of the skeletons of various vertebrates and how they evolved.

8354. Milan, Manuel, and Keane, William. *Fact and Fancy in American Wildlife* (4–6). Illustrated. 1969, Houghton $5.95. Maxims and proverbs about animals are explored.

8355. Palazzo, Tony. *Animals of the Night* (4–6). Illus. by author. 1970, Lion $5.98. Interesting information about nocturnal denizens from all around the world.

8356. Palazzo, Tony. *Biggest and Littlest Animals* (4–7). Illus. by author. 1970, Lion $5.95; LB $5.49. Many ways of comparing animals are explored, including size and mobility.

8357. Patent, Dorothy. *Sizes and Shapes in Nature: What They Mean* (6–9). Illustrated. 1979, Holiday $7.95. An explanation of how environmental needs have effected structural changes in various animals.

8358. Pringle, Laurence. *Discovering Nature Indoors* (5–7). Illustrated. 1970, Natural Hist. Pr. $4.95. Subtitle: *A Nature and Science Guide to Investigations with Small Animals.*

8359. Roth, Charles E. *Walking Catfish and Other Aliens* (5–7). Illustrated. 1973, Addison $5.95. A discussion of animals who are now, but were not originally, inhabitants of the United States. Also use: *Misplaced Animals, and Other Living Creatures* by Alice L. Hopf (1975, McGraw $5.72).

8360. Russell, Solveig P. *Coats and Covers* (4–6). Illus. by Frank O'Leary. 1970, Steck $3.25. How humans and animals are protected by their outer coverings and how these often must be supplemented.

8361. Scott, Jack. *The Survivors: Enduring Animals of North America* (5–9). Illus. by Daphne Gillen. 1975, Harcourt $7.50. In separate chapters, the author describes 12 different animals that have not become endangered. Some examples: chipmunk, coyote, porcupine, and raccoon.

8362. Selsam, Millicent E. *When an Animal Grows* (1–3). Illus. by John Kaufmann. 1966, Harper $5.95. A simple introduction to growth patterns among different species.

8363. Selsam, Millicent E., and Hunt, Joyce. *First Look at Mammals* (1–3). Illus. by Harriet Springer. 1973, Walker paper $.95. A question-and-answer approach to the life and structure of a number of mammals. For an older group use: *Mammals and How They Live* by Robert M. McClung (1963, Random $4.39).

8364. Simon, Seymour. *Animal Fact/Animal Fable* (2–3). Illus. by Diane deGroat. 1978, Crown $7.95; paper $3.95. Fact and fallacies about animals entertainingly presented.

8365. Stephen, David, ed. *Encyclopedia of Animals* (6–9). Illustrated. 1974, St. Martins $12.95. An excellent reference or browsing book originally written by 2 Czech zoologists, now edited by an English scientist, and published with all its wealth of illustrations and text. Also use: *Mice, Men and Elephants: A Book about Mammals* by Herbert S. Zim (1942, Harcourt $5.95).

8366. Tee-Van, Helen D. *Small Mammals Are Where You Find Them* (5–7). Illus. by author. 1966, Knopf $5.39. Seven small species of mammals from the United States are introduced with maps and identifying data.

8367. Wildsmith, Brian. *Brian Wildsmith's Wild Animals* (1–3). Illus. by author. 1967, Watts $4.95. A lavishly illustrated book that deals with groups of animals.

8368. Wise, William. *The Amazing Animals of North America* (1–3). Illus. by Joseph Sibal. 1971, Putnam $3.96. Several interesting native animals, such as the grizzly and mountain goat, are introduced, as well as a narrative on how humans have adversely affected their existence.

8369. Zim, Herbert S. *Mammals* (4–6). Illustrated. 1955, Golden $5.95; paper $1.95. Subtitle: *A Guide to Familiar Species.* Also use: *The First Book of Mammals* by Margaret Williamson (1957, Watts $4.47).

8370. Zim, Herbert S. *What's Inside of Animals?* (3–6). Illus. by Herschel Wartik. 1953, Morrow $5.49. This well-organized account introduces the comparative anatomy of various animals. Also use: *Skeletons: An Inside Look at Animals* by Madeleine Liraudais (1972, Walker $4.95; LB $5.85).

Habits and Behavior

8371. Anthony, Patricia A. *Animals Grow* (1–3). Illus. by Leonard Shortall. 1970, Putnam $3.86. The elements that produce animal and plant growth—food, air and water—are analyzed.

8372. Bendick, Jeanne. *How Animals Behave* (2–4). 1976, Parents $5.41. The author explains that animals, acting through the instinct for self-preservation or in reaction to the behavior of others, are behaving in a natural manner. For an older group use: *Watcher in the Wilds* by Daniel Cohen (1971, Little $5.95).

8373. Berrill, Jacquelyn. *Wonders of How Animals Learn* (5–7). Illus. by author. 1979, Dodd $5.95. Animal intelligence and various learning processes are described in this account.

8374. Clarkson, Jan Nagel. *Tricks Animals Play* (K–4). Illustrated. 1975, National Geographic $6.95. "Playing dead" and other tricks that animals have learned in order to survive.

8375. Ford, Barbara. *Animals That Use Tools* (5–7). Illustrated. 1978, Messner $7.29. A survey of the use of tools by animals, ranging from the crab to chimps.

8376. Ford, Barbara. *Why Does a Turtle Dove Live Longer Than a Dog?* (5–7). 1980, Morrow $6.95; LB $6.67. Subtitle: *A Report on Animal Longevity.*

8377. Fox, Charles Philip. *When Winter Comes* (K–1). Illustrated. 1962, Reilly & Lee $4.50. How small animals live in winter.

8378. Freedman, Russell. *Animal Games* (K–4). Illus. by St. Tamara. 1976, Holiday $4.95. Sixteen common animals and the games they play.

8379. Hartman, Jane E. *Animals That Live in Groups* (6–8). Illustrated. 1979, Holiday $6.95. A description of animal societies from termites to elephants.

8380. Hornblow, Leonora, and Hornblow, Arthur. *Animals Do the Strangest Things* (1–3). Illus. by Michael K. Frith. 1964, Random $2.95; LB $3.99. Interesting facts and habits of such animals as the camel, lion, and polar bear. Also use: *Animals and More Animals* by Illa Podendorf (1970, Childrens Press $6.00).

8381. Kohl, Judith, and Kohl, Herbert. *The View from the Oak: The Private Worlds of Other Creatures* (6–8). Illus. by Roger Bayless. 1977, Scribner $8.95; paper $4.95. An exciting exploration of the animal world as animals experience it.

8382. Leskowitz, Irving, and Stone, A. Harris. *Animals Are Like This* (4–6). Illus. by Peter P. Plasencia. 1968, Prentice-Hall $5.95. A description of how the environment has conditioned animal behavior.

8383. Mason, George F. *Animal Vision* (4–7). Illus. by author. 1968, Morrow $5.52. Known and little-known facts about how animals see. Also in this series (all LB $5.52): *Animal Tails* (1958), *Animal Habits* (1959), and *Animal Baggage* (1961).

8384. Peck, Robert Newton. *Path of Hunters: Animal Struggle in a Meadow* (4–6). Illus. by Betty Fraser. 1973, Knopf $4.95; LB $5.99. Life-styles of several forms of wild life—from brown beetle to skunk—are described.

8385. Pringle, Laurence. *Animals and Their Niches: How Species Share Resources* (4–6). Illus. by Leslie Morrill. 1979, Morrow $6.67. A fascinating study of how various animals share their food and homes. Also use: *How Animals Live Together* by Millicent E. Selsam (1979, Morrow $6.67).

8386. Selsam, Millicent E. *Courtship of Animals* (4–6). Illus. by John Kaufmann. 1964, Morrow $6.43. An account of how animals attract one another.

8387. Selsam, Millicent E. *How Animals Tell Time* (4–6). Illustrated. 1967, Morrow $6.43. A simple discussion of the built-in biological clocks that enable animals to regulate their activities.

8388. Simon, Seymour. *Life in the Dark: How Animals Survive at Night* (4–6). Illus. by Arabelle Wheatley. 1974, Watts $4.90. In a lucid and informative book, the author discusses the many forms of life that live by night and their adjustments to this environment.

Babies

8389. Berrill, Jacquelyn. *Wonders of Animal Nurseries* (3–5). 1968, Dodd paper $4.50. Various kinds of animal babies and how they are cared for.

8390. Freedman, Russell. *Animal Fathers* (2–4). Illus. by Joseph Cellini. 1976, Holiday $4.95. Material about 15 animal fathers and how they help care for their children.

8391. Freedman, Russell. *Hanging On* (2–4). Illustrated. 1977, Holiday $5.95. The carrying and nurturing of 22 different animal babies described with photographs and text.

8392. Hudson, Robert G. *Nature's Nursery: Baby Mammals* (4–6). Illustrated. 1969, Day $4.50. From birth to maturity with a number of baby mammals, including humans.

8393. May, Julian. *Living Things and Their Young* (4–6). Illustrated. 1969, Follett $3.48. The process of reproduction in several animals.

8394. Pfloog, Jan. *Wild Animals and Their Babies* (2–4). Illustrated. 1971, Golden $6.95. A heavily illustrated account of several animals, their offspring and surroundings.

8395. Selsam, Millicent E. *All Kinds of Babies* (K–3). 1969, Four Winds $5.95; paper $1.25. A variety of young animals are introduced.

8396. Weber, William J. *Wild Orphan Babies— Mammals and Birds: Caring for Them/Setting Them Free* (6–9). Illustrated. 1978, Holt $6.95. A practical handbook that updates the 1975 edition.

Camouflage

8397. Carthy, John. *Animal Camouflage* (3–5). Illus. by Colin Threadgall. 1974, McGraw $5.72. The disguises that animals assume are described with interesting text and attractive illustrations. Also use: *Animals That Hide, Imitate and Bluff* by Lilo Hess (1970, Scribner $6.95) and, for a younger group, *Can You Find the Animal?* by Wilda S. Ross (1974, Coward $4.49).

8398. Hopf, Alice L. *Nature's Pretenders* (6–9). Illustrated. 1979, Putnam $8.95. Animal camouflage as found in both plants and animals is well covered.

8399. McClung, Robert M. *How Animals Hide* (1–3). Illustrated. 1973, National Geographic $6.95. In simple text and color photographs, the concept of animal camouflage is introduced and developed. Also use: *Hidden Animals* by Millicent E. Selsam (1969, Harper $4.95; LB $4.79).

8400. Shuttlesworth, Dorothy E. *Animal Camouflage* (4–7). Illus. by Matthew Kalmenoff. 1966, Natural Hist. Pr. $4.95. Illustrations enhance the text, which shows how coloration and shading can help animals protect themselves.

Communication

8401. Cosgrove, Margaret. *Messages and Voices: The Communication of Animals* (5–8). Illus. by author. 1974, Dodd $4.95. An examination of the variety of ways in which animals send signals. Also use: *Secret Languages of Animals* by Francine Jacobs (1976, Morrow $4.95; LB $4.59) and, for a younger group, *What Is That Alligator Saying?* by Ruth Belov Gross (1972, Hastings $4.95).

8402. Dean, Anabel. *How Animals Communicate* (4–6). Illus. by Haris Petie. 1977, Messner $6.64. A discussion of why animals communicate, as well as the methods used to convey their signals.

8403. Friedman, Judi. *Noises in the Woods* (1–3). Illus. by John Hamberger. 1979, Dutton $5.95. Tips on how to look and listen for wild things in the woods are given in this easily read account.

8404. Ricciuti, Edward R. *Sounds of Animals at Night* (4–7). Illustrated. 1977, Harper $5.95; LB $5.79. How frogs, birds, and other animals make noises at night and what these sounds mean. Also use: *Animal Sounds* by George F. Mason (1948, Morrow $5.09).

8405. Selsam, Millicent E. *The Language of Animals* (4–6). Illus. by Kathleen Elgin. 1962, Morrow $6.43. How animals communicate by sound, sight, and smell. Also use: *How to Understand Animal Talk* by Vinson Brown (1958, Little $4.95).

8406. Van Woerkom, Dorothy O. *Hidden Messages* (2–4). Illus. by Lynne Cherry. 1979, Crown $6.95. A book on animal communication in the animal kingdom, particularly as practiced by ants.

8407. Winter, Ruth. *Scent Talk among Animals* (4–6). Illus. by Richard Cuffari. 1977, Lippincott $6.95. Communication by scent and its implications for mating and survival are explored in this unusual nature book.

Defenses

8408. Brenner, Barbara. *Beware! These Animals Are Poison* (3–5). Illus. by James Spanfeller. 1979, McCann $7.95. Venomous creatures and their potential danger.

8409. Dean, Anabel. *Animal Defenses* (4–6). Illus. by Haris Petie. 1978, Messner $6.97. How all sorts of animals manage to survive with the use of amazing ploys.

8410. Freedman, Russell. *How Animals Defend Their Young* (4–6). Illustrated. 1978, Dutton $7.95.

The defense tactics used by a variety of birds, insects, fish, and animals are described.

8411. Freedman, Russell. *Tooth and Claw: A Look at Animal Weapons* (3–4). Illustrated. 1980, Holiday $7.95. An overview of how animals protect themselves.

8412. Gilbreath, Alice. *Antlers to Radar: How Animals Defend Themselves* (3–5). Illustrated. 1978, McKay $6.95. Eighteen different means of defense—from claws to camouflage—are described.

8413. Hutchins, Ross E. *How Animals Survive* (3–6). Illustrated. 1974, Parents $5.41. An account of how animals defend themselves. Also use: *Animal Weapons* by George F. Mason (1949, Morrow $5.09).

8414. Schlein, Miriam. *Snake Fights, Rabbit Fights and More* (2–4). Illus. by Sue Thompson. 1979, Crown $6.95. An explanation of how and why animals fight each other.

8415. Shuttlesworth, Dorothy E. *How Wild Animals Fight* (4–7). Illustrated. 1976, Doubleday $5.95. A description of the ways that animals fight for food, territory, survival, or a mate.

Hibernation

8416. Barker, Will. *Winter-Sleeping Wildlife* (5–7). Illus. by Carl Burger. 1958, Harper $8.79. An exploration of animals that hibernate.

8417. Coins, Ellen H. *The Long Winter Sleep: The Story of Mammal Hibernation* (4–6). Illus. by author. 1978, McKay $5.95. A well-illustrated account of how some animals survive the winter.

8418. Cosgrove, Margaret. *Wintertime for Animals* (3–5). Illus. by author. 1975, Dodd $4.95. How all kinds of life, including insects and reptiles, adjust to winter. Also use: *Winter-Sleepers* by Phyllis Sarasy (1962, Prentice-Hall $4.95).

Homes

8419. Batherman, Muriel. *Animals Live Here* (1–3). Illustrated. 1979, Greenwillow $5.95. An examination of animals arranged by where they live.

8420. Cartwright, Sally. *Animal Homes* (1–3). Illus. by Ben Stahl. 1973, Coward $4.49. A variety of homes in the forest that are the habitat of squirrels, porcupine, and others.

8421. Cohen, Daniel. *Animal Territories* (5–8). Illustrated. 1975, Hastings $5.95. How animals stake out and defend their territories, as well as implications for humans.

8422. Nussbaum, Hedda. *Animals Build Amazing Homes* (2–5). Illus. by Christopher Santore. 1979, Random $3.95; LB $3.99. Fifteen examples are presented in easy-to-read text.

8423. Shapp, Charles, and Shapp, Martha. *Let's Find Out about Animal Homes* (1–3). Illus. by Peter Costanza. 1962, Watts $4.47. A useful book that teaches the basic facts about animal homes.

8424. Wood, Frances, and Wood, Dorothy. *At Home in the Wild* (5–7). Illustrated. 1977, Dodd $5.95: A useful book that emphasizes how animals adapt to their environment.

Migration

8425. Buck, Margaret Waring. *Where They Go in Winter* (5–7). Illustrated. 1968, Abingdon $4.95; paper $1.95. The mysteries of animal migration and instinctive behavior are explored with text and detailed drawings.

8426. von Frisch, Otto. *Animal Migration* (6–8). Illustrated. 1969, McGraw $5.72. Seasonal movements of birds, fish, insects, and reptiles are well presented in this informative book.

8427. Walker, Michael J. *Migrating Animals: North America's Wild Travelers* (5–7). Illustrated. 1979, McKay $7.95. The migration patterns of 31 animals are detailed.

Tracks

8428. Arnosky, Jim. *Crinkleroot's Book of Animal Tracks and Wildlife Signs* (4–6). Illustrated. 1979, Putnam $7.95. A chatty introduction to wildlife signs and their meanings.

8429. Branley, Franklyn M. *Big Tracks, Little Tracks* (1–3). 1960, Crowell $6.89; 1975, Scholastic paper $.95. A simple guide to types of animal tracks.

8430. Mason, George F. *Animal Tracks* (4–6). Illustrated. 1943, Morrow $5.09. A nature guidebook that gives information on the tracks of more than 40 North American animals. Also use: *Track Watching* by David Webster (1972, Watts $5.88).

Ape Family

8431. Allen, Martha Dickson. *Meet the Monkeys* (3–6). Illus. by author. 1979, Prentice-Hall $6.95. Thirty-three types of monkeys are described and pictured.

8432. Amon, Aline. *Reading, Writing, Chattering, Chimps* (5–7). Illus. by author. 1975, Atheneum $7.95. A concise survey of experiments teaching chimps to communicate, including the famous case of Washoe, who learned simple sentences using hand gestures.

8433. Borea, Phyllis. *Seymour, a Gibbon: About Apes and Other Animals and How You Can Help to Keep Them Alive* (4–6). Illustrated. 1973, Atheneum $5.25. Through the story of Seymour, the author introduces principles of evolution and tells how to care for animals in captivity.

8434. Conklin, Gladys. *Little Apes* (1–3). Illus. by Joseph Cellini. 1970, Holiday $5.95. An average day in the life of 4 different kinds of young apes. Also use: *Chimps and Baboons* by Emily d'Aulaire (1974, National Wildlife $2.50).

8435. Cook, David, and Hughes, Jill. *A Closer Look at Apes* (5–7). Illustrated. 1976, Watts $2.95; LB $4.90. An examination, chiefly through color drawings, of various kinds of apes.

8436. Fenner, Carol. *Gorilla Gorilla* (3–5). Illus. by Symeon Shimin. 1973, Random $4.95; LB $5.99. An informational book that traces the life of a male gorilla from birth to maturity and eventual capture to be sent to a zoo.

8437. Gardner, Richard. *The Baboon* (5–7). Illustrated. 1972, Macmillan $5.95. History and physical characteristics of baboons are presented in this well-organized account. For a younger group use: *Baboons* by Sarel Eimerl (1968, Simon & Schuster $3.95).

8438. Hurd, Edith Thacher. *The Mother Chimpanzee* (PS–3). Illus. by Clement Hurd. 1978, Little $5.95. The daily life in the growing up of a baby chimp under the watchful eyes of her mother.

8439. Kevles, Bettyann. *Watching the Wild Apes: The Primate Studies of Goodall, Fossey and Galdikos* (6–9). 1976, Dutton $7.95. A thorough, fascinating survey of the people, methodology, and findings involved in 3 important studies of primates.

8440. McDearmon, Kay. *Gorillas* (4–6). Illustrated. 1979, Dodd $4.95. The life, habits, and society of the gorilla in text and photographs.

8441. Michel, Anna. *The Story of Nim* (3–6). Illustrated. 1980, Knopf $6.95. A narrative about a chimpanzee who learned language.

8442. Napier, Prue. *Chimpanzees* (4–5). Illus. by Douglas Bowness. 1976, McGraw $5.72. A clear and direct text complemented nicely by diagrams that describe many aspects of a chimpanzee's life. For a younger group use: *Growing Up Chimpanzee* by Eugenia Alston (1975, Crowell $5.50; LB $6.50).

8443. Pluckrose, Henry, ed. *Apes* (2–4). Illus. by Richard Orr. 1979, Watts $2.95; LB $4.90. A simple introduction to the life-styles of these primates.

8444. Schick, Alice. *Kongo and Kumba: Two Gorillas* (3–5). Illus. by Joseph Cellini. 1974, Dial $4.95; LB $4.58. Alternating chapters describe the first five years in the lives of 2 gorillas, one in captivity and the other in the wild.

8445. Schick, Alice. *The Siamang Gibbons: An Ape Family* (4–6). Illustrated. 1976, Raintree $5.95; LB $5.97. The life of a Siamang gibbon, first in his native habitat in Sumatra and then in captivity.

8446. Selsam, Millicent E., and Hunt, Joyce. *A First Look at Monkeys and Apes* (1–3). Illus. by Harriett Springer. 1979, Walker $7.95. An introductory account that emphasizes principles of classification.

8447. Teleki, Geza, and others. *Aerial Apes: Gibbons of Asia* (3–5). Illustrated. 1979, Coward $7.50. The habits and life-style of these unusual airborne apes are well presented.

8448. Teleki, Geza. *Goblin, A Wild Chimpanzee* (5–8). Illustrated. 1977, Dutton $7.95. The daily life of a chimp in the Gombe National Park of Tanzania.

8449. Teleki, Geza, and others. *Leakey the Elder: A Chimpanzee and His Community* (5–7). Illustrated. 1980, Dutton $9.95. The authors focus attention on an elderly male chimp in Tanzania's Gombe National Park.

8450. Zim, Herbert S. *Monkeys* (4–7). Illustrated. 1955, Morrow $5.09. Information on various kinds of monkeys, as well as how to raise one as a pet. Also use: *Wonders of the Monkey World* by Jacquelyn Berrill (1967, Dodd $4.50).

Bats

8451. Freschet, Berniece. *Wufu: The Story of Little Brown Bat* (2–4). Illus. by Albert Michini. 1975,

Putnam $5.95. The life cycle of a bat told sensitively in text and black-and-white etchings.

8452. Kaufmann, John. *Bats in the Dark* (2–3). Illustrated. 1972, Crowell $4.50; LB $5.95. A succinct discussion of a variety of bats, their nocturnal habits and food-gathering techniques.

8453. Lauber, Patricia. *Bats: Wings in the Night* (4–6). 1968, Random $2.95; LB $4.99. Based on scientific studies, lucid descriptions of the habits and distinctive features of the more than 800 varieties of this flying mammal.

8454. Leen, Nina. *The Bat* (4–7). Illustrated. 1976, Holt $6.95. Annotated photographs that explore the life-style and usefulness of the bat.

8455. Pitt, Valerie. *Bats* (4–6). Illustrated. 1976, Watts $4.90. A simple account of the life and habits of bats and the many myths about them. Also use: *Wonders of the Bat World* by Sigmund A. Levine (1969, Dodd $4.50).

Bears

8456. Bailey, Bernadine. *Wonders of the World of Bears* (4–6). Illustrated. 1975, Dodd $4.95. An explanation of the various kinds of bears and how they live.

8457. Dixon, Paige. *The Young Grizzly* (4–6). Illustrated. 1974, Atheneum $6.95. A nicely presented look at the life of the growing grizzly.

8458. McClung, Robert M. *Samson: Last of the California Grizzlies* (4–6). Illus. by Bob Hines. 1973, Morrow $5.95; LB $5.49. The life story of a member of a now extinct species—the golden bear that is depicted on the California state flag.

8459. McDearmon, Kay. *Polar Bear* (3–5). Illustrated. 1976, Dodd $4.50. The life cycle of the polar bear, including material on defense mechanisms, mating habits, and how they are studied by humans. Also use: *Biography of a Polar Bear* by Barbara A. Steiner (1972, Putnam $4.97).

8460. Morey, Walt. *Operation Blue Bear: A True Story* (4–6). Illustrated. 1975, Dutton $7.95. An expert nature writer tells about a group of Alaskan Coastguardsmen who tried to save a rare blue bear who was raiding their garbage cans. Also use: *Monarch of Dead Man Bay: The Life and Death of a Kodiak Bear* by Roger Caras (1969, Little, paper $1.95).

8461. Patent, Dorothy. *Bears of the World* (5–7). Illustrated. 1980, Holiday $8.95. A thorough and interesting account of 7 present-day species of bears. Also use: *The Bear Family* by Dorothy Wood (1966, Harvey House $5.39).

8462. Pluckrose, Henry. *Bears* (2–4). Illus. by Richard Orr. 1978, Gloucester $4.90. An easily read book that will interest children. Also use: *Bears Live Here* by Irmengarde Eberle (1966, Doubleday $4.95).

Big Cats

8463. Adamson, Joy. *Born Free* (6–9). Illustrated. 1960, Pantheon $5.95; LB $6.99. A lioness is raised among people and then retrained to return to the wilds of Kenya. Sequels from Harcourt: *Living Free: The Story of Elsa and Her Cubs* (1961, $9.50) and *Forever Free* (1963, $9.50; Bantam, paper $1.25). For a younger group use: *Elsa* (1963, Pantheon $4.99).

8464. Boorer, Michael. *Wild Cats* (4–6). Illus. by Peter Warner. 1970, Grosset $4.49. The cat family, its evolution and behavior patterns.

8465. Bronson, Wilfrid S. *Cats* (4–6). Illus. by author. 1950, Harcourt $5.50. All about cats, from stray tomcats to the cats of the jungle. Also use: *The Big Cats* by Herbert S. Zim (1976, Morrow $5.09).

8466. Conklin, Gladys. *Cheetahs, the Swift Hunters* (2–4). Illustrated. 1976, Holiday $6.95. The life of a mother cheetah during the first 18 months of her cub's life. For a slightly older group use: *Pippa: The Cheetah and Her Cubs* by Joy Adamson (1970, Harcourt $6.95).

8467. Conklin, Gladys. *Lion Family* (1–3). Illus. by Joseph Cellini. 1973, Holiday $5.95. A description of the activities of a family of lions living in East Africa's Serengeti region. Also use: *Lions and Tigers* by Jocelyn Arundel (1974, National Wildlife $2.50).

8468. McDearmon, Kay. *Cougar* (3–5). Illustrated. 1977, Dodd $4.95. Two years in the lives of 2 cougar cubs are described graphically in text and photographs.

8469. Michel, Anna. *Little Wild Lion Cub* (1–3). Illus. by Tony Chen. 1980, Pantheon $4.95; LB $4.99. An introductory account of the habits of lions.

8470. Pluckrose, Henry. *Lions and Tigers* (2–4). Illus. by Eric Tenney and Maurice Wilson. 1979, Watts $2.95; LB $4.90. A brief description of habits and behavior is supplied, plus a basic guide to the various species.

8471. Schaller, George B., and Selsam, Millicent E. *The Tiger: Its Life in the Wild* (5–8). Illus. by Richard Keane and S. Schauer. 1969, Harper $6.89. Fascinating observations of the world's largest cat, which the author studied and photographed in India's Kanha Park.

8472. Schaller, George B., and Schaller, Kay. *Wonders of Lions* (5–8). Illustrated. 1977, Dodd $5.95. A thorough, enjoyable book about the habits and habitats of these big cats.

8473. Schick, Alice. *Serengeti Cats* (6–8). Illus. by Joel Schick. 1977, Lippincott $6.95. The hunting, mating, and rearing habits of types of cats that live in the Serengeti National Park in Tanzania.

8474. Voight, Virginia F. *Bobcat* (3–5). Illustrated. 1978, Dodd $5.95. A typical year in the life of a bobcat.

8475. Zim, Herbert S. *Little Cats* (2–4). Illustrated. 1978, Morrow $5.95. Included in this simple account is information on such cats as the lynx and the bobcat.

Elephants

8476. Conklin, Gladys. *Elephants of Africa* (2–4). Illus. by Joseph Cellini. 1972, Holiday $5.95. A factual description of African elephants and their group life, stressing the need for protection of this diminishing species.

8477. Eberle, Irmengarde. *Elephants Live Here* (4–6). Illustrated. 1970, Doubleday $4.50. Life in an elephant herd in Africa told primarily through photographs. For a younger group use: *Elephants* by Robert Gray (1974, National Wildlife $2.50).

8478. Jurmain, Suzanne. *From Trunk to Tail: Elephants Legendary and Real* (6–8). Illustrated. 1978, Harcourt $6.95. The elephant in fact, fiction, and legend.

8479. Lavine, Sigmund A., and Scuro, Vincent. *Wonders of Elephants* (5–8). Illustrated. 1980, Dodd $5.95. The structure and living habits of both African and Indian elephants are presented in a lively way.

8480. Michel, Anna. *Little Wild Elephant* (PS–1). Illus. by Peter Parnall and Virginia Parnall. 1979, Pantheon $3.95; LB $4.99. The first 4 years of an elephant's life told in simple text.

8481. Pluckrose, Henry. *Small World of Elephants* (1–4). Illus. by Peter Barrett. 1979, Watts $2.95. A simple, clear treatment of the history and habits of elephants.

8482. Van Wormer, Joe. *Elephants* (5–8). Illustrated. 1976, Dutton $7.50. Excellent photographs highlight this book, which contains only short passages of text. Also use: *Elephants* by Herbert S. Zim (1946, Morrow $5.09).

Giraffes

8483. Brown, Louise C. *Giraffes* (3–5). Illus. by Audrey Ross. 1980, Dodd $4.95. A clear and straightforward account on the world's tallest animal.

8484. Cooke, Ann. *Giraffes at Home* (1–3). Illus. by Robert Quackenbush. 1972, Crowell $4.50; LB $5.95. An easy-to-read account of structure, behavior, and habitat. Also use: *Giraffe Lives in Africa* by Gladys Conklin (1971, Holiday $4.50).

8485. Hopf, Alice L. *Biography of a Giraffe* (2–4). Illus. by Patricia Collins. 1978, Putnam $5.49. A fine introduction to the life cycle of a giraffe.

8486. Schlein, Miriam. *Giraffe, the Silent Giant* (3–6). Illus. by Betty Fraser. 1976, Four Winds $6.95. The habits, behavior, and appearance of giraffes, with some of their changes through the ages and their interaction with humans. Also use: *Natural History of Giraffes* by Dorcas MacClintock (1973, Scribner $7.95).

8487. Schlein, Miriam. *On the Track of The Mystery Animal: The Story of the Discovery of the Okapi* (4–6). Illus. by Ruth Sanderson. 1978, Four Winds $6.95. The story of the British naturalist Sir Harry Johnston and his quest for the Okapi.

Deer Family

8488. Bergman-Sucksdorff, Astrid. *Roe Deer* (3–5). Illus. by author. 1969, Harcourt $5.95. A year in the animal's life, told simply, with excellent photographs.

8489. Berry, William D. *Doneki: An Alaskan Moose* (4–6). Illus. by author. 1965, Macmillan $4.50. The first year in the life of a moose living in the Mount McKinley region of Alaska.

8490. Hopf, Alice L. *Biography of an American Reindeer* (4–7). Illus. by John Groth. 1976, Putnam $4.97. The life cycle of the reindeer and its amazing adaption to Arctic climate and vegetation.

8491. Jenkins, Marie M. *Deer, Moose, Elk and Their Family* (6–9). Illus. by Matthew Kalmenoff. 1979, Holiday $7.95. A comprehensive introduction to the life and habits of various antlered animals.

8492. Reardon, Jim. *Wonders of Caribou* (5–8). 1976, Dodd $4.95. The life and habits of these northern relatives of the deer, along with general material on the tundra.

8493. Rue, Leonard Lee. *The World of the White-Tailed Deer* (4–6). Illustrated. 1966, Lippincott $8.95. A year in the life of a white-tailed deer, beautifully illustrated with photographs. Also use: *The Deer Family* by Dorothy Wood (1969, Harvey House $4.69).

8494. Ryden, Hope. *The Little Deer of the Florida Keys* (4–6). Illustrated. 1978, Putnam $7.95. A photographic essay on these tiny animals and efforts to save them. For a younger group use: *Mother Deer* by Edith Thacher Hurd (1972, Little $5.95).

Marsupials

8495. Freschet, Berniece. *Possum Baby* (2–3). Illus. by Jim Arnosky. 1978, Putnam $5.29. An easily read narrative of the birth and early life of an opossum.

8496. Harris, Susan. *Creatures with Pockets* (2–4). Illus. by Franki Coventry. 1980, Watts $5.90. Twelve different marsupials, chiefly from Australia, are described.

8497. Hurd, Edith Thacher. *The Mother Kangaroo* (K–3). Illustrated. 1976, Little $5.95. How a mother kangaroo cares for its offspring.

8498. Jenkins, Marie M. *Kangaroos, Opossums and Other Marsupials* (5–7). 1975, Holiday $6.95. The origins, living habits, and survival problems of marsupials.

8499. Lauber, Patricia. *The Surprising Kangaroos and Other Pouched Animals* (3–6). Illustrated. 1965, Random $4.39. A look at the interesting habits of marsupials.

8500. Lavine, Sigmund A. *Wonders of Marsupials* (5–8). Illustrated. 1979, Dodd $5.95. The physical appearance and living habits of several of the most important species are covered.

8501. McClung, Robert M. *Possum* (2–4). Illus. by author. 1963, Morrow $6.01. The story of an opossum and her life until she bears her own family and carries them in her pouch. Also use with a younger group: *Opossum* by Kazue Mizumura (1974, Crowell $5.95).

8502. Noguere, Suzanne, and Chen, Tony. *Little Koala* (1–3). Illus. by Tony Chen. 1979, Holt $6.95. The early months in the life of this Australian marsupial. Also use: *Koalas Live Here* by Irmengarde Eberle (1967, Doubleday $4.50).

8503. Rabinowich, Ellen. *Kangaroos, Koalas and Other Marsupials* (4–6). Illustrated. 1978, Watts $4.90. A brief overview illustrated by photographs.

8504. Rau, Margaret. *The Gray Kangaroo at Home* (4–7). Illustrated. 1978, Knopf $5.95. A year in the life of a kangaroo doe.

8505. Sherman, Geraldine. *Animals with Pouches —the Marsupials* (2–4). Illus. by Lorence Bjorklund. 1978, Holiday $5.95. Seventeen marsupials, including kangaroos, koalas, and opossums, are described.

Pandas

8506. Bonners, Susan. *Panda* (3–5). Illustrated. 1978, Delacorte $6.95. The birth and life of a giant panda in text and pictures.

8507. Eberle, Irmengarde. *Pandas Live Here* (3–5). Illustrated. 1973, Doubleday $4.95. Information about the habits and way of life of pandas told in text and photographs.

8508. Gross, Ruth Belov. *A Book About Pandas* (2–4). Illustrated. 1973, Dial $4.95; LB $4.58; paper $.95. This excellent introduction to the panda's habits and way of life contains many photographs. Also use: *The Giant Panda Book* by Anthony Hiss (1973, Golden $5.95).

8509. Rau, Margaret. *The Giant Panda at Home* (4–6). Illus. by Eva Hulsmann. 1977, Knopf $4.95; LB $5.99. Beautiful full-page drawings illustrate this account of physical characteristics and habits of the panda.

Rodents

8510. Brady, Irene. *Beaver Year* (3–5). Illus. by author. 1976, Houghton $5.95. The story of 2 young beavers from birth to founding their own colony, told convincingly and with authenticity. For a slightly younger group use: *The Mother Beaver* by Edith Thacher Hurd (1971, Little $4.95).

8511. Brady, Irene. *A Mouse Named Mus* (2–5). Illus. by author. 1972, Houghton $4.95; LB

$4.23. Drawings and text give with explicit details the life cycle of the common house mouse.

8512. Brady, Irene. *Wild Mouse* (2–4). Illus. by author. 1976, Scribner $5.95. Told in diary form, this is the story of the first 16 days of 3 white-footed mice. Also use: *The Tale of Whitefoot* by Carl T. Brandhorst (1968, Simon & Schuster $3.50; LB $3.39).

8513. Chace, G. Earl. *Wonders of Prairie Dogs* (4–6). Illus. by author. 1976, Dodd $4.95. In narrative form the author explores the life of this amazingly social animal. Also use: *Owl and the Prairie Dog* by Berniece Freschet (1969, Scribner $3.95).

8514. Eberle, Irmengarde. *Prairie Dogs in Prairie Dog Town* (3–5). Illus. by John Hamberger. 1974, Crowell $6.95. By concentrating on one prairie dog family, the author reveals interesting facts about the habits and communal life of these small animals.

8515. Edmonds, Walter. *Beaver Valley* (4–6). Illus. by Leslie Morrill. 1971, Little $5.50. What happens to a valley when a den of beavers moves in.

8516. Freschet, Berniece. *Bear Mouse* (2–4). Illus. by Donald Carrick. 1973, Scribner $6.95. A winter day in the life of a meadow mouse, her search for food and the dangers she encounters.

8517. George, Jean Craighead. *The Moon of the Moles* (4–6). Illus. by Robert Levering. 1970, Crowell $3.95; LB $4.95. The mole's life beneath the soil and its special adaptations for survival.

8518. Hess, Lilo. *Mouse and Company* (3–5). Illus. by author. 1972, Scribner $5.95. The life cycle of the door mouse, plus a description of other types and a section on mice as pets.

8519. Hogan, Paula Z. *The Beaver* (K–3). Illus. by Yoshi Miyake. 1979, Raintree $7.99. The life cycle and habits of the beaver in a simple narrative.

8520. Kohn, Bernice. *Chipmunks* (3–4). Illus. by John Hamberger. 1970, Prentice-Hall $4.95. A brief, direct text tells all the essentials. Also use: *A Chipmunk Lives Here* by Irmengarde Eberle (1966, Doubleday $4.95).

8521. Laycock, George. *Squirrels* (4–6). Illustrated. 1975, Four Winds $5.95. Common and unusual facts reveal the habits and characteristics of various kinds of squirrels.

8522. McNulty, Faith. *Woodchuck* (1–3). Illustrated. 1974, Harper $4.95; LB $4.79. The life cycle of the woodchuck told in text and pictures. For an older group use: *The World of the Woodchuck* by W. J. Schoonmaker (1966, Lippincott $7.82).

8523. Melianby, Kenneth. *Talpa: The Story of a Mole* (3–5). Illus. by Bert Kitchen. 1977, World $5.95. A fictionalized but accurate story that tells of the first year in the life of a mole. Also use: *Moles and Shrews* by Charles L. Ripper (1957, Morrow $6.00).

8524. Miles, Miska. *Beaver Moon* (2–5). Illus. by John Schoenherr. 1978, Little $5.95. An old beaver survives many dangers to build a new home.

8525. Newton, James R. *The March of the Lemmings* (2–4). Illus. by Charles Robinson. 1976, Crowell $5.95. When the lemming community becomes overpopulated, the rodents become restless and hostile and embark on their march across the land to the sea, where they drown—a mystery still to scientists.

8526. Oxford Scientific Films. *House Mouse* (4–8). Illustrated. 1978, Putnam $5.95. Large captioned photographs form the body of this most attractive work.

8527. Rounds, Glen. *The Beaver: How He Works* (2–4). Illus. by author. 1976, Holiday $4.95. Highlights the construction feats of the beaver. Also use: *Junior Science Book of Beavers* by Alexander L. Crosby (1960, Garrard $5.90).

8528. Schwartz, Elizabeth, and Schwartz, Charles. *Cottontail Rabbit* (4–6). Illustrated. 1957, Holiday $4.50. The life cycle of a wild rabbit. For a younger group use: *Biography of a Cottontail* by Lucille W. Trost (1971, Putnam $4.97).

8529. Scott, Jack. *Little Dogs of the Prairie* (5–9). Illustrated. 1977, Putnam $7.95. The habits and homes of prairie dogs and their place in the ecological scheme.

8530. Sheehan, Angela. *The Beaver* (2–3). Illus. by Graham Allen. 1979, Watts $2.50; LB $4.90. Various aspects of beaver life, such as food gathering and home building, are described.

8531. Shuttlesworth, Dorothy E. *The Story of Rodents* (4–6). Illus. by Lydia Rosier. 1971, Doubleday $4.95. A survey of the various species of rodents, concentrating on those in North America; special section on rodents as pets.

8532. Silverstein, Alvin, and Silverstein, Virginia B. *Rats and Mice: Friends and Foes of Man* (4–6). Illus. by Joseph Cellini. 1968, Lothrop $5.95. The beneficial and destructive roles of these rodents are emphasized, along with the amazing lore that has surrounded them through history.

8533. Steiner, Barbara A. *Biography of a Kangaroo Rat* (3–5). Illus. by Linda Powell. 1977, Putnam $4.97. A narrative treatment that still manages to convey all the pertinent information about kangaroo rats and how they live.

8534. Tunis, Edwin. *Chipmunks on the Doorstep* (5–7). Illus. by author. 1971, Crowell $5.95; LB $6.95. Text and pictures convey, with humor and charm, information about these engaging animals.

8535. Van Wormer, Joe. *Squirrels* (4–6). Illustrated. 1978, Dutton $6.95. All sorts of members of the squirrel family are presented in text and many black-and-white photographs.

8536. Whitehead, Robert. *Rabbits and Hares* (4–6). 1976, Watts $4.47. A beginning book for those interested in learning about the life and habits of rabbits and how to raise them.

8537. Wildsmith, Brian. *Squirrels* (K–3). Illus. by author. 1975, Watts $5.95. Various aspects of squirrels, including the many uses they make of their tails, are portrayed in brilliant illustrations.

Sheep and Goats

8538. Adrian, Mary. *The North American Bighorn Sheep* (4–6). Illustrated. 1966, Hastings $4.95. The life cycle of a bighorn sheep is told in an account that stresses conservation.

8539. Jenkins, Marie M. *Goats, Sheep and How They Live* (5–7). Illus. by Matthew Kalmenoff. 1978, Holiday $7.95. The characteristics, habitat and various species are among the topics treated.

8540. McDearmon, Kay. *Rocky Mountain Bighorns* (3–5). Illustrated. 1980, Dodd $4.95. The life and habits of these sturdy acrobatic mountain animals are detailed.

8541. Scott, Jack. *The Book of the Goat* (4–6). Illustrated. 1979, Putnam $8.95. A lively account that reveals interesting facts about this often ridiculed animal.

Wolves, Foxes, and Coyotes

8542. Barry, Scott. *The Kingdom of the Wolves* (4–6). Illustrated. 1979, Putnam $8.95. A sympathetic view of the life and habits of the wolf enhanced by the author's photographs.

8543. Fox, Michael. *Sundance Coyote* (5–7). 1974, Coward $5.95. A psychologist who specializes in animal behavior has written another fine re-creation of nature in the life history of a coyote from birth to finding a mate.

8544. Fox, Michael. *Vixie: The Story of a Little Fox* (4–6). Illus. by Jennifer Perrott. 1973, Coward $5.95. A narrative of a young fox's life is filled with accurate animal life as well as lessons on conservation and the balance of nature.

8545. Fox, Michael. *The Wolf* (5–8). Illus. by Charles Frace. 1973, Coward $5.95. One year in the lives of 2 wolves, Shadow and Silver.

8546. Graham, Ada, and Graham, Frank. *Coyote Song* (6–8). Illustrated. 1978, Delacorte $6.95. An account that stresses the present ecological plight of the coyote.

8547. Johnston, Johanna. *The Fabulous Fox* (4–6). Illustrated. 1979, Dodd $5.95. From Aesop's fables to contemporary nonfiction accounts, this is a fine collection of material about the fox.

8548. Pringle, Laurence. *The Controversial Coyote* (6–8). Illustrated. 1977, Harcourt $5.95. The "pros" and "cons" of the coyote in the ecological cycle are explored.

8549. Rockwell, Jane. *Wolves* (3–6). Illustrated. 1977, Watts $4.90. The myth of the "big, bad wolf" is exposed in this interesting account. Also use: *Silver Wolf* by Paige Dixon (1973, Atheneum, paper $1.95).

Other Animals

8550. Arundel, Jocelyn. *Little Stripe: An African Zebra* (2–3). Illus. by John Kaufmann. 1967, Hastings $4.95. The hazardous life of an African zebra in an account that stresses conservation.

8551. Burkett, Molly. *The Year of the Badger* (4–6). Illus. by Pamela Johnson. 1974, Lippincott $4.95. The story of a British family that nursed Nikki, a badger, back to health.

8552. Blassingame, Wyatt. *Wonders of Raccoons* (5–7). Illustrated. 1977, Dodd $5.95. An affectionate but not coy description of the life-style and habits of this mischievous creature.

8553. Catherall, Arthur. *A Zebra Came to Drink* (5–6). Illus. by John Schoenherr. 1967, Dutton $6.25. A graphic account of a mother zebra's valiant fight for survival and how she struggles to protect her newborn foal after being separated from their herd. Also use: *Land of the Zebra* by Jocelyn Arundel (1974, National Wildlife $2.50).

8554. Conklin, Gladys. *Llamas of South America* (3–5). Illus. by Lorence Bjorklund. 1975, Holiday $5.95. The history, characteristics, and uses of llamas, as well as related animals such as alpacas and vicunas. Also use: *Camels and Llamas* by Olive L. Earle (1961, Morrow $5.09).

8555. Costello, David F. *The World of the Porcupine* (6–8). 1966, Lippincott $6.82. A fine introduction to this unusual animal.

8556. Freschet, Berniece. *Porcupine Baby* (K–2). Illus. by Jim Arnosky. 1978, Putnam $5.29. A first month in the life of a porcupine.

8557. Freschet, Berniece. *Skunk Baby* (2–4). Illus. by Kazue Mizumura. 1973, Crowell $4.95. A simply written description of the adventures of a baby skunk and his first encounter with a fox. Also use: *Misunderstood Skunk* by Lilo Hess (1969, Scribner $6.95).

8558. Goodall, Daphne Machin. *Zebras* (2–4). Illustrated. 1978, Raintree $5.95. Good introductory material on this frequently misunderstood animal.

8559. Griffiths, Gordon Douglas. *Mattie: The Story of a Hedgehog* (4–6). Illus. by Norman Adams. 1977, Delacorte $5.95; LB $5.47. The life story of a hedgehog—6 years from birth to death—is told with warmth and simplicity.

8560. Harris, Lorle. *Biography of a River Otter* (4–6). Illus. by Ruth Kirschner. 1979, Putnam $5.49. A life-cycle story involving an otter and her cub.

8561. Hartman, Jane E. *Armadillos, Anteaters, and Sloths: How They Live* (4–6). Illustrated. 1980, Holiday $7.95. An introductory source on 3 of the New World's most unusual animals.

8562. Hess, Lilo. *The Curious Raccoons* (2–4). Illus. by author. 1968, Scribner $5.95. Excellent photographs enliven this book devoted to raccoon antics.

8563. Hoke, John. *Discovering the World of the Three-Toed Sloth* (4–6). Illustrated. 1976, Watts $4.47. A delightful account of one of the world's slowest animals.

8564. Hopf, Alice L. *Biography of a Rhino* (2–4). Illus. by Kiyo Komoda. 1972, Putnam $4.97. The life of a white rhinoceros on an African preserve, until she is killed by poachers.

8565. Hopf, Alice L. *Biography of an Armadillo* (2–4). Illus. by Jean Zallinger. 1976, Putnam $4.97. An informative and authoritative description of the life cycle of an armadillo, including its habitat and diet.

8566. Hopf, Alice L. *Pigs Wild and Tame* (6–8). Illustrated. 1979, Holiday $7.95. Domestic breeds are discussed as well as such wild varieties as the warthog and peccary.

8567. Hopf, Alice L. *Wild Cousins of the Horse* (6–9). Illustrated. 1977, Putnam $6.50. All kinds of equine-related species are discussed with a view of their ecological future. Companion to *Wild Cousins of the Dog* (1973, $4.49).

8568. Lavine, Sigmund A. *Wonders of Camels* (5–8). Illustrated. 1979, Dodd $5.95. A well-rounded picture of camels, their environment, and their place in art as well as history.

8569. Lavine, Sigmund A., and Scuro, Vincent. *Wonders of Donkeys* (5–8). Illustrated. 1979, Dodd $5.95. The history and habits of this much misunderstood animal.

8570. Patent, Dorothy. *Raccoons, Coatimundis and Their Family* (4–7). Illustrated. 1979, Holiday $7.95. An authoritative account of this mammal family, including pandas.

8571. Pringle, Laurence. *Follow a Fisher* (2–4). Illus. by Tony Chen. 1973, Crowell $4.95. Interesting facts about this little-known member of the weasel family that was almost extinct by the 1930s. Also use: *Weasels, Otters, Skunks and Their Families* by Dorothy Patent (1973, Holiday $5.95).

8572. Rau, Margaret. *Musk Oxen: Bearded Ones of the Arctic* (3–7). Illus. by Patricia Collins. 1976, Crowell $5.95. A fine introduction to the habits and living problems of these huge arctic beasts.

8573. Schlein, Miriam. *Lucky Porcupine!* (PS). Illus. by Martha Weston. 1980, Scholastic $7.95. A simple text and expressive drawings are used to introduce the porcupine.

8574. Scott, Jack. *Return of the Buffalo* (5–9). Illus. by Ozzie Sweet. 1976, Putnam $6.95. A history of the shameful treatement this animal has received in the past and a detailed account of the buffalo's life-style.

8575. Sheehan, Angela. *The Otter* (2–3). Illus. by Bernard Robinson. 1979, Watts $2.50; LB $4.90. Basic information is covered in text and full-color illustrations.

8576. Waters, John F. *Camels: Ships of the Desert* (1–3). Illus. by Reynold Ruffins. 1974, Crowell $4.50; LB $5.95. A simple text that concentrates on how the camel can withstand harsh desert life.

Oceanography, Marine and Freshwater Life

Oceanography

8577. Berger, Melvin. *Oceanography Lab* (4–6). Illustrated. 1973, John Day $5.95. The work of oceanographers and their laboratories are described in simple, clear language.

8578. Boyer, Robert E. *The Story of Oceanography* (6–8). 1975, Harvey House $5.89. An introduction to various forms of plant and animal life in the sea.

8579. Carson, Rachel. *The Sea Around Us* (6–8). Illustrated. 1958, Golden $11.95. A special, well-illustrated edition of the adult title. Also use: *The Sea for Sam* by W. Maxwell Reed (1960, Harcourt $7.95).

8580. Coombs, Charles. *Deep-Sea World: The Story of Oceanography* (5–7). 1966, Morrow $7.35. A survey of this rapidly growing science that explores and cultivates our oceans and the life they sustain. Also use: *Oceanography* by Jerome Williams (1972, Watts $4.47).

8581. Davies, Eryl. *Ocean Frontiers* (4–8). Illustrated. 1980, Viking $5.95. All kinds of equipment like diving suits are described and pictured in this book.

8582. Goldin, Augusta. *The Bottom of the Sea* (1–3). Illus. by Ed Emberley. 1966, Crowell $6.95. A description of the plants and animals that live on the bottom of the ocean. Also use: *The Sunlit Sea* (1968, Crowell $6.95).

8583. Limburg, Peter R., and Sweeney, James B. *102 Questions and Answers about the Sea* (4–6). Illustrated. 1975, Messner $7.29. Both the usual and bizarre aspects of oceans and sea life are explored. For a younger group use: *Let's Find Out about the Ocean* by David C. Knight (1970, Watts $4.47).

8584. May, Julian. *The Land beneath the Sea* (3–5). Illus. by Leonard Everett Fisher. 1971, Holiday $4.50. A vivid introduction to the land formations on the ocean floor.

8585. Pick, Christopher C. *The Young Scientist Book of the Undersea* (4–7). Illustrated. 1978, EMC $5.95. Essential information is covered interestingly in this British import.

8586. Robonson, Bruce H. *Lurkers of the Deep: Life within the Ocean Depths* (5–8). Illustrated. 1978, McKay $6.95. A guide to the strange sea life found in the lower depths of the ocean.

8587. Selsam, Millicent E. *See Through the Sea* (3–6). Illus. by Winifred Lubell. 1955, Harper $5.79. A basic, easily read description of ocean and shore plants and animals.

8588. Shannon, Terry. *Windows in the Sea: New Vehicles That Scan the Ocean Depths* (5–8). Illustrated. 1973, Childrens Press $6.60. This book supplies details on the various machines that explore the animal and plant life of the world's waters. Also use: *All about Undersea Explorations* by Ruth Brindze (1960, Random $4.39).

8589. Simon, Seymour. *Science at Work: Projects in Oceanography* (5–7). Illus. by Lynn Sweat. 1972, Watts $4.90. A series of experiments that explain various aspects of the ocean.

Waves, Tides, and Currents

8590. Brindze, Ruth. *The Gulf Stream* (5–7). Illus. by Helene Carter. 1945, Vanguard $5.95. An examination of water currents, and the Gulf Stream and its importance.

8591. Cartwright, Sally. *The Tide* (1–3). Illus. by Marilyn Miller. 1971, Coward $4.49. The principles behind tidal movements are presented in simple text with pictures.

8592. Clemons, Elizabeth. *Waves, Tides and Currents* (5–6). Illustrated. 1967, Knopf $3.75; LB $4.99. An explanation of what tides are, the part gravity plays in their formation, and their differences, including size and range. Also use: *The Rise and Fall of the Seas* by Ruth Brindze (1964, Harcourt $5.95).

8593. Milne, Lorus F., and Milne, Margery. *When the Tide Goes Far Out* (4–8). Illus. by Kenneth Gosner. 1970, Atheneum $4.25. A description of the shore plants and animals that are alternately covered and uncovered by the tide.

8594. Zim, Herbert S. *Waves* (3–5). Illus. by Rene Martin. 1967, Morrow $5.09. The origins, characteristics, and measurements of ocean waves.

Sea Mammals

8595. Brady, Irene. *Elephants on the Beach* (3–5). Illus. by author. 1979, Scribner $7.95. An informal account of the habits and habitat of the elephant seal.

8596. Brown, Joseph E. *Wonders of Seals and Sea Lions* (5–7). Illustrated. 1976, Dodd $4.95. An excellent introduction to the various types of these sea animals and how they live. Also use: *Seals and Walruses* by Louis Darling (1955, Morrow $6.01).

8597. Brown, Louise C. *Elephant Seals* (3–4). Illustrated. 1979, Dodd $4.95. A simple introduction to the habits and life-style of elephant seals.

8598. Burton, Robert. *Seals* (5–7). Illus. by Timothy Bramfitt. 1980, McGraw $7.95. Real seals are illustrated, plus coverage on allied types like sea lions and walruses.

8599. Harris, Susan. *Swimming Mammals* (1–2). Illus. by Reginald Davis. 1977, Watts $4.90. Sea-oriented mammals are introduced in simple text with good illustrations.

8600. Johnson, William Weber. *Story of Sea Otters* (5–8). Illustrated. 1973, Random $5.69. The life and habits of sea otters told through pictures and simple text. Also use: *Day in the Life of a Sea Otter* by Kay McDearmon (1973, Dodd $3.50).

8601. May, Julian. *Sea Otter* (3–5). Illus. by William Barss. 1972, Creative Education $4.95. The habits of sea otters and a discussion of the way in which they are threatened with extinction and are now a protected species.

8602. Scheffer, Victor B. *A Natural History of Marine Mammals* (6–9). Illus. by Peter Parnall. 1976, Scribner $7.95. Six marine mammals, including sea otters and 2 types of seals, are thoroughly described.

8603. Shaw, Evelyn. *Elephant Seal Island* (1–2). Illus. by Cherryl Pape. 1978, Harper $4.95; LB $5.95. A simple account of seal life told in story form.

8604. Shaw, Evelyn. *Sea Otters* (1–3). Illus. by Cherryl Pape. 1980, Harper $5.95; LB $6.89. An easily read account of a mother sea otter and how she cares for her son.

Dolphins

8605. Lauber, Patricia. *The Friendly Dolphins* (3–4). Illus. by Jean Simpson. 1963, Random $3.95; LB $4.39. Scientific facts and deductions, drawings, diagrams, and photographs are explained. Also use: *Dolphins* by Mickie Compere (1970, Scholastic, paper 95¢).

8606. Malone, Margaret Gay. *Dolly the Dolphin* (4–6). Illustrated. 1978, Messner $7.29. The true story of a Florida family's experiences with a pet dolphin.

8607. Moffett, Martha. *Dolphins* (5–7). 1971, Watts $4.90. An interesting account that combines background information on the structure, habits, and evolution of the dolphin.

8608. Morris, Robert A. *Dolphin* (K–3). Illus. by Mamoru Funai. 1975, Harper $4.95; LB $4.79. A simple account of the first 5 months of this lovable sea mammal. Also use: *The Playful Dolphins* by Linda McCarter Bridge (1976, National Geographic $4.25).

Whales

8609. Cook, Joseph J, and Wisner, William L. *The Blue Whale: Vanishing Leviathan* (4–7). Illustrated. 1973, Dodd $4.95. An examination of the world's largest mammal and its possible extinction.

8610. Fisher, Ronald. *Namu: Making Friends with a Killer Whale* (1–3). Illustrated. 1973, National Geographic $4.25. The true story of a killer whale that was brought to the Seattle aquarium for observation.

8611. Graham, Ada, and Graham, Frank. *Whale Watch* (6–8). Illustrated. 1978, Delacorte $6.95. A history of the whale with emphasis on its present precarious position.

8612. Harris, Susan. *Whales* (2–4). Illus. by Jim Channell. 1980, Watts $5.90. A well-organized introductory narrative that covers basic material thoroughly.

8613. Hoke, Helen, and Pitt, Valerie. *Whales* (4–7). Illus. by Thomas R. Funderburk. 1973, Watts $4.90. An introduction to the types, characteristics, and habits of whales, porpoises, and dolphins. Also use: *All about Whales* by Roy Chapman Andrews (1954, Random $4.39).

8614. Hurd, Edith Thacher. *The Mother Whale* (2–3). Illus. by Clement Hurd. 1973, Little $4.95. This simple informative description of the life cycle of the sperm whale begins with the birth of a calf and its gradual growth to independence; attractively illustrated with block prints.

8615. Jacobs, Francine. *Sounds in the Sea* (4–6). Illus. by Jean Zallinger. 1977, Morrow $5.95; LB $5.49. The noisy sea is examined, with special attention to the language of the whale and porpoise. Also use: *There's a Sound in the Sea: A Child's Eye-View of the Whale* by Tamar Griggs (1975, Scrimshaw $10.95; paper $5.95).

8616. McClung, Robert M. *Thor: Last of the Sperm Whales* (3–5). Illus. by Bob Hines. 1971, Morrow $5.49. Modern hunting techniques in the whaling industry are discussed in this account of a sperm whale; mating, birth, food habits, behavior, and travel patterns detailed.

8617. McGovern, Ann. *Little Whale* (2–4). Illus. by John Hamberger. 1979, Scholastic $7.95. The life of a humpback whale from birth to adulthood.

8618. Mizumura, Kazue. *The Blue Whale* (2–3). Illustrated. 1971, Crowell $5.95. An easy-to-read book about the blue whale, its habits, and how it is threatened by humans. Also use: *Catch a Whale by the Tail* by Edward R. Ricciuti (1969, Harper $5.95; LB $4.79).

8619. Pluckrose, Henry. *Whales* (2–4). Illus. by Norman Weaver. 1979, Gloucester $4.90. An introduction for young readers to these giants of the sea.

8620. Shebar, Sharon Sigmond. *Whaling for Glory!* (4–6). Illustrated. 1978, Messner $7.29. The American whaling industry in mid-nineteenth century is explored through a description of a three-year voyage of a whaling ship.

8621. Simon, Seymour. *Killer Whales* (4–6). Illustrated. 1978, Lippincott $6.95. A realistic account that helps dispel the myths associated with this mammal.

8622. Steiner, Barbara A. *Biography of a Killer Whale* (3–5). Illus. by Bette J. Davis. 1978, Putnam $5.49. The life cycle of Karok, a killer whale.

8623. Stonehouse, Bernard. *A Closer Look at Whales and Dolphins* (4–6). Illustrated. 1978, Watts $5.90; paper $1.95. Various facets of the structure and behavioral patterns of many types of whales are discussed.

8624. Watson, Jane W. *Whales, Friendly Dolphins and Mighty Giants of the Sea* (4–7). Illus. by Richard E. Amundsen. 1975, Western $4.95; LB $6.95. Like the subject, this book is oversize, and it contains much interesting information about a variety of large sea animals. Also use: *Whales, Their Life in the Sea* by Faith McNulty (1975, Harper $5.95; LB $5.79).

8625. Zim, Herbert S. *The Great Whales* (4–7). Illus. by James G. Irving. 1951, Morrow $5.09. Kinds of whales and how they live. Also use: *In the Wake of the Whale* by John A. Barbour (1969, Macmillan $3.95).

Fish

8626. Brown, Anne Ensign. *Wonders of Sea Horses* (5–7). Illustrated. 1979, Dodd $5.95. A well-organized account that includes a section on the care and raising of sea horses.

8627. Cook, Joseph J. *The Incredible Atlantic Herring* (5–9). Illustrated. 1979, Dodd $5.95. The life cycle, history, and uses of the most valuable food fish in the North Atlantic.

8628. Fegely, Thomas D. *The World of Freshwater Fish* (6–9). Illustrated. 1978, Dodd $5.95. A general overview of the structure and environments of the many freshwater species of fish.

8629. Fletcher, Alan M. *Fishes and Their Young* (2–4). Illus. by Allan Eitzen. 1974, Addison $5.95. The birth and nurturing of young fish with various species described.

8630. Fletcher, Alan M. *Fishes Dangerous to Man* (4–6). Illustrated. 1959, Addison $5.95. About 25 fish—including the stingray, shark, and piranha—are described.

8631. Friedman, Judi. *The Eels' Strange Journey* (2–3). Illus. by Gail Owens. 1976, Crowell $5.95. An account of the puzzling migrations of Atlantic Coast eels. Also use: *The Mysterious Eel* by John F. Waters (1973, Hastings $4.95).

8632. Hogan, Paula Z. *The Salmon* (1–3). Illus. by Yoshi Miyake. 1979, Raintree $5.99. The life cycle of the salmon in very simple text and pictures.

8633. Morris, Robert A. *Sea Horse* (1–3). Illus. by Arnold Lobel. 1972, Harper $4.95; LB $4.79. A simply written explanation of the habits of the Atlantic sea horse.

8634. Overbeck, Cynthia. *The Fish Book* (3–5). Illus. by Sharon Lerner. 1978, Lerner $3.95. An introduction to 12 varieties of tropical fish found in aquariums. Also use: *All about Fish* by Carl Burger (1960, Random $4.39).

8635. Oxford Scientific Films. *The Stickleback Cycle* (4–8). 1979, Putnam $6.95. Large color photographs tell the story of mating and birth of this unusual fish.

8636. Phleger, Fred. *Red Tag Comes Back* (1–3). Illus. by Arnold Lobel. 1961, Harper $6.89. The life cycle of a salmon in an easily read, charmingly illustrated account.

8637. Pringle, Laurence. *The Minnow Family: Chubs, Dace, Minnows and Shiners* (3–5). Illus. by Dot Barlowe and Sy Barlowe. 1976, Morrow $4.95; LB $4.59. The whys and wherefores of the world's largest fish family.

8638. Ricciuti, Edward R. *Donald and the Fish That Walked* (1–2). Illus. by Syd Hoff. 1974, Harper $4.95. Donald insisted that he had seen a bright pink fish walking, and indeed he had—a walking catfish!

8639. Selsam, Millicent E. *Animals of the Sea* (2–3). Illus. by John Hamberger. 1976, Four Winds $4.95. Interesting authoritative facts about many aspects of marine life, describing how each animal moves, what it eats, and how it survives.

8640. Selsam, Millicent E., and Hunt, Joyce. *First Look at Fish* (1–3). Illus. by Harriett Springer. 1972, Walker $5.50; LB $5.39. The anatomy of fish and an introduction to the most important species are 2 of the topics discussed in this elementary treatment. Also use: *Let's Find Out about Fishes* by Martha Shapp (1965, Watts $4.90).

8641. Van Dulm, Sacha. *The Stickleback* (3–5). Illus. by Jan Riem. 1979, Barron's $4.95. Simple text and stunning watercolor illustrations highlight this account of a most unusual fish.

8642. Wildsmith, Brian. *Brian Wildsmith's Fishes* (K–3). Illus. by author. 1968, Watts $5.95. A colorfully illustrated picture book about various common fish.

8643. Zim, Herbert S., and Shoemaker, Hurst H. *Fishes* (5–8). Illus. by James Gordon Irving. 1957, Golden $6.95; paper $1.95. Subtitle: *A Guide to Fresh and Saltwater Species.* Also use: *Wondrous World of Fishes* by the National Geographic Society (1965, $4.25).

Sharks

8644. Blumberg, Rhoda. *A First Book of Sharks* (4–6). 1976, Watts $4.90. An excellent introduction to sharks, their food, habits, and enemies.

Also use: *The Nightmare World of the Shark* by Joseph J. Cook (1968, Dodd $4.95).

8645. Bunting, Eve. *The Sea World Book of Sharks* (4–9). Illustrated. 1979, Sea World $6.98. A profile of the structure, life, and habits of sharks.

8646. Carrick, Carol. *Sand Tiger Shark* (2–4). Illus. by Donald Carrick. 1977, Seabury $6.95. An informative and dramatic account of tiger sharks and other marine creatures—hungry, hostile, predatory, and solitary. Also use: *Hungry Sharks* by John F. Waters (1973, Crowell $5.95).

8647. Copps, Dale. *Savage Survivor: 300 Million Years of the Shark* (6–8). 1976, Follett $5.95; LB $5.97. A description of the shark's system and behavior, which have enabled it to survive through the centuries.

8648. McGovern, Ann. *Sharks* (K–3). Illus. by Murray Tinkelman. 1976, Four Winds $5.95. In question-and-answer format, the author gives introductory information about sharks, their habitat and eating habits.

8649. McGowen, Tom. *Album of Sharks* (4–6). Illus. by Rod Ruth. 1977, Rand $5.95; LB $5.97. Eleven types of sharks, with material on structure, habits, size, and stories surrounding each. Also use: *Sharks* by Herbert S. Zim (1966, Morrow $5.50; LB $5.09).

8650. Selsam, Millicent E., and Hunt, Joyce. *A First Look at Sharks* (1–3). Illus. by Harriett Springer. 1979, Walker $7.85. The physical characteristics and behavior of the shark are covered in this beginning account.

Lobsters and Other Crustaceans

8651. Carrick, Carol, and Carrick, Donald. *Blue Lobster: A Life Cycle* (1–3). Illustrated. 1975, Dial $6.95. A simple, accurate account of the life of this underwater species.

8652. Cook, Joseph J. *The Nocturnal World of the Lobster* (5–9). Illus. by Jan Cook. 1972, Dodd $4.50. A fascinating glimpse into the life of lobsters and crayfish with material on their habits, types, bodily structure, and conservation.

8653. Hawes, Judy. *Shrimps* (1–3). Illus. by Joseph Low. 1966, Crowell $4.50; LB $5.95. The life cycle of the shrimp, its growth and habits, and its ability to travel remarkable distances are described accurately and simply.

8654. Russell, Solveig P. *Crusty Ones: A First Look at Crustaceans* (2–5). Illus. by Laurence Di Fiori.

1974, Walck $5.95. An introduction that includes lobsters, crabs, shrimp, and barnacles.

8655.   Taylor, Herb. *Lobster: Its Life Cycle* (5–7). Illustrated. 1975, Sterling $5.95; LB $5.89. The life story of lobsters with valuable material on how pollution has endangered their once large population.

8656.   Waters, John F. *Crab from Yesterday: The Life Cycle of a Horseshoe Crab* (4–6). Illus. by W. T. Mars. 1970, Warne $3.95. For 300 million years, this creature has survived; this account tells why.

8657.   Zim, Herbert S., and Krantz, Lucretia. *Crabs* (4–6). Illus. by Rene Martin. 1974, Morrow $5.50. The anatomy, habits, and commercial value of crabs are described in this well-organized account.

Oysters, Sponges, Starfish

8658.   Grayson, Fred N. *Oysters* (4–6). Illustrated. 1974, Messner $6.64. The life-style, uses, and characteristics of this sea creature.

8659.   Jacobson, Morris K, and Pong, Rosemary. *Wonders of Sponges* (5–8). Illustrated. 1976, Dodd $4.95. An explanation of the life and habits of sponges, well illustrated with photographs.

8660.   Jacobson, Morris K, and Emerson, William K. *Wonders of Starfish* (5–7). Illustrated. 1977, Dodd $4.95. The types of starfish are discussed, along with feeding habits, and the growth and reproduction processes. Also use: *Sea Stars and Their Kin* by Herbert S. Zim (1976, Morrow $4.59).

8661.   McClung, Robert M. *Sea Star* (2–4). Illus. by author. 1975, Morrow $5.49. The structure of the starfish, its eating habits, and its reproductive pattern are simply explained as the reader follows one starfish through its yearly cycle. Also use: *Starfish* by Edith Thacher Hurd (1962, Crowell $5.95).

8662.   Silverstein, Alvin, and Silverstein, Virginia B. *Star in the Sea* (2–4). Illus. by Symeon Shimin. 1969, Warne $3.95. The simple account of the life cycle of the starfish.

Octopus

8663.   Carrick, Carol. *Octopus* (2–4). Illus. by Donald Carrick. 1978, Seabury $6.95. The day-to-day life of a female octopus that ends with the egg-laying process.

8664.   Conklin, Gladys P. *The Octopus and Other Cephalopods* (5–6). Illustrated. 1977, Holiday $5.95. A brief, informative discussion of structure and living habits of octopus, squid, cuttlefish, and similar species. Also use: *The Phantom World of the Octopus and Squid* by Joseph J. Cook (1965, Dodd $4.50).

8665.   Hopf, Alice L. *Biography of an Octopus* (2–4). Illus. by Mamoru Funai. 1971, Putnam $4.97. The life of an octopus from birth to maturity with information on its structure, the way its eggs are laid and guarded, and its eating habits.

8666.   Shaw, Evelyn. *Octopus* (1–2). Illus. by Ralph Carpentier. 1971, Harper $4.79. How an octopus hunts for food, avoids predators, finds a home, and lays eggs, described simply and clearly.

8667.   Vevers, Henry Gwynne. *Octopus, Cuttlefish and Squid* (4–6). Illustrated. 1978, McGraw $6.95. Basic information on 3 members of the mollusk family in well-presented text and drawings.

Corals and Jellyfish

8668.   Berger, Gilda. *The Coral Reef: What Lives There* (2–4). Illus. by Murray Tinkelman. 1977, Coward $5.29. How coral reefs are formed and their wildlife are 2 of the topics in this book. For an older group use: *Exploring the Coral Reef* by Robert F. Burgess (1972, Macmillan $4.95).

8669.   Jacobson, Morris K, and Franz, David R. *Wonders of Jellyfish* (6–9). Illustrated. 1978, Dodd $5.95. A detailed and fascinating account of the structure and behavioral patterns of this primitive animal.

8670.   Jacobson, Morris K, and Franz, David R. *Wonders of Corals and Coral Reefs* (6–9). Illustrated. 1979, Dodd $5.95. A well-researched and thorough account of coral reefs and their inhabitants.

8671.   May, Julian. *These Islands Are Alive* (3–5). Illus. by Rod Ruth. 1971, Hawthorn $4.50. In this fascinating description of the Florida Keys, the author includes much incidental information about the varieties of coral and building of coral colonies.

8672.   Ronai, Lili. *Corals* (2–3). Illus. by Arabelle Wheatley. 1976, Crowell $5.95. An excellent first book on corals, describing how reefs are formed, how corals eat and regenerate, and the different kinds of coral. For a slightly older group use: *Corals* by Herbert S. Zim (1966, Morrow $5.09).

8673.   Shepherd, Elizabeth. *Jellyfishes* (4–6). Illus. by Howard Berelson. 1969, Lothrop $5.09. The anatomy and habits of several jellyfish are discussed, as well as directions to produce a jellyfish model.

8674. Waters, John F. *A Jellyfish Is Not a Fish* (2–3). Illus. by Kazue Mizumura. 1979, Crowell $6.95; LB $6.89. A simple introduction to the life and habits of jellyfish.

Shells

8675. Clemons, Elizabeth. *Shells Are Where You Find Them* (2–4). Illus. by Joe Gault. 1960, Knopf $4.99. A basic guide to types of shells and shell collecting.

8676. Goudey, Alice E. *Houses from the Sea* (K–3). Illus. by Adrienne Adams. 1959, Scribner $8.95; paper $.95. A picture story book about shells.

8677. Jacobson, Morris K, and Emerson, William K. *Wonders of the World of Shells: Sea, Land and Fresh-Water* (6–8). Illustrated. 1971, Dodd $4.50. The authors describe how each of the 6 major classes of mollusks lives, reproduces, and fends off enemies; includes guide to collecting shells. Also use: *Sea Shells of the World: A Guide to the Better-Known Species* by R. Tucker Abbott (1962, Golden $5.95; paper $1.95).

8678. Rogers, Julia Ellen. *The Shell Book* (6–9). 1951, Branford $11.50. An excellent introduction to various shells for mature readers.

Seashores

8679. Buck, Margaret Waring. *Along the Seashore* (4–6). Illus. by author. 1964, Abingdon $5.95; paper $1.95. Everything from algae to flowers, shells, fish, and birds of the shore.

8680. Carson, Rachel. *The Edge of the Sea* (6–8). Illus. by Bob Hines. 1955, Houghton $7.95. Various types of coastal habitats are described with outstanding photographs of the Atlantic Coast. Also use: *Beachcomber's Book* by Bernice Kohn (1970, Viking $4.95; Penguin, paper $1.95).

8681. Cooper, Elizabeth K. *Science on the Shores and Banks* (6–9). 1960, Harcourt $4.95; paper $1.50. Animal and plant life in or near water. Also use: *Tide Pools and Beaches* by Elizabeth Clemons (1974, Knopf $2.95; LB $4.99).

8682. Kirkpatrick, Rena K. *Look at Shore Life* (K–2). Illustrated. 1978, Raintree $5.49. A very superficial introduction that is suitable for browsing purposes.

8683. List, Ilka. *Questions and Answers about Seashore Life* (1–4). Illus. by A and Arabelle Wheatley. 1971, Four Winds $6.95. A clearly written and well-illustrated introduction to seashore life.

8684. Zim, Herbert S., and Ingle, Lester. *Seashores* (5–8). Illustrated. 1955, Golden $5.95; paper $1.95. Subtitle: *A Guide to Animals and Plants along the Beaches.*

Zoos and Marine Aquariums

8685. Bridges, William. *Zoo Doctor* (5–6). Illustrated. 1957, Morrow $5.95. Teaching seals to drink and making formula for lion cubs are part of the day.

8686. Buchenholz, Bruce. *Doctor in the Zoo* (6–9). 1976, Pengui. paper $12.95. Although written for adults, this account of a zoo veterinarian's typical week will intrigue a younger audience.

8687. Chaplina, Vera. *True Stories from the Moscow Zoo* (5–8). Illus. by Mel Hunter. 1970, Prentice-Hall $4.50. A zookeeper tells about her experiences with animals, including a lion cub she raised in her apartment.

8688. Halmi, Robert. *Zoos of the World* (5–7). Illustrated. 1975, Four Winds $6.95. By using examples of zoos in history and some of the good and bad zoos of today, the author reviews criteria in construction and management that must be met to insure an animal's comfort and safety. Also use: *Zoos of the World* by James Fisher (1967, Natural Hist. Pr. $6.95).

8689. Hewett, Joan. *Watching Them Grow: Inside a Zoo Nursery* (4–6). Illustrated. 1979, Little $7.95. The care and feeding of baby zoo animals during a period from November to March.

8690. McCoy, Joseph J. *Our Captive Animals* (5–7). Illustrated. 1971, Seabury $6.95. A discussion of zoo animals and how captivity affects their welfare. Also use: *Zoo Animals* by Donald Hoffmeister (1967, Western, paper $1.95).

8691. Paige, David. *Behind the Scenes at the Aquarium* (4–6). Illustrated. 1979, Whitman $6.95; LB $5.21. An absorbing view of the administration and management of an aquarium such as the Shedd Aquarium in Chicago.

8692. Paige, David. *Behind the Scenes at the Zoo* (5–7). Illustrated. 1978, Whitman $6.25. How zoos initiate and carry out the best care possible for their charges.

8693. Perry, John. *A First Book of Zoos* (3–6). Illustrated. 1971, Watts $.90. The design and functions of zoos are described, as well as their maintenance and administration.

8694. Schick, Alice, and Friedman, Sara Ann. *Zoo Year* (4–6). Illus. by Joel Schick. 1978, Lippincott $8.95. Events such as the birth of a giraffe and a roundup of pelicans are described in this view of the Bronx Zoo.

8695. Scott, Jack. *City of Birds and Beasts* (4–7). Illustrated. 1978, Putnam $8.95. Subtitle: *Behind the Scenes at the Bronx Zoo.*

8696. Shannon, Terry, and Payzant, Charles. *New at the Zoo* (5–7). 1972, Golden $6.60. A charming, brief book that describes the care and feeding of a variety of zoo offspring.

8697. Shuttlesworth, Dorothy E. *Zoos in the Making* (5–7). Illustrated. 1977, Dutton $8.50. Important zoos and animal parks are identified and described; a discussion of how zoos are designed; well-illustrated with photographs.

Pets

General

8698. Caputo, Robert. *More than Just Pets: Why People Study Animals* (PS–1). Illustrated. 1980, Coward $7.95. The author explains what we can learn from animals and how this can help us.

8699. Caras, Roger. *A Zoo in Your Room* (5–8). Illus. by Pamela Johnson. 1975, Harcourt $5.95. An overview of the care and feeding of a variety of household pets.

8700. Case, Marshall T. *Look What I Found* (4–6). Illustrated. 1971, Chatham $.95. A description of how to catch, house, and care for small wildlife. Also use: *Problem Pets* by Lilo Hess (1972, Scribner $5.95; paper 95¢).

8701. Chrystie, Frances. *Pets: A Complete Handbook on the Care, Understanding and Appreciation of All Kinds of Animal Pets* (5–9). Illus. by Gillett Good Griffin. 1974, Little $6.95. A perennial favorite, particularly comprehensive in the great variety of pets discussed. Also use: *A Pet Book for Boys and Girls* by Alfred P. Morgan (1949, Scribner $6.95).

8702. McCoy, Joseph J. *Pet Safety* (4–6). Illus. by Bette J. Davis. 1979, Watts $6.90. A narrative on special kinds of pet care.

8703. Reynolds, Michelle. *Critters's Kitchen* (4–6). 1979, Atheneum $4.66. A seventh-grade student gives recipes for 32 foods that her pets and other animals like.

8704. Sabin, Francene, and Sabin, Louis. *Perfect Pets* (5–7). Illustrated. 1978, Putnam $7.95. All kinds of pets—from insects to hamsters—are introduced.

8705. Simon, Seymour. *Pets in a Jar: Collecting and Caring for Small Wild Animals* (4–6). Illus. by Betty Fraser. 1975, Viking $6.95. How to catch and care for such small wild creatures as snails, toads, and ants. Also use: *Shelf Pets: How to Take Care of Small Wild Animals* by Edward R. Ricciuti (1971, Harper $5.95; LB $5.79).

8706. Stevens, Carla. *Your First Pet and How to Take Care of It* (2–4). Illus. by Lisl Weil. 1974, Macmillan $4.95. Gerbils, other rodents, goldfish, dogs, and cats are among the pets covered.

8707. Vandivert, Rita. *Understanding Animals as Pets* (4–6). Illus. by William Vandivert. 1976, Warne $5.95. A comprehensive text for country and city children on how to care for a variety of pets from dogs and gerbils to snakes and horses.

8708. Weber, William J. *Care of Uncommon Pets* (4–8). Illustrated. 1979, Holt $7.95. Chickens, lizards, rabbits, canaries, tortoises, and 15 other animals are presented.

Cats

8709. Besser, Marianne. *The Cat Book* (4–6). Illus. by Shannon Stirnweis. 1967, Hastings $5.95. The evolution, characteristics, behavior, and kinds of domestic cats. Also use: *All about Cats* by Carl Burger (1966, Random $2.95; LB $4.39).

8710. Hess, Lilo. *Listen to Your Kitten Purr* (4–6). Illustrated. 1980, Scribner $8.95. A lesson concerning the need for being responsible for one's pets is presented in this photo documentary.

8711. Holman, Michael. *Cats* (1–3). Illus. by Jilly Lovat. 1976, Watts $4.90. A brief survey that touches on history, breeds, and characteristics of cats.

8712. Levitin, Sonia. *Reigning Cats and Dogs* (6–8). Illus. by Joan Berg Victor. 1978, Atheneum $7.95. A memoir of the author's life with numerous animals.

8713. Rockwell, Jane. *Cats and Kittens* (4–7). Illustrated. 1974, Watts $4.90. The anatomy and personalities of cats are discussed, as well as care and feeding. Also use: *Catnip: Selecting and Training Your Cat* by Kurt Unkelbach (1970, Prentice-Hall $5.95; paper 95¢).

8714. Selsam, Millicent E. *How Kittens Grow* (1–2). Illus. by Esther Bubley. 1975, Four Winds $4.95. Photographs and simply written text describe the stages in a kitten's growth.

8715. Silverstein, Alvin, and Silverstein, Virginia B. *Cats: All about Them* (3–5). Illustrated. 1978, Lothrop $6.95; LB $6.43. A compendium of information about cats, their history, and domestication.

8716. Stevens, Carla. *The Birth of Sunset's Kittens* (K–3). Illus. by Leonard Stevens. 1969, Addison $6.95. Appealing photographs show the birth process of a litter of kittens.

8717. Tabor, Anthony. *Cats' Eyes* (all ages). Illustrated. 1978, Dutton $9.95. The life of Tiger, a cat, as seen through detailed pencil drawings.

8718. Unkelbach, Kurt. *Tiger Up a Tree: Knowing and Training Your Kitten* (2–5). Illus. by Paul Frame. 1972, Prentice-Hall $5.95. Sensible advice about training, feeding, and caring for a kitten, which puts the responsibility for a pet squarely in a child's hands.

Dogs

8719. Bethell, Jean. *How to Care for Your Dog* (2–4). Illus. by Norman Birdwell. 1967, Four Winds $5.50; Scholastic paper $.95. A simple guide that includes sections on illnesses, housebreaking and grooming. Also use: *A Puppy for You* by Lilo Hess (1975, Scribner $6.95).

8720. Broderick, Dorothy M. *Training a Companion Dog* (4–7). Illus. by Haris Petie. 1965, Prentice-Hall $4.95. How to train one's dog to be an obedient companion; analogies between human and animal behavior that children will appreciate. Also use: *Newer and Better Dog Obedience Training* by Byron G. Wels (1974, Putnam $5.95).

8721. Bronson, Wilfrid S. *Dogs: Best Breeds for Young People* (4–7). Illus. by author. 1969, Marcourt $5.95. All the important information that should be known before owning a dog is covered with wit and clarity.

8722. Caras, Roger, and Graham, Pamela C. *Dogs: Records, Stars, Feats and Facts* (4–6). Illustrated. 1979, Harcourt $2.95. Six recognized breeds are described with accompanying charts and photographs.

8723. Clover, Harry. *The Book of Dogs* (6–9). Illustrated. 1970, Viking $4.95. The British-oriented text is divided by the 6 main types of dogs (e.g, hounds, gundogs); well illustrated with several pictures in color. Also use: *Dogs of America* by Francene Sabin (1967, Putnam $5.69).

8724. Fichter, George S. *Working Dogs* (5–7). Illustrated. 1979, Watts $5.45. An overview of the work that dogs do, from herding sheep to aiding the blind.

8725. Fox, Michael, and Gates, Wende Devlin. *What Is Your Dog Saying?* (4–6). 1978, Coward $5.33. A narrative that tells how to recognize and understand dog language.

8726. Haggerty, Arthur J, and Benjamin, Carol Lee. *Dog Tricks* (4–6). Illus. by Carol Lee Benjamin. 1978, Doubleday $3.32. Various dog tricks are described.

8727. Hall, Lynn. *Kids and Dog Shows* (5–9). Illustrated. 1975, Follett $5.95; LB $5.97. How to train, groom, and show dogs is the central focus of this useful, well-organized book.

8728. Henry, Marguerite. *Album of Dogs* (3–6). Illus. by Wesley Dennis. 1970, Rand $4.95; LB $4.97. More than 25 breeds are discussed and pictured.

8729. Hess, Lilo. *A Dog by Your Side* (3–6). Illustrated. 1977, Scribner $6.95. A basic introduction to the various breeds of dogs, as well as material on how to care for a trained dog. Also use: *Both Ends of the Leash* by Kurt Unkelbach (1968, Prentice-Hall $4.95; paper 95¢).

8730. Hess, Lilo. *Life Begins for Puppies* (2–5). Illustrated. 1978, Scribner $6.95. The birth and first 4 weeks of life of sheepdog puppies. Also use: *My Puppy Is Born* by Joanna Cole (1973, Morrow $5.50; LB $5.09).

8731. Huntington, Harriet E. *Let's Look at Dogs* (4–6). Illustrated. 1980, Doubleday $6.95. An introduction to the most common breeds, plus such useful information as the reasons for dog licensing.

8732. Kay, Helen. *Man and Mastiff* (4–6). Illustrated. 1967, Macmillan $3.95. An interesting account of the development of the St. Bernard and its present characteristics and use. Also use: *Barry: The Story of a Brave St. Bernard* by Bettina Hurlimann (1967, Harcourt $5.75).

8733. McCloy, James. *Dogs at Work* (4–6). Illus. by Shelia Beatty. 1979, Crown $7.95. In brief sections, the author describes various breeds of working dogs and their uses.

8734. Pfloog, Jan. *Puppies* (PS). Illus. by author. 1979, Random $2.50. The behavior and needs of puppies and how to care for them are briefly covered. A companion to *Kittens* (1977, $2.50).

8735. Pinkwater, Jill, and Pinkwater, D. Manus. *Superpuppy* (4–6). Illustrated. 1977, Seabury $9.95. All one needs to know about choosing and rearing the "best possible" dog. Also use: *Bringing*

Up Puppies by Jane W. Levin (1958, Harcourt $5.95).

8736. Putnam, Peter. *The Triumph of the Seeing Eye* (5–7). Illustrated. 1963, Harper $5.79. The story of Morris Frank, pioneer worker with guide dogs and the Seeing Eye organization.

8737. Selsam, Millicent E. *How Puppies Grow* (1–2). Illus. by Esther Bubley. 1972, Four Winds $4.95. The stages in a puppy's life from birth, through walking, seeing, eating, and playing, described in excellent photographs and simple text.

8738. Sendak, Maurice, and Margolis, Matthew. *Some Swell Pup: Or Are You Sure You Want a Dog?* (K–4). Illus. by author. 1976, Farrar $5.95. Cartoon-style illustrations introduce children to the responsibility of having and caring for a pet.

8739. Simon, Seymour. *Discovering What Puppies Do* (3–5). Illus. by Susan Bonners. 1977, McGraw $5.72. The choosing, care, and training of puppies presented in an easily read treatment. Also use: *How to Bring Up Your Pet Dog* by Kurt Unkelbach (1972, Dodd $4.95).

8740. Unkelbach, Kurt. *How to Teach an Old Dog New Tricks* (5–7). Illus. by Sam Savitt. 1979, Dodd $6.95. A fine guide on how to retrain a pet dog.

8741. Unkelbach, Kurt. *You're a Good Dog, Joe: Knowing and Training Your Puppy* (2–4). Illus. by Paul Frame. 1971, Prentice-Hall $5.95. A comprehensive and useful book on all aspects of dog training and care.

8742. Wolf, Bernard. *Connie's New Eyes* (5–8). Illustrated. 1976, Lippincott $8.95. The training of a seeing eye dog from birth to use with a blind owner.

8743. Wolters, Richard A. *Kid's Dog: A Training Book* (3–5). Illustrated. 1978, Doubleday $5.95. How to select and train a dog, illustrated with fine photographs.

Horses

8744. Adler, Larry. *Famous Horses in America* (4–6). 1979, McKay $5.33. Profiles of famous horses in history. Also use: *Famous Horses and Their People* by Edna H. Green (1975, Stephen Green Pr. $7.95).

8745. Amaral, Anthony. *Movie Horses* (4–6). Illustrated. 1967, Bobbs-Merrill $5.50. The training and treatment of horses used in films and television.

8746. Berry, Barbara J. *Horse Happy: A Complete Guide to Owning Your First Horse* (5–8). Illustrated. 1978, Bobbs-Merrill $8.95; paper $5.95. A sensible, detailed account of horse buying and owning.

8747. Brady, Irene. *America's Horses and Ponies* (5–7). Illus. by author. 1969, Houghton $10.95; paper $6.95. Background information on all sorts of equines in a lucid, well-organized account. Also use: *C. W. Anderson's Complete Book of Horses and Horsemanship* (1963, Macmillan $6.95).

8748. Darling, Lois, and Darling, Louis. *Sixty Million Years of Horses* (4–7). Illustrated. 1960, Morrow $5.09. The horse, its relatives and usefulness in the past and present.

8749. Demuth, Jack, and Demuth, Patricia. *City Horse* (4–6). Illustrated. 1979, Dodd $6.95. Various aspects of the life of a New York City policeman's horse are described.

8750. Ford, Barbara. *The Island Ponies: An Environmental Study of Their Life on Assateague* (6–8). 1979, Morrow $6.95. An introduction to these famous wild horses.

8751. Freedman, Russell. *Getting Born* (3–4). Illustrated. 1978, Holiday $6.95. Photographs and text describe the birth of a pony.

8752. Hall, Lynn. *A Horse Called Dragon* (5–7). Illus. by Joseph Cellini. 1971, Follett $3.95; LB $4.98. A nonfiction account of the Mexican mustang that was eventually brought to Texas to help establish the "Pony of the Americas" breed.

8753. Henry, Marguerite. *All about Horses* (5–8). Illus. by Wesley Dennis. 1963, Random $4.39. From prehistoric beginnings to present-day breeds, including the horse's place in history. Also use: *Album of Horses* (1951, Rand $4.96; LB $4.79).

8754. Hess, Lilo. *A Pony to Love* (4–6). Illus. by author. 1975, Scribner $8.95. The purchase, care, and handling of a pony described in clear, direct prose and illustrated with photographs.

8755. Hess, Lilo. *Shetland Ponies* (1–3). Illus. by author. 1964, Crowell $4.50. The life of 2 Shetland ponies from birth to their first master forms the basis for this text and the touching illustrations.

8756. Hogner, Dorothy Childs. *The Horse Family* (3–6). Illustrated. 1953, Walck $4.95. Covers such topics as the horse in history, art, and mythology. For an older group use: *The Story of Horses* by Dorothy Shuttlesworth (n.d. Doubleday $4.95).

8757. Ipcar, Dahlov. *World Full of Horses* (1–3). Illus. by author. 1955, Doubleday $4.95. Beautiful picture book of horses in America, yesterday and today. For a slightly older group use: *Questions and Answers about Horses* by Millicent E. Selsam (1973, Four Winds, paper 95¢).

8758. Krueger, Bob. *The Wild Mustangs* (6–8). Illustrated. 1980, McKay $7.95. The story of wild horses and the beneficial effects of the 1971 Horse and Burro Act.

8759. May, Julian. *Horses: How They Came to Be* (2–4). Illus. by Lorence Bjorklund. 1968, Holiday $4.95. A history of the horse, plus material on today's species and how they are cared for.

8760. Miller, Jane. *Birth of a Foal* (1–4). Illus. by author. 1977, Lippincott $6.95. Pictures illustrate this sensitive account of birth and maternal love. Also use: *A Foal Is Born* by Hans-Heinrich Isenbart (1976, Putnam $5.95).

8761. Phillips, Betty Lou. *The American Quarter Horse* (6–8). Illustrated. 1979, McKay $8.95. The history and husbandry of this breed.

8762. Rabinowich, Ellen. *Horses and Foals* (3–4). Illustrated. 1979, Watts $5.90. Through concentration on a mare and a foal, a discussion of the structure and characteristics of horses is introduced. Also use: *Twenty Gallant Horses* by Clarence W. Anderson (1965, Macmillan $7.95).

8763. Richards, Jane. *A Horse Grows Up* (K–3). Illus. by Bert Hardy. 1972, Walker $4.50. Lovely illustrations and simple text tell the story of a colt.

8764. Robertson, Alden. *The Wild Horse Gatherers* (6–9). Illustrated. 1978, Scribner $10.95. A vivid description of a wild horse roundup on government rangelands.

8765. Rounds, Glen. *Wild Horses on the Red Desert* (2–4). Illus. by author. 1969, Holiday $5.95. An account of how wild horses live in the Badlands of South Dakota.

8766. Ryden, Hope. *Wild Colt: The Life of a Young Mustang* (4–6). Illustrated. 1972, Coward $6.95. A beautifully photographed picture study of a young colt growing up.

8767. Scott, Jack. *Island of Wild Horses* (5–9). Illustrated. 1978, Putnam $7.95. The horses of Assateague examined in simple text and impressive photographs.

8768. Slaughter, Jean. *Pony Care* (5–7). Illustrated. 1961, Knopf $4.50; LB $5.69. A detailed account of how to handle and care for a pony, with tips on purchasing and housing.

8769. Sutton, Felix. *Horses of America* (4–6). Illus. by Walter Wilwerding. 1964, Putnam $5.69. The distinguished ancestry of each American horse breed is traced to its "foundation sire." Also use:

The Book of Horses by Glenn Balch (1967, Four Winds $5.95; paper 95¢).

8770. Thompson, Neil. *A Closer Look at Horses* (5–8). Illustrated. 1978, Gloucester $5.90. A basic introduction is given to the structure, behavior, and evolution of the horse.

Fish

8771. Axelrod, Herbert R. *Tropical Fish as a Hobby* (5–7). Illustrated. 1969, McGraw $12.50. A guide to selection, care, and breeding. Also use: *Tropical Fish in Your Home* (1960, Sterling $6.95).

8772. Cole, Joanna, and Wexler, Jerome. *A Fish Hatches* (3–5). Illustrated. 1978, Morrow $6.95. The story in text and photographs of a trout from egg to fully grown fish.

8773. Hoke, John. *The First Book of Aquariums* (4–7). 1975, Watts $4.90. A detailed and very useful guide for the beginner.

8774. Morgan, Alfred P. *Aquarium Book for Boys and Girls* (5–8). Illustrated. 1959, Scribner $4.95. A comprehensive introduction to all aspects of aquarium maintenance.

8775. Patent, Dorothy. *Fish and How They Reproduce* (6–9). Illus. by Matthew Kalmenoff. 1976, Holiday $6.95. After introductory chapters on the types of fish and their adaptations, there is a detailed account of mating habits, spawning, and other related topics.

8776. Sarnoff, Jane, and Ruffins, Reynold. *A Great Aquarium Book: The Putting-It-Together Guide for Beginners* (4–8). Illustrated. 1977, Scribner $7.95; paper $3.95. Straightforward explanations presented with verse in a readable manual.

8777. Selsam, Millicent E. *Plenty of Fish* (K–3). Illus. by Erik Blegvad. 1960, Harper $4.79. A good book for the beginning reader on goldfish and their care.

8778. Selsam, Millicent E. *Underwater Zoos* (4–6). Illus. by Kathleen Elgin. 1961, Morrow $5.49. How to collect unusual pets from fresh and salt water.

8779. Simon, Seymour. *What Do You Want to Know about Guppies?* (2–5). Illus. by Susan Bonners. 1977, Four Winds $6.95. Guppies, from how they got their name to how they reproduce.

8780. Villiard, Paul. *Exotic Fish as Pets* (5–7). Illustrated. 1978, Doubleday $4.95. This book has 2 parts—various fish species and setting up an aquarium.

8781. Wong, Herbert H., and Vessel, Matthew F. *My Goldfish* (1–3). Illus. by Arvis Stewart. 1969, Addison $5.95. With fictional overtones, this account describes the habits of a goldfish.

8782. Zim, Herbert S. *Goldfish* (2–5). Illus. by Jay Buba. 1947, Morrow $5.09. An interesting account of the types of goldfish, their needs, and how to care for them.

Other Pets

8783. Cooper, Kay. *All about Rabbits as Pets* (3–6). Illustrated. 1974, Messner $6.29. In addition to background material, the author gives excellent coverage on the care, raising, and feeding of rabbits.

8784. Dobrin, Arnold. *Gerbils* (3–6). Illus. by author. 1970, Lothrop $5.49. An interesting account of how to care for this popular pet. Also use: *Gerbils and Other Small Pets* by Dorothy E. Shuttlesworth (1970, Dutton $6.95).

8785. Fichter, George S. *Keeping Amphibians and Reptiles as Pets* (4–6). 1979, Watts $5.90. Practical tips on how to care for such animals as frogs, snakes, and turtles.

8786. Headstrom, Richard. *Lizards as Pets* (6–8). Illustrated. 1971, Lippincott $5.95; LB $5.82. How to care for and make a pet of this fascinating reptile.

8787. Hoke, John. *The First Book of Turtles and Their Care* (6–8). Illus. by Barbara Wolff. 1970, Watts $4.90. The turtle's anatomy, species, and living habits, as well as information on how to keep them as pets.

8788. Hooks, William H. *The 17 Gerbils of Class 4A* (3–6). Illus. by Joel Schick. 1976, Coward $5.95. Taking care of gerbils can be lots of fun for a fourth-grade class. Also use: *Discovering What Gerbils Do* by Seymour Simon (1971, McGraw $5.72).

8789. Joseph, Joan. *Pet Birds* (5–8). Illus. by John Hamberger. 1975, Watts $4.90. How to train talking birds, what to feed various varieties, and how to diagnose illnesses are only 3 of the many topics covered. Also use: *Birds as Pets* by Paul Villiard (1974, Doubleday $5.95).

8790. Overbeck, Cynthia. *Curly the Piglet* (2–4). Illustrated. 1976, Carolrhoda $3.95. Two children on a farm observe the growth of a small pig.

8791. Selsam, Millicent E. *Let's Get Turtles* (1–3). Illus. by Arnold Lobel. 1965, Harper $4.79. Simple information about caring for turtles as seen through the experiences of 2 small boys.

8792. Silverstein, Alvin, and Silverstein, Virginia B. *Gerbils: All about Them* (5–8). 1976, Lippincott $6.95. The most extensive work for young readers on the subject.

8793. Silverstein, Alvin, and Silverstein, Virginia B. *Guinea Pigs: All about Them* (3–6). Illustrated. 1972, Lothrop $5.95; LB $5.49. The history, life cycle, and habits of, and tips on caring for these rodents as pets.

8794. Silverstein, Alvin, and Silverstein, Virginia B. *Hamsters: All about Them* (4–7). Illustrated. 1974, Lothrop $5.49. A basic manual for the hamster owner, full of excellent photographs. Also use: *Golden Hamsters* by Herbert S. Zim (1951, Morrow $5.52).

8795. Silverstein, Alvin, and Silverstein, Virginia B. *Rabbits* (3–6). Illustrated. 1973, Lothrop $6.01. A well-organized account that explores many facets about rabbit life, with a section on legends and lore. Also use: *Rabbits* by Herbert S. Zim (1948, Morrow $5.09).

8796. Villiard, Paul. *Insects as Pets* (6–8). Illustrated. 1973, Doubleday $4.95. A description of a number of insects that can be caught and studied at home. Also use: *Insect Zoo: How to Collect and Care for Insects* by Constance Ewbank (1973, Walker $4.95; LB $5.95).

8797. Villiard, Paul. *Reptiles as Pets* (4–6). Illustrated. 1969, Doubleday $5.95. A concise, instructive guide to keeping reptiles as pets.

8798. Zappler, Georg, and Zappler, Lisbeth. *Amphibians as Pets* (6–8). Illustrated. 1973, Doubleday $5.95. The structure and living habits of amphibians, as well as information on the care and raising of them.

8799. Zim, Herbert S. *Homing Pigeons* (6–9). Illus. by James G. Irving. 1949, Morrow $5.09. A guide to the raising and flying of homing pigeons.

8800. Zim, Herbert S. *Parrakeets* (4–6). Illus. by Larry Kettelkamp. 1953, Morrow $5.09. Everything a young person needs to know about caring for these pets.

Technology and Engineering

General

8801. Buehr, Walter. *The Magic of Paper* (4–7). Illus. by author. 1966, Morrow $5.49. The past, present, and future of paper with an interesting section on the varieties being produced today.

8802. Cohn, Angelo. *The Wonderful World of Paper* (4–7). Illustrated. 1967, Abelard $7.95. As well as the many uses of paper, this account discusses the manufacturing processes as they have changed through history.

8803. Colby, C. B. *Space Age Fire Fighters: New Weapons in the Fireman's Arsenal* (3–6). Illustrated. 1974, Coward $5.19. New and innovative techniques for fighting fires.

8804. Cooke, David C. *Inventions That Made History* (5–7). Illustrated. 1968, Putnam $4.89. Thirty-two inventions that have changed human life.

8805. Gottlieb, Leonard. *Factory Made: How Things Are Made* (5–8). Illustrated. 1978, Houghton $7.95. The stories behind the manufacture of 13 commonplace objects.

8806. Hahn, James, and Hahn, Lynn. *Plastics* (5–7). Illustrated. 1974, Watts $4.90. A fine overview of the types, history, and many uses of plastics. Also use: *Plastics* by C. P. Vale (1971, John Day $4.47).

8807. Pratt, Fletcher. *All about Famous Inventors and Their Inventions* (4–7). Illustrated. 1957, Random $4.30. From the spinning jenny to the audion tube.

8808. Sullivan, George. *How Do They Make It?* (4–6). Illustrated. 1965, Westminster $5.25. For a number of products, the history, composition, and present methods of manufacture are given.

8809. Torbert, Floyd James. *Fire Fighters the World Over* (2–4). Illus. by author. 1967, Hastings $4.25; LB $3.96. How 17 countries face different problems in fire fighting and how they have tried to solve them.

8810. Weiss, Harvey. *What Holds It Together* (5–8). Illus. by author. 1977, Atlantic $6.95.

Clamps, glue, cement, and thread are only a few of the ways by which we hold objects together.

Transportation

8811. Ancona, George. *Monsters on Wheels* (4–6). Illus. by author. 1974, Dutton $7.50. A description in text and photos of 17 huge machines.

8812. Barton, Byron. *Wheels* (PS–K). Illus. by author. 1979, Crowell $6.95; LB $6.89. A history of wheels and their importance through the ages.

8813. Billout, Guy. *By Camel or by Car* (2–3). 1979, Prentice-Hall $5.96. A simple discussion of how various vehicles can move across different surfaces.

8814. Dalgliesh, Alice. *America Travels* (4–7). 1961, Macmillan $4.95. Modes of travel up to the rocket age. Also use: *Transportation in Today's World* by Etta Schneider Ress (1965, Creative Education $6.95).

8815. Hellman, Hal. *Transportation in the World of the Future* (5–7). Illustrated. 1974, Evans $6.95. A fascinating glimpse of possible future modes of transporation. Also use: *Cars, Boats, Trains and Planes of Today and Tomorrow* by Thomas G. Aylesworth (1975, Walker $6.85).

8816. Hirsch, S. Carl. *On Course!* (5–7). Illus. by William Steinel. 1967, Viking $4.95. Subtitle: *Navigation in Sea, Air and Space.*

8817. Italiano, Carlo. *Sleighs: The Gentle Transportation* (4–7). Illustrated. 1978, Tundra $9.95. A nostalgic look at the part sleighs have played in our lives, and still do.

8818. Jupo, Frank. *No Place Too Far: The Story of Travel through the Ages* (4–5). Illus. by author. 1967, Dodd $4.50. Methods of travel and vehicles in the past and present.

8819. Kaufmann, John. *Streamlined* (2–4). Illus. by author. 1974, Crowell $5.95. The streamlined shapes of birds and fish help them move through air and water more rapidly. People have designed many of our vehicles to take account of this principle. The clear, lucid writing makes this an excellent first science book.

8820. McLeod, Sterling, and others. *How Will We Move all the People? Transportation for Tomorrow's World* (6–8). Illustrated. 1971, Messner $4.29. A look at the problems and possible solutions to our future transportation needs.

8821. Miller, Lisa. *Wheels* (2–4). Illus. by Tomie de Paola. 1965, Coward $4.49. The various ways in which wheels affect our lives, from essential items to recreational devices, are outlined in a well-organized text.

8822. Reck, Franklin M. *The Romance of American Transportation* (6–8). 1962, Crowell $7.95. The story of how we have traveled around our country.

8823. Sullivan, George. *How Does It Get There?* (5–8). 1973, Macmillan $5.95. A description of the various ways goods and materials are shipped, from supertankers to zoo transports.

8824. Tunis, Edwin. *Wheels: A Pictorial History* (6–8). 1977, Crowell $9.95. Through carefully executed drawings, a history of transportation is presented.

Aeronautics

8825. Ault, Philip H. *By the Seat of Their Pants: The Story of Early Aviation* (6–8). Illustrated. 1978, Dodd $6.95. A lively volume that highlights such pioneers as Amelia Earhart, the Wright Brothers, and Lindberg.

8826. Bendick, Jeanne. *The First Book of Airplanes* (3–5). Illus. by author. 1976, Watts $4.90. In simple text and illustrations, why planes fly and a brief history of flight.

8827. Burchard, Peter. *Balloons: From Paper Bags to Sky Hooks* (3–6). Illus. by author. 1960, Macmillan $5.95. The history of balloons from earliest attempts to the present.

8828. Coombs, Charles. *Skyhooks: The Story of Helicopters* (5–9). Illustrated. 1967, Morrow $6.25. Through a detailed description of the many uses of helicopters, the author also tells about their history and construction.

8829. Corbett, Scott. *What Makes a Plane Fly?* (3–6). Illus. by Len Darwin. 1967, Little $5.95. The principles of flight clearly described with suggested experiments for added clarification. Also use: *Why Airplanes Fly* by Don Dwiggins (1976, Childrens Press $6.50).

8830. Dahnsen, Alan. *Aircraft* (2–4). Illustrated. 1978, Watts $4.90. In simple terms, the characteristics and uses of major modern aircraft are explained.

8831. Dean, Anabel. *Up, Up, and Away!* (5–8). Illustrated. 1980, Westminster $8.95. The history of ballooning from a sport to today's practical uses.

8832. Delear, Frank J. *Famous First Flights across the Atlantic* (6–9). Illustrated. 1979, Dodd $8.95. Ten early trans-Atlantic flights are highlighted in this account.

8833. Delear, Frank J. *Helicopters and Airplanes of the U.S. Army* (4–9). Illustrated. 1977, Dodd $5.95. A statistical rundown with photographs of the present and past aircraft used by the U.S. Army.

8834. Freeman, Tony. *Blimps* (3–6). Illustrated. 1979, Childrens Press $5.95. Background information is given through a visit to the airship *Columbia*.

8835. Harris, Susan. *Helicopters* (2–4). Illus. by E. Smart. 1979, Watts $5.90. The history of helicopters, their many varieties, and how they operate are covered in this simple account.

8836. Hewish, Mark. *The Young Scientist Book of Jets* (4–7). Illustrated. 1978, EMC $5.95. An attractive semi-comic book format is used to cover basic material.

8837. Jacobs, Lou, Jr. *The Jumbo Jets* (5–7). Illustrated. 1976, Bobbs-Merrill $6.95. An introduction in text and pictures to these large carriers.

8838. Kanetzke, Howard W. *Airplanes and Balloons* (2–4). Illustrated. 1978, Raintree $5.49. Principles of flight are explained simply with many concrete examples.

8839. Mohn, Peter B. *The Thunderbirds* (4–6). Illustrated. 1980, Childrens Press $6.50. The story of the Air Force's crack flying team. Also use: *Blue Angels* (1977, Childrens Press $7.95).

8840. Navarra, John Gabriel. *Flying Today and Tomorrow* (4–6). Illustrated. 1972, Doubleday $4.95. The future of air travel is discussed in terms of such aircraft as STOLs and SSTs. Also use: *Jetport* by Norma Richard (1973, Doubleday $4.95).

8841. Navarra, John Gabriel. *Superplanes* (7–9). Illustrated. 1979, Doubleday $6.95. A narrative on high-speed planes and their many uses.

8842. Olney, Ross R. *Air Traffic Control* (6–8). Illustrated. 1972, Nelson $5.25. Many aspects of air traffic control and the personnel involved are described in this account that emphasizes safety.

Also use: *Cleared for Takeoff* by Charles Coombs (1969, Morrow $6.01).

8843. Place, Marian T. *New York to Nome: The First International Cross-Country Flight* (4–7). 1972, Macmillan $3.95. The excitement and danger of this daring mission are conveyed in this account of 4 single-engine airplanes and the amazing trip that made aviation history in 1920.

8844. Rutland, Jonathan. *See Inside an Airport* (3–5). Illustrated. 1978, Watts $5.90. Air and ground control devices and services to passengers are 2 of the topics covered. Also use: *Man in Flight: How the Airlines Operate* by Creighton Peet (1972, Macrae $6.25).

8845. Urquhart, David Inglis. *The Airplane and How It Works* (3–5). Illus. by Enrico Arno. 1973, Walck $5.95. Lift, thrust, and drag are 3 concepts explained in this fine account. Also use: *Junior Science Book of Flying* by Rocco V. Feravolo (1960, Garrard $3.58).

8846. Wilson, Mike, and Scagell, Robin. *Jet Journey* (2–7). Illustrated. 1978, Viking $5.95. Many illustrations and easily read text in this account of a trip by jet aircraft.

Automobiles

8847. Barris, George, and Scagnetti, Jack. *Famous Custom and Show Cars* (5–7). Illustrated. 1973, Dutton $7.50. A fascinating album of famous novelty automobiles. Also use: *Classic Cars* by Robert B. Jackson (1974, Walck $6.95).

8848. Bendick, Jeanne. *The First Book of Automobiles* (3–5). Illus. by author. 1978, Watts $4.90. Different types of cars are presented with special material on traffic problems and pollution. Also use: *Wheels on the Road* by David Hebb (1966, Macmillan $2.95).

8849. Berger, Melvin. *Automobile Factory* (4–6). Illustrated. 1977, Watts $4.90. The most important steps in the manufacture of the automobile are explained in this noncritical introduction. Also use: *Behind the Scenes in a Car Factory* by Leon Harris (1972, Lippincott $4.95).

8850. Bergere, Thea. *Automobiles of Yesteryear* (4–7). Illustrated. 1962, Dodd $4.50. Subtitle: *A Pictorial Record of Motor Cars That Made History— Pioneer Antique, Classic and Sports Models.*

8851. Colby, C. B. *Trucks on the Highway* (4–6). Illustrated. 1964, Coward $5.19. Simple text and many photographs introduce several kinds of trucks.

8852. Cooke, David C. *How Automobiles Are Made* (4–6). Illustrated. 1971, Dodd $4.95. A well-illustrated account that begins with design planning and ends with the finished product.

8853. Corbett, Scott. *What Makes a Car Go?* (3–5). Illus. by Len Darwin. 1963, Little $5.95. Simple text and lucid diagrams reveal the mysteries of auto engines.

8854. Dexler, Paul R. *Yesterday's Cars* (6–9). Illustrated. 1979, Lerner $5.95. A fine browsing book of some of this world's most elegant old automobiles.

8855. Foster, Genevieve. *The Year of the Horseless Carriage* (5–6). Illus. by author. 1975, Scribner $6.95. The work of Trevithick, Fulton and Stephenson on developing steam-driven vehicles is described within the context of the world in which they lived.

8856. Harding, Anthony, ed. *Car Facts and Feats* (6–9). Illustrated. 1977, Sterling $14.95; LB $12.69. Records involving the fastest, biggest, etc.

8857. Jackson, Robert B. *Antique Cars* (4–7). Illustrated. 1976, Walck $5.95. A history of automobiles with examples that cover 1893–1932. Also use: *The Early Days of Automobiles* by Elizabeth Janeway (1956, Random $4.39).

8858. Jackson, Robert B. *Big Book of Old Cars* (4–6). Illustrated. 1978, McKay $7.95. A combination of 3 previously published books, *Antique Cars*, *Classic Cars*, and *The Steam Cars of the Classic Twins*.

8859. Kanetzke, Howard. *The Story of Cars* (2–4). Illustrated. 1978, Raintree $5.49. A brief history of cars plus material on their parts and construction.

8860. Koren, Edward. *Behind the Wheel* (2–4). 1972, Holt $4.95; paper $1.25. What you see from the driver's seat if you sit in a steamshovel, ship, crane, helicopter, car, or trailer.

8861. Knudson, Richard L. *Classic Sports Cars* (5–9). Illustrated. 1979, Lerner $5.95. A collection of sports cars such as MG, Jaguar, and Mercedes-Benz.

8862. Lord, Beman. *Look at Cars* (3–6). Illustrated. 1971, Walck $5.95. An introduction to many different types of cars, including sports cars. Also use: *Sports Cars* by Robert B. Jackson (1972, Walck $6.95).

8863. Marston, Hope Irvin. *Big Rigs* (6–9). Illustrated. 1960, Dodd $5.95. A description of the kinds and uses of tractor trailers, the largest trucks on the highway.

8864. Navarra, John Gabriel. *Supercars* (5–9). Illustrated. 1975, Doubleday $5.95. A series of brief chapters on a number of new or experimental cars that represent advances from standard models. Also use: *The X Cars: Detroit's One-of-a-Kind Autos* by Henry B. Lent (1971, Putnam $4.97).

8865. Radlauer, Edward. *Dune Buggies* (3–5). Illustrated. 1968, Bowmar $3.95. Slight text and many photographs introduce this interesting vehicle. Also use: *Dune Buggies* by Gary Gladstone (1972, Lippincott $3.95).

8866. Radlauer, Edward. *Some Basics about Vans* (4–8). Illustrated. 1978, Childrens Press $5.50. A beginning work for reluctant readers, with many photographs.

8867. Rich, Mark J. *Diesel Trucks* (3–6). Illustrated. 1978, Childrens Press $5.50. A simple introduction to various kinds of diesel trucks and the work they do. Also use: *The Trucks That Haul by Night* by Leonard A. Stevens (1966, Crowell $6.79).

8868. Stambler, Irwin. *New Automobiles of the Future* (6–9). Illustrated. 1978, Putnam $7.95. A discussion of future automobile design that reflects changes in availability of energy.

8869. Stambler, Irwin. *Unusual Automobiles of Today and Tomorrow* (6–9). Illustrated. 1972, Putnam $4.89. A description of strange autos that have been manufactured or might be in the future.

8870. Waitley, Douglas. *The Roads We Traveled: An Amusing History of the Automobile* (6–9). Illustrated. 1979, Messner $8.29. An entertaining history that ends about 1930.

8871. Zim, Herbert S., and Skelly, James R. *Trucks* (4–6). Illus. by Stan Riernacki. 1970, Morrow $5.52. All kinds of trucks are described and their specific uses. Also use: *Tractors* (1972, Morrow $5.52).

Railroads

8872. Ault, Philip H. *All Aboard! The Story of Passenger Trains in America* (5–7). Illustrated. 1976, Dodd $5.95. A history of American passenger trains that concentrates on the unusual and bizarre.

8873. Brown, Dee. *Lonesome Whistle* (6–9). Illustrated. 1980, Holt $8.95. The story of the first transcontinental railroad. Also use: *The Railroads* by Leonard Everett Fisher (1979, Holiday $6.95).

8874. Crews, Donald. *Freight Train* (PS–K). Illus. by author. 1978, Greenwillow $6.95; LB $6.67. A description in text and pictures of the various cars included in a freight train, from engine to caboose.

8875. Ditzel, Paul C. *Railroad Yard* (3–6). Illustrated. 1978, Messner $6.64. The design and function of a railway yard and a freight train.

8876. Holbrook, Stewart. *The Golden Age of Railroads* (6–9). 1960, Random $4.39. A history of railroads in the United States from 1830 to the internal combusion engine in the 1920s.

8877. Kanetzke, Howard. *Trains and Railroads* (2–4). Illustrated. 1978, Raintree $5.49. A good overview of the subject, with simple explanations.

8878. Latham, Frank B. *The Transcontinental Railroad, 1862–69: A Great Engineering Feat Links America, Coast to Coast* (5–7). Illustrated. 1973, Watts $4.90. The construction of the first railroad across the United States and its impact on people and on national growth.

8879. Navarra, John Gabriel. *Supertrains* (4–7). Illustrated. 1975, Doubleday $5.95. In a world beset with dwindling energy sources, the author explores one alternate for mass transportation and the developments that have occurred worldwide with train transportation.

8880. Scarry, Huck. *Huck Scarry's Steam Train Journey* (K–2). Illustrated. 1979, Collins $5.95; LB $5.91. A slim thread of a story holds together this picture book on old-time trains.

8881. Snow, Richard. *The Iron Road: A Portrait of American Railroading* (4–8). Illustrated. 1978, Four Winds $8.95. The story of our railroads and how they affect our lives.

8882. Stein, R. Conrad. *The Story of the Golden Spike* (3–6). Illustrated. 1978, Childrens Press $4.95. The building and completion in 1869 of the transcontinental railroad.

Ships and Boats

8883. Adkins, Jan. *Wooden Ship* (4–6). Illustrated. 1978, Houghton $6.96. An explanation in text and pictures of how a ship was built in the 1870s.

8884. Berenstain, Michael. *The Ship Book* (2–4). Illustrated. 1978, McKay $6.95. A brief overview of ships and boats through the ages.

8885. Coombs, Charles. *Tankers: Giants of the Sea* (5–7). Illustrated. 1979, Morrow $6.95; LB $6.67.

The history, design, and functions of oil-carrying vessels are covered.

8886. Hancock, Ralph. *Supermachines* (2–7). A heavily illustrated account of such machines as the hydrofoil, supertanker, and bathyscaphe.

8887. Harris, Susan. *Boats and Ships* (3–4). 1979, Watts $5.90. A survey of boats from canoes to large passenger liners and oil tankers.

8888. Lasky, Kathryn. *Tall Ships* (5–9). Illustrated. 1978, Scribner $9.95. A re-creation of the era of sailing ships and the accompanying seafaring life.

8889. Lewis, Thomas P. *Clipper Ship* (1–3). Illustrated. 1978, Harper $5.95; LB $6.89. An easily read account of our sailing ships.

8890. Limburg, Peter R., and Sweeney, James B. *Vessels for Underwater Exploration* (4–6). Illustrated. 1973, Crown $7.95. Story of the machines, including submarines, used to explore the oceans.

8891. Oppenheim, Joanne. *Have You Seen Boats?* (1–3). Illustrated. 1971, Addison $5.50. A very simple survey with black-and-white photographs of ships and boats. For older readers use: *Ships of Commerce* by C. B. Colby (1963, Coward $5.19).

8892. Plowden, David. *Tugboat* (5–8). Illus. by author. 1976, Macmillan $7.95. Life aboard the *Julia C. Moran*, a New York City harbor tugboat, as explored in text and photographs.

8893. Rutland, Jonathan. *See Inside a Galleon* (3–5). Illustrated. 1978, Watts $5.90. Topics covered include a glimpse into these sixteenth-century vessels and a look at life at sea.

8894. Sullivan, George. *Supertanker: The Story of the World's Biggest Ships* (6–9). Illustrated. 1978, Dodd $6.95. A thorough account that also sheds light on the world's oil situation.

8895. Tunis, Edwin. *Oars, Sails and Steam: A Picture Book of Ships* (2–4). 1977, Crowell $8.95. A beautifully illustrated account of the development of water transportation. Also use: *Ships through History* by Ralph T. Ward (1973, Bobbs-Merrill $7.95).

8896. Van Orden, M. D. *The Book of United States Navy Ships* (5–8). Illustrated. 1979, Dodd $5.95. A rundown on ships of the navy, plus a special section on ships of the future.

8897. Wyckoff, James. *Who Really Invented the Submarine?* (4–6). Illustrated. 1965, Putnam $4.29. An informal and interesting account of submarine history. Also use: *The First Book of Submarines* by J. B. Icenhower (1970, Watts $4.90).

8898. Zim, Herbert S., and Skelly, James R. *Cargo Ships* (3–6). Illus. by Richard Cuffari. 1970, Morrow $5.52. An account of the design, construction, and uses of today's cargo ships.

Construction

General

8899. Barker, Albert. *From Settlement to City* (4–8). Illustrated. 1978, Messner $6.97. Using an imaginary city as a case study, the author traces a city's growth from the days of wagon trains to the present. Also use: *Cities Old and New* by William Wise (1973, Parents $5.41).

8900. Bate, Norman. *Who Built the Bridge?* (K–3). Illustrated. 1954, Scribner $5.95. A picture story of the building of a bridge and of all the people and machinery that helped. Also use: *The First Book of Bridges* by Creighton Peet (1966, Watts $4.90).

8901. Berenstain, Michael. *The Lighthouse Book* (3–4). Illustrated. 1979, McKay $6.95. Excellent diagrams plus an informative text make this an interesting work.

8902. Berger, Melvin. *Building Construction* (4–6). Illustrated. 1978, Watts $4.90. Various kinds of work and workers involved in the building industry in the United States are presented.

8903. Boardman, Fon W. *Canals* (5–7). Illustrated. 1959, Walck $7.95. A history of the building of canals, with separate chapters on the Erie, Suez, and Panama canals.

8904. Corbett, Scott. *Bridges* (5–7). Illustrated. 1978, Four Winds $6.95. Beginning with the ancient Romans, this account traces the history of bridges and their architectural characteristics.

8905. Farb, Peter. *The Story of Dams: An Introduction to Hydrology* (5–7). Illus. by George Kanelous. 1961, Harvey House $6.29. Harnessing water for farming and hydroelectric power.

8906. Franchere, Ruth. *Westward by Canal* (5–8). Illustrated. 1972, Macmillan $4.95. A history of the Erie Canal from the complex maneuvers that preceded the construction to the many attempts to copy its success.

8907. Humphrey, Henry. *What's Inside?* (3–5). Illustrated. 1971, Simon & Schuster $4.95. Chiefly by photographs, the interiors of various types of structures, such as a lighthouse and a bank vault, are explored.

8908. Kelly, James E., and Park, William R. *The Dam Builders* (2–3). Illus. by Herbert E. Lake. 1977, Addison $6.95. The planning, equipment, and actual construction involved are covered in simple terms, together with a mention of environmental concerns.

8909. Kelly, James E., and Park, William R. *Roadbuilding* (2–4). Illustrated. 1973, Addison $5.95. The process of road building is covered from planning stages to eventual upkeep and maintenance.

8910. Kelly, James E. *The Tunnel Builders* (2–5). Illus. by Herbert E. Lake. 1976, Addison $5.95. A fine introduction to the many techniques used for building street tunnels, as well as tunnels under mountains and rivers.

8911. Lewis, Alan. *Super Structures* (6–9). Illustrated. 1980, Viking $5.95. An explanation of construction techniques and an examination of such buildings as the Empire State and Sydney Opera House.

8912. Macaulay, David. *Underground* (5–8). Illus. by author. 1976, Houghton $9.95. An exploration in text and detailed drawings of the intricate network of systems under city streets.

8913. Olney, Ross R. *They Said It Couldn't Be Done* (5–7). Illustrated. 1979, Dutton $9.95. Ten enterprises—from the building of the Brooklyn Bridge to the moon landing—that seemed impossible at the time.

8914. Paradis, Adrian. *From Trails to Superhighways: The Story of America's Roads* (6–8). Illus. by Russell Hoover. 1971, Messner $5.64. A history of the development of U.S. roads. For a younger group use: *Have You Seen Roads?* by Joanne Oppenheim (1969, Addison $5.50).

8915. Russell, Solveig P. *The Big Ditch Waterways: The Story of Canals* (3–5). Illus. by Don Sibley. 1977, Parents $5.41. A discussion of the construction and present status of the major canals of the world, including the Panama, the St. Lawrence Seaway, and the Erie.

8916. Salvadori, Mario. *Building: The Fight against Gravity* (6–8). Illus. by Saralinda Hooker and Christopher Ragus. 1979, Atheneum $11.95. The principles of building and architecture are explained in simple terms.

8917. Sullivan, George. *How Do They Build It?* (5–8). Illustrated. 1972, Westminster $5.95. Describes the techniques and tools used to build bridges, highways, tunnels, and various kinds of buildings.

8918. Sullivan, George. *New World of Construction Engineering* (6–8). 1968, Westminster $4.50. The present and future of engineering.

8919. Urquhart, David Inglis. *Central Heating and How It Works* (3–6). Illus. by Patricia F. Korbet. 1972, Walck $5.95. The story of heating, its history, and contemporary pollution problems are emphasized in this account.

8920. Zim, Herbert S., and Skelly, James R. *Pipes and Plumbing Systems* (3–6). Illustrated. 1974, Morrow $5.75; paper $1.25. The history of plumbing and contemporary methods, manufacture and use of pipes, pumps, etc., are discussed in this basic account. Also use: *Plumbing and How It Works* by David Inglis Urquhart (1973, Walck $4.95).

Houses

8921. Adler, Irving. *Houses* (2–4). Illustrated. 1964, Day $6.89. A description of the ways houses are built and of their parts.

8922. Huntington, Lee Pennock. *Simple Shelters* (4–6). Illus. by Stefen Bernath. 1979, Coward $5.64. Eighteen dwellings from various places and historical periods are described.

8923. Myller, Rolf. *From Idea into House* (5–9). Illus. by Henry K. Szwarce. 1974, Atheneum $7.95. A detailed, fascinating account of an architect's steps in planning a house according to a particular family's specifications. For a younger group use: *Building on Your Street* by Seymour Simon (1973, Holiday $3.95).

8924. Siberell, Anne. *Houses: Shelters from Pre-Historic Times to Today* (1–3). Illus. by author. 1979, Holt $6.95. A survey that covers homes from caves to solar-heated houses.

8925. Sobol, Harriet Langsam. *Pete's House* (2–4). Illustrated. 1978, Macmillan $7.95. Through detailed photographs, the process of house building is explored from blueprints to finished product.

8926. Shapp, Martha, and Shapp, Charles. *Let's Find Out about Houses* (1–3). Illus. by Tomie de Paola. 1975, Watts $4.90. A guided tour to the parts of a house and their uses.

Machinery

Engines and Machines

8927. Aylesworth, Thomas G. *It Works Like This* (4–6). Illustrated. 1968, Doubleday $4.95. This simple account gives an explanation of the workings of 33 common machines, such as the sewing machine.

8928. Corbett, Scott. *What about the Wankel Engine?* (4–6). Illus. by Jerome Kuhl. 1974, Four Winds $6.95. The author describes clearly the characteristics of the Wankel engine and other possible successors to the internal-combustion engine of today.

8929. Lodewijk, T. *The Way Things Work: An Illustrated Encyclopedia of Technology* (6–9). Illustrated. 1973, Simon & Schuster $12.95. An excellent adaptation for young readers of the adult work that explains the workings of common machines and appliances. Also use: *How It Works* by Martin L. Keen (1972, Grosset $5.95).

8930. Pollard, Michael. *How Things Work* (4–7). Illustrated. 1979, Larousse $7.95. Simple explanations are given on the workings of many machines, such as computers, television sets, and oil rigs.

8931. Renner, Al G. *How to Make and Use Electric Motors* (5–7). Illustrated. 1974, Putnam $5.49. Clear, detailed instructions are given for the construction of 3 different battery-powered engines.

8932. Schneider, Herman. *Everyday Machines and How They Work* (5–8). Illus. by Jeanne Bendick. 1950, McGraw $5.72. A basic introduction to machinery.

8933. Urquhart, David Inglis. *The Refrigerator and How It Works* (3–5). Illus. by Allan Eitzen. 1972, Walck $4.95. The development and scientific principles of operation are described.

8934. Watson, Aldren. *The Source of Everyday Things* (2–3). Illus. by author. 1978, Grosset $4.41. The origins of many familiar objects.

8935. Weiss, Harvey. *Motors and Engines and How They Work* (5–8). Illus. by author. 1969, Crowell $7.95. A lucid demonstration of the basic technology of water, wind, steam, electric, and jet rocket engines. Also use: *Engines* by Peter R. Limburg (1970, Watts $4.90) and *Jet and Rocket Engines: How They Work* by I. G. Edmonds (1973, Putnam $4.29).

8936. Zim, Herbert S., and Skelly, James R. *Machine Tools* (3–6). Illus. by Gary Ruse. 1969, Morrow $5.52; paper $1.25. Descriptions, explanations, and diagrammatic illustrations of the mechanisms common to the machinist's trade.

8937. Zim, Herbert S. *What's Inside of Engines?* (4–7). Illus. by Raymond Perlman. 1953, Morrow $5.49. A simple explanation of how engines work.

Heavy Machinery

8938. Hahn, Christine. *Amusement Park Machines* (2–4). Illustrated. 1979, Raintree $5.99. Very simple text and many photographs on such machines as the roller coaster.

8939. Pick, Christopher C. *Oil Machines* (2–4). Illustrated. 1979, Raintree $5.99. Drilling rigs are included in this well-illustrated account.

8940. Pick, Christopher C. *Undersea Machines* (2–4). Illustrated. 1979, Raintree $5.99. All kinds of devices used to explore the ocean and the sea bottom are described.

8941. Rutland, Jonathan. *See Inside an Oil Rig and Tanker* (5–7). Illustrated. 1979, Watts $6.90. How the world gets its oil is revealed in text and pictures.

8942. Stone, William. *Earth Moving Machines* (2–4). Illustrated. 1979, Raintree $5.99. All sorts of tractors and various other machines are featured in text and pictures.

8943. Zim, Herbert S., and Skelly, James R. *Hoists, Cranes and Derricks* (3–6). Illus. by Gary Ruse. 1969, Morrow $5.52; paper $1.25. An introduction to the 3 basic types of lifting machines.

Electronics

8944. Bendick, Jeanne, and Lefkowitz, R. J. *Electronics for Young People* (5–7). Illustrated. 1973, McGraw $5.72. Subtitle: *Automation, Computers, Communications, Microcircuits, Lasers and More.* Also use: *Electronics* by Robert Irving (1961, Knopf $5.39).

8945. Branley, Franklyn M. *The Electromagnetic Spectrum* (5–8). Illus. by Leonard D. Dank. 1979, Crowell $8.95; LB $8.79. How we are able to investigate our universe and communicate over long distances.

8946. Englebardt, Stanley L. *Miracle Chip: The Microelectronic Revolution* (5–8). Illustrated. 1979, Lothrop $6.95; LB $6.67. The story of silicon chips and their many uses, primarily in information storage and retrieval.

Telephone and Telegraph

8947. Branley, Franklyn M. *Timmy and the Tin-Can Telephone* (1–3). Illus. by Paul Galdone. 1959, Crowell $2.95. The principles of sound transmission explained in words and pictures with easy directions for making a telephone. Also use: *Let's Find Out about Telephones* by David C. Knight (1967, Watts $4.47).

8948. Darwin, Len. *What Makes a Telephone Work?* (3–6). Illus. by author. 1970, Little $4.50. A thorough introduction that covers the field from tin can telephones to the complex instrument of today.

8949. Nathan, Adele Gutman. *The First Transatlantic Cable* (5–7). Illus. by Denver Gillen. 1959, Random $4.27. The account of the laying of the cable that allowed telephone communication between Europe and America.

8950. O'Connor, Jerome J. *The Telephone, How It Works* (5–7). Illustrated. 1971, Putnam $4.29. An interesting introduction to parts of the telephone and other ways of transmitting sound. Also use: *Your Telephone and How It Works* by Herman Schneider and Nina Schneider (1965, McGraw $5.72).

Television, Radio, and Recording

8951. Bendick, Jeanne, and Bendick, Robert. *Television Works like This* (6–9). Illus. by Jeanne Bendick. 1965, McGraw $5.72. One of the best simplified books about television.

8952. Berger, Melvin. *The Stereo-Hi Fi Handbook* (6–8). Illustrated. 1979, Lothrop $6.95; LB $6.67. Valuable basic information about sound systems and pieces of equipment.

8953. Corbett, Scott. *What Makes TV Work?* (4–6). Illus. by Len Darwin. 1965, Little $5.95. The sequence of steps necessary to transmit a television picture from the studio to the home receiver. Also use: *Television* by Edward Stoddard (1970, Watts $4.47).

8954. Edmunds, Alice. *Who Puts the Grooves in the Record?* (4–6). 1976, Random $2.25. Various people connected with the record industry describe their jobs. Also use: *Playback: The Story of Recording Devices* by Robert K. Krishef (1974, Lerner $3.95).

8955. Morgan, Alfred P. *The First Book of Radio and Electronics for Boys and Girls* (4–6). Illustrated.

1977, Scribner $2.95. A fine up-to-date introduction that concentrates on basics.

8956. Olney, Ross R. *Sound All Around: How Hi-Fi and Stereo Work* (4–6). Illus. by Lewis Zacks. 1967, Prentice-Hall $4.95. Clear, simple explanation of the working components of high fidelity and stereo systems with tips for young fans on how to assemble equipment from kits.

Metals

8957. Burt, Olive W. *The First Book of Copper* (4–7). Illustrated. 1968, Watts $4.90. A well-organized text that explores many facets of the production and use of copper through history to the present.

8958. Fisher, Douglas Alan. *Steel: From the Iron Age to the Space Age* (6–8). Illustrated. 1967, Harper $7.89. A history of steel with emphasis on present-day uses and manufacturing techniques.

8959. Markun, Patricia Maloney. *The First Book of Mining* Illus. by Mildred Waltrip. (4–6). 1959, Watts $4.90. A brief history of mining and a discussion of present-day methods.

8960. O'Donnell, James J. *Gold: The Noble Metal* (6–9). Illus. by Barbara Sealing. 1978, Doubleday $4.95. The history, uses, and legends connected with this metal are outlined.

8961. Smith, Norman F. *If It Shines, Clangs and Bends, Its Metal* (3–5). Illus. by Tom Huffman. 1980, Coward $5.99. A first look at metals that describes their origin, properties, and uses.

8962. Stwertka, Eve, and Stwertka, Albert. *Steel Mill* (5–7). Illustrated. 1978, Watts $4.90. An interesting explanation of the process of steel making and the occupations this involves.

Weapons and the Armed Forces

8963. Ambrus, Victor G. *Horses in Battle* (5–7). Illus. by author. 1978, Oxford $8.95. A history of the cavalry from ancient Egypt to World War I.

8964. Anderson, Madelyn Klein. *Sea Raids and Rescues: The United States Coast Guard* (6–9). Illustrated. 1979, McKay $7.95. A history of the Coast Guard from its formation in 1790 to the present. Also use: *What Does a Coastguardsman Do?* by Grant Compton (1968, Dodd $4.50).

8965. Berenstain, Michael. *The Armor Book* (3–6). Illustrated. 1979, McKay $6.95. The history and usefulness of armor are chronicled and directions for building one's own armor are included.

8966. Berger, Michael L. *Firearms in American History* (6–9). Illustrated. 1979, Watts $5.45. A survey from colonialists' firearms to the development of the Colt .45.

8967. Colby, C. B. *Annapolis: Cadets, Training, and Equipment* (4–6). Illustrated. 1964, Coward $5.19. The training of a naval cadet, told in simple text and many pictures. Also use: *Our Space Age Navy: Carriers, Aircraft, Submarines and Missiles* (1962, Coward $5.19).

8968. Colby, C. B. *Countdown: Rockets and Missiles for National Defense* (4–7). Illustrated. 1970, Coward $5.19. Pictures accompanied by brief text introduce many kinds of missiles.

8969. Colby, C. B. *Firearms by Winchester: A Part of United States History* (4 up). Illustrated. 1957, Coward $5.19. A brief history and description of Winchester rifles and the firm that manufactures them.

8970. Colby, C. B. *Leathernecks* (4–6). 1957, Coward $5.19. The training, weapons, and equipment of the United States Marine Corps.

8971. Colby, C. B. *Two Centuries of Weapons: 1776–1976* (4–6). Illustrated. 1976, Coward $5.19. Typical weapons of 1776, 1876, and 1976 are pictured and briefly discussed.

8972. Cooke, David C. *Famous U.S. Air Force Bombers* (5–7). Illustrated. 1973, Dodd $4.95. About 30 planes from 1918 to 1956 are pictured and discussed. Also use: *Famous U.S. Navy Fighter Planes* (1972, Dodd $4.95).

8973. Dolan, Edward F. *Gun Control: A Decision for Americans* (6–9). 1978, Watts $4.90. Both sides of this controversial question are presented fairly and with good balance.

8974. Haines, Gail Kay. *Explosives* (K–3). Illus. by Mike Eagle. 1976, Morrow $4.95; LB $4.59. A picture book on various explosives from gunpowder to nuclear fission.

8975. Lord, Beman. *Look at the Army* (4–7). Illustrated. 1965, Walck $5.95. An introduction to the organization and functions of the Army. Also use (Coward, ea. $5.19): *Our Space Age Army* (1961), *West Point Cadets: Training and Equipment* (1963) and *Special Forces: The U.S. Army's Experts in Unconventional Warfare* (1964) all by C. B. Colby.

8976. Morrison, Sean. *Armor* (6–9). Illus. by author. 1963, Crowell $8.95. Thorough, detailed description of arms and armor from 4000 B.C. to the Renaissance, with a brief chapter on modern armor.

8977. Nickel, Helmut. *Warriors and Worthies: Arms and Armor through the Ages* (6–9). Illustrated. 1969, Atheneum $10.00. A stunning art book, illustrated with photos, introducing the weapons and armor from early Egyptian days to the arms of nineteenth-century American frontier days. Also use: *Weapons: A Pictorial History* by Edwin Tunis (1977, Crowell $12.95).

8978. Peterson, Harold L. *Forts in America* (5–8). Illus. by Daniel D. Feaser. 1964, Scribner $5.95. Illustrated history that traces the development of forts and identifies models or actual sites that can be visited. Also use: *Historic American Forts: From Frontier Stockades to Coastal Fortress* by C. B. Colby (1963, Coward $5.19).

Author/Illustrator Index

Aardema, Verna. Behind the Back of the Mountain: Black Folktales from Southern Africa, 5306; Half-a-Ball-of-Kenki: An Ashanti Tale, 5307; Who's in Rabbit's House? A Masai Tale, 5308; Why Mosquitoes Buzz in Peoples' Ears: A West African Folktale, Retold by Verna Aardema, 5309; The Riddle of the Drum: A Tale from Tizapan, Mexico, 5647; Ji-Nongo Means Riddles, 5915

Aaron, Chester. An American Ghost, 1488; Better Than Laughter, 2969

Abbott, Jacob B., 8254

Abbott, R. Tucker. Sea Shells of the World: A Guide to the Better-Known Species, 8677

Abdul, Raoul. The Magic of Black Poetry, 5083; Famous Black Entertainers of Today, 6749

Abel, Ray, 1828; 3538; 7802

Abercombie, Barbara Mattes. The Other Side of a Poem, 4925

Abrams, Joy. Look Good, Feel Good, through Yoga, Grooming, Nutrition, 7310

Abrams, Lester, 5196

Abrashkin, Raymond. (jt. auth.) 2919; (jt. auth.) 2920

Acheson, Patricia C. Our Federal Government: How It Works, An Introduction to the United States, 7028

Aciato, Jacqueline, 3887

Ackley, Edith F. Dolls to Make for Fun and Profit, 4354; Marionettes: Easy to Make! Fun to Use!, 4894

Ackley, Telka, 4354

Adams, Adrienne. 279; (jt. auth.) 587; 690; 1083; 1239; 1293; 3670; The Christmas Party, 3813; The Easter Egg Artists, 3927; 3928; A Woggle of Witches, 3945; 3946; 3964; Poetry of Earth, 5171; 5217; 5218; 5500; 5502; 5509; 8676

Adams, Barbara. Like It Is: Facts and Feelings about Handicaps from Kids Who Know, 7379

Adams, Florence. Catch a Sunbeam: A Book of Solar Study, 7821

Adams, Mildred. (jt. auth.) 7766

Adams, Norman, 8559

Adams, Richard. Watership Down, 2532

Adams, Samuel H. Pony Express, 6425; The Santa Fe Trail, 6426

Adams, Tom, 4150

Adamson, Joy. Born Free, 8463; Living Free: The Story of Elsa and Her Cubs, 8463; Forever Free, 8463; Elsa, 8463; Pippa: The Cheetah and Her Cubs, 8466

Adamson, Wendy. Saving Lake Superior: A Story of Environmental Action, 6964; (jt. auth.) 7824

Adelson, Leone. Dandelions Don't Bite: The Story of Words, 4715

Adkins, Jan. Luther Tarbox, 2017; The Bakery, 4098; Toolchest, 4365; The Craft of Sail, 4552; Symbols: A Silent Language, 4680; Wooden Ship, 8883

Adkins, Joan, 8048

Adler, Carole S. The Silver Coach, 1646; The Magic of the Glits, 1856; In Our House Scott Is My Brother, 2970

Adler, David A. Cam Jansen and the Mystery of the Stolen Diamonds, 2018; The House on the Roof: A Sukkoth Story, 4014; You Think It's Fun to Be a Clown, 4853; The Children of Chelm, 5621; Base 5, 7445; 3D, 2D, ID, 7446; Redwoods Are the Tallest Trees in the World, 7900

Adler, Irving. The Adler Book of Puzzles and Riddles, 4074; Language and Man, 4703; Your Eyes, 7267; Taste, Touch and Smell, 7273; Numerals: New Dresses for Old Numbers, 7447; Integers: Positive and Negative, 7447; Sets and Numbers for the Very Young, 7448; (jt. auth.) 7511; The Calendar, 7522; Energy, 7541; Fire in Your Life, 7549; Heat and Its Uses, 7550; Color in Your Life, 7563; Dust, 7603; The Stars: Decoding Their Messages, 7624; Petroleum: Gas, Oil and Asphalt, 7801; Atomic Energy, 7812; Food, 7937; Irrigation: Changing Deserts into Gardens, 7988; Houses, 8921

Adler, Joyce. (jt. auth.) 4703

Adler, Larry. Famous Horses in America, 8744

Adler, Peggy, 4074; Geography Puzzles, 4075; Math Puzzles, 7511; 7511; 7937

Adler, Ruth. (jt. auth.) 7267; (jt. auth.) 7447; (jt. auth.) 7448; 7549; (jt. auth.) 7550; (jt. auth.) 7988

Adler, Susan. (jt. auth.) 7334

Adoff, Arnold. Black Is Brown Is Tan, 789; Where Wild Willie, 969; Ma nDa la, 1082; Eats, 4926; It Is the Poem Singing into Your Eyes: Anthology of New Young Poets, 4927; Under the Early Morning Trees, 4928; Black Out Loud: An Anthology of Modern Poems by Black Americans, 5084; I Am the Darker Brother: An Anthology of Modern Poems by Negro Americans, 5084; My Black Me: A Beginning Book of Black Poetry, 5085; Big Sister Tells Me That I'm Black, 5086; Tornado!, 5172; I Am the Running Girl, 5191; Malcolm X, 6568

Adrian, Mary. The Fireball Mystery, 2019; The Mystery of the Dinosaur Bones, 2019; Day and Night in the Arctic, 5891; Wildlife in the Antarctic, 5892; Secret Neighbors: Wildlife in a City Lot, 8086; The American Eagle, 8273; The North American Bighorn Sheep, 8538

Adshead, Gladys L. Brownies—Hush!, 585; Brownies—It's Christmas, 3814; An Inheritance of Poetry, 4929

Aesop. The Caldecott Aesop. A Facsimile of the 1883 Edition, 5547; Fables of Aesop, 5548; The Hare and the Tortoise, 5549; Three Aesop Fox Fables, 5549; The Town Mouse and the Country Mouse, 5549; The

Burnham, Sophy. Buccaneer, 1513; The Dogwalker, 2074

Burningham, John. ABC, 6; The Blanket, 201; Would You Rather . . . , 307; Come Away from the Water, Shirley, 599; Cannonball Simp, 700; Harquin: The Fox Who Went Down to the Valley, 701; Mr. Gumpy's Motor Car, 979; Time to Get Out of the Bath, Shirley, 1145; 2649; Around the World in Eighty Days, 6668

Burns, Aubrey. Bird Watching, 8230

Burns, Marilyn. The Book of Think: Or How to Solve a Problem Twice Your Size, 4077; I Am Not a Short Adult: Getting Good at Being a Kid, 7050; The I Hate Mathematics! Book, 7513; This Book Is about Time, 7523; Good for Me: All about Food in 32 Bites, 8003

Burnstein, John. Slim Goodbody: What Can Go Wrong and How to Be Strong, 7327

Burr, Dane, 5083

Burr, Lonnie. Two for the Show: Great Comedy Teams, 4882

Burroughs, Gail, 2556

Burstein, Chaya M. Rifka Grows Up, 2929; Rifka Bangs the Teakettle, 2929

Burt, Olive W. Black Women of Valor, 6474; Sacajawea, 6594; I Am an American, 7029; The First Book of Copper, 8957

Burton, Hester. In Spite of All Terror, 1670; Beyond the Weir Bridge, 3338; Time of Trial, 3339

Burton, Marilee Robin. The Elephant's Nest: Four Wordless Stories, 228

Burton, Robert. Seals, 8598

Burton, Virginia L. The Little House, 1236; Mike Mulligan and His Steam Shovel, 1258; Katy and the Big Snow, 1258; 2390; Life Story, 7679

Burwell, Ted, 6320

Busch, Phyllis S. A Walk in the Snow, 7855; Cactus in the Desert, 7868; Exploring as You Walk in the City, 8032; Exploring as You Walk in the Meadow, 8032; Living Things That Poison, Itch and Sting, 8033

Bush, Chan. (jt. auth.) 4399; (jt. auth.) 4562

Bush, Terri. (jt. auth.) 5098

Busoni, Rafaello, 3815; 6192

Butler, Joan. (jt. auth.) 4879

Butterfield, Ned, 2357

Butterworth, Oliver. The Narrow Passage, 2075; The Enormous Egg, 2393; The Trouble with Jenny's Ear, 2394

Byard, Carole, 1059; 1127; 5334; 6821

Byars, Betsy. The Last Snail, 308; Go and Hush the Baby, 805; The Midnight Fox, 1514; The Pinballs, 1871; The 18th Emergency, 1971; The Winged Colt of Casa Mia, 2586; After the Goat Man, 3055; The Cartoonist, 3056; Goodbye, Chicken Little, 3057; The House of Wings, 3058; The Night Swimmers, 3059; The Summer of the Swans, 3219; The TV Kid, 3220

Byfield, Barbara. The Haunted Churchbell, 980; The Haunted Ghost, 2395; Andrew and the Alchemist, 2587; The Haunted Tower, 2588

Bygrave, Mike. Motorcycle, 4535

Byrd, Robert, 7955

Cabeen, Richard. Standard Handbook of Stamp Collecting, 4216

Caddell, Foster, 2342; 2348

Cain, Sandra, 4921

Caines, Jeannette Franklin. Abby, 806

Caldecott, Randolph. Randolph Caldecott's John Gilpin and Other Stories, 156; 5547

Caldwell, John C. Let's Visit China Today, 5963; Let's Visit Peru, 6139

Calhoun, Mary. Cross-Country Cat, 309; Hungry Leprechaun, 601; The Witch Who Lost Her Shadow, 602; Wobble the Witch Cat, 603; Euphonia and the Flood, 981; Katie John, 1872; Ownself, 2589; The Horse Comes First, 3060; Medicine Show: Conning People and Making Them Like It, 3593; Jack the Wise and the Cornish Cuckoos, 5405; Old Man Whickutt's Donkey, 5703

Callen, Larry. Pinch, 1515; Sorrow's Song, 1873; The Deadly Mandrake, 2397

Calvin, James, 1734

Cameron, Eleanor. The Terrible Churnadryne, 2076; The Court of the Stone Children, 2590; The Wonderful Flight to the Mushroom Planet, 2863; Time and Mr. Bass, 2863; Julia and the Hand of God, 3061; A Room Made of Windows, 3062; To the Green Mountains, 3063

Cameron, John. If Mice Could Fly, 310

Cameron, Polly. "I Can't" Said the Ant, 5116; The Green Machine, 5116

Campbell, Ann. Start to Draw, 4291

Campbell, Chester W. Will Rogers, 6826

Campbell, Donald Grant. Scotland in Pictures, 6025

Campbell, Elizabeth A. The Carving on the Tree, 6339; Jamestown: The Beginning, 6342

Campbell, Hannah. Why Did They Name It?, 3594

Campbell, Hope. A Peak beneath the Moon, 2077; Peter's Angel, 2592

Caney, Steven. Kids' America, 4222; Steven Caney's Play Book, 4223

Canfield, Dorothy. Understood Betsy, 1671

Cantwell, Mary. St. Patrick's Day, 3773

Capellaro, Helen. (jt. auth.) 7330

Capp, Clifford S. Colonial Georgia, 6337

Caputo, Robert. More than Just Pets: Why People Study Animals, 8698

Caras, Roger. Skunk for a Day, 702; The Bizarre Animals, 8334; On Safari with Roger Caras, 8335; Monarch of Dead Man Bay: The Life and Death of a Kodiak Bear, 8460; A Zoo in Your Room, 8699; Dogs: Records, Stars, Feats and Facts, 8722

Cardy, Wayne C. (jt. auth.) 4219

Carew, Jan. Children of the Sun, 2591; The Third Gift, 5317

Carey, Bonnie. Grasshopper to the Rescue: A Georgian Story, 5584

Carey, M. V. Alfred Hitchcock and the Three Investigators in the Mystery of the Sinister Scarecrow, 2078

Carigiet, Alois, 1092

Carle, Eric. All about Arthur: An Absolutely Absurd Ape, 7; 1, 2, 3 to the Zoo, 50; The Rooster Who Set Out to See the World, 51; A Very Long Tail: A Folding Book, 118; The Very Long Train, 118; Do You Want to Be My Friend?, 229; The Grouchy Ladybug, 311; Have You Seen My Cat?, 703; The Secret Birthday Message, 807; The Rooster Who Set Out to See the World, 982; 1103; The Very Hungry Caterpillar, 1279; My Very First Book of Words, 4722; 5071; 5072; The Tiny Seed, 7862

Carlisle, Laura Mae. (jt. auth.) 4978

Carlson, Bernice W. (jt. auth.) 4307; The Right Play for You, 4888; Act It Out, 4888; Let's Pretend It Happened to You: A Real-People and Storybook-People Approach to Creative Dramatics, 4889; Funny-Bone Dramatics, 4915

Carlson, Dale Bick. Girls Are Equal Too: The Women's Movement for Teenagers, 7051

Carlson, Natalie Savage. Time for the White Egret, 312; Jaky or Dodo, 1517; The Half Sisters, 1672; Ann Aurelia and Dorothy, 1874; Carnival in Paris, 1875; Family under the Bridge, 1876; The Empty Schoolhouse, 1972; Luvvy and the Girls, 1973; Sailors' Choice, 2079; The Happy Orpheline, 3291; A Brother for the Orphelines, 3291; A Pet for the Orphelines, 3291; The Orphelines in the Enchanted Castle, 3291; Alphonse, That Bearded One, 3381; The Night the

William Penn, 6348; Year of Independence 1776, 6394; Sunday in Centerville: The Battle of Bull Run, 1861, 6448; Year of Lincoln, 1861, 6449; Abraham Lincoln's World, 6449; Theodore Roosevelt: An Initial Biography, 6544; The Year of the Horseless Carriage, 8855

Foster, George. (jt. auth.) 6857

Foster, John. A First Poetry Book, 4961

Foster, Laura Louise. Keeping the Plants You Pick, 4238; 4271

Founds, George, 6949

Fowke, Edith. Sally Go Round the Sun: Three Hundred Children's Songs, Rhymes and Games, 4839; Ring around the Moon, 4963

Fowler, H. Waller. Kites: A Practical Guide to Kite Making and Flying, 4532

Fox, Charles Philip. When Winter Comes, 8377

Fox, Elton C., 6714

Fox, Lilla Margaret. Folk Costume of Eastern Europe, 5736; Folk Costume of Western Europe, 5736; Folk Costume of Southern Europe, 5736

Fox, Michael. Ramer and Chennai: Brothers of the Wild, 1547; Whitepaws: A Coyote-Dog, 1548; Wild Dogs Three, 1549; Sundance Coyote, 8543; Vixie: The Story of a Little Fox, 8544; The Wolf, 8545; What Is Your Dog Saying?, 8725

Fox, Paula. Dear Prosper, 1550; The King's Falcon, 1551; Maurice's Room, 1717; How Many Miles to Babylon?, 2146; Blowfish Live in the Sea, 3099; Portrait of Ivan, 3100; The Stone-Faced Boy, 3229; The Slave Dancer, 3443; The Little Swineherd and Other Tales, 5229

Fox, Siv Cedering. The Blue Horse and Other Night Poems, 4962

Fox, Sonny. Jokes and How to Tell Them, 4035

Fox, William. From Bones to Bodies: A Story of Paleontology, 5775; The Amazing Bee, 8119

Frace, Charles, 8545

Fradin, Dennis B. Wisconsin in Words and Pictures, 6226; Arizona in Words and Pictures, 6239; Alaska in Words and Pictures, 6247; California in Words and Pictures, 6248

Frame, Jean. How to Give a Party, 4521

Frame, Paul, 1872; 2182; Drawing Cats and Kittens, 4297; (jt. auth.) 4521; 4521; 5195; 6474; 6534; 6658; 6861; 6900; 8718; 8741

Franchere, Ruth. Cesar Chavez, 6602; Westward by Canal, 8906

Francis, Dorothy B. Run of the Sea Witch, 2993

Franco, Marjorie. So Who Hasn't Got Problems?, 1889

Francoise. Jeanne-Marie Counts Her Sheep, 56; Minou, 1100; Springtime for Jeanne-Marie, 1100; Noel for Jeanne-Marie, 3837

Frank, Anne. The Diary of a Young Girl, 5869

Frank, Phil. Subee Lives on a Houseboat, 6249

Frank, Susan. (jt. auth.) 6249

Frankel, Godfrey. (jt. auth.) 4452

Frankel, Lillian. Bike-Ways (101 Things to Do with a Bike), 4452

Frankenberg, Robert, 1608; 6645

Franklin, Edward, 1011

Franklin, Folsom. Famous Pioneers, 6483

Franklin, Harold, 1573

Franko, Ivan. Fox Mykyta, 5589

Franz, David R. (jt. auth.) 8669; (jt. auth.) 8670

Franzen, Greta. The Great Ship Vasa, 6050

Frascino, Edward, 937; 1906; 2850

Frasconi, Antonio. The House That Jack Built, 163; 357; 3659; See and Say: A Picture Book in Four Languages, 4705; 5054; 5629

Fraser, Betty, 94; 3721; 8384; 8486; 8705

Frazier, Carl. The Lincoln Country in Pictures, 6227

Frazier, Rosalie. (jt. auth.) 6227

Freed, Ruth. (jt. auth.) 5791

Freed, Stanley A. Man from the Beginning, 5791

Freedman, Russell. The Brains of Animals and Man, 7253; How Birds Fly, 8248; Animal Games, 8378; Animal Fathers, 8390; Hanging On, 8391; How Animals Defend Their Young, 8410; Tooth and Claw: A Look at Animal Weapons, 8411; Getting Born, 8751

Freeman, Barbara. A Haunting Air, 2652; The Other Face, 2653; A Pocket of Silence, 2654

Freeman, Don. The Chalk Box Story, 234; Beady Bear, 363; Corduroy, 364; Dandelion, 365; Hattie the Backstage Bat, 366; Norman the Doorman, 367; Penguins, of All People, 368; A Pocket for Corduroy, 369; Will's Quill, 370; Tilly Witch, 615; 699; Fly High, Fly Low, 721; Mop Top, 1157; 1243

Freeman, Dorothy R. How to Read a Highway Map, 5744

Freeman, Grace R. Inside the Synagogue, 3706

Freeman, Ira. (jt. auth.) 7423; (jt. auth.) 7568; The Science of Light and Radiation, 7569; (jt. auth.) 7596; The Science of Chemistry, 7597; (jt. auth.) 7599; (jt. auth.) 7610

Freeman, Mae. Stars and Stripes: The Story of the American Flag, 4700; The Story of Albert Einstein: The Scientist Who Searched Out the Secrets of the Universe, 6722; Fun with Science, 7423; Fun with Scientific Experiments, 7423; Finding Out about Shapes, 7495; Fun and Experiments with Light, 7568; Fun with Chemistry, 7596; The Story of Chemistry, 7599; The Sun, the Moon and the Stars, 7610; Space Base, 7704

Freeman, Mae Bleeker. Finding Out About the Past, 5803

Freeman, Margaret, 4931

Freeman, S. H. Basic Baseball Strategy, 4429

Freeman, Tony. An Introduction to Radio-Controlled Sailplanes, 4385; Blimps, 8834; Columbia, 8834

Freese, Arthur S. The Bionic People Are Here, 7306

Fregosi, Claudia. Are There Spooks in the Dark?, 204; The Happy Horse, 722

French, Fiona, 5265

Frenck, Hal, 888; 6600

Freschet, Berniece. Where's Henrietta's Hen?, 57; Bear Mouse, 371; Bernard of Scotland Yard, 372; Bernard Sees the World, 373; Elephant and Friends, 374; The Happy Dromedary, 375; Little Black Bear Goes for a Walk, 376; Grizzly Bear, 723; Moose Baby, 1367; The Watersnake, 1552; A Year on Muskrat Marsh, 7734; The Ants Go Marching, 8111; The Web in the Grass, 8145; Lizard Lying in the Sun, 8205; Turtle Pond, 8221; Biography of a Buzzard, 8306; Wufu: The Story of Little Brown Bat, 8451; Possum Baby, 8495; Owl and the Prairie Dog, 8513; Bear Mouse, 8516; Porcupine Baby, 8556; Skunk Baby, 8557

Freschet, Gina, 372; 373

Freshman, Shelley, 3843; 7483; 7647

Freuchen, Pipaluk. Eskimo Boy, 3101

Freund, Rudolf, 8210

Frewer, Glyn. Tyto: The Odyssey of an Owl, 8287

Frey, Shaney. The Complete Beginner's Guide to Skin Diving, 4586

Friedland, Ronald. (jt. auth.) 6737

Friedman, Arthur, 5621

Friedman, Frieda. Janitor's Girl, 1718; Ellen and the Gang, 1890

Friedman, Judi. Noises in the Woods, 8403; The Eels' Strange Journey, 8631

Friedman, Marvin, 1515; 1873; 3081

Friedman, Richard. (jt. auth.) 4573

Friedman, Sara Ann. (jt. auth.) 8694

Friedrich, Otto. (jt. auth.) 3928

Friedrich, Priscilla. The Easter Bunny That Overslept, 3928

Friis-Baastad, Babbis. Kristy's Courage, 3230

Friskey, Margaret. Chicken Little, Count to Ten, 58; Seven Diving Ducks, 377

Frith, Michael K., 8235; 8380

Patterson, Lillie. Christmas Feasts and Festivals, 3805; Easter, 3924; Halloween, 3942; Meet Miss Liberty, 6202; Frederick Douglass: Freedom Fighter, 6557; Benjamin Banneker: Genius of Early America, 6707

Patton, A. Rae. (jt. auth.) 7597

Patz, Nancy. Nobody Knows I Have Delicate Toes, 483; Pumpernickel Tickle and Mean Green Cheese, 483

Paul, Aileen. Kids Cooking Complete Meals: Menus, Recipes, Instructions, 4123; Kids Cooking, 4123; Candies, Cookies, Cakes, 4124; Kids Cooking: The Aileen Paul Cooking School Cookbook, 4125; Kids Outdoor Gardening, 4155; Kids Camping, 4469

Paul, Arthur, 4932

Paul, John. (jt. auth.) 5570

Pauli, Hertha. Her Name Was Sojourner Truth, 6574

Paull, Grace, 2071; 3484

Pausen, Gary. Hiking and Backpacking, 4470

Pavey, Peter. One Dragon's Dream, 75

Pavia, Cathy, 4161

Payne, Elizabeth. The Pharoahs of Ancient Egypt, 5820; Meet the North American Indians, 6303; Meet the Pilgrim Fathers, 6358

Payne, Emmy. Katy No-Pocket, 484

Payson, Dale, 965; 1688; 1874; 2548; 3156

Payzant, Charles. (jt. auth.) 8696

Pearce, Ann Philippa. The Battle of Bubble and Squeak, 1614; The Shadow Cage, and Other Tales of the Supernatural, 2774; Tom's Midnight Garden, 2775

Peare, Catherine O. The Herbert Hoover Story, 6528; The FDR Story, 6543; The Helen Keller Story, 6609

Pearl, Richard M. Wonders of Rocks and Minerals, 7771

Pearlman, Moshe. (jt. auth.) 6099

Pearson, Clyde, 1612

Pearson, Michael. Those Yankee Rebels, 6400

Pearson, Susan. Izzie, 485; That's Enough for One Day, J.P.!, 863; Molly Moves Out, 1440

Peck, Anne M. The Pageant of Canadian History, 6168

Peck, Leigh. Pecos Bill and Lightning, 5723

Peck, Richard. Dreamland Lake, 1937; Through a Brief Darkness, 2245; The Ghost Belonged to Me, 2776; Ghosts I Have Been, 2777; Representing Super Doll, 3160; Mindscapes: Poems for the Real World, 5017

Peck, Robert Newton. Soup, 1938; Soup and Me, 1938; Soup for President, 1939; Mr. Little, 2003; Hub, 2497; Rabbits and Redcoats, 3429; Bee Tree and Other Stuff, 6788; Path of Hunters: Animal Struggle in a Meadow, 8384

Peck, Stephen R., 7435

Pedersen, Christian. The International Flag Book in Color, 4701

Peet, Bill. Cowardly Clyde, 486; Eli, 487; Whingdingdilly, 488; Big Bad Bruce, 647; The Caboose Who Got Loose, 1008; Jennifer and Josephine, 1009; The Wump World, 1307

Peet, Creighton. Man in Flight: How the Airlines Operate, 8844; The First Book of Bridges, 8900

Pei, Mario. (jt. auth.) 3621; All about Language, 4713

Pels, Albert, 4901

Pels, Gertrude. Easy Puppets: Making and Using Hand Puppets, 4901

Pelseno, Jo, 2523

Pelta, Kathy. There's a Job for You in Food Service, 7166

Pendle, Alexy, 3365

Pendle, George. Land and People of Chile, 6137; The Land and Peoples of Paraguay and Uruguay, 6143; The Land and People of Peru, 6157

Penner, Lucille Recht. The Colonial Cookbook, 4126

Penney, R. L. Penguins Are Coming, 8295

Penzler, Otto. Hang Gliding, 4394

Peppe, Rodney. Circus Numbers: A Counting Book, 76; Odd One Out, 77; Hey Riddle Diddle!, 181; Three Little Pigs, 5441

Perera, Thomas B. (jt. auth.) 6978; Who Will Clean the Air?, 6979

Peretz, I. L. The Case against the Wind and Other Stories, 2778

Perkins, Carol. I Saw You from Afar: A Visit to the Bushmen of the Kalahari Desert, 5962; The Sound of Boomerangs, 6006

Perkins, Marlin. (jt. auth.) 5962

Perkins, Wilma L. The Fannie Farmer Junior Cookbook, 4127

Perl, Lila. Pieface and Daphne, 1795; That Crazy April, 2004; Dumb Like Me, Olivia Potts, 3013; The Telltale Summer of Tina C., 3014; Don't Ask Miranda, 3161; America Goes to the Fair: All about State and County Fairs in the U.S.A., 3635; Slumps, Grunts and Snickerdoodles: What Colonial America Ate and Why, 4126; The Hamburger Book: All about Hamburgers and Hamburger Cookery, 4128; Hunter's Stew and Hangtown Fry: What Pioneer America Ate and Why, 4129; Ethiopia, Land of the Lion, 5932; East Africa: Kenya, Tanzania, Uganda, 5943; Yugoslavia, Romania, Bulgaria: New Era in the Balkans, 6068; Mexico, Crucible of the Americas, 6112; The Global Food Shortage: Food Scarcity on Our Planet and What We Can Do About It, 6933; New World of Food, 6933

Perl, Susan, 4037

Perlman, Raymond, 5775; 7688; 8937

Permin, Ib. Hokus Pokus: With Wands, Water and Glasses, 4172

Perovskaya, Olga. The Wolf in Olga's Kitchen, 1613

Perrault, Charles. Cinderella, 5474, 5475; Perrault's Complete Fairy Tales, 5476; Puss in Boots, 5477; The Little Red Riding Hood, 5478

Perrine, Mary. Salt Boy, 1064

Perrott, Jennifer, 4343; 8544

Perry, Bill. Our Threatened Wildlife: An Ecological Study, 6956

Perry, John. A First Book of Zoos, 8693

Perry, Patricia. Mommy and Daddy Are Divorced, 7138

Pesek, Ludek. The Earth Is Near, 2908

Pessino, Catherine. (jt. auth.) 4088; (jt. auth.) 5765

Petersen, Grete. (jt. auth.) 4283

Petersen, W. P. Meditation Made Easy, 7321

Petersham, Maud. The Rooster Crows: A Book of American Rhymes and Jingles, 182; The Box with Red Wheels: A Picture Book, 489; The Circus Baby, 490; 3292; David: From the Story Told in the First Book of Samuel and the First Book of Kings, 3743; Joseph and His Brothers, 3744; The Christ Child: As Told by Matthew and Luke, 3762; 3817; The Rooster Crows: A Book of American Rhymes and Jingles, 5150; 5256; The Silver Mace: A Story of Williamsburg, 6366; Let's Learn about Silk, 8025

Petersham, Miska. (jt. auth.) 182; (jt. auth.) 489; (jt. auth.) 490; 3292; (jt. auth.) 3743; (jt. auth.) 3744; (jt. auth.) 3762; 3817; (jt. auth.) 5150; 5256; (jt. auth.) 6366; (jt. auth.) 8025

Peterson, Esther Allen. Frederick's Alligator, 1065

Peterson, Hans. The Big Snowstorm, 7859

Peterson, Harold L. Forts in America, 8978

Peterson, Helen Stone. Oliver Wendell Holmes: Soldier, Lawyer, Supreme Court Justice, 6516; The Making of the United States Constitution, 7027

Peterson, Jeanne Whitehouse. I Have a Sister, My Sister Is Deaf, 864, 1066; That Is That, 1441

Peterson, John. How to Write Codes and Send Secret Messages, 4697

Petie, Haris, 5929; 6343; 7328; 7857; The Seed the Squirrel Dropped, 7862; 8072; 8077; A Book of Big Bugs, 8102; 8338; 8402; 8409; 8720

Petras, John J. (jt. auth.) 7387

Petrides, George A. A Field Guide to Trees and Shrubs, 7904

Petrides, Heidrun, 1124

Petry, Ann. Tituba of Salem Village, 3411; Harriet Tubman: Conductor on the Underground Railroad, 6576

Roth, Arthur. The Iceberg Hermit, 2268; Two for Survival, 2269

Roth, Charles E. The Most Dangerous Animal in the World, 6938; Then There Were None, 6953; Walking Catfish and Other Aliens, 8359

Roth, Henry, 7505

Roth, Laszlo, 4742; 7648

Rothkopf, Carol Z. Austria, 6071; The First Book of the Red Cross, 7371

Rothman, Joel. Secrets with Ciphers and Codes, 4695; At Last to the Ocean, 6973; This Can Lick a Lollipop: Body Riddles for Kids/Esto Goza Chupando un Caramelo, 7232

Rotondo, Pat, 7293

Roughsey, Dick. The Giant Devil-Dingo, 5396

Rounds, Glen, 374; 375; 376; 1137; 1146; 1357; 1370; 1371; 1582; The Blind Colt, 1621; Stolen Pony, 1621; 1666; 1719; The Day the Circus Came to Lone Tree, 2511; 2656; Mr. Yowder and the Giant Bull Snake, 2796; 3048; 3644; 4063; 4086; 4526; Sweet Betsy from Pike, 4796; 4803; Mr. Yowder and the Steamboat, 5725; Mr. Yowder and the Lion Roar Capsules, 5725; Ol' Paul, the Mighty Logger, 5726; 5728; Buffalo Harvest, 6306; 6422; The Cowboy Trade, 6438; The Prairie Schooners, 6439; Wildlife at Your Doorstep, 8051; 8144; 8158; 8205; The Beaver: How He Works, 8527; Wild Horses on the Red Desert, 8765

Rovinson, Charles, 312

Rowand, Phyllis, 1299

Rowe, Gavin, 3880; 7836

Roy, Cal. The Serpent and the Sun, 3668

Roy, Donald. A Thousand Pails of Water, 771

Roy, Jeroo, 3200

Roy, Ron. Three Ducks Went Wandering, 772; Awful Thursday, 1450

Rubel, Nicole, 382; (jt. auth.) 995

Rubel, Reina, 5044

Ruben, Patricia. What is New? What Is Missing? What Is Different?, 4083

Rubenstone, Jessie. Knitting for Beginners, 4349; Crochet for Beginners, 4349

Rubin, Bob. Pete Rose, 6873

Rubin, Eva J., 65

Rubin, Robert. Lou Gehrig: Courageous Star, 6860; Satchel Paige: All-Time Baseball Great, 6869

Ruchlis, Hy. The Wonder of Light, 7577; A Picture Story of How and Why We See, 7577; Your Changing Earth, 7675; How a Rock Came to Be in a Fence on a Road Near a Town, 7773

Rudeen, Kenneth. Roberto Clemente, 6855; Jackie Robinson, 6871; Wilt Chamberlain, 6897

Ruden, Patricia. Apples to Zippers, 38

Rudley, Stephen. The Abominable Snowcreature, 3642

Rudstrom, Lennart. A Family, 6053; A Home, 6054; A Farm, 6054

Rue, Leonard Lee. The World of the White-Tailed Deer, 8493

Ruffins, Reynold. My Brother Never Feeds the Cat, 871; (jt. auth.) 3643; 4059; (jt. auth.) 4060; 4060; 4061; 4062; (jt. auth.) 4457; 4478; 8576; (jt. auth.) 8776

Rumsey, Marian. Lost in the Desert, 2270; Lion on the Run, 2270

Ruse, Gary, 8936; 8943

Ruse, Margaret, 1189

Ruskin, Ariane. History in Art, 4621

Ruskin, John. King of the Golden River, 2797, 2798

Russ, Lavinia. Alec's Sand Castle, 653; The April Age, 3170; Over the Hills and Far Away, 3171

Russel, Helen Ross. Soil, A Field Trip Guide, 7768

Russell, Franklin. The Honeybees, 8128

Russell, Gertrude Barter, 3692

Russell, Solveig P. One, Two, Three and Many: A First Look at Numbers, 7457; Size, Distance, Weight: A First Look at Measuring, 7482; Lines and Shapes: A First Look at Geometry, 7501; Farm, 7997; Like and Unlike: A First Look at Classification, 8052; Coats and Covers, 8360; Crusty Ones: A First Look at Crustaceans, 8654; The Big Ditch Waterways: The Story of Canals, 8915

Russell, Yvonne. Words in My World, 4735

Russo, Susan, 4926; The Moon's the North Wind's Cooky: Night Poems, 5030

Ruth, Rod, 5769; 5770; 7615; 8177; 8649; 8671

Rutherford, Douglas. The Gunshot Grand Prix, 2271

Rutland, Jonathan. See Inside an Ancient Greek Town, 5836; See Inside a Roman Town, 5847; Looking at Israel, 6102; Human Body, 7233; Exploring the World of Speed, 7547; See Inside an Airport, 8844; See Inside a Galleon, 8893; See Inside an Oil Rig and Tanker, 8941

Ryan, Cheli D. Hildilid's Night, 655

Ryan, Edwin H., 2931

Ryan, Martha. Weather, 7836

Rydberg, Ernie. (jt. auth.) 3568

Rydberg, Lou. The Shadow Army, 3568

Ryden, Hope. The Little Deer of the Florida Keys, 8494; Wild Colt: The Life of a Young Mustang, 8766

Ryder, Joanne. Fog in the Meadow, 1309; Snail in the Woods, 8081; Fireflies, 8167

Saari, Kaye. The Kidnapping of the Coffee Pot, 1012

Sabin, Francene. Women Who Win, 6845; Perfect Pets, 8704; Dogs of America, 8723

Sabin, Louis. 100 Great Moments in Sports, 4404; (jt. auth.) 8704

Sachs, Ann, 1810

Sachs, Marilyn. Dorrie's Book, 1810; The Truth about Mary Rose, 1811; Amy and Laura, 2007; The Bears' House, 2008; Marv, 2009; Veronica Ganz, 2010; Peter and Veronica, 2010; A Secret Friend, 3018; A December Tale, 3172; A Summer's Lease, 3173; A Pocket Full of Seeds, 3569

Sackett, S. J. Cowboys and the Songs They Sang, 4797

Saether, Haakon, 3552

Sage, Alison. (jt. auth.) 4111

Sagsoorian, Paul, 2115; 2920

Sahachner, Erwin, 4968

Saint-Exupery, Antoine de. The Little Prince, 2799

St. George, Judith. Mystery at St. Martin's, 2272; The Halo Wind, 3489; The Amazing Voyage of the New Orleans, 6422

St. John, Glory. How to Count like a Martian, 7458

St. John, Wylly Folk. Mystery of the Gingerbread House, 2273; The Ghost Next Door, 2800

St. Tamara, 1591; Asian Crafts, 4253; 8378

Salant, Sam, 8345

Saldutti, Denise, 904

Sale, J. Kirk. The Land and People of Ghana, 5955

Sallis, Susan. An Open Mind, 3253

Salny, Roslyn W. Hobby Collections A-Z, 4093

Salten, Felix. Bambi: A Life in the Woods, 1622

Salvadori, Mario. Building: The Fight against Gravity, 8916

Samson, Joan. Watching the New Baby, 7412

Samson, John G. The Pond: The Life of the Aquatic Plants, Insects, Fish, Amphibians, Reptiles, Mammals and Birds That Inhabit the Pond, 7755

San Souci, Daniel, 5695

San Souci, Robert. The Legend of Scarface: A Blackfeet Indian Tale, 5695

Sanchez, Carlos, 5653

Sandberg, Inger. The Boy with Many Houses, 1120

Sandberg, Lasse, 1120

Sandburg, Carl. The Wedding Procession of the Rag Doll and the Broom Handle and Who Was in It, 656; Wind Song, 5031; Rootabaga Stories, 5256; Abe

Thomas, Patricia. "There Are Rocks in My Socks!" Said the Ox to the Fox, 543

Thompson, Blanche Jennings. All the Silver Pennies, 5043

Thompson, Brenda. Flags, 4702

Thompson, David H. The Penguin: Its Life Cycle, 8298

Thompson, Jean. Don't Forget Michael, 1837; Brother of the Wolves, 3397

Thompson, Neil. A Closer Look at Horses, 8770

Thompson, Sue, 8414

Thompson, Vivian L. Hawaiian Legends of Tricksters and Riddlers, 5398; Hawaiian Tales of Heroes and Champions, 5399; Hawaiian Myths of Earth, Sea and Sky, 5399

Thorndike, Susan. The Electric Radish and Other Jokes, 4068

Thrasher, Crystal. The Dark Didn't Catch Me, 1839

Threadgall, Colin, 8397

Thum, Marcella. Exploring Black America: A History and Guide, 7088

Thurber, James. Thirteen Clocks, 2837; Many Moons, 5260; The Great Quillow, 5260; The White Deer, 5261

Thurman, Judith. The Magic Lantern: How Movies Got to Move, 4886; (jt. auth.) 5012; Flashlight and Other Poems, 5044

Thypin, Marilyn. Try It On, 7004

Tichenor, Tom. Christmas Tree Crafts, 3895

Tidd, Robert, 7271

Tiegreen, Alan, 1677; 1678; 1679; 2749; 3053; 3257

Tierney, Hanne. Where's Your Baby Brother, Becky Bunting?, 1212

Tillyard, Angela. The Land and People of Yugoslavia, 6070

Tinkelman, Murray, 3655; 5903; 8352; 8648; 8668

Tinker, Gene. Let's Learn Ski Touring: Your Guide to Cross-Country Fun, 4569

Tinkle, Lon. The Valiant Few: Crisis at the Alamo, 6415

Tison, Annette. The Adventures of the Three Colors, 112

Titiev, Estelle. How the Moolah Was Taught a Lesson and Other Tales from Russia, 5616

Titus, Eve. Anatole and the Cat, 544; Anatole and the Piano, 544; Anatole and the Thirty Thieves, 544; Anatole in Italy, 544; Anatole and the Pied Piper, 545; Basil and the Pigmy Cats, 2838; Basil in Mexico, 2839; Why the Wind God Wept, 5648

Tobias, Ann. Pot, 7357

Tobias, Tobi. Chasing the Goblins Away, 672; Jane, Wishing, 673; A Day Off, 890; Moving Day, 891; Petey, 1074; The Quitting Deal, 1213; At the Beach, 1314; How Your Mother and Father Met, and What Happened After, 1840; Isamu Noguchi: The Life of a Sculptor, 6771; Marian Anderson, 6805; Arthur Mitchell, 6821; Maria Tallchief, 6828

Todd, Ruthven. Space Cat, 2913; Space Cat Meets Mars, 2913

Tolan, Stephanie S. Grandpa and Me, 1841

Tolkien, John R. The Hobbit, 2840

Tolle, Jean Bahor. The Great Pete Penney, 2373

Tolstoy, Alexei. The Great Big Enormous Turnip, 1214

Tomalin, Ruth. Gone Away, 2841

Tomelty, Roma. (jt. auth.) 2030

Tomes, Jacqueline, 1890

Tomes, Margot, 1476; 1480; 2113; 3409; 3410; 3423; 3424; 5052; 5284; 5515; 5521; 5534; 5586; 5733; 6509; 6513; 6524; 6549; 6807; 7482

Tompert, Ann. Little Fox Goes to the End of the World, 546

Tompkins, Alan, 7257

Toone, Betty L. Appalachia: The Mountains, the Place and the People, 6215

Toppin, Edgar A. (jt. auth.) 6482

Torbert, Floyd James. Park Rangers and Game Wardens

the World Over, 7151; Postmen the World Over, 7170; Fire Fighters the World Over, 8809

Torre, Frank D. Woodworking for Kids, 4371

Torres, Angelo, 6531

Toto, Joe, 4152

Toulmin-Rothe, Ann, 1474

Tousey, Sanford, 6790

Tower, Samuel A. Makers of America; Stamps That Honor Them, 4215

Towle, Faith M. The Magic Cooking Pot, 5386

Towne, Mary. The Glass Room, 1961; First Serve, 2374; Goldenrod, 2842

Towne, Peter. George Washington Carver, 6713

Townsend, John R. Noah's Castle, 1842; The Intruder, 2310; Top of the World, 2311; The Visitors, 2914; Good-Bye to the Jungle, 3029; Pirate's Island, 3029; Trouble in the Jungle, 3029; Modern Poetry, 5045

Towrie, W. (jt. auth.) 5410

Toye, Clive. Soccer, 4579

Toye, William. The Fire Stealer, 5696; The Loon's Necklace, 5697; How Summer Came to Canada, 5697

Traetta, John. Gymnastics Basics, 4496

Traetta, Mary Jean. (jt. auth.) 4496

Trager, Helen G. (jt. auth.) 5387

Trainer, David. A Day in the Life of a TV News Reporter, 7195

Trasher, Crystal. Between Dark and Daylight, 1838

Travers, P. L. Mary Poppins, 2521; Mary Poppins Comes Back, 2521

Trease, Geoffrey. The Baron's Hostage, 3366

Tregarthen, Enys. The Doll Who Came Alive, 5262

Tregaskis, Richard. Guadalcanal Diary, 5890

Trelease, Allen W. Reconstruction: The Great Experiment, 6471

Tremain, Ruthven. Teapot, Switcheroo, and Other Silly Word Games, 4087

Tresselt, Alvin. The Frog in the Well, 547; The World in the Candy Egg, 674; Hi, Mister Robin!, 1315; Johnny Maple Leaf, 1315; Hide and Seek Fog, 1316; It's Time Now!, 1317; Rain Drop Splash, 1318; What Did You Leave Behind?, 1319; White Snow, Bright Snow, 1320; The Mitten, 5617; The Beaver Pond, 7759; The Dead Tree, 7920

Trevino, Elizabeth de. Nacar, the White Deer, 1635; I, Juan de Pareja, 3325

Trier, Walter, 2198

Tripp, Eleanor B. To America, 7078

Tripp, Wallace, 302; 781; 1438; 1564; Sir Toby Jingle's Beastly Journey, 2522; A Great Big Ugly Man Came Up and Tied His Horse to Me: A Book of Nonsense Verse, 5156

Trivas, Irene, 4397

Trivett, Daphne. Time for Clocks, 4261; Shadow Geometry, 7505

Trivett, John. (jt. auth.) 4261

Trost, Lucille W. Biography of a Cottontail, 8528

Troyer, Johannes, 1500; 5177

Tucker, Nicholas. Mother Goose Abroad, 192

Tudor, Bethany. Drawn from New England: Tasha Tudor, 6776

Tudor, Tasha. A Is for Annabelle, 43; 1 is One, 81; Mother Goose, 193; 1571; 1909; 2584; 2585; First Prayers, 3766; First Graces, 3766; Tasha Tudor's Sampler: A Tale for Easter/Pumpkin Moonshine/The Dolls' Christmas, 3800; A Time to Keep, 3801; Take Joy: The Tasha Tudor Christmas Book, 3811; Becky's Christmas, 3879; The Doll's Christmas, 3879; Tasha Tudor's Favorite Christmas Carols, 3903; Tasha Tudor's Old-Fashioned Gifts, 4262; Wings from the Wind, 5046; Tasha Tudor's Bedtime Book, 5304

Tuey, John. (jt. auth.) 4162

Tunis, Edwin. Indians, 6312; Colonial Living, 6380; Colonial Craftsmen: And the Beginnings of American Industry, 6380; Shaw's Fortune: The Picture Story of a Colonial Plantation, 6381; The Tavern at the Ferry,

Welker, Carole E. (jt. auth.) 7955
Wellman, Alice. Tatu and the Honeybird, 965
Wellman, Paul I. The Greatest Cattle Drive, 6445
Wellower, Lucille. Colonial Pennsylvania, 6378
Wells, Haru, 2157; 3280; 3281; 5756
Wells, Rosemary. Max's Toys: A Counting Book, 82;
320; Don't Spill It Again, James, 570; Max's First
Word, 571; Max's Ride, 571; Max's New Suit, 571;
Noisy Nora, 572; Stanley and Rhoda, 573; 877;
Unfortunately Harriet, 898; Abdul, 1222; 1577; Leave
Well Enough Alone, 1848; Morris's Disappearing Bag:
A Christmas Story, 3882; 4529
Wels, Byron G. Here Is Your Hobby: Amateur Radio,
4096; Here Is Your Hobby: Magic, 4178; Newer and
Better Dog Obedience Training, 8720
Welty, Susan F. Birds with Bracelets: The Story of Bird-
Banding, 8242
Wenning, Elizabeth. The Christmas Mouse, 3883
Werenskiold, Erik, 5530
Wernecke, H. H. Celebrating Christmas around the
World, 3812
Werner, Honi, 4139
Werstein, Irving. The Many Faces of the Civil War, 6455
Werth, Kurt, 1052; 2717; 3839; 3885; 3914; 3972; 5281;
6367
Wessells, Katharine Tyler. The Golden Song Book, 4848
Wesson, Lisa C., 3708
Westall, Robert. The Machine Gunners, 1964; The
Watch House, 2323; The Devil on the Road, 2847;
The Wind Eye, 2848
Westcott, Nadine, 2444; I Know an Old Lady Who
Swallowed a Fly, 4804
Westervelt, Virginia. Pearl Buck: A Biographical Novel,
6782
Westman, Wesley C. The Drug Epidemic: What It Means
and How to Combat It, 7349
Weston, Martha, 4077; 4146; 7050; 7420; 8059; 8573
Wetterer, Margaret K. Patrick and the Fairy Thief, 5454
Wexler, Jerome, 7887; (jt. auth.) 7890; 7918; 7957;
7981; 7984; (jt. auth.) 8089; (jt. auth.) 8772
Weyl, Nancy, 4522
Wezel, Peter. The Good Bird, 270
Whatley, Jo Ann. Banking and Finance Careers, 7176
Wheatley, Arabelle, 6948; 7255; 8115; 8149; 8388; 8672;
8683
Wheeler, Cindy. A Good Day, A Good Night, 102
Wheeler, Opal. Edward MacDowell and His Cabin in the
Pines, 6802
Whipple, Addison. Famous Pirates of the New World,
6659
Whitaker, George O. Dinosaur Hunt, 5781
White, Ann S. Divorce, 7146
White, Anne H. Junket, 1641
White, Anne Terry. Prehistoric America, 5800; The St.
Lawrence: Seaway of North America, 6173; Windows
on the World, 7278; All about Great Rivers of the
World, 7760; All about Mountains, 7761
White, David Omar, 2117
White, Dori. Sarah and Katie, 1965
White, E. B. Charlotte's Web, 2849; The Trumpet of the
Swan, 2850
White, Florence Meiman. Escape: The Life of Harry
Houdini, 6818
White, Jack, 7834
White, Jon Manchip. Everyday Life in Ancient Egypt,
5829
White, Laurence B. The Trick Book, 4071; (jt. auth.)
4167; Science Puzzles, 7424; Investigating Science
with Nails, 7438; Investigating Science with Coins,
7438; Investigating Science with Rubber Bands, 7438;
Investigating Science with Paper, 7438
White, Paul. Janet at School, 1080
White, Percival. (jt. auth.) 6174
White, Robb. Deathwatch, 2324; Fire Storm, 2325
White, Sara Jane. (jt. auth.) 8169

White, William Jr. A Mosquito Is Born, 8169
Whitehead, Robert. Rabbits and Hares, 8536
Whitlock, Ralph. A Closer Look at Butterflies and Moths,
8142
Whitman, Walt. Overhead the Sun: Lines from Walt
Whitman, 5054; Leaves of Grass, 5054
Whitney, Alma Marshak. Just Awful, 966
Whitney, Alex. American Indian Clothes and How to
Make Them, 4290
Whitney, David C. The First Book of Facts and How to
Find Them, 4752; Easy Book of Fractions, 7453; Easy
Book of Numbers and Numerals, 7463; Easy Book of
Sets, 7464; Let's Find Out about Subtraction, 7465
Whitney, Phyllis A. Mystery of the Haunted Pool, 2326;
Secret of the Tiger's Eye, 2326; Secret of the Emerald
Star, 2327; Secret of the Spotted Shell, 2327; Secret of
the Stone Face, 2328
Whitney, Thomas P. In a Certain Kingdom: Twelve
Russian Fairy Tales, 5618
Whitridge, Arnold. Simon Bolivar: The Great Liberator,
6627
Wibberley, Leonard. Flint's Island, 2329; Perilous Gold,
2330; The Crime of Martin Coverly, 2851; The Mouse
on the Moon, 2852; John Treegate's Musket, 3432;
Sea Captain from Salem, 3432; The Last Battle, 3462;
The Leopard's Prey, 3462; Red Pawns, 3462;
Guarneri: Story of a Genius, 6798
Wiberg, Harald, 1112; 3862; 7859
Wickers, David. How to Make Things Grow, 4162
Wicks, Keith. Stars and Planets, 7623
Wiener, Norman. (jt. auth.) 7174
Wier, Esther. King of the Mountain, 1642; The Loner,
3201
Wiese, Kurt, 695; 1099; 1140; 1629; 2391; 3283; You
Can Write Chinese, 4714; 5723; 6027; 6190; 6205;
6206; 6207; 6222; 6223; 6230; 6237; 6244; 7786
Wiesenthal, Eleanor. Let's Find Out about Eskimos, 5909
Wiesenthal, Ted. (jt. auth.) 5909
Wiesner, William, 3958; 4048; The Riddle Pot, 4072; A
Pocketful of Riddles, 4072; 5427
Wiess, Ellen. Millicent Maybe, 1481
Wiggin, Kate Douglas. Rebecca of Sunnybrook Farm,
1849; The Birds' Christmas Carol, 3884; Arabian
Nights: Their Best Known Tales, 5645
Wiggins, Lee, 1248
Wikland, Ilon, 1182; 3861
Wikler, Janet. How to Study and Learn, 4758
Wilber, Donald N. The Land and People of Ceylon, 5996
Wilbur, Richard. Opposites, 4739
Wild, Jocelyn. (jt. auth.) 83
Wild, Robin. The Bears' Counting Book, 83
Wilde, Carol, 7122
Wilde, Oscar. The Birthday of the Infanta, 5263; The
Selfish Giant, 5264; The Star Child: A Fairy Tale,
5265
Wilder, Cherry. The Luck of Brin's Five, 2917
Wilder, Laura Ingalls. Little House in the Big Woods,
1850; Farmer Boy, 1850; Little House on the Prairie,
1850; On the Banks of Plum Creek, 1850; By the
Shores of Silver Lake, 1850; Little Town on the
Prairie, 1850; Long Winter, 1850; These Happy
Golden Years, 1850; West from Home: Letters of
Laura Ingalls Wilder, San Francisco, 1851
Wilding-White, Ted. All about UFO's, 3651
Wildsmith, Brian. Brian Wildsmith's ABC, 44; 1,2,3's,
81; What the Moon Saw, 144; Brian Wildsmith's
Mother Goose: A Collection of Nursery Rhymes, 194;
Hunter and His Dog, 574; The Lazy Bear, 575; The
Little Wood Duck, 576; The Owl and the
Woodpecker, 577; Python's Party, 578; 3749; Brian
Wildsmith's the Twelve Days of Christmas, 3904;
Brian Wildsmith's Circus, 4862; 4937; Brian
Wildsmith's Birds, 8243; Brian Wildsmith's Wild
Animals, 8367; Squirrels, 8537; Brian Wildsmith's
Fishes, 8642

Title Index

Biographical Subjects

NOTE: References are to entry number, not page number.

Subject Index

Subjects are listed according to entry numbers, not page numbers.